The Almanac of American Education

2021

The Almanac of American Education

2021

Thirteenth Edition
Edited by Hannah Anderson Krog

Bernan Press

Lanham • Boulder • New York • London

Published in the United States of America
by Bernan Press, a wholly owned subsidiary of
The Rowman & Littlefield Publishing Group, Inc.
4501 Forbes Boulevard, Suite 200
Lanham, Maryland 20706

Bernan Press
800-462-6420
www.rowman.com

ISBN: 978-1-64143-493-5
e-ISBN: 978-1-64143-494-2

♾™ The paper used in this publication meets the minimum requirements of American National Standard for Information Sciences—Permanence of Paper for Printed Library Materials, ANSI/NISO Z39.48-1992.

Manufactured in the United States of America.

Contents

Tables

PART A—NATIONAL EDUCATION STATISTICS

ENROLLMENT TABLES

HISTORICAL ENROLLMENT TABLES

ATTAINMENT TABLES

HISTORICAL ATTAINMENT TABLES

PART B—REGION AND STATE EDUCATION STATISTICS

ATTAINMENT TABLES

POPULATION, SCHOOL, AND STUDENT CHARACTERISTICS TABLES

PART C—COUNTY EDUCATION STATISTICS

POPULATION CHARACTERISTICS, ENROLLMENT, AND ATTAINMENT TABLES

Figures

PART C—COUNTY EDUCATION STATISTICS

Preface

The *Almanac of American Education* serves as a guide to understanding and comparing the quality of education at the national, state, and county levels. Compiled from data released by the U.S. Census Bureau and the National Center for Education Statistics (NCES), *The Almanac* contains historical and current data, insightful analysis, and useful graphics that provide a detailed picture of the state of education in the United States.

The 13th edition of the *Almanac* includes tables and figures updated from the 12th edition alongside several new tables.

The Almanac is organized into three sections: Part A—National Education Statistics; Part B—Region and State Education Statistics; and Part C—County Education Statistics. Most of the data presented in Part A are no longer available in print form from the Census Bureau. Additional tables in Part A are excerpted from the *Digest of Education Statistics* from the NCES, providing an overview of higher education in the United States. The data in Parts B and C have been specially tabulated for this publication from data obtained from the NCES and the Census Bureau.

The Almanac's content allows users to ask—and answer—important questions about historic and current trends in U.S. education, including:

- Is the earnings gap between high-school graduates and college graduates growing or shrinking?

- What are the racial disparities in educational attainment, and are these disparities growing or shrinking over time?
- Which states have the highest and lowest high-school dropout rates?
- Is there a relationship between childhood poverty rates and state-level expenditures per student?
- Which states have the largest county-to-county variation in high-school graduation rates?

The data in this volume meet the publication standards of the federal statistical agencies from which they were obtained. Every effort has been made to select accurate, meaningful, and useful data. All statistical data are subject to error arising from sampling variability, reporting errors, incomplete coverage, imputation, and other causes. The responsibility of the editor and publisher of this volume is limited to reasonable care in the reproduction and presentation of data obtained from established sources.

Hannah Anderson Krog edits several titles for Bernan Press including *State Profiles: The Population and Economy of Each U.S. State* and *Patterns of Economic Change*. She earned her bachelor of arts in journalism from the University of Maryland.

Much appreciation is due to the federal agency personnel who prepared the original data and generously responded to our requests for assistance.

PART A
NATIONAL EDUCATION STATISTICS

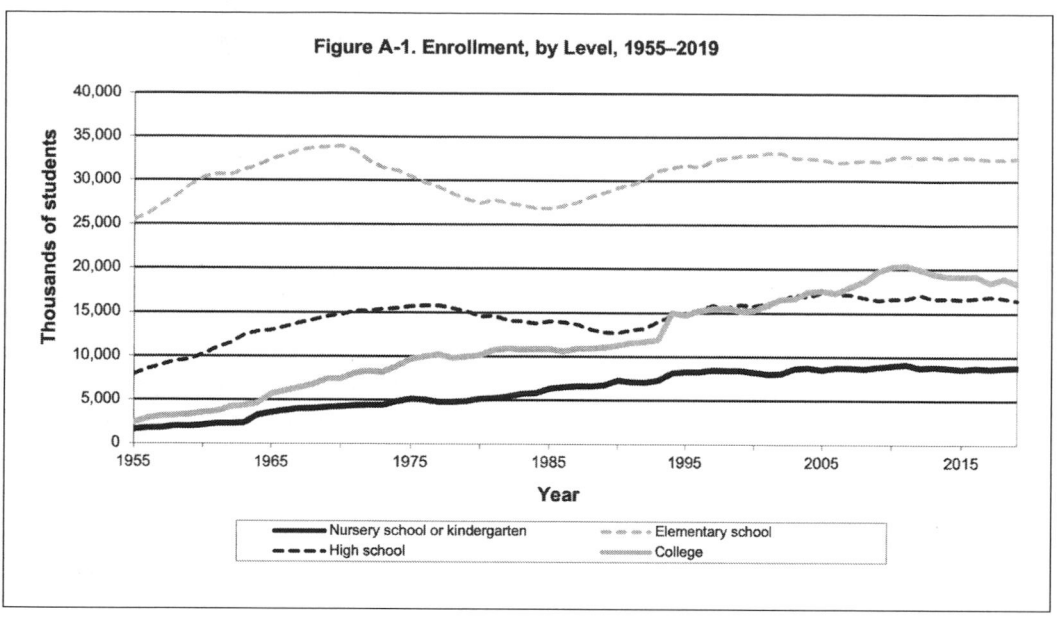

Figure A-1. Enrollment, by Level, 1955–2019

More than 76.1 million people were enrolled in school in 2019. Total school enrollment decreased in the late 1970s and early 1980s, but it began to rise again by 1985. Enrollment peaked in 2011, with more than 79 million students enrolled in school. Enrollment has been trending downward since then, decreasing again in 2019. College enrollment had peaked at 20.4 million students in 2011. Elementary school enrollment has remained between 32.0 and 33.2 million since 1997 (32.6 million in 2019), similar to the baby boom levels of the 1960s but never quite reaching the 33.9 million elementary school enrollees of 1970. High-school enrollment in 2019 was 16.4 million students. High-school enrollment has hovered around 16.5 million since 2013. College enrollment decreased by 619,000 students from 2018 to 2019, with public colleges experiencing a 3.2 percent decrease in enrollment and private colleges experiencing a 3.6 percent decrease. (Table A-10)

In 2019, 24.3 percent of people age 3 years and over were enrolled in school. For the population 3 to 4 years old, 53.7 percent were enrolled in nursery school or kindergarten, and 46.3 percent were not enrolled in school. Among the population 18 to 24 years old, 46.9 percent were enrolled in school, as were 11.0 percent of 25- to 29-year-olds. The proportion of 30- to 34-year-olds enrolled in school was 6.0 percent. (Table A-1)

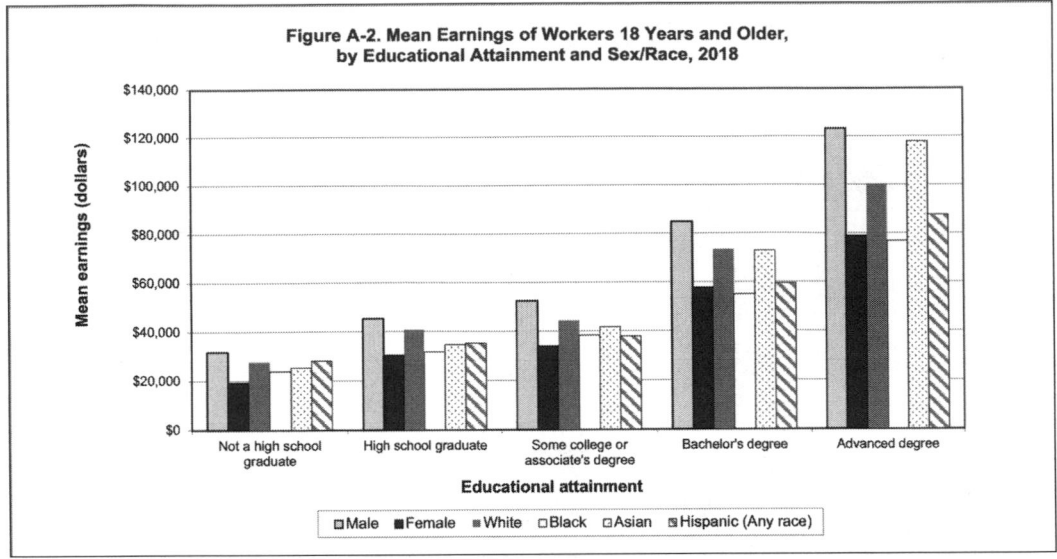

In 2018, the wage gap between males and females age 18 years and older was seen for all levels of educational attainment. On average, women earned 30.6 percent less than men with the same level of educational attainment. The largest gap was between males and females with less than a high school diploma: the mean earnings for women without a high school diploma were 40.1 percent less than men who had that level of educational attainment ($19,068 versus $31,846).

The wage gap between racial/ethnic groups was also seen across most levels of educational attainment. Among people age 18 years and older with a bachelor's degree, the mean earnings of those who identified as black were 25.1 percent less than the mean earnings of people who identified as white. People age 18 years and older with a bachelor's degree who identified as Hispanic earned 20.8 percent less than those who identified as non-Hispanic white. (Table A-34)

In 2019, the median annual earnings for men 25 years old and over was $49,647; for women it was $31,773, with half of the men or women earning more than this amount and half earning less. For those who attended but did not finish high school, the median annual earnings were $25,598 for men, $15,694 for women. For high school graduates, including those with a GED, median earnings were $37,144 for men and $22,052 for women. Men with bachelor's degrees had median earnings of $69,505 while women with bachelor's degrees had median earnings of $45,942. Workers with a professional degree had the highest median earnings, $127,625 for men and $82,093 for women. Men continued to earn at least 30 percent more than women at all levels of educational attainment, except for the doctorate degree level, where the median earnings for women ($86,047) was 19.2 percent less than for men ($106,472). (Table A-35)

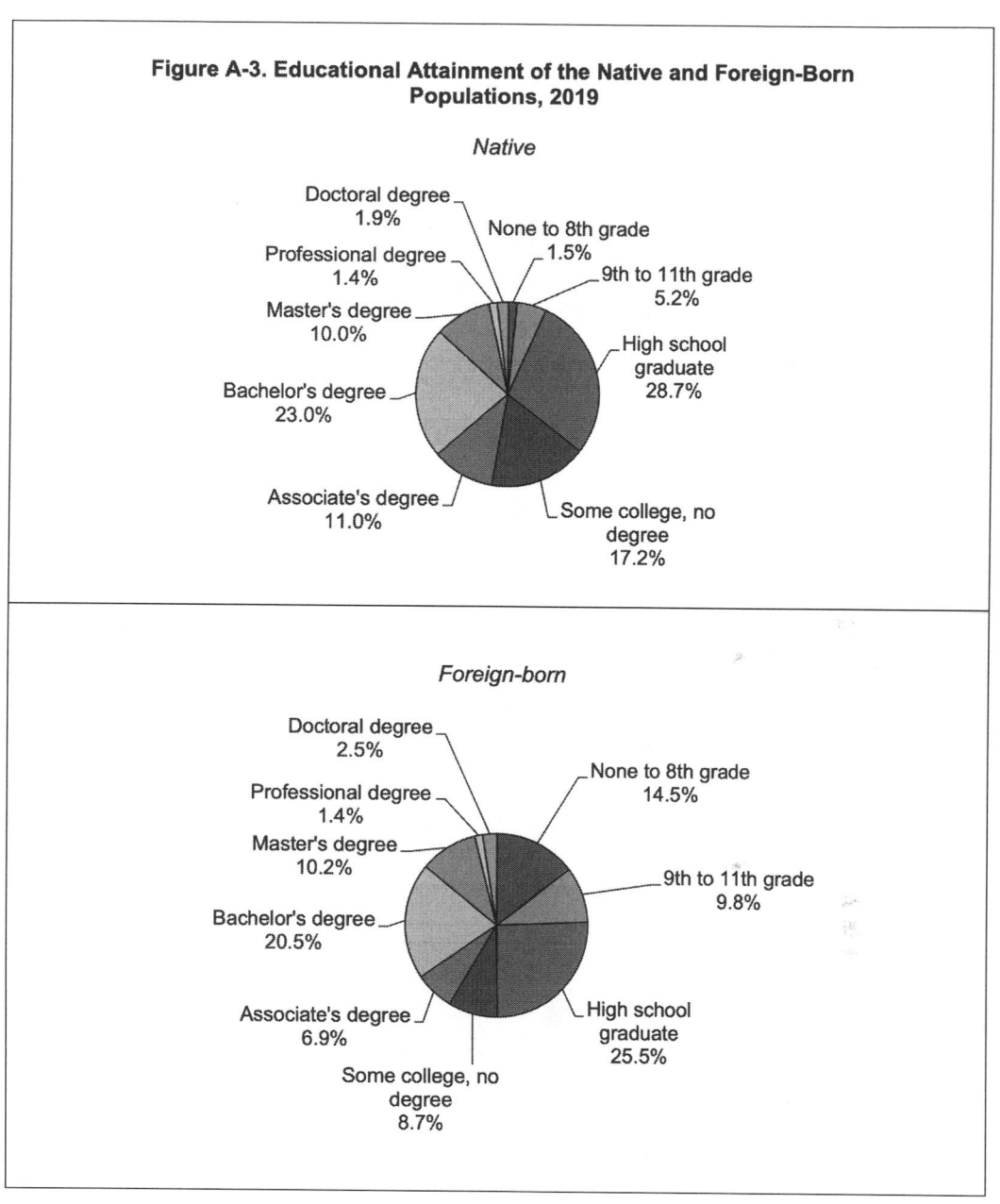

Figure A-3. Educational Attainment of the Native and Foreign-Born Populations, 2019

Native

- Doctoral degree 1.9%
- Professional degree 1.4%
- Master's degree 10.0%
- Bachelor's degree 23.0%
- Associate's degree 11.0%
- None to 8th grade 1.5%
- 9th to 11th grade 5.2%
- High school graduate 28.7%
- Some college, no degree 17.2%

Foreign-born

- Doctoral degree 2.5%
- Professional degree 1.4%
- Master's degree 10.2%
- Bachelor's degree 20.5%
- Associate's degree 6.9%
- None to 8th grade 14.5%
- 9th to 11th grade 9.8%
- High school graduate 25.5%
- Some college, no degree 8.7%

In 2019, 81.9 percent of the population age 25 years and older in the United States was native-born, and 18.1 percent of the population was foreign-born. The foreign-born population had a much larger proportion of people with less than a 9th-grade education, with 14.5 percent of the foreign-born population was in this category, compared to 1.5 percent of the native population. However, the foreign-born population also had a higher percent of people with doctoral degrees than the native population (2.5 percent, compared to 1.9 percent of natives). (Table A-30)

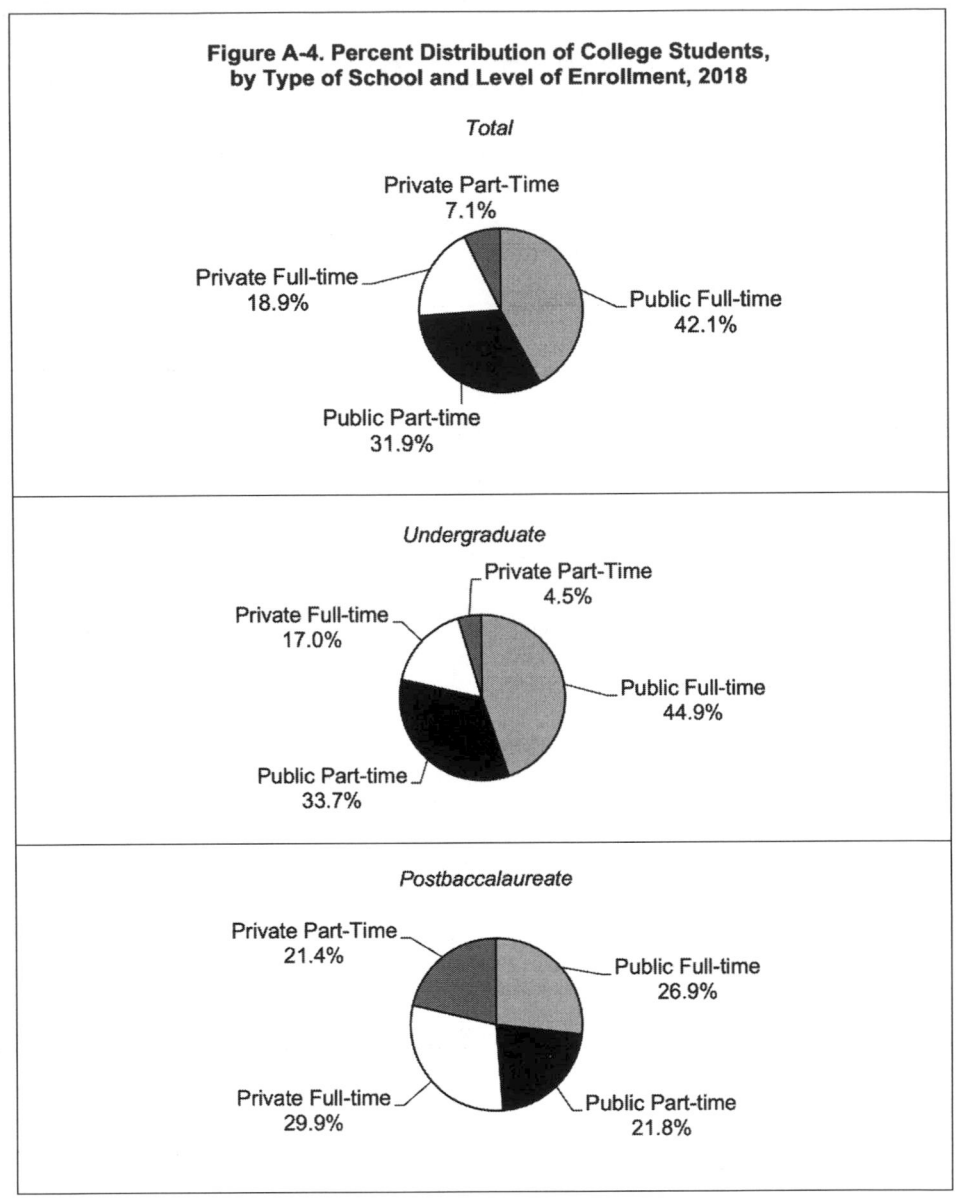

Figure A-4. Percent Distribution of College Students, by Type of School and Level of Enrollment, 2018

Total

Private Part-Time 7.1%
Private Full-time 18.9%
Public Full-time 42.1%
Public Part-time 31.9%

Undergraduate

Private Part-Time 4.5%
Private Full-time 17.0%
Public Full-time 44.9%
Public Part-time 33.7%

Postbaccalaureate

Private Part-Time 21.4%
Public Full-time 26.9%
Private Full-time 29.9%
Public Part-time 21.8%

In 2019, 18.3 million students 15 years old and over were enrolled in colleges and universities. Approximately 14.6 million of them were undergraduates. A higher percent of undergraduates attending four-year colleges were full-time students (84.5 percent) compared to those attending two-year colleges (64.9 percent full-time). The proportion of full-time to part-time college students decreased as age increased. Among students 15 to 19 years old enrolled in college, 93.0 percent were full-time students, followed by 83.3 percent of 20- to 24-year-olds, 61.7 percent of 25- to 34-year-olds, and 41.3 percent of students age 35 years and older. Among graduate students, 64.0 percent were full-time students in 2019. Since 2008 there have been more full-time graduate students than part-time, but prior to 2008 the reverse was usually true: part-time students outnumbered full-time in graduate programs most years. (Table A-5 and A-17)

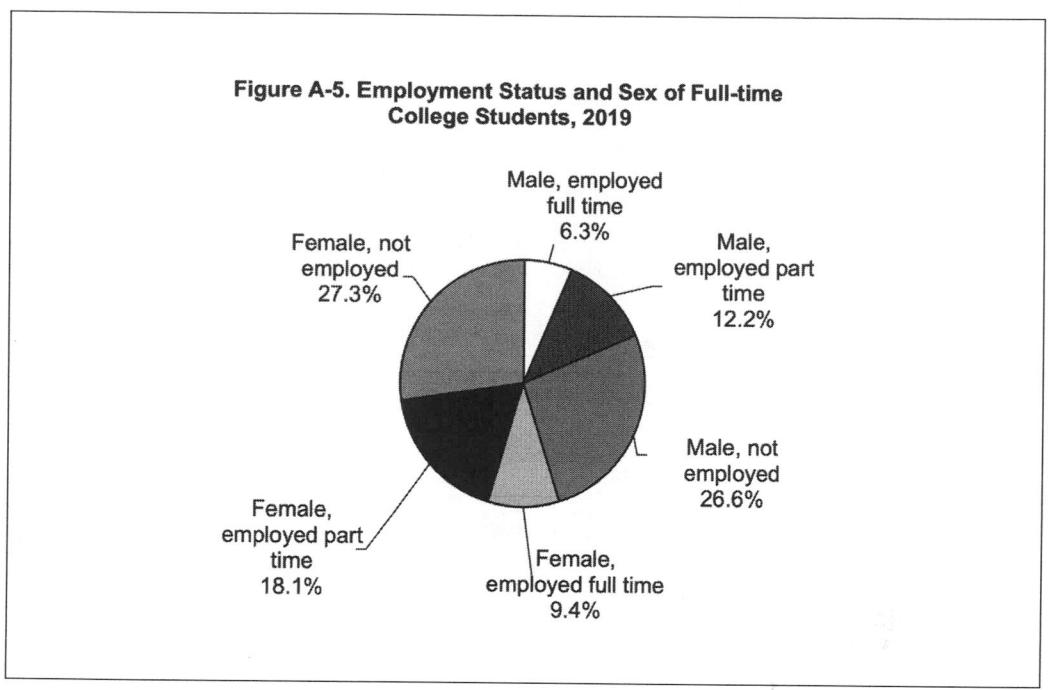

Figure A-5. Employment Status and Sex of Full-time College Students, 2019

In 2019, women made up 55.0 percent of all undergraduate students. By contrast, only 42.2 percent of all undergraduate students in 1970 were women. By the end of the 1970s, the proportions of men and women were more equal; since then, women's share has steadily increased, staying above 55 percent in most years since the early 1990s and reaching its highest levels of 56.9 percent in 2005 and 56.8 percent in 2012. (Table A-17)

In 2018, 63.5 percent of college students who identified as Black were female. Among Hispanic college students, 58.6 percent were female, and females comprised 53.8 percent of the Asian/Pacific Islander college population. Among graduate students, women accounted for 59.9 percent of enrollment in 2018. (Table A-22)

In 2019, 46.1 percent of full-time college students were employed—either full- or part-time–and 84.9 percent of part-time college students were employed. Among those who were enrolled in vocational courses, 72.2 percent were employed, either full-time or part-time. (Tables A–5 and A-6)

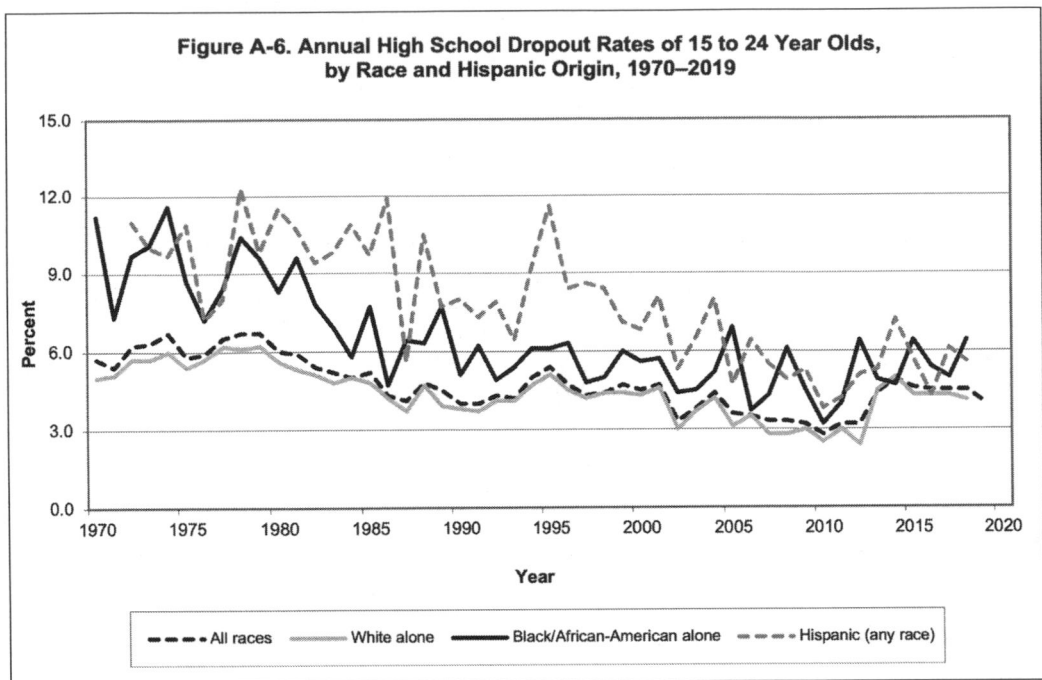

Figure A-6. Annual High School Dropout Rates of 15 to 24 Year Olds, by Race and Hispanic Origin, 1970–2019

The annual high school dropout rate for all students in grades 10 through 12 was 4.0 percent in 2019. The percent of dropouts increased with grade level: 1.6 percent of students dropped out during 10th grade; 3.3 percent of students dropped out during 11th grade; and 7.7 percent of students dropped out during 12th grade. The annual dropout rate was higher for students who identified as Hispanic, with 5.3 percent of Hispanic students in grades 10 though 12 dropping out (students of Hispanic origin can be of any race). (Table A-13)

In 1940, only one in four people in the U.S. had completed high school. By 1966, the ratio had only increased to 1 in 2 – 49.9 percent of the U.S. population 25 years old and older had completed high school. For those who identified as Black, it wasn't until 1980 that more than half of the population age 25 and older had completed high school (51.2 percent). As of 2019, 90.1 percent of the total population age 25 years and over and 87.5 percent of the Black population age 25 years and older were high-school graduates. (Table A-32)

The percentage of college graduates, which constituted just 4.6 percent of the population in 1940, had risen to 9.8 percent by 1966. In 2019, college graduates constituted 36.0 percent of the population 25 years old and over. There are more women than men who have graduated from college. In 2019, 35.4 percent of males and 36.6 percent of females age 25 and over were college graduates. (Table A-32)

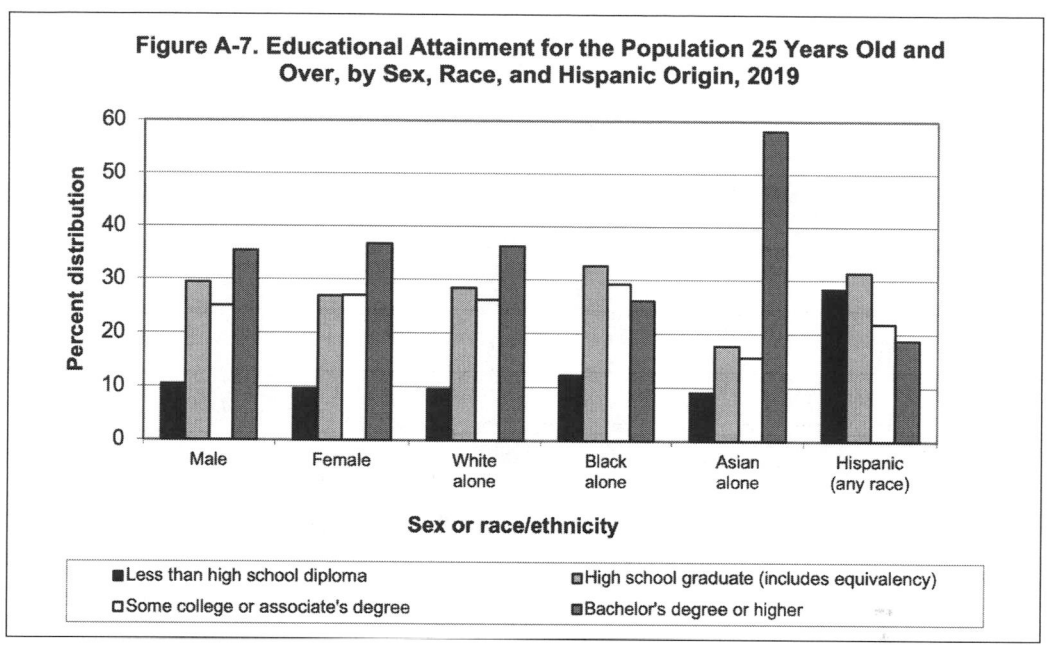

Figure A-7. Educational Attainment for the Population 25 Years Old and Over, by Sex, Race, and Hispanic Origin, 2019

In 2019, 90.1 percent of Americans 25 years old and over had completed high school, and 36.0 percent had completed college. For people age 25 to 29 years, 93.5 percent had completed high school and 38.7 percent had completed college. Women 25 years of age and older had slightly higher rates of high school attainment and college attainment, at 90.5 percent and 36.6 percent, respectively. For women age 25 to 29 years, 94.3 percent had completed high school and 41.8 percent had completed college. Among race and ethnic groups (age 25 and older) in 2019, those who identified as non-Hispanic White had the highest high school completion rate (94.6 percent), followed by Asian (91.2 percent), White (90.5 percent), Black (87.9 percent), and Hispanic (71.8 percent) individuals. More than half (58.1 percent) of those identified as Asian had completed college, followed by those who identified as non-Hispanic White (40.1 percent), White (36.3 percent), Black (26.1 percent), and Hispanic (18.8 percent – people who identified as Hispanic may be of any race.) (Tables A-32)

In 2019, 60.9 percent of the population 25 years and older were employed, 3.2 percent were unemployed, and 35.9 percent were not in the labor force. Of people age 25 and older with bachelor's degrees as their highest level of educational attainment, 71.2 percent were employed, 2.2 percent were unemployed, and 26.6 percent were not in the labor force. (Table A-27)

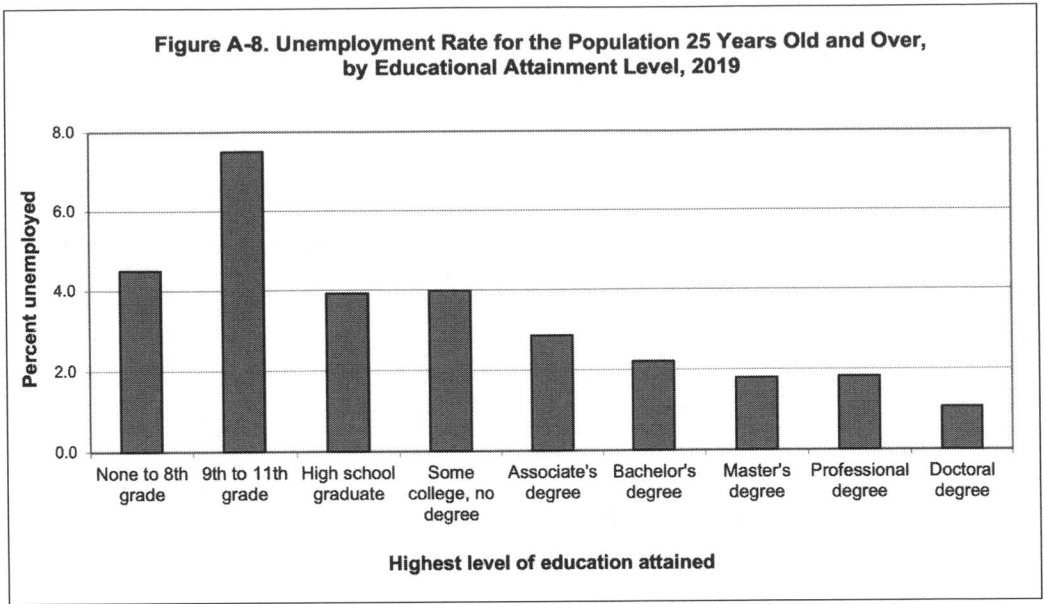

Figure A-8. Unemployment Rate for the Population 25 Years Old and Over, by Educational Attainment Level, 2019

Unemployment data for 2019 show once again that the more education a person has obtained, the less likely he or she will be unemployed. The unemployment rate for the population age 25 and over with a 9th to 11th grade education was 7.5 percent in 2019. For high-school graduates, the rate of unemployment was 3.9 percent; for civilians with a bachelor's degree, it was 2.2 percent. With a professional degree, this percentage dropped to 1.8; and the lowest unemployment rate was for those with a doctoral degree (1.1 percent). The overall unemployment rate in 2019 was 3.2 percent. The unemployment rate for men (3.4 percent) was higher than that for women (3.0 percent). However, there were fewer women than men in the work force. In 2019, the labor force participation rate was 70.6 percent for men, and 58.1 percent for women. (Table A-27)

For persons 25 years old and over, professional and related occupations provided the most jobs in 2019. This category includes teachers, lawyers, scientists, artists, doctors, nurses, and other healthcare professionals. Of individuals employed in professional and related occupations, 75.1 percent held a bachelor's degree or more. In contrast, 10.2 percent of those employed in farming, forestry and fishing, construction, maintenance, production, and transportation occupations had a bachelor's degree or more. Farming, forestry, and fishing employed the greatest percent of people without a high-school diploma (42.6 percent), and service occupations employed the highest number of people without a high-school diploma (3 million). (Table A-28)

The educational and health services industry was the largest employer in the United States and employed nearly 33.1 million people in 2019. More than half (57.8 percent) of the population in the education and health services industry held a bachelor's degree or higher, and 30.6 percent of workers in this field had a master's degree or higher. Mining was the smallest industry in terms of employment, with 704,000 workers, of whom 31.0 percent held a bachelor's degree or higher. (Table A-29)

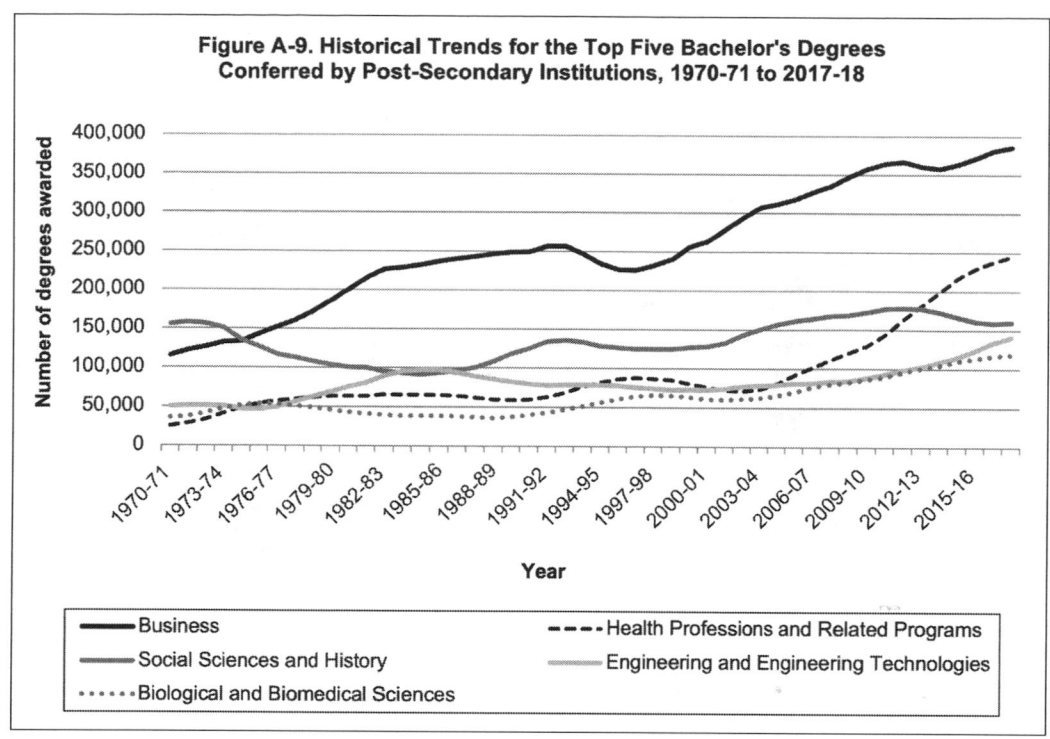

Figure A-9. Historical Trends for the Top Five Bachelor's Degrees Conferred by Post-Secondary Institutions, 1970-71 to 2017-18

The top five bachelor's degrees conferred by post-secondary institutions in the United States during the 2017-2018 school year were: business (386,201 bachelor's degrees conferred), health professions and related programs (159,967 bachelor's degrees), social sciences and history (159,099 bachelor's degrees), engineering and engineering technologies (140,683 bachelor's degrees), and biological and biomedical sciences (118,663 bachelor's degrees). The top three master's degrees granted in 2017-2018 were in: business (192,184 master's degrees conferred), education (146,367 master's degrees conferred), and health professions and related programs (125,216 master's degrees conferred). (Table A-37)

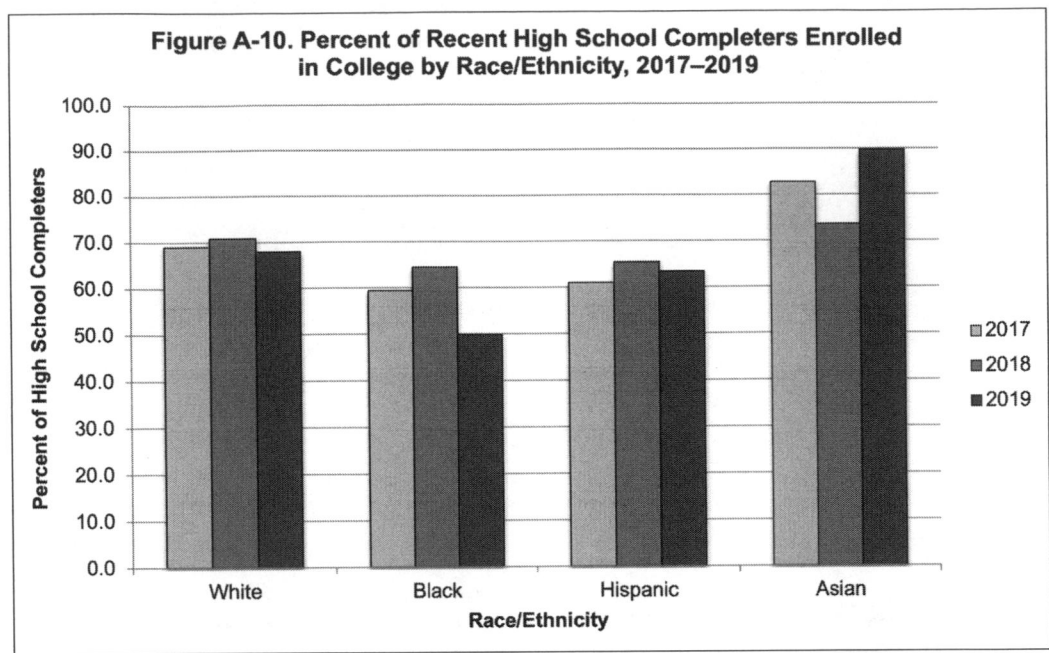

Figure A-10. Percent of Recent High School Completers Enrolled in College by Race/Ethnicity, 2017–2019

The past three years saw an increase in the percent of Hispanic and Asian college students, and a decrease in the percent of college students who identified as White or Black. In 2016, 56.9 percent of college students identified as White, 13.7 percent identified as Black, 18.2 percent identified as Hispanic, and 6.7 percent identified as Asian. In 2018, the proportions were 55.2 percent White, 13.4 percent Black, 19.5 percent Hispanic, and 7.0 percent Asian. (Table A-22)

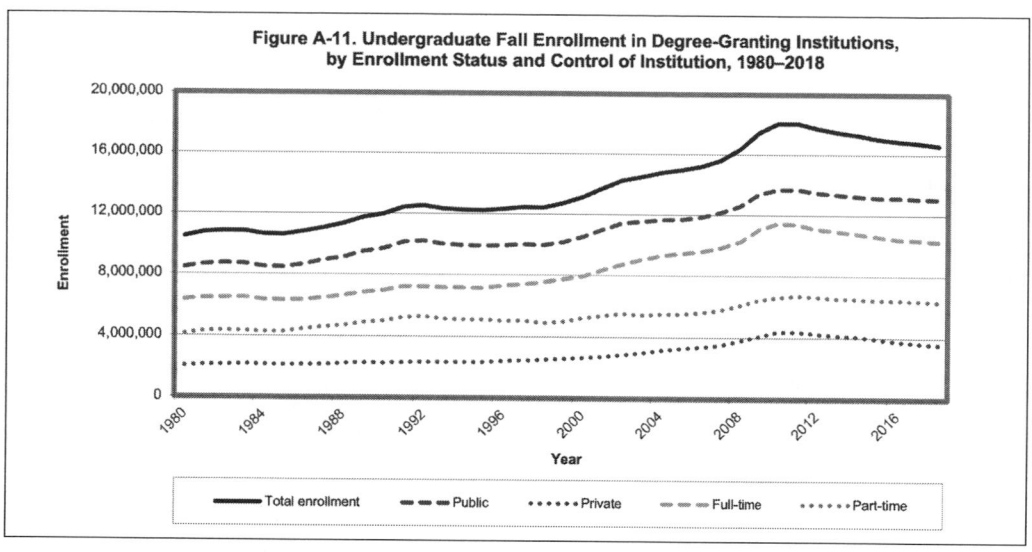

Figure A-11. Undergraduate Fall Enrollment in Degree-Granting Institutions, by Enrollment Status and Control of Institution, 1980–2018

College enrollment increased 37.3 percent between 2000 and 2010, but it has decreased each year since 2010. In 2018, 19.7 million students were enrolled in college, with 14.5 million of them enrolled in public institutions. Enrollment in private colleges peaked at nearly 5.9 million students in 2011, but enrollment has decreased each year since then. There were about 5.1 million students enrolled in private colleges in 2018. Public 4-year colleges continued to enroll the most students, with 9 million students enrolled in 2018. Both public and private 2-year colleges saw a decrease in enrollment from 2017 to 2018, with 170,756 fewer students enrolled in public, 2-year colleges and 36,807 fewer students enrolled in private, 2-year colleges. There have been more females than males enrolled in college since 1978. Women comprised 57.0 percent of college students in 2018. The percentage of females reached its peak of 57.4 percent in 2005. (Tables A-18 and A-19)

PART A

NATIONAL EDUCATION STATISTICS

■ **Enrollment Tables**

Table A-1. Enrollment Status of the Population 3 Years Old and Over, by Sex, Age, Race, Hispanic Origin, Foreign Born, and Foreign-Born Parentage, October 2019

(Numbers in thousands; percent; civilian noninstitutionalized population.)

| Age, sex, race, Hispanic origin, and nativity | Population | Enrolled in school | | | | | | | |
| | | Total | | Nursery or kindergarten | | Elementary | | High school | |
	Number	Number	Percent	Number	Percent	Number	Percent	Number	Percent
ALL RACES									
Both Sexes									
Total	3,13,097	76,089	24.3	8,785	2.8	32,619	10.4	16,395	5.2
3 and 4 years old	8,074	4,334	53.7	4,334	53.7	*	*	*	*
5 and 6 years old	8,016	7,506	93.6	4,368	54.5	3,137	39.1	*	*
7 to 9 years old	12,232	11,930	97.5	83	0.7	11,847	96.9	*	*
10 to 13 years old	16,617	16,282	98.0	*	*	16,067	96.7	215	1.3
14 and 15 years old	8,314	8,141	97.9	*	*	1,410	17.0	6,696	80.5
16 and 17 years old	8,391	7,778	92.7	*	*	56	0.7	7,506	89.5
18 and 19 years old	8,306	5,586	67.3	*	*	3	*	1,579	19.0
20 and 21 years old	8,678	4,641	53.5	*	*	17	0.2	129	1.5
22 to 24 years old	12,360	3,537	28.6	*	*	26	0.2	75	0.6
25 to 29 years old	22,900	2,517	11.0	*	*	6	*	55	0.2
30 to 34 years old	22,054	1,319	6.0	*	*	18	0.1	11	0.1
35 to 44 years old	41,120	1,341	3.3	*	*	7	*	50	0.1
45 to 54 years old	40,309	820	2.0	*	*	24	0.1	63	0.2
55 years old and over	95,728	359	0.4	*	*	*	*	16	*
Male									
Total	152,910	37,773	24.7	4,521	3.0	16,776	11.0	8,409	5.5
3 and 4 years old	4,159	2,217	53.3	2,217	53.3	*	*	*	*
5 and 6 years old	4,090	3,860	94.4	2,266	55.4	1,594	39.0	*	*
7 to 9 years old	6,260	6,149	98.2	38	0.6	6,111	97.6	*	*
10 to 13 years old	8,479	8,290	97.8	*	*	8,200	96.7	90	1.1
14 and 15 years old	4,236	4,153	98.0	*	*	777	18.4	3,360	79.3
16 and 17 years old	4,263	3,948	92.6	*	*	28	0.6	3,833	89.9
18 and 19 years old	4,182	2,746	65.7	*	*	2	*	922	22.1
20 and 21 years old	4,407	2,208	50.1	*	*	13	0.3	72	1.6
22 to 24 years old	6,112	1,549	25.4	*	*	24	0.4	29	0.5
25 to 29 years old	11,465	1,159	10.1	*	*	6	0.1	19	0.2
30 to 34 years old	10,969	521	4.7	*	*	10	0.1	3	*
35 to 44 years old	20,227	501	2.5	*	*	3	*	28	0.1
45 to 54 years old	19,710	322	1.6	*	*	7	*	43	0.2
55 years old and over	44,353	150	0.3	*	*	*	*	10	*
Female									
Total	160,188	38,316	23.9	4,263	2.7	15,843	9.9	7,986	5.0
3 and 4 years old	3,916	2,116	54.0	2,116	54.0	*	*	*	*
5 and 6 years old	3,926	3,645	92.8	2,102	53.5	1,543	39.3	*	*
7 to 9 years old	5,972	5,781	96.8	45	0.8	5,736	96.0	*	*
10 to 13 years old	8,138	7,992	98.2	*	*	7,867	96.7	124	1.5
14 and 15 years old	4,078	3,988	97.8	*	*	632	15.5	3,336	81.8
16 and 17 years old	4,127	3,830	92.8	*	*	29	0.7	3,673	89.0
18 and 19 years old	4,124	2,839	68.9	*	*	2	*	657	15.9
20 and 21 years old	4,271	2,433	57.0	*	*	4	0.1	57	1.3
22 to 24 years old	6,248	1,987	31.8	*	*	2	*	46	0.7
25 to 29 years old	11,435	1,358	11.9	*	*	*	*	36	0.3
30 to 34 years old	11,085	798	7.2	*	*	7	0.1	9	0.1
35 to 44 years old	20,893	840	4.0	*	*	4	*	22	0.1
45 to 54 years old	20,599	498	2.4	*	*	17	0.1	20	0.1
55 years old and over	51,375	209	0.4	*	*	*	*	6	*
WHITE ALONE OR IN COMBINATION									
Both Sexes									
Total	246,868	57,879	23.4	6,744	2.7	25,033	10.1	12,727	5.2
3 and 4 years old	6,167	3,273	53.1	3,273	53.1	*	*	*	*
5 and 6 years old	6,202	5,831	94.0	3,405	54.9	2,426	39.1	*	*
7 to 9 years old	9,379	9,167	97.7	66	0.7	9,101	97.0	*	*
10 to 13 years old	12,766	12,497	97.9	*	*	12,374	96.9	122	1.0
14 and 15 years old	6,448	6,305	97.8	*	*	1,041	16.1	5,242	81.3
16 and 17 years old	6,497	6,037	92.9	*	*	33	0.5	5,860	90.2
18 and 19 years old	6,425	4,331	67.4	*	*	3	*	1,228	19.1
20 and 21 years old	6,646	3,520	53.0	*	*	8	0.1	76	1.1
22 to 24 years old	9,510	2,593	27.3	*	*	22	0.2	67	0.7
25 to 29 years old	17,165	1,685	9.8	*	*	*	*	27	0.2

* = Quantity equals zero or rounds to zero.

Table A-1. Enrollment Status of the Population 3 Years Old and Over, by Sex, Age, Race, Hispanic Origin, Foreign Born, and Foreign-Born Parentage, October 2019—*Continued*

(Numbers in thousands; percent; civilian noninstitutionalized population.)

Age, sex, race, Hispanic origin, and nativity	Enrolled in school — College undergraduate or graduate Number	Percent	Not enrolled in school — Total Number	Percent	High school graduate Number	Percent	Not high school graduate Number	Percent
ALL RACES								
Both Sexes								
Total	18,289	5.8	2,37,009	75.7	2,09,502	66.9	27,507	8.8
3 and 4 years old	*	*	3,741	46.3	*	*	3,741	46.3
5 and 6 years old	*	*	510	6.4	*	*	510	6.4
7 to 9 years old	*	*	302	2.5	*	*	302	2.5
10 to 13 years old	*	*	335	2.0	*	*	335	2.0
14 and 15 years old	36	0.4	173	2.1	3	*	170	2.0
16 and 17 years old	215	2.6	613	7.3	157	1.9	456	5.4
18 and 19 years old	4,004	48.2	2,720	32.7	2,238	26.9	481	5.8
20 and 21 years old	4,495	51.8	4,036	46.5	3,587	41.3	450	5.2
22 to 24 years old	3,436	27.8	8,823	71.4	8,240	66.7	583	4.7
25 to 29 years old	2,456	10.7	20,384	89.0	19,055	83.2	1,329	5.8
30 to 34 years old	1,290	5.8	20,735	94.0	19,144	86.8	1,591	7.2
35 to 44 years old	1,283	3.1	39,779	96.7	36,065	87.7	3,713	9.0
45 to 54 years old	732	1.8	39,489	98.0	35,819	88.9	3,670	9.1
55 years old and over	343	0.4	95,370	99.6	85,195	89.0	10,175	10.6
Male								
Total	8,067	5.3	115,137	75.3	101,234	66.2	13,903	9.1
3 and 4 years old	*	*	1,941	46.7	*	*	1,941	46.7
5 and 6 years old	*	*	229	5.6	*	*	229	5.6
7 to 9 years old	*	*	111	1.8	*	*	111	1.8
10 to 13 years old	*	*	189	2.2	*	*	189	2.2
14 and 15 years old	15	0.4	83	2.0	3	0.1	81	1.9
16 and 17 years old	87	2.0	316	7.4	98	2.3	218	5.1
18 and 19 years old	1,822	43.6	1,435	34.3	1,165	27.9	270	6.5
20 and 21 years old	2,123	48.2	2,199	49.9	1,945	44.1	254	5.8
22 to 24 years old	1,497	24.5	4,562	74.6	4,188	68.5	374	6.1
25 to 29 years old	1,133	9.9	10,306	89.9	9,545	83.3	761	6.6
30 to 34 years old	508	4.6	10,448	95.3	9,644	87.9	805	7.3
35 to 44 years old	469	2.3	19,726	97.5	17,678	87.4	2,048	10.1
45 to 54 years old	271	1.4	19,388	98.4	17,457	88.6	1,931	9.8
55 years old and over	140	0.3	44,203	99.7	39,511	89.1	4,692	10.6
Female								
Total	10,223	6.4	121,872	76.1	108,268	67.6	13,604	8.5
3 and 4 years old	*	*	1,799	46.0	*	*	1,799	46.0
5 and 6 years old	*	*	281	7.2	*	*	281	7.2
7 to 9 years old	*	*	191	3.2	*	*	191	3.2
10 to 13 years old	*	*	146	1.8	*	*	146	1.8
14 and 15 years old	20	0.5	90	2.2	*	*	90	2.2
16 and 17 years old	128	3.1	297	7.2	59	1.4	238	5.8
18 and 19 years old	2,181	52.9	1,285	31.1	1,073	26.0	211	5.1
20 and 21 years old	2,372	55.5	1,838	43.0	1,641	38.4	196	4.6
22 to 24 years old	1,939	31.0	4,261	68.2	4,052	64.8	209	3.3
25 to 29 years old	1,322	11.6	10,078	88.1	9,509	83.2	568	5.0
30 to 34 years old	782	7.1	10,287	92.8	9,500	85.7	787	7.1
35 to 44 years old	814	3.9	20,053	96.0	18,387	88.0	1,666	8.0
45 to 54 years old	461	2.2	20,101	97.6	18,362	89.1	1,739	8.4
55 years old and over	202	0.4	51,167	99.6	45,684	88.9	5,483	10.7
WHITE ALONE OR IN COMBINATION								
Both Sexes								
Total	13,375	5.4	188,989	76.6	167,590	67.9	21,399	8.7
3 and 4 years old	*	*	2,894	46.9	*	*	2,894	46.9
5 and 6 years old	*	*	370	6.0	*	*	370	6.0
7 to 9 years old	*	*	212	2.3	*	*	212	2.3
10 to 13 years old	*	*	270	2.1	*	*	270	2.1
14 and 15 years old	22	0.3	142	2.2	3	*	140	2.2
16 and 17 years old	145	2.2	460	7.1	118	1.8	342	5.3
18 and 19 years old	3,100	48.3	2,094	32.6	1,732	26.9	363	5.6
20 and 21 years old	3,436	51.7	3,126	47.0	2,798	42.1	327	4.9
22 to 24 years old	2,504	26.3	6,917	72.7	6,463	68.0	454	4.8
25 to 29 years old	1,657	9.7	15,480	90.2	14,436	84.1	1,044	6.1

* = Quantity equals zero or rounds to zero.

Table A-1. Enrollment Status of the Population 3 Years Old and Over, by Sex, Age, Race, Hispanic Origin, Foreign Born, and Foreign-Born Parentage, October 2019—*Continued*

(Numbers in thousands; percent; civilian noninstitutionalized population.)

| | | Enrolled in school | | | | | | | |
| | Population | Total | | Nursery or kindergarten | | Elementary | | High school | |
Age, sex, race, Hispanic origin, and nativity	Number	Number	Percent	Number	Percent	Number	Percent	Number	Percent
30 to 34 years old	16,698	881	5.3	*	*	14	0.1	9	0.1
35 to 44 years old	31,617	945	3.0	*	*	*	*	44	0.1
45 to 54 years old	31,717	577	1.8	*	*	11	*	44	0.1
55 years old and over	79,632	237	0.3	*	*	*	*	8	*
Male									
Total	121,592	28,760	23.7	3,423	2.8	12,899	10.6	6,535	5.4
3 and 4 years old	3,147	1,648	52.4	1,648	52.4	*	*	*	*
5 and 6 years old	3,194	3,029	94.8	1,750	54.8	1,278	40.0	*	*
7 to 9 years old	4,770	4,690	98.3	24	0.5	4,666	97.8	*	*
10 to 13 years old	6,514	6,355	97.6	*	*	6,303	96.8	51	0.8
14 and 15 years old	3,287	3,212	97.7	*	*	596	18.1	2,608	79.3
16 and 17 years old	3,310	3,078	93.0	*	*	16	0.5	3,014	91.1
18 and 19 years old	3,240	2,114	65.3	*	*	2	*	724	22.3
20 and 21 years old	3,421	1,686	49.3	*	*	4	0.1	41	1.2
22 to 24 years old	4,698	1,133	24.1	*	*	20	0.4	27	0.6
25 to 29 years old	8,660	771	8.9	*	*	*	*	18	0.2
30 to 34 years old	8,438	368	4.4	*	*	10	0.1	*	*
35 to 44 years old	15,807	360	2.3	*	*	*	*	22	0.1
45 to 54 years old	15,782	225	1.4	*	*	4	*	28	0.2
55 years old and over	37,324	91	0.2	*	*	*	*	2	*
Female									
Total	125,276	29,119	23.2	3,321	2.7	12,134	9.7	6,192	4.9
3 and 4 years old	3,020	1,625	53.8	1,625	53.8	*	*	*	*
5 and 6 years old	3,007	2,803	93.2	1,655	55.0	1,147	38.2	*	*
7 to 9 years old	4,609	4,477	97.1	41	0.9	4,435	96.2	*	*
10 to 13 years old	6,252	6,142	98.2	*	*	6,071	97.1	71	1.1
14 and 15 years old	3,161	3,094	97.9	*	*	445	14.1	2,634	83.3
16 and 17 years old	3,187	2,959	92.8	*	*	16	0.5	2,846	89.3
18 and 19 years old	3,185	2,217	69.6	*	*	2	*	504	15.8
20 and 21 years old	3,225	1,834	56.9	*	*	4	0.1	35	1.1
22 to 24 years old	4,812	1,460	30.3	*	*	2	0.1	40	0.8
25 to 29 years old	8,504	914	10.7	*	*	*	*	10	0.1
30 to 34 years old	8,260	513	6.2	*	*	4	*	9	0.1
35 to 44 years old	15,810	585	3.7	*	*	*	*	22	0.1
45 to 54 years old	15,935	352	2.2	*	*	7	*	16	0.1
55 years old and over	42,308	146	0.3	*	*	*	*	6	*
BLACK ALONE OR IN COMBINATION									
Both Sexes									
Total	45,274	13,679	30.2	1,671	3.7	6,015	13.3	2,852	6.3
3 and 4 years old	1,586	899	56.7	899	56.7	*	*	*	*
5 and 6 years old	1,460	1,366	93.5	755	51.7	610	41.8	*	*
7 to 9 years old	2,316	2,240	96.7	17	0.7	2,223	96.0	*	*
10 to 13 years old	2,965	2,902	97.9	*	*	2,846	96.0	55	1.9
14 and 15 years old	1,457	1,429	98.1	*	*	306	21.0	1,113	76.4
16 and 17 years old	1,464	1,348	92.0	*	*	8	0.5	1,306	89.2
18 and 19 years old	1,373	846	61.6	*	*	*	*	255	18.5
20 and 21 years old	1,476	704	47.7	*	*	6	0.4	62	4.2
22 to 24 years old	2,027	575	28.3	*	*	4	0.2	7	0.3
25 to 29 years old	3,853	531	13.8	*	*	*	*	25	0.7
30 to 34 years old	3,371	268	7.9	*	*	3	0.1	3	0.1
35 to 44 years old	5,829	279	4.8	*	*	4	0.1	5	0.1
45 to 54 years old	5,480	195	3.6	*	*	4	0.1	16	0.3
55 years old and over	10,615	100	0.9	*	*	*	*	4	*
Male									
Total	21,284	6,726	31.6	895	4.2	3,048	14.3	1,474	6.9
3 and 4 years old	823	472	57.3	472	57.3	*	*	*	*
5 and 6 years old	747	700	93.7	410	54.8	291	38.9	*	*
7 to 9 years old	1,177	1,156	98.2	13	1.1	1,142	97.1	*	*
10 to 13 years old	1,508	1,479	98.1	*	*	1,452	96.3	28	1.8
14 and 15 years old	740	732	98.9	*	*	151	20.3	574	77.6
16 and 17 years old	748	683	91.3	*	*	3	0.4	663	88.7
18 and 19 years old	677	417	61.6	*	*	*	*	150	22.1

* = Quantity equals zero or rounds to zero.

Table A-1. Enrollment Status of the Population 3 Years Old and Over, by Sex, Age, Race, Hispanic Origin, Foreign Born, and Foreign-Born Parentage, October 2019—*Continued*

(Numbers in thousands; percent; civilian noninstitutionalized population.)

Age, sex, race, Hispanic origin, and nativity	Enrolled in school		Not enrolled in school					
	College undergraduate or graduate		Total		High school graduate		Not high school graduate	
	Number	Percent	Number	Percent	Number	Percent	Number	Percent
30 to 34 years old	858	5.1	15,817	94.7	14,532	87.0	1,284	7.7
35 to 44 years old	901	2.8	30,672	97.0	27,666	87.5	3,007	9.5
45 to 54 years old	522	1.6	31,140	98.2	28,150	88.8	2,990	9.4
55 years old and over	229	0.3	79,395	99.7	71,692	90.0	7,703	9.7
Male								
Total	5,903	4.9	92,832	76.3	81,729	67.2	11,103	9.1
3 and 4 years old	*	*	1,499	47.6	*	*	1,499	47.6
5 and 6 years old	*	*	166	5.2	*	*	166	5.2
7 to 9 years old	*	*	80	1.7	*	*	80	1.7
10 to 13 years old	*	*	159	2.4	*	*	159	2.4
14 and 15 years old	8	0.2	75	2.3	3	0.1	73	2.2
16 and 17 years old	48	1.5	231	7.0	73	2.2	158	4.8
18 and 19 years old	1,389	42.9	1,126	34.7	908	28.0	218	6.7
20 and 21 years old	1,641	48.0	1,734	50.7	1,546	45.2	188	5.5
22 to 24 years old	1,086	23.1	3,564	75.9	3,276	69.7	288	6.1
25 to 29 years old	753	8.7	7,889	91.1	7,262	83.8	628	7.3
30 to 34 years old	358	4.2	8,070	95.6	7,376	87.4	693	8.2
35 to 44 years old	337	2.1	15,448	97.7	13,747	87.0	1,701	10.8
45 to 54 years old	194	1.2	15,557	98.6	13,975	88.6	1,582	10.0
55 years old and over	89	0.2	37,233	99.8	33,563	89.9	3,670	9.8
Female								
Total	7,471	6.0	96,157	76.8	85,861	68.5	10,296	8.2
3 and 4 years old	*	*	1,395	46.2	*	*	1,395	46.2
5 and 6 years old	*	*	205	6.8	*	*	205	6.8
7 to 9 years old	*	*	132	2.9	*	*	132	2.9
10 to 13 years old	*	*	110	1.8	*	*	110	1.8
14 and 15 years old	14	0.4	67	2.1	*	*	67	2.1
16 and 17 years old	96	3.0	229	7.2	45	1.4	184	5.8
18 and 19 years old	1,712	53.7	969	30.4	824	25.9	145	4.5
20 and 21 years old	1,795	55.7	1,391	43.1	1,252	38.8	139	4.3
22 to 24 years old	1,418	29.5	3,353	69.7	3,186	66.2	166	3.5
25 to 29 years old	904	10.6	7,590	89.3	7,175	84.4	416	4.9
30 to 34 years old	500	6.1	7,747	93.8	7,156	86.6	591	7.2
35 to 44 years old	563	3.6	15,224	96.3	13,919	88.0	1,306	8.3
45 to 54 years old	329	2.1	15,583	97.8	14,176	89.0	1,408	8.8
55 years old and over	140	0.3	42,161	99.7	38,129	90.1	4,033	9.5
BLACK ALONE OR IN COMBINATION								
Both Sexes								
Total	3,142	6.9	31,595	69.8	27,455	60.6	4,140	9.1
3 and 4 years old	*	*	687	43.3	*	*	687	43.3
5 and 6 years old	*	*	94	6.5	*	*	94	6.5
7 to 9 years old	*	*	76	3.3	*	*	76	3.3
10 to 13 years old	*	*	64	2.1	*	*	64	2.1
14 and 15 years old	10	0.7	28	1.9	*	*	28	1.9
16 and 17 years old	34	2.3	117	8.0	27	1.9	89	6.1
18 and 19 years old	591	43.0	528	38.4	444	32.4	84	6.1
20 and 21 years old	636	43.1	772	52.3	687	46.6	85	5.7
22 to 24 years old	564	27.8	1,453	71.7	1,334	65.8	119	5.9
25 to 29 years old	506	13.1	3,322	86.2	3,105	80.6	217	5.6
30 to 34 years old	261	7.8	3,103	92.1	2,916	86.5	187	5.6
35 to 44 years old	269	4.6	5,550	95.2	5,134	88.1	416	7.1
45 to 54 years old	175	3.2	5,285	96.4	4,826	88.0	460	8.4
55 years old and over	96	0.9	10,515	99.1	8,981	84.6	1,535	14.5
Male								
Total	1,309	6.2	14,558	68.4	12,607	59.2	1,952	9.2
3 and 4 years old	*	*	351	42.7	*	*	351	42.7
5 and 6 years old	*	*	47	6.3	*	*	47	6.3
7 to 9 years old	*	*	21	1.8	*	*	21	1.8
10 to 13 years old	*	*	29	1.9	*	*	29	1.9
14 and 15 years old	7	1.0	8	1.1	*	*	8	1.1
16 and 17 years old	17	2.2	65	8.7	16	2.2	49	6.5
18 and 19 years old	267	39.4	260	38.4	218	32.2	42	6.2

* = Quantity equals zero or rounds to zero.

Table A-1. Enrollment Status of the Population 3 Years Old and Over, by Sex, Age, Race, Hispanic Origin, Foreign Born, and Foreign-Born Parentage, October 2019—*Continued*

(Numbers in thousands; percent; civilian noninstitutionalized population.)

Age, sex, race, Hispanic origin, and nativity	Population Number	Enrolled in school							
		Total		Nursery or kindergarten		Elementary		High school	
		Number	Percent	Number	Percent	Number	Percent	Number	Percent
20 and 21 years old	723	351	48.5	*	*	6	0.9	35	4.8
22 to 24 years old	975	223	22.9	*	*	4	0.4	*	*
25 to 29 years old	1,842	224	12.1	*	*	*	*	*	*
30 to 34 years old	1,598	90	5.6	*	*	*	*	3	0.2
35 to 44 years old	2,652	89	3.4	*	*	*	*	5	0.2
45 to 54 years old	2,516	60	2.4	*	*	*	*	12	0.5
55 years old and over	4,558	51	1.1	*	*	*	*	4	0.1
Female									
Total	23,990	6,954	29.0	777	3.2	2,967	12.4	1,378	5.7
3 and 4 years old	763	427	56.0	427	56.0	*	*	*	*
5 and 6 years old	712	665	93.4	346	48.5	320	44.9	*	*
7 to 9 years old	1,139	1,085	95.2	4	0.3	1,081	94.9	*	*
10 to 13 years old	1,457	1,422	97.6	*	*	1,395	95.7	28	1.9
14 and 15 years old	717	697	97.2	*	*	156	21.7	539	75.1
16 and 17 years old	716	665	92.8	*	*	5	0.6	643	89.8
18 and 19 years old	696	429	61.6	*	*	*	*	105	15.0
20 and 21 years old	753	354	47.0	*	*	*	*	28	3.7
22 to 24 years old	1,053	351	33.4	*	*	*	*	7	0.6
25 to 29 years old	2,011	308	15.3	*	*	*	*	25	1.3
30 to 34 years old	1,773	178	10.0	*	*	3	0.2	*	*
35 to 44 years old	3,177	190	6.0	*	*	4	0.1	*	*
45 to 54 years old	2,964	135	4.6	*	*	4	0.1	4	0.1
55 years old and over	6,057	49	0.8	*	*	*	*	*	*
ASIAN ALONE OR IN COMBINATION									
Both Sexes									
Total	21,336	6,094	28.6	663	3.1	2,253	10.6	1,178	5.5
3 and 4 years old	569	329	57.8	329	57.8	*	*	*	*
5 and 6 years old	611	569	93.0	334	54.7	235	38.4	*	*
7 to 9 years old	836	825	98.6	*	*	825	98.6	*	*
10 to 13 years old	1,164	1,151	98.9	*	*	1,111	95.5	40	3.4
14 and 15 years old	557	555	99.6	*	*	53	9.4	499	89.5
16 and 17 years old	625	591	94.6	*	*	20	3.2	528	84.5
18 and 19 years old	546	470	86.2	*	*	*	*	102	18.7
20 and 21 years old	669	526	78.6	*	*	*	*	1	0.2
22 to 24 years old	923	419	45.4	*	*	*	*	*	*
25 to 29 years old	1,906	326	17.1	*	*	*	*	*	*
30 to 34 years old	1,841	181	9.8	*	*	*	*	*	*
35 to 44 years old	3,350	89	2.7	*	*	3	0.1	1	*
45 to 54 years old	2,843	47	1.6	*	*	7	0.2	3	0.1
55 years old and over	4,896	15	0.3	*	*	*	*	4	0.1
Male									
Total	10,159	3,052	30.0	352	3.5	1,163	11.4	560	5.5
3 and 4 years old	313	184	58.7	184	58.7	*	*	*	*
5 and 6 years old	290	279	96.3	168	57.9	111	38.3	*	*
7 to 9 years old	446	439	98.4	*	*	439	98.4	*	*
10 to 13 years old	584	582	99.6	*	*	573	98.2	9	1.5
14 and 15 years old	271	271	100.0	*	*	25	9.1	247	90.9
16 and 17 years old	283	272	96.1	*	*	8	2.9	241	85.3
18 and 19 years old	255	226	88.8	*	*	*	*	54	21.3
20 and 21 years old	322	257	79.9	*	*	*	*	1	0.5
22 to 24 years old	463	210	45.4	*	*	*	*	*	*
25 to 29 years old	970	174	17.9	*	*	*	*	*	*
30 to 34 years old	900	81	9.0	*	*	*	*	*	*
35 to 44 years old	1,575	33	2.1	*	*	3	0.2	1	*
45 to 54 years old	1,326	37	2.8	*	*	4	0.3	3	0.2
55 years old and over	2,161	7	0.3	*	*	*	*	4	0.2
Female									
Total	11,177	3,042	27.2	312	2.8	1,090	9.8	618	5.5
3 and 4 years old	257	145	56.7	145	56.7	*	*	*	*
5 and 6 years old	321	290	90.2	166	51.8	123	38.4	*	*
7 to 9 years old	390	386	98.9	*	*	386	98.9	*	*
10 to 13 years old	580	570	98.2	*	*	538	92.8	31	5.4

* = Quantity equals zero or rounds to zero.

Table A-1. Enrollment Status of the Population 3 Years Old and Over, by Sex, Age, Race, Hispanic Origin, Foreign Born, and Foreign-Born Parentage, October 2019—*Continued*

(Numbers in thousands; percent; civilian noninstitutionalized population.)

Age, sex, race, Hispanic origin, and nativity	Enrolled in school		Not enrolled in school					
	College undergraduate or graduate		Total		High school graduate		Not high school graduate	
	Number	Percent	Number	Percent	Number	Percent	Number	Percent
20 and 21 years old	310	42.8	373	51.5	328	45.3	45	6.2
22 to 24 years old	220	22.5	751	77.1	669	68.7	82	8.4
25 to 29 years old	224	12.1	1,618	87.9	1,504	81.6	114	6.2
30 to 34 years old	87	5.4	1,508	94.4	1,454	91.0	54	3.4
35 to 44 years old	84	3.2	2,563	96.6	2,373	89.5	189	7.1
45 to 54 years old	47	1.9	2,456	97.6	2,185	86.9	271	10.8
55 years old and over	47	1.0	4,507	98.9	3,858	84.6	649	14.2
Female								
Total	1,833	7.6	17,037	71.0	14,848	61.9	2,189	9.1
3 and 4 years old	*	*	336	44.0	*	*	336	44.0
5 and 6 years old	*	*	47	6.6	*	*	47	6.6
7 to 9 years old	*	*	55	4.8	*	*	55	4.8
10 to 13 years old	*	*	35	2.4	*	*	35	2.4
14 and 15 years old	3	0.4	20	2.8	*	*	20	2.8
16 and 17 years old	17	2.4	51	7.2	11	1.5	40	5.6
18 and 19 years old	324	46.5	268	38.4	226	32.5	42	6.0
20 and 21 years old	326	43.3	399	53.0	359	47.7	40	5.3
22 to 24 years old	345	32.7	701	66.6	665	63.1	37	3.5
25 to 29 years old	282	14.0	1,703	84.7	1,601	79.6	102	5.1
30 to 34 years old	174	9.8	1,595	90.0	1,462	82.5	133	7.5
35 to 44 years old	186	5.8	2,988	94.0	2,761	86.9	227	7.1
45 to 54 years old	127	4.3	2,829	95.4	2,640	89.1	189	6.4
55 years old and over	49	0.8	6,009	99.2	5,123	84.6	886	14.6
ASIAN ALONE OR IN COMBINATION								
Both Sexes								
Total	1,999	9.4	15,242	71.4	13,558	63.5	1,685	7.9
3 and 4 years old	*	*	240	42.2	*	*	240	42.2
5 and 6 years old	*	*	43	7.0	*	*	43	7.0
7 to 9 years old	*	*	11	1.4	*	*	11	1.4
10 to 13 years old	*	*	12	1.1	*	*	12	1.1
14 and 15 years old	4	0.7	2	0.4	*	*	2	0.4
16 and 17 years old	43	6.9	34	5.4	11	1.8	23	3.6
18 and 19 years old	368	67.5	75	13.8	53	9.7	22	4.1
20 and 21 years old	525	78.4	143	21.4	129	19.3	14	2.1
22 to 24 years old	419	45.4	504	54.6	499	54.1	5	0.5
25 to 29 years old	326	17.1	1,579	82.9	1,508	79.1	71	3.7
30 to 34 years old	181	9.8	1,660	90.2	1,573	85.4	87	4.7
35 to 44 years old	85	2.5	3,261	97.3	3,043	90.8	218	6.5
45 to 54 years old	37	1.3	2,796	98.4	2,612	91.9	184	6.5
55 years old and over	11	0.2	4,881	99.7	4,128	84.3	753	15.4
Male								
Total	977	9.6	7,107	70.0	6,426	63.3	681	6.7
3 and 4 years old	*	*	129	41.3	*	*	129	41.3
5 and 6 years old	*	*	11	3.7	*	*	11	3.7
7 to 9 years old	*	*	7	1.6	*	*	7	1.6
10 to 13 years old	*	*	2	0.4	*	*	2	0.4
14 and 15 years old	*	*	*	*	*	*	*	*
16 and 17 years old	22	7.9	11	3.9	7	2.5	4	1.4
18 and 19 years old	172	67.5	29	11.2	21	8.3	7	2.9
20 and 21 years old	256	79.4	65	20.1	55	17.2	10	3.0
22 to 24 years old	210	45.4	252	54.6	250	54.0	3	0.6
25 to 29 years old	174	17.9	797	82.1	771	79.5	26	2.7
30 to 34 years old	81	9.0	819	91.0	781	86.7	39	4.3
35 to 44 years old	29	1.9	1,542	97.9	1,446	91.8	96	6.1
45 to 54 years old	30	2.3	1,289	97.2	1,205	90.9	84	6.3
55 years old and over	3	0.2	2,154	99.7	1,890	87.4	265	12.2
Female								
Total	1,022	9.1	8,135	72.8	7,132	63.8	1,004	9.0
3 and 4 years old	*	*	111	43.3	*	*	111	43.3
5 and 6 years old	*	*	32	9.8	*	*	32	9.8
7 to 9 years old	*	*	4	1.1	*	*	4	1.1
10 to 13 years old	*	*	10	1.8	*	*	10	1.8

* = Quantity equals zero or rounds to zero.

Table A-1. Enrollment Status of the Population 3 Years Old and Over, by Sex, Age, Race, Hispanic Origin, Foreign Born, and Foreign-Born Parentage, October 2019—*Continued*

(Numbers in thousands; percent; civilian noninstitutionalized population.)

		Enrolled in school							
	Population	Total		Nursery or kindergarten		Elementary		High school	
Age, sex, race, Hispanic origin, and nativity	Number	Number	Percent	Number	Percent	Number	Percent	Number	Percent
14 and 15 years old	286	283	99.2	*	*	28	9.7	252	88.1
16 and 17 years old	342	319	93.3	*	*	12	3.4	287	83.8
18 and 19 years old	291	244	83.9	*	*	*	*	48	16.4
20 and 21 years old	347	269	77.4	*	*	*	*	*	*
22 to 24 years old	460	209	45.4	*	*	*	*	*	*
25 to 29 years old	935	153	16.3	*	*	*	*	*	*
30 to 34 years old	940	100	10.6	*	*	*	*	*	*
35 to 44 years old	1,775	56	3.2	*	*	*	*	*	*
45 to 54 years old	1,517	10	0.6	*	*	3	0.2	*	*
55 years old and over	2,735	8	0.3	*	*	*	*	*	*
HISPANIC (OF ANY RACE)									
Both Sexes									
Total	57,582	18,204	31.6	2,153	3.7	8,396	14.6	4,101	7.1
3 and 4 years old	2,100	1,046	49.8	1,046	49.8	*	*	*	*
5 and 6 years old	2,047	1,909	93.3	1,089	53.2	820	40.1	*	*
7 to 9 years old	3,240	3,136	96.8	18	0.6	3,118	96.2	*	*
10 to 13 years old	4,266	4,159	97.5	*	*	4,101	96.1	58	1.4
14 and 15 years old	2,106	2,052	97.4	*	*	315	14.9	1,733	82.3
16 and 17 years old	1,987	1,802	90.7	*	*	13	0.7	1,753	88.2
18 and 19 years old	2,032	1,294	63.7	*	*	*	*	422	20.8
20 and 21 years old	1,896	912	48.1	*	*	*	*	46	2.4
22 to 24 years old	2,883	765	26.5	*	*	2	0.1	33	1.1
25 to 29 years old	4,864	498	10.2	*	*	6	0.1	7	0.1
30 to 34 years old	4,537	243	5.4	*	*	11	0.2	4	0.1
35 to 44 years old	8,622	243	2.8	*	*	*	*	27	0.3
45 to 54 years old	7,159	112	1.6	*	*	9	0.1	17	0.2
55 years old and over	9,843	33	0.3	*	*	*	*	3	*
Male									
Total	28,839	9,087	31.5	1,094	3.8	4,332	15.0	2,102	7.3
3 and 4 years old	1,082	560	51.8	560	51.8	*	*	*	*
5 and 6 years old	1,042	974	93.5	531	51.0	443	42.5	*	*
7 to 9 years old	1,653	1,627	98.4	2	0.1	1,624	98.3	*	*
10 to 13 years old	2,164	2,092	96.6	*	*	2,069	95.6	22	1.0
14 and 15 years old	1,083	1,049	96.9	*	*	169	15.6	879	81.2
16 and 17 years old	1,019	925	90.7	*	*	10	0.9	906	88.9
18 and 19 years old	1,014	644	63.5	*	*	*	*	235	23.2
20 and 21 years old	973	436	44.8	*	*	*	*	28	2.9
22 to 24 years old	1,437	314	21.8	*	*	*	*	4	0.3
25 to 29 years old	2,484	222	8.9	*	*	6	0.3	4	0.2
30 to 34 years old	2,352	81	3.4	*	*	7	0.3	*	*
35 to 44 years old	4,398	112	2.6	*	*	*	*	10	0.2
45 to 54 years old	3,583	52	1.5	*	*	4	0.1	13	0.4
55 years old and over	4,556	*	*	*	*	*	*	*	*
Female									
Total	28,744	9,117	31.7	1,059	3.7	4,063	14.1	1,999	7.0
3 and 4 years old	1,019	485	47.6	485	47.6	*	*	*	*
5 and 6 years old	1,005	935	93.1	558	55.5	378	37.6	*	*
7 to 9 years old	1,587	1,509	95.1	16	1.0	1,493	94.1	*	*
10 to 13 years old	2,102	2,067	98.3	*	*	2,032	96.7	35	1.7
14 and 15 years old	1,024	1,002	97.9	*	*	146	14.2	854	83.4
16 and 17 years old	968	878	90.7	*	*	4	0.4	848	87.6
18 and 19 years old	1,018	650	63.9	*	*	*	*	187	18.4
20 and 21 years old	922	476	51.6	*	*	*	*	17	1.9
22 to 24 years old	1,446	451	31.2	*	*	2	0.2	29	2.0
25 to 29 years old	2,380	276	11.6	*	*	*	*	2	0.1
30 to 34 years old	2,185	163	7.4	*	*	4	0.2	4	0.2
35 to 44 years old	4,224	130	3.1	*	*	*	*	17	0.4
45 to 54 years old	3,576	60	1.7	*	*	5	0.1	3	0.1
55 years old and over	5,288	33	0.6	*	*	*	*	3	0.1

* = Quantity equals zero or rounds to zero.

Table A-1. Enrollment Status of the Population 3 Years Old and Over, by Sex, Age, Race, Hispanic Origin, Foreign Born, and Foreign-Born Parentage, October 2019—*Continued*

(Numbers in thousands; percent; civilian noninstitutionalized population.)

Age, sex, race, Hispanic origin, and nativity	Enrolled in school		Not enrolled in school					
	College undergraduate or graduate		Total		High school graduate		Not high school graduate	
	Number	Percent	Number	Percent	Number	Percent	Number	Percent
14 and 15 years old	4	1.3	2	0.8	*	*	2	0.8
16 and 17 years old	21	6.0	23	6.7	4	1.2	19	5.5
18 and 19 years old	196	67.5	47	16.1	32	10.9	15	5.2
20 and 21 years old	269	77.4	78	22.6	74	21.3	5	1.3
22 to 24 years old	209	45.4	251	54.6	249	54.2	2	0.4
25 to 29 years old	153	16.3	783	83.7	737	78.8	45	4.9
30 to 34 years old	100	10.6	840	89.4	792	84.2	48	5.1
35 to 44 years old	56	3.2	1,719	96.8	1,597	90.0	122	6.9
45 to 54 years old	7	0.4	1,507	99.4	1,407	92.8	100	6.6
55 years old and over	8	0.3	2,727	99.7	2,239	81.9	488	17.8
HISPANIC (OF ANY RACE)								
Both Sexes								
Total	3,555	6.2	39,378	68.4	28,104	48.8	11,274	19.6
3 and 4 years old	*	*	1,055	50.2	*	*	1,055	50.2
5 and 6 years old	*	*	138	6.7	*	*	138	6.7
7 to 9 years old	*	*	104	3.2	*	*	104	3.2
10 to 13 years old	*	*	107	2.5	*	*	107	2.5
14 and 15 years old	4	0.2	55	2.6	3	0.1	52	2.5
16 and 17 years old	36	1.8	185	9.3	37	1.9	148	7.4
18 and 19 years old	872	42.9	738	36.3	568	27.9	170	8.4
20 and 21 years old	867	45.7	983	51.9	849	44.8	134	7.1
22 to 24 years old	730	25.3	2,118	73.5	1,913	66.4	205	7.1
25 to 29 years old	485	10.0	4,366	89.8	3,741	76.9	625	12.9
30 to 34 years old	229	5.0	4,294	94.6	3,419	75.4	875	19.3
35 to 44 years old	216	2.5	8,379	97.2	6,149	71.3	2,230	25.9
45 to 54 years old	86	1.2	7,047	98.4	5,049	70.5	1,998	27.9
55 years old and over	30	0.3	9,810	99.7	6,376	64.8	3,434	34.9
Male								
Total	1,559	5.4	19,751	68.5	13,947	48.4	5,804	20.1
3 and 4 years old	*	*	521	48.2	*	*	521	48.2
5 and 6 years old	*	*	68	6.5	*	*	68	6.5
7 to 9 years old	*	*	26	1.6	*	*	26	1.6
10 to 13 years old	*	*	73	3.4	*	*	73	3.4
14 and 15 years old	1	0.1	33	3.1	3	0.2	31	2.8
16 and 17 years old	9	0.9	95	9.3	26	2.6	68	6.7
18 and 19 years old	409	40.4	370	36.5	268	26.5	102	10.0
20 and 21 years old	408	41.9	537	55.2	476	48.9	61	6.3
22 to 24 years old	310	21.6	1,123	78.2	1,007	70.1	116	8.1
25 to 29 years old	211	8.5	2,262	91.1	1,875	75.5	387	15.6
30 to 34 years old	73	3.1	2,272	96.6	1,801	76.6	470	20.0
35 to 44 years old	102	2.3	4,285	97.4	3,021	68.7	1,264	28.7
45 to 54 years old	35	1.0	3,531	98.5	2,512	70.1	1,019	28.4
55 years old and over	*	*	4,556	100.0	2,958	64.9	1,598	35.1
Female								
Total	1,996	6.9	19,627	68.3	14,157	49.3	5,470	19.0
3 and 4 years old	*	*	533	52.4	*	*	533	52.4
5 and 6 years old	*	*	70	6.9	*	*	70	6.9
7 to 9 years old	*	*	78	4.9	*	*	78	4.9
10 to 13 years old	*	*	35	1.7	*	*	35	1.7
14 and 15 years old	3	0.3	21	2.1	*	*	21	2.1
16 and 17 years old	26	2.7	90	9.3	11	1.1	79	8.2
18 and 19 years old	463	45.5	368	36.1	299	29.4	69	6.7
20 and 21 years old	459	49.7	446	48.4	373	40.4	73	7.9
22 to 24 years old	420	29.1	995	68.8	906	62.7	89	6.1
25 to 29 years old	274	11.5	2,104	88.4	1,866	78.4	238	10.0
30 to 34 years old	155	7.1	2,022	92.6	1,618	74.0	405	18.5
35 to 44 years old	114	2.7	4,094	96.9	3,127	74.0	966	22.9
45 to 54 years old	52	1.4	3,516	98.3	2,538	71.0	979	27.4
55 years old and over	30	0.6	5,255	99.4	3,419	64.7	1,836	34.7

* = Quantity equals zero or rounds to zero.

Table A-1. Enrollment Status of the Population 3 Years Old and Over, by Sex, Age, Race, Hispanic Origin, Foreign Born, and Foreign-Born Parentage, October 2019—*Continued*

(Numbers in thousands; percent; civilian noninstitutionalized population.)

Age, sex, race, Hispanic origin, and nativity	Population	Enrolled in school								
		Total		Nursery or kindergarten		Elementary		High school	
	Number	Number	Percent	Number	Percent	Number	Percent	Number	Percent
FOREIGN–BORN									
Both Sexes									
Total	44,408	4,920	11.1	245	0.6	1,381	3.1	1,004	2.3
3 and 4 years old	211	109	51.9	109	51.9	*	*	*	*
5 and 6 years old	280	265	94.8	132	47.2	133	47.6	*	*
7 to 9 years old	492	475	96.6	3	0.7	472	96.0	*	*
10 to 13 years old	697	675	96.8	*	*	665	95.5	10	1.4
14 and 15 years old	456	438	96.2	*	*	79	17.3	356	78.1
16 and 17 years old	471	410	87.2	*	*	*	*	384	81.6
18 and 19 years old	592	449	75.9	*	*	*	*	171	28.9
20 and 21 years old	823	453	55.0	*	*	3	0.3	32	3.9
22 to 24 years old	1,379	394	28.6	*	*	*	*	14	1.0
25 to 29 years old	3,409	430	12.6	*	*	*	*	5	0.1
30 to 34 years old	4,131	281	6.8	*	*	11	0.3	1	*
35 to 44 years old	9,034	286	3.2	*	*	3	*	18	0.2
45 to 54 years old	8,742	174	2.0	*	*	14	0.2	7	0.1
55 years old and over	13,694	81	0.6	*	*	*	*	7	0.1
Male									
Total	21,477	2,472	11.5	140	0.7	677	3.2	538	2.5
3 and 4 years old	110	63	56.9	63	56.9	*	*	*	*
5 and 6 years old	152	148	97.4	75	49.7	72	47.7	*	*
7 to 9 years old	242	238	98.1	2	0.9	236	97.2	*	*
10 to 13 years old	344	338	98.1	*	*	332	96.6	5	1.5
14 and 15 years old	249	239	96.1	*	*	19	7.7	219	88.1
16 and 17 years old	252	217	86.1	*	*	*	*	192	76.3
18 and 19 years old	298	227	76.2	*	*	*	*	79	26.7
20 and 21 years old	432	213	49.4	*	*	3	0.7	15	3.6
22 to 24 years old	743	200	26.9	*	*	*	*	*	*
25 to 29 years old	1,653	234	14.1	*	*	*	*	4	0.3
30 to 34 years old	2,151	130	6.0	*	*	7	0.3	1	*
35 to 44 years old	4,485	113	2.5	*	*	3	0.1	11	0.2
45 to 54 years old	4,220	88	2.1	*	*	4	0.1	7	0.2
55 years old and over	6,146	24	0.4	*	*	*	*	4	0.1
Female									
Total	22,931	2,449	10.7	104	0.5	704	3.1	465	2.0
3 and 4 years old	101	47	46.5	47	46.5	*	*	*	*
5 and 6 years old	128	117	91.7	56	44.2	61	47.5	*	*
7 to 9 years old	249	237	95.2	1	0.4	236	94.7	*	*
10 to 13 years old	352	337	95.6	*	*	333	94.4	4	1.2
14 and 15 years old	207	199	96.4	*	*	60	28.8	136	66.0
16 and 17 years old	219	194	88.4	*	*	*	*	192	87.6
18 and 19 years old	295	222	75.5	*	*	*	*	92	31.2
20 and 21 years old	391	240	61.3	*	*	*	*	17	4.2
22 to 24 years old	636	194	30.5	*	*	*	*	14	2.1
25 to 29 years old	1,756	196	11.2	*	*	*	*	*	*
30 to 34 years old	1,981	151	7.6	*	*	4	0.2	*	*
35 to 44 years old	4,549	173	3.8	*	*	*	*	7	0.2
45 to 54 years old	4,521	86	1.9	*	*	11	0.2	*	*
55 years old and over	7,547	56	0.7	*	*	*	*	3	*
CHILDREN OF FOREIGN–BORN PARENTS									
Both Sexes									
Total	81,167	20,997	25.9	2,218	2.7	8,494	10.5	4,610	5.7
3 and 4 years old	2,027	1,129	55.7	1,129	55.7	*	*	*	*
5 and 6 years old	2,080	1,933	92.9	1,074	51.6	859	41.3	*	*
7 to 9 years old	3,134	3,061	97.7	15	0.5	3,046	97.2	*	*
10 to 13 years old	4,358	4,275	98.1	*	*	4,205	96.5	70	1.6
14 and 15 years old	2,321	2,264	97.6	*	*	305	13.1	1,956	84.3
16 and 17 years old	2,274	2,096	92.1	*	*	23	1.0	1,988	87.4
18 and 19 years old	2,310	1,665	72.1	*	*	*	*	446	19.3
20 and 21 years old	2,369	1,384	58.4	*	*	9	0.4	56	2.4
22 to 24 years old	3,488	1,138	32.6	*	*	2	0.1	30	0.9
25 to 29 years old	6,701	914	13.6	*	*	6	0.1	11	0.2

* = Quantity equals zero or rounds to zero.

Table A-1. Enrollment Status of the Population 3 Years Old and Over, by Sex, Age, Race, Hispanic Origin, Foreign Born, and Foreign-Born Parentage, October 2019—*Continued*

(Numbers in thousands; percent; civilian noninstitutionalized population.)

Age, sex, race, Hispanic origin, and nativity	Enrolled in school		Not enrolled in school					
	College undergraduate or graduate		Total		High school graduate		Not high school graduate	
	Number	Percent	Number	Percent	Number	Percent	Number	Percent
FOREIGN–BORN								
Both Sexes								
Total	2,291	5.2	39,488	88.9	30,078	67.7	9,410	21.2
3 and 4 years old	*	*	101	48.1	*	*	101	48.1
5 and 6 years old	*	*	15	5.2	*	*	15	5.2
7 to 9 years old	*	*	17	3.4	*	*	17	3.4
10 to 13 years old	*	*	22	3.2	*	*	22	3.2
14 and 15 years old	4	0.8	17	3.8	*	*	17	3.8
16 and 17 years old	26	5.6	60	12.8	19	4.0	41	8.8
18 and 19 years old	278	47.0	143	24.1	105	17.8	37	6.3
20 and 21 years old	418	50.8	370	45.0	315	38.3	55	6.7
22 to 24 years old	381	27.6	985	71.4	837	60.7	148	10.7
25 to 29 years old	425	12.5	2,979	87.4	2,527	74.1	453	13.3
30 to 34 years old	268	6.5	3,851	93.2	3,147	76.2	704	17.0
35 to 44 years old	265	2.9	8,748	96.8	6,683	74.0	2,064	22.9
45 to 54 years old	153	1.8	8,568	98.0	6,599	75.5	1,968	22.5
55 years old and over	74	0.5	13,613	99.4	9,845	71.9	3,768	27.5
Male								
Total	1,116	5.2	19,005	88.5	14,392	67.0	4,613	21.5
3 and 4 years old	*	*	47	43.1	*	*	47	43.1
5 and 6 years old	*	*	4	2.6	*	*	4	2.6
7 to 9 years old	*	*	5	1.9	*	*	5	1.9
10 to 13 years old	*	*	7	1.9	*	*	7	1.9
14 and 15 years old	1	0.2	10	3.9	*	*	10	3.9
16 and 17 years old	25	9.8	35	13.9	15	6.1	20	7.8
18 and 19 years old	148	49.6	71	23.8	41	13.8	30	10.0
20 and 21 years old	195	45.2	218	50.6	196	45.5	22	5.1
22 to 24 years old	200	26.9	543	73.1	451	60.7	92	12.4
25 to 29 years old	229	13.9	1,419	85.9	1,146	69.3	273	16.5
30 to 34 years old	122	5.7	2,021	94.0	1,663	77.3	358	16.7
35 to 44 years old	99	2.2	4,372	97.5	3,241	72.3	1,131	25.2
45 to 54 years old	78	1.8	4,132	97.9	3,125	74.1	1,007	23.9
55 years old and over	20	0.3	6,122	99.6	4,514	73.4	1,608	26.2
Female								
Total	1,175	5.1	20,483	89.3	15,686	68.4	4,797	20.9
3 and 4 years old	*	*	54	53.5	*	*	54	53.5
5 and 6 years old	*	*	11	8.3	*	*	11	8.3
7 to 9 years old	*	*	12	4.8	*	*	12	4.8
10 to 13 years old	*	*	16	4.4	*	*	16	4.4
14 and 15 years old	3	1.5	7	3.6	*	*	7	3.6
16 and 17 years old	2	0.8	25	11.6	4	1.6	22	10.0
18 and 19 years old	131	44.3	72	24.5	64	21.8	8	2.6
20 and 21 years old	223	57.0	152	38.7	119	30.3	33	8.4
22 to 24 years old	180	28.4	442	69.5	386	60.8	55	8.7
25 to 29 years old	195	11.1	1,560	88.8	1,381	78.6	180	10.2
30 to 34 years old	147	7.4	1,830	92.4	1,484	74.9	346	17.5
35 to 44 years old	166	3.6	4,376	96.2	3,442	75.7	933	20.5
45 to 54 years old	76	1.7	4,435	98.1	3,474	76.8	961	21.3
55 years old and over	53	0.7	7,491	99.3	5,331	70.6	2,160	28.6
CHILDREN OF FOREIGN–BORN PARENTS								
Both Sexes								
Total	5,675	7.0	60,170	74.1	48,104	59.3	12,066	14.9
3 and 4 years old	*	*	898	44.3	*	*	898	44.3
5 and 6 years old	*	*	147	7.1	*	*	147	7.1
7 to 9 years old	*	*	73	2.3	*	*	73	2.3
10 to 13 years old	*	*	82	1.9	*	*	82	1.9
14 and 15 years old	4	0.2	56	2.4	3	0.1	53	2.3
16 and 17 years old	85	3.7	179	7.9	28	1.2	151	6.6
18 and 19 years old	1,220	52.8	645	27.9	509	22.0	135	5.9
20 and 21 years old	1,319	55.7	985	41.6	855	36.1	129	5.5
22 to 24 years old	1,106	31.7	2,350	67.4	2,121	60.8	229	6.6
25 to 29 years old	896	13.4	5,787	86.4	5,178	77.3	609	9.1

* = Quantity equals zero or rounds to zero.

Table A-1. Enrollment Status of the Population 3 Years Old and Over, by Sex, Age, Race, Hispanic Origin, Foreign Born, and Foreign-Born Parentage, October 2019—*Continued*

(Numbers in thousands; percent; civilian noninstitutionalized population.)

| Age, sex, race, Hispanic origin, and nativity | Population | Enrolled in school | | | | | | | |
| | | Total | | Nursery or kindergarten | | Elementary | | High school | |
	Number	Number	Percent	Number	Percent	Number	Percent	Number	Percent
30 to 34 years old	6,570	432	6.6	*	*	11	0.2	4	0.1
35 to 44 years old	12,642	379	3.0	*	*	7	0.1	28	0.2
45 to 54 years old	11,080	227	2.0	*	*	20	0.2	14	0.1
55 years old and over	19,813	99	0.5	*	*	*	*	7	*
Male									
Total	39,793	10,486	26.4	1,196	3.0	4,388	11.0	2,319	5.8
3 and 4 years old	1,068	600	56.2	600	56.2	*	*	*	*
5 and 6 years old	1,105	1,035	93.7	594	53.7	442	40.0	*	*
7 to 9 years old	1,623	1,606	99.0	2	0.1	1,604	98.8	*	*
10 to 13 years old	2,245	2,192	97.6	*	*	2,158	96.1	33	1.5
14 and 15 years old	1,144	1,121	97.9	*	*	138	12.1	982	85.8
16 and 17 years old	1,144	1,052	92.0	*	*	12	1.1	1,005	87.8
18 and 19 years old	1,128	809	71.7	*	*	*	*	238	21.1
20 and 21 years old	1,196	664	55.5	*	*	9	0.8	27	2.2
22 to 24 years old	1,766	519	29.4	*	*	*	*	4	0.2
25 to 29 years old	3,324	429	12.9	*	*	6	0.2	4	0.1
30 to 34 years old	3,325	188	5.6	*	*	7	0.2	1	*
35 to 44 years old	6,269	125	2.0	*	*	3	0.1	11	0.2
45 to 54 years old	5,397	115	2.1	*	*	7	0.1	11	0.2
55 years old and over	9,060	32	0.4	*	*	*	*	4	*
Female									
Total	41,373	10,511	25.4	1,022	2.5	4,106	9.9	2,291	5.5
3 and 4 years old	959	529	55.1	529	55.1	*	*	*	*
5 and 6 years old	975	897	92.1	480	49.3	417	42.8	*	*
7 to 9 years old	1,511	1,455	96.3	13	0.8	1,442	95.4	*	*
10 to 13 years old	2,113	2,084	98.6	*	*	2,047	96.9	37	1.8
14 and 15 years old	1,176	1,144	97.2	*	*	167	14.2	974	82.8
16 and 17 years old	1,131	1,044	92.3	*	*	11	0.9	983	86.9
18 and 19 years old	1,181	856	72.5	*	*	*	*	208	17.6
20 and 21 years old	1,173	720	61.4	*	*	*	*	29	2.5
22 to 24 years old	1,723	619	36.0	*	*	2	0.1	26	1.5
25 to 29 years old	3,377	485	14.4	*	*	*	*	7	0.2
30 to 34 years old	3,245	244	7.5	*	*	4	0.1	4	0.1
35 to 44 years old	6,373	255	4.0	*	*	4	0.1	17	0.3
45 to 54 years old	5,683	112	2.0	*	*	12	0.2	3	0.1
55 years old and over	10,753	67	0.6	*	*	*	*	3	*

* = Quantity equals zero or rounds to zero.

Table A-1. **Enrollment Status of the Population 3 Years Old and Over, by Sex, Age, Race, Hispanic Origin, Foreign Born, and Foreign-Born Parentage, October 2019**—*Continued*

(Numbers in thousands; percent; civilian noninstitutionalized population.)

Age, sex, race, Hispanic origin, and nativity	Enrolled in school		Not enrolled in school					
	College undergraduate or graduate		Total		High school graduate		Not high school graduate	
	Number	Percent	Number	Percent	Number	Percent	Number	Percent
30 to 34 years old	416	6.3	6,138	93.4	5,274	80.3	864	13.1
35 to 44 years old	344	2.7	12,263	97.0	9,972	78.9	2,291	18.1
45 to 54 years old	192	1.7	10,853	98.0	8,718	78.7	2,135	19.3
55 years old and over	92	0.5	19,714	99.5	15,445	78.0	4,269	21.5
Male								
Total	2,582	6.5	29,308	73.6	23,333	58.6	5,974	15.0
3 and 4 years old	*	*	467	43.8	*	*	467	43.8
5 and 6 years old	*	*	69	6.3	*	*	69	6.3
7 to 9 years old	*	*	17	1.0	*	*	17	1.0
10 to 13 years old	*	*	53	2.4	*	*	53	2.4
14 and 15 years old	1	0.1	24	2.1	3	0.2	21	1.8
16 and 17 years old	35	3.1	92	8.0	24	2.1	68	5.9
18 and 19 years old	571	50.6	319	28.3	250	22.2	69	6.1
20 and 21 years old	628	52.5	532	44.5	478	39.9	55	4.6
22 to 24 years old	515	29.2	1,247	70.6	1,097	62.2	149	8.4
25 to 29 years old	418	12.6	2,895	87.1	2,530	76.1	365	11.0
30 to 34 years old	179	5.4	3,137	94.4	2,682	80.7	455	13.7
35 to 44 years old	110	1.8	6,144	98.0	4,893	78.1	1,251	20.0
45 to 54 years old	96	1.8	5,282	97.9	4,192	77.7	1,090	20.2
55 years old and over	28	0.3	9,029	99.6	7,185	79.3	1,844	20.4
Female								
Total	3,093	7.5	30,862	74.6	24,771	59.9	6,091	14.7
3 and 4 years old	*	*	431	44.9	*	*	431	44.9
5 and 6 years old	*	*	78	7.9	*	*	78	7.9
7 to 9 years old	*	*	56	3.7	*	*	56	3.7
10 to 13 years old	*	*	29	1.4	*	*	29	1.4
14 and 15 years old	3	0.3	33	2.8	*	*	33	2.8
16 and 17 years old	50	4.4	87	7.7	4	0.4	83	7.3
18 and 19 years old	648	54.9	325	27.5	259	22.0	66	5.6
20 and 21 years old	691	59.0	452	38.6	378	32.2	75	6.4
22 to 24 years old	591	34.3	1,103	64.0	1,024	59.4	80	4.6
25 to 29 years old	478	14.2	2,892	85.6	2,648	78.4	244	7.2
30 to 34 years old	237	7.3	3,001	92.5	2,592	79.9	408	12.6
35 to 44 years old	234	3.7	6,119	96.0	5,079	79.7	1,040	16.3
45 to 54 years old	96	1.7	5,571	98.0	4,526	79.6	1,045	18.4
55 years old and over	64	0.6	10,686	99.4	8,260	76.8	2,425	22.6

* = Quantity equals zero or rounds to zero.

Table A-2. Single Grade of Enrollment and High School Graduation Status for Population 3 Years Old and Over, by Sex, Age (Single Years for 3 to 24 Years), Race, and Hispanic Origin, October 2019

(Numbers in thousands; percent; civilian noninstitutionalized population.)

Age, sex, race, and Hispanic origin	Population[1]	Enrolled		Nursery	Kinder-garten	Enrolled								
		Number	Percent			Elementary grades								
						1	2	3	4	5	6	7	8
ALL RACES														
Both Sexes														
Total	313,097	76,089	24.3	4,728	4,057	3,859	4,072	4,112	3,986	4,115	4,249	4,078	4,148
3 years old	4,021	1,721	42.8	1,674	47	*	*	*	*	*	*	*	*
4 years old	4,053	2,612	64.5	2,275	338	*	*	*	*	*	*	*	*
5 years old	4,092	3,713	90.7	705	2,802	191	14	*	*	*	*	*	*
6 years old	3,924	3,793	96.7	74	787	2,687	199	46	*	*	*	*	*
7 years old	4,074	3,966	97.4	*	83	939	2,705	220	19	*	*	*	*
8 years old	4,000	3,875	96.9	*	*	38	997	2,631	171	38	*	*	*
9 years old	4,158	4,088	98.3	*	*	4	131	1,073	2,683	182	16	*	*
10 years old	4,019	3,910	97.3	*	*	*	27	115	1,000	2,561	188	19	*
11 years old	4,202	4,133	98.4	*	*	*	*	26	105	1,143	2,704	148	6
12 years old	4,177	4,104	98.3	*	*	*	*	*	8	141	1,078	2,663	190
13 years old	4,219	4,134	98.0	*	*	*	*	*	*	51	135	1,011	2,747
14 years old	4,154	4,052	97.5	*	*	*	*	*	*	*	75	133	1,047
15 years old	4,160	4,089	98.3	*	*	*	*	*	*	*	6	27	122
16 years old	4,154	3,860	92.9	*	*	*	*	*	*	*	2	11	16
17 years old	4,237	3,918	92.5	*	*	*	*	*	*	*	*	18	10
18 years old	4,055	2,907	71.7	*	*	*	*	*	*	*	*	*	2
19 years old	4,251	2,679	63.0	*	*	*	*	*	*	*	*	2	*
20 years old	4,374	2,426	55.5	*	*	*	*	*	*	*	6	11	*
21 years old	4,303	2,216	51.5	*	*	*	*	*	*	*	*	*	*
22 years old	4,097	1,558	38.0	*	*	*	*	*	*	*	*	17	*
23 years old	4,149	1,065	25.7	*	*	*	*	*	*	*	*	5	*
24 years old	4,114	913	22.2	*	*	*	*	*	*	*	*	*	4
25 to 29 years old	22,900	2,517	11.0	*	*	*	*	*	*	*	6	*	*
30 to 34 years old	22,054	1,319	6.0	*	*	*	*	*	*	*	16	1	*
35 to 39 years old	21,395	827	3.9	*	*	*	*	*	*	*	*	3	*
40 to 44 years old	19,725	513	2.6	*	*	*	*	*	*	*	*	4	*
45 to 49 years old	20,062	500	2.5	*	*	*	*	*	*	*	12	4	4
50 to 54 years old	20,247	320	1.6	*	*	*	*	*	*	*	4	*	*
55 to 59 years old	21,571	169	0.8	*	*	*	*	*	*	*	*	*	*
60 to 64 years old	20,731	92	0.4	*	*	*	*	*	*	*	*	*	*
65 years and over	53,426	97	0.2	*	*	*	*	*	*	*	*	*	*
Male														
Total	152,910	37,773	24.7	2,501	2,020	1,998	2,124	2,102	2,031	2,080	2,156	2,060	2,225
3 years old	2,076	880	42.4	862	18	*	*	*	*	*	*	*	*
4 years old	2,082	1,337	64.2	1,175	162	*	*	*	*	*	*	*	*
5 years old	2,135	1,961	91.9	414	1,411	132	3	*	*	*	*	*	*
6 years old	1,955	1,900	97.2	49	391	1,355	84	20	*	*	*	*	*
7 years old	2,091	2,061	98.6	*	38	486	1,412	116	9	*	*	*	*
8 years old	2,071	2,025	97.8	*	*	23	532	1,357	95	18	*	*	*
9 years old	2,098	2,063	98.3	*	*	2	78	528	1,360	83	11	*	*
10 years old	2,041	1,980	97.0	*	*	*	15	71	511	1,285	92	6	*
11 years old	2,152	2,106	97.9	*	*	*	*	10	54	592	1,376	69	6
12 years old	2,102	2,065	98.2	*	*	*	*	*	2	64	563	1,315	103
13 years old	2,184	2,139	97.9	*	*	*	*	*	*	38	58	529	1,442
14 years old	2,111	2,064	97.7	*	*	*	*	*	*	*	29	77	574
15 years old	2,124	2,089	98.3	*	*	*	*	*	*	*	1	17	80
16 years old	2,106	1,976	93.8	*	*	*	*	*	*	*	*	5	3
17 years old	2,158	1,972	91.4	*	*	*	*	*	*	*	*	10	9
18 years old	2,041	1,454	71.3	*	*	*	*	*	*	*	*	*	2
19 years old	2,141	1,292	60.4	*	*	*	*	*	*	*	*	*	*
20 years old	2,252	1,175	52.2	*	*	*	*	*	*	*	6	7	*
21 years old	2,155	1,033	47.9	*	*	*	*	*	*	*	*	*	*
22 years old	2,061	732	35.5	*	*	*	*	*	*	*	*	15	*
23 years old	2,060	451	21.9	*	*	*	*	*	*	*	*	5	*
24 years old	1,991	366	18.4	*	*	*	*	*	*	*	*	*	4
25 to 29 years old	11,465	1,159	10.1	*	*	*	*	*	*	*	6	*	*
30 to 34 years old	10,969	521	4.7	*	*	*	*	*	*	*	9	1	*
35 to 39 years old	10,551	319	3.0	*	*	*	*	*	*	*	*	3	*
40 to 44 years old	9,676	181	1.9	*	*	*	*	*	*	*	*	*	*
45 to 49 years old	9,806	192	2.0	*	*	*	*	*	*	*	4	*	4
50 to 54 years old	9,903	130	1.3	*	*	*	*	*	*	*	*	*	*
55 to 59 years old	10,434	70	0.7	*	*	*	*	*	*	*	*	*	*

* = Quantity zero or rounds to zero.

Table A-2. Single Grade of Enrollment and High School Graduation Status for Population 3 Years Old and Over, by Sex, Age (Single Years for 3 to 24 Years), Race, and Hispanic Origin, October 2019—*Continued*

(Numbers in thousands; percent; civilian noninstitutionalized population.)

Age, sex, race, and Hispanic origin	Enrolled High school 9	10	11	12	Undergraduate college 1	2	3	4	Graduate school 1	2+	Not enrolled H.S. grad	Not grad	Not enrolled Number	Percent
ALL RACES														
Both Sexes														
Total	3,991	4,068	4,037	4,299	4,201	4,167	3,602	2,615	1,362	2,342	209,502	27,507	237,009	75.7
3 years old	*	*	*	*	*	*	*	*	*	*	*	2,300	2,300	57.2
4 years old	*	*	*	*	*	*	*	*	*	*	*	1,441	1,441	35.5
5 years old	*	*	*	*	*	*	*	*	*	*	*	380	380	9.3
6 years old	*	*	*	*	*	*	*	*	*	*	*	131	131	3.3
7 years old	*	*	*	*	*	*	*	*	*	*	*	108	108	2.6
8 years old	*	*	*	*	*	*	*	*	*	*	*	125	125	3.1
9 years old	*	*	*	*	*	*	*	*	*	*	*	70	70	1.7
10 years old	*	*	*	*	*	*	*	*	*	*	*	108	108	2.7
11 years old	*	*	*	*	*	*	*	*	*	*	*	69	69	1.6
12 years old	24	*	*	*	*	*	*	*	*	*	*	73	73	1.7
13 years old	166	25	*	*	*	*	*	*	*	*	*	85	85	2.0
14 years old	2,588	191	19	*	*	*	*	*	*	*	*	102	102	2.5
15 years old	1,008	2,509	338	44	7	25	3	*	*	*	3	68	71	1.7
16 years old	118	1,077	2,341	247	23	*	9	*	14	3	58	236	293	7.1
17 years old	30	172	1,107	2,415	143	3	4	*	17	*	99	220	319	7.5
18 years old	16	36	117	1,185	1,454	74	21	*	*	2	899	249	1,148	28.3
19 years old	1	14	27	184	1,007	1,185	230	23	7	*	1,339	233	1,572	37.0
20 years old	*	9	19	36	426	829	1,011	59	19	1	1,698	251	1,949	44.5
21 years old	8	2	28	27	184	485	625	688	67	102	1,889	199	2,088	48.5
22 years old	*	11	8	15	101	262	349	525	166	104	2,337	202	2,539	62.0
23 years old	*	*	*	8	76	144	215	285	194	139	2,868	216	3,084	74.3
24 years old	6	*	3	24	55	111	187	234	121	168	3,035	165	3,200	77.8
25 to 29 years old	5	3	3	43	202	471	418	356	308	700	19,055	1,329	20,384	89.0
30 to 34 years old	*	7	4	1	183	186	219	166	142	394	19,144	1,591	20,735	94.0
35 to 39 years old	14	3	4	16	122	114	108	113	99	232	18,676	1,892	20,568	96.1
40 to 44 years old	*	*	7	6	72	95	68	52	65	144	17,389	1,822	19,211	97.4
45 to 49 years old	3	8	9	14	54	80	74	54	53	131	17,768	1,794	19,562	97.5
50 to 54 years old	*	*	4	25	31	43	40	39	42	92	18,050	1,876	19,927	98.4
55 to 59 years old	*	*	*	*	36	28	15	12	18	60	19,365	2,038	21,402	99.2
60 to 64 years old	4	2	*	*	10	19	5	4	15	33	18,758	1,880	20,638	99.6
65 years and over	*	*	*	10	16	13	*	5	16	37	47,072	6,257	53,329	99.8
Male														
Total	2,029	2,068	2,121	2,191	1,833	1,922	1,667	1,145	507	993	101,234	13,903	115,137	75.3
3 years old	*	*	*	*	*	*	*	*	*	*	*	1,196	1,196	57.6
4 years old	*	*	*	*	*	*	*	*	*	*	*	745	745	35.8
5 years old	*	*	*	*	*	*	*	*	*	*	*	174	174	8.1
6 years old	*	*	*	*	*	*	*	*	*	*	*	56	56	2.8
7 years old	*	*	*	*	*	*	*	*	*	*	*	30	30	1.4
8 years old	*	*	*	*	*	*	*	*	*	*	*	46	46	2.2
9 years old	*	*	*	*	*	*	*	*	*	*	*	35	35	1.7
10 years old	*	*	*	*	*	*	*	*	*	*	*	61	61	3.0
11 years old	*	*	*	*	*	*	*	*	*	*	*	46	46	2.1
12 years old	18	*	*	*	*	*	*	*	*	*	*	37	37	1.8
13 years old	66	6	*	*	*	*	*	*	*	*	*	45	45	2.1
14 years old	1,262	114	8	*	*	*	*	*	*	*	*	48	48	2.3
15 years old	573	1,232	157	14	4	8	3	*	*	*	3	33	35	1.7
16 years old	62	567	1,213	98	10	*	4	*	11	3	33	96	130	6.2
17 years old	7	101	621	1,164	44	3	*	*	13	*	64	122	186	8.6
18 years old	11	23	75	685	615	31	12	*	*	2	452	135	587	28.7
19 years old	1	6	10	111	506	528	112	13	5	*	713	135	848	39.6
20 years old	*	4	5	28	199	429	483	9	5	1	926	151	1,077	47.8
21 years old	8	2	11	15	76	242	323	269	37	50	1,019	103	1,122	52.1
22 years old	*	*	4	10	40	136	156	291	46	35	1,198	131	1,329	64.5
23 years old	*	*	*	4	35	71	90	128	71	48	1,461	148	1,609	78.1
24 years old	*	*	*	10	29	23	69	100	53	77	1,530	95	1,625	81.6
25 to 29 years old	*	*	1	18	86	197	212	177	124	338	9,545	761	10,306	89.9
30 to 34 years old	*	2	*	1	59	73	92	63	36	185	9,644	805	10,448	95.3
35 to 39 years old	14	3	*	2	47	48	41	35	22	103	9,211	1,021	10,232	97.0
40 to 44 years old	*	*	7	2	16	33	24	22	25	52	8,468	1,027	9,494	98.1
45 to 49 years old	3	5	9	8	24	48	25	10	17	35	8,683	932	9,615	98.0
50 to 54 years old	*	*	*	18	18	22	15	18	21	18	8,775	999	9,773	98.7
55 to 59 years old	*	*	*	*	18	11	8	10	4	19	9,311	1,053	10,364	99.3

* = Quantity zero or rounds to zero.

Table A-2. Single Grade of Enrollment and High School Graduation Status for Population 3 Years Old and Over, by Sex, Age (Single Years for 3 to 24 Years), Race, and Hispanic Origin, October 2019—*Continued*

(Numbers in thousands; percent; civilian noninstitutionalized population.)

Age, sex, race, and Hispanic origin	Population[1]	Enrolled		Enrolled									
					Kinder-garten	Elementary grades							
		Number	Percent	Nursery		1	2	3	4	5	6	7	8
60 to 64 years old	9,935	36	0.4	*	*	*	*	*	*	*	*	*	*
65 years and over	23,985	44	0.2	*	*	*	*	*	*	*	*	*	*
Female													
Total	160,188	38,316	23.9	2,227	2,037	1,862	1,948	2,010	1,955	2,035	2,093	2,018	1,923
3 years old	1,945	841	43.3	812	29	*	*	*	*	*	*	*	*
4 years old	1,971	1,275	64.7	1,099	176	*	*	*	*	*	*	*	*
5 years old	1,957	1,752	89.5	291	1,391	59	11	*	*	*	*	*	*
6 years old	1,969	1,893	96.2	25	396	1,332	115	26	10	*	*	*	*
7 years old	1,983	1,906	96.1	*	45	453	1,293	105	10	*	*	*	*
8 years old	1,929	1,850	95.9	*	*	15	465	1,274	76	20	*	*	*
9 years old	2,060	2,025	98.3	*	*	2	53	545	1,322	99	5	*	*
10 years old	1,978	1,931	97.6	*	*	*	11	44	489	1,276	97	13	*
11 years old	2,050	2,027	98.9	*	*	*	*	17	52	551	1,328	79	*
12 years old	2,075	2,039	98.3	*	*	*	*	*	6	76	515	1,349	88
13 years old	2,035	1,995	98.0	*	*	*	*	*	*	13	76	481	1,305
14 years old	2,043	1,988	97.3	*	*	*	*	*	*	*	46	55	473
15 years old	2,035	2,000	98.3	*	*	*	*	*	*	*	5	11	42
16 years old	2,048	1,884	92.0	*	*	*	*	*	*	*	2	5	13
17 years old	2,079	1,946	93.6	*	*	*	*	*	*	*	*	8	1
18 years old	2,014	1,452	72.1	*	*	*	*	*	*	*	*	*	*
19 years old	2,110	1,387	65.7	*	*	*	*	*	*	*	*	2	*
20 years old	2,122	1,250	58.9	*	*	*	*	*	*	*	*	4	*
21 years old	2,149	1,183	55.0	*	*	*	*	*	*	*	*	*	*
22 years old	2,036	826	40.6	*	*	*	*	*	*	*	*	2	*
23 years old	2,089	614	29.4	*	*	*	*	*	*	*	*	*	*
24 years old	2,123	548	25.8	*	*	*	*	*	*	*	*	*	*
25 to 29 years old	11,435	1,358	11.9	*	*	*	*	*	*	*	*	*	*
30 to 34 years old	11,085	798	7.2	*	*	*	*	*	*	*	7	*	*
35 to 39 years old	10,844	508	4.7	*	*	*	*	*	*	*	*	*	*
40 to 44 years old	10,049	332	3.3	*	*	*	*	*	*	*	*	4	*
45 to 49 years old	10,256	309	3.0	*	*	*	*	*	*	*	8	4	*
50 to 54 years old	10,343	190	1.8	*	*	*	*	*	*	*	4	*	*
55 to 59 years old	11,138	99	0.9	*	*	*	*	*	*	*	*	*	*
60 to 64 years old	10,796	56	0.5	*	*	*	*	*	*	*	*	*	*
65 years and over	29,442	53	0.2	*	*	*	*	*	*	*	*	*	*
WHITE ALONE NON-HISPANIC													
Both Sexes													
Total	188,587	38,673	20.5	2,399	1,963	1,936	1,971	2,051	1,949	2,063	2,070	2,069	2,077
3 years old	1,926	819	42.6	809	11	*	*	*	*	*	*	*	*
4 years old	1,952	1,289	66.0	1,162	126	*	*	*	*	*	*	*	*
5 years old	1,982	1,826	92.1	397	1,352	72	4	*	*	*	*	*	*
6 years old	1,974	1,894	96.0	32	426	1,358	71	8	12	*	*	*	*
7 years old	1,984	1,936	97.6	*	47	477	1,310	90	12	*	*	*	*
8 years old	1,997	1,952	97.7	*	*	27	537	1,315	50	22	*	*	*
9 years old	2,009	1,994	99.2	*	*	2	31	564	1,294	97	7	*	*
10 years old	2,012	1,964	97.6	*	*	*	18	57	1,251	70	11	*	*
11 years old	2,080	2,052	98.6	*	*	*	16	36	575	1,365	60	*	*
12 years old	2,111	2,072	98.2	*	*	*	*	3	84	525	1,352	93	*
13 years old	2,091	2,051	98.1	*	*	*	*	*	34	60	554	1,350	*
14 years old	2,136	2,094	98.0	*	*	*	*	*	*	31	46	561	*
15 years old	2,142	2,097	97.9	*	*	*	*	*	*	*	5	9	61
16 years old	2,211	2,069	93.6	*	*	*	*	*	*	*	2	1	9
17 years old	2,148	2,002	93.2	*	*	*	*	*	*	*	*	6	1
18 years old	2,220	1,576	71.0	*	*	*	*	*	*	*	*	*	2
19 years old	2,190	1,429	65.3	*	*	*	*	*	*	*	*	2	8
20 years old	2,370	1,350	57.0	*	*	*	*	*	*	*	*	*	*
21 years old	2,264	1,171	51.7	*	*	*	*	*	*	*	*	15	*
22 years old	2,267	817	36.1	*	*	*	*	*	*	*	*	5	*
23 years old	2,165	564	26.1	*	*	*	*	*	*	*	*	*	*
24 years old	2,160	442	20.5	*	*	*	*	*	*	*	*	*	*
25 to 29 years old	12,251	1,195	9.8	*	*	*	*	*	*	*	*	*	*
30 to 34 years old	12,175	629	5.2	*	*	*	*	*	*	*	3	*	*
35 to 39 years old	12,007	434	3.6	*	*	*	*	*	*	*	*	*	*

* = Quantity zero or rounds to zero.

Table A-2. Single Grade of Enrollment and High School Graduation Status for Population 3 Years Old and Over, by Sex, Age (Single Years for 3 to 24 Years), Race, and Hispanic Origin, October 2019—*Continued*

(Numbers in thousands; percent; civilian noninstitutionalized population.)

Age, sex, race, and Hispanic origin	Enrolled High school 9	10	11	12	Enrolled Undergraduate college 1	2	3	4	Enrolled Graduate school 1	2+	Not enrolled H.S. grad	Not grad	Not enrolled Number	Percent
60 to 64 years old	4	2	*	*	3	8	*	*	12	8	8,994	904	9,898	99.6
65 years and over	*	*	*	4	5	12	*	*	4	19	21,205	2,736	23,941	99.8
Female														
Total	1,962	2,000	1,916	2,108	2,368	2,245	1,935	1,470	855	1,349	108,268	13,604	121,872	76.1
3 years old	*	*	*	*	*	*	*	*	*	*	*	1,103	1,103	56.7
4 years old	*	*	*	*	*	*	*	*	*	*	*	696	696	35.3
5 years old	*	*	*	*	*	*	*	*	*	*	*	206	206	10.5
6 years old	*	*	*	*	*	*	*	*	*	*	*	75	75	3.8
7 years old	*	*	*	*	*	*	*	*	*	*	*	78	78	3.9
8 years old	*	*	*	*	*	*	*	*	*	*	*	79	79	4.1
9 years old	*	*	*	*	*	*	*	*	*	*	*	35	35	1.7
10 years old	*	*	*	*	*	*	*	*	*	*	*	47	47	2.4
11 years old	*	*	*	*	*	*	*	*	*	*	*	23	23	1.1
12 years old	6	*	*	*	*	*	*	*	*	*	*	36	36	1.7
13 years old	100	19	*	*	*	*	*	*	*	*	*	40	40	2.0
14 years old	1,326	77	11	*	*	*	*	*	*	*	*	54	54	2.7
15 years old	435	1,276	181	29	3	17	*	*	*	*	*	35	35	1.7
16 years old	56	511	1,127	149	13	*	5	*	2	*	24	140	164	8.0
17 years old	23	71	486	1,251	100	*	4	*	4	*	35	98	133	6.4
18 years old	5	13	42	500	839	44	9	*	*	*	448	114	561	27.9
19 years old	*	7	17	73	501	657	119	10	2	*	626	98	723	34.3
20 years old	*	5	14	8	227	399	528	50	14	*	772	100	871	41.1
21 years old	*	*	17	12	108	243	302	419	29	52	870	96	966	45.0
22 years old	*	11	4	5	61	127	193	235	121	69	1,139	71	1,210	59.4
23 years old	*	*	4	4	41	73	125	157	123	91	1,408	68	1,475	70.6
24 years old	6	*	3	14	26	87	118	134	68	91	1,505	70	1,576	74.2
25 to 29 years old	5	3	2	26	116	275	206	180	184	362	9,509	568	10,078	88.1
30 to 34 years old	*	5	4	*	124	113	127	103	105	209	9,500	787	10,287	92.8
35 to 39 years old	*	*	4	14	75	65	67	78	77	129	9,465	871	10,336	95.3
40 to 44 years old	*	*	*	4	56	62	44	30	40	92	8,922	795	9,717	96.7
45 to 49 years old	*	3	*	6	29	33	49	43	36	96	9,086	862	9,948	97.0
50 to 54 years old	*	*	4	7	13	21	25	21	20	74	9,276	878	10,154	98.2
55 to 59 years old	*	*	*	*	18	18	7	2	14	41	10,053	985	11,039	99.1
60 to 64 years old	*	*	*	*	7	12	5	4	4	24	9,764	976	10,740	99.5
65 years and over	*	*	*	6	11	1	*	5	12	18	25,867	3,522	29,389	99.8
WHITE ALONE NON-HISPANIC														
Both Sexes														
Total	2,057	2,059	2,038	2,293	2,012	2,094	1,978	1,480	802	1,311	139,347	10,568	149,914	79.5
3 years old	*	*	*	*	*	*	*	*	*	*	*	1,106	1,106	57.4
4 years old	*	*	*	*	*	*	*	*	*	*	*	663	663	34.0
5 years old	*	*	*	*	*	*	*	*	*	*	*	156	156	7.9
6 years old	*	*	*	*	*	*	*	*	*	*	*	80	80	4.0
7 years old	*	*	*	*	*	*	*	*	*	*	*	47	47	2.4
8 years old	*	*	*	*	*	*	*	*	*	*	*	45	45	2.3
9 years old	*	*	*	*	*	*	*	*	*	*	*	15	15	0.8
10 years old	*	*	*	*	*	*	*	*	*	*	*	48	48	2.4
11 years old	*	*	*	*	*	*	*	*	*	*	*	29	29	1.4
12 years old	15	*	*	*	*	*	*	*	*	*	*	39	39	1.8
13 years old	47	6	*	*	*	*	*	*	*	*	*	39	39	1.9
14 years old	1,367	81	8	*	*	*	*	*	*	*	*	42	42	2.0
15 years old	548	1,291	150	16	7	9	2	*	*	*	*	46	46	2.1
16 years old	55	577	1,280	121	15	*	*	*	7	3	32	110	142	6.4
17 years old	11	59	505	1,342	64	3	4	*	8	*	59	86	146	6.8
18 years old	8	17	64	640	785	49	12	*	*	*	505	139	644	29.0
19 years old	*	6	16	83	481	695	136	4	7	*	672	89	761	34.7
20 years old	*	4	5	8	163	478	641	38	5	*	913	107	1,020	43.0
21 years old	*	*	4	1	82	204	354	452	36	38	984	110	1,093	48.3
22 years old	*	*	4	9	41	110	187	291	119	41	1,340	109	1,449	63.9
23 years old	*	*	*	4	33	68	111	141	119	83	1,514	87	1,601	73.9
24 years old	2	*	*	15	24	43	57	116	76	110	1,648	69	1,718	79.5
25 to 29 years old	*	3	*	17	82	209	197	184	140	364	10,624	431	11,055	90.2
30 to 34 years old	*	5	*	*	66	72	87	85	85	227	11,104	442	11,546	94.8
35 to 39 years old	5	3	*	5	58	39	65	65	64	131	11,084	490	11,574	96.4

* = Quantity zero or rounds to zero.

Table A-2. Single Grade of Enrollment and High School Graduation Status for Population 3 Years Old and Over, by Sex, Age (Single Years for 3 to 24 Years), Race, and Hispanic Origin, October 2019—Continued

(Numbers in thousands; percent; civilian noninstitutionalized population.)

| Age, sex, race, and Hispanic origin | Population[1] | Enrolled | | Nursery | Kinder-garten | Elementary grades | | | | | | | |
		Number	Percent			1	2	3	4	5	6	7	8
40 to 44 years old	11,176	280	2.5	*	*	*	*	*	*	*	*	*	*
45 to 49 years old	11,939	275	2.3	*	*	*	*	*	*	*	*	2	*
50 to 54 years old	12,797	194	1.5	*	*	*	*	*	*	*	*	*	*
55 to 59 years old	14,676	103	0.7	*	*	*	*	*	*	*	*	*	*
60 to 64 years old	14,651	47	0.3	*	*	*	*	*	*	*	*	*	*
65 years and over	40,524	54	0.1	*	*	*	*	*	*	*	*	*	*
Male													
Total	92,485	19,209	20.8	1,256	966	994	1,060	1,038	952	1,078	1,079	1,027	1,123
3 years old	996	393	39.5	392	1	*	*	*	*	*	*	*	*
4 years old	1,013	653	64.5	616	38	*	*	*	*	*	*	*	*
5 years old	1,013	954	94.2	226	690	38	*	*	*	*	*	*	*
6 years old	1,012	975	96.4	22	215	697	38	3	*	*	*	*	*
7 years old	1,020	999	97.9	*	22	243	691	33	9	*	*	*	*
8 years old	1,023	1,003	98.0	*	*	15	293	665	21	8	*	*	*
9 years old	1,034	1,022	98.8	*	*	2	22	298	645	51	4	*	*
10 years old	1,024	994	97.1	*	*	*	15	33	265	638	40	3	*
11 years old	1,070	1,046	97.7	*	*	*	6	12	309	691	28	*	*
12 years old	1,088	1,068	98.2	*	*	*	*	*	46	294	653	60	*
13 years old	1,059	1,046	98.8	*	*	*	*	25	25	280	702	*	*
14 years old	1,089	1,064	97.7	*	*	*	*	*	22	26	323	*	*
15 years old	1,101	1,084	98.5	*	*	*	*	*	*	9	35	*	*
16 years old	1,125	1,059	94.2	*	*	*	*	*	*	6	1	*	*
17 years old	1,101	1,015	92.2	*	*	*	*	*	*	*	2	*	*
18 years old	1,137	786	69.1	*	*	*	*	*	*	*	*	*	*
19 years old	1,125	693	61.6	*	*	*	*	*	*	*	*	*	*
20 years old	1,211	646	53.4	*	*	*	*	*	*	*	4	*	*
21 years old	1,166	537	46.1	*	*	*	*	*	*	*	*	*	*
22 years old	1,175	383	32.6	*	*	*	*	*	*	*	15	*	*
23 years old	1,031	245	23.7	*	*	*	*	*	*	*	5	*	*
24 years old	1,077	203	18.8	*	*	*	*	*	*	*	*	*	*
25 to 29 years old	6,176	535	8.7	*	*	*	*	*	*	*	*	*	*
30 to 34 years old	6,072	274	4.5	*	*	*	*	*	*	3	*	*	*
35 to 39 years old	5,942	152	2.6	*	*	*	*	*	*	*	*	*	*
40 to 44 years old	5,575	102	1.8	*	*	*	*	*	*	*	*	*	*
45 to 49 years old	5,910	100	1.7	*	*	*	*	*	*	*	*	*	*
50 to 54 years old	6,338	87	1.4	*	*	*	*	*	*	*	*	*	*
55 to 59 years old	7,165	53	0.7	*	*	*	*	*	*	*	*	*	*
60 to 64 years old	7,130	17	0.2	*	*	*	*	*	*	*	*	*	*
65 years and over	18,489	21	0.1	*	*	*	*	*	*	*	*	*	*
Female													
Total	96,102	19,464	20.3	1,144	997	942	911	1,013	997	985	991	1,042	954
3 years old	930	427	45.9	417	10	*	*	*	*	*	*	*	*
4 years old	939	635	67.7	546	89	*	*	*	*	*	*	*	*
5 years old	969	871	90.0	171	662	34	4	*	*	*	*	*	*
6 years old	962	919	95.5	10	211	661	33	5	*	*	*	*	*
7 years old	964	938	97.3	*	25	234	619	57	3	*	*	*	*
8 years old	974	949	97.4	*	*	12	243	650	29	14	*	*	*
9 years old	975	972	99.7	*	*	*	9	266	649	45	3	*	*
10 years old	988	969	98.1	*	*	*	3	24	290	614	31	8	*
11 years old	1,010	1,006	99.6	*	*	10	24	266	674	32	*	*	*
12 years old	1,023	1,004	98.1	*	*	*	3	38	231	700	33	*	*
13 years old	1,032	1,006	97.5	*	*	*	*	9	35	275	648	*	*
14 years old	1,047	1,030	98.4	*	*	*	*	*	8	20	238	*	*
15 years old	1,042	1,013	97.2	*	*	*	*	*	*	5	9	*	*
16 years old	1,086	1,010	93.0	*	*	*	*	*	*	2	1	*	*
17 years old	1,047	987	94.3	*	*	*	*	*	*	*	*	*	*
18 years old	1,083	790	73.0	*	*	*	*	*	*	*	2	*	*
19 years old	1,065	736	69.1	*	*	*	*	*	*	*	4	*	*
20 years old	1,160	704	60.7	*	*	*	*	*	*	*	*	*	*
21 years old	1,098	634	57.7	*	*	*	*	*	*	*	*	*	*
22 years old	1,092	434	39.8	*	*	*	*	*	*	*	*	*	*
23 years old	1,134	319	28.2	*	*	*	*	*	*	*	*	*	*
24 years old	1,083	240	22.1	*	*	*	*	*	*	*	*	*	*
25 to 29 years old	6,075	661	10.9	*	*	*	*	*	*	*	*	*	*
30 to 34 years old	6,103	355	5.8	*	*	*	*	*	*	*	*	*	*

* = Quantity zero or rounds to zero.

Table A-2. Single Grade of Enrollment and High School Graduation Status for Population 3 Years Old and Over, by Sex, Age (Single Years for 3 to 24 Years), Race, and Hispanic Origin, October 2019—*Continued*

(Numbers in thousands; percent; civilian noninstitutionalized population.)

Age, sex, race, and Hispanic origin	Enrolled										Not enrolled		Not enrolled	
	High school				Undergraduate college				Graduate school		H.S. grad	Not grad	Number	Percent
	9	10	11	12	1	2	3	4	1	2+				
40 to 44 years old	*	*	3	2	30	42	42	28	45	88	10,478	418	10,896	97.5
45 to 49 years old	*	5	*	10	30	44	47	31	36	71	11,168	496	11,664	97.7
50 to 54 years old	*	*	*	17	18	16	23	29	28	63	12,007	596	12,603	98.5
55 to 59 years old	*	*	*	*	22	9	9	12	8	43	13,810	762	14,573	99.3
60 to 64 years old	*	2	*	*	6	*	5	*	11	23	13,904	699	14,603	99.7
65 years and over	*	*	*	3	6	5	*	3	9	27	37,498	2,971	40,470	99.9
Male														
Total	1,019	1,070	1,082	1,203	860	1,003	914	697	259	527	67,705	5,572	73,277	79.2
3 years old	*	*	*	*	*	*	*	*	*	*	*	603	603	60.5
4 years old	*	*	*	*	*	*	*	*	*	*	*	359	359	35.5
5 years old	*	*	*	*	*	*	*	*	*	*	*	59	59	5.8
6 years old	*	*	*	*	*	*	*	*	*	*	*	37	37	3.6
7 years old	*	*	*	*	*	*	*	*	*	*	*	21	21	2.1
8 years old	*	*	*	*	*	*	*	*	*	*	*	20	20	2.0
9 years old	*	*	*	*	*	*	*	*	*	*	*	13	13	1.2
10 years old	*	*	*	*	*	*	*	*	*	*	*	30	30	2.9
11 years old	*	*	*	*	*	*	*	*	*	*	*	24	24	2.3
12 years old	15	*	*	*	*	*	*	*	*	*	*	19	19	1.8
13 years old	14	*	*	*	*	*	*	*	*	*	*	13	13	1.2
14 years old	647	42	3	*	*	*	*	*	*	*	*	25	25	2.3
15 years old	304	652	70	6	3	2	2	*	*	*	*	17	17	1.5
16 years old	31	302	666	47	5	*	*	*	4	3	18	48	65	5.8
17 years old	*	40	281	661	16	3	*	*	7	*	36	50	86	7.8
18 years old	3	15	44	376	321	18	8	*	*	*	277	74	352	30.9
19 years old	*	4	10	54	259	289	68	4	5	*	376	56	432	38.4
20 years old	*	4	*	6	59	263	306	4	1	*	487	77	564	46.6
21 years old	*	*	*	*	40	118	168	169	19	22	573	56	629	53.9
22 years old	*	*	4	9	21	52	82	164	27	10	712	80	792	67.4
23 years old	*	*	*	4	18	40	59	62	31	26	736	51	787	76.3
24 years old	*	*	*	6	19	11	25	63	26	52	831	44	874	81.2
25 to 29 years old	*	*	*	13	26	103	77	114	44	157	5,390	251	5,641	91.3
30 to 34 years old	*	*	*	*	15	28	49	40	26	114	5,555	243	5,797	95.5
35 to 39 years old	5	3	*	*	19	14	23	28	21	38	5,521	270	5,790	97.4
40 to 44 years old	*	*	3	2	6	8	15	15	15	38	5,225	248	5,473	98.2
45 to 49 years old	*	5	*	4	6	34	15	10	8	17	5,541	269	5,810	98.3
50 to 54 years old	*	*	*	14	8	11	15	14	14	12	5,911	339	6,251	98.6
55 to 59 years old	*	*	*	*	13	3	3	10	4	19	6,681	431	7,113	99.3
60 to 64 years old	*	2	*	*	3	*	*	*	7	5	6,741	372	7,113	99.8
65 years and over	*	*	*	*	*	5	*	*	1	15	17,095	1,374	18,469	99.9
Female														
Total	1,038	989	956	1,090	1,152	1,091	1,064	782	543	784	71,642	4,996	76,638	79.7
3 years old	*	*	*	*	*	*	*	*	*	*	*	504	504	54.1
4 years old	*	*	*	*	*	*	*	*	*	*	*	304	304	32.3
5 years old	*	*	*	*	*	*	*	*	*	*	*	97	97	10.0
6 years old	*	*	*	*	*	*	*	*	*	*	*	43	43	4.5
7 years old	*	*	*	*	*	*	*	*	*	*	*	26	26	2.7
8 years old	*	*	*	*	*	*	*	*	*	*	*	25	25	2.6
9 years old	*	*	*	*	*	*	*	*	*	*	*	3	3	0.3
10 years old	*	*	*	*	*	*	*	*	*	*	*	19	19	1.9
11 years old	*	*	*	*	*	*	*	*	*	*	*	5	5	0.4
12 years old	*	*	*	*	*	*	*	*	*	*	*	19	19	1.9
13 years old	33	6	*	*	*	*	*	*	*	*	*	26	26	2.5
14 years old	720	39	4	*	*	*	*	*	*	*	*	17	17	1.6
15 years old	244	639	80	9	3	8	*	*	*	*	*	29	29	2.8
16 years old	24	274	613	73	10	*	*	*	2	*	15	62	76	7.0
17 years old	11	19	224	681	47	*	4	*	1	*	24	36	60	5.7
18 years old	5	2	20	264	465	32	4	*	*	*	228	64	292	27.0
19 years old	*	2	6	28	222	406	69	*	2	*	296	33	329	30.9
20 years old	*	*	5	3	104	215	335	34	4	*	426	30	456	39.3
21 years old	*	*	4	1	41	85	185	283	17	16	411	54	464	42.3
22 years old	*	*	*	*	21	58	105	127	92	32	628	30	657	60.2
23 years old	*	*	*	*	15	28	52	79	88	57	778	36	815	71.8
24 years old	2	*	*	9	5	32	32	53	50	58	818	26	844	77.9
25 to 29 years old	*	3	*	4	56	105	119	69	96	207	5,234	180	5,414	89.1
30 to 34 years old	*	5	*	*	51	44	38	45	59	113	5,550	199	5,748	94.2

* = Quantity zero or rounds to zero.

Table A-2. Single Grade of Enrollment and High School Graduation Status for Population 3 Years Old and Over, by Sex, Age (Single Years for 3 to 24 Years), Race, and Hispanic Origin, October 2019—Continued

(Numbers in thousands; percent; civilian noninstitutionalized population.)

Age, sex, race, and Hispanic origin	Population[1]	Enrolled Number	Enrolled Percent	Nursery	Kinder-garten	Elementary grades 1	2	3	4	5	6	7	8
35 to 39 years old	6,065	282	4.6	*	*	*	*	*	*	*	*	*	*
40 to 44 years old	5,601	178	3.2	*	*	*	*	*	*	*	*	*	*
45 to 49 years old	6,029	174	2.9	*	*	*	*	*	*	*	2	*	*
50 to 54 years old	6,459	107	1.7	*	*	*	*	*	*	*	*	*	*
55 to 59 years old	7,510	50	0.7	*	*	*	*	*	*	*	*	*	*
60 to 64 years old	7,520	30	0.4	*	*	*	*	*	*	*	*	*	*
65 years and over	22,034	33	0.2	*	*	*	*	*	*	*	*	*	*
BLACK ALONE													
Both Sexes													
Total	41,267	11,551	28.0	714	642	568	630	665	580	567	715	628	639
3 years old	689	327	47.4	309	18	*	*	*	*	*	*	*	*
4 years old	611	393	64.3	318	75	*	*	*	*	*	*	*	*
5 years old	631	560	88.7	83	422	55	*	*	*	*	*	*	*
6 years old	550	539	98.0	4	111	362	47	15	3	*	*	*	*
7 years old	662	633	95.7	*	17	147	421	45	*	*	*	*	*
8 years old	604	571	94.4	*	*	4	105	416	46	*	*	*	*
9 years old	632	619	98.0	*	*	*	58	146	396	19	*	*	*
10 years old	575	558	97.1	*	*	*	*	39	116	346	53	4	*
11 years old	678	662	97.7	*	*	*	*	3	14	178	425	42	*
12 years old	590	577	97.8	*	*	*	*	*	5	13	183	348	25
13 years old	676	664	98.2	*	*	*	*	*	12	22	185	399	—
14 years old	614	591	96.1	*	*	*	*	*	*	22	31	181	—
15 years old	604	599	99.3	*	*	*	*	*	*	*	7	30	—
16 years old	562	495	88.2	*	*	*	*	*	*	*	3	*	—
17 years old	642	605	94.1	*	*	*	*	*	*	*	*	*	*
18 years old	551	371	67.4	*	*	*	*	*	*	*	*	*	*
19 years old	701	389	55.4	*	*	*	*	*	*	*	*	*	*
20 years old	611	286	46.8	*	*	*	*	*	*	*	6	*	*
21 years old	653	322	49.4	*	*	*	*	*	*	*	*	*	*
22 years old	555	169	30.3	*	*	*	*	*	*	*	*	*	*
23 years old	628	170	27.0	*	*	*	*	*	*	*	*	*	*
24 years old	644	171	26.6	*	*	*	*	*	*	*	*	*	4
25 to 29 years old	3,544	487	13.7	*	*	*	*	*	*	*	*	*	*
30 to 34 years old	3,126	244	7.8	*	*	*	*	*	*	*	3	*	*
35 to 39 years old	2,871	172	6.0	*	*	*	*	*	*	*	*	*	*
40 to 44 years old	2,630	94	3.6	*	*	*	*	*	*	*	*	4	*
45 to 49 years old	2,619	122	4.7	*	*	*	*	*	*	*	*	4	*
50 to 54 years old	2,596	63	2.4	*	*	*	*	*	*	*	*	*	*
55 to 59 years old	2,519	44	1.8	*	*	*	*	*	*	*	*	*	*
60 to 64 years old	2,601	35	1.3	*	*	*	*	*	*	*	*	*	*
65 years and over	5,099	21	0.4	*	*	*	*	*	*	*	*	*	*
Male													
Total	19,302	5,618	29.1	389	353	288	289	337	319	299	329	304	337
3 years old	366	172	47.0	166	6	*	*	*	*	*	*	*	*
4 years old	328	217	66.2	159	58	*	*	*	*	*	*	*	*
5 years old	359	314	87.5	61	212	41	*	*	*	*	*	*	*
6 years old	237	237	100.0	4	63	158	1	11	*	*	*	*	*
7 years old	338	331	98.1	*	13	86	193	39	*	*	*	*	*
8 years old	321	312	97.2	*	*	3	57	221	31	*	*	*	*
9 years old	305	300	98.1	*	*	*	37	42	212	9	*	*	*
10 years old	302	293	97.1	*	*	*	*	23	68	173	26	3	*
11 years old	331	324	97.7	*	*	*	*	*	7	103	186	28	*
12 years old	286	279	97.5	*	*	*	*	*	1	2	91	166	15
13 years old	355	353	99.3	*	*	*	*	*	12	20	90	207	—
14 years old	310	306	98.8	*	*	*	*	*	*	*	8	89	—
15 years old	304	299	98.6	*	*	*	*	*	*	*	7	22	—
16 years old	288	255	88.3	*	*	*	*	*	*	*	3	*	—
17 years old	312	286	91.7	*	*	*	*	*	*	*	*	*	*
18 years old	259	175	67.7	*	*	*	*	*	*	*	*	*	*
19 years old	358	196	54.7	*	*	*	*	*	*	*	*	*	*
20 years old	299	140	46.7	*	*	*	*	*	*	*	6	*	*
21 years old	317	148	46.7	*	*	*	*	*	*	*	*	*	*
22 years old	266	78	29.4	*	*	*	*	*	*	*	*	*	*
23 years old	368	87	23.6	*	*	*	*	*	*	*	*	*	*

* = Quantity zero or rounds to zero.

Table A-2. Single Grade of Enrollment and High School Graduation Status for Population 3 Years Old and Over, by Sex, Age (Single Years for 3 to 24 Years), Race, and Hispanic Origin, October 2019—*Continued*

(Numbers in thousands; percent; civilian noninstitutionalized population.)

Age, sex, race, and Hispanic origin	Enrolled High school 9	10	11	12	Undergraduate college 1	2	3	4	Graduate school 1	2+	Not enrolled H.S. grad	Not grad	Not enrolled Number	Percent
35 to 39 years old	*	*	*	5	38	24	42	37	42	94	5,563	221	5,783	95.4
40 to 44 years old	*	*	*	1	23	34	28	13	30	50	5,253	170	5,423	96.8
45 to 49 years old	*	*	*	6	23	10	32	21	28	53	5,627	228	5,855	97.1
50 to 54 years old	*	*	*	3	10	5	7	16	14	51	6,096	256	6,352	98.3
55 to 59 years old	*	*	*	*	8	6	6	2	4	23	7,129	331	7,460	99.3
60 to 64 years old	*	*	*	*	3	*	5	*	4	18	7,163	328	7,490	99.6
65 years and over	*	*	*	3	6	*	*	3	8	12	20,403	1,598	22,001	99.8
BLACK ALONE														
Both Sexes														
Total	536	587	598	634	723	736	434	418	186	350	25,891	3,825	29,716	72.0
3 years old	*	*	*	*	*	*	*	*	*	*	*	362	362	52.6
4 years old	*	*	*	*	*	*	*	*	*	*	*	218	218	35.7
5 years old	*	*	*	*	*	*	*	*	*	*	*	71	71	11.3
6 years old	*	*	*	*	*	*	*	*	*	*	*	11	11	2.0
7 years old	*	*	*	*	*	*	*	*	*	*	*	29	29	4.3
8 years old	*	*	*	*	*	*	*	*	*	*	*	34	34	5.6
9 years old	*	*	*	*	*	*	*	*	*	*	*	13	13	2.0
10 years old	*	*	*	*	*	*	*	*	*	*	*	17	17	2.9
11 years old	*	*	*	*	*	*	*	*	*	*	*	16	16	2.3
12 years old	4	*	*	*	*	*	*	*	*	*	*	13	13	2.2
13 years old	33	13	*	*	*	*	*	*	*	*	*	12	12	1.8
14 years old	320	36	*	*	*	*	*	*	*	*	*	24	24	3.9
15 years old	126	362	61	4	1	9	*	*	*	*	*	4	4	0.7
16 years old	31	138	275	43	1	*	1	*	4	*	16	50	66	11.8
17 years old	*	34	206	337	22	*	*	*	5	*	7	31	38	5.9
18 years old	8	*	13	165	180	4	*	*	*	2	148	32	180	32.6
19 years old	*	*	*	35	167	153	19	15	*	*	261	51	313	44.6
20 years old	*	*	10	18	92	85	69	5	*	*	281	44	325	53.2
21 years old	*	2	14	7	19	93	69	86	15	16	297	34	331	50.6
22 years old	*	*	4	*	20	33	26	57	12	18	363	24	387	69.7
23 years old	*	*	*	*	19	25	38	51	11	25	408	51	459	73.0
24 years old	*	*	3	*	9	37	51	53	12	2	437	35	473	73.4
25 to 29 years old	5	*	*	20	38	116	75	73	57	101	2,863	194	3,057	86.3
30 to 34 years old	*	2	*	1	54	47	41	38	23	35	2,696	187	2,882	92.2
35 to 39 years old	5	*	*	*	39	36	16	11	18	46	2,524	175	2,698	94.0
40 to 44 years old	*	*	*	*	31	21	7	11	1	19	2,331	205	2,536	96.4
45 to 49 years old	*	*	9	4	9	27	10	4	8	47	2,311	186	2,497	95.3
50 to 54 years old	*	*	4	*	4	12	7	10	6	20	2,305	228	2,533	97.6
55 to 59 years old	*	*	*	*	14	11	5	*	6	8	2,220	255	2,475	98.2
60 to 64 years old	4	*	*	*	*	18	*	4	4	4	2,234	332	2,566	98.7
65 years and over	*	*	*	*	4	6	*	*	4	7	4,189	889	5,078	99.6
Male														
Total	321	281	307	294	309	302	198	163	70	128	11,899	1,785	13,684	70.9
3 years old	*	*	*	*	*	*	*	*	*	*	*	194	194	53.0
4 years old	*	*	*	*	*	*	*	*	*	*	*	111	111	33.8
5 years old	*	*	*	*	*	*	*	*	*	*	*	45	45	12.5
6 years old	*	*	*	*	*	*	*	*	*	*	*	*	*	*
7 years old	*	*	*	*	*	*	*	*	*	*	*	6	6	1.9
8 years old	*	*	*	*	*	*	*	*	*	*	*	9	9	2.8
9 years old	*	*	*	*	*	*	*	*	*	*	*	6	6	1.9
10 years old	*	*	*	*	*	*	*	*	*	*	*	9	9	2.9
11 years old	*	*	*	*	*	*	*	*	*	*	*	7	7	2.3
12 years old	4	*	*	*	*	*	*	*	*	*	*	7	7	2.5
13 years old	18	6	*	*	*	*	*	*	*	*	*	2	2	0.7
14 years old	178	31	*	*	*	*	*	*	*	*	*	4	4	1.2
15 years old	84	162	17	*	1	7	*	*	*	*	*	4	4	1.4
16 years old	21	66	146	14	1	*	*	*	4	*	9	25	34	11.7
17 years old	*	11	116	148	9	*	*	*	2	*	4	22	26	8.3
18 years old	8	*	8	97	60	*	*	*	*	2	67	17	84	32.3
19 years old	*	*	*	15	85	76	10	9	*	*	138	24	162	45.3
20 years old	*	*	5	16	36	49	29	*	*	*	146	14	159	53.3
21 years old	*	2	6	1	8	29	38	44	15	5	145	24	169	53.3
22 years old	*	*	*	*	11	23	5	31	2	5	170	17	188	70.6
23 years old	*	*	*	*	12	16	13	28	6	13	236	45	281	76.4

* = Quantity zero or rounds to zero.

Table A-2. Single Grade of Enrollment and High School Graduation Status for Population 3 Years Old and Over, by Sex, Age (Single Years for 3 to 24 Years), Race, and Hispanic Origin, October 2019—*Continued*

(Numbers in thousands; percent; civilian noninstitutionalized population.)

Age, sex, race, and Hispanic origin	Population[1]	Enrolled				Enrolled									
									Elementary grades						
		Number	Percent	Nursery	Kinder-garten	1	2	3	4	5	6	7	8
24 years old	243	38	15.7	*	*	*	*	*	*	*	*	*	4
25 to 29 years old	1,714	208	12.1	*	*	*	*	*	*	*	*	*	*
30 to 34 years old	1,466	72	4.9	*	*	*	*	*	*	*	*	*	*
35 to 39 years old	1,318	71	5.4	*	*	*	*	*	*	*	*	*	*
40 to 44 years old	1,189	16	1.3	*	*	*	*	*	*	*	*	*	*
45 to 49 years old	1,181	41	3.5	*	*	*	*	*	*	*	*	*	*
50 to 54 years old	1,185	19	1.6	*	*	*	*	*	*	*	*	*	*
55 to 59 years old	1,166	17	1.5	*	*	*	*	*	*	*	*	*	*
60 to 64 years old	1,156	16	1.4	*	*	*	*	*	*	*	*	*	*
65 years and over	2,072	18	0.9	*	*	*	*	*	*	*	*	*	*
Female													
Total	21,965	5,933	27.0	325	290	280	340	328	260	268	386	324	303
3 years old	323	155	47.8	143	11	*	*	*	*	*	*	*	*
4 years old	283	176	62.1	159	17	*	*	*	*	*	*	*	*
5 years old	272	246	90.4	22	210	13	*	*	*	*	*	*	*
6 years old	313	302	96.5	*	48	204	46	4	*	*	*	*	*
7 years old	324	301	93.1	*	4	62	227	5	3	*	*	*	*
8 years old	283	258	91.3	*	*	1	47	195	15	*	*	*	*
9 years old	326	319	97.9	*	*	*	20	105	184	10	*	*	*
10 years old	273	265	97.1	*	*	*	*	16	47	173	27	2	*
11 years old	347	338	97.7	*	*	*	*	3	7	75	239	14	*
12 years old	304	298	98.1	*	*	*	*	*	3	10	92	182	10
13 years old	321	311	97.0	*	*	*	*	*	*	*	2	96	192
14 years old	304	284	93.4	*	*	*	*	*	*	*	22	23	92
15 years old	300	300	100.0	*	*	*	*	*	*	*	*	*	8
16 years old	273	241	88.1	*	*	*	*	*	*	*	*	*	*
17 years old	330	318	96.5	*	*	*	*	*	*	*	*	*	*
18 years old	292	196	67.2	*	*	*	*	*	*	*	*	*	*
19 years old	344	193	56.2	*	*	*	*	*	*	*	*	*	*
20 years old	312	146	46.8	*	*	*	*	*	*	*	*	*	*
21 years old	336	174	51.8	*	*	*	*	*	*	*	*	*	*
22 years old	290	90	31.2	*	*	*	*	*	*	*	*	*	*
23 years old	260	83	31.8	*	*	*	*	*	*	*	*	*	*
24 years old	401	133	33.2	*	*	*	*	*	*	*	*	*	*
25 to 29 years old	1,829	279	15.2	*	*	*	*	*	*	*	*	*	*
30 to 34 years old	1,660	172	10.4	*	*	*	*	*	*	*	3	*	*
35 to 39 years old	1,553	101	6.5	*	*	*	*	*	*	*	*	*	*
40 to 44 years old	1,440	78	5.4	*	*	*	*	*	*	*	*	4	*
45 to 49 years old	1,438	81	5.6	*	*	*	*	*	*	*	*	4	*
50 to 54 years old	1,411	44	3.1	*	*	*	*	*	*	*	*	*	*
55 to 59 years old	1,353	27	2.0	*	*	*	*	*	*	*	*	*	*
60 to 64 years old	1,445	19	1.3	*	*	*	*	*	*	*	*	*	*
65 years and over	3,026	3	0.1	*	*	*	*	*	*	*	*	*	*
ASIAN ALONE													
Both Sexes													
Total	19,347	5,023	26.0	260	256	222	239	211	216	185	231	258	238
3 years old	210	102	48.7	99	3	*	*	*	*	*	*	*	*
4 years old	226	152	67.2	125	27	*	*	*	*	*	*	*	*
5 years old	272	245	90.2	32	190	20	4	*	*	*	*	*	*
6 years old	215	205	95.4	5	36	146	19	*	*	*	*	*	*
7 years old	227	226	99.7	*	*	54	149	20	3	*	*	*	*
8 years old	239	231	96.8	*	*	3	67	148	9	4	*	*	*
9 years old	194	191	98.5	*	*	*	*	36	150	5	*	*	*
10 years old	201	201	100.0	*	*	*	*	7	42	132	20	*	*
11 years old	237	237	100.0	*	*	*	*	*	12	44	158	23	*
12 years old	206	206	100.0	*	*	*	*	*	*	*	45	135	20
13 years old	273	273	100.0	*	*	*	*	*	*	*	1	71	177
14 years old	248	248	100.0	*	*	*	*	*	*	*	*	11	33
15 years old	214	212	98.9	*	*	*	*	*	*	*	*	*	4
16 years old	249	229	92.1	*	*	*	*	*	*	*	*	4	*
17 years old	241	231	95.9	*	*	*	*	*	*	*	*	10	5
18 years old	249	203	81.7	*	*	*	*	*	*	*	*	*	*
19 years old	224	204	91.1	*	*	*	*	*	*	*	*	*	*
20 years old	250	210	84.2	*	*	*	*	*	*	*	*	*	*

* = Quantity zero or rounds to zero.

Table A-2. Single Grade of Enrollment and High School Graduation Status for Population 3 Years Old and Over, by Sex, Age (Single Years for 3 to 24 Years), Race, and Hispanic Origin, October 2019—*Continued*

(Numbers in thousands; percent; civilian noninstitutionalized population.)

Age, sex, race, and Hispanic origin	High school 9	10	11	12	Undergraduate college 1	2	3	4	Graduate school 1	2+	Not enrolled H.S. grad	Not grad	Not enrolled Number	Percent
24 years old	*	*	*	*	*	2	23	6	4	*	194	11	205	84.3
25 to 29 years old	*	*	*	*	21	29	60	25	24	47	1,411	96	1,507	87.9
30 to 34 years old	*	2	*	1	25	15	2	15	5	7	1,341	53	1,394	95.1
35 to 39 years old	5	*	*	*	17	16	7	*	1	26	1,176	71	1,247	94.6
40 to 44 years old	*	*	*	*	4	9	*	*	*	3	1,068	106	1,174	98.7
45 to 49 years old	*	*	9	4	9	6	6	*	*	9	1,034	106	1,140	96.5
50 to 54 years old	*	*	*	*	4	4	*	4	*	7	1,036	130	1,166	98.4
55 to 59 years old	*	*	*	*	5	8	5	*	*	*	1,025	124	1,149	98.5
60 to 64 years old	4	*	*	*	*	8	*	*	4	*	988	153	1,140	98.6
65 years and over	*	*	*	*	4	6	*	*	4	5	1,712	342	2,054	99.1
Female														
Total	215	307	291	340	413	434	236	255	116	222	13,992	2,040	16,032	73.0
3 years old	*	*	*	*	*	*	*	*	*	*	*	168	168	52.2
4 years old	*	*	*	*	*	*	*	*	*	*	*	107	107	37.9
5 years old	*	*	*	*	*	*	*	*	*	*	*	26	26	9.6
6 years old	*	*	*	*	*	*	*	*	*	*	*	11	11	3.5
7 years old	*	*	*	*	*	*	*	*	*	*	*	22	22	6.9
8 years old	*	*	*	*	*	*	*	*	*	*	*	25	25	8.7
9 years old	*	*	*	*	*	*	*	*	*	*	*	7	7	2.1
10 years old	*	*	*	*	*	*	*	*	*	*	*	8	8	2.9
11 years old	*	*	*	*	*	*	*	*	*	*	*	8	8	2.3
12 years old	*	*	*	*	*	*	*	*	*	*	*	6	6	1.9
13 years old	15	7	*	*	*	*	*	*	*	*	*	10	10	3.0
14 years old	142	5	*	*	*	*	*	*	*	*	*	20	20	6.6
15 years old	42	200	43	4	*	3	*	*	*	*	*	*	*	*
16 years old	10	72	129	28	*	*	1	*	*	*	7	25	33	11.9
17 years old	*	23	91	189	13	*	*	*	3	*	3	9	12	3.5
18 years old	*	*	5	68	119	4	*	*	*	*	81	15	96	32.8
19 years old	*	*	*	21	82	77	8	5	*	*	124	27	151	43.8
20 years old	*	*	5	3	56	37	40	5	*	*	135	31	166	53.2
21 years old	*	*	8	7	11	64	31	41	*	11	152	9	162	48.2
22 years old	*	*	4	*	9	10	20	25	10	13	193	7	199	68.8
23 years old	*	*	*	*	8	9	25	23	5	12	172	6	178	68.2
24 years old	*	*	3	*	9	35	29	47	8	2	243	25	268	66.8
25 to 29 years old	5	*	*	20	17	87	15	48	33	53	1,452	99	1,550	84.8
30 to 34 years old	*	*	*	*	29	32	39	23	18	28	1,355	133	1,488	89.6
35 to 39 years old	*	*	*	*	23	20	10	11	17	20	1,348	104	1,451	93.5
40 to 44 years old	*	*	*	*	27	12	7	11	1	16	1,263	99	1,362	94.6
45 to 49 years old	*	*	*	*	*	22	4	4	8	39	1,277	80	1,357	94.4
50 to 54 years old	*	*	4	*	*	9	7	5	6	13	1,269	98	1,367	96.9
55 to 59 years old	*	*	*	*	10	4	*	*	6	8	1,195	131	1,326	98.0
60 to 64 years old	*	*	*	*	*	11	*	4	*	4	1,246	179	1,426	98.7
65 years and over	*	*	*	*	*	*	*	*	*	3	2,477	547	3,023	99.9
ASIAN ALONE														
Both Sexes														
Total	255	227	234	222	332	315	330	243	197	352	12,737	1,587	14,324	74.0
3 years old	*	*	*	*	*	*	*	*	*	*	*	108	108	51.3
4 years old	*	*	*	*	*	*	*	*	*	*	*	74	74	32.8
5 years old	*	*	*	*	*	*	*	*	*	*	*	27	27	9.8
6 years old	*	*	*	*	*	*	*	*	*	*	*	10	10	4.6
7 years old	*	*	*	*	*	*	*	*	*	*	*	1	1	0.3
8 years old	*	*	*	*	*	*	*	*	*	*	*	8	8	3.2
9 years old	*	*	*	*	*	*	*	*	*	*	*	3	3	1.5
10 years old	*	*	*	*	*	*	*	*	*	*	*	*	*	*
11 years old	*	*	*	*	*	*	*	*	*	*	*	*	*	*
12 years old	6	*	*	*	*	*	*	*	*	*	*	*	*	*
13 years old	24	*	*	*	*	*	*	*	*	*	*	*	*	*
14 years old	188	6	11	*	*	*	*	*	*	*	*	*	*	*
15 years old	32	155	14	4	*	4	*	*	*	*	*	2	2	1.1
16 years old	3	53	150	16	3	*	*	*	*	*	3	16	20	7.9
17 years old	*	12	42	132	26	*	*	*	4	*	4	6	10	4.1
18 years old	*	1	12	61	125	5	*	*	*	*	23	22	45	18.3
19 years old	*	*	6	6	63	106	23	*	*	*	20	*	20	8.9
20 years old	*	*	*	*	57	48	99	1	5	1	30	10	39	15.8

* = Quantity zero or rounds to zero.

Table A-2. Single Grade of Enrollment and High School Graduation Status for Population 3 Years Old and Over, by Sex, Age (Single Years for 3 to 24 Years), Race, and Hispanic Origin, October 2019—*Continued*

(Numbers in thousands; percent; civilian noninstitutionalized population.)

| | | | | | | Enrolled | | | | | | | | |
| | | Enrolled | | | | Elementary grades | | | | | | | | |
Age, sex, race, and Hispanic origin	Population[1]	Number	Percent	Nursery	Kinder-garten	1	2	3	4	5	6	7	8
21 years old	298	219	73.5	*	*	*	*	*	*	*	*	*	*
22 years old	269	185	68.8	*	*	*	*	*	*	*	*	*	*
23 years old	284	105	37.1	*	*	*	*	*	*	*	*	*	*
24 years old	252	88	35.0	*	*	*	*	*	*	*	*	*	*
25 to 29 years old	1,711	302	17.6	*	*	*	*	*	*	*	*	*	*
30 to 34 years old	1,737	166	9.5	*	*	*	*	*	*	*	*	*	*
35 to 39 years old	1,671	40	2.4	*	*	*	*	*	*	*	*	3	*
40 to 44 years old	1,492	48	3.2	*	*	*	*	*	*	*	*	*	*
45 to 49 years old	1,456	37	2.5	*	*	*	*	*	*	*	7	*	*
50 to 54 years old	1,266	10	0.8	*	*	*	*	*	*	*	*	*	*
55 to 59 years old	1,134	7	0.6	*	*	*	*	*	*	*	*	*	*
60 to 64 years old	1,038	3	0.3	*	*	*	*	*	*	*	*	*	*
65 years and over	2,565	5	0.2	*	*	*	*	*	*	*	*	*	*
Male													
Total	9,189	2,532	27.6	132	131	109	127	118	112	81	129	150	116
3 years old	116	47	40.2	44	3	*	*	*	*	*	*	*	*
4 years old	118	84	71.1	68	16	*	*	*	*	*	*	*	*
5 years old	131	127	96.9	16	100	11	*	*	*	*	*	*	*
6 years old	99	92	93.1	5	12	69	8	*	*	*	*	*	*
7 years old	118	118	100.0	*	*	27	80	11	*	*	*	*	*
8 years old	130	126	96.9	*	*	3	39	75	9	*	*	*	*
9 years old	109	106	97.3	*	*	*	*	25	78	3	*	*	*
10 years old	91	91	100.0	*	*	*	*	7	15	61	7	*	*
11 years old	124	124	100.0	*	*	*	*	*	8	18	96	2	*
12 years old	95	95	100.0	*	*	*	*	*	*	*	22	72	1
13 years old	163	163	100.0	*	*	*	*	*	*	*	1	59	94
14 years old	117	117	100.0	*	*	*	*	*	*	*	*	9	16
15 years old	114	114	100.0	*	*	*	*	*	*	*	*	*	*
16 years old	105	99	93.7	*	*	*	*	*	*	*	*	*	*
17 years old	119	119	99.4	*	*	*	*	*	*	*	*	4	5
18 years old	121	103	84.9	*	*	*	*	*	*	*	*	*	*
19 years old	112	105	93.5	*	*	*	*	*	*	*	*	*	*
20 years old	132	100	76.3	*	*	*	*	*	*	*	*	*	*
21 years old	127	105	82.7	*	*	*	*	*	*	*	*	*	*
22 years old	125	98	78.0	*	*	*	*	*	*	*	*	*	*
23 years old	177	51	28.9	*	*	*	*	*	*	*	*	*	*
24 years old	111	37	33.3	*	*	*	*	*	*	*	*	*	*
25 to 29 years old	858	162	18.9	*	*	*	*	*	*	*	*	*	*
30 to 34 years old	826	71	8.6	*	*	*	*	*	*	*	*	*	*
35 to 39 years old	813	18	2.3	*	*	*	*	*	*	*	*	3	*
40 to 44 years old	671	15	2.2	*	*	*	*	*	*	*	*	*	*
45 to 49 years old	697	29	4.2	*	*	*	*	*	*	*	4	*	*
50 to 54 years old	579	8	1.4	*	*	*	*	*	*	*	*	*	*
55 to 59 years old	487	*	*	*	*	*	*	*	*	*	*	*	*
60 to 64 years old	497	3	0.7	*	*	*	*	*	*	*	*	*	*
65 years and over	1,105	4	0.4	*	*	*	*	*	*	*	*	*	*
Female													
Total	10,158	2,491	24.5	128	125	113	112	93	104	104	102	109	122
3 years old	94	56	59.2	56	*	*	*	*	*	*	*	*	*
4 years old	108	68	62.8	57	11	*	*	*	*	*	*	*	*
5 years old	141	118	83.9	16	90	9	4	*	*	*	*	*	*
6 years old	116	113	97.3	*	24	77	12	*	*	*	*	*	*
7 years old	109	108	99.4	*	*	27	69	9	3	*	*	*	*
8 years old	109	105	96.6	*	*	*	28	73	*	4	*	*	*
9 years old	84	84	100.0	*	*	*	*	10	71	3	*	*	*
10 years old	110	110	100.0	*	*	*	*	*	26	71	12	*	*
11 years old	113	113	100.0	*	*	*	*	*	4	26	62	21	*
12 years old	111	111	100.0	*	*	*	*	*	*	*	23	63	19
13 years old	110	110	100.0	*	*	*	*	*	*	*	1	12	82
14 years old	131	131	100.0	*	*	*	*	*	*	*	*	3	17
15 years old	101	98	97.6	*	*	*	*	*	*	*	*	*	4
16 years old	143	130	90.9	*	*	*	*	*	*	*	*	4	*
17 years old	122	112	92.4	*	*	*	*	*	*	*	*	6	*
18 years old	127	100	78.7	*	*	*	*	*	*	*	*	*	*
19 years old	112	99	88.7	*	*	*	*	*	*	*	*	*	*

* = Quantity zero or rounds to zero.

Table A-2. Single Grade of Enrollment and High School Graduation Status for Population 3 Years Old and Over, by Sex, Age (Single Years for 3 to 24 Years), Race, and Hispanic Origin, October 2019—*Continued*

(Numbers in thousands; percent; civilian noninstitutionalized population.)

Age, sex, race, and Hispanic origin	Enrolled										Not enrolled		Not enrolled	
	High school				Undergraduate college				Graduate school		H.S. grad	Not grad	Number	Percent
	9	10	11	12	1	2	3	4	1	2+				
21 years old	*	*	*	*	17	41	67	49	15	31	75	5	79	26.5
22 years old	*	*	*	*	4	31	43	66	23	18	82	2	84	31.2
23 years old	*	*	*	*	*	15	14	28	39	9	176	3	178	62.9
24 years old	*	*	*	*	9	*	11	27	26	15	164	*	164	65.0
25 to 29 years old	*	*	*	*	4	28	33	43	52	142	1,349	60	1,409	82.4
30 to 34 years old	*	*	*	*	15	15	30	11	18	76	1,484	87	1,571	90.5
35 to 39 years old	*	*	*	*	*	5	6	7	2	18	1,508	123	1,631	97.6
40 to 44 years old	*	*	*	1	1	8	3	10	5	21	1,352	92	1,444	96.8
45 to 49 years old	3	*	*	*	2	6	*	*	5	13	1,321	98	1,419	97.5
50 to 54 years old	*	*	*	*	5	*	*	*	3	2	1,175	81	1,256	99.2
55 to 59 years old	*	*	*	*	*	4	*	*	*	3	1,023	105	1,128	99.4
60 to 64 years old	*	*	*	*	*	*	*	*	*	3	891	145	1,035	99.7
65 years and over	*	*	*	4	*	*	*	1	*	*	2,059	501	2,560	99.8
Male														
Total	118	120	104	115	173	142	162	110	94	190	6,012	645	6,657	72.4
3 years old	*	*	*	*	*	*	*	*	*	*	*	69	69	59.8
4 years old	*	*	*	*	*	*	*	*	*	*	*	34	34	28.9
5 years old	*	*	*	*	*	*	*	*	*	*	*	4	4	3.1
6 years old	*	*	*	*	*	*	*	*	*	*	*	7	7	6.9
7 years old	*	*	*	*	*	*	*	*	*	*	*	*	*	*
8 years old	*	*	*	*	*	*	*	*	*	*	*	4	4	3.1
9 years old	*	*	*	*	*	*	*	*	*	*	*	3	3	2.7
10 years old	*	*	*	*	*	*	*	*	*	*	*	*	*	*
11 years old	*	*	*	*	*	*	*	*	*	*	*	*	*	*
12 years old	*	*	*	*	*	*	*	*	*	*	*	*	*	*
13 years old	9	*	*	*	*	*	*	*	*	*	*	*	*	*
14 years old	87	2	4	*	*	*	*	*	*	*	*	*	*	*
15 years old	19	92	3	*	*	*	*	*	*	*	*	*	*	*
16 years old	*	18	70	8	3	*	*	*	*	*	3	3	7	6.3
17 years old	*	9	16	66	15	*	*	*	4	*	*	1	1	0.6
18 years old	*	*	11	31	59	3	*	*	*	*	11	7	18	15.1
19 years old	*	*	*	6	30	57	12	*	*	*	7	*	7	6.5
20 years old	*	*	*	*	30	25	45	*	*	1	22	10	31	23.7
21 years old	*	*	*	*	8	21	43	17	3	12	22	*	22	17.3
22 years old	*	*	*	*	4	9	30	36	7	13	28	*	28	22.0
23 years old	*	*	*	*	*	9	*	15	23	5	123	3	126	71.1
24 years old	*	*	*	*	*	*	*	12	17	7	74	*	74	66.7
25 to 29 years old	*	*	*	*	4	8	17	22	26	84	675	21	696	81.1
30 to 34 years old	*	*	*	*	12	5	13	*	6	36	716	39	754	91.4
35 to 39 years old	*	*	*	*	*	*	2	*	*	13	740	54	795	97.7
40 to 44 years old	*	*	*	1	*	*	*	7	*	7	617	39	657	97.8
45 to 49 years old	3	*	*	1	2	6	*	*	5	9	614	54	668	95.8
50 to 54 years old	*	*	*	*	5	*	*	*	3	*	543	28	571	98.6
55 to 59 years old	*	*	*	*	*	*	*	*	*	*	449	38	487	100.0
60 to 64 years old	*	*	*	*	*	*	*	*	*	3	440	53	494	99.3
65 years and over	*	*	*	4	*	*	*	*	*	*	927	173	1,101	99.6
Female														
Total	138	106	131	107	159	173	168	133	103	162	6,725	942	7,667	75.5
3 years old	*	*	*	*	*	*	*	*	*	*	*	38	38	40.8
4 years old	*	*	*	*	*	*	*	*	*	*	*	40	40	37.2
5 years old	*	*	*	*	*	*	*	*	*	*	*	23	23	16.1
6 years old	*	*	*	*	*	*	*	*	*	*	*	3	3	2.7
7 years old	*	*	*	*	*	*	*	*	*	*	*	1	1	0.6
8 years old	*	*	*	*	*	*	*	*	*	*	*	4	4	3.4
9 years old	*	*	*	*	*	*	*	*	*	*	*	*	*	*
10 years old	*	*	*	*	*	*	*	*	*	*	*	*	*	*
11 years old	*	*	*	*	*	*	*	*	*	*	*	*	*	*
12 years old	6	*	*	*	*	*	*	*	*	*	*	*	*	*
13 years old	15	*	*	*	*	*	*	*	*	*	*	*	*	*
14 years old	101	4	7	*	*	*	*	*	*	*	*	*	*	*
15 years old	13	62	11	4	*	4	*	*	*	*	*	2	2	2.4
16 years old	3	36	80	8	*	*	*	*	*	*	*	13	13	9.1
17 years old	*	4	26	66	11	*	*	*	*	*	4	5	9	7.6
18 years old	*	1	1	30	66	3	*	*	*	*	12	15	27	21.3
19 years old	*	*	6	*	33	49	11	*	*	*	12	*	13	11.3

* = Quantity zero or rounds to zero.

Table A-2. Single Grade of Enrollment and High School Graduation Status for Population 3 Years Old and Over, by Sex, Age (Single Years for 3 to 24 Years), Race, and Hispanic Origin, October 2019—*Continued*

(Numbers in thousands; percent; civilian noninstitutionalized population.)

Age, sex, race, and Hispanic origin	Population[1]	Enrolled		Nursery	Kindergarten	Elementary grades							
		Number	Percent			1	2	3	4	5	6	7	8
20 years old	118	110	93.0	*	*	*	*	*	*	*	*	*	*
21 years old	171	114	66.6	*	*	*	*	*	*	*	*	*	*
22 years old	144	87	60.7	*	*	*	*	*	*	*	*	*	*
23 years old	107	54	50.9	*	*	*	*	*	*	*	*	*	*
24 years old	141	51	36.3	*	*	*	*	*	*	*	*	*	*
25 to 29 years old	853	140	16.4	*	*	*	*	*	*	*	*	*	*
30 to 34 years old	911	94	10.4	*	*	*	*	*	*	*	*	*	*
35 to 39 years old	858	22	2.5	*	*	*	*	*	*	*	*	*	*
40 to 44 years old	821	34	4.1	*	*	*	*	*	*	*	*	*	*
45 to 49 years old	759	8	1.0	*	*	*	*	*	*	*	3	*	*
50 to 54 years old	687	2	0.3	*	*	*	*	*	*	*	*	*	*
55 to 59 years old	648	7	1.0	*	*	*	*	*	*	*	*	*	*
60 to 64 years old	541	*	*	*	*	*	*	*	*	*	*	*	*
65 years and over	1,460	1	0.1	*	*	*	*	*	*	*	*	*	*
HISPANIC (OF ANY RACE)													
Both Sexes													
Total	57,582	18,204	31.6	1,115	1,038	958	1,102	1,046	1,071	1,120	1,131	941	1,027
3 years old	1,052	423	40.2	407	15	*	*	*	*	*	*	*	*
4 years old	1,049	623	59.4	520	104	*	*	*	*	*	*	*	*
5 years old	1,048	936	89.3	154	734	42	6	*	*	*	*	*	*
6 years old	999	973	97.4	34	166	678	77	18	*	*	*	*	*
7 years old	1,067	1,038	97.2	*	18	232	723	63	2	*	*	*	*
8 years old	1,066	1,025	96.2	*	*	4	257	675	78	12	*	*	*
9 years old	1,106	1,073	97.0	*	*	2	31	277	695	59	9	*	*
10 years old	1,017	983	96.6	*	*	*	8	6	265	658	42	4	*
11 years old	1,128	1,107	98.2	*	*	*	*	7	30	351	686	27	6
12 years old	1,123	1,104	98.3	*	*	*	*	*	1	36	305	717	46
13 years old	997	964	96.6	*	*	*	*	*	*	4	48	137	716
14 years old	1,043	1,007	96.5	*	*	*	*	*	*	*	19	43	222
15 years old	1,063	1,044	98.3	*	*	*	*	*	*	*	1	6	23
16 years old	954	878	92.1	*	*	*	*	*	*	*	*	2	7
17 years old	1,033	924	89.4	*	*	*	*	*	*	*	*	1	3
18 years old	976	702	71.9	*	*	*	*	*	*	*	*	*	*
19 years old	1,057	593	56.1	*	*	*	*	*	*	*	*	*	*
20 years old	984	493	50.1	*	*	*	*	*	*	*	*	*	*
21 years old	912	419	46.0	*	*	*	*	*	*	*	*	*	*
22 years old	947	369	39.0	*	*	*	*	*	*	*	*	2	*
23 years old	956	212	22.2	*	*	*	*	*	*	*	*	*	*
24 years old	980	183	18.7	*	*	*	*	*	*	*	*	*	*
25 to 29 years old	4,864	498	10.2	*	*	*	*	*	*	*	6	*	*
30 to 34 years old	4,537	243	5.4	*	*	*	*	*	*	*	10	1	*
35 to 39 years old	4,475	162	3.6	*	*	*	*	*	*	*	*	*	*
40 to 44 years old	4,147	81	1.9	*	*	*	*	*	*	*	*	*	*
45 to 49 years old	3,824	74	1.9	*	*	*	*	*	*	*	3	*	4
50 to 54 years old	3,335	38	1.1	*	*	*	*	*	*	*	2	*	*
55 to 59 years old	2,940	13	0.4	*	*	*	*	*	*	*	*	*	*
60 to 64 years old	2,204	5	0.2	*	*	*	*	*	*	*	*	*	*
65 years and over	4,699	16	0.3	*	*	*	*	*	*	*	*	*	*
Male													
Total	28,839	9,087	31.5	604	490	513	601	527	555	529	575	483	549
3 years old	540	234	43.3	227	7	*	*	*	*	*	*	*	*
4 years old	542	327	60.2	279	47	*	*	*	*	*	*	*	*
5 years old	527	469	89.0	79	345	42	3	*	*	*	*	*	*
6 years old	515	505	98.0	19	88	353	43	1	*	*	*	*	*
7 years old	541	538	99.6	*	2	116	391	29	*	*	*	*	*
8 years old	558	546	97.8	*	*	2	146	349	39	10	*	*	*
9 years old	554	542	97.9	*	*	*	19	140	357	19	7	*	*
10 years old	516	495	96.1	*	*	*	*	3	144	324	26	*	*
11 years old	590	576	97.6	*	*	*	*	4	14	167	366	19	6
12 years old	535	526	98.4	*	*	*	*	*	1	9	144	348	25
13 years old	524	494	94.3	*	*	*	*	*	*	13	77	382	
14 years old	535	516	96.5	*	*	*	*	*	*	7	35	108	
15 years old	548	533	97.4	*	*	*	*	*	*	1	*	19	
16 years old	495	458	92.6	*	*	*	*	*	*	*	2	3	

* = Quantity zero or rounds to zero.

Table A-2. Single Grade of Enrollment and High School Graduation Status for Population 3 Years Old and Over, by Sex, Age (Single Years for 3 to 24 Years), Race, and Hispanic Origin, October 2019—*Continued*

(Numbers in thousands; percent; civilian noninstitutionalized population.)

Age, sex, race, and Hispanic origin	Enrolled										Not enrolled		Not enrolled	
	High school				Undergraduate college				Graduate school		H.S. grad	Not grad	Number	Percent
	9	10	11	12	1	2	3	4	1	2+				
20 years old	*	*	*	*	27	23	54	1	5	*	8	*	8	7.0
21 years old	*	*	*	*	9	19	23	31	12	19	53	5	57	33.4
22 years old	*	*	*	*	1	22	14	30	16	5	54	2	56	39.3
23 years old	*	*	*	*	*	6	14	13	16	4	52	*	52	49.1
24 years old	*	*	*	*	9	*	11	15	9	8	90	*	90	63.7
25 to 29 years old	*	*	*	*	*	19	15	21	26	58	674	39	713	83.6
30 to 34 years old	*	*	*	*	3	11	17	11	13	40	768	48	817	89.6
35 to 39 years old	*	*	*	*	*	5	4	7	2	5	767	69	836	97.5
40 to 44 years old	*	*	*	*	1	8	3	3	5	14	734	53	787	95.9
45 to 49 years old	*	*	*	*	*	*	*	*	*	5	707	44	751	99.0
50 to 54 years old	*	*	*	*	*	*	*	*	*	2	632	53	684	99.7
55 to 59 years old	*	*	*	*	*	4	*	*	*	3	574	67	641	99.0
60 to 64 years old	*	*	*	*	*	*	*	*	*	*	450	91	541	100.0
65 years and over	*	*	*	*	*	*	*	1	*	*	1,131	328	1,459	99.9
HISPANIC (OF ANY RACE)														
Both Sexes														
Total	1,038	1,054	960	1,048	960	952	801	394	167	200	20,104	11,274	39,378	68.4
3 years old	*	*	*	*	*	*	*	*	*	*	*	629	629	59.8
4 years old	*	*	*	*	*	*	*	*	*	*	*	426	426	40.6
5 years old	*	*	*	*	*	*	*	*	*	*	*	112	112	10.7
6 years old	*	*	*	*	*	*	*	*	*	*	*	26	26	2.6
7 years old	*	*	*	*	*	*	*	*	*	*	*	30	30	2.8
8 years old	*	*	*	*	*	*	*	*	*	*	*	41	41	3.8
9 years old	*	*	*	*	*	*	*	*	*	*	*	33	33	3.0
10 years old	*	*	*	*	*	*	*	*	*	*	*	34	34	3.4
11 years old	*	*	*	*	*	*	*	*	*	*	*	21	21	1.8
12 years old	*	*	*	*	*	*	*	*	*	*	*	19	19	1.7
13 years old	58	*	*	*	*	*	*	*	*	*	*	34	34	3.4
14 years old	650	72	1	*	*	*	*	*	*	*	*	36	36	3.5
15 years old	255	624	111	20	*	3	1	*	*	*	3	16	18	1.7
16 years old	33	265	495	63	3	*	8	*	3	*	13	63	76	7.9
17 years old	18	54	293	533	22	*	*	*	*	*	24	85	109	10.6
18 years old	8	14	25	305	324	16	10	*	*	*	207	67	274	28.1
19 years old	1	7	4	57	256	205	52	10	*	*	360	104	464	43.9
20 years old	*	5	4	9	87	216	148	14	9	*	401	90	491	49.9
21 years old	8	*	5	14	56	123	123	70	*	21	448	44	493	54.0
22 years old	*	11	*	5	30	101	91	93	10	26	515	63	578	61.0
23 years old	*	*	*	4	18	25	68	54	21	22	672	71	744	77.8
24 years old	4	*	*	9	6	31	72	38	6	17	726	70	796	81.3
25 to 29 years old	*	*	1	6	68	112	116	43	63	83	3,741	625	4,366	89.8
30 to 34 years old	*	*	4	*	39	48	53	26	16	48	3,419	875	4,294	94.6
35 to 39 years old	4	*	4	11	20	29	19	28	10	35	3,226	1,087	4,313	96.4
40 to 44 years old	*	*	4	3	11	19	12	3	13	16	2,923	1,143	4,066	98.1
45 to 49 years old	*	3	9	*	8	7	22	14	4	*	2,726	1,023	3,750	98.1
50 to 54 years old	*	*	*	5	4	15	7	*	5	1	2,323	974	3,297	98.9
55 to 59 years old	*	*	*	*	*	*	1	*	3	8	2,041	887	2,928	99.6
60 to 64 years old	*	*	*	*	4	1	*	*	*	*	1,509	691	2,200	99.8
65 years and over	*	*	*	3	5	1	*	*	3	3	2,827	1,856	4,683	99.7
Male														
Total	529	512	537	524	417	459	348	138	82	115	13,947	5,804	19,751	68.5
3 years old	*	*	*	*	*	*	*	*	*	*	*	306	306	56.7
4 years old	*	*	*	*	*	*	*	*	*	*	*	215	215	39.8
5 years old	*	*	*	*	*	*	*	*	*	*	*	58	58	11.0
6 years old	*	*	*	*	*	*	*	*	*	*	*	10	10	2.0
7 years old	*	*	*	*	*	*	*	*	*	*	*	2	2	0.4
8 years old	*	*	*	*	*	*	*	*	*	*	*	12	12	2.2
9 years old	*	*	*	*	*	*	*	*	*	*	*	12	12	2.1
10 years old	*	*	*	*	*	*	*	*	*	*	*	20	20	3.9
11 years old	*	*	*	*	*	*	*	*	*	*	*	14	14	2.4
12 years old	*	*	*	*	*	*	*	*	*	*	*	9	9	1.6
13 years old	22	*	*	*	*	*	*	*	*	*	*	30	30	5.7
14 years old	318	49	1	*	*	*	*	*	*	*	*	19	19	3.5
15 years old	148	286	69	8	*	*	1	*	*	*	3	12	14	2.6
16 years old	14	139	267	27	*	*	4	*	3	*	6	30	37	7.4

* = Quantity zero or rounds to zero.

Table A-2. Single Grade of Enrollment and High School Graduation Status for Population 3 Years Old and Over, by Sex, Age (Single Years for 3 to 24 Years), Race, and Hispanic Origin, October 2019—*Continued*

(Numbers in thousands; percent; civilian noninstitutionalized population.)

Age, sex, race, and Hispanic origin	Population[1]	Enrolled Number	Enrolled Percent	Nursery	Kinder-garten	Elementary grades 1	2	3	4	5	6	7	8
17 years old	524	466	88.9	*	*	*	*	*	*	*	*	1	3
18 years old	498	359	72.1	*	*	*	*	*	*	*	*	*	*
19 years old	517	286	55.3	*	*	*	*	*	*	*	*	*	*
20 years old	519	236	45.5	*	*	*	*	*	*	*	*	*	*
21 years old	454	200	44.0	*	*	*	*	*	*	*	*	*	*
22 years old	482	174	36.0	*	*	*	*	*	*	*	*	*	*
23 years old	452	67	14.9	*	*	*	*	*	*	*	*	*	*
24 years old	503	73	14.5	*	*	*	*	*	*	*	*	*	*
25 to 29 years old	2,484	222	8.9	*	*	*	*	*	*	*	6	*	*
30 to 34 years old	2,352	81	3.4	*	*	*	*	*	*	*	6	1	*
35 to 39 years old	2,298	73	3.2	*	*	*	*	*	*	*	*	*	*
40 to 44 years old	2,100	39	1.9	*	*	*	*	*	*	*	*	*	*
45 to 49 years old	1,910	36	1.9	*	*	*	*	*	*	*	*	*	4
50 to 54 years old	1,673	16	1.0	*	*	*	*	*	*	*	*	*	*
55 to 59 years old	1,468	*	*	*	*	*	*	*	*	*	*	*	*
60 to 64 years old	1,036	*	*	*	*	*	*	*	*	*	*	*	*
65 years and over	2,052			*	*	*	*	*	*	*	*	*	*
Female													
Total	28,744	9,117	31.7	511	548	445	501	519	516	591	556	458	478
3 years old	512	189	36.8	181	8	*	*	*	*	*	*	*	*
4 years old	507	297	58.5	240	56	*	*	*	*	*	*	*	*
5 years old	521	467	89.6	75	389	*	3	*	*	*	*	*	*
6 years old	484	468	96.8	15	79	324	34	17	*	*	*	*	*
7 years old	527	500	94.8	*	16	116	332	33	2	*	*	*	*
8 years old	508	479	94.3	*	*	2	111	325	39	2	*	*	*
9 years old	552	531	96.1	*	*	2	12	137	338	39	2	*	*
10 years old	502	488	97.2	*	*	*	8	3	121	335	16	4	*
11 years old	537	531	98.8	*	*	*	*	3	16	184	320	8	*
12 years old	589	578	98.2	*	*	*	*	*	27	161	369	21	
13 years old	474	470	99.2	*	*	*	*	*	*	4	36	60	335
14 years old	508	491	96.6	*	*	*	*	*	*	*	13	9	114
15 years old	515	511	99.2	*	*	*	*	*	*	*	*	6	4
16 years old	459	420	91.5	*	*	*	*	*	*	*	*	*	4
17 years old	509	458	89.9	*	*	*	*	*	*	*	*	*	*
18 years old	478	343	71.8	*	*	*	*	*	*	*	*	*	*
19 years old	540	307	56.9	*	*	*	*	*	*	*	*	*	*
20 years old	465	257	55.3	*	*	*	*	*	*	*	*	*	*
21 years old	458	219	47.9	*	*	*	*	*	*	*	*	*	*
22 years old	465	196	42.0	*	*	*	*	*	*	*	*	2	*
23 years old	504	145	28.8	*	*	*	*	*	*	*	*	*	*
24 years old	477	111	23.2	*	*	*	*	*	*	*	*	*	*
25 to 29 years old	2,380	276	11.6	*	*	*	*	*	*	*	*	*	*
30 to 34 years old	2,185	163	7.4	*	*	*	*	*	*	*	4	*	*
35 to 39 years old	2,177	89	4.1	*	*	*	*	*	*	*	*	*	*
40 to 44 years old	2,047	42	2.0	*	*	*	*	*	*	*	*	*	*
45 to 49 years old	1,914	39	2.0	*	*	*	*	*	*	*	3	*	*
50 to 54 years old	1,662	21	1.3	*	*	*	*	*	*	*	2	*	*
55 to 59 years old	1,472	13	0.8	*	*	*	*	*	*	*	*	*	*
60 to 64 years old	1,168	5	0.4	*	*	*	*	*	*	*	*	*	*
65 years and over	2,647	16	0.6	*	*	*	*	*	*	*	*	*	*

* = Quantity zero or rounds to zero.

Table A-2. Single Grade of Enrollment and High School Graduation Status for Population 3 Years Old and Over, by Sex, Age (Single Years for 3 to 24 Years), Race, and Hispanic Origin, October 2019—*Continued*

(Numbers in thousands; percent; civilian noninstitutionalized population.)

Age, sex, race, and Hispanic origin	Enrolled										Not enrolled		Not enrolled	
	High school				Undergraduate college				Graduate school		H.S. grad	Not grad	Number	Percent
	9	10	11	12	1	2	3	4	1	2+				
17 years old	6	33	176	245	3	*	*	*	*	*	20	38	58	11.1
18 years old	8	3	12	173	148	10	4	*	*	*	93	46	139	27.9
19 years old	1	2	*	36	116	109	22	*	*	*	176	55	231	44.7
20 years old	*	*	*	6	60	93	67	5	4	*	238	45	283	54.5
21 years old	8	*	*	14	15	60	69	24	*	10	238	16	254	56.0
22 years old	*	*	*	*	11	60	38	49	10	6	279	30	308	64.0
23 years old	*	*	*	*	5	6	18	22	12	4	335	50	385	85.1
24 years old	*	*	*	4	5	10	26	16	6	5	393	36	430	85.5
25 to 29 years old	*	*	*	4	27	44	60	7	29	45	1,875	387	2,262	91.1
30 to 34 years old	*	*	*	*	6	21	20	8	*	17	1,801	470	2,272	96.6
35 to 39 years old	4	*	*	2	9	17	9	8	*	25	1,603	622	2,225	96.8
40 to 44 years old	*	*	4	*	2	15	5	*	10	3	1,418	642	2,060	98.1
45 to 49 years old	*	*	9	*	8	7	4	*	4	*	1,360	515	1,874	98.1
50 to 54 years old	*	*	*	5	*	7	*	*	5	*	1,152	504	1,656	99.0
55 to 59 years old	*	*	*	*	*	*	*	*	*	*	1,015	453	1,468	100.0
60 to 64 years old	*	*	*	*	*	*	*	*	*	*	714	322	1,036	100.0
65 years and over	*	*	*	*	*	*	*	*	*	*	1,228	823	2,052	100.0
Female														
Total	509	543	423	524	544	493	453	255	85	165	14,157	5,470	19,627	68.3
3 years old	*	*	*	*	*	*	*	*	*	*	*	323	323	63.2
4 years old	*	*	*	*	*	*	*	*	*	*	*	210	210	41.5
5 years old	*	*	*	*	*	*	*	*	*	*	*	54	54	10.4
6 years old	*	*	*	*	*	*	*	*	*	*	*	16	16	3.2
7 years old	*	*	*	*	*	*	*	*	*	*	*	27	27	5.2
8 years old	*	*	*	*	*	*	*	*	*	*	*	29	29	5.7
9 years old	*	*	*	*	*	*	*	*	*	*	*	22	22	3.9
10 years old	*	*	*	*	*	*	*	*	*	*	*	14	14	2.8
11 years old	*	*	*	*	*	*	*	*	*	*	*	7	7	1.2
12 years old	*	*	*	*	*	*	*	*	*	*	*	10	10	1.8
13 years old	35	*	*	*	*	*	*	*	*	*	*	4	4	0.8
14 years old	332	24	*	*	*	*	*	*	*	*	*	17	17	3.4
15 years old	106	338	42	12	*	3	*	*	*	*	*	4	4	0.8
16 years old	19	126	228	36	3	*	4	*	*	*	7	32	39	8.5
17 years old	12	21	118	288	19	*	*	*	*	*	4	47	51	10.1
18 years old	*	10	13	132	176	6	5	*	*	*	115	20	135	28.2
19 years old	*	6	4	21	140	96	30	10	*	*	185	48	233	43.1
20 years old	*	5	4	3	27	123	80	9	5	*	163	45	208	44.7
21 years old	*	*	5	*	41	62	54	46	*	11	210	28	238	52.1
22 years old	*	11	*	5	19	41	53	44	*	20	237	33	270	58.0
23 years old	*	*	*	4	13	19	50	33	9	18	337	22	359	71.2
24 years old	4	*	*	5	1	20	45	22	*	12	332	34	367	76.8
25 to 29 years old	*	*	1	2	41	68	57	36	34	38	1,866	238	2,104	88.4
30 to 34 years old	*	*	4	*	32	26	32	18	16	31	1,618	405	2,022	92.6
35 to 39 years old	*	*	4	10	12	13	10	21	10	10	1,623	465	2,088	95.9
40 to 44 years old	*	*	*	3	8	5	6	3	4	13	1,504	501	2,006	98.0
45 to 49 years old	*	3	*	*	*	*	18	14	*	*	1,367	509	1,876	98.0
50 to 54 years old	*	*	*	*	4	7	7	*	*	1	1,171	470	1,641	98.7
55 to 59 years old	*	*	*	*	*	*	1	*	3	8	1,026	433	1,460	99.2
60 to 64 years old	*	*	*	*	4	1	*	*	*	*	794	369	1,163	99.6
65 years and over	*	*	*	3	5	1	*	*	3	3	1,598	1,033	2,631	99.4

* = Quantity zero or rounds to zero.

Table A-3. Nursery and Primary School Enrollment of Population 3 to 6 Years Old, by Control of School, Attendance Status, Age, Race, Hispanic Origin, Mother's Labor Force Status and Education, and Family Income, October 2019

(Numbers in thousands; civilian noninstitutionalized population.)

Characteristic	Total	Not enrolled	Enrolled in nursery school — Total: Total	Part-day	Full-day	Public: Total	Part-day	Full-day	Private: Total	Part-day	Full-day
3 TO 6 YEARS OLD											
Total	16,090	4,251	4,728	2,058	2,670	2,614	1,134	1,480	2,114	924	1,190
Race and Hispanic origin											
White alone	11,481	3,069	3,352	1,558	1,794	1,756	839	917	1,596	719	877
White alone non-Hispanic	7,833	2,005	2,399	1,127	1,273	1,094	539	555	1,306	588	718
Black alone	2,481	663	714	192	522	520	140	380	194	52	142
Asian alone	923	219	260	143	118	118	64	54	142	78	64
Hispanic (of any race)	4,147	1,193	1,115	501	613	775	353	422	340	149	191
Labor force status of mother											
Children not living with mother	1,514	424	430	152	278	325	118	207	104	34	70
Mother employed part-time	2,282	524	690	413	277	336	182	154	354	231	123
Mother employed full-time	7,333	1,645	2,353	838	1,515	1,182	451	731	1,171	387	784
Mother unemployed	430	146	110	55	55	89	41	48	21	13	8
Mother not in the labor force	4,531	1,513	1,146	601	545	682	341	341	464	259	205
Education of mother											
Children not living with mother	1,514	424	430	152	278	325	118	207	104	34	70
Elementary: 0 to 8 years	537	190	93	37	56	85	37	48	8	*	8
High school: 9 to 11 years	838	297	161	76	84	142	68	74	18	8	10
High school graduate	3,311	1,087	855	385	470	626	267	359	229	118	111
Some college or associate's degree	3,907	1,120	1,074	494	580	639	310	329	435	184	251
Bachelor's degree or more	5,984	1,133	2,115	913	1,202	796	334	462	1,319	579	740
Family income											
Less than $20,000	1,506	474	365	132	233	303	109	194	63	24	39
$20,000 to $29,999	1,196	362	327	100	226	234	80	154	92	21	72
$30,000 to $39,999	1,303	426	329	123	206	232	72	159	97	51	46
$40,000 to $49,999	990	318	253	122	131	193	89	104	60	33	28
$50,000 to $74,999	2,068	636	598	288	309	394	183	211	204	105	98
$75,000 and over	5,926	1,180	2,052	949	1,103	759	372	387	1,293	577	716
Not reported	3,102	855	805	344	461	500	230	270	305	114	191
3 AND 4 YEARS OLD											
Total	8,074	3,741	3,949	1,725	2,223	2,124	912	1,212	1,825	814	1,011
Race and Hispanic origin											
White alone	5,729	2,718	2,757	1,287	1,470	1,398	660	738	1,359	627	732
White alone non-Hispanic	3,877	1,769	1,971	931	1,040	874	426	448	1,097	505	592
Black alone	1,300	580	627	185	442	455	133	322	172	52	120
Asian alone	436	182	224	129	95	96	56	39	128	72	56
Hispanic (of any race)	2,100	1,055	927	406	521	615	266	349	312	140	172
Labor force status of mother											
Children not living with mother	785	386	345	132	213	264	107	157	80	25	55
Mother employed part-time	1,106	460	581	348	233	280	149	131	301	199	102
Mother employed full-time	3,629	1,458	2,013	712	1,301	987	357	630	1,026	355	671
Mother unemployed	230	128	100	47	54	80	33	46	21	13	8
Mother not in the labor force	2,323	1,309	910	487	423	513	265	248	396	222	175
Education of mother											
Children not living with mother	785	386	345	132	213	264	107	157	80	25	55
Elementary: 0 to 8 years	256	161	68	26	42	60	26	34	8	*	8
High school: 9 to 11 years	411	259	136	62	74	117	53	64	18	8	10
High school graduate	1,724	927	702	326	376	511	230	281	191	97	95
Some college or associate's degree	1,988	981	901	403	497	522	234	287	379	169	210
Bachelor's degree or more	2,909	1,026	1,797	776	1,021	649	261	388	1,148	515	633
Family income											
Less than $20,000	714	389	294	91	203	245	73	172	49	18	31
$20,000 to $29,999	631	325	273	88	185	186	67	119	87	21	66
$30,000 to $39,999	696	382	284	107	177	187	57	131	97	51	46
$40,000 to $49,999	522	286	198	89	109	149	57	92	49	32	17
$50,000 to $74,999	1,103	556	500	268	232	322	167	155	178	101	77
$75,000 and over	2,885	1,049	1,727	774	953	619	287	332	1,108	487	620
Not reported	1,523	752	672	308	364	415	203	211	258	105	153

* = Quantity zero or rounds to zero.

Table A-3. Nursery and Primary School Enrollment of Population 3 to 6 Years Old, by Control of School, Attendance Status, Age, Race, Hispanic Origin, Mother's Labor Force Status and Education, and Family Income, October 2019—*Continued*

(Numbers in thousands; civilian noninstitutionalized population.)

Characteristic	Enrolled in kindergarten									Enrolled in elementary school		
	Total			Public			Private					
	Total	Part-day	Full-day	Total	Part-day	Full-day	Total	Part-day	Full-day	Total	Public	Private
3 TO 6 YEARS OLD												
Total	3,974	693	3,281	3,464	624	2,840	510	69	441	3,137	2,850	287
Race and Hispanic origin												
White alone	2,830	506	2,324	2,477	453	2,024	353	53	300	2,231	2,005	226
White alone non-Hispanic	1,916	315	1,601	1,640	263	1,378	276	53	223	1,513	1,318	195
Black alone	625	75	551	546	75	471	79	*	79	479	433	45
Asian alone	256	56	200	197	39	158	58	17	42	188	184	5
Hispanic (of any race)	1,020	208	811	926	208	718	93	*	93	820	790	30
Labor force status of mother												
Children not living with mother	404	48	356	366	46	320	38	2	36	256	236	20
Mother employed part-time	617	134	482	536	120	415	81	14	67	452	404	48
Mother employed full-time	1,783	289	1,494	1,522	258	1,264	261	32	229	1,552	1,406	146
Mother unemployed	83	13	70	82	13	70	*	*	*	92	92	*
Mother not in the labor force	1,088	209	879	958	188	771	130	21	108	784	712	73
Education of mother												
Children not living with mother	404	48	356	366	46	320	38	2	36	256	236	20
Elementary: 0 to 8 years	145	29	117	141	29	112	4	*	4	108	92	17
High school: 9 to 11 years	191	50	141	189	50	139	2	*	2	190	177	12
High school graduate	703	126	577	638	121	517	65	5	60	665	636	29
Some college or associate's degree	978	170	808	879	163	716	99	7	92	734	667	67
Bachelor's degree or more	1,553	270	1,282	1,251	216	1,036	301	55	246	1,184	1,043	141
Family income												
Less than $20,000	354	50	304	336	46	290	18	4	14	313	291	21
$20,000 to $29,999	270	37	233	262	37	225	8	*	8	237	228	10
$30,000 to $39,999	287	72	215	263	72	191	24	*	24	261	252	9
$40,000 to $49,999	245	47	198	223	45	177	23	2	21	174	156	18
$50,000 to $74,999	465	101	364	399	86	313	66	15	51	370	344	26
$75,000 and over	1,553	250	1,303	1,285	210	1,075	269	40	229	1,141	987	154
Not reported	800	136	663	697	128	569	103	9	94	642	593	49
3 AND 4 YEARS OLD												
Total	385	100	285	316	85	231	69	15	54	*	*	*
Race and Hispanic origin												
White alone	255	72	183	205	63	141	50	8	42	*	*	*
White alone non-Hispanic	137	44	93	105	36	70	32	8	24	*	*	*
Black alone	93	7	86	84	7	77	9	*	9	*	*	*
Asian alone	30	15	16	20	8	12	10	7	4	*	*	*
Hispanic (of any race)	119	28	91	101	28	73	18	*	18	*	*	*
Labor force status of mother												
Children not living with mother	54	21	33	41	21	20	13	*	13	*	*	*
Mother employed part-time	66	19	47	50	19	31	15	*	15	*	*	*
Mother employed full-time	159	40	119	129	30	99	30	10	20	*	*	*
Mother unemployed	1	*	1	1	*	1	*	*	*	*	*	*
Mother not in the labor force	105	20	85	95	15	79	10	5	5	*	*	*
Education of mother												
Children not living with mother	54	21	33	41	21	20	13	*	13	*	*	*
Elementary: 0 to 8 years	28	4	23	28	4	23	*	*	*	*	*	*
High school: 9 to 11 years	17	2	14	17	2	14	*	*	*	*	*	*
High school graduate	94	16	78	81	16	65	13	*	13	*	*	*
Some college or associate's degree	106	27	79	89	27	62	17	*	17	*	*	*
Bachelor's degree or more	86	29	57	60	14	46	26	15	11	*	*	*
Family income												
Less than $20,000	30	1	29	30	1	29	*	*	*	*	*	*
$20,000 to $29,999	33	7	26	28	7	20	5	*	5	*	*	*
$30,000 to $39,999	30	10	20	30	10	20	*	*	*	*	*	*
$40,000 to $49,999	38	4	34	37	4	33	1	*	1	*	*	*
$50,000 to $74,999	47	17	31	30	13	17	18	4	14	*	*	*
$75,000 and over	108	30	79	75	19	56	33	11	22	*	*	*
Not reported	98	31	67	86	31	55	12	*	12	*	*	*

* = Quantity zero or rounds to zero.

Table A-3. Nursery and Primary School Enrollment of Population 3 to 6 Years Old, by Control of School, Attendance Status, Age, Race, Hispanic Origin, Mother's Labor Force Status and Education, and Family Income, October 2019—*Continued*

(Numbers in thousands; civilian noninstitutionalized population.)

| Characteristic | Total | Not enrolled | Enrolled in nursery school | | | | | | | | |
| | | | Total | | | Public | | | Private | | |
			Total	Part-day	Full-day	Total	Part-day	Full-day	Total	Part-day	Full-day
5 YEARS OLD											
Total	4,092	380	705	296	409	430	188	242	276	108	167
Race and Hispanic origin											
White alone	2,889	245	529	234	295	302	144	157	228	90	138
White alone non-Hispanic	1,982	156	397	181	216	198	100	97	199	81	119
Black alone	631	71	83	7	76	65	7	58	18	*	18
Asian alone	272	27	32	14	18	18	8	10	14	6	8
Hispanic (of any race)	1,048	112	154	74	80	126	65	61	28	9	19
Labor force status of mother											
Children not living with mother	414	34	80	15	65	55	6	50	24	9	15
Mother employed part-time	604	43	109	65	44	56	33	23	53	32	21
Mother employed full-time	1,823	137	302	118	184	169	86	83	133	32	102
Mother unemployed	95	17	7	6	1	7	6	1	*	*	*
Mother not in the labor force	1,156	148	208	93	114	143	58	85	65	36	29
Education of mother											
Children not living with mother	414	34	80	15	65	55	6	50	24	9	15
Elementary: 0 to 8 years	131	23	20	11	9	20	11	9	*	*	*
High school: 9 to 11 years	206	30	19	9	10	19	9	10	*	*	*
High school graduate	808	119	142	56	86	104	34	70	38	22	16
Some college or associate's degree	913	92	148	74	74	94	61	34	54	13	41
Bachelor's degree or more	1,618	82	296	132	164	136	67	69	160	65	95
Family income											
Less than $20,000	401	76	59	33	26	46	27	18	13	6	8
$20,000 to $29,999	288	20	54	13	41	48	13	35	6	*	6
$30,000 to $39,999	305	37	42	16	26	42	16	26	*	*	*
$40,000 to $49,999	251	19	49	27	22	38	26	11	12	1	10
$50,000 to $74,999	483	61	95	20	74	72	16	56	22	5	18
$75,000 and over	1,583	92	306	165	141	125	76	49	181	90	92
Not reported	781	75	101	21	80	60	14	45	41	7	34
6 YEARS OLD											
Total	3,924	131	74	37	37	61	35	26	14	2	11
Race and Hispanic origin											
White alone	2,863	105	66	37	29	56	35	21	10	2	8
White alone non-Hispanic	1,974	80	32	15	17	22	13	9	10	2	8
Black alone	550	11	4	*	4	*	*	*	4	*	4
Asian alone	215	10	5	*	5	5	*	5	*	*	*
Hispanic (of any race)	999	26	34	22	12	34	22	12	*	*	*
Labor force status of mother											
Children not living with mother	314	4	6	6	*	6	6	*	*	*	*
Mother employed part-time	572	21	*	*	*	*	*	*	*	*	*
Mother employed full-time	1,881	50	38	8	30	27	8	19	11	*	11
Mother unemployed	105	*	2	2	*	2	2	*	*	*	*
Mother not in the labor force	1,052	56	28	20	8	26	18	7	3	2	*
Education of mother											
Children not living with mother	314	4	6	6	*	6	6	*	*	*	*
Elementary: 0 to 8 years	149	6	5	*	5	5	*	5	*	*	*
High school: 9 to 11 years	220	8	6	6	*	6	6	*	*	*	*
High school graduate	779	41	11	3	8	11	3	8	*	*	*
Some college or associate's degree	1,005	47	25	17	8	23	15	8	2	2	*
Bachelor's degree or more	1,457	25	22	5	17	11	5	5	11	*	11
Family income											
Less than $20,000	391	9	12	8	4	12	8	4	*	*	*
$20,000 to $29,999	276	17	*	*	*	*	*	*	*	*	*
$30,000 to $39,999	302	8	3	*	3	3	*	3	*	*	*
$40,000 to $49,999	217	12	6	6	*	6	6	*	*	*	*
$50,000 to $74,999	482	19	4	*	4	*	*	*	4	*	4
$75,000 and over	1,459	39	19	9	9	15	9	5	4	*	4
Not reported	798	28	31	14	17	25	12	14	6	2	4

* = Quantity zero or rounds to zero.

Table A-3. Nursery and Primary School Enrollment of Population 3 to 6 Years Old, by Control of School, Attendance Status, Age, Race, Hispanic Origin, Mother's Labor Force Status and Education, and Family Income, October 2019—*Continued*

(Numbers in thousands; civilian noninstitutionalized population.)

Characteristic	Enrolled in kindergarten									Enrolled in elementary school		
	Total			Public			Private					
	Total	Part-day	Full-day	Total	Part-day	Full-day	Total	Part-day	Full-day	Total	Public	Private
5 YEARS OLD												
Total	2,802	427	2,375	2,447	390	2,057	355	37	318	205	197	9
Race and Hispanic origin												
White alone	1,994	310	1,684	1,744	280	1,464	250	30	220	120	115	5
White alone non-Hispanic	1,352	191	1,161	1,149	162	988	203	30	173	76	71	5
Black alone	422	45	377	367	45	322	55	*	55	55	51	3
Asian alone	190	36	153	159	29	130	31	7	24	23	23	*
Hispanic (of any race)	734	130	604	671	130	541	63	*	63	48	48	*
Labor force status of mother												
Children not living with mother	268	23	245	251	21	230	17	2	15	33	33	*
Mother employed part-time	426	83	343	373	75	299	53	8	45	26	23	3
Mother employed full-time	1,283	174	1,108	1,091	157	934	191	18	174	101	97	3
Mother unemployed	64	10	54	63	10	54	*	*	*	7	7	*
Mother not in the labor force	762	136	626	668	127	541	94	9	85	38	36	3
Education of mother												
Children not living with mother	268	23	245	251	21	230	17	2	15	33	33	*
Elementary: 0 to 8 years	87	13	74	83	13	69	4	*	4	1	1	*
High school: 9 to 11 years	145	35	110	143	35	108	2	*	2	12	12	*
High school graduate	496	88	408	458	87	371	38	1	37	51	51	*
Some college or associate's degree	640	88	552	582	82	500	58	6	52	33	33	*
Bachelor's degree or more	1,165	179	987	930	151	778	236	27	208	75	67	9
Family income												
Less than $20,000	250	31	219	232	27	205	18	4	14	16	13	3
$20,000 to $29,999	187	28	158	186	28	158	1	*	1	28	28	*
$30,000 to $39,999	201	47	153	183	47	136	17	*	17	26	26	*
$40,000 to $49,999	176	37	139	156	36	121	19	1	18	6	6	*
$50,000 to $74,999	309	50	259	269	42	227	40	9	32	18	18	*
$75,000 and over	1,136	152	984	941	137	804	195	14	180	48	45	3
Not reported	543	81	463	479	72	407	64	9	56	62	59	3
6 YEARS OLD												
Total	787	167	620	701	150	551	86	17	69	2,932	2,653	278
Race and Hispanic origin												
White alone	581	124	457	528	110	419	53	15	38	2,111	1,891	220
White alone non-Hispanic	426	80	347	385	65	320	41	15	26	1,436	1,247	190
Black alone	111	23	88	95	23	72	16	*	16	424	382	42
Asian alone	36	5	31	19	2	17	17	3	14	165	160	5
Hispanic (of any race)	166	51	116	154	51	104	12	*	12	772	742	30
Labor force status of mother												
Children not living with mother	82	4	78	74	4	70	8	*	8	223	203	20
Mother employed part-time	125	32	93	112	27	85	13	5	7	426	381	45
Mother employed full-time	341	75	266	302	71	231	39	4	35	1,452	1,309	143
Mother unemployed	18	3	15	18	3	15	*	*	*	85	85	*
Mother not in the labor force	222	53	168	196	45	151	26	8	18	746	676	70
Education of mother												
Children not living with mother	82	4	78	74	4	70	8	*	8	223	203	20
Elementary: 0 to 8 years	31	11	20	31	11	20	*	*	*	107	91	17
High school: 9 to 11 years	29	12	17	29	12	17	*	*	*	178	165	12
High school graduate	113	22	91	99	18	81	14	4	10	614	585	29
Some college or associate's degree	232	55	177	207	54	153	24	1	23	701	634	67
Bachelor's degree or more	301	63	239	262	50	211	40	12	27	1,108	976	132
Family income												
Less than $20,000	74	17	56	74	17	56	*	*	*	296	278	18
$20,000 to $29,999	50	1	49	48	1	47	2	*	2	209	200	10
$30,000 to $39,999	56	15	41	49	15	34	7	*	7	235	226	9
$40,000 to $49,999	32	6	26	30	6	24	2	1	2	167	149	18
$50,000 to $74,999	108	34	74	101	32	69	8	2	5	352	326	26
$75,000 and over	309	69	241	268	54	214	41	14	26	1,092	942	150
Not reported	158	25	133	131	25	107	27	*	27	580	533	47

* = Quantity zero or rounds to zero.

Table A-4. Current Grade for People 15 to 24 Years Old Enrolled in School, and Highest Grade Completed for People with Selected Enrollment and Completion Status, by Sex, Age, Race, and Hispanic Origin, October 2019

(Numbers in thousands; civilian noninstitutionalized population.)

Age, sex, race, and Hispanic origin	Total	Enrolled — Current grade							Not enrolled — Enrolled last year — Highest grade completed						Not enrolled last year
		Less than 9th grade	9th grade	10th grade	11th grade	12th grade	College (graduated this year)	Other college	Less than 9th grade	9th grade	10th grade	11th or 12th, no diploma	New HS graduate	Other[1]	
ALL RACES															
Both Sexes															
Total	41,893	258	1,187	3,828	3,988	4,184	2,109	10,076	42	65	141	266	1,075	2,327	12,346
15 years old	4,160	155	1,008	2,509	338	44	7	29	8	6	10	1	*	*	46
16 years old	4,154	28	118	1,077	2,341	247	14	35	12	43	79	37	7	17	98
17 years old	4,237	28	30	172	1,107	2,415	110	57	*	16	24	105	66	7	101
18 years old	4,055	2	16	36	117	1,185	1,182	370	11	*	16	83	547	103	389
19 years old	4,251	2	1	14	27	184	629	1,823	2	*	3	34	290	307	936
20 to 24 years old	21,037	43	14	21	59	110	169	7,762	9	*	9	7	165	1,893	10,776
Male															
Total	21,088	163	662	1,935	2,096	2,139	924	4,620	26	15	69	142	564	1,093	6,637
15 years old	2,124	97	573	1,232	157	14	3	12	3	3	*	1	*	*	28
16 years old	2,106	8	62	567	1,213	98	7	20	6	5	41	10	2	14	52
17 years old	2,158	20	7	101	621	1,164	34	26	*	7	11	51	45	7	64
18 years old	2,041	2	11	23	75	685	492	168	11	*	11	51	275	61	179
19 years old	2,141	*	1	6	10	111	318	846	*	*	3	23	156	150	516
20 to 24 years old	10,518	37	8	6	21	66	71	3,549	6	*	4	6	88	860	5,798
Female															
Total	20,805	95	524	1,893	1,892	2,045	1,185	5,455	17	50	72	124	511	1,234	5,709
15 years old	2,035	58	435	1,276	181	29	3	17	5	2	10	*	*	*	18
16 years old	2,048	20	56	511	1,127	149	6	14	6	38	38	27	5	3	46
17 years old	2,079	9	23	71	486	1,251	76	31	*	10	13	53	21	*	37
18 years old	2,014	*	5	13	42	500	690	202	*	*	5	32	273	42	210
19 years old	2,110	2	*	7	17	73	311	977	2	*	*	10	135	157	420
20 to 24 years old	10,519	6	6	16	38	43	98	4,213	3	*	5	2	78	1,032	4,979
WHITE ALONE															
Total	30,690	156	906	2,781	2,856	3,093	1,592	7,168	27	37	108	208	783	1,692	9,283
15 years old	3,037	94	771	1,804	247	36	7	16	8	6	8	1	*	*	42
16 years old	3,036	17	84	818	1,723	168	11	28	*	22	63	26	6	14	58
17 years old	3,042	12	29	112	756	1,789	64	32	*	10	17	82	51	7	81
18 years old	3,065	2	8	24	87	892	906	256	8	*	9	74	412	82	306
19 years old	3,100	2	1	8	20	131	481	1,306	2	*	3	22	193	224	707
20 to 24 years old	15,409	30	14	14	23	77	124	5,530	9	*	9	3	122	1,365	8,089
WHITE ALONE NON-HISPANIC															
Total	22,138	125	623	1,953	2,028	2,238	1,193	5,359	20	20	75	139	558	1,300	6,508
15 years old	2,142	74	548	1,291	150	16	7	11	5	5	8	*	*	*	28
16 years old	2,211	12	55	577	1,280	121	7	18	*	16	48	13	6	14	46
17 years old	2,148	7	11	59	505	1,342	47	31	*	*	5	47	30	7	57
18 years old	2,220	2	8	17	64	640	682	165	4	*	5	61	290	53	231
19 years old	2,190	2	*	6	16	83	349	974	2	*	*	15	152	146	446
20 to 24 years old	11,227	28	2	4	13	37	101	4,160	9	*	9	3	80	1,081	5,700
BLACK ALONE															
Total	6,151	50	165	536	585	609	222	1,409	10	12	19	38	215	338	1,941
15 years old	604	37	126	362	61	4	*	10	*	*	*	*	*	*	4
16 years old	562	3	31	138	275	43	*	6	10	12	8	8	*	*	27
17 years old	642	*	*	34	206	337	13	14	*	*	4	9	7	*	19
18 years old	551	*	8	*	13	165	116	69	*	*	7	6	97	18	51
19 years old	701	*	*	*	*	35	71	282	*	*	*	11	76	61	164
20 to 24 years old	3,092	10	*	2	31	26	22	1,027	*	*	*	4	35	260	1,676

[1]Other includes people whose response to questions on educational attainment did not fall into one of the listed categories (e.g., completed high school (not last year), but enrolled in college or some other type of school last year).

* = Quantity zero or rounds to zero.

Table A-4. Current Grade for People 15 to 24 Years Old Enrolled in School, and Highest Grade Completed for People with Selected Enrollment and Completion Status, by Sex, Age, Race, and Hispanic Origin, October 2019—*Continued*

(Numbers in thousands; civilian noninstitutionalized population.)

Age, sex, race, and Hispanic origin	Total	Enrolled — Current grade							Not enrolled — Enrolled last year — Highest grade completed						Not enrolled last year
		Less than 9th grade	9th grade	10th grade	11th grade	12th grade	College (graduated this year)	Other college	Less than 9th grade	9th grade	10th grade	11th or 12th, no diploma	New HS graduate	Other[1]	
ASIAN ALONE															
Total..........................	2,530	23	35	221	224	218	170	998	3	*	6	12	19	175	427
15 years old	214	4	32	155	14	4	*	4	*	*	2	*	*	*	*
16 years old	249	4	3	53	150	16	3	*	*	*	3	3	*	*	13
17 years old	241	15	*	12	42	132	23	7	*	*	*	6	4	*	1
18 years old	249	*	*	1	12	61	94	36	3	*	*	3	13	3	23
19 years old	224	*	*	*	6	6	37	155	*	*	*	*	3	1	16
20 to 24 years old	1,353	*	*	*	*	*	12	796	*	*	*	*	*	170	374
HISPANIC (OF ANY RACE)															
Total.................................	9,861	46	327	979	938	1,020	432	2,077	6	28	42	76	249	463	3,177
15 years old	1,063	30	255	624	111	20	*	4	3	1	*	1	*	*	14
16 years old	954	9	33	265	495	63	3	11	*	10	24	12	1	*	28
17 years old	1,033	5	18	54	293	533	21	1	*	16	12	36	21	*	25
18 years old	976	*	8	14	25	305	250	99	3	*	4	13	133	29	91
19 years old	1,057	*	1	7	4	57	134	388	*	*	3	15	53	84	310
20 to 24 years old	4,778	2	12	16	10	41	23	1,574	*	*	*	*	41	351	2,709

[1]Other includes people whose response to questions on educational attainment did not fall into one of the listed categories (e.g., completed high school (not last year), but enrolled in college or some other type of school last year).

* = Quantity zero or rounds to zero.

Table A-5. Type of College and Year Enrolled for College Students 15 Years Old and Over, by Age, Sex, Race, Attendance Status, Control of School, Disability Status, and Enrollment Status, October 2019

(Numbers in thousands; civilian noninstitutionalized population.)

Characteristic	Total enrolled	Undergraduate college								Graduate school	
		All colleges				Two-year college		Four-year college			
		1st year	2nd year	3rd year	4th year	1st year	2nd or higher	1st year	2nd or higher	1st year	2nd or higher
BOTH SEXES	18,289	4,201	4,167	3,602	2,615	1,824	2,506	2,377	7,878	1,362	2,342
Full-Time Students											
Total	13,849	3,357	3,219	2,814	2,090	1,257	1,555	2,100	6,569	904	1,465
Age											
15–19 years old	3,957	2,441	1,204	253	17	794	339	1,647	1,134	37	5
20–24 years old	6,610	593	1,475	2,042	1,584	249	784	344	4,316	463	452
25–34 years old	2,309	176	382	384	349	138	280	38	836	273	745
35 years old and over	973	146	158	136	140	75	151	71	283	130	263
Race											
White alone	9,652	2,344	2,290	2,074	1,454	931	1,136	1,413	4,682	599	890
White alone non-Hispanic	7,410	1,701	1,685	1,577	1,199	634	754	1,067	3,707	487	761
Black alone	2,001	518	511	315	321	190	277	328	869	125	212
Asian alone	1,503	290	269	284	203	60	90	230	666	162	295
Hispanic (of any race)	2,568	709	705	590	285	310	442	400	1,138	125	154
Employment Status											
Full time	2,185	345	436	424	290	155	261	190	889	222	469
Part time	4,192	827	986	1,058	741	348	547	479	2,239	250	330
Not employed	7,471	2,185	1,797	1,332	1,059	754	747	1,431	3,441	432	666
Control of School											
Public	11,172	2,839	2,740	2,320	1,692	1,162	1,474	1,676	5,277	583	999
Private	2,677	518	479	495	398	94	80	424	1,292	320	466
Disability Status											
No disability	13,505	3,235	3,135	2,751	2,063	1,178	1,491	2,057	6,458	875	1,446
Any disability	343	122	84	63	27	78	64	44	111	28	19
Part-Time Students											
Total	4,441	844	948	788	525	567	952	277	1,309	458	877
Age											
15–19 years old	298	193	83	15	6	135	54	58	50	*	*
20–24 years old	1,321	248	355	345	208	165	396	82	512	103	62
25–34 years old	1,436	209	275	254	173	149	266	60	435	177	349
35 years old and over	1,385	194	234	174	138	118	235	77	312	178	467
Race											
White alone	3,131	541	628	573	376	367	608	174	968	357	657
White alone non-Hispanic	2,267	311	409	401	281	211	433	100	658	316	550
Black alone	846	205	226	119	97	131	206	74	235	61	138
Asian alone	265	43	46	45	40	26	67	17	64	35	56
Hispanic (of any race)	987	251	248	211	108	165	229	86	339	42	127
Employment Status											
Full time	2,639	406	495	436	293	268	452	138	772	349	661
Part time	1,133	267	298	256	136	184	351	83	339	60	114
Not employed	669	171	155	96	96	114	149	56	198	49	102
Control of School											
Public	3,574	708	870	684	466	512	905	196	1,115	295	551
Private	866	136	78	104	59	55	47	81	194	163	326
Disability Status											
No disability	4,259	795	897	770	488	538	908	258	1,248	451	857
Any disability	182	49	51	18	37	30	44	19	62	7	20
MALE	8,067	1,833	1,922	1,667	1,145	860	1,181	973	3,553	507	993
Full-Time Students											
Total	6,247	1,479	1,496	1,319	949	599	742	880	3,022	369	635
Age											
15–19 years old	1,777	1,092	519	126	7	396	181	695	470	29	5
20–24 years old	2,998	240	733	948	721	99	376	141	2,027	180	175
25–34 years old	1,107	83	165	206	168	67	111	16	428	118	366
35 years old and over	365	64	79	39	53	36	73	28	97	42	89
Race											
White alone	4,334	1,037	1,085	968	664	439	549	598	2,168	219	361
White alone non-Hispanic	3,307	736	798	745	562	286	367	450	1,738	163	303
Black alone	876	221	233	141	145	89	126	132	393	55	81
Asian alone	749	134	128	143	97	28	36	106	332	87	160
Hispanic (of any race)	1,157	327	340	255	108	154	214	173	489	62	64

* = Quantity zero or rounds to zero.

Table A-5. Type of College and Year Enrolled for College Students 15 Years Old and Over, by Age, Sex, Race, Attendance Status, Control of School, Disability Status, and Enrollment Status, October 2019—*Continued*

(Numbers in thousands; civilian noninstitutionalized population.)

Characteristic	Total enrolled	Undergraduate college								Graduate school	
		All colleges				Two-year college		Four-year college			
		1st year	2nd year	3rd year	4th year	1st year	2nd or higher	1st year	2nd or higher	1st year	2nd or higher
Employment Status											
Full time	879	145	176	189	102	66	111	79	355	76	191
Part time	1,683	312	437	453	295	141	262	171	923	77	110
Not employed	3,685	1,022	883	678	553	392	369	630	1,745	215	334
Control of School											
Public	4,960	1,233	1,255	1,058	773	551	703	682	2,384	231	410
Private	1,287	246	241	261	176	48	40	197	639	138	225
Disability Status											
No disability	6,121	1,436	1,458	1,300	935	574	705	862	2,988	358	634
Any disability	126	43	38	20	14	25	37	18	34	11	1
Part-Time Students											
Total	1,819	354	426	348	196	260	439	93	531	138	358
Age											
15–19 years old	147	86	51	4	6	63	36	23	26	*	*
20–24 years old	622	138	168	172	76	100	223	39	193	32	35
25–34 years old	535	62	104	97	72	50	94	12	180	43	157
35 years old and over	515	68	102	74	43	48	87	19	132	63	166
Race											
White alone	1,327	214	309	262	163	171	307	43	427	115	263
White alone non-Hispanic	954	124	205	170	135	97	211	27	298	96	224
Black alone	295	88	69	57	19	55	85	33	59	15	47
Asian alone	121	39	15	19	12	22	19	17	26	7	29
Hispanic (of any race)	402	90	119	93	31	74	111	16	131	20	50
Employment Status											
Full time	1,102	166	208	219	134	140	231	26	330	84	291
Part time	456	133	135	96	35	83	144	50	122	28	29
Not employed	261	55	83	32	28	38	63	18	79	26	38
Control of School											
Public	1,477	297	380	301	183	231	416	65	449	86	230
Private	342	57	45	47	13	29	23	28	82	52	128
Disability Status											
No disability	1,749	343	392	345	190	253	416	90	511	133	346
Any disability	70	11	33	2	7	7	23	4	20	5	12
FEMALE	10,223	2,368	2,245	1,935	1,470	964	1,325	1,404	4,325	855	1,349
Full-Time Students											
Total	7,601	1,878	1,723	1,495	1,141	657	812	1,221	3,547	535	830
Age											
15–19 years old	2,179	1,350	685	127	10	398	158	952	664	8	*
20–24 years old	3,611	353	742	1,094	862	150	408	203	2,289	283	277
25–34 years old	1,203	93	217	177	181	71	168	22	408	155	379
35 years old and over	608	82	79	97	87	39	78	43	186	88	173
Race											
White alone	5,318	1,308	1,206	1,106	790	493	588	815	2,514	380	529
White alone non-Hispanic	4,102	965	886	833	637	348	386	618	1,969	323	458
Black alone	1,125	296	278	174	176	100	152	196	476	70	131
Asian alone	755	156	142	141	105	32	55	124	334	76	135
Hispanic (of any race)	1,411	382	365	335	177	155	227	227	649	63	89
Employment Status											
Full time	1,306	200	260	235	188	89	149	111	534	146	277
Part time	2,509	515	549	606	447	207	285	308	1,316	173	220
Not employed	3,786	1,163	914	654	506	362	378	801	1,697	216	332
Control of School											
Public	6,212	1,605	1,485	1,261	919	611	772	994	2,893	353	589
Private	1,389	272	238	234	222	46	41	226	653	182	241
Disability Status											
No disability	7,384	1,799	1,677	1,451	1,127	604	785	1,195	3,470	518	812
Any disability	217	79	46	43	14	53	27	26	76	17	18

* = Quantity zero or rounds to zero.

Table A-5. Type of College and Year Enrolled for College Students 15 Years Old and Over, by Age, Sex, Race, Attendance Status, Control of School, Disability Status, and Enrollment Status, October 2019—*Continued*

(Numbers in thousands; civilian noninstitutionalized population.)

| Characteristic | Total enrolled | Undergraduate college | | | | | | | | Graduate school | |
| | | All colleges | | | | Two-year college | | Four-year college | | | |
		1st year	2nd year	3rd year	4th year	1st year	2nd or higher	1st year	2nd or higher	1st year	2nd or higher
Part-Time Students											
Total..	2,621	490	523	440	329	307	513	183	779	320	519
Age											
15–19 years old	150	107	33	10	*	72	19	35	24	*	*
20–24 years old	699	110	187	172	132	66	173	44	319	72	26
25–34 years old	901	147	171	156	101	99	173	47	256	134	192
35 years old and over...............	870	127	132	101	96	69	148	57	180	114	301
Race											
White alone..............................	1,805	327	320	310	213	196	301	131	541	242	394
White alone non-Hispanic.........	1,314	187	205	231	146	114	222	73	359	220	326
Black alone...............................	551	117	157	63	78	76	121	41	176	46	91
Asian alone	143	4	31	26	28	4	47	*	38	27	27
Hispanic (of any race)..............	585	161	129	119	78	91	118	70	208	22	76
Employment Status											
Full time...................................	1,537	240	287	217	159	128	221	112	442	265	370
Part time	676	134	163	160	101	102	207	33	217	32	85
Not employed............................	408	116	72	64	69	77	85	39	119	23	65
Control of School											
Public..	2,097	411	489	383	283	280	489	131	666	210	321
Private.......................................	524	79	33	57	46	26	24	53	113	110	198
Disability Status											
No disability.............................	2,510	453	505	424	299	285	491	168	737	318	511
Any disability............................	112	37	17	16	30	22	22	15	42	2	8

* = Quantity zero or rounds to zero.

Table A-6. Employment Status and Enrollment in Vocational Courses for the Population 15 Years Old and Over, by Sex, Age, Educational Attainment, and College Enrollment, October 2019[1]

(Numbers in thousands; percent; civilian noninstitutionalized population.)

Characteristic	Total			Employed full-time			Employed part-time			Not employed		
	Total	Enrolled in vocational courses		Total	Enrolled in vocational courses		Total	Enrolled in vocational courses		Total	Enrolled in vocational courses	
		Number	Percent		Number	Percent		Number	Percent		Number	Percent
BOTH SEXES												
Total.....................................	264,005	3,720	1.4	132,770	2,010	1.5	27,732	676	2.4	103,503	1,033	1.0
Age												
15 to 19 years old	20,856	302	1.4	1,560	49	3.2	4,014	91	2.3	15,282	162	1.1
20 to 24 years old	21,037	677	3.2	9,455	229	2.4	4,945	170	3.4	6,638	278	4.2
25 to 34 years old	44,954	923	2.1	32,122	607	1.9	4,235	142	3.3	8,596	174	2.0
35 to 44 years old	41,120	653	1.6	30,209	441	1.5	3,485	95	2.7	7,426	117	1.6
45 to 64 years old	82,611	841	1.0	52,623	593	1.1	6,854	92	1.3	23,134	156	0.7
65 years and over	53,426	323	0.6	6,801	90	1.3	4,198	87	2.1	42,427	146	0.3
Educational attainment												
Not a high school graduate	35,905	179	0.5	8,539	73	0.9	3,699	27	0.7	23,667	79	0.3
High school graduate only	72,835	701	1.0	34,933	304	0.9	6,899	148	2.1	31,004	249	0.8
Some college or associate's degree...................................	70,744	1,362	1.9	35,056	647	1.8	9,625	279	2.9	26,063	435	1.7
Bachelor's degree or more	84,521	1,479	1.8	54,243	986	1.8	7,509	223	3.0	22,769	270	1.2
College enrollment												
Enrolled in college....................	18,289	1,133	6.2	4,824	350	7.3	5,325	298	5.6	8,140	486	6.0
Not enrolled in college	245,716	2,587	1.1	127,946	1,660	1.3	22,407	378	1.7	95,363	548	0.6
MALE												
Total.....................................	127,811	1,860	1.5	74,400	1,138	1.5	9,940	254	2.6	43,471	468	1.1
Age												
15 to 19 years old	10,569	185	1.7	883	35	3.9	1,810	52	2.9	7,876	98	1.2
20 to 24 years old	10,518	325	3.1	5,051	128	2.5	2,147	55	2.6	3,321	142	4.3
25 to 34 years old	22,434	531	2.4	18,024	404	2.2	1,348	51	3.8	3,061	76	2.5
35 to 44 years old	20,227	295	1.5	17,141	224	1.3	793	24	3.0	2,293	47	2.1
45 to 64 years old	40,078	390	1.0	29,220	310	1.1	1,866	21	1.1	8,992	58	0.6
65 years and over	23,985	135	0.6	4,081	38	0.9	1,977	50	2.5	17,927	47	0.3
Educational attainment												
Not a high school graduate	18,270	80	0.4	5,814	32	0.6	1,566	4	0.3	10,890	44	0.4
High school graduate only	37,279	394	1.1	21,931	207	0.9	2,667	59	2.2	12,681	128	1.0
Some college or associate's degree...................................	33,045	711	2.2	19,248	383	2.0	3,383	113	3.3	10,414	216	2.1
Bachelor's degree or more	39,217	675	1.7	27,407	516	1.9	2,325	78	3.4	9,485	80	0.8
College enrollment												
Enrolled in college....................	8,067	563	7.0	1,981	195	9.9	2,139	133	6.2	3,946	235	5.9
Not enrolled in college	119,744	1,297	1.1	72,419	943	1.3	7,801	121	1.6	39,525	233	0.6
FEMALE												
Total.....................................	136,194	1,860	1.4	58,370	872	1.5	17,791	423	2.4	60,032	566	0.9
Age												
15 to 19 years old	10,287	117	1.1	677	15	2.2	2,204	38	1.7	7,405	64	0.9
20 to 24 years old	10,519	352	3.3	4,404	101	2.3	2,798	115	4.1	3,317	136	4.1
25 to 34 years old	22,520	393	1.7	14,098	204	1.4	2,887	91	3.2	5,535	98	1.8
35 to 44 years old	20,893	358	1.7	13,068	218	1.7	2,692	71	2.6	5,133	70	1.4
45 to 64 years old	42,533	452	1.1	23,403	283	1.2	4,988	70	1.4	14,142	98	0.7
65 years and over	29,442	187	0.6	2,720	52	1.9	2,222	37	1.6	24,500	99	0.4
Educational attainment												
Not a high school graduate	17,635	99	0.6	2,726	41	1.5	2,133	22	1.1	12,777	35	0.3
High school graduate only	35,556	307	0.9	13,002	97	0.7	4,232	89	2.1	18,322	121	0.7
Some college or associate's degree...................................	37,698	650	1.7	15,807	264	1.7	6,242	166	2.7	15,649	220	1.4
Bachelor's degree or more	45,304	804	1.8	26,836	469	1.7	5,185	145	2.8	13,284	190	1.4
College enrollment												
Enrolled in college....................	10,223	571	5.6	2,843	154	5.4	3,185	165	5.2	4,194	251	6.0
Not enrolled in college	125,971	1,290	1.0	55,527	718	1.3	14,606	257	1.8	55,838	315	0.6

[1]People enrolled in vocational courses are not considered to be enrolled in school for all tables. People enrolled in regular school below the college level are not asked about vocational enrollment in the CPS. They are counted in this table as not enrolled in vocational courses.

Table A-7. Enrollment Status of High School Graduates 15 to 24 Years Old, by Type of School, Attendance Status, and Sex, October 2019

(Numbers in thousands; civilian noninstitutionalized population.)

| | | Enrolled in college or vocational school | | | | | | Not enrolled | |
| | | 2-year college | | 4-year college | | Graduate school | Vocational school | | |
Characteristic	Total	Full-time	Part-time	Full-time	Part-time	Graduate school	Vocational school	Employed	Not employed
ALL RACES									
Both sexes	26,344	2,139	751	7,403	702	1,123	281	10,828	3,115
Graduated this year	3,185	576	111	1,345	63	15	26	614	435
Graduated earlier	23,159	1,563	641	6,058	640	1,108	255	10,214	2,680
Male	12,926	1,053	421	3,316	281	456	154	5,754	1,491
Graduated this year	1,489	287	45	559	22	12	18	290	257
Graduated earlier	11,437	766	377	2,757	259	445	136	5,464	1,234
Female	13,417	1,086	330	4,088	422	667	127	5,075	1,624
Graduated this year	1,696	288	66	787	41	4	8	324	178
Graduated earlier	11,721	797	264	3,301	381	663	119	4,750	1,446
WHITE ALONE									
Both sexes	19,364	1,634	522	5,259	538	761	176	8,314	2,159
Graduated this year	2,375	443	71	1,004	59	15	23	482	278
Graduated earlier	16,989	1,191	451	4,255	480	746	153	7,832	1,882
Male	9,561	795	308	2,355	229	280	108	4,496	990
Graduated this year	1,126	215	34	430	22	12	16	224	174
Graduated earlier	8,435	580	273	1,925	207	268	92	4,272	816
Female	9,803	839	215	2,903	309	481	68	3,818	1,169
Graduated this year	1,249	228	37	574	37	4	7	258	104
Graduated earlier	8,554	611	178	2,330	272	478	61	3,560	1,065
WHITE ALONE, NON-HISPANIC									
Both sexes	14,196	1,094	304	4,149	328	652	144	6,043	1,481
Graduated this year	1,750	307	38	807	31	9	23	350	184
Graduated earlier	12,445	787	266	3,342	297	643	121	5,693	1,297
Male	7,010	536	173	1,870	153	233	82	3,281	681
Graduated this year	853	146	20	351	14	5	16	173	128
Graduated earlier	6,158	390	153	1,519	140	227	67	3,108	553
Female	7,185	558	130	2,279	175	419	62	2,762	800
Graduated this year	897	161	18	457	17	4	7	178	56
Graduated earlier	6,288	397	112	1,823	158	415	54	2,585	744
BLACK ALONE									
Both sexes	3,843	306	131	964	101	122	52	1,560	607
Graduated this year	438	60	22	136	4	*	*	90	125
Graduated earlier	3,406	246	109	828	97	122	52	1,470	482
Male	1,821	140	71	423	21	58	31	772	305
Graduated this year	203	25	10	48	*	*	*	51	70
Graduated earlier	1,618	115	61	376	21	58	31	721	235
Female	2,023	166	60	541	80	64	21	788	302
Graduated this year	234	35	12	89	4	*	*	39	55
Graduated earlier	1,788	131	48	452	76	64	21	749	247
ASIAN ALONE									
Both sexes	1,731	112	23	787	47	186	25	415	137
Graduated this year	189	36	*	134	*	*	2	10	7
Graduated earlier	1,542	77	22	653	47	186	22	405	130
Male	865	60	8	385	30	92	6	195	89
Graduated this year	96	24	*	62	*	*	2	5	4
Graduated earlier	768	36	8	323	30	92	3	191	85
Female	866	53	14	402	17	94	19	219	48
Graduated this year	93	12	*	72	*	*	*	5	4
Graduated earlier	773	41	14	330	17	94	19	214	44
HISPANIC (OF ANY RACE)									
Both sexes	5,857	590	239	1,291	231	135	40	2,535	795
Graduated this year	681	138	33	227	28	6	1	140	108
Graduated earlier	5,176	451	206	1,064	204	129	39	2,395	687
Male	2,915	288	149	561	76	60	26	1,382	373
Graduated this year	290	69	14	86	8	6	*	54	52
Graduated earlier	2,625	219	135	475	68	54	26	1,328	321
Female	2,942	302	90	730	155	75	14	1,153	422
Graduated this year	391	70	18	141	19	*	1	86	56
Graduated earlier	2,551	232	71	590	136	75	13	1,068	366

* = Quantity zero or rounds to zero.

Table A-8. Enrollment Status for Families with Children 5 to 24 Years Old, by Control of School, Race, Type of Family, and Family Income, October 2019

(Numbers in thousands; civilian noninstitutionalized population.)

Characteristic	Total	Families with no dependents 5 to 24 years old[1]	Families with dependents 5 to 24 years old[1]						
			Kindergarten, elementary, and high school enrollment status				College enrollment status		
			None enrolled in elementary or high school	Public only	Public and private	Private only	None enrolled in college	One enrolled in college	Two or more enrolled in college
ALL RACES									
All Families........................	83,702	45,346	8,077	27,385	653	2,240	32,165	5,285	907
Less than $20,000	5,176	2,238	551	2,256	30	103	2,684	235	20
$20,000 to $74,999	27,334	14,768	2,520	9,407	150	488	10,860	1,528	177
$75,000 and over....................	30,756	16,351	2,989	9,926	278	1,211	11,608	2,294	503
Not reported........................	20,436	11,988	2,017	5,796	196	439	7,013	1,227	208
Married-couple families	61,015	36,477	4,638	17,620	503	1,776	20,347	3,498	693
Less than $20,000	1,916	1,254	105	511	7	38	623	35	4
$20,000 to $74,999	17,733	11,023	1,192	5,117	95	306	5,771	808	131
$75,000 and over....................	26,877	14,856	2,238	8,426	266	1,092	9,703	1,888	431
Not reported........................	14,488	9,343	1,103	3,567	135	340	4,250	767	128
Unmarried householder[2]	22,687	8,869	3,439	9,765	150	464	11,818	1,786	214
Less than $20,000	3,260	983	446	1,745	22	64	2,060	200	16
$20,000 to $74,999	9,601	3,745	1,328	4,290	55	182	5,089	720	46
$75,000 and over....................	3,878	1,495	751	1,500	12	120	1,905	406	72
Not reported........................	5,948	2,646	914	2,230	61	98	2,763	460	80
WHITE ALONE									
All Families........................	65,662	36,963	6,069	20,412	487	1,731	24,047	3,967	684
Less than $20,000	3,253	1,466	324	1,394	22	47	1,620	157	10
$20,000 to $74,999	21,310	12,021	1,860	6,957	104	367	8,072	1,110	108
$75,000 and over....................	25,461	13,928	2,418	7,916	236	963	9,300	1,813	419
Not reported........................	15,637	9,548	1,466	4,144	126	354	5,055	887	147
Married-couple families	50,593	30,991	3,799	13,950	412	1,441	16,253	2,798	551
Less than $20,000	1,401	889	73	408	7	23	477	30	4
$20,000 to $74,999	14,772	9,484	949	4,009	73	257	4,564	644	80
$75,000 and over....................	22,701	12,839	1,915	6,844	231	871	7,958	1,528	375
Not reported........................	11,720	7,779	862	2,689	101	290	3,254	596	92
Unmarried householder[2]	15,068	5,972	2,270	6,462	75	290	7,794	1,169	134
Less than $20,000	1,853	577	251	986	15	24	1,143	126	7
$20,000 to $74,999	6,538	2,537	911	2,949	31	111	3,508	466	28
$75,000 and over....................	2,760	1,089	503	1,072	5	91	1,342	285	44
Not reported........................	3,917	1,769	604	1,455	25	64	1,801	291	55
WHITE ALONE NON-HISPANIC									
All Families........................	53,377	32,343	4,596	14,568	398	1,473	17,645	2,839	550
Less than $20,000	2,071	1,043	194	783	14	37	935	86	7
$20,000 to $74,999	15,846	10,084	1,233	4,180	68	280	5,087	614	60
$75,000 and over....................	22,764	12,827	2,084	6,775	208	870	8,062	1,505	371
Not reported........................	12,697	8,390	1,085	2,829	108	286	3,562	634	112
Married-couple families	42,875	27,852	3,015	10,414	352	1,243	12,471	2,091	461
Less than $20,000	931	647	49	211	7	17	266	15	4
$20,000 to $74,999	11,394	8,185	632	2,328	52	198	2,813	349	48
$75,000 and over....................	20,560	11,963	1,685	5,924	204	784	6,977	1,286	334
Not reported........................	9,990	7,058	649	1,951	88	244	2,416	441	76
Unmarried householder[2]	10,502	4,491	1,581	4,154	47	230	5,174	749	89
Less than $20,000	1,139	396	145	572	7	19	669	71	4
$20,000 to $74,999	4,452	1,899	601	1,853	17	82	2,275	265	12
$75,000 and over....................	2,203	864	399	851	3	86	1,085	218	36
Not reported........................	2,708	1,332	436	879	20	42	1,145	194	36
BLACK ALONE									
All Families........................	10,309	4,593	1,199	4,108	110	299	4,919	721	75
Less than $20,000	1,396	509	153	696	7	32	832	51	4
$20,000 to $74,999	3,693	1,631	413	1,525	38	85	1,815	225	22
$75,000 and over....................	2,281	1,038	290	827	6	121	973	251	19
Not reported........................	2,939	1,415	344	1,061	59	61	1,299	194	31

* = Quantity zero or rounds to zero.
[1] Unmarried (or married with spouse absent) child, grandchild, brother/sister or other relative.
[2] No spouse present.
[3] May be of any race.

Table A-8. Enrollment Status for Families with Children 5 to 24 Years Old, by Control of School, Race, Type of Family, and Family Income, October 2019—*Continued*

(Numbers in thousands; civilian noninstitutionalized population.)

| | | | Families with dependents 5 to 24 years old[1] | | | | | | |
| | | | Kindergarten, elementary, and high school enrollment status | | | | College enrollment status | | |
Characteristic	Total	Families with no dependents 5 to 24 years old[1]	None enrolled in elementary or high school	Public only	Public and private	Private only	None enrolled in college	One enrolled in college	Two or more enrolled in college
Married-couple families	4,829	2,628	391	1,606	50	154	1,841	321	39
Less than $20,000	285	193	15	69	*	7	87	5	*
$20,000 to $74,999	1,461	803	109	509	20	20	594	53	11
$75,000 and over	1,643	806	160	573	6	98	630	194	14
Not reported	1,440	825	107	455	24	29	531	69	15
Unmarried householder[2]	5,480	1,965	808	2,502	60	145	3,078	400	36
Less than $20,000	1,111	316	137	626	7	24	745	46	4
$20,000 to $74,999	2,232	828	304	1,016	18	66	1,221	172	11
$75,000 and over	638	232	130	254	*	23	343	57	5
Not reported	1,499	590	237	605	35	32	769	124	16
ASIAN ALONE									
All Families	5,025	2,535	530	1,786	37	137	1,933	437	120
Less than $20,000	202	128	30	36	*	8	64	10	*
$20,000 to $74,999	1,266	650	133	472	2	10	449	125	43
$75,000 and over	2,247	1,047	210	869	24	97	964	181	54
Not reported	1,310	709	158	409	11	22	457	121	23
Married-couple families	4,042	2,055	321	1,507	29	130	1,603	289	95
Less than $20,000	147	108	13	18	*	8	39	*	*
$20,000 to $74,999	970	474	88	396	2	10	375	81	39
$75,000 and over	1,910	935	112	755	17	92	817	121	37
Not reported	1,015	538	108	338	11	21	372	86	19
Unmarried householder[2]	983	480	209	280	7	7	330	149	24
Less than $20,000	55	20	17	18	*	*	25	10	*
$20,000 to $74,999	297	176	45	76	*	*	74	44	3
$75,000 and over	337	112	98	114	7	5	147	60	18
Not reported	295	171	50	72	*	1	85	35	4
HISPANIC[3]									
All Families	13,738	5,171	1,628	6,544	92	302	7,162	1,258	147
Less than $20,000	1,347	493	153	676	8	18	774	77	3
$20,000 to $74,999	6,085	2,169	692	3,089	36	99	3,330	538	48
$75,000 and over	3,087	1,246	374	1,323	28	116	1,419	368	55
Not reported	3,219	1,263	410	1,456	21	69	1,639	275	41
Married-couple families	8,554	3,509	850	3,907	61	227	4,171	778	96
Less than $20,000	530	290	29	205	*	6	224	15	*
$20,000 to $74,999	3,666	1,405	346	1,822	22	71	1,921	307	33
$75,000 and over	2,460	1,008	249	1,071	27	105	1,121	290	41
Not reported	1,898	804	226	809	13	46	905	166	23
Unmarried householder[2]	5,184	1,662	778	2,637	32	75	2,991	480	51
Less than $20,000	817	202	124	471	8	12	550	61	3
$20,000 to $74,999	2,420	764	346	1,267	14	28	1,409	232	15
$75,000 and over	627	238	125	252	1	12	298	78	14
Not reported	1,321	459	183	647	8	23	734	109	19

* = Quantity zero or rounds to zero.
[1]Unmarried (or married with spouse absent) child, grandchild, brother/sister or other relative.
[2]No spouse present.
[3]May be of any race.

Table A-9. Total Fall Enrollment in Degree-Granting Postsecondary Institutions, by Level of Enrollment, Sex of Student, Level and Control of Institution, and Attendance Status of Student, 2018

(Number.)

Level and control of institution and attendance status of student	Total			Undergraduate			Postbaccalaureate		
	Total	Males	Females	Total	Males	Females	Total	Males	Females
Total	19,645,918	8,442,662	11,203,256	16,610,235	7,225,999	9,384,236	3,035,683	1,216,663	1,819,020
Full-time	11,991,721	5,338,934	6,652,787	10,267,135	4,602,752	5,664,383	1,724,586	736,182	988,404
Part-time	7,654,197	3,103,728	4,550,469	6,343,100	2,623,247	3,719,853	1,311,097	480,481	830,616
4-Year	13,900,710	5,990,993	7,909,717	10,865,027	4,774,330	6,090,697	3,035,683	1,216,663	1,819,020
Full-time	9,880,953	4,385,208	5,495,745	8,156,367	3,649,026	4,507,341	1,724,586	736,182	988,404
Part-time	4,019,757	1,605,785	2,413,972	2,708,660	1,125,304	1,583,356	1,311,097	480,481	830,616
2-Year	5,745,208	2,451,669	3,293,539	5,745,208	2,451,669	3,293,539	NA	NA	NA
Full-time	2,110,768	953,726	1,157,042	2,110,768	953,726	1,157,042	NA	NA	NA
Part-time	3,634,440	1,497,943	2,136,497	3,634,440	1,497,943	2,136,497	NA	NA	NA
PUBLIC	14,529,264	6,391,471	8,137,793	13,049,326	5,774,848	7,274,478	1,479,938	616,623	863,315
Full-time	8,268,820	3,787,941	4,480,879	7,451,638	3,427,581	4,024,057	817,182	360,360	456,822
Part-time	6,260,444	2,603,530	3,656,914	5,597,688	2,347,267	3,250,421	662,756	256,263	406,493
Public 4-Year	8,982,560	4,005,748	4,976,812	7,502,622	3,389,125	4,113,497	1,479,938	616,623	863,315
Full-time	6,336,978	2,895,088	3,441,890	5,519,796	2,534,728	2,985,068	817,182	360,360	456,822
Part-time	2,645,582	1,110,660	1,534,922	1,982,826	854,397	1,128,429	662,756	256,263	406,493
Public 2-Year	5,546,704	2,385,723	3,160,981	5,546,704	2,385,723	3,160,981	NA	NA	NA
Full time	1,931,842	892,853	1,038,989	1,931,842	892,853	1,038,989	NA	NA	NA
Part-time	3,614,862	1,492,870	2,121,992	3,614,862	1,492,870	2,121,992	NA	NA	NA
PRIVATE	5,116,654	2,051,191	3,065,463	3,560,909	1,451,151	2,109,758	1,555,745	600,040	955,705
Full-time	3,722,901	1,550,993	2,171,908	2,815,497	1,175,171	1,640,326	907,404	375,822	531,582
Part-time	1,393,753	500,198	893,555	745,412	275,980	469,432	648,341	224,218	424,123
Private 4-Year	4,918,150	1,985,245	2,932,905	3,362,405	1,385,205	1,977,200	1,555,745	600,040	955,705
Full-time	3,543,975	1,490,120	2,053,855	2,636,571	1,114,298	1,522,273	907,404	375,822	531,582
Part-time	1,374,175	495,125	879,050	725,834	270,907	454,927	648,341	224,218	424,123
Private 2-Year	198,504	65,946	132,558	198,504	65,946	132,558	NA	NA	NA
Full-time	178,926	60,873	118,053	178,926	60,873	118,053	NA	NA	NA
Part-time	19,578	5,073	14,505	19,578	5,073	14,505	NA	NA	NA
Nonprofit	4,134,244	1,722,517	2,411,727	2,821,653	1,191,128	1,630,525	1,312,591	531,389	781,202
Full-time	3,126,130	1,337,841	1,788,289	2,321,433	995,083	1,326,350	804,697	342,758	461,939
Part-time	1,008,114	384,676	623,438	500,220	196,045	304,175	507,894	188,631	319,263
Nonprofit 4-year	4,089,090	1,711,257	2,377,833	2,776,499	1,179,868	1,596,631	1,312,591	531,389	781,202
Full-time	3,088,150	1,328,444	1,759,706	2,283,453	985,686	1,297,767	804,697	342,758	461,939
Part-time	1,000,940	382,813	618,127	493,046	194,182	298,864	507,894	188,631	319,263
Nonprofit 2-year	45,154	11,260	33,894	45,154	11,260	33,894	NA	NA	NA
Full-time	37,980	9,397	28,583	37,980	9,397	28,583	NA	NA	NA
Part-time	7,174	1,863	5,311	7,174	1,863	5,311	NA	NA	NA
For-profit	982,410	328,674	653,736	739,256	260,023	479,233	243,154	68,651	174,503
Full-time	596,771	213,152	383,619	494,064	180,088	313,976	102,707	33,064	69,643
Part-time	385,639	115,522	270,117	245,192	79,935	165,257	140,447	35,587	104,860
For-profit 4-year	829,060	273,988	555,072	585,906	205,337	380,569	243,154	68,651	174,503
Full-time	455,825	161,676	294,149	353,118	128,612	224,506	102,707	33,064	69,643
Part-time	373,235	112,312	260,923	232,788	76,725	156,063	140,447	35,587	104,860
For-profit 2-year	153,350	54,686	98,664	153,350	54,686	98,664	NA	NA	NA
Full-time	140,946	51,476	89,470	140,946	51,476	89,470	NA	NA	NA
Part-time	12,404	3,210	9,194	12,404	3,210	9,194	NA	NA	NA

NA = Not applicable
Note: Degree-granting institutions grant associate's or higher degrees and participate in Title IV federal financial aid programs.

PART A
NATIONAL EDUCATION STATISTICS

■ **Historical Enrollment Tables**

Table A-10. School Enrollment of the Population 3 Years Old and Over, by Level and Control of School, Selected Race, and Hispanic Origin, October 1955–2019

(Numbers in thousands; civilian noninstitutionalized population.)

Year, race, and Hispanic origin	Total enrolled	Nursery school Total	Nursery school Public	Nursery school Private	Kindergarten Total	Kindergarten Public	Kindergarten Private	Elementary school Total	Elementary school Public	Elementary school Private
ALL RACES										
2019	76,089	4,728	2,614	2,114	4,057	3,531	525	32,619	29,754	2,866
2018	76,840	4,836	2,763	2,073	3,908	3,529	379	32,483	29,665	2,818
2017	76,409	4,676	2,782	1,894	3,964	3,542	422	32,530	29,873	2,656
2016	77,232	4,746	2,806	1,941	4,017	3,654	364	32,604	29,978	2,627
2015	77,066	4,532	2,610	1,922	4,073	3,644	428	32,826	30,173	2,653
2014	77,214	4,694	2,693	2,001	4,069	3,617	453	32,622	29,805	2,817
2013	77,772	4,682	2,558	2,124	4,150	3,725	425	32,873	30,171	2,702
2012	78,426	4,628	2,732	1,896	4,138	3,684	454	32,683	29,865	2,818
2011	79,043	4,946	2,904	2,042	4,214	3,732	482	32,872	29,965	2,907
2010	78,519	4,835	2,776	2,059	4,172	3,764	408	32,663	29,841	2,822
2009	77,288	4,708	2,744	1,964	4,132	3,767	365	32,238	29,365	2,874
2008	76,353	4,614	2,632	1,982	4,047	3,578	469	32,344	29,162	3,182
2007	75,967	4,628	2,570	2,058	4,132	3,656	476	32,169	29,052	3,117
2006	75,197	4,688	2,519	2,169	4,039	3,552	487	32,089	28,975	3,113
2005	75,780	4,603	2,480	2,123	3,912	3,349	563	32,438	29,072	3,366
2004	75,461	4,739	2,487	2,252	3,992	3,417	575	32,556	29,166	3,389
2003	74,911	4,928	2,567	2,361	3,719	3,098	622	32,565	29,204	3,361
2002	74,046	4,471	2,246	2,225	3,571	2,976	594	33,132	29,658	3,474
2001	73,124	4,289	2,161	2,128	3,737	3,145	591	33,166	29,800	3,366
2000	72,214	4,401	2,217	2,184	3,832	3,173	659	32,898	29,378	3,520
1999	72,395	4,578	2,269	2,309	3,825	3,167	658	32,873	29,264	3,609
1998	72,109	4,577	2,265	2,313	3,828	3,128	700	32,573	29,124	3,449
1997	72,031	4,500	2,254	2,246	3,933	3,271	663	32,369	29,308	3,061
1996	70,297	4,212	1,868	2,344	4,034	3,353	681	31,515	28,153	3,362
1995	69,769	4,399	2,012	2,387	3,877	3,174	704	31,815	28,384	3,431
1994[1]	69,272	4,259	1,940	2,319	3,863	3,278	585	31,512	28,131	3,381
1993r	64,414	3,032	1,258	1,774	4,275	3,589	686	31,219	28,278	2,941
1993	62,730	3,018	1,230	1,788	4,180	3,499	681	30,604	27,688	2,914
1992	62,082	2,899	1,098	1,801	4,130	3,507	623	30,165	27,066	3,102
1991	61,276	2,933	1,094	1,839	4,152	3,531	621	29,591	26,632	2,958
1990	60,588	3,401	1,212	2,188	3,899	3,332	567	29,265	26,591	2,674
1989	59,236	2,877	971	1,906	3,868	3,293	575	28,637	25,897	2,740
1988	58,847	2,639	868	1,770	3,958	3,420	538	28,223	25,443	2,778
1987	58,691	2,587	848	1,739	4,018	3,423	595	27,524	24,760	2,765
1986	58,153	2,554	835	1,719	3,961	3,328	633	27,121	24,163	2,958
1985	58,014	2,491	854	1,637	3,815	3,221	594	26,866	23,803	3,063
1984	57,313	2,354	761	1,593	3,484	2,953	531	26,838	24,120	2,718
1983	57,745	2,350	809	1,541	3,361	2,706	656	27,198	24,203	2,994
1982	57,905	2,153	729	1,423	3,299	2,746	553	27,412	24,381	3,031
1981	58,390	2,058	663	1,396	3,161	2,616	545	27,795	24,758	3,037
1980	57,348	1,987	633	1,354	3,176	2,690	486	27,449	24,398	3,051
1979	57,854	1,869	636	1,233	3,025	2,593	432	27,865	24,756	3,109
1978	58,616	1,824	587	1,237	2,989	2,493	496	28,490	25,252	3,238
1977	60,013	1,618	562	1,056	3,191	2,665	526	29,234	25,983	3,251
1976	60,482	1,526	476	1,050	3,490	2,962	528	29,774	26,698	3,075
1975	60,969	1,748	574	1,174	3,393	2,851	542	30,446	27,166	3,279
1974	60,259	1,607	423	1,184	3,252	2,726	526	31,126	27,956	3,169
1973	59,392	1,324	400	924	3,074	2,582	493	31,469	28,201	3,268
1972	60,142	1,283	402	881	3,135	2,636	499	32,242	28,693	3,549
1971	61,106	1,066	317	749	3,263	2,689	574	33,507	29,829	3,678
1970	60,357	1,096	333	763	3,183	2,647	536	33,950	30,001	3,949
1969	59,913	860	245	615	3,276	2,682	594	33,788	29,825	3,964
1968	58,791	816	262	554	3,268	2,709	559	33,761	29,527	4,234
1967	57,656	713	230	484	3,312	2,678	635	33,440	28,877	4,562
1966	56,167	688	215	473	3,115	2,527	588	32,916	28,208	4,706
1965	54,701	520	127	393	3,057	2,439	618	32,474	27,596	4,878
1964	52,490	471	91	380	2,830	2,349	481	31,734	26,811	4,923
1963	50,356	NA	NA	NA	2,340	1,936	404	31,245	26,502	4,742
1962	48,704	NA	NA	NA	2,319	1,914	405	30,661	26,148	4,513
1961	47,708	NA	NA	NA	2,299	1,926	373	30,718	26,221	4,497
1960	46,260	NA	NA	NA	2,092	1,691	401	30,349	25,814	4,535
1959	44,370	NA	NA	NA	2,032	1,678	354	29,382	24,680	4,702
1958	42,900	NA	NA	NA	1,991	1,569	422	28,184	23,800	4,385
1957	41,166	NA	NA	NA	1,824	1,471	353	27,248	23,076	4,172
1956	39,353	NA	NA	NA	1,758	1,566	192	26,169	22,474	3,695
1955	37,426	NA	NA	NA	1,628	1,365	263	25,458	22,078	3,379

NA = Not available.

r = Revised, controlled to 1990 census based population estimates; previous 1993 data controlled to 1980 census based population estimates.

[1] Prior to 1994, total enrolled does not include the 35 and over population.

[2] Starting in 2003 respondents could identify more than one race. Except as noted, the race data in this table from 2003 onward represent those respondents who indicated only one race category.

[3] Data shown for 1955 to 1966 for the Black population are for Black and Other races.

[4] The data shown prior to 2003 consists of those identifying themselves as "Asian or Pacific Islanders."

Table A-10. School Enrollment of the Population 3 Years Old and Over, by Level and Control of School, Selected Race, and Hispanic Origin, October 1955–2019—*Continued*

(Numbers in thousands; civilian noninstitutionalized population.)

Year, race, and Hispanic origin	High school			College			
	Total	Public	Private	Total	Public	Private	Full-time
ALL RACES							
2019	16,395	15,208	1,187	18,289	14,746	3,543	13,849
2018	16,706	15,519	1,187	18,908	15,234	3,674	14,204
2017	16,841	15,546	1,295	18,398	14,806	3,592	13,606
2016	16,668	15,330	1,338	19,196	14,971	4,225	14,421
2015	16,535	15,358	1,177	19,101	15,175	3,926	14,236
2014	16,654	15,379	1,275	19,175	15,325	3,850	14,400
2013	16,601	15,468	1,133	19,467	15,514	3,953	14,228
2012	17,047	15,704	1,343	19,930	15,778	4,152	14,602
2011	16,613	15,426	1,187	20,397	16,134	4,263	14,903
2010	16,574	15,338	1,236	20,275	16,153	4,122	14,600
2009	16,445	15,269	1,177	19,764	15,722	4,042	14,364
2008	16,715	15,397	1,319	18,632	14,739	3,893	13,245
2007	17,082	15,804	1,278	17,956	14,072	3,884	12,656
2006	17,149	15,617	1,532	17,232	13,466	3,766	12,070
2005	17,354	15,934	1,420	17,472	13,435	4,037	12,237
2004	16,791	15,498	1,293	17,383	13,652	3,731	11,990
2003	17,062	15,785	1,276	16,638	13,109	3,529	11,490
2002	16,374	15,064	1,310	16,497	12,834	3,664	11,141
2001	16,059	14,830	1,230	15,873	12,421	3,452	10,404
2000	15,770	14,431	1,339	15,314	12,008	3,305	10,159
1999	15,916	14,638	1,278	15,203	11,659	3,544	10,112
1998	15,584	14,299	1,285	15,547	11,984	3,563	10,184
1997	15,793	14,634	1,159	15,436	12,091	3,345	10,236
1996	15,309	14,113	1,197	15,226	12,014	3,212	9,839
1995	14,963	13,750	1,213	14,715	11,372	3,343	9,544
1994[1]	14,616	13,539	1,077	15,022	11,694	3,329	9,573
1993r	13,989	12,985	1,004	11,901	9,440	2,461	8,706
1993	13,522	12,542	977	11,409	9,031	2,374	8,308
1992	13,219	12,268	952	11,671	9,282	2,386	8,503
1991	13,010	12,069	945	11,589	9,078	2,511	8,461
1990	12,719	11,818	903	11,306	8,889	2,417	8,154
1989	12,786	11,980	806	11,066	8,576	2,490	7,905
1988	13,093	12,095	998	10,937	8,663	2,278	7,771
1987	13,647	12,577	1,070	10,915	8,556	2,361	7,560
1986	13,912	12,746	1,166	10,605	8,153	2,452	7,507
1985	13,979	12,764	1,215	10,863	8,379	2,483	7,720
1984	13,777	12,721	1,057	10,859	8,467	2,392	7,822
1983	14,010	12,792	1,218	10,825	8,185	2,640	7,711
1982	14,123	13,004	1,118	10,919	8,354	2,565	7,736
1981	14,642	13,523	1,119	10,734	8,159	2,576	7,569
1980	14,556	NA	NA	10,180	NA	NA	7,147
1979	15,116	13,994	1,122	9,978	7,699	2,280	7,010
1978	15,475	14,231	1,244	9,838	7,427	2,410	6,979
1977	15,753	14,505	1,248	10,217	7,925	2,292	7,196
1976	15,742	14,541	1,201	9,950	7,739	2,211	7,176
1975	15,683	14,503	1,180	9,697	7,704	1,994	7,105
1974	15,447	14,275	1,172	8,827	6,905	1,922	6,351
1973	15,347	14,162	1,184	8,179	6,224	1,955	6,089
1972	15,169	14,015	1,155	8,313	6,337	1,976	6,314
1971	15,183	14,057	1,126	8,087	6,271	1,816	6,204
1970	14,715	13,545	1,170	7,413	5,699	1,714	5,763
1969	14,553	13,400	1,153	7,435	5,439	1,995	5,810
1968	14,145	12,793	1,352	6,801	4,948	1,854	5,357
1967	13,790	12,498	1,292	6,401	4,540	1,861	4,976
1966	13,364	11,985	1,377	6,085	4,178	1,908	4,847
1965	12,975	11,517	1,457	5,675	3,840	1,835	4,414
1964	12,812	11,403	1,410	4,643	3,025	1,618	3,556
1963	12,438	11,186	1,251	4,336	2,897	1,439	3,260
1962	11,516	10,431	1,085	4,208	2,820	1,388	3,237
1961	10,959	9,817	1,141	3,731	2,376	1,354	2,902
1960	10,249	9,215	1,033	3,570	2,307	1,262	2,681
1959	9,616	8,571	1,045	3,340	2,120	1,220	2,464
1958	9,482	8,485	998	3,242	2,088	1,155	NA
1957	8,956	8,059	897	3,138	2,054	1,084	NA
1956	8,543	7,668	875	2,883	1,824	1,059	NA
1955	7,961	7,181	780	2,379	1,515	864	NA

NA = Not available.

r = Revised, controlled to 1990 census based population estimates; previous 1993 data controlled to 1980 census based population estimates.

[1]Prior to 1994, total enrolled does not include the 35 and over population.

[2]Starting in 2003 respondents could identify more than one race. Except as noted, the race data in this table from 2003 onward represent those respondents who indicated only one race category.

[3]Data shown for 1955 to 1966 for the Black population are for Black and Other races.

[4]The data shown prior to 2003 consists of those identifying themselves as "Asian or Pacific Islanders."

Table A-10. School Enrollment of the Population 3 Years Old and Over, by Level and Control of School, Selected Race, and Hispanic Origin, October 1955–2019—*Continued*

(Numbers in thousands; civilian noninstitutionalized population.)

Year, race, and Hispanic origin	Total enrolled	Nursery school			Kindergarten			Elementary school		
		Total	Public	Private	Total	Public	Private	Total	Public	Private
WHITE ALONE										
2019	54,352	3,352	1,756	1,596	2,895	2,533	362	23,385	21,129	2,257
2018	55,199	3,509	1,943	1,565	2,831	2,510	321	23,379	21,215	2,164
2017	55,148	3,315	1,885	1,430	2,918	2,580	338	23,411	21,385	2,026
2016	56,007	3,445	1,984	1,461	2,859	2,578	281	23,732	21,786	1,946
2015	56,056	3,230	1,778	1,452	2,970	2,630	340	23,863	21,776	2,088
2014	56,343	3,354	1,814	1,540	2,866	2,557	309	23,886	21,677	2,209
2013	56,914	3,346	1,740	1,606	2,933	2,588	345	24,238	22,090	2,148
2012	57,702	3,393	1,925	1,468	2,940	2,584	355	24,187	21,928	2,260
2011	59,647	3,624	1,997	1,627	3,198	2,806	393	24,864	22,419	2,445
2010	59,236	3,659	1,992	1,668	3,069	2,745	324	24,680	22,395	2,284
2009	58,586	3,404	1,832	1,572	3,154	2,860	293	24,575	22,257	2,319
2008	58,244	3,479	1,830	1,649	3,121	2,748	373	24,552	21,986	2,565
2007	58,021	3,545	1,880	1,665	3,223	2,836	387	24,431	21,869	2,562
2006	57,419	3,624	1,815	1,809	3,084	2,701	382	24,472	21,923	2,549
2005	58,013	3,542	1,767	1,775	3,056	2,611	445	24,652	21,858	2,795
2004	57,585	3,566	1,703	1,863	3,043	2,571	472	24,773	21,889	2,883
2003[2]	57,391	3,909	1,918	1,990	2,866	2,367	499	24,711	21,893	2,818
2002	57,501	3,473	1,613	1,860	2,760	2,240	520	25,625	22,703	2,922
2001	56,649	3,278	1,484	1,794	2,893	2,394	499	25,729	22,848	2,881
2000	56,344	3,392	1,539	1,853	2,998	2,453	545	25,562	22,538	3,024
1999	56,713	3,590	1,571	2,019	2,956	2,422	534	25,628	22,552	3,076
1998	56,515	3,549	1,598	1,951	2,933	2,356	577	25,489	22,547	2,942
1997	56,587	3,489	1,572	1,917	3,078	2,532	546	25,289	22,679	2,610
1996	55,378	3,284	1,314	1,970	3,163	2,596	567	24,692	21,785	2,907
1995	55,186	3,553	1,435	2,118	3,032	2,440	592	24,963	22,010	2,954
1994[1]	54,823	3,376	1,330	2,046	3,010	2,505	505	24,786	21,903	2,883
1993r	51,034	2,434	851	1,583	3,323	2,730	593	24,637	22,078	2,559
1993	49,985	2,447	843	1,604	3,273	2,681	592	24,249	21,714	2,535
1992	49,713	2,387	785	1,602	3,256	2,727	529	23,932	21,213	2,718
1991	49,156	2,447	810	1,637	3,274	2,766	508	23,547	20,948	2,599
1990	48,897	2,830	869	1,961	3,081	2,609	472	23,343	20,984	2,359
1989	47,923	2,393	712	1,681	3,118	2,611	506	22,867	20,468	2,399
1988	47,672	2,234	651	1,583	3,192	2,722	471	22,541	20,086	2,455
1987	47,471	2,204	630	1,574	3,120	2,591	529	22,037	19,538	2,498
1986	47,267	2,144	601	1,543	3,161	2,589	572	21,761	19,090	2,671
1985	47,452	2,087	617	1,470	3,060	2,545	515	21,593	18,817	2,776
1984	46,941	1,915	543	1,372	2,788	2,319	469	21,730	19,282	2,449
1983	47,423	1,932	563	1,369	2,769	2,181	588	22,054	19,340	2,714
1982	47,662	1,783	504	1,279	2,677	2,189	489	22,297	19,583	2,713
1981	48,169	1,685	447	1,238	2,597	2,130	467	22,663	19,924	2,739
1980	47,673	1,637	432	1,205	2,595	2,172	423	22,510	19,743	2,768
1979	48,225	1,537	428	1,110	2,437	2,069	368	22,959	20,174	2,785
1978	48,843	1,456	351	1,105	2,452	2,009	444	23,524	20,551	2,973
1977	50,151	1,314	372	942	2,611	2,153	458	24,262	21,312	2,950
1976	50,761	1,246	318	929	2,881	2,423	457	24,776	21,947	2,829
1975	51,430	1,432	392	1,040	2,845	2,363	483	25,412	22,351	3,059
1974	50,992	1,340	293	1,048	2,745	2,268	477	26,051	23,063	2,990
1973	50,617	1,087	242	845	2,584	2,139	445	26,531	23,506	3,025
1972	51,314	1,079	285	794	2,633	2,185	448	27,185	23,869	3,316
1971	52,081	888	225	664	2,735	2,207	527	28,187	24,720	3,466
1970	51,719	893	198	695	2,706	2,233	473	28,638	24,923	3,715
1969	51,465	676	136	539	2,803	2,289	515	28,572	24,803	3,768
1968	50,608	664	163	501	2,775	2,272	504	28,634	24,580	4,054
1967	49,721	564	134	429	2,840	2,254	587	28,415	24,044	4,371
1966	48,620	564	127	437	2,693	2,163	530	28,012	23,469	4,542
1965	47,451	451	93	358	2,648	2,086	562	27,679	22,976	4,703
1964	44,850	NA	NA	NA	2,157	1,795	362	27,099	22,381	4,718
1963	43,815	NA	NA	NA	2,064	1,699	365	26,709	22,181	4,527
1962	42,501	NA	NA	NA	2,025	1,667	358	26,272	21,922	4,350
1961	42,498	NA	NA	NA	1,968	1,618	350	26,294	22,014	4,281
1960	40,348	NA	NA	NA	1,849	1,485	364	26,035	21,696	4,339
1959	38,857	NA	NA	NA	1,758	1,434	324	25,395	20,854	4,541
1958	37,662	NA	NA	NA	1,769	1,383	386	24,380	20,178	4,203
1957	36,132	NA	NA	NA	1,595	1,258	337	23,610	19,595	4,015
1956	34,641	NA	NA	NA	1,544	1,364	180	22,740	19,186	3,554
1955	32,929	NA	NA	NA	1,484	1,244	240	22,185	18,947	3,238

NA = Not available.

r = Revised, controlled to 1990 census based population estimates; previous 1993 data controlled to 1980 census based population estimates.

[1]Prior to 1994, total enrolled does not include the 35 and over population.

[2]Starting in 2003 respondents could identify more than one race. Except as noted, the race data in this table from 2003 onward represent those respondents who indicated only one race category.

[3]Data shown for 1955 to 1966 for the Black population are for Black and Other races.

[4]The data shown prior to 2003 consists of those identifying themselves as "Asian or Pacific Islanders."

Table A-10. School Enrollment of the Population 3 Years Old and Over, by Level and Control of School, Selected Race, and Hispanic Origin, October 1955–2019—*Continued*

(Numbers in thousands; civilian noninstitutionalized population.)

Year, race, and Hispanic origin	High school			College			
	Total	Public	Private	Total	Public	Private	Full-time
WHITE ALONE							
2019	11,936	11,065	870	12,783	10,217	2,567	9,652
2018	12,157	11,174	983	13,323	10,670	2,653	9,989
2017	12,281	11,306	975	13,224	10,524	2,700	9,623
2016	12,071	11,017	1,053	13,901	10,846	3,054	10,373
2015	12,133	11,199	934	13,859	11,039	2,821	10,254
2014	12,283	11,315	969	13,953	11,227	2,727	10,506
2013	12,157	11,270	887	14,240	11,378	2,862	10,281
2012	12,554	11,494	1,060	14,628	11,530	3,098	10,694
2011	12,548	11,542	1,007	15,412	12,161	3,251	11,205
2010	12,570	11,525	1,045	15,258	12,179	3,079	10,818
2009	12,425	11,419	1,006	15,027	11,948	3,079	10,847
2008	12,687	11,585	1,103	14,405	11,432	2,973	10,256
2007	12,986	11,886	1,100	13,835	10,855	2,979	9,696
2006	12,966	11,694	1,273	13,273	10,338	2,936	9,236
2005	13,296	12,109	1,187	13,466	10,303	3,163	9,392
2004	12,823	11,684	1,138	13,381	10,478	2,904	9,257
2003[2]	13,036	11,939	1,097	12,870	10,101	2,769	8,855
2002	12,862	11,730	1,132	12,781	9,774	3,007	8,613
2001	12,540	11,473	1,067	12,208	9,503	2,705	7,909
2000	12,392	11,259	1,133	11,999	9,364	2,636	7,945
1999	12,487	11,374	1,113	12,053	9,185	2,868	7,886
1998	12,142	11,013	1,130	12,401	9,518	2,883	8,012
1997	12,290	11,287	1,003	12,442	9,713	2,729	8,127
1996	12,052	10,999	1,053	12,188	9,567	2,622	7,849
1995	11,617	10,574	1,042	12,021	9,311	2,711	7,773
1994[1]	11,430	10,514	916	12,222	9,472	2,751	7,722
1993r	10,960	10,124	836	9,685	7,695	1,990	6,996
1993	10,651	9,834	819	9,366	7,428	1,940	6,739
1992	10,480	9,648	833	9,658	7,653	2,001	6,985
1991	10,309	9,467	841	9,579	7,464	2,118	6,919
1990	10,177	9,370	807	9,466	7,411	2,056	6,776
1989	10,172	9,443	730	9,374	7,219	2,158	6,658
1988	10,462	9,571	890	9,245	7,302	1,940	6,488
1987	10,967	10,019	947	9,143	7,113	2,034	6,275
1986	11,259	10,229	1,030	8,943	6,821	2,122	6,253
1985	11,378	10,258	1,120	9,334	7,131	2,203	6,597
1984	11,240	10,266	974	9,269	7,163	2,105	6,672
1983	11,425	10,339	1,086	9,242	6,949	2,293	6,532
1982	11,577	10,541	1,036	9,328	7,102	2,227	6,579
1981	12,062	11,035	1,027	9,162	6,906	2,256	6,452
1980	12,056	NA	NA	8,875	NA	NA	6,212
1979	12,583	11,549	1,033	8,709	6,672	2,037	6,058
1978	12,897	11,741	1,156	8,514	6,368	2,145	5,974
1977	13,152	11,980	1,172	8,812	6,743	2,069	6,165
1976	13,214	12,093	1,121	8,644	6,657	1,987	6,170
1975	13,224	12,112	1,112	8,516	6,724	1,792	6,183
1974	13,073	11,966	1,107	7,781	6,049	1,732	5,575
1973	13,091	11,967	1,124	7,324	5,550	1,773	5,408
1972	12,959	11,876	1,083	7,458	5,644	1,814	5,678
1971	12,998	11,937	1,061	7,273	5,624	1,650	5,560
1970	12,723	11,599	1,124	6,759	5,168	1,591	5,221
1969	12,588	11,502	1,085	6,827	4,967	1,860	5,307
1968	12,280	11,007	1,272	6,255	4,501	1,753	4,919
1967	11,997	10,769	1,228	5,905	4,155	1,750	4,604
1966	11,643	10,312	1,329	5,708	3,914	1,795	4,556
1965	11,356	9,961	1,395	5,317	3,568	1,749	4,111
1964	11,257	9,898	1,359	4,338	2,798	1,540	NA
1963	10,994	9,782	1,212	4,050	2,680	1,370	NA
1962	10,270	9,217	1,053	3,934	2,620	1,314	NA
1961	9,737	8,635	1,102	3,498	2,205	1,293	NA
1960	9,122	8,124	999	3,342	2,126	1,215	NA
1959	8,586	7,572	1,014	3,118	1,960	1,158	NA
1958	8,484	7,501	982	3,030	1,928	1,101	NA
1957	7,995	7,121	874	2,932	1,924	1,006	NA
1956	7,670	6,825	845	2,687	1,704	983	NA
1955	7,036	6,303	733	2,224	1,429	795	NA

NA = Not available.
r = Revised, controlled to 1990 census based population estimates; previous 1993 data controlled to 1980 census based population estimates.
[1] Prior to 1994, total enrolled does not include the 35 and over population.
[2] Starting in 2003 respondents could identify more than one race. Except as noted, the race data in this table from 2003 onward represent those respondents who indicated only one race category.
[3] Data shown for 1955 to 1966 for the Black population are for Black and Other races.
[4] The data shown prior to 2003 consists of those identifying themselves as "Asian or Pacific Islanders."

Table A-10. School Enrollment of the Population 3 Years Old and Over, by Level and Control of School, Selected Race, and Hispanic Origin, October 1955–2019—*Continued*

(Numbers in thousands; civilian noninstitutionalized population.)

Year, race, and Hispanic origin	Total enrolled	Nursery school			Kindergarten			Elementary school		
		Total	Public	Private	Total	Public	Private	Total	Public	Private
WHITE ALONE NON-HISPANIC										
2019	38,673	2,399	1,094	1,306	1,963	1,684	279	16,186	14,265	1,921
2018	39,679	2,550	1,221	1,329	1,972	1,726	246	16,272	14,419	1,854
2017	39,649	2,461	1,211	1,250	1,955	1,699	256	16,272	14,594	1,679
2016	40,606	2,499	1,275	1,224	1,956	1,697	259	16,640	14,939	1,701
2015	41,145	2,410	1,143	1,268	2,022	1,748	273	16,879	15,095	1,783
2014	41,456	2,477	1,159	1,317	1,990	1,726	264	16,904	15,008	1,897
2013	42,025	2,531	1,089	1,442	1,968	1,691	277	17,309	15,379	1,930
2012	42,776	2,509	1,227	1,283	2,011	1,691	320	17,413	15,401	2,012
2011	44,951	2,743	1,332	1,411	2,238	1,903	335	17,830	15,670	2,160
2010	44,968	2,766	1,274	1,492	2,120	1,842	278	17,942	15,960	1,981
2009	45,470	2,575	1,188	1,387	2,252	1,990	262	18,244	16,198	2,046
2008	45,373	2,710	1,213	1,497	2,206	1,884	323	18,349	16,029	2,320
2007	45,334	2,711	1,225	1,486	2,279	1,929	351	18,306	15,998	2,307
2006	45,386	2,769	1,152	1,616	2,288	1,940	348	18,622	16,322	2,301
2005	46,338	2,810	1,211	1,599	2,308	1,936	372	18,858	16,335	2,523
2004	46,095	2,840	1,153	1,687	2,325	1,917	408	19,093	16,447	2,646
2003[2]	46,440	3,184	1,382	1,802	2,245	1,804	440	19,252	16,735	2,517
2002	46,725	2,881	1,172	1,709	2,065	1,585	480	20,124	17,495	2,628
2001	46,110	2,725	1,054	1,671	2,203	1,781	422	20,298	17,693	2,605
2000	46,660	2,854	1,149	1,705	2,346	1,846	500	20,574	17,747	2,827
1999	47,292	3,044	1,146	1,898	2,307	1,839	468	20,779	17,960	2,819
1998	47,386	2,964	1,136	1,828	2,336	1,790	547	20,806	18,107	2,699
1997	47,776	2,956	1,143	1,813	2,456	1,970	486	20,839	18,426	2,413
1996	46,947	2,767	922	1,845	2,590	2,081	509	20,447	17,808	2,639
1995	48,019	3,104	1,129	1,975	2,551	2,047	504	21,256	18,518	2,738
1994[1]	47,679	3,024	1,090	1,934	2,522	2,059	462	21,170	18,555	2,615
1993	43,827	2,277	720	1,557	2,779	2,239	540	20,961	18,617	2,344
BLACK ALONE[3]										
2019	11,551	714	520	194	642	557	85	4,991	4,651	341
2018	11,690	680	459	221	555	541	14	4,991	4,694	297
2017	11,609	754	576	178	507	477	30	5,048	4,739	309
2016	11,684	620	457	163	668	631	37	4,855	4,522	333
2015	11,544	703	501	202	618	596	23	4,883	4,647	236
2014	11,796	746	557	189	690	605	86	4,844	4,587	257
2013	11,824	683	465	218	736	691	46	4,848	4,625	224
2012	11,918	708	516	193	646	598	48	4,856	4,583	273
2011	12,037	794	562	232	559	503	56	4,902	4,658	245
2010	11,969	698	522	175	736	682	54	4,795	4,498	298
2009	11,748	811	640	171	619	578	41	4,749	4,424	325
2008	11,421	706	548	158	601	545	56	4,993	4,665	329
2007	11,475	700	485	215	605	548	56	4,926	4,572	353
2006	11,400	715	513	202	608	536	71	4,952	4,608	344
2005	11,384	719	542	177	538	486	52	5,106	4,747	359
2004	11,540	825	600	224	596	535	61	5,159	4,905	254
2003[2]	11,408	697	484	212	558	495	63	5,245	4,942	302
2002	11,703	725	503	221	598	543	55	5,545	5,210	335
2001	11,630	787	537	250	605	536	69	5,478	5,160	318
2000	11,503	726	531	195	629	547	82	5,481	5,133	347
1999	11,282	729	569	160	632	558	74	5,388	5,002	386
1998	11,411	761	528	233	689	592	97	5,332	5,031	301
1997	11,270	796	582	214	632	571	61	5,332	5,049	284
1996	10,851	702	459	243	634	545	89	5,171	4,846	325
1995	10,753	663	478	185	653	564	89	5,185	4,845	340
1994[1]	10,702	721	513	208	662	603	59	5,086	4,709	378
1993r	9,786	433	320	113	721	649	72	5,009	4,733	276
1993	9,470	414	307	107	687	618	69	4,865	4,599	266
1992	9,150	374	250	124	688	625	63	4,730	4,494	234
1991	9,031	360	244	117	676	598	79	4,672	4,445	229
1990	8,854	431	283	148	636	574	62	4,627	4,428	199
1989	8,707	366	216	150	601	557	44	4,528	4,296	232
1988	8,609	286	168	118	591	547	44	4,538	4,289	250
1987	8,712	277	164	113	699	658	41	4,402	4,206	194

NA = Not available.

r = Revised, controlled to 1990 census based population estimates; previous 1993 data controlled to 1980 census based population estimates.

[1]Prior to 1994, total enrolled does not include the 35 and over population.

[2]Starting in 2003 respondents could identify more than one race. Except as noted, the race data in this table from 2003 onward represent those respondents who indicated only one race category.

[3]Data shown for 1955 to 1966 for the Black population are for Black and Other races.

[4]The data shown prior to 2003 consists of those identifying themselves as "Asian or Pacific Islanders."

Table A-10.   School Enrollment of the Population 3 Years Old and Over, by Level and Control of School, Selected Race, and Hispanic Origin, October 1955–2019—*Continued*

(Numbers in thousands; civilian noninstitutionalized population.)

Year, race, and Hispanic origin	High school			College			
	Total	Public	Private	Total	Public	Private	Full-time
WHITE ALONE NON-HISPANIC							
2019............................	8,447	7,718	729	9,677	7,497	2,180	7,410
2018............................	8,637	7,817	820	10,248	7,973	2,274	7,748
2017............................	8,905	8,051	854	10,055	7,736	2,319	7,404
2016............................	8,760	7,839	921	10,749	8,219	2,530	8,135
2015............................	8,931	8,087	843	10,904	8,526	2,377	8,226
2014............................	9,018	8,155	862	11,068	8,775	2,292	8,456
2013............................	8,869	8,109	760	11,348	8,889	2,459	8,362
2012............................	9,193	8,252	941	11,650	8,977	2,672	8,604
2011............................	9,437	8,535	902	12,703	9,842	2,861	9,333
2010............................	9,528	8,598	930	12,613	9,900	2,713	9,122
2009............................	9,573	8,655	919	12,826	10,022	2,803	9,368
2008............................	9,783	8,798	986	12,324	9,630	2,694	8,925
2007............................	10,171	9,204	966	11,867	9,141	2,726	8,379
2006............................	10,222	9,072	1,150	11,485	8,821	2,664	8,105
2005............................	10,647	9,566	1,081	11,715	8,852	2,863	8,246
2004............................	10,266	9,221	1,044	11,571	8,928	2,643	8,082
2003[2]........................	10,463	9,473	990	11,295	8,742	2,553	7,810
2002............................	10,419	9,388	1,031	11,236	8,488	2,749	7,673
2001............................	10,281	9,331	950	10,602	8,133	2,469	6,980
2000............................	10,250	9,222	1,029	10,636	8,202	2,434	7,105
1999............................	10,344	9,314	1,030	10,818	8,158	2,660	7,162
1998............................	10,170	9,131	1,039	11,109	8,435	2,674	7,251
1997............................	10,280	9,358	922	11,245	8,688	2,558	7,378
1996............................	10,107	9,148	959	11,034	8,584	2,450	7,178
1995............................	10,084	9,094	991	11,024	8,439	2,585	7,194
1994[1]........................	9,786	8,951	835	11,178	8,568	2,610	7,152
1993............................	9,216	8,449	767	8,594	6,772	1,822	6,247
BLACK ALONE[3]							
2019............................	2,355	2,167	189	2,848	2,330	517	2,001
2018............................	2,456	2,380	76	3,009	2,475	534	2,143
2017............................	2,488	2,366	122	2,812	2,414	398	2,034
2016............................	2,656	2,556	100	2,885	2,271	614	2,064
2015............................	2,515	2,420	95	2,826	2,260	566	2,045
2014............................	2,581	2,451	130	2,934	2,284	650	2,055
2013............................	2,699	2,588	111	2,857	2,340	517	2,092
2012............................	2,669	2,528	141	3,038	2,507	531	2,168
2011............................	2,635	2,545	91	3,146	2,541	605	2,279
2010............................	2,657	2,552	105	3,083	2,495	587	2,223
2009............................	2,680	2,592	89	2,889	2,322	567	2,061
2008............................	2,639	2,524	115	2,481	1,975	506	1,690
2007............................	2,743	2,627	116	2,501	1,968	533	1,683
2006............................	2,792	2,628	165	2,334	1,816	518	1,628
2005............................	2,723	2,592	131	2,298	1,800	498	1,526
2004............................	2,660	2,584	76	2,301	1,831	470	1,504
2003[2]........................	2,765	2,691	74	2,144	1,773	371	1,416
2002............................	2,558	2,451	107	2,278	1,868	410	1,468
2001............................	2,531	2,412	119	2,230	1,766	463	1,475
2000............................	2,502	2,350	152	2,164	1,721	443	1,351
1999............................	2,536	2,427	109	1,998	1,587	411	1,372
1998............................	2,614	2,515	99	2,016	1,595	421	1,284
1997............................	2,605	2,516	89	1,903	1,546	357	1,280
1996............................	2,443	2,338	105	1,901	1,519	381	1,179
1995............................	2,481	2,370	111	1,772	1,353	419	1,117
1994[1]........................	2,434	2,313	121	1,800	1,439	361	1,147
1993r..........................	2,317	2,197	120	1,305	1,006	299	951
1993............................	2,244	2,128	115	1,261	973	288	914
1992............................	2,152	2,072	72	1,217	980	237	904
1991............................	2,100	2,044	56	1,220	1,004	217	900
1990............................	1,975	1,909	65	1,188	963	227	869
1989............................	2,069	2,027	42	1,139	932	208	833
1988............................	2,079	2,016	62	1,114	894	220	801
1987............................	2,140	2,056	84	1,193	977	218	852

NA = Not available.

r = Revised, controlled to 1990 census based population estimates; previous 1993 data controlled to 1980 census based population estimates.

[1]Prior to 1994, total enrolled does not include the 35 and over population.

[2]Starting in 2003 respondents could identify more than one race. Except as noted, the race data in this table from 2003 onward represent those respondents who indicated only one race category.

[3]Data shown for 1955 to 1966 for the Black population are for Black and Other races.

[4]The data shown prior to 2003 consists of those identifying themselves as "Asian or Pacific Islanders."

Table A-10.   School Enrollment of the Population 3 Years Old and Over, by Level and Control of School, Selected Race, and Hispanic Origin, October 1955–2019—*Continued*

(Numbers in thousands; civilian noninstitutionalized population.)

Year, race, and Hispanic origin	Total enrolled	Nursery school			Kindergarten			Elementary school		
		Total	Public	Private	Total	Public	Private	Total	Public	Private
1986	8,556	315	200	115	647	600	47	4,326	4,134	193
1985	8,444	332	212	120	625	562	63	4,307	4,131	175
1984	8,226	340	179	161	563	513	51	4,123	3,947	177
1983	8,199	326	215	111	476	427	48	4,153	3,964	189
1982	8,262	305	192	113	508	463	45	4,194	3,974	220
1981	8,350	284	182	102	474	412	62	4,291	4,087	204
1980	8,251	294	180	115	490	440	50	4,259	4,058	202
1979	8,317	278	185	95	497	443	54	4,296	4,053	243
1978	8,416	312	210	102	451	414	38	4,356	4,154	202
1977	8,564	250	171	78	496	447	50	4,387	4,166	221
1976	8,518	226	146	80	542	482	60	4,430	4,256	175
1975	8,400	276	171	105	468	426	42	4,509	4,344	165
1974	8,215	227	121	106	463	416	47	4,585	4,455	131
1973	7,834	210	146	64	423	391	32	4,473	4,277	196
1972	7,959	185	113	72	448	402	46	4,573	4,382	191
1971	8,179	151	90	61	464	422	42	4,877	4,712	165
1970	7,829	178	129	49	426	374	53	4,868	4,668	200
1969	7,680	170	102	68	425	361	64	4,785	4,633	151
1968	7,448	132	89	43	448	397	51	4,716	4,569	146
1967	7,196	140	92	47	418	375	44	4,618	4,444	173
1966	7,547	125	88	37	420	364	56	4,904	4,739	165
1965	7,252	72	37	35	407	353	54	4,796	4,620	176
1964	6,807	NA	NA	NA	312	275	37	4,634	4,430	205
1963	6,541	NA	NA	NA	276	237	39	4,536	4,321	215
1962	6,203	NA	NA	NA	294	247	47	4,389	4,226	163
1961	6,210	NA	NA	NA	331	308	23	4,424	4,207	216
1960	5,910	NA	NA	NA	243	206	37	4,313	4,118	195
1959	5,513	NA	NA	NA	274	244	30	3,987	3,826	161
1958	5,238	NA	NA	NA	222	186	36	3,804	3,621	182
1957	5,034	NA	NA	NA	229	213	16	3,638	3,483	155
1956	4,712	NA	NA	NA	214	202	12	3,429	3,287	142
1955	4,498	NA	NA	NA	144	121	23	3,273	3,131	142
ASIAN ALONE[4]										
2019	5,023	260	118	142	256	197	58	1,800	1,684	116
2018	4,779	263	129	134	220	208	12	1,720	1,551	170
2017	4,636	253	123	130	239	204	35	1,632	1,478	154
2016	4,720	304	138	166	214	188	26	1,781	1,658	123
2015	4,567	244	102	142	215	188	27	1,704	1,552	152
2014	4,449	257	105	152	179	147	32	1,643	1,476	167
2013	4,375	242	113	129	165	149	16	1,576	1,402	174
2012	4,275	208	90	118	224	196	28	1,540	1,388	152
2011	3,779	212	120	92	209	189	21	1,469	1,336	133
2010	3,815	223	97	127	196	181	15	1,488	1,358	130
2009	3,515	239	107	132	167	146	21	1,296	1,170	125
2008	3,545	205	110	95	144	119	24	1,356	1,168	188
2007	3,470	171	77	94	137	112	25	1,421	1,305	115
2006	3,287	143	65	78	162	149	13	1,235	1,105	130
2005	3,377	185	80	105	138	99	39	1,228	1,137	91
2004	3,409	165	72	93	164	152	12	1,239	1,153	86
2003[2]	3,312	138	56	82	122	93	29	1,258	1,122	136
2002	3,787	217	85	132	157	137	20	1,431	1,237	195
2001	3,803	161	91	70	181	161	20	1,409	1,263	146
2000	3,442	222	91	132	152	124	28	1,350	1,257	93
1999	3,621	205	96	109	195	148	47	1,461	1,343	118
1998	3,386	196	77	118	145	120	25	1,380	1,190	189
1997	3,261	168	59	108	161	110	51	1,329	1,186	144
1996	3,258	183	63	120	177	158	19	1,255	1,144	111
1995	1,863	76	28	47	75	62	13	697	622	74
1994[1]	2,057	76	27	50	74	60	14	785	707	78
1993	2,321	100	38	62	139	125	14	1,012	930	82

NA = Not available.

r = Revised, controlled to 1990 census based population estimates; previous 1993 data controlled to 1980 census based population estimates.

[1]Prior to 1994, total enrolled does not include the 35 and over population.

[2]Starting in 2003 respondents could identify more than one race. Except as noted, the race data in this table from 2003 onward represent those respondents who indicated only one race category.

[3]Data shown for 1955 to 1966 for the Black population are for Black and Other races.

[4]The data shown prior to 2003 consists of those identifying themselves as "Asian or Pacific Islanders."

Table A-10. School Enrollment of the Population 3 Years Old and Over, by Level and Control of School, Selected Race, and Hispanic Origin, October 1955–2019—*Continued*

(Numbers in thousands; civilian noninstitutionalized population.)

Year, race, and Hispanic origin	High school			College			
	Total	Public	Private	Total	Public	Private	Full-time
1986........................	2,130	2,040	91	1,138	896	242	859
1985........................	2,131	2,068	63	1,049	860	190	767
1984........................	2,061	2,002	59	1,138	918	220	810
1983........................	2,143	2,057	86	1,102	858	245	806
1982........................	2,128	2,073	55	1,127	865	263	800
1981........................	2,168	2,102	65	1,133	898	235	815
1980........................	2,200	NA	NA	1,007	NA	NA	723
1979........................	2,245	2,171	74	1,002	814	188	748
1978........................	2,276	2,211	65	1,020	822	199	753
1977........................	2,327	2,269	59	1,103	916	187	803
1976........................	2,258	2,187	71	1,062	887	175	817
1975........................	2,199	2,140	59	948	782	166	742
1974........................	2,125	2,072	54	814	659	155	589
1973........................	2,044	1,988	56	685	537	147	536
1972........................	2,025	1,971	54	727	582	145	525
1971........................	2,006	1,951	55	680	532	148	534
1970........................	1,834	1,794	41	522	422	100	427
1969........................	1,808	1,751	57	492	372	120	401
1968........................	1,718	1,656	62	434	359	75	338
1967........................	1,651	1,605	46	370	280	90	271
1966........................	1,721	1,673	48	282	NA	NA	210
1965	1,619	1,556	62	358	272	86	218
1964........................	1,556	1,505	51	306	227	78	NA
1963........................	1,444	1,404	39	286	217	69	NA
1962........................	1,246	1,214	32	274	200	74	NA
1961........................	1,222	1,182	39	233	171	61	NA
1960........................	1,127	1,092	34	227	180	46	NA
1959........................	1,030	999	31	222	160	62	NA
1958........................	998	981	17	212	160	53	NA
1957........................	961	939	22	206	132	74	NA
1956........................	873	843	30	196	120	76	NA
1955........................	926	878	48	155	86	69	NA
ASIAN ALONE[4]							
2019........................	938	901	37	1,768	1,443	325	1,503
2018........................	886	851	34	1,691	1,336	355	1,439
2017........................	931	853	78	1,581	1,219	362	1,330
2016........................	837	776	62	1,585	1,163	421	1,349
2015........................	787	727	60	1,616	1,232	384	1,340
2014........................	827	766	61	1,543	1,202	341	1,247
2013........................	817	741	76	1,576	1,144	432	1,260
2012........................	857	778	79	1,447	1,078	369	1,175
2011........................	685	635	50	1,204	936	268	963
2010........................	586	542	43	1,322	969	353	1,090
2009........................	582	530	53	1,231	950	282	972
2008........................	620	564	56	1,220	918	301	917
2007........................	638	616	23	1,103	841	261	896
2006........................	663	611	51	1,084	862	223	866
2005........................	642	596	46	1,184	904	279	948
2004........................	650	619	31	1,191	928	263	881
2003[2].....................	632	585	47	1,162	833	328	901
2002........................	723	664	59	1,258	1,040	218	951
2001........................	771	736	35	1,280	1,026	254	921
2000........................	668	622	46	1,049	831	218	792
1999........................	719	666	53	1,041	779	261	787
1998........................	650	599	51	1,016	783	233	821
1997........................	656	600	57	947	712	235	721
1996........................	644	606	38	999	816	183	710
1995........................	399	375	24	617	470	147	456
1994[1]	399	365	34	723	548	174	530
1993........................	428	390	37	641	519	122	542

NA = Not available.

r = Revised, controlled to 1990 census based population estimates; previous 1993 data controlled to 1980 census based population estimates.
[1] Prior to 1994, total enrolled does not include the 35 and over population.
[2] Starting in 2003 respondents could identify more than one race. Except as noted, the race data in this table from 2003 onward represent those respondents who indicated only one race category.
[3] Data shown for 1955 to 1966 for the Black population are for Black and Other races.
[4] The data shown prior to 2003 consists of those identifying themselves as "Asian or Pacific Islanders."

Table A-10.   School Enrollment of the Population 3 Years Old and Over, by Level and Control of School, Selected Race, and Hispanic Origin, October 1955–2019—*Continued*

(Numbers in thousands; civilian noninstitutionalized population.)

Year, race, and Hispanic origin	Total enrolled	Nursery school			Kindergarten			Elementary school		
		Total	Public	Private	Total	Public	Private	Total	Public	Private
HISPANIC (OF ANY RACE)										
2019	18,204	1,115	775	340	1,038	939	99	8,396	8,021	375
2018	18,080	1,149	864	285	970	891	79	8,305	7,929	375
2017	17,974	1,007	751	257	1,116	1,032	83	8,340	7,924	416
2016	17,865	1,079	791	287	1,034	1,008	26	8,148	7,835	313
2015	17,362	933	735	198	1,090	1,020	70	8,187	7,824	364
2014	17,122	1,016	769	248	1,044	991	54	8,085	7,699	386
2013	16,971	991	781	210	1,090	1,018	73	7,942	7,680	262
2012	17,043	988	781	206	1,050	1,009	41	7,841	7,566	275
2011	16,131	1,010	766	244	1,042	984	58	7,716	7,401	315
2010	15,670	994	794	200	1,050	1,002	49	7,403	7,052	351
2009	14,528	930	717	213	965	933	32	7,058	6,716	342
2008	13,967	844	668	177	961	910	51	6,742	6,450	292
2007	13,708	905	711	194	990	954	37	6,582	6,299	284
2006	13,111	911	707	205	846	798	48	6,394	6,109	285
2005	12,809	797	601	196	804	725	79	6,330	5,991	339
2004	12,509	787	591	196	769	699	70	6,184	5,895	290
2003	11,929	768	561	206	694	633	61	5,974	5,651	322
2002	11,544	637	476	161	727	688	39	5,909	5,585	324
2001	11,163	593	452	141	728	641	87	5,779	5,478	301
2000	10,163	574	419	154	687	639	48	5,224	5,012	213
1999	9,936	585	458	127	666	594	73	5,088	4,829	259
1998	9,528	618	492	126	639	608	31	4,831	4,568	262
1997	9,220	548	436	112	648	589	59	4,644	4,427	217
1996	8,818	533	403	130	602	539	63	4,443	4,162	281
1995	8,563	510	350	160	558	465	93	4,434	4,165	269
1994[1]	8,183	400	278	122	559	516	43	4,162	3,848	314
1993r	7,651	231	169	62	639	576	63	4,027	3,779	248
1993	6,689	194	142	52	538	484	53	3,534	3,317	217
1992	6,598	209	139	70	554	493	60	3,525	3,271	252
1991	6,306	215	146	69	552	525	27	3,461	3,240	221
1990	6,072	242	153	88	475	446	29	3,301	3,107	197
1989	5,722	181	95	86	404	382	21	3,219	3,031	188
1988	5,588	151	111	40	461	445	16	3,160	2,954	207
1987	5,619	226	138	88	439	399	39	3,048	2,861	187
1986	5,513	179	114	65	465	421	44	2,995	2,787	208
1985	5,070	168	105	63	364	315	49	2,803	2,607	196
1984	4,284	117	78	39	293	267	26	2,384	2,218	166
1983	4,618	108	60	48	335	285	50	2,548	2,323	225
1982	4,478	83	46	37	329	291	37	2,501	2,276	225
1981	4,551	131	68	63	306	282	24	2,474	2,239	235
1980	4,263	146	70	75	263	234	30	2,363	2,134	228
1979	3,608	89	50	39	226	210	16	1,934	1,745	189
1978	3,455	87	47	39	231	198	33	1,893	1,704	188
1977	3,516	75	30	46	220	206	14	1,874	1,654	220
1976	3,623	68	38	30	262	242	20	1,934	1,768	165
1975	3,741	85	47	39	235	218	17	2,062	1,858	204
1974	3,620	85	37	48	225	207	18	2,040	1,780	260
1973	3,171	68	41	27	171	165	6	1,884	1,712	172
1972	3,257	61	43	18	241	227	14	1,879	1,705	173
WHITE ALONE OR IN COMBINATION										
2019	57,879	3,637	1,904	1,732	3,107	2,726	382	25,033	22,672	2,361
2018	58,796	3,785	2,088	1,697	3,034	2,684	350	25,102	22,789	2,313
2017	58,381	3,576	2,022	1,554	3,137	2,780	356	25,040	22,895	2,145
2016	58,973	3,695	2,119	1,576	3,046	2,746	300	25,148	23,034	2,114
2015	59,162	3436	1890	1546	3133	2762	371	25,493	23,271	2223
2014	59,281	3,575	1,942	1,634	3,125	2,791	334	25,391	23,054	2,337
2013	60,066	3,650	1,896	1,754	3,166	2,813	353	25,776	23,510	2,266
2012	60,618	3601	2058	1543	3177	2799	378	25,613	23,244	2369
2011	61,979	3,833	2,132	1,702	3,393	2,988	405	25,989	23,474	2,516
2010	61,498	3,880	2,130	1,749	3,188	2,848	339	25,844	23,469	2,375
2009	60,778	3,582	1,931	1,651	3,271	2,974	298	25,629	23,238	2,391

NA = Not available.

r = Revised, controlled to 1990 census based population estimates; previous 1993 data controlled to 1980 census based population estimates.

[1]Prior to 1994, total enrolled does not include the 35 and over population.

[2]Starting in 2003 respondents could identify more than one race. Except as noted, the race data in this table from 2003 onward represent those respondents who indicated only one race category.

[3]Data shown for 1955 to 1966 for the Black population are for Black and Other races.

[4]The data shown prior to 2003 consists of those identifying themselves as "Asian or Pacific Islanders."

Table A-10. School Enrollment of the Population 3 Years Old and Over, by Level and Control of School, Selected Race, and Hispanic Origin, October 1955–2019—*Continued*

(Numbers in thousands; civilian noninstitutionalized population.)

Year, race, and Hispanic origin	High school			College			
	Total	Public	Private	Total	Public	Private	Full-time
HISPANIC (OF ANY RACE)							
2019	4,101	3,900	201	3,555	3,133	421	2,568
2018	4,082	3,901	181	3,574	3,116	458	2,578
2017	3,936	3,769	167	3,574	3,133	442	2,510
2016	3,943	3,787	156	3,661	3,050	612	2,571
2015	3,777	3,658	120	3,374	2,861	514	2,343
2014	3,681	3,545	136	3,295	2,799	496	2,352
2013	3,729	3,596	133	3,219	2,768	452	2,179
2012	3,765	3,633	131	3,400	2,948	451	2,397
2011	3,410	3,294	116	2,953	2,515	438	2,041
2010	3,344	3,219	125	2,879	2,478	401	1,868
2009	3,142	3,052	90	2,434	2,122	312	1,651
2008	3,192	3,066	126	2,227	1,919	308	1,434
2007	3,058	2,902	156	2,172	1,888	284	1,459
2006	2,990	2,856	134	1,968	1,664	304	1,246
2005	2,937	2,824	113	1,942	1,625	316	1,255
2004	2,793	2,685	108	1,975	1,676	299	1,276
2003	2,779	2,667	112	1,714	1,480	235	1,139
2002	2,614	2,513	101	1,656	1,374	283	1,004
2001	2,363	2,246	117	1,700	1,445	255	1,005
2000	2,253	2,144	108	1,426	1,219	207	873
1999	2,290	2,200	91	1,307	1,093	214	765
1998	2,077	1,978	98	1,363	1,137	226	801
1997	2,119	2,035	84	1,260	1,079	181	797
1996	2,018	1,922	96	1,223	1,031	192	708
1995	1,854	1,772	83	1,207	1,037	170	709
1994[1]	1,874	1,781	92	1,187	1,019	169	640
1993r	1,722	1,653	69	1,029	872	157	686
1993	1,556	1,496	60	867	731	134	573
1992	1,494	1,435	59	813	710	104	487
1991	1,357	1,299	61	721	607	115	481
1990	1,437	1,374	64	617	515	100	380
1989	1,278	1,231	48	642	557	82	416
1988	1,163	1,113	49	654	592	60	414
1987	1,239	1,160	80	668	551	115	414
1986	1,197	1,116	81	677	540	137	418
1985	1,156	1,090	67	579	464	116	381
1984	966	909	57	524	433	91	356
1983	1,104	1,027	77	523	441	82	335
1982	1,072	995	77	493	398	96	312
1981	1,130	1,056	74	510	398	112	343
1980	1,048	NA	NA	443	NA	NA	294
1979	920	875	45	440	365	75	314
1978	868	825	43	377	315	62	231
1977	928	836	92	418	357	60	287
1976	932	867	65	427	354	73	297
1975	948	886	61	411	358	53	287
1974	916	858	59	354	297	57	247
1973	758	707	51	290	247	43	201
1972	834	784	50	242	213	29	178
WHITE ALONE OR IN COMBINATION							
2019	12,727	11,812	915	13,375	10,712	2,662	10,127
2018	12,991	11,928	1,063	13,885	11,123	2,761	10,402
2017	12,926	11,869	1,056	13,703	10,897	2,805	10,029
2016	12,728	11,627	1,102	14,355	11,223	3,132	10,731
2015	12,805	11,813	992	14,295	11,365	2930	10,581
2014	12,879	11,824	1,055	14,310	11,503	2,807	10,778
2013	12,732	11,803	929	14,743	11,768	2,975	10,647
2012	13,110	12,010	1101	15,117	11,919	3198	11,038
2011	12,979	11,952	1,027	15,785	12,449	3,336	11,476
2010	13,001	11,924	1,077	15,586	12,460	3,127	11,062
2009	12,905	11,877	1,029	15,391	12,236	3,155	11,150

NA = Not available.

r = Revised, controlled to 1990 census based population estimates; previous 1993 data controlled to 1980 census based population estimates.

[1] Prior to 1994, total enrolled does not include the 35 and over population.

[2] Starting in 2003 respondents could identify more than one race. Except as noted, the race data in this table from 2003 onward represent those respondents who indicated only one race category.

[3] Data shown for 1955 to 1966 for the Black population are for Black and Other races.

[4] The data shown prior to 2003 consists of those identifying themselves as "Asian or Pacific Islanders."

Table A-10. School Enrollment of the Population 3 Years Old and Over, by Level and Control of School, Selected Race, and Hispanic Origin, October 1955–2019—*Continued*

(Numbers in thousands; civilian noninstitutionalized population.)

Year, race, and Hispanic origin	Total enrolled	Nursery school			Kindergarten			Elementary school		
		Total	Public	Private	Total	Public	Private	Total	Public	Private
2008	60,309	3,642	1,927	1,715	3,247	2,863	385	25,498	22,849	2,649
2007	59,896	3,689	1,959	1,730	3,339	2,946	393	25,321	22,689	2,632
2006	59,391	3,765	1,895	1,871	3,213	2,820	393	25,424	22,809	2,615
2005	60,035	3,642	1,819	1,823	3,179	2,715	463	25,682	22,794	2,888
2004	59,427	3,682	1,762	1,920	3,169	2,670	498	25,691	22,682	3,009
2003	59,184	4,039	1,989	2,050	3,002	2,477	525	25,581	22,686	2,895
BLACK ALONE OR IN COMBINATION										
2019	13,679	911	640	271	761	671	90	6,015	5,638	377
2018	13,654	835	558	277	685	663	22	5,960	5,590	370
2017	13,598	909	663	246	651	615	36	6,087	5,695	391
2016	13,507	792	561	231	797	749	48	5,749	5,332	417
2015	13,248	820	594	226	710	680	29	5,883	5,598	285
2014	13,387	840	624	216	830	739	91	5,720	5,409	312
2013	13,517	852	560	291	855	804	51	5,637	5,378	259
2012	13,534	834	613	221	799	744	55	5,603	5,299	305
2011	13,288	904	649	255	696	628	68	5,524	5,253	271
2010	13,105	798	589	210	809	743	66	5,402	5,069	333
2009	12,825	894	687	206	674	632	42	5,295	4,942	353
2008	12,542	776	589	187	668	609	59	5,593	5,225	368
2007	12,401	788	546	242	673	617	57	5,395	5,030	365
2006	12,261	801	568	234	678	607	71	5,365	5,002	363
2005	12,118	763	563	200	593	531	62	5,504	5,122	382
2004	12,303	864	622	242	676	606	70	5,540	5,251	289
2003	12,144	787	526	262	637	559	78	5,604	5,276	327
ASIAN ALONE OR IN COMBINATION										
2019	6,094	341	142	199	322	249	73	2,253	2,078	175
2018	5,857	339	157	183	273	237	36	2,216	1,955	262
2017	5,708	356	172	184	305	257	48	2,165	1,952	213
2016	5,669	402	170	232	266	233	34	2,207	1,990	217
2015	5,417	334	125	209	256	211	44	2,047	1,830	217
2014	5,353	320	122	198	255	214	41	2,078	1,857	221
2013	5,399	367	157	210	240	214	26	2,026	1,780	246
2012	5,154	268	118	150	270	232	38	1,939	1,733	206
2011	4,571	273	139	134	257	235	22	1,860	1,686	173
2010	4,591	297	132	165	230	212	18	1,876	1,696	180
2009	4,117	316	140	175	195	170	25	1,571	1,410	160
2008	4,122	267	143	123	188	156	32	1,570	1,351	219
2007	4,025	219	94	125	179	151	28	1,664	1,513	151
2006	3,849	189	78	111	203	181	22	1,497	1,331	166
2005	3,964	220	94	126	159	118	41	1,495	1,362	133
2004	3,943	208	82	127	191	169	21	1,497	1,350	148
2003	3,817	164	73	90	148	111	38	1,507	1,346	161

NA = Not available.

r = Revised, controlled to 1990 census based population estimates; previous 1993 data controlled to 1980 census based population estimates.

[1]Prior to 1994, total enrolled does not include the 35 and over population.

[2]Starting in 2003 respondents could identify more than one race. Except as noted, the race data in this table from 2003 onward represent those respondents who indicated only one race category.

[3]Data shown for 1955 to 1966 for the Black population are for Black and Other races.

[4]The data shown prior to 2003 consists of those identifying themselves as "Asian or Pacific Islanders."

Table A-10. School Enrollment of the Population 3 Years Old and Over, by Level and Control of School, Selected Race, and Hispanic Origin, October 1955–2019—*Continued*

(Numbers in thousands; civilian noninstitutionalized population.)

Year, race, and Hispanic origin	High school			College			
	Total	Public	Private	Total	Public	Private	Full-time
2008............................	13,184	12,050	1,133	14,738	11,692	3,046	10,511
2007............................	13,433	12,302	1,131	14,114	11,058	3,056	9,912
2006............................	13,425	12,115	1,309	13,564	10,569	2,995	9,433
2005............................	13,741	12,516	1,225	13,791	10,561	3,230	9,618
2004............................	13,218	12,047	1,170	13,668	10,711	2,957	9,468
2003............................	13,398	12,267	1,131	13,164	10,366	2,798	9,048
BLACK ALONE OR IN COMBINATION							
2019............................	2,852	2,629	222	3,142	2,577	564	2,215
2018............................	2,902	2,802	100	3,272	2,694	579	2,331
2017............................	2,884	2,727	157	3,068	2,609	459	2,261
2016............................	3,090	2,959	131	3,079	2,435	644	2,219
2015............................	2,850	2,730	120	2,985	2,364	621	2,163
2014............................	2,898	2,730	168	3,099	2,405	694	2,185
2013............................	3,055	2,921	134	3,118	2,542	577	2,297
2012............................	2,962	2,816	146	3,335	2,752	583	2,373
2011............................	2,847	2,752	95	3,317	2,676	641	2,401
2010............................	2,846	2,724	122	3,250	2,641	610	2,354
2009............................	2,932	2,836	97	3,030	2,434	596	2,178
2008............................	2,886	2,769	118	2,619	2,065	554	1,779
2007............................	2,915	2,792	122	2,630	2,059	571	1,774
2006............................	2,971	2,798	174	2,444	1,907	537	1,702
2005............................	2,870	2,729	141	2,387	1,866	521	1,585
2004............................	2,811	2,726	85	2,412	1,922	490	1,591
2003............................	2,889	2,800	89	2,227	1,846	381	1,482
ASIAN ALONE OR IN COMBINATION							
2019............................	1,178	1,115	63	1,999	1,642	358	1,711
2018............................	1,109	1,042	67	1,919	1,531	388	1,634
2017............................	1,132	1,015	117	1,750	1,356	394	1,460
2016............................	1,014	922	92	1,780	1,324	455	1,512
2015............................	960	879	81	1,821	1,385	436	1,501
2014............................	988	893	96	1,712	1,337	375	1,392
2013............................	1,000	909	91	1,766	1,295	471	1,412
2012............................	1,060	949	111	1,617	1,201	415	1,300
2011............................	825	757	68	1,356	1,053	302	1,063
2010............................	722	668	54	1,467	1,089	378	1,205
2009............................	701	636	65	1,334	1,033	301	1,061
2008............................	758	690	68	1,340	1,009	331	1,009
2007............................	760	718	42	1,204	917	287	988
2006............................	806	743	63	1,154	918	235	900
2005............................	792	726	67	1,297	993	305	1,036
2004............................	786	743	43	1,260	980	281	936
2003............................	736	674	62	1,262	925	337	965

NA = Not available.

r = Revised, controlled to 1990 census based population estimates; previous 1993 data controlled to 1980 census based population estimates.

[1]Prior to 1994, total enrolled does not include the 35 and over population.

[2]Starting in 2003 respondents could identify more than one race. Except as noted, the race data in this table from 2003 onward represent those respondents who indicated only one race category.

[3]Data shown for 1955 to 1966 for the Black population are for Black and Other races.

[4]The data shown prior to 2003 consists of those identifying themselves as "Asian or Pacific Islanders."

Table A-11. Percentage of the Population 3 Years Old and Over Enrolled in School, by Age, Sex, Race, and Hispanic Origin, October 1947–2019

(Percent; civilian noninstitutionalized population.)

Year, sex, race, and Hispanic origin	Total enrolled 3 to 34 years old	Total enrolled 3 years old and over	Age 3 and 4	5 and 6	7 to 9	10 to 13	14 and 15	16 and 17	18 and 19	20 and 21	22 to 24	25 to 29	30 to 34	35 and over
ALL RACES														
Both Sexes														
2019	54.1	24.3	53.7	93.6	97.5	98.0	97.9	92.7	67.3	53.5	28.6	11.0	6.0	1.4
2018	54.6	24.6	54.0	93.5	97.0	98.2	98.6	92.3	69.1	54.6	28.0	12.7	6.3	1.5
2017	54.6	24.7	53.8	93.5	97.1	97.8	98.2	92.9	68.2	55.0	28.4	12.1	5.9	1.5
2016	55.2	25.1	53.8	93.3	97.8	98.5	98.0	93.0	69.5	55.5	28.8	13.2	6.4	1.5
2015	55.2	25.3	52.7	94.2	97.3	98.0	98.0	93.7	68.5	53.3	28.8	13.2	6.6	1.6
2014	55.2	25.6	54.5	93.4	97.7	97.5	97.8	92.9	68.4	51.4	29.6	13.1	6.4	1.8
2013	55.8	25.9	54.9	93.8	97.9	98.2	98.4	93.7	67.1	52.8	29.7	13.3	6.7	1.8
2012	56.6	26.4	53.5	93.2	98.0	98.0	98.2	95.8	69.0	54.0	30.7	14.0	7.5	1.9
2011	56.8	26.9	52.4	95.1	98.0	98.5	98.6	95.7	71.1	52.7	31.1	14.8	7.7	2.0
2010	56.5	26.9	53.2	94.5	97.7	98.2	98.1	96.1	69.2	52.4	28.9	14.6	8.3	2.1
2009	56.5	26.7	52.4	94.1	97.7	98.5	98.0	94.6	68.9	51.7	30.4	13.5	8.1	2.1
2008	56.2	26.6	52.8	93.8	98.3	98.9	98.6	95.2	66.0	50.1	28.2	13.2	7.3	2.0
2007	56.1	26.6	54.5	94.7	98.1	98.6	98.7	94.3	66.8	48.4	27.3	12.4	7.2	1.9
2006	56.2	26.7	55.7	94.6	98.2	98.3	98.3	94.5	65.5	47.5	26.7	11.7	7.2	1.9
2005	56.5	27.1	53.6	95.4	98.6	98.6	98.0	95.1	67.6	48.7	27.3	11.9	6.9	2.0
2004	56.2	27.2	54.0	95.4	98.1	98.6	98.5	94.5	64.4	48.9	26.3	13.0	6.6	2.0
2003	56.2	27.2	55.1	94.5	98.1	98.4	97.5	94.9	64.5	48.3	27.8	11.8	6.8	1.9
2002	56.1	27.3	54.5	95.2	98.0	98.5	98.4	94.3	63.3	47.8	25.6	12.1	6.6	2.1
2001	55.7	27.2	52.2	95.3	98.2	98.4	98.1	93.4	61.0	45.5	25.1	11.4	6.8	2.0
2000	55.9	27.5	52.1	95.6	98.1	98.3	98.7	92.8	61.2	44.1	24.6	11.4	6.7	1.9
1999	56.0	27.7	54.2	96.0	98.5	98.8	98.2	93.6	60.6	45.3	24.5	11.1	6.2	2.1
1998	55.8	27.9	52.1	95.6	98.8	99.0	98.4	93.9	62.2	44.8	24.9	11.4	6.6	2.1
1997	55.6	28.3	52.6	96.6	98.8	99.3	98.9	94.3	61.5	45.9	26.4	11.8	5.7	2.3
1996	54.1	27.8	48.3	94.0	97.2	98.1	98.0	92.8	61.5	44.4	24.8	11.9	6.1	2.3
1995	53.7	27.8	48.7	96.0	98.7	99.1	98.9	93.6	59.4	44.9	23.2	11.6	6.0	2.2
1994	53.3	27.9	47.3	96.7	99.3	99.4	98.8	94.4	60.2	44.9	24.1	10.8	6.7	2.3
1993r	51.9	NA	40.1	95.3	99.5	99.5	98.9	93.9	61.4	42.6	23.5	10.2	5.9	NA
1993	51.8	26.9	40.4	95.4	99.5	99.5	98.9	94.0	61.6	42.7	23.6	10.2	5.9	2.2
1992	51.4	26.9	39.7	95.5	99.4	99.4	99.1	94.1	61.4	44.0	23.7	9.8	6.1	2.1
1991	50.7	26.9	40.5	95.4	99.6	99.7	98.8	93.3	59.6	42.0	22.2	10.2	6.2	2.2
1990	50.2	26.8	44.4	96.5	99.7	99.6	99.0	92.5	57.3	39.7	21.0	9.7	5.8	2.1
1989	49.1	26.4	39.1	95.2	99.2	99.4	98.8	92.7	56.0	38.5	19.9	9.3	5.7	2.0
1988	48.7	26.5	38.2	96.0	99.6	99.7	98.9	91.6	55.7	39.1	18.3	8.3	5.9	2.1
1987	48.6	26.6	38.3	95.1	99.6	99.5	98.6	91.7	55.6	38.7	17.5	9.0	5.9	1.8
1986	48.2	26.6	39.0	95.3	99.3	99.1	97.6	92.3	54.6	33.0	17.9	8.8	6.0	1.8
1985	48.3	26.8	38.9	96.1	99.1	99.3	98.1	91.7	51.6	35.3	16.9	9.2	6.1	1.7
1984	47.9	26.6	36.3	94.5	99.0	99.4	97.8	91.5	50.1	33.9	17.3	9.1	6.3	1.5
1983	48.4	27.1	37.6	95.4	98.9	99.4	98.3	91.7	50.4	32.5	16.6	9.6	6.4	1.7
1982	48.6	27.4	36.4	95.0	99.2	99.1	98.5	90.6	47.8	34.0	16.8	9.6	6.3	1.6
1981	48.9	27.9	36.0	94.0	99.2	99.3	98.0	90.6	49.0	31.6	16.5	9.0	6.9	1.7
1980	49.7	28.2	36.7	95.7	99.1	99.4	98.2	89.0	46.4	31.0	16.3	9.3	6.5	1.6
1979	50.3	28.7	35.1	95.8	99.2	99.1	98.1	89.2	45.0	30.2	15.8	9.6	6.4	1.7
1978	51.2	29.3	34.2	95.3	99.3	99.0	98.4	89.1	45.4	29.5	16.3	9.4	6.4	1.6
1977	52.5	NA	32.0	95.8	99.5	99.4	98.5	88.9	46.2	31.8	16.5	10.8	6.9	NA
1976	53.1	31.7	31.3	95.5	99.2	99.2	98.2	89.1	46.2	32.0	17.1	10.0	6.0	3.9
1975	53.7	NA	31.5	94.7	99.3	99.3	98.2	89.0	46.9	31.2	16.2	10.1	6.6	NA
1974	53.6	NA	28.8	94.2	99.1	99.5	97.9	87.9	43.1	30.2	15.1	9.6	5.7	NA
1973	53.5	NA	24.2	92.5	99.1	99.2	97.5	88.3	42.9	30.1	14.5	8.5	4.5	NA
1972	54.9	NA	24.4	91.9	99.0	99.3	97.6	88.9	46.3	31.4	14.8	8.6	4.6	NA
1971	56.2	NA	21.2	91.6	99.1	99.2	98.6	90.2	49.2	32.2	15.4	8.0	4.9	NA
1970	56.4	NA	20.5	89.5	99.3	99.2	98.1	90.0	47.7	31.9	14.9	7.5	4.2	NA
1969	57.0	NA	16.1	88.4	99.3	99.1	98.1	89.7	50.2	34.1	15.4	7.9	4.8	NA
1968	56.7	NA	15.7	87.6	99.1	99.1	98.0	90.2	50.4	31.2	13.8	7.0	3.9	NA
1967	56.6	NA	14.2	87.4	99.4	99.1	98.2	88.8	47.6	33.3	13.6	6.6	4.0	NA
1966	56.1	NA	12.5	85.1	99.3	99.3	98.6	88.5	47.2	29.9	13.2	6.5	2.7	NA
1965	55.5	NA	10.6	84.4	99.3	99.4	98.9	87.4	46.3	27.6	13.2	6.1	3.2	NA
1964	54.5	NA	9.5	83.3	99.0	99.0	98.6	87.7	41.6	26.3	9.9	5.2	2.6	NA
1963	58.5	NA	NA	82.7	99.4	99.3	98.4	87.1	40.9	25.0	11.4	4.9	2.5	NA
1962	57.8	NA	NA	82.2	99.2	99.3	98.0	84.3	41.8	23.0	10.3	5.0	2.6	NA

Note: Data shown for 1947 to 1966 for the Black population are for Black and other races. Data for 1947 to 1963 exclude kindergarten. Nursery school was first collected in 1964.

* = Quantity zero or rounds to zero.

NA = Not available.

r = Revised, controlled to 1990 census based population estimates; previous 1993 data controlled to 1980 census based population estimates.

[1]Starting in 2003, respondents could identify more than one race. Except as noted, the race data in this table from 2003 onward represent those respondents who indicated only one race category.

[2]The data shown prior to 2003 consists of those identifying themselves as "Asian or Pacific Islanders."

Table A-11. Percentage of the Population 3 Years Old and Over Enrolled in School, by Age, Sex, Race, and Hispanic Origin, October 1947–2019—*Continued*

(Percent; civilian noninstitutionalized population.)

Year, sex, race, and Hispanic origin	Total enrolled 3 to 34 years old	Total enrolled 3 years old and over	Age											
			3 and 4	5 and 6	7 to 9	10 to 13	14 and 15	16 and 17	18 and 19	20 and 21	22 to 24	25 to 29	30 to 34	35 and over
1961	56.8	NA	NA	81.7	99.4	99.3	97.6	83.6	38.0	21.5	8.4	4.4	2.0	NA
1960	56.4	NA	NA	80.7	99.6	99.5	97.8	82.6	38.4	19.4	8.7	4.9	2.4	NA
1959	55.5	NA	NA	80.0	99.4	99.4	97.5	82.9	36.8	18.8	8.6	5.1	2.2	NA
1958	54.8	NA	NA	80.4	99.5	99.5	96.9	80.6	37.6	------13.4------		5.7	2.2	NA
1957	53.6	NA	NA	78.6	99.5	99.5	97.1	80.5	34.9	------14.0------		5.5	1.8	NA
1956	52.3	NA	NA	77.6	99.4	99.4	96.9	78.4	35.4	------12.8------		5.1	1.9	NA
1955	50.8	NA	NA	78.1	99.2	99.2	95.9	77.4	31.5	------11.1------		4.2	1.6	NA
1954	50.0	NA	NA	77.3	99.2	99.5	95.8	78.0	32.4	------11.2------		4.1	1.5	NA
1953	48.8	NA	NA	55.7	99.4	99.4	96.5	74.7	31.2	------11.1------		2.9	1.7	NA
1952	46.8	NA	NA	54.7	98.7	98.9	96.2	73.4	28.7	-------9.5------		2.6	1.1	NA
1951	45.4	NA	NA	54.5	99.0	99.2	94.8	75.1	26.3	-------8.3------		2.5	NA	NA
1950	44.2	NA	NA	58.2	98.9	98.6	94.7	71.3	29.4	-------9.0------		3.0	NA	NA
1949	43.9	NA	NA	59.3	98.5	98.7	93.5	69.5	25.3	-------9.2------		3.8	1.1	NA
1948	43.1	NA	NA	56.0	98.3	98.0	92.7	71.2	26.9	-------9.7------		2.6	0.9	NA
1947	42.3	NA	NA	58.0	98.4	98.6	91.6	67.6	24.3	------10.2------		3.0	1.0	NA
Male														
2019	53.6	24.7	53.3	94.4	98.2	97.8	98.0	92.6	65.7	50.1	25.4	10.1	4.7	1.2
2018	54.1	25.0	53.6	93.3	97.1	98.1	98.8	93.7	66.1	50.9	26.1	11.2	5.4	1.1
2017	54.0	25.1	53.4	92.8	97.1	97.8	98.2	92.3	65.1	50.8	26.8	10.9	5.2	1.1
2016	54.8	25.6	54.1	92.7	97.5	98.3	98.7	92.7	68.2	51.4	27.6	11.8	5.5	1.2
2015	54.9	25.7	53.6	93.5	97.5	98.3	97.9	93.1	65.7	50.2	27.5	11.7	5.5	1.2
2014	54.8	25.9	53.5	94.0	97.5	96.9	97.5	92.1	64.9	49.1	28.1	12.2	5.3	1.4
2013	55.2	26.2	53.2	93.8	97.9	98.1	98.2	93.3	65.1	48.5	27.6	12.2	5.3	1.4
2012	55.9	26.6	52.7	93.2	97.7	98.2	98.3	95.7	65.8	49.5	29.4	11.9	5.8	1.3
2011	56.2	27.2	52.8	95.1	98.1	98.6	98.4	95.4	68.8	49.2	30.3	12.9	6.4	1.5
2010	55.9	27.1	53.0	93.7	97.6	97.9	98.0	94.9	66.9	49.2	27.0	13.5	6.7	1.6
2009	55.7	26.9	51.6	93.9	97.6	98.6	97.6	94.5	65.0	48.7	29.0	11.7	6.9	1.5
2008	55.6	26.9	52.3	93.8	98.0	98.7	99.0	94.9	64.0	47.4	26.3	12.1	6.3	1.4
2007	55.4	26.9	54.4	94.0	98.1	98.4	98.4	94.4	66.3	43.7	25.4	10.2	6.4	1.5
2006	55.5	27.0	56.0	94.4	98.1	98.2	98.2	94.1	63.6	44.0	25.0	10.4	5.9	1.5
2005	55.8	27.4	52.8	94.8	98.2	98.4	97.5	95.1	66.5	45.3	25.2	9.6	5.9	1.5
2004	55.0	27.6	54.7	95.5	97.8	98.5	98.7	94.9	60.3	46.6	24.1	11.5	5.6	1.6
2003	55.9	27.8	55.9	94.7	97.9	98.3	97.5	95.0	62.4	43.4	26.1	10.8	6.3	1.5
2002	55.8	27.9	54.6	95.3	98.1	98.3	98.4	94.0	61.8	44.8	23.8	10.7	5.5	1.7
2001	55.4	27.8	51.6	95.2	98.5	98.1	98.1	93.0	58.9	44.0	23.8	10.3	5.7	1.5
2000	55.8	28.0	50.8	95.1	98.0	98.3	98.7	92.7	58.3	41.0	23.9	10.0	5.6	1.5
1999	56.6	28.6	53.3	95.9	98.3	98.7	98.0	93.7	60.3	44.7	23.6	10.7	5.8	1.6
1998	55.9	28.6	53.3	95.2	98.7	99.0	98.3	93.5	60.1	42.7	24.6	10.9	5.5	1.6
1997	55.8	28.8	51.9	96.7	98.6	99.4	99.1	94.2	60.6	44.4	25.4	11.7	4.7	1.6
1996	54.4	28.5	46.9	93.8	97.2	98.0	98.5	93.2	60.8	43.9	25.2	11.4	4.9	1.8
1995	54.3	28.7	49.4	95.3	98.9	99.1	99.0	94.5	59.5	44.7	22.8	11.0	5.4	1.8
1994	53.7	28.7	47.6	97.0	99.2	99.4	98.8	94.3	60.4	42.7	24.2	10.5	5.9	1.7
1993r	52.6	NA	41.1	95.5	99.5	99.6	99.0	94.9	61.1	42.3	25.3	9.6	5.2	NA
1993	52.6	27.9	41.5	95.5	99.5	99.6	99.0	95.0	61.6	42.6	25.5	9.6	5.2	1.6
1992	51.9	27.7	40.3	95.7	99.5	99.5	99.2	95.4	61.6	41.7	23.8	9.1	5.2	1.5
1991	51.5	27.9	39.9	95.0	99.7	99.8	99.1	93.7	59.8	41.8	24.0	10.6	5.6	1.6
1990	50.9	27.7	43.9	96.5	99.7	99.6	99.1	92.7	58.2	40.3	22.3	9.2	4.8	1.5
1989	49.7	27.3	38.8	95.1	99.3	99.2	99.2	93.2	56.6	37.3	20.4	9.3	5.0	1.4
1988	49.6	27.6	38.3	95.9	99.6	99.7	98.9	92.1	56.2	39.0	20.5	8.1	5.5	1.5
1987	49.9	27.9	40.0	95.7	99.7	99.7	98.7	92.3	57.9	41.2	18.7	9.1	5.0	1.3
1986	49.3	27.8	38.8	96.0	99.4	98.9	97.6	92.3	57.1	33.4	19.0	9.4	5.6	1.3
1985	49.2	27.9	36.8	95.3	99.1	99.2	98.3	92.4	52.2	36.5	18.8	9.4	5.4	1.3
1984	49.1	28.0	35.9	94.0	98.8	99.3	97.5	91.8	52.4	36.2	20.1	9.6	5.8	1.1
1983	49.7	28.6	38.1	95.1	98.8	99.3	98.4	91.8	50.4	35.2	19.4	10.7	5.8	1.2
1982	49.7	28.8	36.4	94.7	99.2	99.0	98.7	91.3	48.9	35.2	18.5	10.1	5.8	1.2
1981	50.2	29.3	36.8	94.2	98.9	99.2	98.2	90.7	50.5	32.1	19.2	9.6	6.2	1.2
1980	50.9	29.6	37.8	95.0	99.0	99.4	98.7	89.1	47.0	32.6	17.8	9.8	5.9	1.2
1979	51.8	30.2	34.6	96.3	99.0	98.9	98.3	90.8	46.6	31.6	17.6	10.4	6.0	1.3
1978	52.9	31.0	34.0	95.1	99.1	98.8	98.4	89.5	47.8	31.7	19.1	10.9	6.5	1.3
1977	54.3	NA	32.1	94.7	99.5	99.2	98.7	90.0	48.4	34.6	19.7	12.6	7.1	NA
1976	55.1	33.6	30.9	95.6	98.9	99.1	98.6	90.5	48.2	33.6	20.7	13.0	6.8	3.6

Note: Data shown for 1947 to 1966 for the Black population are for Black and other races. Data for 1947 to 1963 exclude kindergarten. Nursery school was first collected in 1964.
* = Quantity zero or rounds to zero.
NA = Not available.
r = Revised, controlled to 1990 census based population estimates; previous 1993 data controlled to 1980 census based population estimates.
[1]Starting in 2003, respondents could identify more than one race. Except as noted, the race data in this table from 2003 onward represent those respondents who indicated only one race category.
[2]The data shown prior to 2003 consists of those identifying themselves as "Asian or Pacific Islanders."

Table A-11. Percentage of the Population 3 Years Old and Over Enrolled in School, by Age, Sex, Race, and Hispanic Origin, October 1947–2019—*Continued*

(Percent; civilian noninstitutionalized population.)

Year, sex, race, and Hispanic origin	Total enrolled 3 to 34 years old	Total enrolled 3 years old and over	Age											
			3 and 4	5 and 6	7 to 9	10 to 13	14 and 15	16 and 17	18 and 19	20 and 21	22 to 24	25 to 29	30 to 34	35 and over
1975	56.0	NA	30.6	94.3	99.2	98.9	98.4	90.7	49.9	35.3	20.0	13.1	7.7	NA
1974	56.0	NA	28.1	94.4	99.1	99.3	98.0	88.6	45.8	34.8	19.4	12.7	6.7	NA
1973	56.1	NA	24.5	92.2	99.0	99.2	97.9	89.4	47.9	34.4	19.1	11.8	5.6	NA
1972	57.8	NA	24.4	91.7	98.9	99.3	97.7	90.2	51.2	37.3	21.3	12.1	5.8	NA
1971	59.3	NA	20.0	90.9	99.0	98.8	98.7	91.7	55.4	38.9	23.3	11.9	6.3	NA
1970	59.7	NA	21.2	88.9	99.3	98.8	98.2	91.3	54.4	42.7	21.2	11.0	5.3	NA
1969	60.5	NA	15.5	87.7	99.0	98.9	98.1	91.6	59.4	46.5	22.9	11.4	5.9	NA
1968	60.4	NA	15.4	87.3	98.9	98.9	98.2	91.7	60.4	45.0	20.5	10.8	5.0	NA
1967	60.0	NA	14.2	86.6	99.4	98.9	98.3	91.0	56.3	44.3	21.0	9.9	5.4	NA
1966	59.7	NA	12.3	84.5	99.2	99.1	98.7	89.9	57.8	41.4	21.3	9.6	3.8	NA
1965	58.8	NA	10.2	84.4	99.3	99.3	99.0	88.0	55.6	37.6	21.1	9.4	4.5	NA
1964	57.5	NA	8.9	83.4	98.7	98.9	99.0	89.8	50.9	34.4	16.1	8.1	3.6	NA
1963	62.3	NA	NA	82.7	99.2	99.0	98.7	89.4	51.0	33.6	19.5	7.8	3.7	NA
1962	61.7	NA	NA	82.6	99.1	99.2	98.7	87.1	51.2	31.3	17.7	8.5	3.9	NA
1961	60.4	NA	NA	82.0	99.5	99.2	98.1	84.7	48.6	29.5	13.9	7.1	2.9	NA
1960	60.0	NA	NA	80.8	99.6	99.4	97.9	84.5	47.8	27.1	15.0	8.4	3.7	NA
1959	59.1	NA	NA	79.5	99.2	99.4	97.8	84.8	45.6	28.3	13.7	8.9	3.3	NA
1958	58.7	NA	NA	80.6	99.6	99.4	96.9	83.8	47.5	------21.0------		9.5	2.9	NA
1957	57.5	NA	NA	78.3	99.4	99.6	98.0	82.8	43.3	------21.3------		9.5	2.6	NA
1956	56.3	NA	NA	77.1	99.2	99.1	97.1	79.9	45.1	------20.6------		8.9	2.7	NA
1955	54.9	NA	NA	78.1	99.1	99.4	95.7	81.1	42.5	------18.1------		7.0	2.1	NA
1954	54.0	NA	NA	76.3	99.0	99.4	96.1	80.9	40.6	------19.1------		6.7	1.9	NA
1953	50.2	NA	NA	55.0	99.3	99.1	96.4	76.5	37.7	------18.5------		5.5	2.0	NA
1952	49.4	NA	NA	54.8	98.6	98.9	96.2	73.9	37.2	------16.9------		4.7	1.7	NA
1951	56.8	NA	NA	55.1	99.1	99.1	95.1	74.3	32.4	------14.3------		4.2	NA	NA
1950	54.8	NA	NA	56.8	98.8	98.7	95.2	72.8	35.7	------14.3------		5.9	NA	NA
1949	45.8	NA	NA	60.1	98.5	98.6	93.9	70.8	31.6	------15.4------		6.8	1.9	NA
1948	44.8	NA	NA	55.1	99.5	98.1	92.0	72.1	34.3	------16.5------		5.1	1.5	NA
1947	44.3	NA	NA	57.4	98.5	98.7	90.3	67.6	31.4	------17.0------		5.8	1.7	NA
Female														
2019	54.6	23.9	54.0	92.8	96.8	98.2	97.8	92.8	68.9	57.0	31.8	11.9	7.2	1.7
2018	55.1	24.3	54.4	93.8	96.9	98.4	98.3	90.8	72.2	58.4	29.9	14.2	7.2	1.8
2017	55.2	24.4	54.1	94.2	97.0	97.8	98.3	93.5	71.3	59.2	30.0	13.4	6.5	1.8
2016	55.6	24.7	53.5	93.8	98.1	98.7	97.3	93.3	70.7	59.7	30.0	14.7	7.2	1.7
2015	55.6	24.9	51.8	94.9	97.2	97.6	98.1	94.4	71.4	56.5	30.1	14.6	7.7	1.9
2014	55.7	25.2	55.5	92.8	97.9	98.1	98.2	93.8	72.1	53.9	31.0	14.0	7.4	2.1
2013	56.4	25.7	56.7	93.7	97.9	98.2	98.6	94.1	69.2	57.3	31.7	14.4	8.1	2.3
2012	57.4	26.2	54.4	93.3	98.4	97.8	98.2	95.9	72.3	58.3	32.1	16.0	9.2	2.3
2011	57.4	26.5	52.1	95.2	97.9	98.4	98.9	96.0	73.5	56.4	32.0	16.8	8.9	2.4
2010	57.4	26.7	53.4	95.3	98.0	98.6	98.3	97.3	71.5	56.0	30.8	15.8	9.9	2.6
2009	57.3	26.6	53.2	94.4	97.9	98.4	98.5	94.7	72.9	54.9	31.8	15.3	9.3	2.7
2008	56.7	26.3	53.3	93.7	98.7	99.2	98.2	95.4	68.1	53.0	30.1	14.3	8.3	2.5
2007	56.8	26.3	54.7	95.3	98.1	98.7	99.0	94.1	67.2	53.3	29.2	14.7	7.9	2.4
2006	56.6	26.3	55.4	94.8	98.3	98.4	98.4	95.0	67.4	51.1	28.5	13.0	8.5	2.3
2005	57.2	26.8	54.4	96.1	99.0	98.9	98.4	95.1	68.8	52.3	29.2	14.2	7.9	2.4
2004	56.5	26.8	53.2	95.3	98.5	98.7	98.3	94.1	68.5	51.3	28.4	14.4	7.7	2.5
2003	56.4	26.6	54.1	94.4	98.3	98.6	97.5	94.8	66.6	52.9	29.5	12.8	7.3	2.2
2002	56.4	26.8	54.4	95.1	97.9	98.7	98.5	94.7	65.0	50.9	27.3	13.5	7.7	2.5
2001	55.9	26.7	52.9	95.4	97.8	98.8	98.2	93.8	63.2	46.9	26.5	13.0	7.9	2.5
2000	56.0	26.9	53.4	96.1	98.2	98.3	98.6	92.9	64.2	47.3	25.3	12.7	7.7	2.3
1999	55.5	27.0	55.2	96.1	98.7	98.9	98.3	93.5	60.9	45.8	25.4	11.4	6.6	2.4
1998	55.6	27.3	50.9	95.9	98.8	99.1	98.5	94.3	64.4	47.2	25.2	12.9	7.7	2.6
1997	55.4	27.6	53.2	96.4	99.1	99.3	98.7	94.4	62.4	47.4	27.4	11.9	6.6	2.9
1996	53.8	27.1	49.8	94.3	97.3	98.2	97.5	92.4	62.2	44.8	24.5	12.5	7.3	2.8
1995	53.2	27.0	48.1	96.8	98.5	99.1	98.8	92.6	59.2	45.1	23.6	12.2	6.5	2.7
1994	52.9	27.2	46.9	96.4	99.5	99.4	98.7	94.4	60.0	47.0	23.9	11.1	7.5	2.8
1993r	51.1	NA	39.0	95.2	99.4	99.5	98.7	92.8	61.7	42.8	21.7	10.8	6.6	NA
1993	51.0	25.9	39.3	95.2	99.4	99.5	98.7	92.9	61.7	42.9	21.8	10.8	6.6	2.6
1992	51.0	26.1	39.1	95.2	99.2	99.2	99.1	92.7	61.2	46.1	23.6	10.5	7.0	2.6
1991	49.9	26.0	41.1	95.8	99.5	99.6	98.4	92.8	59.4	42.2	20.4	9.8	6.8	2.8
1990	49.5	25.9	44.9	96.4	99.6	99.7	98.9	92.4	56.3	39.2	19.9	10.2	6.9	2.7

Note: Data shown for 1947 to 1966 for the Black population are for Black and other races. Data for 1947 to 1963 exclude kindergarten. Nursery school was first collected in 1964.

* = Quantity zero or rounds to zero.

NA = Not available.

r = Revised, controlled to 1990 census based population estimates; previous 1993 data controlled to 1980 census based population estimates.

[1]Starting in 2003, respondents could identify more than one race. Except as noted, the race data in this table from 2003 onward represent those respondents who indicated only one race category.

[2]The data shown prior to 2003 consists of those identifying themselves as "Asian or Pacific Islanders."

Table A-11. Percentage of the Population 3 Years Old and Over Enrolled in School, by Age, Sex, Race, and Hispanic Origin, October 1947–2019—*Continued*

(Percent; civilian noninstitutionalized population.)

Year, sex, race, and Hispanic origin	Total enrolled 3 to 34 years old	Total enrolled 3 years old and over	Age											
			3 and 4	5 and 6	7 to 9	10 to 13	14 and 15	16 and 17	18 and 19	20 and 21	22 to 24	25 to 29	30 to 34	35 and over
1989	48.4	25.5	39.5	95.2	99.2	99.6	98.4	92.2	55.5	39.7	19.5	9.3	6.4	2.5
1988	47.7	25.5	38.1	96.0	99.6	99.7	98.8	91.2	55.2	39.1	16.2	8.6	6.4	2.6
1987	47.4	25.3	36.6	94.5	99.5	99.2	98.4	91.1	53.4	36.4	16.5	9.0	6.7	2.2
1986	47.1	25.4	39.0	94.6	99.2	99.3	97.5	92.3	52.1	32.7	16.8	8.2	6.4	2.2
1985	47.4	25.7	41.2	97.0	99.2	99.4	97.9	90.9	51.0	34.1	15.1	9.1	6.8	2.1
1984	46.6	25.3	36.7	95.1	99.3	99.4	98.2	91.2	48.0	31.7	14.6	8.6	6.7	1.9
1983	47.0	25.7	36.9	95.8	99.0	99.5	98.2	91.6	50.3	29.9	13.9	8.5	7.0	2.0
1982	47.5	26.1	36.4	95.3	99.2	99.3	98.3	89.9	46.8	32.9	15.1	9.0	6.9	1.9
1981	47.7	26.6	35.2	93.8	99.5	99.4	97.7	90.5	47.5	31.2	13.9	8.4	7.5	2.0
1980	48.5	26.9	35.5	96.4	99.2	99.4	97.7	88.8	45.8	29.5	14.9	8.8	7.0	1.9
1979	49.0	27.3	35.6	95.2	99.4	99.4	97.9	87.6	43.4	28.9	14.1	8.8	6.7	2.0
1978	49.5	27.8	34.5	95.5	99.5	99.2	98.4	88.8	43.0	27.5	13.6	7.9	6.2	2.0
1977	50.7	NA	32.0	96.9	99.5	99.6	98.3	87.7	44.0	29.1	13.6	9.1	6.7	NA
1976	51.0	29.8	31.6	95.5	99.4	99.3	97.8	87.7	44.4	30.6	13.8	7.3	5.2	4.2
1975	51.5	NA	32.4	95.2	99.5	99.6	98.0	87.2	44.2	27.4	12.6	7.2	5.6	NA
1974	51.3	NA	29.5	93.9	99.2	99.7	97.9	87.1	40.7	26.0	11.1	6.7	4.6	NA
1973	50.9	NA	23.8	92.9	99.3	99.2	97.1	87.2	38.2	26.3	10.2	5.4	3.6	NA
1972	52.0	NA	24.4	92.2	99.1	99.4	97.5	87.6	41.8	26.3	8.9	5.3	3.6	NA
1971	53.2	NA	22.4	92.3	99.2	99.5	98.5	88.7	43.4	26.8	8.4	4.4	3.6	NA
1970	53.2	NA	19.8	90.2	99.3	99.5	98.0	88.6	41.6	23.6	9.4	4.3	3.1	NA
1969	53.6	NA	16.8	89.1	99.6	99.4	98.2	87.7	41.8	25.3	9.1	4.6	3.8	NA
1968	53.2	NA	16.1	88.0	99.3	99.3	97.8	88.7	41.3	21.5	8.3	3.4	2.9	NA
1967	53.3	NA	14.1	88.2	99.5	99.3	98.2	86.7	40.3	24.9	7.4	3.6	2.8	NA
1966	52.7	NA	12.7	85.7	99.4	99.5	98.4	87.1	37.7	20.9	6.6	3.6	1.7	NA
1965	52.3	NA	10.9	84.4	99.3	99.5	98.7	86.9	37.7	19.5	6.5	3.1	2.1	NA
1964	51.5	NA	10.2	83.2	99.3	99.2	98.2	85.6	33.7	19.5	4.4	2.6	1.6	NA
1963	54.9	NA	NA	82.6	99.6	99.6	98.0	84.8	32.3	17.8	4.4	2.4	1.5	NA
1962	54.0	NA	NA	81.7	99.3	99.4	97.3	81.5	33.7	16.1	3.9	1.8	1.4	NA
1961	53.4	NA	NA	81.4	99.3	99.4	97.2	82.4	28.6	14.9	3.7	1.9	1.2	NA
1960	52.8	NA	NA	80.6	99.6	99.5	97.6	80.6	30.0	13.1	3.4	1.8	1.2	NA
1959	52.0	NA	NA	80.5	99.6	99.5	97.1	81.0	29.2	11.1	4.4	1.7	1.3	NA
1958	51.0	NA	NA	80.2	99.4	99.5	96.9	77.3	29.4	-------7.3------		2.2	1.5	NA
1957	50.0	NA	NA	79.0	99.6	99.5	96.2	78.1	28.1	-------8.2------		1.9	1.1	NA
1956	48.7	NA	NA	78.2	99.5	99.4	96.8	76.9	27.4	-------6.8------		1.7	1.2	NA
1955	47.0	NA	NA	78.1	99.3	99.0	96.1	73.8	22.5	-------6.1------		1.8	1.1	NA
1954	46.3	NA	NA	78.3	99.5	99.7	95.4	75.2	25.4	-------6.0------		1.7	1.1	NA
1953	43.0	NA	NA	56.6	99.5	99.7	96.6	72.9	25.9	-------6.4------		0.5	1.4	NA
1952	41.9	NA	NA	54.6	98.9	98.9	96.6	72.9	22.1	-------4.9------		0.6	0.7	NA
1951	49.1	NA	NA	54.0	98.9	99.3	94.5	75.4	21.3	-------4.3------		1.0	NA	NA
1950	48.4	NA	NA	59.5	99.0	98.4	94.3	69.8	24.3	-------4.6------		0.4	NA	NA
1949	39.2	NA	NA	58.4	98.5	98.8	93.1	68.2	19.9	-------3.7------		1.1	0.4	NA
1948	38.4	NA	NA	56.8	98.2	97.8	93.5	70.3	20.3	-------3.4------		0.4	0.4	NA
1947	38.0	NA	NA	58.7	98.4	98.5	92.8	67.5	18.5	-------3.9------		0.4	0.3	NA
WHITE ALONE														
Both Sexes														
2019	53.3	22.7	52.6	93.9	97.6	97.8	97.7	92.8	66.9	52.9	27.2	9.7	5.2	1.2
2018	53.9	23.1	54.7	93.7	96.8	98.4	98.6	93.3	68.9	53.9	26.8	11.3	5.6	1.3
2017	53.9	23.2	53.4	93.5	96.9	97.5	98.4	93.1	67.8	54.7	26.9	11.5	5.6	1.3
2016	54.7	23.6	53.7	93.8	98.0	98.4	98.4	92.4	69.4	56.2	27.5	12.7	5.9	1.3
2015	54.6	23.8	52.2	94.1	97.5	97.8	97.8	93.8	68.6	53.8	27.7	12.8	6.1	1.4
2014	54.6	24.0	53.6	93.6	97.6	97.5	97.7	93.5	68.3	53.0	28.6	12.4	5.9	1.5
2013	55.0	24.3	54.0	93.9	98.1	98.2	98.4	93.6	67.6	52.2	28.9	12.2	6.4	1.6
2012	55.8	24.8	53.4	93.3	98.2	97.7	98.3	96.0	68.7	54.4	29.5	13.4	6.5	1.6
2011	56.2	25.5	51.4	95.7	98.2	98.6	98.6	95.5	70.3	53.8	30.9	14.0	6.9	1.7
2010	55.8	25.4	52.1	94.2	97.7	98.1	98.0	96.2	70.0	51.6	28.1	13.9	7.8	1.9
2009	55.7	25.3	51.1	94.0	97.9	98.7	98.1	94.4	68.7	52.6	28.9	12.9	7.3	1.9
2008	55.5	25.3	52.0	94.0	98.2	98.9	98.7	95.4	67.1	51.2	28.1	12.3	6.2	1.8
2007	55.5	25.3	54.1	94.8	98.0	98.7	98.7	94.6	67.1	50.1	26.3	11.5	6.6	1.8
2006	55.5	25.3	55.6	95.0	98.4	98.4	98.4	95.0	64.9	48.2	25.5	11.3	6.7	1.7

Note: Data shown for 1947 to 1966 for the Black population are for Black and other races. Data for 1947 to 1963 exclude kindergarten. Nursery school was first collected in 1964.
* = Quantity zero or rounds to zero.
NA = Not available.
r = Revised, controlled to 1990 census based population estimates; previous 1993 data controlled to 1980 census based population estimates.
[1]Starting in 2003, respondents could identify more than one race. Except as noted, the race data in this table from 2003 onward represent those respondents who indicated only one race category.
[2]The data shown prior to 2003 consists of those identifying themselves as "Asian or Pacific Islanders."

Table A-11. Percentage of the Population 3 Years Old and Over Enrolled in School, by Age, Sex, Race, and Hispanic Origin, October 1947–2019—*Continued*

(Percent; civilian noninstitutionalized population.)

Year, sex, race, and Hispanic origin	Total enrolled 3 to 34 years old	Total enrolled 3 years old and over	3 and 4	5 and 6	7 to 9	10 to 13	14 and 15	16 and 17	18 and 19	20 and 21	22 to 24	25 to 29	30 to 34	35 and over
2005	55.9	25.7	54.2	95.3	98.6	98.7	98.3	95.4	68.0	49.3	26.0	11.3	6.2	1.8
2004	55.5	25.7	52.8	95.5	98.1	98.3	98.5	94.2	64.9	49.3	25.3	12.2	6.4	1.8
2003[1]	55.4	25.8	55.3	94.7	98.0	98.4	97.3	95.0	64.4	48.2	26.7	11.0	6.2	1.8
2002	55.4	26.0	53.9	95.1	98.0	98.5	98.5	94.6	63.8	47.4	24.6	11.4	5.9	2.0
2001	54.8	25.8	51.7	94.8	98.3	98.7	98.2	93.5	60.4	45.9	23.3	10.7	6.0	1.8
2000	55.1	26.1	50.2	95.3	98.2	98.3	98.4	92.8	61.3	44.9	23.7	10.4	6.0	1.8
1999	55.2	26.4	53.7	95.6	98.5	98.8	98.2	93.5	60.5	45.6	24.1	10.5	5.8	1.9
1998	55.0	26.6	50.7	95.4	98.8	99.1	98.6	94.1	61.9	44.8	24.1	11.0	6.2	2.0
1997	54.8	26.8	50.9	96.8	98.8	99.3	98.8	94.5	61.5	46.4	25.8	11.3	5.4	2.2
1996	53.4	26.4	47.9	94.8	97.1	98.2	98.0	92.8	62.5	44.9	24.6	11.3	5.7	2.2
1995	53.2	26.6	49.6	96.2	98.9	99.0	98.8	93.7	59.3	46.2	23.1	11.5	5.5	2.1
1994r	52.6	26.6	47.0	96.6	99.2	99.3	98.7	94.3	60.9	46.2	23.5	10.4	6.6	2.2
1993r	51.2	NA	40.4	95.4	99.5	99.5	98.9	93.9	61.4	43.7	23.1	9.7	5.9	NA
1993	51.1	25.7	40.8	95.5	99.5	99.5	98.9	94.1	61.7	44.0	23.3	9.8	5.9	2.1
1992	50.7	NA	40.1	95.4	99.4	99.3	99.2	94.2	61.7	45.3	23.3	9.6	6.0	NA
1991	50.0	NA	41.3	95.3	99.6	99.7	98.7	93.3	59.7	43.2	21.7	9.9	6.0	NA
1990	49.5	NA	44.9	96.5	99.7	99.6	99.1	92.5	57.1	41.0	20.2	9.9	5.9	NA
1989	48.4	NA	39.4	95.2	99.2	99.4	98.8	92.3	56.4	39.5	20.0	9.4	5.6	NA
1988	48.0	NA	38.9	96.1	99.7	99.7	98.8	91.4	55.8	40.2	18.6	8.2	5.9	NA
1987	47.7	NA	38.2	94.8	99.6	99.4	98.5	91.8	55.3	39.6	17.3	8.7	5.7	NA
1986	47.7	NA	39.1	95.3	99.3	97.8	99.0	92.2	55.3	33.9	17.7	9.1	6.2	NA
1985	47.8	NA	38.6	96.4	99.3	99.3	98.1	91.6	52.4	36.1	17.0	9.2	5.9	NA
1984	47.3	NA	36.0	94.6	99.0	99.4	97.8	91.2	51.1	34.3	17.2	9.1	6.2	NA
1983	47.7	NA	37.6	95.7	98.9	99.3	98.4	91.4	50.9	33.4	16.4	9.4	6.1	NA
1982	47.9	NA	35.9	94.9	99.2	99.2	98.6	90.3	47.9	35.1	16.2	9.6	6.2	NA
1981	48.2	NA	35.6	93.9	99.3	99.3	98.1	90.4	48.5	32.6	16.2	8.5	6.1	NA
1980	48.9	NA	36.3	95.8	99.0	99.4	98.3	88.6	46.3	31.9	16.4	9.2	6.3	NA
1979	49.6	NA	33.9	95.8	99.2	·99.2	98.2	89.0	44.5	31.1	15.7	9.7	6.3	NA
1978	50.3	NA	32.7	95.4	99.3	99.0	98.4	88.7	44.9	29.6	16.1	9.4	6.2	NA
1977	51.6	NA	31.1	95.6	99.5	99.4	98.5	88.5	45.5	31.8	16.3	10.6	6.6	NA
1976	52.3	NA	30.4	95.8	99.1	99.2	98.1	89.1	45.4	32.5	17.0	10.0	5.7	NA
1975	53.1	NA	30.9	94.8	99.4	99.3	98.3	89.3	46.5	31.8	16.8	10.0	6.6	NA
1974	53.0	NA	28.6	94.4	99.2	99.4	98.1	87.9	42.6	30.7	15.2	9.6	5.5	NA
1973	53.1	NA	23.2	93.0	99.1	99.3	97.6	88.3	43.4	31.3	14.6	8.7	4.5	NA
1972	54.4	NA	23.8	92.2	99.1	99.3	97.6	88.9	46.6	32.6	15.0	8.7	4.5	NA
1971	55.8	NA	20.9	91.9	99.1	99.2	98.7	90.5	49.4	32.7	15.9	8.1	4.8	NA
1970	56.2	NA	19.9	90.3	99.3	99.1	98.2	90.6	48.7	33.1	15.7	7.7	4.2	NA
1969	56.8	NA	15.1	89.2	99.4	99.2	98.2	90.2	50.9	35.4	16.2	8.2	5.0	NA
1968	56.6	NA	15.0	88.5	99.1	99.1	98.1	90.8	50.9	32.8	14.5	7.4	3.9	NA
1967	56.5	NA	13.3	88.2	99.5	99.2	98.5	89.5	48.4	34.7	14.1	6.7	4.1	NA
1966	56.1	NA	12.3	85.7	99.3	99.3	98.8	89.0	48.2	32.2	14.0	6.9	2.7	NA
1965	55.5	NA	10.3	85.3	99.4	99.4	99.0	87.8	47.1	29.4	14.1	6.5	3.2	NA
1964	54.4	NA	9.3	84.0	99.0	99.0	98.8	88.3	42.3	27.8	10.6	5.4	2.6	NA
1963	58.4	NA	NA	83.7	99.5	99.3	98.5	87.8	41.0	26.2	12.2	5.2	2.6	NA
1962	57.9	NA	NA	83.2	99.3	99.4	98.2	85.9	43.0	24.1	10.9	5.2	2.7	NA
1961	56.9	NA	NA	82.2	99.6	99.5	98.0	84.5	39.0	22.4	9.0	4.6	2.1	NA
1960	56.4	NA	NA	82.0	99.7	99.5	98.1	83.3	38.9	20.6	9.3	5.2	2.6	NA
1959	55.5	NA	NA	81.0	99.5	99.5	97.9	83.8	37.3	19.9	8.9	5.4	2.3	NA
1958	54.9	NA	NA	81.4	------99.6------		------90.0------		38.1	------14.1------		5.9	2.3	NA
1957	53.7	NA	NA	79.3	------99.7------		------90.1------		34.6	------14.7------		5.7	1.9	NA
1956	52.5	NA	NA	78.4	------99.4------		------89.2------		35.9	------13.4------		5.4	2.1	NA
1955	50.8	NA	NA	79.2	------99.3------		------87.5------		32.1	------11.6------		4.2	1.6	NA
1954	50.2	NA	NA	78.6	------99.6------		------88.3------		33.6	------12.0------		4.0	1.5	NA
1953	46.6	NA	NA	67.1	------99.7------		------86.4------		31.7	------11.9------		3.1	1.8	NA
1952	45.4	NA	NA	54.8	------99.1------		------86.1------		28.9	------9.8------		2.7	1.2	NA
1951	52.8	NA	NA	54.5	------99.3------		------86.3------		26.9	------8.8------		2.8	NA	NA
1950	51.6	NA	NA	------------89.0----------			------84.4------		30.5	------9.5------		3.0	NA	NA
1949	42.6	NA	NA	------------88.8----------			------83.0------		25.9	------9.6------		4.0	1.2	NA
1948	41.8	NA	NA	------------87.8----------			------83.9------		27.3	------10.0------		2.8	0.9	NA
1947	41.2	NA	NA	------------88.7----------			------80.2------		24.8	------10.5------		3.0	1.1	NA

Note: Data shown for 1947 to 1966 for the Black population are for Black and other races. Data for 1947 to 1963 exclude kindergarten. Nursery school was first collected in 1964.
* = Quantity zero or rounds to zero.
NA = Not available.
r = Revised, controlled to 1990 census based population estimates; previous 1993 data controlled to 1980 census based population estimates.
[1]Starting in 2003, respondents could identify more than one race. Except as noted, the race data in this table from 2003 onward represent those respondents who indicated only one race category.
[2]The data shown prior to 2003 consists of those identifying themselves as "Asian or Pacific Islanders."

Table A-11. Percentage of the Population 3 Years Old and Over Enrolled in School, by Age, Sex, Race, and Hispanic Origin, October 1947–2019—*Continued*

(Percent; civilian noninstitutionalized population.)

Year, sex, race, and Hispanic origin	Total enrolled 3 to 34 years old	Total enrolled 3 years old and over	3 and 4	5 and 6	7 to 9	10 to 13	14 and 15	16 and 17	18 and 19	20 and 21	22 to 24	25 to 29	30 to 34	35 and over
Male														
2019	52.6	22.9	51.7	94.4	98.2	97.5	97.6	92.8	64.7	48.8	24.3	8.8	4.3	1.0
2018	53.3	23.4	55.4	93.4	97.0	98.5	98.7	93.7	65.5	49.3	25.0	9.9	5.3	1.0
2017	53.2	23.4	52.1	92.9	97.3	97.6	98.4	92.6	65.1	50.8	25.1	10.3	5.1	1.0
2016	54.0	23.9	55.6	93.8	97.9	98.2	98.8	92.2	67.9	51.2	25.8	10.9	4.9	1.0
2015	53.9	24.0	53.0	93.5	97.5	98.0	97.5	92.9	65.1	50.8	25.7	11.5	5.3	1.1
2014	53.9	24.2	52.3	93.7	97.2	96.8	97.3	92.5	64.8	50.4	26.8	11.6	5.0	1.2
2013	54.1	24.4	52.2	93.7	98.0	98.2	98.3	92.8	66.0	47.2	26.1	11.1	5.3	1.2
2012	54.9	24.9	52.9	93.1	98.0	98.0	98.3	95.8	66.0	48.5	28.3	11.6	5.5	1.2
2011	55.5	25.8	52.0	95.5	98.4	98.6	98.5	95.5	67.6	50.3	30.1	12.3	6.0	1.4
2010	54.9	25.5	51.8	93.2	97.3	97.6	98.0	95.0	67.5	48.2	25.9	13.0	6.5	1.5
2009	54.8	25.4	50.0	93.7	97.7	98.9	97.9	94.1	64.6	48.8	28.3	11.2	6.4	1.4
2008	54.8	25.5	51.8	93.8	97.9	98.7	99.0	94.9	64.3	48.4	26.5	11.5	5.5	1.3
2007	54.4	25.4	52.9	94.1	97.9	98.6	98.3	94.5	66.4	44.6	24.2	9.6	5.7	1.4
2006	54.6	25.5	55.9	94.8	98.3	98.4	98.2	94.7	62.7	43.8	24.0	10.2	5.5	1.3
2005	54.9	25.9	53.1	94.6	98.2	98.6	98.3	95.1	66.1	45.1	24.4	8.9	5.5	1.4
2004	54.8	26.0	53.4	95.8	97.9	98.2	98.8	94.5	60.0	46.0	23.3	11.2	5.5	1.4
2003[1]	54.8	26.2	56.2	95.0	97.6	98.7	97.2	95.3	61.7	43.2	25.6	9.9	5.6	1.4
2002	54.9	26.5	54.0	95.0	98.0	98.3	98.4	94.2	62.5	44.1	23.5	10.2	5.0	1.6
2001	54.3	26.2	51.8	94.7	98.6	98.4	98.0	92.8	58.2	43.6	21.5	9.8	5.0	1.4
2000	54.8	26.5	49.1	94.8	97.0	98.3	98.4	93.1	58.5	41.8	23.2	9.5	4.9	1.4
1999	55.5	27.1	53.5	95.4	98.5	98.6	98.2	93.1	60.0	44.5	23.7	10.3	5.4	1.5
1998	54.9	27.1	52.4	94.9	98.8	99.1	98.7	93.3	59.7	42.1	24.5	10.2	5.2	1.6
1997	54.7	27.3	50.4	97.4	98.5	99.4	99.1	94.2	60.0	45.0	24.9	10.8	4.3	1.5
1996	53.3	27.0	46.5	94.6	96.9	98.0	98.6	93.0	60.9	43.6	25.4	10.6	4.3	1.7
1995	53.5	27.3	49.6	95.5	99.0	99.0	98.8	94.2	59.4	46.3	22.7	11.3	5.0	1.7
1994	52.7	27.2	46.2	97.0	99.1	99.3	98.7	94.3	61.3	43.4	23.6	9.9	5.8	1.7
1993r	51.6	NA	41.2	95.1	99.5	99.5	98.9	95.0	60.1	44.4	24.5	9.1	5.2	NA
1993	51.6	26.4	41.7	95.2	99.5	99.5	99.0	95.1	60.6	44.8	24.9	9.1	5.2	1.5
1992	50.8	NA	39.8	95.1	99.5	99.5	99.0	99.5	60.7	44.0	23.6	8.6	5.2	NA
1991	50.4	NA	40.6	94.9	99.7	99.8	98.9	94.2	58.4	42.4	23.3	10.0	5.4	NA
1990	50.0	NA	44.9	96.7	99.7	99.6	99.2	92.3	57.3	41.2	21.8	9.4	4.9	NA
1989	48.9	NA	38.7	95.4	99.3	99.2	99.3	92.6	57.3	39.3	20.4	9.3	5.0	NA
1988	48.7	NA	39.0	96.1	99.7	99.6	98.9	91.6	56.5	40.9	20.7	7.8	5.4	NA
1987	48.8	NA	39.8	95.2	99.6	99.7	98.8	92.5	57.3	42.1	18.4	8.6	5.0	NA
1986	48.6	NA	39.3	95.6	99.4	99.0	99.1	92.1	57.5	34.2	19.2	9.6	5.7	NA
1985	48.5	NA	37.3	95.7	99.3	99.2	98.2	92.5	51.9	37.2	19.0	9.5	5.4	NA
1984	48.3	NA	35.8	94.1	98.7	99.3	97.6	91.5	52.6	36.3	20.2	9.2	5.4	NA
1983	48.9	NA	38.2	95.1	98.8	99.3	98.3	91.6	50.7	36.6	19.2	10.4	5.6	NA
1982	48.9	NA	36.3	94.8	99.2	99.1	99.0	91.0	48.5	36.5	18.0	10.2	5.4	NA
1981	49.2	NA	36.8	94.3	99.1	99.2	98.3	90.5	49.2	33.3	19.1	9.1	5.5	NA
1980	50.0	NA	38.0	95.2	98.8	99.4	98.7	88.8	47.5	33.7	18.2	9.6	5.6	NA
1979	50.7	NA	33.5	96.3	99.0	99.0	98.3	90.3	46.1	32.2	17.6	10.5	5.9	NA
1978	51.9	NA	33.1	95.3	99.2	98.9	98.3	88.9	47.2	32.0	19.2	10.9	6.4	NA
1977	53.3	NA	31.7	94.3	99.6	99.3	98.7	89.5	47.7	34.7	19.4	12.6	6.8	NA
1976	54.2	NA	29.9	95.8	98.8	99.1	98.5	90.6	46.9	34.2	20.4	12.9	6.5	NA
1975	55.4	NA	30.8	94.3	99.2	99.0	98.5	91.0	49.6	36.3	20.5	13.1	7.5	NA
1974	55.2	NA	27.7	94.8	99.1	99.2	98.2	88.2	45.5	35.0	19.2	12.8	6.4	NA
1973	55.6	NA	23.5	92.7	99.0	99.3	98.0	89.4	48.4	35.7	19.6	12.1	5.4	NA
1972	57.3	NA	23.4	91.7	98.9	99.2	97.7	90.4	51.5	38.4	21.6	12.5	5.8	NA
1971	59.0	NA	20.1	91.2	99.0	98.9	98.9	92.0	55.9	39.7	24.6	12.1	6.2	NA
1970	59.6	NA	20.7	89.7	99.3	98.8	98.3	92.2	56.0	45.0	22.6	11.2	5.4	NA
1969	60.5	NA	14.5	88.5	99.1	98.9	98.2	92.2	60.9	48.9	24.2	12.2	6.2	NA
1968	60.4	NA	14.8	87.9	99.0	99.0	98.2	92.1	61.5	47.8	21.9	11.4	5.0	NA
1967	60.0	NA	13.6	87.5	99.5	99.0	98.5	91.4	57.2	46.9	22.0	10.5	5.4	NA
1966	59.8	NA	12.2	85.0	99.2	99.1	98.8	90.3	59.0	44.9	23.0	10.3	3.8	NA
1965	59.0	NA	10.4	84.8	99.3	99.3	99.1	88.6	56.6	39.9	23.3	10.0	4.5	NA
1964	57.6	NA	8.8	84.0	98.8	98.9	99.0	90.4	52.4	36.6	17.7	8.3	3.6	NA
1963	62.3	NA	NA	84.1	99.4	99.0	98.8	89.8	51.6	35.2	21.1	8.2	3.8	NA
1962	61.9	NA	NA	83.9	99.1	99.3	98.7	88.5	52.7	33.7	18.8	8.9	4.2	NA
1961	60.4	NA	NA	82.6	99.7	99.4	98.3	85.5	49.6	31.1	15.0	7.5	3.1	NA
1960	60.3	NA	NA	82.3	99.7	99.5	98.1	85.2	49.5	29.2	16.3	8.9	4.0	NA

Note: Data shown for 1947 to 1966 for the Black population are for Black and other races. Data for 1947 to 1963 exclude kindergarten. Nursery school was first collected in 1964.

* = Quantity zero or rounds to zero.

NA = Not available.

r = Revised, controlled to 1990 census based population estimates; previous 1993 data controlled to 1980 census based population estimates.

[1] Starting in 2003, respondents could identify more than one race. Except as noted, the race data in this table from 2003 onward represent those respondents who indicated only one race category.

[2] The data shown prior to 2003 consists of those identifying themselves as "Asian or Pacific Islanders."

Table A-11. Percentage of the Population 3 Years Old and Over Enrolled in School, by Age, Sex, Race, and Hispanic Origin, October 1947–2019—*Continued*

(Percent; civilian noninstitutionalized population.)

Year, sex, race, and Hispanic origin	Total enrolled 3 to 34 years old	Total enrolled 3 years old and over	3 and 4	5 and 6	7 to 9	10 to 13	14 and 15	16 and 17	18 and 19	20 and 21	22 to 24	25 to 29	30 to 34	35 and over
1959	59.2	NA	NA	80.1	99.3	99.4	98.1	85.9	47.1	30.8	14.1	9.5	3.4	NA
1958	58.8	NA	NA	81.5	------99.6------		------91.1------		48.1	------22.3------		9.9	3.0	NA
1957	57.7	NA	NA	79.1	------99.7------		------91.9------		44.0	------22.9------		9.9	2.7	NA
1956	56.5	NA	NA	78.2	------99.4------		------90.1------		46.4	------21.8------		9.3	2.9	NA
1955	54.9	NA	NA	79.0	------99.4------		------89.1------		43.9	------19.3------		7.1	2.2	NA
1954	54.3	NA	NA	78.0	------99.4------		------89.6------		43.3	------20.5------		6.5	1.9	NA
1953	50.5	NA	NA	56.8	------99.4------		------87.9------		38.1	------20.3------		5.7	2.2	NA
1952	49.4	NA	NA	55.2	------99.1------		------87.0------		38.3	------17.8------		5.0	1.6	NA
1951	56.8	NA	NA	55.4	------99.3------		------86.6------		33.8	------14.9------		4.2	NA	NA
1950	54.7	NA	NA	----------88.6------			------85.0------		37.3	------14.6------		5.9	NA	NA
1949	45.9	NA	NA	----------89.1------			------84.1------		32.1	------15.7------		7.1	2.0	NA
1948	45.3	NA	NA	----------87.6------			------84.4------		35.9	------17.2------		5.3	1.5	NA
1947	44.4	NA	NA	----------88.6------			------79.6------		32.6	------17.4------		5.9	1.8	NA
Female														
2019	54.0	22.5	53.5	93.3	97.0	98.2	97.7	92.8	69.1	57.4	30.1	10.6	6.1	1.4
2018	54.6	22.8	53.9	94.0	96.7	98.2	98.5	92.9	72.5	58.7	28.5	12.8	5.9	1.5
2017	54.6	23.0	54.8	94.2	96.6	97.5	98.4	93.7	70.7	58.6	28.7	12.8	6.2	1.6
2016	55.3	23.4	51.7	93.7	98.0	98.7	97.9	92.7	71.0	61.3	29.3	14.6	7.0	1.5
2015	55.2	23.5	51.4	94.9	97.4	97.5	98.0	94.8	72.2	56.9	29.8	14.1	6.8	1.7
2014	55.4	23.8	55.0	93.6	97.9	98.3	98.1	94.5	72.0	56.1	30.3	13.2	6.9	1.8
2013	55.9	24.3	55.8	94.0	98.1	98.2	98.5	94.5	69.2	57.5	31.6	13.3	7.5	2.0
2012	56.7	24.7	55.1	93.6	98.3	97.4	98.4	96.1	71.6	60.1	30.7	15.2	7.5	2.0
2011	56.9	25.2	50.8	96.0	97.9	98.5	98.8	95.6	73.2	57.5	31.7	15.8	7.9	2.0
2010	56.8	25.3	52.5	95.1	98.0	98.5	98.1	97.4	72.5	55.5	30.2	14.9	9.0	2.2
2009	56.7	25.2	52.2	94.3	98.1	98.4	98.4	94.8	73.0	56.6	29.5	14.7	8.3	2.4
2008	56.3	25.1	52.3	94.2	98.6	99.1	98.5	95.9	69.9	54.3	29.8	13.1	6.9	2.3
2007	56.7	25.2	55.4	95.6	98.1	98.8	99.2	94.7	67.8	55.7	28.5	13.6	7.6	2.2
2006	56.3	25.1	55.3	95.2	98.5	98.5	98.7	95.3	67.2	52.6	27.1	12.4	8.0	2.1
2005	57.0	25.6	55.4	96.0	98.9	98.8	98.4	95.7	70.1	53.8	27.7	13.8	7.0	2.2
2004	56.2	25.4	52.0	95.2	98.4	98.5	98.2	93.9	69.8	52.6	27.4	13.3	7.2	2.2
2003[1]	55.9	25.4	54.3	94.4	98.4	98.6	97.4	94.8	67.3	53.1	27.8	12.1	6.8	2.1
2002	55.8	25.6	53.7	95.1	98.0	98.7	98.5	95.0	65.1	50.8	25.7	12.7	6.9	2.3
2001	55.3	25.4	51.5	94.9	97.9	98.9	98.4	94.3	62.7	48.2	25.1	11.7	7.0	2.2
2000	55.4	25.7	51.4	95.8	98.5	98.4	98.3	92.5	64.2	48.2	24.2	11.3	7.1	2.2
1999	55.0	25.8	53.9	95.8	98.7	98.9	98.3	93.8	60.9	46.8	24.5	10.7	6.3	2.3
1998	55.0	26.0	49.0	96.0	98.8	99.2	98.5	94.9	64.2	47.9	23.8	11.9	7.2	2.4
1997	54.9	26.3	51.3	96.2	99.1	99.2	98.6	94.8	63.1	47.9	26.7	11.8	6.4	2.8
1996	53.5	25.9	49.3	95.0	97.4	98.3	97.3	92.7	64.1	46.1	23.6	12.0	7.1	2.6
1995	52.9	25.8	49.6	96.9	98.8	99.1	98.8	93.3	59.2	46.0	23.6	11.7	6.0	2.6
1994	52.6	26.0	47.9	96.1	99.4	99.4	98.8	94.4	60.5	49.0	23.5	11.0	7.4	2.7
1993r	50.7	NA	39.5	95.7	99.5	99.5	98.9	92.8	62.8	43.0	21.7	10.4	6.5	NA
1993	50.6	24.9	39.9	95.8	99.5	99.5	98.9	93.0	62.9	43.3	21.8	10.4	6.5	2.6
1992	50.5	NA	40.4	95.7	99.2	99.1	99.4	92.8	62.7	46.6	22.9	10.6	6.7	NA
1991	49.5	NA	42.0	95.7	99.5	99.6	98.5	92.5	60.9	43.9	20.2	9.7	6.7	NA
1990	49.0	NA	44.8	96.4	99.7	99.7	98.9	92.8	57.0	40.9	18.7	10.4	6.9	NA
1989	47.8	NA	40.2	94.9	99.2	99.6	98.1	92.1	55.6	39.7	19.6	9.6	6.3	NA
1988	47.2	NA	38.8	96.1	99.6	99.8	98.8	91.1	55.1	39.6	16.5	8.6	6.3	NA
1987	46.7	NA	36.4	94.4	99.5	99.2	98.3	91.0	53.3	37.3	16.2	8.7	6.4	NA
1986	46.8	NA	39.0	94.9	99.1	99.3	98.8	92.2	53.0	33.7	16.2	8.7	6.7	NA
1985	47.0	NA	39.9	97.1	99.3	99.3	97.9	90.8	52.9	35.0	15.0	9.0	6.4	NA
1984	46.3	NA	36.1	95.2	99.3	99.4	98.0	91.0	49.6	32.3	14.2	8.9	6.9	NA
1983	46.6	NA	36.0	96.5	99.0	99.4	98.4	91.2	51.1	30.5	13.6	8.5	6.7	NA
1982	46.9	NA	35.5	95.0	99.2	99.4	98.4	89.6	47.4	33.7	14.5	9.0	6.9	NA
1981	47.1	NA	34.3	93.5	99.5	99.4	97.8	90.4	47.8	31.9	13.4	7.9	6.7	NA
1980	47.9	NA	34.6	96.4	99.2	99.4	97.8	88.4	45.1	30.2	14.8	8.9	7.0	NA
1979	48.4	NA	34.4	95.3	99.5	99.5	98.1	87.7	43.0	30.0	13.9	9.0	6.7	NA
1978	48.7	NA	32.2	95.6	99.5	99.2	98.5	88.4	42.7	27.4	13.0	7.9	6.0	NA
1977	49.9	NA	30.5	96.9	99.5	99.6	98.4	87.4	43.4	29.0	13.3	8.8	6.3	NA
1976	50.4	NA	31.0	95.8	99.5	99.3	97.6	87.7	44.0	30.9	13.7	7.1	4.8	NA
1975	50.9	NA	30.9	95.3	99.5	99.6	98.1	87.5	43.5	27.5	12.2	7.0	5.7	NA
1974	50.9	NA	29.5	94.0	99.3	99.7	97.9	87.6	39.9	26.6	11.4	6.5	4.6	NA

Note: Data shown for 1947 to 1966 for the Black population are for Black and other races. Data for 1947 to 1963 exclude kindergarten. Nursery school was first collected in 1964.

* = Quantity zero or rounds to zero.

NA = Not available.

r = Revised, controlled to 1990 census based population estimates; previous 1993 data controlled to 1980 census based population estimates.

[1]Starting in 2003, respondents could identify more than one race. Except as noted, the race data in this table from 2003 onward represent those respondents who indicated only one race category.

[2]The data shown prior to 2003 consists of those identifying themselves as "Asian or Pacific Islanders."

Table A-11. Percentage of the Population 3 Years Old and Over Enrolled in School, by Age, Sex, Race, and Hispanic Origin, October 1947–2019—*Continued*

(Percent; civilian noninstitutionalized population.)

Year, sex, race, and Hispanic origin	Total enrolled 3 to 34 years old	Total enrolled 3 years old and over	Age											
			3 and 4	5 and 6	7 to 9	10 to 13	14 and 15	16 and 17	18 and 19	20 and 21	22 to 24	25 to 29	30 to 34	35 and over
1973	50.5	NA	22.9	93.2	99.3	99.3	97.1	87.3	38.7	27.4	9.9	5.4	3.6	NA
1972	51.5	NA	24.4	92.7	99.2	99.4	97.5	87.3	41.9	27.5	8.9	5.1	3.2	NA
1971	52.6	NA	21.7	92.6	99.3	99.5	98.4	88.9	43.2	27.0	8.1	4.3	3.5	NA
1970	52.9	NA	19.1	90.9	99.3	99.5	98.1	89.0	41.8	24.1	9.7	4.4	3.1	NA
1969	53.2	NA	15.8	89.8	99.6	99.5	98.2	88.2	41.8	25.8	9.4	4.5	3.7	NA
1968	52.9	NA	15.2	89.0	99.3	99.3	98.0	89.4	41.3	22.3	8.2	3.7	2.8	NA
1967	53.0	NA	13.1	89.0	99.6	99.4	98.5	87.4	41.0	25.6	7.5	3.3	2.9	NA
1966	52.5	NA	12.4	86.4	99.5	99.5	98.7	87.6	38.6	22.3	6.6	3.9	1.7	NA
1965	52.2	NA	10.3	85.7	99.4	99.5	98.9	87.0	38.3	20.9	6.3	3.2	2.0	NA
1964	51.3	NA	9.9	83.9	99.2	99.1	98.6	86.1	33.7	20.3	4.5	2.6	1.6	NA
1963	54.7	NA	NA	83.8	99.7	99.5	98.2	85.7	32.1	18.6	4.4	2.4	1.5	NA
1962	54.0	NA	NA	82.4	99.5	99.5	97.6	83.3	34.6	16.3	4.1	1.8	1.4	NA
1961	53.4	NA	NA	81.7	99.5	99.5	97.7	83.5	29.7	15.3	3.8	2.1	1.3	NA
1960	52.7	NA	NA	81.6	99.7	99.6	98.1	81.4	29.7	13.5	3.5	1.8	1.2	NA
1959	52.0	NA	NA	81.9	99.7	99.6	97.7	81.6	28.8	11.1	4.6	1.7	1.3	NA
1958	51.1	NA	NA	81.2	------99.6------		------88.9------		29.9	------7.5------		2.2	1.6	NA
1957	49.8	NA	NA	79.5	------99.7------		------88.2------		27.0	------8.3------		1.7	1.1	NA
1956	48.6	NA	NA	78.6	------99.5------		------88.2------		27.3	------7.0------		1.8	1.3	NA
1955	46.9	NA	NA	79.5	------99.3------		------85.9------		22.4	------6.2------		1.5	1.0	NA
1954	46.4	NA	NA	79.1	------99.8------		------87.0------		25.3	------6.4------		1.7	1.1	NA
1953	42.9	NA	NA	57.4	------99.9------		------84.9------		26.5	------6.5------		0.6	1.5	NA
1952	41.7	NA	NA	54.3	------99.1------		------85.3------		21.1	------4.3------		0.6	0.7	NA
1951	49.0	NA	NA	53.6	------99.4------		------86.0------		21.7	------4.3------		0.9	NA	NA
1950	48.6	NA	NA	----------89.4------			------83.7------		24.2	------4.8------		0.4	NA	NA
1949	39.4	NA	NA	----------88.6------			------81.9------		20.5	------3.8------		1.2	0.4	NA
1948	38.4	NA	NA	----------87.9------			------83.4------		19.7	------3.5------		0.4	0.4	NA
1947	38.1	NA	NA	----------88.9------			------80.8------		18.3	------4.1------		0.4	0.4	NA
WHITE ALONE NON-HISPANIC														
Both Sexes														
2019	52.7	20.5	54.4	94.0	98.2	98.1	97.9	93.4	68.1	54.4	27.7	9.8	5.2	1.2
2018	53.6	21.0	58.2	93.9	96.7	98.6	98.8	93.9	71.3	57.5	27.5	11.3	5.9	1.2
2017	53.2	21.0	56.0	93.0	97.0	97.8	98.5	93.3	67.8	58.1	27.2	11.3	5.8	1.2
2016	54.1	21.5	55.5	93.9	98.0	98.5	98.7	92.2	70.4	57.3	27.7	13.3	6.6	1.2
2015	54.4	21.8	56.0	94.1	97.5	98.1	98.3	94.4	70.1	55.5	28.9	13.1	6.5	1.3
2014	54.4	21.9	57.6	93.4	97.3	97.5	97.8	93.4	69.3	56.1	29.9	12.9	6.3	1.4
2013	54.7	22.3	57.4	93.6	97.9	98.5	98.4	93.6	69.6	55.2	29.1	12.9	6.5	1.6
2012	55.6	22.7	56.5	93.8	98.1	97.5	98.2	96.4	68.8	55.9	30.2	14.4	6.6	1.6
2011	56.4	23.6	56.2	95.8	98.2	98.5	98.9	95.9	72.1	56.2	32.9	15.2	7.8	1.7
2010	56.1	23.6	56.1	94.2	97.4	98.3	98.0	96.2	71.0	55.5	29.1	14.6	8.5	1.8
2009	56.8	23.9	55.5	94.1	98.4	98.9	98.3	95.0	72.4	56.4	31.1	14.0	8.1	1.9
2008	56.7	23.9	56.0	94.9	98.8	98.9	98.8	95.9	70.0	55.8	30.3	13.3	6.9	1.8
2007	56.6	23.9	56.3	95.0	98.6	98.6	98.8	95.6	69.7	54.5	28.4	12.5	7.4	1.8
2006	56.8	24.0	58.2	95.6	98.5	98.6	98.4	95.9	67.9	52.9	27.4	12.5	7.4	1.7
2005	57.6	24.6	58.5	95.9	99.0	99.0	98.6	96.1	71.6	54.4	27.8	12.5	6.9	1.8
2004	56.9	24.5	56.0	96.2	98.3	98.6	98.5	95.1	68.1	54.0	27.0	13.5	6.7	1.8
2003[1]	57.0	24.7	58.8	95.8	98.2	98.5	97.5	95.6	67.9	51.8	29.4	12.5	6.8	1.8
2002	56.8	24.9	57.8	95.3	98.1	98.6	98.6	95.3	67.1	53.1	27.3	12.2	6.3	1.9
2001	56.2	24.7	55.1	95.3	98.5	98.8	98.2	94.6	64.2	50.8	25.5	11.7	6.4	1.8
2000	56.0	25.0	54.6	95.5	98.4	98.5	98.9	94.0	63.9	49.2	24.9	11.1	6.1	1.8
1999	56.2	25.4	58.6	96.0	98.5	98.9	98.4	94.5	64.1	50.0	26.3	10.9	5.9	1.9
1998	55.9	25.6	54.0	96.1	98.8	99.2	98.9	95.1	66.6	49.2	26.1	11.5	6.3	2.0
1997	55.6	25.9	54.9	96.9	98.9	99.2	98.9	95.1	64.1	49.9	27.8	12.2	5.6	2.2
1996	54.0	25.5	50.3	96.1	97.3	98.3	98.2	93.6	65.5	48.9	25.9	11.8	5.8	2.2
1995	53.8	25.9	52.3*	96.6	99.0	99.0	98.8	94.4	61.8	49.7	24.4	12.3	5.7	2.1
1994	54.5	25.9	50.1	96.7	99.2	99.3	99.2	95.1	62.6	50.1	24.9	10.8	6.7	2.2
1993	51.4	25.0	43.1	95.7	99.5	99.5	99.1	95.0	63.6	46.1	24.9	10.2	6.0	2.1

Note: Data shown for 1947 to 1966 for the Black population are for Black and other races. Data for 1947 to 1963 exclude kindergarten. Nursery school was first collected in 1964.
* = Quantity zero or rounds to zero.
NA = Not available.
r = Revised, controlled to 1990 census based population estimates; previous 1993 data controlled to 1980 census based population estimates.
[1]Starting in 2003, respondents could identify more than one race. Except as noted, the race data in this table from 2003 onward represent those respondents who indicated only one race category.
[2]The data shown prior to 2003 consists of those identifying themselves as "Asian or Pacific Islanders."

Table A-11. Percentage of the Population 3 Years Old and Over Enrolled in School, by Age, Sex, Race, and Hispanic Origin, October 1947–2019—*Continued*

(Percent; civilian noninstitutionalized population.)

Year, sex, race, and Hispanic origin	Total enrolled 3 to 34 years old	Total enrolled 3 years old and over	3 and 4	5 and 6	7 to 9	10 to 13	14 and 15	16 and 17	18 and 19	20 and 21	22 to 24	25 to 29	30 to 34	35 and over
Male														
2019	52.0	20.8	52.1	95.3	98.2	98.0	98.1	93.2	65.4	49.8	25.3	8.7	4.5	0.9
2018	53.2	21.4	58.1	94.0	96.8	98.7	99.0	93.8	68.3	53.4	26.2	9.9	5.5	1.0
2017	52.8	21.3	54.3	92.5	97.2	97.9	98.6	92.8	65.4	54.6	25.9	10.5	5.0	0.9
2016	53.8	21.9	56.6	94.2	98.0	98.3	98.8	91.9	69.4	52.8	26.8	11.7	5.5	1.0
2015	54.1	22.1	57.1	93.2	97.8	98.3	98.3	93.8	67.2	53.3	26.9	12.3	5.9	1.0
2014	54.1	22.3	56.5	93.7	96.9	96.8	97.1	92.7	66.0	55.3	28.3	12.1	5.8	1.1
2013	54.1	22.4	55.2	93.7	97.8	98.4	98.4	92.8	68.6	51.0	26.2	11.4	5.6	1.1
2012	55.0	22.9	55.6	93.6	97.7	97.7	97.9	96.0	65.4	49.7	29.6	13.0	6.1	1.2
2011	56.1	23.9	56.4	95.5	98.3	98.5	98.4	95.8	69.9	53.0	33.1	13.2	7.0	1.3
2010	55.5	23.9	55.9	93.3	97.1	97.7	98.0	94.7	67.8	52.1	27.8	13.8	7.2	1.4
2009	56.2	24.2	54.9	93.3	98.2	99.0	97.9	94.7	68.4	53.2	30.8	12.4	7.1	1.4
2008	56.5	24.3	57.2	94.7	98.5	98.7	99.1	95.5	66.8	52.4	29.1	12.6	6.2	1.3
2007	56.0	24.2	53.8	94.0	98.5	98.5	98.3	95.2	69.3	49.9	26.9	10.6	6.7	1.3
2006	56.4	24.4	58.3	95.9	98.5	98.6	97.9	95.5	65.4	49.2	26.2	11.9	6.3	1.3
2005	57.1	24.9	56.8	95.4	98.9	99.1	98.4	95.9	69.8	50.5	26.4	10.2	6.5	1.3
2004	56.7	25.0	57.2	96.2	98.2	98.4	98.7	95.6	63.8	50.6	25.1	12.7	6.2	1.4
2003[1]	57.1	25.4	60.6	96.2	97.7	98.2	97.4	96.1	65.4	47.9	28.9	11.7	6.3	1.4
2002	56.8	25.5	57.8	94.9	98.1	98.5	98.5	95.2	66.3	49.2	27.6	11.1	5.5	1.6
2001	56.0	25.2	54.4	94.8	98.8	98.4	97.8	94.0	62.7	49.1	23.7	10.8	5.3	1.3
2000	55.8	25.5	54.1	94.5	98.1	98.2	98.8	94.7	61.2	45.8	25.0	10.5	4.7	1.4
1999	56.7	26.2	59.2	96.1	98.4	98.7	98.2	94.3	63.7	48.9	26.8	10.7	5.8	1.5
1998	55.7	26.3	54.8	95.5	98.8	99.0	99.0	94.4	65.2	46.4	27.4	10.9	5.3	1.6
1997	55.9	26.5	54.9	97.4	98.8	99.3	99.0	94.5	63.3	48.5	27.5	12.0	4.6	1.5
1996	54.2	26.1	48.0	95.5	97.2	98.1	98.8	93.5	63.7	48.7	27.3	11.4	4.3	1.6
1995	54.2	26.6	51.1	95.9	99.0	99.0	98.9	95.0	61.9	50.0	24.1	12.2	5.0	1.6
1994	53.5	26.6	49.0	97.1	99.2	99.4	99.4	95.4	62.5	47.6	25.5	10.3	6.0	1.6
1993	52.2	25.9	44.1	95.4	99.5	99.6	99.3	96.2	62.5	47.0	26.7	9.9	5.2	1.5
Female														
2019	53.3	20.3	56.8	92.7	98.2	98.3	97.8	93.6	71.1	59.2	30.0	10.9	5.8	1.4
2018	53.9	20.6	58.2	93.8	96.5	98.5	98.5	94.0	74.3	61.8	28.9	12.8	6.2	1.5
2017	53.6	20.7	57.8	93.5	96.8	97.6	98.4	93.8	70.3	61.8	28.4	12.1	6.6	1.5
2016	54.4	21.1	54.3	93.5	97.9	98.8	98.6	92.5	71.6	62.0	28.5	14.9	7.8	1.4
2015	54.6	21.4	54.8	95.1	97.2	97.9	98.4	95.0	73.1	57.7	30.9	14.0	7.1	1.6
2014	54.7	21.6	58.8	93.1	97.7	98.1	98.5	94.1	72.9	57.0	31.4	13.6	6.9	1.7
2013	55.4	22.1	59.7	93.5	98.0	98.5	98.4	94.5	70.8	59.6	31.9	14.3	7.4	2.0
2012	56.2	22.5	57.4	94.0	98.5	97.3	98.4	96.8	72.3	61.7	30.8	16.2	7.1	2.0
2011	56.8	23.3	56.1	96.1	98.1	98.5	99.3	95.9	74.3	59.5	32.7	17.3	8.5	2.0
2010	56.7	23.4	56.3	95.2	97.7	98.9	98.1	97.8	74.3	59.2	30.4	15.4	9.8	2.2
2009	57.4	23.7	56.2	95.0	98.7	98.7	98.7	95.4	76.5	59.8	31.4	15.6	9.0	2.4
2008	57.0	23.5	54.8	95.0	99.1	99.2	98.4	96.3	73.4	59.5	31.5	14.0	7.6	2.2
2007	57.3	23.7	58.9	96.0	98.8	98.7	99.2	96.0	70.1	59.2	29.9	14.4	8.0	2.2
2006	57.1	23.7	58.1	95.3	98.6	98.5	99.0	96.2	70.5	56.5	28.7	13.2	8.5	2.1
2005	58.0	24.3	60.3	96.3	99.0	98.8	98.7	96.3	73.5	58.5	29.1	14.7	7.4	2.2
2004	57.1	24.1	54.7	96.2	98.5	98.7	98.3	94.5	72.5	57.4	28.8	14.4	7.2	2.1
2003[1]	57.0	24.1	56.9	95.3	98.6	98.8	97.6	95.1	70.3	55.6	29.9	13.2	7.3	2.1
2002	56.8	24.3	57.7	95.6	98.0	98.6	98.6	95.5	67.9	57.0	27.0	13.4	7.2	2.2
2001	56.4	24.2	55.9	95.9	98.3	99.1	98.6	95.3	65.8	52.4	27.3	12.5	7.4	2.2
2000	56.1	24.6	55.2	96.4	98.6	98.8	99.0	93.3	66.7	52.7	24.8	11.8	7.4	2.1
1999	55.7	24.7	57.9	96.0	98.5	99.1	98.6	94.8	64.6	51.1	25.7	11.0	6.1	2.3
1998	55.7	25.0	53.1	96.7	98.7	99.3	98.8	95.7	68.0	52.2	24.8	12.1	7.3	2.4
1997	55.2	25.4	55.0	96.4	99.0	99.1	98.8	95.7	64.9	51.3	28.1	12.4	6.6	2.9
1996	53.8	25.0	52.9	96.7	97.3	98.6	97.7	93.7	67.3	49.0	24.5	12.1	7.3	2.6
1995	53.4	25.1	53.5	97.4	98.9	99.0	98.7	93.8	61.8	49.3	24.8	12.3	6.3	2.5
1994	52.9	25.3	51.3	96.3	99.3	99.3	98.9	94.8	62.7	52.4	24.3	11.4	7.3	2.7
1993	50.6	24.3	42.0	96.0	99.5	99.5	98.9	93.7	64.8	45.2	23.1	10.5	6.7	2.6

Note: Data shown for 1947 to 1966 for the Black population are for Black and other races. Data for 1947 to 1963 exclude kindergarten. Nursery school was first collected in 1964.

* = Quantity zero or rounds to zero.

NA = Not available.

r = Revised, controlled to 1990 census based population estimates; previous 1993 data controlled to 1980 census based population estimates.

[1]Starting in 2003, respondents could identify more than one race. Except as noted, the race data in this table from 2003 onward represent those respondents who indicated only one race category.

[2]The data shown prior to 2003 consists of those identifying themselves as "Asian or Pacific Islanders."

Table A-11. Percentage of the Population 3 Years Old and Over Enrolled in School, by Age, Sex, Race, and Hispanic Origin, October 1947–2019—*Continued*

(Percent; civilian noninstitutionalized population.)

Year, sex, race, and Hispanic origin	Total enrolled 3 to 34 years old	Total enrolled 3 years old and over	Age											
			3 and 4	5 and 6	7 to 9	10 to 13	14 and 15	16 and 17	18 and 19	20 and 21	22 to 24	25 to 29	30 to 34	35 and over
BLACK ALONE														
Both Sexes														
2019	54.1	28.0	55.4	93.0	96.0	97.7	97.7	91.4	60.7	48.1	27.9	13.7	7.8	2.6
2018	55.3	28.6	54.5	93.4	97.1	98.4	97.5	87.9	65.8	52.7	28.1	16.1	8.3	2.6
2017	55.1	28.7	57.7	91.5	96.8	98.9	96.6	90.7	67.0	47.5	27.5	13.5	7.7	2.7
2016	55.4	29.2	50.8	93.5	97.4	98.6	96.1	94.9	67.2	48.2	28.0	12.7	8.7	2.9
2015	55.3	29.2	52.7	93.7	95.4	98.3	98.7	94.4	64.5	43.7	27.5	13.1	8.2	2.8
2014	56.0	30.2	57.5	94.5	98.8	97.7	98.9	91.8	65.2	41.1	24.5	14.6	9.1	3.8
2013	57.2	30.7	57.2	94.4	96.7	97.8	98.7	92.8	64.2	47.9	27.0	16.7	8.6	3.1
2012	58.3	31.4	53.1	91.5	97.2	98.9	97.3	94.2	68.6	49.4	27.9	16.1	12.2	3.2
2011	58.4	32.3	55.2	92.0	97.1	98.5	98.5	95.7	74.1	41.1	31.2	18.1	11.4	3.8
2010	58.4	32.5	56.2	94.3	97.1	98.6	98.5	95.5	62.7	50.2	29.0	16.0	10.9	4.0
2009	58.5	32.4	57.7	93.6	97.4	98.6	97.8	94.1	65.2	44.7	31.9	14.6	11.0	3.7
2008	57.8	31.7	54.6	93.1	98.9	98.0	97.9	94.2	59.2	40.3	24.9	14.7	11.5	2.8
2007	58.4	32.2	58.5	94.0	98.2	97.9	99.0	93.4	61.7	38.7	28.0	15.0	9.4	3.0
2006	58.1	32.3	59.2	92.6	97.1	97.2	97.5	93.3	64.7	39.1	27.2	11.8	8.6	3.1
2005	58.4	32.7	52.2	95.9	98.6	98.6	95.8	93.1	62.8	37.6	28.0	11.7	10.0	3.1
2004	59.0	33.4	59.6	94.1	97.5	99.4	99.0	95.7	59.2	40.0	25.1	14.3	7.2	3.3
2003[1]	59.2	33.4	55.5	94.4	98.3	98.2	97.9	94.3	61.9	41.4	27.4	12.2	8.6	2.8
2002	59.6	34.1	57.5	95.7	98.1	98.1	98.2	93.3	57.7	43.5	23.5	13.6	9.8	3.1
2001	59.5	34.3	58.8	96.0	97.8	97.0	97.6	92.1	59.6	37.2	26.0	12.2	11.5	3.2
2000	59.0	34.0	59.9	96.3	97.5	98.4	99.6	91.4	57.2	36.6	24.2	14.3	9.6	2.6
1999	58.1	33.7	56.3	97.5	98.2	98.7	98.2	93.3	57.4	39.4	21.7	10.4	7.8	2.5
1998	58.9	34.6	58.5	95.3	98.7	98.6	98.9	92.9	60.2	39.2	21.5	13.6	8.5	2.6
1997	58.4	34.6	60.0	95.8	99.2	99.4	99.2	93.4	58.2	35.9	25.4	10.7	6.5	2.8
1996	56.2	33.8	49.9	90.5	97.4	97.4	98.9	92.1	52.8	37.0	21.0	13.7	7.1	3.0
1995	56.1	33.9	47.5	95.5	97.7	99.2	99.0	92.9	57.4	37.4	19.9	10.0	7.8	2.7
1994	56.4	34.4	51.9	97.2	99.7	99.6	99.2	95.4	54.0	34.9	22.6	10.5	7.2	2.9
1993r	53.8	NA	39.8	94.5	99.0	99.8	98.5	94.8	57.6	30.1	18.0	10.4	5.5	NA
1993	53.6	32.4	39.8	94.6	99.0	99.8	98.5	94.7	57.7	30.0	18.1	10.4	5.5	2.6
1992	53.0	NA	38.6	95.9	99.4	99.7	99.4	93.0	56.2	33.3	20.3	7.9	5.3	NA
1991	52.5	NA	37.2	95.8	99.6	100.0	99.1	91.7	55.6	30.0	18.2	8.7	6.5	NA
1990	51.9	NA	41.6	96.3	99.9	99.9	99.2	91.7	55.2	28.4	20.0	6.1	4.4	NA
1989	51.3	NA	38.9	94.9	99.0	99.4	99.4	93.7	50.2	30.7	17.2	6.4	4.9	NA
1988	50.6	NA	33.4	95.5	99.7	99.7	98.9	91.5	50.3	28.1	13.2	7.2	5.6	NA
1987	51.7	NA	36.8	95.8	99.7	99.8	98.3	91.5	53.2	28.7	15.0	9.3	6.0	NA
1986	51.6	NA	38.6	95.4	99.8	99.0	98.3	93.9	50.7	25.6	17.1	8.0	6.2	NA
1985	50.9	NA	42.7	95.7	98.4	99.5	97.9	91.7	44.1	27.7	13.7	7.5	5.9	NA
1984	50.1	NA	38.2	94.1	99.5	99.3	97.9	92.4	44.3	27.7	15.7	7.4	5.1	NA
1983	50.8	NA	36.2	94.7	99.1	99.7	97.8	92.6	46.1	23.4	15.6	7.4	6.5	NA
1982	51.6	NA	38.6	95.4	99.2	98.9	98.1	91.6	43.6	24.3	17.0	7.8	7.6	NA
1981	52.5	NA	36.7	94.5	98.8	99.4	97.1	91.3	48.2	23.4	14.7	8.4	7.0	NA
1980	53.9	NA	38.2	95.4	99.4	99.4	97.9	90.6	45.7	23.4	13.6	8.8	6.8	NA
1979	55.0	NA	40.8	96.0	99.4	98.7	97.4	90.8	46.6	23.7	15.0	7.9	6.8	NA
1978	56.3	NA	41.3	93.9	99.5	98.9	98.5	91.2	46.2	25.6	15.0	8.7	7.9	NA
1977	57.7	NA	35.2	96.5	99.3	99.0	98.8	90.8	48.3	29.5	15.2	11.3	9.0	NA
1976	57.9	NA	34.5	94.0	99.3	98.8	99.0	89.0	50.4	28.2	16.4	9.4	8.1	NA
1975	57.7	NA	33.5	94.3	99.3	99.2	97.4	86.9	47.1	27.1	14.2	9.4	7.1	NA
1974	57.3	NA	29.1	92.8	99.2	99.8	97.0	87.1	44.0	23.4	12.1	8.9	6.9	NA
1973	55.8	NA	28.9	89.9	99.2	99.0	96.7	87.7	37.8	20.5	12.4	6.1	5.0	NA
1972	57.8	NA	28.3	90.0	98.7	99.3	97.4	89.5	42.8	22.0	13.1	6.5	5.9	NA
1971	58.6	NA	21.5	89.8	99.0	98.8	98.4	89.2	46.6	27.3	11.4	6.2	5.2	NA
1970	57.4	NA	22.7	84.9	99.3	99.3	97.6	85.7	40.1	22.8	8.0	4.8	3.4	NA
1969	57.8	NA	21.2	84.1	98.8	99.1	97.9	85.8	44.5	23.3	8.6	4.3	3.4	NA
1968	57.4	NA	18.7	82.7	99.2	99.0	97.7	86.4	45.4	18.2	7.9	3.1	3.3	NA
1967	56.8	NA	17.7	82.2	99.1	98.7	86.1	84.1	40.7	21.2	7.2	5.0	2.4	NA
1966	55.5	NA	13.7	80.8	99.2	99.2	97.4	85.2	37.7	11.6	6.1	2.3	2.3	NA
1965	55.6	NA	11.8	79.1	98.9	99.3	98.1	83.9	39.6	12.8	6.2	2.1	2.4	NA
1964	54.5	NA	10.5	80.3	99.0	99.0	96.9	82.4	35.6	14.0	3.8	3.1	2.9	NA
1963	58.8	NA	NA	76.6	98.5	99.5	97.6	82.0	39.8	16.2	5.5	3.3	2.0	NA
1962	57.1	NA	NA	76.0	98.6	98.8	97.1	73.2	33.4	14.9	6.1	3.8	1.5	NA

Note: Data shown for 1947 to 1966 for the Black population are for Black and other races. Data for 1947 to 1963 exclude kindergarten. Nursery school was first collected in 1964.
* = Quantity zero or rounds to zero.
NA = Not available.
r = Revised, controlled to 1990 census based population estimates; previous 1993 data controlled to 1980 census based population estimates.
[1]Starting in 2003, respondents could identify more than one race. Except as noted, the race data in this table from 2003 onward represent those respondents who indicated only one race category.
[2]The data shown prior to 2003 consists of those identifying themselves as "Asian or Pacific Islanders."

Table A-11. Percentage of the Population 3 Years Old and Over Enrolled in School, by Age, Sex, Race, and Hispanic Origin, October 1947–2019—*Continued*

(Percent; civilian noninstitutionalized population.)

Year, sex, race, and Hispanic origin	Total enrolled 3 to 34 years old	Total enrolled 3 years old and over	Age 3 and 4	5 and 6	7 to 9	10 to 13	14 and 15	16 and 17	18 and 19	20 and 21	22 to 24	25 to 29	30 to 34	35 and over
1961	56.8	NA	NA	79.1	98.0	98.3	95.1	76.8	30.6	15.9	4.3	2.4	1.1	NA
1960	55.9	NA	NA	73.3	99.3	99.0	95.9	76.9	34.6	11.9	4.4	2.9	1.0	NA
1959	55.1	NA	NA	74.3	98.9	99.1	93.9	76.3	33.6	11.6	6.3	2.8	1.3	NA
1958	54.0	NA	NA	73.9	------98.8-----		------82.8------		34.3	------8.7------		3.9	1.3	NA
1957	53.5	NA	NA	74.3	------98.2-----		------84.8-----		36.7	------8.8------		4.6	1.2	NA
1956	51.5	NA	NA	72.8	------98.4-----		------81.2-----		31.8	------8.7------		3.1	0.7	NA
1955	50.7	NA	NA	71.1	------98.2-----		------82.8-----		27.6	------7.2------		4.9	1.8	NA
1954	48.6	NA	NA	68.8	------98.0-----		------78.8-----		24.0	------5.8------		4.8	1.4	NA
1953	45.5	NA	NA	46.3	------97.3-----		------82.3-----		27.6	------5.4------		1.7	0.8	NA
1952	46.4	NA	NA	54.0	------96.4-----		------77.3-----		------------------6.3------------------					NA
1951	53.4	NA	NA	54.9	------97.3-----		------77.1-----		20.8	------6.2------		2.7	NA	NA
1950	51.2	NA	NA	----------86.8----------			------75.5-----		23.3	------6.3------		3.0	NA	NA
1949	40.9	NA	NA	----------83.7----------			------69.5-----		20.0	------6.2------		1.8	0.5	NA
1948	39.2	NA	NA	----------80.1----------			------66.8-----		24.6	------6.3------		1.5	0.6	NA
1947	41.0	NA	NA	----------84.8----------			------71.9-----		20.2	------6.9------		2.5	0.5	NA
Male														
2019	54.0	29.1	56.1	92.4	97.8	98.0	98.7	90.1	60.1	46.7	23.2	12.1	4.9	2.1
2018	54.8	29.3	50.0	92.3	97.2	98.1	98.7	92.0	65.2	52.2	23.8	13.7	4.5	1.7
2017	54.7	29.7	59.7	90.0	96.0	98.8	95.4	89.0	63.2	42.6	24.0	12.3	6.2	2.1
2016	56.0	30.5	46.6	91.2	96.1	98.6	98.9	95.7	66.6	46.2	26.8	12.9	7.4	2.3
2015	55.6	30.3	51.0	92.1	95.8	99.2	99.5	94.7	63.3	39.6	30.4	10.1	4.5	1.8
2014	56.2	31.2	58.0	96.1	98.6	97.3	98.7	92.6	60.3	41.8	22.2	11.6	7.0	2.7
2013	56.8	31.5	54.1	94.4	96.5	97.8	98.8	94.3	59.9	43.2	25.2	13.1	5.2	2.4
2012	58.1	31.9	51.1	92.1	97.0	98.9	98.5	95.5	60.5	48.8	26.8	11.5	7.3	1.9
2011	57.9	33.0	53.4	92.4	97.5	98.5	97.8	94.0	72.6	38.0	29.8	14.2	7.5	2.7
2010	57.9	33.1	55.5	93.7	97.5	98.4	97.7	93.5	60.8	44.5	28.5	13.2	6.5	2.7
2009	58.0	32.9	56.3	93.7	96.8	98.5	96.4	95.2	60.5	42.2	26.6	11.7	7.9	2.2
2008	58.0	32.7	53.3	95.5	98.5	98.5	98.9	94.0	57.9	37.8	23.2	10.6	8.5	1.5
2007	59.5	33.9	59.6	93.9	98.3	97.2	99.2	95.2	61.9	37.8	28.0	10.4	9.4	2.0
2006	58.7	33.7	56.6	93.5	97.2	96.8	97.7	91.8	63.9	38.0	24.2	9.3	6.9	2.5
2005	58.9	34.0	54.0	94.8	97.7	97.7	93.6	93.6	67.2	35.1	23.4	9.3	6.3	2.4
2004	59.2	34.6	61.1	93.7	96.7	99.2	98.8	96.5	58.1	37.8	20.2	8.7	4.0	2.2
2003[1]	60.0	34.9	56.5	92.4	98.8	98.1	98.3	94.0	61.5	34.3	23.5	9.7	7.4	1.9
2002	60.2	35.4	57.5	96.2	99.1	97.9	97.6	92.9	54.9	39.5	16.6	10.1	7.5	2.1
2001	60.1	35.7	55.4	95.6	98.3	96.0	99.0	93.2	57.3	36.2	22.7	8.2	8.3	2.3
2000	59.5	35.3	57.6	95.8	98.3	98.7	99.6	89.1	52.4	30.5	21.8	11.3	8.3	2.2
1999	59.9	35.8	53.0	98.4	97.7	99.0	97.9	94.4	60.3	42.3	16.1	9.0	6.5	2.0
1998	60.1	36.2	57.8	95.0	98.5	98.6	97.7	93.9	58.2	40.7	15.1	12.6	5.6	1.8
1997	59.5	36.2	57.3	94.2	98.7	99.1	99.6	93.9	56.7	34.1	21.5	10.5	5.6	2.0
1996	57.8	35.7	47.0	90.1	98.1	97.2	98.1	93.7	55.2	39.0	18.6	12.8	5.4	2.4
1995	58.3	36.2	51.5	94.7	98.2	99.5	99.6	95.2	59.1	36.1	20.3	6.1	6.7	2.3
1994	58.4	36.5	56.8	97.1	99.6	99.5	99.7	95.3	53.4	33.7	21.3	10.8	5.7	2.1
1993r	56.0	NA	41.6	96.8	99.3	100.0	99.0	96.1	63.4	23.7	19.6	10.4	3.1	NA
1993	55.8	34.8	41.7	96.9	99.3	100.0	99.0	96.0	63.6	23.9	19.6	10.3	3.1	2.0
1992	54.8	NA	41.3	97.6	99.9	99.7	99.9	94.5	60.7	27.1	18.7	7.6	3.3	NA
1991	54.5	NA	35.2	95.4	99.8	100.0	100.0	90.4	62.2	30.1	19.3	8.6	4.8	NA
1990	53.9	NA	38.3	96.1	99.9	99.9	99.7	93.2	60.7	31.1	20.0	4.6	2.3	NA
1989	52.6	NA	40.2	92.9	98.9	98.8	99.3	95.6	51.0	23.2	15.5	5.5	3.2	NA
1988	52.4	NA	34.5	96.0	99.6	100.0	99.1	93.2	49.7	20.7	14.7	6.3	4.1	NA
1987	54.0	NA	39.0	97.4	100.0	99.8	98.1	91.8	58.7	30.3	15.5	8.4	3.4	NA
1986	53.8	NA	38.7	97.1	99.6	98.8	98.4	94.7	54.1	25.4	17.3	7.1	5.9	NA
1985	52.6	NA	34.6	94.6	98.2	99.1	98.2	91.8	49.5	29.7	13.2	6.9	5.7	NA
1984	52.6	NA	37.2	92.8	99.5	99.1	96.9	93.2	48.6	29.7	17.5	5.7	3.9	NA
1983	52.9	NA	37.1	95.8	98.9	99.4	98.4	91.8	46.6	23.5	17.2	9.1	6.6	NA
1982	53.2	NA	37.4	93.9	99.3	98.4	97.8	92.2	46.5	20.9	17.4	8.5	7.1	NA
1981	54.5	NA	34.8	94.5	98.5	99.2	97.3	92.1	51.9	20.6	14.7	8.4	5.6	NA
1980	56.1	NA	36.6	94.1	99.5	99.4	98.5	90.8	42.8	23.0	13.3	10.6	7.3	NA
1979	57.8	NA	40.4	96.6	99.0	98.4	98.5	94.6	48.0	26.9	14.6	8.1	6.3	NA
1978	58.7	NA	37.9	93.2	99.4	98.8	99.0	92.8	50.5	25.2	14.7	9.5	7.8	NA
1977	60.3	NA	32.4	96.0	99.1	98.6	99.0	92.5	50.5	31.0	18.5	12.1	9.2	NA
1976	61.1	NA	36.3	94.4	99.5	98.8	99.5	90.9	54.9	28.0	18.7	11.0	8.8	NA

Note: Data shown for 1947 to 1966 for the Black population are for Black and other races. Data for 1947 to 1963 exclude kindergarten. Nursery school was first collected in 1964.
* = Quantity zero or rounds to zero.
NA = Not available.
r = Revised, controlled to 1990 census based population estimates; previous 1993 data controlled to 1980 census based population estimates.
[1]Starting in 2003, respondents could identify more than one race. Except as noted, the race data in this table from 2003 onward represent those respondents who indicated only one race category.
[2]The data shown prior to 2003 consists of those identifying themselves as "Asian or Pacific Islanders."

Table A-11. Percentage of the Population 3 Years Old and Over Enrolled in School, by Age, Sex, Race, and Hispanic Origin, October 1947–2019—*Continued*

(Percent; civilian noninstitutionalized population.)

Year, sex, race, and Hispanic origin	Total enrolled 3 to 34 years old	Total enrolled 3 years old and over	3 and 4	5 and 6	7 to 9	10 to 13	14 and 15	16 and 17	18 and 19	20 and 21	22 to 24	25 to 29	30 to 34	35 and over
1975	60.3	NA	29.5	94.6	99.3	99.0	97.6	88.2	49.9	28.7	14.7	11.8	8.6	NA
1974	60.7	NA	30.3	91.8	99.5	99.6	96.1	90.1	46.1	27.7	16.0	10.4	9.7	NA
1973	58.6	NA	29.2	89.0	99.2	99.1	96.9	89.0	43.5	24.5	13.9	6.9	6.5	NA
1972	60.9	NA	32.1	90.8	98.4	99.4	97.6	88.9	47.7	27.1	18.4	7.3	5.2	NA
1971	60.4	NA	19.0	88.7	99.1	98.1	97.7	90.0	50.7	31.3	12.9	8.5	6.4	NA
1970	59.5	NA	22.3	84.2	99.2	99.1	98.0	85.4	41.3	27.8	9.6	6.1	3.6	NA
1969	60.0	NA	21.3	83.1	98.3	98.9	98.0	87.4	49.5	28.4	10.7	2.8	2.9	NA
1968	60.0	NA	16.9	84.1	98.8	98.4	98.5	88.5	53.1	23.4	7.5	5.2	3.4	NA
1967	59.2	NA	17.0	81.0	99.0	98.3	96.5	86.7	48.6	24.5	9.0	3.5	3.5	NA
1966	58.1	NA	12.7	80.0	99.1	99.0	98.2	87.4	46.3	14.4	9.1	2.6	2.7	NA
1965	57.7	NA	9.5	81.0	99.3	99.4	98.7	82.2	47.5	18.5	4.3	2.6	2.3	NA
1964	56.8	NA	9.4	80.7	98.2	98.7	98.8	84.3	39.9	14.2	3.8	3.5	4.0	NA
1963	61.9	NA	NA	74.3	97.7	99.2	98.2	85.9	46.5	21.7	7.1	4.7	2.7	NA
1962	60.4	NA	NA	74.5	98.9	98.6	99.1	77.1	40.3	15.0	10.1	5.8	1.7	NA
1961	60.0	NA	NA	78.7	98.4	97.6	96.6	78.6	41.7	19.9	6.1	4.0	1.9	NA
1960	58.3	NA	NA	71.8	99.4	98.7	97.0	79.1	36.9	13.7	6.3	3.9	1.0	NA
1959	58.0	NA	NA	76.0	98.7	99.1	95.8	76.3	35.5	12.5	10.6	4.5	1.8	NA
1958	58.0	NA	NA	74.2	------98.8------		------87.6------		43.4	------11.8------		6.3	2.4	NA
1957	55.9	NA	NA	73.1	------98.2------		------84.7------		38.5	------10.3------		6.0	1.2	NA
1956	54.3	NA	NA	70.4	------97.6------		------81.3------		36.8	------12.5------		5.3	0.9	NA
1955	54.4	NA	NA	72.8	------98.2------		------85.2------		32.9	------9.8------		6.2	1.9	NA
1954	52.0	NA	NA	64.7	------97.5------		------82.8------		21.6	------10.1------		7.9	1.9	NA
1953	47.8	NA	NA	41.6	------97.1------		------79.1------		34.6	------5.8------		3.3	0.9	NA
1952	49.7	NA	NA	51.4	------96.0------		------72.5------		------------6.0------------					NA
1951	56.9	NA	NA	52.8	------98.0------		------74.9------		23.6	------9.0------		4.3	NA	NA
1950	56.0	NA	NA	----------87.0----------			------79.3------		19.9	------11.1------		6.1	NA	NA
1949	45.0	NA	NA	----------83.1----------			------68.8------		26.1	------11.8------		3.3	1.1	NA
1948	40.4	NA	NA	----------78.9----------			------63.9------		24.0	------10.5------		2.5	1.4	NA
1947	45.1	NA	NA	----------84.6----------			------72.6------		20.7	------12.3------		5.1	0.8	NA
Female														
2019	54.2	27.0	54.5	93.7	94.2	97.5	96.7	92.7	61.2	49.4	32.2	15.2	10.4	3.0
2018	55.7	28.1	58.6	94.5	97.1	98.8	96.3	83.8	66.4	53.1	32.2	18.3	11.7	3.4
2017	55.4	27.9	55.4	93.1	97.7	98.9	97.8	92.5	70.7	52.5	30.7	14.7	8.9	3.1
2016	54.9	28.0	55.1	95.9	98.7	98.6	93.2	94.0	67.8	50.3	29.0	12.5	9.8	3.4
2015	55.0	28.3	54.6	95.3	94.9	97.4	97.8	94.1	65.6	47.7	24.8	15.7	11.2	3.6
2014	55.7	29.4	57.0	92.9	98.9	98.0	99.1	91.0	70.1	40.5	26.8	17.2	10.8	4.6
2013	57.6	30.0	60.2	94.4	96.8	97.8	98.6	91.3	68.3	52.1	28.7	19.8	11.5	3.6
2012	58.6	30.9	55.1	90.9	97.3	98.9	96.1	92.8	76.6	50.0	28.9	20.0	16.1	4.2
2011	58.9	31.7	57.1	91.5	96.8	98.6	99.3	97.3	75.6	44.6	32.2	21.7	14.7	4.8
2010	58.8	31.9	56.8	95.0	96.8	98.8	99.3	97.5	64.5	55.4	29.6	18.5	14.6	4.9
2009	58.9	31.9	59.0	93.6	98.0	98.8	99.3	92.9	69.7	47.3	36.2	17.2	13.5	4.8
2008	57.6	30.9	55.8	90.8	99.4	99.4	96.9	94.4	60.5	42.6	26.3	18.3	13.8	3.8
2007	57.4	30.8	57.3	94.2	98.1	98.6	98.8	91.7	61.6	39.5	27.9	18.9	9.4	3.8
2006	57.6	31.1	61.5	91.7	96.9	97.6	97.2	94.7	65.4	40.2	30.0	14.0	9.9	3.6
2005	57.9	31.5	50.6	97.1	99.5	99.5	98.0	92.5	58.5	40.1	31.8	13.8	13.0	3.6
2004	58.7	32.3	57.7	94.5	98.2	99.6	99.1	94.8	60.2	41.9	29.5	19.0	9.8	4.2
2003[1]	58.4	32.1	54.5	96.4	97.7	98.3	97.5	94.6	62.2	47.4	30.8	14.2	9.6	3.5
2002	59.1	33.0	55.4	95.2	97.2	98.3	98.8	93.7	60.6	47.1	28.8	16.3	11.7	3.8
2001	58.9	33.1	62.1	96.5	97.2	98.1	96.2	91.0	62.0	37.9	29.0	15.3	14.0	3.9
2000	58.7	32.9	62.3	96.8	96.8	98.2	99.6	93.8	61.5	41.3	26.4	16.5	10.7	2.9
1999	56.5	32.0	59.1	96.5	98.7	98.6	98.5	92.1	54.7	36.9	25.9	11.5	8.9	2.9
1998	57.8	33.2	59.1	95.6	98.9	98.7	100.0	91.8	62.2	37.8	26.2	14.4	10.9	3.2
1997	57.4	33.3	62.9	97.2	99.8	99.7	98.9	92.9	59.6	37.3	28.7	10.8	7.2	3.5
1996	54.7	32.2	52.6	90.8	96.7	97.6	99.6	90.4	50.5	35.5	23.2	14.4	8.6	3.5
1995	54.1	31.9	43.6	96.3	97.2	99.0	98.3	90.4	55.9	38.5	19.5	13.0	8.7	3.0
1994	54.4	32.5	47.0	97.2	99.7	99.7	98.6	95.5	54.6	35.9	23.6	10.3	8.5	3.4
1993r	51.6	NA	37.9	92.0	98.7	99.7	97.9	93.4	52.0	35.3	16.6	10.5	7.4	NA
1993	51.6	30.4	37.8	92.1	98.7	99.7	97.9	93.4	51.9	35.1	16.7	10.5	7.5	3.0
1992	51.3	NA	35.8	94.1	98.9	99.6	98.8	91.5	51.8	38.6	21.6	8.2	6.9	NA
1991	50.6	NA	39.5	96.1	99.5	100.0	98.2	93.1	49.4	29.9	17.3	8.8	7.9	NA

Note: Data shown for 1947 to 1966 for the Black population are for Black and other races. Data for 1947 to 1963 exclude kindergarten. Nursery school was first collected in 1964.

* = Quantity zero or rounds to zero.

NA = Not available.

r = Revised, controlled to 1990 census based population estimates; previous 1993 data controlled to 1980 census based population estimates.

[1]Starting in 2003, respondents could identify more than one race. Except as noted, the race data in this table from 2003 onward represent those respondents who indicated only one race category.

[2]The data shown prior to 2003 consists of those identifying themselves as "Asian or Pacific Islanders."

Table A-11.　Percentage of the Population 3 Years Old and Over Enrolled in School, by Age, Sex, Race, and Hispanic Origin, October 1947–2019—*Continued*

(Percent; civilian noninstitutionalized population.)

Year, sex, race, and Hispanic origin	Total enrolled 3 to 34 years old	Total enrolled 3 years old and over	3 and 4	5 and 6	7 to 9	10 to 13	14 and 15	16 and 17	18 and 19	20 and 21	22 to 24	25 to 29	30 to 34	35 and over
1990	50.1	NA	45.0	96.5	99.8	99.8	98.7	90.2	50.0	26.0	20.1	7.3	6.2	NA
1989	50.1	NA	37.6	97.1	99.2	99.9	99.5	91.7	49.4	37.3	18.6	7.1	6.3	NA
1988	49.0	NA	32.3	94.9	99.8	99.3	98.6	89.8	50.9	34.3	11.9	7.9	6.9	NA
1987	49.6	NA	34.4	94.1	99.3	99.7	98.6	91.2	48.2	27.4	14.6	10.0	8.1	NA
1986	49.5	NA	38.6	93.7	100.0	99.3	98.2	93.1	47.6	25.7	16.9	8.6	6.5	NA
1985	49.4	NA	50.2	97.1	98.7	99.9	97.6	91.6	39.0	26.0	14.1	7.9	6.1	NA
1984	47.8	NA	39.2	95.3	99.5	99.4	99.0	91.7	40.3	25.9	14.1	8.8	6.2	NA
1983	48.8	NA	35.2	93.6	99.3	100.0	97.1	93.4	45.7	23.3	14.2	6.0	6.5	NA
1982	50.2	NA	39.8	97.0	99.1	99.5	98.3	91.0	41.0	27.2	16.6	7.2	8.0	NA
1981	50.6	NA	38.7	94.4	99.1	99.6	97.0	90.5	44.9	25.7	14.7	8.4	8.1	NA
1980	52.0	NA	39.7	96.7	99.3	99.3	97.4	90.4	48.2	23.7	13.9	7.4	6.5	NA
1979	52.5	NA	41.2	95.5	99.7	99.0	96.4	87.1	45.4	21.1	15.3	7.7	7.3	NA
1978	54.1	NA	44.8	94.7	99.6	99.1	98.0	89.6	42.4	26.0	15.2	8.1	8.0	NA
1977	55.4	NA	38.1	97.0	99.4	99.4	98.5	89.1	46.3	28.2	12.6	10.7	8.9	NA
1976	55.0	NA	32.6	93.6	99.1	98.8	98.4	87.0	46.4	28.4	14.5	8.1	7.6	NA
1975	55.3	NA	37.6	93.9	99.3	99.4	97.2	85.6	44.7	25.8	13.8	7.5	5.9	NA
1974	54.2	NA	28.0	93.8	98.9	100.0	97.9	84.2	42.1	20.1	9.0	7.7	4.8	NA
1973	53.3	NA	28.5	90.9	99.2	98.9	96.5	86.4	32.8	17.3	11.1	5.5	3.8	NA
1972	54.9	NA	24.5	89.1	99.0	99.3	97.3	90.1	38.7	17.9	8.5	5.9	6.5	NA
1971	56.9	NA	24.1	90.9	98.9	99.4	99.0	88.4	43.1	24.1	10.1	4.2	4.2	NA
1970	55.5	NA	23.2	85.7	99.5	99.5	97.2	85.9	38.9	18.9	6.7	3.6	3.3	NA
1969	55.8	NA	21.1	85.0	99.4	99.2	97.7	84.3	40.1	19.6	6.9	5.5	3.7	NA
1968	54.9	NA	20.5	81.3	99.7	99.5	96.9	84.3	38.6	14.5	8.3	1.5	3.2	NA
1967	54.6	NA	18.5	83.4	99.2	99.0	95.8	81.6	34.0	18.5	5.6	6.1	1.5	NA
1966	53.2	NA	14.7	81.6	99.3	99.4	96.5	83.1	30.3	9.3	3.6	2.0	2.0	NA
1965	53.6	NA	14.1	77.3	98.6	99.2	97.6	85.6	32.5	8.0	7.8	1.7	2.4	NA
1964	52.5	NA	11.7	79.9	99.9	99.3	95.0	80.6	31.7	13.7	3.8	2.8	2.0	NA
1963	56.0	NA	NA	79.0	99.2	99.8	96.9	78.2	33.9	11.5	4.3	2.2	1.5	NA
1962	54.1	NA	NA	77.5	98.3	99.1	95.2	69.5	27.3	14.9	3.0	2.2	1.3	NA
1961	53.8	NA	NA	79.5	97.6	99.0	93.5	75.1	20.6	12.4	2.7	1.0	0.4	NA
1960	53.7	NA	NA	74.9	99.1	99.3	94.8	74.7	32.2	10.4	2.8	2.1	1.0	NA
1959	52.4	NA	NA	72.5	99.2	99.1	92.0	76.4	31.9	10.8	2.7	1.4	1.0	NA
1958	50.3	NA	NA	73.7	------98.7------		------78.1------		26.4	------6.0------		1.9	0.4	NA
1957	51.3	NA	NA	75.6	------98.2------		------85.0------		35.1	------7.6------		3.5	1.1	NA
1956	49.0	NA	NA	75.2	------99.1------		------81.1------		27.5	------5.7------		1.3	0.6	NA
1955	47.4	NA	NA	69.4	------98.1------		------80.5------		23.1	------5.5------		3.8	1.7	NA
1954	45.6	NA	NA	73.0	------98.6------		------74.7------		25.7	------2.9------		2.3	0.9	NA
1953	43.5	NA	NA	51.1	------97.6------		------85.5------		21.6	------5.0------		0.3	0.7	NA
1952	43.6	NA	NA	56.3	------97.0------		------82.3------		------------6.4------------					NA
1951	50.3	NA	NA	57.1	------96.5------		------79.2------		17.9	------4.3------		1.5	NA	NA
1950	47.0	NA	NA	------86.5------			------71.9------		25.7	------3.0------		0.6	NA	NA
1949	37.3	NA	NA	------84.5------			------70.0------		14.5	------1.9------		0.7	-	NA
1948	38.2	NA	NA	------81.3------			------69.6------		25.2	------2.7------		0.6	-	NA
1947	37.3	NA	NA	------84.9------			------71.3------		19.9	------2.5------		0.3	0.3	NA
ASIAN[2]														
Both Sexes														
2019	55.8	26.0	58.3	92.5	98.3	100.0	99.5	94.0	86.2	78.4	47.0	17.6	9.5	1.4
2018	53.9	25.2	50.9	90.4	99.0	97.1	100.0	90.0	79.1	74.4	45.5	18.7	9.2	1.5
2017	55.1	25.4	56.5	94.8	98.2	98.5	100.0	93.8	82.4	79.7	50.5	16.7	5.8	1.1
2016	54.7	25.9	62.8	89.5	97.8	98.5	97.9	94.2	77.1	75.6	46.5	21.0	6.4	1.4
2015	56.4	26.6	56.2	95.4	97.4	98.3	99.7	86.8	83.7	83.8	49.7	20.2	8.6	1.5
2014	55.8	26.9	53.9	90.5	96.3	97.5	95.5	94.5	88.1	75.8	56.5	19.2	5.4	1.9
2013	56.6	27.4	57.5	91.7	96.9	98.8	98.8	96.8	83.8	81.7	47.3	18.9	8.0	2.1
2012	57.2	27.6	54.1	93.5	99.9	98.3	98.7	97.3	81.0	74.6	53.0	18.8	8.6	1.8
2011	56.8	26.9	51.8	96.7	97.4	96.7	97.9	97.2	84.5	79.0	42.6	16.4	8.3	2.0
2010	58.6	27.9	61.8	96.5	98.5	98.4	97.6	95.3	82.3	80.2	46.5	20.9	10.3	1.8
2009	57.8	26.9	52.4	94.7	96.4	95.4	96.2	96.6	94.1	73.0	56.7	19.3	10.8	2.0
2008	57.3	27.4	55.8	90.8	98.0	99.5	98.7	92.4	85.4	81.1	43.1	23.4	11.5	2.4
2007	55.6	26.9	53.4	94.3	98.2	99.2	99.8	92.6	86.5	66.5	47.4	19.0	9.9	1.7
2006	54.7	26.9	48.3	96.7	99.1	99.2	99.5	92.2	83.0	74.7	44.8	17.8	8.7	2.2

Note: Data shown for 1947 to 1966 for the Black population are for Black and other races. Data for 1947 to 1963 exclude kindergarten. Nursery school was first collected in 1964.
* = Quantity zero or rounds to zero.
NA = Not available.
r = Revised, controlled to 1990 census based population estimates; previous 1993 data controlled to 1980 census based population estimates.
[1]Starting in 2003, respondents could identify more than one race. Except as noted, the race data in this table from 2003 onward represent those respondents who indicated only one race category.
[2]The data shown prior to 2003 consists of those identifying themselves as "Asian or Pacific Islanders."

Table A-11. Percentage of the Population 3 Years Old and Over Enrolled in School, by Age, Sex, Race, and Hispanic Origin, October 1947–2019—*Continued*

(Percent; civilian noninstitutionalized population.)

Year, sex, race, and Hispanic origin	Total enrolled 3 to 34 years old	Total enrolled 3 years old and over	Age											
			3 and 4	5 and 6	7 to 9	10 to 13	14 and 15	16 and 17	18 and 19	20 and 21	22 to 24	25 to 29	30 to 34	35 and over
2005	55.6	28.2	55.0	94.7	99.5	97.6	98.8	98.3	88.3	80.5	42.7	21.0	9.3	2.2
2004	56.8	29.3	58.3	97.2	99.9	99.1	97.5	98.6	82.6	79.7	46.8	21.5	9.5	2.6
2003[1]	56.8	29.3	54.5	89.4	99.0	99.3	99.0	97.6	87.3	79.8	48.1	22.5	9.2	2.2
2002	57.3	30.8	56.1	95.6	96.9	98.8	98.4	94.9	78.9	72.8	49.5	18.3	8.3	2.4
2001	57.7	31.7	41.9	99.4	96.3	99.6	98.4	95.7	84.0	72.6	50.8	22.6	7.8	2.2
2000	58.3	32.6	56.0	97.6	97.8	97.6	99.6	98.4	78.8	66.2	45.3	18.7	8.9	2.8
1999	60.9	34.3	55.8	98.9	99.6	100.0	95.8	97.3	78.5	61.7	45.6	20.3	7.8	3.0
1998	59.9	34.2	53.4	97.9	97.9	98.1	95.3	95.6	83.3	70.6	49.0	21.3	8.7	2.6
1997	60.6	34.6	60.2	94.0	97.7	100.0	99.4	94.7	80.2	73.2	41.8	24.2	9.6	2.7
1996	58.6	35.0	50.4	95.7	98.9	99.3	96.8	94.3	78.3	65.8	39.5	18.6	9.9	3.6
1995	57.3	32.5	42.1	95.9	99.5	99.8	100.0	95.9	83.1	63.4	46.7	21.2	11.1	3.2
1994	60.9	33.1	42.3	97.8	99.5	99.7	100.0	97.3	81.8	67.4	53.5	23.8	8.4	2.7
1993	62.2	34.7	39.6	97.1	99.7	100.0	99.9	91.1	82.5	76.1	55.3	21.0	8.6	3.4
Male														
2019	56.6	27.6	55.8	95.3	98.0	100.0	100.0	96.7	89.0	79.4	45.0	18.9	8.6	1.6
2018	54.0	26.4	51.1	91.0	98.1	94.7	100.0	95.0	75.3	73.9	47.4	18.7	7.9	1.4
2017	55.5	26.7	53.7	93.3	97.7	98.0	100.0	94.4	78.2	78.6	54.5	16.3	4.4	0.8
2016	56.2	27.8	60.5	86.4	98.0	98.8	98.8	91.7	75.1	77.6	51.4	22.3	7.0	1.7
2015	57.1	27.6	60.4	97.8	97.6	98.4	99.7	85.3	80.5	81.8	47.2	20.2	8.4	1.1
2014	57.4	28.7	53.9	91.2	97.8	97.2	94.7	93.3	87.5	74.0	62.2	22.0	3.7	1.8
2013	58.4	29.0	60.1	94.5	97.7	99.0	98.0	95.2	83.0	86.6	48.4	22.3	6.1	1.7
2012	57.9	28.8	48.7	93.0	99.7	97.9	97.5	97.4	83.1	74.8	52.8	19.9	7.0	1.5
2011	57.7	28.0	51.6	96.9	96.8	98.2	98.4	96.5	89.2	80.5	39.4	15.8	8.1	1.3
2010	59.8	29.4	63.2	97.5	98.8	97.8	97.1	96.0	77.6	82.9	42.7	22.8	10.8	1.8
2009	58.0	28.2	51.9	94.2	95.6	94.5	97.3	95.1	92.6	71.8	56.9	19.6	9.5	2.3
2008	57.1	27.9	54.2	91.1	96.8	99.1	100.0	96.0	89.0	74.1	38.0	25.2	10.3	1.9
2007	57.2	28.6	56.7	96.9	99.0	99.0	99.7	93.5	91.8	67.6	46.0	18.1	10.3	1.9
2006	55.5	28.3	56.7	96.8	98.3	98.8	99.4	91.0	79.7	76.1	42.2	16.3	8.5	2.4
2005	56.9	29.7	53.2	96.8	99.8	96.9	97.8	97.8	85.2	84.0	42.6	21.1	10.3	2.0
2004	59.3	31.9	58.3	96.0	99.7	99.8	96.5	99.0	85.9	84.2	49.8	24.1	11.4	2.9
2003[1]	59.6	31.8	53.3	90.8	97.9	99.9	97.8	100.0	90.4	77.0	47.8	28.9	11.9	2.3
2002	58.7	32.3	54.1	97.7	95.6	98.4	99.4	94.3	80.0	70.2	50.1	20.6	9.5	2.4
2001	59.1	33.6	35.9	99.6	96.0	100.0	97.1	94.5	83.3	74.9	58.9	22.9	10.6	1.7
2000	60.5	35.0	56.0	96.8	99.5	97.0	99.3	97.8	75.5	67.2	49.1	16.0	10.2	2.7
1999	62.0	35.8	53.5	97.9	99.2	100.0	93.7	98.7	74.4	59.6	50.5	21.4	10.6	3.1
1998	60.8	35.2	51.5	100.0	97.9	98.5	95.0	96.8	74.8	68.0	51.3	21.4	11.1	2.2
1997	63.4	36.6	61.3	89.7	99.4	100.0	98.6	95.5	88.2	71.6	46.9	31.0	10.6	2.5
1996	62.1	38.0	51.0	94.0	99.0	99.6	97.9	93.7	81.0	70.7	37.3	24.4	14.4	3.6
1995	60.0	35.6	38.0	94.5	98.9	99.6	100.0	96.9	81.9	60.3	47.8	24.8	15.7	3.5
1994	64.7	35.8	45.5	98.2	99.0	100.0	100.0	96.9	81.5	70.9	57.0	31.3	10.7	2.1
1993	65.9	37.9	43.0	95.9	99.8	99.9	100.0	93.4	79.4	78.5	65.4	21.0	11.2	3.4
Female														
2019	55.1	24.5	61.1	90.0	98.6	100.0	99.0	91.6	83.4	77.4	49.3	16.4	10.4	1.3
2018	53.8	24.1	50.7	89.8	100.0	99.7	100.0	86.2	83.1	75.1	43.6	18.7	10.4	1.5
2017	54.7	24.3	59.4	96.3	98.7	99.0	100.0	93.3	86.8	80.8	46.4	17.0	7.1	1.4
2016	53.3	24.2	51.9	92.8	97.5	98.2	97.1	96.3	79.3	73.7	41.2	19.5	5.9	1.2
2015	55.7	25.7	51.9	92.6	97.1	98.2	99.7	88.2	86.9	85.6	52.5	20.1	8.9	1.9
2014	54.2	25.4	53.8	89.8	94.9	97.8	96.3	95.5	88.7	77.8	50.7	16.7	7.0	2.0
2013	54.9	26.0	54.6	88.8	96.2	98.5	99.6	98.0	84.6	76.3	46.0	15.7	9.6	2.5
2012	56.5	26.6	59.0	94.0	100.0	98.6	100.0	97.3	78.7	74.4	53.3	17.7	10.0	2.1
2011	55.9	25.9	52.0	96.5	98.0	95.3	97.3	98.0	79.2	77.5	46.0	17.0	8.5	2.5
2010	57.3	26.5	60.5	95.6	98.2	99.0	98.1	94.3	87.2	77.8	50.3	19.1	9.9	1.8
2009	57.5	25.8	53.1	95.3	97.3	96.2	94.5	98.3	95.8	74.1	56.5	19.1	10.2	1.8
2008	57.4	26.8	57.8	90.4	99.0	100.0	97.5	88.7	81.8	89.5	47.5	21.7	12.7	2.9
2007	54.0	25.3	49.1	91.9	97.3	99.5	100.0	91.7	81.0	65.4	48.5	19.8	9.6	1.5
2006	53.8	25.6	39.1	96.5	100.0	99.5	99.0	93.3	87.3	72.9	47.0	19.1	8.9	2.0
2005	54.4	26.8	56.8	92.3	99.3	98.3	100.0	98.8	91.7	75.9	42.9	20.9	8.4	2.4
2004	54.1	26.9	58.4	99.1	100.0	98.2	98.5	98.1	79.0	74.7	43.9	19.1	7.6	2.4
2003[1]	54.0	27.1	55.8	87.4	100.0	98.4	100.0	94.9	84.6	82.5	48.3	16.6	6.7	2.1
2002	56.1	29.5	58.1	93.4	97.9	99.2	97.5	95.5	77.9	75.8	48.9	16.1	7.2	2.3

Note: Data shown for 1947 to 1966 for the Black population are for Black and other races. Data for 1947 to 1963 exclude kindergarten. Nursery school was first collected in 1964.
* = Quantity zero or rounds to zero.
NA = Not available.
r = Revised, controlled to 1990 census based population estimates; previous 1993 data controlled to 1980 census based population estimates.
[1]Starting in 2003, respondents could identify more than one race. Except as noted, the race data in this table from 2003 onward represent those respondents who indicated only one race category.
[2]The data shown prior to 2003 consists of those identifying themselves as "Asian or Pacific Islanders."

Table A-11. Percentage of the Population 3 Years Old and Over Enrolled in School, by Age, Sex, Race, and Hispanic Origin, October 1947–2019—*Continued*

(Percent; civilian noninstitutionalized population.)

Year, sex, race, and Hispanic origin	Total enrolled 3 to 34 years old	Total enrolled 3 years old and over	Age											
			3 and 4	5 and 6	7 to 9	10 to 13	14 and 15	16 and 17	18 and 19	20 and 21	22 to 24	25 to 29	30 to 34	35 and over
2001	56.2	29.9	47.7	99.1	96.6	99.2	100.0	97.2	84.6	70.0	42.5	22.3	5.1	2.6
2000	56.0	30.4	55.9	98.6	96.2	98.2	100.0	99.1	82.0	65.1	41.7	20.6	7.5	2.9
1999	59.8	32.9	57.8	100.0	100.0	100.0	97.6	95.8	82.0	63.7	42.2	19.4	5.2	2.9
1998	59.0	33.2	55.0	95.6	97.8	97.7	95.6	94.4	91.5	73.6	46.6	21.2	6.5	3.0
1997	57.9	32.7	59.5	98.4	95.5	100.0	100.0	93.8	71.6	74.3	36.5	17.4	8.8	2.9
1996	54.9	32.0	49.5	97.9	98.8	99.0	95.5	95.0	75.4	80.8	42.2	13.5	6.1	3.7
1995	54.5	29.6	46.0	98.1	100.0	100.0	100.0	94.8	84.4	67.0	46.2	17.8	6.8	3.1
1994	57.3	30.6	39.0	97.4	100.0	99.4	100.0	97.7	81.9	64.2	49.3	16.9	6.7	3.2
1993	58.6	31.9	36.1	98.5	99.6	100.0	99.8	88.7	87.0	74.5	43.4	20.9	6.3	3.4
HISPANIC ORIGIN (OF ANY RACE)														
Both Sexes														
2019	55.7	31.6	49.8	93.3	96.8	97.5	97.4	90.7	63.7	48.1	26.5	10.2	5.4	1.5
2018	55.7	31.9	47.9	93.5	96.9	97.8	98.1	91.7	63.5	46.0	24.8	12.0	4.9	1.6
2017	56.4	32.6	47.9	95.0	97.0	97.3	98.4	92.7	67.2	46.0	25.9	12.3	4.8	1.8
2016	56.8	32.9	49.5	93.0	97.0	98.4	97.6	93.6	68.4	51.7	26.7	11.3	4.7	1.6
2015	55.8	32.7	44.1	93.7	97.9	97.1	96.7	92.6	65.2	48.8	25.2	11.2	4.6	1.7
2014	55.4	33.1	45.5	94.4	98.2	97.3	97.1	92.2	64.7	44.7	24.0	10.7	5.3	1.9
2013	55.5	33.4	45.4	93.9	98.4	97.7	98.3	93.9	59.3	43.9	26.7	10.4	5.7	2.0
2012	56.4	34.2	46.3	92.1	98.1	98.3	98.5	94.8	68.1	49.5	27.1	9.4	6.2	1.8
2011	55.6	34.0	41.6	95.6	98.2	98.5	98.2	94.6	65.2	45.7	23.6	10.5	4.5	1.6
2010	55.1	33.8	44.2	94.3	98.5	97.3	97.9	96.0	66.2	37.0	23.8	11.4	5.7	2.3
2009	52.8	32.3	41.9	93.7	96.5	98.0	97.9	92.6	57.1	37.2	20.4	9.5	5.6	2.2
2008	51.9	31.9	43.6	91.8	97.1	98.6	98.7	93.8	55.1	32.1	19.8	9.2	4.2	2.2
2007	51.7	32.1	48.2	94.3	96.3	99.0	98.4	90.6	57.2	32.3	18.8	8.3	4.5	2.1
2006	51.3	31.9	48.8	93.4	98.1	98.2	98.4	91.1	53.4	30.6	17.9	7.3	5.3	1.8
2005	50.9	32.1	43.0	93.8	97.4	97.9	97.3	92.6	54.3	30.0	19.5	7.8	4.2	2.0
2004	50.7	32.4	43.9	93.0	97.6	97.5	98.2	90.2	50.1	32.2	19.4	8.1	5.3	2.2
2003	49.6	31.6	43.7	91.6	97.5	98.3	96.7	92.1	50.5	33.7	16.1	6.2	4.6	1.8
2002	49.9	32.3	41.0	94.4	97.9	98.1	98.1	90.9	50.6	24.6	15.3	8.4	4.4	2.4
2001	49.5	32.4	39.7	93.6	97.4	98.3	97.8	88.2	45.5	27.9	15.5	7.7	4.4	2.5
2000	51.3	32.6	35.9	94.3	97.5	97.4	96.2	87.0	49.5	26.1	18.2	7.4	5.6	2.0
1999	51.1	32.9	36.9	93.9	99.0	98.3	97.6	88.1	44.5	22.6	15.0	9.1	5.6	2.3
1998	50.4	32.6	36.7	98.2	98.8	99.1	96.8	89.1	40.3	25.6	16.3	8.7	5.5	2.3
1997	50.8	32.7	36.6	96.6	98.6	99.6	98.4	91.1	49.4	28.9	16.4	7.3	3.7	1.8
1996	50.3	32.8	38.1	89.5	96.6	97.6	96.6	88.7	47.0	25.3	17.6	8.6	5.0	2.5
1995	49.7	32.9	36.9	93.9	98.5	99.2	98.9	88.2	46.1	27.1	15.6	7.1	4.7	2.7
1994	49.0	32.6	30.8	96.1	99.2	99.4	96.1	88.3	51.4	24.9	15.1	8.1	5.7	2.7
1993r	48.6	NA	26.8	93.6	99.6	99.2	97.6	88.1	50.0	31.8	13.8	7.7	5.1	NA
1993	48.9	31.6	26.8	93.8	99.6	99.2	97.6	88.3	50.0	31.8	13.7	7.7	5.1	1.9
1992	49.2	NA	28.8	96.0	99.5	99.1	98.8	87.2	53.7	30.1	14.5	6.7	6.0	NA
1991	47.9	NA	30.6	92.4	99.9	99.4	97.2	82.6	47.9	26.4	11.6	6.9	5.9	NA
1990	47.4	NA	29.8	94.8	99.6	99.2	99.0	85.4	44.1	27.2	9.9	6.3	3.1	NA
1989	45.8	NA	23.8	92.8	98.0	99.3	96.5	86.4	44.6	18.8	12.0	6.6	3.5	NA
1988	46.0	NA	24.5	95.7	99.6	99.8	98.8	78.8	44.1	16.7	12.1	5.8	6.2	NA
1987	47.2	NA	30.7	93.0	99.2	99.4	97.6	87.1	39.1	26.5	12.3	7.5	4.9	NA
1986	48.2	NA	28.8	93.7	99.4	99.3	97.2	84.0	46.0	21.4	13.7	9.2	5.6	NA
1985	47.7	NA	27.0	94.5	98.4	99.4	96.1	84.5	41.8	24.0	11.6	8.6	5.6	NA
1984	47.7	NA	24.2	93.9	98.7	99.4	94.9	85.7	39.9	28.1	11.3	6.6	7.5	NA
1983	49.3	NA	23.5	95.1	98.5	99.7	96.0	88.6	44.3	24.0	12.5	7.1	5.7	NA
1982	49.4	NA	21.8	92.2	98.7	98.8	96.9	85.5	39.2	22.7	10.4	8.2	4.4	NA
1981	49.0	NA	24.5	90.4	99.2	99.1	94.0	82.8	37.8	20.6	12.3	8.0	4.7	NA
1980	49.8	NA	28.5	94.5	98.4	99.7	94.3	81.8	37.8	19.5	11.7	6.9	4.1	NA
1979	48.6	NA	22.5	92.5	98.7	99.0	96.3	82.3	39.9	22.6	10.0	7.8	7.1	NA
1978	48.3	NA	22.5	91.4	99.5	98.0	95.2	83.0	35.7	16.8	11.8	8.0	4.1	NA
1977	50.8	NA	19.5	93.7	99.0	99.3	97.6	83.6	40.6	23.1	10.8	9.3	5.6	NA
1976	51.8	NA	22.2	95.0	97.5	99.1	95.4	81.3	45.2	24.0	14.8	7.9	2.7	NA
1975	54.8	NA	27.3	92.1	99.6	99.2	95.6	86.2	44.0	27.5	14.1	8.3	4.1	NA
1974	54.3	NA	25.3	92.1	98.8	99.2	96.1	78.3	45.2	23.2	11.3	6.7	2.2	NA
1973	52.8	NA	18.8	90.7	98.7	99.1	94.4	80.2	39.2	21.5	10.0	6.8	1.3	NA

Note: Data shown for 1947 to 1966 for the Black population are for Black and other races. Data for 1947 to 1963 exclude kindergarten. Nursery school was first collected in 1964.

* = Quantity zero or rounds to zero.

NA = Not available.

r = Revised, controlled to 1990 census based population estimates; previous 1993 data controlled to 1980 census based population estimates.

[1]Starting in 2003, respondents could identify more than one race. Except as noted, the race data in this table from 2003 onward represent those respondents who indicated only one race category.

[2]The data shown prior to 2003 consists of those identifying themselves as "Asian or Pacific Islanders."

Table A-11. Percentage of the Population 3 Years Old and Over Enrolled in School, by Age, Sex, Race, and Hispanic Origin, October 1947–2019—*Continued*

(Percent; civilian noninstitutionalized population.)

Year, sex, race, and Hispanic origin	Total enrolled 3 to 34 years old	Total enrolled 3 years old and over	Age											
			3 and 4	5 and 6	7 to 9	10 to 13	14 and 15	16 and 17	18 and 19	20 and 21	22 to 24	25 to 29	30 to 34	35 and over
1972	53.0	NA	20.5	90.0	98.7	99.1	96.7	83.9	41.4	17.0	9.9	5.2	3.5	NA
Male														
2019	54.7	31.5	51.8	93.5	98.4	96.6	96.9	90.7	63.5	44.8	21.8	8.9	3.4	1.3
2018	54.7	31.8	48.2	92.8	96.8	97.9	97.8	93.4	59.4	42.1	21.4	10.7	5.1	1.4
2017	55.0	32.1	47.1	94.6	97.5	97.4	98.2	91.7	63.3	40.9	23.0	9.9	5.0	1.4
2016	55.4	32.6	50.7	91.8	96.3	98.1	98.4	93.4	66.3	46.0	23.4	9.3	3.6	1.3
2015	54.4	32.4	44.3	93.6	97.5	97.3	96.0	91.7	59.9	44.4	24.2	9.2	3.3	1.6
2014	53.6	32.6	43.1	94.6	97.8	96.7	97.8	89.3	61.6	37.4	21.5	10.0	3.2	1.9
2013	54.0	33.1	44.2	93.6	98.6	97.7	97.9	93.5	55.4	38.0	24.4	10.8	3.9	1.6
2012	54.7	33.9	45.4	92.2	98.2	98.6	98.9	95.1	65.7	44.4	24.7	7.4	3.3	1.8
2011	54.1	33.9	43.6	95.9	98.8	98.8	98.7	94.6	61.0	43.1	21.0	9.9	3.4	1.6
2010	52.9	32.8	43.3	93.4	98.1	96.9	97.5	96.0	64.9	34.0	18.6	9.6	4.9	1.9
2009	50.9	31.3	39.4	94.1	96.2	98.8	98.1	92.5	51.8	32.1	18.6	7.8	5.2	1.6
2008	50.0	31.1	40.5	91.0	96.7	98.6	98.6	93.1	54.7	30.8	16.6	8.2	4.1	1.6
2007	49.4	31.1	50.7	94.1	96.4	99.0	97.8	91.1	55.2	24.6	14.4	6.7	3.1	1.8
2006	49.0	30.9	49.1	91.7	97.7	97.9	99.0	91.7	51.5	24.1	16.0	5.4	3.5	1.2
2005	48.4	31.0	43.0	92.4	96.0	97.2	97.8	92.5	51.8	25.2	17.5	5.6	2.6	1.6
2004	48.5	31.5	43.8	93.9	97.2	97.5	99.0	89.2	43.9	30.6	17.2	6.7	3.3	1.5
2003	47.3	30.8	42.9	91.3	97.5	98.4	96.7	90.4	47.0	27.2	13.3	4.9	3.8	1.3
2002	48.1	31.9	41.7	95.1	97.8	97.6	90.2	88.8	48.4	24.5	11.5	7.0	3.1	2.2
2001	48.4	32.2	42.9	94.9	97.9	98.6	98.4	87.8	40.0	24.4	14.6	6.5	3.5	2.2
2000	50.5	32.5	31.9	95.4	96.6	98.4	96.9	85.7	48.0	24.2	15.2	5.1	5.7	1.4
1999	50.3	32.9	33.5	92.8	98.8	98.5	98.1	87.9	45.3	21.5	11.2	8.6	3.9	2.0
1998	49.0	32.4	44.9	92.8	98.8	99.3	97.0	88.0	33.7	24.6	12.9	6.9	4.7	1.8
1997	49.0	32.3	35.5	97.7	97.7	99.8	99.5	92.5	45.4	27.6	14.0	5.9	2.7	1.6
1996	49.2	33.0	39.6	91.0	95.4	97.9	98.0	90.4	46.8	19.5	16.2	6.8	4.3	2.6
1995	49.1	33.1	40.8	93.6	98.8	98.8	98.4	88.4	47.4	24.8	14.8	5.6	4.5	2.1
1994	48.0	32.5	32.6	96.5	98.6	99.3	94.6	86.6	54.2	23.7	14.0	7.1	4.2	2.3
1993r	46.6	NA	26.9	93.4	99.8	98.8	96.9	88.7	47.8	31.6	13.0	5.5	5.4	NA
1993	47.4	31.5	27.0	93.6	99.8	98.8	96.9	89.1	47.7	31.6	12.8	5.5	5.4	1.5
1992	47.9	NA	24.9	96.5	100.0	99.2	98.1	89.2	52.6	24.3	13.8	5.3	3.5	NA
1991	46.4	NA	30.7	92.3	99.8	99.7	97.8	83.6	42.1	20.8	9.9	6.8	3.3	NA
1990	47.1	NA	27.3	95.6	99.5	99.0	99.1	85.5	40.7	21.7	11.2	4.6	4.0	NA
1989	45.8	NA	21.3	92.5	97.7	98.6	98.0	88.7	44.2	17.1	12.2	7.3	4.1	NA
1988	46.2	NA	27.9	96.7	99.2	100.0	98.1	80.9	44.7	21.6	12.5	4.5	5.0	NA
1987	47.8	NA	30.5	92.8	99.7	100.0	98.1	90.9	42.3	30.1	11.4	7.8	5.1	NA
1986	47.3	NA	29.4	93.0	100.0	99.4	96.8	85.0	45.8	19.2	13.0	9.1	4.4	NA
1985	47.5	NA	26.4	95.3	98.9	99.1	96.2	88.9	38.6	20.3	12.6	8.7	3.8	NA
1984	48.6	NA	20.0	93.6	98.2	100.0	95.7	85.1	38.8	27.5	12.3	8.2	4.0	NA
1983	50.7	NA	25.0	91.9	98.8	99.6	97.8	88.2	40.4	26.2	15.1	6.9	4.6	NA
1982	50.4	NA	25.2	90.3	99.6	98.4	96.8	87.8	39.7	21.6	11.2	10.8	3.1	NA
1981	49.6	NA	25.5	89.6	98.8	99.0	92.3	84.5	36.0	24.4	11.4	8.3	4.3	NA
1980	49.9	NA	30.1	94.0	97.7	99.4	96.7	81.5	36.9	21.4	10.7	6.8	6.2	NA
1979	51.0	NA	22.8	93.8	98.7	99.0	96.6	85.1	42.6	24.0	12.4	8.7	6.1	NA
1978	50.5	NA	22.6	93.2	99.1	97.8	94.0	80.4	40.0	18.1	13.6	9.5	4.4	NA
1977	54.2	NA	23.2	91.4	100.0	98.7	99.1	89.4	43.1	22.8	16.0	13.1	6.4	NA
1976	55.0	NA	22.1	94.6	97.4	98.5	97.3	85.5	46.3	27.1	18.6	11.4	5.6	NA
1975	58.1	NA	26.7	89.7	99.6	98.8	97.4	88.3	51.9	31.3	15.9	11.9	7.2	NA
1974	56.0	NA	23.5	93.1	98.3	98.5	97.9	78.6	46.8	22.3	14.5	8.4	7.4	NA
1973	55.5	NA	23.1	92.4	99.1	99.1	96.5	86.6	45.8	23.8	10.8	9.9	6.7	NA
1972	54.7	NA	20.4	90.3	98.8	99.1	98.1	87.8	40.5	20.0	13.9	5.8	2.5	NA
Female														
2019	56.8	31.7	47.6	93.1	95.1	98.3	97.9	90.7	63.9	51.6	31.2	11.6	7.4	1.7
2018	56.9	32.0	47.6	94.3	96.9	97.7	98.3	90.1	67.9	50.0	28.2	13.3	4.7	1.8
2017	57.8	33.0	48.8	95.5	96.5	97.3	98.6	93.6	71.1	50.7	29.2	14.7	4.6	2.2
2016	58.3	33.2	48.2	94.2	97.6	98.8	96.8	93.9	70.5	57.5	30.2	13.3	5.9	1.9
2015	55.7	32.9	44.0	93.9	98.4	96.9	97.4	93.7	70.1	53.2	26.3	13.2	5.9	1.8
2014	57.4	33.6	47.8	94.2	98.6	97.9	96.4	95.3	67.8	53.8	26.3	11.5	7.6	2.0
2013	57.0	33.7	46.7	94.1	98.2	97.7	98.8	94.3	63.2	50.6	29.1	10.0	7.6	2.3
2012	58.2	34.5	47.1	92.1	98.1	98.0	98.1	94.5	70.7	55.0	29.7	11.5	9.3	1.9

Note: Data shown for 1947 to 1966 for the Black population are for Black and other races. Data for 1947 to 1963 exclude kindergarten. Nursery school was first collected in 1964.
* = Quantity zero or rounds to zero.
NA = Not available.
r = Revised, controlled to 1990 census based population estimates; previous 1993 data controlled to 1980 census based population estimates.
[1]Starting in 2003, respondents could identify more than one race. Except as noted, the race data in this table from 2003 onward represent those respondents who indicated only one race category.
[2]The data shown prior to 2003 consists of those identifying themselves as "Asian or Pacific Islanders."

Table A-11. Percentage of the Population 3 Years Old and Over Enrolled in School, by Age, Sex, Race, and Hispanic Origin, October 1947–2019—*Continued*

(Percent; civilian noninstitutionalized population.)

Year, sex, race, and Hispanic origin	Total enrolled 3 to 34 years old	Total enrolled 3 years old and over	Age 3 and 4	5 and 6	7 to 9	10 to 13	14 and 15	16 and 17	18 and 19	20 and 21	22 to 24	25 to 29	30 to 34	35 and over
2011	57.2	34.1	39.6	95.3	97.6	98.2	97.6	94.6	70.3	48.8	26.6	11.2	5.8	1.6
2010	57.4	34.8	45.0	95.2	98.9	97.7	98.3	96.0	67.6	40.5	29.2	13.6	6.6	2.7
2009	55.0	33.3	44.4	93.2	96.7	97.2	97.6	92.6	62.5	43.1	22.2	11.6	6.0	2.8
2008	53.9	32.8	46.9	92.6	97.4	98.7	98.8	94.5	55.5	33.5	23.4	10.4	4.4	2.7
2007	54.3	33.1	45.6	94.5	96.2	99.0	99.1	90.0	59.2	41.0	23.7	10.3	6.1	2.3
2006	53.9	33.1	48.5	95.3	98.5	98.6	97.7	90.4	55.4	37.5	20.1	9.7	7.3	2.3
2005	58.0	33.3	43.0	95.3	98.8	98.6	96.7	92.6	57.2	35.3	21.8	10.4	6.1	2.4
2004	53.1	33.3	44.0	92.2	97.9	97.5	97.5	91.3	56.9	34.0	22.0	9.7	7.5	2.8
2003	52.2	32.5	44.7	92.0	97.5	98.2	96.8	93.8	54.4	41.1	19.4	7.9	5.6	2.2
2002	51.8	32.8	40.3	93.8	98.1	98.7	97.9	92.8	53.2	24.6	20.2	9.9	6.0	2.7
2001	50.6	32.6	36.3	92.4	96.9	98.1	97.2	88.7	51.1	31.6	16.7	9.1	5.3	2.8
2000	52.2	32.8	40.0	93.1	98.4	96.4	95.4	88.3	51.1	28.1	21.6	9.5	5.5	2.6
1999	52.1	32.8	40.5	95.0	99.3	98.0	96.9	88.3	43.6	23.6	19.2	9.5	7.3	2.7
1998	51.9	32.8	34.3	93.7	98.8	98.9	96.7	90.5	46.8	26.8	20.0	10.6	6.5	2.8
1997	52.7	33.0	37.7	95.7	99.6	99.5	97.3	89.6	53.9	30.4	19.2	8.8	4.9	2.0
1996	51.4	32.7	36.8	87.8	97.9	97.4	95.0	86.9	47.2	31.1	19.3	10.5	5.7	2.5
1995	50.3	32.7	32.7	94.3	98.2	99.6	99.4	88.0	44.8	29.2	16.6	8.7	4.9	3.2
1994	50.2	32.7	28.9	95.7	99.8	99.4	97.6	90.2	48.6	26.4	16.5	9.1	7.3	3.0
1993r	50.7	NA	26.7	93.9	99.4	99.6	98.2	87.3	51.9	31.9	14.7	10.2	4.7	NA
1993	50.6	31.6	26.7	93.9	99.4	99.6	98.2	87.4	51.9	32.0	14.5	10.2	4.8	2.2
1992	50.6	NA	32.7	95.4	99.0	99.1	99.6	85.0	54.9	35.6	15.4	8.2	6.0	NA
1991	49.5	NA	30.5	92.6	100.0	99.2	96.6	81.5	53.7	32.0	13.6	7.0	5.9	NA
1990	47.7	NA	32.3	93.9	99.7	99.4	98.8	85.3	47.2	33.1	8.4	8.1	3.1	NA
1989	45.9	NA	26.5	93.3	98.3	100.0	95.1	83.7	45.0	20.8	11.9	5.8	3.5	NA
1988	45.8	NA	20.7	94.6	100.0	99.6	99.6	76.6	43.5	11.2	11.5	7.2	6.2	NA
1987	46.5	NA	30.8	93.2	98.7	98.9	97.1	82.6	36.2	22.0	13.2	7.3	4.9	NA
1986	49.0	NA	28.2	94.4	98.7	99.2	97.5	83.0	46.2	23.7	14.5	9.2	5.6	NA
1985	47.9	NA	27.7	93.7	98.0	99.7	96.0	80.0	44.7	27.4	10.4	8.6	5.6	NA
1984	46.8	NA	28.2	94.2	99.2	98.7	94.0	86.3	40.8	28.7	10.4	4.9	7.5	NA
1983	48.0	NA	22.0	98.3	98.1	99.8	94.1	89.1	47.6	21.7	10.1	7.4	5.7	NA
1982	48.4	NA	16.3	93.9	97.8	99.2	97.1	82.8	38.7	23.7	9.7	5.7	4.4	NA
1981	48.4	NA	23.4	91.3	99.6	99.3	95.7	80.8	39.4	16.8	13.1	7.7	4.7	NA
1980	49.8	NA	26.6	94.9	99.0	99.9	92.1	82.2	38.8	17.6	12.6	6.9	4.1	NA
1979	46.3	NA	22.3	91.1	98.7	98.9	95.9	79.5	37.1	21.5	7.8	7.0	7.1	NA
1978	46.2	NA	22.5	89.4	100.0	98.2	96.6	86.2	31.9	15.7	10.1	6.5	4.1	NA
1977	47.6	NA	15.8	96.3	97.9	99.9	95.9	77.4	38.5	23.4	6.2	5.9	5.6	NA
1976	48.8	NA	22.3	95.5	97.6	99.7	93.6	77.6	44.2	21.4	12.1	4.8	2.7	NA
1975	51.7	NA	27.9	94.4	99.5	99.7	93.8	84.0	37.1	24.3	12.5	5.3	4.1	NA
1974	52.5	NA	27.4	91.1	99.2	100.0	94.1	77.9	43.7	23.9	8.4	4.9	2.2	NA
1973	50.1	NA	14.0	88.9	98.3	99.1	92.5	74.9	32.9	19.4	9.2	3.9	1.3	NA
1972	51.4	NA	20.5	89.7	98.5	99.0	95.4	80.0	42.4	14.6	6.8	4.7	3.5	NA
WHITE ALONE OR IN COMBINATION														
Both Sexes														
2019	54.0	23.4	53.1	94.0	97.7	97.9	97.8	92.9	67.4	53.0	27.3	9.8	5.3	1.2
2018	54.6	23.9	54.5	93.7	97.0	98.3	98.6	93.2	69.2	53.9	26.7	11.4	5.6	1.3
2017	54.5	23.9	53.2	93.7	97.0	97.6	98.4	93.3	68.1	54.6	26.8	11.5	5.6	1.3
2016	55.2	24.2	53.8	93.7	98.0	98.5	98.4	92.6	69.7	56.0	27.4	12.7	5.9	1.3
2015	55.2	24.4	52.1	94.2	97.6	97.9	97.9	94.0	68.5	53.4	27.7	12.7	6.1	1.4
2014	55.1	24.6	54.0	93.4	97.7	97.5	97.7	93.4	68.1	52.3	28.6	12.3	5.9	1.5
2013	55.5	25.0	54.4	93.9	98.2	98.2	98.5	93.7	67.0	52.3	29.1	12.2	6.3	1.6
2012	56.2	25.4	53.6	93.7	98.1	97.8	98.3	96.1	68.4	54.0	29.5	13.3	6.7	1.7
2011	56.5	25.9	51.6	95.6	98.2	98.6	98.7	95.7	70.2	53.7	30.8	14.1	7.0	1.7
2010	56.1	25.8	52.3	94.3	97.8	98.1	98.1	96.2	70.0	51.4	28.0	14.0	7.7	1.9
2009	56.0	25.7	51.3	94.2	98.0	98.7	98.1	94.6	68.4	52.5	28.8	13.0	7.4	1.9
2008	55.9	25.7	52.4	94.0	98.2	98.9	98.7	95.5	67.0	51.0	28.1	12.4	6.3	1.8
2007	55.7	25.7	54.0	94.8	98.0	98.7	98.7	94.6	67.1	49.7	26.2	16.2	9.4	1.8
2006	55.8	25.7	55.5	94.8	98.4	98.5	98.4	94.9	65.0	47.9	25.6	11.4	6.8	1.7
2005	56.2	26.1	53.9	95.3	98.6	98.7	98.3	95.3	67.7	49.3	26.2	11.3	6.2	1.8
2004	55.7	26.1	52.7	95.5	98.2	98.4	98.5	94.0	64.8	49.4	25.2	12.2	6.4	1.8

Note: Data shown for 1947 to 1966 for the Black population are for Black and other races. Data for 1947 to 1963 exclude kindergarten. Nursery school was first collected in 1964.

* = Quantity zero or rounds to zero.

NA = Not available.

r = Revised, controlled to 1990 census based population estimates; previous 1993 data controlled to 1980 census based population estimates.

[1]Starting in 2003, respondents could identify more than one race. Except as noted, the race data in this table from 2003 onward represent those respondents who indicated only one race category.

[2]The data shown prior to 2003 consists of those identifying themselves as "Asian or Pacific Islanders."

Table A-11. Percentage of the Population 3 Years Old and Over Enrolled in School, by Age, Sex, Race, and Hispanic Origin, October 1947–2019—*Continued*

(Percent; civilian noninstitutionalized population.)

Year, sex, race, and Hispanic origin	Total enrolled 3 to 34 years old	Total enrolled 3 years old and over	Age											
			3 and 4	5 and 6	7 to 9	10 to 13	14 and 15	16 and 17	18 and 19	20 and 21	22 to 24	25 to 29	30 to 34	35 and over
2003.............................	55.6	26.1	55.2	94.8	98.0	98.4	97.4	95.0	64.2	48.3	26.8	11.0	6.3	1.7
Male														
2019.............................	53.3	23.7	52.4	94.8	98.3	97.6	97.7	93.0	65.3	49.3	24.1	8.9	4.4	1.0
2018.............................	53.9	24.1	54.8	93.6	97.2	98.5	98.8	93.9	65.8	49.2	25.0	10.0	5.3	1.0
2017.............................	53.8	24.1	52.2	93.2	97.2	97.7	98.5	92.9	65.5	50.5	25.0	10.2	5.1	1.0
2016.............................	54.5	24.5	55.3	93.7	97.9	98.2	98.7	92.2	68.4	51.0	25.7	10.7	4.9	1.0
2015.............................	54.6	24.7	53.4	93.4	97.7	98.1	97.6	93.2	65.3	50.6	25.4	11.5	5.3	1.1
2014.............................	54.4	24.9	52.6	93.8	97.4	96.8	97.3	92.4	64.6	49.4	26.7	11.5	5.1	1.2
2013.............................	54.7	25.1	52.7	93.9	98.1	98.2	98.4	93.0	65.4	47.4	26.6	11.2	5.2	1.2
2012.............................	55.3	25.5	52.8	93.6	97.8	98.1	98.2	95.9	65.6	48.2	28.2	11.5	5.6	1.3
2011.............................	55.9	26.3	52.5	95.6	98.4	98.7	98.5	95.6	67.4	50.3	30.1	12.5	6.2	1.4
2010.............................	55.2	26.0	52.2	93.4	97.4	97.7	98.1	95.0	67.5	48.2	25.9	13.1	6.4	1.5
2009.............................	55.1	25.8	50.5	93.8	97.8	98.9	97.8	94.3	64.3	49.2	27.9	11.3	6.5	1.4
2008.............................	55.2	25.9	52.1	93.6	97.9	98.7	99.0	95.0	64.4	48.1	26.4	11.6	5.7	1.3
2007.............................	54.6	25.8	53.2	94.0	97.9	98.6	98.3	94.4	66.4	44.1	24.0	12.9	9.4	1.4
2006.............................	54.9	25.9	56.0	94.5	98.3	98.4	98.2	94.7	62.7	43.5	24.1	10.3	5.6	1.3
2005.............................	55.2	26.2	52.6	94.7	98.2	98.6	98.3	95.2	65.7	45.1	24.6	8.9	5.4	1.4
2004.............................	55.0	26.3	53.4	95.8	98.0	98.2	98.8	94.3	59.9	46.5	23.2	11.1	5.5	1.4
2003.............................	55.0	26.5	55.9	95.2	97.7	98.2	97.3	95.1	61.6	43.4	25.5	9.8	5.7	1.4
Female														
2019.............................	54.7	23.2	53.8	93.2	97.1	98.2	97.9	92.8	69.6	56.9	30.3	10.7	6.2	1.5
2018.............................	55.3	23.6	54.2	93.8	96.8	98.2	98.5	92.5	72.8	58.7	28.4	12.8	5.9	1.5
2017.............................	55.1	23.7	54.2	94.2	96.7	97.4	98.4	93.7	70.7	58.9	28.7	12.8	6.1	1.6
2016.............................	55.9	24.0	52.3	93.7	98.2	98.8	98.0	93.0	71.0	61.2	29.0	14.8	6.9	1.5
2015.............................	55.7	24.2	50.9	95.1	97.6	97.6	98.1	94.8	71.8	56.2	30.0	14.0	6.9	1.7
2014.............................	55.8	24.3	55.4	92.9	98.0	98.2	98.1	94.4	71.7	55.7	30.3	13.1	6.8	1.8
2013.............................	56.4	24.9	56.1	94.0	98.3	98.3	98.6	94.5	68.8	57.6	31.7	13.2	7.4	2.0
2012.............................	57.2	25.3	54.5	93.8	98.4	97.5	98.5	96.3	71.4	59.6	31.0	15.1	7.8	2.0
2011.............................	57.2	25.6	50.7	95.7	98.0	98.5	98.8	95.7	73.1	57.4	31.6	15.9	7.9	2.0
2010.............................	57.1	25.7	52.5	95.2	98.1	98.5	98.1	97.4	72.5	55.0	30.1	15.0	9.1	2.3
2009.............................	57.0	25.7	52.1	94.5	98.1	98.4	98.4	94.8	72.7	56.0	29.7	14.8	8.3	2.4
2008.............................	56.6	25.5	52.7	94.4	98.6	99.1	98.5	96.0	69.7	54.0	29.8	13.2	7.0	2.3
2007.............................	56.9	25.6	54.9	95.6	98.1	98.7	99.2	94.9	67.9	55.5	28.4	19.2	9.4	2.2
2006.............................	56.6	25.5	55.0	95.2	98.5	98.5	98.6	95.2	67.3	52.4	27.1	12.4	8.1	2.1
2005.............................	57.4	26.0	55.3	96.0	98.9	98.8	98.4	95.5	70.0	53.8	27.9	13.8	7.1	2.3
2004.............................	56.5	25.8	51.9	95.3	98.4	98.5	98.2	93.8	69.7	52.4	27.1	13.4	7.3	2.2
2003.............................	56.3	25.7	54.4	94.5	98.3	98.7	97.5	94.9	66.8	53.1	28.1	12.2	7.0	2.1
BLACK ALONE OR IN COMBINATION														
Both Sexes														
2019.............................	56.1	30.2	56.7	93.5	96.7	97.9	98.1	92.0	61.6	47.7	28.3	13.8	7.9	2.6
2018.............................	56.5	30.5	53.3	93.4	97.3	98.1	97.7	88.5	67.1	50.9	28.0	15.6	7.9	2.7
2017.............................	56.9	30.9	56.7	92.1	97.1	98.8	96.8	91.4	66.9	47.9	27.6	13.6	7.3	2.7
2016.............................	57.1	31.1	52.4	93.2	97.7	98.8	96.3	95.0	67.2	47.6	27.2	12.6	8.7	2.9
2015.............................	56.6	31.0	51.2	93.7	96.2	98.5	98.3	95	64.7	42.4	26.8	12.6	8.3	2.8
2014.............................	57.1	31.8	56.9	94.6	98.8	97.8	98.7	91.7	64.8	39.7	24.7	14.2	9.0	3.7
2013.............................	58.5	32.5	58.4	94.3	97.1	98.0	98.7	92.9	64.0	49.1	27.4	16.7	8.2	3.0
2012.............................	59.5	33.2	51.8	92.4	96.7	99.0	97.6	94.6	68.7	49.6	29.3	15.7	12.2	3.3
2011.............................	59.3	33.6	53.9	92.1	97.3	98.5	98.7	96.0	74.1	41.8	31.0	18.1	11.3	3.8
2010.............................	59.2	33.6	55.8	94.8	97.5	98.7	98.6	95.7	63.2	49.9	28.9	16.0	10.8	3.9
2009.............................	59.4	33.5	57.1	93.8	97.4	98.6	97.7	94.4	64.7	44.2	31.6	14.7	11.3	3.7
2008.............................	58.8	33.0	54.5	92.9	98.8	99.1	98.1	94.5	59.7	40.4	24.8	15.1	11.4	2.8
2007.............................	59.0	33.2	58.2	94.2	98.2	98.0	99.1	93.7	62.0	38.1	27.3	15.3	9.6	3.0
2006.............................	58.8	33.3	59.0	92.4	96.9	97.2	97.4	93.2	64.9	38.9	27.8	11.9	8.9	3.2
2005.............................	59.0	33.5	51.3	96.1	98.5	98.6	95.9	92.9	62.5	38.1	27.8	11.7	9.9	3.1
2004.............................	59.6	34.3	58.6	94.5	97.4	99.4	98.6	95.3	59.7	40.8	25.3	14.8	7.0	3.3
2003.............................	59.8	34.2	56.5	94.6	98.1	98.3	98.0	94.2	60.9	42.1	27.2	12.4	8.4	2.8

Note: Data shown for 1947 to 1966 for the Black population are for Black and other races. Data for 1947 to 1963 exclude kindergarten. Nursery school was first collected in 1964.
* = Quantity zero or rounds to zero.
NA = Not available.
r = Revised, controlled to 1990 census based population estimates; previous 1993 data controlled to 1980 census based population estimates.
[1]Starting in 2003, respondents could identify more than one race. Except as noted, the race data in this table from 2003 onward represent those respondents who indicated only one race category.
[2]The data shown prior to 2003 consists of those identifying themselves as "Asian or Pacific Islanders."

Table A-11. Percentage of the Population 3 Years Old and Over Enrolled in School, by Age, Sex, Race, and Hispanic Origin, October 1947–2019—*Continued*

(Percent; civilian noninstitutionalized population.)

Year, sex, race, and Hispanic origin	Total enrolled 3 to 34 years old	Total enrolled 3 years old and over	Age											
			3 and 4	5 and 6	7 to 9	10 to 13	14 and 15	16 and 17	18 and 19	20 and 21	22 to 24	25 to 29	30 to 34	35 and over
Male														
2019	56.5	31.6	57.3	93.7	98.2	98.1	98.9	91.3	61.6	48.5	22.9	12.1	5.6	2.1
2018	55.8	31.2	48.4	93.1	97.7	97.8	98.9	93.4	66.9	50.9	23.4	13.1	4.6	1.7
2017	56.3	31.8	58.3	91.2	96.0	98.8	95.9	90.7	62.8	41.4	23.8	12.1	6.0	2.2
2016	57.4	32.4	48.1	90.8	96.6	98.8	98.5	95.4	66.9	44.2	25.8	12.3	7.3	2.2
2015	57.2	32.2	50.6	92.4	96.5	99.3	99.1	95.2	64.6	39.4	29.3	9.7	4.6	1.8
2014	57.4	32.8	56.4	95.7	98.8	97.8	98.4	91.7	61.1	39.2	21.9	11.6	7.2	2.6
2013	58.5	33.5	55.4	94.6	97.0	97.8	98.6	95.0	59.4	44.6	26.2	13.7	4.9	2.4
2012	59.0	33.7	48.8	93.5	95.8	99.1	98.7	95.6	61.4	49.4	27.2	11.1	7.2	2.1
2011	59.0	34.5	52.8	92.8	97.5	98.6	97.9	94.5	71.6	38.9	30.0	14.1	7.7	2.7
2010	58.8	34.4	55.0	94.2	97.7	98.6	97.8	93.8	62.0	44.9	28.0	12.9	6.3	2.7
2009	58.9	34.0	57.4	93.8	97.2	98.3	95.9	95.6	60.4	42.3	25.7	11.5	8.1	2.2
2008	58.8	34.0	53.1	94.0	98.3	98.7	99.0	94.3	58.0	38.1	22.7	11.0	8.6	1.6
2007	60.1	35.0	60.5	93.9	98.1	97.5	99.2	95.2	61.5	37.8	27.8	10.7	9.7	2.0
2006	59.5	34.8	57.0	92.5	97.0	97.1	97.8	91.9	64.1	38.8	25.6	9.5	7.0	2.5
2005	59.2	34.6	52.5	95.1	97.5	97.9	93.8	93.8	66.2	34.9	23.9	9.3	6.1	2.3
2004	59.7	35.3	59.9	93.9	96.8	99.2	98.8	96.3	57.9	38.2	21.0	9.3	3.9	2.2
2003	60.6	35.7	57.6	93.2	98.8	98.2	98.3	93.8	61.1	35.6	23.4	9.4	7.2	1.9
Female														
2019	55.8	29.0	56.0	93.4	95.2	97.6	97.2	92.8	61.6	47.0	33.4	15.3	10.0	3.1
2018	57.1	29.9	58.0	93.8	97.0	98.4	96.4	83.6	67.4	50.9	32.5	18.0	11.0	3.5
2017	57.4	30.2	54.9	93.1	98.1	98.7	97.6	92.1	70.9	54.6	31.1	15.0	8.5	3.0
2016	56.8	29.9	56.6	95.6	98.9	98.8	93.9	94.6	67.6	51.1	28.5	12.8	9.9	3.4
2015	56.1	29.9	51.9	94.9	95.8	97.6	97.6	94.8	64.8	45.2	24.6	15.1	11.5	3.6
2014	56.8	31.0	57.4	93.6	98.9	97.9	99.1	91.6	68.4	40.1	27.5	16.4	10.5	4.5
2013	58.6	31.7	61.2	94.0	97.3	98.1	98.8	91.0	68.4	53.1	28.6	11.1	10.9	3.5
2012	59.9	32.7	54.7	91.3	97.7	99.0	96.5	93.7	76.4	49.7	31.2	19.6	16.3	4.3
2011	59.5	32.8	55.0	91.3	97.2	98.4	99.4	97.5	76.5	45.0	31.7	21.7	14.4	4.7
2010	59.6	33.0	56.7	95.4	97.2	98.8	99.4	97.6	64.3	54.2	29.7	18.7	14.5	4.9
2009	59.8	33.0	56.9	93.9	97.6	98.9	99.4	93.1	68.9	46.1	36.5	17.5	13.5	4.8
2008	58.8	32.1	55.7	91.7	99.4	99.5	97.2	94.7	61.3	42.5	26.6	18.6	13.8	3.8
2007	57.9	31.7	55.7	94.5	98.2	98.4	98.9	92.2	62.6	38.5	26.8	19.4	9.5	3.8
2006	58.2	32.0	60.9	92.3	96.9	97.4	97.0	94.6	65.6	39.0	29.8	14.0	10.5	3.6
2005	58.8	32.4	50.0	97.1	99.4	99.3	97.8	92.0	59.1	41.3	31.1	13.8	12.8	3.7
2004	59.6	33.4	57.0	95.0	98.1	99.6	98.4	94.2	61.3	43.1	29.3	19.3	9.5	4.2
2003	59.1	32.9	55.3	95.9	97.3	98.4	97.6	94.5	60.7	47.5	30.7	14.7	9.4	3.5
ASIAN ALONE OR IN COMBINATION														
Both Sexes														
2019	58.0	28.6	57.8	93.0	98.6	98.9	99.6	94.6	86.2	78.6	45.4	17.1	9.8	1.4
2018	56.5	28.1	51.8	91.7	98.0	97.6	100.0	91.8	80.9	74.3	43.0	19.2	8.7	1.5
2017	57.6	28.5	54.9	96.0	98.1	98.6	100.0	94.5	83.1	77.0	49.0	16.6	6.1	1.2
2016	57.0	28.6	63.2	90.7	98.1	98.8	98.2	94.0	78.4	73.7	46.7	20.6	6.4	1.4
2015	58.0	28.8	59.9	95.6	97.8	98.2	98.2	88.1	83.3	83.1	48.4	19.8	9.0	1.5
2014	57.4	29.4	54.2	89.3	97.0	97.7	96.3	93.8	85.9	73.7	53.9	19.5	5.6	2.0
2013	58.7	30.3	57.4	92.5	97.7	98.5	99.0	97.4	83.0	80.3	46.2	18.1	7.8	2.2
2012	59.1	30.1	56.7	93.9	99.9	98.6	99.0	97.8	79.4	72.8	52.2	18.5	8.4	1.8
2011	58.8	29.7	55.4	96.6	97.9	97.4	98.2	97.6	80.4	77.1	41.4	17.2	9.1	2.1
2010	60.5	30.6	62.4	96.7	98.9	98.4	98.0	96.1	81.9	76.9	46.5	21.3	10.1	1.8
2009	59.3	29.0	55.3	95.6	97.2	95.8	96.8	97.0	90.1	73.6	53.5	18.7	10.8	2.1
2008	59.2	29.5	57.4	92.6	98.3	99.6	98.8	93.5	85.9	79.4	43.0	23.0	11.9	2.5
2007	57.0	28.8	54.1	93.9	98.4	99.3	99.7	93.4	86.3	64.3	45.9	19.6	9.5	1.8
2006	56.3	29.0	51.5	94.6	99.0	99.3	99.6	92.0	82.3	72.2	43.1	17.3	8.8	2.2
2005	57.6	30.5	54.4	95.5	99.6	97.5	98.7	98.2	86.2	77.1	44.4	20.9	9.4	2.3
2004	58.5	31.4	57.7	97.6	99.9	99.2	98.0	97.1	79.9	77.7	46.2	20.8	9.3	2.7
2003	58.2	31.3	51.4	89.3	99.2	99.4	99.1	95.7	87.1	77.0	48.1	21.6	9.4	2.2

Note: Data shown for 1947 to 1966 for the Black population are for Black and other races. Data for 1947 to 1963 exclude kindergarten. Nursery school was first collected in 1964.

* = Quantity zero or rounds to zero.

NA = Not available.

r = Revised, controlled to 1990 census based population estimates; previous 1993 data controlled to 1980 census based population estimates.

¹Starting in 2003, respondents could identify more than one race. Except as noted, the race data in this table from 2003 onward represent those respondents who indicated only one race category.

²The data shown prior to 2003 consists of those identifying themselves as "Asian or Pacific Islanders."

Table A-11. Percentage of the Population 3 Years Old and Over Enrolled in School, by Age, Sex, Race, and Hispanic Origin, October 1947–2019—*Continued*

(Percent; civilian noninstitutionalized population.)

Year, sex, race, and Hispanic origin	Total enrolled 3 to 34 years old	Total enrolled 3 years old and over	Age											
			3 and 4	5 and 6	7 to 9	10 to 13	14 and 15	16 and 17	18 and 19	20 and 21	22 to 24	25 to 29	30 to 34	35 and over
Male														
2019	58.4	30.0	58.7	96.3	98.4	99.6	100.0	96.1	88.8	79.9	45.4	17.9	9.0	1.5
2018	56.2	29.1	51.0	92.9	96.3	95.5	100.0	95.6	76.6	73.3	45.5	19.0	7.3	1.4
2017	58.2	29.8	53.7	94.7	98.3	98.2	100.0	94.7	80.0	76.0	53.0	15.6	5.6	1.0
2016	58.7	30.6	60.1	87.5	98.2	98.9	99.0	91.1	76.3	76.9	52.1	21.4	7.2	1.6
2015	58.5	29.8	65.2	96.6	98.0	98.6	97.9	87.5	81.4	82.3	44.7	19.8	8.4	1.1
2014	59.0	31.1	55.3	92.0	98.3	97.7	95.6	94.0	85.2	71.3	59.2	21.6	4.1	1.9
2013	59.6	31.3	57.8	94.1	98.2	98.3	98.3	96.1	82.4	84.2	47.9	20.4	5.6	1.6
2012	59.5	31.2	57.8	94.2	99.8	98.3	98.0	97.8	82.3	72.6	49.4	19.6	6.3	1.5
2011	59.4	30.7	55.9	97.4	97.3	98.6	98.6	96.9	83.3	79.5	39.1	17.0	9.5	1.4
2010	61.5	32.2	63.1	97.9	99.0	98.0	97.6	96.5	78.1	80.7	43.1	23.5	10.3	1.7
2009	59.5	30.5	54.9	95.3	96.6	95.3	97.8	96.1	91.4	74.3	51.5	17.9	9.7	2.3
2008	59.4	30.2	56.1	92.8	97.3	99.2	100.0	96.4	89.7	74.2	39.0	24.5	11.3	2.0
2007	58.6	30.4	58.9	95.4	99.1	99.1	99.7	93.5	90.6	62.7	47.0	19.5	9.8	2.1
2006	57.0	30.2	60.4	94.7	98.2	98.6	99.0	90.1	78.1	74.6	43.0	14.9	8.5	2.4
2005	58.3	31.7	51.1	97.4	99.7	96.5	98.0	97.3	83.6	82.1	42.2	20.2	9.9	2.0
2004	60.8	33.9	57.2	96.5	99.8	99.9	97.1	96.9	83.5	83.6	49.6	23.0	10.9	2.9
2003	60.2	33.4	49.3	91.9	98.2	99.9	98.2	95.9	89.6	74.0	47.3	27.9	12.1	2.4
Female														
2019	57.6	27.2	56.7	90.2	98.9	98.2	99.2	93.3	83.9	77.4	45.4	16.3	10.6	1.2
2018	56.9	27.2	52.6	90.6	99.8	99.7	100.0	88.8	85.5	75.3	40.4	19.4	9.9	1.5
2017	56.9	27.3	56.1	97.2	98.0	98.9	100.0	94.4	86.4	78.0	44.8	17.5	6.6	1.4
2016	55.3	26.8	66.4	94.0	98.0	98.6	96.7	80.4	70.6	40.4	40.4	15.8	5.8	1.2
2015	57.4	28.0	54.4	94.4	97.5	97.8	98.5	88.7	85.2	83.8	52.5	19.8	9.6	1.9
2014	55.8	27.9	53.2	86.4	95.6	97.8	97.1	93.6	86.5	76.2	48.6	17.6	7.0	2.0
2013	57.8	29.4	57.0	90.5	97.2	98.7	99.7	98.4	83.6	76.0	44.4	15.8	9.6	2.7
2012	58.7	29.2	55.5	93.7	100.0	98.8	100.0	97.9	76.3	72.9	55.3	17.5	10.2	2.1
2011	58.3	28.7	54.9	95.7	98.5	96.2	97.9	98.3	77.1	74.8	44.0	17.4	8.7	2.6
2010	59.4	29.1	61.7	95.5	98.7	98.9	98.4	95.7	86.2	73.1	50.0	19.1	9.9	2.0
2009	59.2	27.7	55.8	95.9	97.8	96.3	95.2	98.1	88.8	73.0	55.6	19.5	11.9	1.9
2008	58.9	28.8	59.1	92.3	99.2	100.0	97.5	90.8	82.4	85.7	46.8	21.7	12.5	2.9
2007	55.5	27.4	48.3	92.5	97.6	99.5	99.7	93.2	82.2	66.1	45.0	19.7	9.2	1.5
2006	55.7	27.9	41.4	94.5	100.0	99.6	99.1	93.6	87.8	69.4	43.2	19.4	9.0	2.1
2005	57.0	29.3	57.5	93.2	99.5	98.5	99.7	99.1	89.2	71.2	46.2	21.6	8.9	2.5
2004	56.1	29.0	58.4	99.2	99.9	98.5	98.9	97.2	76.3	71.5	42.9	18.8	7.8	2.5
2003	56.2	29.3	54.2	86.0	100.0	98.7	100.0	95.4	85.1	79.7	48.8	15.8	6.9	2.1

Note: Data shown for 1947 to 1966 for the Black population are for Black and other races. Data for 1947 to 1963 exclude kindergarten. Nursery school was first collected in 1964.

* = Quantity zero or rounds to zero.

NA = Not available.

r = Revised, controlled to 1990 census based population estimates; previous 1993 data controlled to 1980 census based population estimates.

[1]Starting in 2003, respondents could identify more than one race. Except as noted, the race data in this table from 2003 onward represent those respondents who indicated only one race category.

[2]The data shown prior to 2003 consists of those identifying themselves as "Asian or Pacific Islanders."

Table A-12. Population 6 to 17 Years Old Enrolled Below Modal Grade, 1971–2019

(Numbers in thousands; percent; civilian noninstitutionalized population.)

Year, sex, race, and Hispanic origin	Percent below modal grade				Dropout rate, 15 to 17 years	Population in age group			
	6 to 8 years	9 to 11 years	12 to 14 years	15 to 17 years		6 to 8 years	9 to 11 years	12 to 14 years	15 to 17 years
ALL RACES									
Both Sexes									
2019	25.1	29.9	29.9	31.4	4.2	11,998	12,378	12,551	12,551
2018	25.5	30.0	29.4	33.1	4.4	12,231	12,353	12,474	12,547
2017	24.7	30.2	30.1	33.6	3.6	12,196	12,463	12,363	12,687
2016	24.6	30.0	30.1	31.9	3.8	12,152	12,497	12,326	12,663
2015	24.0	29.7	31.0	32.0	3.2	12,182	12,520	12,361	12,663
2014	23.3	28.6	30.8	32.7	4.1	12,320	12,286	12,433	12,502
2013	23.0	26.5	31.1	32.9	3.7	12,405	12,246	12,448	12,422
2012	24.0	28.2	30.7	34.5	2.4	12,185	12,236	12,435	12,554
2011	22.8	28.8	29.8	32.5	2.3	12,643	12,408	11,834	12,282
2010	18.8	25.1	29.1	29.8	2.2	12,618	12,190	11,963	12,273
2009	19.4	26.8	30.1	30.8	3.0	12,305	11,819	12,030	12,391
2008	20.2	27.3	31.3	31.7	2.7	12,104	11,793	12,128	12,746
2007	20.1	26.2	27.9	30.0	2.9	12,011	11,805	12,398	12,857
2006	20.1	26.1	27.9	30.5	3.0	11,776	11,902	12,473	12,926
2005	20.7	25.4	28.3	30.6	2.8	11,784	11,998	12,689	13,204
2004	21.7	25.4	28.2	32.0	3.5	11,799	12,034	12,870	12,766
2003	21.3	28.1	28.8	30.6	3.2	11,866	12,124	12,951	12,753
2002	18.0	25.5	27.1	30.1	3.3	12,029	12,421	12,592	12,187
2001	18.6	23.7	25.9	29.7	3.8	11,972	12,738	12,357	12,031
2000	19.2	24.0	27.8	30.2	4.3	12,079	12,713	12,003	11,933
1999	17.4	25.3	26.5	30.8	4.0	12,159	12,537	11,921	12,048
1998	19.0	23.8	26.7	31.9	3.8	12,364	12,098	11,739	11,850
1997	18.6	24.2	28.5	32.1	3.6	12,325	11,866	11,650	11,953
1996	17.9	23.3	28.8	31.0	4.8	12,191	11,845	11,653	11,617
1995	17.5	25.6	30.8	32.8	4.1	11,728	11,812	11,582	11,401
1994	18.9	26.2	31.3	30.9	3.8	11,601	11,528	11,462	10,560
1993r	18.7	28.1	31.0	32.3	3.8	11,363	11,283	10,981	10,247
1993	18.7	28.0	30.8	32.0	3.7	11,363	11,283	10,981	10,247
1992	19.4	28.4	30.9	30.5	3.6	11,260	11,183	10,723	10,114
1991	21.2	26.9	29.6	30.0	4.6	11,120	11,099	10,440	9,923
1990	21.5	27.6	31.0	30.1	4.7	11,015	10,914	10,152	9,912
1989	21.4	29.0	31.8	28.0	4.5	11,007	10,673	9,928	10,020
1988	20.4	28.4	28.7	26.2	5.1	10,906	10,350	9,869	10,379
1987	20.9	26.7	27.6	24.8	5.1	10,702	10,053	9,795	10,944
1986	19.2	26.5	27.3	25.8	4.9	10,389	9,959	9,908	11,149
1985	17.9	24.9	25.7	25.5	5.1	10,076	9,673	10,442	11,024
1984	16.6	23.9	27.0	24.6	5.3	9,707	9,594	10,858	10,711
1983	15.4	24.4	24.8	23.7	5.2	9,605	9,730	11,123	10,768
1982	16.6	22.8	23.9	23.0	5.4	9,492	10,169	10,989	11,131
1981	14.4	23.3	23.0	23.8	6.1	9,519	10,657	10,712	11,757
1980	14.3	20.3	22.6	22.5	6.6	9,350	10,681	10,537	11,835
1979	13.0	20.2	20.3	21.6	6.5	9,804	10,545	10,886	12,190
1978	12.4	19.5	19.2	21.8	6.5	10,246	10,448	11,391	12,346
1977	10.7	18.9	18.9	21.2	6.4	10,449	10,537	11,826	12,472
1976	10.6	18.1	19.8	22.2	6.3	10,334	10,872	12,137	12,550
1975	11.1	17.4	21.3	22.5	6.4	10,256	11,343	12,372	12,531
1974	10.3	17.8	21.7	21.6	7.1	10,343	11,789	12,415	12,566
1973	10.7	18.4	21.5	21.3	7.1	10,614	11,946	12,542	12,309
1972	10.7	19.6	21.9	22.3	6.6	11,119	12,152	12,451	12,283
1971	11.1	19.7	22.0	22.5	5.7	11,938	12,648	12,429	11,906
Male									
2019	25.4	30.3	30.9	34.1	3.9	6,117	6,290	6,398	6,388
2018	27.7	31.7	31.6	36.8	3.6	6,288	6,277	6,335	6,396
2017	25.6	31.7	32.4	36.8	4.1	6,244	6,341	6,295	6,460
2016	26.0	31.3	33.5	35.4	4.1	6,197	6,358	6,296	6,413
2015	24.8	31.0	31.5	35.6	3.3	6,201	6,398	6,302	6,464
2014	24.7	30.3	33.3	35.6	4.7	6,269	6,316	6,346	6,375
2013	24.3	30.0	34.0	37.0	3.9	6,264	6,272	6,347	6,328
2012	26.4	31.1	34.9	38.5	2.6	6,252	6,251	6,347	6,423
2011	25.2	32.2	32.7	37.1	2.4	6,478	6,326	6,067	6,256
2010	20.7	28.1	31.3	32.9	2.9	6,451	6,213	6,104	6,300
2009	20.5	30.2	33.0	34.8	3.2	6,260	6,058	6,144	6,334
2008	22.5	28.9	34.4	34.6	2.8	6,174	6,005	6,220	6,502
2007	23.0	28.1	29.8	33.7	2.9	6,159	6,031	6,310	6,572

* = Quantity zero or rounds to zero.
r = Revised, controlled to 1990 census based population estimates; previous 1993 data controlled to 1980 census based population estimates.
[1]Starting in 2003, respondents could identify more than one race. Except as noted, the race data in this table from 2003 onward represent those respondents who indicated only one race category.
[2]The data shown prior to 2003 consists of those identifying themselves as "Asian or Pacific Islanders."

Table A-12. Population 6 to 17 Years Old Enrolled Below Modal Grade, 1971–2019—*Continued*

(Numbers in thousands; percent; civilian noninstitutionalized population.)

Year, sex, race, and Hispanic origin	Percent below modal grade				Dropout rate, 15 to 17 years	Population in age group			
	6 to 8 years	9 to 11 years	12 to 14 years	15 to 17 years		6 to 8 years	9 to 11 years	12 to 14 years	15 to 17 years
2006............................	21.7	28.2	31.1	35.0	3.3	5,991	6,115	6,374	6,574
2005............................	23.2	28.6	30.7	34.3	3.0	6,014	6,126	6,523	6,645
2004............................	23.9	28.2	31.7	36.8	3.5	6,075	6,120	6,685	6,395
2003............................	23.9	32.0	31.8	35.1	3.4	6,198	6,331	6,426	6,569
2002............................	20.3	29.2	31.0	35.6	3.5	6,156	6,349	6,436	6,210
2001............................	22.1	26.1	28.7	34.0	4.3	6,147	6,540	6,311	6,182
2000............................	22.1	27.2	31.3	34.3	4.5	6,181	6,504	6,148	6,136
1999............................	18.8	28.9	30.2	36.2	3.9	6,211	6,471	6,048	6,195
1998............................	21.4	26.6	30.4	37.4	4.1	6,341	6,206	5,971	6,082
1997............................	21.9	27.7	33.4	37.8	3.7	6,295	6,112	5,932	6,126
1996............................	20.7	26.0	33.9	36.9	4.5	6,268	6,043	5,934	5,985
1995............................	20.2	28.0	35.2	38.5	3.5	5,999	6,027	5,930	5,840
1994............................	21.1	28.0	35.6	35.7	3.9	5,894	6,026	5,874	5,640
1993r..........................	21.2	32.1	35.4	40.3	3.3	5,837	5,736	5,629	5,262
1993............................	21.1	32.0	35.0	38.7	3.1	5,837	5,736	5,629	5,262
1992............................	21.6	32.6	37.0	35.2	2.7	5,738	5,742	5,502	5,166
1991............................	24.0	30.7	34.7	35.5	4.3	5,674	5,704	5,343	5,085
1990............................	23.9	32.0	36.2	35.3	4.6	5,629	5,603	5,200	5,078
1989............................	25.1	32.9	36.7	33.4	4.3	5,632	5,472	5,088	5,151
1988............................	23.5	33.2	33.7	30.6	4.8	5,580	5,298	5,065	5,286
1987............................	23.7	31.8	31.8	29.2	4.6	5,496	5,147	5,036	5,535
1986............................	22.9	30.4	32.2	30.2	4.9	5,311	5,113	5,066	5,697
1985............................	20.6	28.3	29.0	30.2	4.9	5,159	4,946	5,340	5,623
1984............................	18.8	27.7	31.1	30.2	5.5	4,963	4,905	5,521	5,469
1983............................	17.8	28.7	30.3	28.5	5.3	4,913	4,974	5,690	5,463
1982............................	19.2	26.4	28.0	27.9	5.2	4,852	5,198	5,566	5,688
1981............................	17.2	27.9	25.6	28.1	6.2	4,866	5,447	5,510	5,914
1980............................	16.4	23.4	27.3	26.8	6.4	4,774	5,453	5,282	6,067
1979............................	15.5	23.4	24.1	27.4	5.9	5,004	5,379	5,555	6,174
1978............................	14.7	22.9	22.9	26.2	6.7	5,227	5,326	5,797	6,265
1977............................	12.5	22.4	22.6	25.3	6.1	5,327	5,371	6,044	6,297
1976............................	12.5	20.9	23.4	27.5	5.7	5,265	5,540	6,185	6,356
1975............................	12.6	21.2	25.8	26.8	5.7	5,223	5,782	6,336	6,309
1974............................	12.2	21.2	25.9	26.3	7.0	5,267	6,011	6,329	6,352
1973............................	12.8	20.8	25.2	26.4	6.8	5,403	6,082	6,397	6,215
1972............................	12.5	23.3	26.8	26.8	6.2	5,662	6,188	6,322	6,232
1971............................	13.5	22.8	26.1	27.2	5.0	6,088	6,440	6,293	6,019
Female									
2019............................	24.8	29.5	28.9	28.6	4.4	5,880	6,088	6,153	6,163
2018............................	23.2	28.4	27.1	29.1	5.2	5,943	6,076	6,139	6,150
2017............................	23.7	28.8	27.8	30.3	3.1	5,952	6,122	6,068	6,227
2016............................	23.2	28.7	26.5	28.3	3.5	5,955	6,140	6,030	6,250
2015............................	23.1	28.3	30.6	28.3	3.0	5,981	6,123	6,060	6,199
2014............................	21.8	26.9	28.1	29.8	3.4	6,050	5,970	6,087	6,126
2013............................	21.6	22.8	28.0	28.7	3.4	6,141	5,974	6,100	6,095
2012............................	21.5	25.2	26.4	30.3	2.1	5,933	5,985	6,087	6,132
2011............................	20.4	25.2	26.8	27.8	2.1	6,165	6,082	5,767	6,026
2010............................	16.8	22.1	26.9	26.6	1.5	6,166	5,977	5,860	5,973
2009............................	18.2	23.2	27.2	26.7	2.8	6,046	5,761	5,886	6,057
2008............................	17.9	25.8	28.1	28.7	2.7	5,930	5,787	5,908	6,244
2007............................	17.2	24.1	25.9	26.2	2.9	5,852	5,773	6,088	6,285
2006............................	18.4	23.9	24.6	25.9	2.6	5,785	5,787	6,099	6,352
2005............................	18.2	22.0	25.8	26.8	2.6	5,769	5,872	6,167	6,559
2004............................	19.4	22.5	24.4	27.1	3.5	5,724	5,914	6,185	6,371
2003............................	18.5	23.8	25.8	25.8	3.0	5,668	5,793	6,524	6,184
2002............................	15.6	21.7	23.0	24.4	3.1	5,872	6,072	6,156	5,977
2001............................	14.9	21.3	23.0	25.2	3.3	5,825	6,197	6,046	5,849
2000............................	16.1	20.6	24.2	25.8	4.2	5,897	6,209	5,855	5,797
1999............................	16.1	21.6	22.7	25.1	4.2	5,948	6,066	5,872	5,852
1998............................	16.5	20.9	22.8	26.2	3.5	6,023	5,892	5,768	5,768
1997............................	15.1	20.4	23.3	26.1	3.5	6,030	5,754	5,718	5,827
1996............................	14.9	20.4	23.4	24.7	5.3	5,923	5,802	5,719	5,632
1995............................	14.6	23.1	26.0	26.7	4.4	5,728	5,786	5,653	5,552
1994............................	16.5	24.2	26.7	24.8	3.6	5,705	5,644	5,666	5,384
1993r..........................	16.3	24.0	26.4	26.4	4.4	5,526	5,545	5,353	4,984
1993............................	16.1	23.9	26.2	24.9	4.3	5,526	5,545	5,353	4,984
1992............................	17.1	23.5	24.6	25.6	4.5	5,523	5,441	5,220	4,947

* = Quantity zero or rounds to zero.
r = Revised, controlled to 1990 census based population estimates; previous 1993 data controlled to 1980 census based population estimates.
[1]Starting in 2003, respondents could identify more than one race. Except as noted, the race data in this table from 2003 onward represent those respondents who indicated only one race category.
[2]The data shown prior to 2003 consists of those identifying themselves as "Asian or Pacific Islanders."

Table A-12. Population 6 to 17 Years Old Enrolled Below Modal Grade, 1971–2019—*Continued*

(Numbers in thousands; percent; civilian noninstitutionalized population.)

Year, sex, race, and Hispanic origin	Percent below modal grade				Dropout rate, 15 to 17 years	Population in age group			
	6 to 8 years	9 to 11 years	12 to 14 years	15 to 17 years		6 to 8 years	9 to 11 years	12 to 14 years	15 to 17 years
1991	18.2	22.8	24.6	24.2	5.1	5,445	5,395	5,098	4,838
1990	19.1	23.2	25.7	24.7	4.7	5,387	5,312	4,951	4,834
1989	18.1	22.6	26.6	22.3	4.6	5,375	5,201	4,840	4,869
1988	17.3	23.6	23.4	21.7	5.4	5,327	5,052	4,803	5,093
1987	17.8	21.5	23.2	20.2	5.6	5,206	4,906	4,759	5,408
1986	15.2	22.4	22.1	21.1	4.9	5,078	4,846	4,842	5,452
1985	15.1	21.4	22.1	20.6	5.5	4,917	4,727	5,102	5,401
1984	14.2	19.8	22.9	18.7	5.1	4,744	4,689	5,337	5,242
1983	12.9	19.9	19.1	18.6	5.2	4,692	4,756	5,433	5,305
1982	13.8	19.0	19.7	17.9	5.7	4,640	4,971	5,423	5,443
1981	11.6	18.4	20.1	19.6	6.1	4,653	5,210	5,202	5,843
1980	12.1	17.0	17.8	18.0	6.7	4,576	5,228	5,255	5,768
1979	10.4	16.9	16.4	15.6	7.1	4,800	5,166	5,331	6,016
1978	10.1	16.0	15.3	17.2	6.4	5,019	5,122	5,594	6,081
1977	8.9	15.2	15.0	17.1	6.6	5,122	5,166	5,782	6,175
1976	8.6	15.1	16.0	16.8	7.0	5,069	5,332	5,952	6,194
1975	9.4	13.5	16.7	18.2	7.2	5,033	5,561	6,036	6,222
1974	8.3	14.4	17.4	16.8	7.1	5,076	5,778	6,086	6,214
1973	8.7	15.8	16.5	16.1	7.4	5,211	5,864	6,145	6,094
1972	8.9	15.7	17.0	17.7	7.1	5,457	5,964	6,129	6,051
1971	8.7	12.3	17.8	17.6	6.5	5,850	6,208	6,136	5,887
WHITE ALONE									
Both Sexes									
2019	25.9	30.6	29.6	31.3	4.2	8,673	8,834	9,111	9,115
2018	25.1	30.1	30.0	32.6	3.8	8,723	8,925	9,095	9,147
2017	25.4	30.0	30.3	33.3	3.6	8,720	9,036	9,077	9,210
2016	25.2	30.1	30.6	32.2	4.1	8,772	9,060	9,073	9,267
2015	24.5	30.0	31.4	32.0	3.2	8,865	9,038	9,095	9,271
2014	24.0	28.3	29.9	31.9	3.9	8,983	9,035	9,181	9,220
2013	23.2	27.1	31.8	33.3	3.7	9,014	9,034	9,236	9,228
2012	24.4	28.3	31.3	33.7	2.4	9,006	9,067	9,247	9,291
2011	23.6	28.7	30.6	32.5	2.2	9,488	9,401	9,020	9,337
2010	19.7	25.3	28.8	29.4	2.3	9,455	9,276	9,110	9,344
2009	19.6	26.7	29.4	29.9	3.3	9,377	9,006	9,167	9,495
2008	20.8	27.5	29.7	30.8	2.6	9,288	8,967	9,250	9,658
2007	21.3	26.2	27.6	28.3	2.8	9,118	9,021	9,432	9,834
2006	20.6	25.5	26.8	29.9	3.0	8,981	9,074	9,542	9,813
2005	21.4	23.8	28.0	29.5	2.6	8,929	9,194	9,680	10,131
2004	22.4	25.6	27.6	30.7	3.8	9,051	9,173	9,853	9,784
2003[1]	21.5	27.6	28.3	29.4	3.2	9,102	9,112	9,875	9,889
2002	18.1	25.7	26.2	29.6	3.1	9,230	9,682	9,832	9,520
2001	19.2	22.7	25.2	28.9	3.8	9,330	9,826	9,651	9,480
2000	19.4	23.7	26.3	29.7	4.5	9,404	9,937	9,368	9,449
1999	18.3	24.6	25.8	30.0	4.2	9,539	9,768	9,323	9,428
1998	19.5	23.5	25.8	30.5	3.8	9,624	9,508	9,219	9,341
1997	18.8	24.0	27.9	30.3	3.5	9,555	9,390	9,167	9,352
1996	18.1	22.6	27.6	30.1	4.9	9,458	9,420	9,184	9,135
1995	17.7	24.9	29.2	31.0	3.9	9,221	9,340	9,130	8,933
1994	19.4	25.8	30.1	29.6	3.7	9,087	9,261	9,121	8,668
1993r	18.8	27.3	29.4	31.2	3.9	9,018	8,967	8,728	8,160
1993	18.7	27.2	29.2	29.7	3.6	9,074	9,017	8,783	8,159
1992	19.5	27.5	29.6	28.1	3.5	8,956	8,996	8,520	8,031
1991	21.3	25.7	27.7	27.2	4.7	8,874	8,840	8,328	7,903
1990	21.9	26.8	28.4	27.3	4.6	8,860	8,752	8,140	7,909
1989	22.4	26.8	29.9	25.7	4.6	8,858	8,527	7,994	8,026
1988	21.0	27.6	27.2	23.9	5.4	8,758	8,323	7,929	8,353
1987	21.1	25.9	26.0	22.7	5.1	8,606	8,117	7,846	8,887
1986	19.1	25.1	25.3	23.7	5.0	8,395	8,000	8,054	9,037
1985	18.0	23.3	23.3	23.0	5.3	8,136	7,840	8,429	9,045
1984	16.3	22.1	24.7	22.7	5.6	7,915	7,781	8,827	8,853
1983	15.5	22.4	23.1	21.1	5.4	7,821	7,906	9,152	8,831
1982	16.4	21.8	22.1	21.1	5.6	7,729	8,294	9,035	9,184
1981	14.7	22.2	21.0	21.6	6.1	7,782	8,741	8,813	9,762
1980	14.1	19.0	21.1	19.3	6.7	7,635	8,823	8,739	10,132
1979	12.9	18.4	18.5	19.4	6.5	8,041	8,747	9,026	10,239
1978	12.4	18.0	17.9	19.3	6.8	8,460	8,686	9,522	10,358

* = Quantity zero or rounds to zero.
r = Revised, controlled to 1990 census based population estimates; previous 1993 data controlled to 1980 census based population estimates.
[1]Starting in 2003, respondents could identify more than one race. Except as noted, the race data in this table from 2003 onward represent those respondents who indicated only one race category.
[2]The data shown prior to 2003 consists of those identifying themselves as "Asian or Pacific Islanders."

Table A-12. Population 6 to 17 Years Old Enrolled Below Modal Grade, 1971–2019—*Continued*

(Numbers in thousands; percent; civilian noninstitutionalized population.)

Year, sex, race, and Hispanic origin	Percent below modal grade				Dropout rate, 15 to 17 years	Population in age group			
	6 to 8 years	9 to 11 years	12 to 14 years	15 to 17 years		6 to 8 years	9 to 11 years	12 to 14 years	15 to 17 years
1977	10.6	17.7	17.5	19.3	6.6	8,675	8,771	9,918	10,510
1976	10.5	17.2	18.7	19.7	6.3	8,612	9,066	10,187	10,622
1975	11.0	16.0	20.0	20.4	6.3	8,566	9,486	10,466	10,583
1974	10.2	16.5	19.7	19.4	6.9	8,656	9,912	10,508	10,678
1973	10.6	17.3	19.9	19.1	7.0	8,929	10,117	10,704	10,481
1972	10.3	18.2	20.1	20.0	6.6	9,359	10,313	10,606	10,506
1971	10.5	18.3	20.4	19.9	5.5	9,988	10,692	10,682	10,231
Male									
2019	26.0	31.0	31.1	33.6	3.8	4,440	4,517	4,662	4,655
2018	27.8	32.7	31.6	36.6	3.6	4,465	4,564	4,656	4,671
2017	26.9	32.7	32.7	35.7	4.0	4,460	4,622	4,643	4,704
2016	27.2	31.0	33.5	36.7	4.3	4,486	4,637	4,639	4,737
2015	26.3	31.5	32.2	35.7	3.6	4,535	4,628	4,650	4,742
2014	25.5	30.0	32.3	35.2	4.5	4,600	4,629	4,703	4,721
2013	25.6	30.6	34.7	37.2	4.2	4,618	4,626	4,733	4,726
2012	26.2	30.9	36.0	38.2	2.8	4,615	4,642	4,741	4,764
2011	26.2	31.9	33.5	37.7	2.2	4,861	4,816	4,626	4,809
2010	22.1	28.0	30.9	32.4	3.0	4,825	4,746	4,666	4,805
2009	20.9	29.8	32.2	33.4	3.5	4,816	4,611	4,697	4,866
2008	23.1	29.8	32.9	34.2	2.7	4,764	4,568	4,748	4,966
2007	24.3	28.4	29.5	31.8	2.9	4,671	4,620	4,851	5,022
2006	22.5	27.0	29.8	34.2	3.3	4,596	4,652	4,900	5,011
2005	24.3	27.4	31.0	33.2	2.7	4,576	4,715	4,995	5,116
2004	24.9	28.0	31.4	35.2	3.8	4,706	4,647	5,168	4,905
2003[1]	24.4	31.6	31.2	34.0	3.4	4,785	4,795	4,961	5,026
2002	21.7	29.5	30.4	34.7	3.2	4,737	4,965	5,044	4,875
2001	22.7	25.3	28.3	32.8	4.4	4,789	5,040	4,949	4,862
2000	22.5	27.6	29.6	34.0	4.4	4,815	5,094	4,798	4,861
1999	19.9	28.2	29.7	35.8	4.2	4,883	5,009	4,777	4,851
1998	21.9	26.4	30.2	36.2	4.4	4,930	4,879	4,728	4,815
1997	22.3	27.8	32.7	37.0	3.8	4,897	4,819	4,702	4,821
1996	20.8	25.9	32.3	36.5	4.5	4,849	4,836	4,706	4,694
1995	20.5	28.0	33.4	36.5	3.8	4,727	4,797	4,680	4,592
1994	22.0	27.9	34.4	35.2	4.0	4,659	4,758	4,679	4,457
1993r	21.4	31.8	33.8	37.6	3.2	4,625	4,601	4,476	4,178
1993	21.4	31.6	33.6	36.1	3.1	4,662	4,614	4,485	4,178
1992	21.5	31.8	35.8	32.4	2.8	4,602	4,607	4,359	4,115
1991	24.4	29.1	32.5	32.5	4.2	4,556	4,568	4,270	4,047
1990	24.6	31.3	33.3	32.6	4.8	4,555	4,482	4,186	4,054
1989	26.0	32.1	35.0	30.8	4.6	4,544	4,378	4,112	4,107
1988	24.7	32.8	32.2	28.8	5.1	4,493	4,272	4,062	4,281
1987	24.6	30.5	30.4	26.6	4.5	4,415	4,167	4,069	4,504
1986	22.9	28.9	30.1	27.9	5.2	4,307	4,108	4,125	4,624
1985	21.1	26.5	26.7	28.0	4.9	4,175	4,024	4,307	4,634
1984	18.1	25.8	28.7	28.1	5.8	4,061	3,994	4,501	4,542
1983	18.1	26.3	28.0	26.3	5.6	4,002	4,054	4,697	4,481
1982	19.3	26.2	26.2	26.1	5.3	3,956	4,260	4,591	4,711
1981	17.3	26.9	24.2	25.4	6.3	3,990	4,480	4,556	4,937
1980	16.3	21.9	25.7	23.9	6.7	3,907	4,517	4,399	5,066
1979	15.4	20.8	22.3	24.8	6.2	4,114	4,475	4,616	5,201
1978	14.7	21.2	22.0	23.1	7.2	4,328	4,441	4,843	5,287
1977	12.5	21.1	21.2	23.5	6.3	4,436	4,484	5,079	5,325
1976	12.6	20.2	22.1	24.8	5.6	4,402	4,632	5,200	5,398
1975	12.9	19.7	24.7	24.7	5.4	4,376	4,848	5,385	5,332
1974	12.1	19.5	23.7	23.8	7.0	4,422	5,066	5,383	5,402
1973	12.5	19.6	23.1	24.0	6.6	4,559	5,165	5,469	5,319
1972	12.2	21.9	24.6	24.3	6.1	4,778	5,266	5,410	5,340
1971	12.6	21.6	23.9	24.4	4.6	5,106	5,461	5,455	5,185
Female									
2019	25.8	30.2	28.1	28.8	4.5	4,233	4,317	4,449	4,461
2018	22.3	27.3	28.4	28.4	4.0	4,259	4,361	4,440	4,476
2017	23.8	27.2	27.7	30.9	3.1	4,260	4,414	4,434	4,506
2016	23.1	29.2	27.6	27.5	3.9	4,286	4,423	4,434	4,530
2015	22.7	28.4	30.6	28.1	2.7	4,330	4,410	4,445	4,529
2014	22.3	26.4	27.5	28.5	3.4	4,383	4,406	4,479	4,500
2013	20.6	23.4	28.7	29.2	3.1	4,397	4,408	4,502	4,502

* = Quantity zero or rounds to zero.

r = Revised, controlled to 1990 census based population estimates; previous 1993 data controlled to 1980 census based population estimates.

[1]Starting in 2003, respondents could identify more than one race. Except as noted, the race data in this table from 2003 onward represent those respondents who indicated only one race category.

[2]The data shown prior to 2003 consists of those identifying themselves as "Asian or Pacific Islanders."

Table A-12. Population 6 to 17 Years Old Enrolled Below Modal Grade, 1971–2019—*Continued*

(Numbers in thousands; percent; civilian noninstitutionalized population.)

Year, sex, race, and Hispanic origin	Percent below modal grade				Dropout rate, 15 to 17 years	Population in age group			
	6 to 8 years	9 to 11 years	12 to 14 years	15 to 17 years		6 to 8 years	9 to 11 years	12 to 14 years	15 to 17 years
2012............	22.6	25.6	26.3	29.0	2.0	4,392	4,425	4,506	4,527
2011............	20.8	25.4	27.6	27.0	2.2	4,627	4,585	4,394	4,528
2010............	17.3	22.5	26.6	26.3	1.4	4,630	4,530	4,444	4,539
2009............	18.2	23.3	26.5	26.2	3.0	4,561	4,394	4,470	4,629
2008............	18.4	25.0	26.3	27.2	2.4	4,524	4,398	4,502	4,692
2007............	18.2	23.9	25.7	24.6	2.7	4,447	4,401	4,582	4,812
2006............	18.6	24.0	23.8	25.5	2.6	4,385	4,422	4,643	4,801
2005............	18.3	20.1	24.8	25.8	2.5	4,353	4,479	4,685	5,015
2004	19.7	23.3	23.4	26.1	3.8	4,345	4,527	4,686	4,878
2003[1]........	18.3	23.1	25.3	24.7	3.0	4,317	4,317	4,914	4,863
2002............	14.4	21.7	21.9	24.3	3.0	4,493	4,717	4,788	4,645
2001............	15.5	20.0	21.8	24.9	3.1	4,541	4,786	4,701	4,618
2000............	16.1	19.7	22.9	25.2	4.5	4,587	4,843	4,570	4,588
1999............	16.7	20.7	21.8	23.9	4.1	4,655	4,579	4,546	4,578
1998............	16.9	20.5	21.2	24.4	3.2	4,694	4,629	4,491	4,527
1997............	15.1	20.0	22.7	23.2	3.3	4,658	4,571	4,464	4,530
1996............	15.3	19.2	22.7	23.2	5.3	4,609	4,583	4,477	4,441
1995............	14.7	21.6	24.8	25.0	4.1	4,494	4,543	4,449	4,342
1994............	16.7	23.5	25.7	23.6	3.4	4,427	4,504	4,443	4,212
1993r...........	15.9	22.6	24.8	24.4	4.3	4,393	4,366	4,252	3,982
1993............	15.8	22.5	24.6	23.1	4.2	4,412	4,404	4,298	3,982
1992............	17.3	22.9	23.2	23.6	4.3	4,354	4,389	4,161	3,916
1991............	18.1	22.1	22.6	21.5	5.2	4,318	4,272	4,058	3,856
1990............	19.0	22.2	23.2	21.8	4.5	4,305	4,270	3,954	3,855
1989............	18.6	21.3	24.5	20.3	4.7	4,314	4,149	3,882	3,919
1988............	17.1	22.2	21.9	18.8	5.6	4,265	4,051	3,867	4,072
1987............	17.3	21.0	21.3	18.7	5.8	4,191	3,950	3,777	4,383
1986............	15.0	21.1	20.2	19.3	4.8	4,088	3,892	3,929	4,413
1985............	14.8	19.9	19.7	17.6	5.7	3,961	3,816	4,122	4,411
1984............	14.3	18.3	20.5	17.0	5.4	3,854	3,787	4,326	4,311
1983............	12.7	18.3	17.9	15.8	5.2	3,819	3,852	4,455	4,350
1982............	13.4	17.2	17.8	15.8	6.0	3,773	4,034	4,444	4,473
1981............	11.9	17.3	17.6	17.6	5.9	3,792	4,261	4,257	4,825
1980............	11.7	16.0	16.5	14.7	6.6	3,728	4,306	4,340	5,066
1979............	10.3	15.8	14.5	13.8	6.9	3,927	4,272	4,410	5,038
1978............	10.0	14.7	13.7	15.2	6.4	4,132	4,245	4,679	5,071
1977............	8.5	14.1	13.7	14.9	6.8	4,239	4,287	4,839	5,185
1976............	8.4	14.1	15.1	14.5	6.9	4,210	4,434	4,987	5,224
1975............	9.1	12.2	15.1	16.0	7.1	4,190	4,638	5,081	5,251
1974............	8.2	13.4	15.5	15.0	6.7	4,234	4,846	5,125	5,276
1973............	8.5	14.8	16.5	14.0	7.4	4,370	4,952	5,235	5,162
1972............	8.3	14.2	15.4	15.5	7.2	4,581	5,047	5,196	5,166
1971............	8.4	14.9	16.6	15.2	6.3	4,882	5,231	5,227	5,046
WHITE ALONE NON-HISPANIC									
Both Sexes									
2019............	26.7	30.8	30.5	30.0	3.7	5,955	6,102	6,338	6,501
2018............	25.4	31.8	31.2	30.8	3.5	5,998	6,188	6,394	6,594
2017............	26.3	32.0	28.4	33.5	3.3	5,968	6,291	6,497	6,739
2016............	25.6	29.8	30.8	31.4	4.4	6,038	6,340	6,533	6,757
2015............	25.6	29.9	30.8	30.8	2.7	6,185	6,411	6,574	6,806
2014............	24.6	28.6	29.5	30.7	4.0	6,300	6,443	6,656	6,829
2013............	23.2	25.8	30.9	32.1	3.6	6,287	6,489	6,752	6,865
2012............	25.2	28.1	31.5	32.3	2.2	6,366	6,552	6,812	6,916
2011............	25.0	29.0	31.1	30.8	1.8	6,648	6,765	6,750	7,033
2010............	21.0	25.3	28.5	27.6	2.2	6,707	6,836	6,821	7,243
2009............	19.9	26.6	29.7	29.0	2.8	6,768	6,755	6,989	7,437
2008............	21.6	28.0	29.8	29.4	2.2	6,798	6,768	7,008	7,534
2007............	21.3	25.3	26.5	26.8	2.1	6,763	6,783	7,182	7,784
2006............	20.5	24.5	25.1	28.6	2.3	6,748	6,887	7,368	7,827
2005............	22.4	23.2	26.3	29.0	2.1	6,728	7,052	7,584	8,150
2004............	22.7	25.1	27.0	29.8	3.3	6,878	7,090	7,768	7,892
2003[1]........	21.8	27.1	27.3	28.7	2.8	7,006	7,102	7,889	7,980
2002............	18.9	24.9	25.8	28.1	2.5	7,118	7,627	7,913	7,803
2001............	19.9	23.1	25.3	28.1	3.1	7,325	7,726	7,773	7,829
2000............	19.4	23.7	26.1	28.8	3.5	7,418	8,045	7,727	7,852

* = Quantity zero or rounds to zero.
r = Revised, controlled to 1990 census based population estimates; previous 1993 data controlled to 1980 census based population estimates.
[1]Starting in 2003, respondents could identify more than one race. Except as noted, the race data in this table from 2003 onward represent those respondents who indicated only one race category.
[2]The data shown prior to 2003 consists of those identifying themselves as "Asian or Pacific Islanders."

Table A-12. Population 6 to 17 Years Old Enrolled Below Modal Grade, 1971–2019—*Continued*

(Numbers in thousands; percent; civilian noninstitutionalized population.)

Year, sex, race, and Hispanic origin	Percent below modal grade				Dropout rate, 15 to 17 years	Population in age group			
	6 to 8 years	9 to 11 years	12 to 14 years	15 to 17 years		6 to 8 years	9 to 11 years	12 to 14 years	15 to 17 years
1999...................	18.9	24.2	25.3	28.9	3.6	7,717	7,938	7,669	7,879
1998...................	20.5	23.7	26.0	28.9	3.0	7,755	7,794	7,697	7,859
1997...................	19.7	24.6	27.3	28.4	3.2	7,729	7,775	7,789	7,866
1996...................	18.8	22.7	26.2	28.6	4.2	7,803	7,792	7,731	7,716
1995...................	18.2	24.5	28.0	29.2	3.4	7,853	8,000	7,872	7,795
1994...................	19.8	25.6	30.0	28.0	3.1	7,779	7,864	7,845	7,490
1993...................	18.8	27.2	28.8	29.5	3.0	7,736	7,802	7,600	7,022
Male									
2019...................	27.3	31.4	32.8	31.9	3.5	3,055	3,128	3,235	3,327
2018...................	27.9	35.4	33.4	34.3	3.5	3,104	3,176	3,276	3,383
2017...................	28.8	34.6	31.2	36.9	3.6	3,064	3,225	3,323	3,447
2016...................	28.2	31.7	33.2	35.0	4.9	3,086	3,251	3,360	3,467
2015...................	28.3	32.3	31.3	34.4	2.9	3,150	3,289	3,390	3,479
2014...................	25.8	29.6	32.3	33.4	4.6	3,218	3,303	3,412	3,487
2013...................	25.5	29.0	33.6	36.8	4.2	3,232	3,320	3,474	3,515
2012...................	26.6	31.7	36.9	37.7	2.8	3,264	3,371	3,518	3,545
2011...................	28.7	32.8	34.4	36.9	1.9	3,394	3,473	3,472	3,619
2010...................	24.3	28.5	31.2	31.7	3.1	3,414	3,498	3,487	3,728
2009...................	22.4	30.3	32.4	33.4	3.1	3,489	3,453	3,593	3,793
2008...................	24.8	30.3	33.6	33.0	2.4	3,485	3,459	3,599	3,862
2007...................	24.1	28.4	28.1	30.3	2.2	3,457	3,473	3,715	3,970
2006...................	23.1	26.0	27.6	32.4	2.9	3,449	3,537	3,775	3,984
2005...................	25.4	26.8	28.2	32.5	2.2	3,450	3,618	3,902	4,136
2004...................	25.0	27.9	30.6	35.0	3.4	3,548	3,605	4,054	3,994
2003¹..................	24.6	31.7	30.7	33.4	2.9	3,668	3,725	3,960	4,101
2002...................	22.7	29.0	30.7	33.6	2.4	3,667	3,969	4,005	4,038
2001...................	23.1	26.2	28.5	31.6	3.7	3,808	3,971	3,920	4,020
2000...................	22.5	27.7	30.0	33.4	3.4	3,795	4,135	3,970	4,034
1999...................	20.3	27.7	29.7	35.1	3.5	3,955	4,076	3,913	4,058
1998...................	23.1	26.5	30.8	34.3	3.6	4,016	4,003	3,894	3,981
1997...................	24.1	29.0	32.5	35.3	3.8	3,977	3,971	3,996	4,020
1996...................	22.5	25.9	30.8	35.1	4.1	3,964	4,035	3,957	3,959
1995...................	22.1	27.3	31.9	34.9	3.1	4,038	4,094	4,017	4,010
1994...................	22.8	28.0	34.3	33.6	2.9	3,993	4,010	4,030	3,866
1993...................	22.0	31.5	33.2	35.6	2.4	3,952	4,021	3,889	3,578
Female									
2019...................	26.2	30.3	28.2	27.9	4.0	2,900	2,973	3,102	3,175
2018...................	22.7	28.0	28.9	27.1	3.5	2,894	3,011	3,118	3,211
2017...................	23.6	29.2	25.5	29.9	3.0	2,904	3,066	3,173	3,293
2016...................	22.9	27.7	28.2	27.6	3.9	2,952	3,089	3,173	3,290
2015...................	22.7	27.4	30.2	27.2	2.6	3,035	3,122	3,184	3,327
2014...................	23.4	27.5	26.7	28.0	3.3	3,082	3,141	3,245	3,342
2013...................	20.7	22.4	28.1	27.3	3.0	3,055	3,169	3,279	3,350
2012...................	23.8	24.4	25.7	26.8	1.5	3,102	3,181	3,295	3,371
2011...................	21.1	24.9	27.5	24.3	1.7	3,254	3,292	3,278	3,414
2010...................	17.6	22.0	25.8	23.4	1.3	3,294	3,338	3,334	3,515
2009...................	17.3	22.8	26.8	24.4	2.4	3,280	3,301	3,396	3,644
2008...................	18.3	25.5	25.7	25.6	2.1	3,313	3,309	3,408	3,673
2007...................	18.4	22.0	24.7	23.1	2.0	3,306	3,310	3,467	3,814
2006...................	17.6	22.8	22.6	24.6	1.8	3,299	3,350	3,593	3,843
2005...................	19.2	19.4	24.2	25.3	2.0	3,277	3,434	3,682	4,014
2004...................	20.3	22.2	23.1	24.5	3.3	3,330	3,485	3,714	3,898
2003¹..................	18.6	22.2	24.0	23.7	2.6	3,337	3,377	3,929	3,878
2002...................	14.8	20.4	20.9	22.2	2.6	3,451	3,658	3,908	3,765
2001...................	16.4	19.8	22.0	24.4	2.6	3,517	3,755	3,853	3,809
2000...................	16.2	19.6	21.9	23.9	3.7	3,623	3,910	3,757	3,818
1999...................	17.4	20.5	20.8	22.3	3.6	3,761	3,864	3,757	3,840
1998...................	17.6	20.8	21.2	23.5	2.5	3,740	3,791	3,803	3,878
1997...................	15.0	19.9	21.8	21.3	2.6	3,752	3,804	3,793	3,846
1996...................	15.0	19.3	21.3	21.7	4.3	3,839	3,757	3,773	3,757
1995...................	14.1	21.5	23.8	23.1	3.8	3,815	3,906	3,854	3,784
1994...................	16.6	23.1	25.5	22.1	3.2	3,786	3,854	3,814	3,624
1993...................	15.4	22.6	24.2	23.1	3.6	3,784	3,782	3,710	3,444

* = Quantity zero or rounds to zero.
r = Revised, controlled to 1990 census based population estimates; previous 1993 data controlled to 1980 census based population estimates.
¹Starting in 2003, respondents could identify more than one race. Except as noted, the race data in this table from 2003 onward represent those respondents who indicated only one race category.
²The data shown prior to 2003 consists of those identifying themselves as "Asian or Pacific Islanders."

Table A-12. Population 6 to 17 Years Old Enrolled Below Modal Grade, 1971–2019—*Continued*

(Numbers in thousands; percent; civilian noninstitutionalized population.)

Year, sex, race, and Hispanic origin	Percent below modal grade				Dropout rate, 15 to 17 years	Population in age group			
	6 to 8 years	9 to 11 years	12 to 14 years	15 to 17 years		6 to 8 years	9 to 11 years	12 to 14 years	15 to 17 years
BLACK ALONE									
Both Sexes									
2019	22.3	30.1	35.7	33.8	4.7	1,816	1,884	1,881	1,807
2018	28.5	32.0	28.3	37.4	7.5	1,862	1,901	1,847	1,830
2017	23.8	32.8	32.7	37.4	4.4	1,962	1,814	1,818	1,873
2016	24.2	33.9	30.9	33.2	2.8	1,877	1,878	1,817	1,895
2015	22.3	28.9	32.3	35.6	3.1	1,794	1,913	1,831	1,899
2014	22.2	32.2	35.5	38.1	5.2	1,772	1,822	1,871	1,869
2013	24.7	28.0	32.2	36.0	4.6	1,885	1,781	1,892	1,865
2012	25.3	28.5	35.6	38.3	2.6	1,719	1,828	1,897	1,879
2011	20.9	30.6	29.4	33.6	2.7	1,882	1,831	1,773	1,855
2010	17.2	26.8	33.4	32.7	2.2	1,871	1,710	1,809	1,911
2009	20.5	31.6	33.1	36.5	2.7	1,692	1,814	1,801	1,943
2008	19.1	27.6	41.6	39.4	3.1	1,781	1,797	1,851	1,994
2007	17.7	28.1	33.0	39.2	3.0	1,797	1,770	1,937	2,021
2006	19.1	29.9	35.7	35.7	3.1	1,813	1,811	1,960	2,059
2005	20.8	35.6	34.1	38.8	4.2	1,806	1,826	2,011	2,085
2004	19.8	27.4	34.1	40.1	2.3	1,775	1,906	2,034	1,992
2003[1]	22.7	34.2	33.9	37.4	3.7	1,760	2,043	2,110	1,950
2002	19.6	28.6	32.8	36.2	3.9	2,017	2,048	2,036	1,943
2001	17.3	29.7	31.1	35.6	4.0	1,937	2,144	1,998	1,823
2000	19.6	26.9	37.8	34.6	4.7	1,976	2,082	1,961	1,852
1999	16.1	30.2	31.7	34.8	3.5	1,948	2,108	1,912	1,911
1998	18.3	26.6	31.4	38.4	3.6	2,068	1,968	1,868	1,892
1997	18.4	26.1	33.5	40.0	3.8	2,061	1,908	1,845	1,938
1996	18.4	29.2	36.8	36.9	4.8	2,054	1,847	1,839	1,858
1995	16.8	31.1	38.3	41.3	4.1	1,909	1,890	1,822	1,851
1994	18.4	35.1	36.1	37.7	3.3	1,912	1,795	1,835	1,809
1993r	20.0	33.6	34.8	45.1	3.6	1,767	1,763	1,747	1,641
1993	19.9	33.4	38.8	43.3	3.6	1,709	1,710	1,695	1,642
1992	20.6	28.7	38.0	40.6	4.2	1,761	1,635	1,686	1,621
1991	21.0	34.3	40.7	43.4	5.3	1,674	1,701	1,643	1,574
1990	21.9	33.1	46.1	42.9	5.2	1,645	1,712	1,574	1,571
1989	19.6	34.0	41.3	39.3	3.9	1,642	1,682	1,554	1,618
1988	18.6	33.1	37.6	38.4	4.7	1,680	1,629	1,545	1,637
1987	19.8	33.1	35.6	35.3	5.1	1,679	1,554	1,552	1,654
1986	12.7	34.6	38.5	38.3	4.6	1,611	1,542	1,530	1,692
1985	18.0	33.9	37.9	37.7	4.6	1,568	1,498	1,635	1,627
1984	17.9	32.3	38.1	34.6	4.1	1,445	1,442	1,652	1,536
1983	15.3	34.9	34.4	35.8	4.7	1,429	1,450	1,601	1,617
1982	17.2	27.1	32.5	32.6	4.6	1,765	1,874	1,953	1,947
1981	13.9	26.2	33.7	36.1	6.3	1,437	1,594	1,615	1,679
1980	14.9	27.8	30.5	37.6	5.1	1,460	1,606	1,568	1,728
1979	12.5	29.5	29.2	34.3	6.4	1,515	1,576	1,636	1,722
1978	12.6	27.8	26.6	35.4	5.7	1,557	1,523	1,664	1,764
1977	11.3	24.9	26.3	32.2	5.4	1,552	1,558	1,698	1,754
1976	10.5	23.2	26.1	35.6	6.7	1,493	1,633	1,724	1,726
1975	11.9	26.1	29.2	34.9	8.0	1,489	1,656	1,720	1,760
1974	11.6	26.2	33.2	34.4	8.2	1,509	1,684	1,750	1,682
1973	12.0	25.8	31.7	35.4	8.2	1,525	1,650	1,671	1,671
1972	13.2	30.5	33.1	37.3	6.6	1,585	1,638	1,691	1,636
1971	14.2	27.9	34.7	40.2	7.0	1,794	1,787	1,638	1,533
Male									
2019	25.7	30.7	33.4	39.2	5.7	896	939	951	905
2018	31.8	31.2	32.5	39.7	5.0	950	960	934	917
2017	23.8	31.6	35.9	43.0	5.4	990	908	919	939
2016	22.2	36.2	36.6	31.0	2.4	962	931	918	952
2015	18.9	30.1	33.9	39.4	2.2	903	971	927	954
2014	23.2	34.1	38.3	40.2	4.6	883	959	948	939
2013	22.1	30.2	36.8	41.8	3.8	921	905	961	936
2012	29.3	33.6	37.7	40.3	1.4	918	911	963	943
2011	21.5	35.7	32.9	36.3	4.1	977	902	898	927
2010	17.4	31.5	35.2	37.0	3.0	954	856	912	961
2009	19.4	35.8	35.1	44.4	2.6	805	954	911	980
2008	19.8	26.6	47.0	43.1	3.4	917	908	934	992
2007	22.7	31.6	35.4	43.5	2.2	946	886	964	1,027

* = Quantity zero or rounds to zero.
r = Revised, controlled to 1990 census based population estimates; previous 1993 data controlled to 1980 census based population estimates.
[1]Starting in 2003, respondents could identify more than one race. Except as noted, the race data in this table from 2003 onward represent those respondents who indicated only one race category.
[2]The data shown prior to 2003 consists of those identifying themselves as "Asian or Pacific Islanders."

Table A-12. Population 6 to 17 Years Old Enrolled Below Modal Grade, 1971–2019—*Continued*

(Numbers in thousands; percent; civilian noninstitutionalized population.)

Year, sex, race, and Hispanic origin	Percent below modal grade				Dropout rate, 15 to 17 years	Population in age group			
	6 to 8 years	9 to 11 years	12 to 14 years	15 to 17 years	15 to 17 years	6 to 8 years	9 to 11 years	12 to 14 years	15 to 17 years
2006	20.3	35.1	40.3	43.9	3.3	929	920	991	1,032
2005	22.6	37.9	35.8	43.0	5.2	912	913	1,011	1,041
2004	21.0	31.4	37.8	46.5	2.0	885	992	1,012	1,009
2003[1]	23.6	36.8	38.7	43.4	3.9	927	1,059	975	1,047
2002	17.5	32.5	37.0	44.7	5.0	1,044	1,036	1,012	973
2001	21.1	31.1	33.3	42.8	3.5	978	1,108	1,010	924
2000	20.8	27.5	43.3	37.0	6.4	1,003	1,057	994	941
1999	15.9	34.2	36.3	37.6	3.0	964	1,085	969	992
1998	20.9	29.3	33.3	41.9	3.0	1,054	994	946	968
1997	21.3	29.3	39.4	43.8	3.1	1,019	994	934	979
1996	21.3	30.4	45.1	43.2	4.5	1,054	925	931	943
1995	18.8	31.2	45.0	47.5	2.9	982	944	922	952
1994	19.4	30.3	39.9	39.8	3.2	951	928	928	898
1993r	21.8	36.5	44.3	53.0	2.5	903	884	891	832
1993	21.6	36.5	44.2	51.8	2.5	864	857	867	832
1992	24.5	28.7	44.5	47.0	2.8	864	862	860	813
1991	22.9	39.6	46.2	50.6	5.4	846	878	839	798
1990	23.2	37.3	52.7	49.1	4.3	828	877	791	795
1989	21.7	38.8	44.8	46.7	2.8	831	858	785	828
1988	18.9	37.2	43.7	41.4	4.1	851	828	780	828
1987	21.6	41.1	39.7	42.3	4.9	861	779	802	818
1986	15.0	39.0	45.2	45.9	4.0	806	792	770	855
1985	19.5	38.2	41.4	40.3	5.4	778	775	830	816
1984	24.1	38.1	42.5	42.8	4.2	729	727	832	769
1983	16.8	42.0	43.1	40.6	4.4	721	723	808	799
1982	18.8	27.5	36.2	36.9	4.8	898	937	975	977
1981	17.7	34.2	33.3	42.4	5.4	723	811	814	832
1980	16.8	31.8	36.2	43.3	4.9	736	807	770	876
1979	14.7	37.3	33.8	43.6	4.0	762	796	828	853
1978	15.4	33.0	30.3	43.1	4.1	774	767	847	870
1977	12.1	29.8	31.1	35.3	4.8	776	782	858	868
1976	11.5	26.1	30.9	43.3	5.7	755	816	870	855
1975	12.8	30.7	32.5	40.2	7.6	743	849	845	879
1974	13.5	31.0	40.9	41.1	7.2	747	858	861	849
1973	14.1	29.5	38.0	42.0	8.5	752	831	837	824
1972	14.5	36.8	41.3	43.8	6.6	787	828	836	818
1971	18.1	30.9	38.5	47.6	7.4	890	900	810	757
Female									
2019	18.7	29.5	38.1	28.6	3.8	920	945	929	903
2018	25.1	32.8	23.9	34.9	9.9	912	941	914	913
2017	23.8	33.9	29.5	31.9	3.3	972	906	899	933
2016	26.2	31.6	25.0	35.6	3.3	915	947	899	943
2015	25.8	27.6	30.7	31.8	3.9	891	942	905	945
2014	21.2	30.1	32.7	36.0	5.8	890	863	923	930
2013	27.1	25.7	27.5	29.9	5.4	964	877	931	929
2012	20.7	23.4	33.4	36.2	3.9	801	917	934	935
2011	20.2	25.5	25.8	31.0	1.4	905	930	875	928
2010	16.9	22.0	31.6	28.6	1.4	917	853	897	951
2009	21.5	26.9	31.1	28.5	2.8	887	860	891	963
2008	18.3	28.6	36.0	35.8	2.9	864	889	917	1,003
2007	12.2	24.7	30.5	34.5	3.9	851	885	972	993
2006	17.7	24.7	31.0	27.5	2.8	884	891	968	1,027
2005	19.0	33.3	32.4	34.7	3.3	893	913	999	1,044
2004	18.6	23.1	30.5	33.4	2.6	890	914	1,022	983
2003[1]	21.7	31.5	39.8	30.3	3.4	833	983	1,135	903
2002	22.0	24.7	28.7	27.8	2.8	973	1,012	1,024	970
2001	13.3	28.2	29.0	27.9	4.5	959	1,036	988	900
2000	18.2	26.4	32.0	32.3	2.9	974	1,025	968	911
1999	16.3	25.8	27.0	31.6	4.0	984	1,022	944	919
1998	15.6	23.8	29.6	34.6	4.3	1,014	974	922	924
1997	15.9	22.8	27.4	36.0	4.5	1,041	915	911	959
1996	13.4	28.1	28.4	30.3	4.9	1,000	922	909	915
1995	14.8	23.6	30.9	34.6	5.3	928	946	901	898
1994	17.5	29.1	32.3	35.4	3.6	961	867	908	911
1993r	18.0	30.8	33.1	36.6	4.7	864	879	856	809
1993	18.1	30.3	33.2	34.6	4.7	844	854	828	809
1992	16.7	28.7	31.2	34.2	5.6	897	773	826	808

* = Quantity zero or rounds to zero.
r = Revised, controlled to 1990 census based population estimates; previous 1993 data controlled to 1980 census based population estimates.
[1]Starting in 2003, respondents could identify more than one race. Except as noted, the race data in this table from 2003 onward represent those respondents who indicated only one race category.
[2]The data shown prior to 2003 consists of those identifying themselves as "Asian or Pacific Islanders."

Table A-12. Population 6 to 17 Years Old Enrolled Below Modal Grade, 1971–2019—*Continued*

(Numbers in thousands; percent; civilian noninstitutionalized population.)

Year, sex, race, and Hispanic origin	Percent below modal grade				Dropout rate, 15 to 17 years	Population in age group			
	6 to 8 years	9 to 11 years	12 to 14 years	15 to 17 years		6 to 8 years	9 to 11 years	12 to 14 years	15 to 17 years
1991	19.0	28.6	35.0	36.0	5.2	828	823	804	776
1990	20.7	28.7	39.3	36.6	6.1	817	835	783	776
1989	17.5	29.0	37.7	31.5	5.1	811	824	769	790
1988	18.2	28.8	31.4	35.2	5.3	829	801	765	809
1987	18.0	25.2	31.3	28.5	5.3	818	775	750	836
1985	16.6	29.3	34.2	35.1	3.8	790	723	805	811
1984	11.5	26.4	33.5	26.3	4.0	716	715	820	767
1983	13.8	27.8	25.5	31.2	5.0	708	727	793	818
1982	15.5	26.7	28.7	28.1	4.3	867	937	978	970
1981	10.1	17.9	34.2	29.9	7.1	714	783	801	847
1980	12.8	23.8	25.1	31.7	5.3	724	799	798	852
1979	10.4	21.5	24.5	25.2	8.7	753	780	808	869
1978	9.8	22.6	22.6	27.9	7.2	783	756	817	894
1977	10.6	20.0	21.3	29.1	6.0	776	776	840	886
1976	9.5	20.3	21.2	28.1	7.7	738	817	854	871
1975	11.0	21.3	25.9	29.6	8.3	746	807	875	881
1974	9.7	21.3	25.8	27.5	9.2	762	826	889	833
1973	10.0	22.1	25.4	28.9	7.9	773	819	834	847
1972	11.9	24.1	25.1	30.9	6.6	798	810	855	818
1971	10.4	24.9	31.0	33.1	6.7	904	887	828	776
ASIAN ALONE[2]									
Both Sexes									
2019	24.7	22.4	22.2	24.7	3.5	680	631	727	704
2018	20.6	25.9	22.4	22.8	5.5	713	605	651	684
2017	20.3	30.0	22.7	26.8	3.8	602	664	632	717
2016	21.8	22.5	22.9	27.3	2.9	642	700	628	681
2015	25.2	22.2	22.5	25.5	4.8	605	691	619	644
2014	13.0	25.1	26.7	28.1	1.4	618	611	625	650
2013	15.1	15.0	21.3	18.7	1.2	606	630	542	615
2012	17.1	19.1	17.6	30.5	1.6	590	560	591	624
2011	17.4	23.7	25.0	26.5	2.4	602	582	481	536
2010	9.1	20.5	22.7	19.9	3.1	618	575	495	424
2009	9.3	12.2	26.8	20.6	1.5	522	491	448	421
2008	17.8	23.0	26.8	20.1	4.4	491	517	482	507
2007	11.3	21.9	17.0	24.2	3.7	545	534	497	463
2006	15.2	19.7	20.9	23.0	3.2	425	472	490	476
2005	12.8	12.2	16.3	19.1	1.2	502	429	486	457
2004	12.1	11.4	20.9	23.6	1.7	417	468	490	491
2003[1]	7.5	13.6	19.7	24.5	1.6	486	453	459	458
2002	11.1	12.3	20.4	18.6	2.7	602	490	530	553
2001	11.9	17.9	20.3	21.0	2.8	503	565	523	565
2000	10.7	15.5	17.5	22.2	0.6	524	490	490	475
1999	7.5	16.5	17.9	25.5	3.2	533	496	560	555
Male									
2019	25.2	23.2	28.3	21.0	1.2	347	324	376	338
2018	20.2	23.3	24.4	21.0	2.7	367	328	301	340
2017	24.5	29.0	21.3	30.8	3.5	298	353	318	356
2016	24.0	28.0	25.4	29.2	3.3	337	360	313	307
2015	22.4	20.6	17.2	26.1	4.9	299	352	285	327
2014	18.5	25.0	31.6	30.6	2.9	316	306	323	303
2013	13.0	18.5	23.9	21.5	1.4	297	298	281	287
2012	19.2	19.3	17.0	30.2	2.4	300	259	307	327
2011	17.1	25.8	25.3	29.7	2.3	324	293	249	266
2010	8.1	20.2	24.4	21.8	2.6	327	296	247	237
2009	9.7	13.2	26.6	22.0	0.7	272	232	227	233
2008	25.1	20.8	24.5	17.9	2.4	227	257	249	253
2007	7.6	20.5	18.2	26.0	4.0	278	272	240	246
2006	14.3	18.4	23.5	21.7	3.3	206	256	264	227
2005	12.3	13.8	13.2	18.1	1.6	261	202	265	228
2004	10.9	16.0	20.9	23.5	2.4	220	216	282	231
2003[1]	7.3	15.9	20.3	19.3	-	226	223	261	231
2002	9.6	12.4	23.3	18.9	1.7	274	239	267	287
2001	15.2	16.6	19.0	22.2	4.9	265	294	256	313
2000	14.7	14.2	16.1	30.3	1.0	286	243	267	261
1999	8.4	16.4	17.6	30.3	2.2	277	269	246	276

* = Quantity zero or rounds to zero.
r = Revised, controlled to 1990 census based population estimates; previous 1993 data controlled to 1980 census based population estimates.
[1]Starting in 2003, respondents could identify more than one race. Except as noted, the race data in this table from 2003 onward represent those respondents who indicated only one race category.
[2]The data shown prior to 2003 consists of those identifying themselves as "Asian or Pacific Islanders."

Table A-12. Population 6 to 17 Years Old Enrolled Below Modal Grade, 1971–2019—*Continued*

(Numbers in thousands; percent; civilian noninstitutionalized population.)

Year, sex, race, and Hispanic origin	Percent below modal grade				Dropout rate, 15 to 17 years	Population in age group			
	6 to 8 years	9 to 11 years	12 to 14 years	15 to 17 years		6 to 8 years	9 to 11 years	12 to 14 years	15 to 17 years
Female									
2019	24.2	21.5	15.7	28.2	5.6	333	307	351	366
2018	21.0	28.9	20.7	24.6	8.2	346	276	350	344
2017	16.1	31.1	24.1	22.9	4.0	304	311	314	362
2016	19.3	16.6	20.5	25.8	2.5	305	340	315	374
2015	27.9	24.0	26.8	24.8	4.8	305	339	334	318
2014	7.1	25.3	21.5	25.9	0.1	302	306	302	346
2013	17.2	12.0	18.6	16.3	1.0	309	332	262	327
2012	15.0	18.8	18.3	30.9	0.7	290	301	284	296
2011	17.6	21.5	24.6	23.3	2.6	278	289	232	270
2010	10.4	20.7	20.9	17.5	3.7	290	279	248	187
2009	8.7	11.4	27.0	18.9	2.4	251	259	220	188
2008	11.7	25.1	29.3	22.4	6.5	264	260	233	254
2007	15.2	23.5	15.8	22.2	3.4	268	263	257	217
2006	16.1	21.2	17.9	24.2	3.1	218	216	226	249
2005	13.4	10.8	20.0	20.1	0.9	241	227	221	229
2004	13.5	7.3	20.8	23.7	1.1	196	253	208	260
2003[1]	7.6	11.3	18.8	29.9	3.2	259	230	198	227
2002	12.4	12.2	17.5	18.2	3.7	327	251	263	266
2001	8.3	19.3	21.4	19.6	0.2	238	270	268	252
2000	5.9	16.7	19.2	12.3	0.1	239	247	224	215
1999	6.6	16.7	18.5	20.6	4.0	256	227	314	278
HISPANIC (OF ANY RACE)									
Both Sexes									
2019	23.5	30.9	26.5	33.7	5.4	3,132	3,251	3,164	3,050
2018	23.7	26.4	26.7	36.7	4.8	3,196	3,205	3,161	2,933
2017	22.9	25.6	34.2	33.6	3.9	3,164	3,215	2,999	2,913
2016	24.1	29.6	29.1	34.3	3.0	3,104	3,173	2,956	2,978
2015	21.5	30.7	31.5	34.4	4.0	3,134	3,165	2,909	2,871
2014	22.0	27.5	30.5	34.4	4.5	3,159	2,967	2,901	2,703
2013	22.5	29.8	32.9	36.0	3.6	3,117	2,926	2,868	2,662
2012	22.8	28.6	29.0	38.2	3.0	3,025	2,954	2,791	2,661
2011	20.2	28.4	29.0	37.8	3.3	3,161	2,847	2,496	2,502
2010	16.0	24.0	28.5	35.5	2.5	3,046	2,681	2,494	2,307
2009	18.6	26.7	28.9	34.1	4.7	2,893	2,524	2,418	2,254
2008	18.4	25.8	29.4	35.8	3.5	2,690	2,402	2,422	2,321
2007	20.9	28.9	31.1	34.0	5.7	2,541	2,414	2,418	2,211
2006	20.6	29.2	32.6	35.3	5.7	2,441	2,382	2,361	2,165
2005	18.1	26.2	33.2	32.1	4.9	2,390	2,317	2,322	2,202
2004	21.5	28.1	30.0	34.6	6.1	2,382	2,250	2,283	2,072
2003	20.2	28.7	31.3	32.7	5.2	2,280	2,221	2,167	2,063
2002	15.5	28.4	27.9	35.6	5.9	2,258	2,204	2,079	1,841
2001	16.7	22.1	25.0	34.6	6.9	2,143	2,198	2,011	1,733
2000	19.4	23.2	27.3	34.4	8.8	2,067	1,965	1,744	1,671
1999	15.7	25.9	27.9	36.5	7.3	1,902	1,922	1,734	1,653
1998	15.4	23.2	24.6	33.8	7.6	1,940	1,767	1,561	1,549
1997	15.2	21.5	31.0	41.4	5.5	1,909	1,666	1,444	1,575
1996	14.9	22.9	35.5	39.0	8.4	1,711	1,680	1,550	1,478
1995	14.4	26.1	38.5	43.6	7.4	1,597	1,628	1,496	1,373
1994	16.8	28.4	32.3	39.9	8.8	1,526	1,593	1,442	1,347
1993r	18.9	29.2	33.2	42.2	8.2	1,390	1,255	1,204	1,225
1993	18.9	29.2	32.7	38.3	7.9	1,455	1,295	1,243	1,226
1992	16.2	25.3	34.3	39.9	8.1	1,272	1,371	1,141	1,110
1991	21.8	30.7	35.8	38.4	11.3	1,290	1,356	1,088	1,023
1990	21.5	34.8	37.7	39.8	9.0	1,270	1,230	1,095	1,062
1989	21.9	33.8	39.9	39.5	10.6	1,257	1,154	1,079	1,001
1988	23.2	37.0	45.0	36.8	13.7	1,248	1,107	1,052	953
1987	16.9	31.2	38.9	37.3	9.1	1,181	1,054	1,063	981
1986	19.1	33.3	42.5	35.5	11.0	1,067	1,119	1,025	1,018
1985	18.7	32.4	35.8	35.7	11.3	1,035	1,047	957	946
1984	20.2	32.7	34.7	38.5	10.7	901	829	806	816
1983	20.2	32.7	39.5	38.0	8.3	903	909	949	860
1982	21.9	32.6	37.3	37.0	10.9	923	875	924	883
1981	17.9	34.7	34.9	34.9	13.3	882	939	866	963
1980	20.8	26.1	34.8	35.8	12.6	881	949	863	889

* = Quantity zero or rounds to zero.
r = Revised, controlled to 1990 census based population estimates; previous 1993 data controlled to 1980 census based population estimates.
[1]Starting in 2003, respondents could identify more than one race. Except as noted, the race data in this table from 2003 onward represent those respondents who indicated only one race category.
[2]The data shown prior to 2003 consists of those identifying themselves as "Asian or Pacific Islanders."

Table A-12. Population 6 to 17 Years Old Enrolled Below Modal Grade, 1971–2019—*Continued*

(Numbers in thousands; percent; civilian noninstitutionalized population.)

Year, sex, race, and Hispanic origin	Percent below modal grade				Dropout rate, 15 to 17 years	Population in age group			
	6 to 8 years	9 to 11 years	12 to 14 years	15 to 17 years		6 to 8 years	9 to 11 years	12 to 14 years	15 to 17 years
1979............................	18.2	33.6	33.0	30.3	10.9	729	712	697	755
1978............................	19.8	29.1	33.6	37.8	12.3	723	684	666	751
1977............................	13.0	24.1	25.1	35.2	11.0	676	693	662	773
Male									
2019............................	23.5	30.4	25.5	37.4	5.1	1,613	1,660	1,593	1,567
2018............................	26.1	27.0	27.4	42.2	4.0	1,639	1,619	1,629	1,463
2017............................	22.6	27.2	36.1	35.2	5.1	1,641	1,604	1,559	1,461
2016............................	25.3	28.5	32.4	41.0	2.7	1,570	1,620	1,507	1,530
2015............................	21.0	31.0	32.1	37.3	4.6	1,595	1,608	1,492	1,512
2014............................	23.8	31.2	31.8	38.1	5.5	1,594	1,510	1,481	1,402
2013............................	24.5	34.7	35.3	38.4	4.0	1,579	1,507	1,458	1,373
2012............................	26.4	29.5	32.2	40.7	2.7	1,571	1,513	1,408	1,382
2011............................	21.0	30.7	30.5	39.6	3.0	1,605	1,465	1,290	1,294
2010............................	16.7	24.9	29.1	35.0	3.1	1,544	1,381	1,290	1,178
2009............................	16.8	28.4	32.3	34.5	4.9	1,458	1,322	1,216	1,165
2008............................	18.4	27.4	31.2	38.1	3.7	1,377	1,218	1,233	1,198
2007............................	24.3	28.5	34.1	37.4	5.9	1,302	1,252	1,217	1,130
2006............................	20.0	31.0	37.7	40.6	4.9	1,251	1,214	1,208	1,111
2005............................	20.5	29.2	39.2	37.0	4.7	1,219	1,192	1,202	1,087
2004	25.2	28.8	34.3	36.6	6.4	1,247	1,142	1,202	1,001
2003	23.0	31.2	32.3	35.9	6.2	1,205	1,178	1,081	1,020
2002............................	17.4	31.6	28.7	38.5	7.4	1,140	1,090	1,137	911
2001............................	21.2	23.4	27.8	40.8	7.7	1,065	1,128	1,093	895
2000............................	23.1	26.7	27.7	36.9	9.0	1,048	993	875	872
1999............................	17.9	29.5	29.7	38.9	7.6	973	990	893	854
1998............................	16.8	26.6	26.9	44.9	8.1	950	900	849	869
1997............................	15.3	22.3	33.7	45.8	3.7	969	863	735	836
1996............................	13.5	25.8	40.5	45.1	6.8	914	808	798	764
1995............................	11.4	31.1	42.4	47.6	7.5	794	839	776	697
1994............................	16.4	27.5	36.3	45.1	11.4	778	845	721	676
1993r...........................	19.1	35.1	37.2	50.4	7.6	722	612	618	658
1993............................	19.1	34.3	36.9	46.0	7.3	778	637	648	658
1992............................	15.6	27.2	42.5	46.2	6.8	636	687	602	576
1991............................	22.7	31.5	43.9	42.6	10.7	651	691	544	521
1990............................	22.2	36.4	40.2	43.8	9.0	676	616	590	564
1989............................	23.7	36.1	40.0	45.2	7.8	642	584	560	511
1988............................	26.9	42.0	53.8	40.5	12.4	676	566	470	523
1987............................	19.8	31.7	44.8	38.7	6.4	600	524	569	517
1986............................	22.2	38.0	49.3	37.8	10.8	544	555	535	471
1985............................	16.7	36.8	38.4	43.4	7.8	521	527	502	449
1984............................	18.3	35.7	33.1	42.8	10.0	443	420	423	432
1983............................	22.2	38.8	45.7	41.8	8.2	445	479	479	428
1982............................	23.1	36.4	39.1	43.4	10.1	428	426	466	477
1981............................	19.9	39.8	38.0	40.0	14.3	438	480	439	495
1980............................	22.5	29.9	40.5	40.7	13.5	418	481	415	445
1979............................	19.0	34.6	36.4	31.3	8.8	368	358	349	386
1978............................	23.5	29.9	33.9	37.3	13.6	388	335	339	413
1977............................	11.5	31.4	23.3	38.4	6.7	365	325	330	406
Female									
2019............................	23.5	31.5	27.5	29.9	5.6	1,519	1,591	1,571	1,483
2018............................	21.3	25.8	25.9	31.1	5.5	1,557	1,586	1,532	1,470
2017............................	23.1	24.0	32.2	32.1	2.6	1,524	1,611	1,440	1,452
2016............................	22.8	30.8	25.7	27.2	3.3	1,534	1,553	1,449	1,448
2015............................	22.0	30.4	30.8	31.3	3.4	1,539	1,556	1,417	1,359
2014............................	20.2	23.7	29.2	30.5	3.5	1,565	1,457	1,420	1,301
2013............................	20.5	24.5	30.5	33.4	3.0	1,539	1,420	1,410	1,289
2012............................	18.9	27.6	25.8	35.5	3.3	1,454	1,441	1,382	1,279
2011............................	19.5	25.9	27.4	35.8	3.7	1,556	1,382	1,206	1,209
2010............................	15.2	23.0	27.9	36.1	2.0	1,502	1,301	1,204	1,129
2009............................	20.5	24.9	25.4	33.6	4.6	1,435	1,202	1,202	1,089
2008............................	18.4	24.1	27.5	33.3	3.2	1,313	1,184	1,189	1,123
2007............................	17.3	29.4	28.2	30.5	5.4	1,239	1,162	1,202	1,080
2006............................	21.3	27.4	27.3	29.5	6.5	1,190	1,168	1,153	1,054
2005............................	15.6	23.0	26.7	27.3	5.1	1,171	1,126	1,119	1,115
2004	17.6	27.3	25.1	32.8	5.7	1,135	1,108	1,080	1,070
2003	17.1	25.7	30.3	29.7	4.3	1,075	1,043	1,086	1,042

* = Quantity zero or rounds to zero.

r = Revised, controlled to 1990 census based population estimates; previous 1993 data controlled to 1980 census based population estimates.

[1]Starting in 2003, respondents could identify more than one race. Except as noted, the race data in this table from 2003 onward represent those respondents who indicated only one race category.

[2]The data shown prior to 2003 consists of those identifying themselves as "Asian or Pacific Islanders."

Table A-12. Population 6 to 17 Years Old Enrolled Below Modal Grade, 1971–2019—*Continued*

(Numbers in thousands; percent; civilian noninstitutionalized population.)

Year, sex, race, and Hispanic origin	Percent below modal grade				Dropout rate, 15 to 17 years	Population in age group			
	6 to 8 years	9 to 11 years	12 to 14 years	15 to 17 years		6 to 8 years	9 to 11 years	12 to 14 years	15 to 17 years
2002	13.6	25.3	27.0	32.7	4.5	1,118	1,115	942	930
2001	12.2	20.8	21.6	28.0	6.0	1,078	1,070	918	838
2000	15.7	19.7	26.9	31.8	8.6	1,020	974	869	800
1999	13.5	22.0	26.1	33.8	6.9	930	932	841	800
1998	14.1	19.7	21.8	31.1	7.0	990	867	712	680
1997	15.0	20.4	28.8	36.1	7.4	939	803	710	739
1996	16.6	20.3	30.4	32.4	10.4	798	871	753	712
1995	17.5	20.6	34.5	39.5	7.2	802	789	721	677
1994	17.2	29.2	28.5	34.9	6.1	748	747	722	671
1993r	18.9	24.2	29.0	32.3	8.7	667	643	586	567
1993	18.7	24.3	28.3	29.3	8.6	678	658	597	567
1992	16.8	23.4	25.0	33.1	9.6	636	684	539	534
1991	20.8	29.8	27.6	34.1	12.0	639	665	544	502
1990	20.7	33.2	34.9	35.3	9.0	594	614	505	498
1989	20.0	31.4	39.7	33.5	13.5	615	570	519	490
1988	18.7	31.8	37.8	32.3	15.3	572	541	582	430
1987	13.8	30.8	32.2	35.8	12.1	581	530	494	464
1986	15.9	28.7	35.1	33.5	11.2	523	564	490	547
1985	20.8	27.9	33.0	28.8	14.5	514	520	455	497
1984	22.1	29.6	36.6	33.6	11.5	458	409	383	384
1983	18.1	25.8	33.2	34.3	8.3	458	430	470	432
1982	20.8	29.0	35.6	29.6	11.8	495	449	458	406
1981	16.0	29.4	31.6	29.5	12.2	444	459	427	468
1980	19.2	22.2	29.5	30.9	11.7	463	468	448	444
1979	17.5	32.5	29.6	29.3	13.0	361	354	348	369
1978	15.5	28.4	33.3	38.5	10.7	335	349	327	338
1977	14.8	17.7	26.8	31.6	15.8	311	368	332	367
WHITE ALONE OR IN COMBINATION									
Both Sexes									
2019	25.4	30.1	29.3	31.2	4.1	9,268	9,497	9,686	9,730
2018	25.0	30.0	30.0	32.7	3.7	9,361	9,594	9,736	9,762
2017	25.1	29.7	30.3	33.3	3.4	9,320	9,694	9,618	9,720
2016	24.9	29.8	30.5	32.0	4.0	9,274	9,615	9,586	9,779
2015	24.4	30.3	31.2	31.9	3.1	9,492	9,632	9,658	9,802
2014	24.2	28.2	29.9	32.1	3.9	9,623	9,586	9,679	9,679
2013	23.1	27.3	31.3	33.1	3.6	9,664	9,574	9,754	9,681
2012	24.4	28.5	30.8	33.6	2.4	9,607	9,630	9,685	9,740
2011	23.6	28.8	30.4	32.6	2.1	9,956	9,824	9,378	9,652
2010	19.6	25.2	28.6	29.4	2.2	9,935	9,712	9,435	9,699
2009	19.7	26.7	29.6	30.0	3.2	9,887	9,345	9,515	9,832
2008	20.6	27.5	29.6	30.7	2.5	9,680	9,298	9,577	10,043
2007	21.1	26.1	27.4	28.5	2.8	9,502	9,326	9,734	10,169
2006	20.6	25.6	26.7	29.9	3.0	9,346	9,444	9,850	10,175
2005	21.1	23.9	27.9	29.4	2.6	9,314	9,588	10,026	10,479
2004	22.4	25.6	27.4	30.5	3.9	9,422	9,506	10,175	10,079
2003	21.7	27.4	28.1	29.4	3.2	9,447	9,446	10,194	10,151
Male									
2019	25.2	30.5	30.7	33.8	3.8	4,759	4,823	4,937	4,961
2018	27.3	32.5	31.7	37.1	3.4	4,780	4,858	4,977	4,969
2017	26.3	31.8	32.5	35.7	3.9	4,758	4,943	4,921	4,968
2016	26.8	30.7	33.4	36.5	4.3	4,731	4,923	4,922	4,998
2015	26.2	31.8	31.8	35.7	3.4	4,855	4,935	4,968	5,003
2014	25.6	29.7	32.3	35.4	4.6	4,945	4,931	4,960	4,948
2013	25.6	31.0	34.0	36.8	4.1	4,911	4,940	4,965	4,951
2012	26.5	31.1	35.6	37.9	2.8	4,898	4,966	4,935	4,979
2011	26.3	31.9	33.2	37.6	2.1	5,089	5,042	4,820	4,956
2010	22.0	28.0	30.7	32.3	3.0	5,039	4,970	4,824	4,996
2009	21.1	29.8	32.8	33.3	3.4	5,072	4,776	4,866	5,039
2008	22.8	29.7	32.6	33.7	2.7	4,963	4,744	4,934	5,163
2007	24.0	28.2	29.1	32.0	2.9	4,857	4,770	4,997	5,203
2006	22.4	27.2	29.6	34.1	3.4	4,769	4,842	5,042	5,193
2005	23.9	27.3	30.9	33.1	2.7	4,751	4,925	5,151	5,268
2004	24.9	28.1	31.2	35.1	3.9	4,876	4,823	5,318	5,043
2003	24.5	31.6	31.0	33.8	3.4	4,965	4,946	5,108	5,172

* = Quantity zero or rounds to zero.
r = Revised, controlled to 1990 census based population estimates; previous 1993 data controlled to 1980 census based population estimates.
[1]Starting in 2003, respondents could identify more than one race. Except as noted, the race data in this table from 2003 onward represent those respondents who indicated only one race category.
[2]The data shown prior to 2003 consists of those identifying themselves as "Asian or Pacific Islanders."

Table A-12. Population 6 to 17 Years Old Enrolled Below Modal Grade, 1971–2019—*Continued*

(Numbers in thousands; percent; civilian noninstitutionalized population.)

Year, sex, race, and Hispanic origin	Percent below modal grade				Dropout rate, 15 to 17 years	Population in age group			
	6 to 8 years	9 to 11 years	12 to 14 years	15 to 17 years	15 to 17 years	6 to 8 years	9 to 11 years	12 to 14 years	15 to 17 years
Female									
2019	25.6	29.7	27.9	28.4	4.5	4,509	4,674	4,749	4,768
2018	22.6	27.4	28.1	28.1	4.0	4,581	4,736	4,760	4,793
2017	23.9	27.5	28.1	30.7	3.0	4,562	4,750	4,697	4,753
2016	22.9	28.8	27.3	27.4	3.7	4,543	4,692	4,664	4,782
2015	22.6	28.6	30.5	27.9	2.8	4,636	4,697	4,690	4,799
2014	22.8	26.6	27.3	28.8	3.2	4,678	4,655	4,718	4,731
2013	20.6	23.3	28.5	29.3	3.1	4,753	4,633	4,789	4,729
2012	22.2	25.7	25.7	29.1	1.9	4,709	4,664	4,751	4,761
2011	20.8	25.5	27.4	27.3	2.2	4,867	4,782	4,558	4,696
2010	17.1	22.4	26.5	26.4	1.4	4,896	4,743	4,610	4,703
2009	18.2	23.4	26.3	26.5	2.9	4,815	4,569	4,649	4,792
2008	18.3	25.3	26.3	27.5	2.4	4,717	4,554	4,643	4,880
2007	18.1	23.9	25.5	24.7	2.7	4,646	4,555	4,737	4,966
2006	18.7	23.8	23.6	25.5	2.6	4,577	4,602	4,808	4,982
2005	18.2	20.2	24.7	25.7	2.6	4,563	4,663	4,875	5,211
2004	19.6	23.0	23.2	25.9	3.9	4,545	4,683	4,857	5,037
2003	18.6	22.7	25.2	24.8	3.0	4,482	4,500	5,086	4,979
BLACK ALONE OR IN COMBINATION									
Both Sexes									
2019	22.3	28.6	34.0	33.4	4.3	2,210	2,303	2,188	2,201
2018	27.8	31.6	27.8	37.6	6.8	2,253	2,289	2,179	2,175
2017	23.0	31.8	32.6	36.9	4.0	2,395	2,245	2,098	2,187
2016	24.2	33.4	30.6	32.8	2.8	2,217	2,212	2,130	2,238
2015	22.4	30.4	32.3	35.6	2.7	2,146	2,321	2,148	2,144
2014	23.0	31.7	35.1	37.9	5.2	2,157	2,130	2,131	2,133
2013	24.2	28.2	30.9	35.7	4.5	2,235	2,055	2,163	2,145
2012	25.9	28.8	33.7	38.1	2.4	2,066	2,094	2,139	2,113
2011	21.6	30.7	28.6	34.2	2.5	2,186	2,061	1,945	2,003
2010	17.4	26.3	32.7	32.7	2.1	2,122	1,938	1,971	2,067
2009	21.2	30.9	33.2	36.4	2.5	1,939	2,006	2,001	2,116
2008	18.7	27.2	40.0	38.6	3.0	2,026	2,002	2,036	2,179
2007	17.6	27.3	32.1	38.8	2.8	1,998	1,950	2,071	2,146
2006	18.9	28.3	34.8	35.0	3.1	1,982	1,988	2,074	2,202
2005	20.3	34.8	33.4	37.9	4.4	1,970	1,982	2,137	2,194
2004	20.3	27.0	33.2	39.1	2.5	1,950	2,022	2,174	2,107
2003	23.2	33.5	33.4	36.8	3.8	1,921	2,183	2,220	2,034
Male									
2019	23.7	28.9	32.6	39.4	4.7	1,093	1,170	1,107	1,122
2018	29.3	31.4	32.1	41.1	4.2	1,171	1,118	1,102	1,086
2017	21.2	29.2	34.3	42.2	4.7	1,210	1,115	1,049	1,090
2016	22.4	36.2	35.5	31.8	2.7	1,138	1,093	1,083	1,135
2015	20.2	30.9	33.3	39.3	2.0	1,058	1,187	1,105	1,075
2014	22.6	33.7	38.5	40.1	5.3	1,055	1,122	1,097	1,053
2013	22.0	31.3	35.3	39.9	3.3	1,088	1,050	1,100	1,061
2012	31.0	32.4	36.1	39.4	1.4	1,095	1,061	1,085	1,047
2011	23.6	35.4	32.2	36.8	3.8	1,135	1,017	991	994
2010	17.3	30.9	34.5	36.1	3.0	1,085	961	978	1,041
2009	21.4	34.1	36.9	43.3	2.4	934	1,042	1,006	1,059
2008	20.2	26.0	45.4	41.3	3.3	1,026	1,020	1,032	1,090
2007	21.7	29.9	34.4	42.6	2.1	1,053	983	1,034	1,086
2006	20.0	33.5	39.0	42.8	3.5	1,013	1,018	1,050	1,094
2005	22.1	37.0	35.5	41.8	5.0	981	999	1,061	1,082
2004	21.1	30.6	37.3	45.3	1.9	966	1,042	1,065	1,056
2003	24.2	36.6	38.5	42.9	4.0	1,014	1,116	1,033	1,083
Female									
2019	20.8	28.2	35.4	27.3	3.7	1,117	1,133	1,081	1,079
2018	26.2	31.8	23.4	33.7	9.3	1,082	1,170	1,077	1,089
2017	24.8	34.3	30.9	31.7	3.4	1,184	1,130	1,050	1,097
2016	25.9	30.7	25.6	33.8	2.8	1,079	1,119	1,047	1,103
2015	24.5	29.9	31.4	31.8	3.5	1,088	1,134	1,044	1,069
2014	23.4	29.5	31.6	35.8	5.1	1,102	1,008	1,033	1,080
2013	26.3	24.8	26.4	31.5	5.6	1,147	1,005	1,063	1,085
2012	20.2	25.1	31.2	36.8	3.4	971	1,032	1,054	1,066

* = Quantity zero or rounds to zero.
r = Revised, controlled to 1990 census based population estimates; previous 1993 data controlled to 1980 census based population estimates.
[1]Starting in 2003, respondents could identify more than one race. Except as noted, the race data in this table from 2003 onward represent those respondents who indicated only one race category.
[2]The data shown prior to 2003 consists of those identifying themselves as "Asian or Pacific Islanders."

Table A-12. Population 6 to 17 Years Old Enrolled Below Modal Grade, 1971–2019—*Continued*

(Numbers in thousands; percent; civilian noninstitutionalized population.)

Year, sex, race, and Hispanic origin	Percent below modal grade				Dropout rate, 15 to 17 years	Population in age group			
	6 to 8 years	9 to 11 years	12 to 14 years	15 to 17 years		6 to 8 years	9 to 11 years	12 to 14 years	15 to 17 years
2011	19.5	26.0	24.8	31.7	1.3	1,051	1,044	954	1,009
2010	17.4	21.8	31.0	29.4	1.3	1,037	977	993	1,026
2009	21.0	27.5	29.5	29.5	2.5	1,004	965	995	1,058
2008	17.2	28.3	34.4	35.9	2.7	1,000	982	1,004	1,089
2007	13.2	24.6	29.9	34.8	3.6	945	967	1,037	1,061
2006	17.8	23.0	30.6	27.3	2.7	969	969	1,024	1,108
2005	18.6	32.6	31.4	34.1	3.7	990	983	1,076	1,112
2004	17.8	23.0	30.6	27.3	2.7	969	969	1,024	1,108
2003	22.0	30.4	29.0	29.8	3.4	907	1,067	1,187	951
ASIAN ALONE OR IN COMBINATION									
Both Sexes									
2019	23.5	22.0	21.4	26.4	2.8	848	844	885	888
2018	19.8	26.5	23.1	24.8	4.5	898	782	838	847
2017	19.7	26.8	22.9	25.3	3.4	802	866	817	869
2016	23.3	21.2	22.5	25.3	3.0	784	890	761	813
2015	26.1	23.7	22.1	24.0	4.5	761	793	765	772
2014	15.5	23.9	25.5	28.1	1.3	801	783	756	760
2013	17.2	16.5	21.3	18.8	1.0	825	772	693	734
2012	17.0	19.2	17.7	30.9	1.3	751	707	738	768
2011	17.5	22.5	25.7	27.8	2.0	744	718	614	650
2010	10.9	19.8	22.5	19.9	2.5	779	728	603	532
2009	9.5	13.6	26.9	19.8	1.2	690	563	513	508
2008	16.9	23.7	24.8	20.8	3.9	599	587	558	603
2007	11.4	20.6	15.6	25.3	3.6	650	613	600	548
2006	15.0	19.9	19.2	22.2	3.2	528	574	574	603
2005	13.0	12.3	16.5	18.4	1.2	600	531	576	581
2004	13.9	12.4	20.3	24.6	2.6	494	576	585	599
2003	8.8	14.9	18.4	23.5	2.4	579	548	552	543
Male									
2019	21.9	23.0	25.7	24.4	0.9	426	434	431	421
2018	18.1	26.4	24.3	23.8	2.5	457	422	393	412
2017	21.9	26.1	23.9	28.3	3.5	411	444	414	437
2016	24.7	26.6	24.9	25.9	3.9	411	460	389	382
2015	24.0	22.1	17.4	25.0	4.1	377	402	358	388
2014	20.5	21.1	30.0	31.6	2.5	414	395	373	348
2013	16.3	19.8	22.2	21.1	1.2	383	373	339	343
2012	18.9	20.6	17.5	32.9	2.0	376	341	368	397
2011	17.5	23.0	27.0	30.8	2.0	380	368	324	300
2010	9.7	19.6	25.2	21.8	2.1	397	385	309	291
2009	10.5	16.9	26.8	20.6	0.6	363	269	271	285
2008	22.3	23.0	20.6	15.9	2.1	285	291	299	289
2007	8.4	20.2	16.7	28.4	4.3	316	307	287	289
2006	15.4	15.4	15.4	15.4	4.1	259	311	291	285
2005	12.5	13.2	14.5	16.5	1.6	318	254	307	286
2004	12.4	16.2	19.3	22.3	3.6	254	278	324	286
2003	9.3	19.8	19.4	19.2	1.8	263	268	299	277
Female									
2019	25.1	20.9	17.2	28.4	4.5	421	410	454	467
2018	21.5	26.8	22.1	25.9	6.5	441	360	445	435
2017	17.5	27.6	22.0	22.2	3.3	391	422	403	432
2016	21.7	15.5	19.9	24.7	2.2	373	430	372	432
2015	28.2	25.5	26.1	22.9	4.9	383	392	407	384
2014	10.2	26.9	21.2	25.1	0.3	388	389	383	411
2013	18.1	13.6	20.4	16.7	0.8	442	400	354	391
2012	15.1	17.9	18.0	28.8	0.5	376	366	370	371
2011	17.4	22.0	24.3	25.2	2.0	364	350	290	350
2010	12.1	20.0	19.6	17.6	2.9	382	344	294	242
2009	8.4	10.6	27.0	18.8	2.1	326	293	242	223
2008	12.2	24.4	29.6	25.6	5.5	314	295	259	314
2007	14.3	21.1	14.6	21.8	2.9	334	306	314	259
2006	14.6	20.6	15.4	22.2	2.4	269	263	283	318
2005	13.7	11.5	18.8	20.2	0.9	282	276	269	295
2004	15.5	8.8	21.6	26.7	1.6	241	298	261	313
2003	8.4	10.3	17.2	28.0	3.1	316	280	253	266

* = Quantity zero or rounds to zero.
r = Revised, controlled to 1990 census based population estimates; previous 1993 data controlled to 1980 census based population estimates.
[1]Starting in 2003, respondents could identify more than one race. Except as noted, the race data in this table from 2003 onward represent those respondents who indicated only one race category.
[2]The data shown prior to 2003 consists of those identifying themselves as "Asian or Pacific Islanders."

Table A-13. Annual High School Dropout Rates of 15 to 24 Year Olds by Sex, Race, Grade, and Hispanic Origin, October 1967–2019

(Numbers in thousands; percent; civilian noninstitutionalized population.)

Year, grade, race, and Hispanic origin	Total[1]			Male			Female		
	Total students	Dropouts	Dropout rate	Total students	Dropouts	Dropout rate	Total students	Dropouts	Dropout rate
ALL RACES									
Grades 10–12									
2019	11,694	473	4.0	5,859	227	3.9	5,835	246	4.2
2018	11,638	518	4.5	5,973	236	4.0	5,665	282	5.0
2017	11,719	523	4.5	5,971	307	5.1	5,748	215	3.7
2016	11,807	532	4.5	5,939	305	5.1	5,868	227	3.9
2015	11,646	535	4.6	5,894	283	4.8	5,752	252	4.4
2014	11,634	567	4.9	5,932	300	5.1	5,702	267	4.7
2013	11,495	508	4.4	5,844	267	4.6	5,651	241	4.3
2012	11,962	386	3.2	5,997	201	3.4	5,965	184	3.1
2011	11,726	375	3.2	6,010	206	3.4	5,716	169	2.9
2010	11,647	326	2.8	6,006	172	2.9	5,641	154	2.7
2009	11,651	373	3.2	5,798	189	3.3	5,853	184	3.1
2008	11,750	390	3.3	5,999	174	2.9	5,751	216	3.8
2007	11,584	383	3.3	5,879	206	3.5	5,705	177	3.1
2006	11,604	407	3.5	5,932	227	3.8	5,672	180	3.2
2005	11,494	414	3.6	5,843	233	4.0	5,651	181	3.2
2004	11,166	486	4.4	5,624	266	4.7	5,542	220	4.0
2003	11,378	429	3.8	5,705	225	4.0	5,674	203	3.6
2002	10,989	367	3.3	5,504	193	3.5	5,484	174	3.2
2001	10,777	507	4.7	5,534	293	5.3	5,243	214	4.1
2000	10,773	488	4.5	5,417	280	5.2	5,356	208	3.9
1999	11,067	520	4.7	5,659	243	4.3	5,411	277	5.1
1998	10,791	479	4.4	5,486	237	4.3	5,305	243	4.6
1997	10,645	454	4.3	5,330	251	4.7	5,313	203	3.8
1996	10,249	485	4.7	5,175	240	4.6	5,072	244	4.8
1995	10,106	544	5.4	5,161	297	5.8	4,946	247	5.0
1994	9,922	497	5.0	5,048	249	4.9	4,873	247	5.1
1993r	9,430	404	4.3	4,787	211	4.4	4,640	192	4.1
1993	9,021	382	4.2	4,570	199	4.4	4,452	183	4.1
1992	8,939	384	4.3	4,580	175	3.8	4,357	207	4.8
1991	8,612	348	4.0	4,380	167	3.8	4,231	180	4.3
1990	8,679	347	4.0	4,356	177	4.1	4,323	170	3.9
1989	8,974	404	4.5	4,519	203	4.5	4,453	199	4.5
1988	9,590	461	4.8	4,960	256	5.2	4,628	206	4.5
1987	9,802	403	4.1	4,921	215	4.4	4,879	187	3.8
1986	9,829	421	4.3	4,910	213	4.3	4,917	208	4.2
1985	9,704	504	5.2	4,831	259	5.4	4,874	245	5.0
1984	10,041	507	5.0	4,986	268	5.4	5,054	238	4.7
1983	10,331	535	5.2	5,130	294	5.7	5,200	241	4.6
1982	10,611	577	5.4	5,310	305	5.7	5,301	271	5.1
1981	10,868	639	5.9	5,379	322	6.0	5,487	316	5.8
1980	10,891	658	6.0	5,445	362	6.6	5,448	296	5.4
1979	11,136	744	6.7	5,479	369	6.7	5,658	377	6.7
1978	11,116	743	6.7	5,558	415	7.5	5,558	328	5.9
1977	11,300	734	6.5	5,657	392	6.9	5,643	342	6.1
1976	10,996	644	5.9	5,534	360	6.5	5,463	285	5.2
1975	11,033	639	5.8	5,485	296	5.4	5,548	343	6.2
1974	11,026	742	6.7	5,421	402	7.4	5,605	340	6.1
1973	10,851	683	6.3	5,407	370	6.8	5,444	313	5.7
1972	10,664	659	6.2	5,305	317	6.0	5,358	341	6.4
1971	10,451	562	5.4	5,193	297	5.7	5,258	266	5.1
1970	10,281	588	5.7	5,145	288	5.6	5,138	302	5.9
1969	10,212	551	5.4	5,069	273	5.4	5,142	278	5.4
1968	9,814	506	5.2	4,831	247	5.1	4,983	259	5.2
1967	9,350	486	5.2	4,605	237	5.1	4,745	249	5.2
Grade 10									
2019	3,964	65	1.6	2,059	15	0.7	1,905	50	2.6
2018	3,950	66	1.7	2,045	23	1.1	1,905	43	2.3
2017	3,975	41	1.0	2,153	35	1.6	1,822	6	0.3
2016	3,985	69	1.7	2,013	36	1.8	1,972	33	1.7
2015	3,994	61	1.5	2,016	24	1.2	1,979	37	1.9
2014	4,026	73	1.8	2,095	58	2.8	1,931	16	0.8
2013	3,971	35	0.9	1,996	19	0.9	1,976	16	0.8

* = Quantity zero or rounds to zero.
r = Revised, controlled to 1990 census based population estimates; previous 1993 data controlled to 1980 census based population estimates.
[1]Starting in 2003 respondents could identify more than one race. Except as noted, the race data in this table from 2003 onward represent those respondents who indicated only one race category.
[2]The data shown prior to 2003 consists of those identifying themselves as "Asian or Pacific Islanders."

Table A-13. Annual High School Dropout Rates of 15 to 24 Year Olds by Sex, Race, Grade, and Hispanic Origin, October 1967–2019—*Continued*

(Numbers in thousands; percent; civilian noninstitutionalized population.)

Year, grade, race, and Hispanic origin	Total[1]			Male			Female		
	Total students	Dropouts	Dropout rate	Total students	Dropouts	Dropout rate	Total students	Dropouts	Dropout rate
2012	4,226	34	0.8	2,104	20	1.0	2,122	14	0.7
2011	3,998	48	1.2	2,009	26	1.3	1,989	22	1.1
2010	3,983	27	0.7	2,008	17	0.8	1,976	10	0.5
2009	3,983	50	1.2	1,993	28	1.4	1,989	22	1.1
2008	4,154	56	1.4	2,104	25	1.2	2,050	31	1.5
2007	4,064	63	1.6	2,027	32	1.6	2,037	31	1.5
2006	4,179	31	0.7	2,053	19	0.9	2,126	12	0.5
2005	4,483	72	1.6	2,244	49	2.2	2,239	23	1.0
2004	4,028	99	2.5	2,096	56	2.7	1,931	42	2.2
2003	4,107	64	1.6	2,111	26	1.2	1,995	37	1.9
2002	3,896	55	1.4	1,963	36	1.8	1,934	19	1.0
2001	3,900	90	2.3	1,988	50	2.5	1,913	41	2.1
2000	3,957	77	1.9	2,036	48	2.4	1,920	28	1.5
1999	3,910	104	2.7	2,036	54	2.7	1,875	50	2.7
1998	3,883	90	2.3	1,971	36	1.8	1,911	54	2.8
1997	3,738	79	2.1	1,894	44	2.3	1,843	35	1.9
1996	3,691	94	2.5	1,906	50	2.6	1,784	43	2.4
1995	3,552	88	2.5	1,823	40	2.2	1,728	47	2.7
1994	3,474	76	2.2	1,793	45	2.5	1,681	31	1.8
1993r	3,265	86	2.6	1,696	52	3.1	1,567	33	2.1
1993	3,139	81	2.6	1,627	50	3.1	1,513	31	2.0
1992	3,197	81	2.5	1,657	37	2.2	1,539	43	2.8
1991	3,132	105	3.4	1,571	46	2.9	1,561	59	3.8
1990	3,215	90	2.8	1,660	43	2.6	1,555	47	3.0
1989	3,071	99	3.2	1,567	56	3.6	1,504	43	2.9
1988	3,308	112	3.4	1,716	63	3.7	1,592	49	3.1
1987	3,492	106	3.0	1,818	45	2.5	1,674	61	3.6
1986	3,555	119	3.3	1,820	56	3.1	1,734	63	3.6
1985	3,491	143	4.1	1,797	74	4.1	1,695	69	4.1
1984	3,415	135	4.0	1,735	76	4.4	1,680	59	3.5
1983	3,468	129	3.7	1,755	70	4.0	1,713	59	3.4
1982	3,540	144	4.1	1,792	69	3.9	1,747	74	4.2
1981	3,735	144	3.9	1,816	65	3.6	1,918	78	4.1
1980	3,817	166	4.3	1,957	95	4.9	1,861	71	3.8
1979	3,920	217	5.5	1,985	102	5.1	1,934	114	5.9
1978	3,878	185	4.8	1,943	96	4.9	1,935	89	4.6
1977	3,970	177	4.5	2,021	96	4.8	1,949	81	4.2
1976	3,914	145	3.7	1,960	79	4.0	1,955	67	3.4
1975	3,983	183	4.6	2,017	87	4.3	1,967	97	4.9
1974	3,901	223	5.7	1,951	122	6.3	1,949	101	5.2
1973	3,899	210	5.4	1,930	112	5.8	1,969	98	5.0
1972	3,868	203	5.2	1,940	106	5.5	1,928	97	5.0
1971	3,762	174	4.6	1,925	95	4.9	1,838	79	4.3
1970	3,686	186	5.0	1,865	90	4.8	1,822	97	5.3
1969	3,485	159	4.6	1,756	84	4.8	1,729	75	4.3
1968	3,615	151	4.2	1,849	75	4.1	1,767	76	4.3
1967	3,370	129	3.8	1,726	64	3.7	1,644	65	4.0
Grade 11									
2019	4,290	141	3.3	2,194	69	3.2	2,096	72	3.4
2018	4,210	140	3.3	2,137	49	2.3	2,074	91	4.4
2017	4,510	137	3.0	2,327	86	3.7	2,183	51	2.3
2016	4,261	126	3.0	2,191	78	3.6	2,070	48	2.3
2015	4,338	137	3.2	2,198	63	2.9	2,140	74	3.4
2014	4,274	151	3.5	2,189	89	4.1	2,085	63	3.0
2013	4,232	149	3.5	2,172	89	4.1	2,060	60	2.9
2012	4,378	66	1.5	2,228	28	1.2	2,150	39	1.8
2011	4,358	84	1.9	2,234	52	2.3	2,124	32	1.5
2010	4,247	84	2.0	2,201	50	2.3	2,046	34	1.7
2009	4,444	106	2.4	2,226	51	2.3	2,218	55	2.5
2008	4,186	96	2.3	2,113	60	2.9	2,073	36	1.7
2007	4,388	118	2.7	2,280	64	2.8	2,108	55	2.6
2006	4,323	112	2.6	2,271	62	2.7	2,053	50	2.4
2005	4,080	72	1.8	2,184	46	2.1	1,896	26	1.4
2004	4,010	141	3.5	2,012	76	3.8	1,998	65	3.3
2003	4,327	117	2.7	2,158	68	3.2	2,169	49	2.3

* = Quantity zero or rounds to zero.

r = Revised, controlled to 1990 census based population estimates; previous 1993 data controlled to 1980 census based population estimates.

[1] Starting in 2003 respondents could identify more than one race. Except as noted, the race data in this table from 2003 onward represent those respondents who indicated only one race category.

[2] The data shown prior to 2003 consists of those identifying themselves as "Asian or Pacific Islanders."

Table A-13. Annual High School Dropout Rates of 15 to 24 Year Olds by Sex, Race, Grade, and Hispanic Origin, October 1967–2019—*Continued*

(Numbers in thousands; percent; civilian noninstitutionalized population.)

Year, grade, race, and Hispanic origin	Total[1]			Male			Female		
	Total students	Dropouts	Dropout rate	Total students	Dropouts	Dropout rate	Total students	Dropouts	Dropout rate
2002..........................	4,137	99	2.4	2,111	54	2.6	2,026	45	2.2
2001..........................	4,114	139	3.4	2,134	72	3.4	1,979	67	3.4
2000..........................	3,833	170	4.4	1,933	78	4.0	1,901	93	4.9
1999..........................	4,036	150	3.7	2,052	69	3.4	1,984	81	4.0
1998..........................	3,735	110	2.9	1,902	55	2.9	1,833	55	3.0
1997..........................	3,882	142	3.7	1,957	71	3.6	1,925	71	3.7
1996..........................	3,606	138	3.8	1,828	76	4.2	1,778	62	3.5
1995..........................	3,568	159	4.5	1,846	89	4.8	1,724	71	4.1
1994..........................	3,587	132	3.7	1,864	61	3.3	1,722	70	4.1
1993r........................	3,375	106	3.1	1,725	43	2.5	1,650	63	3.8
1993..........................	3,218	100	3.1	1,643	40	2.4	1,575	60	3.8
1992..........................	3,213	120	3.7	1,642	52	3.2	1,570	67	4.3
1991..........................	3,083	101	3.3	1,598	42	2.6	1,484	58	3.9
1990..........................	2,976	98	3.3	1,462	57	3.9	1,514	41	2.7
1989..........................	3,302	125	3.8	1,683	67	4.0	1,618	57	3.5
1988..........................	3,447	161	4.7	1,819	89	4.9	1,627	72	4.4
1987..........................	3,566	122	3.4	1,766	71	4.0	1,800	51	2.8
1986..........................	3,433	116	3.4	1,700	51	3.0	1,733	65	3.8
1985..........................	3,274	139	4.2	1,618	70	4.3	1,656	69	4.2
1984..........................	3,328	163	4.9	1,682	87	5.2	1,646	76	4.6
1983..........................	3,601	162	4.5	1,825	87	4.8	1,775	75	4.2
1982..........................	3,694	218	5.9	1,872	122	6.5	1,822	96	5.3
1981..........................	3,787	262	6.9	1,937	144	7.4	1,850	118	6.4
1980..........................	3,670	225	6.1	1,832	120	6.6	1,839	105	5.7
1979..........................	3,718	229	6.2	1,840	102	5.5	1,879	128	6.8
1978..........................	3,708	230	6.2	1,905	113	5.9	1,803	117	6.5
1977..........................	3,832	244	6.4	1,964	133	6.8	1,867	110	5.9
1976..........................	3,786	227	6.0	1,955	123	6.3	1,831	104	5.7
1975..........................	3,596	230	6.4	1,828	103	5.6	1,767	126	7.1
1974..........................	3,721	237	6.4	1,819	123	6.8	1,902	114	6.0
1973..........................	3,631	237	6.5	1,877	126	6.7	1,754	111	6.3
1972..........................	3,581	241	6.7	1,825	107	5.9	1,756	134	7.6
1971..........................	3,585	185	5.2	1,772	82	4.6	1,811	103	5.7
1970..........................	3,456	198	5.7	1,750	96	5.5	1,706	102	6.0
1969..........................	3,489	190	5.4	1,779	100	5.6	1,710	90	5.3
1968..........................	3,255	179	5.5	1,640	91	5.5	1,614	88	5.5
1967..........................	3,068	169	5.5	1,557	76	4.9	1,511	93	6.2
Grade 12									
2019..........................	3,440	266	7.7	1,606	142	8.8	1,835	124	6.8
2018..........................	3,478	312	9.0	1,791	164	9.2	1,687	148	8.8
2017..........................	3,234	344	10.6	1,491	186	12.5	1,744	158	9.1
2016..........................	3,561	337	9.5	1,735	191	11.0	1,826	146	8.0
2015..........................	3,315	337	10.2	1,680	196	11.7	1,634	141	8.6
2014..........................	3,334	343	10.3	1,648	154	9.3	1,686	189	11.2
2013..........................	3,291	325	9.9	1,675	159	9.5	1,615	166	10.3
2012..........................	3,358	285	8.5	1,665	154	9.2	1,693	131	7.7
2011..........................	3,370	243	7.2	1,767	129	7.3	1,603	114	7.1
2010..........................	3,417	215	6.3	1,798	106	5.9	1,620	110	6.8
2009..........................	3,224	217	6.7	1,578	109	6.9	1,646	108	6.5
2008..........................	3,409	237	7.0	1,781	89	5.0	1,628	149	9.1
2007..........................	3,133	202	6.4	1,572	111	7.0	1,561	91	5.8
2006..........................	3,101	265	8.5	1,608	146	9.1	1,492	119	8.0
2005..........................	2,931	270	9.2	1,415	138	9.7	1,516	132	8.7
2004..........................	3,130	247	7.9	1,516	133	8.8	1,614	114	7.1
2003..........................	2,945	248	8.4	1,435	131	9.1	1,510	117	7.7
2002..........................	2,956	214	7.2	1,432	104	7.3	1,524	110	7.2
2001..........................	2,762	277	10.0	1,411	171	12.1	1,351	106	7.8
2000..........................	2,983	241	8.1	1,447	154	10.6	1,535	87	5.7
1999..........................	3,121	266	8.5	1,571	120	7.6	1,552	146	9.4
1998..........................	3,173	279	8.8	1,613	146	9.0	1,560	133	8.5
1997..........................	3,025	233	7.7	1,479	136	9.2	1,545	97	6.3
1996..........................	2,952	253	8.6	1,441	114	7.9	1,510	139	9.2
1995..........................	2,986	297	9.9	1,492	168	11.3	1,494	129	8.6
1994..........................	2,861	289	10.1	1,391	143	10.3	1,470	146	9.9
1993r........................	2,790	212	7.6	1,366	116	8.5	1,423	96	6.7

* = Quantity zero or rounds to zero.
r = Revised, controlled to 1990 census based population estimates; previous 1993 data controlled to 1980 census based population estimates.
[1]Starting in 2003 respondents could identify more than one race. Except as noted, the race data in this table from 2003 onward represent those respondents who indicated only one race category.
[2]The data shown prior to 2003 consists of those identifying themselves as "Asian or Pacific Islanders."

Table A-13. Annual High School Dropout Rates of 15 to 24 Year Olds by Sex, Race, Grade, and Hispanic Origin, October 1967–2019—*Continued*

(Numbers in thousands; percent; civilian noninstitutionalized population.)

Year, grade, race, and Hispanic origin	Total[1]			Male			Female		
	Total students	Dropouts	Dropout rate	Total students	Dropouts	Dropout rate	Total students	Dropouts	Dropout rate
1993	2,664	201	7.5	1,300	109	8.4	1,364	92	6.7
1992	2,529	183	7.2	1,281	86	6.7	1,248	97	7.8
1991	2,397	142	5.9	1,211	79	6.5	1,186	63	5.3
1990	2,488	159	6.4	1,234	77	6.2	1,254	82	6.5
1989	2,601	180	6.9	1,269	80	6.3	1,331	99	7.4
1988	2,835	188	6.6	1,425	104	7.3	1,409	85	6.0
1987	2,744	175	6.4	1,337	99	7.4	1,405	75	5.3
1986	2,841	186	6.5	1,390	106	7.6	1,450	80	5.5
1985	2,939	222	7.6	1,416	115	8.1	1,523	107	7.0
1984	3,298	209	6.3	1,569	105	6.7	1,728	103	6.0
1983	3,262	244	7.5	1,550	137	8.8	1,712	107	6.3
1982	3,377	215	6.4	1,646	114	6.9	1,732	101	5.8
1981	3,346	233	7.0	1,626	113	6.9	1,719	120	7.0
1980	3,404	267	7.8	1,656	147	8.9	1,748	120	6.9
1979	3,498	298	8.5	1,654	164	9.9	1,845	135	7.3
1978	3,530	328	9.3	1,710	206	12.0	1,820	122	6.7
1977	3,498	313	8.9	1,672	163	9.7	1,827	151	8.3
1976	3,296	272	8.3	1,619	158	9.8	1,677	114	6.8
1975	3,454	226	6.5	1,640	106	6.5	1,814	120	6.6
1974	3,404	282	8.3	1,651	157	9.5	1,754	125	7.1
1973	3,321	236	7.1	1,600	132	8.3	1,721	104	6.0
1972	3,215	215	6.7	1,540	104	6.8	1,674	110	6.6
1971	3,104	203	6.5	1,496	120	8.0	1,609	84	5.2
1970	3,139	204	6.5	1,530	102	6.7	1,610	103	6.4
1969	3,238	202	6.2	1,534	89	5.8	1,703	113	6.6
1968	2,944	176	6.0	1,342	81	6.0	1,602	95	5.9
1967	2,912	188	6.5	1,322	97	7.3	1,590	91	5.7
WHITE ALONE									
Grades 10–12									
2019	8,562	353	4.1	4,334	169	3.9	4,228	185	4.4
2018	8,428	348	4.1	4,293	175	4.1	4,135	173	4.2
2017	8,528	369	4.3	4,401	209	4.8	4,126	159	3.9
2016	8,541	371	4.3	4,303	211	4.9	4,238	159	3.8
2015	8,605	369	4.3	4,382	213	4.9	4,223	156	3.7
2014	8,594	434	5.0	4,379	218	5.0	4,215	216	5.1
2013	8,501	386	4.5	4,391	216	4.9	4,110	171	4.2
2012	8,767	207	2.4	4,479	126	2.8	4,288	81	1.9
2011	8,815	261	3.0	4,559	145	3.2	4,256	116	2.7
2010	8,793	221	2.5	4,592	127	2.8	4,201	94	2.2
2009	8,886	269	3.0	4,459	146	3.3	4,427	123	2.8
2008	8,942	246	2.8	4,588	123	2.7	4,353	123	2.8
2007	8,927	246	2.8	4,518	126	2.8	4,409	120	2.7
2006	8,924	311	3.5	4,568	177	3.9	4,355	133	3.1
2005	8,855	271	3.1	4,472	151	3.4	4,382	120	2.7
2004	8,585	359	4.2	4,344	211	4.9	4,241	148	3.5
2003[1]	8,781	321	3.7	4,434	172	3.9	4,347	148	3.4
2002	8,636	259	3.0	4,371	133	3.0	4,265	126	3.0
2001	8,490	388	4.6	4,363	230	5.3	4,126	158	3.8
2000	8,540	371	4.3	4,368	204	4.7	4,172	167	4.0
1999	8,665	380	4.4	4,426	180	4.1	4,238	198	4.7
1998	8,487	371	4.4	4,306	188	4.4	4,181	183	4.4
1997	8,402	355	4.2	4,220	208	4.9	4,180	145	3.5
1996	8,005	361	4.5	4,077	198	4.8	3,928	163	4.1
1995	7,926	402	5.1	4,079	220	5.4	3,849	183	4.8
1994	7,862	371	4.7	4,014	184	4.6	3,848	188	4.9
1993r	7,442	306	4.1	3,790	157	4.1	3,654	150	4.1
1993	7,152	290	4.1	3,623	147	4.1	3,530	143	4.1
1992	7,077	292	4.1	3,646	140	3.8	3,430	151	4.4
1991	6,856	254	3.7	3,514	127	3.6	3,343	128	3.8
1990	6,984	266	3.8	3,522	144	4.1	3,462	122	3.5
1989	7,243	286	3.9	3,653	149	4.1	3,589	136	3.8
1988	7,727	362	4.7	4,016	203	5.1	3,712	161	4.3
1987	7,979	299	3.7	4,023	163	4.1	3,953	135	3.4
1986	8,011	333	4.2	4,007	168	4.2	4,007	166	4.1

* = Quantity zero or rounds to zero.
r = Revised, controlled to 1990 census based population estimates; previous 1993 data controlled to 1980 census based population estimates.
[1]Starting in 2003 respondents could identify more than one race. Except as noted, the race data in this table from 2003 onward represent those respondents who indicated only one race category.
[2]The data shown prior to 2003 consists of those identifying themselves as "Asian or Pacific Islanders."

Table A-13. Annual High School Dropout Rates of 15 to 24 Year Olds by Sex, Race, Grade, and Hispanic Origin, October 1967–2019—*Continued*

(Numbers in thousands; percent; civilian noninstitutionalized population.)

Year, grade, race, and Hispanic origin	Total[1] Total students	Dropouts	Dropout rate	Male Total students	Dropouts	Dropout rate	Female Total students	Dropouts	Dropout rate
1985	7,967	384	4.8	3,963	195	4.9	4,003	188	4.7
1984	8,221	410	5.0	4,119	220	5.3	4,101	190	4.6
1983	8,531	410	4.8	4,264	232	5.4	4,264	177	4.2
1982	8,769	444	5.1	4,381	231	5.3	4,390	214	4.9
1981	9,067	478	5.3	4,532	254	5.6	4,536	224	4.9
1980	9,177	517	5.6	4,624	294	6.4	4,554	224	4.9
1979	9,437	588	6.2	4,694	311	6.6	4,742	277	5.8
1978	9,360	574	6.1	4,747	329	6.9	4,611	244	5.3
1977	9,536	594	6.2	4,766	327	6.9	4,770	267	5.6
1976	9,362	532	5.7	4,708	297	6.3	4,654	235	5.0
1975	9,440	507	5.4	4,709	234	5.0	4,732	274	5.8
1974	9,403	566	6.0	4,650	326	7.0	4,754	241	5.1
1973	9,359	537	5.7	4,708	288	6.1	4,649	248	5.3
1972	9,173	520	5.7	4,588	247	5.4	4,583	272	5.9
1971	9,140	470	5.1	4,577	244	5.3	4,562	226	5.0
1970	8,959	449	5.0	4,496	212	4.7	4,462	237	5.3
1969	8,878	429	4.8	4,438	208	4.7	4,439	221	5.0
1968	8,580	387	4.5	4,246	190	4.5	4,331	196	4.5
1967	8,186	379	4.6	4,060	189	4.7	4,126	190	4.6
WHITE ALONE, NON-HISPANIC									
Grades 10–12									
2019	6,198	234	3.8	3,161	115	3.6	3,037	119	3.9
2018	6,097	213	3.5	3,112	113	3.6	2,984	100	3.3
2017	6,224	235	3.8	3,231	132	4.1	2,993	103	3.4
2016	6,230	273	4.4	3,234	164	5.1	2,996	109	3.6
2015	6,382	233	3.6	3,289	145	4.4	3,092	87	2.8
2014	6,397	285	4.5	3,288	154	4.7	3,109	131	4.2
2013	6,268	256	4.1	3,236	144	4.5	3,031	112	3.7
2012	6,436	95	1.5	3,257	61	1.9	3,179	34	1.1
2011	6,647	171	2.6	3,404	89	2.6	3,243	82	2.5
2010	6,851	150	2.2	3,568	97	2.7	3,284	53	1.6
2009	6,944	160	2.3	3,491	91	2.6	3,453	68	2.0
2008	7,079	156	2.2	3,638	83	2.3	3,441	73	2.1
2007	7,274	155	2.1	3,684	82	2.2	3,590	73	2.0
2006	7,171	200	2.8	3,693	120	3.2	3,478	80	2.3
2005	7,227	196	2.7	3,652	103	2.8	3,575	93	2.6
2004	7,015	245	3.5	3,582	130	3.6	3,434	115	3.4
2003[1]	7,139	214	3.0	3,665	116	3.2	3,474	98	2.8
2002	7,124	173	2.4	3,620	84	2.3	3,504	89	2.6
2001	7,070	272	3.8	3,647	173	4.7	3,423	98	2.9
2000	7,159	276	3.9	3,648	150	4.1	3,511	126	3.6
1999	7,265	274	3.8	3,744	130	3.5	3,523	145	4.1
1998	7,174	266	3.7	3,605	130	3.6	3,570	137	3.8
1997	7,090	242	3.4	3,533	140	4.0	3,558	103	2.9
1996	6,850	267	3.9	3,511	145	4.1	3,337	121	3.6
1995	6,905	296	4.3	3,564	164	4.6	3,341	131	3.9
1994	6,839	274	4.0	3,496	137	3.9	3,343	137	4.1
1993	6,277	237	3.8	3,229	128	4.0	3,047	108	3.5
BLACK ALONE									
Grades 10–12									
2019	1,710	70	4.1	815	34	4.1	894	36	4.1
2018	1,769	113	6.4	946	41	4.3	823	73	8.8
2017	1,784	88	5.0	879	58	6.6	905	31	3.4
2016	1,815	98	5.4	919	49	5.3	897	49	5.5
2015	1,735	112	6.4	842	49	5.8	893	63	7.0
2014	1,757	83	4.7	905	44	4.9	852	39	4.5
2013	1,791	88	4.9	859	37	4.3	931	51	5.5
2012	1,949	124	6.4	897	49	5.5	1,052	75	7.1
2011	1,944	78	4.0	965	54	5.6	978	24	2.4
2010	1,898	62	3.2	946	36	3.8	952	26	2.7
2009	1,797	81	4.5	870	38	4.4	927	42	4.6
2008	1,868	114	6.1	925	42	4.6	943	72	7.6

* = Quantity zero or rounds to zero.
r = Revised, controlled to 1990 census based population estimates; previous 1993 data controlled to 1980 census based population estimates.
[1]Starting in 2003 respondents could identify more than one race. Except as noted, the race data in this table from 2003 onward represent those respondents who indicated only one race category.
[2]The data shown prior to 2003 consists of those identifying themselves as "Asian or Pacific Islanders."

Table A-13. Annual High School Dropout Rates of 15 to 24 Year Olds by Sex, Race, Grade, and Hispanic Origin, October 1967–2019—*Continued*

(Numbers in thousands; percent; civilian noninstitutionalized population.)

Year, grade, race, and Hispanic origin	Total[1]			Male			Female		
	Total students	Dropouts	Dropout rate	Total students	Dropouts	Dropout rate	Total students	Dropouts	Dropout rate
2007	1,781	76	4.3	914	45	4.9	867	31	3.6
2006	1,767	65	3.7	902	29	3.2	864	37	4.3
2005	1,763	122	6.9	943	71	7.5	820	51	6.2
2004	1,716	90	5.2	833	40	4.8	883	50	5.7
2003[1]	1,698	76	4.5	812	33	4.1	886	43	4.9
2002	1,664	73	4.4	782	40	5.1	882	33	3.8
2001	1,655	95	5.7	828	51	6.2	827	45	5.4
2000	1,706	96	5.6	819	62	7.6	888	34	3.8
1999	1,794	107	6.0	925	48	5.2	870	59	6.8
1998	1,759	88	5.0	918	42	4.6	841	46	5.5
1997	1,678	80	4.8	813	33	4.1	866	49	5.7
1996	1,704	107	6.3	803	37	4.6	901	70	7.8
1995	1,598	97	6.1	797	63	7.9	802	35	4.4
1994	1,559	96	6.1	763	50	6.5	795	45	5.7
1993r	1,499	80	5.3	740	43	5.8	758	37	4.9
1993	1,447	78	5.4	724	41	5.7	722	36	5.0
1992	1,422	70	4.9	702	23	3.3	720	48	6.7
1991	1,366	85	6.2	685	38	5.5	683	48	7.0
1990	1,303	66	5.1	636	26	4.1	666	40	6.0
1989	1,384	106	7.7	684	47	6.9	701	60	8.6
1988	1,468	93	6.3	751	50	6.7	717	43	6.0
1987	1,463	93	6.4	730	45	6.2	732	47	6.4
1986	1,449	68	4.7	711	34	4.8	737	34	4.6
1985	1,422	110	7.7	703	58	8.3	719	52	7.2
1984	1,524	88	5.8	711	44	6.2	813	43	5.3
1983	1,498	103	6.9	687	48	7.0	810	55	6.8
1982	1,553	121	7.8	786	71	9.0	767	50	6.5
1981	1,516	146	9.6	704	66	9.4	815	83	10.2
1980	1,496	124	8.3	714	57	8.0	781	66	8.5
1979	1,479	142	9.6	679	51	7.5	802	92	11.5
1978	1,542	160	10.4	706	78	11.0	835	81	9.7
1977	1,588	133	8.4	746	62	8.3	789	71	9.0
1976	1,449	105	7.2	729	62	8.5	721	45	6.2
1975	1,416	123	8.7	673	56	8.3	743	67	9.0
1974	1,441	167	11.6	679	73	10.8	761	93	12.2
1973	1,372	138	10.1	650	78	12.0	725	61	8.4
1972	1,373	133	9.7	644	65	10.1	756	68	9.0
1971	1,195	87	7.3	552	51	9.2	643	37	5.8
1970	1,192	133	11.2	587	74	12.6	606	60	9.9
1969	1,209	113	9.3	562	58	10.3	646	55	8.5
1968	1,123	113	10.1	523	52	9.9	600	61	10.2
1967	1,066	106	9.9	485	47	9.7	578	58	10.0
ASIAN[2]									
Grades 10–12									
2019	630	18	2.8	313	7	2.3	317	11	3.3
2018	617	28	4.5	310	9	3.0	308	19	6.1
2017	657	42	6.3	323	22	6.8	334	20	5.9
2016	594	20	3.3	281	11	3.9	313	9	2.8
2015	552	34	6.2	263	20	7.5	288	14	5.0
2014	566	5	0.9	259	3	1.2	307	2	0.6
2013	604	10	1.7	279	4	1.5	324	6	1.8
2012	592	19	3.2	331	9	2.7	261	10	3.8
2011	495	17	3.5	272	4	1.5	223	13	6.0
2010	419	12	2.8	220	6	2.9	199	5	2.6
2009	426	7	1.7	215	2	0.8	210	5	2.6
2008	429	17	3.9	219	-	0.2	210	16	7.8
2007	404	30	7.5	202	13	6.6	202	17	8.3
2006	445	19	4.2	237	11	4.5	208	8	3.7
2005	425	6	1.5	219	5	2.4	206	1	0.5
2004	452	4	0.9	233	-	-	219	4	1.9
2003[1]	457	11	2.4	237	3	1.4	221	7	3.4
2002	515	12	2.3	266	8	3.0	249	4	1.6
2001	470	10	2.1	274	9	3.3	197	1	0.5
2000	399	13	3.3	178	12	6.7	221	1	0.5
1999	523	25	4.8	269	13	4.8	253	12	4.7

* = Quantity zero or rounds to zero.
r = Revised, controlled to 1990 census based population estimates; previous 1993 data controlled to 1980 census based population estimates.
[1] Starting in 2003 respondents could identify more than one race. Except as noted, the race data in this table from 2003 onward represent those respondents who indicated only one race category.
[2] The data shown prior to 2003 consists of those identifying themselves as "Asian or Pacific Islanders."

Table A-13. Annual High School Dropout Rates of 15 to 24 Year Olds by Sex, Race, Grade, and Hispanic Origin, October 1967–2019—*Continued*

(Numbers in thousands; percent; civilian noninstitutionalized population.)

Year, grade, race, and Hispanic origin	Total[1]			Male			Female		
	Total students	Dropouts	Dropout rate	Total students	Dropouts	Dropout rate	Total students	Dropouts	Dropout rate
HISPANIC ORIGIN (OF ANY RACE)									
Grades 10–12									
2019.............................	2,744	147	5.3	1,395	72	5.2	1,350	74	5.5
2018.............................	2,736	153	5.6	1,385	67	4.8	1,351	86	6.4
2017.............................	2,650	161	6.1	1,357	104	7.7	1,293	56	4.4
2016.............................	2,747	118	4.3	1,331	67	5.1	1,416	51	3.6
2015.............................	2,599	148	5.7	1,314	67	5.1	1,285	80	6.3
2014.............................	2,490	179	7.2	1,254	86	6.8	1,236	93	7.5
2013.............................	2,509	132	5.3	1,291	71	5.5	1,218	61	5.0
2012.............................	2,671	136	5.1	1,377	76	5.5	1,294	60	4.6
2011.............................	2,376	100	4.2	1,260	56	4.4	1,116	44	4.0
2010.............................	2,130	80	3.8	1,113	30	2.7	1,018	51	5.0
2009.............................	2,129	114	5.3	1,039	55	5.3	1,090	59	5.4
2008.............................	2,062	101	4.9	1,052	44	4.2	1,011	57	5.6
2007.............................	1,785	99	5.5	904	49	5.5	882	49	5.6
2006.............................	1,923	124	6.4	958	61	6.3	965	63	6.6
2005.............................	1,814	86	4.7	910	51	5.6	904	35	3.9
2004	1,723	138	8.0	842	97	11.5	881	40	4.6
2003	1,792	116	6.5	846	65	7.7	945	51	5.4
2002.............................	1,614	86	5.3	801	50	6.2	814	36	4.4
2001.............................	1,487	121	8.1	755	57	7.5	732	64	8.7
2000.............................	1,465	100	6.8	761	54	7.1	704	46	6.5
1999.............................	1,482	105	7.1	729	50	6.9	751	55	7.3
1998.............................	1,368	115	8.4	731	63	8.6	637	52	8.2
1997.............................	1,377	119	8.6	710	74	10.4	668	45	6.7
1996.............................	1,195	100	8.4	588	54	9.2	608	46	7.6
1995.............................	1,251	145	11.6	644	70	10.9	608	76	12.5
1994.............................	1,179	109	9.2	607	51	8.4	572	58	10.1
1993r............................	1,061	69	6.5	488	25	5.1	573	44	7.5
1993.............................	943	60	6.4	436	21	4.8	508	39	7.7
1992.............................	917	72	7.9	468	27	5.8	441	38	8.6
1991.............................	809	59	7.3	396	41	10.4	417	20	4.8
1990.............................	811	65	8.0	379	33	8.7	428	31	7.2
1989.............................	762	59	7.7	394	30	7.6	366	28	7.7
1988.............................	730	77	10.5	398	49	12.3	333	28	8.4
1987.............................	769	43	5.6	380	19	5.0	389	24	6.2
1986.............................	764	91	11.9	376	44	11.7	388	48	12.4
1985.............................	729	71	9.7	333	31	9.3	396	39	9.8
1984.............................	706	77	10.9	311	38	12.2	396	40	10.1
1983.............................	691	68	9.8	351	48	13.7	340	21	6.2
1982.............................	692	65	9.4	370	35	9.5	321	29	9.0
1981.............................	717	77	10.7	350	37	10.6	367	40	10.9
1980.............................	646	74	11.5	295	50	16.9	350	24	6.9
1979.............................	593	58	9.8	295	30	10.2	298	27	9.1
1978.............................	567	70	12.3	295	46	15.6	271	23	8.5
1977.............................	627	50	8.0	341	35	10.3	287	15	5.2
1976.............................	638	46	7.2	300	22	7.3	336	23	6.8
1975.............................	614	67	10.9	317	32	10.1	294	34	11.6
1974.............................	547	53	9.7	271	34	12.5	278	20	7.2
1973.............................	499	50	10.0	240	19	7.9	259	31	12.0
1972.............................	498	55	11.0	253	28	11.1	247	27	10.9
WHITE ALONE OR IN COMBINATION									
Grades 10–12									
2019.............................	9,098	374	4.1	4,582	177	3.9	4,516	197	4.4
2018.............................	8,983	364	4.0	4,553	180	4.0	4,430	184	4.1
2017.............................	8,968	375	4.2	4,619	212	4.6	4,348	163	3.7
2016.............................	9,054	385	4.3	4,566	224	4.9	4,488	161	3.6
2015.............................	9,037	378	4.2	4,610	213	4.6	4,427	165	3.7
2014.............................	9,005	446	5.0	4,580	229	5.0	4,424	217	4.9
2013.............................	8,854	404	4.6	4,577	226	4.9	4,276	178	4.2
2012.............................	9,101	220	2.4	4,629	137	3.0	4,473	83	1.9

* = Quantity zero or rounds to zero.
r = Revised, controlled to 1990 census based population estimates; previous 1993 data controlled to 1980 census based population estimates.
[1]Starting in 2003 respondents could identify more than one race. Except as noted, the race data in this table from 2003 onward represent those respondents who indicated only one race category.
[2]The data shown prior to 2003 consists of those identifying themselves as "Asian or Pacific Islanders."

Table A-13. Annual High School Dropout Rates of 15 to 24 Year Olds by Sex, Race, Grade, and Hispanic Origin, October 1967–2019—*Continued*

(Numbers in thousands; percent; civilian noninstitutionalized population.)

Year, grade, race, and Hispanic origin	Total[1] Total students	Dropouts	Dropout rate	Male Total students	Dropouts	Dropout rate	Female Total students	Dropouts	Dropout rate
2011	9,087	272	3.0	4,696	145	3.1	4,391	127	2.9
2010	9,112	242	2.7	4,764	130	2.7	4,348	112	2.6
2009	9,216	280	3.0	4,610	148	3.2	4,606	132	2.9
2008	9,277	257	2.8	4,766	129	2.7	4,511	128	2.8
2007	9,199	251	2.7	4,664	131	2.8	4,535	120	2.7
2006	9,212	320	3.5	4,695	185	3.9	4,517	136	3.0
2005	9,158	281	3.1	4,610	155	3.4	4,548	126	2.8
2004	8,821	382	4.3	4,464	222	5.0	4,357	160	3.7
2003	9,045	335	3.7	4,573	183	4.0	4,471	151	3.4
BLACK ALONE OR IN COMBINATION									
Grades 10–12									
2019	2,000	76	3.8	962	36	3.7	1,038	41	3.9
2018	2,085	129	6.2	1,093	41	3.7	992	88	8.9
2017	2,084	95	4.6	1,022	58	5.7	1,062	37	3.4
2016	2,142	106	4.9	1,077	56	5.2	1,066	49	4.6
2015	1,950	112	5.7	951	49	5.1	999	63	6.3
2014	2,012	95	4.7	1,019	55	5.4	993	40	4.0
2013	1,989	98	4.9	962	42	4.3	1,027	56	5.4
2012	2,124	129	6.1	976	52	5.3	1,148	77	6.7
2011	2,051	82	4.0	1,024	54	5.3	1,027	28	2.8
2010	2,038	76	3.7	1,021	38	3.7	1,017	39	3.8
2009	1,985	86	4.3	958	40	4.2	1,026	46	4.5
2008	2,033	121	5.9	1,012	46	4.5	1,021	75	7.3
2007	1,900	78	4.1	977	47	4.8	923	31	3.4
2006	1,891	66	3.5	952	29	3.0	939	38	4.0
2005	1,870	129	6.9	979	71	7.3	890	58	6.5
2004	1,797	99	5.5	869	40	4.6	928	59	6.3
2003	1,808	79	4.4	853	36	4.2	955	43	4.5
ASIAN ALONE OR IN COMBINATION									
Grades 10–12									
2019	783	19	2.4	370	7	1.9	413	11	2.7
2018	758	30	3.9	372	11	3.0	386	19	4.8
2017	796	44	5.5	397	24	6.2	398	20	4.9
2016	731	25	3.4	353	16	4.4	378	9	2.3
2015	661	38	5.7	312	20	6.3	349	18	5.2
2014	660	5	0.8	300	3	1.0	361	2	0.5
2013	744	10	1.4	339	4	1.2	405	6	1.5
2012	696	19	2.7	368	9	2.5	328	10	3.1
2011	579	17	3.0	303	4	1.3	275	13	4.9
2010	520	16	3.2	270	6	2.4	250	10	4.0
2009	525	8	1.4	255	2	0.8	270	5	2.0
2008	511	17	3.3	256	-	0.2	255	16	6.4
2007	483	30	6.2	233	13	5.8	250	17	6.7
2006	542	23	4.2	279	15	5.4	263	8	3.0
2005	525	8	1.5	270	6	2.3	255	2	0.6
2004	516	8	1.6	273	3	1.2	243	5	2.1
2003	533	17	3.1	278	8	3.0	254	8	3.3

* = Quantity zero or rounds to zero.

r = Revised, controlled to 1990 census based population estimates; previous 1993 data controlled to 1980 census based population estimates.

[1] Starting in 2003 respondents could identify more than one race. Except as noted, the race data in this table from 2003 onward represent those respondents who indicated only one race category.

[2] The data shown prior to 2003 consists of those identifying themselves as "Asian or Pacific Islanders."

Table A-14. Population 14 to 24 Years Old, by High School Graduate Status, College Enrollment, Attainment, Sex, Race, and Hispanic Origin, October 1967–2019

(Numbers in thousands; percent; civilian noninstitutionalized population.)

| Year, race, and Hispanic origin | Population 18 to 24 years old | | | | | | | | High school graduates, 14 to 24 years old | | |
| | | High school graduates | | Percent | | | High school dropouts | | | Percent | |
	Total	Total	Enrolled in college	High school graduates	Enrolled in college	Of high school graduates enrolled in college	Number	Percent	All graduates	Enrolled in college	Enrolled or completed some college
ALL RACES											
Both Sexes											
2019............................	29,343	25,999	11,934	88.6	40.7	45.9	1,515	5.2	26,410	46.1	71.1
2018............................	29,553	26,039	12,097	88.1	40.9	46.5	1,673	5.7	26,412	46.6	72.2
2017............................	29,538	25,831	11,937	87.5	40.4	46.2	1,772	6.0	26,248	46.4	72.0
2016............................	29,893	26,123	12,320	87.4	41.2	47.2	1,911	6.4	26,571	47.3	72.3
2015............................	30,037	26,248	12,152	87.4	40.5	46.3	1,917	6.4	26,673	46.4	72.2
2014............................	30,304	26,311	12,132	86.8	40.0	46.1	2,090	6.9	26,700	46.3	72.0
2013............................	30,556	26,317	12,202	86.1	39.9	46.4	2,215	7.3	26,734	46.8	71.8
2012............................	30,377	25,866	12,456	85.1	41.0	48.2	2,319	7.6	26,255	48.5	72.9
2011............................	29,943	25,435	12,570	84.9	42.0	49.4	2,481	8.3	25,765	49.6	73.1
2010............................	29,659	25,224	12,213	85.0	41.2	48.4	2,590	8.7	25,564	48.7	72.6
2009............................	29,223	24,647	12,073	84.3	41.3	49.0	2,733	9.4	25,015	49.1	72.0
2008............................	28,950	24,568	11,466	84.9	39.6	46.7	2,702	9.3	24,922	47.0	70.6
2007............................	28,778	24,146	11,161	83.9	38.8	46.2	2,937	10.2	24,491	46.3	69.7
2006............................	28,372	23,430	10,586	82.6	37.3	45.2	3,128	11.0	23,800	45.4	69.3
2005............................	27,855	23,103	10,834	82.9	38.9	46.9	3,154	11.3	23,445	47.0	69.8
2004............................	27,948	23,086	10,611	82.6	38.0	46.0	3,836	12.1	23,379	46.2	69.0
2003............................	27,404	22,603	10,364	82.5	37.8	45.9	3,228	11.8	22,898	45.9	68.8
2002............................	27,367	22,319	10,033	81.6	36.7	45.0	3,375	12.3	22,639	45.2	67.6
2001............................	26,965	21,836	9,629	81.0	35.7	44.1	3,519	13.0	22,136	44.1	66.7
2000............................	26,658	21,822	9,452	81.9	35.5	43.3	3,315	12.4	22,080	43.5	66.7
1999............................	26,041	21,127	9,259	81.1	35.6	43.8	3,413	13.1	21,390	44.0	67.2
1998............................	25,507	20,567	9,322	80.6	36.6	45.3	3,544	13.9	20,775	45.5	68.0
1997............................	24,973	20,338	9,204	81.4	36.9	45.2	3,236	13.0	20,577	45.6	67.3
1996............................	24,671	20,131	8,767	81.6	35.5	43.5	3,147	12.8	20,465	44.0	67.2
1995............................	24,900	20,125	8,539	80.8	34.3	42.4	3,471	13.9	20,359	42.7	67.1
1994............................	25,254	20,581	8,729	81.5	34.6	42.4	3,365	13.3	20,779	42.7	66.9
1993r............................	25,522	20,844	8,630	81.7	33.8	41.4	3,349	13.1	21,060	41.6	65.3
1993............................	24,100	19,772	8,193	82.0	34.0	41.4	3,070	12.7	19,979	41.6	65.4
1992............................	24,278	19,921	8,343	82.1	34.4	41.9	3,083	12.7	20,194	42.3	65.6
1991............................	24,572	19,883	8,172	80.9	33.3	41.1	3,486	14.2	20,065	41.4	60.7
1990............................	24,852	20,311	7,964	82.3	32.0	39.1	3,379	13.6	20,571	39.6	58.9
1989............................	25,261	20,461	7,804	81.0	30.9	38.1	3,644	14.4	20,749	38.5	57.9
1988............................	25,733	20,900	7,791	81.2	30.3	37.3	3,749	14.6	21,204	37.6	57.4
1987............................	25,950	21,118	7,693	81.4	29.6	36.4	3,751	14.5	21,477	36.9	56.2
1986............................	26,512	21,768	7,477	82.1	28.2	34.3	3,687	13.9	22,086	34.8	55.0
1985............................	27,122	22,349	7,537	82.4	27.8	33.7	3,687	13.9	22,722	34.3	54.3
1984............................	28,031	22,870	7,591	81.6	27.1	33.2	4,142	14.8	23,252	33.7	53.0
1983............................	28,580	22,988	7,477	80.4	26.2	32.5	4,410	15.4	23,359	33.1	52.8
1982............................	28,846	23,291	7,678	80.7	26.6	33.0	4,500	15.6	23,708	33.5	52.7
1981............................	28,965	23,343	7,575	80.6	26.2	32.5	4,520	15.6	23,705	32.9	51.7
1980............................	28,957	23,413	7,400	80.9	25.6	31.6	4,515	15.6	23,856	32.1	51.1
1979............................	27,974	22,421	6,991	80.1	25.0	31.2	4,560	16.3	22,911	31.9	51.6
1978............................	27,647	22,309	6,995	80.7	25.3	31.4	4,388	15.9	22,759	31.9	51.4
1977............................	27,331	22,008	7,142	80.5	26.1	32.5	4,313	15.8	22,499	33.0	52.0
1976............................	26,919	21,677	7,181	80.5	26.7	33.1	4,276	15.9	22,158	33.7	53.4
1975............................	26,387	21,326	6,935	80.8	26.3	32.5	4,110	15.6	21,824	33.1	52.5
1974............................	25,670	20,725	6,316	80.7	24.6	30.5	4,070	15.9	21,267	31.2	51.3
1973............................	25,237	20,377	6,055	80.7	24.0	29.7	3,973	15.7	20,895	30.4	50.7
1972............................	24,579	19,618	6,257	79.8	25.5	31.9	4,068	16.6	20,107	32.6	52.9
1971............................	23,668	18,691	6,210	79.0	26.2	33.2	4,025	17.0	19,130	33.9	53.1
1970............................	22,552	17,768	5,805	78.8	25.7	32.7	3,908	17.3	18,218	33.5	52.3
1969............................	21,362	16,703	5,840	78.2	27.3	35.0	3,769	17.6	17,152	35.7	52.5
1968............................	20,562	15,683	5,356	76.3	26.0	34.2	3,929	19.1	16,165	35.2	51.5
1967............................	20,009	15,114	5,100	75.5	25.5	33.7	3,967	19.8	15,642	34.9	50.5

r = Revised, controlled to 1990 census based population estimates; previous 1993 data controlled to 1980 census based population estimates.
Note: The change in the educational attainment question and the college completion categories from "4 or more years of college" to "at least some college," in 1992 caused an increase in the proportion of 14-to-24-year-old high school graduates enrolled in college or completed some college, of approximately 5 percentage points. High school graduates are people who have completed 4 years of high school or more, for 1967 to 1991. Beginning in 1992, they were people whose highest degree was a high school diploma (including equivalency) or higher.
[1] Starting in 2003 respondents could identify more than one race. Except as noted, the race data in this table from 2003 onward represent those respondents who indicated only one race category.
[2] The data shown prior to 2003 consists of those identifying themselves as "Asian or Pacific Islanders."

Table A-14. Population 14 to 24 Years Old, by High School Graduate Status, College Enrollment, Attainment, Sex, Race, and Hispanic Origin, October 1967–2019—*Continued*

(Numbers in thousands; percent; civilian noninstitutionalized population.)

Year, race, and Hispanic origin	Population 18 to 24 years old								High school graduates, 14 to 24 years old		
		High school graduates		Percent			High school dropouts			Percent	
	Total	Total	Enrolled in college	High school graduates	Enrolled in college	Of high school graduates enrolled in college	Number	Percent	All graduates	Enrolled in college	Enrolled or completed some college
Male											
2019	14,700	12,741	5,442	86.7	37.0	42.7	898	6.1	12,943	42.8	66.2
2018	14,845	12,816	5,586	86.3	37.6	43.6	995	6.7	12,956	43.8	67.5
2017	14,833	12,697	5,460	85.6	36.8	43.0	1,019	6.9	12,873	43.1	67.8
2016	15,042	12,851	5,800	85.4	38.6	45.1	1,134	7.5	13,014	45.2	68.1
2015	15,074	13,031	5,694	86.5	37.8	43.7	1,034	6.9	13,256	43.8	68.0
2014	15,234	13,019	5,676	85.5	37.3	43.6	1,132	7.4	13,225	43.9	67.7
2013	15,379	13,051	5,630	84.9	36.6	43.1	1,183	7.7	13,254	43.6	67.0
2012	15,252	12,753	5,731	83.6	37.6	44.9	1,300	8.5	12,940	45.3	68.4
2011	15,211	12,659	5,953	83.2	39.1	47.0	1,374	9.0	12,834	47.2	69.0
2010	14,887	12,371	5,698	83.1	38.3	46.1	1,473	9.9	12,540	46.2	68.4
2009	14,677	12,111	5,640	82.5	38.4	46.6	1,568	10.7	12,277	46.7	68.5
2008	14,559	12,181	5,383	83.7	37.0	44.2	1,445	9.9	12,374	44.6	66.7
2007	14,515	11,825	5,156	81.5	35.5	43.6	1,680	11.6	11,972	43.7	66.0
2006	14,300	11,508	4,874	80.5	34.1	42.4	1,741	12.2	11,659	42.5	65.1
2005	14,077	11,182	4,973	79.4	35.3	44.5	1,852	13.2	11,330	44.4	65.9
2004	14,018	11,258	4,865	80.3	34.7	43.2	1,942	13.9	11,364	43.5	65.0
2003	13,681	10,919	4,697	79.8	34.3	43.0	1,875	13.7	11,040	43.1	65.0
2002	13,744	10,823	4,629	78.7	33.7	42.8	1,925	14.0	10,975	42.9	64.6
2001	13,434	10,461	4,437	77.9	33.0	42.4	2,028	15.1	10,587	42.4	63.9
2000	13,338	10,622	4,343	79.6	32.6	40.9	1,837	13.8	10,736	41.0	63.1
1999	12,905	10,201	4,396	79.1	34.0	43.1	1,818	14.9	10,331	43.3	64.5
1998	12,764	9,915	4,403	77.7	34.5	44.4	2,018	15.8	10,006	44.5	64.9
1997	12,513	9,933	4,374	79.4	35.0	44.0	1,765	14.1	10,025	44.2	64.9
1996	12,285	9,815	4,187	80.0	34.1	42.6	1,628	13.2	9,960	43.0	65.6
1995	12,351	9,789	4,089	79.3	33.1	41.8	1,791	14.5	9,884	42.1	64.2
1994	12,557	9,970	4,152	79.4	33.1	41.6	1,804	14.4	10,051	41.9	64.9
1993r	12,712	10,142	4,237	79.8	33.3	41.8	1,745	13.7	10,229	42.0	63.9
1993	11,898	9,541	3,994	80.2	33.6	41.9	1,575	13.2	9,625	42.0	64.1
1992	11,965	9,576	3,912	80.0	32.7	40.9	1,617	13.5	9,706	41.3	64.1
1991	12,036	9,493	3,954	78.9	32.9	41.7	1,810	15.0	9,564	41.9	59.2
1990	12,134	9,778	3,922	80.6	32.3	40.1	1,689	13.9	9,894	40.5	58.0
1989	12,325	9,700	3,717	78.7	30.2	38.3	1,941	15.7	9,810	38.6	57.2
1988	12,491	9,832	3,770	78.7	30.2	38.3	1,950	15.6	9,947	38.5	56.5
1987	12,626	10,030	3,867	79.4	30.6	38.6	1,948	15.4	10,207	39.0	56.0
1986	12,921	10,338	3,702	80.0	28.7	35.8	1,924	14.9	10,465	36.2	54.4
1985	13,199	10,614	3,749	80.4	28.4	35.3	2,015	15.3	10,784	36.0	54.6
1984	13,744	10,914	3,929	79.4	28.6	36.0	2,184	15.9	11,052	36.4	53.6
1983	14,003	10,906	3,820	77.9	27.3	35.0	2,379	17.0	10,959	35.5	52.7
1982	14,083	11,120	3,837	79.0	27.2	34.5	2,329	16.5	11,295	35.0	53.0
1981	14,127	11,052	3,833	78.2	27.1	34.7	2,424	17.2	11,203	35.1	52.1
1980	14,107	11,125	3,717	78.9	26.3	33.4	2,390	16.9	11,309	33.7	51.4
1979	13,571	10,657	3,508	78.5	25.8	32.9	2,320	17.1	10,838	33.6	52.4
1978	13,385	10,614	3,621	79.3	27.1	34.1	2,200	16.4	10,789	34.5	52.6
1977	13,218	10,440	3,712	79.0	28.1	35.6	2,170	16.4	10,626	36.0	54.2
1976	13,012	10,312	3,673	79.2	28.2	35.6	2,109	16.2	10,492	36.0	55.7
1975	12,724	10,214	3,693	80.3	29.0	36.2	1,928	15.2	10,415	36.7	56.1
1974	12,315	9,835	3,411	79.9	27.7	34.7	1,958	15.9	10,073	35.3	55.6
1973	12,111	9,716	3,360	80.2	27.7	34.6	1,853	15.3	9,908	35.1	55.4
1972	11,712	9,247	3,534	79.0	30.2	38.2	1,898	16.2	9,461	38.8	59.0
1971	11,092	8,669	3,599	78.2	32.4	41.5	1,865	16.8	8,855	42.1	60.1
1970	10,385	8,087	3,331	77.9	32.1	41.2	1,746	16.8	8,279	41.8	59.2
1969	9,649	7,445	3,392	77.2	35.2	45.6	1,640	17.0	7,609	46.2	61.2
1968	9,251	6,864	3,152	74.2	34.1	45.9	1,777	19.2	8,038	46.7	61.1
1967	8,999	6,678	2,982	74.2	33.1	44.7	1,804	20.0	6,829	45.1	58.8

r = Revised, controlled to 1990 census based population estimates; previous 1993 data controlled to 1980 census based population estimates.
Note: The change in the educational attainment question and the college completion categories from "4 or more years of college" to "at least some college," in 1992 caused an increase in the proportion of 14-to-24-year-old high school graduates enrolled in college or completed some college, of approximately 5 percentage points. High school graduates are people who have completed 4 years of high school or more, for 1967 to 1991. Beginning in 1992, they were people whose highest degree was a high school diploma (including equivalency) or higher.
[1] Starting in 2003 respondents could identify more than one race. Except as noted, the race data in this table from 2003 onward represent those respondents who indicated only one race category.
[2] The data shown prior to 2003 consists of those identifying themselves as "Asian or Pacific Islanders."

Table A-14. Population 14 to 24 Years Old, by High School Graduate Status, College Enrollment, Attainment, Sex, Race, and Hispanic Origin, October 1967–2019—*Continued*

(Numbers in thousands; percent; civilian noninstitutionalized population.)

Year, race, and Hispanic origin	Population 18 to 24 years old								High school graduates, 14 to 24 years old		
		High school graduates		Percent			High school dropouts			Percent	
	Total	Total	Enrolled in college	High school graduates	Enrolled in college	Of high school graduates enrolled in college	Number	Percent	All graduates	Enrolled in college	Enrolled or completed some college
Female											
2019............................	14,643	13,258	6,492	90.5	44.3	49.0	617	4.2	13,466	49.3	75.7
2018............................	14,708	13,223	6,511	89.9	44.3	49.2	679	4.6	13,456	49.3	76.8
2017............................	14,705	13,134	6,477	89.3	44.0	49.3	754	5.1	13,375	49.6	76.1
2016............................	14,851	13,273	6,521	89.4	43.9	49.1	778	5.2	13,557	49.3	76.4
2015............................	14,963	13,217	6,459	88.3	43.2	48.9	883	5.9	13,418	49.0	76.3
2014............................	15,070	13,293	6,456	88.2	42.8	48.6	958	6.4	13,475	48.7	76.3
2013............................	15,177	13,266	6,573	87.4	43.3	49.5	1,033	6.8	13,480	49.9	76.6
2012............................	15,125	13,113	6,725	86.7	44.5	51.3	1,019	6.7	13,316	51.6	77.2
2011............................	14,732	12,776	6,617	86.7	44.9	51.8	1,107	7.5	12,930	51.9	77.2
2010............................	14,772	12,854	6,515	87.0	44.1	50.7	1,116	7.6	13,024	51.1	76.7
2009............................	14,546	12,536	6,432	86.2	44.2	51.3	1,165	8.0	12,738	51.4	75.5
2008............................	14,391	12,387	6,083	86.1	42.3	49.1	1,257	8.7	12,548	49.3	74.5
2007............................	14,263	12,321	6,005	86.4	42.1	48.7	1,256	8.8	12,519	48.8	73.3
2006............................	14,073	11,922	5,712	84.7	40.6	47.9	1,387	9.9	12,141	48.1	73.3
2005............................	13,778	11,921	5,861	86.5	42.5	49.2	1,302	9.5	12,115	49.4	73.4
2004............................	13,930	11,828	5,746	84.9	41.2	48.6	1,444	10.4	12,015	48.8	72.8
2003............................	13,724	11,684	5,667	85.1	41.3	48.5	1,354	9.9	11,858	48.5	72.2
2002............................	13,623	11,496	5,404	84.4	39.7	47.0	1,450	10.6	11,664	47.3	70.3
2001............................	13,531	11,375	5,192	84.1	38.4	45.7	1,491	11.0	11,549	45.7	69.4
2000............................	13,319	11,200	5,109	84.1	38.4	45.6	1,478	11.1	11,344	45.8	70.1
1999............................	13,136	10,926	4,863	83.2	37.0	44.5	1,594	12.1	11,058	44.6	69.8
1998............................	12,743	10,651	4,919	83.6	38.6	46.2	1,526	12.0	10,768	46.4	70.7
1997............................	12,460	10,403	4,829	83.5	38.8	46.4	1,471	11.8	10,549	46.8	69.6
1996............................	12,386	10,317	4,582	83.3	37.0	44.4	1,519	12.3	10,507	44.9	68.6
1995............................	12,548	10,338	4,452	82.4	35.5	43.1	1,679	13.4	10,477	43.4	69.8
1994............................	12,696	10,611	4,576	83.6	36.0	43.1	1,561	12.3	10,729	43.4	68.7
1993r............................	12,810	10,702	4,393	83.5	34.3	41.0	1,604	12.5	10,831	41.3	66.6
1993............................	12,202	10,232	4,199	83.9	34.4	41.0	1,494	12.2	10,355	41.2	66.7
1992............................	12,313	10,344	4,429	84.0	36.0	42.8	1,466	11.9	10,486	43.3	66.9
1991............................	12,536	10,391	4,218	82.9	33.6	40.6	1,676	13.4	10,502	41.0	62.1
1990............................	12,718	10,533	4,042	82.8	31.8	38.4	1,690	13.3	10,676	38.7	59.8
1989............................	12,936	10,758	4,085	83.2	31.6	38.0	1,702	13.2	10,936	38.4	58.6
1988............................	13,242	11,068	4,021	83.6	30.4	36.3	1,799	13.5	11,257	36.8	58.2
1987............................	13,324	11,086	3,826	83.2	28.7	34.5	1,803	13.5	11,268	35.0	56.4
1986............................	13,591	11,430	3,775	84.1	27.8	33.0	1,751	12.9	11,623	33.5	55.5
1985............................	13,923	11,736	3,788	84.3	27.2	32.3	1,804	13.0	11,937	32.8	54.0
1984............................	14,287	11,956	3,662	83.7	25.6	30.6	1,958	13.7	12,199	31.3	52.4
1983............................	14,577	12,082	3,657	82.9	25.1	30.3	2,031	13.9	12,294	31.0	52.8
1982............................	14,763	12,171	3,841	82.4	26.0	31.6	2,171	14.7	12,411	32.1	52.4
1981............................	14,838	12,290	3,741	82.8	25.2	30.4	2,097	14.1	12,503	31.0	51.3
1980............................	14,851	12,287	3,682	82.7	24.8	30.0	2,124	14.3	12,547	30.6	50.8
1979............................	14,403	11,763	3,482	81.7	24.2	29.6	2,240	15.6	12,074	30.4	50.8
1978............................	14,262	11,694	3,373	82.0	23.7	28.8	2,188	15.3	11,969	29.6	50.3
1977............................	14,113	11,569	3,431	82.0	24.3	29.7	2,143	15.2	11,875	30.3	50.0
1976............................	13,907	11,365	3,508	81.7	25.2	30.9	2,168	15.6	11,666	31.6	51.4
1975............................	13,663	11,113	3,243	81.3	23.7	29.2	2,181	16.0	11,407	29.9	49.2
1974............................	13,355	10,889	2,905	81.5	21.8	26.7	2,112	15.8	11,194	27.4	47.5
1973............................	13,126	10,663	2,696	81.2	20.5	25.3	2,119	16.1	10,986	26.1	46.5
1972............................	12,867	10,371	2,724	80.6	21.2	26.3	2,170	16.9	10,644	27.0	47.4
1971............................	12,576	10,020	2,610	79.7	20.8	26.0	2,159	17.2	10,272	26.9	47.1
1970............................	12,167	9,680	2,474	79.6	20.3	25.6	2,163	17.8	9,908	26.3	46.6
1969............................	11,713	9,259	2,448	79.0	20.9	26.4	2,128	18.2	9,499	27.1	45.7
1968............................	11,311	8,820	2,205	78.0	19.5	25.0	2,150	19.0	9,072	25.9	44.4
1967............................	11,011	8,436	2,117	76.6	19.2	25.1	2,162	19.6	8,694	26.0	44.7

r = Revised, controlled to 1990 census based population estimates; previous 1993 data controlled to 1980 census based population estimates.
Note: The change in the educational attainment question and the college completion categories from "4 or more years of college" to "at least some college," in 1992 caused an increase in the proportion of 14-to-24-year-old high school graduates enrolled in college or completed some college, of approximately 5 percentage points. High school graduates are people who have completed 4 years of high school or more, for 1967 to 1991. Beginning in 1992, they were people whose highest degree was a high school diploma (including equivalency) or higher.
[1] Starting in 2003 respondents could identify more than one race. Except as noted, the race data in this table from 2003 onward represent those respondents who indicated only one race category.
[2] The data shown prior to 2003 consists of those identifying themselves as "Asian or Pacific Islanders."

Table A-14. Population 14 to 24 Years Old, by High School Graduate Status, College Enrollment, Attainment, Sex, Race, and Hispanic Origin, October 1967–2019—*Continued*

(Numbers in thousands; percent; civilian noninstitutionalized population.)

Year, race, and Hispanic origin	Population 18 to 24 years old								High school graduates, 14 to 24 years old		
		High school graduates		Percent			High school dropouts			Percent	
	Total	Total	Enrolled in college	High school graduates	Enrolled in college	Of high school graduates enrolled in college	Number	Percent	All graduates	Enrolled in college	Enrolled or completed some college
WHITE ALONE											
Both Sexes											
2019	21,574	19,132	8,603	88.7	39.9	45.0	1,109	5.1	19,409	45.1	70.0
2018	21,717	19,133	8,771	88.1	40.4	45.8	1,284	5.9	19,413	46.1	71.8
2017	21,789	19,069	8,690	87.5	39.9	45.6	1,358	6.2	19,351	45.7	72.1
2016	22,018	19,373	9,106	88.0	41.4	47.0	1,381	6.3	19,673	47.1	72.7
2015	22,244	19,451	8,969	87.4	40.3	46.1	1,430	6.4	19,747	46.2	72.6
2014	22,507	19,541	9,077	86.8	40.3	46.4	1,599	7.1	19,786	46.6	72.1
2013	22,658	19,660	9,049	86.8	39.9	46.0	1,599	7.1	19,985	46.5	72.1
2012	22,712	19,555	9,302	86.1	41.0	47.6	1,641	7.2	19,831	47.9	73.5
2011	23,089	19,760	9,813	85.6	42.5	49.7	1,885	8.2	20,007	49.8	74.0
2010	22,851	19,517	9,325	85.4	40.8	47.8	1,941	8.5	19,741	48.0	73.0
2009	22,606	19,241	9,327	85.1	41.3	48.5	2,059	9.1	19,512	48.6	72.1
2008	22,530	19,334	9,141	85.8	40.6	47.3	1,991	8.8	19,586	47.5	71.6
2007	22,392	18,913	8,780	84.5	39.2	46.4	2,248	10.0	19,170	46.5	70.3
2006	22,169	18,489	8,298	83.4	37.4	44.9	2,399	10.8	18,751	45.1	69.9
2005	21,777	18,130	8,498	83.3	39.0	46.9	2,466	11.3	18,352	46.9	70.0
2004	21,896	18,213	8,351	82.6	38.0	45.9	2,599	11.9	18,414	46.1	69.1
2003[1]	21,502	17,901	8,150	83.3	37.9	45.5	2,489	11.6	18,123	45.5	69.1
2002	21,704	17,793	7,921	82.0	36.5	44.5	2,641	12.2	17,995	44.6	67.5
2001	21,372	17,348	7,548	81.2	35.3	43.5	2,865	13.4	17,547	43.5	67.0
2000	21,257	17,512	7,566	82.4	35.6	43.2	2,598	12.2	17,714	43.4	66.9
1999	20,866	17,052	7,447	81.7	35.7	43.7	2,680	12.8	17,220	43.8	67.5
1998	20,465	16,701	7,541	81.6	36.9	45.2	2,810	13.7	16,855	45.3	68.3
1997	20,020	16,557	7,495	82.7	37.4	45.3	2,476	12.4	16,733	45.6	67.7
1996	19,676	16,199	7,123	82.3	36.2	44.0	2,458	12.5	16,436	44.3	68.4
1995	19,866	16,269	7,011	81.9	35.3	43.1	2,711	13.6	16,439	43.4	68.3
1994	20,171	16,670	7,118	82.6	35.3	42.7	2,553	12.7	16,814	42.9	67.6
1993r	20,493	16,989	7,074	82.9	34.5	41.6	2,595	12.7	17,161	41.8	66.5
1993	19,430	16,196	6,763	83.4	34.8	41.8	2,369	12.2	16,361	41.9	66.7
1992	19,671	16,379	6,916	83.3	35.2	42.2	2,398	12.2	16,586	42.7	67.0
1991	19,980	16,324	6,813	81.7	34.1	41.7	2,845	14.2	16,467	42.0	62.3
1990	20,393	16,823	6,635	82.5	32.5	39.4	2,751	13.5	17,022	39.8	60.1
1989	20,825	17,089	6,631	82.1	31.8	38.8	2,926	14.1	17,329	39.1	58.9
1988	21,261	17,491	6,659	82.3	31.3	38.1	3,012	14.2	17,720	38.4	58.5
1987	21,493	17,689	6,483	82.3	30.2	36.6	3,042	14.2	17,982	37.1	56.8
1986	22,020	18,291	6,307	83.1	28.6	34.5	2,961	13.4	18,554	34.9	55.5
1985	22,632	18,916	6,500	83.6	28.7	34.4	3,050	13.5	19,229	35.0	55.3
1984	23,347	19,373	6,526	83.0	28.0	33.7	3,281	14.1	19,686	34.2	53.8
1983	23,899	19,643	6,463	82.2	27.0	32.9	3,428	14.3	19,948	33.5	53.4
1982	24,206	19,944	6,694	82.4	27.2	33.1	3,523	14.6	20,292	33.6	53.1
1981	24,486	20,123	6,549	82.2	26.7	32.5	3,590	14.7	20,439	33.0	52.1
1980	24,482	20,214	6,423	82.6	26.2	31.8	3,525	14.4	20,583	32.3	51.4
1979	23,895	19,616	6,120	82.1	25.6	31.2	3,571	14.9	20,033	31.8	51.7
1978	23,650	19,526	6,077	82.6	25.7	31.1	3,464	14.6	19,911	31.7	51.3
1977	23,430	19,291	6,209	82.3	26.5	32.2	3,445	14.7	19,712	32.6	52.1
1976	23,119	19,045	6,276	82.4	27.1	33.0	3,407	14.7	19,462	33.5	53.5
1975	22,703	18,883	6,116	83.2	26.9	32.4	3,149	13.9	19,298	33.0	52.7
1974	22,141	18,318	5,589	82.7	25.2	30.5	3,212	14.5	18,794	31.2	51.7
1973	21,766	18,023	5,438	82.8	25.0	30.2	3,085	14.2	18,470	30.8	51.6
1972	21,315	17,410	5,624	81.7	26.4	32.3	3,241	15.2	17,838	33.0	53.9
1971	20,533	16,593	5,594	81.3	27.2	33.5	3,156	15.4	17,087	34.2	54.1
1970	19,608	15,960	5,305	81.4	27.1	33.2	2,974	15.2	16,334	33.9	53.4
1969	18,606	15,031	5,347	80.8	28.7	35.6	2,915	15.7	15,383	36.2	53.5
1968	17,951	14,127	4,929	78.7	27.5	34.9	3,107	17.3	14,506	35.7	52.5
1967	17,500	13,657	4,708	78.0	26.9	34.5	3,141	17.9	14,022	35.2	51.4

r = Revised, controlled to 1990 census based population estimates; previous 1993 data controlled to 1980 census based population estimates.
Note: The change in the educational attainment question and the college completion categories from "4 or more years of college" to "at least some college," in 1992 caused an increase in the proportion of 14-to-24-year-old high school graduates enrolled in college or completed some college, of approximately 5 percentage points. High school graduates are people who have completed 4 years of high school or more, for 1967 to 1991. Beginning in 1992, they were people whose highest degree was a high school diploma (including equivalency) or higher.
[1] Starting in 2003 respondents could identify more than one race. Except as noted, the race data in this table from 2003 onward represent those respondents who indicated only one race category.
[2] The data shown prior to 2003 consists of those identifying themselves as "Asian or Pacific Islanders."

Table A-14. Population 14 to 24 Years Old, by High School Graduate Status, College Enrollment, Attainment, Sex, Race, and Hispanic Origin, October 1967–2019—*Continued*

(Numbers in thousands; percent; civilian noninstitutionalized population.)

Year, race, and Hispanic origin	Population 18 to 24 years old								High school graduates, 14 to 24 years old		
		High school graduates		Percent			High school dropouts			Percent	
	Total	Total	Enrolled in college	High school graduates	Enrolled in college	Of high school graduates enrolled in college	Number	Percent	All graduates	Enrolled in college	Enrolled or completed some college
Male											
2019	10,880	9,440	3,922	86.8	36.0	41.5	666	6.1	9,573	41.6	64.8
2018	10,972	9,478	4,045	86.4	36.9	42.7	765	7.0	9,588	42.8	66.3
2017	11,012	9,408	3,973	85.4	36.1	42.2	780	7.1	9,536	42.3	67.6
2016	11,139	9,614	4,267	86.3	38.3	44.4	818	7.3	9,734	44.4	67.7
2015	11,251	9,714	4,189	86.3	37.2	43.1	791	7.0	9,875	43.2	67.6
2014	11,397	9,781	4,296	85.8	37.7	43.9	866	7.6	9,904	44.1	67.4
2013	11,475	9,792	4,131	85.3	36.0	42.2	855	7.5	9,956	42.6	66.7
2012	11,499	9,692	4,261	84.3	37.1	44.0	937	8.1	9,810	44.3	68.0
2011	11,850	9,928	4,685	83.8	39.5	47.2	1,077	9.1	10,061	47.3	70.0
2010	11,579	9,651	4,369	83.3	37.7	45.3	1,124	9.7	9,754	45.4	68.6
2009	11,449	9,535	4,404	83.3	38.5	46.2	1,201	10.5	9,662	46.4	68.3
2008	11,432	9,646	4,340	84.4	38.0	45.0	1,122	9.8	9,784	45.2	67.8
2007	11,387	9,311	4,040	81.8	35.5	43.4	1,333	11.7	9,430	43.5	66.0
2006	11,264	9,139	3,842	81.1	34.1	42.0	1,396	12.4	9,237	42.2	66.0
2005	11,116	8,885	3,924	79.9	35.3	44.1	1,469	13.2	8,986	44.1	65.9
2004	11,107	9,001	3,855	81.0	34.7	42.8	1,524	13.7	9,067	43.1	64.4
2003[1]	10,885	8,763	3,726	80.5	34.2	42.5	1,452	13.3	8,862	42.6	65.1
2002	10,986	8,717	3,701	79.4	33.7	42.5	1,506	13.7	8,833	42.5	64.6
2001	10,817	8,490	3,521	78.5	32.6	41.5	1,659	15.3	8,582	41.5	64.0
2000	10,739	8,603	3,522	80.1	32.8	40.9	1,450	13.5	8,690	41.1	63.5
1999	10,532	8,382	3,585	79.6	34.0	42.7	1,462	13.9	8,457	42.8	64.8
1998	10,400	8,194	3,634	78.8	34.9	44.3	1,628	15.7	8,256	44.4	65.5
1997	10,173	8,204	3,633	80.6	35.7	44.3	1,406	13.8	8,274	44.5	65.3
1996	9,897	8,000	3,419	80.8	34.5	42.7	1,275	12.9	8,104	43.0	66.0
1995	9,980	8,001	3,398	80.2	34.0	42.5	1,430	14.3	8,067	42.7	65.3
1994	10,123	8,168	3,406	80.7	33.6	41.7	1,377	13.6	8,227	41.9	65.4
1993r	10,294	8,338	3,498	81.0	34.0	42.0	1,388	13.5	8,411	42.1	65.1
1993	9,641	7,857	3,313	81.5	34.4	42.2	1,379	12.9	7,926	42.3	65.4
1992	9,744	7,911	3,291	81.2	33.8	41.6	1,300	13.3	8,016	42.1	65.8
1991	9,896	7,843	3,270	79.3	33.0	41.7	1,520	15.4	7,899	41.9	59.9
1990	10,053	8,157	3,292	81.1	32.7	40.3	1,430	14.2	8,246	40.7	58.8
1989	10,240	8,177	3,223	79.9	31.5	39.4	1,572	15.4	8,271	39.7	58.5
1988	10,380	8,268	3,260	79.7	31.4	39.4	1,594	15.4	8,365	39.6	57.8
1987	10,549	8,498	3,289	80.6	31.2	38.7	1,593	15.1	8,647	39.2	56.4
1986	10,814	8,780	3,168	81.2	29.3	36.1	1,575	14.6	8,886	36.4	55.1
1985	11,108	9,077	3,254	81.7	29.3	35.8	1,637	14.7	9,229	36.6	55.5
1984	11,521	9,348	3,406	81.1	29.6	36.4	1,744	15.1	9,459	36.8	54.2
1983	11,787	9,411	3,335	79.8	28.3	35.4	1,865	15.8	9,534	35.9	53.5
1982	11,874	9,611	3,308	80.9	27.9	34.4	1,810	15.2	9,761	34.9	53.2
1981	12,040	9,619	3,340	79.9	27.7	34.7	1,960	16.3	9,754	35.1	52.8
1980	12,011	9,686	3,275	80.6	27.3	33.8	1,883	15.7	9,838	34.1	51.8
1979	11,721	9,457	3,104	80.7	26.5	32.8	1,830	15.6	9,615	33.4	52.7
1978	11,572	9,438	3,195	81.6	27.6	33.9	1,722	14.9	9,582	34.3	52.5
1977	11,445	9,263	3,286	80.9	28.7	35.5	1,779	15.5	9,422	35.8	54.5
1976	11,279	9,186	3,250	81.4	28.8	35.4	1,691	15.0	9,340	35.7	55.9
1975	11,050	9,139	3,326	82.7	30.1	36.4	1,490	13.5	9,310	36.9	56.6
1974	10,722	8,768	3,035	81.8	28.3	34.6	1,579	14.7	8,980	35.2	55.9
1973	10,511	8,637	3,032	82.2	28.8	35.1	1,453	13.8	8,817	35.6	56.5
1972	10,212	8,278	3,195	81.1	31.3	38.6	1,506	14.7	8,462	39.2	60.1
1971	9,653	7,807	3,284	80.9	34.0	42.1	1,429	14.8	7,978	42.6	61.4
1970	9,053	7,324	3,096	80.9	34.2	42.3	1,297	14.3	7,496	42.9	60.9
1969	8,420	6,740	3,146	80.0	37.4	46.7	1,248	14.8	6,882	47.3	62.8
1968	8,084	6,221	2,949	77.0	36.5	47.4	1,401	17.3	6,372	48.1	62.7
1967	7,864	6,073	2,761	77.2	35.1	45.5	1,391	17.7	6,210	45.9	60.0

r = Revised, controlled to 1990 census based population estimates; previous 1993 data controlled to 1980 census based population estimates.

Note: The change in the educational attainment question and the college completion categories from "4 or more years of college" to "at least some college," in 1992 caused an increase in the proportion of 14-to-24-year-old high school graduates enrolled in college or completed some college, of approximately 5 percentage points. High school graduates are people who have completed 4 years of high school or more, for 1967 to 1991. Beginning in 1992, they were people whose highest degree was a high school diploma (including equivalency) or higher.

[1] Starting in 2003 respondents could identify more than one race. Except as noted, the race data in this table from 2003 onward represent those respondents who indicated only one race category.

[2] The data shown prior to 2003 consists of those identifying themselves as "Asian or Pacific Islanders."

Table A-14. Population 14 to 24 Years Old, by High School Graduate Status, College Enrollment, Attainment, Sex, Race, and Hispanic Origin, October 1967–2019—*Continued*

(Numbers in thousands; percent; civilian noninstitutionalized population.)

| | Population 18 to 24 years old | | | | | | | | High school graduates, 14 to 24 years old | | |
| | High school graduates | | | Percent | | | High school dropouts | | | Percent | |
Year, race, and Hispanic origin	Total	Total	Enrolled in college	High school graduates	Enrolled in college	Of high school graduates enrolled in college	Number	Percent	All graduates	Enrolled in college	Enrolled or completed some college
Female											
2019	10,694	9,692	4,680	90.6	43.8	48.3	443	4.1	9,837	48.6	75.1
2018	10,744	9,655	4,725	89.9	44.0	48.9	518	4.8	9,825	49.2	77.2
2017	10,777	9,661	4,717	89.6	43.8	48.8	578	5.4	9,814	49.0	76.4
2016	10,879	9,759	4,839	89.7	44.5	49.6	563	5.2	9,939	49.8	77.5
2015	10,993	9,736	4,780	88.6	43.5	49.1	639	5.8	9,872	49.1	77.5
2014	11,110	9,760	4,780	87.9	43.0	49.0	733	6.6	9,882	49.2	76.8
2013	11,183	9,868	4,919	88.2	44.0	49.8	744	6.7	10,029	50.2	77.5
2012	11,214	9,863	5,041	88.0	45.0	51.1	704	6.3	10,021	51.5	78.8
2011	11,238	9,832	5,128	87.5	45.6	51.8	808	7.2	9,946	52.2	78.0
2010	11,271	9,867	4,956	87.5	44.0	50.2	817	7.2	9,987	50.6	77.3
2009	11,157	9,706	4,923	87.0	44.1	50.7	858	7.7	9,850	50.8	75.8
2008	11,098	9,688	4,801	87.3	43.3	49.6	869	7.8	9,802	49.9	75.4
2007	11,005	9,603	4,741	87.3	43.1	49.4	915	8.3	9,741	49.5	74.4
2006	10,905	9,350	4,456	85.7	40.9	47.7	1,003	9.2	9,513	47.9	73.7
2005	10,661	9,245	4,574	86.7	42.9	49.5	997	9.4	9,366	49.7	73.9
2004	10,789	9,212	4,496	85.4	41.7	48.8	1,075	10.0	9,347	49.0	73.5
2003[1]	10,617	9,138	4,424	86.1	41.7	48.4	1,037	9.8	9,260	48.3	72.9
2002	10,718	9,075	4,220	84.7	39.4	46.5	1,135	10.6	9,162	46.6	70.4
2001	10,555	8,859	4,027	83.9	38.1	45.5	1,206	11.4	8,965	45.5	69.8
2000	10,517	8,909	4,044	84.7	38.5	45.4	1,148	10.9	9,024	45.6	70.2
1999	10,334	8,671	3,862	83.9	37.4	44.5	1,218	11.8	8,763	44.7	70.1
1998	10,065	8,507	3,907	84.5	38.8	45.9	1,181	11.7	8,599	46.2	71.0
1997	9,847	8,352	3,863	84.8	39.2	46.3	1,072	10.9	8,458	46.6	70.1
1996	9,778	8,200	3,705	83.9	37.9	45.2	1,182	12.1	8,333	45.6	70.7
1995	9,886	8,271	3,615	83.7	36.6	43.7	1,281	13.0	8,376	44.0	71.3
1994	10,048	8,503	3,714	84.6	37.0	43.7	1,175	11.7	8,588	43.9	69.7
1993r	10,199	8,651	3,576	84.8	35.1	41.3	1,207	11.8	8,750	41.5	67.9
1993	9,790	8,339	3,450	85.2	35.2	41.4	1,125	11.5	8,435	41.6	68.0
1992	9,928	8,468	3,625	85.3	36.5	42.8	1,098	11.1	8,569	43.2	68.1
1991	10,119	8,481	3,544	83.8	35.0	41.8	1,324	13.1	8,568	42.1	64.5
1990	10,340	8,666	3,344	83.8	32.3	38.6	1,322	12.8	8,775	38.9	61.4
1989	10,586	8,913	3,409	84.2	32.2	38.2	1,354	12.8	9,059	38.6	59.2
1988	10,881	9,223	3,399	84.8	31.2	36.9	1,418	13.0	9,355	37.3	59.1
1987	10,944	9,189	3,192	84.0	29.2	34.7	1,449	13.2	9,334	36.2	57.2
1986	11,205	9,509	3,139	84.9	28.0	33.0	1,388	12.4	9,667	33.6	55.8
1985	11,524	9,840	3,247	85.4	28.2	33.0	1,413	12.3	10,001	33.6	55.2
1984	11,826	10,026	3,120	84.8	26.4	31.1	1,535	13.0	10,089	31.8	53.4
1983	12,112	10,233	3,129	84.5	25.8	30.6	1,563	12.9	10,233	31.3	53.4
1982	12,332	10,333	3,285	83.8	26.6	31.8	1,713	13.0	10,530	32.3	52.9
1981	12,446	10,504	3,208	84.4	25.8	30.5	1,629	13.1	10,687	31.1	51.6
1980	12,471	10,528	3,147	84.4	25.2	29.9	1,642	13.2	10,749	30.6	50.9
1979	12,174	10,157	3,015	83.4	24.8	29.7	1,741	14.3	10,417	30.3	50.8
1978	12,078	10,088	2,882	83.5	23.9	28.6	1,742	14.4	10,327	29.3	50.3
1977	11,985	10,029	2,923	83.7	24.4	29.1	1,666	13.9	10,292	29.7	50.0
1976	11,840	9,860	3,026	83.3	25.6	30.7	1,717	14.5	10,118	31.4	51.3
1975	11,653	9,743	2,790	83.6	23.9	28.6	1,658	14.2	9,986	29.4	49.1
1974	11,419	9,551	2,555	83.6	22.4	26.8	1,633	14.3	9,811	27.5	47.8
1973	11,255	9,387	2,406	83.4	21.4	25.6	1,632	14.5	9,653	26.4	47.1
1972	11,103	9,132	2,428	82.2	21.9	26.6	1,735	15.6	9,377	27.4	48.3
1971	10,880	8,887	2,310	81.7	21.2	26.0	1,726	15.9	9,107	26.8	47.7
1970	10,555	8,634	2,209	81.8	20.9	25.6	1,675	15.9	8,837	26.3	47.2
1969	10,186	8,291	2,200	81.4	21.6	26.5	1,668	16.4	8,501	27.2	46.3
1968	9,866	7,906	1,980	80.1	20.1	25.0	1,706	17.3	8,135	26.0	45.1
1967	9,637	7,586	1,949	78.7	20.2	25.7	1,750	18.2	7,815	26.6	45.7

r = Revised, controlled to 1990 census based population estimates; previous 1993 data controlled to 1980 census based population estimates.
Note: The change in the educational attainment question and the college completion categories from "4 or more years of college" to "at least some college," in 1992 caused an increase in the proportion of 14-to-24-year-old high school graduates enrolled in college or completed some college, of approximately 5 percentage points. High school graduates are people who have completed 4 years of high school or more, for 1967 to 1991. Beginning in 1992, they were people whose highest degree was a high school diploma (including equivalency) or higher.
[1] Starting in 2003 respondents could identify more than one race. Except as noted, the race data in this table from 2003 onward represent those respondents who indicated only one race category.
[2] The data shown prior to 2003 consists of those identifying themselves as "Asian or Pacific Islanders."

Table A-14. Population 14 to 24 Years Old, by High School Graduate Status, College Enrollment, Attainment, Sex, Race, and Hispanic Origin, October 1967–2019—*Continued*

(Numbers in thousands; percent; civilian noninstitutionalized population.)

Year, race, and Hispanic origin	Population 18 to 24 years old								High school graduates, 14 to 24 years old		
		High school graduates		Percent			High school dropouts			Percent	
	Total	Total	Enrolled in college	High school graduates	Enrolled in college	Of high school graduates enrolled in college	Number	Percent	All graduates	Enrolled in college	Enrolled or completed some college
WHITE ALONE NON-HISPANIC											
Both Sexes											
2019	15,637	14,007	6,430	89.6	41.1	45.9	710	4.5	14,220	46.1	72.0
2018	15,789	14,183	6,671	89.8	42.3	47.0	704	4.5	14,374	47.2	73.8
2017	15,945	14,251	6,544	89.4	41.0	45.9	747	4.7	14,442	45.9	74.3
2016	16,363	14,641	6,895	89.5	42.1	47.1	822	5.0	14,816	47.1	74.6
2015	16,615	14,812	6,938	89.1	41.8	46.8	816	4.9	15,025	46.9	74.6
2014	16,723	14,877	7,054	89.0	42.2	47.4	890	5.3	15,066	47.6	74.9
2013	16,962	15,135	7,065	89.2	41.6	46.7	876	5.2	15,394	47.1	75.0
2012	17,072	15,216	7,189	89.1	42.1	47.2	819	4.8	15,421	47.6	75.0
2011	17,627	15,565	7,882	88.3	44.7	50.6	1,002	5.7	15,752	50.7	76.2
2010	17,693	15,761	7,663	89.1	43.3	48.6	1,003	5.7	15,927	48.8	75.4
2009	17,750	15,839	7,983	89.2	45.0	50.4	1,029	5.8	16,051	50.5	75.2
2008	17,839	16,038	7,894	89.9	44.2	49.2	960	5.4	16,224	49.4	74.2
2007	17,669	15,727	7,533	89.0	42.6	47.9	1,064	6.0	15,921	48.0	72.9
2006	17,565	15,452	7,200	88.0	41.0	46.6	1,189	6.8	15,642	46.8	72.5
2005	17,293	15,187	7,393	87.8	42.8	48.7	1,216	7.0	15,368	48.7	72.6
2004	17,326	15,224	7,228	87.9	41.7	47.5	1,313	7.6	15,382	47.7	71.8
2003[1]	17,158	15,070	7,129	87.8	41.6	47.3	1,267	7.4	15,255	47.3	71.5
2002	17,131	14,910	7,004	87.0	40.9	47.0	1,289	7.5	15,089	47.1	70.4
2001	16,721	14,480	6,565	86.6	39.3	45.3	1,390	8.3	14,646	45.3	69.7
2000	17,327	15,187	6,709	87.7	38.7	44.2	1,316	7.6	15,344	44.3	69.0
1999	17,080	14,812	6,735	86.7	39.4	45.5	1,404	8.2	14,952	45.6	70.2
1998	16,634	14,402	6,757	86.6	40.6	46.9	1,491	9.0	14,542	47.0	70.6
1997	16,575	14,414	6,728	87.0	40.6	46.7	1,432	8.6	14,527	46.9	70.0
1996	16,339	14,288	6,447	87.5	39.5	45.1	1,303	8.0	14,501	45.5	70.7
1995	16,867	14,523	6,393	86.1	37.9	44.0	1,647	9.8	14,672	44.3	70.2
1994	17,114	14,916	6,521	87.2	38.1	43.7	1,505	8.8	15,049	44.0	69.2
1993	16,895	14,665	6,221	86.8	36.8	42.4	1,524	9.0	14,801	42.6	68.1
Male											
2019	7,922	6,920	2,929	87.4	37.0	42.3	438	5.5	7,019	42.4	66.8
2018	7,977	7,044	3,123	88.3	39.1	44.3	416	5.2	7,125	44.5	68.3
2017	8,096	7,098	3,057	87.7	37.8	43.1	409	5.1	7,187	43.0	69.8
2016	8,259	7,279	3,288	88.1	39.8	45.2	463	5.6	7,348	45.2	69.6
2015	8,401	7,396	3,284	88.0	39.1	44.4	451	5.4	7,512	44.4	69.7
2014	8,446	7,426	3,391	87.9	40.2	45.7	485	5.7	7,526	45.8	70.5
2013	8,562	7,526	3,260	87.9	38.1	43.3	462	5.4	7,658	43.8	70.2
2012	8,598	7,552	3,290	87.8	38.3	43.6	455	5.3	7,637	43.9	69.5
2011	8,864	7,697	3,754	86.8	42.4	48.8	554	6.2	7,794	48.9	72.7
2010	8,919	7,808	3,617	87.5	40.6	46.3	569	6.4	7,884	46.4	70.9
2009	8,957	7,818	3,787	87.3	42.3	48.4	632	7.1	7,915	48.5	71.9
2008	9,032	8,028	3,766	88.9	41.7	46.9	546	6.0	8,126	47.1	70.4
2007	8,940	7,786	3,541	87.1	39.6	45.5	622	7.0	7,883	45.5	68.8
2006	8,842	7,660	3,354	86.6	37.9	43.8	647	7.3	7,734	43.9	68.4
2005	8,700	7,443	3,429	85.5	39.4	46.1	685	7.9	7,526	46.0	68.6
2004	8,644	7,527	3,322	87.1	38.4	44.1	691	8.0	7,576	44.4	66.7
2003[2]	8,538	7,325	3,291	85.8	38.5	44.9	721	8.4	7,401	45.0	68.5
2002	8,453	7,244	3,287	85.7	38.9	45.4	668	7.9	7,352	45.5	67.9
2001	8,343	7,112	3,094	85.3	37.1	43.4	741	8.9	7,191	43.4	67.1
2000	8,670	7,493	3,136	86.4	36.2	41.9	677	7.8	7,556	42.0	65.4
1999	8,580	7,301	3,284	85.1	38.3	45.0	753	8.8	7,369	45.0	67.7
1998	8,380	7,094	3,300	84.7	39.4	46.5	826	9.9	7,151	46.6	68.2
1997	8,326	7,112	3,276	85.4	39.3	46.1	797	9.6	7,154	46.3	68.1

r = Revised, controlled to 1990 census based population estimates; previous 1993 data controlled to 1980 census based population estimates.

Note: The change in the educational attainment question and the college completion categories from "4 or more years of college" to "at least some college," in 1992 caused an increase in the proportion of 14-to-24-year-old high school graduates enrolled in college or completed some college, of approximately 5 percentage points. High school graduates are people who have completed 4 years of high school or more, for 1967 to 1991. Beginning in 1992, they were people whose highest degree was a high school diploma (including equivalency) or higher.

[1] Starting in 2003 respondents could identify more than one race. Except as noted, the race data in this table from 2003 onward represent those respondents who indicated only one race category.

[2] The data shown prior to 2003 consists of those identifying themselves as "Asian or Pacific Islanders."

Table A-14. Population 14 to 24 Years Old, by High School Graduate Status, College Enrollment, Attainment, Sex, Race, and Hispanic Origin, October 1967–2019—*Continued*

(Numbers in thousands; percent; civilian noninstitutionalized population.)

| Year, race, and Hispanic origin | Population 18 to 24 years old | | | | | | | | High school graduates, 14 to 24 years old | | |
| | High school graduates | | | Percent | | | High school dropouts | | | Percent | |
	Total	Total	Enrolled in college	High school graduates	Enrolled in college	Of high school graduates enrolled in college	Number	Percent	All graduates	Enrolled in college	Enrolled or completed some college
1996	8,168	7,050	3,130	86.3	38.3	44.4	651	8.0	7,143	44.7	68.6
1995	8,399	7,089	3,105	84.4	37.0	43.8	883	10.5	7,147	44.0	67.3
1994	8,457	7,261	3,126	85.9	37.0	43.1	777	9.2	7,317	43.3	67.0
1993	8,403	7,138	3,071	84.9	36.6	43.0	811	9.7	7,191	43.2	67.1
Female											
2019	7,715	7,087	3,502	91.9	45.4	49.4	272	3.5	7,201	49.7	77.0
2018	7,812	7,139	3,549	91.4	45.4	49.7	287	3.7	7,250	49.9	79.3
2017	7,849	7,154	3,487	91.1	44.4	48.7	338	4.3	7,255	48.8	78.8
2016	8,104	7,362	3,606	90.8	44.5	49.0	360	4.4	7,468	49.0	79.5
2015	8,215	7,416	3,654	90.3	44.5	49.3	365	4.4	7,513	49.3	79.5
2014	8,278	7,451	3,663	90.0	44.2	49.2	404	4.9	7,541	49.3	79.3
2013	8,400	7,609	3,804	90.6	45.3	50.0	414	4.9	7,736	50.4	79.8
2012	8,474	7,664	3,899	90.4	46.0	50.9	364	4.3	7,784	51.2	80.5
2011	8,763	7,868	4,128	89.8	47.1	52.5	448	5.1	7,958	52.5	79.6
2010	8,774	7,953	4,046	90.6	46.1	50.9	434	4.9	8,044	51.2	79.8
2009	8,793	8,021	4,195	91.2	47.7	52.3	398	4.5	8,136	52.4	78.3
2008	8,808	8,010	4,127	90.9	46.9	51.5	414	4.7	8,099	51.7	78.0
2007	8,728	7,941	3,992	91.0	45.7	50.3	442	5.1	8,039	50.4	76.9
2006	8,724	7,791	3,846	89.3	44.1	49.4	542	6.2	7,908	49.5	76.4
2005	8,593	7,744	3,964	90.1	46.1	51.2	531	6.2	7,842	51.4	76.4
2004	8,628	7,697	3,906	89.2	45.3	50.7	622	7.2	7,805	50.9	76.8
2003[1]	8,620	7,745	3,838	89.9	44.5	49.6	546	6.3	7,854	49.5	74.4
2002	8,678	7,666	3,717	88.3	42.8	48.5	621	7.2	7,736	48.6	72.8
2001	8,378	7,368	3,471	87.9	41.4	47.2	648	7.7	7,455	47.2	72.3
2000	8,657	7,693	3,573	88.9	41.3	46.4	638	7.4	7,789	46.6	72.5
1999	8,500	7,510	3,451	88.4	40.6	46.0	651	7.7	7,583	46.2	72.5
1998	8,254	7,308	3,457	88.5	41.9	47.3	665	8.1	7,391	47.5	73.0
1997	8,249	7,302	3,452	88.5	41.9	47.3	636	7.7	7,373	47.5	71.9
1996	8,171	7,238	3,317	88.6	40.6	45.8	652	8.0	7,358	46.3	72.8
1995	8,467	7,433	3,288	87.8	38.8	44.2	764	9.0	7,525	44.6	73.1
1994	8,657	7,655	3,395	88.4	39.2	44.4	728	8.4	7,732	44.6	71.3
1993	8,492	7,527	3,150	88.6	37.1	41.9	714	8.4	7,610	42.0	69.1
BLACK ALONE											
Both Sexes											
2019	4,344	3,784	1,588	87.1	36.5	42.0	270	6.2	3,850	42.4	66.4
2018	4,415	3,852	1,670	87.2	37.8	43.3	216	4.9	3,894	43.3	67.8
2017	4,458	3,807	1,595	85.4	35.8	41.9	270	6.1	3,885	41.9	65.4
2016	4,551	3,857	1,644	84.7	36.1	42.6	314	6.9	3,937	42.5	65.6
2015	4,635	3,971	1,636	85.7	35.3	41.2	347	7.5	4,019	41.3	64.5
2014	4,704	3,993	1,528	84.9	32.5	38.3	345	7.3	4,061	39.0	65.9
2013	4,746	3,885	1,600	81.9	33.7	41.2	393	8.3	3,929	41.5	65.7
2012	4,714	3,754	1,689	79.6	35.8	45.0	467	9.9	3,816	45.0	66.6
2011	4,503	3,649	1,639	81.0	36.4	44.9	399	8.9	3,702	45.3	66.3
2010	4,457	3,669	1,692	82.3	38.0	46.1	450	10.1	3,731	46.2	66.2
2009	4,346	3,458	1,604	79.6	36.9	46.4	505	11.6	3,532	46.4	67.5
2008	4,265	3,387	1,349	79.4	31.6	40.0	548	12.1	3,445	40.2	60.7
2007	4,182	3,423	1,396	81.8	33.4	40.8	425	10.2	3,483	40.9	61.4
2006	4,085	3,156	1,321	77.3	32.3	41.9	532	13.0	3,224	41.9	60.8
2005	3,964	3,137	1,297	79.1	32.7	41.3	512	12.9	3,212	41.3	63.5
2004	3,940	3,050	1,238	77.4	31.4	40.6	596	15.1	3,112	41.1	63.2
2003[1]	3,837	2,948	1,225	76.8	31.9	41.6	545	14.2	2,997	41.8	62.5
2002	3,924	3,040	1,226	77.5	31.3	40.3	571	14.5	3,117	41.1	61.2
2001	3,916	3,016	1,206	77.0	30.8	40.0	540	13.8	3,095	40.0	59.0
2000	4,013	3,090	1,216	77.0	30.3	39.4	615	15.3	3,129	39.5	61.0

r = Revised, controlled to 1990 census based population estimates; previous 1993 data controlled to 1980 census based population estimates.

Note: The change in the educational attainment question and the college completion categories from "4 or more years of college" to "at least some college," in 1992 caused an increase in the proportion of 14-to-24-year-old high school graduates enrolled in college or completed some college, of approximately 5 percentage points. High school graduates are people who have completed 4 or more years of high school or more, for 1967 to 1991. Beginning in 1992, they were people whose highest degree was a high school diploma (including equivalency) or higher.

[1] Starting in 2003 respondents could identify more than one race. Except as noted, the race data in this table from 2003 onward represent those respondents who indicated only one race category.

[2] The data shown prior to 2003 consists of those identifying themselves as "Asian or Pacific Islanders."

Table A-14. Population 14 to 24 Years Old, by High School Graduate Status, College Enrollment, Attainment, Sex, Race, and Hispanic Origin, October 1967–2019—*Continued*

(Numbers in thousands; percent; civilian noninstitutionalized population.)

Year, race, and Hispanic origin	Population 18 to 24 years old								High school graduates, 14 to 24 years old		
		High school graduates		Percent			High school dropouts			Percent	
	Total	Total	Enrolled in college	High school graduates	Enrolled in college	Of high school graduates enrolled in college	Number	Percent	All graduates	Enrolled in college	Enrolled or completed some college
1999............................	3,827	2,911	1,145	76.1	29.9	39.4	613	16.0	2,985	39.9	60.4
1998............................	3,745	2,747	1,116	73.4	29.8	40.6	642	17.1	2,790	40.8	61.8
1997............................	3,650	2,725	1,085	74.7	29.7	39.8	611	16.7	2,762	40.2	60.0
1996............................	3,637	2,738	983	75.3	27.0	35.9	581	16.0	2,805	36.6	54.6
1995............................	3,625	2,788	988	76.9	27.3	35.4	522	14.4	2,828	35.8	58.0
1994............................	3,661	2,818	1,001	77.0	27.3	35.5	568	15.5	2,859	36.3	59.2
1993r..........................	3,666	2,747	897	74.9	24.5	32.7	600	16.4	2,771	32.8	54.0
1993............................	3,516	2,629	861	74.8	24.5	32.8	578	16.4	2,653	32.9	53.9
1992............................	3,521	2,625	886	74.6	25.2	33.8	575	16.3	2,668	34.3	53.3
1991............................	3,504	2,630	828	75.1	23.6	31.5	545	15.6	2,658	31.8	46.0
1990............................	3,520	2,710	894	77.0	25.4	33.0	530	15.1	2,759	33.7	48.0
1989............................	3,559	2,708	835	76.1	23.5	30.8	583	16.4	2,750	31.5	49.2
1988............................	3,568	2,680	752	75.1	21.1	28.1	631	17.7	2,741	28.6	46.3
1987............................	3,603	2,739	823	76.0	22.8	30.0	611	17.0	2,790	30.6	48.1
1986............................	3,653	2,795	812	76.5	22.2	29.1	617	16.8	2,837	29.3	47.8
1985............................	3,716	2,810	734	75.6	19.8	26.1	655	17.6	2,848	26.5	43.8
1984............................	3,862	2,885	786	74.7	20.4	27.2	712	18.4	2,950	28.0	45.2
1983............................	3,865	2,740	741	70.9	19.2	27.0	832	21.5	2,790	27.7	45.0
1982............................	3,872	2,744	767	70.9	19.8	28.0	851	22.0	2,793	28.2	45.5
1981............................	3,778	2,678	750	70.9	19.9	28.0	821	21.7	2,718	28.7	44.8
1980............................	3,721	2,592	715	69.7	19.2	27.6	876	23.5	2,656	28.1	45.9
1979............................	3,510	2,356	696	67.1	19.8	29.5	895	25.5	2,415	30.6	48.4
1978............................	3,452	2,340	694	67.8	20.1	29.7	850	24.6	2,396	30.6	47.8
1977............................	3,387	2,286	721	67.5	21.3	31.5	808	23.9	2,342	32.4	46.9
1976............................	3,315	2,239	749	67.5	22.6	33.5	803	24.2	2,291	34.2	50.4
1975............................	3,213	2,081	665	64.8	20.7	32.0	877	27.3	2,149	32.6	48.1
1974............................	3,105	2,083	555	67.1	17.9	26.6	780	25.1	2,145	27.5	44.8
1973............................	3,114	2,079	498	66.8	16.0	24.0	826	26.5	2,139	25.0	41.6
1972............................	2,986	1,992	540	66.7	18.1	27.1	782	26.2	2,044	28.0	42.0
1971............................	2,866	1,789	522	62.4	18.2	29.2	825	28.8	1,833	30.0	42.3
1970............................	2,692	1,602	416	59.5	15.5	26.0	897	33.3	1,635	26.7	39.4
1969............................	2,542	1,497	407	58.9	16.0	27.2	828	32.6	1,547	27.5	40.1
1968............................	2,421	1,399	352	57.8	14.5	25.2	799	33.0	1,432	26.0	38.1
1967............................	2,283	1,276	297	55.9	13.0	23.3	788	34.5	1,316	23.7	35.0
Male											
2019............................	2,109	1,790	695	84.9	32.9	38.8	152	7.2	1,826	39.3	63.1
2018............................	2,148	1,819	736	84.7	34.2	40.4	129	6.0	1,827	40.6	63.2
2017............................	2,172	1,821	695	83.8	32.0	38.2	163	7.5	1,857	38.1	60.4
2016............................	2,218	1,774	728	80.0	32.8	41.0	204	9.2	1,795	41.2	61.4
2015............................	2,257	1,923	779	85.2	34.5	40.5	165	7.3	1,947	40.6	63.3
2014............................	2,289	1,889	633	82.5	27.6	33.5	166	7.3	1,934	34.7	61.1
2013............................	2,303	1,847	690	80.2	30.0	37.4	221	9.6	1,865	38.0	61.7
2012............................	2,278	1,787	760	78.4	33.4	42.5	258	11.3	1,820	42.7	63.8
2011............................	2,165	1,701	717	78.6	33.1	42.2	205	9.5	1,732	42.7	60.9
2010............................	2,140	1,692	734	79.1	34.3	43.4	258	12.1	1,730	43.2	61.4
2009............................	2,082	1,592	673	76.5	32.3	42.3	289	13.9	1,617	42.0	63.5
2008............................	2,045	1,641	595	80.2	29.1	36.3	210	10.2	1,668	36.9	54.8
2007............................	2,011	1,622	649	80.6	32.3	40.0	202	10.0	1,642	40.1	59.3
2006............................	1,959	1,488	541	76.0	27.6	36.4	219	11.2	1,519	36.3	53.4
2005............................	1,897	1,393	530	73.4	27.9	38.0	280	14.8	1,420	37.9	58.4
2004	1,852	1,341	479	72.4	25.9	35.7	331	17.9	1,363	36.1	60.9
2003¹..........................	1,801	1,331	499	73.9	27.7	37.5	300	16.7	1,346	37.8	57.1
2002............................	1,843	1,354	475	73.5	25.8	35.1	311	16.9	1,372	35.6	56.1
2001............................	1,818	1,287	470	70.8	25.8	36.4	308	16.9	1,310	36.4	53.1
2000............................	1,885	1,389	470	73.7	24.9	33.8	329	17.4	1,409	34.1	53.5
1999............................	1,747	1,292	501	73.9	28.7	38.8	285	16.3	1,336	40.2	57.7

r = Revised, controlled to 1990 census based population estimates; previous 1993 data controlled to 1980 census based population estimates.
Note: The change in the educational attainment question and the college completion categories from "4 or more years of college" to "at least some college," in 1992 caused an increase in the proportion of 14-to-24-year-old high school graduates enrolled in college or completed some college, of approximately 5 percentage points. High school graduates are people who have completed 4 years of high school or more, for 1967 to 1991. Beginning in 1992, they were people whose highest degree was a high school diploma (including equivalency) or higher.
¹ Starting in 2003 respondents could identify more than one race. Except as noted, the race data in this table from 2003 onward represent those respondents who indicated only one race category.
² The data shown prior to 2003 consists of those identifying themselves as "Asian or Pacific Islanders."

Table A-14. Population 14 to 24 Years Old, by High School Graduate Status, College Enrollment, Attainment, Sex, Race, and Hispanic Origin, October 1967–2019—*Continued*

(Numbers in thousands; percent; civilian noninstitutionalized population.)

| Year, race, and Hispanic origin | Population 18 to 24 years old | | | | | | | | High school graduates, 14 to 24 years old | | |
| | | High school graduates | | Percent | | | High school dropouts | | | Percent | |
	Total	Total	Enrolled in college	High school graduates	Enrolled in college	Of high school graduates enrolled in college	Number	Percent	All graduates	Enrolled in college	Enrolled or completed some college
1998	1,724	1,163	445	67.5	25.8	38.2	354	20.5	1,186	38.5	57.5
1997	1,701	1,214	425	71.4	25.0	35.0	297	17.5	1,232	35.1	56.3
1996	1,682	1,199	422	71.3	25.1	35.2	292	17.4	1,225	35.8	53.7
1995	1,660	1,247	430	75.1	25.9	34.4	235	14.2	1,262	35.1	56.2
1994	1,733	1,277	440	73.7	25.4	34.5	303	17.5	1,293	35.3	57.9
1993r	1,703	1,240	387	72.8	22.7	31.2	266	15.6	1,247	31.4	50.1
1993	1,659	1,207	379	72.8	22.8	31.4	258	15.6	1,214	31.5	50.0
1992	1,676	1,211	356	72.3	21.2	29.4	259	15.5	1,226	29.7	49.4
1991	1,635	1,174	378	71.8	23.1	32.2	252	15.4	1,188	32.4	47.0
1990	1,634	1,240	426	75.9	26.1	34.4	223	13.6	1,260	35.1	48.8
1989	1,654	1,195	324	72.2	19.6	27.1	307	18.6	1,207	27.5	45.8
1988	1,653	1,189	297	71.9	18.0	25.0	312	18.9	1,205	25.1	42.5
1987	1,666	1,188	377	71.3	22.6	31.7	312	18.7	1,209	32.3	48.0
1986	1,687	1,220	349	72.3	20.7	28.6	300	17.8	1,239	29.1	44.4
1985	1,720	1,244	345	72.3	20.1	27.7	323	18.8	1,258	28.2	43.6
1984	1,811	1,272	367	70.2	20.3	28.9	362	20.2	1,295	29.6	45.2
1983	1,807	1,202	331	66.5	18.3	27.5	435	24.1	1,228	27.9	43.6
1982	1,786	1,171	331	65.6	18.5	28.3	458	25.6	1,188	28.6	44.5
1981	1,730	1,154	325	66.7	18.8	28.2	419	24.2	1,165	28.5	42.3
1980	1,690	1,115	293	66.0	17.3	26.3	440	26.0	1,141	26.9	44.1
1979	1,577	973	304	61.7	19.3	31.2	457	29.0	988	32.0	46.7
1978	1,554	956	305	61.5	19.6	31.9	451	29.0	981	32.4	49.3
1977	1,528	970	309	63.5	20.2	31.9	369	24.1	991	33.0	47.6
1976	1,503	936	331	62.3	22.0	35.4	393	26.1	952	35.9	50.3
1975	1,451	897	294	61.8	20.3	32.8	404	27.8	923	33.4	50.5
1974	1,396	919	280	65.8	20.1	30.5	346	24.8	941	31.1	47.3
1973	1,434	952	266	66.4	18.5	27.9	371	25.9	962	28.4	44.2
1972	1,373	870	287	63.4	20.9	33.0	373	27.2	897	34.0	47.4
1971	1,318	769	262	58.3	19.9	34.1	416	31.6	783	34.9	45.8
1970	1,220	668	192	54.8	15.7	28.7	436	35.7	684	29.5	41.4
1969	1,141	631	202	55.3	17.7	32.0	383	33.6	653	32.5	44.6
1968	1,087	582	170	53.5	15.6	29.2	370	34.0	600	30.3	43.2
1967	1,032	525	167	50.9	16.2	31.8	397	38.5	539	32.3	41.6
Female											
2019	2,235	1,993	893	89.2	40.0	44.8	118	5.3	2,023	45.1	69.5
2018	2,267	2,034	934	89.7	41.2	45.9	86	3.8	2,067	45.6	71.9
2017	2,286	1,986	900	86.9	39.3	45.3	107	4.7	2,028	45.4	70.1
2016	2,333	2,083	916	89.3	39.3	44.0	111	4.7	2,142	43.6	69.1
2015	2,378	2,048	857	86.1	36.1	41.9	182	7.7	2,071	42.0	65.6
2014	2,415	2,104	895	87.2	37.1	42.5	179	7.4	2,128	42.9	70.2
2013	2,442	2,038	909	83.4	37.2	44.6	173	7.1	2,064	44.7	69.3
2012	2,436	1,967	929	80.8	38.1	47.2	209	8.6	1,996	47.0	69.2
2011	2,339	1,949	921	83.3	39.4	47.3	194	8.3	1,970	47.6	71.0
2010	2,317	1,977	958	85.3	41.3	48.4	192	8.3	2,001	48.8	70.4
2009	2,263	1,865	931	82.4	41.1	49.9	216	9.5	1,915	50.1	70.9
2008	2,220	1,746	754	78.7	34.0	43.2	304	13.7	1,777	43.3	66.2
2007	2,171	1,801	747	82.9	34.4	41.5	223	10.3	1,841	41.5	63.3
2006	2,126	1,668	780	78.5	36.7	46.7	313	14.7	1,705	46.9	67.3
2005	2,067	1,745	767	84.4	37.1	44.0	232	11.2	1,793	44.0	67.5
2004	2,088	1,709	759	81.8	36.3	44.4	266	12.7	1,749	44.9	65.0
2003[1]	2,035	1,618	726	79.5	35.7	44.9	245	12.0	1,652	45.1	66.8
2002	2,081	1,686	751	81.0	36.1	44.5	260	12.5	1,745	45.5	65.2
2001	2,098	1,729	736	82.4	35.1	42.7	232	11.0	1,785	42.7	63.3
2000	2,128	1,700	747	79.9	35.1	43.9	287	13.5	1,720	43.9	67.1
1999	2,080	1,619	644	77.9	31.0	39.8	327	15.7	1,650	39.6	62.6
1998	2,021	1,584	671	78.4	33.2	42.4	288	14.3	1,604	42.4	65.0

r = Revised, controlled to 1990 census based population estimates; previous 1993 data controlled to 1980 census based population estimates.
Note: The change in the educational attainment question and the college completion categories from "4 or more years of college" to "at least some college," in 1992 caused an increase in the proportion of 14-to-24-year-old high school graduates enrolled in college or completed some college, of approximately 5 percentage points. High school graduates are people who have completed 4 years of high school or more, for 1967 to 1991. Beginning in 1992, they were people whose highest degree was a high school diploma (including equivalency) or higher.
[1] Starting in 2003 respondents could identify more than one race. Except as noted, the race data in this table from 2003 onward represent those respondents who indicated only one race category.
[2] The data shown prior to 2003 consists of those identifying themselves as "Asian or Pacific Islanders."

Table A-14. Population 14 to 24 Years Old, by High School Graduate Status, College Enrollment, Attainment, Sex, Race, and Hispanic Origin, October 1967–2019—*Continued*

(Numbers in thousands; percent; civilian noninstitutionalized population.)

Year, race, and Hispanic origin	Population 18 to 24 years old								High school graduates, 14 to 24 years old		
		High school graduates		Percent			High school dropouts			Percent	
	Total	Total	Enrolled in college	High school graduates	Enrolled in college	Of high school graduates enrolled in college	Number	Percent	All graduates	Enrolled in college	Enrolled or completed some college
1997............	1,949	1,511	659	77.5	33.8	43.6	314	16.1	1,529	43.1	63.0
1996............	1,956	1,539	561	78.7	28.7	36.4	288	14.7	1,580	37.3	55.3
1995............	1,965	1,541	558	78.4	28.4	36.2	287	14.6	1,566	36.3	59.5
1994............	1,928	1,542	561	80.0	29.1	36.4	265	13.7	1,567	37.1	60.3
1993r............	1,965	1,508	511	76.7	26.0	33.9	337	17.2	1,526	34.1	57.2
1993............	1,857	1,425	484	76.7	26.1	34.0	319	17.2	1,441	34.1	57.1
1992............	1,845	1,417	531	76.8	28.8	37.5	315	17.1	1,446	38.2	56.6
1991............	1,869	1,455	450	77.8	24.1	30.9	296	15.8	1,468	31.4	45.2
1990............	1,886	1,468	467	77.8	24.8	31.8	306	16.2	1,498	32.4	47.3
1989............	1,905	1,511	511	79.3	26.8	33.8	277	14.5	1,541	34.7	51.8
1988............	1,915	1,492	455	77.9	23.8	30.5	318	16.6	1,538	31.3	49.2
1987............	1,937	1,550	445	80.0	23.0	28.7	298	15.4	1,579	29.4	48.9
1986............	1,966	1,574	462	80.1	23.5	29.4	306	15.6	1,598	29.3	50.4
1985............	1,996	1,565	389	78.4	19.5	24.9	332	16.6	1,592	25.1	44.0
1984............	2,052	1,613	419	78.6	20.4	26.0	349	17.0	1,655	26.8	45.1
1983............	2,058	1,539	411	74.8	20.0	26.7	398	19.3	1,561	27.5	46.3
1982............	2,086	1,572	436	75.4	20.9	27.7	393	18.8	1,604	27.9	46.3
1981............	2,049	1,526	424	74.5	20.7	27.8	402	19.6	1,554	28.8	46.6
1980............	2,031	1,475	422	72.6	20.8	28.6	436	21.5	1,511	29.1	47.4
1979............	1,934	1,383	392	71.5	20.3	28.3	439	22.7	1,426	29.7	49.8
1978............	1,897	1,384	390	73.0	20.6	28.2	398	21.0	1,415	29.3	46.7
1977............	1,859	1,317	413	70.8	22.2	31.4	439	23.6	1,354	31.9	46.2
1976............	1,813	1,302	417	71.8	23.0	32.0	410	22.6	1,338	32.9	50.3
1975............	1,761	1,182	372	67.1	21.1	31.5	473	26.9	1,224	32.0	46.4
1974............	1,709	1,167	277	68.3	16.2	23.7	434	25.4	1,207	24.8	42.9
1973............	1,681	1,125	231	66.9	13.7	20.5	456	27.1	1,177	22.2	39.4
1972............	1,613	1,123	253	69.6	15.7	22.5	408	25.3	1,150	23.2	37.9
1971............	1,547	1,019	259	65.9	16.7	25.4	409	26.4	1,049	26.4	39.8
1970............	1,471	935	225	63.6	15.3	24.1	461	31.3	955	24.7	39.3
1969............	1,402	867	206	61.8	14.7	23.8	444	31.7	896	24.0	38.6
1968............	1,334	819	183	61.4	13.7	22.3	430	32.2	834	22.9	35.9
1967............	1,249	751	130	60.1	10.4	17.3	391	31.3	778	17.9	33.2
ASIAN ALONE[2]											
Both Sexes											
2019............	1,826	1,700	1,131	93.1	61.9	66.5	41	2.3	1,744	66.9	93.6
2018............	1,842	1,719	1,079	93.3	58.6	62.8	51	2.8	1,742	63.0	88.4
2017............	1,753	1,658	1,101	94.6	62.8	66.4	28	1.6	1,694	66.9	90.6
2016............	1,768	1,628	1,003	92.1	56.7	61.6	53	3.0	1,661	61.5	87.7
2015............	1,634	1,514	1,026	92.6	62.8	67.8	38	2.3	1,560	67.1	91.9
2014............	1,590	1,504	1,023	94.6	64.3	68.0	17	1.1	1,541	67.6	91.7
2013............	1,639	1,495	1,001	91.2	61.1	66.9	61	3.7	1,530	67.4	86.8
2012............	1,537	1,385	915	90.1	59.5	66.0	54	3.5	1,418	66.3	84.9
2011............	1,252	1,123	748	89.8	59.7	66.5	65	5.2	1,149	66.9	88.1
2010............	1,303	1,193	811	91.5	62.2	68.0	64	4.9	1,232	68.4	89.8
2009............	1,181	1,080	768	91.4	65.0	71.1	26	2.2	1,096	71.0	91.8
2008............	1,113	1,021	655	91.8	58.9	64.1	42	3.8	1,056	64.6	90.4
2007............	1,165	1,010	658	86.7	56.4	65.1	86	7.4	1,026	65.1	91.6
2006............	1,148	1,046	661	91.1	57.6	63.2	46	4.0	1,064	63.0	87.0
2005............	1,145	1,072	693	93.6	60.5	64.6	34	3.0	1,098	65.1	87.0
2004............	1,152	1,066	695	92.5	60.3	65.2	49	4.3	1,090	65.7	89.1
2003[1]............	1,144	1,030	693	90.1	60.6	67.3	56	4.9	1,046	67.7	88.2
2002............	1,339	1,230	803	91.8	60.0	65.3	57	4.2	1,265	65.7	86.9
2001............	1,312	1,197	794	91.2	60.5	66.5	47	3.6	1,218	66.5	87.6
2000............	1,143	1,038	639	90.8	55.9	61.6	52	4.6	1,053	61.8	83.9
1999............	1,130	1,019	626	90.2	55.4	61.4	58	5.1	1,035	62.0	85.5

r = Revised, controlled to 1990 census based population estimates; previous 1993 data controlled to 1980 census based population estimates.
Note: The change in the educational attainment question and the college completion categories from "4 or more years of college" to "at least some college," in 1992 caused an increase in the proportion of 14-to-24-year-old high school graduates enrolled in college or completed some college, of approximately 5 percentage points. High school graduates are people who have completed 4 years of high school or more, for 1967 to 1991. Beginning in 1992, they were people whose highest degree was a high school diploma (including equivalency) or higher.
[1] Starting in 2003 respondents could identify more than one race. Except as noted, the race data in this table from 2003 onward represent those respondents who indicated only one race category.
[2] The data shown prior to 2003 consists of those identifying themselves as "Asian or Pacific Islanders."

Table A-14. Population 14 to 24 Years Old, by High School Graduate Status, College Enrollment, Attainment, Sex, Race, and Hispanic Origin, October 1967–2019—*Continued*

(Numbers in thousands; percent; civilian noninstitutionalized population.)

| | Population 18 to 24 years old | | | | | | | | High school graduates, 14 to 24 years old | | |
| | High school graduates | | | Percent | | | High school dropouts | | | Percent | |
Year, race, and Hispanic origin	Total	Total	Enrolled in college	High school graduates	Enrolled in college	Of high school graduates enrolled in college	Number	Percent	All graduates	Enrolled in college	Enrolled or completed some college
Male											
2019	906	839	552	92.6	60.9	65.8	20	2.2	865	66.4	91.1
2018	950	888	558	93.5	58.8	62.9	27	2.8	901	63.4	89.1
2017	895	842	561	94.1	62.7	66.7	12	1.3	849	66.9	89.4
2016	914	842	533	92.1	58.3	63.3	21	2.3	854	63.0	87.1
2015	819	758	493	92.6	60.2	65.0	24	2.9	783	64.2	90.0
2014	809	771	549	95.3	67.9	71.2	13	1.6	793	71.0	91.1
2013	859	795	534	92.5	62.2	67.2	18	2.1	806	67.2	86.1
2012	776	695	455	89.6	58.6	65.4	21	2.6	713	65.9	84.7
2011	639	573	379	89.6	59.3	66.2	30	4.7	582	66.1	87.6
2010	651	597	390	91.7	59.9	65.3	29	4.5	619	65.7	87.5
2009	590	546	383	92.4	64.9	70.2	7	1.2	559	69.9	90.1
2008	547	487	295	89.1	53.9	60.5	21	3.9	510	62.0	89.9
2007	560	481	318	85.8	56.9	66.3	38	6.8	483	66.4	91.8
2006	591	525	338	88.8	57.2	64.4	34	5.8	536	64.0	84.0
2005	590	552	366	93.5	62.0	66.3	17	2.9	565	66.4	88.2
2004	586	549	373	93.7	63.6	67.9	15	2.5	561	68.4	88.2
2003[1]	543	483	337	88.9	62.0	69.8	43	7.8	486	69.9	90.0
2002	707	637	417	90.0	59.0	65.5	38	5.4	652	65.3	86.7
2001	661	583	417	88.1	63.1	72.0	35	5.3	594	72.0	88.9
2000	571	521	337	91.1	58.9	64.7	34	6.0	527	64.7	85.6
1999	505	443	284	87.8	56.2	64.0	39	7.7	454	64.9	82.5
Female											
2019	920	861	579	93.6	62.9	67.2	22	2.4	880	67.5	96.1
2018	892	831	520	93.1	58.3	62.6	24	2.7	841	62.5	87.7
2017	859	816	540	95.0	62.8	66.1	17	1.9	844	66.9	91.9
2016	854	787	469	92.2	55.0	59.7	32	3.8	808	60.0	88.3
2015	816	756	533	92.6	65.4	70.6	14	1.7	776	70.0	93.8
2014	780	732	473	93.9	60.6	64.6	4	0.5	748	63.9	92.3
2013	780	700	467	89.8	59.8	66.6	43	5.5	723	67.5	87.5
2012	761	690	460	90.7	60.4	66.6	33	4.3	704	66.8	85.1
2011	612	551	369	89.9	60.2	66.9	35	5.8	567	67.8	88.7
2010	653	596	422	91.3	64.6	70.7	35	5.3	614	71.2	92.1
2009	591	534	384	90.4	65.1	72.0	19	3.3	538	72.2	93.7
2008	566	534	360	94.4	63.7	67.5	21	3.6	546	67.0	90.9
2007	605	529	339	87.4	56.0	64.1	48	7.9	543	63.9	91.5
2006	557	521	324	93.6	58.1	62.2	11	2.1	528	61.9	90.0
2005	555	521	327	93.8	58.9	62.8	17	3.0	533	63.7	85.8
2004	567	517	323	91.3	56.9	62.4	35	6.1	529	62.8	90.0
2003[1]	601	547	356	91.2	59.3	65.1	13	2.2	561	65.9	86.7
2002	632	593	386	93.8	61.0	65.1	19	2.9	613	66.1	87.2
2001	651	614	377	94.3	57.9	61.3	12	1.8	625	61.3	86.3
2000	572	517	302	90.4	52.9	58.5	18	3.1	526	58.9	82.3
1999	626	576	342	92.1	54.7	59.4	19	3.1	582	59.7	87.8
HISPANIC (OF ANY RACE)											
Both Sexes											
2019	6,811	5,799	2,469	85.1	36.3	42.6	509	7.5	5,879	42.7	64.7
2018	6,762	5,661	2,430	83.7	35.9	42.9	656	9.7	5,755	43.2	66.6
2017	6,653	5,457	2,410	82.0	36.2	44.2	703	10.6	5,571	44.7	65.9
2016	6,539	5,477	2,565	83.8	39.2	46.8	648	9.9	5,608	47.3	67.2
2015	6,464	5,366	2,368	83.0	36.6	44.1	669	10.3	5,460	44.2	66.6
2014	6,568	5,324	2,282	81.1	34.7	42.9	777	11.8	5,409	43.1	62.8

r = Revised, controlled to 1990 census based population estimates; previous 1993 data controlled to 1980 census based population estimates.
Note: The change in the educational attainment question and the college completion categories from "4 or more years of college" to "at least some college," in 1992 caused an increase in the proportion of 14-to-24-year-old high school graduates enrolled in college or completed some college, of approximately 5 percentage points. High school graduates are people who have completed 4 years of high school or more, for 1967 to 1991. Beginning in 1992, they were people whose highest degree was a high school diploma (including equivalency) or higher.
[1] Starting in 2003 respondents could identify more than one race. Except as noted, the race data in this table from 2003 onward represent those respondents who indicated only one race category.
[2] The data shown prior to 2003 consists of those identifying themselves as "Asian or Pacific Islanders."

Table A-14. Population 14 to 24 Years Old, by High School Graduate Status, College Enrollment, Attainment, Sex, Race, and Hispanic Origin, October 1967–2019—*Continued*

(Numbers in thousands; percent; civilian noninstitutionalized population.)

Year, race, and Hispanic origin	Population 18 to 24 years old								High school graduates, 14 to 24 years old		
	Total	High school graduates		Percent			High school dropouts			Percent	
		Total	Enrolled in college	High school graduates	Enrolled in college	Of high school graduates enrolled in college	Number	Percent	All graduates	Enrolled in college	Enrolled or completed some college
2013	6,489	5,118	2,193	78.9	33.8	42.8	889	13.7	5,190	43.1	62.3
2012	6,416	4,902	2,403	76.4	37.5	49.0	972	15.1	4,987	49.4	68.1
2011	5,974	4,569	2,079	76.5	34.8	45.5	975	16.3	4,630	45.7	65.4
2010	5,685	4,138	1,814	72.8	31.9	43.8	1,050	18.5	4,199	44.2	63.2
2009	5,332	3,747	1,465	70.3	27.5	39.1	1,112	20.8	3,813	39.6	57.8
2008	5,176	3,618	1,338	69.9	25.8	37.0	1,155	22.3	3,691	37.7	58.7
2007	5,175	3,487	1,375	67.4	26.6	39.4	1,310	25.3	3,553	39.9	58.0
2006	5,006	3,301	1,182	65.9	23.6	35.8	1,313	26.2	3,379	36.6	57.2
2005	4,898	3,230	1,215	66.0	24.8	37.6	1,335	27.3	3,280	38.0	57.3
2004	4,941	3,244	1,221	65.6	24.7	37.7	1,386	28.0	3,287	37.9	55.9
2003	4,754	3,096	1,115	65.1	23.5	36.0	1,353	28.4	3,135	36.0	56.5
2002	4,918	3,078	979	62.6	19.9	31.8	1,479	30.1	3,109	32.0	53.1
2001	4,892	3,031	1,035	62.0	21.1	34.2	1,548	31.7	3,068	34.2	52.8
2000	4,134	2,462	899	59.6	21.7	36.5	1,335	32.3	2,509	36.8	53.1
1999	3,953	2,325	739	58.8	18.7	31.8	1,340	33.9	2,359	31.7	49.6
1998	4,014	2,403	820	59.8	20.4	34.1	1,383	34.4	2,419	34.3	53.2
1997	3,606	2,236	806	62.0	22.4	36.0	1,103	30.6	2,302	37.1	54.3
1996	3,510	2,019	706	57.5	20.1	35.0	1,210	34.5	2,046	34.5	52.5
1995	3,603	2,112	745	58.6	20.7	35.3	1,250	34.7	2,142	35.7	55.8
1994	3,523	1,995	662	56.6	18.8	33.2	1,224	34.7	2,009	33.4	54.3
1993r	3,363	2,049	728	60.9	21.6	35.5	1,103	32.8	2,081	35.8	55.6
1993	2,772	1,682	602	60.7	21.7	35.8	907	32.7	1,712	36.0	55.8
1992	2,754	1,579	586	57.3	21.3	37.1	936	33.9	1,603	37.6	55.0
1991	2,874	1,498	516	52.1	18.0	34.4	1,139	39.6	1,519	34.6	47.6
1990	2,749	1,498	435	54.5	15.8	29.0	1,025	37.3	1,523	29.4	44.7
1989	2,818	1,576	453	55.9	16.1	28.7	1,062	37.7	1,600	29.4	43.6
1988	2,642	1,458	450	55.2	17.0	30.9	1,046	39.6	1,481	31.3	47.0
1987	2,592	1,597	455	61.6	17.6	28.5	849	32.8	1,612	28.7	44.0
1986	2,514	1,507	458	59.9	18.2	30.4	864	34.4	1,535	30.9	45.6
1985	2,221	1,396	375	62.9	16.9	26.9	700	31.5	1,419	27.6	46.7
1984	2,018	1,212	362	60.1	17.9	29.9	691	34.2	1,223	30.0	46.0
1983	2,025	1,110	349	54.8	17.2	31.4	759	37.5	1,134	32.3	48.4
1982	2,001	1,153	337	57.6	16.8	29.2	740	37.0	1,173	30.0	47.3
1981	2,052	1,144	342	55.8	16.7	29.9	790	38.5	1,166	30.5	45.8
1980	2,033	1,099	327	54.1	16.1	29.8	820	40.3	1,117	30.1	47.3
1979	1,754	968	292	55.2	16.6	30.2	687	39.2	1,001	31.2	45.7
1978	1,672	935	254	55.9	15.2	27.2	656	39.2	965	28.0	43.2
1977	1,609	880	277	54.7	17.2	31.5	622	38.7	900	32.4	43.8
1976	1,551	862	309	55.6	19.9	35.8	566	36.5	891	36.3	48.9
1975	1,446	832	295	57.5	20.4	35.5	505	34.9	849	36.5	50.8
1974	1,506	842	272	55.9	18.1	32.3	558	37.1	858	33.1	47.8
1973	1,285	709	206	55.2	16.0	29.1	500	38.9	732	30.3	43.0
1972	1,338	694	179	51.9	13.4	25.8	541	40.4	709	27.2	36.7
Male											
2019	3,424	2,878	1,127	84.1	32.9	39.1	279	8.1	2,918	39.0	59.4
2018	3,442	2,787	1,089	81.0	31.6	39.1	406	11.8	2,816	39.3	61.9
2017	3,355	2,648	1,045	78.9	31.1	39.5	429	12.8	2,690	40.0	62.1
2016	3,291	2,674	1,148	81.3	34.9	42.9	395	12.0	2,729	43.1	63.0
2015	3,246	2,661	1,063	82.0	32.8	40.0	360	11.1	2,711	40.1	61.3
2014	3,354	2,667	1,016	79.5	30.3	38.1	429	12.8	2,700	38.1	57.7
2013	3,329	2,564	968	77.0	29.1	37.7	491	14.7	2,597	38.0	55.7
2012	3,311	2,455	1,109	74.1	33.5	45.2	560	16.9	2,496	45.5	63.2
2011	3,250	2,421	1,006	74.5	31.0	41.6	568	17.5	2,458	41.9	60.2
2010	2,930	2,034	819	69.4	27.9	40.2	623	21.3	2,065	40.6	58.5
2009	2,741	1,894	663	69.1	24.2	35.0	616	22.5	1,925	35.6	51.3

r = Revised, controlled to 1990 census based population estimates; previous 1993 data controlled to 1980 census based population estimates.

Note: The change in the educational attainment question and the college completion categories from "4 or more years of college" to "at least some college," in 1992 caused an increase in the proportion of 14-to-24-year-old high school graduates enrolled in college or completed some college, of approximately 5 percentage points. High school graduates are people who have completed 4 years of high school or more, for 1967 to 1991. Beginning in 1992, they were people whose highest degree was a high school diploma (including equivalency) or higher.

[1] Starting in 2003 respondents could identify more than one race. Except as noted, the race data in this table from 2003 onward represent those respondents who indicated only one race category.

[2] The data shown prior to 2003 consists of those identifying themselves as "Asian or Pacific Islanders."

Table A-14. Population 14 to 24 Years Old, by High School Graduate Status, College Enrollment, Attainment, Sex, Race, and Hispanic Origin, October 1967–2019—*Continued*

(Numbers in thousands; percent; civilian noninstitutionalized population.)

Year, race, and Hispanic origin	Population 18 to 24 years old								High school graduates, 14 to 24 years old		
		High school graduates		Percent			High school dropouts			Percent	
	Total	Total	Enrolled in college	High school graduates	Enrolled in college	Of high school graduates enrolled in college	Number	Percent	All graduates	Enrolled in college	Enrolled or completed some college
2008	2,675	1,797	615	67.2	23.0	34.2	649	24.3	1,841	35.1	54.4
2007	2,706	1,689	560	62.4	20.7	33.1	790	29.2	1,711	33.6	52.2
2006	2,618	1,600	523	61.1	20.0	32.7	812	31.0	1,628	33.2	53.2
2005	2,613	1,569	540	60.1	20.7	34.4	838	32.1	1,589	34.6	52.4
2004	2,648	1,597	574	60.3	21.7	36.0	888	33.5	1,614	35.9	53.0
2003	2,541	1,548	465	60.9	18.3	30.0	805	31.7	1,571	30.0	48.7
2002	2,707	1,562	439	57.7	16.2	28.1	914	33.8	1,572	28.1	48.4
2001	2,596	1,455	449	56.1	17.3	31.0	962	37.1	1,468	31.0	48.1
2000	2,171	1,172	401	54.0	18.5	34.2	800	36.8	1,197	34.5	50.8
1999	2,045	1,122	322	54.9	15.8	28.7	746	36.4	1,131	28.7	45.7
1998	2,109	1,146	346	54.3	16.4	30.2	838	39.7	1,153	30.0	47.2
1997	1,937	1,140	371	58.9	19.2	32.5	643	33.2	1,168	33.0	49.2
1996	1,815	994	300	54.8	16.5	30.2	657	36.2	1,005	30.6	48.8
1995	1,907	1,106	356	58.0	18.7	32.2	653	34.2	1,022	36.2	52.3
1994	1,896	1,021	312	53.8	16.5	30.6	685	36.1	1,026	30.7	52.7
1993r	1,710	1,005	338	58.8	19.8	33.6	591	34.6	1,023	33.7	51.2
1993	1,354	786	266	58.1	19.6	33.8	470	34.7	803	33.9	51.1
1992	1,384	720	247	52.0	17.8	34.3	531	38.4	736	34.8	52.2
1991	1,503	719	211	47.8	14.0	29.3	668	44.4	728	29.7	42.2
1990	1,403	753	214	53.7	15.3	28.4	559	39.8	770	29.4	46.5
1989	1,439	756	211	52.5	14.7	27.9	580	40.3	767	28.2	42.7
1988	1,375	724	228	52.7	16.6	31.5	553	40.2	736	32.2	48.3
1987	1,337	795	247	59.5	18.5	31.1	461	34.5	803	31.1	45.1
1986	1,339	769	233	57.4	17.4	30.3	499	37.3	776	30.5	44.4
1985	1,132	659	168	58.2	14.8	25.5	405	35.8	675	26.4	44.9
1984	956	549	154	57.4	16.1	28.1	338	35.4	554	28.2	45.7
1983	968	476	152	49.2	15.7	31.9	396	40.9	489	33.1	47.4
1982	944	519	141	55.0	14.9	27.2	347	36.8	525	28.0	44.8
1981	988	498	164	50.4	16.6	32.9	428	43.3	506	33.6	48.6
1980	1,012	518	160	51.2	15.8	30.9	431	42.6	521	31.1	49.5
1979	837	454	153	54.2	18.3	33.7	328	39.2	469	34.3	49.5
1978	781	420	126	53.8	16.1	30.0	313	40.1	438	30.4	46.3
1977	754	396	139	52.5	18.4	35.1	295	39.1	404	35.9	46.5
1976	701	378	150	53.9	21.4	39.7	253	36.1	403	39.8	51.8
1975	678	383	145	56.5	21.4	37.9	221	32.6	390	37.9	55.4
1974	720	390	141	54.2	19.6	36.2	279	38.8	401	36.7	51.4
1973	625	348	105	55.7	16.8	30.2	228	36.5	361	32.1	45.4
1972	609	301	92	49.4	15.1	30.6	253	41.5	309	32.0	44.3
Female											
2019	3,386	2,920	1,342	86.2	39.6	46.0	230	6.8	2,961	46.3	70.0
2018	3,320	2,874	1,342	86.6	40.4	46.7	250	7.5	2,939	47.1	71.1
2017	3,298	2,810	1,365	85.2	41.4	48.6	274	8.3	2,881	49.1	69.4
2016	3,248	2,803	1,417	86.3	43.6	50.6	253	7.8	2,879	51.3	71.2
2015	3,218	2,704	1,305	84.0	40.5	48.2	309	9.6	2,750	48.2	71.9
2014	3,214	2,657	1,265	82.7	39.4	47.6	348	10.8	2,709	48.2	67.9
2013	3,160	2,554	1,225	80.8	38.8	48.0	398	12.6	2,593	48.1	69.0
2012	3,105	2,447	1,294	78.8	41.7	52.9	411	13.2	2,491	53.3	72.9
2011	2,724	2,147	1,073	78.8	39.4	50.0	407	15.0	2,173	50.0	71.4
2010	2,755	2,104	995	76.4	36.1	47.3	426	15.5	2,134	47.7	67.8
2009	2,591	1,853	803	71.5	31.0	43.3	496	19.1	1,888	43.6	64.5
2008	2,501	1,821	723	72.8	28.9	39.7	506	20.2	1,850	40.3	63.1
2007	2,469	1,798	816	72.8	33.0	45.4	520	21.1	1,842	45.6	63.4
2006	2,388	1,701	660	71.2	27.6	38.8	501	21.0	1,751	39.7	61.0
2005	2,285	1,661	675	72.7	29.5	40.6	498	21.8	1,691	41.2	62.0
2004	2,293	1,647	647	71.8	28.2	39.3	498	21.7	1,673	39.8	58.6

r = Revised, controlled to 1990 census based population estimates; previous 1993 data controlled to 1980 census based population estimates.
Note: The change in the educational attainment question and the college completion categories from "4 or more years of college" to "at least some college," in 1992 caused an increase in the proportion of 14-to-24-year-old high school graduates enrolled in college or completed some college, of approximately 5 percentage points. High school graduates are people who have completed 4 years of high school or more, for 1967 to 1991. Beginning in 1992, they were people whose highest degree was a high school diploma (including equivalency) or higher.
[1] Starting in 2003 respondents could identify more than one race. Except as noted, the race data in this table from 2003 onward represent those respondents who indicated only one race category.
[2] The data shown prior to 2003 consists of those identifying themselves as "Asian or Pacific Islanders."

Table A-14. Population 14 to 24 Years Old, by High School Graduate Status, College Enrollment, Attainment, Sex, Race, and Hispanic Origin, October 1967–2019—*Continued*

(Numbers in thousands; percent; civilian noninstitutionalized population.)

	Population 18 to 24 years old								High school graduates, 14 to 24 years old		
		High school graduates		Percent			High school dropouts			Percent	
Year, race, and Hispanic origin	Total	Total	Enrolled in college	High school graduates	Enrolled in college	Of high school graduates enrolled in college	Number	Percent	All graduates	Enrolled in college	Enrolled or completed some college
2003	2,213	1,548	651	69.9	29.4	42.1	548	24.7	1,563	41.9	64.4
2002	2,211	1,516	540	68.6	24.4	35.6	565	25.6	1,537	35.9	57.9
2001	2,296	1,576	585	68.6	25.5	37.1	586	25.5	1,600	37.1	57.0
2000	1,963	1,290	498	65.7	25.4	38.6	535	27.3	1,312	38.9	55.2
1999	1,908	1,203	417	63.0	21.8	34.7	593	31.1	1,228	34.4	53.3
1998	1,906	1,257	474	66.0	24.9	37.7	545	28.6	1,266	38.2	58.7
1997	1,669	1,097	436	65.7	26.1	39.7	460	27.6	1,135	41.4	59.6
1996	1,694	1,026	406	60.6	24.0	39.6	554	32.7	1,043	40.4	56.0
1995	1,696	1,011	389	59.6	22.9	38.4	598	35.4	1,022	38.6	59.6
1994	1,628	973	350	59.8	21.5	36.0	539	33.1	983	36.2	55.9
1993r	1,652	1,045	390	63.3	23.6	37.3	510	30.9	1,059	37.8	60.1
1993	1,418	895	336	63.1	23.7	37.5	439	31.0	907	38.0	60.4
1992	1,369	860	339	62.8	24.8	39.4	405	29.6	867	39.9	57.4
1991	1,372	780	305	56.9	22.2	39.1	473	34.5	791	39.2	52.5
1990	1,346	745	221	55.3	16.4	29.7	465	34.5	753	29.5	43.0
1989	1,377	823	244	59.8	17.7	29.6	482	35.0	836	30.5	44.5
1988	1,267	736	224	58.1	17.7	30.4	492	38.8	747	30.5	45.8
1987	1,256	801	208	63.8	16.6	26.0	387	30.8	808	26.4	43.2
1986	1,175	739	226	62.9	19.2	30.6	365	31.1	759	31.4	46.8
1985	1,091	734	205	67.3	18.8	27.9	295	27.0	743	28.4	48.0
1984	1,061	661	207	62.3	19.5	31.3	353	33.2	667	31.5	46.6
1983	1,057	634	198	60.0	18.7	31.2	363	34.3	644	31.8	49.7
1982	1,056	634	196	60.0	18.6	30.9	393	37.2	640	31.0	49.2
1981	1,064	646	178	60.7	16.7	27.6	362	34.0	662	28.2	43.4
1980	1,021	579	165	56.7	16.2	28.5	389	38.1	595	29.1	45.4
1979	917	516	140	56.3	15.3	27.1	358	39.0	534	28.1	42.3
1978	891	516	128	57.9	14.4	24.8	343	38.5	528	25.8	40.0
1977	855	483	139	56.5	16.3	28.8	326	38.1	495	29.7	41.6
1976	850	483	160	56.8	18.8	33.1	313	36.8	489	33.5	46.5
1975	769	449	150	58.4	19.5	33.4	283	36.8	460	34.8	46.7
1974	786	451	129	57.4	16.4	28.6	280	35.6	459	29.2	43.4
1973	658	362	102	55.0	15.5	28.2	272	41.3	372	28.8	41.1
1972	728	394	88	54.1	12.1	22.3	288	39.6	402	23.6	31.1
WHITE ALONE OR IN COMBINATION											
Both Sexes											
2019	22,581	20,033	9,041	88.7	40.0	45.1	1,144	5.1	20,321	45.3	70.3
2018	22,681	19,953	9,174	88.0	40.5	46.0	1,356	6.0	20,259	46.2	71.9
2017	22,651	19,846	9,048	87.6	39.9	45.6	1,390	6.1	20,145	45.7	72.0
2016	22,830	20,100	9,446	88.0	41.4	47.0	1,419	6.2	20,416	47.2	72.6
2015	23,067	20,193	9,268	87.5	40.2	45.9	1,464	6.3	20,507	46.0	72.5
2014	23,327	20,258	9,329	86.8	40.0	46.1	1,638	7.0	20,520	46.2	72.0
2013	23,539	20,436	9,422	86.8	40.0	46.1	1,679	7.1	20,773	46.5	72.1
2012	23,516	20,257	9,614	86.1	40.9	47.5	1,710	7.3	20,546	47.8	73.4
2011	23,679	20,256	10,043	85.5	42.4	49.6	1,941	8.2	20,504	49.7	73.9
2010	23,381	19,949	9,524	85.3	40.7	47.7	2,013	8.6	20,180	48.0	72.9
2009	23,256	19,784	9,562	85.1	41.1	48.3	2,127	9.1	20,060	48.5	72.0
2008	23,120	19,810	9,360	85.7	40.5	47.2	2,072	9.0	20,067	47.5	71.6
2007	22,928	19,330	8,958	84.3	39.1	46.3	2,338	10.2	19,595	46.5	70.3
2006	22,670	18,882	8,465	83.3	37.3	44.8	2,458	10.8	19,153	45.1	69.9
2005	22,345	18,583	8,721	83.2	39.0	47.1	2,539	11.4	18,818	47.0	70.0
2004	22,411	18,663	8,544	83.3	38.1	45.8	2,639	11.8	18,868	46.0	69.0
2003	22,029	18,335	8,358	83.2	37.9	45.6	2,558	11.6	18,565	45.6	69.0

r = Revised, controlled to 1990 census based population estimates; previous 1993 data controlled to 1980 census based population estimates.
Note: The change in the educational attainment question and the college completion categories from "4 or more years of college" to "at least some college," in 1992 caused an increase in the proportion of 14-to-24-year-old high school graduates enrolled in college or completed some college, of approximately 5 percentage points. High school graduates are people who have completed 4 years of high school or more, for 1967 to 1991. Beginning in 1992, they were people whose highest degree was a high school diploma (including equivalency) or higher.
[1] Starting in 2003 respondents could identify more than one race. Except as noted, the race data in this table from 2003 onward represent those respondents who indicated only one race category.
[2] The data shown prior to 2003 consists of those identifying themselves as "Asian or Pacific Islanders."

Table A-14. Population 14 to 24 Years Old, by High School Graduate Status, College Enrollment, Attainment, Sex, Race, and Hispanic Origin, October 1967–2019—*Continued*

(Numbers in thousands; percent; civilian noninstitutionalized population.)

Year, race, and Hispanic origin	Population 18 to 24 years old								High school graduates, 14 to 24 years old		
		High school graduates		Percent			High school dropouts			Percent	
	Total	Total	Enrolled in college	High school graduates	Enrolled in college	Of high school graduates enrolled in college	Number	Percent	All graduates	Enrolled in college	Enrolled or completed some college
Male											
2019............................	11,358	9,846	4,116	86.7	36.2	41.8	694	6.1	9,978	41.8	65.1
2018............................	11,446	9,872	4,225	86.2	36.9	42.8	809	7.1	9,989	43.0	66.5
2017............................	11,424	9,769	4,116	85.5	36.0	42.1	796	7.0	9,898	42.2	67.5
2016............................	11,534	9,967	4,432	86.4	38.4	44.5	845	7.3	10,093	44.5	67.9
2015............................	11,635	10,059	4,319	86.5	37.1	42.9	812	7.0	10,224	43.0	67.6
2014............................	11,801	10,108	4,397	85.7	37.3	43.5	900	7.6	10,237	43.7	67.4
2013............................	11,921	10,185	4,323	85.4	36.3	42.4	896	7.5	10,357	42.9	66.7
2012............................	11,925	10,045	4,399	84.2	36.9	43.8	991	8.3	10,174	44.2	68.1
2011............................	12,153	10,175	4,789	83.7	39.4	47.1	1,105	9.1	10,308	47.2	69.7
2010............................	11,832	9,869	4,472	83.4	37.8	45.3	1,152	9.7	9,976	45.4	68.5
2009............................	11,774	9,824	4,513	83.4	38.3	45.9	1,224	10.4	9,952	46.1	68.3
2008............................	11,738	9,891	4,444	84.3	37.9	44.9	1,165	9.9	10,031	45.2	67.8
2007............................	11,670	9,511	4,116	81.5	35.3	43.3	1,397	12.0	9,634	43.4	66.0
2006............................	11,502	9,331	3,923	81.1	34.1	42.0	1,427	12.4	9,435	42.2	66.1
2005............................	11,394	9,086	4,018	79.7	35.3	43.5	1,519	13.3	9,193	44.2	60.0
2004............................	11,371	9,227	3,956	81.1	34.8	42.9	1,548	13.6	9,296	43.1	64.4
2003............................	11,147	8,967	3,815	80.4	34.2	42.5	1,493	13.4	9,070	42.6	65.1
Female											
2019............................	11,223	10,187	4,925	90.8	43.9	48.3	450	4.0	10,343	48.7	75.3
2018............................	11,234	10,081	4,950	89.7	44.1	49.1	547	4.9	10,270	49.3	77.0
2017............................	11,228	10,077	4,931	89.8	43.9	48.9	593	5.3	10,248	49.1	76.4
2016............................	11,296	10,133	5,014	89.7	44.4	49.5	574	5.1	10,323	49.7	77.3
2015............................	11,433	10,134	4,949	88.6	43.3	48.8	653	5.7	10,283	48.9	77.4
2014............................	11,526	10,151	4,932	88.1	42.8	48.6	739	6.4	10,283	48.8	76.5
2013............................	11,617	10,251	5,099	88.2	43.9	49.7	783	6.7	10,415	50.1	77.4
2012............................	11,590	10,212	5,215	88.1	45.0	51.1	719	6.2	10,372	51.4	78.5
2011............................	11,525	10,081	5,254	87.5	45.6	52.1	836	7.3	10,196	52.1	78.1
2010............................	11,549	10,080	5,052	87.3	43.7	50.1	861	7.5	10,204	50.5	77.1
2009............................	11,482	9,960	5,049	86.7	44.0	50.7	903	7.9	10,108	50.8	75.6
2008............................	11,381	9,919	4,916	87.2	43.2	49.6	908	8.0	10,036	49.9	75.4
2007............................	11,258	9,820	4,842	87.2	43.0	49.3	941	8.4	9,960	49.4	74.4
2006............................	11,168	9,551	4,542	85.5	40.7	47.6	1,032	9.2	9,718	47.8	73.6
2005............................	10,952	9,497	4,702	86.7	42.9	49.4	1,020	9.3	9,625	49.7	73.9
2004............................	11,040	9,436	4,588	85.5	41.6	48.6	1,091	9.9	9,572	48.8	73.5
2003............................	10,882	9,367	4,543	86.1	41.7	48.5	1,065	9.8	9,495	48.5	72.7
BLACK ALONE OR IN COMBINATION											
Both Sexes											
2019............................	4,877	4,257	1,791	87.3	36.7	42.1	287	5.9	4,327	42.4	67.2
2018............................	4,865	4,214	1,840	86.6	37.8	43.7	270	5.5	4,275	43.6	68.6
2017............................	4,935	4,219	1,782	85.5	36.1	42.2	296	6.0	4,314	42.4	65.7
2016............................	4,978	4,216	1,782	84.7	35.8	42.3	342	6.9	4,305	42.2	65.5
2015............................	5,032	4,316	1,741	85.8	34.6	40.3	359	7.1	4,367	40.5	64.2
2014............................	5,121	4,352	1,645	85.0	32.1	37.8	366	7.1	4,426	38.4	65.7
2013............................	5,199	4,297	1,806	82.7	34.7	42.0	422	8.1	4,345	42.4	66.4
2012............................	5,142	4,119	1,891	80.1	36.8	45.9	500	9.7	4,187	45.9	67.2
2011............................	4,793	3,902	1,759	81.4	36.7	45.1	424	8.8	3,955	45.5	67.3
2010............................	4,745	3,898	1,808	82.1	38.1	46.4	493	10.4	3,965	46.6	66.7
2009............................	4,623	3,688	1,699	79.8	36.8	46.1	532	11.5	3,766	46.0	67.2
2008............................	4,531	3,588	1,435	79.2	31.7	40.0	548	12.1	3,646	40.3	60.9
2007............................	4,425	3,603	1,468	81.4	33.2	40.7	477	10.8	3,671	40.9	61.8
2006............................	4,264	3,287	1,387	77.1	32.5	42.2	560	13.1	3,359	42.2	61.1

r = Revised, controlled to 1990 census based population estimates; previous 1993 data controlled to 1980 census based population estimates.
Note: The change in the educational attainment question and the college completion categories from "4 or more years of college" to "at least some college," in 1992 caused an increase in the proportion of 14-to-24-year-old high school graduates enrolled in college or completed some college, of approximately 5 percentage points. High school graduates are people who have completed 4 years of high school or more, for 1967 to 1991. Beginning in 1992, they were people whose highest degree was a high school diploma (including equivalency) or higher.
[1] Starting in 2003 respondents could identify more than one race. Except as noted, the race data in this table from 2003 onward represent those respondents who indicated only one race category.
[2] The data shown prior to 2003 consists of those identifying themselves as "Asian or Pacific Islanders."

Table A-14. Population 14 to 24 Years Old, by High School Graduate Status, College Enrollment, Attainment, Sex, Race, and Hispanic Origin, October 1967–2019—*Continued*

(Numbers in thousands; percent; civilian noninstitutionalized population.)

Year, race, and Hispanic origin	Population 18 to 24 years old								High school graduates, 14 to 24 years old		
		High school graduates		Percent			High school dropouts			Percent	
	Total	Total	Enrolled in college	High school graduates	Enrolled in college	Of high school graduates enrolled in college	Number	Percent	All graduates	Enrolled in college	Enrolled or completed some college
2005...............	4,158	3,303	1,371	79.4	33.0	31.7	530	12.7	3,378	41.5	63.5
2004...............	4,115	3,190	1,318	77.5	32.0	41.3	620	15.1	3,253	41.8	63.5
2003...............	4,016	3,091	1,285	77.0	32.0	41.6	563	14.0	3,141	41.9	62.0
Male											
2019...............	2,375	2,012	796	84.7	33.5	39.6	169	7.1	2,052	40.0	64.3
2018...............	2,385	2,016	822	84.5	34.5	40.8	155	6.5	2,029	41.1	65.0
2017...............	2,413	2,032	767	84.2	31.8	37.8	176	7.3	2,068	37.7	60.2
2016...............	2,407	1,924	777	79.9	32.3	40.4	226	9.4	1,948	40.6	61.2
2015...............	2,421	2,067	833	85.4	34.4	40.3	172	7.1	2,094	40.5	63.2
2014...............	2,451	2,008	660	81.9	26.9	32.8	183	7.4	2,055	34.0	60.6
2013...............	2,491	2,020	780	81.1	31.3	38.6	230	9.2	2,042	39.3	62.5
2012...............	2,500	1,972	859	78.9	34.4	43.6	279	11.2	2,009	43.8	65.0
2011...............	2,289	1,800	762	78.6	33.3	42.4	218	9.5	1,831	42.9	61.4
2010...............	2,250	1,781	779	79.2	34.6	43.7	269	11.9	1,823	43.7	61.9
2009...............	2,211	1,702	712	76.9	32.2	41.9	301	13.6	1,726	41.6	63.7
2008...............	2,190	1,743	633	79.6	28.9	36.3	235	10.7	1,770	36.9	54.9
2007...............	2,132	1,703	686	79.9	32.2	40.3	234	11.0	1,728	40.4	59.6
2006...............	2,032	1,545	577	76.0	28.4	37.3	225	11.0	1,576	37.2	54.5
2005...............	1,988	1,466	557	73.7	28.0	38.0	290	14.6	1,492	37.9	58.2
2004...............	1,951	1,418	521	72.7	26.7	36.7	347	17.8	1,442	37.0	61.3
2003...............	1,868	1,382	525	74.0	28.1	38.0	311	16.6	1,397	38.3	57.4
Female											
2019...............	2,502	2,244	994	89.7	39.7	44.3	118	4.7	2,275	44.6	69.9
2018...............	2,481	2,198	1,017	88.6	41.0	46.3	115	4.6	2,245	45.9	71.8
2017...............	2,522	2,187	1,014	86.7	40.2	46.4	120	4.8	2,246	46.7	70.7
2016...............	2,571	2,292	1,004	89.1	39.1	43.8	116	4.5	2,357	43.5	69.1
2015...............	2,612	2,249	908	86.1	34.8	40.4	188	7.2	2,273	40.6	65.2
2014...............	2,670	2,344	985	87.8	36.9	42.0	183	6.9	2,371	42.3	70.1
2013...............	2,708	2,277	1,026	84.1	37.9	45.0	192	7.1	2,303	45.1	69.9
2012...............	2,642	2,147	1,032	81.3	39.1	48.1	221	8.4	2,178	47.9	69.4
2011...............	2,504	2,102	997	84.0	39.8	47.4	206	8.2	2,124	47.7	72.3
2010...............	2,495	2,117	1,029	84.8	41.3	48.6	224	9.0	2,142	49.0	70.7
2009...............	2,411	1,987	987	82.4	40.9	49.7	231	9.6	2,040	49.8	70.1
2008...............	2,341	1,845	802	78.8	34.2	43.5	313	13.4	1,876	43.5	66.5
2007...............	2,293	1,900	782	82.9	34.1	41.2	243	10.6	1,942	41.3	63.7
2006...............	2,232	1,742	810	78.1	36.3	46.5	335	15.0	1,783	46.5	66.8
2005...............	2,170	1,837	814	84.7	37.5	44.4	240	11.1	1,885	44.3	67.7
2004...............	2,164	1,772	797	81.9	36.8	45.0	272	12.6	1,811	45.5	65.3
2003...............	2,148	1,708	760	79.5	35.4	44.5	252	11.7	1,744	44.7	65.7
ASIAN ALONE OR IN COMBINATION											
Both Sexes											
2019...............	2,138	1,993	1,312	93.2	61.4	65.8	41	1.9	2,051	66.2	92.6
2018...............	2,180	2,036	1,265	93.4	58.0	62.2	58	2.6	2,059	62.4	88.1
2017...............	1,989	1,875	1,223	94.2	61.5	65.2	33	1.6	1,910	65.7	90.1
2016...............	2,025	1,867	1,161	92.2	57.3	62.2	61	3.0	1,903	62.1	87.3
2015...............	1,889	1,747	1,182	92.5	62.6	67.7	52	2.8	1,795	67.0	91.5
2014...............	1,844	1,737	1,132	94.2	61.4	65.2	17	0.9	1,781	64.6	90.2
2013...............	1,947	1,765	1,156	90.6	59.4	65.5	70	3.6	1,801	65.9	86.5
2012...............	1,780	1,610	1,043	90.5	58.6	64.8	61	3.4	1,650	65.2	85.2
2011...............	1,435	1,295	833	90.2	58.0	64.3	67	4.6	1,321	64.7	88.1
2010...............	1,465	1,338	904	91.3	61.7	67.6	80	5.5	1,382	68.0	88.9

r = Revised, controlled to 1990 census based population estimates; previous 1993 data controlled to 1980 census based population estimates.

Note: The change in the educational attainment question and the college completion categories from "4 or more years of college" to "at least some college," in 1992 caused an increase in the proportion of 14-to-24-year-old high school graduates enrolled in college or completed some college, of approximately 5 percentage points. High school graduates are people who have completed 4 years of high school or more, for 1967 to 1991. Beginning in 1992, they were people whose highest degree was a high school diploma (including equivalency) or higher.

[1] Starting in 2003 respondents could identify more than one race. Except as noted, the race data in this table from 2003 onward represent those respondents who indicated only one race category.

[2] The data shown prior to 2003 consists of those identifying themselves as "Asian or Pacific Islanders."

Table A-14. Population 14 to 24 Years Old, by High School Graduate Status, College Enrollment, Attainment, Sex, Race, and Hispanic Origin, October 1967–2019—*Continued*

(Numbers in thousands; percent; civilian noninstitutionalized population.)

| Year, race, and Hispanic origin | Population 18 to 24 years old | | | | | | | | High school graduates, 14 to 24 years old | | |
| | | High school graduates | | Percent | | | High school dropouts | | | Percent | |
	Total	Total	Enrolled in college	High school graduates	Enrolled in college	Of high school graduates enrolled in college	Number	Percent	All graduates	Enrolled in college	Enrolled or completed some college
2009	1,345	1,231	844	91.5	62.8	68.5	29	2.1	1,249	68.5	90.8
2008	1,251	1,153	738	92.1	59.0	64.0	42	3.4	1,188	64.4	89.7
2007	1,293	1,126	720	87.1	55.7	63.9	94	7.3	1,143	63.9	90.3
2006	1,270	1,158	705	91.2	55.5	60.9	49	3.9	1,180	60.6	86.1
2005	1,299	1,214	773	93.5	59.5	63.7	38	2.9	1,243	64.2	86.0
2004	1,263	1,167	750	92.5	59.4	64.3	53	4.2	1,191	64.6	87.6
2003	1,280	1,162	774	90.8	60.5	66.6	56	4.4	1,184	66.9	87.8
Male											
2019	1,039	964	638	92.8	61.4	66.2	20	1.9	994	66.5	90.3
2018	1,114	1,033	641	92.7	57.6	62.1	33	3.0	1,046	62.5	88.4
2017	1,003	934	613	93.1	61.1	65.6	16	1.6	941	65.8	89.3
2016	1,045	969	624	92.7	59.7	64.4	25	2.3	984	64.1	87.3
2015	937	869	561	92.8	59.9	64.6	30	3.2	896	63.9	89.2
2014	932	882	600	94.6	64.3	68.0	13	1.4	904	67.9	89.8
2013	1,009	927	612	91.9	60.7	66.1	22	2.2	939	66.1	84.8
2012	900	807	510	89.7	56.7	63.2	28	3.1	832	63.9	84.5
2011	747	673	429	90.1	57.4	63.7	31	4.2	682	63.7	87.6
2010	750	685	453	91.4	60.4	66.1	40	5.3	711	66.5	87.4
2009	673	624	418	92.8	62.2	67.0	7	1.1	637	66.8	89.8
2008	626	560	340	89.4	54.4	60.8	22	3.4	582	62.2	89.2
2007	560	481	318	85.8	56.9	66.3	38	6.8	483	66.4	91.8
2006	649	578	362	89.1	55.8	62.7	34	5.3	591	62.3	83.8
2005	653	603	392	92.4	59.9	65.0	20	3.1	621	65.1	86.3
2004	634	588	398	92.8	62.7	67.7	18	2.9	601	68.0	87.8
2003	609	545	370	89.5	60.8	67.9	43	7.1	551	67.7	88.7
Female											
2019	1,098	1,029	674	93.7	61.4	65.5	22	2.0	1,058	66.0	94.8
2018	1,066	1,003	624	94.1	58.6	62.2	24	2.3	1,014	62.1	87.9
2017	986	941	611	95.4	61.9	64.9	17	1.7	969	65.6	90.9
2016	980	898	536	91.6	54.7	59.7	36	3.7	919	60.0	87.3
2015	952	878	621	92.2	65.2	70.7	22	2.3	899	70.2	93.8
2014	911	855	533	93.8	58.5	62.3	4	0.5	877	61.3	90.6
2013	938	838	544	89.3	58.0	64.9	48	5.1	861	65.7	88.4
2012	880	803	533	91.2	60.6	66.4	33	3.7	817	66.5	85.8
2011	688	622	403	90.4	58.7	64.9	35	5.1	638	65.7	88.7
2010	715	652	451	91.2	63.1	69.1	41	5.7	671	69.7	90.4
2009	673	607	426	90.3	63.3	70.1	21	3.2	611	70.2	91.8
2008	625	593	397	94.9	63.6	67.0	21	3.3	605	66.5	90.3
2007	605	529	339	87.4	56.0	64.1	48	7.9	543	63.9	91.5
2006	621	580	343	93.4	55.3	59.2	14	2.3	589	58.8	88.5
2005	645	610	381	94.6	59.1	62.5	17	2.7	622	63.3	85.8
2004	628	579	352	92.1	56.0	60.8	35	5.5	591	61.2	87.5
2003	671	617	404	92.0	60.2	65.5	13	1.9	633	66.3	87.0

r = Revised, controlled to 1990 census based population estimates; previous 1993 data controlled to 1980 census based population estimates.

Note: The change in the educational attainment question and the college completion categories from "4 or more years of college" to "at least some college," in 1992 caused an increase in the proportion of 14-to-24-year-old high school graduates enrolled in college or completed some college, of approximately 5 percentage points. High school graduates are people who have completed 4 years of high school or more, for 1967 to 1991. Beginning in 1992, they were people whose highest degree was a high school diploma (including equivalency) or higher.

[1] Starting in 2003 respondents could identify more than one race. Except as noted, the race data in this table from 2003 onward represent those respondents who indicated only one race category.

[2] The data shown prior to 2003 consists of those identifying themselves as "Asian or Pacific Islanders."

Table A-15. Population 18 and 19 Years Old, by School Enrollment Status, Sex, Race, and Hispanic Origin, October 1967–2019

(Numbers in thousands; percent; civilian noninstitutionalized population.)

Year, race, and Hispanic origin	Total	Population 18 and 19 years old							
		Still in high school	Percent	Dropped out	Percent	High school graduate only	Percent	In college	Percent
ALL RACES									
Both Sexes									
2019............................	8,306	1,582	19.1	481	5.8	2,238	26.9	4,004	48.2
2018............................	8,359	1,556	18.6	528	6.3	2,055	24.6	4,220	50.5
2017............................	8,222	1,663	20.2	568	6.9	2,049	24.9	3,943	48.0
2016............................	8,266	1,570	19.0	532	6.4	1,993	24.1	4,171	50.5
2015............................	8,158	1,613	19.8	611	7.5	1,957	24.0	3,978	48.8
2014............................	8,261	1,618	19.6	588	7.1	2,019	24.4	4,036	48.9
2013............................	8,473	1,736	20.5	529	6.2	2,257	26.6	3,951	46.6
2012............................	8,484	1,840	21.7	605	7.1	2,025	23.9	4,015	47.3
2011............................	8,465	1,775	21.0	545	6.4	1,903	22.5	4,242	50.1
2010............................	8,529	1,540	18.1	622	7.3	2,003	23.5	4,364	51.2
2009............................	8,615	1,645	19.1	736	8.5	1,944	22.6	4,289	49.8
2008............................	8,492	1,481	17.4	750	8.8	2,134	25.1	4,126	48.6
2007............................	8,338	1,491	17.9	675	8.1	2,097	25.2	4,075	48.9
2006............................	8,102	1,560	19.3	743	9.2	2,053	25.3	3,746	46.2
2005............................	7,559	1,372	18.1	661	8.7	1,694	22.4	3,727	49.3
2004............................	7,701	1,266	16.4	840	10.9	1,910	24.8	3,685	47.8
2003............................	7,533	1,345	17.9	817	10.8	1,859	24.7	3,512	46.6
2002............................	7,907	1,427	18.0	884	11.2	2,015	25.5	3,581	45.3
2001............................	7,985	1,394	17.5	1,034	12.9	2,079	26.0	3,478	43.6
2000............................	8,045	1,327	16.5	1,012	12.6	2,107	26.2	3,599	44.7
1999............................	7,991	1,321	16.5	1,047	13.1	2,103	26.3	3,520	44.0
1998............................	7,902	1,244	15.7	1,104	14.0	1,884	23.8	3,670	46.4
1997............................	7,510	1,256	16.7	1,038	13.8	1,854	24.7	3,362	44.8
1996............................	7,376	1,230	16.7	940	12.7	1,897	25.7	3,309	44.9
1995............................	7,198	1,173	16.3	1,051	14.6	1,873	26.0	3,101	43.1
1994............................	6,946	1,129	16.3	929	13.4	1,837	26.4	3,051	43.9
1993............................	6,594	1,137	17.2	778	11.8	1,753	26.6	2,926	44.4
1992............................	6,535	1,121	17.2	780	11.9	1,742	26.7	2,892	44.3
1991............................	6,664	1,040	15.6	889	13.3	1,806	27.1	2,929	44.0
1990............................	7,064	1,024	14.5	1,003	14.2	2,018	28.6	3,019	42.7
1989............................	7,361	1,058	14.4	1,033	14.0	2,204	29.9	3,066	41.7
1988............................	7,294	1,013	13.9	1,063	14.6	2,172	29.8	3,046	41.8
1987............................	7,160	937	13.1	954	13.3	2,224	31.1	3,045	42.5
1986............................	7,095	930	13.1	872	12.3	2,351	33.1	2,942	41.5
1985............................	7,204	809	11.2	1,031	14.3	2,457	34.1	2,907	40.4
1984............................	7,428	857	11.5	1,129	15.2	2,575	34.7	2,867	38.6
1983............................	7,819	999	12.8	1,132	14.5	2,748	35.1	2,940	37.6
1982............................	8,023	908	11.3	1,336	16.7	2,850	35.5	2,929	36.5
1981............................	8,115	932	11.5	1,299	16.0	2,840	35.0	3,044	37.5
1980............................	8,160	855	10.5	1,284	15.7	3,088	37.8	2,933	35.9
1979............................	8,214	849	10.3	1,382	16.8	3,139	38.2	2,844	34.6
1978............................	8,153	801	9.8	1,361	16.7	3,092	37.9	2,899	35.6
1977............................	8,151	849	10.4	1,355	16.6	3,034	37.2	2,913	35.7
1976............................	8,148	831	10.2	1,355	16.6	3,025	37.1	2,937	36.0
1975............................	8,024	822	10.2	1,286	16.0	2,973	37.1	2,943	36.7
1974............................	7,822	777	9.9	1,302	16.6	3,146	40.2	2,597	33.2
1973............................	7,649	766	10.0	1,228	16.1	3,138	41.0	2,517	32.9
1972............................	7,462	778	10.4	1,100	14.7	2,904	38.9	2,680	35.9
1971............................	7,231	830	11.5	1,108	15.3	2,567	35.5	2,726	37.7
1970............................	6,958	728	10.5	1,125	16.2	2,511	36.1	2,594	37.3
1969............................	6,677	749	11.2	1,007	15.1	2,320	34.7	2,601	39.0
1968............................	6,587	816	12.4	1,033	15.7	2,237	34.0	2,501	38.0
1967............................	6,358	741	11.7	1,086	17.1	2,245	35.3	2,286	36.0
Male									
2019............................	4,182	924	22.1	270	6.5	1,165	27.9	1,822	43.6
2018............................	4,233	886	20.9	340	8.0	1,097	25.9	1,911	45.1
2017............................	4,153	957	23.1	346	8.3	1,103	26.6	1,746	42.1
2016............................	4,192	916	21.9	303	7.2	1,028	24.5	1,944	46.4
2015............................	4,106	860	20.9	359	8.7	1,050	25.6	1,838	44.7
2014............................	4,183	935	22.4	323	7.7	1,146	27.4	1,779	42.5

* = Quantity zero or rounds to zero.
Note: High school graduates are people who have completed 4 years of high school or more, for 1967 to 1991. Beginning in 1992, they were people whose highest degree was a high school diploma (including equivalency) or higher.
[1] Starting in 2003 respondents could identify more than one race. Except as noted, the race data in this table from 2003 onward represent those respondents who indicated only one race category.
[2] The data shown prior to 2003 consists of those identifying themselves as "Asian or Pacific Islanders."

Table A-15. Population 18 and 19 Years Old, by School Enrollment Status, Sex, Race, and Hispanic Origin, October 1967–2019—*Continued*

(Numbers in thousands; percent; civilian noninstitutionalized population.)

Year, race, and Hispanic origin	Total	Population 18 and 19 years old							
		Still in high school	Percent	Dropped out	Percent	High school graduate only	Percent	In college	Percent
2013	4,319	1,004	23.2	272	6.3	1,235	28.6	1,809	41.9
2012	4,310	1,033	23.7	359	8.3	1,114	25.9	1,803	41.8
2011	4,341	1,038	23.9	293	6.8	1,060	24.4	1,949	44.9
2010	4,296	867	20.2	347	8.1	1,073	25.0	2,009	46.8
2009	4,352	899	20.7	410	9.4	1,114	25.6	1,928	44.3
2008	4,289	834	19.5	376	8.8	1,169	27.3	1,909	44.5
2007	4,222	895	21.2	354	8.4	1,070	25.3	1,903	45.1
2006	4,103	907	22.1	414	10.1	1,079	26.3	1,703	41.5
2005	3,880	899	23.2	392	10.1	914	23.6	1,675	43.2
2004	3,861	714	18.5	522	13.5	1,015	26.3	1,610	41.7
2003	3,764	781	20.7	480	12.8	935	24.8	1,568	41.7
2002	4,042	862	21.3	523	12.9	1,022	25.3	1,635	40.5
2001	4,027	801	19.9	614	15.2	1,042	25.9	1,570	39.0
2000	4,037	783	19.4	571	14.1	1,113	27.6	1,570	38.9
1999	4,026	780	19.4	550	13.7	1,048	26.0	1,648	40.9
1998	3,994	732	18.3	611	15.3	984	24.6	1,667	41.7
1997	3,816	750	19.7	585	15.3	920	24.1	1,561	40.9
1996	3,711	769	20.7	488	13.2	965	26.0	1,489	40.1
1995	3,611	719	19.9	532	14.7	929	25.7	1,431	39.6
1994	3,485	688	19.7	499	14.3	882	25.3	1,416	40.6
1993	3,329	712	21.4	403	12.1	877	26.3	1,337	40.2
1992	3,275	694	21.2	400	12.2	856	26.1	1,325	40.5
1991	3,307	650	19.7	453	13.7	878	26.5	1,326	40.1
1990	3,503	595	17.0	512	14.6	953	27.2	1,443	41.2
1989	3,640	640	17.6	531	14.6	1,047	28.8	1,422	39.1
1988	3,618	666	18.4	566	15.6	1,021	28.2	1,365	37.7
1987	3,537	564	15.9	493	13.9	997	28.2	1,483	41.9
1986	3,502	594	17.0	459	13.1	1,045	29.8	1,404	40.1
1985	3,550	503	14.2	580	16.3	1,118	31.5	1,349	38.0
1984	3,674	551	15.0	594	16.2	1,156	31.5	1,373	37.4
1983	3,877	616	15.9	630	16.2	1,291	33.3	1,340	34.6
1982	3,961	562	14.2	709	17.9	1,314	33.2	1,376	34.7
1981	3,996	567	14.2	706	17.7	1,273	31.9	1,450	36.3
1980	3,993	510	12.8	673	16.9	1,441	36.1	1,369	34.3
1979	4,023	533	13.2	739	18.4	1,410	35.0	1,341	33.3
1978	3,975	511	12.9	692	17.4	1,381	34.7	1,391	35.0
1977	3,961	522	13.2	702	17.7	1,341	33.9	1,396	35.2
1976	3,957	516	13.0	684	17.3	1,366	34.5	1,391	35.2
1975	3,891	514	13.2	603	15.5	1,348	34.6	1,426	36.6
1974	3,782	469	12.4	706	18.7	1,345	35.6	1,262	33.4
1973	3,720	490	13.2	589	15.8	1,348	36.2	1,293	34.8
1972	3,630	492	13.6	555	15.3	1,217	33.5	1,366	37.6
1971	3,503	496	14.2	551	15.7	1,012	28.9	1,444	41.2
1970	3,349	485	14.5	537	16.0	981	29.3	1,346	40.2
1969	3,173	489	15.4	473	14.9	814	25.7	1,397	44.0
1968	3,133	535	17.1	485	15.5	756	24.1	1,357	43.3
1967	2,908	438	15.1	500	17.2	772	26.5	1,198	41.2
Female									
2019	4,124	658	16.0	211	5.1	1,073	26.0	2,181	52.9
2018	4,126	671	16.3	188	4.5	958	23.2	2,309	56.0
2017	4,070	705	17.3	222	5.5	946	23.2	2,197	54.0
2016	4,075	654	16.0	229	5.6	965	23.7	2,227	54.7
2015	4,052	752	18.6	252	6.2	907	22.4	2,141	52.8
2014	4,079	683	16.7	265	6.5	873	21.4	2,257	55.3
2013	4,154	732	17.6	257	6.2	1,022	24.6	2,142	51.6
2012	4,174	807	18.9	245	5.9	911	21.8	2,212	53.0
2011	4,124	737	17.9	252	6.1	843	20.4	2,293	55.6
2010	4,233	673	15.9	275	6.5	930	22.0	2,355	55.6
2009	4,263	746	17.5	325	7.6	830	19.5	2,361	55.4
2008	4,203	647	15.4	374	8.9	965	23.0	2,217	52.7
2007	4,116	595	14.5	321	7.8	1,027	25.0	2,172	52.8
2006	3,999	654	16.3	328	8.2	974	24.4	2,043	51.1
2005	3,679	472	12.8	269	7.3	886	24.1	2,052	55.8

* = Quantity zero or rounds to zero.

Note: High school graduates are people who have completed 4 years of high school or more, for 1967 to 1991. Beginning in 1992, they were people whose highest degree was a high school diploma (including equivalency) or higher.

[1] Starting in 2003 respondents could identify more than one race. Except as noted, the race data in this table from 2003 onward represent those respondents who indicated only one race category.

[2] The data shown prior to 2003 consists of those identifying themselves as "Asian or Pacific Islanders."

Table A-15. Population 18 and 19 Years Old, by School Enrollment Status, Sex, Race, and Hispanic Origin, October 1967–2019—*Continued*

(Numbers in thousands; percent; civilian noninstitutionalized population.)

Year, race, and Hispanic origin	Total	Population 18 and 19 years old								
		Still in high school	Percent	Dropped out	Percent	High school graduate only	Percent	In college	Percent
2004	3,840	553	14.4	318	8.3	895	23.3	2,074	54.0
2003	3,769	565	15.0	337	8.9	923	24.5	1,944	51.6
2002	3,865	565	14.6	361	9.3	993	25.7	1,946	50.3
2001	3,958	594	15.0	420	10.6	1,037	26.2	1,907	48.2
2000	4,008	544	13.6	440	11.0	995	24.8	2,029	50.6
1999	3,965	540	13.6	497	12.5	1,056	26.6	1,872	47.2
1998	3,908	513	13.1	492	12.6	900	23.0	2,003	51.3
1997	3,694	506	13.7	453	12.3	934	25.3	1,801	48.8
1996	3,665	460	12.6	452	12.3	932	25.4	1,821	49.7
1995	3,587	453	12.6	519	14.5	944	26.3	1,671	46.6
1994	3,461	440	12.7	430	12.4	956	27.6	1,635	47.2
1993	3,265	425	13.0	375	11.5	877	26.9	1,588	48.6
1992	3,260	428	13.1	380	11.7	886	27.2	1,566	48.0
1991	3,357	389	11.6	436	13.0	929	27.7	1,603	47.8
1990	3,561	429	12.0	491	13.8	1,065	29.9	1,576	44.3
1989	3,721	421	11.3	501	13.5	1,156	31.1	1,643	44.2
1988	3,676	346	9.4	497	13.5	1,151	31.3	1,682	45.8
1987	3,623	374	10.3	461	12.7	1,226	33.8	1,562	43.1
1986	3,593	337	9.4	413	11.5	1,306	36.3	1,537	42.8
1985	3,654	304	8.3	451	12.3	1,340	36.7	1,559	42.7
1984	3,754	306	8.2	535	14.3	1,419	37.8	1,494	39.8
1983	3,942	383	9.7	502	12.7	1,457	37.0	1,600	40.6
1982	4,062	346	8.5	627	15.4	1,536	37.8	1,553	38.2
1981	4,119	364	8.8	594	14.4	1,567	38.0	1,594	38.7
1980	4,167	345	8.3	611	14.7	1,646	39.5	1,565	37.6
1979	4,191	317	7.6	643	15.3	1,728	41.2	1,503	35.9
1978	4,178	291	7.0	669	16.0	1,711	41.0	1,507	36.1
1977	4,190	326	7.8	654	15.6	1,693	40.4	1,517	36.2
1976	4,191	314	7.5	672	16.0	1,659	39.6	1,546	36.9
1975	4,133	308	7.5	683	16.5	1,625	39.3	1,517	36.7
1974	4,040	309	7.6	596	14.8	1,800	44.6	1,335	33.0
1973	3,929	276	7.0	638	16.2	1,791	45.6	1,224	31.2
1972	3,832	287	7.5	545	14.2	1,686	44.0	1,314	34.3
1971	3,728	337	9.0	556	14.9	1,554	41.7	1,281	34.4
1970	3,609	253	7.0	589	16.3	1,519	42.1	1,248	34.6
1969	3,504	260	7.4	534	15.2	1,506	43.0	1,204	34.4
1968	3,454	281	8.1	548	15.9	1,481	42.9	1,144	33.1
1967	3,450	302	8.8	586	17.0	1,474	42.7	1,088	31.5
WHITE									
Both Sexes									
2019	6,165	1,174	19.0	356	5.8	1,685	27.3	2,949	47.8
2018	6,198	1,092	17.6	419	6.8	1,509	24.3	3,178	51.3
2017	6,153	1,192	19.4	450	7.3	1,529	24.8	2,982	48.5
2016	6,144	1,097	17.9	370	6.0	1,506	24.5	3,170	51.6
2015	6,147	1,159	18.9	474	7.7	1,456	23.7	3,057	49.7
2014	6,213	1,182	19.0	451	7.3	1,517	24.4	3,064	49.3
2013	6,294	1,219	19.4	390	6.2	1,652	26.2	3,033	48.2
2012	6,372	1,303	20.1	418	6.6	1,575	24.7	3,077	48.3
2011	6,501	1,274	19.6	449	6.9	1,480	22.8	3,298	50.7
2010	6,523	1,168	17.9	435	6.7	1,522	23.3	3,398	52.1
2009	6,594	1,194	18.1	526	8.0	1,536	23.3	3,337	50.6
2008	6,589	1,067	16.2	558	8.5	1,611	24.4	3,353	50.9
2007	6,446	1,083	16.8	517	8.0	1,605	24.9	3,242	50.3
2006	6,321	1,121	17.7	600	9.5	1,619	25.6	2,982	47.2
2005	5,893	1,023	17.4	515	8.7	1,383	23.5	2,972	50.4
2004	6,043	963	15.9	634	10.5	1,500	24.8	2,946	48.8
2003[1]	5,915	979	16.6	659	11.1	1,444	24.4	2,833	47.9
2002	6,252	1,096	17.5	663	10.6	1,602	25.6	2,891	46.2
2001	6,254	1,022	16.3	843	13.5	1,634	26.1	2,755	44.1
2000	6,399	1,010	15.8	795	12.4	1,680	26.3	2,914	45.5
1999	6,383	1,009	15.8	810	12.7	1,715	26.9	2,849	44.6
1998	6,266	884	14.1	848	13.5	1,540	24.6	2,994	47.8

* = Quantity zero or rounds to zero.
Note: High school graduates are people who have completed 4 years of high school or more, for 1967 to 1991. Beginning in 1992, they were people whose highest degree was a high school diploma (including equivalency) or higher.
[1] Starting in 2003 respondents could identify more than one race. Except as noted, the race data in this table from 2003 onward represent those respondents who indicated only one race category.
[2] The data shown prior to 2003 consists of those identifying themselves as "Asian or Pacific Islanders."

Table A-15. Population 18 and 19 Years Old, by School Enrollment Status, Sex, Race, and Hispanic Origin, October 1967–2019—*Continued*

(Numbers in thousands; percent; civilian noninstitutionalized population.)

Year, race, and Hispanic origin	Total	Population 18 and 19 years old								
		Still in high school	Percent	Dropped out	Percent	High school graduate only	Percent	In college	Percent
1997.............................	5,995	896	14.9	816	13.6	1,491	24.9	2,792	46.6
1996.............................	5,833	914	15.7	735	12.6	1,453	24.9	2,731	46.8
1995.............................	5,698	803	14.1	809	14.2	1,509	26.5	2,577	45.2
1994.............................	5,559	817	14.7	681	12.3	1,493	26.9	2,568	46.2
1993.............................	5,252	786	15.0	628	12.0	1,382	26.3	2,456	46.8
1992.............................	5,203	793	15.2	582	11.2	1,409	27.1	2,419	46.5
1991.............................	5,358	709	13.2	722	13.5	1,440	26.9	2,487	46.4
1990.............................	5,725	724	12.6	799	14.0	1,654	28.9	2,548	44.5
1989.............................	6,013	744	12.4	819	13.6	1,802	30.0	2,648	44.0
1988.............................	5,981	699	11.7	855	14.3	1,788	29.9	2,639	44.1
1987.............................	5,845	667	11.4	762	13.0	1,852	31.7	2,564	43.9
1986.............................	5,825	669	11.5	693	11.9	1,940	33.3	2,523	43.3
1985.............................	5,922	566	9.6	815	13.8	2,002	33.8	2,539	42.9
1984.............................	6,139	594	9.7	913	14.9	2,091	34.1	2,541	41.4
1983.............................	6,452	688	10.7	884	13.7	2,283	35.4	2,597	40.3
1982.............................	6,666	647	9.7	1,051	15.8	2,419	36.3	2,549	38.2
1981.............................	6,794	656	9.7	1,054	15.5	2,445	36.0	2,639	38.8
1980.............................	6,913	621	9.0	1,032	14.9	2,682	38.8	2,578	37.3
1979.............................	6,980	607	8.7	1,115	16.0	2,760	39.5	2,498	35.8
1978.............................	6,933	560	8.1	1,082	15.6	2,738	39.5	2,553	36.8
1977.............................	6,944	581	8.4	1,103	15.9	2,681	38.6	2,579	37.1
1976.............................	6,951	581	8.4	1,131	16.3	2,662	38.3	2,577	37.1
1975.............................	6,855	572	8.3	1,005	14.7	2,665	38.9	2,613	38.1
1974.............................	6,707	551	8.2	1,045	15.6	2,803	41.8	2,308	34.4
1973.............................	6,559	568	8.7	962	14.7	2,748	41.9	2,281	34.8
1972.............................	6,424	582	9.1	857	13.3	2,574	40.1	2,411	37.5
1971.............................	6,243	596	9.5	875	14.0	2,287	36.6	2,485	39.8
1970.............................	6,009	563	9.4	845	14.1	2,240	37.3	2,361	39.3
1969.............................	5,762	557	9.7	772	13.4	2,056	35.7	2,377	41.3
1968.............................	5,692	614	10.8	822	14.4	1,972	34.6	2,284	40.1
1967.............................	5,506	558	10.1	875	15.9	1,968	35.7	2,105	38.2
Male									
2019.............................	3,122	687	22.0	211	6.8	890	28.5	1,334	42.7
2018.............................	3,147	630	20.0	281	8.9	806	25.6	1,430	45.4
2017.............................	3,123	717	22.9	273	8.7	816	26.1	1,317	42.2
2016.............................	3,119	649	20.8	202	6.5	798	25.6	1,470	47.1
2015.............................	3,123	621	19.9	282	9.0	806	25.8	1,414	45.3
2014.............................	3,165	653	20.6	236	7.5	879	27.8	1,397	44.1
2013.............................	3,212	732	22.8	196	6.1	898	27.9	1,386	43.2
2012.............................	3,259	763	23.1	237	7.3	872	26.8	1,387	42.6
2011.............................	3,352	748	22.3	240	7.2	845	25.2	1,520	45.3
2010.............................	3,316	667	20.1	246	7.4	830	25.0	1,573	47.4
2009.............................	3,349	652	19.5	291	8.7	894	26.7	1,511	45.1
2008.............................	3,350	589	17.6	299	8.9	896	26.7	1,566	46.7
2007.............................	3,277	668	20.4	281	8.6	819	25.0	1,508	46.0
2006.............................	3,211	645	20.1	351	10.9	848	26.4	1,367	42.6
2005.............................	3,049	665	21.8	304	10.0	737	24.2	1,343	44.1
2004	3,062	524	17.1	406	13.3	824	26.9	1,308	42.7
2003[1]...........................	3,003	594	19.8	381	12.7	770	25.6	1,258	41.9
2002.............................	3,186	661	20.7	366	11.5	830	26.1	1,329	41.7
2001.............................	3,192	585	18.3	494	15.5	840	26.3	1,273	39.9
2000.............................	3,248	612	18.8	447	13.8	900	27.7	1,289	39.7
1999.............................	3,242	609	18.8	423	13.0	874	27.0	1,336	41.2
1998.............................	3,197	533	16.7	472	14.8	816	25.5	1,376	43.0
1997.............................	3,060	523	17.1	473	15.5	750	24.5	1,314	42.9
1996.............................	2,953	575	19.5	382	12.9	773	26.2	1,223	41.4
1995.............................	2,886	519	18.0	408	14.1	764	26.5	1,195	41.4
1994.............................	2,813	512	18.2	355	12.6	734	26.1	1,212	43.1
1993.............................	2,641	497	18.8	338	12.8	703	26.6	1,103	41.8
1992.............................	2,608	482	18.5	304	11.7	720	27.6	1,102	42.3
1991.............................	2,677	451	16.8	381	14.2	733	27.4	1,112	41.5
1990.............................	2,852	416	14.6	421	14.8	797	27.9	1,218	42.7
1989.............................	2,997	463	15.4	433	14.4	848	28.3	1,253	41.8

* = Quantity zero or rounds to zero.
Note: High school graduates are people who have completed 4 years of high school or more, for 1967 to 1991. Beginning in 1992, they were people whose highest degree was a high school diploma (including equivalency) or higher.
[1] Starting in 2003 respondents could identify more than one race. Except as noted, the race data in this table from 2003 onward represent those respondents who indicated only one race category.
[2] The data shown prior to 2003 consists of those identifying themselves as "Asian or Pacific Islanders."

Table A-15. Population 18 and 19 Years Old, by School Enrollment Status, Sex, Race, and Hispanic Origin, October 1967–2019—*Continued*

(Numbers in thousands; percent; civilian noninstitutionalized population.)

Year, race, and Hispanic origin	Total	Population 18 and 19 years old							
		Still in high school	Percent	Dropped out	Percent	High school graduate only	Percent	In college	Percent
1988.............................	2,976	487	16.4	461	15.5	834	28.0	1,194	40.1
1987.............................	2,906	404	13.9	400	13.8	842	29.0	1,260	43.4
1986.............................	2,888	411	14.2	370	12.8	866	30.0	1,241	43.0
1985.............................	2,937	349	11.9	478	16.3	934	31.8	1,176	40.0
1984.............................	3,047	378	12.4	480	15.8	965	31.7	1,224	40.2
1983.............................	3,216	434	13.5	500	15.5	1,085	33.7	1,197	37.2
1982.............................	3,301	412	12.5	549	16.6	1,151	34.9	1,189	36.0
1981.............................	3,356	394	11.7	599	17.8	1,104	32.9	1,259	37.5
1980.............................	3,407	385	11.3	549	16.1	1,241	36.4	1,232	36.2
1979.............................	3,445	395	11.5	610	17.7	1,248	36.2	1,192	34.6
1978.............................	3,405	368	10.8	554	16.3	1,244	36.5	1,239	36.4
1977.............................	3,396	348	10.2	577	17.0	1,199	35.3	1,272	37.5
1976.............................	3,393	348	10.3	582	17.2	1,219	35.9	1,244	36.7
1975.............................	3,343	374	11.2	458	13.7	1,228	36.7	1,283	38.4
1974.............................	3,265	343	10.5	568	17.4	1,211	37.1	1,143	35.0
1973.............................	3,208	375	11.7	454	14.2	1,202	37.5	1,177	36.7
1972.............................	3,137	374	11.9	423	13.5	1,098	35.0	1,242	39.6
1971.............................	3,035	367	12.1	432	14.2	908	29.9	1,328	43.8
1970.............................	2,901	374	12.9	384	13.2	892	30.7	1,251	43.1
1969.............................	2,745	374	13.6	345	12.6	728	26.5	1,298	47.3
1968.............................	2,710	403	14.9	387	14.3	658	24.3	1,262	46.6
1967.............................	2,511	340	13.5	386	15.4	688	27.4	1,097	43.7
Female									
2019.............................	3,043	488	16.0	145	4.8	795	26.1	1,615	53.1
2018.............................	3,051	462	15.2	137	4.5	703	23.0	1,749	57.3
2017.............................	3,029	476	15.7	177	5.8	712	23.5	1,665	54.9
2016.............................	3,025	448	14.8	168	5.6	709	23.4	1,700	56.2
2015.............................	3,024	538	17.8	192	6.3	650	21.5	1,644	54.4
2014.............................	3,049	529	17.4	215	7.1	638	20.9	1,667	54.7
2013.............................	3,083	487	15.8	195	6.3	754	24.5	1,646	53.4
2012.............................	3,113	540	16.9	181	5.8	702	22.6	1,690	54.3
2011.............................	3,148	526	16.7	209	6.6	635	20.2	1,779	56.5
2010.............................	3,206	501	15.6	188	5.9	692	21.6	1,825	56.9
2009.............................	3,245	542	16.7	235	7.2	642	19.8	1,826	56.3
2008.............................	3,239	478	14.8	259	8.0	715	22.1	1,787	55.2
2007.............................	3,169	414	13.1	235	7.4	785	24.8	1,734	54.7
2006.............................	3,111	476	15.3	249	8.0	771	24.8	1,615	51.9
2005.............................	2,844	358	12.6	210	7.4	647	22.7	1,629	57.3
2004.............................	2,980	440	14.7	227	7.6	675	22.7	1,638	55.0
2003¹.............................	2,913	385	13.2	279	9.6	674	23.1	1,575	54.1
2002.............................	3,066	435	14.2	297	9.7	772	25.2	1,562	50.9
2001.............................	3,062	438	14.3	349	11.4	794	25.9	1,481	48.4
2000.............................	3,151	397	12.6	348	11.0	781	24.8	1,625	51.6
1999.............................	3,141	400	12.7	387	12.3	841	26.8	1,513	48.2
1998.............................	3,069	351	11.4	376	12.3	724	23.6	1,618	52.7
1997.............................	2,934	371	12.6	344	11.7	740	25.2	1,479	50.4
1996.............................	2,879	338	11.7	353	12.3	680	23.6	1,508	52.4
1995.............................	2,812	283	10.1	401	14.3	745	26.5	1,383	49.2
1994.............................	2,746	305	11.1	325	11.8	759	27.6	1,357	49.4
1993.............................	2,611	289	11.1	290	11.1	679	26.0	1,353	51.8
1992.............................	2,595	311	12.0	278	10.7	689	26.6	1,317	50.8
1991.............................	2,681	259	9.7	341	12.7	706	26.3	1,375	51.3
1990.............................	2,873	307	10.7	378	13.2	857	29.8	1,331	46.3
1989.............................	3,016	281	9.3	386	12.8	954	31.6	1,395	46.3
1988.............................	3,005	212	7.1	394	13.1	954	31.7	1,445	48.1
1987.............................	2,939	263	8.9	362	12.3	1,010	34.4	1,304	44.4
1986.............................	2,937	257	8.8	323	11.0	1,074	36.6	1,283	43.7
1985.............................	2,985	217	7.3	337	11.3	1,068	35.8	1,363	45.7
1984.............................	3,092	216	7.0	432	14.0	1,127	36.4	1,317	42.6
1983.............................	3,236	255	7.9	383	11.8	1,198	37.0	1,400	43.3
1982.............................	3,365	234	7.0	502	14.9	1,269	37.7	1,360	40.4
1981.............................	3,438	262	7.6	454	13.2	1,342	39.0	1,380	40.1
1980.............................	3,506	237	6.8	483	13.8	1,440	41.1	1,346	38.4

* = Quantity zero or rounds to zero.
Note: High school graduates are people who have completed 4 years of high school or more, for 1967 to 1991. Beginning in 1992, they were people whose highest degree was a high school diploma (including equivalency) or higher.
¹ Starting in 2003 respondents could identify more than one race. Except as noted, the race data in this table from 2003 onward represent those respondents who indicated only one race category.
² The data shown prior to 2003 consists of those identifying themselves as "Asian or Pacific Islanders."

Table A-15. Population 18 and 19 Years Old, by School Enrollment Status, Sex, Race, and Hispanic Origin, October 1967–2019—*Continued*

(Numbers in thousands; percent; civilian noninstitutionalized population.)

Year, race, and Hispanic origin	Total	Population 18 and 19 years old								
		Still in high school	Percent	Dropped out	Percent	High school graduate only	Percent	In college	Percent
1979............................	3,535	213	6.0	505	14.3	1,511	42.7	1,306	36.9
1978............................	3,528	193	5.5	528	15.0	1,493	42.3	1,314	37.2
1977............................	3,548	232	6.5	526	14.8	1,483	41.8	1,307	36.8
1976............................	3,558	230	6.5	550	15.5	1,444	40.6	1,334	37.5
1975............................	3,512	199	5.7	547	15.6	1,436	40.9	1,330	37.9
1974............................	3,442	207	6.0	477	13.9	1,592	46.3	1,166	33.9
1973............................	3,351	192	5.7	508	15.2	1,547	46.2	1,104	32.9
1972............................	3,287	208	6.3	434	13.2	1,476	44.9	1,169	35.6
1971............................	3,208	229	7.1	442	13.8	1,380	43.0	1,157	36.1
1970............................	3,108	190	6.1	460	14.8	1,348	43.4	1,110	35.7
1969............................	3,017	183	6.1	427	14.2	1,328	44.0	1,079	35.8
1968............................	2,981	210	7.0	435	14.6	1,314	44.1	1,022	34.3
1967............................	2,996	218	7.3	489	16.3	1,280	42.7	1,009	33.7
WHITE NON-HISPANIC									
Both Sexes									
2019............................	4,410	836	19.0	228	5.2	1,177	26.7	2,169	49.2
2018............................	4,404	756	17.2	222	5.0	1,043	23.7	2,382	54.1
2017............................	4,400	853	19.4	294	6.7	1,124	25.5	2,129	48.4
2016............................	4,563	775	17.0	242	5.3	1,106	24.2	2,439	53.5
2015............................	4,575	839	18.3	305	6.7	1,063	23.2	2,368	51.8
2014............................	4,555	860	18.9	290	6.4	1,106	24.3	2,299	50.5
2013............................	4,645	856	18.4	248	5.3	1,162	25.0	2,379	51.2
2012............................	4,748	905	18.6	249	5.2	1,232	26.0	2,363	49.8
2011............................	4,889	937	19.2	291	5.9	1,074	22.0	2,588	52.9
2010............................	4,935	804	16.3	277	5.6	1,156	23.4	2,699	54.7
2009............................	5,068	826	16.3	288	5.7	1,112	21.9	2,842	56.1
2008............................	5,185	780	15.0	296	5.7	1,258	24.3	2,850	55.0
2007............................	5,067	793	15.7	283	5.6	1,252	24.7	2,739	54.1
2006............................	5,018	843	16.8	361	7.2	1,251	24.9	2,564	51.1
2005............................	4,770	790	16.6	297	6.2	1,065	22.3	2,618	54.9
2004............................	4,885	731	15.0	363	7.4	1,195	24.5	2,596	53.1
2003[1].......................	4,780	758	15.9	379	7.9	1,157	24.2	2,486	52.0
2002............................	5,016	817	16.3	369	7.4	1,281	25.5	2,549	50.8
2001............................	4,928	780	15.8	467	9.5	1,298	26.3	2,383	48.4
2000............................	5,221	757	14.5	500	9.6	1,384	26.5	2,580	49.4
1999............................	5,228	779	14.9	491	9.4	1,384	26.5	2,574	49.2
1998............................	5,080	691	13.6	475	9.4	1,211	23.8	2,703	53.2
Male									
2019............................	2,262	508	22.4	131	5.8	653	28.9	971	42.9
2018............................	2,239	443	19.8	152	6.8	557	24.9	1,086	48.5
2017............................	2,262	528	23.4	174	7.7	608	26.9	952	42.1
2016............................	2,351	463	19.7	123	5.2	597	25.4	1,168	49.7
2015............................	2,350	460	19.6	181	7.7	589	25.1	1,121	47.7
2014............................	2,334	490	21.0	147	6.3	646	27.7	1,050	45.0
2013............................	2,392	516	21.6	123	5.2	629	26.3	1,124	47.0
2012............................	2,412	527	21.4	124	5.1	710	29.4	1,051	43.6
2011............................	2,470	543	22.0	145	5.9	599	24.2	1,184	47.9
2010............................	2,516	470	18.7	166	6.6	645	25.6	1,236	49.1
2009............................	2,573	473	18.4	173	6.7	641	24.9	1,286	50.0
2008............................	2,649	423	16.0	170	6.4	709	26.8	1,346	50.8
2007............................	2,587	496	19.2	150	5.8	643	24.9	1,298	50.2
2006............................	2,553	501	19.6	204	8.0	679	26.6	1,168	45.7
2005............................	2,449	515	21.0	168	6.9	573	23.4	1,193	48.7
2004............................	2,443	408	16.7	204	8.4	681	27.9	1,150	47.1
2003[1].......................	2,407	460	19.1	230	9.6	602	25.0	1,115	46.3
2002............................	2,502	481	19.2	182	7.3	660	26.4	1,179	47.1
2001............................	2,526	453	17.9	257	10.2	685	27.1	1,131	44.8
2000............................	2,628	471	17.9	274	10.4	745	28.3	1,138	43.3
1999............................	2,648	473	17.9	255	9.6	706	26.7	1,214	45.8
1998............................	2,613	432	16.5	254	9.7	653	25.0	1,274	48.8

* = Quantity zero or rounds to zero.
Note: High school graduates are people who have completed 4 years of high school or more, for 1967 to 1991. Beginning in 1992, they were people whose highest degree was a high school diploma (including equivalency) or higher.
[1] Starting in 2003 respondents could identify more than one race. Except as noted, the race data in this table from 2003 onward represent those respondents who indicated only one race category.
[2] The data shown prior to 2003 consists of those identifying themselves as "Asian or Pacific Islanders."

Table A-15. Population 18 and 19 Years Old, by School Enrollment Status, Sex, Race, and Hispanic Origin, October 1967–2019—*Continued*

(Numbers in thousands; percent; civilian noninstitutionalized population.)

Year, race, and Hispanic origin	Total	Population 18 and 19 years old								
		Still in high school	Percent	Dropped out	Percent	High school graduate only	Percent	In college	Percent
Female									
2019.............................	1,252	221	17.7	83	6.6	409	32.7	538	43.0
2018.............................	2,165	312	14.4	70	3.2	486	22.5	1,296	59.9
2017.............................	2,138	325	15.2	120	5.6	515	24.1	1,178	55.1
2016.............................	2,212	312	14.1	119	5.4	510	23.1	1,271	57.5
2015.............................	2,225	379	17.1	124	5.6	474	21.3	1,248	56.1
2014.............................	2,222	370	16.6	143	6.4	460	20.7	1,249	56.2
2013.............................	2,253	340	15.1	125	5.5	533	23.7	1,254	55.7
2012.............................	2,336	377	15.7	125	5.3	522	22.3	1,312	56.2
2011.............................	2,419	394	16.3	146	6.0	475	19.6	1,404	58.1
2010.............................	2,419	334	13.8	111	4.6	511	21.1	1,463	60.5
2009.............................	2,495	353	14.1	115	4.6	471	18.9	1,556	62.4
2008.............................	2,536	357	14.1	126	5.0	549	21.7	1,504	59.3
2007.............................	2,480	298	12.0	132	5.3	609	24.6	1,441	58.1
2006.............................	2,466	341	13.8	157	6.4	571	23.2	1,396	56.6
2005.............................	2,321	275	11.9	129	5.6	491	21.2	1,425	61.4
2004	2,441	323	13.2	159	6.5	513	21.0	1,446	59.2
2003[1]	2,373	298	12.6	149	6.3	555	23.4	1,371	57.8
2002.............................	2,514	336	13.4	187	7.4	621	24.7	1,370	54.5
2001.............................	2,402	328	13.7	209	8.7	613	25.5	1,252	52.1
2000.............................	2,593	286	11.0	225	8.7	639	24.6	1,443	55.6
1999.............................	2,580	307	11.9	236	9.1	677	26.2	1,360	52.7
1998.............................	2,467	259	10.5	221	9.0	558	22.6	1,429	57.9
BLACK									
Both Sexes									
2019.............................	1,252	221	17.7	83	6.6	409	32.7	538	43.0
2018.............................	1,264	302	23.9	71	5.6	361	28.6	530	42.0
2017.............................	1,246	310	24.9	64	5.2	346	27.8	525	42.1
2016.............................	1,244	305	24.5	87	7.0	321	25.8	530	42.6
2015.............................	1,233	286	23.2	84	6.8	354	28.7	509	41.3
2014.............................	1,251	307	24.5	94	7.5	341	27.3	510	40.7
2013.............................	1,305	386	29.6	92	7.1	375	28.8	451	34.6
2012.............................	1,356	400	29.2	110	8.1	315	23.2	531	39.1
2011.............................	1,316	396	30.1	60	4.5	281	21.3	580	44.0
2010.............................	1,336	271	20.3	144	10.8	355	26.5	567	42.4
2009.............................	1,346	319	23.7	180	13.4	288	21.4	559	41.5
2008.............................	1,335	311	23.3	145	10.8	400	30.0	479	35.9
2007.............................	1,284	300	23.4	112	8.7	380	29.6	492	38.3
2006.............................	1,230	332	27.0	103	8.3	332	27.0	464	37.7
2005.............................	1,126	256	22.7	110	9.8	309	27.4	451	40.0
2004	1,112	218	19.6	162	14.5	292	26.3	440	39.6
2003[1]	1,052	277	26.3	128	12.2	273	26.0	374	35.6
2002.............................	1,181	251	21.3	180	15.2	320	27.1	430	36.4
2001.............................	1,246	299	24.0	152	12.2	351	28.2	444	35.6
2000.............................	1,251	262	20.9	187	14.9	348	27.8	454	36.3
1999.............................	1,199	259	21.6	190	15.8	320	26.7	430	35.9
1998.............................	1,246	290	23.3	224	18.0	271	21.7	461	37.0
1997.............................	1,133	278	24.5	172	15.2	302	26.7	381	33.6
1996.............................	1,161	268	23.1	175	15.1	373	32.1	345	29.7
1995.............................	1,099	287	26.1	177	16.1	291	26.5	344	31.3
1994.............................	1,017	239	23.5	199	19.6	269	26.5	310	30.5
1993.............................	1,040	290	27.9	133	12.8	306	29.4	311	29.9
1992.............................	1,007	275	27.3	166	16.5	275	27.3	291	28.9
1991.............................	1,041	276	26.5	146	14.0	316	30.4	303	29.1
1990.............................	1,079	246	22.8	178	16.5	306	28.4	349	32.3
1989.............................	1,078	239	22.2	194	18.0	343	31.8	302	28.0
1988.............................	1,057	251	23.7	189	17.9	336	31.8	281	26.6
1987.............................	1,043	213	20.4	166	15.9	323	31.0	341	32.7
1986.............................	1,048	212	20.2	156	14.9	374	35.7	306	29.2
1985.............................	1,072	213	19.9	186	17.4	414	38.6	259	24.2
1984.............................	1,092	218	20.0	186	17.0	423	38.7	265	24.3
1983.............................	1,134	265	23.4	199	17.5	412	36.3	258	22.8

* = Quantity zero or rounds to zero.
Note: High school graduates are people who have completed 4 years of high school or more, for 1967 to 1991. Beginning in 1992, they were people whose highest degree was a high school diploma (including equivalency) or higher.
[1] Starting in 2003 respondents could identify more than one race. Except as noted, the race data in this table from 2003 onward represent those respondents who indicated only one race category.
[2] The data shown prior to 2003 consists of those identifying themselves as "Asian or Pacific Islanders."

Table A-15. Population 18 and 19 Years Old, by School Enrollment Status, Sex, Race, and Hispanic Origin, October 1967–2019—*Continued*

(Numbers in thousands; percent; civilian noninstitutionalized population.)

Year, race, and Hispanic origin	Total	Population 18 and 19 years old							
		Still in high school	Percent	Dropped out	Percent	High school graduate only	Percent	In college	Percent
1982	1,146	226	19.7	253	22.1	393	34.3	274	23.9
1981	1,128	238	21.1	218	19.3	366	32.4	306	27.1
1980	1,081	211	19.5	229	21.2	358	33.1	283	26.2
1979	1,072	221	20.6	246	22.9	326	30.4	279	26.0
1978	1,065	221	20.8	258	24.2	316	29.7	270	25.4
1977	1,072	249	23.2	235	21.9	319	29.8	269	25.1
1976	1,055	230	21.8	211	20.0	312	29.6	302	28.6
1975	1,030	225	21.8	262	25.4	283	27.5	260	25.2
1974	1,004	209	20.8	235	23.4	327	32.6	233	23.2
1973	997	182	18.3	252	25.3	369	37.0	194	19.5
1972	958	181	18.9	229	23.9	319	33.3	229	23.9
1971	908	219	24.1	219	24.1	266	29.3	204	22.5
1970	878	161	18.3	274	31.2	252	28.7	191	21.8
1969	837	179	21.4	227	27.1	238	28.4	193	23.1
1968	830	195	23.5	202	24.3	251	30.2	182	21.9
1967	780	175	22.4	203	26.0	261	33.5	141	18.1
Male									
2019	616	128	20.7	41	6.7	205	33.2	243	39.4
2018	623	173	27.7	31	5.0	186	29.8	234	37.5
2017	615	155	25.3	45	7.4	181	29.4	234	38.0
2016	612	193	31.5	56	9.2	148	24.2	215	35.1
2015	606	155	25.5	49	8.0	173	28.6	229	37.8
2014	617	197	31.9	56	9.1	189	30.6	175	28.4
2013	646	201	31.1	58	8.9	201	31.1	186	28.9
2012	673	201	29.9	87	12.9	179	26.6	206	30.6
2011	645	226	35.0	39	6.0	138	21.4	242	37.6
2010	654	159	24.4	83	12.6	174	26.5	238	36.4
2009	659	174	26.4	102	15.5	158	24.0	225	34.1
2008	653	173	26.5	53	8.1	222	34.0	205	31.4
2007	628	161	25.7	54	8.6	186	29.6	227	36.2
2006	600	210	35.0	42	7.0	174	29.0	174	28.9
2005	552	178	32.2	60	10.9	121	21.9	193	35.0
2004	519	137	26.4	91	17.6	126	24.3	165	31.7
2003[1]	502	143	28.5	77	15.3	116	23.1	166	33.1
2002	608	155	25.5	123	20.2	151	24.8	179	29.4
2001	624	179	28.7	97	15.5	169	27.1	179	28.7
2000	593	148	25.0	105	17.7	177	29.8	163	27.5
1999	586	144	24.6	97	16.6	136	23.2	209	35.7
1998	613	163	26.6	128	20.9	128	20.9	194	31.6
1997	554	172	31.0	90	16.2	150	27.1	142	25.6
1996	564	167	29.6	90	16.0	162	28.7	145	25.7
1995	519	162	31.2	94	18.1	118	22.7	145	27.9
1994	497	134	27.0	116	23.3	115	23.1	132	26.6
1993	517	181	35.0	53	10.3	135	26.1	148	28.6
1992	499	180	36.1	82	16.4	114	22.8	123	24.6
1991	504	176	34.9	62	12.3	129	25.6	137	27.2
1990	520	152	29.2	80	15.4	124	23.8	164	31.5
1989	516	137	26.6	90	17.4	163	31.6	126	24.4
1988	510	145	28.4	92	18.0	165	32.4	108	21.2
1987	501	140	27.9	80	16.0	127	25.3	154	30.7
1986	506	149	29.4	74	14.6	165	32.6	118	23.3
1985	518	135	26.1	92	17.8	170	32.8	121	23.4
1984	524	143	27.3	103	19.7	166	31.7	112	21.4
1983	539	158	29.3	106	19.7	182	33.8	93	17.3
1982	549	132	24.0	145	26.4	148	27.0	124	22.6
1981	538	145	27.0	102	19.0	158	29.4	133	24.7
1980	503	118	23.5	114	22.7	173	34.4	98	19.5
1979	497	128	25.8	122	24.5	137	27.6	110	22.1
1978	493	135	27.4	127	25.8	117	23.7	114	23.1
1977	496	161	32.5	118	23.8	127	25.6	90	18.1
1976	499	153	30.7	96	19.2	129	25.9	121	24.2
1975	476	127	26.7	132	27.7	106	22.3	111	23.3
1974	474	116	24.5	128	27.0	128	27.0	102	21.5

* = Quantity zero or rounds to zero.
Note: High school graduates are people who have completed 4 years of high school or more, for 1967 to 1991. Beginning in 1992, they were people whose highest degree was a high school diploma (including equivalency) or higher.
[1] Starting in 2003 respondents could identify more than one race. Except as noted, the race data in this table from 2003 onward represent those respondents who indicated only one race category.
[2] The data shown prior to 2003 consists of those identifying themselves as "Asian or Pacific Islanders."

Table A-15. Population 18 and 19 Years Old, by School Enrollment Status, Sex, Race, and Hispanic Origin, October 1967–2019—*Continued*

(Numbers in thousands; percent; civilian noninstitutionalized population.)

Year, race, and Hispanic origin	Population 18 and 19 years old								
	Total	Still in high school	Percent	Dropped out	Percent	High school graduate only	Percent	In college	Percent
1973................	467	106	22.7	130	27.8	135	28.9	96	20.6
1972................	445	110	24.7	121	27.2	112	25.2	102	22.9
1971................	423	120	28.4	110	26.0	99	23.4	94	22.2
1970................	414	98	23.7	151	36.5	92	22.2	73	17.6
1969................	394	109	27.7	124	31.5	75	19.0	86	21.8
1968................	390	124	31.8	93	23.8	90	23.1	83	21.3
1967................	356	95	26.7	109	30.6	74	20.8	78	21.9
Female									
2019................	636	94	14.7	42	6.5	205	32.2	295	46.5
2018................	640	129	20.2	39	6.1	176	27.4	296	46.3
2017................	631	155	24.6	19	3.1	165	26.2	291	46.1
2016................	631	112	17.8	31	4.9	173	27.4	316	50.0
2015................	627	131	20.9	36	5.7	180	28.8	280	44.6
2014................	635	110	17.4	38	6.0	152	24.0	334	52.7
2013................	659	186	28.2	35	5.2	174	26.4	265	40.1
2012................	683	198	28.5	23	3.4	136	20.0	325	47.6
2011................	671	170	25.4	21	3.1	143	21.3	337	50.3
2010................	682	111	16.3	61	9.0	181	26.5	329	48.2
2009................	687	145	21.1	78	11.3	130	19.0	334	48.6
2008................	681	138	20.3	92	13.5	178	26.1	274	40.2
2007................	655	139	21.2	58	8.8	194	29.6	265	40.4
2006................	631	122	19.3	60	9.6	158	25.0	291	46.1
2005................	574	78	13.6	49	8.6	189	32.9	258	44.9
2004................	593	81	13.7	70	11.9	167	28.2	275	46.5
2003[1].............	550	133	24.2	51	9.3	157	28.5	209	38.0
2002................	574	97	16.9	57	9.9	169	29.4	251	43.7
2001................	623	122	19.6	54	8.7	182	29.2	265	42.5
2000................	658	113	17.2	82	12.5	172	26.1	291	44.2
1999................	613	114	18.6	94	15.3	184	30.0	221	36.1
1998................	633	127	20.1	96	15.2	143	22.6	267	42.2
1997................	579	107	18.5	82	14.2	152	26.3	238	41.1
1996................	597	102	17.1	85	14.2	211	35.3	199	33.3
1995................	581	126	21.7	83	14.3	173	29.8	199	34.3
1994................	520	105	20.2	83	16.0	154	29.6	178	34.2
1993................	523	108	20.7	80	15.3	172	32.9	163	31.2
1992................	508	95	18.7	84	16.5	161	31.7	168	33.1
1991................	537	99	18.4	85	15.8	187	34.8	166	30.9
1990................	559	95	17.0	98	17.5	181	32.4	185	33.1
1989................	562	102	18.1	104	18.5	180	32.0	176	31.3
1988................	547	105	19.2	97	17.7	172	31.4	173	31.6
1987................	542	75	13.8	85	15.7	196	36.2	186	34.3
1986................	542	62	11.4	83	15.3	209	38.6	188	34.7
1985................	554	78	14.1	94	17.0	244	44.0	138	24.9
1984................	568	76	13.4	82	14.4	257	45.2	153	26.9
1983................	595	108	18.2	93	15.6	230	38.7	164	27.6
1982................	597	95	15.9	108	18.1	244	40.9	150	25.1
1981................	590	93	15.8	116	19.7	209	35.4	172	29.2
1980................	578	93	16.1	115	19.9	185	32.0	185	32.0
1979................	576	93	16.1	125	21.7	189	32.8	169	29.3
1978................	572	88	15.4	130	22.7	199	34.8	155	27.1
1977................	576	88	15.3	117	20.3	192	33.3	179	31.1
1976................	556	77	13.8	115	20.7	183	32.9	181	32.6
1975................	553	97	17.5	130	23.5	176	31.8	150	27.1
1974................	530	92	17.4	107	20.2	200	37.7	131	24.7
1973................	530	77	14.5	122	23.0	234	44.2	97	18.3
1972................	513	71	13.8	108	21.1	207	40.4	127	24.8
1971................	485	100	20.6	109	22.5	167	34.4	109	22.5
1970................	464	62	13.4	124	26.7	160	34.5	118	25.4
1969................	443	70	15.8	102	23.0	163	36.8	108	24.4
1968................	439	69	15.7	109	24.8	161	36.7	100	22.8
1967................	424	81	19.1	93	21.9	187	44.1	63	14.9

* = Quantity zero or rounds to zero.
Note: High school graduates are people who have completed 4 years of high school or more, for 1967 to 1991. Beginning in 1992, they were people whose highest degree was a high school diploma (including equivalency) or higher.
[1] Starting in 2003 respondents could identify more than one race. Except as noted, the race data in this table from 2003 onward represent those respondents who indicated only one race category.
[2] The data shown prior to 2003 consists of those identifying themselves as "Asian or Pacific Islanders."

Table A-15. Population 18 and 19 Years Old, by School Enrollment Status, Sex, Race, and Hispanic Origin, October 1967–2019—*Continued*

(Numbers in thousands; percent; civilian noninstitutionalized population.)

Year, race, and Hispanic origin	Total	Population 18 and 19 years old								
		Still in high school	Percent	Dropped out	Percent	High school graduate only	Percent	In college	Percent
ASIAN ALONE[2]									
Both Sexes									
2019	473	85	17.9	22	4.8	43	9.1	323	68.2
2018	439	57	13.0	11	2.5	81	18.4	291	66.1
2017	376	49	13.1	11	3.0	55	14.6	260	69.3
2016	405	57	14.1	16	4.1	76	18.9	255	63.0
2015	358	65	18.1	17	4.7	41	11.5	235	65.6
2014	352	40	11.3	*	*	42	11.9	270	76.8
2013	442	68	15.5	4	0.9	68	15.3	302	68.3
2012	388	61	15.7	23	5.8	51	13.1	253	65.3
2011	337	44	13.2	13	3.7	40	11.8	240	71.3
2010	331	38	11.5	12	3.7	46	14.0	234	70.8
2009	327	64	19.7	2	0.7	17	5.2	243	74.4
2008	259	49	19.0	7	2.7	31	12.0	172	66.4
2007	296	55	18.4	12	4.2	27	9.3	201	68.1
2006	297	43	14.4	9	3.0	41	14.0	204	68.6
2005	251	34	13.4	4	1.5	25	10.0	188	74.9
2004	257	31	11.9	10	3.8	34	13.2	182	70.7
2003[1]	286	41	14.3	3	1.0	33	11.5	209	73.1
2002	353	42	11.9	14	4.0	61	17.3	236	66.9
2001	353	50	14.2	18	5.1	38	10.8	247	70.0
2000	326	45	13.8	17	5.2	52	16.0	212	65.0
1999	339	43	12.7	22	6.5	51	15.0	223	65.8
Male									
2019	233	47	20.2	7	3.1	18	7.8	161	68.8
2018	221	27	12.2	8	3.6	47	21.1	139	63.1
2017	194	30	15.5	3	1.5	39	20.2	122	62.7
2016	215	27	12.6	10	4.4	44	20.5	135	62.5
2015	178	31	17.4	14	8.0	20	11.5	112	63.1
2014	177	19	11.0	*	*	22	12.5	136	76.5
2013	230	37	16.2	1	0.3	38	16.7	154	66.9
2012	200	37	18.7	14	7.1	20	9.7	129	64.5
2011	178	28	15.4	*	*	19	10.8	131	73.7
2010	170	16	9.6	8	5.0	30	17.4	116	68.1
2009	178	31	17.6	*	*	13	7.4	134	75.0
2008	128	39	30.2	6	5.1	8	5.9	75	58.9
2007	150	33	22.1	2	1.1	11	7.1	104	69.7
2006	167	20	12.2	8	4.7	26	15.7	113	67.5
2005	131	21	16.3	3	2.0	17	13.0	90	68.9
2004	133	22	16.7	1	0.7	18	13.5	92	69.3
2003[1]	129	14	10.9	3	2.3	9	7.0	103	79.8
2002	179	22	12.3	10	5.6	26	14.5	121	67.6
2001	168	27	16.1	14	8.3	14	8.3	113	67.3
2000	162	14	8.6	14	8.6	26	16.0	108	66.7
1999	156	23	14.7	17	10.9	23	14.7	93	59.6
Female									
2019	239	38	15.7	15	6.3	25	10.3	162	67.7
2018	218	30	13.8	3	1.3	34	15.7	151	69.3
2017	182	19	10.5	8	4.6	16	8.7	138	76.3
2016	189	30	15.7	7	3.6	32	17.0	120	63.6
2015	180	34	18.7	3	1.5	21	11.6	123	68.2
2014	175	20	11.6	*	*	20	11.3	134	77.0
2013	212	31	14.8	3	1.6	29	13.8	148	69.8
2012	188	24	12.6	8	4.5	32	16.8	124	66.2
2011	158	17	10.7	13	7.9	20	12.8	109	68.6
2010	161	22	13.6	4	2.4	17	10.4	118	73.6
2009	149	33	22.2	2	1.6	4	2.7	109	73.6
2008	132	11	8.0	*	0.4	24	17.9	97	73.7
2007	146	21	14.6	11	7.5	17	11.5	97	66.4
2006	130	23	17.3	1	0.9	15	11.8	91	70.0
2005	120	12	10.3	1	0.9	9	7.5	98	81.4

* = Quantity zero or rounds to zero.
Note: High school graduates are people who have completed 4 years of high school or more, for 1967 to 1991. Beginning in 1992, they were people whose highest degree was a high school diploma (including equivalency) or higher.
[1] Starting in 2003 respondents could identify more than one race. Except as noted, the race data in this table from 2003 onward represent those respondents who indicated only one race category.
[2] The data shown prior to 2003 consists of those identifying themselves as "Asian or Pacific Islanders."

Table A-15. Population 18 and 19 Years Old, by School Enrollment Status, Sex, Race, and Hispanic Origin, October 1967–2019—*Continued*

(Numbers in thousands; percent; civilian noninstitutionalized population.)

Year, race, and Hispanic origin	Total	Population 18 and 19 years old								
		Still in high school	Percent	Dropped out	Percent	High school graduate only	Percent	In college	Percent
2004	124	8	6.8	9	7.1	18	14.5	89	72.2
2003[1]	157	26	16.6	*	*	24	15.3	107	68.2
2002	173	20	11.6	3	1.7	35	20.2	115	66.5
2001	185	23	12.4	4	2.2	24	13.0	134	72.4
2000	164	30	18.3	4	2.4	26	15.9	104	63.4
1999	183	20	10.9	5	2.7	28	15.3	130	71.0

HISPANIC (OF ANY RACE)

Both Sexes

2019	2,032	422	20.8	170	8.4	568	27.9	872	42.9
2018	2,006	383	19.1	209	10.4	523	26.1	890	44.4
2017	1,965	390	19.9	181	9.2	463	23.6	931	47.4
2016	1,825	364	19.9	146	8.0	430	23.6	884	48.5
2015	1,760	372	21.1	181	10.3	432	24.5	776	44.1
2014	1,908	377	19.8	183	9.6	491	25.7	857	44.9
2013	1,889	393	20.8	184	9.7	585	31.0	727	38.5
2012	1,871	449	23.8	222	11.9	374	20.0	827	44.2
2011	1,743	371	21.3	166	9.5	441	25.3	765	43.9
2010	1,768	389	22.0	179	10.1	418	23.6	783	44.3
2009	1,680	409	24.3	261	15.5	460	27.4	550	32.7
2008	1,539	320	20.8	296	19.3	395	25.7	528	34.3
2007	1,523	311	20.4	254	16.7	399	26.2	559	36.7
2006	1,406	307	21.8	253	18.0	402	28.6	444	31.6
2005	1,253	272	21.7	227	18.1	348	27.8	406	32.4
2004	1,270	244	19.2	296	23.3	346	27.2	384	30.2
2003	1,214	229	18.9	291	24.0	315	25.9	379	31.2
2002	1,309	303	23.1	310	23.7	336	25.7	360	27.5
2001	1,391	246	17.7	399	28.7	359	25.8	387	27.8
2000	1,248	268	21.5	311	24.9	320	25.6	349	28.0
1999	1,220	246	20.2	337	27.6	340	27.9	297	24.3
1998	1,209	199	16.5	402	33.3	320	26.5	288	23.8
1997	1,087	221	20.3	274	25.2	276	25.4	316	29.1
1996	1,000	229	22.9	295	29.5	236	23.6	240	24.0
1995	1,012	203	20.1	312	30.8	233	23.0	264	26.1
1994	925	250	27.0	237	25.6	213	23.0	225	24.3
1993	710	159	22.4	201	28.3	155	21.8	195	27.5
1992	778	188	24.2	197	25.3	163	21.0	230	29.6
1991	823	206	25.0	269	32.7	160	19.4	188	22.8
1990	746	181	24.3	255	34.2	162	21.7	148	19.8
1989	733	150	20.5	205	28.0	201	27.4	177	24.1
1988	734	121	16.5	229	31.2	181	24.7	203	27.7
1987	699	121	17.3	195	27.9	231	33.0	152	21.7
1986	614	114	18.6	164	26.7	171	27.9	165	26.9
1985	570	111	19.5	175	30.7	157	27.5	127	22.3
1984	561	88	15.7	146	26.0	191	34.0	136	24.2
1983	573	119	20.8	166	29.0	154	26.9	134	23.4
1982	600	92	15.3	198	33.0	167	27.8	143	23.8
1981	606	100	16.5	220	36.3	157	25.9	129	21.3
1980	597	89	14.9	233	39.0	138	23.1	137	22.9
1979	507	78	15.4	157	31.0	148	29.2	124	24.5
1978	478	61	12.8	183	38.3	125	26.2	109	22.8
1977	515	86	16.7	168	32.6	138	26.8	123	23.9
1976	534	98	18.4	164	30.7	129	24.2	143	26.8
1975	489	97	19.8	147	30.1	127	26.0	118	24.1
1974	467	99	21.2	139	29.8	117	25.1	112	24.0
1973	387	70	18.1	142	36.7	93	24.0	82	21.2
1972	381	88	23.1	117	30.7	106	27.8	70	18.4

Male

2019	1,014	235	23.2	102	10.0	268	26.5	409	40.4
2018	1,036	222	21.5	139	13.4	282	27.2	392	37.9
2017	982	209	21.3	113	11.5	247	25.1	413	42.0

* = Quantity zero or rounds to zero.
Note: High school graduates are people who have completed 4 years of high school or more, for 1967 to 1991. Beginning in 1992, they were people whose highest degree was a high school diploma (including equivalency) or higher.
[1] Starting in 2003 respondents could identify more than one race. Except as noted, the race data in this table from 2003 onward represent those respondents who indicated only one race category.
[2] The data shown prior to 2003 consists of those identifying themselves as "Asian or Pacific Islanders."

Table A-15. Population 18 and 19 Years Old, by School Enrollment Status, Sex, Race, and Hispanic Origin, October 1967–2019—*Continued*

(Numbers in thousands; percent; civilian noninstitutionalized population.)

Year, race, and Hispanic origin	Total	Population 18 and 19 years old								
		Still in high school	Percent	Dropped out	Percent	High school graduate only	Percent	In college	Percent
2016	894	210	23.4	90	10.0	212	23.7	383	42.8
2015	849	194	22.8	108	12.8	232	27.3	315	37.1
2014	958	206	21.5	105	10.9	263	27.4	385	40.2
2013	953	233	24.4	98	10.3	326	34.2	295	31.0
2012	950	252	26.5	143	15.1	183	19.2	372	39.2
2011	952	229	24.1	102	10.7	269	28.3	351	36.9
2010	896	201	22.4	97	10.9	217	24.2	381	42.5
2009	853	200	23.4	129	15.2	282	33.0	242	28.4
2008	779	190	24.4	141	18.1	212	27.2	236	30.3
2007	780	185	23.7	145	18.5	205	26.3	246	31.5
2006	708	152	21.4	150	21.2	193	27.3	213	30.1
2005	663	166	25.1	144	21.7	180	27.1	173	26.2
2004	668	117	17.5	214	32.0	166	24.9	171	25.6
2003	635	142	22.4	161	25.4	179	28.2	153	24.1
2002	716	191	26.7	200	27.9	169	23.6	156	21.8
2001	701	131	18.7	254	36.2	167	23.8	149	21.3
2000	656	154	23.5	183	27.9	159	24.2	160	24.4
1999	642	148	23.1	180	28.0	171	26.6	143	22.3
1998	598	104	17.4	234	39.1	163	27.3	97	16.2
1997	579	130	22.5	162	28.0	154	26.6	133	23.0
1996	506	139	27.5	154	30.4	115	22.7	98	19.4
1995	535	132	24.7	145	27.1	137	25.6	121	22.6
1994	454	157	34.6	118	26.0	90	19.8	89	19.6
1993	325	86	26.5	105	32.3	65	20.0	69	21.2
1992	385	110	28.6	99	25.7	83	21.6	93	24.2
1991	416	107	25.7	161	38.7	80	19.2	68	16.3
1990	358	76	21.2	141	39.4	71	19.8	70	19.6
1989	371	89	24.0	96	25.9	111	29.9	75	20.2
1988	364	88	24.2	128	35.2	73	20.1	75	20.6
1987	333	66	19.8	105	31.5	86	25.8	76	22.8
1986	326	58	17.8	95	29.1	86	26.4	87	26.7
1985	275	62	22.5	116	42.2	53	19.3	44	16.0
1984	249	55	22.1	65	26.1	87	34.9	42	16.9
1983	266	66	24.8	87	32.7	72	27.1	41	15.4
1982	304	69	22.7	106	34.9	77	25.3	52	17.1
1981	288	47	16.3	127	44.1	57	19.8	57	19.8
1980	310	46	14.8	134	43.2	62	20.0	68	21.9
1979	256	42	16.4	89	34.8	58	22.7	67	26.2
1978	221	35	15.8	81	36.7	52	23.5	53	24.0
1977	238	49	20.6	80	33.6	55	23.1	54	22.7
1976	258	51	19.8	82	31.8	56	21.7	69	26.7
1975	229	66	28.8	60	26.2	50	21.8	53	23.1
1974	222	49	22.1	78	35.1	40	18.0	55	24.8
1973	190	48	25.3	62	32.6	41	21.6	39	20.5
1972	190	49	25.8	67	35.3	46	24.2	28	14.7
Female									
2019	1,018	187	18.4	69	6.7	299	29.4	463	45.5
2018	970	161	16.6	70	7.2	241	24.9	498	51.3
2017	983	181	18.4	67	6.9	216	22.0	518	52.7
2016	930	154	16.6	56	6.1	218	23.5	501	53.9
2015	912	179	19.6	72	7.9	200	21.9	461	50.5
2014	950	172	18.1	78	8.2	228	24.0	472	49.7
2013	936	160	17.1	86	9.1	259	27.6	432	46.2
2012	921	197	21.0	79	8.6	191	20.7	454	49.3
2011	791	142	17.9	64	8.1	172	21.7	414	52.4
2010	872	188	21.5	82	9.4	201	23.0	402	46.1
2009	827	209	25.3	132	15.9	179	21.6	308	37.2
2008	760	130	17.1	156	20.5	183	24.0	292	38.4
2007	743	126	17.0	109	14.7	193	26.1	313	42.2
2006	698	156	22.3	102	14.7	209	30.0	231	33.1
2005	591	105	17.8	83	14.0	171	28.9	232	39.3
2004	602	127	21.1	82	13.6	180	29.9	213	35.4
2003	579	87	15.0	130	22.5	136	23.5	226	39.0

* = Quantity zero or rounds to zero.
Note: High school graduates are people who have completed 4 years of high school or more, for 1967 to 1991. Beginning in 1992, they were people whose highest degree was a high school diploma (including equivalency) or higher.
[1] Starting in 2003 respondents could identify more than one race. Except as noted, the race data in this table from 2003 onward represent those respondents who indicated only one race category.
[2] The data shown prior to 2003 consists of those identifying themselves as "Asian or Pacific Islanders."

Table A-15. Population 18 and 19 Years Old, by School Enrollment Status, Sex, Race, and Hispanic Origin, October 1967–2019—*Continued*

(Numbers in thousands; percent; civilian noninstitutionalized population.)

Year, race, and Hispanic origin	Total	Population 18 and 19 years old							
		Still in high school	Percent	Dropped out	Percent	High school graduate only	Percent	In college	Percent
2002............................	593	112	18.9	110	18.5	167	28.2	204	34.4
2001............................	691	116	16.8	145	21.0	192	27.8	238	34.4
2000............................	591	114	19.3	128	21.7	161	27.2	188	31.8
1999............................	577	99	17.2	157	27.2	168	29.1	153	26.5
1998............................	611	95	15.5	169	27.7	156	25.5	191	31.3
1997............................	508	91	17.9	112	22.0	122	24.0	183	36.0
1996............................	494	91	18.4	140	28.3	121	24.5	142	28.7
1995............................	478	71	14.9	167	34.9	97	20.3	143	29.9
1994............................	471	93	19.7	119	25.3	123	26.1	136	28.9
1993............................	385	74	19.2	96	24.9	89	23.1	126	32.7
1992............................	393	78	19.8	98	24.9	80	20.4	137	34.9
1991............................	407	98	24.1	109	26.8	80	19.7	120	29.5
1990............................	388	105	27.1	114	29.4	91	23.5	78	20.1
1989............................	362	60	16.6	108	29.8	91	25.1	103	28.5
1988............................	370	32	8.6	101	27.3	108	29.2	129	34.9
1987............................	367	58	15.8	89	24.3	144	39.2	76	20.7
1986............................	288	54	18.8	69	24.0	86	29.9	79	27.4
1985............................	296	51	17.2	59	19.9	104	35.1	82	27.7
1984............................	311	33	10.6	81	26.0	103	33.1	94	30.2
1983............................	307	53	17.3	79	25.7	82	26.7	93	30.3
1982............................	296	23	7.8	92	31.1	90	30.4	91	30.7
1981............................	318	53	16.7	93	29.2	100	31.4	72	22.6
1980............................	287	44	15.3	99	34.5	76	26.5	68	23.7
1979............................	251	35	13.9	68	27.1	90	35.9	58	23.1
1978............................	257	26	10.1	102	39.7	73	28.4	56	21.8
1977............................	277	37	13.4	88	31.8	82	29.6	70	25.3
1976............................	276	49	17.8	81	29.3	72	26.1	74	26.8
1975............................	261	32	12.3	87	33.3	77	29.5	65	24.9
1974............................	245	50	20.4	62	25.3	77	31.4	56	22.9
1973............................	197	21	10.7	80	40.6	52	26.4	44	22.3
1972............................	191	37	19.4	50	26.2	61	31.9	43	22.5
WHITE ALONE OR IN COMBINATION									
Both Sexes									
2019............................	6,425	1,231	19.2	363	5.6	1,732	26.9	3,100	48.3
2018............................	6,488	1,157	17.8	432	6.7	1,563	24.1	3,336	51.4
2017............................	6,408	1,241	19.4	461	7.2	1,585	24.7	3,121	48.7
2016............................	6,392	1,139	17.8	383	6.0	1,554	24.3	3,316	51.9
2015............................	6,376	1,204	18.9	489	7.7	1,519	23.8	3,163	49.6
2014............................	6,450	1,238	19.2	467	7.2	1,592	24.7	3,154	48.9
2013............................	6,502	1,235	19.0	414	6.4	1,728	26.6	3,124	48.0
2012............................	6,539	1,331	20.0	437	6.7	1,627	24.9	3,144	48.1
2011............................	6,686	1,309	19.6	455	6.8	1,540	23.0	3,381	50.6
2010............................	6,679	1,195	17.9	450	6.7	1,556	23.3	3,478	52.1
2009............................	6,780	1,227	18.1	538	7.9	1,601	23.6	3,414	50.3
2008............................	6,762	1,093	16.2	581	8.6	1,647	24.4	3,440	50.9
2007............................	6,595	1,108	16.8	525	8.0	1,644	24.9	3,318	50.3
2006............................	6,466	1,160	17.9	615	9.5	1,648	25.5	3,043	47.1
2005............................	6,078	1,064	17.5	537	8.8	1,434	23.6	3,043	50.1
2004............................	6,191	988	16.0	643	10.4	1,548	25.0	3,012	48.7
2003............................	6,093	994	16.3	675	11.1	1,519	24.9	2,905	47.7
Male									
2019............................	3,240	726	22.4	218	6.7	908	28.0	1,389	42.9
2018............................	3,299	661	20.0	289	8.8	839	25.4	1,510	45.8
2017............................	3,233	747	23.1	276	8.5	839	26.0	1,370	42.4
2016............................	3,233	664	20.5	209	6.5	813	25.1	1,547	47.8
2015............................	3,232	639	19.8	289	8.9	832	25.7	1,472	45.5
2014............................	3,292	694	21.1	252	7.7	913	27.7	1,433	43.5
2013............................	3,327	743	22.3	209	6.3	943	28.3	1,433	43.1
2012............................	3,364	779	22.9	254	7.5	902	26.8	1,429	42.5
2011............................	3,457	776	22.4	247	7.1	881	25.5	1,554	44.9

* = Quantity zero or rounds to zero.
Note: High school graduates are people who have completed 4 years of high school or more, for 1967 to 1991. Beginning in 1992, they were people whose highest degree was a high school diploma (including equivalency) or higher.
[1] Starting in 2003 respondents could identify more than one race. Except as noted, the race data in this table from 2003 onward represent those respondents who indicated only one race category.
[2] The data shown prior to 2003 consists of those identifying themselves as "Asian or Pacific Islanders."

Table A-15. Population 18 and 19 Years Old, by School Enrollment Status, Sex, Race, and Hispanic Origin, October 1967–2019—*Continued*

(Numbers in thousands; percent; civilian noninstitutionalized population.)

Year, race, and Hispanic origin	Total	Still in high school	Percent	Dropped out	Percent	High school graduate only	Percent	In college	Percent
2010.............................	3,396	674	19.8	251	7.4	852	25.1	1,620	47.7
2009.............................	3,422	665	19.4	297	8.7	925	27.0	1,535	44.9
2008.............................	3,435	605	17.6	305	8.9	917	26.7	1,607	46.8
2007.............................	3,350	684	20.4	284	8.5	842	25.1	1,540	46.0
2006.............................	3,278	657	20.0	357	10.9	864	26.4	1,399	42.7
2005.............................	3,149	692	22.0	321	10.2	765	24.3	1,371	43.5
2004.............................	3,129	538	17.2	415	13.3	845	27.0	1,331	42.5
2003.............................	3,078	604	19.6	390	12.7	801	26.0	1,283	41.7
Female									
2019.............................	3,185	505	15.9	145	4.5	824	25.9	1,712	53.7
2018.............................	3,189	496	15.5	143	4.5	724	22.7	1,826	57.3
2017.............................	3,174	494	15.6	185	5.8	745	23.5	1,751	55.1
2016.............................	3,159	475	15.0	174	5.5	741	23.5	1,770	56.0
2015.............................	3,144	565	18.0	200	6.4	687	21.9	1,691	53.8
2014.............................	3,159	544	17.2	215	6.8	679	21.5	1,720	54.5
2013.............................	3,174	492	15.5	206	6.5	786	24.7	1,691	53.3
2012.............................	3,175	552	16.9	183	5.8	725	22.8	1,715	54.0
2011.............................	3,228	533	16.5	209	6.5	659	20.4	1,828	56.6
2010.............................	3,282	521	15.9	200	6.1	704	21.4	1,858	56.6
2009.............................	3,358	562	16.7	242	7.2	676	20.1	1,879	55.9
2008.............................	3,328	488	14.7	277	8.3	730	21.9	1,833	55.1
2007.............................	3,245	424	13.1	241	7.4	801	24.7	1,779	54.8
2006.............................	3,188	503	15.8	258	8.1	784	24.6	1,643	51.5
2005.............................	2,929	372	12.7	216	7.4	669	22.8	1,672	57.1
2004.............................	3,062	450	14.7	228	7.4	702	22.9	1,682	54.9
2003.............................	3,015	390	12.9	284	9.4	719	23.8	1,622	53.8
BLACK ALONE OR IN COMBINATION									
Both Sexes									
2019.............................	1,373	255	18.5	84	6.1	444	32.4	591	43.0
2018.............................	1,411	336	23.8	76	5.4	388	27.5	611	43.3
2017.............................	1,414	349	24.7	78	5.5	391	27.6	597	42.2
2016.............................	1,399	338	24.2	99	7.1	360	25.7	602	43.1
2015.............................	1,370	326	23.8	90	6.5	394	28.8	560	40.8
2014.............................	1,384	345	24.9	106	7.7	380	27.5	553	39.9
2013.............................	1,420	399	28.1	101	7.1	411	29.0	509	35.9
2012.............................	1,461	426	28.9	117	8.0	340	23.3	579	39.6
2011.............................	1,381	409	29.6	65	4.7	292	21.2	615	44.5
2010.............................	1,439	287	20.0	158	11.0	371	25.8	622	43.2
2009.............................	1,450	335	23.1	191	13.1	321	22.1	604	41.7
2008.............................	1,431	339	23.7	155	10.8	422	29.5	515	36.0
2007.............................	1,347	306	22.7	116	8.6	395	29.3	530	39.3
2006.............................	1,287	343	26.6	111	8.6	341	26.5	492	38.2
2005.............................	1,195	266	22.3	112	9.4	336	28.1	481	40.2
2004.............................	1,163	229	19.7	163	14.0	305	26.2	466	40.1
2003.............................	1,129	288	25.5	131	11.6	310	27.5	400	35.4
Male									
2019.............................	677	150	22.1	42	6.2	218	32.2	267	39.4
2018.............................	692	186	26.9	31	4.5	198	28.6	277	40.0
2017.............................	701	172	24.5	53	7.5	208	29.7	269	38.3
2016.............................	686	208	30.4	64	9.3	163	23.8	250	36.5
2015.............................	661	167	25.3	49	7.4	186	28.1	259	39.2
2014.............................	679	222	32.8	66	9.7	198	29.2	192	28.4
2013.............................	700	206	29.4	62	8.9	222	31.7	210	30.0
2012.............................	744	213	28.6	94	12.6	194	26.0	244	32.7
2011.............................	681	238	35.0	44	6.5	149	21.9	250	36.6
2010.............................	700	170	24.3	86	12.3	180	25.7	264	37.7
2009.............................	708	182	25.8	110	15.5	171	24.1	245	34.6
2008.............................	706	191	27.0	58	8.3	238	33.7	219	31.1
2007.............................	657	164	25.0	56	8.5	197	30.0	240	36.5

* = Quantity zero or rounds to zero.

Note: High school graduates are people who have completed 4 years of high school or more, for 1967 to 1991. Beginning in 1992, they were people whose highest degree was a high school diploma (including equivalency) or higher.

[1] Starting in 2003 respondents could identify more than one race. Except as noted, the race data in this table from 2003 onward represent those respondents who indicated only one race category.

[2] The data shown prior to 2003 consists of those identifying themselves as "Asian or Pacific Islanders."

Table A-15.　Population 18 and 19 Years Old, by School Enrollment Status, Sex, Race, and Hispanic Origin, October 1967–2019—*Continued*

(Numbers in thousands; percent; civilian noninstitutionalized population.)

Year, race, and Hispanic origin	Total	Population 18 and 19 years old							
		Still in high school	Percent	Dropped out	Percent	High school graduate only	Percent	In college	Percent
2006............................	623	213	34.3	45	7.3	178	28.6	186	29.8
2005............................	586	187	31.8	62	10.7	136	23.2	201	34.3
2004............................	549	142	25.9	93	17.0	139	25.3	175	31.9
2003............................	525	146	27.8	81	15.4	123	23.4	175	33.3
Female									
2019............................	696	105	15.0	42	6.0	226	32.5	324	46.5
2018............................	719	150	20.8	45	6.2	190	26.4	334	46.5
2017............................	713	177	24.9	25	3.5	182	25.6	328	46.0
2016............................	713	130	18.2	35	4.9	197	27.6	352	49.3
2015............................	709	159	22.4	41	5.8	209	29.5	300	42.3
2014............................	705	122	17.3	41	5.7	182	25.8	360	51.1
2013............................	720	193	26.8	38	5.3	189	26.3	299	41.6
2012............................	717	213	29.1	23	3.2	146	20.4	335	46.7
2011............................	699	170	24.3	21	3.0	143	20.5	365	52.2
2010............................	739	117	15.9	72	9.8	192	25.9	358	48.4
2009............................	742	152	20.5	81	11.3	150	20.2	359	48.4
2008............................	724	148	20.5	96	13.3	184	25.4	296	40.8
2007............................	690	142	20.6	61	8.8	198	28.6	290	42.0
2006............................	665	130	19.5	66	9.9	163	24.5	307	46.1
2005............................	609	80	13.1	49	8.1	200	32.8	280	45.9
2004............................	615	86	14.0	70	11.4	169	27.5	290	47.2
2003............................	604	142	23.5	51	8.4	186	30.8	225	37.3
ASIAN ALONE OR IN COMBINATION									
Both Sexes									
2019............................	546	102	18.7	22	4.1	53	9.7	368	67.5
2018............................	523	63	12.0	11	2.1	89	17.0	360	68.9
2017............................	433	63	14.5	11	2.6	62	14.3	297	68.7
2016............................	487	69	14.2	17	3.6	88	18.1	313	64.2
2015............................	430	71	16.5	24	5.6	48	11.1	287	66.8
2014............................	407	53	13.0	*	*	58	14.1	296	72.8
2013............................	529	89	16.7	9	1.7	81	15.4	350	66.2
2012............................	436	71	16.4	23	5.2	67	15.4	274	63.0
2011............................	399	55	13.6	13	3.1	66	16.4	267	66.8
2010............................	369	39	10.5	13	3.6	53	14.4	264	71.5
2009............................	384	74	19.3	3	0.9	35	9.0	271	70.8
2008............................	309	52	16.8	7	2.3	37	11.8	214	69.1
2007............................	336	58	17.2	12	3.7	34	10.0	232	69.1
2006............................	318	47	14.8	9	2.8	47	14.9	215	67.5
2005............................	286	42	14.7	4	1.3	36	12.6	204	71.5
2004............................	299	36	12.0	14	4.5	46	15.4	203	67.9
2003............................	320	43	13.4	3	1.1	38	11.9	236	73.8
Male									
2019............................	255	54	21.3	7	2.9	21	8.3	172	67.5
2018............................	268	33	12.2	8	3.0	55	20.5	172	64.3
2017............................	220	43	19.4	3	1.3	41	18.7	133	60.6
2016............................	244	27	11.2	10	3.9	48	19.8	159	65.2
2015............................	213	32	15.1	18	8.3	22	10.3	141	66.3
2014............................	206	29	14.3	*	*	30	14.8	146	71.0
2013............................	265	48	18.0	1	0.2	46	17.3	171	64.5
2012............................	225	42	18.6	14	6.3	26	11.4	143	63.7
2011............................	214	33	15.5	*	*	36	16.7	145	67.9
2010............................	196	17	8.6	9	4.6	34	17.2	136	69.5
2009............................	188	34	18.3	1	0.3	16	8.3	138	73.2
2008............................	150	41	27.6	6	4.3	9	6.0	93	62.1
2007............................	161	33	20.7	2	1.0	14	8.4	113	69.9
2006............................	179	22	12.4	8	4.3	31	17.5	118	65.8
2005............................	152	30	19.5	3	1.7	22	14.5	97	64.1
2004............................	149	27	18.1	5	3.2	20	13.4	97	65.1
2003............................	144	17	11.8	3	2.3	12	8.3	112	77.8

* = Quantity zero or rounds to zero.
Note: High school graduates are people who have completed 4 years of high school or more, for 1967 to 1991. Beginning in 1992, they were people whose highest degree was a high school diploma (including equivalency) or higher.
[1] Starting in 2003 respondents could identify more than one race. Except as noted, the race data in this table from 2003 onward represent those respondents who indicated only one race category.
[2] The data shown prior to 2003 consists of those identifying themselves as "Asian or Pacific Islanders."

Table A-15. Population 18 and 19 Years Old, by School Enrollment Status, Sex, Race, and Hispanic Origin, October 1967–2019—*Continued*

(Numbers in thousands; percent; civilian noninstitutionalized population.)

Year, race, and Hispanic origin	Total	Population 18 and 19 years old							
		Still in high school	Percent	Dropped out	Percent	High school graduate only	Percent	In college	Percent
Female									
2019.............................	291	48	16.4	15	5.2	32	10.9	196	67.5
2018.............................	255	30	11.8	3	1.1	34	13.4	187	73.7
2017.............................	213	20	9.4	8	3.9	21	9.7	164	77.1
2016.............................	243	42	17.2	8	3.2	40	16.3	153	63.3
2015.............................	217	39	18.0	6	2.9	26	11.9	146	67.3
2014.............................	201	24	11.8	*	*	27	13.5	150	74.7
2013.............................	263	41	15.5	8	3.1	35	13.4	179	68.0
2012.............................	210	30	14.1	8	4.0	41	19.7	131	62.2
2011.............................	186	21	11.6	13	6.8	30	16.1	122	65.6
2010.............................	174	22	12.6	4	2.5	20	11.3	128	73.7
2009.............................	196	40	20.4	3	1.5	19	9.7	134	68.4
2008.............................	159	11	6.6	*	0.3	28	17.3	121	75.8
2007.............................	174	24	13.9	11	6.3	20	11.5	119	68.3
2006.............................	139	25	18.0	1	0.8	16	11.4	97	69.7
2005.............................	134	12	9.2	1	0.9	14	10.4	107	80.0
2004.............................	150	8	5.3	9	5.9	27	18.0	106	70.7
2003.............................	176	25	14.2	*	*	27	15.3	124	70.5

* = Quantity zero or rounds to zero.

Note: High school graduates are people who have completed 4 years of high school or more, for 1967 to 1991. Beginning in 1992, they were people whose highest degree was a high school diploma (including equivalency) or higher.

[1] Starting in 2003 respondents could identify more than one race. Except as noted, the race data in this table from 2003 onward represent those respondents who indicated only one race category.

[2] The data shown prior to 2003 consists of those identifying themselves as "Asian or Pacific Islanders."

Table A-16. Age Distribution of College Students 14 Years Old and Over, by Sex, October 1947–2019

(Numbers in thousands; civilian noninstitutionalized population.)

Year, sex, race, and Hispanic origin	All students								Male							
	Total	14 to 17 years	18 and 19 years	20 and 21 years	22 to 24 years	25 to 29 years	30 to 34 years	35 years and over	Total	14 to 17 years	18 and 19 years	20 and 21 years	22 to 24 years	25 to 29 years	30 to 34 years	35 years and over
ALL RACES																
2019	18,289	251	4,004	4,495	3,436	2,456	1,290	2,358	8,067	102	1,822	2,123	1,497	1,133	508	880
2018	18,908	212	4,220	4,396	3,481	2,862	1,338	2,399	8,373	86	1,911	2,076	1,600	1,280	562	858
2017	18,398	236	3,943	4,367	3,627	2,674	1,207	2,346	8,112	85	1,746	2,025	1,688	1,188	526	853
2016	19,196	241	4,171	4,417	3,733	2,882	1,336	2,417	8,644	80	1,944	2,085	1,771	1,264	574	927
2015	19,101	222	3,978	4,505	3,669	2,805	1,370	2,551	8,484	108	1,838	2,113	1,743	1,238	565	878
2014	19,175	234	4,036	4,218	3,878	2,722	1,267	2,820	8,629	126	1,779	2,090	1,808	1,283	509	1,036
2013	19,467	308	3,951	4,326	3,925	2,715	1,351	2,891	8,536	148	1,809	2,001	1,819	1,253	522	983
2012	19,930	269	4,015	4,562	3,879	2,817	1,516	2,871	8,602	130	1,803	2,049	1,878	1,194	576	972
2011	20,397	203	4,242	4,459	3,869	3,066	1,551	3,007	9,132	108	1,949	2,127	1,877	1,343	643	1,084
2010	20,275	229	4,364	4,348	3,501	2,992	1,632	3,210	9,007	94	2,009	2,108	1,580	1,396	659	1,160
2009	19,764	206	4,289	4,034	3,749	2,769	1,524	3,193	8,642	89	1,928	1,943	1,770	1,194	649	1,069
2008	18,632	241	4,126	3,920	3,420	2,657	1,356	2,911	8,311	133	1,909	1,908	1,566	1,229	577	989
2007	17,956	186	4,075	3,794	3,292	2,496	1,342	2,772	7,826	76	1,903	1,729	1,524	1,029	596	968
2006	17,232	212	3,746	3,675	3,166	2,312	1,346	2,776	7,506	79	1,703	1,682	1,489	1,033	537	982
2005	17,472	181	3,727	3,945	3,162	2,291	1,309	2,857	7,539	62	1,675	1,878	1,420	923	562	1,019
2004	17,383	198	3,685	3,777	3,149	2,403	1,287	2,884	7,575	75	1,610	1,811	1,444	1,068	533	1,033
2003¹	16,638	150	3,512	3,533	3,320	2,164	1,330	2,630	7,318	61	1,568	1,551	1,578	982	607	970
2002	16,497	195	3,581	3,525	2,927	2,093	1,308	2,867	7,240	80	1,635	1,640	1,354	918	542	1,071
2001	15,873	138	3,478	3,421	2,731	2,084	1,337	2,685	6,875	54	1,570	1,579	1,287	917	559	908
2000	15,314	149	3,599	3,169	2,683	1,962	1,244	2,507	6,682	61	1,570	1,472	1,300	844	517	918
1999	15,203	151	3,520	3,120	2,620	1,940	1,155	2,697	6,956	78	1,648	1,525	1,224	911	547	1,023
1998	15,546	123	3,670	3,092	2,561	2,148	1,266	2,685	6,905	48	1,667	1,517	1,219	979	521	953
1997	15,436	171	3,362	3,143	2,699	2,154	1,116	2,791	6,843	59	1,561	1,521	1,292	1,052	457	899
1996	15,226	237	3,309	2,907	2,551	2,215	1,228	2,778	6,820	97	1,489	1,379	1,319	1,038	485	1,013
1995	14,715	158	3,101	2,940	2,498	2,143	1,206	2,669	6,703	68	1,431	1,423	1,235	1,008	553	985
1994²	15,022	150	3,051	3,028	2,650	2,026	1,393	2,725	6,764	65	1,416	1,414	1,322	972	617	958
1993r	14,394	130	3,070	2,892	2,668	1,914	1,226	2,493	6,599	55	1,407	1,405	1,425	892	534	880
1993	13,898	123	2,926	2,734	2,533	1,867	1,227	2,488	6,324	52	1,337	1,312	1,345	872	534	873
1992	14,035	205	2,892	2,938	2,512	1,829	1,296	2,364	6,192	97	1,325	1,344	1,243	845	547	789
1991	14,057	132	2,929	2,939	2,304	1,983	1,302	2,468	6,439	49	1,326	1,390	1,238	1,018	587	832
1990	13,621	178	3,019	2,767	2,178	1,927	1,235	2,319	6,192	86	1,443	1,364	1,115	910	502	772
1989	13,180	183	3,066	2,570	2,168	1,889	1,192	2,112	5,950	73	1,422	1,228	1,067	926	517	716
1988	13,116	182	3,046	2,681	2,064	1,735	1,228	2,179	5,950	58	1,365	1,295	1,110	835	560	727
1987	12,719	239	3,045	2,642	2,006	1,826	1,159	1,802	6,030	116	1,483	1,350	1,034	921	500	625
1986	12,651	201	2,967	2,374	2,136	1,860	1,245	1,867	5,957	82	1,421	1,161	1,120	968	577	628
1985	12,524	262	2,907	2,616	2,014	1,884	1,180	1,661	5,906	131	1,349	1,313	1,087	942	522	561
1984	12,304	253	2,867	2,597	2,127	1,857	1,158	1,445	5,989	91	1,373	1,337	1,219	965	527	476
1983	12,320	260	2,940	2,495	2,042	1,921	1,167	1,495	6,010	108	1,340	1,310	1,170	1,055	521	506
1982	12,308	254	2,929	2,689	2,060	1,859	1,129	1,389	5,899	112	1,376	1,346	1,115	968	492	490
1981	12,127	232	3,044	2,545	1,986	1,717	1,211	1,393	5,825	96	1,450	1,239	1,144	909	533	453
1980	11,387	249	2,933	2,423	1,870	1,641	1,062	1,207	5,430	96	1,369	1,246	989	853	472	405
1979	11,380	311	2,844	2,353	1,794	1,679	996	1,402	5,480	129	1,341	1,192	975	893	463	487
1978	11,141	274	2,899	2,298	1,798	1,619	950	1,303	5,580	106	1,391	1,202	1,028	922	474	457
1977	11,546	274	2,913	2,430	1,799	1,809	992	1,329	5,889	112	1,396	1,280	1,036	1,035	511	520
1976	11,139	281	2,937	2,398	1,846	1,686	803	1,189	5,785	105	1,391	1,209	1,073	1,067	451	489
1975	10,880	293	2,943	2,313	1,679	1,616	853	1,183	5,911	128	1,426	1,256	1,011	1,025	496	569
1974	9,852	309	2,597	2,192	1,527	1,482	720	1,025	5,402	145	1,262	1,206	943	951	420	476
1973	8,966	295	2,517	2,073	1,465	1,278	551	787	5,048	121	1,293	1,130	937	867	329	371
1972	9,096	295	2,680	2,116	1,461	1,229	531	783	5,218	141	1,366	1,170	998	848	330	365
1971	8,087	284	2,726	1,997	1,487	1,067	527	NA	4,850	129	1,444	1,090	1,065	787	334	NA
1970	7,413	260	2,594	1,857	1,354	939	410	NA	4,401	130	1,346	1,083	902	684	256	NA
1969	7,435	242	2,601	1,945	1,294	918	435	NA	4,448	120	1,397	1,112	883	671	265	NA
1968	6,801	281	2,501	1,826	1,029	790	373	NA	4,124	134	1,357	1,093	702	603	236	NA
1967	6,401	239	2,286	1,816	998	707	356	NA	3,841	96	1,198	1,066	718	524	239	NA
1966	6,085	254	2,440	1,472	987	679	254	NA	3,749	105	1,355	899	722	494	174	NA
1965	5,675	264	2,215	1,326	940	614	316	NA	3,503	113	1,218	804	699	458	211	NA
1964	4,643	291	1,616	1,287	670	523	256	NA	2,888	165	866	769	510	396	182	NA
1963	4,336	180	1,504	1,212	717	482	241	NA	2,742	99	796	734	574	365	174	NA

NA = Not available.

r = Revised, controlled to 1990 census based population estimates; previous 1993 data controlled to 1980 census based population estimates.

¹ Starting in 2003 respondents could identify more than one race. Except as noted, the race data in this table from 2003 onward represent those respondents who indicated only one race category.

² The data shown prior to 2003 consists of those identifying themselves as "Asian or Pacific Islanders."

³ Total excludes age groups where "NA" appears in the column. This applies to people 35 and over prior to 1972 for the total population, prior to 1973 for the White alone population and the Black alone population, and prior to 1986 for the Hispanic population. Data for 1950 exclude persons aged 30 and over.

⁴ Data for 1955 to 1963 are for Black and other races.

⁵ This series was discontinued in 2006.

Table A-16. Age Distribution of College Students 14 Years Old and Over, by Sex, October 1947–2019—*Continued*

(Numbers in thousands; civilian noninstitutionalized population.)

Year, sex, race, and Hispanic origin	Female							
	Total	14 to 17 years	18 and 19 years	20 and 21 years	22 to 24 years	25 to 29 years	30 to 34 years	35 years and over
ALL RACES								
2019	10,223	149	2,181	2,372	1,939	1,322	782	1,478
2018	10,534	126	2,309	2,320	1,881	1,582	776	1,540
2017	10,287	151	2,197	2,341	1,939	1,486	681	1,492
2016	10,551	161	2,227	2,331	1,962	1,618	762	1,490
2015	10,617	113	2,141	2,392	1,927	1,567	805	1,673
2014	10,546	108	2,257	2,128	2,070	1,439	758	1,784
2013	10,931	159	2,142	2,325	2,105	1,462	829	1,908
2012	11,327	139	2,212	2,513	2,001	1,623	940	1,900
2011	11,266	95	2,293	2,333	1,992	1,722	908	1,923
2010	11,268	135	2,355	2,240	1,920	1,596	973	2,049
2009	11,123	116	2,361	2,091	1,980	1,575	875	2,124
2008	10,321	108	2,217	2,013	1,854	1,428	779	1,922
2007	10,130	109	2,172	2,065	1,768	1,466	746	1,804
2006	9,726	133	2,043	1,993	1,677	1,278	809	1,793
2005	9,934	119	2,052	2,067	1,742	1,368	747	1,838
2004	9,808	123	2,074	1,966	1,705	1,335	753	1,850
2003[1]	9,319	89	1,944	1,982	1,742	1,181	723	1,660
2002	9,258	116	1,946	1,885	1,573	1,175	766	1,797
2001	8,998	84	1,907	1,841	1,444	1,167	778	1,776
2000	8,631	88	2,029	1,697	1,383	1,118	728	1,589
1999	8,247	73	1,872	1,595	1,396	1,029	608	1,674
1998	8,641	74	2,003	1,574	1,342	1,170	745	1,732
1997	8,593	112	1,801	1,622	1,406	1,102	658	1,892
1996	8,406	140	1,821	1,528	1,233	1,177	743	1,765
1995	8,013	90	1,671	1,518	1,263	1,135	653	1,684
1994[2]	8,258	85	1,635	1,613	1,328	1,054	776	1,766
1993r	7,795	75	1,663	1,487	1,243	1,022	692	1,613
1993	7,574	71	1,588	1,422	1,189	995	693	1,616
1992	7,844	107	1,566	1,594	1,269	984	748	1,575
1991	7,618	83	1,603	1,549	1,066	965	715	1,636
1990	7,429	91	1,576	1,403	1,063	1,017	732	1,546
1989	7,231	110	1,643	1,342	1,100	964	675	1,396
1988	7,166	124	1,682	1,386	953	900	668	1,452
1987	6,689	123	1,562	1,292	972	905	659	1,176
1986	6,694	120	1,546	1,213	1,016	892	667	1,240
1985	6,618	129	1,559	1,303	926	941	658	1,100
1984	6,315	161	1,494	1,260	908	892	630	970
1983	6,310	153	1,600	1,185	872	865	645	989
1982	6,410	141	1,553	1,343	945	891	637	900
1981	6,303	136	1,594	1,305	842	808	677	940
1980	5,957	153	1,565	1,178	882	788	590	802
1979	5,900	183	1,503	1,161	818	786	533	914
1978	5,559	168	1,507	1,096	770	697	476	845
1977	5,657	162	1,517	1,151	763	774	481	809
1976	5,354	176	1,546	1,189	773	619	352	700
1975	4,969	164	1,517	1,058	668	590	357	614
1974	4,449	165	1,335	986	584	531	300	548
1973	3,918	174	1,224	944	528	411	222	416
1972	3,877	153	1,314	946	464	381	200	418
1971	3,236	154	1,281	906	423	280	192	NA
1970	3,013	130	1,248	774	452	255	154	NA
1969	2,987	122	1,204	833	411	247	171	NA
1968	2,677	147	1,144	733	328	187	138	NA
1967	2,560	143	1,088	749	280	183	117	NA
1966	2,337	149	1,085	573	265	185	80	NA
1965	2,172	151	997	522	241	156	105	NA
1964	1,755	126	750	518	160	127	74	NA
1963	1,594	81	708	478	143	117	67	NA

NA = Not available.

r = Revised, controlled to 1990 census based population estimates; previous 1993 data controlled to 1980 census based population estimates.

[1] Starting in 2003 respondents could identify more than one race. Except as noted, the race data in this table from 2003 onward represent those respondents who indicated only one race category.

[2] The data shown prior to 2003 consists of those identifying themselves as "Asian or Pacific Islanders."

[3] Total excludes age groups where "NA" appears in the column.This applies to people 35 and over prior to 1972 for the total population, prior to 1973 for the White alone population and the Black alone population, and prior to 1986 for the Hispanic population.Data for 1950 exclude persons aged 30 and over.

[4] Data for 1955 to 1963 are for Black and other races.

[5] This series was discontinued in 2006.

Table A-16. Age Distribution of College Students 14 Years Old and Over, by Sex, October 1947–2019—*Continued*

(Numbers in thousands; civilian noninstitutionalized population.)

Year, sex, race, and Hispanic origin	All students Total	14 to 17 years	18 and 19 years	20 and 21 years	22 to 24 years	25 to 29 years	30 to 34 years	35 years and over	Male Total	14 to 17 years	18 and 19 years	20 and 21 years	22 to 24 years	25 to 29 years	30 to 34 years	35 years and over
1962	4,208	233	1,612	996	630	486	251	NA	2,742	125	891	617	508	406	195	NA
1961	3,731	213	1,470	892	507	437	212	NA	2,356	84	834	554	393	337	154	NA
1960	3,570	222	1,299	790	509	491	259	NA	2,339	99	734	503	411	399	193	NA
1959	3,340	210	1,175	739	489	503	224	NA	2,187	92	651	501	355	422	166	NA
1958	3,242	167	1,114	----1,221----		534	206	NA	2,129	73	621	----850----		439	146	NA
1957	3,138	176	989	----1,236----		553	184	NA	2,028	77	538	----827----		459	127	NA
1956	2,883	167	934	----1,105----		494	183	NA	1,932	77	512	----781----		429	133	NA
1955	2,379	147	745	----931----		406	150	NA	1,579	57	432	----647----		337	107	NA
1950	2,175	180	733	----939----		324	NA	NA	1,474	74	395	----692----		314	NA	NA
1947	2,311	188	620	----1,088----		321	94	NA	1,687	87	343	----872----		301	84	NA
WHITE ALONE																
2019	12,783	157	2,949	3,262	2,391	1,587	824	1,613	5,661	56	1,334	1,539	1,050	723	343	616
2018	13,323	169	3,178	3,154	2,438	1,862	875	1,647	5,980	61	1,430	1,485	1,130	830	414	629
2017	13,224	156	2,982	3,178	2,530	1,845	861	1,672	5,864	64	1,317	1,484	1,172	825	396	606
2016	13,901	166	3,170	3,289	2,647	2,041	925	1,663	6,222	55	1,470	1,549	1,247	872	385	644
2015	13,859	149	3,057	3,308	2,604	2,021	945	1,776	6,253	78	1,414	1,586	1,189	920	415	651
2014	13,953	148	3,064	3,232	2,781	1,942	888	1,898	6,398	67	1,397	1,621	1,278	927	374	733
2013	14,240	234	3,033	3,160	2,857	1,879	970	2,107	6,241	115	1,386	1,452	1,292	867	406	721
2012	14,628	204	3,077	3,427	2,798	2,048	1,002	2,072	6,392	87	1,387	1,497	1,377	892	428	725
2011	15,412	141	3,298	3,545	2,970	2,254	1,085	2,120	7,054	78	1,520	1,679	1,486	1,013	470	808
2010	15,258	154	3,398	3,297	2,629	2,217	1,197	2,366	6,883	59	1,573	1,624	1,172	1,051	511	893
2009	15,027	160	3,337	3,205	2,784	2,066	1,097	2,377	6,681	77	1,511	1,533	1,360	904	483	814
2008	14,405	171	3,353	3,119	2,669	1,952	907	2,234	6,570	85	1,566	1,524	1,250	938	413	794
2007	13,835	141	3,242	3,053	2,485	1,817	952	2,144	6,050	62	1,508	1,359	1,172	770	413	766
2006	13,273	161	2,982	2,958	2,358	1,740	985	2,090	5,829	57	1,367	1,344	1,131	799	396	734
2005	13,466	116	2,972	3,176	2,350	1,708	939	2,205	5,843	38	1,343	1,488	1,092	685	420	777
2004	13,381	134	2,946	3,016	2,389	1,776	974	2,146	5,944	49	1,308	1,437	1,110	837	421	782
2003[1]	12,870	100	2,833	2,796	2,521	1,585	960	2,075	5,714	48	1,258	1,236	1,232	723	435	783
2002	12,781	109	2,891	2,810	2,220	1,582	933	2,236	5,719	57	1,329	1,306	1,066	712	394	855
2001	12,208	88	2,755	2,774	2,019	1,514	956	2,103	5,383	36	1,273	1,305	943	693	401	731
2000	11,999	117	2,914	2,590	2,062	1,433	906	1,978	5,311	47	1,289	1,225	1,008	662	367	713
1999	12,053	87	2,849	2,520	2,077	1,475	870	2,174	5,562	33	1,336	1,226	1,024	715	414	816
1998	12,401	93	2,994	2,537	2,011	1,604	964	2,199	5,602	30	1,376	1,256	1,002	746	396	795
1997	12,442	127	2,792	2,602	2,101	1,666	856	2,298	5,552	48	1,314	1,289	1,030	802	345	725
1996	12,189	167	2,731	2,362	2,030	1,704	940	2,254	5,453	70	1,223	1,117	1,079	797	357	811
1995	12,021	116	2,577	2,437	1,997	1,745	941	2,208	5,535	44	1,195	1,201	1,002	857	432	804
1994[2]	12,222	101	2,568	2,459	2,091	1,592	1,143	2,267	5,524	44	1,212	1,140	1,054	749	512	815
1993r	11,735	103	2,566	2,356	2,152	1,507	1,003	2,049	5,403	44	1,157	1,196	1,145	705	451	705
1993	11,434	98	2,456	2,243	2,064	1,490	1,015	2,068	5,222	41	1,103	1,120	1,090	699	457	711
1992	11,710	158	2,419	2,466	2,031	1,512	1,070	2,053	5,210	82	1,102	1,162	1,027	689	471	678
1991	11,686	104	2,487	2,449	1,877	1,598	1,063	2,107	5,304	41	1,112	1,146	1,012	809	480	703
1990	11,488	132	2,548	2,341	1,746	1,638	1,060	2,023	5,235	63	1,218	1,151	923	782	434	665
1989	11,243	147	2,648	2,170	1,813	1,611	986	1,868	5,136	63	1,253	1,070	900	789	438	623
1988	11,140	137	2,639	2,270	1,750	1,425	1,023	1,896	5,078	50	1,194	1,114	952	685	470	613
1987	10,731	194	2,564	2,254	1,665	1,483	985	1,584	5,104	97	1,260	1,156	873	740	436	541
1986	10,707	173	2,549	2,015	1,743	1,580	1,037	1,609	5,074	69	1,254	982	932	835	475	528
1985	10,781	229	2,539	2,257	1,704	1,590	1,014	1,448	5,103	120	1,176	1,137	941	812	449	468
1984	10,520	209	2,541	2,206	1,779	1,566	967	1,252	5,111	73	1,224	1,143	1,039	796	434	402
1983	10,565	214	2,597	2,161	1,705	1,603	961	1,324	5,162	87	1,197	1,149	989	875	421	444
1982	10,551	216	2,549	2,348	1,697	1,581	938	1,222	5,077	95	1,189	1,188	931	831	415	428
1981	10,353	197	2,639	2,239	1,671	1,390	1,027	1,190	5,010	86	1,259	1,104	977	745	448	391
1980	9,925	212	2,578	2,131	1,625	1,413	915	1,051	4,804	79	1,232	1,114	878	735	400	366
1979	9,956	256	2,498	2,079	1,543	1,474	859	1,247	4,823	110	1,192	1,058	854	788	398	423
1978	9,661	229	2,553	1,993	1,531	1,399	808	1,148	4,913	90	1,239	1,056	900	810	413	405
1977	9,962	227	2,579	2,099	1,531	1,550	827	1,149	5,156	91	1,272	1,124	890	907	433	439
1976	9,679	237	2,577	2,108	1,591	1,458	673	1,035	5,084	89	1,244	1,073	933	936	382	427
1975	9,546	252	2,613	2,042	1,461	1,410	737	1,031	5,263	111	1,283	1,134	909	911	426	489
1974	8,689	271	2,308	1,940	1,341	1,308	613	908	4,782	128	1,143	1,067	825	855	350	414

NA = Not available.

r = Revised, controlled to 1990 census based population estimates; previous 1993 data controlled to 1980 census based population estimates.

[1] Starting in 2003 respondents could identify more than one race. Except as noted, the race data in this table from 2003 onward represent those respondents who indicated only one race category.

[2] The data shown prior to 2003 consists of those identifying themselves as "Asian or Pacific Islanders."

[3] Total excludes age groups where "NA" appears in the column. This applies to people 35 and over prior to 1972 for the total population, prior to 1973 for the White alone population and the Black alone population, and prior to 1986 for the Hispanic population. Data for 1950 exclude persons aged 30 and over.

[4] Data for 1955 to 1963 are for Black and other races.

[5] This series was discontinued in 2006.

Table A-16. Age Distribution of College Students 14 Years Old and Over, by Sex, October 1947–2019—*Continued*

(Numbers in thousands; civilian noninstitutionalized population.)

Year, sex, race, and Hispanic origin	Female							
	Total	14 to 17 years	18 and 19 years	20 and 21 years	22 to 24 years	25 to 29 years	30 to 34 years	35 years and over
1962.........................	1,466	108	721	379	122	80	56	NA
1961.........................	1,375	129	636	338	114	100	58	NA
1960.........................	1,231	123	565	287	98	92	66	NA
1959.........................	1,153	118	524	238	134	81	58	NA
1958.........................	1,113	94	493	----371----		95	60	NA
1957.........................	1,110	99	451	----409----		94	57	NA
1956.........................	951	90	422	----324----		65	50	NA
1955.........................	800	90	313	----285----		69	43	NA
1950.........................	701	106	338	----247----		10	NA	NA
1947.........................	624	101	277	----216----		20	10	NA
WHITE ALONE								
2019.........................	7,123	101	1,615	1,724	1,341	863	482	997
2018.........................	7,343	108	1,749	1,668	1,308	1,032	460	1,018
2017.........................	7,360	92	1,665	1,695	1,358	1,020	465	1,066
2016.........................	7,678	112	1,700	1,740	1,400	1,169	540	1,019
2015.........................	7,607	71	1,644	1,721	1,415	1,101	530	1,124
2014.........................	7,555	81	1,667	1,611	1,502	1,015	514	1,165
2013.........................	7,999	119	1,646	1,707	1,565	1,011	564	1,386
2012.........................	8,236	117	1,690	1,930	1,421	1,156	574	1,347
2011.........................	8,358	63	1,779	1,866	1,484	1,241	615	1,311
2010.........................	8,375	95	1,825	1,673	1,458	1,166	686	1,472
2009.........................	8,346	84	1,826	1,672	1,424	1,162	614	1,564
2008.........................	7,835	85	1,787	1,595	1,419	1,014	493	1,440
2007.........................	7,785	80	1,734	1,694	1,313	1,047	539	1,378
2006.........................	7,445	104	1,615	1,613	1,227	941	588	1,355
2005.........................	7,624	79	1,629	1,688	1,258	1,024	519	1,428
2004.........................	7,438	86	1,638	1,579	1,279	939	553	1,364
2003[1].........................	7,155	53	1,575	1,560	1,289	862	525	1,291
2002.........................	7,062	52	1,562	1,504	1,154	870	539	1,381
2001.........................	6,826	52	1,481	1,468	1,077	820	555	1,372
2000.........................	6,689	70	1,625	1,365	1,054	770	539	1,266
1999.........................	6,491	55	1,513	1,296	1,053	760	455	1,359
1998.........................	6,799	63	1,618	1,281	1,008	858	567	1,405
1997.........................	6,890	79	1,479	1,313	1,071	864	511	1,573
1996.........................	6,735	97	1,508	1,246	951	906	583	1,443
1995.........................	6,486	72	1,383	1,237	995	887	508	1,404
1994[2].........................	6,698	57	1,357	1,320	1,037	844	631	1,453
1993r.........................	6,331	59	1,409	1,160	1,007	802	552	1,344
1993.........................	6,212	57	1,353	1,123	974	791	558	1,357
1992.........................	6,499	76	1,317	1,303	1,005	823	599	1,376
1991.........................	6,382	63	1,375	1,304	865	789	583	1,404
1990.........................	6,253	69	1,331	1,190	823	856	627	1,358
1989.........................	6,107	84	1,395	1,101	913	822	548	1,245
1988.........................	6,063	87	1,445	1,156	798	740	554	1,283
1987.........................	5,627	97	1,304	1,097	791	743	550	1,044
1986.........................	5,632	105	1,295	1,033	811	745	562	1,081
1985.........................	5,679	110	1,363	1,120	764	778	565	979
1984.........................	5,410	136	1,317	1,063	740	770	533	851
1983.........................	5,404	127	1,400	1,012	717	728	540	880
1982.........................	5,472	120	1,360	1,159	766	749	523	795
1981.........................	5,342	111	1,380	1,134	694	646	578	799
1980.........................	5,121	133	1,346	1,017	747	678	514	686
1979.........................	5,131	146	1,306	1,021	688	686	461	823
1978.........................	4,748	139	1,314	937	631	590	395	742
1977.........................	4,806	135	1,307	975	641	643	394	711
1976.........................	4,593	147	1,334	1,034	658	521	291	608
1975.........................	4,284	141	1,330	908	552	500	311	542
1974.........................	3,907	143	1,166	873	516	453	263	493

NA = Not available.

r = Revised, controlled to 1990 census based population estimates; previous 1993 data controlled to 1980 census based population estimates.

[1] Starting in 2003 respondents could identify more than one race. Except as noted, the race data in this table from 2003 onward represent those respondents who indicated only one race category.

[2] The data shown prior to 2003 consists of those identifying themselves as "Asian or Pacific Islanders."

[3] Total excludes age groups where "NA" appears in the column. This applies to people 35 and over prior to 1972 for the total population, prior to 1973 for the White alone population and the Black alone population, and prior to 1986 for the Hispanic population. Data for 1950 exclude persons aged 30 and over.

[4] Data for 1955 to 1963 are for Black and other races.

[5] This series was discontinued in 2006.

Table A-16. Age Distribution of College Students 14 Years Old and Over, by Sex, October 1947–2019—Continued

(Numbers in thousands; civilian noninstitutionalized population.)

Year, sex, race, and Hispanic origin	All students								Male							
	Total	14 to 17 years	18 and 19 years	20 and 21 years	22 to 24 years	25 to 29 years	30 to 34 years	35 years and over	Total	14 to 17 years	18 and 19 years	20 and 21 years	22 to 24 years	25 to 29 years	30 to 34 years	35 years and over
1973	8,014	253	2,281	1,865	1,292	1,152	481	690	4,218	111	1,177	1,017	838	789	286	NA
1972	7,458	259	2,411	1,917	1,296	1,119	456	NA	4,395	120	1,242	1,062	891	784	296	NA
1971	7,273	251	2,485	1,758	1,351	965	463	NA	4,407	117	1,328	964	992	712	293	NA
1970	6,759	230	2,361	1,684	1,260	853	371	NA	4,066	117	1,251	995	850	622	231	NA
1969	6,827	222	2,377	1,762	1,208	855	404	NA	4,146	110	1,298	1,021	827	637	252	NA
1968	6,255	251	2,284	1,691	954	741	333	NA	3,843	117	1,262	1,021	666	564	213	NA
1967	5,905	220	2,105	1,688	915	646	329	NA	3,560	88	1,097	998	666	494	217	NA
1966	5,708	233	2,293	----2,313-----		-----869------		NA	3,536	93	1,281	----1,541----		-----621----		NA
1965	5,317	233	2,074	----2,139-----		-----871-----		NA	3,326	104	1,152	----1,441----		-----629----		NA
1964	4,337	257	1,519	----1,850-----		-----711-----		NA	2,720	147	823	----1,226----		-----524----		NA
1963	4,050	171	1,391	----1,817-----		-----671-----		NA	2,593	94	746	----1,246----		-----507----		NA
1962	3,934	217	1,509	----1,517-----		-----691-----		NA	2,586	120	836	----1,066----		-----564----		NA
1961	3,498	204	1,388	----1,296-----		-----610-----		NA	2,208	79	786	------883----		------460----		NA
1960	3,342	214	1,211	----1,209-----		-----709-----		NA	2,214	97	691	------859----		------567----		NA
1959	3,118	193	1,101	----1,134-----		-----690-----		NA	2,067	88	620	------798----		------561----		NA
1958	3,030	155	1,044	----1,136-----		-----695-----		NA	1,999	68	577	------802----		------552----		NA
1957	2,932	161	921	----1,165-----		-----685-----		NA	1,938	68	510	------797----		------563----		NA
1956	2,687	152	869	----1,025-----		-----641-----		NA	1,808	68	474	------733----		------533----		NA
1955	2,224	125	715	------880-----		----504-----		NA	1,495	47	418	------621----		------409----		NA
WHITE ALONE NON-HISPANIC																
2019	9,677	121	2,169	2,491	1,770	1,175	621	1,329	4,261	46	971	1,170	787	521	271	494
2018	10,248	116	2,382	2,420	1,869	1,384	684	1,392	4,616	45	1,086	1,161	875	611	315	522
2017	10,055	89	2,129	2,510	1,905	1,379	691	1,351	4,518	34	952	1,206	899	637	304	486
2016	10,749	82	2,439	2,465	1,990	1,615	789	1,368	4,879	30	1,168	1,168	952	702	327	531
2015	10,904	106	2,368	2,517	2,053	1,593	777	1,489	4,970	54	1,121	1,234	930	744	353	534
2014	11,068	113	2,299	2,545	2,209	1,545	742	1,613	5,115	58	1,050	1,310	1,031	728	337	600
2013	11,348	193	2,379	2,456	2,230	1,529	764	1,798	4,944	97	1,124	1,135	1,001	668	322	597
2012	11,650	150	2,363	2,620	2,207	1,734	778	1,799	5,074	61	1,051	1,126	1,113	761	356	606
2011	12,703	105	2,588	2,867	2,427	1,892	936	1,888	5,731	55	1,184	1,349	1,221	817	417	689
2010	12,613	114	2,699	2,813	2,152	1,818	996	2,022	5,673	39	1,236	1,395	986	854	416	747
2009	12,826	120	2,842	2,755	2,385	1,736	913	2,074	5,709	54	1,286	1,327	1,174	765	397	706
2008	12,324	121	2,850	2,734	2,309	1,625	779	1,906	5,602	58	1,346	1,322	1,098	766	347	664
2007	11,867	104	2,739	2,677	2,117	1,509	816	1,904	5,269	45	1,298	1,223	1,021	639	370	674
2006	11,485	114	2,564	2,606	2,030	1,494	830	1,848	5,085	41	1,168	1,208	979	702	347	640
2005	11,715	93	2,618	2,769	2,006	1,445	806	1,977	5,114	30	1,193	1,308	928	590	373	692
2004	11,571	111	2,596	2,618	2,014	1,513	814	1,905	5,146	44	1,150	1,242	930	710	372	698
2003[1]	11,295	90	2,486	2,419	2,225	1,371	832	1,872	5,067	41	1,115	1,082	1,094	639	386	710
2002	11,236	97	2,549	2,525	1,931	1,317	812	2,007	5,060	57	1,179	1,162	947	596	350	770
2001	10,602	74	2,383	2,450	1,732	1,283	827	1,854	4,691	30	1,131	1,170	794	587	348	632
2000	10,636	92	2,580	2,333	1,796	1,275	770	1,790	4,716	35	1,138	1,109	890	603	296	646
1999	10,818	80	2,574	2,324	1,837	1,283	755	1,965	5,033	30	1,214	1,141	929	627	368	722
1998	11,109	84	2,715	2,281	1,760	1,408	840	2,020	5,084	30	1,280	1,123	897	668	348	738
1997	11,246	81	2,491	2,361	1,876	1,504	779	2,153	5,024	33	1,184	1,161	930	732	314	669
1996	11,034	147	2,504	2,156	1,788	1,514	834	2,091	4,961	61	1,136	1,039	955	727	303	740
1995	11,024	103	2,372	2,226	1,796	1,618	859	2,051	5,068	36	1,111	1,103	892	799	380	749
1994[2]	11,178	93	2,362	2,255	1,904	1,444	1,018	2,101	5,053	41	1,132	1,039	955	689	457	741
1993	10,554	83	2,270	2,026	1,924	1,367	923	1,960	4,838	36	1,038	1,016	1,017	663	399	670
BLACK ALONE[4]																
2019	2,848	43	538	550	499	461	238	518	1,171	24	243	252	199	208	69	176
2018	3,009	15	530	600	540	561	246	518	1,183	6	234	282	220	228	63	151
2017	2,812	35	525	546	524	455	219	509	1,175	13	234	251	210	193	81	192
2016	2,885	30	530	572	542	405	247	559	1,217	12	215	276	237	192	97	188
2015	2,826	25	509	575	553	404	223	537	1,147	12	229	252	298	145	57	154
2014	2,934	54	510	537	482	414	242	695	1,132	38	175	244	214	162	79	220
2013	2,857	32	451	633	515	461	225	539	1,116	18	186	268	236	172	54	182

NA = Not available.

r = Revised, controlled to 1990 census based population estimates; previous 1993 data controlled to 1980 census based population estimates.

[1] Starting in 2003 respondents could identify more than one race. Except as noted, the race data in this table from 2003 onward represent those respondents who indicated only one race category.

[2] The data shown prior to 2003 consists of those identifying themselves as "Asian or Pacific Islanders."

[3] Total excludes age groups where "NA" appears in the column. This applies to people 35 and over prior to 1972 for the total population, prior to 1973 for the White alone population and the Black alone population, and prior to 1986 for the Hispanic population. Data for 1950 exclude persons aged 30 and over.

[4] Data for 1955 to 1963 are for Black and other races.

[5] This series was discontinued in 2006.

Table A-16. Age Distribution of College Students 14 Years Old and Over, by Sex, October 1947–2019—*Continued*

(Numbers in thousands; civilian noninstitutionalized population.)

Year, sex, race, and Hispanic origin	Female							
	Total	14 to 17 years	18 and 19 years	20 and 21 years	22 to 24 years	25 to 29 years	30 to 34 years	35 years and over
1973........................	3,107	142	1,104	848	454	363	196	NA
1972........................	3,061	138	1,169	855	404	334	160	NA
1971........................	2,867	134	1,157	794	359	252	170	NA
1970........................	2,693	113	1,110	689	410	231	140	NA
1969........................	2,681	112	1,079	741	380	218	151	NA
1968........................	2,412	134	1,022	670	288	177	120	NA
1967........................	2,345	133	1,009	690	250	152	112	NA
1966........................	2,172	140	1,012	-----772-----		-----248-----		NA
1965........................	1,991	129	922	-----698-----		-----242-----		NA
1964........................	1,617	110	696	-----624-----		-----187-----		NA
1963........................	1,457	77	645	-----571-----		-----164-----		NA
1962........................	1,348	97	673	-----451-----		-----127-----		NA
1961........................	1,290	125	602	-----413-----		-----150-----		NA
1960........................	1,128	117	520	-----350-----		-----142-----		NA
1959........................	1,051	105	481	-----336-----		-----129-----		NA
1958........................	1,031	87	467	-----334-----		-----143-----		NA
1957........................	994	93	411	-----368-----		-----122-----		NA
1956........................	879	84	395	-----292-----		-----108-----		NA
1955........................	729	78	297	-----259-----		------95-----		NA
WHITE ALONE NON-HISPANIC								
2019........................	5,416	76	1,198	1,321	982	653	350	835
2018........................	5,632	71	1,296	1,258	994	773	370	870
2017........................	5,537	55	1,178	1,304	1,006	742	387	865
2016........................	5,870	52	1,271	1,297	1,038	913	463	837
2015........................	5,934	52	1,248	1,283	1,123	849	424	954
2014........................	5,953	55	1,249	1,235	1,179	817	405	1,013
2013........................	6,404	95	1,254	1,321	1,229	861	442	1,201
2012........................	6,575	88	1,312	1,494	1,094	973	422	1,193
2011........................	6,972	50	1,404	1,517	1,206	1,075	519	1,199
2010........................	6,940	75	1,463	1,417	1,166	964	581	1,275
2009........................	7,116	66	1,556	1,429	1,211	971	516	1,368
2008........................	6,722	63	1,504	1,412	1,211	859	432	1,242
2007........................	6,598	59	1,441	1,455	1,096	870	447	1,230
2006........................	6,400	73	1,396	1,398	1,051	792	483	1,208
2005........................	6,601	63	1,425	1,461	1,078	855	433	1,285
2004........................	6,425	67	1,446	1,375	1,085	803	442	1,207
2003[1]	6,228	49	1,371	1,337	1,130	732	446	1,163
2002........................	6,177	40	1,370	1,364	984	721	462	1,237
2001........................	5,912	44	1,252	1,280	938	695	479	1,222
2000........................	5,921	57	1,443	1,224	906	672	474	1,145
1999........................	5,785	49	1,360	1,183	908	656	387	1,241
1998........................	6,025	54	1,435	1,158	863	740	493	1,282
1997........................	6,222	48	1,307	1,200	946	771	465	1,485
1996........................	6,073	86	1,367	1,117	833	787	531	1,352
1995........................	5,956	67	1,261	1,123	904	819	479	1,302
1994[2]	6,124	53	1,229	1,216	950	755	561	1,361
1993........................	5,715	48	1,232	1,010	907	704	524	1,290
BLACK ALONE[4]								
2019........................	1,676	20	295	298	300	253	169	342
2018........................	1,826	9	296	318	320	332	183	367
2017........................	1,637	22	291	295	314	262	138	316
2016........................	1,669	18	316	296	305	212	151	372
2015........................	1,679	13	280	323	255	259	166	383
2014........................	1,802	17	334	293	268	252	164	475
2013........................	1,740	14	265	365	280	289	171	357

NA = Not available.

r = Revised, controlled to 1990 census based population estimates; previous 1993 data controlled to 1980 census based population estimates.

[1] Starting in 2003 respondents could identify more than one race. Except as noted, the race data in this table from 2003 onward represent those respondents who indicated only one race category.

[2] The data shown prior to 2003 consists of those identifying themselves as "Asian or Pacific Islanders."

[3] Total excludes age groups where "NA" appears in the column. This applies to people 35 and over prior to 1972 for the total population, prior to 1973 for the White alone population and the Black alone population, and prior to 1986 for the Hispanic population. Data for 1950 exclude persons aged 30 and over.

[4] Data for 1955 to 1963 are for Black and other races.

[5] This series was discontinued in 2006.

Table A-16. Age Distribution of College Students 14 Years Old and Over, by Sex, October 1947–2019—*Continued*

(Numbers in thousands; civilian noninstitutionalized population.)

Year, sex, race, and Hispanic origin	All students								Male							
	Total	14 to 17 years	18 and 19 years	20 and 21 years	22 to 24 years	25 to 29 years	30 to 34 years	35 years and over	Total	14 to 17 years	18 and 19 years	20 and 21 years	22 to 24 years	25 to 29 years	30 to 34 years	35 years and over
2012	3,038	27	531	636	522	443	326	553	1,152	18	206	316	238	142	85	148
2011	3,146	38	580	489	570	511	307	651	1,212	23	242	243	232	189	92	191
2010	3,083	33	567	622	503	438	277	643	1,185	14	238	262	234	180	77	180
2009	2,889	34	559	495	550	410	253	587	1,058	5	225	237	212	151	81	147
2008	2,481	36	479	463	408	377	269	451	919	21	205	217	174	115	82	106
2007	2,501	27	492	436	468	400	229	449	1,016	10	227	213	209	126	102	130
2006	2,334	30	464	416	441	303	199	480	896	10	174	182	186	112	70	163
2005	2,217	28	431	393	435	282	217	430	832	6	182	178	153	99	64	150
2004	2,301	40	440	398	400	352	170	501	776	13	165	169	146	92	41	151
2003[1]	2,144	28	374	415	435	289	214	388	798	10	166	153	180	100	84	105
2002	2,278	56	430	418	379	301	241	454	802	14	179	175	121	97	83	133
2001	2,230	33	444	383	379	283	279	429	781	7	179	137	153	88	90	126
2000	2,164	19	454	375	387	325	242	361	815	10	163	137	169	110	92	133
1999	1,998	45	430	389	325	254	199	354	833	34	210	193	98	93	79	123
1998	2,016	22	461	354	300	328	211	340	770	12	194	162	88	140	67	105
1997	1,903	24	381	321	383	258	165	372	723	7	142	137	146	110	65	117
1996	1,901	45	345	346	292	337	182	354	764	17	145	155	122	142	64	120
1995	1,772	24	344	339	305	233	193	334	710	13	145	142	143	65	80	122
1994	1,800	36	310	347	344	256	184	323	745	16	132	161	147	118	72	99
1993r	1,599	13	322	311	264	253	143	293	652	4	151	109	127	118	36	107
1993	1,545	13	311	297	253	245	141	284	636	4	148	107	124	116	36	102
1992	1,424	28	291	316	279	170	132	208	527	8	123	114	119	73	37	54
1991	1,477	18	303	302	223	216	157	257	629	7	137	138	103	99	55	90
1990	1,393	35	349	287	258	150	108	207	587	16	164	151	111	52	26	65
1989	1,287	32	302	290	243	156	119	146	480	8	126	104	94	65	37	47
1988	1,321	33	281	273	198	188	142	206	494	6	108	90	99	75	48	68
1987	1,351	32	341	264	218	220	121	155	587	13	154	124	99	99	37	62
1986	1,359	19	308	242	262	187	143	198	580	12	120	111	118	81	64	74
1985	1,263	21	259	274	201	183	112	213	552	10	121	140	84	64	40	93
1984	1,332	40	265	274	247	182	131	193	618	16	112	129	126	99	62	74
1983	1,273	31	258	242	241	179	151	171	560	12	93	112	126	91	64	62
1982	1,294	22	274	242	251	196	142	167	544	9	124	92	115	91	51	62
1981	1,335	31	306	232	212	219	132	203	566	7	133	92	100	115	57	62
1980	1,163	30	283	225	180	176	113	156	476	14	98	101	79	92	53	39
1979	1,156	43	279	224	193	150	112	155	498	12	110	110	84	71	47	64
1978	1,175	38	270	238	186	167	121	155	504	13	114	106	85	82	52	52
1977	1,284	37	269	262	190	210	136	180	571	18	90	115	104	101	62	81
1976	1,217	34	302	252	195	171	109	154	551	11	121	113	97	90	57	62
1975	1,099	34	260	237	168	151	97	152	523	14	111	107	76	82	53	80
1974	930	34	233	190	132	136	88	117	485	13	102	100	78	70	60	62
1973	781	37	194	164	140	89	60	97	358	7	96	93	77	49	36	NA
1972	727	32	229	168	143	87	68	NA	384	18	102	91	94	49	30	NA
1971	680	29	204	199	119	79	50	NA	363	11	94	106	62	58	31	NA
1970	522	21	191	152	73	54	31	NA	253	10	73	81	38	33	19	NA
1969	492	19	193	149	65	39	26	NA	236	10	86	75	41	15	10	NA
1968	434	20	182	112	58	33	29	NA	221	12	83	61	26	27	13	NA
1967	370	16	141	105	51	42	15	NA	199	7	78	57	32	15	11	NA
1966	282	17	112	-----112-----		-----41-----		NA	154	10	47	-----72-----		-----25-----		NA
1965	274	30	111	------99-----		------34-----		NA	126	8	52	-----47-----		-----19-----		NA
1964	234	30	78	------79-----		------47-----		NA	120	16	35	-----36-----		-----33-----		NA
1963	286	9	113	-----112-----		------52-----		NA	149	5	50	-----62-----		-----32-----		NA
1962	274	16	103	-----109-----		------46-----		NA	156	5	55	-----59-----		-----37-----		NA
1961	233	9	82	-----103-----		------39-----		NA	148	5	48	-----64-----		-----31-----		NA
1960	227	8	88	------90-----		------41-----		NA	125	2	43	-----55-----		-----25-----		NA
1959	222	17	74	------94-----		------37-----		NA	120	4	31	-----58-----		-----27-----		NA
1958	212	12	70	------85-----		------45-----		NA	130	5	44	-----48-----		-----33-----		NA
1957	206	15	68	------71-----		------52-----		NA	90	9	28	-----30-----		-----23-----		NA
1956	196	15	65	------80-----		------36-----		NA	124	9	38	-----48-----		-----29-----		NA
1955	155	21	31	------51-----		------52-----		NA	84	9	15	-----25-----		-----35-----		NA

NA = Not available.

r = Revised, controlled to 1990 census based population estimates; previous 1993 data controlled to 1980 census based population estimates.

[1] Starting in 2003 respondents could identify more than one race. Except as noted, the race data in this table from 2003 onward represent those respondents who indicated only one race category.

[2] The data shown prior to 2003 consists of those identifying themselves as "Asian or Pacific Islanders."

[3] Total excludes age groups where "NA" appears in the column. This applies to people 35 and over prior to 1972 for the total population, prior to 1973 for the White alone population and the Black alone population, and prior to 1986 for the Hispanic population. Data for 1950 exclude persons aged 30 and over.

[4] Data for 1955 to 1963 are for Black and other races.

[5] This series was discontinued in 2006.

Table A-16. Age Distribution of College Students 14 Years Old and Over, by Sex, October 1947–2019—*Continued*

(Numbers in thousands; civilian noninstitutionalized population.)

Year, sex, race, and Hispanic origin				Female			
	Total	14 to 17 years	18 and 19 years	20 and 21 years	22 to 24 years	25 to 29 years	30 to 34 years	35 years and over
2012	1,886	10	325	320	284	301	241	406
2011	1,934	16	337	246	338	322	215	460
2010	1,898	20	329	360	269	258	199	463
2009	1,831	29	334	258	338	259	172	441
2008	1,562	15	274	246	234	261	188	345
2007	1,485	18	265	223	259	274	127	320
2006	1,438	20	291	234	255	191	130	318
2005	1,385	22	249	215	282	183	153	281
2004	1,525	27	275	229	254	259	130	350
2003[1]	1,346	19	209	262	255	188	130	283
2002	1,476	42	251	243	257	204	158	321
2001	1,449	26	265	245	226	195	190	302
2000	1,349	9	291	238	218	215	150	228
1999	1,164	10	221	196	227	161	120	229
1998	1,247	9	267	192	212	188	144	234
1997	1,180	17	238	184	237	149	100	255
1996	1,136	28	199	192	170	195	119	234
1995	1,062	11	199	197	162	168	113	212
1994	1,054	21	178	186	197	138	112	224
1993r	947	9	172	202	137	135	107	186
1993	909	8	163	191	130	129	106	182
1992	897	21	168	202	161	97	95	154
1991	848	11	166	164	120	118	102	167
1990	807	19	185	136	146	98	82	141
1989	807	24	176	186	149	91	82	99
1988	827	27	173	183	99	113	94	138
1987	764	19	186	140	119	121	84	93
1986	779	7	187	131	144	106	79	124
1985	712	11	138	134	117	119	72	121
1984	714	24	153	145	121	83	69	119
1983	714	19	164	131	116	88	87	109
1982	750	12	150	150	136	105	92	105
1981	769	24	172	140	112	105	75	141
1980	686	16	185	124	101	84	60	116
1979	659	31	169	114	109	79	66	91
1978	671	25	155	133	102	85	68	103
1977	712	19	179	147	87	108	74	98
1976	665	23	181	139	97	81	52	92
1975	577	20	150	130	92	69	44	72
1974	448	22	131	91	55	66	28	55
1973	325	30	97	71	63	40	24	NA
1972	343	14	127	77	49	38	38	NA
1971	317	18	109	93	57	21	19	NA
1970	269	11	118	71	36	22	11	NA
1969	256	9	108	74	24	25	17	NA
1968	213	8	100	51	32	7	15	NA
1967	171	9	63	48	19	27	4	NA
1966	128	7	65	-----40-----		-----16-----		NA
1965	148	22	59	-----52-----		-----15-----		NA
1964	114	14	43	-----43-----		-----14-----		NA
1963	137	4	63	-----50-----		-----20-----		NA
1962	118	11	48	-----50-----		------9-----		NA
1961	85	4	34	-----39-----		------8-----		NA
1960	102	6	45	-----35-----		-----16-----		NA
1959	102	13	43	-----36-----		-----10-----		NA
1958	82	7	26	-----37-----		-----12-----		NA
1957	116	6	40	-----41-----		-----29-----		NA
1956	72	6	27	-----32-----		------7-----		NA
1955	71	12	16	-----26-----		-----17-----		NA

NA = Not available.

r = Revised, controlled to 1990 census based population estimates; previous 1993 data controlled to 1980 census based population estimates.

[1] Starting in 2003 respondents could identify more than one race. Except as noted, the race data in this table from 2003 onward represent those respondents who indicated only one race category.

[2] The data shown prior to 2003 consists of those identifying themselves as "Asian or Pacific Islanders."

[3] Total excludes age groups where "NA" appears in the column. This applies to people 35 and over prior to 1972 for the total population, prior to 1973 for the White alone population and the Black alone population, and prior to 1986 for the Hispanic population. Data for 1950 exclude persons aged 30 and over.

[4] Data for 1955 to 1963 are for Black and other races.

[5] This series was discontinued in 2006.

Table A-16. Age Distribution of College Students 14 Years Old and Over, by Sex, October 1947–2019—*Continued*

(Numbers in thousands; civilian noninstitutionalized population.)

Year, sex, race, and Hispanic origin	All students								Male							
	Total	14 to 17 years	18 and 19 years	20 and 21 years	22 to 24 years	25 to 29 years	30 to 34 years	35 years and over	Total	14 to 17 years	18 and 19 years	20 and 21 years	22 to 24 years	25 to 29 years	30 to 34 years	35 years and over
BLACK ALONE NON-HISPANIC[5]																
2005	2,217	28	431	393	435	282	217	430	832	6	182	178	153	99	64	150
2004	2,231	40	430	392	379	344	163	483	760	13	161	166	143	92	38	147
2003[1]	2,090	28	368	399	423	282	205	385	773	10	166	145	177	93	80	102
2002	2,217	56	428	410	358	293	233	439	782	14	177	174	113	95	83	126
2001	2,173	33	430	373	375	263	275	423	759	7	174	137	150	78	90	123
2000	2,119	19	439	373	370	321	242	355	798	10	154	137	164	110	92	130
1999	1,952	45	413	390	320	250	192	342	811	35	192	193	99	91	76	125
1998	1,971	22	453	351	282	322	211	331	752	12	194	159	83	134	67	102
1997	1,868	21	371	314	378	253	161	369	712	7	138	137	143	105	65	117
1996	1,863	41	342	342	281	329	176	350	750	17	142	155	122	134	64	117
1995	1,745	24	332	337	302	231	189	330	699	13	136	142	143	65	80	120
1994	1,783	36	308	347	342	253	182	314	734	16	131	161	145	116	72	93
1993	1,505	13	310	291	246	232	134	279	615	4	149	105	121	104	33	100
ASIAN[2]																
2019	1,768	37	323	430	379	302	166	133	870	22	161	205	186	162	71	63
2018	1,691	19	291	414	374	314	152	128	846	13	139	226	193	166	61	48
2017	1,581	32	260	430	411	262	90	95	750	7	122	213	227	127	30	25
2016	1,585	19	255	358	390	328	108	127	835	4	135	177	222	177	53	68
2015	1,616	20	235	421	370	291	135	143	752	10	112	193	188	138	61	49
2014	1,543	19	270	305	447	273	80	148	797	14	136	158	255	149	26	59
2013	1,576	30	302	340	359	261	111	174	789	8	154	188	193	151	38	58
2012	1,447	26	253	289	372	247	116	143	700	15	129	140	185	131	44	55
2011	1,204	21	240	281	227	189	99	147	567	6	131	141	107	92	45	45
2010	1,322	32	234	308	269	237	117	126	647	17	116	150	124	126	58	57
2009	1,231	11	243	216	308	197	114	141	613	8	134	97	153	96	53	73
2008	1,220	27	172	247	236	245	137	156	567	22	75	123	96	132	61	58
2007	1,103	10	201	204	252	206	123	105	533	2	104	106	108	98	60	54
2006	1,084	8	204	215	242	187	103	125	535	5	113	121	104	80	51	61
2005	1,184	22	188	272	234	226	114	129	605	10	90	163	113	110	61	58
2004	1,191	20	182	245	269	217	113	146	636	11	92	135	145	116	65	71
2003[1]	1,162	16	209	219	264	228	108	116	606	3	103	104	130	141	67	59
2002	1,258	28	236	269	299	182	105	140	649	8	121	137	160	101	56	67
2001	1,280	17	247	245	302	265	90	115	664	10	113	127	177	134	63	40
2000	1,049	12	212	200	227	188	81	130	517	4	108	109	120	66	51	60
1999	1,041	16	223	192	211	187	71	142	506	11	93	95	96	97	47	67
HISPANIC (OF ANY RACE)																
2019	3,555	40	872	867	730	485	229	333	1,559	11	409	408	310	211	73	137
2018	3,574	58	890	885	656	562	218	306	1,613	17	392	405	292	261	116	131
2017	3,574	80	931	769	710	530	187	368	1,529	30	413	311	321	219	104	132
2016	3,661	89	884	948	732	491	191	326	1,582	28	383	437	327	210	76	120
2015	3,374	43	776	930	663	459	189	315	1,484	23	315	421	327	192	69	136
2014	3,295	52	857	797	628	441	189	332	1,441	11	385	356	275	222	47	144
2013	3,219	43	727	773	692	417	222	345	1,438	19	295	352	321	237	84	130
2012	3,400	61	827	912	664	365	257	313	1,510	26	372	421	316	155	72	148
2011	2,953	36	765	740	574	407	175	256	1,438	23	351	376	279	212	67	130
2010	2,879	41	783	517	514	424	228	373	1,302	19	381	242	196	197	108	159
2009	2,434	43	550	482	433	373	217	336	1,080	23	242	221	200	159	108	127
2008	2,227	53	528	407	402	359	141	337	1,042	31	236	210	169	186	76	135
2007	2,172	41	559	412	404	332	155	269	880	16	246	154	160	145	57	102
2006	1,968	54	444	386	353	271	190	271	808	19	213	146	164	109	64	94
2005	1,942	31	406	420	389	288	150	257	804	10	173	183	183	111	52	92
2004	1,975	23	384	431	407	280	179	271	852	5	171	212	191	131	53	89

NA = Not available.

r = Revised, controlled to 1990 census based population estimates; previous 1993 data controlled to 1980 census based population estimates.

[1] Starting in 2003 respondents could identify more than one race. Except as noted, the race data in this table from 2003 onward represent those respondents who indicated only one race category.

[2] The data shown prior to 2003 consists of those identifying themselves as "Asian or Pacific Islanders."

[3] Total excludes age groups where "NA" appears in the column. This applies to people 35 and over prior to 1972 for the total population, prior to 1973 for the White alone population and the Black alone population, and prior to 1986 for the Hispanic population. Data for 1950 exclude persons aged 30 and over.

[4] Data for 1955 to 1963 are for Black and other races.

[5] This series was discontinued in 2006.

Table A-16. Age Distribution of College Students 14 Years Old and Over, by Sex, October 1947–2019—*Continued*

(Numbers in thousands; civilian noninstitutionalized population.)

Year, sex, race, and Hispanic origin	Female							
	Total	14 to 17 years	18 and 19 years	20 and 21 years	22 to 24 years	25 to 29 years	30 to 34 years	35 years and over
BLACK ALONE NON-HISPANIC[5]								
2005.........................	1,385	22	249	215	282	183	153	281
2004	1,471	27	268	227	237	251	125	336
2003[1]	1,317	19	202	254	246	188	125	283
2002.........................	1,435	42	251	237	244	198	150	313
2001.........................	1,414	26	256	236	226	186	185	300
2000.........................	1,321	9	285	235	206	211	150	225
1999.........................	1,141	10	221	196	221	159	117	218
1998.........................	1,219	9	259	192	199	188	144	229
1997.........................	1,156	14	233	177	235	149	96	252
1996.........................	1,113	25	199	188	160	195	113	234
1995.........................	1,046	11	196	195	159	167	109	210
1994.........................	1,049	21	178	186	197	138	109	221
1993.........................	890	8	161	186	125	128	102	179
ASIAN[2]								
2019.........................	898	14	162	224	193	140	94	70
2018.........................	844	6	151	188	181	148	91	80
2017.........................	831	25	138	217	184	135	60	71
2016.........................	749	15	120	181	168	151	55	59
2015.........................	864	10	123	229	182	153	74	94
2014.........................	746	5	134	147	192	124	55	89
2013.........................	787	22	148	152	166	110	73	116
2012.........................	747	11	124	148	187	116	72	88
2011.........................	637	16	109	140	120	97	54	101
2010.........................	676	15	118	158	145	111	59	69
2009.........................	619	4	109	120	155	101	61	68
2008.........................	653	5	97	123	140	113	76	98
2007.........................	569	8	97	98	144	108	63	51
2006.........................	549	3	91	94	139	107	52	64
2005.........................	579	12	98	109	120	116	53	71
2004	556	9	89	110	124	101	48	75
2003[1]	556	13	107	115	134	88	42	57
2002.........................	609	19	115	132	139	82	49	73
2001.........................	616	6	134	118	125	131	27	75
2000.........................	532	8	104	91	107	122	30	69
1999.........................	534	5	130	97	115	89	24	74
HISPANIC (OF ANY RACE)								
2019.........................	1,996	29	463	459	420	274	155	195
2018.........................	1,960	41	498	480	364	301	102	175
2017.........................	2,045	50	518	457	390	312	83	236
2016.........................	2,079	60	501	511	405	281	115	206
2015.........................	1,890	20	461	508	336	267	120	179
2014.........................	1,855	40	472	441	352	219	142	188
2013.........................	1,781	24	432	421	371	180	138	215
2012.........................	1,890	35	454	491	348	211	185	166
2011.........................	1,515	13	414	364	294	196	108	126
2010.........................	1,576	21	402	275	319	227	119	213
2009.........................	1,354	20	308	261	234	214	108	209
2008.........................	1,185	23	292	197	233	173	65	202
2007.........................	1,292	25	313	258	244	187	98	167
2006.........................	1,161	36	231	240	189	162	126	177
2005.........................	1,137	21	232	237	206	178	98	165
2004	1,123	19	213	219	216	150	126	182

NA = Not available.

r = Revised, controlled to 1990 census based population estimates; previous 1993 data controlled to 1980 census based population estimates.

[1] Starting in 2003 respondents could identify more than one race. Except as noted, the race data in this table from 2003 onward represent those respondents who indicated only one race category.

[2] The data shown prior to 2003 consists of those identifying themselves as "Asian or Pacific Islanders."

[3] Total excludes age groups where "NA" appears in the column. This applies to people 35 and over prior to 1972 for the total population, prior to 1973 for the White alone population and the Black alone population, and prior to 1986 for the Hispanic population. Data for 1950 exclude persons aged 30 and over.

[4] Data for 1955 to 1963 are for Black and other races.

[5] This series was discontinued in 2006.

Table A-16. Age Distribution of College Students 14 Years Old and Over, by Sex, October 1947–2019—Continued

(Numbers in thousands; civilian noninstitutionalized population.)

Year, sex, race, and Hispanic origin	All students								Male							
	Total	14 to 17 years	18 and 19 years	20 and 21 years	22 to 24 years	25 to 29 years	30 to 34 years	35 years and over	Total	14 to 17 years	18 and 19 years	20 and 21 years	22 to 24 years	25 to 29 years	30 to 34 years	35 years and over
2003	1,714	12	379	407	329	224	156	207	703	7	153	167	145	93	61	77
2002	1,656	15	360	303	316	274	140	249	705	3	156	151	132	118	49	97
2001	1,700	14	387	342	306	255	136	260	731	6	149	145	156	116	57	102
2000	1,426	24	349	268	282	167	142	194	619	12	160	118	123	61	75	70
1999	1,307	7	297	197	247	207	127	225	568	2	143	84	96	94	54	95
1998	1,363	9	288	263	269	206	130	198	550	—	97	139	110	86	54	64
1997	1,260	49	316	254	236	174	80	151	555	15	133	132	106	78	31	60
1996	1,223	22	240	213	253	198	112	184	529	8	98	78	124	79	54	90
1995	1,207	20	264	245	236	153	97	193	568	14	121	111	124	71	55	73
1994	1,187	9	225	230	207	180	132	205	529	3	89	115	108	73	55	86
1993r	1,169	17	222	299	207	178	106	139	539	7	81	154	103	71	67	56
1993	995	15	195	241	166	149	100	129	442	6	69	118	79	57	63	51
1992	918	17	230	200	156	124	90	102	388	9	93	80	74	57	35	40
1991	830	10	188	203	125	124	72	109	347	5	68	79	64	64	30	37
1990	748	13	148	188	99	109	59	130	364	12	70	80	64	39	30	67
1989	754	17	177	134	142	112	58	114	353	5	75	66	70	63	31	42
1988	747	13	203	110	137	118	73	93	355	9	75	76	77	48	29	43
1987	739	8	152	155	148	137	67	73	390	3	76	100	71	77	42	21
1986	794	16	171	146	141	164	67	89	377	4	92	67	74	80	26	34
1985	580	16	127	128	120	111	78	NA	279	10	44	53	71	72	29	NA
1984	524	5	136	133	93	100	57	NA	231	2	42	63	49	49	26	NA
1983	521	17	134	124	91	114	41	NA	253	10	41	61	50	74	17	NA
1982	494	16	143	104	90	94	47	NA	216	6	52	47	42	49	20	NA
1981	510	15	129	123	90	103	50	NA	258	6	57	68	39	55	33	NA
1980	443	10	137	94	84	69	49	NA	222	2	68	52	34	36	30	NA
1979	439	18	124	95	73	73	56	NA	225	8	67	43	43	39	25	NA
1978	377	15	109	68	77	78	30	NA	196	7	53	30	43	49	14	NA
1977	417	14	123	95	59	81	45	NA	224	6	54	45	40	56	23	NA
1976	426	13	143	83	83	73	31	NA	223	3	69	39	42	50	20	NA
1975	411	13	118	101	76	68	35	NA	218	3	53	52	40	45	25	NA
1974	354	11	112	96	64	39	32	NA	195	6	55	44	42	24	24	NA
1973	289	15	82	69	55	45	23	NA	168	11	39	37	29	32	20	NA
1972	242	14	70	60	49	34	15	NA	126	7	28	35	29	20	7	NA

WHITE ALONE OR IN COMBINATION

Year, sex, race, and Hispanic origin	All students								Male							
	Total	14 to 17 years	18 and 19 years	20 and 21 years	22 to 24 years	25 to 29 years	30 to 34 years	35 years and over	Total	14 to 17 years	18 and 19 years	20 and 21 years	22 to 24 years	25 to 29 years	30 to 34 years	35 years and over
2019	13,375	167	3,100	3,436	2,504	1,657	858	1,652	5,903	56	1,389	1,641	1,086	753	358	619
2018	13,885	178	3,336	3,316	2,522	1,935	900	1,697	6,229	67	1,510	1,543	1,172	866	424	647
2017	13,703	168	3,121	3,306	2,621	1,904	885	1,698	6,059	64	1,370	1,533	1,212	847	409	623
2016	14,355	180	3,316	3,418	2,712	2,099	942	1,687	6,415	60	1,547	1,602	1,284	876	396	651
2015	14,295	165	3,163	3,416	2,689	2,072	972	1,818	6,425	81	1,472	1,627	1,220	942	423	658
2014	14,310	154	3,154	3,299	2,877	1,982	910	1,935	6,549	73	1,433	1,646	1,318	947	385	748
2013	14,743	246	3,124	3,292	3,005	1,942	988	2,145	6,500	123	1,433	1,521	1,369	905	411	738
2012	15,117	216	3,144	3,574	2,897	2,099	1,058	2,130	6,612	98	1,429	1,547	1,423	915	442	759
2011	15,785	141	3,381	3,631	3,031	2,316	1,124	2,160	7,239	78	1,554	1,719	1,517	1,046	496	830
2010	15,586	157	3,478	3,359	2,687	2,287	1,220	2,399	7,030	60	1,620	1,656	1,196	1,080	516	902
2009	15,391	160	3,414	3,289	2,859	2,125	1,133	2,411	6,848	77	1,535	1,591	1,387	930	501	826
2008	14,738	175	3,440	3,181	2,738	2,003	936	2,264	6,730	87	1,607	1,550	1,286	966	426	807
2007	14,114	147	3,318	3,111	2,529	1,857	978	2,174	6,169	64	1,540	1,390	1,186	789	425	774
2006	13,564	166	3,043	3,006	2,416	1,791	1,016	2,125	5,966	61	1,399	1,363	1,161	827	411	744
2005	13,791	125	3,043	3,244	2,433	1,740	954	2,251	5,978	43	1,371	1,519	1,128	696	424	796
2004	13,668	135	3,012	3,106	2,425	1,807	989	2,192	6,068	49	1,331	1,494	1,131	847	425	792
2003	13,164	106	2,905	2,868	2,584	1,613	989	2,099	5,837	48	1,283	1,274	1,257	730	446	798

BLACK ALONE OR IN COMBINATION

Year, sex, race, and Hispanic origin	All students								Male							
	Total	14 to 17 years	18 and 19 years	20 and 21 years	22 to 24 years	25 to 29 years	30 to 34 years	35 years and over	Total	14 to 17 years	18 and 19 years	20 and 21 years	22 to 24 years	25 to 29 years	30 to 34 years	35 years and over
2019	3,142	43	591	636	564	506	261	540	1,309	24	267	310	220	224	87	178
2018	3,272	23	611	643	586	595	258	557	1,305	11	277	305	241	243	73	156

NA = Not available.

r = Revised, controlled to 1990 census based population estimates; previous 1993 data controlled to 1980 census based population estimates.

[1] Starting in 2003 respondents could identify more than one race. Except as noted, the race data in this table from 2003 onward represent those respondents who indicated only one race category.

[2] The data shown prior to 2003 consists of those identifying themselves as "Asian or Pacific Islanders."

[3] Total excludes age groups where "NA" appears in the column. This applies to people 35 and over prior to 1972 for the total population, prior to 1973 for the White alone population and the Black alone population, and prior to 1986 for the Hispanic population. Data for 1950 exclude persons aged 30 and over.

[4] Data for 1955 to 1963 are for Black and other races.

[5] This series was discontinued in 2006.

Table A-16. Age Distribution of College Students 14 Years Old and Over, by Sex, October 1947–2019—*Continued*

(Numbers in thousands; civilian noninstitutionalized population.)

Year, sex, race, and Hispanic origin	Female							
	Total	14 to 17 years	18 and 19 years	20 and 21 years	22 to 24 years	25 to 29 years	30 to 34 years	35 years and over
2003	1,011	5	226	240	185	131	95	130
2002	951	12	204	152	184	156	92	152
2001	969	8	238	197	150	139	80	157
2000	807	13	188	150	160	106	67	124
1999	739	5	154	113	151	113	73	130
1998	814	9	191	124	159	120	77	134
1997	704	34	183	123	130	96	49	91
1996	693	15	142	136	128	119	59	95
1995	639	6	143	134	112	82	42	120
1994	659	6	136	115	99	106	78	119
1993r	630	10	141	145	104	107	40	83
1993	553	9	126	123	87	93	38	78
1992	530	7	137	120	82	67	55	62
1991	483	5	120	124	61	59	42	72
1990	384	1	78	108	35	70	29	63
1989	401	11	103	69	72	49	27	71
1988	391	4	129	35	60	70	43	51
1987	349	5	76	56	76	60	25	51
1986	417	12	79	80	67	84	41	54
1985	299	6	82	75	48	39	49	NA
1984	292	3	94	70	43	51	31	NA
1983	270	7	93	64	41	40	25	NA
1982	278	10	91	57	48	45	27	NA
1981	252	9	72	55	51	48	17	NA
1980	221	8	63	42	50	33	20	NA
1979	215	10	58	52	30	34	31	NA
1978	181	8	56	38	34	29	16	NA
1977	194	8	70	50	19	25	22	NA
1976	203	9	74	45	41	23	11	NA
1975	193	10	65	49	36	23	10	NA
1974	157	5	56	51	22	15	8	NA
1973	123	5	44	33	25	13	3	NA
1972	117	7	43	25	20	14	8	NA
WHITE ALONE OR IN COMBINATION								
2019	7,471	111	1,712	1,795	1,418	904	500	1,032
2018	7,655	111	1,826	1,773	1,350	1,069	476	1,050
2017	7,644	104	1,751	1,772	1,408	1,057	476	1,076
2016	7,940	121	1,770	1,816	1,428	1,224	546	1,036
2015	7,870	84	1,691	1,789	1,469	1,129	548	1,160
2014	7,761	81	1,720	1,653	1,559	1,036	525	1,187
2013	8,243	123	1,691	1,771	1,637	1,037	577	1,407
2012	8,505	119	1,715	2,027	1,473	1,184	615	1,372
2011	8,545	63	1,828	1,912	1,514	1,270	627	1,330
2010	8,556	97	1,858	1,702	1,491	1,207	703	1,497
2009	8,544	84	1,879	1,698	1,473	1,195	631	1,585
2008	8,008	88	1,833	1,631	1,452	1,037	510	1,457
2007	7,945	82	1,779	1,721	1,343	1,068	553	1,400
2006	7,598	105	1,643	1,643	1,255	964	605	1,382
2005	7,813	82	1,672	1,725	1,305	1,044	530	1,454
2004	7,600	86	1,682	1,612	1,295	960	564	1,401
2003	7,328	57	1,622	1,594	1,327	883	543	1,302
BLACK ALONE OR IN COMBINATION								
2019	1,833	20	324	326	345	282	174	362
2018	1,968	12	334	338	345	352	185	401

NA = Not available.

r = Revised, controlled to 1990 census based population estimates; previous 1993 data controlled to 1980 census based population estimates.

[1] Starting in 2003 respondents could identify more than one race. Except as noted, the race data in this table from 2003 onward represent those respondents who indicated only one race category.

[2] The data shown prior to 2003 consists of those identifying themselves as "Asian or Pacific Islanders."

[3] Total excludes age groups where "NA" appears in the column. This applies to people 35 and over prior to 1972 for the total population, prior to 1973 for the White alone population and the Black alone population, and prior to 1986 for the Hispanic population. Data for 1950 exclude persons aged 30 and over.

[4] Data for 1955 to 1963 are for Black and other races.

[5] This series was discontinued in 2006.

Table A-16. Age Distribution of College Students 14 Years Old and Over, by Sex, October 1947–2019—*Continued*

(Numbers in thousands; civilian noninstitutionalized population.)

Year, sex, race, and Hispanic origin	All students								Male							
	Total	14 to 17 years	18 and 19 years	20 and 21 years	22 to 24 years	25 to 29 years	30 to 34 years	35 years and over	Total	14 to 17 years	18 and 19 years	20 and 21 years	22 to 24 years	25 to 29 years	30 to 34 years	35 years and over
2017	3,068	47	597	606	579	493	225	520	1,273	13	269	267	231	208	82	203
2016	3,079	35	602	607	572	430	261	572	1,283	14	250	280	247	195	102	194
2015	2,985	28	560	602	580	421	244	551	1,216	14	259	269	305	150	63	156
2014	3,099	56	553	562	530	432	259	707	1,181	40	192	244	223	173	88	220
2013	3,118	36	509	716	581	499	228	550	1,238	22	210	306	263	192	54	190
2012	3,335	33	579	721	592	465	348	598	1,292	22	244	353	263	149	89	174
2011	3,317	39	615	540	605	533	321	665	1,279	23	250	264	249	196	100	198
2010	3,250	38	622	653	533	463	286	655	1,241	19	264	271	244	186	78	180
2009	3,030	34	604	520	574	428	268	601	1,109	5	245	250	217	155	88	149
2008	2,619	36	515	490	429	400	278	470	983	21	219	229	184	127	85	116
2007	2,630	33	530	459	479	432	243	455	1,077	12	240	229	217	139	110	130
2006	2,444	30	492	423	471	318	217	493	951	10	186	186	206	120	74	170
2005	2,387	31	481	428	462	299	229	458	895	9	201	189	167	109	66	154
2004	2,412	40	466	436	416	371	170	512	827	13	175	187	159	100	41	153
2003	2,227	30	400	440	445	303	214	395	826	10	175	165	186	100	84	107
ASIAN ALONE OR IN COMBINATION																
2019	1,999	47	368	525	419	326	181	134	977	22	172	256	210	174	81	63
2018	1,919	19	360	504	402	350	152	133	951	13	172	258	211	182	61	53
2017	1,750	32	297	488	438	286	101	108	822	7	133	236	243	131	40	32
2016	1,780	22	313	421	427	346	118	133	937	7	159	211	254	178	59	70
2015	1,821	21	287	488	407	315	156	147	840	11	141	218	202	151	67	49
2014	1,712	19	296	347	490	310	90	161	878	14	146	175	278	166	30	68
2013	1,766	31	350	394	412	274	117	188	872	8	171	221	221	153	38	60
2012	1,617	33	274	348	421	266	124	151	774	21	143	165	202	140	44	58
2011	1,356	21	267	323	243	220	121	161	658	6	145	162	123	110	60	53
2010	1,467	37	264	343	298	268	125	133	740	20	136	177	141	149	61	57
2009	1,334	11	271	242	330	207	122	150	656	8	138	115	165	98	57	76
2008	1,340	27	214	265	259	260	149	167	632	22	93	134	113	135	70	65
2007	1,204	11	232	220	268	232	126	116	592	2	113	116	123	113	61	64
2006	1,154	9	215	227	263	198	110	131	566	6	118	122	122	81	55	62
2005	1,297	25	204	292	277	240	122	137	640	13	97	170	124	113	63	60
2003	1,262	19	236	248	290	232	117	121	649	3	112	115	143	142	72	61

NA = Not available.

r = Revised, controlled to 1990 census based population estimates; previous 1993 data controlled to 1980 census based population estimates.

[1] Starting in 2003 respondents could identify more than one race. Except as noted, the race data in this table from 2003 onward represent those respondents who indicated only one race category.

[2] The data shown prior to 2003 consists of those identifying themselves as "Asian or Pacific Islanders."

[3] Total excludes age groups where "NA" appears in the column. This applies to people 35 and over prior to 1972 for the total population, prior to 1973 for the White alone population and the Black alone population, and prior to 1986 for the Hispanic population. Data for 1950 exclude persons aged 30 and over.

[4] Data for 1955 to 1963 are for Black and other races.

[5] This series was discontinued in 2006.

Table A-16. Age Distribution of College Students 14 Years Old and Over, by Sex, October 1947–2019—*Continued*

(Numbers in thousands; civilian noninstitutionalized population.)

Year, sex, race, and Hispanic origin	Female							
	Total	14 to 17 years	18 and 19 years	20 and 21 years	22 to 24 years	25 to 29 years	30 to 34 years	35 years and over
2017......................	1,794	34	328	339	347	286	144	317
2016......................	1,797	21	352	328	325	234	159	378
2015......................	1,770	14	300	332	275	271	181	396
2014......................	1,919	17	360	318	307	259	171	486
2013......................	1,880	14	299	409	317	306	174	360
2012......................	2,043	11	335	368	329	316	259	424
2011......................	2,037	16	365	276	356	337	221	467
2010......................	2,009	20	358	383	289	277	208	474
2009......................	1,921	29	359	270	357	274	180	451
2008......................	1,636	15	296	261	245	272	193	354
2007......................	1,553	20	290	230	263	292	133	325
2006......................	1,493	20	307	238	265	198	143	323
2005......................	1,493	22	280	239	295	190	164	303
2004......................	1,584	27	290	249	258	271	130	359
2003......................	1,401	20	225	275	260	203	130	288
ASIAN ALONE OR IN COMBINATION								
2019......................	1,022	24	196	269	209	153	100	71
2018......................	968	6	187	246	191	168	91	80
2017......................	928	25	164	252	195	155	60	76
2016......................	843	15	153	209	174	169	60	63
2015......................	981	10	146	270	205	164	88	98
2014......................	834	5	150	171	212	145	60	92
2013......................	894	22	179	173	191	121	78	128
2012......................	843	11	131	183	219	126	80	94
2011......................	697	16	122	161	121	110	61	108
2010......................	727	17	128	166	157	119	63	76
2009......................	678	4	134	127	165	109	65	74
2008......................	708	5	121	131	146	125	79	102
2007......................	612	9	119	104	145	118	65	52
2006......................	588	3	97	105	141	117	55	69
2005......................	657	12	107	122	153	128	59	77
2003......................	613	16	124	133	147	89	44	60

NA = Not available.

r = Revised, controlled to 1990 census based population estimates; previous 1993 data controlled to 1980 census based population estimates.

[1] Starting in 2003 respondents could identify more than one race. Except as noted, the race data in this table from 2003 onward represent those respondents who indicated only one race category.

[2] The data shown prior to 2003 consists of those identifying themselves as "Asian or Pacific Islanders."

[3] Total excludes age groups where "NA" appears in the column.This applies to people 35 and over prior to 1972 for the total population, prior to 1973 for the White alone population and the Black alone population, and prior to 1986 for the Hispanic population.Data for 1950 exclude persons aged 30 and over.

[4] Data for 1955 to 1963 are for Black and other races.

[5] This series was discontinued in 2006.

Table A-17. College Enrollment of Students 14 Years Old and Over, by Type of College, Attendance Status, Age, and Sex, October 1970–2019

(Numbers in thousands; civilian noninstitutionalized population.)

Year and type of college	All students Total	14 to 19 years	20 to 21 years	22 to 24 years	25 to 34 years	35 years and over	Public	Private	Male Total	Full-time	Part-time	Female Total	Full-time	Part-time
ALL UNDERGRADUATES														
2019	14,586	4,212	4,307	2,543	2,202	1,322	12,317	2,268	6,567	5,244	1,323	8,019	6,237	1,782
2018	14,827	4,393	4,237	2,607	2,322	1,269	12,457	2,370	6,727	5,494	1,233	8,100	6,231	1,869
2017	14,589	4,126	4,261	2,615	2,295	1,293	12,236	2,353	6,581	5,210	1,371	8,008	6,125	1,884
2016	15,497	4,369	4,295	2,916	2,489	1,427	12,523	2,974	7,075	5,630	1,445	8,422	6,486	1,936
2015	15,433	4,165	4,371	2,774	2,570	1,553	12,762	2,671	7,002	5,477	1,525	8,431	6,438	1,992
2014	15,498	4,249	4,075	2,978	2,438	1,759	12,877	2,620	7,071	5,713	1,358	8,427	6,524	1,903
2013	15,738	4,202	4,159	3,052	2,598	1,727	13,129	2,609	7,097	5,606	1,492	8,641	6,507	2,133
2012	16,170	4,236	4,420	3,025	2,783	1,706	13,451	2,719	7,107	5,603	1,505	9,063	6,789	2,274
2011	16,625	4,435	4,368	3,000	3,019	1,802	13,816	2,809	7,515	5,830	1,685	9,110	6,908	2,202
2010	16,354	4,546	4,225	2,671	2,912	2,000	13,701	2,653	7,300	5,582	1,718	9,054	6,773	2,282
2009	16,012	4,463	3,965	2,849	2,737	1,999	13,356	2,656	7,121	5,632	1,488	8,891	6,686	2,205
2008	14,955	4,347	3,862	2,600	2,430	1,716	12,340	2,616	6,737	5,220	1,517	8,218	6,158	2,060
2007	14,365	4,237	3,732	2,513	2,277	1,605	11,811	2,554	6,405	5,053	1,353	7,959	5,813	2,146
2006	13,854	3,940	3,591	2,437	2,178	1,709	11,269	2,585	6,135	4,686	1,450	7,719	5,695	2,024
2005	14,169	3,901	3,847	2,588	2,142	1,690	11,292	2,876	6,189	4,799	1,391	7,979	5,852	2,127
2004	14,004	3,863	3,700	2,431	2,257	1,753	11,384	2,620	6,156	4,714	1,442	7,848	5,704	2,144
2003	13,370	3,633	3,449	2,687	2,094	1,506	10,980	2,389	5,902	4,476	1,425	7,468	5,391	2,077
2002	13,426	3,743	3,457	2,355	2,106	1,764	10,830	2,595	5,929	4,462	1,467	7,497	5,273	2,223
2001	12,552	3,568	3,329	2,136	1,979	1,540	10,188	2,364	5,522	4,057	1,464	7,030	4,949	2,082
2000	12,401	3,710	3,093	2,113	1,988	1,498	10,044	2,357	5,520	4,059	1,461	6,881	4,832	2,049
1999	12,046	3,625	3,043	2,000	1,885	1,493	9,689	2,357	5,554	4,143	1,411	6,492	4,548	1,945
1998	12,509	3,749	3,019	2,025	2,101	1,616	10,100	2,410	5,621	4,051	1,570	6,888	4,765	2,123
1997	12,409	3,504	3,080	2,137	1,970	1,718	10,074	2,335	5,539	4,165	1,375	6,870	4,752	2,118
1996	12,305	3,526	2,856	2,017	2,226	1,680	10,121	2,183	5,533	4,032	1,502	6,772	4,502	2,269
1995	11,966	3,251	2,881	2,033	2,151	1,651	9,570	2,396	5,413	3,911	1,501	6,554	4,433	2,121
1994	12,410	3,192	3,006	2,099	2,281	1,832	9,983	2,427	5,526	3,969	1,557	6,883	4,480	2,404
1993r	11,959	3,197	2,879	2,131	2,118	1,634	9,706	2,253	5,442	4,020	1,422	6,517	4,346	2,171
1993	11,507	3,045	2,721	2,020	2,088	1,633	9,330	2,176	5,194	3,812	1,382	6,313	4,182	2,130
1992	11,643	3,097	2,902	2,004	2,090	1,550	9,519	2,124	5,091	3,724	1,365	6,553	4,338	2,214
1991	11,374	3,061	2,902	1,757	2,120	1,534	9,257	2,117	5,120	3,724	1,395	6,254	4,145	2,109
1990	11,108	3,194	2,740	1,681	2,067	1,425	9,031	2,076	5,030	3,628	1,402	6,077	3,967	2,109
1989	10,661	3,250	2,529	1,658	1,921	1,304	8,633	2,027	4,730	3,436	1,295	5,931	3,880	2,051
1988	10,605	3,229	2,645	1,600	1,865	1,266	8,617	1,988	4,763	3,441	1,322	5,842	3,816	2,026
1987	10,304	3,283	2,585	1,512	1,848	1,076	8,306	1,998	4,878	3,476	1,403	5,426	3,445	1,981
1986	10,036	3,158	2,298	1,583	1,932	1,065	7,955	2,081	4,663	3,350	1,312	5,373	3,474	1,899
1985	10,097	3,169	2,586	1,475	1,884	984	8,042	2,055	4,667	3,454	1,213	5,430	3,578	1,852
1984	9,910	3,120	2,564	1,547	1,826	852	7,944	1,966	4,725	3,573	1,152	5,185	3,419	1,766
1983	9,925	3,200	2,464	1,475	1,873	914	7,808	2,117	4,759	3,472	1,287	5,166	3,424	1,742
1982	9,952	3,183	2,657	1,526	1,745	843	7,908	2,044	4,703	3,485	1,218	5,249	3,480	1,769
1981	9,969	3,276	2,511	1,458	1,808	916	7,789	2,180	4,724	3,452	1,273	5,245	3,490	1,755
1980	9,279	3,182	2,393	1,316	1,598	791	NA	NA	4,353	3,247	1,105	4,927	3,210	1,717
1979	9,193	3,156	2,308	1,297	1,526	905	7,331	1,861	4,387	3,219	1,168	4,805	3,163	1,642
1978	8,947	3,173	2,246	1,233	1,505	790	7,008	1,939	4,445	3,269	1,176	4,502	3,031	1,471
1977[1]	8,408	3,184	2,376	1,206	1,640	NA	6,683	1,724	4,372	3,304	1,068	4,027	3,002	1,025
1976	8,988	3,216	2,358	1,224	1,472	718	7,196	1,787	4,569	3,353	1,213	4,419	3,166	1,253
1975	8,108	3,237	2,255	1,072	1,546	NA	6,598	1,510	4,393	3,394	999	3,715	2,902	813
1974	7,338	2,906	2,131	1,028	1,272	NA	5,843	1,494	4,030	3,128	902	3,307	2,561	746
1973	6,794	2,812	2,031	924	1,028	NA	5,279	1,516	3,791	3,035	756	3,004	2,423	581
1972	6,992	2,974	2,065	944	1,011	NA	5,460	1,532	3,982	3,231	751	3,010	2,445	565
1971	6,895	3,008	1,936	1,019	931	NA	5,472	1,423	4,017	3,240	777	2,878	2,348	530
1970	6,274	2,854	1,803	866	750	NA	4,910	1,363	3,627	3,045	582	2,646	2,164	482
TWO-YEAR COLLEGE STUDENTS														
2019	4,330	1,323	991	604	833	579	4,053	277	2,041	1,342	699	2,289	1,469	820
2018	4,272	1,488	878	558	818	530	3,986	285	1,828	1,246	582	2,444	1,512	932
2017	4,272	1,292	956	644	888	491	3,979	293	1,988	1,317	671	2,284	1,372	912
2016	4,346	1,363	876	692	903	512	4,054	293	2,040	1,350	690	2,306	1,432	875
2015	4,717	1,433	1,104	632	912	637	4,344	373	2,124	1,379	745	2,593	1,669	924
2014	4,841	1,432	989	734	973	714	4,410	431	2,056	1,363	693	2,786	1,839	946
2013	5,270	1,502	1,052	938	1,008	770	4,920	350	2,390	1,617	772	2,881	1,865	1,016
2012	5,830	1,624	1,307	892	1,205	802	5,377	453	2,509	1,665	844	3,321	2,119	1,201

* = Quantity equals zero or rounds to zero.
NA = Not available.
r = Revised, controlled to 1990 census based population estimates; previous 1993 data controlled to 1980 census based population estimates.
[1]Data for 1970–1975 and 1977 do not include people ages 35 and over.

Table A-17. College Enrollment of Students 14 Years Old and Over, by Type of College, Attendance Status, Age, and Sex, October 1970–2019—*Continued*

(Numbers in thousands; civilian noninstitutionalized population.)

Year and type of college	Full time						Part time					
	Total	14 to 19 years	20 to 21 years	22 to 24 years	25 to 34 years	35 years and over	Total	14 to 19 years	20 to 21 years	22 to 24 years	25 to 34 years	35 years and over
ALL UNDERGRADUATES												
2019	11,480	3,915	3,739	1,955	1,291	580	3,105	298	568	588	911	741
2018	11,725	4,062	3,746	2,024	1,283	611	3,102	331	491	583	1,039	658
2017	11,334	3,768	3,832	1,962	1,268	505	3,255	358	429	654	1,027	788
2016	12,116	4,011	3,757	2,314	1,398	637	3,381	359	539	602	1,091	790
2015	11,915	3,751	3,848	2,170	1,424	722	3,518	414	523	604	1,146	831
2014	12,237	3,943	3,620	2,338	1,542	794	3,260	306	455	640	895	964
2013	12,113	3,823	3,627	2,250	1,608	805	3,625	379	532	802	990	922
2012	12,391	3,820	3,804	2,369	1,675	723	3,779	416	616	655	1,109	983
2011	12,738	4,059	3,855	2,235	1,758	832	3,887	376	514	766	1,261	970
2010	12,354	4,032	3,653	2,071	1,674	924	4,000	514	572	599	1,237	1,077
2009	12,318	4,128	3,534	2,276	1,547	833	3,694	335	431	573	1,189	1,165
2008	11,378	3,999	3,445	2,017	1,240	676	3,577	347	417	583	1,190	1,040
2007	10,866	3,879	3,282	1,858	1,285	562	3,499	358	450	656	992	1,043
2006	10,380	3,567	3,150	1,810	1,242	612	3,474	373	441	627	936	1,097
2005	10,651	3,540	3,369	1,977	1,139	625	3,518	360	479	611	1,003	1,065
2004	10,418	3,533	3,251	1,836	1,150	648	3,586	330	449	595	1,107	1,105
2003	9,868	3,299	2,992	1,948	1,081	547	3,502	334	457	739	1,013	959
2002	9,735	3,356	3,058	1,737	1,073	511	3,690	387	399	619	1,033	1,253
2001	9,006	3,190	2,840	1,524	976	476	3,546	378	489	612	1,003	1,064
2000	8,891	3,368	2,658	1,479	930	457	3,510	342	435	633	1,058	1,041
1999	8,691	3,280	2,625	1,485	888	412	3,355	345	418	514	997	1,081
1998	8,816	3,327	2,619	1,461	956	452	3,693	421	400	563	1,145	1,164
1997	8,917	3,144	2,704	1,576	960	532	3,492	360	376	560	1,010	1,186
1996	8,534	3,131	2,460	1,516	990	437	3,771	394	396	501	1,236	1,243
1995	8,344	2,902	2,462	1,444	1,004	533	3,622	349	419	589	1,147	1,118
1994	8,449	2,843	2,585	1,455	981	586	3,961	350	421	644	1,300	1,245
1993r	8,366	2,866	2,513	1,513	941	533	3,593	332	366	619	1,176	1,102
1993	7,994	2,732	2,380	1,429	927	527	3,513	314	342	590	1,161	1,106
1992	8,063	2,838	2,506	1,427	834	458	3,580	259	396	578	1,255	1,092
1991	7,869	2,809	2,534	1,248	878	400	3,505	252	368	509	1,242	1,134
1990	7,597	2,912	2,333	1,165	824	363	3,511	282	408	515	1,244	1,062
1989	7,314	2,989	2,209	1,122	655	341	3,346	260	321	536	1,266	963
1988	7,257	2,925	2,275	1,079	691	285	3,348	303	371	521	1,173	981
1987	6,920	2,892	2,179	1,005	610	235	3,384	391	406	507	1,238	841
1986	6,825	2,880	1,973	1,055	680	237	3,212	278	324	528	1,254	828
1985	7,033	2,900	2,237	1,017	701	178	3,065	269	349	457	1,184	806
1984	6,992	2,846	2,221	1,067	689	170	2,918	274	344	480	1,139	683
1983	6,896	2,895	2,124	993	718	166	3,029	305	340	482	1,153	748
1982	6,965	2,880	2,286	979	662	159	2,987	302	372	547	1,083	684
1981	6,942	2,983	2,157	986	613	202	3,027	293	353	471	1,195	715
1980	6,457	2,897	2,107	810	500	142	2,822	283	287	505	1,098	649
1979	6,383	2,892	1,994	815	523	158	2,810	264	314	482	1,003	748
1978	6,300	2,872	1,918	820	559	132	2,647	302	328	412	947	658
1977[1]	6,304	2,855	2,075	775	598	NA	2,104	329	301	431	1,042	NA
1976	6,519	2,963	2,033	821	563	138	2,466	253	325	403	909	577
1975	6,296	2,987	1,958	696	655	NA	1,812	250	297	376	891	NA
1974	5,689	2,661	1,842	697	488	NA	1,649	245	289	331	784	NA
1973	5,460	2,629	1,801	630	398	NA	1,334	183	230	294	630	NA
1972	5,678	2,797	1,845	624	412	NA	1,314	177	220	320	599	NA
1971	5,588	2,801	1,729	700	357	NA	1,307	207	207	319	574	NA
1970	5,208	2,685	1,628	591	301	NA	1,066	169	175	275	449	NA
TWO-YEAR COLLEGE STUDENTS												
2019	2,811	1,133	672	361	418	227	1,519	190	319	242	415	353
2018	2,758	1,280	612	317	351	199	1,513	208	266	241	467	332
2017	2,689	1,039	732	391	405	122	1,583	253	225	253	483	369
2016	2,782	1,125	587	416	446	207	1,565	238	290	276	457	304
2015	3,048	1,142	792	403	457	254	1,669	291	312	229	454	383
2014	3,202	1,225	665	474	559	279	1,639	207	324	259	415	434
2013	3,482	1,254	748	571	535	374	1,788	249	305	367	472	396
2012	3,784	1,312	938	568	631	336	2,046	312	369	324	574	466

* = Quantity equals zero or rounds to zero.
NA = Not available.
r = Revised, controlled to 1990 census based population estimates; previous 1993 data controlled to 1980 census based population estimates.
[1]Data for 1970–1975 and 1977 do not include people ages 35 and over.

Table A-17. College Enrollment of Students 14 Years Old and Over, by Type of College, Attendance Status, Age, and Sex, October 1970–2019—*Continued*

(Numbers in thousands; civilian noninstitutionalized population.)

Year and type of college	Total	14 to 19 years	20 to 21 years	22 to 24 years	25 to 34 years	35 years and over	Public	Private	Male Total	Male Full-time	Male Part-time	Female Total	Female Full-time	Female Part-time
2011	5,705	1,596	1,187	845	1,237	840	5,265	440	2,453	1,664	790	3,252	2,053	1,199
2010	5,904	1,754	1,230	836	1,170	915	5,450	454	2,693	1,803	890	3,211	2,066	1,144
2009	5,551	1,636	960	813	1,221	920	5,095	456	2,363	1,573	790	3,188	2,060	1,128
2008	5,345	1,731	1,001	726	1,095	792	5,006	339	2,331	1,487	844	3,014	1,910	1,104
2007	4,814	1,496	856	774	963	725	4,418	396	2,061	1,322	739	2,753	1,666	1,087
2006	4,294	1,367	788	573	836	731	3,878	416	1,788	1,169	620	2,506	1,531	975
2005	4,327	1,259	833	603	882	751	3,890	437	1,866	1,197	669	2,462	1,436	1,026
2004	4,340	1,243	802	568	898	829	3,939	401	1,756	1,141	615	2,584	1,461	1,123
2003	4,384	1,178	746	843	834	784	3,999	385	1,782	1,055	726	2,603	1,507	1,095
2002	4,378	1,227	777	656	880	838	3,948	431	1,884	1,102	783	2,494	1,363	1,131
2001	4,159	1,200	776	605	832	746	3,749	410	1,802	1,057	745	2,357	1,252	1,105
2000	3,881	1,232	710	525	673	741	3,590	291	1,655	969	686	2,226	1,224	1,002
1999	3,794	1,187	715	460	683	749	3,482	312	1,637	949	688	2,157	1,157	1,000
1998	4,234	1,301	701	619	839	774	3,865	369	1,845	1,049	796	2,389	1,287	1,103
1997	4,078	1,178	760	528	806	807	3,780	298	1,663	983	680	2,415	1,307	1,108
1996	4,174	1,223	669	515	922	845	3,890	284	1,752	974	778	2,423	1,235	1,187
1995	3,882	1,028	608	593	892	761	3,553	330	1,626	898	728	2,256	1,124	1,132
1994	4,208	1,063	623	621	1,011	890	3,846	362	1,704	937	766	2,504	1,234	1,270
1993r	4,345	1,131	745	648	978	843	4,024	321	1,825	1,061	764	2,520	1,317	1,203
1993	4,196	1,077	696	614	965	844	3,884	311	1,748	1,006	742	2,448	1,268	1,179
1992	4,239	1,084	789	581	988	797	3,937	302	1,688	936	751	2,551	1,268	1,283
1991	4,277	1,120	732	560	1,084	781	4,025	252	1,798	973	825	2,479	1,239	1,239
1990	3,965	1,059	689	475	967	775	3,689	276	1,624	849	775	2,340	1,103	1,237
1989	3,627	1,048	557	467	880	676	3,382	245	1,464	777	688	2,163	949	1,214
1988	3,837	1,134	665	497	879	662	3,609	228	1,542	847	695	2,295	1,054	1,241
1987	3,648	1,111	624	457	851	605	3,405	243	1,522	780	742	2,127	937	1,190
1986	3,391	1,023	506	427	875	559	3,089	302	1,466	752	714	1,924	856	1,068
1985	3,289	959	558	403	851	518	3,009	281	1,336	702	634	1,954	914	1,040
1984	3,172	994	525	442	795	417	2,875	298	1,436	834	601	1,738	829	909
1983	3,416	1,050	595	405	882	485	3,136	280	1,498	807	691	1,919	897	1,022
1982	3,448	1,088	604	494	826	437	3,164	283	1,477	854	623	1,971	961	1,011
1981	3,347	1,144	566	414	768	455	3,091	255	1,475	837	638	1,872	909	963
1980	3,107	1,079	450	417	721	441	NA	NA	1,331	768	563	1,777	798	979
1979	2,897	933	403	407	664	490	2,710	187	1,251	684	567	1,646	725	921
1978	2,904	966	427	391	670	451	2,686	218	1,368	698	669	1,537	701	835
1977[1]	2,510	933	455	380	741	NA	2,362	148	1,253	681	572	1,256	691	565
1976	2,854	907	444	367	718	419	2,688	165	1,400	760	640	1,454	743	711
1975	2,561	1,024	431	354	752	NA	2,437	123	1,412	850	562	1,148	717	431
1974	2,072	834	369	305	565	NA	1,917	154	1,172	709	463	899	528	371
1973	1,797	816	278	254	449	NA	1,669	128	1,012	629	383	785	471	314
1972	1,910	883	334	267	426	NA	1,816	94	1,125	770	355	785	484	301
1971	1,830	928	307	263	331	NA	1,726	105	1,087	726	361	743	473	270
1970	1,692	895	281	234	283	NA	1,559	133	1,001	726	275	691	452	239
GRADUATE STUDENTS														
2019	3,704	42	188	893	1,544	1,037	2,429	1,275	1,500	1,004	496	2,204	1,365	839
2018	4,080	38	159	875	1,878	1,130	2,777	1,304	1,646	1,048	598	2,434	1,431	1,003
2017	3,809	53	105	1,012	1,586	1,053	2,570	1,239	1,531	994	537	2,278	1,278	1,000
2016	3,699	42	121	817	1,729	990	2,448	1,251	1,569	1,071	498	2,130	1,234	896
2015	3,668	35	134	895	1,605	998	2,413	1,255	1,482	1,043	439	2,186	1,278	908
2014	3,677	22	143	900	1,551	1,061	2,447	1,230	1,559	957	602	2,119	1,205	913
2013	3,729	57	168	873	1,468	1,164	2,385	1,344	1,439	933	506	2,291	1,182	1,108
2012	3,760	48	142	854	1,550	1,165	2,327	1,433	1,495	910	585	2,265	1,301	964
2011	3,773	11	91	868	1,598	1,205	2,318	1,454	1,617	905	712	2,156	1,261	895
2010	3,921	47	123	830	1,712	1,209	2,453	1,468	1,708	1,050	658	2,214	1,196	1,017
2009	3,752	32	70	901	1,556	1,194	2,366	1,386	1,521	852	669	2,232	1,194	1,038
2008	3,676	20	58	819	1,583	1,195	2,399	1,277	1,574	880	694	2,103	987	1,116
2007	3,591	24	62	779	1,560	1,166	2,261	1,330	1,420	819	601	2,171	971	1,200
2006	3,378	18	84	729	1,480	1,067	2,197	1,181	1,371	692	678	2,007	998	1,009
2005	3,304	7	98	574	1,458	1,167	2,143	1,161	1,349	711	638	1,955	875	1,079
2004	3,378	20	77	718	1,433	1,131	2,267	1,111	1,419	726	693	1,959	845	1,114
2003	3,268	29	84	632	1,399	1,123	2,129	1,139	1,416	774	643	1,852	849	1,003
2002	3,072	33	68	572	1,296	1,104	2,003	1,068	1,311	632	679	1,761	774	987
2001	3,321	48	91	595	1,442	1,145	2,233	1,088	1,353	614	739	1,968	784	1,184

* = Quantity equals zero or rounds to zero.
NA = Not available.
r = Revised, controlled to 1990 census based population estimates; previous 1993 data controlled to 1980 census based population estimates.
[1] Data for 1970–1975 and 1977 do not include people ages 35 and over.

Table A-17. College Enrollment of Students 14 Years Old and Over, by Type of College, Attendance Status, Age, and Sex, October 1970–2019—Continued

(Numbers in thousands; civilian noninstitutionalized population.)

Year and type of college	Full time Total	14 to 19 years	20 to 21 years	22 to 24 years	25 to 34 years	35 years and over	Part time Total	14 to 19 years	20 to 21 years	22 to 24 years	25 to 34 years	35 years and over
2011	3,716	1,341	882	458	672	363	1,989	255	306	387	564	477
2010	3,870	1,422	868	554	654	372	2,034	332	362	282	516	542
2009	3,633	1,409	689	540	641	354	1,918	227	271	274	580	566
2008	3,397	1,450	763	455	466	263	1,948	281	239	271	628	529
2007	2,988	1,276	627	425	443	219	1,826	221	230	349	520	506
2006	2,699	1,145	600	312	401	241	1,595	221	188	261	435	490
2005	2,632	1,031	605	373	393	231	1,695	228	228	230	489	520
2004	2,602	1,027	553	327	425	269	1,738	216	249	241	472	560
2003	2,563	973	516	386	429	258	1,822	205	230	457	404	526
2002	2,464	975	571	344	374	200	1,914	252	206	312	506	638
2001	2,310	951	529	301	307	222	1,850	250	247	304	524	525
2000	2,193	993	507	278	230	184	1,688	239	202	247	444	557
1999	2,105	955	498	261	230	161	1,688	231	217	199	453	588
1998	2,336	1,024	495	331	302	184	1,899	277	206	288	537	591
1997	2,290	947	522	283	327	212	1,788	231	238	245	479	595
1996	2,209	995	457	271	315	171	1,965	227	212	244	607	674
1995	2,022	810	397	298	321	195	1,860	218	211	295	571	565
1994	2,172	848	407	319	341	256	2,036	215	216	302	669	634
1993r	2,378	891	515	348	365	259	1,967	240	230	300	613	585
1993	2,274	850	483	325	360	256	1,922	227	213	288	605	588
1992	2,205	897	528	287	304	188	2,034	187	261	294	683	609
1991	2,212	915	476	269	361	191	2,065	205	256	291	723	589
1990	1,953	847	408	227	310	160	2,012	212	281	247	657	615
1989	1,725	860	368	160	210	128	1,902	188	189	307	669	548
1988	1,901	926	410	209	227	128	1,936	207	256	288	651	534
1987	1,716	839	368	192	212	105	1,932	272	256	264	639	500
1986	1,608	814	296	170	223	105	1,783	209	210	257	652	454
1985	1,615	779	341	174	244	78	1,674	180	217	229	607	440
1984	1,663	812	330	190	247	84	1,509	182	195	252	548	333
1983	1,703	855	374	159	250	65	1,713	195	221	245	631	420
1982	1,814	883	381	214	260	77	1,634	205	223	280	566	356
1981	1,745	927	357	170	188	102	1,601	217	209	243	579	353
1980	1,566	884	287	160	167	67	1,542	195	163	256	554	374
1979	1,408	749	251	156	185	68	1,489	184	152	251	480	423
1978	1,400	776	243	157	167	57	1,505	190	184	234	503	394
1977[1]	1,372	718	283	162	208	NA	1,138	216	172	218	533	NA
1976	1,503	764	261	177	228	74	1,351	143	183	190	490	346
1975	1,567	865	274	155	274	NA	994	159	157	199	478	NA
1974	1,237	702	233	151	152	NA	835	132	136	154	413	NA
1973	1,100	702	164	121	111	NA	697	114	113	133	338	NA
1972	1,255	772	223	134	126	NA	655	111	111	133	300	NA
1971	1,199	797	209	124	70	NA	631	131	98	139	261	NA
1970	1,177	786	197	114	80	NA	515	109	84	120	203	NA
GRADUATE STUDENTS												
2019	2,368	42	161	755	1,018	392	1,335	*	27	138	526	644
2018	2,479	38	134	684	1,184	439	1,601	*	26	190	693	691
2017	2,272	53	85	837	946	351	1,537	*	20	175	640	702
2016	2,305	42	95	693	1,103	372	1,394	*	26	123	627	618
2015	2,321	35	105	749	1,051	381	1,347	*	29	146	555	617
2014	2,163	22	111	739	911	380	1,515	*	32	161	640	682
2013	2,115	38	143	702	866	366	1,614	18	25	171	602	798
2012	2,211	45	122	699	924	420	1,549	3	21	155	625	745
2011	2,165	6	77	684	955	444	1,607	5	14	185	643	761
2010	2,246	35	120	697	1,027	367	1,675	12	4	133	685	842
2009	2,046	26	49	704	916	351	1,707	6	20	197	641	843
2008	1,867	20	53	646	851	296	1,810	*	5	173	732	899
2007	1,790	23	59	569	815	324	1,801	1	4	210	745	842
2006	1,690	16	70	542	809	254	1,688	3	14	187	671	813
2005	1,587	4	98	423	767	294	1,717	3	*	150	691	873
2004	1,571	20	76	548	675	252	1,807	*	1	170	757	878
2003	1,622	26	76	479	738	304	1,646	3	8	153	662	820
2002	1,406	31	61	432	631	251	1,666	2	6	140	666	852
2001	1,398	38	77	455	630	197	1,923	10	14	139	812	947

* = Quantity equals zero or rounds to zero.
NA = Not available.
r = Revised, controlled to 1990 census based population estimates; previous 1993 data controlled to 1980 census based population estimates.
[1] Data for 1970–1975 and 1977 do not include people ages 35 and over.

Table A-17. College Enrollment of Students 14 Years Old and Over, by Type of College, Attendance Status, Age, and Sex, October 1970–2019—*Continued*

(Numbers in thousands; civilian noninstitutionalized population.)

Year and type of college	All students								Male			Female		
	Total	14 to 19 years	20 to 21 years	22 to 24 years	25 to 34 years	35 years and over	Public	Private	Total	Full-time	Part-time	Total	Full-time	Part-time
2000	2,913	38	77	571	1,218	1,009	1,965	948	1,162	546	616	1,750	722	1,028
1999	3,157	45	77	620	1,211	1,205	1,970	1,188	1,403	699	703	1,755	722	1,033
1998	3,037	45	73	536	1,313	1,070	1,884	1,153	1,284	614	669	1,753	758	995
1997	3,027	30	63	562	1,299	1,073	2,016	1,010	1,304	651	653	1,723	668	1,055
1996	2,922	21	52	534	1,217	1,098	1,893	1,029	1,288	650	638	1,634	655	979
1995	2,749	8	60	465	1,198	1,018	1,802	947	1,290	646	644	1,459	554	905
1994	2,613	9	21	551	1,138	893	1,710	902	1,238	619	619	1,375	505	870
1993r	2,435	3	14	537	1,022	859	1,611	824	1,156	601	555	1,278	458	820
1993	2,391	3	13	514	1,006	856	1,580	812	1,130	579	551	1,261	446	815
1992	2,392	*	36	508	1,035	814	1,546	846	1,102	606	496	1,291	521	770
1991	2,683	*	37	547	1,165	934	1,824	859	1,320	688	631	1,364	491	872
1990	2,514	2	27	497	1,095	893	1,722	792	1,162	569	593	1,352	531	820
1989	2,520	*	40	509	1,161	809	1,662	857	1,219	626	594	1,300	515	786
1988	2,511	*	36	464	1,098	913	1,716	795	1,187	522	666	1,324	435	889
1987	2,415	1	57	494	1,137	725	1,655	760	1,152	579	573	1,263	462	801
1986	2,365	*	44	530	1,057	732	1,624	741	1,184	596	589	1,181	479	702
1985	2,427	*	31	540	1,179	678	1,652	775	1,239	607	632	1,188	395	793
1984	2,395	*	32	580	1,190	594	1,648	747	1,263	654	610	1,132	440	692
1983	2,442	*	32	568	1,214	629	1,614	829	1,279	665	614	1,163	438	725
1982	2,393	1	31	534	1,244	584	1,587	806	1,216	626	590	1,178	421	756
1981	2,205	*	34	528	1,120	523	1,478	726	1,127	546	581	1,078	347	731
1980	2,173	2	31	554	1,104	481	NA	NA	1,106	526	581	1,066	372	694
1979	2,214	*	45	497	1,149	523	1,537	678	1,105	503	602	1,109	355	754
1978	2,217	*	51	565	1,064	536	1,454	762	1,149	516	633	1,068	366	702
1977[1]	1,810	2	53	593	1,161	NA	1,241	568	995	548	447	813	338	475
1976	2,152	*	40	622	1,017	472	1,516	634	1,216	576	638	937	292	644
1975	1,590	*	59	607	923	NA	1,105	484	949	542	407	640	267	373
1974	1,490	*	61	499	930	NA	1,061	428	897	457	440	593	205	388
1973	1,385	*	42	541	801	NA	945	439	887	467	420	498	163	335
1972	1,320	1	52	517	749	NA	877	443	872	481	391	450	155	295
1971	1,192	1	60	468	663	NA	799	393	833	480	353	359	136	223
1970	1,140	*	54	488	599	NA	789	351	774	432	342	366	123	243

* = Quantity equals zero or rounds to zero.
NA = Not available.
r = Revised, controlled to 1990 census based population estimates; previous 1993 data controlled to 1980 census based population estimates.
[1]Data for 1970–1975 and 1977 do not include people ages 35 and over.

Table A-17. College Enrollment of Students 14 Years Old and Over, by Type of College, Attendance Status, Age, and Sex, October 1970–2019—*Continued*

(Numbers in thousands; civilian noninstitutionalized population.)

Year and type of college	Full time						Part time					
	Total	14 to 19 years	20 to 21 years	22 to 24 years	25 to 34 years	35 years and over	Total	14 to 19 years	20 to 21 years	22 to 24 years	25 to 34 years	35 years and over
2000	1,268	32	67	414	544	211	1,645	6	10	156	674	798
1999	1,421	38	71	487	539	287	1,736	8	6	133	672	918
1998	1,372	45	58	429	579	262	1,665	*	15	107	734	808
1997	1,319	26	57	401	605	229	1,708	3	6	160	694	844
1996	1,305	18	42	420	570	254	1,617	3	9	114	647	844
1995	1,199	8	43	352	571	225	1,550	*	17	112	627	793
1994	1,124	9	19	377	544	175	1,489	*	2	174	594	718
1993r	1,059	3	11	376	482	186	1,376	*	3	161	540	673
1993	1,025	3	10	358	469	184	1,366	*	3	156	536	672
1992	1,126	*	33	387	478	228	1,266	*	3	120	557	586
1991	1,180	*	29	423	539	188	1,504	*	8	124	626	746
1990	1,100	2	25	376	518	180	1,413	*	2	121	577	714
1989	1,140	*	33	375	525	208	1,380	*	7	135	637	601
1988	956	*	31	304	465	157	1,555	*	5	160	634	756
1987	1,041	1	52	343	477	167	1,374	*	5	151	660	558
1986	1,074	*	40	412	465	157	1,291	*	4	120	593	575
1985	1,002	*	27	385	449	141	1,424	*	4	155	728	537
1984	1,093	*	27	427	544	95	1,302	*	6	153	644	498
1983	1,103	*	32	420	530	121	1,339	*	*	148	685	507
1982	1,047	*	28	381	522	116	1,346	1	4	153	721	467
1981	893	*	28	355	447	64	1,312	*	6	173	673	459
1980	898	2	24	403	403	66	1,275	*	6	152	702	415
1979	858	*	32	358	397	72	1,356	*	14	140	752	451
1978	882	*	38	396	376	71	1,335	*	14	169	688	465
1977[1]	886	2	43	382	459	NA	922	*	10	211	702	NA
1976	869	*	35	405	355	73	1,282	*	5	217	662	398
1975	809	*	43	382	386	NA	780	*	16	225	537	NA
1974	662	*	41	289	330	NA	828	*	20	210	600	NA
1973	630	*	33	350	248	NA	755	*	9	191	553	NA
1972	636	1	44	332	262	NA	686	*	8	185	487	NA
1971	616	1	57	299	261	NA	576	*	3	169	402	NA
1970	555	*	42	304	212	NA	585	*	12	184	387	NA

* = Quantity equals zero or rounds to zero.
NA = Not available.
r = Revised, controlled to 1990 census based population estimates; previous 1993 data controlled to 1980 census based population estimates.
[1]Data for 1970–1975 and 1977 do not include people ages 35 and over.

Table A-18. Total Fall Enrollment in Degree-Granting Institutions, by Attendance Status, Sex of Student, and Control of Institution, Selected Years, 1947–2018

(Number; percent.)

Year	Total enrolled	Attendance status			Sex of student			Control of institution			
		Full-time	Part-time	Percent part-time	Male	Female	Percent Female	Public	Private		
									Total	Nonprofit	For-profit
2018.............	19,645,918	11,991,721	7,654,197	39.0	8,442,662	11,203,256	57.0	14,529,264	5,116,654	4,134,244	982,410
2017.............	19,778,151	12,076,141	7,702,010	38.9	8,571,314	11,206,837	56.7	14,571,739	5,206,412	4,108,489	1,097,923
2016.............	19,846,904	12,125,314	7,721,590	38.9	8,638,422	11,208,482	56.5	14,585,840	5,261,064	4,078,956	1,182,108
2015.............	19,988,204	12,287,512	7,700,692	38.5	8,723,819	11,264,385	56.4	14,572,843	5,415,361	4,065,891	1,349,470
2014.............	20,209,092	12,454,464	7,754,628	38.4	8,797,530	11,411,562	56.5	14,654,660	5,554,432	3,997,249	1,557,183
2013.............	20,376,677	12,596,610	7,780,067	38.2	8,861,197	11,515,480	56.5	14,746,848	5,629,829	3,971,390	1,658,439
2012.............	20,644,478	12,734,404	7,910,074	38.3	8,919,006	11,725,472	56.8	14,884,667	5,759,811	3,951,388	1,808,423
2011.............	21,010,590	13,002,531	8,008,059	38.1	9,034,256	11,976,334	57.0	15,116,303	5,894,287	3,926,819	1,967,468
2010.............	21,019,438	13,087,182	7,932,256	37.7	9,045,759	11,973,679	57.0	15,142,171	5,877,267	3,854,482	2,022,785
2009.............	20,313,594	12,605,355	7,708,239	37.9	8,732,953	11,580,641	57.0	14,810,768	5,502,826	3,767,672	1,735,154
2008	19,102,814	11,747,743	7,355,071	38.5	8,188,895	10,913,919	57.1	13,972,153	5,130,661	3,661,519	1,469,142
2007	18,248,128	11,269,892	6,978,236	38.2	7,815,914	10,432,214	57.2	13,490,780	4,757,348	3,571,150	1,186,198
2006	17,758,870	10,957,305	6,801,565	38.3	7,574,815	10,184,055	57.3	13,180,133	4,578,737	3,512,866	1,065,871
2005	17,487,475	10,797,011	6,690,464	38.3	7,455,925	10,031,550	57.4	13,021,834	4,465,641	3,454,692	1,010,949
2004	17,272,044	10,610,177	6,661,867	38.6	7,387,262	9,884,782	57.2	12,980,112	4,291,932	3,411,685	880,247
2003	16,911,481	10,326,133	6,585,348	38.9	7,260,264	9,651,217	57.1	12,858,698	4,052,783	3,341,048	711,735
2002	16,611,711	9,946,359	6,665,352	40.1	7,202,116	9,409,595	56.6	12,751,993	3,859,718	3,265,476	594,242
2001	15,927,987	9,447,502	6,480,485	40.7	6,960,815	8,967,172	56.3	12,233,156	3,694,831	3,167,330	527,501
2000	15,312,289	9,009,600	6,302,689	41.2	6,721,769	8,590,520	56.1	11,752,786	3,559,503	3,109,419	450,084
1999	14,849,691	8,803,139	6,046,552	40.7	6,515,164	8,334,527	56.1	11,375,739	3,473,952	3,055,029	418,923
1998	14,506,967	8,563,338	5,943,629	41.0	6,369,265	8,137,702	56.1	11,137,769	3,369,198	3,004,925	364,273
1997	14,502,334	8,438,062	6,064,272	41.8	6,396,028	8,106,306	55.9	11,196,119	3,306,215	2,977,614	328,601
1996	14,367,520	8,302,953	6,064,567	42.2	6,352,825	8,014,695	55.8	11,120,499	3,247,021	2,942,556	304,465
1995	14,261,781	8,128,802	6,132,979	43.0	6,342,539	7,919,242	55.5	11,092,374	3,169,407	2,929,044	240,363
1994	14,278,790	8,137,776	6,141,014	43.0	6,371,898	7,906,892	55.4	11,133,680	3,145,110	2,910,107	235,003
1993	14,304,803	8,127,618	6,177,185	43.2	6,427,450	7,877,353	55.1	11,189,088	3,115,715	2,888,897	226,818
1992	14,487,359	8,162,118	6,325,241	43.7	6,523,989	7,963,370	55.0	11,384,567	3,102,792	2,872,523	230,269
1991	14,358,953	8,115,329	6,243,624	43.5	6,501,844	7,857,109	54.7	11,309,563	3,049,390	2,819,041	230,349
1990	13,818,637	7,820,985	5,997,652	43.4	6,283,909	7,534,728	54.5	10,844,717	2,973,920	2,760,227	213,693
1989	13,538,560	7,660,950	5,877,610	43.4	6,190,015	7,348,545	54.3	10,577,963	2,960,597	2,731,174	229,423
1988	13,055,337	7,436,768	5,618,569	43.0	6,001,896	7,053,441	54.0	10,161,388	2,893,949	2,673,567	220,382
1987	12,766,642	7,231,085	5,535,557	43.4	5,932,056	6,834,586	53.5	9,973,254	2,793,388	2,602,350	191,038[3]
1986	12,503,511	7,119,550	5,383,961	43.1	5,884,515	6,618,996	52.9	9,713,893	2,789,618	2,572,479	217,139[3]
1985	12,247,055	7,075,221	5,171,834	42.2	5,818,450	6,428,605	52.5	9,479,273	2,767,782	2,571,791	195,991
1984	12,241,940	7,098,388	5,143,552	42.0	5,863,574	6,378,366	52.1	9,477,370	2,764,570	2,574,419	190,151
1983	12,464,661	7,261,050	5,203,611	41.7	6,023,725	6,440,936	51.7	9,682,734	2,781,927	2,589,187	192,740
1982	12,425,780	7,220,618	5,205,162	41.9	6,031,384	6,394,396	51.5	9,696,087	2,729,693	2,552,739	176,954[2]
1981	12,371,672	7,181,250	5,190,422	42.0	5,975,056	6,396,616	51.7	9,647,032	2,724,640	2,572,405	152,235[2]
1980	12,096,895	7,097,958	4,998,937	41.3	5,874,374	6,222,521	51.4	9,457,394	2,639,501	2,527,787	152,235[2]
1979	11,569,899	6,794,039	4,775,860	41.3	5,682,877	5,887,022	50.9	9,036,822	2,533,077	2,461,773	71,304
1978	11,260,092	6,667,657	4,592,435	40.8	5,640,998	5,619,094	49.9	8,785,893	2,474,199	2,408,331	65,868
1977	11,285,787	6,792,925	4,492,862	39.8	5,789,016	5,496,771	48.7	8,846,993	2,438,794	2,386,652	52,142
1976	11,012,137	6,717,058	4,295,079	39.0	5,810,828	5,201,309	47.2	8,653,477	2,358,660	2,314,298	44,362
1975	11,184,859	6,841,334	4,343,525	38.8	6,148,997	5,035,862	45.0	8,834,508	2,350,351	2,311,448	38,903
1974	10,223,729	6,370,273	3,853,456	37.7	5,622,429	4,601,300	45.0	7,988,500	2,235,229	2,200,963	34,266
1973	9,602,123	6,189,493	3,412,630	35.5	5,371,052	4,231,071	44.1	7,419,516	2,182,607	2,148,784	33,823
1972	9,214,860	6,072,389	3,142,471	34.1	5,238,757	3,976,103	43.1	7,070,635	2,144,225	2,123,245	20,980
1971	8,948,644	6,077,232	2,871,412	32.1	5,207,004	3,741,640	41.8	6,804,309	2,144,335	2,121,913	22,422
1970	8,580,887	5,816,290	2,764,597	32.2	5,043,642	3,537,245	41.2	6,428,134	2,152,753	2,134,420	18,333
1969	8,004,660	5,498,883	2,505,777	31.3	4,746,201	3,258,459	40.7	5,896,868	2,107,792	2,087,653	20,139
1968	7,513,091	5,210,155	2,302,936	30.7	4,477,649	3,035,442	40.4	5,430,652	2,082,439	2,061,211	21,228
1967	6,911,748	4,793,128	2,118,620	30.7	4,132,800	2,778,948	40.2	4,816,028	2,095,720	2,074,041	21,679
1966.............	6,389,872	4,438,606	1,951,266	30.5	3,856,216	2,533,656	39.7	4,348,917	2,040,955	NA	NA
1965.............	5,920,864	4,095,728	1,825,136	30.8	3,630,020	2,290,844	38.7	3,969,596	1,951,268	NA	NA
1964.............	5,280,020	3,573,238	1,706,782	32.3	3,248,713	2,031,307	38.5	3,467,708	1,812,312	NA	NA
1963.............	4,779,609	3,183,833	1,595,776	33.4	2,961,540	1,818,069	38.0	3,081,279	1,698,330	NA	NA
1961.............	4,145,065	2,785,133	1,359,932	32.8	2,585,821	1,559,244	37.6	2,561,447	1,583,618	NA	NA

Note: Data through 1995 are for institutions of higher education, while later data are for degree-granting institutions. Degree-granting institutions grant associate's or higher degrees and participate in Title IV federal financial aid programs. The degree-granting classification is very similar to the earlier higher education classification, but it includes more 2-year colleges and excludes a few higher education institutions that did not grant degrees. Some data have been revised from previously published figures.
NA = Not available..

Table A-18.   Total Fall Enrollment in Degree-Granting Institutions, by Attendance Status, Sex of Student, and Control of Institution, Selected Years, 1947–2018—*Continued*

(Number; percent.)

Year	Total enrolled	Attendance status			Sex of student			Control of institution			
		Full-time	Part-time	Percent part-time	Male	Female	Percent Female	Public	Private		
									Total	Nonprofit	For-profit
1959...............	3,639,847	2,421,016	1,218,831	33.5	2,332,617	1,307,230	35.9	2,180,982	1,458,865	NA	NA
1957	3,323,783	NA	NA	NA	2,170,765	1,153,018	34.7	1,972,673	1,351,110	NA	NA
1956...............	2,918,212	NA	NA	NA	1,911,458	1,006,754	34.5	1,656,402	1,261,810	NA	NA
1955...............	2,653,034	NA	NA	NA	1,733,184	919,850	34.7	1,476,282	1,176,752	NA	NA
1954...............	2,446,693	NA	NA	NA	1,563,382	883,311	36.1	1,353,531	1,093,162	NA	NA
1953...............	2,231,054	NA	NA	NA	1,422,598	808,456	36.2	1,185,876	1,045,178	NA	NA
1952...............	2,134,242	NA	NA	NA	1,380,357	753,885	35.3	1,101,240	1,033,002	NA	NA
1951...............	2,101,962	NA	NA	NA	1,390,740	711,222	33.8	1,037,938	1,064,024	NA	NA
1950...............	2,281,298	NA	NA	NA	1,560,392	720,906	31.6	1,139,699	1,141,599	NA	NA
1949...............	2,444,900	NA	NA	NA	1,721,572	723,328	29.6	1,207,151	1,237,749	NA	NA
1948...............	2,403,396	NA	NA	NA	1,709,367	694,029	28.9	1,185,588	1,217,808	NA	NA
1947...............	2,338,226	NA	NA	NA	1,659,249	678,977	29.0	1,152,377	1,185,849	NA	NA

Note: Data through 1995 are for institutions of higher education, while later data are for degree-granting institutions. Degree-granting institutions grant associate's or higher degrees and participate in Title IV federal financial aid programs. The degree-granting classification is very similar to the earlier higher education classification, but it includes more 2-year colleges and excludes a few higher education institutions that did not grant degrees. Some data have been revised from previously published figures.

NA = Not available..

Table A-19. Total Fall Enrollment in Degree-Granting Institutions, by Control and Type of Institution, 1970–2018

(Numbers in thousands.)

Year	All institutions			Public institutions			Private institutions		
	Total	4-year	2-year	Total	4-year	2-year	Total	4-year	2-year
2018	19,646	13,901	5,745	14,529	8,983	5,547	5,117	4,918	199
2017	19,778	13,825	5,953	14,572	8,854	5,717	5,206	4,971	235
2016	19,847	13,754	6,092	14,586	8,743	5,843	5,261	5,012	250
2015	19,988	13,489	6,499	14,573	8,349	6,224	5,415	5,140	275
2014	20,209	13,494	6,715	14,655	8,257	6,398	5,554	5,237	317
2013	20,377	13,406	6,971	14,747	8,120	6,626	5,630	5,286	344
2012	20,644	13,477	7,168	14,885	8,093	6,792	5,760	5,384	376
2011	21,011	13,499	7,511	15,116	8,048	7,068	5,894	5,451	443
2010	21,019	13,336	7,684	15,142	7,924	7,218	5,877	5,412	466
2009	20,314	12,791	7,523	14,811	7,709	7,102	5,503	5,082	421
2008	19,103	12,131	6,971	13,972	7,332	6,640	5,131	4,800	331
2007	18,248	11,630	6,618	13,491	7,167	6,324	4,757	4,464	294
2006	17,759	11,240	6,519	13,180	6,955	6,225	4,579	4,285	293
2005	17,487	10,999	6,488	13,022	6,838	6,184	4,466	4,162	304
2004	17,272	10,726	6,546	12,980	6,737	6,244	4,292	3,990	302
2003	16,911	10,417	6,494	12,859	6,649	6,209	4,053	3,768	285
2002	16,612	10,082	6,529	12,752	6,482	6,270	3,860	3,601	259
2001	15,928	9,677	6,251	12,233	6,236	5,997	3,695	3,441	254
2000	15,312	9,364	5,948	11,753	6,055	5,697	3,560	3,308	251
1999	14,850	9,196	5,654	11,376	5,978	5,398	3,474	3,218	255
1998	14,507	9,018	5,489	11,138	5,892	5,246	3,369	3,126	243
1997	14,502	8,897	5,606	11,196	5,835	5,361	3,306	3,061	245
1996	14,368	8,804	5,563	11,120	5,806	5,314	3,247	2,998	249
1995	14,262	8,769	5,493	11,092	5,815	5,278	3,169	2,955	215
1994	14,279	8,749	5,530	11,134	5,825	5,308	3,145	2,924	221
1993	14,305	8,739	5,566	11,189	5,852	5,337	3,116	2,887	229
1992	14,487	8,765	5,722	11,385	5,900	5,485	3,103	2,865	238
1991	14,359	8,707	5,652	11,310	5,905	5,405	3,049	2,802	247
1990	13,819	8,579	5,240	10,845	5,848	4,996	2,974	2,730	244
1989	13,539	8,388	5,151	10,578	5,694	4,884	2,961	2,693	267
1988	13,055	8,180	4,875	10,161	5,546	4,615	2,894	2,634	260
1987	12,767	7,990	4,776	9,973	5,432	4,541	2,793	2,558	235[2]
1986	12,504	7,824	4,680	9,714	5,300	4,414	2,790	2,524	265[2]
1985	12,247	7,716	4,531	9,479	5,210	4,270	2,768	2,506	261
1984	12,242	7,711	4,531	9,477	5,198	4,279	2,765	2,513	252
1983	12,465	7,741	4,723	9,683	5,223	4,459	2,782	2,518	264
1982	12,426	7,654	4,772	9,696	5,176	4,520	2,730	2,478	264[1]
1981	12,372	7,655	4,716	9,647	5,166	4,481	2,725	2,489	264[1]
1980	12,097	7,571	4,526	9,457	5,129	4,329	2,640	2,442	264[1]
1979	11,570	7,353	4,217	9,037	4,980	4,057	2,533	2,373	160
1978	11,260	7,232	4,028	8,786	4,912	3,874	2,474	2,319	155
1977	11,286	7,243	4,043	8,847	4,945	3,902	2,439	2,298	141
1976	11,012	7,129	3,883	8,653	4,902	3,752	2,359	2,227	132
1975	11,185	7,215	3,970	8,835	4,998	3,836	2,350	2,217	134
1974	10,224	6,820	3,404	7,989	4,703	3,285	2,235	2,117	119
1973	9,602	6,590	3,012	7,420	4,530	2,890	2,183	2,060	122
1972	9,215	6,459	2,756	7,071	4,430	2,641	2,144	2,029	115
1971	8,949	6,369	2,579	6,804	4,347	2,457	2,144	2,022	122
1970	8,581	6,262	2,319	6,428	4,233	2,195	2,153	2,029	124

Note: Data through 1995 are for institutions of higher education, while later data are for degree-granting institutions. Degree-granting institutions grant associate's or higher degrees and participate in Title IV federal financial aid programs. The degree-granting classification is very similar to the earlier higher education classification, but it includes more 2-year colleges and excludes a few higher education institutions that did not grant degrees. A university is an institution of higher education consisting of a liberal arts college, a diverse graduate program, and usually two or more professional schools or faculties. It is empowered to confer degrees in various fields of study; for purposes of maintaining trend data in this publication, the selection of university institutions has not been revised since 1982. Some data have been revised from previously published figures.

[1] Large increases are due to the addition of schools accredited by the Accrediting Commission of Career Schools and Colleges of Technology.

[2] Because of imputation techniques, data are not consistent with figures for other years.

Table A-20. Total Undergraduate Fall Enrollment in Degree-Granting Four-Year Institutions, by Attendance Status, Sex of Student, and Control of Institution, Selected Years 1970–2018

(Number.)

Year	Total	Full-time	Part-time	Males	Females	Males	
						Full-time	Part-time
2018	16,610,235	10,267,135	6,343,100	7,225,999	9,384,236	4,602,752	2,623,247
2017	16,773,036	10,371,863	6,401,173	7,351,259	9,421,777	4,683,715	2,667,544
2016	16,874,649	10,430,068	6,444,581	7,416,859	9,457,790	4,725,510	2,691,349
2015	17,046,673	10,603,030	6,443,643	7,502,254	9,544,419	4,809,098	2,693,156
2014	17,294,136	10,784,392	6,509,744	7,586,299	9,707,837	4,877,531	2,708,768
2013	17,476,304	10,939,276	6,537,028	7,660,140	9,816,164	4,950,210	2,709,930
2012	17,735,638	11,097,092	6,638,546	7,714,938	10,020,700	4,984,389	2,730,549
2011	18,077,303	11,365,175	6,712,128	7,822,992	10,254,311	5,070,553	2,752,439
2010	18,082,427	11,457,040	6,625,387	7,836,282	10,246,145	5,118,975	2,717,307
2009	17,464,179	11,038,275	6,425,904	7,563,176	9,901,003	4,942,120	2,621,056
2008	16,365,738	10,254,930	6,110,808	7,066,623	9,299,115	4,577,431	2,489,192
2007	15,603,771	9,840,978	5,762,793	6,727,600	8,876,171	4,396,868	2,330,732
2006	15,184,302	9,571,079	5,613,223	6,513,756	8,670,546	4,264,606	2,249,150
2005	14,963,964	9,446,430	5,517,534	6,408,871	8,555,093	4,200,863	2,208,008
2004	14,780,630	9,284,336	5,496,294	6,340,048	8,440,582	4,140,628	2,199,420
2003	14,480,364	9,045,253	5,435,111	6,227,372	8,252,992	4,048,682	2,178,690
2002	14,257,077	8,734,252	5,522,825	6,192,390	8,064,687	3,934,168	2,258,222
2001	13,715,610	8,327,640	5,387,970	6,004,431	7,711,179	3,768,630	2,235,801
2000	13,155,393	7,922,926	5,232,467	5,778,268	7,377,125	3,588,246	2,190,022
1999	12,739,445	7,753,548	4,985,897	5,584,234	7,155,211	3,524,586	2,059,648
1998	12,436,937	7,538,711	4,898,226	5,446,133	6,990,804	3,428,161	2,017,972
1997	12,450,587	7,418,598	5,031,989	5,468,532	6,982,055	3,379,597	2,088,935
1996	12,326,948	7,298,839	5,028,109	5,420,672	6,906,276	3,339,108	2,081,564
1995	12,231,719	7,145,268	5,086,451	5,401,130	6,830,589	3,296,610	2,104,520
1994	12,262,608	7,168,706	5,093,902	5,422,113	6,840,495	3,341,591	2,080,522
1993	12,323,959	7,179,482	5,144,477	5,483,682	6,840,277	3,381,997	2,101,685
1992	12,537,700	7,244,442	5,293,258	5,582,936	6,954,764	3,424,739	2,158,197
1991	12,439,287	7,221,412	5,217,875	5,571,003	6,868,284	3,435,526	2,135,477
1990	11,959,106	6,976,030	4,983,076	5,379,759	6,579,347	3,336,535	2,043,224
1989	11,742,531	6,840,696	4,901,835	5,310,990	6,431,541	3,278,647	2,032,343
1988	11,316,548	6,642,428	4,674,120	5,137,644	6,178,904	3,206,442	1,931,202
1987	11,046,235	6,462,549	4,583,686	5,068,457	5,977,778	3,163,676	1,904,781
1986	10,797,975	6,352,073	4,445,902	5,017,505	5,780,470	3,146,330	1,871,175
1985	10,596,674	6,319,592	4,277,082	4,962,080	5,634,594	3,156,446	1,805,634
1984	10,618,071	6,347,653	4,270,418	5,006,813	5,611,258	3,194,930	1,811,883
1983	10,845,995	6,514,034	4,331,961	5,158,300	5,687,695	3,304,247	1,854,053
1982	10,825,062	6,483,805	4,341,257	5,170,494	5,654,568	3,299,436	1,871,058
1981	10,754,522	6,449,068	4,305,454	5,108,271	5,646,251	3,260,473	1,847,798
1980	10,475,055	6,361,744	4,113,311	5,000,177	5,474,878	3,226,857	1,773,320
1975	9,679,455	6,168,396	3,511,059	5,257,005	4,422,450	3,459,328	1,797,677
1970	7,368,644	5,280,064	2,088,580	4,249,702	3,118,942	3,096,371	1,153,331

NA = Not available.

Note: Data include unclassified undergraduate students. Data through 1995 are for institutions of higher education, while later data are for degree-granting institutions. Degree-granting institutions grant associate's or higher degrees and participate in Title IV federal financial aid programs. The degree-granting classification is very similar to the earlier higher education classification, but it includes more 2-year colleges and excludes a few higher education institutions that did not grant degrees. Some data have been revised from previously published figures. Details may not sum to totals because of rounding.

Table A-20. Total Undergraduate Fall Enrollment in Degree-Granting Four-Year Institutions, by Attendance Status, Sex of Student, and Control of Institution, Selected Years 1970–2018—*Continued*

(Number.)

Year	Females		Public	Private		
	Full-time	Part-time		Total	Nonprofit	For-profit
2018	5,664,383	3,719,853	13,049,326	3,560,909	2,821,653	739,256
2017	5,688,148	3,733,629	13,112,594	3,660,442	2,819,080	841,362
2016	5,704,558	3,753,232	13,143,979	3,730,670	2,813,742	916,928
2015	5,793,932	3,750,487	13,150,823	3,895,850	2,822,122	1,073,728
2014	5,906,861	3,800,976	13,244,533	4,049,603	2,772,065	1,277,538
2013	5,989,066	3,827,098	13,348,292	4,128,012	2,755,463	1,372,549
2012	6,112,703	3,907,997	13,478,100	4,257,538	2,744,400	1,513,138
2011	6,294,622	3,959,689	13,694,899	4,382,404	2,718,923	1,663,481
2010	6,338,065	3,908,080	13,703,000	4,379,427	2,652,993	1,726,434
2009	6,096,155	3,804,848	13,386,375	4,077,804	2,595,171	1,482,633
2008	5,677,499	3,621,616	12,591,217	3,774,521	2,536,532	1,237,989
2007	5,444,110	3,432,061	12,137,583	3,466,188	2,470,327	995,861
2006	5,306,473	3,364,073	11,847,426	3,336,876	2,448,240	888,636
2005	5,245,567	3,309,526	11,697,730	3,266,234	2,418,368	847,866
2004	5,143,708	3,296,874	11,650,580	3,130,050	2,389,366	740,684
2003	4,996,571	3,256,421	11,523,103	2,957,261	2,346,673	610,588
2002	4,800,084	3,264,603	11,432,855	2,824,222	2,306,091	518,131
2001	4,559,010	3,152,169	10,985,871	2,729,739	2,257,718	472,021
2000	4,334,680	3,042,445	10,539,322	2,616,071	2,213,180	402,891
1999	4,228,962	2,926,249	10,174,228	2,565,217	2,185,290	379,927
1998	4,110,550	2,880,254	9,950,212	2,486,725	2,152,655	334,070
1997	4,039,001	2,943,054	10,007,479	2,443,108	2,139,824	303,284
1996	3,959,731	2,946,545	9,935,283	2,391,665	2,112,318	279,347
1995	3,848,658	2,981,931	9,903,626	2,328,093	2,104,693	223,400
1994	3,827,115	3,013,380	9,945,128	2,317,480	2,100,465	217,015
1993	3,797,485	3,042,792	10,011,787	2,312,172	2,099,197	212,975
1992	3,819,703	3,135,061	10,216,297	2,321,403	2,101,721	219,682
1991	3,785,886	3,082,398	10,147,957	2,291,330	2,072,354	218,976
1990	3,639,495	2,939,852	9,709,596	2,249,510	2,043,407	206,103
1989	3,562,049	2,869,492	9,487,742	2,254,789	NA	NA
1988	3,435,986	2,742,918	9,103,146	2,213,402	NA	NA
1987	3,298,873	2,678,905	8,918,589	2,127,646	1,939,942	187,704
1986	3,205,743	2,574,727	8,660,716	2,137,259	1,928,294	208,965
1985	3,163,146	2,471,448	8,477,125	2,119,549	1,928,996	190,553
1984	3,152,723	2,458,535	8,493,491	2,124,580	1,940,310	184,270
1983	3,209,787	2,477,908	8,697,118	2,148,877	1,961,076	187,801
1982	3,184,369	2,470,199	8,713,073	2,111,989	1,939,389	172,600
1981	3,188,595	2,457,656	8,648,363	2,106,159	1,958,848	147,311
1980	3,134,887	2,339,991	8,441,955	2,033,100	1,926,703	106,397
1975	2,709,068	1,713,382	7,826,032	1,853,423	1,814,844	38,579
1970	2,183,693	935,249	5,620,255	1,748,389	1,730,133	18,256

NA = Not available.
Note: Data include unclassified undergraduate students. Data through 1995 are for institutions of higher education, while later data are for degree-granting institutions. Degree-granting institutions grant associate's or higher degrees and participate in Title IV federal financial aid programs. The degree-granting classification is very similar to the earlier higher education classification, but it includes more 2-year colleges and excludes a few higher education institutions that did not grant degrees. Some data have been revised from previously published figures. Details may not sum to totals because of rounding.

Table A-21. Total Postbaccalaureate Fall Enrollment in Degree-granting Institutions, by Attendance Status, Sex of Student, and Control of Institution, 1967–2018

(Number.)

Year	Total	Full-time	Part-time	Males	Females	Males Full-time	Males Part-time
2018	3,035,683	1,724,586	1,311,097	1,216,663	1,819,020	736,182	480,481
2017	3,005,115	1,704,278	1,300,837	1,220,055	1,785,060	740,240	479,815
2016	2,972,255	1,695,246	1,277,009	1,221,563	1,750,692	747,288	474,275
2015	2,941,531	1,684,482	1,257,049	1,221,565	1,719,966	749,349	472,216
2014	2,914,956	1,670,072	1,244,884	1,211,231	1,703,725	742,247	468,984
2013	2,900,373	1,657,334	1,243,039	1,201,057	1,699,316	732,112	468,945
2012	2,908,840	1,637,312	1,271,528	1,204,068	1,704,772	724,017	480,051
2011	2,933,287	1,637,356	1,295,931	1,211,264	1,722,023	722,265	488,999
2010	2,937,011	1,630,142	1,306,869	1,209,477	1,727,534	719,408	490,069
2009	2,849,415	1,567,080	1,282,335	1,169,777	1,679,638	689,977	479,800
2008	2,737,076	1,492,813	1,244,263	1,122,272	1,614,804	656,926	465,346
2007	2,644,357	1,428,914	1,215,443	1,088,314	1,556,043	632,576	455,738
2006	2,574,568	1,386,226	1,188,342	1,061,059	1,513,509	614,709	446,350
2005	2,523,511	1,350,581	1,172,930	1,047,054	1,476,457	602,525	444,529
2004	2,491,414	1,325,841	1,165,573	1,047,214	1,444,200	598,727	448,487
2003	2,431,117	1,280,880	1,150,237	1,032,892	1,398,225	589,190	443,702
2002	2,354,634	1,212,107	1,142,527	1,009,726	1,344,908	566,930	442,796
2001	2,212,377	1,119,862	1,092,515	956,384	1,255,993	531,260	425,124
2000	2,156,896	1,086,674	1,070,222	943,501	1,213,395	522,847	420,654
1999	2,110,246	1,049,591	1,060,655	930,930	1,179,316	508,930	422,000
1998	2,070,030	1,024,627	1,045,403	923,132	1,146,898	505,492	417,640
1997	2,051,747	1,019,464	1,032,283	927,496	1,124,251	510,845	416,651
1996	2,040,572	1,004,114	1,036,458	932,153	1,108,419	512,100	420,053
1995	2,030,062	983,534	1,046,528	941,409	1,088,653	510,782	430,627
1994	2,016,182	969,070	1,047,112	949,785	1,066,397	513,592	436,193
1993	1,980,844	948,136	1,032,708	943,768	1,037,076	508,574	435,194
1992	1,949,659	917,676	1,031,983	941,053	1,008,606	502,166	438,887
1991	1,919,666	893,917	1,025,749	930,841	988,825	493,849	436,992
1990	1,859,531	844,955	1,014,576	904,150	955,381	471,217	432,933
1989	1,796,029	820,254	975,775	879,025	917,004	461,596	417,429
1988	1,738,789	794,340	944,449	864,252	874,537	455,337	408,915
1987	1,720,407	768,536	951,871	863,599	856,808	447,212	416,387
1986	1,705,536	767,477	938,059	867,010	838,526	452,717	414,293
1985	1,650,381	755,629	894,752	856,370	794,011	451,274	405,096
1984	1,623,869	750,735	873,134	856,761	767,108	452,579	404,182
1983	1,618,666	747,016	871,650	865,425	753,241	455,540	409,885
1982	1,600,718	736,813	863,905	860,890	739,828	453,519	407,371
1981	1,617,150	732,182	884,968	866,785	750,365	452,364	414,421
1980	1,621,840	736,214	885,626	874,197	747,643	462,387	411,810
1979	1,571,922	714,624	857,298	862,754	709,168	456,197	406,557
1978	1,575,693	704,831	870,862	879,931	695,762	458,865	421,066
1977	1,569,084	698,902	870,182	891,819	677,265	462,038	429,781
1976	1,577,546	683,825	893,721	904,551	672,995	459,286	445,265
1975	1,505,404	672,938	832,466	891,992	613,412	467,425	424,567
1974	1,425,001	643,927	781,074	856,847	568,154	454,706	402,141
1973	1,342,452	610,935	731,517	833,453	508,999	444,219	389,234
1972	1,272,421	583,299	689,122	810,164	462,257	436,533	373,631
1971	1,204,390	564,236	640,154	789,131	415,259	428,167	360,964
1970	1,212,243	536,226	676,017	793,940	418,303	407,724	386,216
1969	1,120,175	506,833	613,342	738,673	381,502	383,630	355,043
1968	1,037,377	469,747	567,630	696,649	340,728	358,686	337,963
1967	896,065	448,238	447,827	630,701	265,364	354,628	276,073

NA = Not available.

Note: Data include unclassified graduate students. Data through 1995 are for institutions of higher education, while later data are for degree-granting institutions. Degree-granting institutions grant associate's or higher degrees and participate in Title IV federal financial aid programs. The degree-granting classification is very similar to the earlier higher education classification, but it includes more 2-year colleges and excludes a few higher education institutions that did not grant degrees. Some data have been revised from previously published figures.

Table A-21. Total Postbaccalaureate Fall Enrollment in Degree-granting Institutions, by Attendance Status, Sex of Student, and Control of Institution, 1967–2018—*Continued*

(Number.)

Year	Females		Public	Private		
	Full-time	Part-time		Total	Nonprofit	For-profit
2018	988,404	830,616	1,479,938	1,555,745	1,312,591	243,154
2017	964,038	821,022	1,459,145	1,545,970	1,289,409	256,561
2016	947,958	802,734	1,441,861	1,530,394	1,265,214	265,180
2015	935,133	784,833	1,422,020	1,519,511	1,243,769	275,742
2014	927,825	775,900	1,410,127	1,504,829	1,225,184	279,645
2013	925,222	774,094	1,398,556	1,501,817	1,215,927	285,890
2012	913,295	791,477	1,406,567	1,502,273	1,206,988	295,285
2011	915,091	806,932	1,421,404	1,511,883	1,207,896	303,987
2010	910,734	816,800	1,439,171	1,497,840	1,201,489	296,351
2009	877,103	802,535	1,424,393	1,425,022	1,172,501	252,521
2008	835,887	778,917	1,380,936	1,356,140	1,124,987	231,153
2007	796,338	759,705	1,353,197	1,291,160	1,100,823	190,337
2006	771,517	741,992	1,332,707	1,241,861	1,064,626	177,235
2005	748,056	728,401	1,324,104	1,199,407	1,036,324	163,083
2004	727,114	717,086	1,329,532	1,161,882	1,022,319	139,563
2003	691,690	706,535	1,335,595	1,095,522	994,375	101,147
2002	645,177	699,731	1,319,138	1,035,496	959,385	76,111
2001	588,602	667,391	1,247,285	965,092	909,612	55,480
2000	563,827	649,568	1,213,464	943,432	896,239	47,193
1999	540,661	638,655	1,201,511	908,735	869,739	38,996
1998	519,135	627,763	1,187,557	882,473	852,270	30,203
1997	508,619	615,632	1,188,640	863,107	837,790	25,317
1996	492,014	616,405	1,185,216	855,356	830,238	25,118
1995	472,752	615,901	1,188,748	841,314	824,351	16,963
1994	455,478	610,919	1,188,552	827,630	809,642	17,988
1993	439,562	597,514	1,177,301	803,543	789,700	13,843
1992	415,510	593,096	1,168,270	781,389	770,802	10,587
1991	400,068	588,757	1,161,606	758,060	746,687	11,373
1990	373,738	581,643	1,135,121	724,410	716,820	7,590
1989	358,658	558,346	1,090,221	705,808	NA	NA
1988	339,003	535,534	1,058,242	680,547	NA	NA
1987	321,324	535,484	1,054,665	665,742	662,408	3,334
1986	314,760	523,766	1,053,177	652,359	644,185	8,174
1985	304,355	489,656	1,002,148	648,233	642,795	5,438
1984	298,156	468,952	983,879	639,990	634,109	5,881
1983	291,476	461,765	985,616	633,050	628,111	4,939
1982	283,294	456,534	983,014	617,704	613,350	4,354
1981	279,818	470,547	998,669	618,481	613,557	4,924
1980	273,827	473,816	1,015,439	606,401	601,084	5,317
1979	258,427	450,741	989,991	581,931	578,425	3,506
1978	245,966	449,796	998,608	577,085	573,563	3,522
1977	236,864	440,401	1,004,013	565,071	561,384	3,687
1976	224,539	448,456	1,033,115	544,431	541,064	3,367
1975	205,513	407,899	1,008,476	496,928	496,604	324
1974	189,221	378,933	956,770	468,231	467,950	281
1973	166,716	342,283	897,104	445,348	445,205	143
1972	146,766	315,491	848,031	424,390	424,278	112
1971	136,069	279,190	796,516	407,874	407,804	70
1970	128,502	289,801	807,879	404,364	404,287	77
1969	123,203	258,299	738,551	381,624	381,558	66
1968	111,061	229,667	648,657	388,720	388,681	39
1967	93,610	171,754	522,623	373,442	373,336	106

NA = Not available.
Note: Data include unclassified graduate students. Data through 1995 are for institutions of higher education, while later data are for degree-granting institutions. Degree-granting institutions grant associate's or higher degrees and participate in Title IV federal financial aid programs. The degree-granting classification is very similar to the earlier higher education classification, but it includes more 2-year colleges and excludes a few higher education institutions that did not grant degrees. Some data have been revised from previously published figures.

This page is intentionally left blank

Table A-22. Total Fall Enrollment in Degree-Granting Institutions, by Race/Ethnicity, Sex, Attendance Status, and Level of Student, Selected Years 1976–2018

(Numbers in thousands; percent.)

Race/ethnicity, sex, attendance status, and level of student	1976		1990		2000		2010		2013	
	Number	Percent	Number	Percent	Number	Percent	Number	Percent	Number	Percent
All students, total	10,986	100.0	13,819	100.0	15,312	100.0	21,019	100.0	20,377	100.0
White	9,076	84.3	10,722	79.9	10,462	70.8	12,721	62.6	11,589	59.3
Black	1,033	9.6	1,247	9.3	1,730	11.7	3,039	15.0	2,872	14.7
Hispanic	384	3.6	782	5.8	1,462	9.9	2,749	13.5	3,093	15.8
Asian/Pacific Islander	198	1.8	572	4.3	978	6.6	1,282	6.3	1,260	6.4
Asian	NA	NA	NA	NA	NA	NA	1,218	6.0	1,199	6.1
Pacific Islander	NA	NA	NA	NA	NA	NA	64	0.3	61	0.3
American Indian/Alaska Native	76	0.7	103	0.8	151	1.0	196	1.0	162	0.8
Two or more races	NA	NA	NA	NA	NA	NA	325	1.6	560	2.9
Nonresident alien	219	X	391	X	529	X	708	X	840	X
Male	5,794	100.0	6,284	100.0	6,722	100.0	9,046	100.0	8,861	100.0
White	4,814	85.3	4,861	80.5	4,635	72.1	5,606	64.7	5,132	61.1
Black	470	8.3	485	8.0	635	9.9	1,089	12.6	1,065	12.7
Hispanic	210	3.7	354	5.9	627	9.8	1,158	13.4	1,308	15.6
Asian/Pacific Islander	108	1.9	295	4.9	466	7.3	601	6.9	594	7.1
Asian	NA	NA	NA	NA	NA	NA	572	6.6	567	6.8
Pacific Islander	NA	NA	NA	NA	NA	NA	29	0.3	27	0.3
American Indian/Alaska Native	39	0.7	43	0.7	61	1.0	79	0.9	65	0.8
Two or more races	NA	NA	NA	NA	NA	NA	134	1.6	237	2.8
Nonresident alien	154	X	246	X	297	X	380	X	460	X
Female	5,191	100.0	7,535	100.0	8,591	100.0	11,974	100.0	11,515	100.0
White	4,262	83.1	5,861	79.3	5,827	69.7	7,115	61.1	6,457	58.0
Black	563	11.0	762	10.3	1,095	13.1	1,950	16.7	1,807	16.2
Hispanic	174	3.4	429	5.8	835	10.0	1,591	13.7	1,785	16.0
Asian/Pacific Islander	89	1.7	278	3.8	512	6.1	681	5.8	665	6.0
Asian	NA	NA	NA	NA	NA	NA	646	5.5	632	5.7
Pacific Islander	NA	NA	NA	NA	NA	NA	35	0.3	34	0.3
American Indian/Alaska Native	38	0.7	60	0.8	90	1.1	118	1.0	98	0.9
Two or more races	NA	NA	NA	NA	NA	NA	191	1.6	323	2.9
Nonresident alien	65	X	145	X	231	X	328	X	380	X
Full-time	6,704	100.0	7,821	100.0	9,010	100.0	13,087	100.0	12,597	100.0
White	5,513	84.2	6,016	79.9	6,231	72.5	8,053	64.3	7,238	60.8
Black	659	10.1	718	9.5	983	11.4	1,811	14.5	1,669	14.0
Hispanic	211	3.2	395	5.2	710	8.3	1,501	12.0	1,702	14.3
Asian/Pacific Islander	118	1.8	347	4.6	591	6.9	821	6.6	821	6.9
Asian	NA	NA	NA	NA	NA	NA	783	6.3	786	6.6
Pacific Islander	NA	NA	NA	NA	NA	NA	38	0.3	36	0.3
American Indian/Alaska Native	43	0.7	54	0.7	84	1.0	118	0.9	94	0.8
Two or more races	NA	NA	NA	NA	NA	NA	217	1.7	378	3.2
Nonresident alien	160	X	290	X	410	X	565	X	695	X
Part-time	4,282	100.0	5,998	100.0	6,303	100.0	7,932	100.0	7,780	100.0
White	3,563	84.4	4,706	79.8	4,231	68.4	4,667	59.9	4,352	57.0
Black	374	8.9	529	9.0	748	12.1	1,228	15.8	1,203	15.8
Hispanic	173	4.1	388	6.6	751	12.2	1,248	16.0	1,391	18.2
Asian/Pacific Islander	80	1.9	225	3.8	387	6.3	461	5.9	438	5.7
Asian	NA	NA	NA	NA	NA	NA	435	5.6	413	5.4
Pacific Islander	NA	NA	NA	NA	NA	NA	26	0.3	25	0.3
American Indian/Alaska Native	33	0.8	48	0.8	67	1.1	78	1.0	68	0.9
Two or more races	NA	NA	NA	NA	NA	NA	108	1.4	183	2.4
Nonresident alien	59	X	102	X	119	X	142	X	145	X
Undergraduate, total	9,419	100.0	11,959	100.0	13,155	100.0	18,082	100.0	17,476	100.0
White	7,740	83.4	9,273	79.0	8,983	69.8	10,896	61.6	9,898	58.2
Black	943	10.2	1,147	9.8	1,549	12.0	2,677	15.1	2,505	14.7
Hispanic	353	3.8	725	6.2	1,351	10.5	2,551	14.4	2,872	16.9

NA = Not available.

X = Not applicable.

Note: Race categories exclude persons of Hispanic ethnicity. Because of underreporting and nonreporting of racial/ethnic data, some figures are slightly lower than corresponding data in other tables. Data through 1990 are for institutions of higher education, while later data are for degree-granting institutions. Degree-granting institutions grant associate's or higher degrees and participate in Title IV federal financial aid programs. The degree-granting classification is very similar to the earlier higher education classification, but it includes more 2-year colleges and excludes a few higher education institutions that did not grant degrees. Some data have been revised from previously published figures. Detail may not sum to totals because of rounding.

Table A-22. Total Fall Enrollment in Degree-Granting Institutions, by Race/Ethnicity, Sex, Attendance Status, and Level of Student, Selected Years 1976–2018—*Continued*

(Numbers in thousands; percent.)

Race/ethnicity, sex, attendance status, and level of student	2014 Number	2014 Percent	2015 Number	2015 Percent	2016 Number	2016 Percent	2017 Number	2017 Percent	2018 Number	2018 Percent
All students, total	20,209	100.0	19,988	100.0	19,847	100.0	19,778	100.0	19,646	100.0
White	11,239	58.3	10,939	57.6	10,717	56.9	10,517	56.0	10,301	55.2
Black	2,793	14.5	2,681	14.1	2,589	13.7	2,550	13.6	2,493	13.4
Hispanic	3,192	16.5	3,298	17.4	3,428	18.2	3,546	18.9	3,645	19.5
Asian/Pacific Islander	1,272	6.6	1,284	6.8	1,307	6.9	1,328	7.1	1,353	7.3
Asian	1,214	6.3	1,229	6.5	1,253	6.7	1,276	6.8	1,302	7.0
Pacific Islander	58	0.3	55	0.3	53	0.3	52	0.3	51	0.3
American Indian/Alaska Native	153	0.8	146	0.8	142	0.8	137	0.7	134	0.7
Two or more races	642	3.3	658	3.5	666	3.5	700	3.7	728	3.9
Nonresident alien	918	X	982	X	998	X	1,000	X	992	X
Male	8,798	100.0	8,724	100.0	8,638	100.0	8,571	100.0	8,443	100.0
White	4,974	60.0	4,848	59.3	4,736	58.6	4,632	57.8	4,500	57.0
Black	1,035	12.5	999	12.2	959	11.9	942	11.7	910	11.5
Hispanic	1,348	16.3	1,389	17.0	1,439	17.8	1,479	18.4	1,508	19.1
Asian/Pacific Islander	599	7.2	603	7.4	610	7.5	617	7.7	626	7.9
Asian	573	6.9	578	7.1	586	7.3	594	7.4	603	7.6
Pacific Islander	26	0.3	25	0.3	24	0.3	23	0.3	22	0.3
American Indian/Alaska Native	61	0.7	58	0.7	56	0.7	54	0.7	52	0.7
Two or more races	270	3.3	278	3.4	282	3.5	295	3.7	305	3.9
Nonresident alien	510	X	549	X	556	X	552	X	543	X
Female	11,412	100.0	11,264	100.0	11,208	100.0	11,207	100.0	11,203	100.0
White	6,265	56.9	6,091	56.2	5,981	55.6	5,885	54.7	5,801	53.9
Black	1,758	16.0	1,682	15.5	1,630	15.1	1,607	14.9	1,584	14.7
Hispanic	1,844	16.8	1,908	17.6	1,989	18.5	2,067	19.2	2,137	19.9
Asian/Pacific Islander	673	6.1	681	6.3	697	6.5	710	6.6	727	6.8
Asian	641	5.8	651	6.0	667	6.2	682	6.3	699	6.5
Pacific Islander	32	0.3	30	0.3	30	0.3	29	0.3	28	0.3
American Indian/Alaska Native	92	0.8	88	0.8	86	0.8	84	0.8	82	0.8
Two or more races	373	3.4	380	3.5	384	3.6	405	3.8	423	3.9
Nonresident alien	408	X	434	X	443	X	448	X	449	X
Full-time	12,454	100.0	12,288	100.0	12,125	100.0	12,076	100.0	11,992	100.0
White	6,983	59.7	6,784	59.1	6,611	58.5	6,482	57.6	6,359	56.9
Black	1,600	13.7	1,537	13.4	1,470	13.0	1,454	12.9	1,416	12.7
Hispanic	1,748	14.9	1,786	15.6	1,843	16.3	1,914	17.0	1,965	17.6
Asian/Pacific Islander	832	7.1	844	7.4	857	7.6	870	7.7	888	7.9
Asian	798	6.8	812	7.1	827	7.3	841	7.5	860	7.7
Pacific Islander	34	0.3	32	0.3	30	0.3	29	0.3	28	0.3
American Indian/Alaska Native	88	0.8	83	0.7	80	0.7	76	0.7	74	0.7
Two or more races	440	3.8	440	3.8	435	3.9	455	4.0	471	4.2
Nonresident alien	763	X	813	X	828	X	825	X	818	X
Part-time	7,755	100.0	7,701	100.0	7,722	100.0	7,702	100.0	7,654	100.0
White	4,256	56.0	4,155	55.2	4,105	54.4	4,035	53.6	3,942	52.7
Black	1,192	15.7	1,144	15.2	1,120	14.8	1,096	14.6	1,077	14.4
Hispanic	1,444	19.0	1,511	20.1	1,585	21.0	1,632	21.7	1,680	22.5
Asian/Pacific Islander	440	5.8	440	5.8	449	5.9	458	6.1	465	6.2
Asian	416	5.5	417	5.5	427	5.6	435	5.8	443	5.9
Pacific Islander	24	0.3	24	0.3	23	0.3	23	0.3	22	0.3
American Indian/Alaska Native	65	0.9	63	0.8	62	0.8	61	0.8	60	0.8
Two or more races	202	2.7	217	2.9	230	3.1	245	3.3	256	3.4
Nonresident alien	155	X	169	X	170	X	175	X	174	X
Undergraduate, total	17,294	100.0	17,047	100.0	16,875	100.0	16,773	100.0	16,610	100.0
White	9,583	57.2	9,304	56.4	9,086	55.7	8,883	54.8	8,665	54.0
Black	2,427	14.5	2,317	14.1	2,226	13.7	2,184	13.5	2,128	13.3
Hispanic	2,962	17.7	3,055	18.5	3,168	19.4	3,271	20.2	3,353	20.9

NA = Not available.

X = Not applicable.

Note: Race categories exclude persons of Hispanic ethnicity. Because of underreporting and nonreporting of racial/ethnic data, some figures are slightly lower than corresponding data in other tables. Data through 1990 are for institutions of higher education, while later data are for degree-granting institutions. Degree-granting institutions grant associate's or higher degrees and participate in Title IV federal financial aid programs. The degree-granting classification is very similar to the earlier higher education classification, but it includes more 2-year colleges and excludes a few higher education institutions that did not grant degrees. Some data have been revised from previously published figures. Detail may not sum to totals because of rounding.

Table A-22. Total Fall Enrollment in Degree-Granting Institutions, by Race/Ethnicity, Sex, Attendance Status, and Level of Student, Selected Years 1976–2018—*Continued*

(Numbers in thousands; percent.)

Race/ethnicity, sex, attendance status, and level of student	1976 Number	1976 Percent	1990 Number	1990 Percent	2000 Number	2000 Percent	2010 Number	2010 Percent	2013 Number	2013 Percent
Asian/Pacific Islander	169	1.8	500	4.3	846	6.6	1,087	6.1	1,064	6.3
Asian	NA	NA	NA	NA	NA	NA	1,030	5.8	1,010	5.9
Pacific Islander	NA	NA	NA	NA	NA	NA	58	0.3	54	0.3
American Indian/Alaska Native	70	0.8	95	0.8	139	1.1	179	1.0	147	0.9
Two or more races	NA	NA	NA	NA	NA	NA	294	1.7	506	3.0
Nonresident alien	143	X	219	X	288	X	398	X	484	X
Undergraduate, male	4,897	100.0	5,380	100.0	5,778	100.0	7,836	100.0	7,660	100.0
White	4,052	84.4	4,184	79.6	4,010	71.3	4,861	63.7	4,439	60.0
Black	431	9.0	448	8.5	577	10.3	983	12.9	955	12.9
Hispanic	192	4.0	327	6.2	583	10.4	1,083	14.2	1,224	16.5
Asian/Pacific Islander	91	1.9	254	4.8	402	7.1	513	6.7	507	6.9
Asian	NA	NA	NA	NA	NA	NA	487	6.4	483	6.5
Pacific Islander	NA	NA	NA	NA	NA	NA	26	0.3	25	0.3
American Indian/Alaska Native	35	0.7	40	0.8	56	1.0	72	0.9	59	0.8
Two or more races	NA	NA	NA	NA	NA	NA	122	1.6	217	2.9
Nonresident alien	96	X	126	X	150	X	201	X	258	X
Undergraduate, female	4,522	100.0	6,579	100.0	7,377	100.0	10,246	100.0	9,816	100.0
White	3,688	82.4	5,088	78.4	4,973	68.7	6,035	60.1	5,459	56.9
Black	513	11.5	699	10.8	972	13.4	1,694	16.9	1,549	16.2
Hispanic	161	3.6	398	6.1	768	10.6	1,468	14.6	1,648	17.2
Asian/Pacific Islander	78	1.7	246	3.8	444	6.1	574	5.7	557	5.8
Asian	NA	NA	NA	NA	NA	NA	542	5.4	527	5.5
Pacific Islander	NA	NA	NA	NA	NA	NA	32	0.3	30	0.3
American Indian/Alaska Native	35	0.8	56	0.9	82	1.1	107	1.1	88	0.9
Two or more races	NA	NA	NA	NA	NA	NA	171	1.7	289	3.0
Nonresident alien	47	X	93	X	138	X	197	X	225	X
Postbaccalaureate, total	1,567	100.0	1,860	100.0	2,157	100.0	2,937	100.0	2,900	100.0
White	1,336	89.6	1,450	86.0	1,479	77.2	1,825	69.4	1,691	66.5
Black	90	6.0	100	5.9	181	9.5	362	13.8	367	14.4
Hispanic	31	2.1	58	3.4	111	5.8	198	7.5	221	8.7
Asian/Pacific Islander	29	1.9	72	4.3	133	6.9	194	7.4	195	7.7
Asian	NA	NA	NA	NA	NA	NA	188	7.1	188	7.4
Pacific Islander	NA	NA	NA	NA	NA	NA	6	0.2	7	0.3
American Indian/Alaska Native	6	0.4	7	0.4	13	0.7	17	0.7	15	0.6
Two or more races	NA	NA	NA	NA	NA	NA	32	1.2	54	2.1
Nonresident alien	75	X	173	X	241	X	309	X	357	X
Postbaccalaureate, male	898	100.0	904	100.0	944	100.0	1,209	100.0	1,201	100.0
White	762	90.7	677	86.3	625	78.4	745	72.2	693	69.4
Black	39	4.7	37	4.7	58	7.3	106	10.3	110	11.0
Hispanic	18	2.2	27	3.4	45	5.6	75	7.2	84	8.4
Asian/Pacific Islander	17	2.1	40	5.2	64	8.0	87	8.5	87	8.7
Asian	NA	NA	NA	NA	NA	NA	85	8.2	84	8.4
Pacific Islander	NA	NA	NA	NA	NA	NA	3	0.2	3	0.3
American Indian/Alaska Native	4	0.4	3	0.4	5	0.6	6	0.6	5	0.5
Two or more races	NA	NA	NA	NA	NA	NA	12	1.2	21	2.1
Nonresident alien	58	X	120	X	147	X	178	X	202	X
Postbaccalaureate, female	669	100.0	955	100.0	1,213	100.0	1,728	100.0	1,699	100.0
White	574	88.1	773	85.6	854	76.3	1,080	67.7	998	64.6
Black	50	7.7	63	7.0	123	11.0	256	16.0	258	16.7
Hispanic	13	2.0	31	3.4	66	5.9	123	7.7	137	8.9
Asian/Pacific Islander	11	1.7	32	3.5	69	6.1	107	6.7	108	7.0
Asian	NA	NA	NA	NA	NA	NA	103	6.5	104	6.7
Pacific Islander	NA	NA	NA	NA	NA	NA	4	0.2	4	0.3
American Indian/Alaska Native	3	0.4	4	0.5	8	0.7	11	0.7	9	0.6
Two or more races	NA	NA	NA	NA	NA	NA	20	1.2	34	2.2
Nonresident alien	18	X	53	X	94	X	131	X	155	X

NA = Not available.

X = Not applicable.

Note: Race categories exclude persons of Hispanic ethnicity. Because of underreporting and nonreporting of racial/ethnic data, some figures are slightly lower than corresponding data in other tables. Data through 1990 are for institutions of higher education, while later data are for degree-granting institutions. Degree-granting institutions grant associate's or higher degrees and participate in Title IV federal financial aid programs. The degree-granting classification is very similar to the earlier higher education classification, but it includes more 2-year colleges and excludes a few higher education institutions that did not grant degrees. Some data have been revised from previously published figures. Detail may not sum to totals because of rounding.

Table A-22.   Total Fall Enrollment in Degree-Granting Institutions, by Race/Ethnicity, Sex, Attendance Status, and Level of Student, Selected Years 1976–2018—*Continued*

(Numbers in thousands; percent.)

Race/ethnicity, sex, attendance status, and level of student	2014 Number	2014 Percent	2015 Number	2015 Percent	2016 Number	2016 Percent	2017 Number	2017 Percent	2018 Number	2018 Percent
Asian/Pacific Islander	1,075	6.4	1,084	6.6	1,100	6.7	1,114	6.9	1,132	7.1
Asian	1,023	6.1	1,035	6.3	1,053	6.5	1,068	6.6	1,087	6.8
Pacific Islander	52	0.3	49	0.3	47	0.3	46	0.3	45	0.3
American Indian/Alaska Native	139	0.8	132	0.8	129	0.8	124	0.8	120	0.7
Two or more races	580	3.5	590	3.6	595	3.7	624	3.9	647	4.0
Nonresident alien	529	X	565	X	570	X	574	X	567	X
Undergraduate, male	7,586	100.0	7,502	100.0	7,417	100.0	7,351	100.0	7,226	100.0
White	4,299	58.9	4,188	58.2	4,087	57.5	3,990	56.7	3,867	55.9
Black	925	12.7	888	12.3	849	12.0	832	11.8	800	11.6
Hispanic	1,262	17.3	1,298	18.0	1,343	18.9	1,379	19.6	1,403	20.3
Asian/Pacific Islander	512	7.0	515	7.2	521	7.3	525	7.5	531	7.7
Asian	488	6.7	492	6.8	499	7.0	504	7.2	511	7.4
Pacific Islander	24	0.3	23	0.3	21	0.3	21	0.3	20	0.3
American Indian/Alaska Native	56	0.8	53	0.7	52	0.7	49	0.7	47	0.7
Two or more races	246	3.4	252	3.5	255	3.6	267	3.8	275	4.0
Nonresident alien	287	X	307	X	310	X	309	X	302	X
Undergraduate, female	9,708	100.0	9,544	100.0	9,458	100.0	9,422	100.0	9,384	100.0
White	5,283	55.8	5,116	55.1	4,999	54.3	4,893	53.4	4,797	52.6
Black	1,502	15.9	1,428	15.4	1,377	15.0	1,352	14.8	1,327	14.6
Hispanic	1,701	18.0	1,757	18.9	1,825	19.8	1,892	20.7	1,950	21.4
Asian/Pacific Islander	563	6.0	569	6.1	580	6.3	588	6.4	600	6.6
Asian	535	5.6	543	5.8	554	6.0	563	6.2	576	6.3
Pacific Islander	29	0.3	26	0.3	26	0.3	25	0.3	25	0.3
American Indian/Alaska Native	83	0.9	79	0.9	77	0.8	75	0.8	73	0.8
Two or more races	334	3.5	338	3.6	340	3.7	357	3.9	372	4.1
Nonresident alien	242	X	258	X	261	X	265	X	264	X
Postbaccalaureate, total	2,915	100.0	2,942	100.0	2,972	100.0	3,005	100.0	3,036	100.0
White	1,657	65.6	1,635	64.8	1,631	64.1	1,635	63.4	1,637	62.7
Black	366	14.5	364	14.4	363	14.3	365	14.2	365	14.0
Hispanic	229	9.1	243	9.6	260	10.2	275	10.7	292	11.2
Asian/Pacific Islander	197	7.8	200	7.9	206	8.1	214	8.3	221	8.5
Asian	191	7.6	194	7.7	200	7.9	208	8.1	215	8.2
Pacific Islander	6	0.3	6	0.2	6	0.2	6	0.2	6	0.2
American Indian/Alaska Native	14	0.6	14	0.6	14	0.5	14	0.5	14	0.5
Two or more races	63	2.5	67	2.7	71	2.8	76	2.9	81	3.1
Nonresident alien	388	X	417	X	428	X	426	X	425	X
Postbaccalaureate, male	1,211	100.0	1,222	100.0	1,222	100.0	1,220	100.0	1,217	100.0
White	675	68.3	660	67.4	649	66.5	642	65.7	633	64.9
Black	110	11.1	111	11.3	110	11.3	110	11.3	109	11.2
Hispanic	86	8.7	91	9.3	96	9.8	100	10.3	105	10.7
Asian/Pacific Islander	87	8.8	88	9.0	89	9.2	92	9.4	94	9.6
Asian	85	8.6	86	8.7	87	8.9	90	9.2	92	9.4
Pacific Islander	3	0.3	2	0.2	2	0.2	2	0.2	2	0.2
American Indian/Alaska Native	5	0.5	5	0.5	5	0.5	5	0.5	5	0.5
Two or more races	24	2.4	26	2.6	27	2.7	28	2.9	30	3.1
Nonresident alien	223	X	241	X	246	X	242	X	240	X
Postbaccalaureate, female	1,704	100.0	1,720	100.0	1,751	100.0	1,785	100.0	1,819	100.0
White	981	63.8	975	63.1	982	62.6	992	62.0	1,004	61.4
Black	256	16.6	254	16.4	253	16.1	255	15.9	256	15.7
Hispanic	143	9.3	152	9.8	164	10.4	175	10.9	187	11.5
Asian/Pacific Islander	110	7.1	112	7.3	117	7.5	122	7.6	127	7.8
Asian	106	6.9	109	7.0	113	7.2	118	7.4	123	7.5
Pacific Islander	4	0.3	4	0.2	4	0.2	4	0.2	4	0.2
American Indian/Alaska Native	9	0.6	9	0.6	9	0.6	9	0.6	9	0.6
Two or more races	39	2.5	42	2.7	44	2.8	48	3.0	51	3.1
Nonresident alien	165	X	176	X	182	X	184	X	185	X

NA = Not available.

X = Not applicable.

Note: Race categories exclude persons of Hispanic ethnicity. Because of underreporting and nonreporting of racial/ethnic data, some figures are slightly lower than corresponding data in other tables. Data through 1990 are for institutions of higher education, while later data are for degree-granting institutions. Degree-granting institutions grant associate's or higher degrees and participate in Title IV federal financial aid programs. The degree-granting classification is very similar to the earlier higher education classification, but it includes more 2-year colleges and excludes a few higher education institutions that did not grant degrees. Some data have been revised from previously published figures. Detail may not sum to totals because of rounding.

Table A-23. Percentage of Recent High School Completers Enrolled in College, by Race/Ethnicity, 1972–2019

(Percent.)

Year	Percent of recent high school completers[1] enrolled in college[2] (annual data)					3-year moving averages[3] Percent of recent high school completers enrolled in college					Difference between percent enrolled		
	Total	White	Black	Hispanic	Asian[4]	Total	White	Black	Hispanic	Asian[4]	White-Black	White-Hispanic	White-Asian[4]
2019	66.2	68.0	49.8	63.4	89.8	67.7	69.4	57.5	64.5	81.8	12.0	NA	-12.3
2018	69.1	70.9	64.5	65.4	73.6	67.4	69.3	58.1	63.4	82.1	11.2	5.9	-12.7
2017	66.7	69.1	59.4	61.0	82.7	68.6	69.9	60.7	66.5	82.0	9.2	NA	-12.1
2016	69.8	69.7	57.3	72.0	91.9	68.6	70.1	57.5	67.6	85.7	12.6	NA	-15.7
2015	69.2	71.3	55.6	68.9	83.2	69.1	69.6	60.8	69.0	88.5	8.8	NA	-18.9
2014	68.4	67.7	70.2	65.2	90.9	67.8	69.3	60.6	64.7	84.2	8.8	NA	-14.9
2013	65.9	68.8	56.7	59.8	80.1	66.8	67.4	60.7	65.5	83.6	6.7	NA	-16.2
2012	66.2	65.7	56.4	70.3	81.5	66.8	67.6	60.5	65.9	82.3	7.1	NA	-14.7
2011	68.2	68.3	67.1	66.6	86.1	67.5	68.2	62.1	66.1	83.9	6.1	NA	-15.7
2010	68.1	70.5	62.0	59.7	84.7	68.8	70.1	66.1	62.3	87.4	NA	7.8	-17.3
2009	70.1	71.3	69.5	59.3	92.1	68.9	71.2	62.4	60.9	88.1	8.8	10.3	-16.9
2008	68.6	71.7	55.7	63.9	88.4	68.6	70.8	60.3	62.3	90.1	10.5	8.6	-19.2
2007	67.2	69.5	55.7	64.0	88.8	67.3	70.0	55.7	62.0	85.8	14.3	8.0	-15.8
2006	66.0	68.5	55.5	57.9	82.3	67.2	70.4	55.6	58.5	85.1	14.7	11.9	-14.7
2005	68.6	73.2	55.7	54.0	86.7	67.1	70.2	58.2	57.5	80.9	12.0	12.6	-10.7
2004	66.7	68.8	62.5	61.8	75.6	66.4	69.4	58.8	57.7	81.6	10.6	11.7	-12.2
2003[5]	63.9	66.2	57.5	58.6	84.1	65.3	68.0	59.9	57.7	74.2	8.1	10.3	NA
2002	65.2	69.1	59.4	53.6	63.7	63.7	66.5	57.3	54.8	71.9	9.3	11.7	NA
2001	61.8	64.3	55.0	51.7	73.8	63.5	66.3	56.4	52.8	78.4	10.0	13.5	-12.0
2000	63.3	65.7	54.9	52.9	81.0	62.7	65.4	56.4	48.6	81.3	9.1	16.9	-15.8
1999	62.9	66.3	58.9	42.3	78.3	64.0	66.8	58.6	47.4	81.1	8.3	19.5	-14.3
1998	65.6	68.5	61.9	47.4	85.5	65.2	67.7	59.8	51.9	83.8	7.9	15.7	-16.1
1997	67.0	68.2	58.5	65.6	80.5	65.9	68.1	58.8	55.3	83.0	9.3	12.8	-15.0
1996	65.0	67.4	56.0	50.8	85.3	64.7	66.6	55.4	57.6	82.7	11.3	9.0	-16.0
1995	61.9	64.3	51.2	53.7	83.0	63.0	65.4	52.9	51.6	82.7	12.5	13.8	-17.3
1994	61.9	64.5	50.8	49.1	78.3	62.1	64.0	52.4	55.0	82.2	11.5	NA	-18.2
1993	62.6	62.9	55.6	62.2	86.2	62.1	63.9	51.3	55.7	82.5	12.6	NA	-18.6
1992	61.9	64.3	48.2	55.0	81.7	62.3	64.2	50.0	58.2	80.9	14.2	NA	-16.7
1991	62.5	65.4	46.4	57.2	78.9	61.5	64.2	47.2	52.6	80.6	17.0	11.7	-16.3
1990	60.1	63.0	46.8	42.7	81.7	60.7	63.0	48.9	52.5	81.4	14.0	NA	-18.5
1989	59.6	60.7	53.4	55.1	81.1	59.5	61.6	48.0	52.7	81.4	13.6	NA	-19.8
1988	58.9	61.1	44.4	57.1	NA	58.4	60.1	49.7	48.5	NA	10.4	11.6	NA
1987	56.8	58.6	52.2	33.5	NA	56.5	58.8	44.2	45.0	NA	14.6	13.8	NA
1986	53.8	56.8	36.9	44.0	NA	56.1	58.5	43.5	42.3	NA	15.0	16.2	NA
1985	57.7	60.1	42.2	51.0	NA	55.5	58.6	39.5	46.1	NA	19.1	12.5	NA
1984	55.2	59.0	39.8	44.3	NA	55.1	57.9	39.9	49.3	NA	18.0	NA	NA
1983	52.7	55.0	38.2	54.2	NA	52.8	55.5	38.0	46.7	NA	17.5	NA	NA
1982	50.6	52.7	35.8	43.2	NA	52.4	54.2	38.8	49.4	NA	15.4	NA	NA
1981	53.9	54.9	42.7	52.1	NA	51.3	52.4	40.3	48.7	NA	12.2	NA	NA
1980	49.3	49.8	42.7	52.3	NA	50.8	51.5	44.0	49.6	NA	7.5	NA	NA
1979	49.3	49.9	46.7	45.0	NA	49.6	50.1	45.2	46.3	NA	NA	NA	NA
1978	50.1	50.5	46.4	42.0	NA	50.0	50.4	47.5	46.1	NA	NA	NA	NA
1977	50.6	50.8	49.5	50.8	NA	49.9	50.1	46.8	48.8	NA	NA	NA	NA
1976	48.8	48.8	44.4	52.7	NA	50.1	50.3	45.3	53.6	NA	NA	NA	NA
1975	50.7	51.1	41.7	58.0	NA	49.1	49.1	44.5	52.7	NA	NA	NA	NA
1974	47.6	47.2	47.2	46.9	NA	48.3	48.7	40.5	53.1	NA	8.3	NA	NA
1973	46.6	47.8	32.5	54.1	NA	47.8	48.2	41.4	48.8	NA	6.8	NA	NA
1972	49.2	49.7	44.6	45.0	NA	49.7	50.5	38.4	49.9	NA	12.1	NA	NA

NA = Not available.

[1] Individuals ages 16 to 24 who graduated from high school or completed a GED or other high school equivalency credential.

[2] Enrollment in college as of October of each year for individuals ages 16 to 24 who had completed high school earlier in the calendar year.

[3] A 3-year moving average is a weighted average of the year indicated, the year immediately preceding, and the year immediately following. For the first and final years of available data, a 2-year moving average is used: The moving average for 1960 reflects an average of 1960 and 1961; for Black and Hispanic data, the moving average for 1972 reflects an average of 1972 and 1973; for Asian-only data, the moving average for 2003 reflects an average of 2003 and 2004; and the moving average for 2019 reflects an average of 2018 and 2019. Moving averages are used to produce more stable estimates.

[4] Prior to 2003, Asian data include Pacific Islanders.

[5] After 2002, White, Black, and Asian data exclude persons of Two or more races.

PART A
NATIONAL EDUCATION STATISTICS

■ **Attainment Tables**

Table A-24. Educational Attainment of the Population 18 Years Old and Over, by Age, Sex, Race, and Hispanic Origin, 2019

(Numbers in thousands; civilian noninstitutionalized population.[1])

Age, sex, race, and Hispanic origin	Total	None	1st to 4th grade	5th to 6th grade	7th to 8th grade	9th grade	10th grade	11th grade[2]	High school graduate
ALL RACES									
Both Sexes									
18 years old and over.........	250,563	834	1,469	3,163	3,413	3,604	3,958	10,118	70,947
18 to 24 years old.........	29,085	66	57	52	101	240	562	3,508	8,688
25 years old and over.........	221,478	769	1,412	3,111	3,312	3,365	3,397	6,611	62,259
25 to 29 years old.........	23,277	72	41	112	132	233	254	667	6,089
30 to 34 years old.........	21,932	42	77	212	223	250	275	675	5,549
35 to 39 years old.........	21,443	63	118	274	229	390	343	598	5,184
40 to 44 years old.........	19,584	76	107	339	293	367	258	550	4,990
45 to 49 years old.........	20,345	75	114	334	268	342	251	589	5,299
50 to 54 years old.........	20,355	62	102	298	274	335	270	665	5,831
55 to 59 years old.........	21,163	54	151	347	283	311	366	700	6,374
60 to 64 years old.........	20,592	65	140	318	289	273	318	640	6,423
65 to 69 years old.........	17,356	68	121	243	264	251	278	439	4,927
70 to 74 years old.........	14,131	55	143	168	247	178	261	383	4,130
75 years old and over.........	21,301	137	298	466	809	435	522	705	7,462
Male									
18 years old and over.........	121,301	410	743	1,653	1,653	1,769	2,014	5,377	36,076
18 to 24 years old.........	14,605	32	38	29	47	148	291	1,928	4,819
25 years old and over.........	106,695	378	705	1,624	1,607	1,621	1,723	3,449	31,257
25 to 29 years old.........	11,792	39	28	60	83	123	138	387	3,416
30 to 34 years old.........	10,935	39	41	119	117	120	155	380	3,178
35 to 39 years old.........	10,629	33	75	149	115	217	198	330	2,951
40 to 44 years old.........	9,628	51	69	180	128	184	161	266	2,740
45 to 49 years old.........	9,993	36	54	178	142	188	126	348	2,940
50 to 54 years old.........	9,930	27	42	156	154	159	141	372	3,057
55 to 59 years old.........	10,046	31	68	214	146	164	197	388	3,116
60 to 64 years old.........	9,819	19	66	175	135	111	149	325	3,171
65 to 69 years old.........	8,198	32	49	115	121	130	118	211	2,212
70 to 74 years old.........	6,691	10	66	80	113	72	119	153	1,753
75 years old and over.........	9,034	60	145	197	353	153	219	290	2,724
Female									
18 years old and over.........	129,262	425	726	1,510	1,760	1,836	1,945	4,742	34,872
18 to 24 years old.........	14,479	34	19	23	55	92	271	1,580	3,870
25 years old and over.........	114,783	391	707	1,487	1,705	1,744	1,674	3,162	31,002
25 to 29 years old.........	11,485	33	12	52	49	110	116	281	2,674
30 to 34 years old.........	10,997	3	36	93	106	129	120	295	2,372
35 to 39 years old.........	10,814	29	43	125	115	173	145	268	2,232
40 to 44 years old.........	9,956	24	37	158	165	183	97	284	2,250
45 to 49 years old.........	10,351	39	60	156	126	153	126	241	2,359
50 to 54 years old.........	10,425	35	60	142	120	176	129	293	2,774
55 to 59 years old.........	11,117	24	83	133	137	147	169	312	3,258
60 to 64 years old.........	10,773	46	75	143	154	163	168	315	3,252
65 to 69 years old.........	9,158	36	72	128	143	121	160	228	2,715
70 to 74 years old.........	7,440	45	77	88	134	106	142	231	2,377
75 years old and over.........	12,267	77	153	269	457	283	303	416	4,739
WHITE ALONE									
Both Sexes									
18 years old and over.........	194,871	489	1,150	2,652	2,683	2,830	2,873	7,231	55,094
18 to 24 years old.........	21,419	40	32	44	89	180	421	2,586	6,270
25 years old and over.........	173,452	449	1,118	2,608	2,594	2,649	2,453	4,645	48,825
25 to 29 years old.........	16,889	38	30	101	114	173	180	420	4,505
30 to 34 years old.........	16,286	29	63	182	194	218	207	490	4,062
35 to 39 years old.........	16,136	35	102	245	205	306	250	400	3,894
40 to 44 years old.........	14,768	60	85	308	232	303	186	400	3,818
45 to 49 years old.........	15,552	58	92	303	217	292	187	442	3,983
50 to 54 years old.........	15,916	31	81	268	208	260	194	450	4,514
55 to 59 years old.........	16,924	25	130	286	217	233	264	520	5,055

* = Quantity zero or rounds to zero.
[1]Civilian noninstitutionalized population, plus armed forces living off post or with their families on post.
[2]Population who attained the 12th grade but received no diploma are included in this category.

Table A-24. Educational Attainment of the Population 18 Years Old and Over, by Age, Sex, Race, and Hispanic Origin, 2019—*Continued*

(Numbers in thousands; civilian noninstitutionalized population.[1])

Age, sex, race, and Hispanic origin	Educational attainment						
	Some college, no degree	Associate's degree, occupational	Associate's degree, academic	Bachelor's degree	Master's degree	Professional degree	Doctoral degree
ALL RACES							
Both Sexes							
18 years old and over......................	45,028	10,381	14,168	53,312	22,459	3,150	4,557
18 to 24 years old	10,338	641	1,171	3,375	245	14	28
25 years old and over......................	34,690	9,741	12,998	49,937	22,214	3,136	4,529
25 to 29 years old	4,243	978	1,438	6,823	1,803	171	221
30 to 34 years old	3,287	1,018	1,305	5,904	2,294	360	461
35 to 39 years old	2,984	1,009	1,265	5,515	2,643	299	530
40 to 44 years old	2,737	834	1,215	4,671	2,361	330	455
45 to 49 years old	3,000	935	1,327	4,785	2,229	313	484
50 to 54 years old	3,059	936	1,270	4,492	2,075	295	393
55 to 59 years old	3,370	1,007	1,307	4,348	1,908	266	370
60 to 64 years old	3,223	924	1,355	4,051	1,867	329	375
65 to 69 years old	3,042	776	1,009	3,495	1,775	262	404
70 to 74 years old	2,346	556	765	2,693	1,560	240	405
75 years old and over..................	3,398	767	740	3,160	1,699	271	431
Male							
18 years old and over......................	21,500	4,809	5,949	25,206	9,721	1,827	2,596
18 to 24 years old	4,909	321	501	1,421	100	7	16
25 years old and over......................	16,591	4,488	5,448	23,785	9,621	1,820	2,580
25 to 29 years old	2,227	436	644	3,302	734	80	96
30 to 34 years old	1,632	454	547	2,841	858	216	238
35 to 39 years old	1,512	501	516	2,566	1,068	141	255
40 to 44 years old	1,350	413	580	2,136	966	161	241
45 to 49 years old	1,472	456	605	2,070	985	141	253
50 to 54 years old	1,514	425	519	2,072	901	155	237
55 to 59 years old	1,443	484	507	2,065	854	162	206
60 to 64 years old	1,487	438	533	1,949	817	223	220
65 to 69 years old	1,489	335	384	1,779	790	184	248
70 to 74 years old	1,099	257	329	1,459	769	146	266
75 years old and over..................	1,366	290	285	1,545	877	211	321
Female							
18 years old and over......................	23,528	5,572	8,220	28,106	12,738	1,324	1,960
18 to 24 years old	5,429	320	670	1,954	145	7	12
25 years old and over......................	18,099	5,252	7,550	26,151	12,593	1,317	1,948
25 to 29 years old	2,015	542	795	3,521	1,069	91	125
30 to 34 years old	1,655	565	758	3,063	1,436	145	223
35 to 39 years old	1,472	507	749	2,949	1,574	158	275
40 to 44 years old	1,388	421	635	2,535	1,395	170	213
45 to 49 years old	1,527	479	723	2,716	1,244	172	232
50 to 54 years old	1,545	511	752	2,420	1,174	139	156
55 to 59 years old	1,927	522	801	2,282	1,054	103	164
60 to 64 years old	1,736	486	822	2,102	1,050	106	156
65 to 69 years old	1,554	442	625	1,716	985	79	156
70 to 74 years old	1,247	300	436	1,235	791	94	138
75 years old and over..................	2,033	477	455	1,614	822	59	111
WHITE ALONE							
Both Sexes							
18 years old and over......................	34,755	8,397	11,186	42,131	17,347	2,563	3,490
18 to 24 years old	7,693	509	923	2,476	124	5	28
25 years old and over......................	27,062	7,888	10,262	39,655	17,223	2,558	3,462
25 to 29 years old	3,008	729	1,070	5,099	1,160	111	153
30 to 34 years old	2,327	788	1,002	4,453	1,651	287	333
35 to 39 years old	2,181	761	944	4,277	1,940	231	363
40 to 44 years old	2,068	666	945	3,500	1,661	243	293
45 to 49 years old	2,238	761	1,042	3,684	1,657	252	346
50 to 54 years old	2,372	764	950	3,708	1,599	218	299
55 to 59 years old	2,690	833	1,036	3,557	1,573	228	278

* = Quantity zero or rounds to zero.
[1]Civilian noninstitutionalized population, plus armed forces living off post or with their families on post.
[2]Population who attained the 12th grade but received no diploma are included in this category.

Table A-24. Educational Attainment of the Population 18 Years Old and Over, by Age, Sex, Race, and Hispanic Origin, 2019—Continued

(Numbers in thousands; civilian noninstitutionalized population.[1])

Age, sex, race, and Hispanic origin	Total	None	1st to 4th grade	5th to 6th grade	7th to 8th grade	9th grade	10th grade	11th grade[2]	High school graduate
60 to 64 years old	16,674	32	121	269	213	202	230	440	5,150
65 to 69 years old	14,286	43	83	179	187	185	185	285	4,012
70 to 74 years old	11,785	26	102	124	194	147	185	256	3,387
75 years old and over	18,236	72	229	342	613	331	386	542	6,443
Male									
18 years old and over	95,463	292	604	1,391	1,316	1,418	1,487	3,872	28,263
18 to 24 years old	10,820	20	25	26	41	121	213	1,416	3,532
25 years old and over	84,643	272	579	1,365	1,275	1,297	1,274	2,455	24,732
25 to 29 years old	8,644	26	26	51	73	84	102	221	2,618
30 to 34 years old	8,264	26	39	100	102	111	127	274	2,393
35 to 39 years old	8,170	23	63	137	103	164	135	227	2,270
40 to 44 years old	7,395	44	56	163	95	145	119	197	2,148
45 to 49 years old	7,756	33	43	165	115	157	102	268	2,260
50 to 54 years old	7,876	17	36	142	118	141	105	265	2,409
55 to 59 years old	8,063	15	61	168	114	120	140	288	2,450
60 to 64 years old	8,152	13	56	150	116	90	113	233	2,587
65 to 69 years old	6,854	22	36	85	85	108	69	143	1,789
70 to 74 years old	5,655	10	47	60	94	62	91	101	1,448
75 years old and over	7,813	43	114	145	262	117	173	238	2,359
Female									
18 years old and over	99,408	197	546	1,261	1,367	1,412	1,386	3,359	26,831
18 to 24 years old	10,598	20	7	18	48	60	208	1,170	2,738
25 years old and over	88,809	177	539	1,243	1,319	1,352	1,178	2,190	24,093
25 to 29 years old	8,245	12	5	50	41	89	78	199	1,887
30 to 34 years old	8,021	3	23	82	92	107	80	216	1,668
35 to 39 years old	7,966	12	39	108	102	142	115	173	1,625
40 to 44 years old	7,372	16	29	145	137	159	67	204	1,670
45 to 49 years old	7,796	25	48	138	102	135	86	173	1,723
50 to 54 years old	8,039	14	45	126	90	119	89	185	2,105
55 to 59 years old	8,861	9	69	118	103	112	124	232	2,605
60 to 64 years old	8,523	19	65	120	98	112	117	207	2,563
65 to 69 years old	7,432	21	47	94	102	78	116	142	2,224
70 to 74 years old	6,130	16	55	64	100	85	94	155	1,939
75 years old and over	10,423	29	114	197	351	214	213	304	4,084
BLACK ALONE									
Both Sexes									
18 years old and over	31,689	141	127	170	405	438	733	2,032	10,533
18 to 24 years old	4,261	15	8	1	9	43	81	566	1,589
25 years old and over	27,428	126	119	168	397	396	652	1,466	8,944
25 to 29 years old	3,603	23	8	4	11	35	54	190	1,047
30 to 34 years old	3,062	11	10	2	20	9	47	116	1,035
35 to 39 years old	2,867	10	*	11	5	41	67	149	841
40 to 44 years old	2,594	7	11	5	35	36	53	107	756
45 to 49 years old	2,630	5	8	8	21	23	40	91	881
50 to 54 years old	2,630	16	6	1	36	48	38	164	866
55 to 59 years old	2,654	9	6	29	31	42	77	131	890
60 to 64 years old	2,343	6	13	17	43	35	64	163	858
65 to 69 years old	1,919	7	12	20	50	48	57	132	638
70 to 74 years old	1,334	3	14	22	22	23	61	91	468
75 years old and over	1,793	27	31	48	123	56	95	132	664
Male									
18 years old and over	14,467	52	61	88	184	200	388	1,032	5,271
18 to 24 years old	2,077	9	3	1	4	18	52	315	843
25 years old and over	12,390	43	58	87	180	182	335	717	4,428
25 to 29 years old	1,759	11	3	4	4	23	24	126	535
30 to 34 years old	1,436	11	2	*	11	*	19	60	565
35 to 39 years old	1,318	1	*	1	*	30	49	85	437
40 to 44 years old	1,172	3	4	1	12	18	36	49	378

* = Quantity zero or rounds to zero.
[1]Civilian noninstitutionalized population, plus armed forces living off post or with their families on post.
[2]Population who attained the 12th grade but received no diploma are included in this category.

Table A-24. Educational Attainment of the Population 18 Years Old and Over, by Age, Sex, Race, and Hispanic Origin, 2019—*Continued*

(Numbers in thousands; civilian noninstitutionalized population.[1])

Age, sex, race, and Hispanic origin	Educational attainment						
	Some college, no degree	Associate's degree, occupational	Associate's degree, academic	Bachelor's degree	Master's degree	Professional degree	Doctoral degree
60 to 64 years old	2,601	790	1,125	3,341	1,533	309	317
65 to 69 years old	2,540	663	856	2,977	1,528	221	342
70 to 74 years old	2,023	461	632	2,279	1,400	218	351
75 years old and over	3,013	672	661	2,781	1,521	240	389
Male							
18 years old and over	16,842	3,954	4,712	20,204	7,512	1,579	2,018
18 to 24 years old	3,642	266	399	1,057	44	3	16
25 years old and over	13,199	3,688	4,312	19,147	7,468	1,577	2,002
25 to 29 years old	1,638	338	468	2,444	435	50	73
30 to 34 years old	1,195	371	437	2,157	590	171	171
35 to 39 years old	1,135	400	402	2,014	804	119	172
40 to 44 years old	1,062	321	449	1,674	645	124	154
45 to 49 years old	1,099	371	473	1,617	740	120	195
50 to 54 years old	1,199	351	369	1,726	695	128	175
55 to 59 years old	1,216	408	390	1,704	686	151	152
60 to 64 years old	1,250	369	454	1,640	676	220	184
65 to 69 years old	1,259	290	327	1,567	701	163	211
70 to 74 years old	940	220	278	1,245	695	140	225
75 years old and over	1,206	249	265	1,359	802	190	292
Female							
18 years old and over	17,913	4,443	6,474	21,927	9,835	984	1,472
18 to 24 years old	4,050	242	524	1,418	80	2	12
25 years old and over	13,862	4,201	5,950	20,508	9,755	982	1,460
25 to 29 years old	1,370	391	602	2,655	724	61	81
30 to 34 years old	1,132	417	564	2,296	1,061	115	162
35 to 39 years old	1,045	361	542	2,263	1,136	112	191
40 to 44 years old	1,005	344	496	1,826	1,016	118	139
45 to 49 years old	1,139	390	569	2,066	918	132	151
50 to 54 years old	1,172	412	581	1,982	904	91	124
55 to 59 years old	1,474	425	646	1,854	887	77	126
60 to 64 years old	1,351	422	671	1,702	857	89	132
65 to 69 years old	1,282	374	529	1,410	827	59	130
70 to 74 years old	1,083	241	354	1,034	706	78	126
75 years old and over	1,808	424	396	1,422	720	50	97
BLACK ALONE							
Both Sexes							
18 years old and over	6,501	1,270	1,817	4,895	2,142	188	297
18 to 24 years old	1,382	82	111	351	23	*	*
25 years old and over	5,119	1,189	1,705	4,544	2,119	188	297
25 to 29 years old	815	163	208	822	201	2	19
30 to 34 years old	662	163	166	557	225	19	17
35 to 39 years old	525	171	203	504	276	19	44
40 to 44 years old	438	110	153	521	285	27	51
45 to 49 years old	491	104	181	452	253	28	42
50 to 54 years old	463	98	219	372	244	37	23
55 to 59 years old	478	113	187	438	173	18	31
60 to 64 years old	424	79	159	293	166	7	16
65 to 69 years old	352	82	97	260	133	10	21
70 to 74 years old	230	48	87	168	68	11	18
75 years old and over	239	58	44	156	96	9	15
Male							
18 years old and over	2,823	562	712	2,178	728	59	129
18 to 24 years old	623	41	54	105	7	*	*
25 years old and over	2,199	521	659	2,072	721	59	129
25 to 29 years old	375	73	80	434	62	*	4
30 to 34 years old	297	58	58	260	79	12	3
35 to 39 years old	240	69	69	235	73	7	21
40 to 44 years old	180	68	67	217	105	8	26

* = Quantity zero or rounds to zero.
[1]Civilian noninstitutionalized population, plus armed forces living off post or with their families on post.
[2]Population who attained the 12th grade but received no diploma are included in this category.

Table A-24. Educational Attainment of the Population 18 Years Old and Over, by Age, Sex, Race, and Hispanic Origin, 2019—*Continued*

(Numbers in thousands; civilian noninstitutionalized population.[1])

Age, sex, race, and Hispanic origin	Total	None	1st to 4th grade	5th to 6th grade	7th to 8th grade	9th grade	10th grade	11th grade[2]	High school graduate
45 to 49 years old	1,182	1	5	5	14	13	19	42	457
50 to 54 years old	1,205	4	3	*	22	13	14	79	431
55 to 59 years old	1,225	5	1	23	15	30	45	75	471
60 to 64 years old	995	2	8	9	13	10	33	71	401
65 to 69 years old	829	2	5	8	26	14	36	57	306
70 to 74 years old	586	*	10	14	7	11	23	30	204
75 years old and over	685	2	18	20	55	20	38	42	242
Female									
18 years old and over	17,222	89	67	82	221	238	346	999	5,262
18 to 24 years old	2,184	6	6	*	5	25	28	250	746
25 years old and over	15,038	83	61	82	216	213	317	749	4,516
25 to 29 years old	1,844	12	5	*	8	11	30	64	512
30 to 34 years old	1,626	*	8	2	9	9	28	56	471
35 to 39 years old	1,550	9	*	9	5	12	18	64	404
40 to 44 years old	1,422	4	7	4	23	17	17	59	378
45 to 49 years old	1,448	4	4	4	6	10	21	48	424
50 to 54 years old	1,425	12	3	1	13	35	24	85	434
55 to 59 years old	1,429	5	5	6	16	13	32	56	419
60 to 64 years old	1,348	4	5	7	30	25	31	92	456
65 to 69 years old	1,090	5	8	12	24	33	21	75	332
70 to 74 years old	748	3	4	8	15	12	38	61	264
75 years old and over	1,108	25	13	28	68	36	57	90	422
ASIAN ALONE									
Both Sexes									
18 years old and over	15,770	157	123	191	220	185	177	359	2,753
18 to 24 years old	1,816	5	14	1	*	8	24	134	302
25 years old and over	13,955	152	109	190	220	177	153	224	2,451
25 to 29 years old	1,696	7	3	*	7	5	10	19	170
30 to 34 years old	1,694	*	2	3	2	4	11	13	215
35 to 39 years old	1,631	7	5	6	18	14	6	18	210
40 to 44 years old	1,542	6	6	10	14	12	2	16	240
45 to 49 years old	1,490	12	12	10	22	18	21	31	227
50 to 54 years old	1,233	15	4	10	21	20	27	26	275
55 to 59 years old	1,069	20	10	15	26	28	10	22	260
60 to 64 years old	1,122	27	7	21	25	22	16	16	247
65 to 69 years old	811	17	13	38	19	11	20	16	169
70 to 74 years old	735	18	21	18	20	5	10	29	185
75 years old and over	933	22	27	58	47	39	22	19	254
Male									
18 years old and over	7,456	43	45	77	93	61	59	188	1,239
18 to 24 years old	924	*	8	*	*	2	11	75	163
25 years old and over	6,532	42	37	77	93	58	48	113	1,077
25 to 29 years old	851	2	*	*	7	2	3	12	84
30 to 34 years old	825	*	*	*	*	4	*	11	108
35 to 39 years old	750	3	4	4	10	3	*	5	102
40 to 44 years old	748	4	6	7	10	7	2	10	116
45 to 49 years old	706	2	4	3	6	12	3	16	111
50 to 54 years old	580	6	*	5	10	*	16	18	115
55 to 59 years old	497	11	6	9	14	9	4	7	110
60 to 64 years old	503	4	2	8	6	7	3	9	111
65 to 69 years old	348	8	2	16	4	5	10	8	67
70 to 74 years old	327	*	6	3	7	*	2	16	65
75 years old and over	399	2	7	21	19	11	5	1	88
Female									
18 years old and over	8,315	115	78	114	127	125	118	171	1,514
18 to 24 years old	892	5	6	1	*	6	13	59	139
25 years old and over	7,423	110	72	113	127	119	105	112	1,375
25 to 29 years old	845	5	3	*	*	3	7	7	86

* = Quantity zero or rounds to zero.
[1]Civilian noninstitutionalized population, plus armed forces living off post or with their families on post.
[2]Population who attained the 12th grade but received no diploma are included in this category.

Table A-24. Educational Attainment of the Population 18 Years Old and Over, by Age, Sex, Race, and Hispanic Origin, 2019—*Continued*

(Numbers in thousands; civilian noninstitutionalized population.[1])

Age, sex, race, and Hispanic origin	Educational attainment						
	Some college, no degree	Associate's degree, occupational	Associate's degree, academic	Bachelor's degree	Master's degree	Professional degree	Doctoral degree
45 to 49 years old	223	48	92	165	75	4	19
50 to 54 years old	207	39	101	169	98	15	9
55 to 59 years old	139	52	75	199	76	4	15
60 to 64 years old	168	41	41	129	57	1	9
65 to 69 years old	153	30	32	103	47	2	6
70 to 74 years old	115	19	34	87	21	1	11
75 years old and over	103	23	8	74	28	5	6
Female							
18 years old and over	3,678	708	1,104	2,717	1,414	129	167
18 to 24 years old	759	40	57	246	15	*	*
25 years old and over	2,919	668	1,047	2,471	1,398	129	167
25 to 29 years old	440	90	128	388	139	2	15
30 to 34 years old	365	105	108	297	146	8	14
35 to 39 years old	285	102	134	270	203	12	23
40 to 44 years old	258	41	86	304	181	18	25
45 to 49 years old	268	56	90	287	179	24	23
50 to 54 years old	257	59	119	202	146	22	14
55 to 59 years old	340	61	111	239	97	15	15
60 to 64 years old	257	38	118	164	109	6	7
65 to 69 years old	198	52	65	157	86	8	15
70 to 74 years old	116	29	53	81	47	10	7
75 years old and over	136	35	35	82	68	4	10
ASIAN ALONE							
Both Sexes							
18 years old and over	1,936	374	671	5,066	2,532	347	681
18 to 24 years old	707	17	86	416	96	7	*
25 years old and over	1,229	357	585	4,650	2,436	340	681
25 to 29 years old	172	36	78	710	393	46	39
30 to 34 years old	126	33	76	700	369	48	93
35 to 39 years old	130	44	62	587	371	46	107
40 to 44 years old	104	29	68	532	345	55	103
45 to 49 years old	141	43	65	521	253	30	84
50 to 54 years old	112	44	62	339	184	37	57
55 to 59 years old	102	32	50	286	135	15	56
60 to 64 years old	108	22	33	373	150	13	43
65 to 69 years old	79	18	41	212	99	20	38
70 to 74 years old	58	34	25	195	72	9	35
75 years old and over	97	20	23	194	64	19	28
Male							
18 years old and over	1,003	170	292	2,294	1,319	162	412
18 to 24 years old	388	4	30	191	47	4	*
25 years old and over	615	166	262	2,103	1,272	158	412
25 to 29 years old	98	14	38	337	211	24	20
30 to 34 years old	72	16	24	328	177	31	54
35 to 39 years old	62	23	24	268	172	12	58
40 to 44 years old	46	12	32	220	192	27	57
45 to 49 years old	72	22	34	233	140	16	33
50 to 54 years old	64	23	30	141	94	12	45
55 to 59 years old	40	13	24	126	82	5	36
60 to 64 years old	53	11	23	161	79	1	26
65 to 69 years old	33	8	16	91	40	11	30
70 to 74 years old	26	13	6	104	44	5	29
75 years old and over	50	12	10	94	41	14	23
Female							
18 years old and over	933	204	379	2,772	1,213	184	269
18 to 24 years old	318	13	56	226	49	2	*
25 years old and over	614	191	324	2,547	1,164	182	269
25 to 29 years old	74	23	40	374	182	22	19

* = Quantity zero or rounds to zero.
[1]Civilian noninstitutionalized population, plus armed forces living off post or with their families on post.
[2]Population who attained the 12th grade but received no diploma are included in this category.

Table A-24. Educational Attainment of the Population 18 Years Old and Over, by Age, Sex, Race, and Hispanic Origin, 2019—*Continued*

(Numbers in thousands; civilian noninstitutionalized population.[1])

Age, sex, race, and Hispanic origin	Total	None	1st to 4th grade	5th to 6th grade	7th to 8th grade	9th grade	10th grade	11th grade[2]	High school graduate
30 to 34 years old	869	*	2	3	2	*	10	2	107
35 to 39 years old	881	4	1	2	8	11	6	13	107
40 to 44 years old	794	2	*	2	4	5	5	7	124
45 to 49 years old	784	10	8	8	15	6	18	15	116
50 to 54 years old	653	9	4	4	11	20	11	8	161
55 to 59 years old	572	10	4	6	12	19	6	15	149
60 to 64 years old	619	23	4	13	19	15	13	7	136
65 to 69 years old	463	8	11	22	15	7	10	9	102
70 to 74 years old	408	18	15	15	13	5	8	13	119
75 years old and over	534	19	20	37	28	29	16	18	166
HISPANIC (OF ANY RACE)									
Both Sexes									
18 years old and over	41,217	416	1,095	2,517	1,455	1,837	1,094	2,717	13,029
18 to 24 years old	6,642	31	21	36	27	117	194	944	2,181
25 years old and over	34,575	385	1,073	2,481	1,428	1,720	901	1,774	10,848
25 to 29 years old	4,963	27	31	92	73	130	73	249	1,693
30 to 34 years old	4,421	22	63	193	125	179	128	258	1,535
35 to 39 years old	4,480	39	89	242	161	263	167	224	1,434
40 to 44 years old	4,097	59	84	321	206	256	115	206	1,293
45 to 49 years old	3,834	41	96	304	172	229	93	238	1,198
50 to 54 years old	3,221	20	93	271	129	187	78	193	989
55 to 59 years old	2,771	21	129	291	140	131	62	141	817
60 to 64 years old	2,244	32	125	253	108	109	50	91	630
65 to 69 years old	1,639	34	85	170	109	80	43	58	463
70 to 74 years old	1,176	29	95	103	88	63	35	42	334
75 years old and over	1,728	61	184	240	115	92	56	72	462
Male									
18 years old and over	20,551	252	560	1,348	701	937	528	1,476	6,998
18 to 24 years old	3,366	15	19	23	19	73	98	529	1,215
25 years old and over	17,184	236	541	1,325	682	863	430	948	5,782
25 to 29 years old	2,603	17	26	50	46	72	42	149	957
30 to 34 years old	2,255	20	39	114	61	87	65	157	846
35 to 39 years old	2,312	28	58	143	78	147	94	115	838
40 to 44 years old	2,068	40	53	169	94	127	65	99	735
45 to 49 years old	1,944	31	48	168	97	134	47	132	645
50 to 54 years old	1,584	11	40	142	60	100	22	100	530
55 to 59 years old	1,336	12	57	177	59	61	30	74	415
60 to 64 years old	1,100	12	61	135	48	44	13	47	298
65 to 69 years old	781	18	36	86	56	37	18	30	205
70 to 74 years old	455	10	40	47	30	24	14	11	121
75 years old and over	746	37	84	95	53	31	19	34	191
Female									
18 years old and over	20,667	164	534	1,169	754	901	566	1,241	6,031
18 to 24 years old	3,276	15	2	13	8	44	95	415	965
25 years old and over	17,391	149	532	1,155	746	857	471	826	5,066
25 to 29 years old	2,360	10	5	43	27	58	31	100	735
30 to 34 years old	2,166	3	23	80	64	92	63	101	689
35 to 39 years old	2,169	11	31	99	84	116	73	109	596
40 to 44 years old	2,029	19	31	152	112	130	49	107	557
45 to 49 years old	1,891	10	49	136	76	95	46	106	554
50 to 54 years old	1,636	9	54	129	69	87	56	93	459
55 to 59 years old	1,435	9	72	114	81	70	33	67	402
60 to 64 years old	1,145	20	64	118	59	65	37	44	332
65 to 69 years old	858	16	49	84	53	43	25	28	259
70 to 74 years old	721	19	55	56	59	39	21	31	212
75 years old and over	982	24	100	145	61	61	36	39	271

* = Quantity zero or rounds to zero.
[1]Civilian noninstitutionalized population, plus armed forces living off post or with their families on post.
[2]Population who attained the 12th grade but received no diploma are included in this category.

Table A-24. Educational Attainment of the Population 18 Years Old and Over, by Age, Sex, Race, and Hispanic Origin, 2019—*Continued*

(Numbers in thousands; civilian noninstitutionalized population.[1])

Age, sex, race, and Hispanic origin	Educational attainment						
	Some college, no degree	Associate's degree, occupational	Associate's degree, academic	Bachelor's degree	Master's degree	Professional degree	Doctoral degree
30 to 34 years old	54	18	51	372	193	17	39
35 to 39 years old	68	22	38	320	199	34	49
40 to 44 years old	58	17	36	312	153	28	45
45 to 49 years old	69	20	32	288	113	14	51
50 to 54 years old	48	21	32	198	89	25	13
55 to 59 years old	62	19	27	160	53	10	20
60 to 64 years old	55	12	10	212	71	12	16
65 to 69 years old	47	11	25	120	59	9	8
70 to 74 years old	32	21	19	91	28	5	5
75 years old and over	47	7	14	100	23	5	4
HISPANIC (OF ANY RACE)							
Both Sexes							
18 years old and over	6,915	1,371	1,865	4,900	1,555	209	243
18 to 24 years old	2,235	162	299	373	22	*	*
25 years old and over	4,680	1,209	1,566	4,527	1,532	209	243
25 to 29 years old	1,042	222	310	853	131	22	14
30 to 34 years old	602	199	245	613	205	30	23
35 to 39 years old	585	175	208	596	244	25	29
40 to 44 years old	473	140	171	500	202	43	30
45 to 49 years old	456	106	175	504	176	11	33
50 to 54 years old	399	105	137	406	171	21	20
55 to 59 years old	358	77	104	341	130	8	21
60 to 64 years old	305	73	73	264	95	16	22
65 to 69 years old	198	38	61	191	68	19	21
70 to 74 years old	122	26	53	109	56	6	15
75 years old and over	140	47	30	152	54	9	14
Male							
18 years old and over	3,341	582	783	2,226	598	105	115
18 to 24 years old	1,010	81	136	141	6	*	*
25 years old and over	2,331	501	647	2,086	592	105	115
25 to 29 years old	547	84	139	416	49	6	3
30 to 34 years old	310	79	88	296	64	15	13
35 to 39 years old	271	80	83	268	82	15	11
40 to 44 years old	228	59	82	204	76	22	15
45 to 49 years old	208	45	92	199	78	4	17
50 to 54 years old	193	40	53	208	66	6	12
55 to 59 years old	164	28	26	163	53	7	11
60 to 64 years old	170	34	34	133	48	10	12
65 to 69 years old	113	28	28	84	27	9	6
70 to 74 years old	61	8	11	49	19	3	8
75 years old and over	64	15	11	66	30	7	9
Female							
18 years old and over	3,574	789	1,083	2,674	956	104	128
18 to 24 years old	1,225	81	164	232	16	*	*
25 years old and over	2,349	708	919	2,442	940	104	128
25 to 29 years old	495	138	171	437	82	16	11
30 to 34 years old	292	120	157	317	141	14	10
35 to 39 years old	314	95	125	328	162	9	18
40 to 44 years old	245	80	89	296	127	20	15
45 to 49 years old	248	61	83	305	99	7	16
50 to 54 years old	205	65	85	197	105	15	9
55 to 59 years old	194	49	78	178	77	*	10
60 to 64 years old	135	39	38	131	47	6	10
65 to 69 years old	85	10	32	107	40	10	15
70 to 74 years old	61	18	42	60	37	3	8
75 years old and over	76	32	19	86	24	2	6

* = Quantity zero or rounds to zero.
[1]Civilian noninstitutionalized population, plus armed forces living off post or with their families on post.
[2]Population who attained the 12th grade but received no diploma are included in this category.

Table A-25. Educational Attainment of the Population 25 Years Old and Over, by Marital Status and Sex, 2019

(Numbers in thousands; percent; civilian noninstitutionalized population.[1])

Sex and marital status	Educational attainment									
	Total		None to 8th grade		9th to 11th grade		High school graduate		Some college, no degree	
	Number	Percent	Number	Percent	Number	Percent	Number	Percent	Number	Percent
BOTH SEXES										
Total...	221,478	100.0	8,603	100.0	13,372	100.0	62,259	100.0	34,690	100.0
Married spouse present	126,768	57.2	4,476	52.0	6,069	45.4	32,493	52.2	18,378	53.0
Married spouse absent, not separated	3,633	1.6	294	3.4	339	2.5	1,063	1.7	468	1.3
Separated..	4,643	2.1	342	4.0	585	4.4	1,618	2.6	759	2.2
Widowed...	14,852	6.7	1,218	14.2	1,414	10.6	5,459	8.8	2,411	7.0
Divorced...	25,235	11.4	697	8.1	1,645	12.3	7,790	12.5	4,815	13.9
Never married	46,348	20.9	1,576	18.3	3,320	24.8	13,836	22.2	7,858	22.7
MALE										
Total...	106,695	100.0	4,313	100.0	6,792	100.0	31,257	100.0	16,591	100.0
Married spouse present	63,541	59.6	2,448	56.8	3,243	47.7	16,857	53.9	9,334	56.3
Married spouse absent, not separated	1,927	1.8	199	4.6	164	2.4	573	1.8	224	1.4
Separated..	1,948	1.8	141	3.3	263	3.9	765	2.4	286	1.7
Widowed...	3,450	3.2	292	6.8	349	5.1	1,135	3.6	568	3.4
Divorced...	10,564	9.9	291	6.7	809	11.9	3,629	11.6	1,939	11.7
Never married	25,266	23.7	941	21.8	1,964	28.9	8,299	26.6	4,240	25.6
FEMALE										
Total...	114,783	100.0	4,290	100.0	6,580	100.0	31,002	100.0	18,099	100.0
Married spouse present	63,227	55.1	2,028	47.3	2,825	42.9	15,636	50.4	9,044	50.0
Married spouse absent, not separated	1,706	1.5	95	2.2	175	2.7	490	1.6	244	1.3
Separated..	2,695	2.3	201	4.7	322	4.9	853	2.8	474	2.6
Widowed...	11,402	9.9	926	21.6	1,066	16.2	4,324	13.9	1,843	10.2
Divorced...	14,671	12.8	405	9.4	835	12.7	4,161	13.4	2,876	15.9
Never married	21,082	18.4	635	14.8	1,356	20.6	5,537	17.9	3,619	20.0

[1]Plus armed forces living off post or with their families on post.

Table A-25. Educational Attainment of the Population 25 Years Old and Over, by Marital Status and Sex, 2019—*Continued*

(Numbers in thousands; percent; civilian noninstitutionalized population.[1])

Sex and marital status	Educational attainment									
	Associate's degree		Bachelor's degree		Master's degree		Professional degree		Doctoral degree	
	Number	Percent	Number	Percent	Number	Percent	Number	Percent	Number	Percent
BOTH SEXES										
Total...	22,738	100.0	49,937	100.0	22,214	100.0	3,136	100.0	4,529	100.0
Married spouse present.......................................	13,410	59.0	31,280	62.6	15,096	68.0	2,240	71.4	3,327	73.5
Married spouse absent, not separated..............	293	1.3	692	1.4	355	1.6	39	1.2	89	2.0
Separated...	454	2.0	617	1.2	206	0.9	34	1.1	28	0.6
Widowed...	1,284	5.6	1,960	3.9	872	3.9	100	3.2	134	3.0
Divorced..	3,038	13.4	4,707	9.4	1,983	8.9	235	7.5	327	7.2
Never married	4,259	18.7	10,681	21.4	3,704	16.7	488	15.6	625	13.8
MALE										
Total...	9,936	100.0	23,785	100.0	9,621	100.0	1,820	100.0	2,580	100.0
Married spouse present.......................................	6,085	61.2	15,215	64.0	6,995	72.7	1,352	74.3	2,011	77.9
Married spouse absent, not separated..............	139	1.4	367	1.5	182	1.9	16	0.9	65	2.5
Separated...	174	1.8	237	1.0	59	0.6	12	0.7	11	0.4
Widowed...	283	2.8	532	2.2	204	2.1	36	2.0	52	2.0
Divorced..	1,120	11.3	1,911	8.0	591	6.1	127	7.0	147	5.7
Never married	2,135	21.5	5,525	23.2	1,591	16.5	277	15.2	295	11.4
FEMALE										
Total...	12,802	100.0	26,151	100.0	12,593	100.0	1,317	100.0	1,948	100.0
Married spouse present.......................................	7,325	57.2	16,065	61.4	8,101	64.3	888	67.4	1,315	67.5
Married spouse absent, not separated..............	154	1.2	326	1.2	173	1.4	24	1.8	25	1.3
Separated...	280	2.2	380	1.5	147	1.2	22	1.7	17	0.9
Widowed...	1,001	7.8	1,428	5.5	668	5.3	64	4.9	82	4.2
Divorced..	1,918	15.0	2,797	10.7	1,392	11.1	108	8.2	180	9.2
Never married	2,124	16.6	5,156	19.7	2,113	16.8	211	16.0	329	16.9

[1] Plus armed forces living off post or with their families on post.

Table A-26. Educational Attainment of the Population 25 Years Old and Over, by Household Relationship and Sex, 2019

(Numbers in thousands; percent; civilian noninstitutionalized population.[1])

Sex and household relationship	Educational attainment									
	Total		None to 8th grade		9th to 11th grade		High school graduate		Some college, no degree	
	Number	Percent	Number	Percent	Number	Percent	Number	Percent	Number	Percent
BOTH SEXES										
Total	221,478	100.0	8,603	100.0	13,372	100.0	62,259	100.0	34,690	100.0
Family householder	80,502	36.3	2,608	30.3	4,497	33.6	20,288	32.6	13,436	38.7
Married spouse present	61,073	75.9	1,865	71.5	2,683	59.7	14,226	70.1	9,613	71.5
Other family householder	19,429	24.1	742	28.5	1,814	40.3	6,062	29.9	3,823	28.5
Nonfamily householder	41973	19.0	1,494	17.4	2,646	19.8	11,553	18.6	7,323	21.1
Living alone	34,952	83.3	1,333	89.2	2,284	86.3	9,880	85.5	6,149	84.0
Living with nonrelatives	7,020	16.7	161	10.8	362	13.7	1,673	14.5	1,174	16.0
Relative of householder	86578	39.1	3,972	46.2	5,399	40.4	26,395	42.4	12,019	34.6
Spouse	61,000	70.5	2,029	51.1	2,897	53.7	16,692	63.2	8,220	68.4
Other	25,577	29.5	1,943	48.9	2,501	46.3	9,703	36.8	3,799	31.6
Nonrelative	12,426	5.6	529	6.1	830	6.2	4,022	6.5	1,912	5.5
MALE										
Total	106,695	100.0	4,313	100.0	6,792	100.0	31,257	100.0	16,591	100.0
Family householder	41,917	18.9	1,418	16.5	2,129	15.9	10,736	17.2	6,607	19.0
Married spouse present	36,350	45.2	1,192	45.7	1,601	35.6	8,779	43.3	5,521	41.1
Other family householder	5,567	6.9	226	8.7	528	11.7	1,957	9.6	1,085	8.1
Nonfamily householder	19,952	9.0	692	8.0	1,291	9.7	5,601	9.0	3,436	9.9
Living alone	15,755	79.0	582	84.1	1,053	81.6	4,540	81.1	2,708	78.8
Living with nonrelatives	4,197	21.0	110	15.9	238	18.4	1061	18.9	728	21.2
Relative of householder	38,205	17.3	1,835	21.3	2,852	21.3	12,650	20.3	5,592	16.1
Spouse	24,826	65.0	950	51.8	1,414	49.6	7,262	57.4	3,515	62.9
Other	13,379	35.0	885	48.2	1,438	50.4	5,388	42.6	2,077	37.1
Nonrelative	6,622	3.0	368	4.3	520	3.9	2,271	3.6	956	2.8
FEMALE										
Total	114,783	100.0	4,290	100.0	6,580	100.0	31,002	100.0	18,099	100.0
Family householder	38,585	17.4	1,190	13.8	2,368	17.7	9,552	15.3	6,829	19.7
Married spouse present	24,723	30.7	674	25.8	1,082	24.1	5,447	26.8	4,092	30.5
Other family householder	13,862	17.2	516	19.8	1,286	28.6	4,105	20.2	2,737	20.4
Nonfamily householder	22,021	9.9	803	9.3	1,355	10.1	5,953	9.6	3,887	11.2
Living alone	19,197	87.2	752	93.6	1,231	90.8	5,340	89.7	3,440	88.5
Living with nonrelatives	2,823	12.8	51	6.4	124	9.2	612	10.3	446	11.5
Relative of householder	48,373	21.8	2,138	24.9	2,547	19.0	13,746	22.1	6,427	18.5
Spouse	36,174	74.8	1,080	50.5	1,483	58.2	9,430	68.6	4,705	73.2
Other	12,199	25.2	1,058	49.5	1,063	41.7	4,315	31.4	1,722	26.8
Nonrelative	5,804	2.6	160	1.9	310	2.3	1,751	2.8	956	2.8

Note. Percentages may not sum to total because of rounding.
[1] Civilian noninstitutionalized population, plus armed forces living off post or with their families on post.

Table A-26. Educational Attainment of the Population 25 Years Old and Over, by Household Relationship and Sex, 2019—*Continued*

(Numbers in thousands; percent; civilian noninstitutionalized population.[1])

Sex and household relationship	Educational attainment									
	Associate degree		Bachelor's degree		Master's degree		Professional degree		Doctoral degree	
	Number	Percent	Number	Percent	Number	Percent	Number	Percent	Number	Percent
BOTH SEXES										
Total..	22,738	100.0	49,937	100.0	22,214	100.0	3,136	100.0	4,529	100.0
Family householder..............................	8,923	39.2	18,642	37.3	9,004	40.5	1,232	39.3	1,872	41.3
Married spouse present....................	6,630	74.3	15,539	83.4	7,705	85.6	1,097	89.0	1,714	91.6
Other family householder...................	2,293	25.7	3,103	16.6	1299	14.4	136	11.0	157	8.4
Nonfamily householder.........................	4,281	18.8	9,321	18.7	4,045	18.2	513	16.4	795	17.6
Living alone....................................	3,552	83.0	7,347	78.8	3,306	81.7	432	84.2	668	84.0
Living with nonrelatives..................	729	17.0	1,974	21.2	739	18.3	82	16.0	127	16.0
Relative of householder	8,459	37.2	19,187	38.4	8,181	36.8	1,266	40.4	1,699	37.5
Spouse...	6,379	75.4	14,984	78.1	7,117	87.0	1,102	87.0	1,579	92.9
Other...	2,081	24.6	4,203	21.9	1064	13.0	163	12.9	121	7.1
Nonrelative...	1,074	4.7	2,786	5.6	985	4.4	125	4.0	162	3.6
MALE										
Total..	9,936	100.0	23,785	100.0	9,621	100.0	1,820	100.0	2,580	100.0
Family householder..............................	4191	18.4	10,128	20.3	4,679	21.1	749	23.9	1,281	28.3
Married spouse present....................	3,608	40.4	9,283	49.8	4,438	49.3	709	57.5	1,218	65.1
Other family householder...................	583	6.5	844	4.5	242	2.7	40	3.2	62	3.3
Nonfamily householder.........................	1,991	8.8	4,600	9.2	1,655	7.5	289	9.2	397	8.0
Living alone....................................	1,559	78.3	3,449	75.0	1289	77.9	244	84.4	331	83.4
Living with nonrelatives..................	431	21.6	1151	25.0	366	22.1	45	15.6	67	16.9
Relative of householder	3,282	14.4	7,646	15.3	2,822	12.7	695	22.2	831	18.3
Spouse...	2,304	70.2	5,561	72.7	2,428	86.0	616	88.6	776	93.4
Other...	978	29.8	2,085	27.3	394	14.0	79	11.4	55	6.6
Nonrelative...	472	2.1	1,411	2.8	465	2.1	87	2.8	72	1.6
FEMALE										
Total..	12,802	100.0	26,151	100.0	12,593	100.0	1,317	100.0	1,948	100.0
Family householder..............................	4,732	20.8	8,514	17.0	4,324	19.5	483	15.4	591	13.0
Married spouse present....................	3,022	33.9	6,256	33.6	3,267	36.3	388	31.5	496	26.5
Other family householder...................	1,710	19.2	2,258	12.1	1,058	11.8	96	7.8	95	5.1
Nonfamily householder.........................	2,290	10.1	4,721	9.5	2,391	10.8	224	7.1	398	8.8
Living alone....................................	1,993	87.0	3,898	82.6	2,017	84.4	188	83.9	338	84.9
Living with nonrelatives..................	297	13.0	823	17.4	373	15.6	36	16.1	60	15.1
Relative of householder	5,177	22.8	11,541	23.1	5,359	24.1	571	18.2	869	19.2
Spouse...	4,074	78.7	9,423	81.6	4,689	87.5	486	85.1	803	92.4
Other...	1,103	21.3	2,117	18.3	670	12.5	84	14.7	66	7.6
Nonrelative...	603	2.7	1,375	2.8	520	2.3	38	1.2	90	2.0

Note. Percentages may not sum to total because of rounding.
[1]Civilian noninstitutionalized population, plus armed forces living off post or with their families on post.

Table A-27. Educational Attainment of the Population 25 years Old and Over, by Labor Force Status and Sex, 2019

(Numbers in thousands; percent; civilian noninstitutionalized population.[1])

Sex and labor force status	Total	Educational attainment								
		None to 8th grade	9th to 11th grade	High school graduate	Some college, no degree	Associate's degree	Bachelor's degree	Master's degree	Professional degree	Doctoral degree
BOTH SEXES										
Total............................	221,478	8,603	13,372	62,259	34,690	22,738	49,937	22,214	3,136	4,529
Employed.........................	137,478	3,597	5,726	34,453	20,731	15,235	35,820	16,050	2,425	3,440
Unemployed.....................	4,531	169	464	1,403	860	450	809	293	45	37
Unemployment rate......	3.2	4.5	7.5	3.9	4.0	2.9	2.2	1.8	1.8	1.1
Not in civilian labor force............................	79,470	4,837	7,182	26,403	13,099	7,053	13,307	5,871	666	1,052
Percent.........................	35.9	56.2	53.7	42.4	37.8	31.0	26.6	26.4	21.2	23.2
MALE										
Total............................	106,695	4,313	6,792	31,257	16,591	9,936	23,785	9,621	1,820	2,580
Employed.........................	72,785	2,411	3,611	20,101	10,941	7,167	18,089	7,116	1,412	1,936
Unemployed.....................	2,556	98	290	857	469	227	445	137	18	14
Unemployment rate......	3.4	3.9	7.4	4.1	4.1	3.1	2.4	1.9	1.3	0.7
Not in civilian labor force............................	31,354	1,803	2,891	10,299	5,181	2,541	5,251	2,369	389	631
Percent.........................	29.4	41.8	42.6	32.9	31.2	25.6	22.1	24.6	21.4	24.5
FEMALE										
Total............................	114,783	4,290	6,580	31,002	18,099	12,802	26,151	12,593	1,317	1,948
Employed.........................	64,693	1,186	2,115	14,352	9,790	8,068	17,731	8,935	1,013	1,504
Unemployed.....................	1,975	71	174	546	392	223	364	156	27	23
Unemployment rate......	3.0	5.6	7.6	3.7	3.8	2.7	2.0	1.7	2.6	1.5
Not in civilian labor force............................	48,116	3,034	4,291	16,104	7,918	4,512	8,056	3,502	277	421
Percent.........................	41.9	70.7	65.2	51.9	43.7	35.2	30.8	27.8	21.0	21.6

Note. Percentages may not sum to total because of rounding.
[1]Civilian noninstitutionalized population, plus armed forces living off post or with their families on post. May be of any race.

This page is intentionally left blank

Table A-28. Educational Attainment of Employed Civilians 25 Years Old and Over, by Occupation and Sex, 2019

(Numbers in thousands; percent; civilian noninstitutionalized population.[1])

Occupation and sex	Total		None to 8th grade		9th to 11th grade		High school graduate		Some college, no degree	
	Number	Percent	Number	Percent	Number	Percent	Number	Percent	Number	Percent
BOTH SEXES										
Total Employed Civilians	137,478	100.0	3,597	100.0	5,726	100.0	34,453	100.0	20,731	100.0
Occupation										
Management, business, and financial occupations	25,465	18.5	170	4.7	329	5.7	3,412	9.9	3,315	16.0
Professional and related occupations	34,622	25.2	37	1.0	117	2.0	2,204	6.4	2,575	12.4
Service occupations..	20,981	15.3	1,191	33.1	1,816	31.7	7,926	23.0	3,913	18.9
Sales and related occupations..........................	12,598	9.2	148	4.1	447	7.8	3,450	10.0	2,388	11.5
Office and administrative occupations	15,040	10.9	95	2.6	331	5.8	4,586	13.3	3,672	17.7
Farming, forestry, and fishing occupations	929	0.7	256	7.1	140	2.4	314	0.9	88	0.4
Construction and extraction occupations..........	7,283	5.3	741	20.6	864	15.1	3,238	9.4	1,016	4.9
Installation, maintenance, and repair occupations	4,132	3.0	119	3.3	250	4.4	1,751	5.1	816	3.9
Production occupations	7,705	5.6	490	13.6	621	10.8	3,496	10.1	1,422	6.9
Transportation and material moving occupations	8,723	6.3	349	9.7	811	14.2	4,078	11.8	1,526	7.4
MALE										
Total Employed Civilians	72,785	100.0	2,411	100.0	3,611	100.0	20,101	100.0	10,941	100.0
Occupation										
Management, business, and financial occupations	14,106	19.4	132	5.5	219	6.1	2,025	10.1	1,894	17.3
Professional and related occupations	14,703	20.2	31	1.3	45	1.2	904	4.5	1,088	9.9
Service occupations..	8,725	12.0	558	23.1	715	19.8	3,204	15.9	1,594	14.6
Sales and related occupations..........................	6,699	9.2	65	2.7	195	5.4	1,668	8.3	1,261	11.5
Office and administrative occupations	4,078	5.6	54	2.2	159	4.4	1,241	6.2	915	8.4
Farming, forestry, and fishing occupations	707	1.0	188	7.8	107	3.0	246	1.2	71	0.6
Construction and extraction occupations..........	7,062	9.7	723	30.0	830	23.0	3,169	15.8	988	9.0
Installation, maintenance, and repair occupations	3,992	5.5	115	4.8	235	6.5	1,694	8.4	798	7.3
Production occupations	5,505	7.6	275	11.4	419	11.6	2,553	12.7	1080	9.9
Transportation and material moving occupations	7,208	9.9	271	11.2	687	19.0	3,398	16.9	1,252	11.4
FEMALE										
Total Employed Civilians	64,693	100.0	1,186	100.0	2,115	100.0	14,352	100.0	9,790	100.0
Occupation										
Management, business, and financial occupations	11,358	17.6	39	3.3	110	5.2	1,386	9.7	1,421	14.5
Professional and related occupations	19,919	30.8	6	0.5	72	3.4	1,300	9.1	1,487	15.2
Service occupations..	12,256	18.9	634	53.5	1,101	52.1	4,722	32.9	2,319	23.7
Sales and related occupations..........................	5,899	9.1	83	7.0	252	11.9	1,782	12.4	1,127	11.5
Office and administrative occupations	10,961	16.9	40	3.4	172	8.1	3,345	23.3	2,757	28.2
Farming, forestry, and fishing occupations	222	0.3	67	5.6	33	1.6	68	0.5	17	0.2
Construction and extraction occupations..........	221	0.3	18	1.5	34	1.6	69	0.5	28	0.3
Installation, maintenance, and repair occupations	140	0.2	4	0.3	15	0.7	57	0.4	18	0.2
Production occupations	2,200	3.4	215	18.1	202	9.6	944	6.6	342	3.5
Transportation and material moving occupations	1,516	2.3	79	6.7	123	5.8	680	4.7	274	2.8

Note. Percentages may not sum to total because of rounding.

* = Quantity zero or rounds to zero.

[1]Civilian noninstitutionalized population plus armed forces living off post or with their families on post.

Table A-28. Educational Attainment of Employed Civilians 25 Years Old and Over, by Occupation and Sex, 2019—*Continued*

(Numbers in thousands; percent; civilian noninstitutionalized population.[1])

Occupation and sex	Educational Attainment									
	Associate's degree		Bachelor's degree		Master's degree		Professional degree		Doctoral degree	
	Number	Percent	Number	Percent	Number	Percent	Number	Percent	Number	Percent
BOTH SEXES										
Total Employed Civilians	15,235	100.0	35,820	100.0	16,050	100.0	2,425	100.0	3,440	100.0
Occupation										
Management, business, and financial occupations	2,342	15.4	10,185	28.4	4,848	30.2	323	13.3	540	15.7
Professional and related occupations	3,677	24.1	12,658	35.3	8,720	54.3	1,914	78.9	2,721	79.1
Service occupations..................................	2,557	16.8	2,940	8.2	525	3.3	61	2.5	52	1.5
Sales and related occupations...........................	1,390	9.1	3,908	10.9	787	4.9	36	1.5	44	1.3
Office and administrative occupations	2,122	13.9	3,385	9.5	768	4.8	30	1.2	51	1.5
Farming, forestry, and fishing occupations	54	0.4	62	0.2	15	0.1	*	*	*	*
Construction and extraction occupations..........	691	4.5	641	1.8	69	0.4	18	0.7	5	0.1
Installation, maintenance, and repair occupations	783	5.1	370	1.0	36	0.2	6	0.2	2	0.1
Production occupations	850	5.6	699	2.0	105	0.7	13	0.5	8	0.2
Transportation and material moving occupations	769	5.0	972	2.7	178	1.1	23	0.9	17	0.5
MALE										
Total Employed Civilians	7,167	100.0	18,089	100.0	7,116	100.0	1,412	100.0	1,936	100.0
Occupation										
Management, business, and financial occupations	1,140	15.9	5,594	30.9	2,576	36.2	198	14.0	328	16.9
Professional and related occupations	1,147	16.0	5,561	30.7	3,300	46.4	1,121	79.4	1,508	77.9
Service occupations..................................	967	13.5	1,416	7.8	247	3.5	9	0.6	15	0.8
Sales and related occupations...........................	685	9.6	2,308	12.8	460	6.5	25	1.8	31	1.6
Office and administrative occupations	490	6.8	979	5.4	210	3.0	5	0.4	26	1.3
Farming, forestry, and fishing occupations	41	0.6	43	0.2	10	0.1	*	*	*	*
Construction and extraction occupations..........	668	9.3	594	3.3	66	0.9	18	1.3	5	0.3
Installation, maintenance, and repair occupations	763	10.6	344	1.9	36	0.5	6	0.4	2	0.1
Production occupations	630	8.8	464	2.6	70	1.0	9	0.6	5	0.3
Transportation and material moving occupations	636	8.9	786	4.3	141	2.0	20	1.4	16	0.8
FEMALE										
Total Employed Civilians	8,068	100.0	17,731	100.0	8,935	100.0	1,013	100.0	1,504	100.0
Occupation										
Management, business, and financial occupations	1,202	14.9	4,592	25.9	2,272	25.4	125	12.3	212	14.1
Professional and related occupations	2,530	31.4	7,097	40.0	5,420	60.7	793	78.3	1,213	80.7
Service occupations..................................	1,590	19.7	1,525	8.6	278	3.1	51	5.0	37	2.5
Sales and related occupations...........................	704	8.7	1,600	9.0	327	3.7	11	1.1	13	0.9
Office and administrative occupations	1,632	20.2	2,406	13.6	558	6.2	25	2.5	25	1.7
Farming, forestry, and fishing occupations	13	0.2	18	0.1	5	0.1	*	*	*	*
Construction and extraction occupations..........	23	0.3	47	0.3	3	0.0	*	*	*	*
Installation, maintenance, and repair occupations	20	0.2	26	0.1	*	*	*	*	*	*
Production occupations	221	2.7	235	1.3	35	0.4	4	0.4	3	0.2
Transportation and material moving occupations	132	1.6	187	1.1	36	0.4	3	0.3	1	0.1

Note. Percentages may not sum to total because of rounding.
* = Quantity zero or rounds to zero.
[1] Civilian noninstitutionalized population plus armed forces living off post or with their families on post.

Table A-29. Educational Attainment of the Population 25 Years Old and Over, by Industry and Sex, 2019

(Numbers in thousands; percent; civilian noninstitutionalized population.[1])

Industry and sex	Total		None to 8th grade		9th to 11th grade		High school graduate		Some college, no degree	
	Number	Percent	Number	Percent	Number	Percent	Number	Percent	Number	Percent
BOTH SEXES										
Total Employed Civilians	137,478	100.0	3,597	100.0	5,726	100.0	34,453	100.0	20,731	100.0
Industry										
Agriculture, forestry, fishing, and hunting	2,017	1.5	297	8.3	194	3.4	657	1.9	254	1.2
Mining	704	0.5	14	0.4	33	0.6	263	0.8	115	0.6
Construction	9,849	7.2	775	21.5	982	17.1	3,948	11.5	1,458	7.0
Manufacturing	14,450	10.5	517	14.4	746	13.0	4,663	13.5	2,203	10.6
Wholesale and retail trade	15,893	11.6	307	8.5	798	13.9	5,240	15.2	3,155	15.2
Transportation and utilities	8,009	5.8	175	4.9	403	7.0	2,972	8.6	1,676	8.1
Information	2,455	1.8	11	0.3	31	0.5	391	1.1	385	1.9
Financial activities	9,847	7.2	43	1.2	120	2.1	1,621	4.7	1,495	7.2
Professional and business services	17,821	13.0	448	12.5	520	9.1	3,009	8.7	2,183	10.5
Educational and health services	33,060	24.0	222	6.2	670	11.7	5,019	14.6	3,756	18.1
Leisure and hospitality	9,980	7.3	503	14.0	755	13.2	3,299	9.6	1,801	8.7
Other services	6,590	4.8	255	7.1	400	7.0	2,223	6.5	1,018	4.9
Public administration	6,802	4.9	29	0.8	73	1.3	1,147	3.3	1,232	5.9
MALE										
Total Employed Civilians	72,785	100.0	2,411	100.0	3,611	100.0	20,101	100.0	10,941	100.0
Industry										
Agriculture, forestry, fishing, and hunting	1,520	2.1	223	9.2	156	4.3	536	2.7	189	1.7
Mining	592	0.8	14	0.6	33	0.9	243	1.2	88	0.8
Construction	8,860	12.2	758	31.4	945	26.2	3,660	18.2	1,301	11.9
Manufacturing	10,213	14.0	304	12.6	543	15.0	3,373	16.8	1,633	14.9
Wholesale and retail trade	8,913	12.2	193	8.0	477	13.2	2,931	14.6	1,767	16.2
Transportation and utilities	6,140	8.4	154	6.4	342	9.5	2,321	11.5	1,220	11.2
Information	1,444	2.0	7	0.3	18	0.5	261	1.3	250	2.3
Financial activities	4,648	6.4	40	1.7	72	2.0	588	2.9	569	5.2
Professional and business services	10,420	14.3	272	11.3	306	8.5	1,738	8.6	1,156	10.6
Educational and health services	8,303	11.4	54	2.2	129	3.6	1097	5.5	701	6.4
Leisure and hospitality	5,072	7.0	267	11.1	380	10.5	1,631	8.1	954	8.7
Other services	3,036	4.2	106	4.4	171	4.7	1,091	5.4	446	4.1
Public administration	3,623	5.0	18	0.7	39	1.1	631	3.1	667	6.1
FEMALE										
Total Employed Civilians	64,693	100.0	1,186	100.0	2,115	100.0	14,352	100.0	9,790	100.0
Industry										
Agriculture, forestry, fishing, and hunting	497	0.8	74	6.2	38	1.8	121	0.8	65	0.7
Mining	111	0.2	-	-	-	-	20	0.1	26	0.3
Construction	989	1.5	17	1.4	37	1.7	288	2.0	157	1.6
Manufacturing	4,237	6.5	213	18.0	203	9.6	1,290	9.0	570	5.8
Wholesale and retail trade	6,981	10.8	114	9.6	322	15.2	2,309	16.1	1,388	14.2
Transportation and utilities	1,869	2.9	20	1.7	61	2.9	651	4.5	456	4.7
Information	1,011	1.6	4	0.3	13	0.6	130	0.9	135	1.4
Financial activities	5,198	8.0	3	0.3	48	2.3	1,033	7.2	925	9.4
Professional and business services	7,401	11.4	176	14.8	214	10.1	1,272	8.9	1,027	10.5
Educational and health services	24,757	38.3	169	14.2	541	25.6	3,921	27.3	3,055	31.2
Leisure and hospitality	4,909	7.6	236	19.9	375	17.7	1,668	11.6	847	8.7
Other services	3,554	5.5	149	12.6	229	10.8	1,132	7.9	573	5.9
Public administration	3,178	4.9	11	0.9	34	1.6	516	3.6	565	5.8

Note. Percentages may not sum to total because of rounding.
* = Quantity zero or rounds to zero.
[1]Civilian noninstitutionalized population plus armed forces living off post or with their families on post.

Table A-29. Educational Attainment of the Population 25 Years Old and Over, by Industry and Sex, 2019—*Continued*

(Numbers in thousands; percent; civilian noninstitutionalized population.[1])

Industry and sex	Educational Attainment										Percent Bachelor's Degree or Higher
	Associate's degree		Bachelor's degree		Master's degree		Professional degree		Doctoral degree		
	Number	Percent	Number	Percent	Number	Percent	Number	Percent	Number	Percent	
BOTH SEXES											
Total Employed Civilians	15,235	100.0	35,820	100.0	16,050	100.0	2,425	100.0	3,440	100.0	42.0
Industry											
Agriculture, forestry, fishing, and hunting.....	193	1.3	317	0.9	80	0.5	6	0.2	18	0.5	20.9
Mining..	60	0.4	142	0.4	65	0.4	-	-	11	0.3	31.0
Construction	956	6.3	1,384	3.9	289	1.8	39	1.6	17	0.5	17.6
Manufacturing....................................	1,608	10.6	3,280	9.2	1,212	7.6	49	2.0	172	5.0	32.6
Wholesale and retail trade......................	1,794	11.8	3,601	10.1	771	4.8	81	3.3	146	4.2	28.9
Transportation and utilities.....................	959	6.3	1,447	4.0	327	2.0	27	1.1	25	0.7	22.8
Information	218	1.4	985	2.7	390	2.4	12	0.5	31	0.9	57.8
Financial activities	979	6.4	4,036	11.3	1,312	8.2	120	4.9	122	3.5	56.8
Professional and business services	1,549	10.2	6,119	17.1	2,689	16.8	724	29.9	579	16.8	56.7
Educational and health services.................	4,281	28.1	9,078	25.3	6,895	43.0	1,102	45.4	2,037	59.2	57.8
Leisure and hospitality...........................	928	6.1	2,143	6.0	500	3.1	34	1.4	17	0.5	27.0
Other services.....................................	862	5.7	1,171	3.3	515	3.2	57	2.4	90	2.6	27.8
Public administration	847	5.6	2,117	5.9	1005	6.3	176	7.3	175	5.1	51.1
MALE											
Total Employed Civilians	7,167	100.0	18,089	100.0	7,116	100.0	1,412	100.0	1,936	100.0	39.2
Industry											
Agriculture, forestry, fishing, and hunting.....	139	1.9	205	1.1	56	0.8	6	0.4	10	0.5	18.2
Mining..	52	0.7	109	0.6	48	0.7	-	-	4	0.2	27.2
Construction	824	11.5	1102	6.1	218	3.1	37	2.6	14	0.7	15.5
Manufacturing....................................	1106	15.4	2,225	12.3	870	12.2	39	2.8	120	6.2	31.9
Wholesale and retail trade......................	935	13.0	2,054	11.4	446	6.3	43	3.0	68	3.5	29.3
Transportation and utilities.....................	761	10.6	1074	5.9	222	3.1	23	1.6	23	1.2	21.9
Information	161	2.2	535	3.0	182	2.6	6	0.4	24	1.2	51.7
Financial activities	360	5.0	2,146	11.9	718	10.1	72	5.1	83	4.3	65.0
Professional and business services	752	10.5	3,703	20.5	1,628	22.9	472	33.4	394	20.4	59.5
Educational and health services.................	759	10.6	2,175	12.0	1,757	24.7	587	41.6	1044	53.9	67.0
Leisure and hospitality...........................	463	6.5	1140	6.3	217	3.0	9	0.6	11	0.6	27.1
Other services.....................................	374	5.2	491	2.7	265	3.7	29	2.1	63	3.3	27.9
Public administration	481	6.7	1,132	6.3	489	6.9	90	6.4	78	4.0	49.4
FEMALE											
Total Employed Civilians	8,068	100.0	17,731	100.0	8,935	100.0	1,013	100.0	1,504	100.0	45.1
Industry											
Agriculture, forestry, fishing, and hunting.....	54	0.7	113	0.6	24	0.3	-	-	9	0.6	29.4
Mining..	9	0.1	33	0.2	17	0.2	-	-	7	0.5	51.4
Construction	132	1.6	282	1.6	71	0.8	2	0.2	2	0.1	36.1
Manufacturing....................................	502	6.2	1,055	6.0	343	3.8	9	0.9	52	3.5	34.4
Wholesale and retail trade......................	859	10.6	1,547	8.7	325	3.6	38	3.8	78	5.2	28.5
Transportation and utilities.....................	197	2.4	373	2.1	105	1.2	4	0.4	2	0.1	25.9
Information	57	0.7	451	2.5	208	2.3	6	0.6	7	0.5	66.5
Financial activities	618	7.7	1,890	10.7	594	6.6	48	4.7	39	2.6	49.5
Professional and business services	798	9.9	2,417	13.6	1,061	11.9	251	24.8	185	12.3	52.9
Educational and health services.................	3,522	43.7	6,903	38.9	5,138	57.5	515	50.8	993	66.0	54.7
Leisure and hospitality...........................	465	5.8	1,003	5.7	283	3.2	25	2.5	6	0.4	26.8
Other services.....................................	489	6.1	680	3.8	249	2.8	28	2.8	26	1.7	27.7
Public administration	366	4.5	985	5.6	516	5.8	86	8.5	98	6.5	53.0

Note. Percentages may not sum to total because of rounding.
* = Quantity zero or rounds to zero.
[1]Civilian noninstitutionalized population plus armed forces living off post or with their families on post.

Table A-30. Educational Attainment of the Population 25 Years Old and Over, by Citizenship, Nativity, Period of Entry, and Sex, 2019

(Numbers in thousands; percent; civilian noninstitutionalized population.[1])

Citizenship, nativity, period of entry, and sex	Total Number	Total Percent	None to 8th grade Number	None to 8th grade Percent	9th to 11th grade Number	9th to 11th grade Percent	High school graduate Number	High school graduate Percent	Some college, no degree Number	Some college, no degree Percent
BOTH SEXES										
Total	221,478	100.0	8,603	3.9	13,372	6.0	62,259	28.1	34,690	15.7
Native	181,283	81.9	2,767	1.5	9,420	5.2	52,024	28.7	31,198	17.2
Foreign-born	40,195	18.1	5,836	14.5	3,952	9.8	10,235	25.5	3,492	8.7
Native										
Native parentage[2]	163,644	90.3	2,382	1.5	8,627	5.3	47,620	29.1	28,126	17.2
Foreign or mixed parentage[3]	17,639	9.7	385	2.2	793	4.5	4,404	25.0	3,072	17.4
Foreign-born										
Naturalized citizen	20,751	51.6	1,856	8.9	1,427	6.9	5,263	25.4	2,246	10.8
Not a citizen	19,444	48.4	3,980	20.5	2,525	13.0	4,972	25.6	1,245	6.4
Year of entry										
2010 or later	7,963	19.8	766	9.6	560	7.0	1,845	23.2	568	7.1
2000-2009	10,252	25.5	1,636	16.0	1,224	11.9	2,732	26.6	747	7.3
1990-1999	9,796	24.4	1,413	14.4	1,086	11.1	2,578	26.3	822	8.4
1980-1989	6,414	16.0	1,064	16.6	692	10.8	1,597	24.9	684	10.7
1970-1979	3,446	8.6	653	18.9	245	7.1	807	23.4	356	10.3
Before 1970	2,324	5.8	303	13.0	146	6.3	676	29.1	314	13.5
MALE										
Total	106,695	100.0	4,313	1.9	6,792	3.1	31,257	14.1	16,591	7.5
Native	87,239	81.8	1,455	1.7	4,832	5.5	26,292	30.1	14,919	17.1
Foreign-born	19,456	18.2	2,858	14.7	1,960	10.1	4,965	25.5	1,672	8.6
Native										
Native parentage[2]	78,475	90.0	1,265	1.6	4,453	5.7	23,977	30.6	13,365	17.0
Foreign or mixed parentage[3]	8,764	10.0	189	2.2	380	4.3	2,314	26.4	1,553	17.7
Foreign-born										
Naturalized citizen	9,632	49.5	805	8.4	652	6.8	2,462	25.6	1,053	10.9
Not a citizen	9,824	50.5	2,053	20.9	1,308	13.3	2,503	25.5	619	6.3
Year of entry										
2010 or later	3,784	9.4	355	9.4	266	7.0	878	23.2	283	7.5
2000-2009	4,869	12.1	796	16.3	594	12.2	1,349	27.7	333	6.8
1990-1999	4,827	12.0	691	14.3	536	11.1	1,291	26.7	434	9.0
1980-1989	3,330	8.3	565	17.0	381	11.4	834	25.0	335	10.1
1970-1979	1,660	4.1	326	19.6	133	8.0	356	21.4	161	9.7
Before 1970	986	2.5	126	12.8	50	5.1	258	26.2	126	12.8
FEMALE										
Total	114,783	100.0	4,290	1.9	6,580	3.0	31,002	14.0	18,099	8.2
Native	94,044	81.9	1,312	1.4	4,588	4.9	25,732	27.4	16,280	17.3
Foreign-born	20,739	18.1	2,978	14.4	1,992	9.6	5,269	25.4	1,819	8.8
Native										
Native parentage[2]	85,169	90.6	1,116	1.3	4,174	4.9	23,643	27.8	14,761	17.3
Foreign or mixed parentage[3]	8,875	9.4	196	2.2	414	4.7	2,090	23.5	1,519	17.1
Foreign-born										
Naturalized citizen	11,119	53.6	1,050	9.4	775	7.0	2,801	25.2	1,193	10.7
Not a citizen	9,620	46.4	1,928	20.0	1,217	12.7	2,468	25.7	626	6.5
Year of entry										
2010 or later	4,179	10.4	411	9.8	294	7.0	967	23.1	285	6.8
2000-2009	5,383	13.4	840	15.6	630	11.7	1,384	25.7	414	7.7
1990-1999	4,968	12.4	722	14.5	550	11.1	1,287	25.9	388	7.8
1980-1989	3,085	7.7	500	16.2	311	10.1	762	24.7	349	11.3
1970-1979	1,786	4.4	327	18.3	111	6.2	451	25.3	195	10.9
Before 1970	1,339	3.3	177	13.2	96	7.2	418	31.2	189	14.1

[1]Civilian noninstitutionalized population plus armed forces living off post or with their families on post.
[2]Native parentage: Both parents born in the United States. Percent: percent of native citizens.
[3]Foreign or mixed parentage: One or both parents born outside of the United States.

Table A-30. Educational Attainment of the Population 25 Years Old and Over, by Citizenship, Nativity, Period of Entry, and Sex, 2019—*Continued*

(Numbers in thousands; percent; civilian noninstitutionalized population.[1])

Citizenship, nativity, period of entry, and sex	Educational attainment									
	Associate degree		Bachelor's degree		Master's degree		Professional degree		Doctoral degree	
	Number	Percent	Number	Percent	Number	Percent	Number	Percent	Number	Percent
BOTH SEXES										
Total	22,738	10.3	49,937	22.5	22,214	10.0	3,136	1.4	4,529	2.0
Native..	19,984	11.0	41,686	23.0	18,120	10.0	2,568	1.4	3,515	1.9
Foreign-born	2,754	6.9	8,250	20.5	4,095	10.2	568	1.4	1,014	2.5
Native										
Native parentage[2]	18,083	11.1	37,290	22.8	16,212	9.9	2,208	1.3	3,096	1.9
Foreign or mixed parentage[3]	1,901	10.8	4,396	24.9	1,907	10.8	361	2.0	419	2.4
Foreign-born										
Naturalized citizen	1,794	8.6	5,036	24.3	2,102	10.1	394	1.9	634	3.1
Not a citizen	960	4.9	3,214	16.5	1,993	10.2	174	0.9	380	2.0
Year of entry										
2010 or later	446	5.6	2,145	26.9	1,329	16.7	96	1.2	207	2.6
2000-2009	620	6.0	1,943	19.0	929	9.1	162	1.6	259	2.5
1990-1999	771	7.9	1,870	19.1	876	8.9	138	1.4	242	2.5
1980-1989	464	7.2	1,208	18.8	480	7.5	82	1.3	142	2.2
1970-1979	238	6.9	672	19.5	311	9.0	51	1.5	112	3.3
Before 1970	216	9.3	412	17.7	168	7.2	38	1.6	52	2.2
MALE										
Total...	9,936	4.5	23,785	10.7	9,621	4.3	1,820	0.8	2,580	1.2
Native..	8,768	10.1	19,920	22.8	7,555	8.7	1,549	1.8	1,950	2.2
Foreign-born	1,168	6.0	3,866	19.9	2,066	10.6	271	1.4	630	3.2
Native										
Native parentage[2]	7,894	10.1	17,764	22.6	6,701	8.5	1,306	1.7	1,749	2.2
Foreign or mixed parentage[3]	874	10.0	2,156	24.6	854	9.7	243	2.8	201	2.3
Foreign-born										
Naturalized citizen	752	7.8	2,296	23.8	1,029	10.7	179	1.9	404	4.2
Not a citizen	416	4.2	1,570	16.0	1,037	10.6	92	0.9	226	2.3
Year of entry										
2010 or later	199	5.3	973	25.7	656	17.3	47	1.2	127	3.4
2000-2009	251	5.2	843	17.3	471	9.7	86	1.8	148	3.0
1990-1999	321	6.7	905	18.7	434	9.0	54	1.1	161	3.3
1980-1989	220	6.6	604	18.1	273	8.2	36	1.1	82	2.5
1970-1979	109	6.6	330	19.9	146	8.8	26	1.6	74	4.5
Before 1970	69	7.0	211	21.4	86	8.7	21	2.1	40	4.1
FEMALE										
Total...	12,802	5.8	26,151	11.8	12,593	5.7	1,317	0.6	1,948	0.9
Native..	11,216	11.9	21,767	23.1	10,565	11.2	1,020	1.1	1,565	1.7
Foreign-born	1,586	7.6	4,384	21.1	2,029	9.8	297	1.4	384	1.9
Native										
Native parentage[2]	10,190	12.0	19,526	22.9	9,511	11.2	902	1.1	1,347	1.6
Foreign or mixed parentage[3]	1027	11.6	2,241	25.3	1,053	11.9	118	1.3	218	2.5
Foreign-born										
Naturalized citizen	1,042	9.4	2,740	24.6	1,073	9.7	215	1.9	229	2.1
Not a citizen	544	5.7	1,644	17.1	956	9.9	82	0.9	154	1.6
Year of entry										
2010 or later	247	5.9	1,172	28.0	673	16.1	49	1.2	80	1.9
2000-2009	369	6.9	1,101	20.5	458	8.5	77	1.4	111	2.1
1990-1999	449	9.0	965	19.4	442	8.9	84	1.7	81	1.6
1980-1989	244	7.9	604	19.6	208	6.7	46	1.5	61	2.0
1970-1979	130	7.3	342	19.1	165	9.2	25	1.4	39	2.2
Before 1970	147	11.0	201	15.0	82	6.1	17	1.3	12	0.9

[1]Civilian noninstitutionalized population plus armed forces living off post or with their families on post.
[2]Native parentage: Both parents born in the United States. Percent: percent of native citizens.
[3]Foreign or mixed parentage: One or both parents born outside of the United States.

Table A-31. Detailed Years of School Completed by People 25 Years Old and Over, by Sex, Age Groups, Race, and Hispanic Origin, 2019

(Numbers in thousands; civilian noninstitutionalized population.[1])

Detailed years of school	All races Number	All races Percent	Males Number	Males Percent	Females Number	Females Percent	25 to 34 years old Number	25 to 34 years old Percent	35 to 54 years old Number	35 to 54 years old Percent
Total...	221,478	100.0	106,695	100.0	114,783	100.0	45,208	100.0	81,727	100.0
Elementary or High school, no diploma										
Less than 1 year, no diploma	769	0.4	378	0.4	391	0.3	114	0.3	275	0.3
1st-4th grade, no diploma....................................	1,412	0.6	705	0.7	707	0.6	118	0.3	440	0.5
5th-6th grade, no diploma	3,111	1.4	1,624	1.5	1,487	1.3	324	0.7	1,245	1.5
7th-8th grade, no diploma	3,312	1.5	1,607	1.5	1,705	1.5	355	0.8	1,065	1.3
9th grade, no diploma...	3,365	1.5	1,621	1.5	1,744	1.5	483	1.1	1,433	1.8
10th grade, no diploma.......................................	3,397	1.5	1,723	1.6	1,674	1.5	529	1.2	1,123	1.4
11th grade, no diploma.......................................	3,940	1.8	2,037	1.9	1,903	1.7	775	1.7	1,419	1.7
12th grade, no diploma.......................................	2,671	1.2	1,412	1.3	1,259	1.1	566	1.3	982	1.2
Elementary or High school, GED										
Less than 1 year, GED..	33	*	14	*	19	*	12	*	14	*
1st-4th grade, GED..	111	0.1	65	0.1	46	*	31	0.1	29	*
5th-6th grade, GED..	48	*	26	*	22	*	8	*	6	*
7th-8th grade, GED..	303	0.1	162	0.2	141	0.1	39	0.1	103	0.1
9th grade, GED..	608	0.3	338	0.3	270	0.2	128	0.3	221	0.3
10th grade, GED..	1,214	0.6	633	0.6	582	0.5	263	0.6	421	0.5
11th grade, GED..	1,982	0.9	1,053	1.0	928	0.8	370	0.8	803	1.0
12th grade, GED..	1,419	0.6	848	0.8	570	0.5	307	0.7	580	0.7
High school diploma	56,542	25.5	28,119	26.4	28,424	24.8	10,481	23.2	19,124	23.4
College, no degree										
Less than 1 year college, no degree......................	4,528	2.0	2,054	1.9	2,473	2.2	961	2.1	1,410	1.7
One year of college, no degree.............................	11,090	5.0	5,144	4.8	5,945	5.2	2,439	5.4	3,670	4.5
Two years of college, no degree...........................	14,333	6.5	6,954	6.5	7,379	6.4	2,878	6.4	4,993	6.1
Three years of college, no degree	3,327	1.5	1,700	1.6	1,627	1.4	850	1.9	1,206	1.5
Four or more years of college, no degree...............	1,412	0.6	738	0.7	674	0.6	402	0.9	502	0.6
Associate's degree, vocational										
Less than 1 year college, vocational/associate's	369	0.2	165	0.2	204	0.2	67	0.2	144	0.2
One year of college, vocational/associate's	1,263	0.6	528	0.5	734	0.6	261	0.6	449	0.6
Two years of college, vocational/associate's	6,341	2.9	2,955	2.8	3,387	3.0	1,223	2.7	2,479	3.0
Three years of college, vocational/associate's........	898	0.4	404	0.4	495	0.4	231	0.5	339	0.4
Four or more years of college, vocational/associate's	869	0.4	436	0.4	433	0.4	214	0.5	303	0.4
Associate's degree, academic										
Less than 1 year college, academic/associate's	122	0.1	53	0.1	69	0.1	25	0.1	60	0.1
One year of college, academic/associate's	579	0.3	248	0.2	331	0.3	102	0.2	213	0.3
Two years of college, academic/associate's	9,138	4.1	3,818	3.6	5,320	4.6	1,818	4.0	3,523	4.3
Three years of college, academic/associate's........	1,624	0.7	688	0.7	936	0.8	395	0.9	651	0.8
Four or more years of college, academic/associate's	1,534	0.7	641	0.6	893	0.8	405	0.9	630	0.8
Bachelor's degree	49,937	22.6	23,785	22.3	26,151	22.8	12,727	28.2	19,463	23.8
Master's degree[2]	22,214	10.0	9,621	9.0	12,593	11.0	4,097	9.1	9,308	11.4
Professional degree	3,136	1.4	1,820	1.7	1,317	1.2	532	1.2	1,237	1.5
Doctorate degree	4,529	2.0	2,580	2.4	1,948	1.7	682	1.5	1,862	2.3

* = Quantity zero or rounds to zero.
[1]Excluding members of the Armed Forces living in barracks.
[2]Detail on graduate school attendance and length of master's degree program, available in previous years, discontinued due to questionnaire changes in 2015.

Table A-31. Detailed Years of School Completed by People 25 Years Old and Over, by Sex, Age Groups, Race, and Hispanic Origin, 2019—*Continued*

(Numbers in thousands; civilian noninstitutionalized population.[1])

Detailed years of school	55 years and older Number	55 years and older Percent	White Number	White Percent	Non-Hispanic White Number	Non-Hispanic White Percent	Black Number	Black Percent	Asian Number	Asian Percent	Hispanic (of any race) Number	Hispanic (of any race) Percent
Total..	94,543	100.0	173,452	100.0	142,557	100.0	27,428	100.0	13,955	100.0	34,575	100.0
Elementary or High school, no diploma												
Less than 1 year, no diploma............................	379	0.4	449	0.3	104	0.1	126	0.5	152	1.1	385	1.1
1st-4th grade, no diploma................................	854	0.9	1,118	0.6	141	0.1	119	0.4	109	0.8	1,073	3.1
5th-6th grade, no diploma................................	1,542	1.6	2,608	1.5	314	0.2	168	0.6	190	1.4	2,481	7.2
7th-8th grade, no diploma................................	1,892	2.0	2,594	1.5	1,297	0.9	397	1.5	220	1.6	1,428	4.1
9th grade, no diploma....................................	1,449	1.5	2,649	1.5	1,124	0.8	396	1.4	177	1.3	1,720	5.0
10th grade, no diploma...................................	1,745	1.9	2,453	1.4	1,645	1.2	652	2.4	153	1.1	901	2.6
11th grade, no diploma...................................	1,746	1.9	2,771	1.6	1,930	1.4	905	3.3	92	0.7	951	2.8
12th grade, no diploma...................................	1,122	1.2	1,874	1.1	1,131	0.8	561	2.1	132	1.0	823	2.4
Elementary or High school, GED												
Less than 1 year, GED....................................	7	*	24	*	12	*	7.0	*	2.0	*	11	*
1st-4th grade, GED.......................................	50	0.1	80	0.1	44	*	13	0.1	10.0	0.1	41	0.1
5th-6th grade, GED.......................................	33	*	36	*	15	0.0	11.0	*	*	*	21	0.1
7th-8th grade, GED.......................................	161	0.2	261	0.2	201	0.1	27	0.1	4	*	69	0.2
9th grade, GED...	259	0.3	473	0.3	393	0.3	94	0.3	7	0.1	95	0.3
10th grade, GED..	530	0.6	976	0.6	843	0.6	143	0.5	13	0.1	171	0.5
11th grade, GED..	809	0.9	1,523	0.9	1,306	0.9	330	1.2	20	0.2	268	0.8
12th grade, GED..	532	0.6	1,129	0.7	815	0.6	214	0.8	22	0.2	340	1.0
High school diploma	26,937	28.5	44,323	25.6	35,464	24.9	8,105	29.6	2,372	17.0	9,831	28.4
College, no degree												
Less than 1 year college, no degree....................	2,157	2.3	3,703	2.1	3,186	2.2	572	2.1	108	0.8	577	1.7
One year of college, no degree.........................	4,980	5.3	8,850	5.1	7,592	5.3	1,538	5.6	289	2.1	1,406	4.1
Two years of college, no degree........................	6,462	6.8	10,887	6.3	9,140	6.4	2,338	8.5	576	4.1	1,998	5.8
Three years of college, no degree	1,271	1.3	2,552	1.5	2,128	1.5	497	1.8	145	1.0	476	1.4
Four or more years of college, no degree.............	508	0.5	1,069	0.6	871	0.6	173	0.6	110	0.8	223	0.6
Associate's degree, vocational												
Less than 1 year college, vocational/associate's .	158	0.2	307	0.2	255	0.2	37	0.1	14	0.1	53	0.2
One year of college, vocational/associate's	552	0.6	1,047	0.6	883	0.6	128	0.5	43	0.3	178	0.5
Two years of college, vocational/associate's	2,640	2.8	5,148	3.0	4,494	3.2	790	2.9	225	1.6	731	2.1
Three years of college, vocational/associate's.....	329	0.4	695	0.4	588	0.4	137	0.5	33	0.2	124	0.4
Four or more years of college, vocational/associate's...	352	0.4	691	0.4	587	0.4	97	0.4	42	0.3	123	0.4
Associate's degree, academic												
Less than 1 year college, academic/associate's ..	38	*	92	0.1	75	0.1	18	0.1	9	0.1	21	0.1
One year of college, academic/associate's	265	0.3	427	0.3	362	0.3	93	0.3	44	0.3	77	0.2
Two years of college, academic/associate's	3,797	4.0	7,262	4.2	6,388	4.5	1,179	4.3	385	2.8	1,010	2.9
Three years of college, academic/associate's......	578	0.6	1,275	0.7	1,075	0.8	225	0.8	64	0.5	236	0.7
Four or more years of college, academic/associate's...	499	0.5	1,207	0.7	1,000	0.7	190	0.7	82	0.6	223	0.7
Bachelor's degree	17,747	18.8	39,655	22.9	35,642	25.0	4,544	16.6	4,650	33.3	4,527	13.1
Master's degree[2]..................................	8,810	9.3	17,223	9.9	15,897	11.2	2,119	7.7	2,436	17.5	1,532	4.4
Professional degree	1,368	1.5	2,558	1.5	2,365	1.7	188	0.7	340	2.4	209	0.6
Doctorate degree	1,985	2.1	3,462	2.0	3,250	2.3	297	1.1	681	4.9	243	0.7

* = Quantity zero or rounds to zero.
[1]Excluding members of the Armed Forces living in barracks.
[2]Detail on graduate school attendance and length of master's degree program, available in previous years, discontinued due to questionnaire changes in 2015.

PART A

NATIONAL EDUCATION STATISTICS

■ **Historical Attainment Tables**

Table A-32. Percent of People 25 Years Old and Over Who Have Completed High School or College, by Race, Hispanic Origin, and Sex, Selected Years, 1940–2019

(Percent; civilian noninstitutionalized population.)

Age and Year	All races Total	Male	Female	White Total	Male	Female	Non-Hispanic White Total	Male	Female	Black[1] Total	Male	Female	Asian Total	Male	Female
25 YEARS AND OLDER															
Completed 4 Years of High School or More															
2019	90.1	89.6	90.5	90.5	89.9	91.0	94.6	94.2	95.0	87.9	87.1	88.6	91.2	92.8	89.8
2018	89.8	89.4	90.2	90.2	89.6	90.8	94.3	93.9	94.7	87.9	87.7	88.1	90.5	92.7	88.6
2017	89.6	89.1	90.0	90.1	89.5	90.6	94.1	93.7	94.5	87.3	86.5	87.9	90.9	92.6	89.4
2016	89.1	88.5	89.6	89.5	88.8	90.1	93.8	93.4	94.3	87.1	86.4	87.7	90.3	91.9	89.0
2015	88.4	88.0	88.8	88.8	88.3	89.3	93.3	93.0	93.5	87.0	86.4	87.6	89.1	91.0	87.4
2014	88.3	87.7	88.9	88.8	88.0	89.6	93.1	92.5	93.7	85.8	85.3	86.2	89.5	91.9	87.4
2013	88.2	87.6	88.6	88.6	88.0	89.2	92.9	92.7	93.2	85.1	84.1	86.0	90.1	91.5	89.0
2012[2]	87.6	87.3	88.0	88.1	87.6	88.5	92.5	92.2	92.7	85.0	84.3	85.5	88.9	90.4	87.6
2011	87.6	87.1	88.0	88.1	87.4	88.6	92.4	92.0	92.8	84.5	83.8	85.0	88.6	90.4	87.1
2010	87.1	86.6	87.6	87.6	86.9	88.2	92.1	91.8	92.3	84.2	83.6	84.6	88.9	91.2	87.0
2009	86.7	86.2	87.1	87.1	86.5	87.7	91.6	91.4	91.9	84.1	84.0	84.1	88.2	90.4	86.2
2008	86.6	85.9	87.2	87.1	86.3	87.8	91.5	91.1	91.8	83.0	81.8	84.0	88.7	90.8	86.9
2007	85.7	85.0	86.4	86.2	85.3	87.1	90.6	90.2	91.0	82.3	81.9	82.6	87.8	89.8	85.9
2006	85.5	85.0	85.9	86.1	85.5	86.7	90.5	90.2	90.8	80.7	80.1	81.2	87.4	89.6	85.5
2005	85.2	84.9	85.5	85.8	85.2	86.2	90.1	89.9	90.3	81.1	81.0	81.2	87.6	90.4	85.2
2004	85.2	84.8	85.4	85.8	85.3	86.3	90.0	89.9	90.1	80.6	80.4	80.8	86.8	88.7	85.0
2003[3]	84.6	84.1	85.0	85.1	84.5	85.7	89.4	89.0	89.7	80.0	79.6	80.3	87.6	89.5	86.0
2002	84.1	83.8	84.4	84.8	84.3	85.2	88.7	88.5	88.9	78.7	78.5	78.9	NA	NA	NA
2001[4]	84.1	84.1	84.2	84.8	84.4	85.1	88.6	88.6	88.6	78.8	79.2	78.5	NA	NA	NA
2000	84.1	84.2	84.0	84.9	84.8	85.0	88.4	88.5	88.4	78.5	78.7	78.3	NA	NA	NA
1999	83.4	83.4	83.4	84.3	84.2	84.3	87.7	87.7	87.7	77.0	76.7	77.2	NA	NA	NA
1998	82.8	82.8	82.9	83.7	83.6	83.8	87.1	87.1	87.1	76.0	75.2	76.7	NA	NA	NA
1997	82.1	82.0	82.2	83.0	82.9	83.2	86.3	86.3	86.3	74.9	73.5	76.0	NA	NA	NA
1996	81.7	81.9	81.6	82.8	82.7	82.8	86.0	86.1	85.9	74.3	74.3	74.2	NA	NA	NA
1995	81.7	81.7	81.6	83.0	83.0	83.0	85.9	86.0	85.8	73.8	73.4	74.1	NA	NA	NA
1994	80.9	81.0	80.7	82.0	82.1	81.9	84.9	85.1	84.7	72.9	71.7	73.8	NA	NA	NA
1993	80.2	80.5	80.0	81.5	81.8	81.3	84.1	84.5	83.8	70.4	69.6	71.1	NA	NA	NA
1992[5]	79.4	79.7	79.2	80.9	81.1	80.7	NA	NA	NA	67.7	67.0	68.2	NA	NA	NA
1991	78.4	78.5	78.3	79.9	79.8	79.9	NA	NA	NA	66.7	66.7	66.7	NA	NA	NA
1990	77.6	77.7	77.5	79.1	79.1	79.0	NA	NA	NA	66.2	65.8	66.5	NA	NA	NA
1989	76.9	77.2	76.6	78.4	78.6	78.2	NA	NA	NA	64.6	64.2	65.0	NA	NA	NA
1988	76.2	76.4	76.0	77.7	77.7	77.6	NA	NA	NA	63.5	63.7	63.4	NA	NA	NA
1987	75.6	76.0	75.3	77.0	77.3	76.7	NA	NA	NA	63.4	63.0	63.7	NA	NA	NA
1986	74.7	75.1	74.4	76.2	76.5	75.9	NA	NA	NA	62.3	61.5	63.0	NA	NA	NA
1985	73.9	74.4	73.5	75.5	76.0	75.1	NA	NA	NA	59.8	58.4	60.8	NA	NA	NA
1984	73.3	73.7	73.0	75.0	75.4	74.6	NA	NA	NA	58.5	57.1	59.7	NA	NA	NA
1983	72.1	72.7	71.5	73.8	74.4	73.3	NA	NA	NA	56.8	56.5	57.1	NA	NA	NA
1982	71.0	71.7	70.3	72.8	73.4	72.3	NA	NA	NA	54.9	55.7	54.3	NA	NA	NA
1981	69.7	70.3	69.1	71.6	72.1	71.2	NA	NA	NA	52.9	53.2	52.6	NA	NA	NA
1980	68.6	69.2	68.1	70.5	71.0	70.1	NA	NA	NA	51.2	51.1	51.3	NA	NA	NA
1979	67.7	68.4	67.1	69.7	70.3	69.2	NA	NA	NA	49.4	49.2	49.5	NA	NA	NA
1978	65.9	66.8	65.2	67.9	68.6	67.2	NA	NA	NA	47.6	47.9	47.3	NA	NA	NA
1977	64.9	65.6	64.4	67.0	67.5	66.5	NA	NA	NA	45.5	45.6	45.4	NA	NA	NA
1976	64.1	64.7	63.5	66.1	66.7	65.5	NA	NA	NA	43.8	42.3	45.0	NA	NA	NA
1975	62.5	63.1	62.1	64.5	65.0	64.1	NA	NA	NA	42.5	41.6	43.3	NA	NA	NA
1974	61.2	61.6	60.9	63.3	63.6	63.0	NA	NA	NA	40.8	39.9	41.5	NA	NA	NA
1973	59.8	60.0	59.6	61.9	62.1	61.7	NA	NA	NA	39.2	38.2	40.1	NA	NA	NA
1972	58.2	58.2	58.2	60.4	60.3	60.5	NA	NA	NA	36.6	35.7	37.2	NA	NA	NA
1971	56.4	56.3	56.6	58.6	58.4	58.8	NA	NA	NA	34.7	33.8	35.4	NA	NA	NA
1970	55.2	55.0	55.4	57.4	57.2	57.6	NA	NA	NA	33.7	32.4	34.8	NA	NA	NA
1969	54.0	53.6	54.4	56.3	55.7	56.7	NA	NA	NA	32.3	31.9	32.6	NA	NA	NA
1968	52.6	52.0	53.2	54.9	54.3	55.5	NA	NA	NA	30.1	28.9	31.0	NA	NA	NA
1967	51.1	50.5	51.7	53.4	52.8	53.8	NA	NA	NA	29.5	27.1	31.5	NA	NA	NA
1966	49.9	49.0	50.8	52.2	51.3	53.0	NA	NA	NA	27.8	25.8	29.5	NA	NA	NA

Note: Starting in 2001, data are from the expanded CPS sample.

NA = Not available

[1]Data in the column labeled "Black" include Black and other races from 1940 to 1962: from 1963 to 2003, data are for the Black population only.

[2]Starting in 2012, data were calculated using population controls based on the 2010 Census.

[3]Starting in 2003, respondents could choose more than one race. The race data in this table for White, non-Hispanic White, Black, and Asian from 2003 onward represent those respondents who indicated only one racial identity. Prior to 2003, Asians were grouped with Pacific Islanders.

[4]Starting in 2001, data were calculated using population controls based on Census 2000.

[5]Begining with data for 1992, a new question results in different categories than for earlier years: Data shown as 'Completed 4 Years of High School or more' is now collected in the category 'High School Graduate.' Data shown as 'College 1 to 3 years' is now collected in the 'Some college' and the two 'Associate degree' categories. Data shown as 'Completed 4 Years of College or more', is now collected in the categories, 'Bachelor's degree,' 'Master's degree,' 'Doctorate degree,' and 'Professional degree'. Due to the change in question format, median years of schooling cannot be derived.

Table A-32. Percent of People 25 Years Old and Over Who Have Completed High School or College, by Race, Hispanic Origin, and Sex, Selected Years, 1940–2019—*Continued*

(Percent; civilian noninstitutionalized population.)

Age and Year	Hispanic (of any race)			White alone or in combination			Non-Hispanic White alone or in combination			Black alone or in combination			Asian alone or in combination		
	Total	Male	Female	Total	Male	Female	Total	Male	Female	Total	Male	Female	Total	Male	Female
25 YEARS AND OLDER															
Completed 4 Years of High School or More															
2019	71.8	70.8	72.8	90.4	89.9	91.0	94.6	94.2	94.9	88.0	87.1	88.8	91.5	92.9	90.1
2018	71.6	70.7	72.5	90.2	89.5	90.7	94.3	93.9	94.6	87.9	87.6	88.2	90.7	92.9	88.8
2017	70.5	69.5	71.6	90.0	89.4	90.5	94.1	93.7	94.5	87.2	86.3	88.0	91.1	92.7	89.7
2016	68.5	67.2	69.7	89.4	88.8	90.1	93.8	93.4	94.3	87.2	86.5	87.7	90.6	92.0	89.4
2015	66.7	65.5	67.8	88.7	88.2	89.2	93.3	93.0	93.5	87.1	86.4	87.6	89.3	91.1	87.7
2014	66.5	65.1	67.9	88.7	87.9	89.5	93.1	92.6	93.7	85.8	85.2	86.3	89.9	92.2	87.9
2013	66.2	64.6	67.9	88.6	88.0	89.2	92.9	92.7	93.1	85.1	84.1	85.9	90.3	91.6	89.2
2012[2]	65.0	64.0	66.0	88.1	87.6	88.5	92.5	92.2	92.7	85.1	84.5	85.6	89.0	90.5	87.8
2011	64.3	63.6	65.1	88.0	87.4	88.6	92.4	92.0	92.7	84.6	83.9	85.1	88.9	90.6	87.4
2010	62.9	61.4	64.4	87.6	86.8	88.2	92.0	91.7	92.3	84.2	83.5	84.8	89.1	91.2	87.3
2009	61.9	60.6	63.3	87.1	86.4	87.7	91.6	91.4	91.8	84.1	83.9	84.2	88.3	90.6	86.4
2008	62.3	60.9	63.7	87.1	86.3	87.8	91.4	91.1	91.8	83.2	81.9	84.1	89.0	90.9	87.2
2007	60.3	58.2	62.5	86.2	85.3	87.0	90.6	90.2	91.0	82.4	82.0	82.6	87.8	89.2	86.5
2006	59.3	58.5	60.1	86.1	85.5	86.7	90.5	90.2	90.8	80.8	80.3	81.2	87.6	89.6	85.8
2005	58.5	57.9	59.1	85.7	85.2	86.2	90.1	89.9	90.3	81.3	81.2	81.3	87.9	90.5	85.6
2004	58.4	57.3	59.5	85.8	85.3	86.2	90.0	89.9	90.1	80.6	80.3	80.9	86.9	88.8	85.2
2003[3]	57.0	56.3	57.8	85.1	84.5	85.7	89.4	89.0	89.6	80.0	79.5	80.3	87.8	89.7	86.1
2002	57.0	56.1	57.9	NA	NA	NA	NA	NA	NA	NA	NA	NA	NA	NA	NA
2001[4]	56.8	55.5	58.0	NA	NA	NA	NA	NA	NA	NA	NA	NA	NA	NA	NA
2000	57.0	56.6	57.5	NA	NA	NA	NA	NA	NA	NA	NA	NA	NA	NA	NA
1999	56.1	56.0	56.3	NA	NA	NA	NA	NA	NA	NA	NA	NA	NA	NA	NA
1998	55.5	55.7	55.3	NA	NA	NA	NA	NA	NA	NA	NA	NA	NA	NA	NA
1997	54.7	54.9	54.6	NA	NA	NA	NA	NA	NA	NA	NA	NA	NA	NA	NA
1996	53.1	53.0	53.3	NA	NA	NA	NA	NA	NA	NA	NA	NA	NA	NA	NA
1995	53.4	52.9	53.8	NA	NA	NA	NA	NA	NA	NA	NA	NA	NA	NA	NA
1994	53.3	53.4	53.2	NA	NA	NA	NA	NA	NA	NA	NA	NA	NA	NA	NA
1993	53.1	52.9	53.2	NA	NA	NA	NA	NA	NA	NA	NA	NA	NA	NA	NA
1992[5]	52.6	53.7	51.5	NA	NA	NA	NA	NA	NA	NA	NA	NA	NA	NA	NA
1991	51.3	51.4	51.2	NA	NA	NA	NA	NA	NA	NA	NA	NA	NA	NA	NA
1990	50.8	50.3	51.3	NA	NA	NA	NA	NA	NA	NA	NA	NA	NA	NA	NA
1989	50.9	51.0	50.7	NA	NA	NA	NA	NA	NA	NA	NA	NA	NA	NA	NA
1988	51.0	52.0	50.0	NA	NA	NA	NA	NA	NA	NA	NA	NA	NA	NA	NA
1987	50.9	51.8	50.0	NA	NA	NA	NA	NA	NA	NA	NA	NA	NA	NA	NA
1986	48.5	49.2	47.8	NA	NA	NA	NA	NA	NA	NA	NA	NA	NA	NA	NA
1985	47.9	48.5	47.4	NA	NA	NA	NA	NA	NA	NA	NA	NA	NA	NA	NA
1984	47.1	48.6	45.7	NA	NA	NA	NA	NA	NA	NA	NA	NA	NA	NA	NA
1983	46.2	48.6	44.2	NA	NA	NA	NA	NA	NA	NA	NA	NA	NA	NA	NA
1982	45.9	48.1	44.1	NA	NA	NA	NA	NA	NA	NA	NA	NA	NA	NA	NA
1981	44.5	45.5	43.6	NA	NA	NA	NA	NA	NA	NA	NA	NA	NA	NA	NA
1980	45.3	46.4	44.1	NA	NA	NA	NA	NA	NA	NA	NA	NA	NA	NA	NA
1979	42.0	42.3	41.7	NA	NA	NA	NA	NA	NA	NA	NA	NA	NA	NA	NA
1978	40.8	42.2	39.6	NA	NA	NA	NA	NA	NA	NA	NA	NA	NA	NA	NA
1977	39.6	42.3	37.2	NA	NA	NA	NA	NA	NA	NA	NA	NA	NA	NA	NA
1976	39.3	41.4	37.3	NA	NA	NA	NA	NA	NA	NA	NA	NA	NA	NA	NA
1975	37.9	39.5	36.7	NA	NA	NA	NA	NA	NA	NA	NA	NA	NA	NA	NA
1974	36.5	38.3	34.9	NA	NA	NA	NA	NA	NA	NA	NA	NA	NA	NA	NA
1973	NA	NA	NA	NA	NA	NA	NA	NA	NA	NA	NA	NA	NA	NA	NA
1972	NA	NA	NA	NA	NA	NA	NA	NA	NA	NA	NA	NA	NA	NA	NA
1971	NA	NA	NA	NA	NA	NA	NA	NA	NA	NA	NA	NA	NA	NA	NA
1970	NA	NA	NA	NA	NA	NA	NA	NA	NA	NA	NA	NA	NA	NA	NA
1969	NA	NA	NA	NA	NA	NA	NA	NA	NA	NA	NA	NA	NA	NA	NA
1968	NA	NA	NA	NA	NA	NA	NA	NA	NA	NA	NA	NA	NA	NA	NA
1967	NA	NA	NA	NA	NA	NA	NA	NA	NA	NA	NA	NA	NA	NA	NA
1966	NA	NA	NA	NA	NA	NA	NA	NA	NA	NA	NA	NA	NA	NA	NA

Note: Starting in 2001, data are from the expanded CPS sample.

NA = Not available

[1]Data in the column labeled "Black" include Black and other races from 1940 to 1962: from 1963 to 2003, data are for the Black population only.

[2]Starting in 2012, data were calculated using population controls based on the 2010 Census.

[3]Starting in 2003, respondents could choose more than one race. The race data in this table for White, non-Hispanic White, Black, and Asian from 2003 onward represent those respondents who indicated only one racial identity. Prior to 2003, Asians were grouped with Pacific Islanders.

[4]Starting in 2001, data were calculated using population controls based on Census 2000.

[5]Begining with data for 1992, a new question results in different categories than for earlier years: Data shown as 'Completed 4 Years of High School or more' is now collected in the category 'High School Graduate.' Data shown as 'College 1 to 3 years' is now collected in the 'Some college' and the two 'Associate degree' categories. Data shown as 'Completed 4 Years of College or more', is now collected in the categories, 'Bachelor's degree,' 'Master's degree,' 'Doctorate degree,' and 'Professional degree'. Due to the change in question format, median years of schooling cannot be derived.

Table A-32. Percent of People 25 Years Old and Over Who Have Completed High School or College, by Race, Hispanic Origin, and Sex, Selected Years, 1940–2019—*Continued*

(Percent; civilian noninstitutionalized population.)

Age and Year	All races			White			Non-Hispanic White			Black[1]			Asian		
	Total	Male	Female	Total	Male	Female	Total	Male	Female	Total	Male	Female	Total	Male	Female
1965	49.0	48.0	49.9	51.3	50.2	52.2	NA	NA	NA	27.2	25.8	28.4	NA	NA	NA
1964	48.0	47.0	48.9	50.3	49.3	51.2	NA	NA	NA	25.7	23.7	27.4	NA	NA	NA
1962	46.3	45.0	47.5	48.7	47.4	49.9	NA	NA	NA	24.8	23.2	26.2	NA	NA	NA
1959	43.7	42.2	45.2	46.1	44.5	47.7	NA	NA	NA	20.7	19.6	21.6	NA	NA	NA
1957	41.6	39.7	43.3	43.2	41.1	45.1	NA	NA	NA	18.4	16.9	19.7	NA	NA	NA
1952	38.8	36.9	40.5	NA	NA	NA	NA	NA	NA	15.0	14.0	15.7	NA	NA	NA
1950	34.3	32.6	36.0	NA	NA	NA	NA	NA	NA	13.7	12.5	14.7	NA	NA	NA
1947	33.1	31.4	34.7	35.0	33.2	36.7	NA	NA	NA	13.6	12.7	14.5	NA	NA	NA
1940	24.5	22.7	26.3	26.1	24.2	28.1	NA	NA	NA	7.7	6.9	8.4	NA	NA	NA
Completed 4 Years of College or More															
2019	36.0	35.4	36.6	36.3	35.7	36.8	40.1	39.9	40.3	26.1	24.1	27.7	58.1	60.4	56.1
2018	35.0	34.6	35.3	35.2	34.9	35.5	38.8	38.9	38.8	25.2	23.2	26.9	56.5	59.3	54.0
2017	34.2	33.7	34.6	34.5	34.0	35.0	38.1	37.8	38.3	23.9	22.1	25.4	54.8	56.6	53.2
2016	33.4	33.2	33.7	33.7	33.4	34.0	37.3	37.2	37.3	23.3	21.7	24.6	55.9	58.8	53.4
2015	32.5	32.3	32.7	32.8	32.6	32.9	36.2	36.3	36.1	22.5	20.6	24.0	53.9	56.8	51.5
2014	32.0	31.9	32.0	32.3	32.3	32.3	35.6	35.9	35.3	22.2	20.4	23.7	52.3	54.7	50.3
2013	31.7	32.0	31.4	32.0	32.4	31.6	35.2	36.0	34.4	21.8	19.8	23.3	53.2	56.1	50.8
2012	30.9	31.4	30.6	31.3	31.9	30.8	34.5	35.5	33.5	21.2	19.2	22.9	51.0	53.7	48.8
2011	30.4	30.8	30.1	31.0	31.5	30.5	34.0	35.0	33.1	19.9	18.0	21.4	50.3	53.4	47.7
2010	29.9	30.3	29.6	30.3	30.8	29.9	33.2	34.2	32.4	19.8	17.7	21.4	52.4	55.6	49.5
2009	29.5	30.1	29.1	29.9	30.6	29.3	32.9	33.9	31.9	19.3	17.8	20.6	52.3	55.7	49.3
2008	29.4	30.1	28.8	29.8	30.5	29.1	32.6	33.8	31.5	19.6	18.7	20.4	52.6	55.8	49.8
2007	28.7	29.5	28.0	29.1	29.9	28.3	31.8	33.2	30.6	18.5	18.0	19.0	52.1	55.2	49.3
2006	28.0	29.2	26.9	28.4	29.7	27.1	31.0	32.8	29.3	18.5	17.2	19.4	49.7	52.5	47.1
2005	27.7	28.9	26.5	28.1	29.4	26.8	30.6	32.4	28.9	17.6	16.0	18.8	50.2	54.0	46.8
2004	27.7	29.4	26.1	28.2	30.0	26.4	30.6	32.9	28.4	17.6	16.6	18.5	49.4	53.7	45.6
2003	27.2	28.9	25.7	27.6	29.4	25.9	30.0	32.3	27.9	17.3	16.7	17.8	49.8	53.9	46.1
2002	26.7	28.5	25.1	27.2	29.1	25.4	29.4	31.7	27.3	17.0	16.4	17.5	NA	NA	NA
2001	26.2	28.2	24.3	26.6	28.7	24.6	28.7	31.3	26.3	15.7	15.3	16.1	NA	NA	NA
2000	25.6	27.8	23.6	26.1	28.5	23.9	28.1	30.8	25.5	16.5	16.3	16.7	NA	NA	NA
1999	25.2	27.5	23.1	25.9	28.5	23.5	27.7	30.6	25.0	15.4	14.2	16.4	NA	NA	NA
1998	24.4	26.5	22.4	25.0	27.3	22.8	26.6	29.3	24.1	14.7	13.9	15.4	NA	NA	NA
1997	23.9	26.2	21.7	24.6	27.0	22.3	26.2	29.0	23.7	13.3	12.5	13.9	NA	NA	NA
1996	23.6	26.0	21.4	24.3	26.9	21.8	25.9	28.8	23.2	13.6	12.4	14.6	NA	NA	NA
1995	23.0	26.0	20.2	24.0	27.2	21.0	25.4	28.9	22.1	13.2	13.6	12.9	NA	NA	NA
1994	22.2	25.1	19.6	22.9	26.1	20.0	24.3	27.8	21.1	12.9	12.8	13.0	NA	NA	NA
1993	21.9	24.8	19.2	22.6	25.7	19.7	23.8	27.2	20.7	12.2	11.9	12.4	NA	NA	NA
1992	21.4	24.3	18.6	22.1	25.2	19.1	NA	NA	NA	11.9	11.9	12.0	NA	NA	NA
1991	21.4	24.3	18.8	22.2	25.4	19.3	NA	NA	NA	11.5	11.4	11.6	NA	NA	NA
1990	21.3	24.4	18.4	22.0	25.3	19.0	NA	NA	NA	11.3	11.9	10.8	NA	NA	NA
1989	21.1	24.5	18.1	21.8	25.4	18.5	NA	NA	NA	11.8	11.7	11.9	NA	NA	NA
1988	20.3	24.0	17.0	20.9	25.0	17.3	NA	NA	NA	11.2	11.1	11.4	NA	NA	NA
1987	19.9	23.6	16.5	20.5	24.5	16.9	NA	NA	NA	10.7	11.0	10.4	NA	NA	NA
1986	19.4	23.2	16.1	20.1	24.1	16.4	NA	NA	NA	10.9	11.2	10.7	NA	NA	NA
1985	19.4	23.1	16.0	20.0	24.0	16.3	NA	NA	NA	11.1	11.2	11.0	NA	NA	NA
1984	19.1	22.9	15.7	19.8	23.9	16.0	NA	NA	NA	10.4	10.4	10.4	NA	NA	NA
1983	18.8	23.0	15.1	19.5	24.0	15.4	NA	NA	NA	9.5	10.0	9.2	NA	NA	NA
1982	17.7	21.9	14.0	18.5	23.0	14.4	NA	NA	NA	8.8	9.1	8.5	NA	NA	NA
1981	17.1	21.1	13.4	17.8	22.2	13.8	NA	NA	NA	8.2	8.2	8.2	NA	NA	NA
1980	17.0	20.9	13.6	17.8	22.1	14.0	NA	NA	NA	7.9	7.7	8.1	NA	NA	NA
1979	16.4	20.4	12.9	17.2	21.4	13.3	NA	NA	NA	7.9	8.3	7.5	NA	NA	NA
1978	15.7	19.7	12.2	16.4	20.7	12.6	NA	NA	NA	7.2	7.3	7.1	NA	NA	NA
1977	15.4	19.2	12.0	16.1	20.2	12.4	NA	NA	NA	7.2	7.0	7.4	NA	NA	NA
1976	14.7	18.6	11.3	15.4	19.6	11.6	NA	NA	NA	6.6	6.3	6.8	NA	NA	NA
1975	13.9	17.6	10.6	14.5	18.4	11.0	NA	NA	NA	6.4	6.7	6.2	NA	NA	NA
1974	13.3	16.9	10.1	14.0	17.7	10.6	NA	NA	NA	5.5	5.7	5.3	NA	NA	NA
1973	12.6	16.0	9.6	13.1	16.8	9.9	NA	NA	NA	6.0	5.9	6.0	NA	NA	NA
1972	12.0	15.4	9.0	12.6	16.2	9.4	NA	NA	NA	5.1	5.5	4.8	NA	NA	NA

Note: Starting in 2001, data are from the expanded CPS sample.

NA = Not available

[1]Data in the column labeled "Black" include Black and other races from 1940 to 1962: from 1963 to 2003, data are for the Black population only.

[2]Starting in 2012, data were calculated using population controls based on the 2010 Census.

[3]Starting in 2003, respondents could choose more than one race. The race data in this table for White, non-Hispanic White, Black, and Asian from 2003 onward represent those respondents who indicated only one racial identity. Prior to 2003, Asians were grouped with Pacific Islanders.

[4]Starting in 2001, data were calculated using population controls based on Census 2000.

[5]Begining with data for 1992, a new question results in different categories than for earlier years: Data shown as 'Completed 4 Years of High School or more' is now collected in the category 'High School Graduate.' Data shown as 'College 1 to 3 years' is now collected in the 'Some college' and the two 'Associate degree' categories. Data shown as 'Completed 4 Years of College or more', is now collected in the categories, 'Bachelor's degree,' 'Master's degree,' 'Doctorate degree,' and 'Professional degree'. Due to the change in question format, median years of schooling cannot be derived.

Table A-32. Percent of People 25 Years Old and Over Who Have Completed High School or College, by Race, Hispanic Origin, and Sex, Selected Years, 1940–2019—*Continued*

(Percent; civilian noninstitutionalized population.)

Age and Year	Hispanic (of any race)			White alone or in combination			Non-Hispanic White alone or in combination			Black alone or in combination			Asian alone or in combination		
	Total	Male	Female	Total	Male	Female	Total	Male	Female	Total	Male	Female	Total	Male	Female
1965	NA	NA	NA	NA	NA	NA	NA	NA	NA	NA	NA	NA	NA	NA	NA
1964	NA	NA	NA	NA	NA	NA	NA	NA	NA	NA	NA	NA	NA	NA	NA
1962	NA	NA	NA	NA	NA	NA	NA	NA	NA	NA	NA	NA	NA	NA	NA
1959	NA	NA	NA	NA	NA	NA	NA	NA	NA	NA	NA	NA	NA	NA	NA
1957	NA	NA	NA	NA	NA	NA	NA	NA	NA	NA	NA	NA	NA	NA	NA
1952	NA	NA	NA	NA	NA	NA	NA	NA	NA	NA	NA	NA	NA	NA	NA
1950	NA	NA	NA	NA	NA	NA	NA	NA	NA	NA	NA	NA	NA	NA	NA
1947	NA	NA	NA	NA	NA	NA	NA	NA	NA	NA	NA	NA	NA	NA	NA
1940	NA	NA	NA	NA	NA	NA	NA	NA	NA	NA	NA	NA	NA	NA	NA
Completed 4 Years of College or More															
2019	18.8	16.9	20.8	36.2	35.5	36.8	40.0	39.8	40.2	26.3	24.3	28.0	57.7	59.6	56.0
2018	18.3	16.6	20.1	35.1	34.7	35.5	38.7	38.8	38.7	25.4	23.2	27.1	56.0	58.6	53.7
2017	17.2	15.8	18.6	34.4	33.9	34.9	38.0	37.8	38.3	24.2	22.3	25.7	54.4	55.9	53.2
2016	16.4	15.4	17.4	33.6	33.3	33.9	37.2	37.1	37.3	23.5	21.8	24.9	55.4	57.9	53.3
2015	15.5	14.3	16.6	32.7	32.5	32.9	36.2	36.2	36.1	22.7	20.7	24.2	53.7	56.2	51.5
2014	15.2	14.2	16.1	32.2	32.2	32.3	35.5	35.8	35.3	22.7	20.6	24.3	52.2	54.2	50.4
2013	15.1	13.9	16.2	31.9	32.3	31.5	35.1	35.9	34.4	22.0	20.0	23.6	52.8	55.5	50.5
2012	14.5	13.3	15.8	31.2	31.8	30.7	34.4	35.4	33.4	21.4	19.4	22.9	50.4	52.6	48.6
2011	14.1	13.1	15.2	30.9	31.4	30.5	33.9	34.9	33.1	20.1	18.2	21.6	49.9	52.8	47.3
2010	13.9	12.9	14.9	30.2	30.7	29.8	33.2	34.1	32.3	19.9	17.7	21.6	51.8	54.7	49.3
2009	13.2	12.5	14.0	29.8	30.4	29.3	32.8	33.8	31.8	19.4	17.8	20.7	51.8	54.8	49.2
2008	13.3	12.6	14.1	29.7	30.3	29.0	32.5	33.6	31.4	19.8	18.8	20.5	52.0	54.6	49.8
2007	12.7	11.8	13.7	29.0	29.8	28.3	31.7	33.0	30.5	18.7	18.2	19.1	47.1	49.1	45.4
2006	12.4	11.9	12.9	28.3	29.6	27.0	30.9	32.7	29.2	18.7	17.4	19.7	49.0	51.4	46.8
2005	12.0	11.8	12.1	28.0	29.3	26.7	30.5	32.3	28.9	17.6	16.0	18.9	49.8	53.3	46.6
2004	12.1	11.8	12.3	28.0	29.9	26.3	30.5	32.8	28.3	17.7	16.5	18.6	48.9	52.8	45.4
2003	11.4	11.2	11.6	27.5	29.3	25.8	29.9	32.2	27.9	17.5	16.8	18.0	49.2	52.7	46.0
2002	11.1	11.0	11.2	NA	NA	NA	NA	NA	NA	NA	NA	NA	NA	NA	NA
2001	11.1	10.8	11.4	NA	NA	NA	NA	NA	NA	NA	NA	NA	NA	NA	NA
2000	10.6	10.7	10.6	NA	NA	NA	NA	NA	NA	NA	NA	NA	NA	NA	NA
1999	10.9	10.7	11.0	NA	NA	NA	NA	NA	NA	NA	NA	NA	NA	NA	NA
1998	11.0	11.1	10.9	NA	NA	NA	NA	NA	NA	NA	NA	NA	NA	NA	NA
1997	10.3	10.6	10.1	NA	NA	NA	NA	NA	NA	NA	NA	NA	NA	NA	NA
1996	9.3	10.3	8.3	NA	NA	NA	NA	NA	NA	NA	NA	NA	NA	NA	NA
1995	9.3	10.1	8.4	NA	NA	NA	NA	NA	NA	NA	NA	NA	NA	NA	NA
1994	9.1	9.6	8.6	NA	NA	NA	NA	NA	NA	NA	NA	NA	NA	NA	NA
1993	9.0	9.5	8.5	NA	NA	NA	NA	NA	NA	NA	NA	NA	NA	NA	NA
1992	9.3	10.2	8.5	NA	NA	NA	NA	NA	NA	NA	NA	NA	NA	NA	NA
1991	9.7	10.0	9.4	NA	NA	NA	NA	NA	NA	NA	NA	NA	NA	NA	NA
1990	9.2	9.8	8.7	NA	NA	NA	NA	NA	NA	NA	NA	NA	NA	NA	NA
1989	9.9	11.0	8.8	NA	NA	NA	NA	NA	NA	NA	NA	NA	NA	NA	NA
1988	10.1	12.3	8.1	NA	NA	NA	NA	NA	NA	NA	NA	NA	NA	NA	NA
1987	8.6	9.7	7.5	NA	NA	NA	NA	NA	NA	NA	NA	NA	NA	NA	NA
1986	8.4	9.5	7.4	NA	NA	NA	NA	NA	NA	NA	NA	NA	NA	NA	NA
1985	8.5	9.7	7.3	NA	NA	NA	NA	NA	NA	NA	NA	NA	NA	NA	NA
1984	8.2	9.5	7.0	NA	NA	NA	NA	NA	NA	NA	NA	NA	NA	NA	NA
1983	7.9	9.2	6.8	NA	NA	NA	NA	NA	NA	NA	NA	NA	NA	NA	NA
1982	7.8	9.6	6.2	NA	NA	NA	NA	NA	NA	NA	NA	NA	NA	NA	NA
1981	7.7	9.7	5.9	NA	NA	NA	NA	NA	NA	NA	NA	NA	NA	NA	NA
1980	7.9	9.7	6.2	NA	NA	NA	NA	NA	NA	NA	NA	NA	NA	NA	NA
1979	6.7	8.2	5.3	NA	NA	NA	NA	NA	NA	NA	NA	NA	NA	NA	NA
1978	7.0	8.6	5.7	NA	NA	NA	NA	NA	NA	NA	NA	NA	NA	NA	NA
1977	6.2	8.1	4.4	NA	NA	NA	NA	NA	NA	NA	NA	NA	NA	NA	NA
1976	6.1	8.6	4.0	NA	NA	NA	NA	NA	NA	NA	NA	NA	NA	NA	NA
1975	6.3	8.3	4.6	NA	NA	NA	NA	NA	NA	NA	NA	NA	NA	NA	NA
1974	5.5	7.1	4.0	NA	NA	NA	NA	NA	NA	NA	NA	NA	NA	NA	NA
1973	NA	NA	NA	NA	NA	NA	NA	NA	NA	NA	NA	NA	NA	NA	NA
1972	NA	NA	NA	NA	NA	NA	NA	NA	NA	NA	NA	NA	NA	NA	NA

Note: Starting in 2001, data are from the expanded CPS sample.

NA = Not available

[1]Data in the column labeled "Black" include Black and other races from 1940 to 1962: from 1963 to 2003, data are for the Black population only.

[2]Starting in 2012, data were calculated using population controls based on the 2010 Census.

[3]Starting in 2003, respondents could choose more than one race. The race data in this table for White, non-Hispanic White, Black, and Asian from 2003 onward represent those respondents who indicated only one racial identity. Prior to 2003, Asians were grouped with Pacific Islanders.

[4]Starting in 2001, data were calculated using population controls based on Census 2000.

[5]Begining with data for 1992, a new question results in different categories than for earlier years: Data shown as 'Completed 4 Years of High School or more' is now collected in the category 'High School Graduate.' Data shown as 'College 1 to 3 years' is now collected in the 'Some college' and the two 'Associate degree' categories. Data shown as 'Completed 4 Years of College or more', is now collected in the categories, 'Bachelor's degree,' 'Master's degree,' 'Doctorate degree,' and 'Professional degree'. Due to the change in question format, median years of schooling cannot be derived.

Table A-32. Percent of People 25 Years Old and Over Who Have Completed High School or College, by Race, Hispanic Origin, and Sex, Selected Years, 1940–2019—*Continued*

(Percent; civilian noninstitutionalized population.)

Age and Year	All races			White			Non-Hispanic White			Black[1]			Asian		
	Total	Male	Female	Total	Male	Female	Total	Male	Female	Total	Male	Female	Total	Male	Female
1971	11.4	14.6	8.5	12.0	15.5	8.9	NA	NA	NA	4.5	4.7	4.3	NA	NA	NA
1970	11.0	14.1	8.2	11.6	15.0	8.6	NA	NA	NA	4.5	4.6	4.4	NA	NA	NA
1969	10.7	13.6	8.1	11.2	14.3	8.5	NA	NA	NA	4.6	4.8	4.5	NA	NA	NA
1968	10.5	13.3	8.0	11.0	14.1	8.3	NA	NA	NA	4.3	3.7	4.8	NA	NA	NA
1967	10.1	12.8	7.6	10.6	13.6	7.9	NA	NA	NA	4.0	3.4	4.4	NA	NA	NA
1966	9.8	12.5	7.4	10.4	13.3	7.7	NA	NA	NA	3.8	3.9	3.7	NA	NA	NA
1965	9.4	12.0	7.1	9.9	12.7	7.3	NA	NA	NA	4.7	4.9	4.5	NA	NA	NA
1964	9.1	11.7	6.8	9.6	12.3	7.1	NA	NA	NA	3.9	4.5	3.4	NA	NA	NA
1962	8.9	11.4	6.7	9.5	12.2	7.0	NA	NA	NA	4.0	3.9	4.0	NA	NA	NA
1959	8.1	10.3	6.0	8.6	11.0	6.2	NA	NA	NA	3.3	3.8	2.9	NA	NA	NA
1957	7.6	9.6	5.8	8.0	10.1	6.0	NA	NA	NA	2.9	2.7	3.0	NA	NA	NA
1952	7.0	8.3	5.8	NA	NA	NA	NA	NA	NA	2.4	2.0	2.7	NA	NA	NA
1950	6.2	7.3	5.2	NA	NA	NA	NA	NA	NA	2.3	2.1	2.4	NA	NA	NA
1947	5.4	6.2	4.7	5.7	6.6	4.9	NA	NA	NA	2.5	2.4	2.6	NA	NA	NA
1940	4.6	5.5	3.8	4.9	5.9	4.0	NA	NA	NA	1.3	1.4	1.2	NA	NA	NA

25 TO 29 YEARS

Completed 4 Years of High School or More

Age and Year	All races			White			Non-Hispanic White			Black[1]			Asian		
	Total	Male	Female	Total	Male	Female	Total	Male	Female	Total	Male	Female	Total	Male	Female
2019	93.5	92.7	94.3	93.8	93.3	94.2	96.3	96.2	96.4	91.0	88.9	93.0	97.0	97.0	97.1
2018	92.9	91.9	94.0	92.9	91.7	94.1	95.6	95.0	96.3	92.0	90.7	93.1	97.5	97.6	97.4
2017	92.5	91.5	93.4	92.4	91.2	93.7	95.6	94.8	96.4	91.8	91.2	92.4	96.8	97.7	95.9
2016	91.7	90.9	92.5	91.6	90.6	92.7	95.2	94.8	95.7	90.6	90.8	90.4	96.5	95.9	97.1
2015	91.2	90.5	91.8	90.8	90.0	91.7	95.4	95.1	95.8	92.2	91.4	93.0	95.5	96.3	94.7
2014	90.8	90.1	91.5	90.9	90.2	91.7	95.6	95.4	95.9	89.8	90.2	89.4	96.7	96.3	97.2
2013	89.9	88.3	91.5	89.5	88.0	91.1	94.1	93.3	94.9	89.8	87.3	92.1	94.7	93.6	95.7
2012	89.7	88.4	91.1	89.6	88.3	90.9	94.6	93.8	95.3	88.5	87.1	89.7	95.7	96.2	95.3
2011	89.0	87.5	90.7	88.9	87.1	90.8	94.4	93.4	95.5	87.7	87.6	87.8	95.2	93.6	96.7
2010	88.8	87.4	90.2	88.5	87.3	89.9	94.5	94.6	94.4	89.0	86.7	91.0	93.2	92.3	94.1
2009	88.6	87.5	89.8	88.4	87.0	89.9	94.6	94.4	94.8	88.9	88.6	89.1	95.2	95.6	94.9
2008	87.8	85.8	89.9	87.6	85.5	89.8	93.7	92.6	94.7	87.4	85.4	89.2	95.6	95.4	95.7
2007	87.0	84.9	89.1	86.5	84.2	89.0	93.5	92.7	94.2	87.4	87.0	87.8	97.2	95.8	98.5
2006	86.4	84.4	88.5	86.1	84.1	88.3	93.4	92.3	94.6	85.6	83.1	87.8	96.6	97.2	96.0
2005	86.2	85.0	87.4	85.7	84.3	87.1	92.8	91.8	93.8	86.5	86.4	86.6	95.5	96.7	94.5
2004	86.6	85.2	88.0	85.9	83.7	88.1	93.3	92.1	94.5	87.9	90.1	86.1	96.2	96.9	95.4
2003	86.5	84.9	88.2	85.7	83.8	87.6	93.7	92.8	94.5	87.6	86.4	88.5	97.1	97.4	96.8
2002	86.4	84.7	88.1	85.9	84.1	87.7	93.0	92.1	93.8	86.6	85.0	88.0	NA	NA	NA
2001	86.8	85.3	88.3	86.4	84.6	88.3	93.4	93.1	93.7	86.3	85.4	87.0	NA	NA	NA
2000	88.1	86.7	89.4	88.3	86.6	90.0	94.0	92.9	95.2	85.9	86.6	85.3	NA	NA	NA
1999	87.8	86.1	89.5	87.6	85.8	89.3	93.0	91.9	94.1	88.2	87.7	88.6	NA	NA	NA
1998	88.1	86.6	89.6	88.1	86.3	90.0	93.6	92.5	94.6	87.6	87.6	87.6	NA	NA	NA
1997	87.4	85.8	88.9	87.6	85.8	89.4	92.9	91.7	94.0	86.2	85.2	87.1	NA	NA	NA
1996	87.3	86.5	88.1	87.5	86.3	88.8	92.6	92.0	93.1	85.6	87.2	84.2	NA	NA	NA
1995	86.8	86.3	87.4	87.4	86.6	88.2	92.5	92.0	93.0	86.5	88.1	85.1	NA	NA	NA
1994	86.1	84.5	87.6	86.5	84.7	88.3	91.1	90.0	92.3	84.1	82.9	85.0	NA	NA	NA
1993	86.7	86.0	87.4	87.3	86.1	88.5	91.2	90.6	91.8	82.8	85.0	80.9	NA	NA	NA
1992	86.3	86.1	86.5	87.0	86.5	87.6	NA	NA	NA	80.9	82.5	79.5	NA	NA	NA
1991	85.4	84.9	85.8	85.8	85.1	86.6	NA	NA	NA	81.7	83.5	80.1	NA	NA	NA
1990	85.7	84.4	87.0	86.3	84.6	88.1	NA	NA	NA	81.7	81.5	81.8	NA	NA	NA
1989	85.5	84.4	86.5	86.0	84.8	87.1	NA	NA	NA	82.2	80.6	83.6	NA	NA	NA
1988	85.7	84.4	87.0	86.5	84.8	88.2	NA	NA	NA	80.7	80.6	80.7	NA	NA	NA
1987	86.0	85.5	86.4	86.3	85.6	87.0	NA	NA	NA	83.3	84.8	82.1	NA	NA	NA
1986	86.1	85.9	86.4	86.5	85.6	87.4	NA	NA	NA	83.4	86.5	80.6	NA	NA	NA
1985	86.1	85.9	86.4	86.8	86.4	87.3	NA	NA	NA	80.6	80.8	80.4	NA	NA	NA
1984	85.9	85.6	86.3	86.9	86.8	87.0	NA	NA	NA	78.9	75.9	81.5	NA	NA	NA
1983	86.0	86.0	86.0	86.9	86.9	86.9	NA	NA	NA	79.4	78.9	79.8	NA	NA	NA
1982	86.2	86.3	86.1	86.9	87.0	86.8	NA	NA	NA	80.9	80.5	81.3	NA	NA	NA
1981	86.3	86.5	86.1	87.6	87.6	87.6	NA	NA	NA	77.3	78.4	76.4	NA	NA	NA

Note: Starting in 2001, data are from the expanded CPS sample.

NA = Not available

[1]Data in the column labeled "Black" include Black and other races from 1940 to 1962: from 1963 to 2003, data are for the Black population only.

[2]Starting in 2012, data were calculated using population controls based on the 2010 Census.

[3]Starting in 2003, respondents could choose more than one race. The race data in this table for White, non-Hispanic White, Black, and Asian from 2003 onward represent those respondents who indicated only one racial identity. Prior to 2003, Asians were grouped with Pacific Islanders.

[4]Starting in 2001, data were calculated using population controls based on Census 2000.

[5]Begining with data for 1992, a new question results in different categories than for earlier years: Data shown as 'Completed 4 Years of High School or more' is now collected in the category 'High School Graduate.' Data shown as 'College 1 to 3 years' is now collected in the 'Some college' and the two 'Associate degree' categories. Data shown as 'Completed 4 Years of College or more', is now collected in the categories, 'Bachelor's degree,' 'Master's degree,' 'Doctorate degree,' and 'Professional degree'. Due to the change in question format, median years of schooling cannot be derived.

Table A-32. Percent of People 25 Years Old and Over Who Have Completed High School or College, by Race, Hispanic Origin, and Sex, Selected Years, 1940–2019—*Continued*

(Percent; civilian noninstitutionalized population.)

Age and Year	Hispanic (of any race)			White alone or in combination			Non-Hispanic White alone or in combination			Black alone or in combination			Asian alone or in combination		
	Total	Male	Female	Total	Male	Female	Total	Male	Female	Total	Male	Female	Total	Male	Female
1971	NA	NA	NA	NA	NA	NA	NA	NA	NA	NA	NA	NA	NA	NA	NA
1970	NA	NA	NA	NA	NA	NA	NA	NA	NA	NA	NA	NA	NA	NA	NA
1969	NA	NA	NA	NA	NA	NA	NA	NA	NA	NA	NA	NA	NA	NA	NA
1968	NA	NA	NA	NA	NA	NA	NA	NA	NA	NA	NA	NA	NA	NA	NA
1967	NA	NA	NA	NA	NA	NA	NA	NA	NA	NA	NA	NA	NA	NA	NA
1966	NA	NA	NA	NA	NA	NA	NA	NA	NA	NA	NA	NA	NA	NA	NA
1965	NA	NA	NA	NA	NA	NA	NA	NA	NA	NA	NA	NA	NA	NA	NA
1964	NA	NA	NA	NA	NA	NA	NA	NA	NA	NA	NA	NA	NA	NA	NA
1962	NA	NA	NA	NA	NA	NA	NA	NA	NA	NA	NA	NA	NA	NA	NA
1959	NA	NA	NA	NA	NA	NA	NA	NA	NA	NA	NA	NA	NA	NA	NA
1957	NA	NA	NA	NA	NA	NA	NA	NA	NA	NA	NA	NA	NA	NA	NA
1952	NA	NA	NA	NA	NA	NA	NA	NA	NA	NA	NA	NA	NA	NA	NA
1950	NA	NA	NA	NA	NA	NA	NA	NA	NA	NA	NA	NA	NA	NA	NA
1947	NA	NA	NA	NA	NA	NA	NA	NA	NA	NA	NA	NA	NA	NA	NA
1940	NA	NA	NA	NA	NA	NA	NA	NA	NA	NA	NA	NA	NA	NA	NA

25 TO 29 YEARS

Completed 4 Years of High School or More

Age and Year	Total	Male	Female	Total	Male	Female	Total	Male	Female	Total	Male	Female	Total	Male	Female
2019	86.4	84.6	88.4	93.8	93.3	94.3	96.3	96.2	96.4	91.4	89.3	93.4	96.7	96.2	97.2
2018	85.2	83.4	87.2	92.9	91.7	94.1	95.6	94.9	96.2	92.2	90.8	93.4	97.5	97.6	97.5
2017	82.7	80.7	84.8	92.3	91.2	93.5	95.6	94.8	96.3	91.8	90.9	92.6	96.9	97.9	95.9
2016	80.6	78.3	83.2	91.7	90.7	92.7	95.2	94.9	95.6	90.7	91.0	90.5	96.7	96.2	97.2
2015	77.1	75.7	78.6	90.8	90.0	91.6	95.4	95.2	95.6	92.2	91.5	92.8	95.5	95.8	95.1
2014	74.7	72.4	77.4	90.8	89.9	91.7	95.6	95.4	95.9	89.1	88.9	89.3	96.9	96.3	97.4
2013	75.8	73.1	78.8	89.6	88.1	91.1	94.2	93.4	95.0	89.5	87.0	91.7	94.9	94.0	95.9
2012	75.0	73.3	76.9	89.6	88.2	91.0	94.6	93.8	95.4	88.4	86.8	89.8	95.5	96.1	94.8
2011	71.5	69.2	74.3	88.9	87.1	90.8	94.4	93.3	95.5	87.9	87.6	88.3	94.7	92.8	96.5
2010	69.4	65.7	74.1	88.5	87.3	89.8	94.4	94.5	94.3	89.9	86.5	91.0	93.1	92.3	93.9
2009	68.9	66.2	72.5	88.4	87.0	89.9	94.5	94.4	94.6	88.8	88.5	89.1	95.1	95.7	94.6
2008	68.3	65.6	71.9	87.6	85.5	89.8	93.7	92.6	94.8	87.7	85.6	89.4	95.7	95.5	95.9
2007	65.0	60.5	70.7	86.5	84.2	88.8	93.4	92.7	94.1	87.4	87.0	87.8	96.3	95.8	96.8
2006	63.3	60.6	66.7	86.0	83.9	88.2	93.3	92.2	94.5	85.6	83.2	87.7	96.0	96.4	95.7
2005	63.3	63.2	63.4	85.6	84.2	87.0	92.8	91.7	93.8	86.6	86.4	86.7	95.5	96.7	94.4
2004	62.4	60.1	65.2	85.9	83.9	87.9	93.2	92.1	94.4	87.8	89.9	86.2	95.7	97.0	94.5
2003	61.7	59.6	64.2	85.7	83.9	87.6	93.6	92.8	94.4	87.4	86.4	88.5	97.2	97.5	97.0
2002	62.4	60.2	65.0	NA	NA	NA	NA	NA	NA	NA	NA	NA	NA	NA	NA
2001	62.4	58.3	67.3	NA	NA	NA	NA	NA	NA	NA	NA	NA	NA	NA	NA
2000	62.8	59.2	66.4	NA	NA	NA	NA	NA	NA	NA	NA	NA	NA	NA	NA
1999	61.6	57.4	66.0	NA	NA	NA	NA	NA	NA	NA	NA	NA	NA	NA	NA
1998	62.8	59.9	66.3	NA	NA	NA	NA	NA	NA	NA	NA	NA	NA	NA	NA
1997	61.8	59.2	64.9	NA	NA	NA	NA	NA	NA	NA	NA	NA	NA	NA	NA
1996	61.1	59.7	62.9	NA	NA	NA	NA	NA	NA	NA	NA	NA	NA	NA	NA
1995	57.1	55.7	58.7	NA	NA	NA	NA	NA	NA	NA	NA	NA	NA	NA	NA
1994	60.3	58.0	63.0	NA	NA	NA	NA	NA	NA	NA	NA	NA	NA	NA	NA
1993	60.9	58.3	64.0	NA	NA	NA	NA	NA	NA	NA	NA	NA	NA	NA	NA
1992	60.9	61.1	60.6	NA	NA	NA	NA	NA	NA	NA	NA	NA	NA	NA	NA
1991	56.7	56.4	57.1	NA	NA	NA	NA	NA	NA	NA	NA	NA	NA	NA	NA
1990	58.2	56.6	59.9	NA	NA	NA	NA	NA	NA	NA	NA	NA	NA	NA	NA
1989	61.0	61.0	61.0	NA	NA	NA	NA	NA	NA	NA	NA	NA	NA	NA	NA
1988	62.0	59.4	65.0	NA	NA	NA	NA	NA	NA	NA	NA	NA	NA	NA	NA
1987	59.8	58.6	61.0	NA	NA	NA	NA	NA	NA	NA	NA	NA	NA	NA	NA
1986	59.1	58.2	60.0	NA	NA	NA	NA	NA	NA	NA	NA	NA	NA	NA	NA
1985	60.9	58.6	63.1	NA	NA	NA	NA	NA	NA	NA	NA	NA	NA	NA	NA
1984	58.6	56.8	60.2	NA	NA	NA	NA	NA	NA	NA	NA	NA	NA	NA	NA
1983	58.3	57.8	58.9	NA	NA	NA	NA	NA	NA	NA	NA	NA	NA	NA	NA
1982	60.9	60.7	61.2	NA	NA	NA	NA	NA	NA	NA	NA	NA	NA	NA	NA
1981	59.8	59.1	60.4	NA	NA	NA	NA	NA	NA	NA	NA	NA	NA	NA	NA

Note: Starting in 2001, data are from the expanded CPS sample.

NA = Not available

[1]Data in the column labeled "Black" include Black and other races from 1940 to 1962: from 1963 to 2003, data are for the Black population only.

[2]Starting in 2012, data were calculated using population controls based on the 2010 Census.

[3]Starting in 2003, respondents could choose more than one race. The race data in this table for White, non-Hispanic White, Black, and Asian from 2003 onward represent those respondents who indicated only one racial identity. Prior to 2003, Asians were grouped with Pacific Islanders.

[4]Starting in 2001, data were calculated using population controls based on Census 2000.

[5]Begining with data for 1992, a new question results in different categories than for earlier years: Data shown as 'Completed 4 Years of High School or more' is now collected in the category 'High School Graduate.' Data shown as 'College 1 to 3 years' is now collected in the 'Some college' and the two 'Associate degree' categories. Data shown as 'Completed 4 Years of College or more', is now collected in the categories, 'Bachelor's degree,' 'Master's degree,' 'Doctorate degree,' and 'Professional degree'. Due to the change in question format, median years of schooling cannot be derived.

Table A-32. Percent of People 25 Years Old and Over Who Have Completed High School or College, by Race, Hispanic Origin, and Sex, Selected Years, 1940–2019—*Continued*

(Percent; civilian noninstitutionalized population.)

Age and Year	All races			White			Non-Hispanic White			Black[1]			Asian		
	Total	Male	Female	Total	Male	Female	Total	Male	Female	Total	Male	Female	Total	Male	Female
1980	85.4	85.4	85.5	86.9	86.8	87.0	NA	NA	NA	76.6	74.8	78.1	NA	NA	NA
1979	85.6	86.3	84.9	87.0	87.7	86.4	NA	NA	NA	74.8	73.9	75.4	NA	NA	NA
1978	85.3	86.0	84.6	86.3	86.8	85.8	NA	NA	NA	77.3	78.5	76.3	NA	NA	NA
1977	85.4	86.6	84.2	86.8	87.6	86.0	NA	NA	NA	74.4	77.5	72.0	NA	NA	NA
1976	84.7	86.0	83.5	85.9	87.3	84.6	NA	NA	NA	73.8	72.5	74.9	NA	NA	NA
1975	83.1	84.5	81.8	84.4	85.7	83.2	NA	NA	NA	71.0	72.2	70.1	NA	NA	NA
1974	81.9	83.1	80.8	83.4	84.1	82.7	NA	NA	NA	68.2	71.1	66.0	NA	NA	NA
1973	80.2	80.6	79.8	82.0	82.4	81.6	NA	NA	NA	64.2	63.1	64.9	NA	NA	NA
1972	79.8	80.5	79.2	81.5	82.3	80.8	NA	NA	NA	64.1	61.8	66.2	NA	NA	NA
1971	77.2	78.1	76.4	79.5	80.8	78.3	NA	NA	NA	57.5	54.1	60.7	NA	NA	NA
1970	75.4	76.6	74.2	77.8	79.2	76.4	NA	NA	NA	56.2	54.5	57.9	NA	NA	NA
1969	74.7	75.6	73.8	77.0	77.5	76.6	NA	NA	NA	55.8	59.8	52.3	NA	NA	NA
1968	73.2	73.7	72.7	75.3	75.5	75.0	NA	NA	NA	55.8	58.1	53.6	NA	NA	NA
1967	72.5	72.1	72.9	74.8	74.3	75.3	NA	NA	NA	53.4	51.7	55.0	NA	NA	NA
1966	71.0	70.9	71.2	73.8	73.2	74.4	NA	NA	NA	47.9	48.9	47.0	NA	NA	NA
1965	70.3	70.5	70.1	72.8	72.7	72.8	NA	NA	NA	50.3	50.3	50.4	NA	NA	NA
1964	69.2	68.8	69.5	72.1	71.8	72.4	NA	NA	NA	45.0	41.6	47.9	NA	NA	NA
1962	65.9	65.8	66.1	69.2	69.2	69.3	NA	NA	NA	41.6	38.9	43.8	NA	NA	NA
1959	63.9	63.9	64.0	67.2	66.9	67.4	NA	NA	NA	39.5	40.6	38.6	NA	NA	NA
1957	60.2	57.9	62.4	63.3	60.7	65.7	NA	NA	NA	31.6	27.4	35.2	NA	NA	NA
1952	57.1	55.3	58.7	NA	NA	NA	NA	NA	NA	28.1	27.9	28.3	NA	NA	NA
1950	52.8	50.6	55.0	NA	NA	NA	NA	NA	NA	23.6	21.3	25.5	NA	NA	NA
1947	51.4	49.4	53.3	54.9	52.9	56.8	NA	NA	NA	22.3	19.6	24.7	NA	NA	NA
1940	38.1	36.0	40.1	41.2	38.9	43.4	NA	NA	NA	12.3	10.6	13.6	NA	NA	NA
Completed 4 Years of College or More															
2019	38.7	35.7	41.8	38.6	34.7	42.7	44.9	40.8	49.2	29.0	28.4	29.5	70.1	69.5	70.6
2018	37.0	33.2	40.8	37.9	33.6	42.4	43.5	38.8	48.4	22.3	18.6	25.7	69.5	68.3	70.8
2017	35.7	32.0	39.3	36.4	32.2	40.7	42.1	37.7	46.5	22.2	20.4	23.9	61.9	58.1	65.9
2016	36.1	32.7	39.5	37.0	33.6	40.5	42.9	39.5	46.3	22.7	20.2	25.0	64.7	60.3	68.8
2015	35.6	32.4	38.9	36.7	33.2	40.3	43.0	39.5	46.6	20.5	16.5	24.2	65.0	62.8	67.2
2014	34.0	30.9	37.2	34.8	31.6	38.2	40.8	37.7	43.9	21.5	19.5	23.4	61.7	56.3	66.5
2013	33.6	30.2	37.0	34.3	30.8	37.9	40.4	37.1	43.8	20.1	16.8	23.1	59.0	54.3	63.2
2012	33.5	29.8	37.2	33.7	29.9	37.6	39.8	36.0	43.6	22.7	18.5	26.2	60.8	56.8	64.5
2011	32.2	28.4	36.1	33.1	29.2	37.4	39.2	35.5	43.0	19.6	16.1	22.8	56.2	51.5	60.6
2010	31.7	27.8	35.7	32.7	28.8	37.0	38.6	34.8	42.4	19.0	14.8	22.9	55.4	52.0	58.6
2009	30.6	26.6	34.8	31.3	27.0	36.0	37.2	32.6	42.0	19.0	15.2	22.4	59.3	58.0	60.6
2008	30.8	26.8	34.9	31.1	26.7	35.9	37.1	32.6	41.7	20.6	18.7	22.3	59.4	55.1	63.5
2007	29.6	26.3	33.0	29.8	25.8	34.0	35.5	31.9	39.2	18.9	17.9	19.9	60.9	59.8	62.0
2006	28.4	25.3	31.6	28.3	25.0	31.7	34.3	31.4	37.2	18.6	14.9	21.6	60.9	59.8	61.9
2005	28.8	25.5	32.2	28.9	25.3	32.7	34.5	30.7	38.2	17.4	14.1	20.1	61.6	60.5	62.5
2004	28.7	26.1	31.4	28.9	26.5	31.5	34.5	31.4	37.5	16.9	13.4	19.7	61.4	62.0	60.9
2003	28.4	26.0	30.9	28.3	25.3	31.5	34.2	31.4	37.1	17.2	17.5	17.0	61.6	60.9	62.3
2002	29.3	26.9	31.8	29.7	26.5	33.1	35.9	32.6	39.2	17.5	17.4	17.7	NA	NA	NA
2001	28.4	25.5	31.3	28.5	25.1	32.1	33.7	30.4	36.9	16.8	15.6	17.9	NA	NA	NA
2000	29.1	27.9	30.1	29.6	27.8	31.3	34.0	32.3	35.8	17.5	18.1	17.0	NA	NA	NA
1999	28.2	26.8	29.5	29.3	27.6	30.9	33.6	32.0	35.1	15.0	13.1	16.5	NA	NA	NA
1998	27.3	25.6	29.0	28.4	26.5	30.4	32.3	30.5	34.2	15.8	14.2	17.0	NA	NA	NA
1997	27.8	26.3	29.3	28.9	27.2	30.7	32.6	31.2	34.1	14.4	12.1	16.4	NA	NA	NA
1996	27.1	26.1	28.2	28.1	27.2	29.1	31.6	30.9	32.3	14.6	12.4	16.4	NA	NA	NA
1995	24.7	24.5	24.9	26.0	25.4	26.6	28.8	28.4	29.2	15.3	17.2	13.6	NA	NA	NA
1994	23.3	22.5	24.0	24.2	23.6	24.8	27.1	26.8	27.4	13.7	11.7	15.4	NA	NA	NA
1993	23.7	23.4	23.9	24.7	24.4	25.1	27.2	27.2	27.1	13.2	12.6	13.8	NA	NA	NA
1992	23.6	23.2	24.0	25.0	24.2	25.7	NA	NA	NA	11.3	12.0	10.6	NA	NA	NA
1991	23.2	23.0	23.4	24.6	24.1	25.0	NA	NA	NA	11.0	11.5	10.6	NA	NA	NA
1990	23.2	23.7	22.8	24.2	24.2	24.3	NA	NA	NA	13.4	15.1	11.9	NA	NA	NA
1989	23.4	23.9	22.9	24.4	24.8	24.0	NA	NA	NA	12.7	12.0	13.3	NA	NA	NA
1988	22.5	23.2	21.9	23.5	24.0	22.9	NA	NA	NA	12.2	12.6	11.9	NA	NA	NA
1987	22.0	22.3	21.7	23.0	23.3	22.8	NA	NA	NA	11.4	11.6	11.1	NA	NA	NA

Note: Starting in 2001, data are from the expanded CPS sample.

NA = Not available

[1]Data in the column labeled "Black" include Black and other races from 1940 to 1962: from 1963 to 2003, data are for the Black population only.

[2]Starting in 2012, data were calculated using population controls based on the 2010 Census.

[3]Starting in 2003, respondents could choose more than one race. The race data in this table for White, non-Hispanic White, Black, and Asian from 2003 onward represent those respondents who indicated only one racial identity. Prior to 2003, Asians were grouped with Pacific Islanders.

[4]Starting in 2001, data were calculated using population controls based on Census 2000.

[5]Begining with data for 1992, a new question results in different categories than for earlier years: Data shown as 'Completed 4 Years of High School or more' is now collected in the category 'High School Graduate.' Data shown as 'College 1 to 3 years' is now collected in the 'Some college' and the two 'Associate degree' categories. Data shown as 'Completed 4 Years of College or more', is now collected in the categories, 'Bachelor's degree,' 'Master's degree,' 'Doctorate degree,' and 'Professional degree'. Due to the change in question format, median years of schooling cannot be derived.

Table A-32. Percent of People 25 Years Old and Over Who Have Completed High School or College, by Race, Hispanic Origin, and Sex, Selected Years, 1940–2019—*Continued*

(Percent; civilian noninstitutionalized population.)

Age and Year	Hispanic (of any race) Total	Male	Female	White alone or in combination Total	Male	Female	Non-Hispanic White alone or in combination Total	Male	Female	Black alone or in combination Total	Male	Female	Asian alone or in combination Total	Male	Female
1980	58.6	58.3	58.8	NA	NA	NA	NA	NA	NA	NA	NA	NA	NA	NA	NA
1979	57.0	55.5	58.5	NA	NA	NA	NA	NA	NA	NA	NA	NA	NA	NA	NA
1978	56.6	58.5	54.7	NA	NA	NA	NA	NA	NA	NA	NA	NA	NA	NA	NA
1977	58.1	62.1	54.8	NA	NA	NA	NA	NA	NA	NA	NA	NA	NA	NA	NA
1976	58.1	57.6	58.4	NA	NA	NA	NA	NA	NA	NA	NA	NA	NA	NA	NA
1975	51.7	51.1	52.1	NA	NA	NA	NA	NA	NA	NA	NA	NA	NA	NA	NA
1974	52.5	55.1	49.9	NA	NA	NA	NA	NA	NA	NA	NA	NA	NA	NA	NA
1973	NA	NA	NA	NA	NA	NA	NA	NA	NA	NA	NA	NA	NA	NA	NA
1972	NA	NA	NA	NA	NA	NA	NA	NA	NA	NA	NA	NA	NA	NA	NA
1971	NA	NA	NA	NA	NA	NA	NA	NA	NA	NA	NA	NA	NA	NA	NA
1970	NA	NA	NA	NA	NA	NA	NA	NA	NA	NA	NA	NA	NA	NA	NA
1969	NA	NA	NA	NA	NA	NA	NA	NA	NA	NA	NA	NA	NA	NA	NA
1968	NA	NA	NA	NA	NA	NA	NA	NA	NA	NA	NA	NA	NA	NA	NA
1967	NA	NA	NA	NA	NA	NA	NA	NA	NA	NA	NA	NA	NA	NA	NA
1966	NA	NA	NA	NA	NA	NA	NA	NA	NA	NA	NA	NA	NA	NA	NA
1965	NA	NA	NA	NA	NA	NA	NA	NA	NA	NA	NA	NA	NA	NA	NA
1964	NA	NA	NA	NA	NA	NA	NA	NA	NA	NA	NA	NA	NA	NA	NA
1962	NA	NA	NA	NA	NA	NA	NA	NA	NA	NA	NA	NA	NA	NA	NA
1959	NA	NA	NA	NA	NA	NA	NA	NA	NA	NA	NA	NA	NA	NA	NA
1957	NA	NA	NA	NA	NA	NA	NA	NA	NA	NA	NA	NA	NA	NA	NA
1952	NA	NA	NA	NA	NA	NA	NA	NA	NA	NA	NA	NA	NA	NA	NA
1950	NA	NA	NA	NA	NA	NA	NA	NA	NA	NA	NA	NA	NA	NA	NA
1947	NA	NA	NA	NA	NA	NA	NA	NA	NA	NA	NA	NA	NA	NA	NA
1940	NA	NA	NA	NA	NA	NA	NA	NA	NA	NA	NA	NA	NA	NA	NA
Completed 4 Years of College or More															
2019	20.6	18.2	23.1	38.3	34.6	42.2	44.6	40.7	48.7	29.1	28.3	29.8	67.8	67.4	68.3
2018	20.7	18.4	23.2	37.5	33.2	42.0	43.1	38.4	47.9	22.0	18.0	25.5	67.5	66.3	68.7
2017	18.5	15.0	22.4	36.2	32.1	40.4	41.8	37.5	46.3	22.4	20.6	24.1	61.2	56.9	65.7
2016	18.7	16.2	21.5	36.7	33.2	40.4	42.5	38.9	46.1	22.9	20.1	25.4	63.2	58.3	67.8
2015	16.4	14.5	18.5	36.4	33.0	40.0	42.6	39.1	46.3	20.7	17.0	24.1	63.5	60.6	66.3
2014	15.1	12.4	18.3	34.5	31.2	38.0	40.6	37.4	43.8	21.4	18.7	23.9	60.0	54.4	65.3
2013	15.7	13.1	18.6	34.1	30.6	37.7	40.1	36.8	43.5	19.8	16.6	22.8	58.1	53.7	62.2
2012	14.8	12.5	17.4	33.5	29.8	37.4	39.6	35.9	43.4	22.8	18.1	27.0	59.6	55.7	63.4
2011	12.8	9.6	16.8	33.0	29.0	37.1	39.0	35.4	42.7	19.8	16.3	22.9	55.7	52.0	59.1
2010	13.5	10.8	16.8	32.6	28.6	36.8	38.4	34.6	42.3	19.3	14.8	23.5	53.7	49.6	57.6
2009	12.2	11.0	13.8	31.1	26.8	35.9	37.1	32.4	41.9	19.0	15.0	22.6	58.0	56.7	59.3
2008	12.4	10.0	15.5	31.0	26.6	35.8	36.9	32.4	41.5	20.9	19.3	22.3	57.4	52.9	61.8
2007	11.6	8.6	15.4	29.7	25.7	33.8	35.3	31.7	39.0	19.1	18.1	19.9	59.0	57.8	60.1
2006	9.5	6.9	12.8	28.1	24.8	31.6	34.1	31.2	37.0	18.9	15.0	22.3	59.4	58.4	60.5
2005	11.2	10.2	12.4	28.8	25.3	32.5	34.3	30.6	38.1	17.6	14.6	20.3	60.3	59.0	61.5
2004	10.9	9.6	12.4	28.7	25.7	31.8	34.2	31.2	37.2	16.8	13.4	19.5	59.9	61.1	58.9
2003	10.0	8.4	12.0	28.2	25.2	31.4	34.0	31.2	36.9	17.3	17.4	17.3	60.3	58.8	61.7
2002	8.9	8.3	9.7	NA	NA	NA	NA	NA	NA	NA	NA	NA	NA	NA	NA
2001	10.5	8.2	13.3	NA	NA	NA	NA	NA	NA	NA	NA	NA	NA	NA	NA
2000	9.7	8.3	11.0	NA	NA	NA	NA	NA	NA	NA	NA	NA	NA	NA	NA
1999	8.9	7.5	10.4	NA	NA	NA	NA	NA	NA	NA	NA	NA	NA	NA	NA
1998	10.4	9.5	11.3	NA	NA	NA	NA	NA	NA	NA	NA	NA	NA	NA	NA
1997	11.0	9.6	10.1	NA	NA	NA	NA	NA	NA	NA	NA	NA	NA	NA	NA
1996	10.0	10.2	9.8	NA	NA	NA	NA	NA	NA	NA	NA	NA	NA	NA	NA
1995	8.9	7.8	10.1	NA	NA	NA	NA	NA	NA	NA	NA	NA	NA	NA	NA
1994	8.0	6.6	9.8	NA	NA	NA	NA	NA	NA	NA	NA	NA	NA	NA	NA
1993	8.3	7.1	9.8	NA	NA	NA	NA	NA	NA	NA	NA	NA	NA	NA	NA
1992	9.5	8.8	10.3	NA	NA	NA	NA	NA	NA	NA	NA	NA	NA	NA	NA
1991	9.2	8.1	10.4	NA	NA	NA	NA	NA	NA	NA	NA	NA	NA	NA	NA
1990	8.1	7.3	9.1	NA	NA	NA	NA	NA	NA	NA	NA	NA	NA	NA	NA
1989	10.1	9.6	10.6	NA	NA	NA	NA	NA	NA	NA	NA	NA	NA	NA	NA
1988	11.4	12.1	10.6	NA	NA	NA	NA	NA	NA	NA	NA	NA	NA	NA	NA
1987	8.7	9.2	8.2	NA	NA	NA	NA	NA	NA	NA	NA	NA	NA	NA	NA

Note: Starting in 2001, data are from the expanded CPS sample.

NA = Not available

[1]Data in the column labeled "Black" include Black and other races from 1940 to 1962: from 1963 to 2003, data are for the Black population only.

[2]Starting in 2012, data were calculated using population controls based on the 2010 Census.

[3]Starting in 2003, respondents could choose more than one race. The race data in this table for White, non-Hispanic White, Black, and Asian from 2003 onward represent those respondents who indicated only one racial identity. Prior to 2003, Asians were grouped with Pacific Islanders.

[4]Starting in 2001, data were calculated using population controls based on Census 2000.

[5]Begining with data for 1992, a new question results in different categories than for earlier years: Data shown as 'Completed 4 Years of High School or more' is now collected in the category 'High School Graduate.' Data shown as 'College 1 to 3 years' is now collected in the 'Some college' and the two 'Associate degree' categories. Data shown as 'Completed 4 Years of College or more', is now collected in the categories, 'Bachelor's degree,' 'Master's degree,' 'Doctorate degree,' and 'Professional degree'. Due to the change in question format, median years of schooling cannot be derived.

Table A-32. Percent of People 25 Years Old and Over Who Have Completed High School or College, by Race, Hispanic Origin, and Sex, Selected Years, 1940–2019—*Continued*

(Percent; civilian noninstitutionalized population.)

Age and Year	All races			White			Non-Hispanic White			Black[1]			Asian		
	Total	Male	Female	Total	Male	Female	Total	Male	Female	Total	Male	Female	Total	Male	Female
1986	22.4	22.9	21.9	23.5	24.1	22.9	NA	NA	NA	11.8	10.1	13.3	NA	NA	NA
1985	22.2	23.1	21.3	23.2	24.2	22.2	NA	NA	NA	11.5	10.3	12.6	NA	NA	NA
1984	21.9	23.2	20.7	23.1	24.3	21.9	NA	NA	NA	11.6	12.9	10.5	NA	NA	NA
1983	22.5	23.9	21.1	23.4	25.0	21.8	NA	NA	NA	12.9	13.1	12.8	NA	NA	NA
1982	21.7	23.3	20.2	22.7	24.5	20.9	NA	NA	NA	12.6	11.8	13.2	NA	NA	NA
1981	21.3	23.1	19.6	22.4	24.3	20.5	NA	NA	NA	11.6	12.1	11.1	NA	NA	NA
1980	22.5	24.0	21.0	23.7	25.5	22.0	NA	NA	NA	11.6	10.5	12.5	NA	NA	NA
1979	23.1	25.6	20.5	24.3	27.1	21.5	NA	NA	NA	12.4	13.3	11.7	NA	NA	NA
1978	23.3	26.0	20.6	24.5	27.6	21.4	NA	NA	NA	11.8	10.7	12.6	NA	NA	NA
1977	24.0	27.0	21.1	25.3	28.5	22.1	NA	NA	NA	12.6	12.8	12.4	NA	NA	NA
1976	23.7	27.5	20.1	24.6	28.7	20.6	NA	NA	NA	13.0	12.0	13.6	NA	NA	NA
1975	21.9	25.1	18.7	22.8	26.3	19.4	NA	NA	NA	10.7	11.4	10.1	NA	NA	NA
1974	20.7	23.9	17.6	22.0	25.3	18.8	NA	NA	NA	7.9	8.8	7.2	NA	NA	NA
1973	19.0	21.6	16.4	19.9	22.8	17.0	NA	NA	NA	8.1	7.1	8.8	NA	NA	NA
1972	19.0	22.0	16.0	19.9	23.1	16.7	NA	NA	NA	8.3	7.1	9.4	NA	NA	NA
1971	16.9	20.1	13.8	17.9	21.3	14.6	NA	NA	NA	6.4	6.4	6.5	NA	NA	NA
1970	16.4	20.0	12.9	17.3	21.3	13.3	NA	NA	NA	7.3	6.7	8.0	NA	NA	NA
1969	16.0	19.4	12.8	17.0	20.6	13.4	NA	NA	NA	6.7	8.1	5.5	NA	NA	NA
1968	14.7	18.0	11.6	15.6	19.1	12.3	NA	NA	NA	5.3	5.3	5.3	NA	NA	NA
1967	14.6	17.2	12.1	15.5	18.3	12.7	NA	NA	NA	5.4	4.2	6.3	NA	NA	NA
1966	14.0	16.8	11.3	14.7	17.9	11.8	NA	NA	NA	5.9	5.4	6.4	NA	NA	NA
1965	12.4	15.6	9.5	13.0	16.4	9.8	NA	NA	NA	6.8	7.3	6.8	NA	NA	NA
1964	12.8	16.6	9.2	13.6	17.5	9.9	NA	NA	NA	5.5	7.5	3.9	NA	NA	NA
1962	13.1	17.2	9.2	14.3	18.7	10.0	NA	NA	NA	4.2	5.7	3.0	NA	NA	NA
1959	11.1	14.8	7.6	11.9	15.9	8.1	NA	NA	NA	4.6	5.6	3.7	NA	NA	NA
1957	10.4	13.5	7.5	11.1	14.5	7.8	NA	NA	NA	4.1	3.3	5.0	NA	NA	NA
1952	10.1	13.8	6.7	NA	NA	NA	NA	NA	NA	4.6	3.2	5.8	NA	NA	NA
1950	7.7	9.6	5.9	NA	NA	NA	NA	NA	NA	2.9	2.4	3.2	NA	NA	NA
1947	5.6	5.8	5.4	5.9	6.2	5.7	NA	NA	NA	2.8	2.6	2.9	NA	NA	NA
1940	5.9	6.9	4.9	6.4	7.5	5.3	NA	NA	NA	1.6	1.5	1.7	NA	NA	NA

Note: Starting in 2001, data are from the expanded CPS sample.

NA = Not available

[1]Data in the column labeled "Black" include Black and other races from 1940 to 1962: from 1963 to 2003, data are for the Black population only.

[2]Starting in 2012, data were calculated using population controls based on the 2010 Census.

[3]Starting in 2003, respondents could choose more than one race. The race data in this table for White, non-Hispanic White, Black, and Asian from 2003 onward represent those respondents who indicated only one racial identity. Prior to 2003, Asians were grouped with Pacific Islanders.

[4]Starting in 2001, data were calculated using population controls based on Census 2000.

[5]Begining with data for 1992, a new question results in different categories than for earlier years: Data shown as 'Completed 4 Years of High School or more' is now collected in the category 'High School Graduate.' Data shown as 'College 1 to 3 years' is now collected in the 'Some college' and the two 'Associate degree' categories. Data shown as 'Completed 4 Years of College or more', is now collected in the categories, 'Bachelor's degree,' 'Master's degree,' 'Doctorate degree,' and 'Professional degree'. Due to the change in question format, median years of schooling cannot be derived.

Table A-32. Percent of People 25 Years Old and Over Who Have Completed High School or College, by Race, Hispanic Origin, and Sex, Selected Years, 1940–2019—*Continued*

(Percent; civilian noninstitutionalized population.)

Age and Year	Hispanic (of any race)			White alone or in combination			Non-Hispanic White alone or in combination			Black alone or in combination			Asian alone or in combination		
	Total	Male	Female	Total	Male	Female	Total	Male	Female	Total	Male	Female	Total	Male	Female
1986	9.0	8.9	9.1	NA	NA	NA	NA	NA	NA	NA	NA	NA	NA	NA	NA
1985	11.1	10.9	11.2	NA	NA	NA	NA	NA	NA	NA	NA	NA	NA	NA	NA
1984	10.6	9.6	11.6	NA	NA	NA	NA	NA	NA	NA	NA	NA	NA	NA	NA
1983	10.4	9.6	11.1	NA	NA	NA	NA	NA	NA	NA	NA	NA	NA	NA	NA
1982	9.7	10.7	8.7	NA	NA	NA	NA	NA	NA	NA	NA	NA	NA	NA	NA
1981	7.5	8.6	6.5	NA	NA	NA	NA	NA	NA	NA	NA	NA	NA	NA	NA
1980	7.7	8.4	6.9	NA	NA	NA	NA	NA	NA	NA	NA	NA	NA	NA	NA
1979	7.3	7.9	6.8	NA	NA	NA	NA	NA	NA	NA	NA	NA	NA	NA	NA
1978	9.6	9.6	9.7	NA	NA	NA	NA	NA	NA	NA	NA	NA	NA	NA	NA
1977	6.7	7.2	6.4	NA	NA	NA	NA	NA	NA	NA	NA	NA	NA	NA	NA
1976	7.4	10.3	4.8	NA	NA	NA	NA	NA	NA	NA	NA	NA	NA	NA	NA
1975	8.8	10.0	7.3	NA	NA	NA	NA	NA	NA	NA	NA	NA	NA	NA	NA
1974	5.7	7.2	4.6	NA	NA	NA	NA	NA	NA	NA	NA	NA	NA	NA	NA
1973	NA	NA	NA	NA	NA	NA	NA	NA	NA	NA	NA	NA	NA	NA	NA
1972	NA	NA	NA	NA	NA	NA	NA	NA	NA	NA	NA	NA	NA	NA	NA
1971	NA	NA	NA	NA	NA	NA	NA	NA	NA	NA	NA	NA	NA	NA	NA
1970	NA	NA	NA	NA	NA	NA	NA	NA	NA	NA	NA	NA	NA	NA	NA
1969	NA	NA	NA	NA	NA	NA	NA	NA	NA	NA	NA	NA	NA	NA	NA
1968	NA	NA	NA	NA	NA	NA	NA	NA	NA	NA	NA	NA	NA	NA	NA
1967	NA	NA	NA	NA	NA	NA	NA	NA	NA	NA	NA	NA	NA	NA	NA
1966	NA	NA	NA	NA	NA	NA	NA	NA	NA	NA	NA	NA	NA	NA	NA
1965	NA	NA	NA	NA	NA	NA	NA	NA	NA	NA	NA	NA	NA	NA	NA
1964	NA	NA	NA	NA	NA	NA	NA	NA	NA	NA	NA	NA	NA	NA	NA
1962	NA	NA	NA	NA	NA	NA	NA	NA	NA	NA	NA	NA	NA	NA	NA
1959	NA	NA	NA	NA	NA	NA	NA	NA	NA	NA	NA	NA	NA	NA	NA
1957	NA	NA	NA	NA	NA	NA	NA	NA	NA	NA	NA	NA	NA	NA	NA
1952	NA	NA	NA	NA	NA	NA	NA	NA	NA	NA	NA	NA	NA	NA	NA
1950	NA	NA	NA	NA	NA	NA	NA	NA	NA	NA	NA	NA	NA	NA	NA
1947	NA	NA	NA	NA	NA	NA	NA	NA	NA	NA	NA	NA	NA	NA	NA
1940	NA	NA	NA	NA	NA	NA	NA	NA	NA	NA	NA	NA	NA	NA	NA

Note: Starting in 2001, data are from the expanded CPS sample.

NA = Not available

[1]Data in the column labeled "Black" include Black and other races from 1940 to 1962: from 1963 to 2003, data are for the Black population only.

[2]Starting in 2012, data were calculated using population controls based on the 2010 Census.

[3]Starting in 2003, respondents could choose more than one race. The race data in this table for White, non-Hispanic White, Black, and Asian from 2003 onward represent those respondents who indicated only one racial identity. Prior to 2003, Asians were grouped with Pacific Islanders.

[4]Starting in 2001, data were calculated using population controls based on Census 2000.

[5]Begining with data for 1992, a new question results in different categories than for earlier years: Data shown as 'Completed 4 Years of High School or more' is now collected in the category 'High School Graduate.' Data shown as 'College 1 to 3 years' is now collected in the 'Some college' and the two 'Associate degree' categories. Data shown as 'Completed 4 Years of College or more', is now collected in the categories, 'Bachelor's degree,' 'Master's degree,' 'Doctorate degree,' and 'Professional degree'. Due to the change in question format, median years of schooling cannot be derived.

Table A-33. Years of School Completed by People 25 Years Old and Over, by Age and Sex, Selected Years, 1940–2019

(Numbers in thousands; civilian noninstitutionalized population, except where noted.)

Year, sex, and age	Total	Elementary		High school		College		Median years
		0 to 4 years	5 to 8 years	1 to 3 years	4 years	1 to 3 years	4 years or more	

Years of school completed

25 YEARS OLD AND OVER

Both Sexes

Year, sex, and age	Total	0 to 4 years	5 to 8 years	1 to 3 years	4 years	1 to 3 years	4 years or more	Median years
2019	221,478	2,181	6,422	13,372	62,259	57,428	79,816	NA
2018	219,830	2,129	6,600	13,682	62,685	57,810	76,924	NA
2017	216,921	2,208	6,600	13,734	62,512	57,765	74,103	NA
2016	215,015	2,414	7,078	13,961	62,002	57,660	71,900	NA
2015	212,132	2,601	7,295	14,686	62,575	56,031	68,945	NA
2014	209,287	2,525	7,388	14,545	62,240	55,709	66,879	NA
2013	206,899	2,344	7,578	14,595	61,704	55,173	65,506	NA
2012	204,579	2,484	7,800	14,993	62,113	53,900	63,291	NA
2011	201,543	2,589	7,688	14,763	61,911	53,249	61,343	NA
2010	199,928	2,615	7,836	15,260	62,456	51,920	59,840	NA
2009	198,285	2,785	8,043	15,587	61,626	51,670	58,574	NA
2008	196,305	2,599	8,226	15,516	61,183	50,994	57,787	NA
2007	194,318	2,830	8,462	16,451	61,490	49,243	55,842	NA
2006	191,884	2,951	8,791	16,154	60,898	49,371	53,720	NA
2005	189,367	2,983	8,935	16,099	60,893	48,076	52,381	NA
2004	186,876	2,858	8,888	15,999	59,811	47,571	51,749	NA
2003	185,183	2,915	9,361	16,323	59,292	46,910	50,383	NA
2002	182,142	2,902	9,668	16,378	58,456	46,042	48,696	NA
2001	180,389	2,810	9,518	16,279	58,272	46,281	47,228	NA
2000	175,230	2,742	9,438	15,674	58,086	44,445	44,845	NA
1999	173,754	2,742	9,655	16,443	57,935	43,176	43,803	NA
1998	172,211	2,834	9,948	16,776	58,174	42,506	41,973	NA
1997	170,581	2,840	10,472	17,211	57,586	41,774	40,697	NA
1996	168,323	3,027	10,595	17,102	56,559	41,372	39,668	NA
1995	166,438	3,074	10,873	16,566	56,450	41,249	38,226	NA
1994	164,512	3,156	11,359	16,925	56,515	40,014	36,544	NA
1993	162,826	3,380	11,747	17,067	57,589	37,451	35,590	NA
1992	160,827	3,449	11,989	17,672	57,860	35,520	34,337	NA
1991	158,694	3,803	13,046	17,379	61,272	29,170	34,026	12.7
1990	156,538	3,833	13,758	17,461	60,119	28,075	33,291	12.7
1989	154,155	3,861	14,061	17,719	59,336	26,614	32,565	12.7
1988	151,635	3,714	14,550	17,847	58,940	25,799	30,787	12.7
1987	149,144	3,640	15,301	17,417	57,669	25,479	29,637	12.7
1986	146,606	3,894	15,672	17,484	56,338	24,729	28,489	12.6
1985	143,524	3,873	16,020	17,553	54,866	23,405	27,808	12.6
1984	140,794	3,884	16,258	17,433	54,073	22,281	26,862	12.6
1983	138,020	4,119	16,714	17,681	52,060	21,531	25,915	12.6
1982	135,526	4,119	17,232	18,006	51,426	20,692	24,050	12.6
1981	132,899	4,358	17,868	18,041	49,915	20,042	22,674	12.5
1980	130,409	4,390	18,426	18,086	47,934	19,379	22,193	12.5
1979	125,295	4,324	18,504	17,579	45,915	18,393	20,579	12.5
1978	123,019	4,445	19,309	18,175	44,381	17,379	19,332	12.4
1977	120,870	4,509	19,567	18,318	43,602	16,247	18,627	12.4
1976	118,848	4,601	19,912	18,204	43,157	15,477	17,496	12.4
1975	116,897	4,912	20,633	18,237	42,353	14,518	16,244	12.3
1974	115,005	5,106	21,200	18,274	41,460	13,665	15,300	12.3
1973	112,866	5,100	21,838	18,420	40,448	12,831	14,228	12.3
1972	111,133	5,124	22,503	18,855	39,171	12,117	13,364	12.2
1971	110,627	5,574	24,029	18,601	38,029	11,782	12,612	12.2
1970	109,310	5,747	24,519	18,682	37,134	11,164	12,062	12.2
1969	107,750	6,014	24,976	18,527	36,133	10,564	11,535	12.1
1968	106,469	6,248	25,467	18,724	34,603	10,254	11,171	12.1
1967	104,864	6,400	26,178	18,647	33,173	9,914	10,550	12.0
1966	103,876	6,705	26,478	18,859	32,391	9,235	10,212	12.0
1965	103,245	6,982	27,063	18,617	31,703	9,139	9,742	11.8
1964	102,421	7,295	27,551	18,419	30,728	9,085	9,345	11.7
1962	100,664	7,826	28,438	17,751	28,477	9,170	9,002	11.4
1960	99,465	8,303	31,218	19,140	24,440	8,747	7,617	10.6
1959	97,478	7,816	28,490	17,520	26,219	7,888	7,734	11.0
1957	95,630	8,561	29,316	16,951	24,832	6,985	7,172	10.6

Note: Starting in 2012, data were created using population controls based on 2010 Census data. Starting in 2001, data were created using population controls based on Census 2000 data. Also starting in 2001, data are from the expanded CPS sample. Begining with data for 1992, a new question results in different categories than for earlier years. Data shown as 'High School, 4 years' are now collected in the category 'High School Graduate.' Data shown as 'College 1 to 3 years' are now collected in the 'Some college' and the two 'Associate degree' categories. Data shown as 'College 4 years or more,' are now collected in the categories, 'Bachelor's degree,' 'Master's degree,' 'Doctorate degree,' and 'Professional degree.' Due to the change in question format, median years of schooling cannot be derived. Total includes persons who did not report on years of school completed.

NA = Not available.

Table A-33. Years of School Completed by People 25 Years Old and Over, by Age and Sex, Selected Years, 1940–2019—*Continued*

(Numbers in thousands; civilian noninstitutionalized population, except where noted.)

Year, sex, and age	Total	Years of school completed						Median years
		Elementary		High school		College		
		0 to 4 years	5 to 8 years	1 to 3 years	4 years	1 to 3 years	4 years or more	
1952	88,358	8,004	30,274	15,228	21,074	6,714	6,118	10.1
1950	87,484	9,491	31,617	14,817	17,625	6,246	5,272	9.3
1947	82,578	8,611	32,308	13,487	16,926	5,533	4,424	9.0
1940	74,776	10,105	34,413	11,182	10,552	4,075	3,407	8.6
Male								
2019	106,695	1,082	3,230	6,792	31,257	26,527	37,807	NA
2018	105,862	973	3,284	6,939	31,325	26,668	36,674	NA
2017	104,324	1,090	3,312	6,934	31,296	26,581	35,112	NA
2016	103,372	1,183	3,513	7,144	30,780	26,468	34,283	NA
2015	101,887	1,243	3,669	7,278	30,997	25,778	32,923	NA
2014	100,592	1,184	3,761	7,403	30,718	25,430	32,095	NA
2013	99,305	1,127	3,836	7,314	30,014	25,283	31,731	NA
2012	98,119	1,237	3,879	7,388	30,216	24,632	30,766	NA
2011	97,220	1,234	3,883	7,443	30,370	24,319	29,971	NA
2010	96,325	1,279	3,931	7,705	30,682	23,570	29,158	NA
2009	95,518	1,372	4,027	7,754	30,025	23,634	28,706	NA
2008	94,470	1,310	4,136	7,853	29,491	23,247	28,433	NA
2007	93,421	1,458	4,249	8,294	29,604	22,219	27,596	NA
2006	92,233	1,472	4,395	7,940	29,380	22,136	26,910	NA
2005	90,899	1,505	4,402	7,787	29,151	21,794	26,259	NA
2004	89,558	1,496	4,308	7,766	27,889	21,763	26,336	NA
2003	88,597	1,482	4,566	8,026	27,356	21,568	25,598	NA
2002	86,996	1,457	4,743	7,894	26,947	21,127	24,828	NA
2001	86,096	1,419	4,673	7,615	26,956	21,120	24,313	NA
2000	83,611	1,341	4,577	7,298	26,651	20,493	23,252	NA
1999	82,917	1,339	4,651	7,736	26,368	20,043	22,782	NA
1998	82,376	1,431	4,727	8,017	26,575	19,792	21,832	NA
1997	81,620	1,454	5,023	8,212	26,226	19,332	21,374	NA
1996	80,339	1,537	5,067	7,930	25,649	19,301	20,854	NA
1995	79,463	1,598	5,231	7,691	25,378	18,933	20,631	NA
1994	78,539	1,669	5,427	7,789	25,404	18,544	19,705	NA
1993	77,644	1,709	5,594	7,821	25,766	17,521	19,234	NA
1992	76,579	1,737	5,726	8,085	25,774	16,631	18,627	NA
1991	75,487	2,018	6,299	7,887	27,189	13,720	18,373	12.8
1990	74,421	2,004	6,557	8,000	26,426	13,271	18,164	12.8
1989	73,225	1,956	6,659	8,076	25,897	12,725	17,913	12.8
1988	71,911	1,852	6,849	8,247	25,638	12,057	17,268	12.7
1987	70,677	1,794	7,259	7,909	24,998	12,062	16,654	12.7
1986	69,503	1,978	7,446	7,872	24,260	11,856	16,091	12.7
1985	67,756	1,947	7,629	7,783	23,552	11,164	15,682	12.7
1984	66,350	1,945	7,688	7,837	22,990	10,678	15,211	12.7
1983	65,004	2,103	7,750	7,867	22,048	10,310	14,926	12.7
1982	63,764	2,074	7,987	7,960	21,749	10,020	13,974	12.6
1981	62,509	2,141	8,322	8,084	21,019	9,734	13,208	12.6
1980	61,389	2,212	8,627	8,046	20,080	9,593	12,832	12.6
1979	58,986	2,190	8,785	7,636	19,250	9,100	12,025	12.6
1978	57,922	2,230	9,195	7,821	18,620	8,657	11,398	12.5
1977	56,917	2,296	9,330	7,969	18,290	8,104	10,926	12.5
1976	55,902	2,371	9,463	7,923	18,048	7,699	10,397	12.5
1975	55,036	2,568	9,760	7,985	17,769	7,274	9,679	12.4
1974	54,167	2,637	10,186	7,966	17,488	6,756	9,135	12.4
1973	53,067	2,598	10,488	8,120	17,011	6,376	8,473	12.3
1972	52,351	2,634	10,854	8,413	16,424	5,972	8,055	12.3
1971	52,357	2,933	11,703	8,264	16,008	5,798	7,653	12.2
1970	51,784	3,031	11,925	8,355	15,571	5,580	7,321	12.2
1969	51,031	3,095	12,182	8,398	15,177	5,263	6,917	12.1
1968	50,510	3,261	12,407	8,564	14,613	4,945	6,721	12.1
1967	49,756	3,417	12,736	8,463	14,015	4,755	6,372	12.0
1966	49,410	3,614	12,992	8,611	13,672	4,342	6,180	11.8
1965	49,242	3,774	13,308	8,529	13,334	4,370	5,923	11.7
1964	48,975	3,959	13,467	8,537	12,902	4,394	5,714	11.5
1962	48,283	4,213	13,927	8,399	11,932	4,315	5,497	11.1

Note: Starting in 2012, data were created using population controls based on 2010 Census data. Starting in 2001, data were created using population controls based on Census 2000 data. Also starting in 2001, data are from the expanded CPS sample. Begining with data for 1992, a new question results in different categories than for earlier years. Data shown as 'High School, 4 years' are now collected in the category 'High School Graduate.' Data shown as 'College 1 to 3 years' are now collected in the 'Some college' and the two 'Associate degree' categories. Data shown as 'College 4 years or more,' are now collected in the categories, 'Bachelor's degree,' 'Master's degree,' 'Doctorate degree,' and 'Professional degree.' Due to the change in question format, median years of schooling cannot be derived. Total includes persons who did not report on years of school completed.
NA = Not available.

Table A-33. Years of School Completed by People 25 Years Old and Over, by Age and Sex, Selected Years, 1940–2019—*Continued*

(Numbers in thousands; civilian noninstitutionalized population, except where noted.)

| Year, sex, and age | Total | Years of school completed ||||||| Median years |
| | | Elementary || High school || College ||| |
		0 to 4 years	5 to 8 years	1 to 3 years	4 years	1 to 3 years	4 years or more	
1960	47,997	4,522	15,562	8,988	10,175	4,127	4,626	10.3
1959	47,041	4,257	14,039	8,326	10,870	3,801	4,765	10.7
1957	46,208	4,610	14,634	8,003	10,230	3,347	4,359	10.3
1952	42,368	4,396	14,876	7,048	8,760	3,164	3,480	9.7
1950	42,627	5,074	15,852	6,974	7,511	2,888	3,008	9.0
1947	40,483	4,615	16,086	6,535	7,353	2,625	2,478	8.9
1940	37,463	5,550	17,639	5,333	4,507	1,824	2,021	8.6
Female								
2019	114,783	1,098	3,192	6,580	31,002	30,902	42,009	NA
2018	113,969	1,156	3,316	6,743	31,360	31,142	40,251	NA
2017	112,597	1,117	3,288	6,799	31,216	31,185	38,991	NA
2016	111,643	1,231	3,565	6,817	31,221	31,192	37,617	NA
2015	110,245	1,358	3,626	7,408	31,578	30,253	36,021	NA
2014	108,695	1,341	3,627	7,142	31,522	30,279	34,784	NA
2013	107,594	1,217	3,741	7,282	31,690	29,890	33,775	NA
2012	106,460	1,246	3,920	7,604	31,898	29,267	32,524	NA
2011	104,323	1,355	3,806	7,320	31,541	28,930	31,372	NA
2010	103,603	1,336	3,904	7,555	31,774	28,350	30,683	NA
2009	102,767	1,413	4,016	7,833	31,601	28,036	29,868	NA
2008	101,835	1,289	4,090	7,663	31,692	27,747	29,354	NA
2007	100,897	1,371	4,213	8,157	31,887	27,024	28,245	NA
2006	99,651	1,479	4,395	8,215	31,518	27,234	26,810	NA
2005	98,467	1,477	4,532	8,311	31,742	26,283	26,122	NA
2004	97,319	1,363	4,580	8,233	31,921	25,808	25,413	NA
2003	96,586	1,433	4,795	8,297	31,936	25,342	24,784	NA
2002	95,146	1,445	4,926	8,484	31,509	24,915	23,868	NA
2001	94,293	1,392	4,845	8,664	31,316	25,161	22,915	NA
2000	91,620	1,400	4,861	8,378	31,435	23,953	21,594	NA
1999	90,837	1,404	5,004	8,707	31,566	23,133	21,021	NA
1998	89,835	1,403	5,220	8,758	31,599	22,714	20,142	NA
1997	88,961	1,387	5,450	8,999	31,360	22,442	19,323	NA
1996	87,984	1,491	5,528	9,171	30,911	22,071	18,813	NA
1995	86,975	1,476	5,642	8,874	31,072	22,317	17,594	NA
1994	85,973	1,487	5,932	9,135	31,111	21,470	16,838	NA
1993	85,181	1,672	6,154	9,246	31,823	19,930	16,357	NA
1992	84,248	1,712	6,263	9,587	32,086	18,889	15,709	NA
1991	83,207	1,784	6,747	9,491	34,083	15,449	15,652	12.7
1990	82,116	1,829	7,200	9,462	33,693	14,806	15,126	12.7
1989	80,930	1,904	7,402	9,643	33,440	13,888	14,652	12.6
1988	79,724	1,862	7,700	9,599	33,303	13,741	13,519	12.6
1987	78,467	1,846	8,042	9,508	32,671	13,417	12,983	12.6
1986	77,102	1,916	8,226	9,612	32,078	12,874	12,399	12.6
1985	75,768	1,926	8,390	9,770	31,314	12,242	12,126	12.6
1984	74,444	1,939	8,571	9,596	31,083	11,603	11,651	12.6
1983	73,016	2,015	8,964	9,814	30,012	11,220	10,990	12.5
1982	71,762	2,045	9,245	10,046	29,677	10,673	10,076	12.5
1981	70,390	2,217	9,545	9,957	28,896	10,309	9,466	12.5
1980	69,020	2,178	9,800	10,040	27,854	9,786	9,362	12.4
1979	66,309	2,133	9,720	9,945	26,665	9,293	8,554	12.4
1978	65,097	2,214	10,114	10,353	25,761	8,721	7,934	12.4
1977	63,953	2,213	10,236	10,349	25,312	8,142	7,701	12.4
1976	62,946	2,230	10,449	10,281	25,109	7,779	7,098	12.3
1975	61,861	2,344	10,871	10,252	24,584	7,243	6,565	12.3
1974	60,838	2,469	11,015	10,308	23,972	6,910	6,165	12.3
1973	59,799	2,502	11,350	10,300	23,437	6,454	5,755	12.2
1972	58,782	2,490	11,649	10,442	22,746	6,145	5,309	12.2
1971	58,270	2,641	12,327	10,339	22,021	5,984	4,959	12.2
1970	57,527	2,716	12,595	10,327	21,563	5,584	4,743	12.1
1969	56,719	2,919	12,796	10,131	20,955	5,301	4,619	12.1
1968	55,959	2,987	13,060	10,160	19,991	5,309	4,450	12.1
1967	55,107	2,985	13,439	10,185	19,157	5,162	4,178	12.0
1966	54,467	3,090	13,488	10,246	18,719	4,892	4,032	12.0

Note: Starting in 2012, data were created using population controls based on 2010 Census data. Starting in 2001, data were created using population controls based on Census 2000 data. Also starting in 2001, data are from the expanded CPS sample. Begining with data for 1992, a new question results in different categories than for earlier years. Data shown as 'High School, 4 years' are now collected in the category 'High School Graduate.' Data shown as 'College 1 to 3 years' are now collected in the 'Some college' and the two 'Associate degree' categories. Data shown as 'College 4 years or more,' are now collected in the categories, 'Bachelor's degree,' 'Master's degree,' 'Doctorate degree,' and 'Professional degree.' Due to the change in question format, median years of schooling cannot be derived. Total includes persons who did not report on years of school completed.

NA = Not available.

Table A-33. Years of School Completed by People 25 Years Old and Over, by Age and Sex, Selected Years, 1940–2019—*Continued*

(Numbers in thousands; civilian noninstitutionalized population, except where noted.)

Year, sex, and age	Total	Elementary		High school		College		Median years
		0 to 4 years	5 to 8 years	1 to 3 years	4 years	1 to 3 years	4 years or more	
1965	54,004	3,207	13,753	10,085	18,369	4,767	3,820	12.0
1964	53,447	3,333	14,086	9,881	17,825	4,686	3,629	11.8
1962	52,381	3,613	14,511	9,352	16,545	4,855	3,505	11.6
1960	51,468	3,781	15,656	10,151	14,267	4,620	2,991	10.9
1959	50,437	3,559	14,451	9,194	15,349	4,087	2,969	11.2
1957	49,422	3,951	14,682	8,948	14,602	3,638	2,813	10.9
1952	45,990	3,608	15,398	8,180	12,314	3,550	2,638	10.4
1950	44,857	4,417	15,824	7,843	10,114	3,358	2,264	9.6
1947	42,095	3,996	16,222	6,952	9,573	2,908	1,946	8.9
1940	37,313	4,554	16,773	5,849	6,044	2,251	1,386	8.7

25 TO 34 YEARS

Both Sexes

Year, sex, and age	Total	0 to 4 years	5 to 8 years	1 to 3 years	4 years	1 to 3 years	4 years or more	Median years
2019	45,208	232	679	2,353	11,639	12,269	18,037	NA
2018	44,854	182	776	2,435	11,460	12,501	17,501	NA
2017	44,250	218	732	2,532	11,494	12,792	16,482	NA
2016	43,763	210	858	2,656	11,224	12,609	16,207	NA
2015	43,006	292	863	2,938	10,965	12,420	15,528	NA
2014	42,466	286	946	3,018	11,040	12,178	14,997	NA
2013	41,797	260	1,035	3,116	10,950	11,955	14,481	NA
2012	41,219	273	1,063	3,079	10,974	11,765	14,065	NA
2011	41,584	318	1,140	3,098	11,250	12,046	13,731	NA
2010	41,085	323	1,169	3,271	11,186	11,655	13,480	NA
2009	40,520	321	1,226	3,202	11,351	11,409	13,010	NA
2008	40,146	282	1,189	3,296	11,297	11,113	12,969	NA
2007	39,868	380	1,283	3,462	11,408	10,961	12,375	NA
2006	39,481	359	1,410	3,375	11,302	11,229	11,806	NA
2005	39,310	414	1,375	3,422	11,269	10,865	11,965	NA
2004	39,201	430	1,399	3,239	11,244	11,044	11,844	NA
2003	39,242	370	1,370	3,336	11,392	10,986	11,791	NA
2002	38,670	433	1,393	3,245	10,988	10,776	11,834	NA
2001	38,865	380	1,317	3,202	11,294	11,146	11,526	NA
2000	37,786	287	1,135	3,052	11,546	10,700	11,066	NA
1999	38,474	280	1,142	3,296	11,826	10,893	11,040	NA
1998	39,354	319	1,207	3,228	12,569	11,220	10,811	NA
1997	40,256	334	1,163	3,624	12,710	11,524	10,892	NA
1996	40,919	418	1,169	3,780	13,087	11,624	10,841	NA
1995	41,388	394	1,264	3,667	14,061	11,659	10,342	NA
1994	41,946	367	1,297	4,057	14,483	11,913	9,829	NA
1993	41,864	382	1,223	3,894	15,036	11,361	9,968	NA
1992	42,493	433	1,250	4,071	16,021	10,860	9,861	NA
1991	42,905	465	1,322	4,178	17,503	9,283	10,153	12.9
1990	43,240	505	1,413	4,041	17,653	9,320	10,326	12.9
1989	43,240	446	1,352	4,013	17,901	9,072	10,454	12.9
1988	42,953	430	1,308	4,095	17,887	9,076	10,155	12.9
1987	42,635	390	1,360	3,995	17,539	9,157	10,196	12.9
1986	42,053	387	1,359	3,797	17,311	9,104	10,094	12.9
1985	40,858	362	1,328	3,703	16,748	8,980	9,737	12.9
1984	40,173	404	1,371	3,638	16,431	8,555	9,771	12.9
1983	39,342	376	1,324	3,664	15,804	8,567	9,605	12.9
1982	38,703	337	1,371	3,598	15,893	8,304	9,200	12.9
1981	37,828	337	1,428	3,665	15,419	8,198	8,782	12.9
1980	36,615	362	1,424	3,571	14,481	7,942	8,836	12.9
1979	34,053	370	1,381	3,452	13,338	7,415	8,096	12.9
1978	33,120	325	1,459	3,515	12,993	7,008	7,821	12.9
1977	32,284	269	1,383	3,715	12,845	6,398	7,676	12.8
1976	31,148	247	1,508	3,619	12,920	5,813	7,041	12.8
1975	30,092	313	1,644	3,743	12,544	5,403	6,443	12.7
1974	28,972	352	1,654	3,763	12,362	5,056	5,785	12.7
1973	27,793	333	1,850	3,915	12,194	4,454	5,047	12.6
1972	26,517	285	1,791	3,981	11,635	4,090	4,734	12.6
1971	25,545	327	2,011	3,986	11,232	3,822	4,169	12.6

Note: Starting in 2012, data were created using population controls based on 2010 Census data. Starting in 2001, data were created using population controls based on Census 2000 data. Also starting in 2001, data are from the expanded CPS sample. Begining with data for 1992, a new question results in different categories than for earlier years. Data shown as 'High School, 4 years' are now collected in the category 'High School Graduate.' Data shown as 'College 1 to 3 years' are now collected in the 'Some college' and the two 'Associate degree' categories. Data shown as 'College 4 years or more,' are now collected in the categories, 'Bachelor's degree,' 'Master's degree,' 'Doctorate degree,' and 'Professional degree.' Due to the change in question format, median years of schooling cannot be derived. Total includes persons who did not report on years of school completed.
NA = Not available.

Table A-33. Years of School Completed by People 25 Years Old and Over, by Age and Sex, Selected Years, 1940–2019—*Continued*

(Numbers in thousands; civilian noninstitutionalized population, except where noted.)

Year, sex, and age	Total	Years of school completed						Median years
		Elementary		High school		College		
		0 to 4 years	5 to 8 years	1 to 3 years	4 years	1 to 3 years	4 years or more	
1970	24,865	329	1,937	4,251	10,929	3,491	3,926	12.5
1969	24,072	359	2,086	4,140	10,592	3,202	3,693	12.5
1968	23,285	350	2,246	4,129	10,157	2,989	3,413	12.5
1967	22,388	319	2,293	4,017	9,645	2,946	3,169	12.5
1966	22,023	430	2,208	4,158	9,546	2,647	3,037	12.4
1965	21,980	543	2,437	4,058	9,500	2,561	2,880	12.4
1964	21,997	502	2,591	4,176	9,370	2,529	2,830	12.4
1962	22,130	597	2,936	4,371	8,815	2,552	2,859	12.4
1960	22,821	709	3,738	5,135	8,166	2,572	2,499	12.4
1959	22,922	761	3,348	4,741	8,979	2,398	2,480	12.3
1957	23,437	750	3,971	4,965	8,927	2,275	2,351	12.2
1952	23,138	844	4,362	4,898	8,620	2,220	2,052	12.2
1950	23,626	1,147	5,308	5,050	7,660	2,198	1,252	11.9
1947	22,627	1,015	5,523	4,997	7,630	1,908	1,378	11.9
1940	21,339	1,377	7,676	4,553	4,702	1,554	1,288	10.0
Male								
2019	22,726	147	379	1,303	6,593	5,939	8,365	NA
2018	22,490	95	432	1,431	6,530	6,047	7,955	NA
2017	22,121	135	390	1,410	6,456	6,267	7,464	NA
2016	21,845	116	468	1,427	6,386	6,015	7,432	NA
2015	21,427	166	488	1,584	6,198	5,920	7,071	NA
2014	21,217	151	512	1,611	6,323	5,910	6,710	NA
2013	20,816	161	582	1,747	6,058	5,749	6,519	NA
2012	20,464	161	579	1,707	6,127	5,619	6,270	NA
2011	20,985	190	657	1,791	6,444	5,750	6,151	NA
2010	20,689	186	641	1,866	6,458	5,587	5,951	NA
2009	20,440	184	695	1,806	6,495	5,508	5,752	NA
2008	20,210	172	714	1,874	6,356	5,277	5,816	NA
2007	20,024	246	757	1,930	6,361	5,137	5,593	NA
2006	19,827	218	834	1,835	6,233	5,336	5,371	NA
2005	19,677	241	769	1,827	6,216	5,198	5,426	NA
2004	19,598	280	793	1,723	6,020	5,286	5,495	NA
2003	19,564	216	771	1,831	6,028	5,252	5,466	NA
2002	19,234	280	809	1,782	5,751	5,131	5,480	NA
2001	19,330	233	748	1,677	6,099	5,161	5,411	NA
2000	18,563	155	593	1,637	5,989	4,870	5,318	NA
1999	18,294	157	616	1,724	6,114	5,052	5,260	NA
1998	19,526	190	654	1,735	6,592	5,233	5,125	NA
1997	20,039	193	629	2,007	6,482	5,477	5,249	NA
1996	20,390	225	601	2,055	6,701	5,536	5,274	NA
1995	20,589	229	708	1,930	7,176	5,373	5,174	NA
1994	20,873	230	716	2,134	7,408	5,510	4,873	NA
1993	20,856	237	679	1,986	7,604	5,308	5,041	NA
1992	21,125	231	682	2,057	8,113	5,116	4,927	NA
1991	21,319	270	694	2,095	8,810	4,441	5,009	12.9
1990	21,462	295	759	2,153	8,649	4,392	5,215	12.9
1989	21,461	251	698	2,129	8,659	4,391	5,335	12.9
1988	21,277	237	651	2,227	8,569	4,273	5,319	12.9
1987	21,142	223	698	2,030	8,544	4,384	5,263	12.9
1986	20,956	227	715	1,887	8,359	4,488	5,279	12.9
1985	20,184	194	700	1,823	7,955	4,433	5,080	12.9
1984	19,876	231	721	1,739	7,798	4,238	5,150	12.9
1983	19,438	213	659	1,724	7,351	4,284	5,207	13.0
1982	19,090	182	659	1,654	7,380	4,162	5,053	13.0
1981	18,625	176	733	1,679	6,991	4,185	4,863	13.0
1980	18,051	198	699	1,639	6,393	4,166	4,957	13.0
1979	16,719	197	695	1,476	5,852	3,862	4,637	13.0
1978	16,263	154	717	1,526	5,701	3,698	4,471	13.1
1977	15,863	134	672	1,625	5,634	3,403	4,396	13.0
1976	15,266	134	724	1,566	5,672	3,085	4,087	12.9
1975	14,776	177	815	1,605	5,508	2,915	3,757	12.9

Note: Starting in 2012, data were created using population controls based on 2010 Census data. Starting in 2001, data were created using population controls based on Census 2000 data. Also starting in 2001, data are from the expanded CPS sample. Begining with data for 1992, a new question results in different categories than for earlier years. Data shown as 'High School, 4 years' are now collected in the category 'High School Graduate.' Data shown as 'College 1 to 3 years' are now collected in the 'Some college' and the two 'Associate degree' categories. Data shown as 'College 4 years or more,' are now collected in the categories, 'Bachelor's degree,' 'Master's degree,' 'Doctorate degree,' and 'Professional degree.' Due to the change in question format, median years of schooling cannot be derived. Total includes persons who did not report on years of school completed.
NA = Not available.

Table A-33. Years of School Completed by People 25 Years Old and Over, by Age and Sex, Selected Years, 1940–2019—*Continued*

(Numbers in thousands; civilian noninstitutionalized population, except where noted.)

Year, sex, and age	Total	Years of school completed						Median years
		Elementary		High school		College		
		0 to 4 years	5 to 8 years	1 to 3 years	4 years	1 to 3 years	4 years or more	
1974	14,222	211	859	1,617	5,491	2,672	3,372	12.8
1973	13,638	204	966	1,760	5,363	2,416	2,927	12.7
1972	13,030	157	927	1,796	5,150	2,191	2,809	12.7
1971	12,596	170	1,092	1,771	5,049	2,005	2,506	12.6
1970	12,236	189	1,063	1,896	4,833	1,842	2,412	12.6
1969	11,788	204	1,121	1,849	4,652	1,719	2,241	12.6
1968	11,381	193	1,192	1,880	4,473	1,505	2,136	12.5
1967	10,876	170	1,209	1,814	4,187	1,522	1,973	12.5
1966	10,701	241	1,162	1,839	4,191	1,374	1,894	12.5
1965	10,693	325	1,240	1,802	4,188	1,316	1,822	12.5
1964	10,729	297	1,344	1,962	4,008	1,306	1,812	12.4
1962	10,762	334	1,569	2,008	3,700	1,309	1,842	12.4
1960	11,184	420	2,026	2,441	3,356	1,316	1,624	12.2
1959	11,226	416	1,822	2,238	3,682	1,256	1,658	12.3
1957	11,368	423	2,097	2,446	3,542	1,181	1,556	12.2
1952	10,936	502	2,202	2,268	3,458	1,118	1,268	12.1
1950	11,454	631	2,705	2,426	3,250	1,117	1,037	11.5
1947	10,894	544	2,665	2,494	3,337	993	738	11.7
1940	10,521	779	3,932	2,220	2,049	692	744	9.7
Female								
2019	22,482	84	300	1,051	5,045	6,330	9,671	NA
2018	22,364	87	344	1,004	4,930	6,454	9,547	NA
2017	22,129	84	342	1,122	5,037	6,526	9,018	NA
2016	21,918	93	390	1,229	4,838	6,594	8,774	NA
2015	21,579	126	375	1,354	4,767	6,500	8,457	NA
2014	21,248	135	435	1,407	4,717	6,267	8,287	NA
2013	20,981	99	454	1,369	4,892	6,205	7,962	NA
2012	20,755	112	484	1,372	4,847	6,145	7,795	NA
2011	20,599	128	483	1,307	4,806	6,296	7,580	NA
2010	20,396	137	527	1,405	4,728	6,068	7,530	NA
2009	20,079	137	531	1,395	4,856	5,901	7,258	NA
2008	19,937	111	475	1,421	4,941	5,836	7,153	NA
2007	19,843	134	527	1,532	5,047	5,824	6,781	NA
2006	19,654	140	577	1,538	5,069	5,894	6,435	NA
2005	19,633	173	607	1,594	5,053	5,667	6,539	NA
2004	19,603	150	606	1,516	5,224	5,758	6,349	NA
2003	19,679	153	598	1,503	5,364	5,734	6,325	NA
2002	19,436	153	584	1,463	5,237	5,645	6,353	NA
2001	19,536	147	569	1,525	5,195	5,985	6,115	NA
2000	19,222	130	542	1,415	5,557	5,831	5,750	NA
1999	19,551	122	525	1,572	5,712	5,842	5,779	NA
1998	19,828	130	553	1,493	5,977	5,986	5,688	NA
1997	20,217	149	533	1,615	6,227	6,047	5,643	NA
1996	20,528	195	569	1,734	6,386	6,090	5,568	NA
1995	20,800	165	556	1,738	6,885	6,286	5,170	NA
1994	21,073	138	581	1,923	7,075	6,404	4,953	NA
1993	21,007	143	543	1,907	7,432	6,054	4,928	NA
1992	21,368	203	567	2,014	7,908	5,744	4,933	NA
1991	21,586	195	629	2,085	8,693	4,841	5,143	12.9
1990	21,779	209	653	1,889	8,986	4,927	5,112	12.9
1989	21,777	195	654	1,885	9,242	4,681	5,119	12.9
1988	21,675	193	657	1,869	9,319	4,801	4,836	12.9
1987	21,494	168	662	1,965	8,995	4,772	4,932	12.9
1986	21,097	160	644	1,910	8,952	4,616	4,813	12.9
1985	20,673	168	627	1,880	8,794	4,547	4,657	12.9
1984	20,297	173	649	1,904	8,634	4,319	4,621	12.9
1983	19,903	161	665	1,941	8,452	4,285	4,398	12.9
1982	19,614	155	713	1,942	8,512	4,140	4,148	12.8
1981	19,203	161	698	1,986	8,427	4,013	3,918	12.8
1980	18,565	164	725	1,932	8,087	3,777	3,879	12.8
1979	17,334	173	685	1,977	7,486	3,553	3,460	12.8

Note: Starting in 2012, data were created using population controls based on 2010 Census data. Starting in 2001, data were created using population controls based on Census 2000 data. Also starting in 2001, data are from the expanded CPS sample. Begining with data for 1992, a new question results in different categories than for earlier years. Data shown as 'High School, 4 years' are now collected in the category 'High School Graduate.' Data shown as 'College 1 to 3 years' are now collected in the 'Some college' and the two 'Associate degree' categories. Data shown as 'College 4 years or more,' are now collected in the categories, 'Bachelor's degree,' 'Master's degree,' 'Doctorate degree,' and 'Professional degree.' Due to the change in question format, median years of schooling cannot be derived. Total includes persons who did not report on years of school completed.
NA = Not available.

Table A-33. Years of School Completed by People 25 Years Old and Over, by Age and Sex, Selected Years, 1940–2019—*Continued*

(Numbers in thousands; civilian noninstitutionalized population, except where noted.)

Year, sex, and age	Total	Elementary		High school		College		Median years
		0 to 4 years	5 to 8 years	1 to 3 years	4 years	1 to 3 years	4 years or more	
1978	16,857	172	742	1,989	7,292	3,311	3,351	12.6
1977	16,421	136	710	2,088	7,212	2,995	3,280	12.7
1976	15,882	112	784	2,054	7,248	2,731	2,954	12.7
1975	15,316	135	833	2,139	7,037	2,489	2,686	12.6
1974	14,750	142	796	2,145	6,871	2,383	2,413	12.6
1973	14,155	129	884	2,154	6,830	2,037	2,121	12.6
1972	13,487	128	862	2,184	6,485	1,899	1,926	12.5
1971	12,950	156	919	2,212	6,183	1,816	1,663	12.5
1970	12,629	140	876	2,355	6,096	1,648	1,512	12.5
1969	12,285	155	965	2,291	5,941	1,481	1,451	12.4
1968	11,904	157	1,053	2,246	5,684	1,484	1,278	12.4
1967	11,512	149	1,084	2,200	5,458	1,426	1,195	12.4
1966	11,322	186	1,047	2,319	5,355	1,273	1,134	12.4
1965	11,284	218	1,197	2,256	5,310	1,244	1,060	12.4
1964	11,269	202	1,248	2,216	5,362	1,221	1,018	12.4
1962	11,368	263	1,367	2,363	5,115	1,243	1,017	12.3
1960	11,637	289	1,712	2,694	4,810	1,256	875	12.2
1959	11,696	345	1,526	2,503	5,297	1,142	822	12.3
1957	12,069	327	1,874	2,519	5,385	1,094	795	12.2
1952	12,202	342	2,160	2,630	5,162	1,102	784	12.2
1950	12,172	516	2,603	2,624	4,410	1,081	714	12.1
1947	11,733	471	2,858	2,503	4,293	915	640	12.0
1940	10,818	598	3,744	2,333	2,653	862	544	10.3

35 TO 54 YEARS

Both Sexes

Year, sex, and age	Total	0 to 4 years	5 to 8 years	1 to 3 years	4 years	1 to 3 years	4 years or more	Median years
2019	81,727	716	2,309	4,957	21,303	20,572	31,869	NA
2018	82,196	690	2,289	4,974	21,680	21,340	31,223	NA
2017	82,072	709	2,403	5,059	22,103	21,621	30,176	NA
2016	82,571	799	2,636	5,296	22,298	22,070	29,473	NA
2015	82,715	862	2,742	5,471	23,153	21,826	28,660	NA
2014	82,687	875	2,612	5,433	23,238	22,472	28,057	NA
2013	83,324	778	2,611	5,437	23,708	22,831	27,959	NA
2012	83,883	863	2,762	5,569	24,608	22,792	27,288	NA
2011	83,796	899	2,474	5,682	25,039	22,796	26,907	NA
2010	84,834	852	2,549	5,937	26,145	22,911	26,440	NA
2009	85,688	909	2,716	6,046	26,121	23,384	26,513	NA
2008	86,067	905	2,742	5,882	26,108	23,504	26,926	NA
2007	86,224	874	2,720	6,310	26,675	22,777	26,869	NA
2006	85,918	965	2,769	6,274	26,636	23,317	25,958	NA
2005	85,311	954	2,757	5,892	27,232	23,129	25,347	NA
2004	84,642	963	2,582	5,938	26,649	23,093	25,417	NA
2003	84,308	957	2,620	6,112	26,346	23,039	25,234	NA
2002	83,829	941	2,636	5,874	26,740	23,148	24,489	NA
2001	83,286	886	2,612	5,899	26,356	23,271	24,262	NA
2000	81,435	932	2,521	5,702	26,481	22,618	23,183	NA
1999	79,976	872	2,535	6,052	26,367	21,561	22,589	NA
1998	78,520	890	2,613	6,164	26,079	21,267	21,506	NA
1997	76,973	867	2,686	6,045	26,054	20,684	20,635	NA
1996	74,661	968	2,710	5,803	24,924	20,105	20,152	NA
1995	73,028	927	2,561	5,664	24,070	19,926	19,878	NA
1994	71,049	987	2,680	5,415	23,804	19,210	18,956	NA
1993	68,845	942	2,486	5,538	23,927	17,984	17,970	NA
1992	66,594	899	2,608	5,845	23,442	16,658	17,144	NA
1991	64,351	995	3,057	5,522	24,815	13,348	16,614	12.9
1990	62,499	980	3,104	5,529	24,434	12,553	15,899	12.9
1989	60,494	999	3,315	5,800	23,334	11,627	15,417	12.9
1988	58,555	958	3,272	5,889	23,049	11,017	14,369	12.8
1987	56,650	842	3,398	5,656	22,820	10,523	13,409	12.8
1986	55,170	896	3,614	5,769	22,151	10,110	12,629	12.8
1985	53,697	899	3,639	5,978	21,600	9,217	12,363	12.8

Note: Starting in 2012, data were created using population controls based on 2010 Census data. Starting in 2001, data were created using population controls based on Census 2000 data. Also starting in 2001, data are from the expanded CPS sample. Begining with data for 1992, a new question results in different categories than for earlier years. Data shown as 'High School, 4 years' are now collected in the category 'High School Graduate.' Data shown as 'College 1 to 3 years' are now collected in the 'Some college' and the two 'Associate degree' categories. Data shown as 'College 4 years or more,' are now collected in the categories, 'Bachelor's degree,' 'Master's degree,' 'Doctorate degree,' and 'Professional degree.' Due to the change in question format, median years of schooling cannot be derived. Total includes persons who did not report on years of school completed.
NA = Not available.

Table A-33. Years of School Completed by People 25 Years Old and Over, by Age and Sex, Selected Years, 1940–2019—*Continued*

(Numbers in thousands; civilian noninstitutionalized population, except where noted.)

Year, sex, and age	Total	Years of school completed						Median years
		Elementary		High school		College		
		0 to 4 years	5 to 8 years	1 to 3 years	4 years	1 to 3 years	4 years or more	
1984	52,297	893	3,754	6,158	21,290	8,702	11,500	12.7
1983	50,956	973	4,044	6,313	20,788	8,045	10,795	12.7
1982	49,722	963	4,320	6,657	20,445	7,580	9,756	12.6
1981	48,680	1,038	4,531	6,773	20,032	7,115	9,181	12.6
1980	48,124	1,034	4,676	7,063	19,584	6,943	8,822	12.6
1979	47,437	1,030	4,895	7,132	19,488	6,655	8,237	12.5
1978	46,921	1,107	5,262	7,590	19,012	6,286	7,667	12.5
1977	46,409	1,192	5,445	7,781	18,781	6,013	7,196	12.5
1976	46,271	1,245	5,729	7,671	18,893	5,957	6,776	12.5
1975	46,193	1,296	5,942	7,765	19,010	5,673	6,506	12.4
1974	46,217	1,293	6,244	7,896	19,038	5,375	6,372	12.4
1973	45,910	1,344	6,519	8,001	18,651	5,318	6,076	12.4
1972	45,956	1,367	7,004	8,521	18,400	5,074	5,589	12.3
1971	46,294	1,439	7,588	8,393	18,334	5,082	5,460	12.3
1970	46,319	1,461	7,935	8,555	18,200	4,875	5,294	12.3
1969	46,255	1,644	8,313	8,586	17,773	4,749	5,190	12.3
1968	46,396	1,654	8,698	8,838	17,362	4,642	5,200	12.2
1967	46,321	1,771	9,036	9,138	16,906	4,525	4,947	12.2
1966	46,313	1,837	9,528	9,309	16,605	4,230	4,805	12.1
1965	46,296	1,827	9,812	9,266	16,359	4,384	4,647	12.1
1964	46,089	1,905	10,259	9,289	15,760	4,397	4,482	12.1
1962	45,287	2,181	10,795	8,938	14,668	4,452	4,253	12.0
1960	44,742	2,424	12,536	9,502	12,517	4,123	3,639	11.3
1959	43,989	2,303	11,657	8,719	13,244	3,715	3,709	11.8
1957	42,645	2,658	12,349	8,384	12,041	3,248	3,360	11.3
1952	39,014	2,606	13,274	7,348	9,374	3,148	2,802	10.5
1950	38,432	3,404	14,420	6,976	7,262	2,878	2,516	9.7
1947	36,717	3,203	15,184	6,311	6,715	2,622	2,221	9.0
1940	33,845	4,549	16,270	4,972	4,217	1,836	1,540	8.6
Male								
2019	40,180	388	1,202	2,690	11,688	9,863	14,348	NA
2018	40,411	356	1,182	2,657	11,753	9,991	14,472	NA
2017	40,303	395	1,305	2,711	12,032	10,026	13,834	NA
2016	40,539	443	1,336	2,903	12,021	10,217	13,620	NA
2015	40,565	469	1,416	2,987	12,401	9,996	13,296	NA
2014	40,525	489	1,459	2,992	12,246	10,199	13,139	NA
2013	40,868	409	1,464	2,962	12,417	10,473	13,142	NA
2012	41,167	462	1,525	2,927	12,869	10,439	12,944	NA
2011	41,209	447	1,292	3,027	13,250	10,339	12,854	NA
2010	41,858	446	1,367	3,227	13,824	10,311	12,682	NA
2009	42,263	500	1,458	3,278	13,644	10,670	12,713	NA
2008	42,419	507	1,490	3,228	13,625	10,711	12,858	NA
2007	42,476	491	1,433	3,480	13,737	10,359	12,976	NA
2006	42,344	549	1,472	3,356	13,660	10,608	12,701	NA
2005	42,024	547	1,476	3,063	14,017	10,429	12,491	NA
2004	41,612	577	1,323	3,157	13,238	10,636	12,682	NA
2003	41,340	538	1,372	3,282	12,903	10,622	12,622	NA
2002	41,154	513	1,333	3,063	13,133	10,739	12,373	NA
2001	40,858	488	1,368	2,974	12,784	10,827	12,417	NA
2000	40,024	479	1,288	2,845	12,845	10,716	11,854	NA
1999	39,300	470	1,290	3,101	12,544	10,233	11,664	NA
1998	38,654	486	1,333	3,284	12,239	10,098	11,214	NA
1997	37,912	486	1,370	3,143	12,326	9,713	10,870	NA
1996	36,596	520	1,319	2,877	11,749	9,514	10,526	NA
1995	35,994	529	1,368	2,781	11,223	9,305	10,784	NA
1994	34,998	545	1,383	2,621	11,009	9,073	10,369	NA
1993	33,751	478	1,316	2,660	10,983	8,624	9,687	NA
1992	32,619	472	1,368	2,750	10,670	7,968	9,389	NA
1991	31,460	530	1,624	2,612	11,092	6,430	9,169	13.0
1990	30,623	527	1,658	2,573	10,790	6,169	8,905	13.0
1989	29,597	504	1,762	2,628	10,235	5,719	8,749	13.0

Note: Starting in 2012, data were created using population controls based on 2010 Census data. Starting in 2001, data were created using population controls based on Census 2000 data. Also starting in 2001, data are from the expanded CPS sample. Begining with data for 1992, a new question results in different categories than for earlier years. Data shown as 'High School, 4 years' are now collected in the category 'High School Graduate.' Data shown as 'College 1 to 3 years' are now collected in the 'Some college' and the two 'Associate degree' categories. Data shown as 'College 4 years or more,' are now collected in the categories, 'Bachelor's degree,' 'Master's degree,' 'Doctorate degree,' and 'Professional degree.' Due to the change in question format, median years of schooling cannot be derived. Total includes persons who did not report on years of school completed.
NA = Not available.

Table A-33. Years of School Completed by People 25 Years Old and Over, by Age and Sex, Selected Years, 1940–2019—*Continued*

(Numbers in thousands; civilian noninstitutionalized population, except where noted.)

Year, sex, and age	Total	Elementary		High school		College		Median years
		0 to 4 years	5 to 8 years	1 to 3 years	4 years	1 to 3 years	4 years or more	
1988	28,645	498	1,725	2,654	10,100	5,327	8,340	12.9
1987	27,680	412	1,801	2,617	9,781	5,173	7,895	12.9
1986	26,925	475	1,919	2,699	9,393	5,013	7,426	12.9
1985	26,181	501	1,928	2,726	9,210	4,502	7,314	12.9
1984	25,460	506	2,014	2,831	8,926	4,257	6,929	12.8
1983	24,796	548	2,108	2,862	8,795	3,884	6,601	12.8
1982	24,164	530	2,302	2,989	8,609	3,757	5,977	12.7
1981	23,646	572	2,425	3,112	8,431	3,519	5,588	12.7
1980	23,373	590	2,492	3,202	8,278	3,442	5,370	12.7
1979	22,976	545	2,612	3,194	8,232	3,306	5,090	12.6
1978	22,719	609	2,779	3,377	8,001	3,136	4,817	12.6
1977	22,445	661	2,889	3,554	7,822	3,000	4,520	12.5
1976	22,403	730	3,004	3,473	7,904	2,969	4,323	12.5
1975	22,358	763	3,100	3,510	7,952	2,879	4,153	12.5
1974	22,367	733	3,286	3,532	8,004	2,730	4,081	12.6
1973	22,166	716	3,413	3,586	7,836	2,714	3,901	12.4
1972	22,200	749	3,674	3,917	7,663	2,564	3,631	12.4
1971	22,474	849	3,985	3,823	7,674	2,578	3,567	12.3
1970	22,475	834	4,208	3,876	7,612	2,555	3,390	12.3
1969	22,420	889	4,359	4,012	7,427	2,456	3,277	12.3
1968	22,521	931	4,487	4,160	7,324	2,364	3,257	12.2
1967	22,482	1,000	4,700	4,270	7,143	2,244	3,128	12.2
1966	22,508	1,085	4,886	4,455	6,990	2,029	3,063	12.1
1965	22,534	1,081	5,076	4,462	6,815	2,161	2,937	12.1
1964	22,457	1,158	5,226	4,416	6,657	2,212	2,789	12.2
1962	22,081	1,235	5,545	4,359	6,202	2,142	2,598	11.9
1960	21,919	1,397	6,415	4,579	5,364	1,957	2,206	11.1
1959	21,511	1,350	5,781	4,329	5,604	1,827	2,250	11.5
1957	20,873	1,491	6,293	3,987	5,195	1,558	1,972	11.0
1952	18,888	1,466	6,512	3,462	4,040	1,518	1,576	10.3
1950	18,896	1,834	7,338	3,339	3,151	1,271	1,403	9.6
1947	18,165	1,678	7,765	3,102	2,907	1,168	1,258	8.6
1940	17,127	2,480	8,458	2,388	1,798	819	917	8.5
Female								
2019	41,547	327	1,107	2,267	9,616	10,709	17,521	NA
2018	41,785	334	1,107	2,317	9,927	11,349	16,751	NA
2017	41,769	314	1,098	2,348	10,072	11,595	16,342	NA
2016	42,031	356	1,300	2,393	10,276	11,853	15,853	NA
2015	42,150	394	1,326	2,484	10,752	11,830	15,364	NA
2014	42,163	385	1,153	2,440	10,993	12,273	14,919	NA
2013	42,456	369	1,147	2,475	11,290	12,358	14,817	NA
2012	42,716	400	1,237	2,642	11,739	12,352	14,345	NA
2011	42,587	452	1,183	2,654	11,789	12,457	14,053	NA
2010	42,976	406	1,181	2,710	12,321	12,600	13,758	NA
2009	43,424	409	1,258	2,768	12,476	12,713	13,800	NA
2008	43,648	398	1,253	2,654	12,483	12,792	14,067	NA
2007	43,748	382	1,288	2,830	12,938	12,419	13,892	NA
2006	43,573	417	1,298	2,915	12,976	12,710	13,255	NA
2005	43,287	407	1,280	2,829	13,215	12,700	12,856	NA
2004	43,030	386	1,259	2,781	13,411	12,458	12,736	NA
2003	42,968	419	1,248	2,830	13,443	12,417	12,611	NA
2002	42,675	428	1,303	2,811	13,607	12,410	12,116	NA
2001	42,428	398	1,244	2,926	13,572	12,444	11,844	NA
2000	41,411	452	1,235	2,858	13,635	11,905	11,330	NA
1999	40,676	402	1,248	2,950	13,825	11,326	10,925	NA
1998	39,866	403	1,279	2,879	13,841	11,168	10,293	NA
1997	39,061	381	1,319	2,902	13,726	10,969	9,766	NA
1996	38,065	449	1,301	2,924	13,174	10,592	9,623	NA
1995	37,034	396	1,192	2,881	12,846	10,623	9,096	NA
1994	36,051	443	1,298	2,792	12,795	10,140	8,587	NA
1993	35,093	462	1,169	2,877	12,944	9,358	8,283	NA

Note: Starting in 2012, data were created using population controls based on 2010 Census data. Starting in 2001, data were created using population controls based on Census 2000 data. Also starting in 2001, data are from the expanded CPS sample. Begining with data for 1992, a new question results in different categories than for earlier years. Data shown as 'High School, 4 years' are now collected in the category 'High School Graduate.' Data shown as 'College 1 to 3 years' are now collected in the 'Some college' and the two 'Associate degree' categories. Data shown as 'College 4 years or more,' are now collected in the categories, 'Bachelor's degree,' 'Master's degree,' 'Doctorate degree,' and 'Professional degree.' Due to the change in question format, median years of schooling cannot be derived. Total includes persons who did not report on years of school completed.
NA = Not available.

Table A-33. Years of School Completed by People 25 Years Old and Over, by Age and Sex, Selected Years, 1940–2019—*Continued*

(Numbers in thousands; civilian noninstitutionalized population, except where noted.)

Year, sex, and age	Total	Elementary		High school		College		Median years
		0 to 4 years	5 to 8 years	1 to 3 years	4 years	1 to 3 years	4 years or more	
1992	33,975	427	1,240	3,096	12,770	8,687	7,756	NA
1991	32,891	464	1,431	2,910	13,723	6,919	7,443	12.8
1990	31,876	454	1,448	2,955	13,643	6,383	6,997	12.8
1989	30,898	498	1,552	3,171	13,099	5,908	6,669	12.8
1988	29,908	462	1,547	3,234	12,949	5,689	6,029	12.7
1987	28,969	430	1,598	3,039	13,038	5,349	5,513	12.7
1986	28,244	420	1,694	3,071	12,759	5,098	5,202	12.7
1985	27,516	398	1,710	3,252	12,391	4,715	5,049	12.7
1984	26,838	389	1,740	3,331	12,364	4,444	4,570	12.6
1983	26,161	427	1,935	3,450	11,993	4,161	4,193	12.6
1982	25,555	433	2,017	3,666	11,833	3,827	3,778	12.6
1981	25,034	467	2,105	3,661	11,599	3,605	3,595	12.5
1980	24,751	444	2,186	3,862	11,307	3,501	3,452	12.5
1979	24,461	486	2,282	3,935	11,258	3,353	3,147	12.5
1978	24,202	497	2,483	4,212	11,012	3,149	2,849	12.5
1977	23,964	534	2,557	4,227	10,959	3,014	2,678	12.4
1976	23,868	517	2,721	4,198	10,989	2,988	2,455	12.4
1975	23,835	533	2,842	4,256	11,058	2,793	2,352	12.4
1974	23,850	559	2,956	4,364	11,033	2,647	2,290	12.4
1973	23,744	628	3,106	4,415	10,815	2,603	2,174	12.3
1972	23,756	618	3,330	4,604	10,736	2,509	1,958	12.3
1971	23,821	590	3,604	4,570	10,660	2,505	1,894	12.3
1970	23,845	629	3,728	4,679	10,588	2,318	1,903	12.3
1969	23,834	755	3,953	4,575	10,349	2,293	1,913	12.3
1968	23,874	725	4,212	4,676	10,038	2,281	1,943	12.2
1967	23,839	773	4,334	4,868	9,762	2,282	1,819	12.2
1966	23,806	752	4,644	4,853	9,615	2,200	1,741	12.2
1965	23,765	746	4,735	4,803	9,545	2,223	1,712	12.2
1964	23,632	748	5,033	4,871	9,103	2,183	1,691	12.1
1962	23,206	946	5,250	4,579	8,466	2,310	1,655	12.1
1960	22,823	1,027	6,121	4,923	7,153	2,166	1,433	11.6
1959	22,478	953	5,876	4,390	7,640	1,888	1,459	12.0
1957	21,772	1,167	6,056	4,397	6,846	1,690	1,388	11.5
1952	20,126	1,140	6,762	3,886	5,334	1,630	1,226	10.7
1950	19,536	1,570	7,082	3,637	4,111	1,607	1,113	9.7
1947	18,552	1,525	7,419	3,209	3,808	1,454	963	9.3
1940	16,718	2,070	7,812	2,584	2,419	1,017	623	8.7
55 YEARS AND OVER								
Both Sexes								
2019	94,543	1,233	3,434	6,062	29,317	24,587	29,910	NA
2018	92,780	1,258	3,535	6,273	29,545	23,970	28,200	NA
2017	90,599	1,280	3,465	6,143	28,916	23,351	27,444	NA
2016	88,682	1,406	3,584	6,009	28,481	22,981	26,221	NA
2015	86,411	1,447	3,690	6,276	28,457	21,785	24,756	NA
2014	84,134	1,365	3,829	6,094	27,962	21,059	23,825	NA
2013	81,778	1,306	3,931	6,043	27,046	20,387	23,066	NA
2012	79,478	1,348	3,974	6,344	26,531	19,343	21,937	NA
2011	76,163	1,372	4,073	5,983	25,622	18,408	20,705	NA
2010	74,008	1,440	4,118	6,051	25,125	17,354	19,920	NA
2009	72,077	1,555	4,101	6,338	24,154	16,877	19,051	NA
2008	70,092	1,411	4,294	6,338	23,779	16,378	17,892	NA
2007	68,226	1,576	4,458	6,680	23,408	15,505	16,599	NA
2006	66,485	1,628	4,610	6,508	22,961	14,824	15,956	NA
2005	64,745	1,614	4,803	6,784	22,392	14,083	15,069	NA
2004	63,034	1,465	4,907	6,821	21,918	13,434	14,488	NA
2003	61,633	1,589	5,372	6,876	21,554	12,884	13,358	NA
2002	59,644	1,528	5,639	7,258	20,728	12,117	12,374	NA
2001	58,238	1,544	5,589	7,178	20,622	11,864	11,440	NA
2000	56,008	1,524	5,780	6,921	20,059	11,126	10,598	NA
1999	55,303	1,589	5,978	7,096	19,742	10,722	10,174	NA

Note: Starting in 2012, data were created using population controls based on 2010 Census data. Starting in 2001, data were created using population controls based on Census 2000 data. Also starting in 2001, data are from the expanded CPS sample. Begining with data for 1992, a new question results in different categories than for earlier years. Data shown as 'High School, 4 years' are now collected in the category 'High School Graduate.' Data shown as 'College 1 to 3 years' are now collected in the 'Some college' and the two 'Associate degree' categories. Data shown as 'College 4 years or more,' are now collected in the categories, 'Bachelor's degree,' 'Master's degree,' 'Doctorate degree,' and 'Professional degree.' Due to the change in question format, median years of schooling cannot be derived. Total includes persons who did not report on years of school completed.
NA = Not available.

Table A-33. Years of School Completed by People 25 Years Old and Over, by Age and Sex, Selected Years, 1940–2019—*Continued*

(Numbers in thousands; civilian noninstitutionalized population, except where noted.)

Year, sex, and age	Total	Elementary 0 to 4 years	Elementary 5 to 8 years	High school 1 to 3 years	High school 4 years	College 1 to 3 years	College 4 years or more	Median years
1998	54,337	1,624	6,126	7,385	19,526	10,022	9,654	NA
1997	53,352	1,628	6,622	7,543	18,823	9,565	9,169	NA
1996	52,742	1,642	6,716	7,520	18,549	9,642	8,677	NA
1995	52,022	1,755	7,048	7,232	18,320	9,662	8,005	NA
1994	51,516	1,802	7,382	7,454	18,228	8,890	7,761	NA
1993	52,117	2,058	8,038	7,637	18,626	8,106	7,652	NA
1992	51,740	2,118	8,133	7,756	18,397	8,005	7,332	NA
1991	51,439	2,341	8,668	7,675	18,954	6,540	7,258	12.6
1990	50,798	2,349	9,239	7,893	18,050	6,202	7,064	12.3
1989	50,421	2,412	9,395	7,907	18,102	5,914	6,693	12.3
1988	50,128	2,325	9,969	7,860	18,004	5,705	6,263	12.3
1987	49,858	2,408	10,544	7,766	17,310	5,799	6,033	12.2
1986	49,383	2,611	10,699	7,917	16,876	5,515	5,767	12.2
1985	48,969	2,612	11,052	7,872	16,516	5,208	5,708	12.2
1984	48,324	2,584	11,131	7,636	16,353	5,026	5,593	12.2
1983	47,723	2,769	11,348	7,703	15,470	4,915	5,514	12.1
1982	47,102	2,818	11,541	7,751	15,091	4,807	5,095	12.1
1981	46,391	2,983	11,909	7,600	14,464	4,721	4,711	12.0
1980	45,670	2,994	12,326	7,451	13,869	4,494	4,535	12.0
1979	43,806	2,924	12,230	6,999	13,088	4,321	4,245	12.0
1978	42,977	3,013	12,593	7,069	12,376	4,086	3,843	11.6
1977	42,176	3,047	12,740	6,823	11,977	3,835	3,754	11.3
1976	41,429	3,107	12,674	6,915	11,346	3,709	3,677	11.1
1975	40,613	3,303	13,045	6,730	10,798	3,442	3,295	10.8
1974	39,817	3,461	13,302	6,615	10,060	3,233	3,145	10.4
1973	39,163	3,424	13,467	6,504	9,604	3,060	3,105	10.2
1972	38,659	3,471	13,706	6,351	9,136	2,952	3,042	10.0
1971	38,787	3,808	14,430	6,225	8,463	2,878	2,982	9.6
1970	38,126	3,957	14,647	5,877	8,005	2,797	2,843	9.2
1969	37,424	4,012	14,576	5,801	7,768	2,615	2,653	9.1
1968	36,789	4,244	14,522	5,760	7,085	2,624	2,558	8.9
1967	36,155	4,310	14,849	5,495	6,622	2,443	2,434	8.7
1966	35,540	4,438	14,742	5,392	6,240	2,358	2,370	8.6
1965	34,969	4,612	14,814	5,293	5,844	2,194	2,215	8.5
1964	34,335	4,888	14,701	4,954	5,598	2,159	2,033	8.3
1962	33,247	5,048	14,707	4,442	4,994	2,166	1,890	8.1
1960	31,902	5,169	14,944	4,503	3,757	2,051	1,479	8.5
1959	30,567	4,752	13,485	4,060	3,996	1,775	1,545	8.1
1957	29,548	5,153	12,996	3,602	3,864	1,462	1,461	8.0
1952	26,206	4,554	12,638	2,982	3,080	1,346	1,264	7.7
1950	25,427	4,940	11,947	2,791	2,704	1,170	1,005	8.3
1947	23,234	4,393	11,601	2,179	2,581	1,003	825	7.5
1940	19,592	4,178	10,467	1,656	1,633	685	579	8.2
Male								
2019	43,789	547	1,649	2,800	12,976	10,724	15,093	NA
2018	42,961	522	1,670	2,851	13,041	10,630	14,247	NA
2017	41,901	561	1,617	2,813	12,808	10,288	13,814	NA
2016	40,988	624	1,708	2,814	12,374	10,236	13,231	NA
2015	39,895	608	1,765	2,707	12,398	9,863	12,556	NA
2014	38,850	544	1,790	2,800	12,150	9,320	12,246	NA
2013	37,621	557	1,790	2,605	11,539	9,060	12,070	NA
2012	36,489	614	1,775	2,754	11,220	8,574	11,552	NA
2011	35,027	597	1,934	2,625	10,676	8,230	10,966	NA
2010	33,778	647	1,923	2,611	10,399	7,672	10,525	NA
2009	32,814	689	1,874	2,669	9,886	7,456	10,241	NA
2008	31,841	631	1,932	2,751	9,510	7,259	9,759	NA
2007	30,920	721	2,060	2,884	9,505	6,723	9,026	NA
2006	30,060	705	2,090	2,784	9,488	6,193	8,837	NA
2005	29,198	717	2,157	2,896	8,918	6,167	8,341	NA
2004	28,347	639	2,192	2,885	8,631	5,841	8,159	NA
2003	27,694	729	2,423	2,912	8,425	5,694	7,510	NA

Note: Starting in 2012, data were created using population controls based on 2010 Census data. Starting in 2001, data were created using population controls based on Census 2000 data. Also starting in 2001, data are from the expanded CPS sample. Begining with data for 1992, a new question results in different categories than for earlier years. Data shown as 'High School, 4 years' are now collected in the category 'High School Graduate.' Data shown as 'College 1 to 3 years' are now collected in the 'Some college' and the two 'Associate degree' categories. Data shown as 'College 4 years or more,' are now collected in the categories, 'Bachelor's degree,' 'Master's degree,' 'Doctorate degree,' and 'Professional degree.' Due to the change in question format, median years of schooling cannot be derived. Total includes persons who did not report on years of school completed.

NA = Not available.

Table A-33. Years of School Completed by People 25 Years Old and Over, by Age and Sex, Selected Years, 1940–2019—*Continued*

(Numbers in thousands; civilian noninstitutionalized population, except where noted.)

Year, sex, and age	Total	Elementary		High school		College		Median years
		0 to 4 years	5 to 8 years	1 to 3 years	4 years	1 to 3 years	4 years or more	
2002	26,608	664	2,601	3,048	8,063	5,257	6,975	NA
2001	25,908	697	2,558	2,964	8,073	5,131	6,485	NA
2000	25,023	706	2,696	2,817	7,816	4,906	6,079	NA
1999	24,694	712	2,746	2,911	7,712	4,756	5,856	NA
1998	24,197	755	2,740	3,000	7,745	4,461	5,496	NA
1997	23,668	773	3,026	3,060	7,417	4,139	5,255	NA
1996	23,352	795	3,058	2,998	7,198	4,254	5,055	NA
1995	22,881	839	3,153	2,980	6,980	4,254	4,675	NA
1994	22,669	894	3,327	3,037	6,987	3,962	4,462	NA
1993	23,038	992	3,595	3,174	7,178	3,587	4,508	NA
1992	22,836	1,033	3,676	3,277	6,991	3,549	4,312	NA
1991	22,708	1,217	3,980	3,183	7,287	2,850	4,193	12.4
1990	22,337	1,182	4,141	3,274	6,986	2,707	4,046	12.4
1989	22,167	1,202	4,198	3,317	7,003	2,616	3,829	12.3
1988	21,989	1,117	4,471	3,366	6,968	2,455	3,609	12.3
1987	21,855	1,160	4,762	3,261	6,673	2,504	3,496	12.3
1986	21,622	1,275	4,813	3,286	6,509	2,355	3,385	12.2
1985	21,391	1,252	5,001	3,234	6,387	2,229	3,289	12.2
1984	21,014	1,209	4,951	3,270	6,265	2,185	3,132	12.2
1983	20,769	1,343	4,986	3,282	5,906	2,141	3,117	12.1
1982	20,508	1,362	5,026	3,313	5,759	2,102	2,946	12.1
1981	20,237	1,394	5,165	3,292	5,597	2,032	2,758	12.0
1980	19,967	1,424	5,436	3,206	5,409	1,986	2,506	11.9
1979	19,292	1,446	5,479	2,964	5,167	1,935	2,301	11.8
1978	18,939	1,467	5,701	2,919	4,919	1,824	2,110	11.4
1977	18,608	1,502	5,770	2,787	4,835	1,700	2,011	11.2
1976	18,233	1,507	5,733	2,884	4,473	1,646	1,989	11.0
1975	17,903	1,628	5,845	2,871	4,308	1,480	1,768	10.5
1974	17,579	1,693	6,042	2,817	3,993	1,356	1,682	10.1
1973	17,263	1,678	6,111	2,774	3,811	1,245	1,645	9.9
1972	17,120	1,728	6,252	2,698	3,612	1,215	1,614	9.6
1971	17,288	1,913	6,629	2,668	3,285	1,214	1,579	9.1
1970	17,074	2,011	6,655	2,583	3,127	1,182	1,516	9.0
1969	16,822	2,003	6,701	2,536	3,099	1,086	1,397	8.8
1968	16,609	2,137	6,728	2,523	2,816	1,078	1,328	8.7
1967	16,398	2,247	6,827	2,379	2,685	989	1,271	8.5
1966	16,201	2,288	6,944	2,317	2,491	939	1,223	8.3
1965	16,015	2,368	6,992	2,265	2,331	893	1,164	8.2
1964	15,789	2,504	6,897	2,159	2,237	876	1,113	8.1
1962	15,440	2,644	6,813	2,032	2,030	864	1,057	8.0
1960	14,895	2,704	7,121	1,969	1,453	853	796	8.4
1959	14,304	2,491	6,436	1,759	1,584	718	857	7.9
1957	13,967	2,696	6,244	1,570	1,493	608	831	7.7
1952	12,544	2,428	6,162	1,318	1,262	528	636	7.5
1950	12,277	2,609	5,808	1,209	1,111	500	569	8.2
1947	11,424	2,393	5,656	939	1,109	464	482	7.3
1940	9,815	2,293	5,249	724	660	313	361	8.1
Female								
2019	50,755	687	1,786	3,262	16,341	13,862	14,817	NA
2018	49,819	736	1,865	3,422	16,504	13,340	13,953	NA
2017	48,698	719	1,849	3,329	16,107	13,063	13,630	NA
2016	47,694	782	1,875	3,195	16,107	12,745	12,990	NA
2015	46,516	839	1,925	3,570	16,059	11,922	12,201	NA
2014	45,284	821	2,039	3,295	15,812	11,739	11,578	NA
2013	44,158	749	2,141	3,438	15,507	11,327	10,996	NA
2012	42,989	734	2,199	3,590	15,311	10,769	10,384	NA
2011	41,136	775	2,140	3,358	14,946	10,178	9,739	NA
2010	40,230	793	2,195	3,440	14,725	9,682	9,395	NA
2009	39,263	867	2,228	3,669	14,268	9,421	8,810	NA
2008	38,251	780	2,362	3,588	14,269	9,119	8,133	NA
2007	37,306	855	2,398	3,796	13,902	8,781	7,573	NA

Note: Starting in 2012, data were created using population controls based on 2010 Census data. Starting in 2001, data were created using population controls based on Census 2000 data. Also starting in 2001, data are from the expanded CPS sample. Begining with data for 1992, a new question results in different categories than for earlier years. Data shown as 'High School, 4 years' are now collected in the category 'High School Graduate.' Data shown as 'College 1 to 3 years' are now collected in the 'Some college' and the two 'Associate degree' categories. Data shown as 'College 4 years or more,' are now collected in the categories, 'Bachelor's degree,' Master's degree,' 'Doctorate degree,' and 'Professional degree.' Due to the change in question format, median years of schooling cannot be derived. Total includes persons who did not report on years of school completed.
NA = Not available.

Table A-33. Years of School Completed by People 25 Years Old and Over, by Age and Sex, Selected Years, 1940–2019—*Continued*

(Numbers in thousands; civilian noninstitutionalized population, except where noted.)

Year, sex, and age	Total	Elementary		High school		College		Median years
		0 to 4 years	5 to 8 years	1 to 3 years	4 years	1 to 3 years	4 years or more	
2006	36,425	922	2,521	3,761	13,472	8,630	7,119	NA
2005	35,547	897	2,645	3,887	13,474	7,916	6,728	NA
2004	34,687	826	2,715	3,936	13,287	7,593	6,329	NA
2003	33,939	860	2,949	3,964	13,129	7,190	5,848	NA
2002	33,035	864	3,038	4,210	12,664	6,860	5,399	NA
2001	32,329	847	3,032	4,213	12,549	6,733	4,956	NA
2000	30,985	817	3,085	4,105	12,243	6,218	4,517	NA
1999	30,609	879	3,232	4,186	12,031	5,965	4,319	NA
1998	30,140	868	3,386	4,386	11,780	5,560	4,160	NA
1997	29,684	855	3,596	4,483	11,407	5,427	3,916	NA
1996	29,390	848	3,659	4,523	11,350	5,387	3,623	NA
1995	29,142	915	3,894	4,255	11,340	5,410	3,330	NA
1994	28,848	909	4,054	4,419	11,242	4,926	3,298	NA
1993	29,080	1,066	4,442	4,462	11,447	4,519	3,149	NA
1992	28,904	1,084	4,456	4,478	11,409	4,455	3,021	NA
1991	28,729	1,125	4,687	4,495	11,667	3,690	3,066	12.3
1990	28,461	1,167	5,098	4,619	11,063	3,495	3,019	12.3
1989	28,255	1,211	5,195	4,587	11,099	3,300	2,863	12.3
1988	28,139	1,208	5,498	4,495	11,034	3,250	2,655	12.3
1987	28,004	1,248	5,782	4,504	10,637	3,294	2,539	12.2
1986	27,762	1,336	5,886	4,630	10,367	3,160	2,382	12.2
1985	27,578	1,360	6,052	4,638	10,129	2,979	2,420	12.2
1984	27,309	1,377	6,183	4,363	10,086	2,843	2,459	12.2
1983	26,954	1,428	6,364	4,423	9,567	2,774	2,398	12.1
1982	26,593	1,458	6,511	4,435	9,330	2,705	2,150	12.1
1981	26,152	1,589	6,742	4,308	8,868	2,690	1,954	12.0
1980	25,703	1,571	6,889	4,245	8,460	2,509	2,030	12.0
1979	24,514	1,474	6,750	4,034	7,920	2,389	1,944	12.0
1978	24,038	1,545	6,889	4,149	7,457	2,263	1,733	11.6
1977	23,568	1,546	6,972	4,034	7,141	2,135	1,742	11.0
1976	23,196	1,602	6,942	4,029	6,871	2,063	1,690	11.0
1975	22,710	1,675	7,198	3,858	6,490	1,962	1,527	10.9
1974	22,238	1,762	7,261	3,799	6,068	1,880	1,463	10.7
1973	21,900	1,746	7,359	3,729	5,790	1,814	1,461	10.5
1972	21,539	1,743	7,455	3,654	5,526	1,737	1,425	10.3
1971	21,500	1,896	7,805	3,556	5,179	1,665	1,402	9.9
1970	21,052	1,946	7,993	3,292	4,879	1,615	1,327	9.5
1969	20,601	2,009	7,878	3,264	4,669	1,526	1,255	9.4
1968	20,180	2,106	7,795	3,237	4,269	1,544	1,229	9.2
1967	19,756	2,063	8,021	3,117	3,937	1,454	1,164	8.9
1966	19,339	2,152	7,797	3,074	3,749	1,419	1,147	8.9
1965	18,955	2,243	7,821	3,026	3,514	1,300	1,048	8.7
1964	18,546	2,383	7,805	2,794	3,360	1,282	920	8.5
1962	17,807	2,404	7,894	2,410	2,964	1,302	833	8.3
1960	17,007	2,465	7,823	2,534	2,304	1,198	683	8.6
1959	16,263	2,261	7,049	2,301	2,412	1,057	688	8.3
1957	15,581	2,457	6,752	2,032	2,371	854	630	8.2
1952	13,662	2,126	6,476	1,664	1,818	818	628	7.9
1950	13,150	2,331	6,139	1,582	1,593	670	436	8.4
1947	11,810	2,000	5,945	1,240	1,472	539	343	7.6
1940	9,777	1,886	5,217	932	973	372	219	8.3

Note: Starting in 2012, data were created using population controls based on 2010 Census data. Starting in 2001, data were created using population controls based on Census 2000 data. Also starting in 2001, data are from the expanded CPS sample. Begining with data for 1992, a new question results in different categories than for earlier years. Data shown as 'High School, 4 years' are now collected in the category 'High School Graduate.' Data shown as 'College 1 to 3 years' are now collected in the 'Some college' and the two 'Associate degree' categories. Data shown as 'College 4 years or more,' are now collected in the categories, 'Bachelor's degree,' 'Master's degree,' 'Doctorate degree,' and 'Professional degree.' Due to the change in question format, median years of schooling cannot be derived. Total includes persons who did not report on years of school completed.
NA = Not available.

This page is intentionally left blank

Table A-34. Mean Earnings of Workers 18 Years Old and Over, by Educational Attainment, Race, Hispanic Origin, and Sex, 1975–2018

(Dollars except as noted.)

Race, sex, year, and Hispanic origin	Total		Not a high school graduate		High school graduate	
	Mean earnings	Number of workers (thousands)	Mean earnings	Number of workers (thousands)	Mean earnings	Number of workers (thousands)
ALL RACES						
Both Sexes						
2018	55,619	165,179	27,037	12,058	38,936	42,882
2017	53,536	163,871	26,832	12,240	38,145	42,816
2016	51,893	162,218	27,800	12,281	36,702	42,897
2015	49,994	161,074	25,315	13,159	35,615	42,404
2014	47,653	158,000	25,236	13,197	34,099	42,529
2013	46,187	156,031	23,755	12,961	32,881	42,433
2012	45,598	155,148	21,622	13,030	32,630	41,915
2011[2]	44,729	152,711	21,107	13,594	32,493	42,129
2010	42,956	151,747	20,935	13,540	30,999	42,650
2009	42,469	152,707	20,241	14,083	30,627	44,396
2008	42,588	155,989	21,023	15,217	31,283	45,182
2007	42,064	155,738	21,484	15,330	31,286	45,393
2006	41,412	154,438	20,873	16,652	31,071	45,936
2005	39,579	152,215	19,915	16,317	29,448	45,652
2004	37,899	150,096	19,169	16,373	28,645	45,545
2003[3]	37,046	148,660	18,734	16,282	27,915	45,064
2002	36,308	148,492	18,826	16,931	27,280	45,407
2001	35,805	147,829	18,793	17,293	26,795	45,641
2000[4]	34,514	147,966	17,738	17,425	25,692	45,977
1999	32,359	146,212	16,127	17,224	24,551	46,531
1998	30,928	142,053	16,053	16,742	23,594	45,987
1997	29,514	140,367	16,124	16,962	22,895	45,976
1996	28,106	138,703	15,011	17,075	22,154	45,908
1995	26,792	136,221	14,013	16,990	21,431	44,546
1994	25,852	135,096	13,697	16,479	20,248	44,614
1993	24,674	133,119	12,820	16,575	19,422	44,779
1992	23,036	131,891	12,685	17,055	18,637	45,600
1991	22,332	130,371	12,613	17,553	18,261	46,508
1990	21,793	130,080	12,582	18,698	17,820	51,977
1989	21,414	129,094	12,242	19,137	17,594	51,846
1988	20,060	127,564	11,889	19,635	16,750	51,297
1987	19,016	124,874	11,824	19,748	15,939	50,815
1986	18,149	122,757	11,203	19,665	15,120	50,104
1985	17,181	120,651	10,726	19,692	14,457	49,674
1984	16,083	118,183	10,384	20,206	13,893	48,452
1983	15,137	115,095	9,853	20,020	13,044	47,560
1982	14,351	113,451	9,387	20,789	12,560	46,584
1981	13,624	113,301	9,357	22,296	12,109	47,332
1980	12,665	111,919	8,845	23,028	11,314	46,795
1979	11,795	110,826	8,420	23,783	10,624	45,497
1978	10,812	106,436	7,759	23,787	9,834	43,510
1977	9,887	103,119	7,066	24,854	9,013	41,696
1976	9,180	100,510	6,720	25,035	8,393	40,570
1975	8,552	97,881	6,198	24,916	7,843	39,827
Male						
2018	65,058	86,913	31,846	7,520	45,259	24,992
2017	62,662	86,872	31,688	7,597	44,466	25,137
2016	61,232	85,718	32,463	7,695	43,534	24,908
2015	58,944	85,263	30,230	8,210	41,942	24,647
2014	56,701	83,402	29,618	8,256	39,874	24,468
2013	54,658	82,576	27,586	8,286	37,763	24,327
2012	54,118	81,979	24,955	8,183	38,454	23,783
2011[2]	52,273	80,502	25,155	8,359	38,679	23,800
2010	50,855	79,949	24,560	8,428	36,281	24,076
2009	50,186	80,799	23,036	8,851	35,468	25,143
2008	51,148	82,727	24,831	9,596	36,753	25,290
2007	50,110	82,932	24,985	9,780	36,839	25,396
2006	49,647	82,310	24,072	10,541	37,356	25,489

[1]For data prior to 1991, "Some college/Associate degree" equals 1 to 3 years of college completed; "Bachelor's degree" equals 4 years of college; "Advanced degree" equals 5 or more years of college completed.
[2]Starting in 2011, earnings data were created using population controls based on Census 2010 data.
[3]Starting in 2003, respondents could choose more than one race. The race data in this table from 2003 onward represent respondents who indicated only one race.
[4]Beginning in 2000, earnings data are from the expanded Current Population Survey (CPS) sample and were calculated using population controls based on Census 2000.
[5]May be of any race.
… = Not available.

Table A-34.   Mean Earnings of Workers 18 Years Old and Over, by Educational Attainment, Race, Hispanic Origin, and Sex, 1975–2018—*Continued*

(Dollars except as noted.)

Race, sex, year, and Hispanic origin	Some college or associate's degree[1]		Bachelor's degree[1]		Advanced degree[1]	
	Mean earnings	Number of workers (thousands)	Mean earnings	Number of workers (thousands)	Mean earnings	Number of workers (thousands)
ALL RACES						
Both Sexes						
2018........................	43,053	46,887	71,155	40,231	99,919	23,118
2017........................	41,507	47,382	67,763	39,153	98,369	22,277
2016........................	40,201	48,128	67,267	37,272	95,203	21,639
2015........................	38,943	47,961	65,482	36,348	92,525	21,199
2014........................	37,945	47,023	62,466	35,305	88,056	19,944
2013........................	36,428	46,952	59,661	34,422	90,304	19,261
2012........................	35,943	47,469	60,159	33,948	89,253	18,783
2011[2].....................	35,585	45,999	59,415	33,188	87,981	17,800
2010........................	34,469	45,604	57,619	32,371	83,930	17,582
2009........................	34,773	45,239	56,665	32,127	85,818	16,860
2008........................	34,808	46,663	58,613	31,890	83,144	17,035
2007........................	35,138	46,577	57,181	31,832	80,977	16,604
2006........................	34,650	45,073	56,788	31,006	82,320	15,769
2005........................	33,496	45,434	54,689	29,658	79,946	15,152
2004........................	32,012	44,381	51,554	29,050	78,093	14,746
2003[3].....................	31,498	44,048	51,206	28,672	74,602	14,592
2002........................	31,046	43,776	51,194	28,257	72,824	14,119
2001........................	30,782	43,214	50,623	27,980	72,869	13,700
2000[4].....................	29,939	43,874	49,595	27,488	71,194	13,200
1999........................	28,469	43,019	45,644	26,490	67,756	12,949
1998........................	27,566	41,412	43,782	25,818	63,473	12,095
1997........................	26,235	40,802	40,478	25,035	63,229	11,591
1996........................	25,181	40,410	38,112	24,028	61,317	11,281
1995........................	23,862	40,142	36,980	23,285	56,667	11,258
1994........................	22,226	40,135	37,224	22,712	56,105	11,155
1993........................	21,539	39,429	35,121	21,815	55,789	10,521
1992........................	20,680	37,730	32,525	21,080	48,548	10,426
1991........................	20,551	35,732	31,323	20,475	46,038	10,103
1990........................	20,694	28,993	31,112	18,128	41,458	12,285
1989........................	20,255	28,078	30,736	17,767	41,019	12,265
1988........................	19,066	27,217	28,344	17,308	37,724	12,109
1987........................	18,054	26,404	26,919	16,497	35,968	11,411
1986........................	17,073	26,113	26,511	15,788	34,787	11,087
1985........................	16,349	25,402	24,877	15,373	32,909	10,510
1984........................	14,936	24,463	23,072	14,653	30,192	10,410
1983........................	14,245	23,208	21,532	13,929	28,333	10,377
1982........................	13,503	22,602	20,272	13,425	26,915	10,051
1981........................	13,176	21,759	19,006	12,579	25,281	9,336
1980........................	12,409	21,384	18,075	12,115	23,308	8,535
1979........................	11,377	21,174	16,514	11,751	21,874	8,621
1978........................	10,357	20,121	15,291	11,001	20,173	8,017
1977........................	9,607	18,905	14,207	10,357	19,077	7,309
1976........................	8,813	17,786	13,033	10,132	17,911	6,985
1975........................	8,388	16,917	12,332	9,764	16,725	6,457
Male						
2018........................	52,460	23,286	84,803	20,083	123,215	11,029
2017........................	50,012	23,606	81,607	19,657	119,590	10,871
2016........................	48,123	23,891	82,089	18,627	116,617	10,595
2015........................	46,154	23,578	79,927	18,287	113,279	10,539
2014........................	46,137	23,057	76,169	17,725	110,645	9,895
2013........................	43,841	23,112	72,124	17,203	115,282	9,647
2012........................	43,593	23,267	72,546	17,175	110,501	9,570
2011[2].....................	43,239	22,469	71,162	16,769	109,063	9,102
2010........................	41,214	21,978	69,764	16,486	103,488	8,980
2009........................	41,773	21,895	69,479	16,226	105,636	8,683
2008........................	42,221	22,830	72,868	16,100	103,980	8,909
2007........................	41,709	22,916	70,898	16,109	100,550	8,730
2006........................	41,521	21,952	69,818	15,769	101,441	8,556

[1]For data prior to 1991, "Some college/Associate degree" equals 1 to 3 years of college completed; "Bachelor's degree" equals 4 years of college; "Advanced degree" equals 5 or more years of college completed.
[2]Starting in 2011, earnings data were created using population controls based on Census 2010 data.
[3]Starting in 2003, respondents could choose more than one race. The race data in this table from 2003 onward represent respondents who indicated only one race.
[4]Beginning in 2000, earnings data are from the expanded Current Population Survey (CPS) sample and were calculated using population controls based on Census 2000.
[5]May be of any race.
... = Not available.

Table A-34. Mean Earnings of Workers 18 Years Old and Over, by Educational Attainment, Race, Hispanic Origin, and Sex, 1975–2018—*Continued*

(Dollars except as noted.)

Race, sex, year, and Hispanic origin	Total		Not a high school graduate		High school graduate	
	Mean earnings	Number of workers (thousands)	Mean earnings	Number of workers (thousands)	Mean earnings	Number of workers (thousands)
2005	48,034	81,258	23,222	10,273	35,248	25,348
2004	45,989	79,776	22,512	10,191	34,054	25,186
2003[3]	44,726	78,869	21,447	10,173	33,266	24,292
2002	44,310	78,757	22,091	10,526	32,673	24,174
2001	43,648	78,342	21,508	10,572	32,363	24,239
2000[4]	42,772	78,319	21,007	10,535	31,446	24,439
1999	40,222	77,118	18,769	10,294	30,363	24,456
1998	38,134	75,213	19,155	10,085	28,742	24,155
1997	36,556	74,596	19,575	10,348	28,307	24,152
1996	34,705	73,955	17,826	10,583	27,642	23,966
1995	33,251	72,634	16,748	10,312	26,333	23,473
1994	32,087	72,246	16,633	9,981	25,038	23,418
1993	30,568	71,183	14,946	10,151	23,973	23,388
1992	28,148	71,138	14,747	10,661	22,811	23,816
1991	27,494	70,145	15,056	10,679	22,663	24,110
1990	27,164	70,218	14,991	11,412	22,378	26,753
1989	27,025	69,798	14,727	11,774	22,508	26,469
1988	25,344	69,006	14,551	11,993	21,481	26,080
1987	24,015	67,951	14,544	12,117	20,364	25,981
1986	23,057	67,189	13,703	12,208	19,453	25,562
1985	21,823	66,439	13,124	12,137	18,575	25,496
1984	20,452	65,005	12,775	12,325	18,016	24,827
1983	19,175	63,816	12,052	12,376	16,728	24,449
1982	18,244	63,489	11,513	12,868	16,160	24,059
1981	17,542	63,547	11,668	13,701	15,900	24,435
1980	16,382	62,825	11,042	14,273	15,002	24,023
1979	15,430	62,464	10,628	14,711	14,317	23,318
1978	14,154	60,586	9,894	14,550	13,188	22,650
1977	12,888	59,441	8,939	15,369	12,092	21,846
1976	11,923	58,419	8,522	15,634	11,189	21,499
1975	11,091	57,297	7,843	15,613	10,475	21,347
Female						
2018	45,136	78,265	19,068	4,537	30,103	17,889
2017	43,240	76,999	18,885	4,643	29,158	17,679
2016	41,429	76,500	19,974	4,586	27,242	17,988
2015	39,929	75,811	17,162	4,949	26,832	17,756
2014	37,538	74,597	17,915	4,941	26,275	18,060
2013	36,664	73,454	16,964	4,675	26,322	18,106
2012	36,052	73,169	15,995	4,847	24,991	18,132
2011[2]	35,205	72,209	14,643	5,234	24,460	18,328
2010	34,160	71,799	14,959	5,112	24,153	18,574
2009	33,797	71,907	15,514	5,232	24,304	19,253
2008	32,922	73,262	14,521	5,621	24,329	19,892
2007	32,899	72,805	15,315	5,550	24,234	19,997
2006	32,015	72,128	15,352	6,110	23,236	20,447
2005	29,897	70,956	14,294	6,044	22,208	20,304
2004	28,722	70,320	13,658	6,182	21,954	20,359
2003[3]	28,367	69,790	14,214	6,108	21,659	20,772
2002	27,271	69,735	13,459	6,404	21,141	21,233
2001	26,962	69,487	14,524	6,720	20,489	21,402
2000[4]	25,228	69,647	12,739	6,890	19,162	21,538
1999	23,584	69,094	12,203	6,929	18,112	22,075
1998	22,818	66,840	11,353	6,657	17,898	21,832
1997	21,528	65,771	10,725	6,614	16,906	21,824
1996	20,570	64,748	10,421	6,492	16,161	21,942
1995	19,414	63,587	9,790	6,678	15,970	21,073
1994	18,684	62,850	9,189	6,498	14,955	21,195
1993	17,900	61,937	9,462	6,425	14,446	21,391
1992	17,050	60,753	9,248	6,394	14,073	21,783
1991	16,320	60,226	8,818	6,875	13,523	22,398
1990	15,493	59,862	8,808	7,286	12,986	25,224
1989	14,809	59,296	8,268	7,363	12,468	25,377

[1]For data prior to 1991, "Some college/Associate degree" equals 1 to 3 years of college completed; "Bachelor's degree" equals 4 years of college; "Advanced degree" equals 5 or more years of college completed.
[2]Starting in 2011, earnings data were created using population controls based on Census 2010 data.
[3]Starting in 2003, respondents could choose more than one race. The race data in this table from 2003 onward represent respondents who indicated only one race.
[4]Beginning in 2000, earnings data are from the expanded Current Population Survey (CPS) sample and were calculated using population controls based on Census 2000.
[5]May be of any race.
… = Not available.

Table A-34. Mean Earnings of Workers 18 Years Old and Over, by Educational Attainment, Race, Hispanic Origin, and Sex, 1975–2018—*Continued*

(Dollars except as noted.)

Race, sex, year, and Hispanic origin	Some college or associate's degree[1]		Bachelor's degree[1]		Advanced degree[1]	
	Mean earnings	Number of workers (thousands)	Mean earnings	Number of workers (thousands)	Mean earnings	Number of workers (thousands)
2005........................	40,995	22,173	67,980	15,217	100,379	8,245
2004........................	39,488	21,477	63,697	14,877	97,702	8,044
2003[3]	38,451	21,534	63,084	14,849	91,831	8,019
2002........................	38,377	21,599	63,503	14,667	90,761	7,788
2001........................	37,429	21,390	63,354	14,507	90,130	7,631
2000[4]	37,372	21,526	62,609	14,375	88,077	7,442
1999........................	35,455	21,211	57,669	13,810	84,065	7,347
1998........................	34,179	20,545	55,057	13,486	77,217	6,942
1997........................	32,641	20,359	50,056	13,008	78,032	6,728
1996........................	31,426	20,208	46,702	12,562	74,406	6,636
1995........................	29,851	19,918	46,111	12,251	69,588	6,679
1994........................	27,636	19,859	46,278	12,324	67,032	6,663
1993........................	26,614	19,532	43,499	11,810	68,221	6,302
1992........................	25,366	19,009	39,912	11,340	58,166	6,312
1991........................	25,345	18,075	38,484	11,126	54,448	6,154
1990........................	26,120	14,844	38,901	9,807	49,768	7,402
1989........................	25,555	14,384	38,692	9,737	50,144	7,434
1988........................	23,827	14,019	35,906	9,466	45,677	7,449
1987........................	22,781	13,433	33,677	9,286	43,140	7,134
1986........................	21,784	13,502	33,376	8,908	41,836	7,009
1985........................	20,698	13,385	31,433	8,794	39,768	6,627
1984........................	18,863	12,818	29,203	8,387	35,804	6,648
1983........................	18,052	12,261	27,239	8,010	33,635	6,719
1982........................	17,108	12,103	25,758	7,865	32,109	6,594
1981........................	16,870	11,784	24,353	7,393	30,072	6,235
1980........................	15,871	11,663	23,340	7,132	27,846	5,733
1979........................	14,716	11,781	21,482	6,889	26,411	5,765
1978........................	13,382	11,352	19,861	6,611	24,274	5,422
1977........................	12,393	10,848	18,187	6,341	22,786	5,038
1976........................	11,376	10,282	16,714	6,135	21,202	4,868
1975........................	10,805	9,851	15,758	5,960	19,672	4,526
Female						
2018........................	33,771	23,600	57,551	20,148	78,664	12,088
2017........................	33,063	23,775	53,804	19,495	78,142	11,405
2016........................	32,391	24,236	52,461	18,645	74,656	11,043
2015........................	31,970	24,382	50,856	18,061	72,006	10,660
2014........................	30,064	23,966	48,650	17,580	65,814	10,049
2013........................	29,242	23,840	47,209	17,218	65,242	9,614
2012........................	28,588	24,202	47,477	16,773	67,182	9,213
2011[2]	28,275	23,529	47,418	16,419	65,915	8,697
2010........................	28,195	23,626	45,015	15,885	63,515	8,602
2009........................	28,207	23,344	43,589	15,900	64,771	8,176
2008........................	27,708	23,833	44,078	15,789	60,301	8,126
2007........................	28,773	23,660	43,127	15,722	59,273	7,873
2006........................	28,126	23,121	43,302	15,237	59,636	7,213
2005........................	26,348	23,260	40,684	14,440	55,553	6,906
2004........................	25,003	22,904	38,806	14,173	54,559	6,702
2003[3]	24,848	22,514	38,447	13,823	53,579	6,572
2002........................	23,905	22,176	37,909	13,589	50,756	6,330
2001........................	24,268	21,824	36,913	13,472	51,160	6,068
2000[4]	22,779	22,348	35,328	13,113	49,368	5,757
1999........................	21,675	21,808	32,547	12,680	46,369	5,602
1998........................	21,056	20,867	31,452	12,332	44,954	5,153
1997........................	19,856	20,442	30,119	12,027	42,744	4,863
1996........................	18,933	20,202	28,701	11,466	42,625	4,646
1995........................	17,962	20,224	26,841	11,034	37,813	4,578
1994........................	16,928	20,276	26,483	10,388	39,905	4,493
1993........................	16,555	19,897	25,232	10,005	37,212	4,218
1992........................	15,922	18,721	23,926	9,741	33,791	4,114
1991........................	15,643	17,657	22,800	9,349	32,932	3,949
1990........................	15,002	14,149	21,933	8,321	28,862	4,883
1989........................	14,688	13,694	21,089	8,030	26,977	4,831

[1]For data prior to 1991, "Some college/Associate degree" equals 1 to 3 years of college completed; "Bachelor's degree" equals 4 years of college; "Advanced degree" equals 5 or more years of college completed.
[2]Starting in 2011, earnings data were created using population controls based on Census 2010 data.
[3]Starting in 2003, respondents could choose more than one race. The race data in this table from 2003 onward represent respondents who indicated only one race.
[4]Beginning in 2000, earnings data are from the expanded Current Population Survey (CPS) sample and were calculated using population controls based on Census 2000.
[5]May be of any race.
… = Not available.

Table A-34. Mean Earnings of Workers 18 Years Old and Over, by Educational Attainment, Race, Hispanic Origin, and Sex, 1975–2018—*Continued*

(Dollars except as noted.)

Race, sex, year, and Hispanic origin	Total		Not a high school graduate		High school graduate	
	Mean earnings	Number of workers (thousands)	Mean earnings	Number of workers (thousands)	Mean earnings	Number of workers (thousands)
1988	13,833	58,558	7,711	7,642	11,857	25,217
1987	13,049	56,923	7,504	7,631	11,309	24,834
1986	12,214	55,568	7,109	7,457	10,606	24,542
1985	11,493	54,212	6,874	7,555	10,115	24,178
1984	10,742	53,178	6,644	7,881	9,561	23,625
1983	10,111	51,279	6,292	7,644	9,147	23,111
1982	9,403	49,962	5,932	7,921	8,715	22,525
1981	8,619	49,754	5,673	8,595	8,063	22,897
1980	7,909	49,094	5,263	8,755	7,423	22,772
1979	7,099	48,362	4,840	9,072	6,741	22,179
1978	6,396	45,850	4,397	9,237	6,192	20,860
1977	5,804	43,678	4,032	9,485	5,624	19,850
1976	5,373	42,091	3,723	9,401	5,240	19,071
1975	4,968	40,584	3,438	9,303	4,802	18,480

WHITE

Both Sexes

Race, sex, year, and Hispanic origin	Total		Not a high school graduate		High school graduate	
2018	57,035	128,742	27,675	9,470	40,744	33,256
2017	54,838	128,070	27,220	9,696	39,781	33,308
2016	53,178	127,241	28,489	9,615	38,326	33,491
2015	51,183	127,291	26,441	10,404	37,106	33,342
2014	48,971	125,227	26,065	10,553	35,528	33,616
2013	47,452	124,663	24,363	10,220	34,192	33,746
2012	46,844	124,316	22,048	10,491	33,928	33,498
2011[2]	46,053	123,044	21,704	10,891	33,719	33,803
2010	44,257	122,556	21,540	10,753	32,132	34,288
2009	43,337	125,151	20,457	11,507	31,429	36,125
2008	43,666	127,552	21,590	12,379	32,126	36,819
2007	43,139	127,413	22,289	12,363	32,223	37,058
2006	42,395	126,570	21,464	13,582	32,083	37,362
2005	40,717	124,870	20,264	13,157	30,569	37,122
2004	38,946	123,452	19,367	13,290	29,605	37,115
2003[3]	38,053	122,599	19,110	13,094	28,708	36,951
2002	37,376	122,699	19,264	13,740	28,145	37,380
2001	36,844	122,930	19,120	14,012	27,700	37,969
2000[4]	35,527	123,039	18,285	14,172	26,444	38,133
1999	33,342	121,518	16,651	13,912	25,267	38,622
1998	32,057	119,201	16,474	13,531	24,409	38,397
1997	30,515	117,985	16,596	13,780	23,618	38,409
1996	28,844	117,230	15,358	13,972	22,782	38,463
1995	27,556	115,636	14,234	13,869	22,154	37,802
1994	26,696	114,586	13,941	13,119	20,911	37,562
1993	25,440	113,342	13,171	13,480	19,918	37,826
1992	23,739	112,406	13,046	13,863	19,171	38,704
1991	22,998	111,842	12,914	14,041	18,766	39,769
1990	22,401	111,972	12,773	15,191	18,257	44,635
1989	22,035	111,243	12,654	15,628	18,011	44,726
1988	20,616	110,159	12,236	16,042	17,183	44,399
1987	19,599	108,407	12,502	16,165	16,339	44,235
1986	18,698	106,384	11,605	16,094	15,514	43,593
1985	17,709	104,818	11,115	16,149	14,815	43,347
1984	16,546	103,022	10,732	16,559	14,274	42,547
1983	15,556	101,035	10,239	16,568	13,357	42,007
1982	14,767	99,488	9,719	17,132	12,854	41,157
1981	14,027	99,510	9,737	18,298	12,355	42,080
1980	13,040	98,358	9,743	18,925	11,524	41,600
1979	12,155	97,544	8,827	19,504	10,431	40,458
1978	11,135	94,002	8,135	19,516	10,020	38,915
1977	10,191	91,254	7,415	20,492	9,173	37,521
1976	9,469	89,090	7,018	20,625	8,559	36,523
1975	8,815	86,894	6,438	20,696	8,005	35,799

[1]For data prior to 1991, "Some college/Associate degree" equals 1 to 3 years of college completed; "Bachelor's degree" equals 4 years of college; "Advanced degree" equals 5 or more years of college completed.
[2]Starting in 2011, earnings data were created using population controls based on Census 2010 data.
[3]Starting in 2003, respondents could choose more than one race. The race data in this table from 2003 onward represent respondents who indicated only one race.
[4]Beginning in 2000, earnings data are from the expanded Current Population Survey (CPS) sample and were calculated using population controls based on Census 2000.
[5]May be of any race.
… = Not available.

Table A-34. Mean Earnings of Workers 18 Years Old and Over, by Educational Attainment, Race, Hispanic Origin, and Sex, 1975–2018—*Continued*

(Dollars except as noted.)

Race, sex, year, and Hispanic origin	Some college or associate's degree[1]		Bachelor's degree[1]		Advanced degree[1]	
	Mean earnings	Number of workers (thousands)	Mean earnings	Number of workers (thousands)	Mean earnings	Number of workers (thousands)
1988	14,009	13,198	19,216	7,842	25,010	4,660
1987	13,158	12,971	18,217	7,211	24,004	4,277
1986	12,029	12,611	17,623	6,880	22,672	4,078
1985	11,504	12,017	16,114	6,579	21,202	3,883
1984	10,614	11,645	14,865	6,266	20,275	3,762
1983	9,981	10,947	13,808	5,919	18,593	3,658
1982	9,348	10,499	12,511	5,560	17,009	3,457
1981	8,811	9,975	11,384	5,186	15,647	3,101
1980	8,256	9,721	10,628	5,043	14,022	2,802
1979	7,190	9,393	9,474	4,862	12,717	2,856
1978	6,441	8,769	8,408	4,390	11,603	2,595
1977	5,856	8,057	7,923	4,016	10,848	2,271
1976	5,301	7,504	7,383	3,997	10,345	2,117
1975	5,019	7,066	6,963	3,804	9,818	1,931

WHITE

Both Sexes

Race, sex, year, and Hispanic origin	Some college or associate's degree[1]		Bachelor's degree[1]		Advanced degree[1]	
2018	44,379	36,543	73,348	31,770	100,195	17,702
2017	42,859	36,748	69,284	31,127	99,044	17,190
2016	41,583	37,481	68,538	29,950	95,647	16,701
2015	39,959	37,686	66,926	29,216	92,640	16,640
2014	39,590	36,920	63,422	28,313	88,835	15,823
2013	37,528	37,388	60,962	27,869	91,369	15,439
2012	36,943	37,706	61,527	27,651	90,948	14,967
2011[2]	36,204	36,861	61,253	27,096	90,060	14,391
2010	35,330	36,609	59,285	26,579	85,255	14,326
2009	35,634	37,035	57,762	26,595	86,188	13,887
2008	35,622	37,891	59,866	26,487	84,739	13,973
2007	35,685	37,988	58,652	26,310	82,384	13,692
2006	35,338	36,878	57,932	25,763	83,185	12,983
2005	34,326	37,409	55,785	24,652	81,697	12,527
2004	32,764	36,551	52,877	24,061	78,963	12,435
2003[3]	32,346	36,318	52,259	24,010	75,638	12,226
2002	31,878	36,023	52,479	23,638	73,870	11,916
2001	31,482	35,722	51,631	23,531	74,398	11,694
2000[4]	30,638	36,334	50,969	23,110	71,983	11,288
1999	29,225	35,575	46,914	22,382	68,418	11,027
1998	28,318	34,540	44,852	22,266	65,379	10,467
1997	26,906	34,274	41,439	21,528	65,058	9,994
1996	25,511	34,087	38,936	20,846	61,779	9,861
1995	24,349	33,850	37,711	20,203	57,054	9,914
1994	22,648	34,006	37,996	19,917	56,475	9,981
1993	21,924	33,728	35,846	18,922	56,964	9,386
1992	21,178	32,164	33,007	18,422	49,315	9,254
1991	21,013	30,977	31,837	18,035	46,496	9,019
1990	21,095	25,105	31,626	15,993	41,908	11,049
1989	20,678	24,212	31,266	15,723	41,610	10,952
1988	19,384	23,643	28,886	15,221	38,129	10,854
1987	18,265	23,083	27,741	14,624	36,175	10,300
1986	17,371	22,653	27,061	14,055	35,265	9,987
1985	16,701	22,131	25,376	13,670	33,401	9,522
1984	15,197	21,451	23,472	13,056	30,515	9,409
1983	14,486	20,452	21,914	12,577	28,532	9,430
1982	13,799	19,967	20,760	12,103	27,040	9,127
1981	13,424	19,102	19,389	11,450	25,564	8,582
1980	12,677	18,888	18,434	11,067	23,466	7,876
1979	11,574	18,835	16,758	10,807	22,085	7,940
1978	10,504	18,022	15,463	10,171	20,531	7,376
1977	9,771	16,968	14,462	9,534	19,337	6,739
1976	8,958	16,127	13,279	9,325	18,153	6,498
1975	8,525	15,423	12,597	8,955	16,920	6,021

[1]For data prior to 1991, "Some college/Associate degree" equals 1 to 3 years of college completed; "Bachelor's degree" equals 4 years of college; "Advanced degree" equals 5 or more years of college completed.
[2]Starting in 2011, earnings data were created using population controls based on Census 2010 data.
[3]Starting in 2003, respondents could choose more than one race. The race data in this table from 2003 onward represent respondents who indicated only one race.
[4]Beginning in 2000, earnings data are from the expanded Current Population Survey (CPS) sample and were calculated using population controls based on Census 2000.
[5]May be of any race.
… = Not available.

Table A-34. Mean Earnings of Workers 18 Years Old and Over, by Educational Attainment, Race, Hispanic Origin, and Sex, 1975–2018—*Continued*

(Dollars except as noted.)

Race, sex, year, and Hispanic origin	Total		Not a high school graduate		High school graduate	
	Mean earnings	Number of workers (thousands)	Mean earnings	Number of workers (thousands)	Mean earnings	Number of workers (thousands)
Male						
2018	66,977	69,057	32,458	6,098	47,199	19,815
2017	64,266	69,222	32,096	6,277	46,284	19,933
2016	62,680	68,496	33,153	6,255	45,390	19,941
2015	60,652	68,610	31,336	6,755	43,711	19,807
2014	58,387	67,466	30,342	6,858	41,492	19,815
2013	56,215	67,148	28,253	6,773	39,191	19,796
2012	55,802	66,906	25,725	6,809	40,070	19,390
2011[2]	55,013	66,151	25,819	6,917	40,247	19,524
2010	52,646	65,828	25,311	6,896	37,684	19,685
2009	51,287	67,464	23,353	7,426	36,418	20,855
2008	52,672	68,816	25,386	8,113	37,852	20,899
2007	51,781	69,099	25,886	8,170	38,214	21,129
2006	51,013	68,752	24,579	8,932	38,833	21,090
2005	49,611	67,874	23,556	8,582	36,753	20,914
2004	47,389	66,714	22,596	8,592	35,362	20,761
2003[3]	46,114	66,199	21,791	8,500	34,224	20,238
2002	45,793	66,202	22,539	8,841	33,920	20,156
2001	45,071	66,216	22,006	8,833	33,545	20,465
2000[4]	44,181	66,222	21,561	8,859	32,528	20,553
1999	41,622	65,134	19,279	8,549	31,289	20,579
1998	39,638	64,181	19,632	8,430	29,782	20,388
1997	37,933	63,738	20,071	8,670	29,298	20,426
1996	35,821	63,532	18,246	8,899	28,591	20,329
1995	34,276	62,520	17,032	8,660	27,467	19,982
1994	33,292	62,029	16,835	8,133	26,125	19,833
1993	31,719	61,356	15,295	8,430	24,781	19,835
1992	29,201	61,270	15,180	8,776	23,677	20,333
1991	28,516	60,770	15,499	8,720	23,475	20,765
1990	28,105	60,676	15,319	9,476	23,135	23,088
1989	28,013	60,877	15,217	9,805	23,291	23,029
1988	26,184	60,221	14,943	10,008	22,216	22,707
1987	24,898	59,468	15,303	10,132	21,012	22,682
1986	23,892	58,932	14,168	10,239	20,128	22,392
1985	22,604	58,385	13,579	10,163	19,203	22,357
1984	21,174	57,362	13,248	10,280	18,681	21,989
1983	19,812	56,641	12,573	10,387	17,281	21,733
1982	18,859	56,364	11,952	10,816	16,662	21,436
1981	18,141	56,397	12,094	11,523	16,352	21,809
1980	16,945	55,772	11,539	11,937	15,382	21,453
1979	15,971	55,556	11,127	12,291	13,916	20,834
1978	14,627	54,113	10,358	12,141	13,534	20,328
1977	13,329	53,174	9,366	12,903	12,377	19,773
1976	12,342	52,312	8,867	13,117	11,497	19,446
1975	11,448	51,510	8,110	13,191	10,726	19,361
Female						
2018	45,531	59,684	19,024	3,371	31,228	13,441
2017	43,749	58,847	18,270	3,419	30,089	13,374
2016	42,098	58,744	19,807	3,360	27,929	13,549
2015	40,112	58,680	17,379	3,649	27,440	13,535
2014	37,971	57,761	18,129	3,695	26,965	13,800
2013	37,222	57,515	16,718	3,446	27,097	13,949
2012	36,404	57,409	15,250	3,682	25,487	14,107
2011[2]	35,635	56,892	14,541	3,974	24,793	14,279
2010	34,521	56,728	14,799	3,857	24,648	14,603
2009	34,040	57,687	15,187	4,080	24,615	15,270
2008	33,115	58,735	14,370	4,265	24,610	15,919
2007	32,899	58,313	15,278	4,192	24,276	15,929
2006	32,148	57,818	15,483	4,650	23,334	16,272
2005	30,125	56,995	14,086	4,575	22,590	16,208
2004	29,018	56,738	13,461	4,698	22,296	16,354

[1]For data prior to 1991, "Some college/Associate degree" equals 1 to 3 years of college completed; "Bachelor's degree" equals 4 years of college; "Advanced degree" equals 5 or more years of college completed.
[2]Starting in 2011, earnings data were created using population controls based on Census 2010 data.
[3]Starting in 2003, respondents could choose more than one race. The race data in this table from 2003 onward represent respondents who indicated only one race.
[4]Beginning in 2000, earnings data are from the expanded Current Population Survey (CPS) sample and were calculated using population controls based on Census 2000.
[5]May be of any race.
… = Not available.

Table A-34. Mean Earnings of Workers 18 Years Old and Over, by Educational Attainment, Race, Hispanic Origin, and Sex, 1975–2018—*Continued*

(Dollars except as noted.)

Race, sex, year, and Hispanic origin	Some college or associate's degree[1]		Bachelor's degree[1]		Advanced degree[1]	
	Mean earnings	Number of workers (thousands)	Mean earnings	Number of workers (thousands)	Mean earnings	Number of workers (thousands)
Male						
2018..........................	54,482	18,546	87,842	16,080	125,533	8,516
2017..........................	51,974	18,724	83,478	15,913	122,160	8,373
2016..........................	50,063	18,951	84,069	15,136	116,854	8,211
2015..........................	47,900	18,905	82,495	14,884	115,094	8,257
2014..........................	48,405	18,518	78,348	14,409	112,351	7,864
2013..........................	45,403	18,729	74,018	14,113	117,959	7,735
2012..........................	45,049	18,825	74,594	14,268	114,150	7,612
2011[2]	44,155	18,279	73,630	13,978	112,515	7,451
2010..........................	42,479	18,019	72,241	13,845	106,142	7,383
2009..........................	42,884	18,273	71,286	13,740	106,571	7,168
2008..........................	43,463	18,849	75,053	13,596	107,099	7,356
2007..........................	42,903	18,995	73,477	13,577	103,293	7,227
2006..........................	42,684	18,340	71,735	13,326	103,340	7,063
2005..........................	42,206	18,583	69,852	12,900	103,144	6,893
2004..........................	40,617	18,005	65,583	12,582	99,899	6,774
2003[3]	39,594	18,060	65,264	12,665	94,017	6,734
2002..........................	39,605	18,068	65,439	12,512	92,733	6,623
2001..........................	38,501	17,957	65,046	12,396	92,304	6,562
2000[4]	38,476	18,179	64,831	12,271	89,812	6,359
1999..........................	36,757	17,831	59,672	11,869	85,405	6,307
1998..........................	35,277	17,407	56,620	11,874	79,734	6,083
1997..........................	33,691	17,423	51,678	11,340	80,322	5,879
1996..........................	32,238	17,418	48,014	11,065	75,481	5,821
1995..........................	30,529	17,136	47,016	10,851	70,155	5,891
1994..........................	28,240	17,091	47,575	10,992	67,629	5,979
1993..........................	27,297	16,959	44,505	10,452	70,000	5,680
1992..........................	26,095	16,468	40,802	10,040	59,297	5,651
1991..........................	26,090	15,873	39,547	9,893	55,256	5,519
1990..........................	26,841	13,003	39,780	8,770	50,385	6,731
1989..........................	26,260	12,582	39,654	8,750	51,031	6,710
1988..........................	24,462	12,277	36,637	8,467	46,181	6,762
1987..........................	23,310	11,771	34,865	8,384	43,440	6,499
1986..........................	22,303	11,846	34,273	8,041	42,480	6,413
1985..........................	21,240	11,831	32,165	7,970	40,358	6,064
1984..........................	19,344	11,387	29,781	7,624	36,219	6,081
1983..........................	18,388	10,974	27,726	7,379	33,981	6,168
1982..........................	17,571	10,822	26,404	7,242	32,266	6,047
1981..........................	17,303	10,448	24,943	6,824	30,396	5,794
1980..........................	16,313	10,400	23,803	6,618	27,991	5,363
1979..........................	15,043	10,572	21,785	6,464	26,645	5,395
1978..........................	13,589	10,350	20,085	6,205	24,635	5,088
1977..........................	12,657	9,853	18,521	5,941	23,093	4,704
1976..........................	11,616	9,394	16,995	5,765	21,490	4,589
1975..........................	11,028	9,096	16,079	5,587	19,858	4,275
Female						
2018..........................	33,968	17,996	58,494	15,690	76,703	9,185
2017..........................	33,390	18,023	54,436	15,213	77,089	8,816
2016..........................	32,911	18,530	52,669	14,814	75,138	8,490
2015..........................	31,966	18,781	50,759	14,332	70,520	8,382
2014..........................	30,718	18,401	47,954	13,904	65,599	7,959
2013..........................	29,622	18,658	47,565	13,755	64,670	7,704
2012..........................	28,861	18,881	47,596	13,383	66,934	7,355
2011[2]	28,383	18,581	48,064	13,117	65,952	6,940
2010..........................	28,400	18,590	45,200	12,735	63,046	6,943
2009..........................	28,573	16,762	43,309	12,855	64,441	6,718
2008..........................	27,859	19,041	43,848	12,891	59,877	6,616
2007..........................	28,466	18,993	42,846	12,733	59,006	6,464
2006..........................	28,069	18,537	43,142	12,437	59,141	5,920
2005..........................	26,547	18,825	40,344	11,751	55,461	5,634
2004..........................	25,140	18,546	38,950	11,479	53,910	5,661

[1]For data prior to 1991, "Some college/Associate degree" equals 1 to 3 years of college completed; "Bachelor's degree" equals 4 years of college; "Advanced degree" equals 5 or more years of college completed.
[2]Starting in 2011, earnings data were created using population controls based on Census 2010 data.
[3]Starting in 2003, respondents could choose more than one race. The race data in this table from 2003 onward represent respondents who indicated only one race.
[4]Beginning in 2000, earnings data are from the expanded Current Population Survey (CPS) sample and were calculated using population controls based on Census 2000.
[5]May be of any race.
... = Not available.

Table A-34. Mean Earnings of Workers 18 Years Old and Over, by Educational Attainment, Race, Hispanic Origin, and Sex, 1975–2018—*Continued*

(Dollars except as noted.)

Race, sex, year, and Hispanic origin	Total		Not a high school graduate		High school graduate	
	Mean earnings	Number of workers (thousands)	Mean earnings	Number of workers (thousands)	Mean earnings	Number of workers (thousands)
2003[3]	28,591	56,400	14,149	4,593	22,028	16,712
2002	27,512	56,496	13,354	4,898	21,388	17,224
2001	27,240	56,714	14,197	5,178	20,866	17,503
2000[4]	25,441	56,816	12,823	5,313	19,330	17,579
1999	23,778	56,385	12,463	5,364	18,400	18,044
1998	23,213	55,020	11,255	5,102	18,327	18,009
1997	21,779	54,247	10,700	5,111	17,166	17,983
1996	20,590	53,697	10,290	5,073	16,270	18,134
1995	19,647	53,117	9,582	5,208	16,196	17,820
1994	18,912	52,557	9,220	4,987	15,078	17,729
1993	18,028	51,986	9,624	5,050	14,557	17,991
1992	17,194	51,137	9,363	5,087	14,184	18,370
1991	16,431	51,072	8,677	5,321	13,621	19,004
1990	15,559	50,905	8,725	5,715	13,031	21,547
1989	14,810	50,366	8,338	5,823	12,406	21,697
1988	13,902	49,938	7,747	6,034	11,915	21,692
1987	13,161	48,939	7,798	6,033	11,421	21,553
1986	12,247	47,452	7,123	5,855	10,641	21,201
1985	11,555	46,433	6,931	5,986	10,142	20,990
1984	10,732	45,660	6,614	6,279	9,561	20,558
1983	10,126	44,394	6,317	6,181	9,150	20,274
1982	9,419	43,124	5,896	6,316	8,714	19,721
1981	8,646	43,113	5,727	6,775	8,054	20,271
1980	7,926	42,586	6,675	6,988	7,415	20,147
1979	7,105	41,988	4,909	7,213	6,731	19,624
1978	6,398	39,889	4,476	7,375	6,176	18,587
1977	5,808	38,080	4,097	7,589	5,604	17,748
1976	5,383	36,787	3,788	7,508	5,214	17,077
1975	4,982	35,384	3,500	7,505	4,800	16,438
NON-HISPANIC WHITE						
Both Sexes						
2018	61,057	103,357	27,707	3,784	42,466	25,039
2017	58,601	103,373	27,145	4,032	41,289	25,484
2016	56,574	103,334	27,014	3,981	39,265	25,971
2015	54,352	103,957	26,974	4,394	38,588	25,921
2014	52,171	102,756	29,080	4,344	36,826	26,583
2013	50,604	102,814	26,750	4,136	35,595	27,119
2012	49,981	102,974	23,126	4,503	35,399	26,822
2011[2]	49,147	102,365	22,642	4,849	35,365	27,313
2010	47,033	102,462	22,584	4,822	33,360	28,045
2009	45,939	105,137	21,229	5,216	32,562	29,860
2008	46,179	107,294	21,765	5,798	33,159	30,598
2007	45,542	107,434	23,015	5,908	33,094	30,855
2006	44,813	106,828	22,206	6,876	32,931	31,345
2005	42,963	106,337	21,134	6,603	31,445	31,484
2004	40,943	105,506	19,742	6,755	30,197	31,793
2003[3]	40,094	105,214	19,769	6,768	29,571	31,831
2002	39,220	105,706	19,423	7,380	28,756	32,365
2001	38,711	106,384	19,659	7,812	28,426	33,050
2000[4]	37,346	106,709	19,147	7,957	27,122	33,231
1999	35,010	106,139	17,098	8,171	25,924	33,983
1998	33,336	105,523	16,837	8,488	24,801	34,344
Male						
2018	72,737	54,698	33,657	2,360	49,509	14,761
2017	69,548	55,091	32,263	2,530	48,476	15,170
2016	67,180	54,893	31,668	2,543	46,416	15,315
2015	65,206	55,185	33,263	2,799	45,748	15,274
2014	63,100	54,432	35,105	2,752	43,312	15,583

[1]For data prior to 1991, "Some college/Associate degree" equals 1 to 3 years of college completed; "Bachelor's degree" equals 4 years of college; "Advanced degree" equals 5 or more years of college completed.
[2]Starting in 2011, earnings data were created using population controls based on Census 2010 data.
[3]Starting in 2003, respondents could choose more than one race. The race data in this table from 2003 onward represent respondents who indicated only one race.
[4]Beginning in 2000, earnings data are from the expanded Current Population Survey (CPS) sample and were calculated using population controls based on Census 2000.
[5]May be of any race.
… = Not available.

Table A-34. Mean Earnings of Workers 18 Years Old and Over, by Educational Attainment, Race, Hispanic Origin, and Sex, 1975–2018—*Continued*

(Dollars except as noted.)

Race, sex, year, and Hispanic origin	Some college or associate's degree[1]		Bachelor's degree[1]		Advanced degree[1]	
	Mean earnings	Number of workers (thousands)	Mean earnings	Number of workers (thousands)	Mean earnings	Number of workers (thousands)
2003[3]	25,177	18,258	37,739	11,344	53,102	5,492
2002	24,101	17,954	37,903	11,126	50,270	5,293
2001	24,387	17,764	36,698	11,135	51,499	5,131
2000[4]	22,790	18,155	35,273	10,838	48,982	4,929
1999	21,655	17,744	32,510	10,513	45,722	4,720
1998	21,246	17,132	31,406	10,393	45,462	4,384
1997	19,892	16,852	30,041	10,188	43,236	4,114
1996	18,482	16,669	28,667	9,781	42,049	4,041
1995	18,011	16,714	26,916	9,352	37,864	4,022
1994	16,998	16,915	26,198	8,925	39,816	4,002
1993	16,490	16,769	25,161	8,470	36,988	3,705
1992	16,018	15,695	23,670	8,382	33,655	3,602
1991	15,677	15,104	22,469	8,143	32,685	3,501
1990	14,922	12,102	21,725	7,223	28,694	4,318
1989	14,640	11,630	20,741	6,973	26,709	4,242
1988	13,898	11,366	19,169	6,754	24,824	4,092
1987	13,015	11,312	18,170	6,240	23,753	3,801
1986	11,964	10,807	17,418	6,014	22,320	3,574
1985	11,488	10,300	15,883	5,700	21,202	3,458
1984	10,504	10,064	14,617	5,432	20,092	3,328
1983	9,969	9,478	13,664	5,198	18,230	3,262
1982	9,336	9,145	12,352	4,861	16,779	3,080
1981	8,740	8,654	11,196	4,626	15,523	2,788
1980	8,221	8,488	10,447	4,449	13,809	2,513
1979	7,135	8,263	9,275	4,343	12,420	2,545
1978	6,342	7,672	8,231	3,966	11,404	2,288
1977	5,774	7,115	7,750	3,593	10,655	2,035
1976	5,250	6,733	7,262	3,560	10,131	1,909
1975	4,926	6,327	6,822	3,368	9,728	1,746
NON-HISPANIC WHITE						
Both Sexes						
2018	45,772	29,939	74,950	28,312	101,350	16,281
2017	43,996	30,141	71,054	27,773	100,150	15,941
2016	42,932	30,953	70,220	26,916	96,689	15,510
2015	40,812	31,693	67,636	26,508	93,599	15,438
2014	40,487	31,236	64,462	25,783	89,735	14,808
2013	38,371	31,688	61,913	25,437	92,569	14,432
2012	37,942	32,362	62,537	25,246	91,627	14,039
2011[2]	36,992	31,780	62,389	24,891	90,659	13,529
2010	36,079	31,698	60,257	24,425	86,040	13,473
2009	36,249	32,430	58,487	24,533	86,770	13,095
2008	36,158	33,221	60,866	24,445	85,017	13,230
2007	36,290	33,431	59,727	24,366	82,900	12,871
2006	35,872	32,403	58,917	23,855	83,785	12,347
2005	34,866	33,355	56,462	23,013	82,205	11,879
2004	33,217	32,560	53,411	22,545	79,355	11,853
2003[3]	32,825	32,460	52,856	22,474	76,200	11,680
2002	32,318	32,344	53,185	22,221	74,122	11,395
2001	31,905	32,118	52,300	22,204	74,932	11,198
2000[4]	31,217	32,836	51,351	21,824	72,356	10,859
1999	29,765	32,155	47,480	21,261	68,946	10,569
1998	23,897	31,459	45,342	21,175	65,461	10,059
Male						
2018	56,700	15,278	90,455	14,407	126,583	7,890
2017	53,779	15,353	85,885	14,239	123,866	7,797
2016	51,782	15,718	86,312	13,676	118,068	7,639
2015	49,241	15,920	83,548	13,498	116,321	7,692
2014	49,712	15,606	80,075	13,117	113,515	7,372

[1]For data prior to 1991, "Some college/Associate degree" equals 1 to 3 years of college completed; "Bachelor's degree" equals 4 years of college; "Advanced degree" equals 5 or more years of college completed.
[2]Starting in 2011, earnings data were created using population controls based on Census 2010 data.
[3]Starting in 2003, respondents could choose more than one race. The race data in this table from 2003 onward represent respondents who indicated only one race.
[4]Beginning in 2000, earnings data are from the expanded Current Population Survey (CPS) sample and were calculated using population controls based on Census 2000.
[5]May be of any race.
… = Not available.

Table A-34. Mean Earnings of Workers 18 Years Old and Over, by Educational Attainment, Race, Hispanic Origin, and Sex, 1975–2018—*Continued*

(Dollars except as noted.)

Race, sex, year, and Hispanic origin	Total		Not a high school graduate		High school graduate	
	Mean earnings	Number of workers (thousands)	Mean earnings	Number of workers (thousands)	Mean earnings	Number of workers (thousands)
2013...........................	60,804	54,529	32,329	2,717	40,991	15,819
2012...........................	60,396	54,569	28,026	2,784	42,157	15,388
2011[2]	59,584	54,244	27,872	2,978	42,772	15,644
2010...........................	56,719	54,268	27,427	2,989	39,449	15,938
2009...........................	55,318	55,638	25,695	3,187	38,160	17,015
2008...........................	56,538	56,822	26,479	3,654	39,405	17,206
2007...........................	55,662	57,080	27,874	3,716	39,764	17,309
2006...........................	54,843	56,843	26,100	4,289	40,180	17,470
2005...........................	53,263	56,675	25,511	4,127	38,134	17,507
2004...........................	50,597	55,930	23,590	4,204	36,324	17,568
2003[3]	49,386	55,774	22,957	4,224	35,589	17,225
2002...........................	48,817	55,994	23,250	4,580	34,909	17,218
2001...........................	47,973	56,528	23,096	4,749	34,627	17,672
2000[4]	47,084	56,675	23,296	4,763	33,669	17,733
1999...........................	44,403	56,071	20,502	4,787	32,532	17,844
1998...........................	41,612	56,246	20,781	5,152	30,429	18,048
Female						
2018...........................	47,928	48,659	17,849	1,424	32,350	10,277
2017...........................	46,110	48,282	18,522	1,502	30,718	10,313
2016...........................	44,556	48,441	18,777	1,437	28,989	10,656
2015...........................	42,070	48,771	15,942	1,595	28,315	10,646
2014...........................	39,860	48,324	18,662	1,591	27,637	10,999
2013...........................	39,084	48,284	16,062	1,418	28,041	11,300
2012...........................	38,240	48,405	15,189	1,718	26,303	11,433
2011[2]	37,382	48,120	14,314	1,870	25,435	11,669
2010...........................	36,125	48,194	14,687	1,833	25,343	12,107
2009...........................	35,396	49,498	14,216	2,029	25,147	12,845
2008...........................	34,517	50,471	13,730	2,144	25,133	13,391
2007...........................	34,069	50,353	14,779	2,192	24,570	13,546
2006...........................	33,407	49,984	15,751	2,857	23,805	13,875
2005...........................	31,208	49,661	13,837	2,476	23,004	13,977
2004...........................	30,051	49,576	13,401	2,551	22,631	14,225
2003[3]	29,613	49,439	14,475	2,543	22,473	14,605
2002...........................	28,410	49,712	13,163	2,800	21,762	15,146
2001...........................	28,210	49,856	14,328	3,062	21,301	15,378
2000[4]	26,315	50,034	12,962	3,194	19,631	15,498
1999...........................	24,492	50,068	12,283	3,384	18,618	16,139
1998...........................	23,891	49,277	10,746	3,336	18,568	16,295
BLACK						
Both Sexes						
2018...........................	42,382	20,439	23,817	1,466	31,675	6,338
2017...........................	41,570	20,112	23,690	1,329	31,889	6,293
2016...........................	40,767	19,755	24,054	1,496	30,131	6,150
2015...........................	39,394	19,150	19,783	1,582	29,211	6,015
2014...........................	37,012	18,657	22,353	1,420	28,439	5,905
2013...........................	35,817	18,023	21,403	1,590	26,670	5,689
2012...........................	34,800	17,838	18,889	1,486	26,625	5,639
2011[2]	34,755	17,295	17,488	1,613	27,562	5,539
2010...........................	32,900	17,016	17,849	1,643	25,781	5,557
2009...........................	33,362	16,744	18,936	1,618	26,970	5,803
2008...........................	32,874	17,509	18,123	1,748	27,265	6,060
2007...........................	33,333	17,453	17,439	1,854	27,179	5,996
2006...........................	32,443	17,234	17,823	1,943	26,368	6,159
2005...........................	30,472	17,000	17,216	2,025	23,904	6,101
2004...........................	29,096	16,632	17,827	2,044	23,498	6,139
2003[3]	28,838	16,389	16,201	2,095	23,777	5,941
2002...........................	28,179	16,352	16,516	2,148	22,823	5,822
2001...........................	27,031	16,683	17,248	2,382	21,743	5,729
2000[4]	26,204	16,756	15,201	2,434	21,789	6,020

[1]For data prior to 1991, "Some college/Associate degree" equals 1 to 3 years of college completed; "Bachelor's degree" equals 4 years of college; "Advanced degree" equals 5 or more years of college completed.
[2]Starting in 2011, earnings data were created using population controls based on Census 2010 data.
[3]Starting in 2003, respondents could choose more than one race. The race data in this table from 2003 onward represent respondents who indicated only one race.
[4]Beginning in 2000, earnings data are from the expanded Current Population Survey (CPS) sample and were calculated using population controls based on Census 2000.
[5]May be of any race.
... = Not available.

Table A-34. Mean Earnings of Workers 18 Years Old and Over, by Educational Attainment, Race, Hispanic Origin, and Sex, 1975–2018—*Continued*

(Dollars except as noted.)

Race, sex, year, and Hispanic origin	Some college or associate's degree[1]		Bachelor's degree[1]		Advanced degree[1]	
	Mean earnings	Number of workers (thousands)	Mean earnings	Number of workers (thousands)	Mean earnings	Number of workers (thousands)
2013........................	46,713	15,873	75,345	12,910	120,004	7,208
2012........................	46,477	16,175	75,826	13,080	115,598	7,139
2011[2]	45,443	15,675	75,168	12,900	113,244	7,045
2010........................	43,567	15,564	73,425	12,791	107,361	6,987
2009........................	43,802	15,981	72,305	12,708	107,872	6,746
2008........................	44,237	16,439	76,613	12,562	107,498	6,960
2007........................	43,835	16,684	75,214	12,597	104,317	6,772
2006........................	43,589	16,024	73,376	12,321	104,031	6,738
2005........................	43,137	16,456	70,932	12,048	104,107	6,535
2004........................	41,467	15,952	66,527	11,739	100,533	6,467
2003[3]	40,316	16,048	66,390	11,849	95,029	6,427
2002........................	40,368	16,121	66,638	11,764	93,686	6,309
2001........................	39,133	16,114	66,196	11,692	92,954	6,299
2000[4]	39,379	16,435	65,459	11,594	90,150	6,149
1999........................	37,651	16,087	60,564	11,283	86,004	6,070
1998........................	29,555	15,849	57,346	11,335	79,524	5,862
Female						
2018........................	34,384	14,661	58,885	13,904	77,623	8,391
2017........................	33,840	14,788	55,450	13,533	77,446	8,144
2016........................	33,801	15,235	53,598	13,240	75,942	7,871
2015........................	32,304	15,772	51,126	13,009	71,035	7,746
2014........................	31,276	15,630	48,291	12,665	66,161	7,436
2013........................	29,999	15,815	48,070	12,526	65,190	7,223
2012........................	29,413	16,187	48,247	12,165	66,824	6,900
2011[2]	28,766	16,105	48,640	11,990	66,120	6,484
2010........................	28,856	16,134	45,779	11,634	63,074	6,486
2009........................	28,911	16,448	43,636	11,825	64,351	6,349
2008........................	28,244	16,781	44,220	11,883	60,063	6,270
2007........................	28,772	16,746	43,150	11,769	59,121	6,099
2006........................	28,322	16,379	43,473	11,534	59,458	5,608
2005........................	26,812	16,899	40,562	10,964	55,422	5,344
2004........................	25,294	16,609	39,161	10,805	53,927	5,386
2003[3]	25,499	16,411	37,761	10,624	53,164	5,253
2002........................	24,318	16,222	38,049	10,457	49,845	5,085
2001........................	24,628	16,004	36,844	10,512	51,756	4,898
2000[4]	23,038	16,401	35,362	10,230	49,126	4,710
1999........................	21,869	16,067	32,687	9,979	45,934	4,499
1998........................	18,198	15,610	31,516	9,840	45,805	4,196
BLACK						
Both Sexes						
2018........................	38,299	6,651	54,959	3,837	76,871	2,145
2017........................	36,777	6,816	53,938	3,740	78,350	1,932
2016........................	34,740	6,841	57,409	3,394	80,903	1,873
2015........................	34,653	6,606	55,506	3,220	80,976	1,725
2014........................	32,074	6,605	51,983	3,084	72,257	1,642
2013........................	32,137	6,228	49,904	2,997	72,496	1,517
2012........................	31,730	6,398	48,972	2,854	68,329	1,459
2011[2]	32,891	5,964	45,477	2,796	70,140	1,380
2010........................	30,592	5,969	44,502	2,593	71,127	1,255
2009........................	30,520	5,577	47,799	2,583	66,923	1,162
2008........................	30,248	5,933	46,527	2,550	66,198	1,216
2007........................	32,787	5,813	46,502	2,682	64,247	1,107
2006........................	31,234	5,581	47,903	2,503	64,834	1,045
2005........................	28,848	5,390	47,101	2,412	63,664	1,071
2004........................	27,779	5,192	42,342	2,348	65,538	909
2003[3]	27,187	5,119	42,968	2,321	64,164	911
2002........................	27,626	5,255	42,285	2,275	59,944	851
2001........................	26,907	5,481	40,165	2,212	55,771	877
2000[4]	26,324	5,431	41,513	2,060	52,373	809

[1]For data prior to 1991, "Some college/Associate degree" equals 1 to 3 years of college completed; "Bachelor's degree" equals 4 years of college; "Advanced degree" equals 5 or more years of college completed.
[2]Starting in 2011, earnings data were created using population controls based on Census 2010 data.
[3]Starting in 2003, respondents could choose more than one race. The race data in this table from 2003 onward represent respondents who indicated only one race.
[4]Beginning in 2000, earnings data are from the expanded Current Population Survey (CPS) sample and were calculated using population controls based on Census 2000.
[5]May be of any race.
... = Not available.

Table A-34. Mean Earnings of Workers 18 Years Old and Over, by Educational Attainment, Race, Hispanic Origin, and Sex, 1975–2018—*Continued*

(Dollars except as noted.)

Race, sex, year, and Hispanic origin	Total		Not a high school graduate		High school graduate	
	Mean earnings	Number of workers (thousands)	Mean earnings	Number of workers (thousands)	Mean earnings	Number of workers (thousands)
1999	24,930	17,107	13,505	2,451	21,008	6,188
1998	22,829	16,201	13,672	2,402	19,236	6,053
1997	21,909	15,873	13,185	2,437	18,980	5,964
1996	21,978	15,255	13,110	2,383	18,722	5,844
1995	20,537	14,847	12,956	2,389	17,072	5,453
1994	19,772	14,754	12,705	2,290	16,446	5,596
1993	18,614	14,315	11,065	2,352	16,122	5,521
1992	17,397	14,087	11,091	2,444	15,230	5,498
1991	16,809	13,865	11,248	2,860	15,060	5,512
1990	16,627	13,731	11,184	2,853	14,794	6,049
1989	16,072	13,600	10,066	2,883	14,613	5,894
1988	15,318	13,356	10,202	2,970	13,835	5,760
1987	14,136	13,023	9,976	3,015	12,862	5,699
1986	13,494	12,729	9,365	3,028	12,276	5,470
1985	12,926	12,427	9,116	3,009	11,791	5,223
1984	12,002	11,948	8,725	3,127	10,882	4,927
1983	11,299	11,296	7,867	3,035	10,557	4,692
1982	10,612	11,081	7,799	3,188	10,287	4,591
1981	10,117	11,088	7,520	3,514	9,994	4,388
1980	11,085	5,576	8,421	2,054	11,563	2,119
1979	8,720	10,856	6,424	3,776	8,723	4,267
1978	7,981	10,420	5,918	3,841	8,152	3,944
1977	7,271	10,014	5,406	3,946	7,553	3,604
1976	6,716	9,744	5,304	4,008	6,805	3,515
1975	6,190	9,368	4,989	3,922	6,281	3,495
Male						
2018	46,402	9,484	28,044	754	36,716	3,358
2017	46,085	9,427	27,150	656	36,451	3,406
2016	46,686	9,231	26,919	769	34,968	3,235
2015	43,781	8,979	23,846	796	33,881	3,158
2014	42,454	8,645	25,516	746	32,836	3,036
2013	40,785	8,348	26,346	843	29,893	2,887
2012	38,244	8,293	19,497	800	30,276	2,891
2011[2]	38,633	7,951	21,035	812	31,219	2,811
2010	35,828	7,801	19,893	884	29,560	2,888
2009	37,553	7,657	21,828	861	30,723	2,996
2008	36,057	8,116	22,344	866	30,985	3,166
2007	35,668	8,088	19,705	985	29,640	2,994
2006	36,045	7,932	21,294	982	30,122	3,067
2005	34,165	7,836	19,890	1,056	27,360	3,050
2004	33,020	7,669	22,796	1,030	26,608	3,120
2003[3]	32,545	7,469	17,915	1,039	28,102	2,910
2002	31,790	7,483	19,294	1,072	25,582	2,832
2001	30,502	7,727	18,543	1,210	25,037	2,759
2000[4]	30,109	7,700	17,992	1,235	25,219	2,942
1999	28,533	8,032	16,109	1,258	25,680	3,024
1998	26,090	7,488	16,013	1,190	22,698	2,974
1997	25,080	7,370	15,423	1,304	22,440	2,862
1996	25,067	7,125	15,461	1,290	22,267	2,836
1995	23,876	7,090	14,877	1,280	19,514	2,812
1994	22,614	7,009	15,984	1,191	18,527	2,818
1993	21,108	6,833	13,074	1,305	18,668	2,775
1992	19,317	6,922	12,748	1,439	16,963	2,744
1991	18,607	6,830	12,845	1,624	17,352	2,731
1990	18,859	6,781	13,031	1,563	17,046	3,013
1989	18,108	6,654	11,827	1,614	16,658	2,848
1988	17,782	6,593	12,439	1,671	16,345	2,795
1987	16,171	6,505	11,899	1,711	14,800	2,769
1986	15,441	6,326	11,248	1,691	14,214	2,666
1985	14,932	6,237	10,802	1,716	13,721	2,572
1984	13,560	5,899	10,216	1,780	12,382	2,339

[1]For data prior to 1991, "Some college/Associate degree" equals 1 to 3 years of college completed; "Bachelor's degree" equals 4 years of college; "Advanced degree" equals 5 or more years of college completed.
[2]Starting in 2011, earnings data were created using population controls based on Census 2010 data.
[3]Starting in 2003, respondents could choose more than one race. The race data in this table from 2003 onward represent respondents who indicated only one race.
[4]Beginning in 2000, earnings data are from the expanded Current Population Survey (CPS) sample and were calculated using population controls based on Census 2000.
[5]May be of any race.
… = Not available.

Table A-34. Mean Earnings of Workers 18 Years Old and Over, by Educational Attainment, Race, Hispanic Origin, and Sex, 1975–2018—*Continued*

(Dollars except as noted.)

Race, sex, year, and Hispanic origin	Some college or associate's degree[1]		Bachelor's degree[1]		Advanced degree[1]	
	Mean earnings	Number of workers (thousands)	Mean earnings	Number of workers (thousands)	Mean earnings	Number of workers (thousands)
1999........................	25,169	5,437	37,362	2,155	52,516	876.836
1998........................	23,927	4,559	36,373	1,897	44,760	764
1997........................	22,899	4,902	32,062	1,846	42,791	724
1996........................	23,628	4,783	31,955	1,655	48,731	590
1995........................	21,824	4,727	29,666	1,684	46,654	595
1994........................	19,631	4,610	30,938	1,679	48,653	579
1993........................	18,867	4,279	29,953	1,638	41,221	525
1992........................	17,702	4,151	27,365	1,463	39,014	530
1991........................	17,598	3,581	25,630	1,383	36,735	528
1990........................	18,209	3,004	26,448	1,217	32,962	607
1989........................	17,385	3,008	25,357	1,121	32,740	694
1988........................	16,760	2,802	23,689	1,204	30,802	621
1987........................	15,491	2,617	20,805	1,097	29,163	596
1986........................	14,743	2,662	21,403	1,004	27,503	564
1985........................	13,805	2,615	20,533	1,046	26,246	535
1984........................	12,890	2,396	19,330	937	24,072	561
1983........................	12,426	2,206	17,207	828	23,506	535
1982........................	11,119	2,067	15,152	747	22,959	488
1981........................	11,456	2,078	14,587	708	19,463	398
1980........................	12,393	964	15,616	283	19,960	353
1979........................	9,895	1,826	13,473	622	18,182	366
1978........................	9,026	1,689	12,870	557	15,076	389
1977........................	8,321	1,578	11,088	532	14,749	354
1976........................	7,331	1,370	10,331	547	15,013	305
1975........................	7,212	1,193	9,473	517	12,333	241
Male						
2018........................	44,903	2,887	58,970	1,740	85,193	743
2017........................	41,410	3,002	61,434	1,628	92,812	733
2016........................	39,407	3,004	70,026	1,531	103,465	691
2015........................	39,459	2,874	63,477	1,466	88,699	683
2014........................	37,116	2,831	60,458	1,376	91,652	653
2013........................	38,126	2,696	57,304	1,312	88,641	608
2012........................	36,043	2,804	53,983	1,210	81,253	585
2011[2]	38,029	2,654	49,390	1,155	85,528	518
2010........................	34,405	2,479	48,560	1,067	81,674	483
2009........................	35,889	2,301	55,655	1,030	78,574	467
2008........................	34,209	2,505	51,691	1,059	73,948	518
2007........................	34,035	2,492	53,029	1,155	74,351	459
2006........................	34,750	2,334	52,569	1,086	74,507	460
2005........................	33,544	2,273	52,070	1,011	77,210	444
2004........................	32,367	2,176	47,746	957	79,168	387
2003[3]	31,556	2,156	45,635	966	76,871	397
2002........................	32,764	2,283	47,018	974	75,050	321
2001........................	31,084	2,457	46,511	943	67,007	356
2000[4]	30,966	2,291	49,270	880	60,207	349
1999........................	28,278	2,388	42,170	993	59,255	368
1998........................	26,586	2,215	42,539	792	51,198	318
1997........................	27,215	2,108	35,792	818	49,940	278
1996........................	26,365	2,047	35,558	700	65,981	253
1995........................	26,846	2,047	36,026	659	57,186	293
1994........................	23,748	1,959	34,073	758	52,829	281
1993........................	21,734	1,804	35,147	721	47,372	228
1992........................	20,550	1,835	30,920	657	43,795	246
1991........................	19,974	1,571	26,075	650	41,313	255
1990........................	21,152	1,372	29,471	564	39,104	269
1989........................	20,253	1,352	27,493	515	38,166	326
1988........................	19,265	1,311	28,506	533	36,452	283
1987........................	18,081	1,250	23,345	482	34,073	294
1986........................	17,419	1,226	23,412	480	31,054	263
1985........................	16,415	1,230	23,818	477	31,947	243
1984........................	14,960	1,106	21,986	424	27,893	250

[1]For data prior to 1991, "Some college/Associate degree" equals 1 to 3 years of college completed; "Bachelor's degree" equals 4 years of college; "Advanced degree" equals 5 or more years of college completed.
[2]Starting in 2011, earnings data were created using population controls based on Census 2010 data.
[3]Starting in 2003, respondents could choose more than one race. The race data in this table from 2003 onward represent respondents who indicated only one race.
[4]Beginning in 2000, earnings data are from the expanded Current Population Survey (CPS) sample and were calculated using population controls based on Census 2000.
[5]May be of any race.
… = Not available.

Table A-34. Mean Earnings of Workers 18 Years Old and Over, by Educational Attainment, Race, Hispanic Origin, and Sex, 1975–2018—*Continued*

(Dollars except as noted.)

Race, sex, year, and Hispanic origin	Total		Not a high school graduate		High school graduate	
	Mean earnings	Number of workers (thousands)	Mean earnings	Number of workers (thousands)	Mean earnings	Number of workers (thousands)
1983	12,789	5,707	9,094	1,768	11,956	2,312
1982	12,203	5,535	9,153	1,798	11,952	2,213
1981	11,937	5,651	9,266	1,925	11,905	2,191
1980	11,085	5,576	8,421	2,054	11,563	2,119
1979	10,403	5,581	7,938	2,138	10,662	2,087
1978	9,651	5,350	7,423	2,156	9,869	1,982
1977	8,710	5,220	6,648	2,230	9,332	1,770
1976	7,991	5,156	6,670	2,289	8,056	1,766
1975	7,541	4,864	6,364	2,247	7,847	1,684
Female						
2018	38,901	10,954	19,333	711	25,994	2,980
2017	37,585	10,684	20,316	672	26,507	2,886
2016	35,576	10,524	21,023	727	24,763	2,915
2015	35,521	10,170	15,665	786	24,047	2,856
2014	32,313	10,012	18,852	674	23,785	2,868
2013	31,531	9,675	15,831	747	23,349	2,801
2012	31,808	9,544	18,178	685	22,783	2,747
2011[2]	31,455	9,343	13,893	801	23,795	2,728
2010	30,421	9,216	15,467	759	21,690	2,668
2009	29,831	9,087	15,644	756	22,964	2,806
2008	29,734	9,392	13,976	881	23,195	2,893
2007	31,317	9,365	14,869	868	24,724	3,001
2006	29,371	9,302	14,277	961	22,643	3,092
2005	27,314	9,163	14,300	968	20,449	3,051
2004	25,738	8,963	12,785	1,015	20,284	3,019
2003[3]	25,735	8,919	14,513	1,056	19,623	3,030
2002	25,131	8,868	13,748	1,075	20,209	2,989
2001	24,036	8,956	15,912	1,172	18,683	2,970
2000[4]	22,884	9,056	12,321	1,198	18,510	3,078
1999	21,742	9,076	10,762	1,194	16,541	3,163
1998	20,026	8,713	11,372	1,212	15,892	3,078
1997	19,161	8,503	10,607	1,132	15,789	3,102
1996	19,271	8,129	10,337	1,094	15,379	3,008
1995	17,485	7,757	10,739	1,108	14,473	2,641
1994	17,200	7,745	9,150	1,099	14,333	2,777
1993	16,336	7,481	8,562	1,048	13,550	2,746
1992	15,542	7,165	8,719	1,005	13,504	2,754
1991	15,064	7,035	9,151	1,237	12,810	2,781
1990	14,449	6,950	8,946	1,290	12,560	3,036
1989	14,122	6,946	7,827	1,269	12,701	3,046
1988	12,916	6,763	7,325	1,299	11,469	2,965
1987	12,106	6,518	7,452	1,304	11,030	2,930
1986	11,571	6,403	6,984	1,337	10,434	2,804
1985	10,904	6,190	6,879	1,293	9,918	2,651
1984	10,482	6,049	6,754	1,347	9,527	2,588
1983	9,778	5,589	6,154	1,267	9,197	2,380
1982	9,024	5,546	6,047	1,390	8,737	2,378
1981	8,225	5,437	5,404	1,589	8,088	2,197
1980	7,684	(NA)	4,685	(NA)	7,508	(NA)
1979	6,940	5,275	4,448	1,638	6,866	2,180
ASIAN						
Both Sexes						
2018	71,116	10,421	25,219	532	34,610	1,605
2017	67,599	10,215	29,306	568	35,164	1,639
2016	63,650	9,941	28,588	536	32,548	1,758
2015	61,603	9,439	23,418	571	34,215	1,533
2014	57,351	9,170	21,969	577	29,809	1,571
2013	54,752	8,732	24,616	588	30,996	1,616
2012	55,151	8,469	23,994	521	30,149	1,445

[1]For data prior to 1991, "Some college/Associate degree" equals 1 to 3 years of college completed; "Bachelor's degree" equals 4 years of college; "Advanced degree" equals 5 or more years of college completed.
[2]Starting in 2011, earnings data were created using population controls based on Census 2010 data.
[3]Starting in 2003, respondents could choose more than one race. The race data in this table from 2003 onward represent respondents who indicated only one race.
[4]Beginning in 2000, earnings data are from the expanded Current Population Survey (CPS) sample and were calculated using population controls based on Census 2000.
[5]May be of any race.
… = Not available.

Table A-34. Mean Earnings of Workers 18 Years Old and Over, by Educational Attainment, Race, Hispanic Origin, and Sex, 1975–2018—*Continued*

(Dollars except as noted.)

Race, sex, year, and Hispanic origin	Some college or associate's degree[1]		Bachelor's degree[1]		Advanced degree[1]	
	Mean earnings	Number of workers (thousands)	Mean earnings	Number of workers (thousands)	Mean earnings	Number of workers (thousands)
1983...............	15,113	996	20,370	363	25,466	268
1982...............	12,926	953	17,658	319	26,452	253
1981...............	13,740	1,002	16,624	327	21,082	205
1980...............	12,393	964	15,616	283	23,346	156
1979...............	11,971	931	16,161	259	21,092	166
1978...............	11,197	770	16,009	260	18,083	181
1977...............	10,023	799	12,978	234	16,385	188
1976...............	8,688	726	12,246	233	17,859	143
1975...............	8,505	599	11,318	213	13,720	121
Female						
2018...............	33,234	3,764	51,630	2,097	72,456	1,401
2017...............	33,131	3,814	48,158	2,111	69,498	1,199
2016...............	31,087	3,837	47,036	1,862	67,707	1,182
2015...............	30,951	3,732	48,842	1,753	75,911	1,041
2014...............	28,290	3,773	45,149	1,707	59,429	988
2013...............	27,564	3,531	44,139	1,684	61,698	909
2012...............	28,363	3,593	45,282	1,644	59,675	874
2011[2]............	28,771	3,310	42,721	1,640	60,889	862
2010...............	27,884	3,491	41,665	1,526	64,532	772
2009...............	26,748	3,276	42,587	1,552	59,073	694
2008...............	27,354	3,428	42,858	1,491	60,430	697
2007...............	31,850	3,320	41,560	1,526	57,076	647
2006...............	28,706	3,246	44,326	1,417	57,206	584
2005...............	25,422	3,116	43,516	1,401	54,044	626
2004...............	24,468	3,015	38,626	1,391	55,436	522
2003[3]............	24,007	2,963	41,066	1,355	54,346	514
2002...............	23,679	2,972	38,741	1,301	50,766	529
2001...............	23,511	3,023	35,448	1,269	48,080	521
2000[4]............	22,937	3,140	35,719	1,179	46,416	459
1999...............	22,733	3,049	33,251	1,162	47,635	508.543
1998...............	20,371	2,870	31,952	1,105	40,214	448
1997...............	19,643	2,794	29,091	1,027	38,392	448
1996...............	21,581	2,736	29,311	954	35,785	337
1995...............	17,985	2,679	25,577	1,025	36,585	304
1994...............	16,589	2,651	28,356	921	44,618	297
1993...............	16,778	2,475	25,865	917	36,485	296
1992...............	15,445	2,316	24,465	806	34,880	285
1991...............	15,742	2,011	25,235	733	32,470	273
1990...............	15,734	1,632	23,837	653	28,074	338
1989...............	15,044	1,656	23,541	606	27,933	368
1988...............	14,557	1,491	19,862	671	26,072	338
1987...............	13,123	1,367	18,815	615	24,383	302
1986...............	12,459	1,436	19,562	524	24,400	301
1985...............	11,488	1,385	17,779	569	21,502	292
1984...............	11,115	1,290	17,134	513	21,000	311
1983...............	10,215	1,210	14,738	465	21,539	267
1982...............	9,574	1,114	13,284	428	19,198	235
1981...............	9,329	1,076	12,839	381	17,743	193
1980...............	8,544	(NA)	12,389	(NA)	17,278	(NA)
1979...............	7,735	895	11,555	363	15,766	200
ASIAN						
Both Sexes						
2018...............	41,595	1,826	72,857	3,660	117,834	2,795
2017...............	38,302	1,894	71,845	3,353	109,714	2,759
2016...............	37,793	1,996	68,610	3,022	105,557	2,627
2015...............	36,914	1,847	65,558	3,056	101,667	2,429
2014...............	32,524	1,792	64,864	3,106	97,309	2,123
2013...............	34,638	1,767	57,841	2,755	96,266	2,003
2012...............	33,239	1,744	59,507	2,717	93,772	2,040

[1]For data prior to 1991, "Some college/Associate degree" equals 1 to 3 years of college completed; "Bachelor's degree" equals 4 years of college; "Advanced degree" equals 5 or more years of college completed.
[2]Starting in 2011, earnings data were created using population controls based on Census 2010 data.
[3]Starting in 2003, respondents could choose more than one race. The race data in this table from 2003 onward represent respondents who indicated only one race.
[4]Beginning in 2000, earnings data are from the expanded Current Population Survey (CPS) sample and were calculated using population controls based on Census 2000.
[5]May be of any race.
... = Not available.

Table A-34. Mean Earnings of Workers 18 Years Old and Over, by Educational Attainment, Race, Hispanic Origin, and Sex, 1975–2018—*Continued*

(Dollars except as noted.)

Race, sex, year, and Hispanic origin	Total		Not a high school graduate		High school graduate	
	Mean earnings	Number of workers (thousands)	Mean earnings	Number of workers (thousands)	Mean earnings	Number of workers (thousands)
2011[2]	51,500	8,014	21,640	563	28,302	1,478
2010	49,263	8,028	20,747	595	28,490	1,520
2009	53,419	7,158	20,461	487	29,312	1,367
2008	51,063	7,118	21,200	540	29,390	1,213
2007	49,571	7,137	21,305	512	28,773	1,241
2006	50,940	7,073	20,573	599	29,426	1,301
2005	45,751	6,684	22,909	598	27,082	1,304
2004	44,361	6,369	19,684	497	28,289	1,192
2003[3]	42,163	6,190	19,558	539	25,704	1,162
2002	40,793	6,086	16,746	536	24,900	1,138
Male						
2018	82,771	5,528	28,683	283	40,718	866
2017	79,440	5,452	35,303	283	41,576	913
2016	75,610	5,258	36,311	267	37,255	933
2015	71,362	5,014	26,616	303	39,038	814
2014	66,326	4,817	26,516	279	33,374	823
2013	64,019	4,690	24,897	288	35,882	881
2012	64,502	4,455	24,256	251	32,794	748
2011[2]	60,397	4,195	25,534	298	32,500	754
2010	57,180	4,196	24,064	315	31,683	766
2009	62,328	3,811	21,167	255	33,080	695
2008	60,007	3,776	23,814	279	34,904	606
2007	57,890	3,731	24,213	244	33,607	630
2006	60,516	3,757	23,311	298	32,528	710
2005	54,257	3,564	28,150	307	30,547	721
2004	52,544	3,440	20,691	235	31,710	676
2003[3]	48,890	3,333	23,745	291	28,522	582
2002	48,934	3,272	17,659	298	29,547	578
Female						
2018	57,945	4,892	21,264	248	27,444	739
2017	54,045	4,763	23,370	285	27,099	725
2016	50,220	4,683	20,875	268	27,217	824
2015	50,544	4,424	19,791	267	28,748	718
2014	47,419	4,353	17,691	297	25,886	748
2013	43,995	4,041	24,346	300	25,129	734
2012	44,770	4,013	23,751	270	27,308	697
2011[2]	41,727	3,819	17,263	265	23,926	723
2010	40,595	3,832	17,016	280	25,246	754
2009	43,270	3,346	19,684	232	25,420	672
2008	40,954	3,341	18,395	260	23,886	607
2007	40,455	3,405	18,643	267	23,785	611
2006	40,089	3,315	17,855	300	25,696	590
2005	36,033	3,119	17,383	291	22,789	582
2004	34,748	2,929	18,780	262	23,802	516
2003[3]	34,315	2,857	14,614	247	22,876	580
2002	31,328	2,814	15,595	237	20,094	559
HISPANIC[5]						
Both Sexes						
2018	40,613	28,535	28,024	6,288	35,105	9,172
2017	38,816	27,827	27,291	6,237	34,472	8,807
2016	38,276	26,936	29,264	6,260	34,751	8,477
2015	37,083	26,263	25,697	6,630	31,647	8,240
2014	33,944	25,254	23,747	6,819	30,329	7,869
2013	32,368	24,393	22,431	6,704	28,415	7,313
2012	31,596	23,811	21,087	6,545	28,097	7,462
2011[2]	30,739	23,027	20,953	6,583	26,681	7,176
2010	29,971	22,326	20,625	6,469	26,314	6,981
2009	29,565	21,551	19,816	6,667	25,998	6,753
2008	30,291	21,853	21,310	6,972	27,020	6,702

[1]For data prior to 1991, "Some college/Associate degree" equals 1 to 3 years of college completed; "Bachelor's degree" equals 4 years of college; "Advanced degree" equals 5 or more years of college completed.
[2]Starting in 2011, earnings data were created using population controls based on Census 2010 data.
[3]Starting in 2003, respondents could choose more than one race. The race data in this table from 2003 onward represent respondents who indicated only one race.
[4]Beginning in 2000, earnings data are from the expanded Current Population Survey (CPS) sample and were calculated using population controls based on Census 2000.
[5]May be of any race.
… = Not available.

Table A-34. Mean Earnings of Workers 18 Years Old and Over, by Educational Attainment, Race, Hispanic Origin, and Sex, 1975–2018—*Continued*

(Dollars except as noted.)

Race, sex, year, and Hispanic origin	Some college or associate's degree[1]		Bachelor's degree[1]		Advanced degree[1]	
	Mean earnings	Number of workers (thousands)	Mean earnings	Number of workers (thousands)	Mean earnings	Number of workers (thousands)
2011[2]	35,034	1,582	57,150	2,645	87,205	1,743
2010	30,519	1,629	56,689	2,576	84,369	1,707
2009	32,958	1,356	55,730	2,376	98,871	1,569
2008	32,671	1,466	58,524	2,298	83,721	1,600
2007	34,423	1,456	54,451	2,354	81,943	1,572
2006	33,238	1,350	56,197	2,268	88,408	1,553
2005	31,460	1,337	51,064	2,108	80,145	1,335
2004	29,524	1,364	47,912	2,119	81,259	1,196
2003[3]	27,209	1,355	48,333	1,878	74,046	1,254
2002	27,340	1,325	46,628	1,911	72,852	1,174
Male						
2018	46,021	967	87,714	1,823	132,138	1,587
2017	45,422	964	86,369	1,694	122,087	1,597
2016	44,013	1,022	78,528	1,520	124,668	1,513
2015	39,272	894	74,452	1,587	116,397	1,414
2014	36,790	903	71,685	1,581	112,262	1,229
2013	37,731	936	66,653	1,417	112,837	1,166
2012	38,417	871	69,657	1,361	105,017	1,222
2011[2]	42,378	810	65,740	1,316	98,812	1,015
2010	34,428	837	64,963	1,285	96,506	992
2009	37,691	722	62,561	1,198	113,711	940
2008	37,283	773	67,088	1,186	97,068	931
2007	41,876	773	60,356	1,156	93,604	926
2006	37,263	658	67,144	1,150	101,676	939
2005	35,401	675	60,739	1,048	92,552	811
2004	33,798	680	56,998	1,079	90,870	770
2003[3]	31,775	673	52,508	992	83,098	793
2002	32,750	664	55,198	971	82,170	758
Female						
2018	36,608	859	58,117	1,837	99,047	1,208
2017	30,923	930	57,009	1,658	92,705	1,162
2016	31,258	973	58,567	1,501	79,613	1,114
2015	34,704	953	55,956	1,469	81,135	1,015
2014	28,185	888	57,793	1,525	76,741	893
2013	31,154	831	48,505	1,337	73,159	836
2012	28,077	873	49,308	1,355	76,942	817
2011[2]	27,328	772	48,647	1,329	71,001	727
2010	26,383	791	48,453	1,291	67,541	715
2009	27,574	634	48,783	1,178	76,637	628
2008	27,528	693	49,380	1,111	65,148	669
2007	25,992	683	48,748	1,197	65,206	645
2006	29,415	692	44,932	1,118	68,084	613
2005	27,439	662	41,494	1,059	60,934	524
2004	25,280	684	38,488	1,040	63,894	426
2003[3]	22,703	682	43,655	885	58,489	461
2002	21,912	661	37,766	939	55,851	415
HISPANIC[5]						
Both Sexes						
2018	37,847	7,523	59,364	3,910	87,619	1,641
2017	37,370	7,587	54,190	3,767	83,067	1,428
2016	35,288	7,404	53,283	3,421	79,831	1,373
2015	35,780	6,887	58,152	3,096	82,499	1,409
2014	33,822	6,541	52,143	2,852	73,952	1,171
2013	32,153	6,524	50,673	2,759	74,926	1,090
2012	30,694	6,042	50,592	2,707	77,985	1,054
2011[2]	31,423	5,773	47,873	2,528	78,606	966
2010	30,826	5,551	47,753	2,390	71,403	935
2009	31,004	5,036	49,017	2,256	74,675	837
2008	31,644	5,149	48,081	2,225	77,630	802

[1]For data prior to 1991, "Some college/Associate degree" equals 1 to 3 years of college completed; "Bachelor's degree" equals 4 years of college; "Advanced degree" equals 5 or more years of college completed.
[2]Starting in 2011, earnings data were created using population controls based on Census 2010 data.
[3]Starting in 2003, respondents could choose more than one race. The race data in this table from 2003 onward represent respondents who indicated only one race.
[4]Beginning in 2000, earnings data are from the expanded Current Population Survey (CPS) sample and were calculated using population controls based on Census 2000.
[5]May be of any race.
… = Not available.

Table A-34. Mean Earnings of Workers 18 Years Old and Over, by Educational Attainment, Race, Hispanic Origin, and Sex, 1975–2018—*Continued*

(Dollars except as noted.)

Race, sex, year, and Hispanic origin	Total		Not a high school graduate		High school graduate	
	Mean earnings	Number of workers (thousands)	Mean earnings	Number of workers (thousands)	Mean earnings	Number of workers (thousands)
2007............................	29,910	21,561	21,303	6,888	27,604	6,682
2006............................	29,155	21,209	20,581	7,134	27,508	6,495
2005............................	27,760	20,025	19,294	6,995	25,659	6,080
2004............................	27,263	19,343	19,025	6,935	25,823	5,741
2003[3]	25,810	18,786	18,349	6,767	23,472	5,517
2002............................	25,824	18,409	18,981	6,748	24,163	5,499
2001............................	24,786	17,575	18,334	6,533	22,866	5,265
2000[4]	23,855	17,161	17,156	6,428	22,009	5,145
1999............................	21,809	16,275	15,991	6,021	20,443	4,907
1998............................	22,117	14,372	15,832	5,281	20,978	4,219
1997............................	20,766	13,972	15,069	5,238	19,558	4,082
1996............................	19,439	13,365	13,287	5,062	18,528	3,783
1995............................	18,262	12,434	13,068	4,784	18,333	3,594
1994............................	18,568	12,035	13,733	4,686	17,323	3,444
1993............................	17,102	11,644	11,852	4,425	16,591	3,367
1992............................	16,501	11,350	11,674	4,426	16,438	3,349
1991............................	16,300	10,006	11,335	3,906	16,142	3,045
1990............................	15,943	9,729	10,368	3,929	15,417	3,282
1989............................	15,714	9,570	11,500	3,985	14,901	3,188
1988............................	15,007	9,226	11,045	3,824	14,667	2,953
1987............................	14,695	8,817	10,961	3,457	13,958	2,982
1986............................	13,558	8,393	9,896	3,379	13,389	2,835
1985............................	13,120	7,840	9,956	3,223	13,044	2,661
1984............................	12,583	7,349	9,671	3,129	12,858	2,457
1983............................	11,901	6,222	9,473	2,674	12,077	2,030
1982............................	11,307	5,914	8,498	2,583	11,539	1,967
1981............................	10,872	5,930	8,645	2,648	11,046	1,966
1980............................	10,062	5,723	8,119	2,649	10,182	1,824
1979............................	9,248	5,545	7,683	2,533	9,338	1,812
1978............................	8,460	4,898	7,138	2,345	8,512	1,554
1977............................	7,761	4,752	6,547	2,306	8,079	1,461
1976............................	7,081	4,303	5,984	2,107	7,580	1,309
1975............................	6,567	4,078	5,462	2,028	6,759	1,293
Male						
2018............................	44,851	16,016	32,348	4,122	40,028	5,594
2017............................	43,300	15,759	31,968	4,104	38,865	5,328
2016............................	44,237	15,189	33,701	4,124	41,541	5,136
2015............................	41,556	14,962	29,719	4,327	36,549	4,982
2014............................	38,152	14,478	27,032	4,478	34,347	4,686
2013............................	35,990	13,980	25,151	4,475	32,070	4,366
2012............................	35,423	13,622	24,012	4,379	32,313	4,460
2011[2]	34,135	13,134	24,189	4,277	29,872	4,272
2010............................	33,274	12,773	23,709	4,263	29,768	4,188
2009............................	32,279	12,643	21,588	4,486	28,908	4,109
2008............................	34,240	12,857	24,340	4,720	30,618	3,990
2007............................	33,040	12,885	23,923	4,726	30,932	4,111
2006............................	32,532	12,711	23,060	4,920	32,148	3,884
2005............................	31,008	12,015	21,623	4,744	29,471	3,667
2004............................	30,828	11,562	21,606	4,633	29,694	3,440
2003[3]	28,806	11,195	20,637	4,556	26,652	3,234
2002............................	29,084	10,979	21,611	4,506	27,992	3,205
2001............................	27,964	10,258	20,614	4,289	26,745	2,985
2000[4]	27,253	9,996	19,501	4,236	25,629	2,940
1999............................	24,381	9,576	17,713	3,944	23,196	2,875
1998............................	25,534	8,288	17,756	3,428	24,739	2,413
1997............................	23,520	8,261	17,447	3,444	22,253	2,391
1996............................	21,870	7,975	14,986	3,382	21,593	2,116
1995............................	20,312	7,337	14,774	3,140	20,882	2,039
1994............................	21,288	7,117	16,355	3,111	19,667	1,937
1993............................	19,460	6,957	13,572	2,928	18,765	1,954
1992............................	18,318	6,811	13,041	2,981	18,884	1,888
1991............................	18,516	5,932	13,134	2,548	18,582	1,705

[1]For data prior to 1991, "Some college/Associate degree" equals 1 to 3 years of college completed; "Bachelor's degree" equals 4 years of college; "Advanced degree" equals 5 or more years of college completed.
[2]Starting in 2011, earnings data were created using population controls based on Census 2010 data.
[3]Starting in 2003, respondents could choose more than one race. The race data in this table from 2003 onward represent respondents who indicated only one race.
[4]Beginning in 2000, earnings data are from the expanded Current Population Survey (CPS) sample and were calculated using population controls based on Census 2000.
[5]May be of any race.
... = Not available.

Table A-34. Mean Earnings of Workers 18 Years Old and Over, by Educational Attainment, Race, Hispanic Origin, and Sex, 1975–2018—*Continued*

(Dollars except as noted.)

Race, sex, year, and Hispanic origin	Some college or associate's degree[1]		Bachelor's degree[1]		Advanced degree[1]	
	Mean earnings	Number of workers (thousands)	Mean earnings	Number of workers (thousands)	Mean earnings	Number of workers (thousands)
2007	31,040	5,000	44,696	2,114	73,111	874
2006	31,380	4,863	45,371	2,038	70,432	678
2005	29,836	4,467	45,933	1,775	70,916	705
2004	29,260	4,369	45,166	1,669	69,839	629
2003[3]	28,494	4,235	43,676	1,663	62,794	603
2002	27,757	4,024	40,949	1,568	67,679	569
2001	27,523	3,842	40,586	1,416	62,194	517
2000[4]	25,276	3,737	44,661	1,395	63,908	455
1999	24,207	3,662	35,704	1,194	55,097	491
1998	23,091	3,289	35,014	1,156	62,583	425
1997	22,001	3,075	33,465	1,140	58,571	437
1996	22,209	3,096	32,955	1,027	49,873	398
1995	19,923	2,856	30,602	866	45,612	334
1994	21,041	2,723	29,165	844	51,898	337
1993	19,043	2,728	30,359	799	45,034	325
1992	18,769	2,515	27,944	767	40,741	293
1991	19,075	2,080	26,623	665	39,609	311
1990	19,206	1,534	25,703	601	38,075	382
1989	18,707	1,513	28,157	535	39,273	349
1988	18,101	1,511	23,745	596	33,843	340
1987	16,899	1,400	23,105	644	34,413	335
1986	16,523	1,411	22,707	471	28,316	295
1985	15,318	1,226	20,878	458	28,357	273
1984	14,359	1,116	19,924	381	26,327	265
1983	13,371	976	17,972	320	24,352	222
1982	13,108	873	18,186	303	28,167	186
1981	12,971	834	16,114	320	24,082	161
1980	11,891	808	15,676	283	21,910	157
1979	10,181	768	14,940	240	18,273	190
1978	9,575	661	13,985	213	17,333	125
1977	8,172	656	12,572	210	16,660	118
1976	7,252	592	11,242	177	14,000	118
1975	7,154	474	10,573	173	15,756	111
Male						
2018	43,825	3,716	64,478	1,892	110,367	689
2017	43,481	3,834	62,469	1,845	95,960	646
2016	42,172	3,652	62,670	1,643	98,834	633
2015	40,672	3,426	69,600	1,570	95,226	655
2014	40,192	3,331	59,791	1,439	92,887	542
2013	37,245	3,222	59,368	1,360	89,624	555
2012	36,238	2,949	60,552	1,308	89,780	525
2011[2]	36,660	2,928	54,936	1,200	96,359	456
2010	35,925	2,756	56,924	1,147	83,343	420
2009	36,071	2,485	58,570	1,122	84,368	439
2008	37,864	2,615	56,980	1,109	96,976	422
2007	35,861	2,510	50,805	1,057	87,195	478
2006	36,217	2,500	51,336	1,066	87,835	340
2005	34,754	2,326	54,700	896	84,033	380
2004	34,447	2,241	53,567	916	84,152	332
2003[3]	34,157	2,193	49,298	867	71,446	344
2002	32,935	2,112	46,115	815	73,836	338
2001	32,595	1,962	45,445	748	75,746	272
2000[4]	30,155	1,873	55,050	722	81,447	223
1999	28,621	1,873	41,740	623	66,191	261
1998	26,483	1,652	40,889	569	83,754	226
1997	25,923	1,598	37,963	557	68,097	272
1996	26,682	1,687	38,130	531	49,307	259
1995	22,171	1,475	35,109	466	50,802	215
1994	24,517	1,410	33,797	450	60,858	210
1993	22,417	1,444	37,554	438	52,441	194
1992	21,266	1,353	32,859	415	45,065	173
1991	21,886	1,132	31,699	356	45,107	192

[1]For data prior to 1991, "Some college/Associate degree" equals 1 to 3 years of college completed; "Bachelor's degree" equals 4 years of college; "Advanced degree" equals 5 or more years of college completed.
[2]Starting in 2011, earnings data were created using population controls based on Census 2010 data.
[3]Starting in 2003, respondents could choose more than one race. The race data in this table from 2003 onward represent respondents who indicated only one race.
[4]Beginning in 2000, earnings data are from the expanded Current Population Survey (CPS) sample and were calculated using population controls based on Census 2000.
[5]May be of any race.
… = Not available.

Table A-34. Mean Earnings of Workers 18 Years Old and Over, by Educational Attainment, Race, Hispanic Origin, and Sex, 1975–2018—*Continued*

(Dollars except as noted.)

Race, sex, year, and Hispanic origin	Total		Not a high school graduate		High school graduate	
	Mean earnings	Number of workers (thousands)	Mean earnings	Number of workers (thousands)	Mean earnings	Number of workers (thousands)
1990..........................	18,320	5,745	13,182	2,562	18,100	1,812
1989..........................	18,087	5,641	13,167	2,632	17,579	1,711
1988..........................	17,357	5,477	12,836	2,517	17,446	1,621
1987..........................	17,048	5,248	12,823	2,281	16,774	1,616
1986..........................	15,624	5,037	11,262	2,262	15,948	1,546
1985..........................	15,293	4,702	11,671	2,111	15,602	1,491
1984..........................	14,957	4,344	11,441	2,022	15,763	1,319
1983..........................	14,265	3,577	11,353	1,678	14,584	1,074
1982..........................	13,484	3,480	10,108	1,622	13,883	1,083
1981..........................	13,052	3,504	10,447	1,686	13,513	1,037
1980..........................	12,310	3,401	9,825	1,707	13,108	961
1979..........................	11,332	3,269	9,393	1,615	11,714	952
1978..........................	10,473	2,915	8,836	1,498	10,940	815
1977..........................	9,655	2,833	8,192	1,460	10,386	776
1976..........................	8,787	2,571	7,440	1,321	9,640	712
1975..........................	8,162	2,456	6,745	1,287	8,546	691
Female						
2018..........................	35,190	12,519	19,793	2,165	27,405	3,577
2017..........................	32,961	12,067	18,292	2,132	27,743	3,478
2016..........................	30,569	11,747	20,694	2,135	24,313	3,340
2015..........................	31,160	11,301	18,138	2,302	24,151	3,258
2014..........................	28,291	10,775	17,461	2,340	24,412	3,183
2013..........................	27,504	10,412	16,971	2,229	22,999	2,946
2012..........................	26,479	10,189	15,174	2,166	21,832	3,001
2011[2]	26,230	9,892	14,949	2,305	21,988	2,904
2010..........................	25,554	9,553	14,667	2,206	21,136	2,793
2009..........................	25,713	8,907	16,170	2,180	21,473	2,644
2008..........................	24,646	8,995	14,960	2,552	21,725	2,712
2007..........................	25,262	8,676	15,574	2,162	22,283	2,570
2006..........................	24,104	8,497	15,072	2,214	20,608	2,611
2005..........................	22,887	8,009	14,365	2,250	19,864	2,413
2004..........................	21,967	7,781	13,830	2,302	20,037	2,301
2003[3]	21,391	7,591	13,632	2,210	18,967	2,283
2002..........................	21,008	7,430	13,694	2,241	18,810	2,293
2001..........................	20,330	7,316	13,976	2,243	17,786	2,279
2000[4]	19,115	7,164	12,622	2,191	17,180	2,204
1999..........................	18,132	6,699	12,722	2,077	16,548	2,032
1998..........................	17,461	6,804	12,273	1,854	15,952	1,806
1997..........................	16,781	5,711	10,503	1,794	15,747	1,691
1996..........................	15,841	5,390	9,867	1,680	14,635	1,667
1995..........................	15,310	5,096	9,809	1,644	14,989	1,555
1994..........................	14,631	4,918	8,559	1,576	14,313	1,508
1993..........................	13,602	4,687	8,489	1,498	13,584	1,413
1992..........................	13,774	4,539	8,854	1,445	13,277	1,461
1991..........................	13,073	4,074	7,960	1,358	13,037	1,339
1990..........................	12,516	3,984	5,093	1,367	12,109	1,470
1989..........................	12,307	3,929	8,256	1,353	11,799	1,477
1988..........................	11,573	3,749	7,597	1,307	11,284	1,332
1987..........................	11,234	3,569	7,350	1,176	10,627	1,366
1986..........................	10,457	3,356	7,130	1,117	10,319	1,289
1985..........................	9,865	3,138	6,699	1,112	9,784	1,170
1984..........................	9,150	3,005	6,438	1,107	9,492	1,138
1983..........................	8,704	2,645	6,305	996	9,261	956
1982..........................	8,195	2,434	5,781	961	8,668	884
1981..........................	7,723	2,426	5,486	962	8,292	929
1980..........................	6,770	2,322	5,028	942	6,923	863
1979..........................	6,255	2,276	4,675	918	6,708	860
1978..........................	5,501	1,983	4,135	847	5,834	739
1977..........................	4,964	1,919	3,707	846	5,466	685
1976..........................	4,548	1,732	3,537	786	5,124	597
1975..........................	4,152	1,622	3,233	741	4,708	602

[1]For data prior to 1991, "Some college/Associate degree" equals 1 to 3 years of college completed; "Bachelor's degree" equals 4 years of college; "Advanced degree" equals 5 or more years of college completed.
[2]Starting in 2011, earnings data were created using population controls based on Census 2010 data.
[3]Starting in 2003, respondents could choose more than one race. The race data in this table from 2003 onward represent respondents who indicated only one race.
[4]Beginning in 2000, earnings data are from the expanded Current Population Survey (CPS) sample and were calculated using population controls based on Census 2000.
[5]May be of any race.
... = Not available.

Table A-34. Mean Earnings of Workers 18 Years Old and Over, by Educational Attainment, Race, Hispanic Origin, and Sex, 1975–2018—*Continued*

(Dollars except as noted.)

Race, sex, year, and Hispanic origin	Some college or associate's degree[1]		Bachelor's degree[1]		Advanced degree[1]	
	Mean earnings	Number of workers (thousands)	Mean earnings	Number of workers (thousands)	Mean earnings	Number of workers (thousands)
1990	22,376	852	31,485	314	47,479	205
1989	22,374	810	32,767	292	49,088	196
1988	21,631	811	26,935	333	40,916	194
1987	19,414	758	26,581	383	39,014	211
1986	19,675	778	27,427	274	32,538	176
1985	18,168	678	24,723	267	32,831	155
1984	17,261	611	23,835	223	30,727	168
1983	16,626	514	21,911	170	28,680	141
1982	15,560	495	22,565	153	34,474	125
1981	15,432	489	19,201	177	27,619	114
1980	14,331	451	19,224	167	24,642	114
1979	12,489	441	18,923	142	21,299	118
1978	11,545	393	16,898	127	20,702	82
1977	9,924	391	15,189	120	19,025	85
1976	8,843	342	13,650	114	16,184	81
1975	8,807	279	12,881	113	17,991	86
Female						
2018	32,013	3,807	54,567	2,018	71,121	951
2017	31,127	3,753	46,237	1,921	72,396	781
2016	28,587	3,752	44,608	1,778	63,592	740
2015	30,937	3,460	46,372	1,525	71,443	754
2014	27,210	3,209	44,347	1,412	57,642	629
2013	27,184	3,302	42,216	1,398	59,686	535
2012	25,408	3,093	41,277	1,398	66,273	528
2011[2]	26,032	2,844	41,483	1,327	62,746	510
2010	25,797	2,795	39,292	1,243	61,673	515
2009	26,065	2,550	39,566	1,134	64,405	398
2008	25,226	2,534	39,231	1,115	56,175	380
2007	26,179	2,489	38,584	1,057	56,129	396
2006	26,260	2,362	38,825	971	52,896	337
2005	24,493	2,141	37,003	879	55,554	324
2004	23,796	2,128	34,949	753	53,887	298
2003[3]	22,411	2,042	37,550	795	51,294	258
2002	22,035	1,911	35,357	753	58,623	230
2001	22,229	1,879	35,142	668	47,176	245
2000[4]	20,372	1,864	33,489	672	47,057	232
1999	19,588	1,789	29,108	570	42,463	229
1998	20,460	1,639	29,317	587	38,422	200
1997	17,759	1,477	29,173	584	43,051	165
1996	16,856	1,409	27,407	495	50,960	139
1995	17,521	1,380	25,338	399	36,255	118
1994	17,309	1,313	23,867	393	37,269	127
1993	15,250	1,284	21,627	361	34,001	131
1992	15,858	1,162	22,144	352	34,457	119
1991	15,720	948	20,791	309	30,713	119
1990	15,245	682	19,378	287	27,184	177
1989	14,482	703	22,617	243	26,700	153
1988	14,012	700	19,707	263	24,444	146
1987	13,929	642	18,003	261	26,584	124
1986	12,648	633	16,142	197	22,071	119
1985	11,791	548	15,503	191	22,480	118
1984	10,848	505	14,404	158	18,706	97
1983	9,750	462	13,507	150	16,817	81
1982	9,896	378	13,719	150	15,244	61
1981	9,483	345	12,292	143	15,503	47
1980	8,808	357	10,568	116	14,668	43
1979	7,069	327	9,168	98	13,313	72
1978	6,686	268	9,684	86	10,908	43
1977	5,588	265	9,082	90	10,569	33
1976	5,075	250	6,884	63	9,218	37
1975	4,790	195	6,226	60	8,067	25

[1]For data prior to 1991, "Some college/Associate degree" equals 1 to 3 years of college completed; "Bachelor's degree" equals 4 years of college; "Advanced degree" equals 5 or more years of college completed.
[2]Starting in 2011, earnings data were created using population controls based on Census 2010 data.
[3]Starting in 2003, respondents could choose more than one race. The race data in this table from 2003 onward represent respondents who indicated only one race.
[4]Beginning in 2000, earnings data are from the expanded Current Population Survey (CPS) sample and were calculated using population controls based on Census 2000.
[5]May be of any race.
… = Not available.

Table A-34. Mean Earnings of Workers 18 Years Old and Over, by Educational Attainment, Race, Hispanic Origin, and Sex, 1975–2018—*Continued*

(Dollars except as noted.)

Race, sex, year, and Hispanic origin	Total		Not a high school graduate		High school graduate	
	Mean earnings	Number of workers (thousands)	Mean earnings	Number of workers (thousands)	Mean earnings	Number of workers (thousands)
WHITE ALONE OR IN COMBINATION						
Both Sexes						
2018............................	56,743	131,740	27,594	9,782	40,561	34,044
2017............................	54,535	130,955	27,180	10,024	39,663	34,025
2016............................	52,885	129,984	28,492	9,901	38,170	34,183
2015............................	50,981	129,762	26,268	10,609	36,948	33,995
2014............................	48,772	127,557	25,894	10,790	35,354	34,216
2013............................	47,280	127,029	24,264	10,470	34,101	34,391
2012............................	46,650	126,527	22,019	10,696	33,803	34,058
2011[2]	45,898	125,256	21,648	11,080	33,584	34,425
2010............................	44,103	124,707	21,427	10,993	32,023	34,908
2009............................	43,213	127,001	20,468	11,708	31,351	36,656
2008............................	43,550	129,419	21,483	12,630	32,072	37,299
2007............................	43,000	129,203	22,245	12,568	32,126	37,570
2006............................	42,249	128,366	21,389	13,800	31,998	37,915
2005............................	40,592	126,882	20,225	13,424	30,494	37,723
2004............................	38,855	125,388	19,365	13,540	29,595	37,639
2003[3]	37,958	124,456	18,734	16,282	27,915	45,064
2002............................	37,290	124,337	19,278	13,957	28,107	37,863
Male						
2018............................	66,592	70,514	32,386	6,295	47,055	20,239
2017............................	63,878	70,702	32,027	6,487	46,168	20,339
2016............................	62,320	69,912	33,197	6,429	45,231	20,309
2015............................	60,364	69,837	31,168	6,866	43,502	20,177
2014............................	58,148	68,611	30,224	6,989	41,291	20,145
2013............................	55,973	68,402	28,083	6,948	39,102	20,165
2012............................	55,544	68,068	25,701	6,940	39,910	19,715
2011[2]	54,835	67,254	25,719	7,030	40,105	19,864
2010............................	52,457	66,903	25,205	7,032	37,540	20,047
2009............................	51,133	68,426	23,327	7,561	36,321	21,162
2008............................	52,502	69,829	25,254	8,263	37,740	21,192
2007............................	51,599	70,073	25,848	8,305	38,072	21,436
2006............................	50,826	69,702	24,524	9,055	38,699	21,401
2005............................	49,437	68,987	23,526	8,740	36,608	21,289
2004............................	47,275	67,758	22,576	8,751	35,348	21,074
2003[3]	45,989	67,198	21,787	8,682	34,225	20,534
2002............................	45,682	67,082	22,601	8,977	33,846	20,430
Female						
2018............................	45,400	61,226	18,941	3,486	31,039	13,805
2017............................	43,571	60,252	18,290	3,537	29,995	13,686
2016............................	41,905	60,071	19,780	3,472	27,833	13,873
2015............................	40,046	59,924	17,281	3,743	27,376	13,817
2014............................	37,859	58,945	17,930	3,801	26,854	14,070
2013............................	37,138	58,627	16,731	3,522	27,011	14,226
2012............................	36,293	58,458	15,217	3,756	25,408	14,343
2011[2]	35,534	58,001	14,581	4,050	24,687	14,561
2010............................	34,434	57,804	14,718	3,960	24,581	14,861
2009............................	33,961	58,574	15,254	4,146	24,561	15,494
2008............................	33,060	59,590	14,345	4,366	24,615	16,107
2007............................	32,810	59,130	15,226	4,263	24,226	16,134
2006............................	32,059	58,663	15,408	4,745	23,313	16,514
2005............................	30,053	57,895	14,066	4,684	22,574	16,434
2004............................	28,954	57,630	13,498	4,788	22,277	16,566
2003[3]	28,532	57,257	14,086	4,684	22,029	16,926
2002............................	27,457	57,254	13,286	4,979	21,381	17,433

[1]For data prior to 1991, "Some college/Associate degree" equals 1 to 3 years of college completed; "Bachelor's degree" equals 4 years of college; "Advanced degree" equals 5 or more years of college completed.
[2]Starting in 2011, earnings data were created using population controls based on Census 2010 data.
[3]Starting in 2003, respondents could choose more than one race. The race data in this table from 2003 onward represent respondents who indicated only one race.
[4]Beginning in 2000, earnings data are from the expanded Current Population Survey (CPS) sample and were calculated using population controls based on Census 2000.
[5]May be of any race.
... = Not available.

Table A-34. Mean Earnings of Workers 18 Years Old and Over, by Educational Attainment, Race, Hispanic Origin, and Sex, 1975–2018—*Continued*

(Dollars except as noted.)

Race, sex, year, and Hispanic origin	Some college or associate's degree[1]		Bachelor's degree[1]		Advanced degree[1]	
	Mean earnings	Number of workers (thousands)	Mean earnings	Number of workers (thousands)	Mean earnings	Number of workers (thousands)
WHITE ALONE OR IN COMBINATION						
Both Sexes						
2018	44,105	37,541	73,115	32,347	100,070	18,024
2017	42,587	37,794	69,035	31,680	98,853	17,429
2016	41,339	38,480	68,292	30,471	95,331	16,947
2015	39,835	38,596	66,733	29,682	92,570	16,877
2014	39,403	37,756	63,404	28,754	88,614	16,039
2013	37,330	38,164	60,859	28,374	91,349	15,627
2012	36,751	38,544	61,399	28,072	90,761	15,154
2011[2]	36,139	37,718	61,173	27,455	89,895	14,575
2010	35,295	37,355	59,122	26,941	85,131	14,511
2009	35,540	37,684	57,662	26,920	86,067	14,031
2008	35,528	38,593	59,824	26,784	84,687	14,111
2007	35,565	38,664	58,565	26,583	82,309	13,816
2006	35,276	37,530	57,807	26,035	83,002	13,084
2005	34,279	38,149	55,758	24,919	81,437	12,665
2004	32,736	37,287	52,790	24,361	78,747	12,560
2003[3]	31,498	44,048	51,206	28,672	74,601	14,592
2002	31,767	36,639	52,509	23,865	73,773	12,011
Male						
2018	54,167	19,000	87,522	16,344	125,050	8,634
2017	51,639	19,232	83,192	16,168	121,690	8,475
2016	49,685	19,464	83,750	15,397	116,488	8,312
2015	47,616	19,353	82,230	15,086	115,139	8,353
2014	48,193	18,921	78,225	14,611	112,251	7,943
2013	45,088	19,129	73,958	14,346	117,941	7,813
2012	44,814	19,246	74,396	14,465	113,877	7,700
2011[2]	44,135	18,674	73,557	14,163	112,265	7,521
2010	42,500	18,359	72,047	14,004	105,955	7,461
2009	42,760	18,567	71,166	13,886	106,451	7,248
2008	43,307	19,210	75,024	13,734	107,065	7,428
2007	42,760	19,343	73,390	13,697	103,214	7,291
2006	42,605	18,686	71,602	13,443	103,097	7,116
2005	42,139	18,954	69,821	13,045	102,904	6,957
2004	40,627	18,362	65,498	12,728	99,543	6,843
2003[3]	39,555	18,421	65,237	12,774	93,792	6,785
2002	39,439	18,377	65,548	12,621	92,575	6,675
Female						
2018	33,793	18,541	58,401	16,002	77,099	9,390
2017	33,208	18,562	54,279	15,511	77,240	8,954
2016	32,797	19,015	52,505	15,074	74,966	8,635
2015	32,010	19,243	50,716	14,596	70,453	8,523
2014	30,572	18,835	48,092	14,143	65,422	8,095
2013	29,534	19,035	47,464	14,028	64,762	7,814
2012	28,709	19,298	47,584	13,607	66,881	7,454
2011[2]	28,299	19,044	47,976	13,292	66,041	7,053
2010	28,332	18,995	45,130	12,937	63,092	7,050
2009	28,528	19,116	43,275	13,034	64,283	6,782
2008	27,819	19,383	43,826	13,050	59,814	6,683
2007	28,362	19,321	42,807	12,886	58,951	6,525
2006	28,008	18,844	43,078	12,591	59,042	5,968
2005	25,518	19,194	40,306	11,873	55,273	5,707
2004	25,079	18,925	38,886	11,633	53,859	5,718
2003[3]	25,093	18,616	37,750	11,476	53,021	5,552
2002	24,046	18,261	37,872	11,243	50,255	5,336

[1]For data prior to 1991, "Some college/Associate degree" equals 1 to 3 years of college completed; "Bachelor's degree" equals 4 years of college; "Advanced degree" equals 5 or more years of college completed.
[2]Starting in 2011, earnings data were created using population controls based on Census 2010 data.
[3]Starting in 2003, respondents could choose more than one race. The race data in this table from 2003 onward represent respondents who indicated only one race.
[4]Beginning in 2000, earnings data are from the expanded Current Population Survey (CPS) sample and were calculated using population controls based on Census 2000.
[5]May be of any race.
… = Not available.

Table A-34. Mean Earnings of Workers 18 Years Old and Over, by Educational Attainment, Race, Hispanic Origin, and Sex, 1975–2018—*Continued*

(Dollars except as noted.)

Race, sex, year, and Hispanic origin	Total		Not a high school graduate		High school graduate	
	Mean earnings	Number of workers (thousands)	Mean earnings	Number of workers (thousands)	Mean earnings	Number of workers (thousands)
NON-HISPANIC WHITE ALONE OR IN COMBINATION						
Both Sexes						
2018............................	60,731	105,563	27,347	3,940	42,274	25,586
2017............................	58,297	105,469	26,904	4,157	41,142	26,003
2016............................	56,249	105,396	27,150	4,117	39,070	26,546
2015............................	54,138	105,849	26,738	4,515	38,446	26,400
2014............................	51,984	104,543	28,791	4,447	36,673	27,032
2013............................	50,424	104,642	26,562	4,238	35,470	27,636
2012............................	49,757	104,714	23,002	4,588	35,260	27,261
2011[2]	48,950	104,217	22,468	4,960	35,205	27,811
2010............................	46,894	104,136	22,408	4,940	33,268	28,501
2009............................	45,813	106,618	21,241	5,331	32,478	30,276
2008............................	46,050	108,823	21,579	5,959	33,105	30,982
2007............................	45,393	108,929	22,945	6,040	32,992	31,288
2006............................	44,652	108,297	22,094	6,995	32,844	31,802
2005............................	42,839	107,945	21,088	6,744	31,367	31,951
2004............................	40,847	107,086	19,667	6,893	30,195	32,217
2003[3]	39,989	106,658	19,764	6,906	29,561	32,225
2002............................	39,135	107,050	19,491	7,516	28,714	32,758
Male						
2018............................	72,324	55,743	33,159	2,457	49,347	15,067
2017............................	69,152	56,133	31,964	2,602	48,321	15,471
2016............................	66,808	55,923	32,056	2,622	46,245	15,570
2015............................	64,884	56,124	33,003	2,862	45,533	15,559
2014............................	62,883	55,277	34,929	2,799	43,134	15,831
2013............................	60,564	55,448	32,072	2,770	40,829	16,130
2012............................	60,103	55,462	27,899	2,824	41,984	15,644
2011[2]	59,346	55,152	27,620	3,049	42,612	15,908
2010............................	56,546	55,081	27,242	3,050	39,332	16,198
2009............................	55,161	56,390	25,612	3,262	38,049	17,253
2008............................	56,357	57,636	26,226	3,743	39,288	17,435
2007............................	55,457	57,886	27,810	3,800	39,602	17,567
2006............................	54,624	57,615	25,996	4,358	40,034	17,723
2005............................	53,084	57,553	25,469	4,213	38,034	17,787
2004............................	50,488	56,762	23,520	4,288	36,323	17,817
2003[3]	49,227	56,549	22,947	4,313	35,550	17,549
2002............................	48,700	56,714	23,426	4,663	34,830	17,446
Female						
2018............................	47,760	49,819	17,716	1,482	32,142	10,518
2017............................	45,948	49,335	18,429	1,554	30,597	10,532
2016............................	44,314	49,473	18,546	1,495	28,808	10,886
2015............................	42,009	49,725	15,893	1,653	28,275	10,840
2014............................	39,755	49,266	18,362	1,647	27,542	11,201
2013............................	38,994	49,193	16,163	1,468	27,957	11,505
2012............................	38,106	49,251	15,161	1,763	26,205	11,617
2011[2]	37,264	49,065	14,246	1,910	25,304	11,902
2010............................	34,434	57,804	14,718	3,960	24,581	14,861
2009............................	35,318	50,227	14,347	2,068	25,096	13,022
2008............................	34,445	51,187	13,726	2,215	25,148	13,547
2007............................	33,979	51,043	14,690	2,239	24,530	13,721
2006............................	33,316	50,682	15,642	2,636	23,794	14,079
2005............................	31,139	50,391	13,793	2,530	22,994	14,163
2004............................	28,954	57,630	13,498	4,788	22,277	16,566
2003[3]	29,564	50,108	14,469	2,592	22,479	14,765
2002............................	28,359	50,335	13,060	2,853	21,745	15,312

[1]For data prior to 1991, "Some college/Associate degree" equals 1 to 3 years of college completed; "Bachelor's degree" equals 4 years of college; "Advanced degree" equals 5 or more years of college completed.
[2]Starting in 2011, earnings data were created using population controls based on Census 2010 data.
[3]Starting in 2003, respondents could choose more than one race. The race data in this table from 2003 onward represent respondents who indicated only one race.
[4]Beginning in 2000, earnings data are from the expanded Current Population Survey (CPS) sample and were calculated using population controls based on Census 2000.
[5]May be of any race.
... = Not available.

Table A-34. Mean Earnings of Workers 18 Years Old and Over, by Educational Attainment, Race, Hispanic Origin, and Sex, 1975–2018—*Continued*

(Dollars except as noted.)

Race, sex, year, and Hispanic origin	Some college or associate's degree[1]		Bachelor's degree[1]		Advanced degree[1]	
	Mean earnings	Number of workers (thousands)	Mean earnings	Number of workers (thousands)	Mean earnings	Number of workers (thousands)
NON-HISPANIC WHITE ALONE OR IN COMBINATION						
Both Sexes						
2018	45,464	30,696	74,740	28,795	101,172	16,544
2017	43,712	30,929	70,848	28,240	100,016	16,138
2016	42,644	31,746	69,962	27,347	96,379	15,729
2015	40,705	32,404	67,469	26,896	93,459	15,633
2014	40,306	31,919	64,462	26,162	89,586	14,981
2013	38,177	32,311	61,814	25,858	92,592	14,598
2012	37,725	33,054	62,395	25,607	91,442	14,202
2011[2]	36,916	32,528	62,300	25,217	90,442	13,699
2010	36,046	32,321	60,111	24,730	85,960	13,644
2009	36,163	32,964	58,398	24,814	86,674	13,231
2008	36,042	33,806	60,818	24,717	84,996	13,358
2007	36,176	33,994	59,637	24,622	82,840	12,983
2006	35,795	32,962	58,785	24,103	83,629	12,433
2005	34,824	33,991	56,441	23,253	81,944	12,003
2004	33,192	33,201	53,335	22,815	79,166	11,961
2003[3]	32,732	33,062	52,823	22,686	76,029	11,777
2002	32,210	32,876	53,244	22,415	74,011	11,482
Male						
2018	56,378	15,607	90,190	14,618	126,140	7,993
2017	53,400	15,721	85,654	14,456	123,474	7,881
2016	51,344	16,121	86,032	13,879	117,742	7,730
2015	48,967	16,271	83,328	13,664	116,296	7,766
2014	49,537	15,922	80,000	13,283	113,429	7,439
2013	46,426	16,176	75,330	13,088	119,984	7,282
2012	46,207	16,520	75,609	13,257	115,320	7,215
2011[2]	45,417	16,018	75,075	13,067	112,884	7,108
2010	43,587	15,845	73,245	12,929	107,217	7,058
2009	43,680	16,218	72,222	12,834	107,782	6,821
2008	44,075	16,739	76,560	12,692	107,540	7,025
2007	43,707	16,973	75,109	12,715	104,236	6,830
2006	43,491	16,320	73,244	12,424	103,794	6,787
2005	43,083	16,769	70,891	12,187	103,850	6,593
2004	41,490	16,260	66,467	11,870	100,220	6,527
2003[3]	40,196	16,358	66,368	11,946	94,830	6,471
2002	40,195	16,390	66,776	11,859	100,412	6,510
Female						
2018	34,175	15,089	58,810	14,177	77,832	8,551
2017	33,698	15,208	55,319	13,783	77,626	8,257
2016	33,667	15,625	53,401	13,468	75,732	7,998
2015	32,372	16,132	51,092	13,232	70,913	7,866
2014	31,118	15,997	48,436	12,879	66,065	7,541
2013	29,907	16,135	47,960	12,769	65,324	7,315
2012	29,250	16,534	48,210	12,349	66,783	6,986
2011[2]	28,668	16,510	48,561	12,150	66,241	6,591
2010	28,332	18,995	45,130	12,937	63,092	7,050
2009	28,882	16,745	43,589	11,980	64,211	6,409
2008	28,163	17,067	44,203	12,025	59,983	6,332
2007	28,665	17,020	43,115	11,907	59,092	6,153
2006	28,248	16,641	43,402	11,678	59,389	5,646
2005	26,782	17,222	40,527	11,065	55,242	5,409
2004	25,079	18,925	38,886	11,633	53,859	5,718
2003[3]	25,422	16,704	37,757	10,739	53,102	5,306
2002	24,271	16,485	38,042	10,556	49,827	5,127

[1]For data prior to 1991, "Some college/Associate degree" equals 1 to 3 years of college completed; "Bachelor's degree" equals 4 years of college; "Advanced degree" equals 5 or more years of college completed.
[2]Starting in 2011, earnings data were created using population controls based on Census 2010 data.
[3]Starting in 2003, respondents could choose more than one race. The race data in this table from 2003 onward represent respondents who indicated only one race.
[4]Beginning in 2000, earnings data are from the expanded Current Population Survey (CPS) sample and were calculated using population controls based on Census 2000.
[5]May be of any race.
… = Not available.

Table A-34. Mean Earnings of Workers 18 Years Old and Over, by Educational Attainment, Race, Hispanic Origin, and Sex, 1975–2018—*Continued*

(Dollars except as noted.)

Race, sex, year, and Hispanic origin	Total		Not a high school graduate		High school graduate	
	Mean earnings	Number of workers (thousands)	Mean earnings	Number of workers (thousands)	Mean earnings	Number of workers (thousands)
BLACK ALONE OR IN COMBINATION						
Both Sexes						
2018............................	42,214	21,858	23,705	1,591	31,505	6,738
2017............................	41,274	21,401	23,937	1,484	31,926	6,656
2016............................	40,580	20,976	24,895	1,638	30,186	6,459
2015............................	39,326	20,228	19,655	1,677	29,060	6,260
2014............................	36,922	19,750	22,204	1,514	28,241	6,204
2013............................	35,571	19,045	20,951	1,726	26,594	5,960
2012............................	34,798	18,798	18,964	1,599	26,408	5,885
2011[2]	34,640	18,098	17,330	1,701	27,323	5,766
2010............................	33,050	17,838	17,525	1,747	25,842	5,786
2009............................	33,294	17,389	18,841	1,691	26,805	5,972
2008............................	32,878	18,157	18,049	1,826	27,123	6,220
2007............................	33,318	18,023	17,555	1,903	27,096	6,149
2006............................	32,384	17,721	17,842	1,995	26,290	6,305
2005............................	30,521	17,540	17,264	2,097	23,810	6,246
2004............................	29,031	17,110	17,821	2,085	23,458	6,299
2003[3]	28,854	16,871	16,238	2,177	23,956	6,082
2002............................	28,255	16,833	17,114	2,217	22,762	5,940
Male						
2018............................	46,264	10,127	27,788	833	36,822	3,544
2017............................	45,864	10,030	27,639	747	36,658	3,602
2016............................	46,496	9,842	28,803	868	35,148	3,389
2015............................	43,773	9,472	23,797	848	33,581	3,287
2014............................	42,302	9,139	25,531	802	32,701	3,179
2013............................	40,318	8,860	25,377	934	29,742	3,044
2012............................	38,147	8,772	19,877	869	29,982	3,033
2011[2]	38,722	8,350	20,704	861	31,081	2,927
2010............................	36,190	8,193	19,428	944	29,801	3,003
2009............................	37,500	7,963	21,585	912	30,541	3,087
2008............................	36,386	8,442	21,894	913	30,690	3,263
2007............................	35,669	8,405	19,932	1,019	29,508	3,083
2006............................	36,026	8,170	21,361	1,006	29,973	3,146
2005............................	34,258	8,127	19,996	1,093	27,189	3,142
2004............................	32,919	7,885	22,755	1,050	26,575	3,202
2003[3]	32,574	7,689	17,982	1,088	28,323	2,981
2002............................	31,967	7,734	20,537	1,114	25,510	2,902
Female						
2018............................	38,718	11,731	19,221	758	25,604	3,193
2017............................	37,224	11,370	20,184	737	26,345	3,054
2016............................	35,351	11,134	20,483	769	24,709	3,069
2015............................	35,411	10,756	15,420	829	24,060	2,972
2014............................	32,288	10,611	18,457	712	23,553	3,025
2013............................	31,442	10,185	15,723	791	23,309	2,916
2012............................	31,867	10,026	17,876	730	22,606	2,851
2011[2]	31,144	9,748	13,869	840	23,449	2,839
2010............................	30,383	9,646	15,292	804	21,570	2,783
2009............................	29,740	9,426	15,631	779	22,805	2,884
2008............................	29,829	9,715	14,204	913	23,187	2,957
2007............................	31,263	9,618	14,816	884	24,669	3,065
2006............................	29,268	9,551	14,257	988	22,622	3,159
2005............................	27,295	9,413	14,289	1,003	20,389	3,104
2004............................	25,707	9,225	12,818	1,035	20,236	3,097
2003[3]	25,739	9,182	14,495	1,089	19,765	3,100
2002............................	25,099	9,098	13,656	1,103	20,137	3,038

[1]For data prior to 1991, "Some college/Associate degree" equals 1 to 3 years of college completed; "Bachelor's degree" equals 4 years of college; "Advanced degree" equals 5 or more years of college completed.
[2]Starting in 2011, earnings data were created using population controls based on Census 2010 data.
[3]Starting in 2003, respondents could choose more than one race. The race data in this table from 2003 onward represent respondents who indicated only one race.
[4]Beginning in 2000, earnings data are from the expanded Current Population Survey (CPS) sample and were calculated using population controls based on Census 2000.
[5]May be of any race.
... = Not available.

Table A-34. Mean Earnings of Workers 18 Years Old and Over, by Educational Attainment, Race, Hispanic Origin, and Sex, 1975–2018—*Continued*

(Dollars except as noted.)

Race, sex, year, and Hispanic origin	Some college or associate's degree[1]		Bachelor's degree[1]		Advanced degree[1]	
	Mean earnings	Number of workers (thousands)	Mean earnings	Number of workers (thousands)	Mean earnings	Number of workers (thousands)
BLACK ALONE OR IN COMBINATION						
Both Sexes						
2018.........................	38,025	7,120	54,482	4,122	77,599	2,285
2017.........................	36,242	7,272	53,964	3,948	77,781	2,039
2016.........................	34,166	7,299	57,751	3,598	79,881	1,981
2015.........................	34,345	7,059	55,584	3,393	81,381	1,837
2014.........................	31,932	7,047	52,652	3,257	71,738	1,725
2013.........................	31,867	6,541	49,351	3,229	72,413	1,587
2012.........................	31,438	6,743	49,385	3,021	69,209	1,548
2011[2]	32,580	6,274	45,809	2,922	70,880	1,433
2010.........................	30,901	6,262	44,743	2,730	71,409	1,313
2009.........................	30,451	5,823	47,773	2,696	67,075	1,205
2008.........................	30,266	6,207	46,983	2,654	66,247	1,248
2007.........................	32,580	6,056	46,555	2,761	64,714	1,152
2006.........................	31,175	5,759	47,740	2,580	64,563	1,080
2005.........................	28,817	5,576	47,641	2,501	63,065	1,118
2004.........................	27,801	5,370	42,131	2,415	64,545	942
2003[3]	27,095	5,296	42,991	2,374	63,966	940
2002.........................	27,582	5,441	42,099	2,340	60,458	884
Male						
2018.........................	44,706	3,105	58,203	1,860	86,444	783
2017.........................	40,854	3,197	61,668	1,708	92,018	775
2016.........................	38,631	3,230	70,663	1,626	101,400	727
2015.........................	39,238	3,084	63,992	1,537	90,477	714
2014.........................	37,034	3,034	60,583	1,446	91,907	675
2013.........................	37,568	2,852	56,800	1,387	88,936	640
2012.........................	35,733	2,973	54,483	1,270	81,457	625
2011[2]	37,776	2,799	50,163	1,218[3]	87,635	543
2010.........................	35,132	2,618	48,948	1,113	82,022	514
2009.........................	35,842	2,409	55,824	1,068	79,551	485
2008.........................	34,159	2,631	52,773	1,103	73,362	530
2007.........................	33,845	2,621	52,951	1,200	75,355	480
2006.........................	34,784	2,417	52,382	1,124	74,769	475
2005.........................	33,449	2,380	53,556	1,049	76,407	462
2004.........................	32,466	2,258	47,448	976	77,648	398
2003[3]	31,591	2,233	45,705	982	76,954	402
2002.........................	32,696	2,375	46,942	1,009	76,003	332
Female						
2018.........................	32,856	4,014	51,423	2,261	72,984	1,502
2017.........................	32,623	4,074	48,089	2,240	69,040	1,263
2016.........................	30,622	4,069	47,094	1,971	67,406	1,254
2015.........................	30,548	3,974	48,620	1,855	75,598	1,123
2014.........................	28,073	4,013	46,315	1,810	58,757	1,050
2013.........................	27,457	3,688	43,738	1,841	61,233	946
2012.........................	28,051	3,769	45,688	1,751	60,912	923
2011[2]	28,395	3,475	42,696	1,704	60,632	889
2010.........................	27,861	3,644	41,846	1,616	64,577	799
2009.........................	26,646	3,414	42,487	1,627	58,664	719
2008.........................	27,399	3,575	42,861	1,550	60,996	718
2007.........................	31,614	3,435	41,636	1,561	57,105	672
2006.........................	28,565	3,342	44,157	1,456	56,541	605
2005.........................	25,366	3,195	43,369	1,452	53,669	656
2004.........................	24,415	3,111	38,522	1,438	54,931	543
2003[3]	23,816	3,063	41,073	1,391	54,265	538
2002.........................	23,621	3,066	38,447	1,339	51,101	552

[1]For data prior to 1991, "Some college/Associate degree" equals 1 to 3 years of college completed; "Bachelor's degree" equals 4 years of college; "Advanced degree" equals 5 or more years of college completed.
[2]Starting in 2011, earnings data were created using population controls based on Census 2010 data.
[3]Starting in 2003, respondents could choose more than one race. The race data in this table from 2003 onward represent respondents who indicated only one race.
[4]Beginning in 2000, earnings data are from the expanded Current Population Survey (CPS) sample and were calculated using population controls based on Census 2000.
[5]May be of any race.
... = Not available.

Table A-34. Mean Earnings of Workers 18 Years Old and Over, by Educational Attainment, Race, Hispanic Origin, and Sex, 1975–2018—*Continued*

(Dollars except as noted.)

Race, sex, year, and Hispanic origin	Total Mean earnings	Total Number of workers (thousands)	Not a high school graduate Mean earnings	Not a high school graduate Number of workers (thousands)	High school graduate Mean earnings	High school graduate Number of workers (thousands)
ASIAN ALONE OR IN COMBINATION						
Both Sexes						
2018	69,591	11,270	25,065	569	35,222	1,738
2017	66,240	10,932	29,126	602	35,168	1,758
2016	62,413	10,599	27,996	567	32,276	1,866
2015	60,892	10,057	23,340	591	33,847	1,652
2014	56,577	9,805	21,960	610	29,376	1,703
2013	54,320	9,367	24,499	613	31,088	1,726
2012	54,277	9,067	23,974	543	30,241	1,555
2011[2]	50,943	8,587	21,649	592	28,304	1,609
2010	48,480	8,563	20,592	620	28,452	1,629
2009	61,575	4,022	20,995	267	32,985	747
2008	50,622	7,553	21,195	569	29,163	1,300
2007	48,865	7,563	21,399	530	28,524	1,331
2006	50,094	7,501	20,142	631	29,502	1,413
2005	45,269	7,131	22,330	629	27,059	1,413
2004	43,856	6,771	19,536	525	27,946	1,292
2003[3]	41,563	6,560	19,548	564	25,554	1,256
2002	40,323	6,424	16,969	559	25,038	1,221
Male						
2018	80,618	5,954	28,661	309	40,956	946
2017	77,742	5,821	34,659	300	41,564	981
2016	74,131	5,602	34,904	289	37,283	984
2015	70,202	5,322	26,205	315	38,246	886
2014	65,545	5,124	26,738	294	32,798	887
2013	63,189	5,032	24,585	302	36,133	951
2012	63,269	4,759	24,720	262	32,762	819
2011[2]	59,326	4,489	25,638	318	32,392	828
2010	56,115	4,461	23,836	330	31,685	820
2009	61,575	4,022	20,995	267	32,985	747
2008	59,565	4,007	23,204	297	34,568	655
2007	56,990	3,945	24,261	254	33,105	685
2006	59,328	3,980	22,631	318	32,716	783
2005	53,761	3,797	27,107	328	30,490	790
2004	52,032	3,634	20,799	252	31,194	730
2003[3]	48,062	3,522	23,122	308	28,514	635
2002	48,128	3,469	18,101	312	29,493	633
Female						
2018	57,238	5,315	20,784	259	28,375	792
2017	53,139	5,111	23,640	302	27,100	777
2016	49,273	4,996	20,803	277	26,695	882
2015	50,426	4,734	20,074	276	28,752	765
2014	46,761	4,681	17,496	315	25,652	815
2013	44,026	4,335	24,416	311	24,895	775
2012	44,342	4,307	23,277	280	27,432	735
2011[2]	41,759	4,097	17,012	274	23,973	781
2010	40,177	4,102	16,895	290	25,175	809
2009	42,848	3,561	20,121	239	25,448	713
2008	40,518	3,546	18,999	272	23,665	644
2007	40,002	3,617	18,753	275	23,660	645
2006	39,652	3,520	17,610	313	25,508	630
2005	35,593	3,333	17,122	301	22,703	622
2004	34,387	3,137	18,375	273	23,721	562
2003[3]	34,031	3,038	15,233	255	22,530	621
2002	31,157	2,954	15,536	247	20,242	588

[1]For data prior to 1991, "Some college/Associate degree" equals 1 to 3 years of college completed; "Bachelor's degree" equals 4 years of college; "Advanced degree" equals 5 or more years of college completed.
[2]Starting in 2011, earnings data were created using population controls based on Census 2010 data.
[3]Starting in 2003, respondents could choose more than one race. The race data in this table from 2003 onward represent respondents who indicated only one race.
[4]Beginning in 2000, earnings data are from the expanded Current Population Survey (CPS) sample and were calculated using population controls based on Census 2000.
[5]May be of any race.
… = Not available.

Table A-34. Mean Earnings of Workers 18 Years Old and Over, by Educational Attainment, Race, Hispanic Origin, and Sex, 1975–2018—*Continued*

(Dollars except as noted.)

Race, sex, year, and Hispanic origin	Some college or associate's degree[1]		Bachelor's degree[1]		Advanced degree[1]	
	Mean earnings	Number of workers (thousands)	Mean earnings	Number of workers (thousands)	Mean earnings	Number of workers (thousands)
ASIAN ALONE OR IN COMBINATION						
Both Sexes						
2018	40,026	2,111	72,079	3,902	116,324	2,948
2017	37,559	2,149	70,857	3,573	109,132	2,848
2016	37,279	2,246	67,706	3,189	104,680	2,729
2015	38,217	2,051	64,314	3,259	101,782	2,501
2014	32,506	1,974	64,665	3,294	96,335	2,222
2013	33,613	1,984	58,218	2,948	96,346	2,094
2012	32,728	1,989	58,891	2,865	93,791	2,113
2011[2]	34,825	1,796	57,118	2,784	87,273	1,804
2010	30,190	1,832	55,988	2,713	84,095	1,770
2009	37,106	793	62,504	1,237	113,267	976
2008	32,577	1,630	58,179	2,403	84,523	1,649
2007	33,846	1,630	54,204	2,454	81,694	1,615
2006	33,050	1,495	55,827	2,375	87,887	1,585
2005	31,332	1,504	51,750	2,204	79,229	1,379
2004	29,377	1,491	47,711	2,226	81,310	1,237
2003[3]	27,083	1,495	47,945	1,948	73,812	1,295
2002	27,146	1,456	46,218	1,984	72,943	1,202
Male						
2018	44,559	1,110	86,473	1,939	130,513	1,649
2017	43,886	1,100	85,215	1,806	121,921	1,633
2016	43,483	1,171	77,744	1,604	124,132	1,554
2015	39,357	1,004	73,370	1,671	117,211	1,444
2014	37,109	998	71,395	1,677	112,206	1,266
2013	36,128	1,060	67,355	1,521	113,152	1,196
2012	37,917	981	68,713	1,439	104,757	1,256
2011[2]	41,887	918	65,569	1,392	98,425	1,032
2010	34,074	935	64,038	1,365	96,127	1,012
2009	37,106	793	62,504	1,237	113,267	976
2008	37,228	865	66,880	1,228	98,718	959
2007	40,965	875	60,606	1,187	93,566	942
2006	37,104	736	66,740	1,191	101,474	950
2005	35,583	758	62,247	1,097	92,170	823
2004	34,237	736	56,581	1,127	91,406	789
2003[3]	31,430	746	52,179	1,024	83,131	807
2002	32,427	744	54,683	1,006	82,134	772
Female						
2018	34,996	1,000	57,864	1,963	98,312	1,299
2017	30,923	1,049	56,176	1,766	91,932	1,214
2016	30,524	1,075	57,544	1,584	78,963	1,175
2015	37,124	1,046	54,785	1,588	80,694	1,056
2014	27,803	976	57,684	1,617	75,320	956
2013	30,727	924	48,470	1,426	73,960	898
2012	27,683	1,008	48,971	1,425	77,697	856
2011[2]	27,441	878	48,660	1,391	72,373	772
2010	26,144	897	47,839	1,348	68,048	759
2009	27,565	717	48,655	1,241	76,052	650
2008	27,315	764	49,076	1,174	64,802	690
2007	25,597	755	48,200	1,266	65,098	673
2006	29,116	759	44,846	1,183	67,514	634
2005	27,007	745	41,350	1,107	60,077	556
2004	24,634	754	38,618	1,099	63,553	448
2003[3]	22,750	748	43,252	924	58,391	487
2002	21,615	711	37,507	978	56,417	429

[1] For data prior to 1991, "Some college/Associate degree" equals 1 to 3 years of college completed; "Bachelor's degree" equals 4 years of college; "Advanced degree" equals 5 or more years of college completed.
[2] Starting in 2011, earnings data were created using population controls based on Census 2010 data.
[3] Starting in 2003, respondents could choose more than one race. The race data in this table from 2003 onward represent respondents who indicated only one race.
[4] Beginning in 2000, earnings data are from the expanded Current Population Survey (CPS) sample and were calculated using population controls based on Census 2000.
[5] May be of any race.
... = Not available.

Table A-35. Median Annual Earnings and Number of Full-Time Year-Round Workers 25 Years Old and Over, by Highest Level of Educational Attainment and Sex, 1991–2019

(Dollars except as noted; people 25 years old and over as of March of the following year; income in current and 2019 CPI-U-RS adjusted dollars.)

				Elementary/secondary					
	Total			Less than 9th Grade			Some high school, no diploma		
Sex and year	Number of persons with earnings who worked full time, year round (thousands)	Median annual earnings		Number of persons with earnings who worked full time, year round (thousands)	Median annual earnings		Number of persons with earnings who worked full time, year round (thousands)	Median annual earnings	
		Current dollars	2019 dollars		Current dollars	2019 dollars		Current dollars	2019 dollars
Male									
2019	103,016	49,647	49,647	3,609	24,420	24,420	5,595	25,598	25,598
2018	101,876	46,680	46,680	3,935	22,678	22,678	6,080	23,649	23,649
2017[1]	101,067	45,399	46,506	3,939	21,393	21,914	6,315	24,293	24,885
2017	101,040	45,256	46,359	3,903	21,899	22,433	6,249	24,085	24,672
2016	99,369	42,747	44,731	4,021	21,263	22,250	6,172	23,165	24,240
2015	98,367	41,886	44,395	4,328	20,877	22,128	6,420	22,214	23,545
2014	96,753	40,846	43,367	4,467	19,553	20,760	6,445	21,701	23,041
2013[2]	95,921	40,328	43,542	4,682	18,503	19,978	6,120	20,021	21,617
2013[3]	95,253	39,602	42,759	4,464	19,701	21,271	6,557	21,417	23,124
2012	94,263	38,428	42,106	4,510	18,002	19,725	6,418	19,780	21,673
2011	93,141	37,653	42,130	4,633	17,505	19,587	6,650	20,437	22,867
2010	92,242	36,852	42,534	4,757	16,384	18,910	6,625	19,356	22,340
2009	91,745	36,801	43,176	4,736	16,473	19,327	6,948	19,720	23,136
2008	91,653	37,463	43,800	4,973	17,043	19,926	7,158	20,845	24,371
2007	90,647	37,828	45,925	5,036	16,625	20,184	7,200	20,643	25,062
2006	89,816	36,847	46,003	5,283	17,169	21,435	7,684	21,184	26,448
2005	88,804	35,758	46,090	5,475	16,321	21,037	7,276	20,934	26,983
2004	87,570	34,823	46,406	5,520	16,171	21,550	7,254	19,593	26,110
2003	86,532	33,517	45,872	5,405	15,461	21,160	7,245	18,990	25,990
2002	85,668	32,471	45,450	5,705	15,130	21,177	7,488	19,802	27,717
2001	84,389	32,494	46,199	5,809	14,594	20,749	7,421	19,434	27,631
2000	83,860	32,155	47,018	5,724	14,131	20,663	7,226	18,915	27,658
1999	82,795	31,545	47,692	5,728	13,529	20,454	7,085	17,653	26,689
1998	80,869	30,654	47,331	5,641	12,571	19,410	7,366	17,462	26,962
1997	80,263	28,919	45,257	5,839	12,157	19,025	7,601	16,818	26,319
1996	79,423	27,248	43,564	6,139	12,174	19,464	7,671	16,058	25,673
1995	78,264	26,346	43,243	6,277	11,723	19,242	7,490	15,791	25,919
1994	77,546	25,465	42,804	6,507	11,324	19,035	7,286	14,584	24,514
1993	76,419	24,605	42,222	6,734	10,895	18,696	7,377	14,550	24,968
1992	75,872	23,894	42,036	7,000	10,374	18,251	7,524	14,218	25,013
1991	75,137	23,686	42,706	7,143	10,319	18,605	7,759	14,736	26,569
Female									
2019	105,587	31,773	31,773	2,903	13,129	13,129	4,960	15,694	15,694
2018	103,733	30,137	30,137	3,082	12,735	12,735	5,201	14,176	14,176
2017[1]	103,240	28,391	29,083	3,270	12,282	12,581	5,433	14,037	14,379
2017	103,352	27,709	28,384	3,294	12,365	12,666	5,471	13,801	14,137
2016	101,906	27,259	28,524	3,212	12,045	12,604	5,471	13,666	14,300
2015	101,006	26,282	27,856	3,569	11,863	12,574	5,508	12,768	13,533
2014	99,193	25,071	26,619	3,644	11,558	12,271	5,934	12,364	13,127
2013[2]	98,670	24,773	26,748	3,664	11,249	12,146	5,692	11,840	12,784
2013[3]	96,915	24,756	26,729	3,633	11,395	12,303	5,677	11,869	12,815
2012	96,256	23,946	26,238	3,674	10,841	11,879	5,898	11,981	13,128
2011	95,404	23,395	26,177	3,839	11,113	12,434	6,235	12,193	13,643
2010	94,679	22,934	26,470	3,897	10,680	12,327	6,003	12,075	13,937
2009	93,426	23,159	27,171	4,036	10,516	12,338	6,175	12,278	14,405
2008	93,143	22,944	26,825	4,201	10,625	12,422	6,413	11,904	13,917
2007	92,075	23,052	27,986	4,070	10,539	12,795	6,286	11,982	14,547
2006	91,315	21,900	27,342	4,257	10,451	13,048	6,750	11,914	14,874
2005	90,762	20,806	26,818	4,579	9,496	12,240	6,812	11,136	14,354
2004	89,794	20,147	26,848	4,742	9,576	12,761	6,982	10,751	14,327
2003	89,118	19,679	26,933	4,734	9,296	12,723	6,965	10,786	14,762
2002	88,903	18,965	26,545	5,015	8,965	12,548	7,103	10,613	14,855
2001	88,075	18,549	26,372	5,196	8,846	12,577	7,376	10,330	14,687
2000	87,619	18,032	26,367	5,195	8,546	12,496	7,565	10,063	14,715
1999	87,229	17,022	25,735	5,397	8,261	12,489	7,525	9,632	14,562
1998	84,819	16,258	25,103	5,419	7,914	12,220	7,559	9,582	14,795
1997	83,821	15,573	24,371	5,647	7,505	11,745	7,661	8,861	13,867
1996	83,056	14,682	23,473	5,775	7,276	11,633	7,929	8,544	13,660
1995	82,457	13,821	22,685	6,020	7,096	11,647	8,122	8,057	13,224
1994	81,829	12,766	21,458	6,183	6,865	11,539	7,943	7,618	12,805
1993	80,898	12,234	20,994	6,423	6,480	11,120	8,152	7,187	12,333
1992	79,854	11,922	20,974	6,921	6,337	11,149	8,248	7,293	12,830
1991	79,383	11,580	20,879	7,065	6,268	11,301	8,561	7,055	12,720

100,000+ = The medians were topcoded. Beginning with 2009 income data, the Census Bureau expanded the upper income interval used to calculate medians and Gini indexes from $100,000 to $250,000.

X = Not available.

[1]Implementation of an updated CPS ASEC processing system.

[2]The 2014 CPS ASEC included redesigned questions for income and health insurance coverage. All of the approximately 98,000 addresses were eligible to receive the redesigned set of health insurance coverage questions. The redesigned income questions were implemented to a subsample of the 98,000 addresses using a probability split panel design. Approximately 68,000 addresses were eligible to receive a set of income questions similar to those used in the 2013 CPS ASEC and the remaining 30,000 addresses were eligible to receive the redesigned income questions. The source of these 2013 estimates is the portion of the CPS ASEC sample which received the redesigned income questions, approximately 30,000 addresses.

[3]The source of these 2013 estimates is the portion of the CPS ASEC sample which received the income questions consistent with the 2013 CPS ASEC, approximately 68,000 addresses.

**Table A-35. Median Annual Earnings and Number of Full-Time Year-Round Workers
25 Years Old and Over, by Highest Level of Educational Attainment and Sex,
1991–2019**—*Continued*

(Dollars except as noted; people 25 years old and over as of March of the following year; income in current and 2019 CPI-U-RS adjusted dollars.)

	Elementary/secondary			College					
	High school graduate (includes equivalency)			Some college, no degree			Associate degree		
	Number of persons with earnings who worked full time, year round (thousands)	Median annual earnings		Number of persons with earnings who worked full time, year round (thousands)	Median annual earnings		Number of persons with earnings who worked full time, year round (thousands)	Median annual earnings	
Sex and year		Current dollars	2019 dollars		Current dollars	2019 dollars		Current dollars	2019 dollars
Male									
2019	29,598	37,144	37,144	15,715	45,639	45,639	10,089	51,250	51,250
2018	29,311	36,476	36,476	16,034	42,379	42,379	9,647	50,034	50,034
2017[1]	29,321	35,143	36,000	16,234	40,718	41,711	9,356	46,852	47,994
2017	29,381	35,276	36,136	16,300	40,912	41,909	9,401	46,518	47,652
2016	29,326	33,516	35,071	16,171	40,232	42,099	9,355	45,987	48,121
2015	28,760	32,307	34,242	16,218	39,823	42,208	9,171	43,785	46,408
2014	28,988	32,080	34,060	15,963	37,865	40,202	8,728	43,871	46,579
2013[2]	29,036	31,188	33,674	16,248	37,741	40,749	8,509	42,717	46,122
2013[3]	28,677	31,288	33,782	15,615	37,424	40,407	8,654	42,176	45,538
2012	28,115	31,064	34,037	15,752	37,062	40,609	8,499	41,731	45,725
2011	28,295	30,616	34,257	15,301	36,552	40,898	8,286	41,916	46,900
2010	28,307	30,250	34,914	15,395	36,226	41,811	7,924	40,974	47,291
2009	28,946	30,303	35,552	15,184	36,693	43,049	7,399	42,163	49,467
2008	28,450	30,879	36,102	15,523	37,297	43,606	7,375	42,608	49,815
2007	27,988	31,337	38,045	15,321	37,447	45,463	7,244	43,006	52,211
2006	28,253	31,009	38,714	14,526	37,271	46,532	6,973	41,807	52,195
2005	28,077	30,134	38,841	14,505	36,930	47,601	7,000	41,903	54,011
2004	27,799	29,332	39,088	14,405	36,162	48,190	6,782	39,765	52,991
2003	26,800	28,763	39,365	14,586	35,073	48,001	6,618	39,015	53,397
2002	26,298	27,526	38,528	14,747	35,023	49,022	6,274	37,970	53,147
2001	25,954	28,343	40,297	14,340	33,777	48,023	6,352	38,870	55,264
2000	26,175	27,480	40,182	14,433	33,319	48,720	6,272	38,026	55,603
1999	26,278	27,188	41,104	14,440	32,575	49,249	5,939	36,558	55,270
1998	25,636	26,542	40,982	13,935	31,627	48,834	5,766	35,962	55,527
1997	25,777	25,453	39,833	13,892	30,536	47,788	5,591	32,930	51,534
1996	25,510	24,814	39,672	13,756	29,160	46,621	5,210	33,065	52,864
1995	24,909	23,365	38,351	13,715	28,004	45,965	5,230	31,027	50,927
1994	24,704	22,387	37,631	13,573	26,768	44,995	5,046	30,643	51,508
1993	24,682	21,782	37,378	13,247	26,323	45,171	4,901	29,736	51,027
1992	25,143	21,645	38,080	12,728	26,318	46,301	4,540	28,791	50,651
1991	25,297	21,546	38,848	12,366	26,591	47,944	4,083	29,358	52,633
Female									
2019	26,755	22,052	22,052	16,314	28,653	28,653	12,478	31,652	31,652
2018	27,264	21,133	21,133	16,616	26,498	26,498	11,924	30,957	30,957
2017[1]	27,595	20,342	20,838	16,915	25,625	26,250	11,935	30,567	31,312
2017	27,672	20,199	20,691	16,919	25,161	25,774	11,905	30,406	31,147
2016	27,483	19,904	20,828	17,033	25,433	26,613	11,870	29,538	30,909
2015	27,607	19,810	20,997	17,437	24,512	25,980	11,409	28,664	30,381
2014	27,688	19,208	20,394	16,851	23,504	24,955	11,069	27,122	28,796
2013[2]	27,640	20,060	21,659	16,776	22,301	24,079	11,265	27,340	29,519
2013[3]	27,482	18,325	19,786	16,805	22,814	24,632	10,887	27,340	29,519
2012	27,717	18,213	19,956	16,625	22,469	24,619	10,757	27,159	29,758
2011	28,051	17,887	20,014	16,427	22,499	25,174	10,353	27,180	30,412
2010	28,314	17,826	20,574	16,661	22,808	26,325	10,197	28,147	32,487
2009	28,154	18,340	21,517	16,208	23,107	27,110	9,936	27,027	31,709
2008	28,217	18,293	21,387	16,329	23,252	27,185	9,662	27,715	32,403
2007	28,134	18,162	22,050	16,600	23,532	28,569	9,166	27,668	33,590
2006	28,538	17,546	21,906	16,099	22,709	28,352	9,043	26,295	32,829
2005	28,409	16,695	21,519	16,402	21,545	27,770	9,070	26,074	33,608
2004	28,561	16,165	21,542	15,791	21,159	28,197	8,861	25,199	33,581
2003	28,976	15,962	21,846	15,691	21,007	28,751	8,523	24,808	33,953
2002	29,161	15,972	22,356	15,616	20,602	28,837	8,323	23,766	33,265
2001	28,945	15,665	22,272	15,420	20,101	28,579	8,177	22,638	32,186
2000	28,968	15,153	22,157	15,825	20,166	29,487	8,108	23,124	33,813
1999	29,798	14,652	22,152	15,693	19,599	29,631	7,482	21,916	33,134
1998	29,330	13,786	21,286	15,173	18,445	28,480	6,931	21,290	32,873
1997	29,332	13,407	20,981	14,677	17,153	26,844	6,914	21,073	32,978
1996	29,212	12,702	20,308	14,528	16,255	25,988	6,839	20,460	32,711
1995	28,785	12,046	19,772	14,619	15,552	25,527	6,642	19,450	31,925
1994	29,110	11,390	19,146	14,911	14,585	24,516	6,573	17,954	30,179
1993	29,171	11,089	19,029	14,390	14,489	24,863	6,282	18,346	31,482
1992	29,596	10,901	19,178	13,615	14,401	25,335	5,539	17,331	30,490
1991	30,149	10,818	19,505	13,013	13,963	25,176	5,236	17,364	31,308

100,000+ = The medians were topcoded. Beginning with 2009 income data, the Census Bureau expanded the upper income interval used to calculate medians and Gini indexes from $100,000 to $250,000.
X = Not available.
[1]Implementation of an updated CPS ASEC processing system.
[2]The 2014 CPS ASEC included redesigned questions for income and health insurance coverage. All of the approximately 98,000 addresses were eligible to receive the redesigned set of health insurance coverage questions. The redesigned income questions were implemented to a subsample of the 98,000 addresses using a probability split panel design. Approximately 68,000 addresses were eligible to receive a set of income questions similar to those used in the 2013 CPS ASEC and the remaining 30,000 addresses were eligible to receive the redesigned income questions. The source of these 2013 estimates is the portion of the CPS ASEC sample which received the redesigned income questions, approximately 30,000 addresses.
[3]The source of these 2013 estimates is the portion of the CPS ASEC sample which received the income questions consistent with the 2013 CPS ASEC, approximately 68,000 addresses.

Table A-35. Median Annual Earnings and Number of Full-Time Year-Round Workers 25 Years Old and Over, by Highest Level of Educational Attainment and Sex, 1991–2019—*Continued*

(Dollars except as noted; people 25 years old and over as of March of the following year; income in current and 2019 CPI-U-RS adjusted dollars.)

	College								
	Bachelor's or higher degree								
	Total			Bachelor's degree			Master's degree		
	Number of persons with earnings who worked full time, year round (thousands)	Median annual earnings		Number of persons with earnings who worked full time, year round (thousands)	Median annual earnings		Number of persons with earnings who worked full time, year round (thousands)	Median annual earnings	
Sex and year		Current dollars	2019 dollars		Current dollars	2019 dollars		Current dollars	2019 dollars
Male									
2019	38,411	77,326	77,326	23,885	69,505	69,505	10,038	88,280	88,280
2018	36,869	74,161	74,161	23,087	65,981	65,981	9,430	85,600	85,600
2017[1]	35,902	72,335	74,098	22,516	64,396	65,966	9,098	82,469	84,479
2017	35,807	72,315	74,078	22,462	65,325	66,917	9,059	82,722	84,738
2016	34,324	70,853	74,141	21,342	63,269	66,205	8,880	80,083	83,799
2015	33,470	70,437	74,656	20,772	62,304	66,036	8,594	78,222	82,908
2014	32,162	67,367	71,525	20,147	60,933	64,694	7,992	76,386	81,101
2013[2]	31,326	69,639	75,190	19,388	60,808	65,655	7,867	75,525	81,545
2013[3]	31,285	65,526	70,749	19,513	58,170	62,807	7,705	75,407	81,418
2012	30,969	63,272	69,327	19,320	56,656	62,078	7,652	71,364	78,194
2011	29,976	62,282	69,688	18,859	56,404	63,111	7,238	71,537	80,044
2010	29,234	61,522	71,000	18,378	55,225	63,740	7,100	69,576	80,303
2009	28,532	61,280	71,895	18,205	54,091	63,461	6,728	69,825	81,920
2008	28,174	63,277	73,980	17,726	57,278	66,966	6,896	70,973	82,978
2007	27,857	62,421	75,782	17,654	56,826	68,990	6,759	71,097	86,315
2006	27,097	61,168	76,367	17,129	54,403	67,921	6,350	67,425	84,179
2005	26,470	58,114	74,906	16,764	51,700	66,639	6,137	64,468	83,096
2004	25,810	56,434	75,205	16,302	51,081	68,071	6,059	63,260	84,301
2003	25,879	55,751	76,302	16,295	50,916	69,684	6,076	61,698	84,441
2002	25,155	55,188	77,246	16,057	50,600	70,825	5,768	60,830	85,144
2001	24,512	54,069	76,873	15,723	49,985	71,067	5,522	61,960	88,092
2000	24,028	53,488	78,212	15,452	49,080	71,767	5,346	59,732	87,342
1999	23,325	52,246	78,988	14,922	47,289	71,494	5,178	59,189	89,485
1998	22,525	50,272	77,622	14,614	45,749	70,639	4,772	55,784	86,133
1997	21,563	47,126	73,750	13,900	41,949	65,648	4,583	52,530	82,207
1996	21,136	44,161	70,604	13,510	39,624	63,350	4,709	50,003	79,944
1995	20,644	43,322	71,107	13,065	39,040	64,079	4,774	49,076	80,552
1994	20,429	42,027	70,644	12,997	38,701	65,053	4,558	46,635	78,389
1993	19,479	41,649	71,470	12,360	37,474	64,306	4,320	45,597	78,245
1992	18,937	40,557	71,351	11,938	36,745	64,645	4,308	44,293	77,924
1991	18,490	39,803	71,766	11,657	36,067	65,030	4,356	43,125	77,755
Female									
2019	42,177	51,766	51,766	26,057	45,942	45,942	12,774	60,601	60,601
2018	39,645	50,385	50,385	24,458	43,951	43,951	12,023	56,545	56,545
2017[1]	38,092	49,395	50,599	23,578	42,174	43,202	11,341	56,945	58,333
2017	38,092	48,223	49,399	23,562	41,827	42,847	11,379	56,806	58,191
2016	36,837	46,788	48,959	22,865	41,045	42,950	11,009	54,571	57,103
2015	35,477	45,170	47,876	22,045	40,115	42,518	10,558	51,494	54,579
2014	34,007	43,330	46,005	21,336	40,033	42,504	9,876	50,255	53,357
2013[2]	33,633	42,063	45,416	21,508	37,424	40,407	9,661	49,731	53,695
2013[3]	32,432	43,115	46,552	20,430	39,201	42,326	9,397	50,507	54,533
2012	31,585	42,027	46,049	20,125	37,285	40,853	9,124	49,703	54,460
2011	30,498	41,338	46,254	19,629	36,812	41,189	8,650	48,738	54,533
2010	29,606	41,112	47,451	18,909	36,359	41,965	8,507	48,488	55,964
2009	28,917	40,766	47,828	18,844	35,972	42,203	7,945	50,576	59,337
2008	28,321	40,801	47,702	18,381	36,294	42,433	7,801	48,000	56,119
2007	27,820	40,712	49,426	18,347	36,167	43,909	7,590	48,077	58,368
2006	26,626	39,450	49,253	17,931	35,094	43,814	6,876	46,250	57,742
2005	25,490	37,055	47,762	17,090	32,668	42,107	6,560	44,385	57,210
2004	24,857	35,726	47,609	16,668	31,585	42,091	6,464	42,243	56,294
2003	24,229	35,125	48,073	16,198	31,309	42,850	6,268	41,334	56,570
2002	23,686	34,292	47,998	16,003	30,788	43,094	6,073	40,939	57,302
2001	22,961	33,842	48,115	15,660	30,973	44,036	5,749	40,744	57,928
2000	21,958	33,148	48,470	15,102	30,418	44,478	5,421	40,619	59,395
1999	21,334	31,604	47,781	14,690	28,520	43,118	5,220	39,712	60,039
1998	20,409	30,692	47,390	14,218	27,415	42,330	4,837	36,888	56,957
1997	19,590	29,781	46,606	13,787	26,401	41,317	4,488	35,882	56,154
1996	18,775	27,556	44,056	13,247	25,192	40,277	4,285	33,302	53,243
1995	18,269	26,843	44,059	12,875	24,065	39,499	4,205	33,509	55,001
1994	17,109	26,237	44,102	11,773	23,405	39,342	4,166	32,069	53,905
1993	16,480	25,246	43,322	11,447	22,452	38,528	4,003	31,389	53,864
1992	15,933	25,093	44,146	11,133	22,383	39,378	3,873	30,169	53,076
1991	15,359	23,627	42,600	10,721	20,967	37,804	3,745	29,747	53,635

100,000+ = The medians were topcoded. Beginning with 2009 income data, the Census Bureau expanded the upper income interval used to calculate medians and Gini indexes from $100,000 to $250,000.

X = Not available.

[1] Implementation of an updated CPS ASEC processing system.

[2] The 2014 CPS ASEC included redesigned questions for income and health insurance coverage. All of the approximately 98,000 addresses were eligible to receive the redesigned set of health insurance coverage questions. The redesigned income questions were implemented to a subsample of the 98,000 addresses using a probability split panel design. Approximately 68,000 addresses were eligible to receive a set of income questions similar to those used in the 2013 CPS ASEC and the remaining 30,000 addresses were eligible to receive the redesigned income questions. The source of these 2013 estimates is the portion of the CPS ASEC sample which received the redesigned income questions, approximately 30,000 addresses.

[3] The source of these 2013 estimates is the portion of the CPS ASEC sample which received the income questions consistent with the 2013 CPS ASEC, approximately 68,000 addresses.

Table A-35. Median Annual Earnings and Number of Full-Time Year-Round Workers 25 Years Old and Over, by Highest Level of Educational Attainment and Sex, 1991–2019—Continued

(Dollars except as noted; people 25 years old and over as of March of the following year; income in current and 2019 CPI-U-RS adjusted dollars.)

	College					
	Bachelor's or higher degree					
	Professional degree			Doctorate degree		
		Median annual earnings			Median annual earnings	
Sex and year	Number of persons with earnings who worked full time, year round (thousands)	Current dollars	2019 dollars	Number of persons with earnings who worked full time, year round (thousands)	Current dollars	2019 dollars
Male						
2019	1,898	127,625	127,625	2,590	106,472	106,472
2018	1,796	120,030	120,030	2,556	100,658	100,658
2017[1]	1,725	121,925	124,897	2,562	104,946	107,504
2017	1,724	110,651	113,348	2,561	102,423	104,920
2016	1,735	107,506	112,495	2,367	101,591	106,305
2015	1,824	111,881	118,583	2,281	91,604	97,091
2014	1,940	107,050	113,658	2,082	91,770	97,435
2013[2]	1,762	102,353	110,511	2,309	101,336	109,413
2013[3]	1,802	101,504	109,595	2,265	93,712	101,182
2012	1,847	100,064	109,640	2,150	91,742	100,522
2011	1,903	98,883	110,641	1,976	82,376	92,171
2010	1,856	96,212	111,046	1,900	86,200	99,491
2009	1,844	102,398	120,136	1,755	89,845	105,408
2008	1,930	100,000+	(X)	1,622	90,575	105,895
2007	1,843	100,000+	(X)	1,601	86,171	104,616
2006	1,969	96,926	121,010	1,649	90,511	113,001
2005	1,912	90,878	117,137	1,656	76,937	99,168
2004	1,876	90,210	120,215	1,573	80,033	106,653
2003	1,901	88,530	121,164	1,606	73,853	101,076
2002	1,816	88,216	123,476	1,514	76,147	106,583
2001	1,779	81,602	116,019	1,488	72,642	103,280
2000	1,711	83,701	122,391	1,520	71,271	104,215
1999	1,774	81,545	123,284	1,451	70,461	106,527
1998	1,695	76,362	117,907	1,443	65,319	100,856
1997	1,741	72,274	113,106	1,338	68,643	107,424
1996	1,702	71,869	114,903	1,215	62,255	99,533
1995	1,657	66,257	108,752	1,149	57,356	94,142
1994	1,691	61,739	103,778	1,183	57,478	96,615
1993	1,650	69,678	119,568	1,149	55,751	95,669
1992	1,639	68,429	120,386	1,053	51,681	90,921
1991	1,547	63,741	114,926	929	51,845	93,478
Female						
2019	1,364	82,093	82,093	1,981	86,047	86,047
2018	1,275	77,868	77,868	1,889	77,412	77,412
2017[1]	1,345	78,121	80,025	1,827	80,081	82,033
2017	1,335	77,090	78,969	1,817	77,766	79,662
2016	1,333	76,523	80,074	1,629	72,018	75,360
2015	1,278	65,012	68,906	1,595	68,887	73,014
2014	1,319	63,353	67,264	1,475	62,388	66,239
2013[2]	1,224	61,224	66,104	1,241	65,673	70,908
2013[3]	1,294	68,826	74,312	1,310	64,001	69,102
2012	1,126	67,428	73,881	1,210	67,057	73,475
2011	1,098	61,206	68,484	1,121	63,913	71,513
2010	1,053	60,477	69,801	1,136	70,417	81,274
2009	1,142	60,259	70,697	987	65,587	76,948
2008	1,197	58,364	68,236	942	60,619	70,872
2007	1,060	61,875	75,119	823	61,554	74,730
2006	1,037	60,463	75,487	782	61,091	76,271
2005	1,090	59,934	77,252	749	56,820	73,238
2004	991	50,311	67,045	734	55,996	74,621
2003	990	48,536	66,427	773	53,003	72,541
2002	946	44,748	62,634	663	52,336	73,255
2001	899	46,635	66,304	653	52,181	74,189
2000	852	46,084	67,386	584	51,460	75,247
1999	824	45,432	68,687	600	46,511	70,318
1998	788	43,490	67,151	567	46,275	71,451
1997	807	45,199	70,735	508	46,545	72,841
1996	715	42,059	67,243	527	42,431	67,838
1995	732	38,588	63,337	457	39,821	65,361
1994	709	35,806	60,187	462	40,793	68,569
1993	583	32,742	56,186	447	42,737	73,337
1992	569	36,640	64,460	358	39,322	69,178
1991	556	34,064	61,418	337	37,242	67,148

100,000+ = The medians were topcoded. Beginning with 2009 income data, the Census Bureau expanded the upper income interval used to calculate medians and Gini indexes from $100,000 to $250,000.
X = Not available.
[1]Implementation of an updated CPS ASEC processing system.
[2]The 2014 CPS ASEC included redesigned questions for income and health insurance coverage. All of the approximately 98,000 addresses were eligible to receive the redesigned set of health insurance coverage questions. The redesigned income questions were implemented to a subsample of the 98,000 addresses using a probability split panel design. Approximately 68,000 addresses were eligible to receive a set of income questions similar to those used in the 2013 CPS ASEC and the remaining 30,000 addresses were eligible to receive the redesigned income questions. The source of these 2013 estimates is the portion of the CPS ASEC sample which received the redesigned income questions, approximately 30,000 addresses.
[3]The source of these 2013 estimates is the portion of the CPS ASEC sample which received the income questions consistent with the 2013 CPS ASEC, approximately 68,000 addresses.

Table A-36. Unemployment Rates of Persons 16 to 64 Years Old, by Age Group and Highest Level of Educational Attainment, Selected Years 1975–2019

(Number; percent.)

Year	16 to 19 years old				20 to 24 years old				
	Unemployment rate for all education levels	Less than high school completion	High school completion	At least some college	Unemployment rate for all education levels	Less than high school completion	High school completion	At least some college	Bachelor's or higher degree
2019	14.5	16.7	14.5	11.1	7.5	15.9	8.8	6.7	3.3
2018	15.4	16.3	16.7	9.5	8.7	19.5	11.1	5.3	5.3
2017	14.8	21.7	12.6	9.2	8.1	16.0	9.7	6.4	4.7
2016	20.2	21.6	22.0	11.8	10.5	17.3	12.2	9.9	4.9
2015	22.5	25.6	23.3	13.2	12.3	19.9	15.8	9.6	5.1
2014	22.9	22.9	25.0	15.1	14.9	25.3	18.9	12.2	6.7
2013	29.4	36.3	29.2	16.2	15.2	29.2	17.5	12.2	7.0
2012	30.6	41.1	28.7	19.6	15.5	27.6	18.3	12.7	6.0
2011	28.8	35.1	28.9	16.2	18.1	30.1	21.6	14.0	8.7
2010	31.9	41.7	29.6	18.1	18.8	32.3	22.3	14.2	7.9
2009	30.3	38.9	29.1	18.1	17.0	29.0	20.3	12.1	7.9
2008	20.9	30.8	17.2	11.3	10.7	19.2	13.0	6.8	4.5
2007	19.5	28.6	15.1	8.9	9.3	18.6	9.4	7.2	3.4
2006	20.6	25.8	17.6	17.7	9.3	15.7	10.4	7.1	3.9
2005	22.8	30.3	19.1	15.8	10.9	18.9	12.0	7.3	5.4
2000	17.2	21.4	15.3	‡	9.2	16.6	10.0	5.2	5.0
1995	21.0	30.3	15.1	12.4	10.7	19.5	12.0	7.3	4.1
1990	17.0	26.2	11.7	‡	8.2	17.4	7.8	4.8	3.1
1985	NA	NA	NA	NA	NA	NA	NA	NA	NA
1980	NA	NA	NA	NA	NA	NA	NA	NA	NA
1975	NA	NA	NA	NA	NA	NA	NA	NA	NA

* = Quantity zero or rounds to zero.
NA = Not available.
‡ = Reporting standards not met.

Table A-36. Unemployment Rates of Persons 16 to 64 Years Old, by Age Group and Highest Level of Educational Attainment, Selected Years 1975–2019—*Continued*

(Number; percent.)

Year	25 to 34 years old					35 to 44 years old				
	Unemployment rate for all education levels	Less than high school completion	High school completion	At least some college	Bachelor's or higher degree	Unemployment rate for all education levels	Less than high school completion	High school completion	At least some college	Bachelor's or higher degree
2019	4.1	9.6	5.6	4.7	2.1	2.9	5.7	4.3	3.1	1.4
2018	4.3	9.1	6.4	4.7	2.0	3.3	5.5	4.9	3.2	2.1
2017	4.9	13.2	7.2	4.4	2.5	4.0	6.9	5.7	4.4	2.3
2016	5.6	13.1	8.6	5.6	2.4	4.1	6.2	6.6	4.5	2.0
2015	5.9	12.5	8.9	6.5	2.4	4.4	8.4	6.3	4.5	2.1
2014	7.4	13.7	10.5	7.8	3.7	5.7	11.5	7.4	6.1	2.8
2013	8.0	15.1	12.1	8.0	3.6	6.4	11.5	8.5	6.7	3.6
2012	9.2	16.8	12.8	10.1	4.1	7.1	14.1	9.1	7.4	3.6
2011	10.0	19.7	14.3	10.1	4.3	8.2	15.9	11.3	7.5	4.6
2010	10.8	20.3	15.9	10.6	4.5	9.2	17.8	11.9	9.2	4.6
2009	10.1	19.9	14.1	9.8	4.5	7.9	15.3	10.6	7.2	4.2
2008	5.9	14.2	8.5	5.0	2.2	4.3	9.1	6.0	3.8	1.9
2007	4.9	10.3	6.2	4.6	2.2	3.7	9.3	4.8	3.0	1.5
2006	5.5	11.0	6.5	5.3	2.8	4.1	8.6	5.1	3.7	2.0
2005	5.8	11.6	7.7	5.4	2.6	4.2	8.7	5.2	3.9	2.0
2000	4.0	10.3	4.8	3.6	1.6	3.5	8.4	3.9	3.1	1.8
1995	5.8	12.9	6.8	5.0	2.7	4.6	10.5	5.1	4.7	2.2
1990	4.8	12.0	5.1	3.8	1.9	3.3	8.3	3.7	2.8	1.6
1985	7.3	15.5	9.1	5.4	2.8	5.6	12.4	6.1	4.8	2.2
1980	6.8	13.7	7.9	6.0	2.5	4.3	9.0	4.2	3.1	1.6
1975	8.6	17.2	9.4	6.7	2.9	6.4	11.2	5.7	4.6	2.3

* = Quantity zero or rounds to zero.
NA = Not available.
‡ = Reporting standards not met.

Table A-36. Unemployment Rates of Persons 16 to 64 Years Old, by Age Group and Highest Level of Educational Attainment, Selected Years 1975–2019—*Continued*

(Number; percent.)

Year	45 to 54 years old					55 to 64 years old				
	Unemployment rate for all education levels	Less than high school completion	High school completion	At least some college	Bachelor's or higher degree	Unemployment rate for all education levels	Less than high school completion	High school completion	At least some college	Bachelor's or higher degree
2019	3.0	5.5	3.3	3.3	2.1	2.6	5.6	2.6	2.6	2.0
2018	3.2	6.5	3.5	3.3	2.2	3.3	5.6	4.0	3.2	2.2
2017	3.3	6.9	4.3	2.9	2.1	3.2	6.0	3.6	3.2	2.4
2016	3.7	6.6	5.0	3.4	2.3	3.9	6.5	4.1	4.1	3.2
2015	4.1	8.6	5.2	4.1	2.2	4.2	6.9	4.4	4.3	3.3
2014	4.9	8.0	6.1	4.8	3.2	5.2	8.2	5.6	5.5	4.0
2013	6.0	12.3	7.8	5.2	3.8	5.7	11.2	6.4	5.8	4.2
2012	6.8	13.5	7.8	6.9	3.9	6.6	11.5	7.1	7.1	4.8
2011	7.5	16.3	9.3	7.1	4.0	6.9	10.0	8.4	7.3	4.9
2010	8.4	15.6	11.0	7.6	4.8	7.3	10.1	9.3	7.7	5.0
2009	7.4	13.6	8.8	7.5	4.3	6.7	12.7	7.8	7.0	4.3
2008	3.9	8.9	4.7	4.0	1.9	3.3	5.6	3.4	3.7	2.4
2007	3.5	7.3	4.0	3.7	1.8	3.1	5.3	3.7	3.5	1.8
2006	3.4	5.9	3.9	3.4	2.3	2.9	6.0	2.9	3.1	2.0
2005	3.9	7.0	4.6	3.7	2.5	3.7	7.5	4.3	3.5	2.3
2000	2.4	6.1	2.7	2.4	1.3	2.8	5.2	3.1	2.8	1.4
1995	3.9	7.9	4.0	3.9	2.4	3.9	6.7	3.4	3.2	3.3
1990	2.5	4.7	2.3	2.6	1.4	2.8	3.9	3.0	2.2	1.8
1985	5.4	10.2	5.4	3.2	2.1	4.6	7.1	4.5	3.0	2.2
1980	3.9	6.6	3.4	3.0	1.3	3.2	5.2	2.7	2.0	‡
1975	5.9	8.5	5.6	4.7	2.0	5.5	7.1	5.1	4.1	1.5

* = Quantity zero or rounds to zero.
NA = Not available.
‡ = Reporting standards not met.

Table A-37. Degrees Conferred by Post-Secondary Institutions, by Level of Degree and Sex of Student, 1970–1971 through 2017–2018

(Number.)

Degree conferred, level of degree, and sex of student (when available)	1970–71	1971–72	1972–73	1973–74	1974–75	1975–76	1976–77	1977–78
Agriculture and Natural Resources								
Bachelor's degrees, total	12,672	13,516	14,756	16,253	17,528	19,402	21,467	22,650
Male	12,136	12,779	13,661	14,684	15,061	15,845	16,690	17,069
Female	536	737	1,095	1,569	2,467	3,557	4,777	5,581
Master's degrees, total	2,457	2,680	2,807	2,928	3,067	3,340	3,724	4,023
Male	2,313	2,490	2,588	2,640	2,703	2,862	3,177	3,268
Female	144	190	219	288	364	478	547	755
Doctor's degrees, total	1,086	971	1,059	930	991	928	893	971
Male	1,055	945	1,031	897	958	867	831	909
Female	31	26	28	33	33	61	62	62
Architecture and Related Services								
Bachelor's degrees, total	5,570	6,440	6,962	7,822	8,226	9,146	9,222	9,250
Male	4,906	5,667	6,042	6,665	6,791	7,396	7,249	7,054
Female	664	773	920	1,157	1,435	1,750	1,973	2,196
Master's degrees, total	1,705	1,899	2,307	2,702	2,938	3,215	3,213	3,115
Male	1,469	1,626	1,943	2,208	2,343	2,545	2,489	2,304
Female	236	273	364	494	595	670	724	811
Doctor's degrees, total	36	50	58	69	69	82	73	73
Male	33	43	54	65	58	69	62	57
Female	3	7	4	4	11	13	11	16
Biological and Biomedical Sciences								
Bachelor's degrees, total	35,705	37,269	42,207	48,244	51,609	54,154	53,464	51,360
Male	25,319	26,314	29,625	33,217	34,580	35,498	34,178	31,673
Female	10,386	10,955	12,582	15,027	17,029	18,656	19,286	19,687
Master's degrees, total	5,625	5,989	6,156	6,408	6,429	6,457	6,953	6,651
Male	3,782	4,056	4,317	4,512	4,554	4,466	4,670	4,353
Female	1,843	1,933	1,839	1,896	1,875	1,991	2,283	2,298
Doctor's degrees, total	3,603	3,587	3,583	3,358	3,334	3,347	3,335	3,255
Male	3,018	2,981	2,892	2,684	2,612	2,631	2,627	2,481
Female	585	606	691	674	722	716	708	774
Biology, Microbiology, and Zoology								
Biology, general								
Bachelor's degree	26,294	27,473	31,185	36,188	38,748	40,163	39,530	37,598
Master's degree	2,665	2,943	2,959	3,186	3,109	3,177	3,322	3,094
Doctor's degree	536	580	627	657	637	624	608	664
Microbiology								
Bachelor's degree	1,475	1,548	1,940	2,311	2,767	2,927	2,884	2,695
Master's degree	456	470	517	505	552	585	659	615
Doctor's degree	365	351	344	384	345	364	325	353
Zoology								
Bachelor's degree	5,721	5,518	5,763	6,128	6,110	6,077	5,574	5,096
Master's degree	1,027	1,040	1,042	1,091	1,039	976	985	958
Doctor's degree	878	836	803	677	697	645	696	624
Business								
Bachelor's degrees, total	115,396	121,917	126,717	132,304	133,639	143,171	152,010	160,775
Male	104,936	110,331	113,337	115,363	111,983	114,986	116,394	117,103
Female	10,460	11,586	13,380	16,941	21,656	28,185	35,616	43,672
Master's degrees, total	26,490	30,509	31,208	32,691	36,315	42,592	46,505	48,347
Male	25,458	29,317	29,689	30,557	33,274	37,654	39,852	40,224
Female	1,032	1,192	1,519	2,134	3,041	4,938	6,653	8,123
Doctor's degrees, total	774	876	917	922	939	906	839	834
Male	753	857	864	873	900	856	785	760
Female	21	19	53	49	39	50	54	74
Communication, Journalism, and Related Programs in Communication Technologies								
Bachelor's degrees, total	10,802	12,340	14,317	17,096	19,248	21,282	23,214	25,400
Male	6,989	7,964	9,074	10,536	11,455	12,458	12,932	13,480
Female	3,813	4,376	5,243	6,560	7,793	8,824	10,282	11,920
Master's degrees, total	1,856	2,200	2,406	2,640	2,794	3,126	3,091	3,296
Male	1,214	1,443	1,546	1,668	1,618	1,818	1,719	1,673
Female	642	757	860	972	1,176	1,308	1,372	1,623
Doctor's degrees, total	145	111	139	175	165	204	171	191
Male	126	96	114	146	119	154	130	138
Female	19	15	25	29	46	50	41	53

Note: Data are for postsecondary institutions participating in Title IV federal financial aid programs.
NA = Not available.
[1]Includes geology/earth science, general; geochemistry; geophysics; paleontology; hydrology; oceanography; and geological and earth sciences, other.
[2]Includes physics, general; atomic/molecular physics; elementary particle physics; nuclear physics; optics; acoustics; theoretical physics; and physics, other.

Table A-37. Degrees Conferred by Post-Secondary Institutions, by Level of Degree and Sex of Student, 1970–1971 through 2017–2018—*Continued*

(Number.)

Degree conferred, level of degree, and sex of student (when available)	1978–79	1979–80	1980–81	1981–82	1982–83	1983–84	1984–85	1985–86
Agriculture and Natural Resources								
Bachelor's degrees, total	23,134	22,802	21,886	21,029	20,909	19,317	18,107	16,823
Male	16,854	16,045	15,154	14,443	14,085	13,206	12,477	11,544
Female	6,280	6,757	6,732	6,586	6,824	6,111	5,630	5,279
Master's degrees, total	3,994	3,976	4,003	4,163	4,254	4,178	3,928	3,801
Male	3,187	3,082	3,061	3,114	3,129	2,989	2,846	2,701
Female	807	894	942	1,049	1,125	1,189	1,082	1,100
Doctor's degrees, total	950	991	1,067	1,079	1,149	1,172	1,213	1,158
Male	877	879	940	925	1,004	1,001	1,036	966
Female	73	112	127	154	145	171	177	192
Architecture and Related Services								
Bachelor's degrees, total	9,273	9,132	9,455	9,728	9,823	9,186	9,325	9,119
Male	6,876	6,596	6,800	6,825	6,403	5,895	6,019	5,824
Female	2,397	2,536	2,655	2,903	3,420	3,291	3,306	3,295
Master's degrees, total	3,113	3,139	3,153	3,327	3,357	3,223	3,275	3,260
Male	2,226	2,245	2,234	2,242	2,224	2,197	2,148	2,129
Female	887	894	919	1,085	1,133	1,026	1,127	1,131
Doctor's degrees, total	96	79	93	80	97	84	89	73
Male	74	66	73	58	74	62	66	56
Female	22	13	20	22	23	22	23	17
Biological and Biomedical Sciences								
Bachelor's degrees, total	48,713	46,254	43,078	41,501	39,924	38,593	38,354	38,395
Male	29,173	26,797	24,124	22,722	21,572	20,565	20,071	20,000
Female	19,540	19,457	18,954	18,779	18,352	18,028	18,283	18,395
Master's degrees, total	6,638	6,339	5,766	5,679	5,711	5,489	5,109	5,064
Male	4,198	4,042	3,602	3,384	3,298	3,123	2,775	2,733
Female	2,440	2,297	2,164	2,295	2,413	2,366	2,334	2,331
Doctor's degrees, total	3,459	3,568	3,640	3,662	3,386	3,496	3,465	3,405
Male	2,593	2,651	2,620	2,611	2,306	2,416	2,335	2,273
Female	866	917	1,020	1,051	1,080	1,080	1,130	1,132
Biology, Microbiology, and Zoology								
Biology, general								
Bachelor's degree	35,962	33,523	31,323	29,651	28,022	27,379	27,593	27,618
Master's degree	3,093	2,911	2,598	2,579	2,354	2,313	2,130	2,173
Doctor's degree	663	718	734	678	521	617	658	574
Microbiology								
Bachelor's degree	2,670	2,631	2,414	2,377	2,324	2,349	2,207	2,257
Master's degree	597	596	482	470	499	505	471	392
Doctor's degree	395	376	370	350	358	388	319	362
Zoology								
Bachelor's degree	4,738	4,301	3,873	3,615	3,407	3,231	3,069	2,894
Master's degree	946	922	881	868	738	700	664	618
Doctor's degree	669	639	613	625	533	521	508	548
Business								
Bachelor's degrees, total	172,392	186,264	200,521	215,190	226,442	229,013	232,282	236,700
Male	119,765	123,639	126,798	130,693	131,451	129,296	127,467	128,415
Female	52,627	62,625	73,723	84,497	94,991	99,717	104,815	108,285
Master's degrees, total	50,397	55,008	57,888	61,251	64,741	66,129	66,981	66,676
Male	40,766	42,744	43,411	44,230	45,987	46,167	46,199	45,927
Female	9,631	12,264	14,477	17,021	18,754	19,962	20,782	20,749
Doctor's degrees, total	852	767	808	826	770	926	827	923
Male	752	650	686	676	638	727	685	720
Female	100	117	122	150	132	199	142	203
Communication, Journalism, and Related Programs in Communication Technologies								
Bachelor's degrees, total	26,457	28,616	31,282	34,222	38,647	40,203	42,102	43,145
Male	13,266	13,656	14,179	14,917	16,213	16,662	17,233	17,681
Female	13,191	14,960	17,103	19,305	22,434	23,541	24,869	25,464
Master's degrees, total	2,882	3,082	3,105	3,327	3,600	3,620	3,657	3,808
Male	1,483	1,527	1,448	1,578	1,660	1,578	1,574	1,603
Female	1,399	1,555	1,657	1,749	1,940	2,042	2,083	2,205
Doctor's degrees, total	192	193	182	200	208	216	232	218
Male	138	121	107	136	123	129	141	116
Female	54	72	75	64	85	87	91	102

Note: Data are for postsecondary institutions participating in Title IV federal financial aid programs.

NA = Not available.

[1]Includes geology/earth science, general; geochemistry; geophysics; paleontology; hydrology; oceanography; and geological and earth sciences, other.

[2]Includes physics, general; atomic/molecular physics; elementary particle physics; nuclear physics; optics; acoustics; theoretical physics; and physics, other.

Table A-37. Degrees Conferred by Post-Secondary Institutions, by Level of Degree and Sex of Student, 1970–1971 through 2017–2018—Continued

(Number.)

Degree conferred, level of degree, and sex of student (when available)	1986–87	1987–88	1988–89	1989–90	1990–91	1991–92	1992–93	1993–94
Agriculture and Natural Resources								
Bachelor's degrees, total	14,991	14,222	13,492	12,900	13,124	15,113	16,769	18,056
Male	10,314	9,744	9,298	8,822	8,832	9,867	11,079	11,746
Female	4,677	4,478	4,194	4,078	4,292	5,246	5,690	6,310
Master's degrees, total	3,522	3,479	3,245	3,382	3,295	3,730	3,959	4,110
Male	2,460	2,427	2,231	2,239	2,160	2,409	2,474	2,512
Female	1,062	1,052	1,014	1,143	1,135	1,321	1,485	1,598
Doctor's degrees, total	1,049	1,142	1,183	1,295	1,185	1,205	1,159	1,262
Male	871	926	950	1,038	953	955	869	969
Female	178	216	233	257	232	250	290	293
Architecture and Related Services								
Bachelor's degrees, total	8,950	8,603	9,150	9,364	9,781	8,753	9,167	8,975
Male	5,617	5,271	5,545	5,703	5,788	5,805	5,940	5,764
Female	3,333	3,332	3,605	3,661	3,993	2,948	3,227	3,211
Master's degrees, total	3,163	3,159	3,383	3,499	3,490	3,640	3,808	3,943
Male	2,086	2,042	2,192	2,228	2,244	2,271	2,376	2,428
Female	1,077	1,117	1,191	1,271	1,246	1,369	1,432	1,515
Doctor's degrees, total	92	98	86	103	135	132	148	161
Male	66	66	63	73	101	93	105	111
Female	26	32	23	30	34	39	43	50
Biological and Biomedical Sciences								
Bachelor's degrees, total	38,074	36,688	36,068	37,304	39,482	42,892	47,009	51,296
Male	19,684	18,267	17,998	18,363	19,418	20,816	22,870	25,071
Female	18,390	18,421	18,070	18,941	20,064	22,076	24,139	26,225
Master's degrees, total	4,995	4,871	5,034	4,941	4,834	4,862	5,026	5,462
Male	2,646	2,530	2,598	2,509	2,417	2,437	2,540	2,681
Female	2,349	2,341	2,436	2,432	2,417	2,425	2,486	2,781
Doctor's degrees, total	3,469	3,688	3,617	3,922	4,152	4,442	4,749	4,891
Male	2,268	2,389	2,299	2,478	2,618	2,749	2,866	2,910
Female	1,201	1,299	1,318	1,444	1,534	1,693	1,883	1,981
Biology, Microbiology, and Zoology								
Biology, general								
Bachelor's degree	27,465	26,838	26,229	27,213	29,285	31,909	34,932	38,103
Master's degree	2,022	1,981	2,097	1,998	1,956	1,995	2,000	2,178
Doctor's degree	537	576	527	551	632	657	671	665
Microbiology								
Bachelor's degree	2,159	2,061	1,833	1,973	1,788	1,750	1,798	1,872
Master's degree	451	404	449	403	343	372	367	359
Doctor's degree	380	442	423	441	443	532	621	591
Zoology								
Bachelor's degree	2,791	2,537	2,549	2,473	2,641	2,811	3,036	3,162
Master's degree	623	629	634	548	551	530	559	658
Doctor's degree	464	492	466	545	516	494	465	503
Business								
Bachelor's degrees, total	240,346	242,859	246,262	248,568	249,165	256,298	256,473	246,265
Male	128,506	129,467	131,098	132,284	131,557	135,263	135,368	128,946
Female	111,840	113,392	115,164	116,284	117,608	121,035	121,105	117,319
Master's degrees, total	67,093	69,230	73,065	76,676	78,255	84,517	89,425	93,285
Male	44,913	45,980	48,540	50,585	50,883	54,609	57,504	59,223
Female	22,180	23,250	24,525	26,091	27,372	29,908	31,921	34,062
Doctor's degrees, total	1,062	1,063	1,100	1,093	1,185	1,242	1,346	1,364
Male	808	810	800	818	876	953	969	980
Female	254	253	300	275	309	289	377	384
Communication, Journalism, and Related Programs in Communication Technologies								
Bachelor's degrees, total	45,521	46,916	48,889	51,572	53,047	55,144	54,907	52,033
Male	18,201	18,672	19,357	20,374	20,806	21,601	22,154	21,484
Female	27,320	28,244	29,532	31,198	32,241	33,543	32,753	30,549
Master's degrees, total	3,881	3,916	4,249	4,353	4,327	4,463	5,179	5,388
Male	1,584	1,568	1,734	1,705	1,711	1,692	1,969	2,088
Female	2,297	2,348	2,515	2,648	2,616	2,771	3,210	3,300
Doctor's degrees, total	275	233	248	272	272	255	301	345
Male	158	133	137	145	150	132	146	174
Female	117	100	111	127	122	123	155	171

Note: Data are for postsecondary institutions participating in Title IV federal financial aid programs.

NA = Not available.

[1] Includes geology/earth science, general; geochemistry; geophysics; paleontology; hydrology; oceanography; and geological and earth sciences, other.

[2] Includes physics, general; atomic/molecular physics; elementary particle physics; nuclear physics; optics; acoustics; theoretical physics; and physics, other.

Table A-37.   Degrees Conferred by Post-Secondary Institutions, by Level of Degree and Sex of Student, 1970–1971 through 2017–2018—*Continued*

(Number.)

Degree conferred, level of degree, and sex of student (when available)	1994–95	1995–96	1996–97	1997–98	1998–99	1999–2000	2000–01	2001–02
Agriculture and Natural Resources								
Bachelor's degrees, total	19,832	21,425	22,597	23,276	24,179	24,238	23,370	23,331
Male	12,686	13,531	13,791	13,806	14,045	13,843	12,840	12,630
Female	7,146	7,894	8,806	9,470	10,134	10,395	10,530	10,701
Master's degrees, total	4,234	4,551	4,505	4,464	4,376	4,360	4,272	4,503
Male	2,541	2,642	2,601	2,545	2,360	2,356	2,251	2,340
Female	1,693	1,909	1,904	1,919	2,016	2,004	2,021	2,163
Doctor's degrees, total	1,256	1,259	1,202	1,290	1,249	1,168	1,127	1,148
Male	955	926	875	924	869	803	741	760
Female	301	333	327	366	380	365	386	388
Architecture and Related Services								
Bachelor's degrees, total	8,756	8,352	7,944	7,652	8,245	8,462	8,480	8,808
Male	5,741	5,340	5,090	4,966	5,145	5,193	5,086	5,224
Female	3,015	3,012	2,854	2,686	3,100	3,269	3,394	3,584
Master's degrees, total	3,923	3,993	4,034	4,347	4,235	4,268	4,302	4,566
Male	2,310	2,361	2,336	2,537	2,435	2,508	2,515	2,606
Female	1,613	1,632	1,698	1,810	1,800	1,760	1,787	1,960
Doctor's degrees, total	141	141	135	131	119	129	153	183
Male	95	96	93	80	76	85	83	117
Female	46	45	42	51	43	44	70	66
Biological and Biomedical Sciences								
Bachelor's degrees, total	55,983	61,014	63,973	65,917	65,310	63,630	60,576	60,309
Male	26,734	28,921	29,562	29,663	28,507	26,579	24,600	23,694
Female	29,249	32,093	34,411	36,254	36,803	37,051	35,976	36,615
Master's degrees, total	5,873	6,593	6,986	6,848	6,966	6,850	7,017	7,011
Male	2,920	3,212	3,419	3,336	3,279	3,171	3,075	3,033
Female	2,953	3,381	3,567	3,512	3,687	3,679	3,942	3,978
Doctor's degrees, total	5,069	5,250	5,313	5,474	5,250	5,463	5,225	5,104
Male	3,012	3,062	3,014	3,123	3,010	3,068	2,923	2,836
Female	2,067	2,188	2,299	2,351	2,240	2,395	2,302	2,268
Biology, Microbiology, and Zoology								
Biology, general								
Bachelor's degree	41,658	44,818	46,632	47,054	46,172	44,982	42,310	42,281
Master's degree	2,350	2,606	2,742	2,617	2,616	2,599	2,582	2,424
Doctor's degree	729	768	693	809	718	727	780	689
Microbiology								
Bachelor's degree	1,992	2,220	2,530	2,926	2,885	3,049	2,779	2,622
Master's degree	326	364	363	401	406	383	334	325
Doctor's degree	572	606	612	585	544	551	553	538
Zoology								
Bachelor's degree	3,149	3,463	3,438	3,653	3,508	3,226	3,045	2,979
Master's degree	586	677	720	685	606	616	560	578
Doctor's degree	487	501	474	465	462	481	380	413
Business								
Bachelor's degrees, total	233,895	226,623	225,934	232,079	239,924	256,070	263,515	278,217
Male	121,663	116,545	116,023	119,379	121,741	128,521	132,275	138,343
Female	112,232	110,078	109,911	112,700	118,183	127,549	131,240	139,874
Master's degrees, total	93,540	93,554	97,204	101,652	106,830	111,532	115,602	119,725
Male	58,931	58,400	59,333	62,357	64,271	67,078	68,471	70,463
Female	34,609	35,154	37,871	39,295	42,559	44,454	47,131	49,262
Doctor's degrees, total	1,391	1,366	1,336	1,290	1,216	1,194	1,180	1,156
Male	1,011	972	947	885	848	812	783	746
Female	380	394	389	405	368	382	397	410
Communication, Journalism, and Related Programs in Communication Technologies								
Bachelor's degrees, total	48,969	48,173	47,894	50,263	52,397	57,058	59,191	64,036
Male	20,501	19,868	19,771	20,103	20,943	22,152	22,542	23,692
Female	28,468	28,305	28,123	30,160	31,454	34,906	36,649	40,344
Master's degrees, total	5,559	5,561	5,552	6,097	5,582	5,525	5,645	5,980
Male	2,086	2,153	1,989	2,369	2,001	2,030	1,964	2,169
Female	3,473	3,408	3,563	3,728	3,581	3,495	3,681	3,811
Doctor's degrees, total	321	345	300	359	348	357	370	383
Male	162	190	155	171	182	168	190	168
Female	159	155	145	188	166	189	180	215

Note: Data are for postsecondary institutions participating in Title IV federal financial aid programs.

NA = Not available.

[1]Includes geology/earth science, general; geochemistry; geophysics; paleontology; hydrology; oceanography; and geological and earth sciences, other.

[2]Includes physics, general; atomic/molecular physics; elementary particle physics; nuclear physics; optics; acoustics; theoretical physics; and physics, other.

Table A-37. Degrees Conferred by Post-Secondary Institutions, by Level of Degree and Sex of Student, 1970–1971 through 2017–2018—*Continued*

(Number.)

Degree conferred, level of degree, and sex of student (when available)	2002–03	2003–04	2004–05	2005–06	2006–07	2007–08	2008–09	2009–10
Agriculture and Natural Resources								
Bachelor's degrees, total	23,348	22,835	23,002	23,053	23,133	24,113	24,982	26,343
Male	12,343	11,889	11,987	12,063	12,309	12,634	13,096	13,524
Female	11,005	10,946	11,015	10,990	10,824	11,479	11,886	12,819
Master's degrees, total	4,492	4,783	4,746	4,640	4,623	4,684	4,878	5,215
Male	2,232	2,306	2,288	2,280	2,174	2,180	2,328	2,512
Female	2,260	2,477	2,458	2,360	2,449	2,504	2,550	2,703
Doctor's degrees, total	1,229	1,185	1,173	1,194	1,272	1,257	1,328	1,149
Male	790	758	763	710	768	742	741	626
Female	439	427	410	484	504	515	587	523
Architecture and Related Services								
Bachelor's degrees, total	9,056	8,838	9,237	9,515	9,717	9,805	10,119	10,051
Male	5,331	5,059	5,222	5,414	5,393	5,579	5,797	5,694
Female	3,725	3,779	4,015	4,101	4,324	4,226	4,322	4,357
Master's degrees, total	4,925	5,424	5,674	5,743	5,951	6,065	6,587	7,280
Male	2,832	3,049	3,180	3,165	3,304	3,252	3,657	4,012
Female	2,093	2,375	2,494	2,578	2,647	2,813	2,930	3,268
Doctor's degrees, total	152	173	179	201	178	199	212	210
Male	83	94	110	108	104	103	113	116
Female	69	79	69	93	74	96	99	94
Biological and Biomedical Sciences								
Bachelor's degrees, total	61,294	62,624	65,915	70,607	76,832	79,829	82,828	86,391
Male	23,356	23,691	25,104	27,183	30,600	32,401	33,707	35,866
Female	37,938	38,933	40,811	43,424	46,232	47,428	49,121	50,525
Master's degrees, total	7,050	7,732	8,284	8,781	8,898	9,689	10,018	10,730
Male	3,015	3,271	3,361	3,709	3,639	4,094	4,250	4,612
Female	4,035	4,461	4,923	5,072	5,259	5,595	5,768	6,118
Doctor's degrees, total	5,268	5,538	5,935	6,162	6,764	7,400	7,499	7,672
Male	2,866	2,975	3,025	3,138	3,440	3,645	3,549	3,603
Female	2,402	2,563	2,910	3,024	3,324	3,755	3,950	4,069
Biology, Microbiology, and Zoology								
Biology, general								
Bachelor's degree	42,699	43,465	45,540	48,855	52,527	54,384	55,859	58,700
Master's degree	2,340	2,529	2,564	2,719	2,679	2,935	2,987	3,087
Doctor's degree	680	681	712	776	788	866	896	919
Microbiology								
Bachelor's degree	2,455	2,365	2,318	2,243	2,347	2,458	2,480	2,449
Master's degree	297	350	390	372	369	353	291	303
Doctor's degree	507	599	610	612	667	734	716	767
Zoology								
Bachelor's degree	2,488	2,454	2,159	2,140	2,223	2,235	2,140	2,147
Master's degree	379	367	384	384	416	381	347	360
Doctor's degree	355	245	268	254	263	281	297	243
Business								
Bachelor's degrees, total	293,391	307,149	311,574	318,042	327,531	335,254	348,056	358,119
Male	145,075	152,513	155,940	159,683	166,350	170,978	177,924	183,272
Female	148,316	154,636	155,634	158,359	161,181	164,276	170,132	174,847
Master's degrees, total	127,685	139,347	142,617	146,406	150,211	155,637	168,404	177,748
Male	75,239	80,858	82,151	83,550	84,115	86,258	91,991	96,742
Female	52,446	58,489	60,466	62,856	66,096	69,379	76,413	81,006
Doctor's degrees, total	1,252	1,481	1,498	1,711	2,029	2,084	2,123	2,249
Male	820	960	901	1,049	1,188	1,250	1,302	1,338
Female	432	521	597	662	841	834	821	911
Communication, Journalism, and Related Programs in Communication Technologies								
Bachelor's degrees, total	69,828	73,002	75,238	76,936	78,420	81,048	83,084	86,062
Male	25,338	25,813	26,926	28,142	29,009	30,384	31,207	32,048
Female	44,490	47,189	48,312	48,794	49,411	50,664	51,877	54,014
Master's degrees, total	6,495	6,900	7,195	7,745	7,272	7,546	7,517	8,093
Male	2,301	2,329	2,535	2,611	2,485	2,580	2,446	2,656
Female	4,194	4,571	4,660	5,134	4,787	4,966	5,071	5,437
Doctor's degrees, total	398	426	468	464	480	496	535	573
Male	179	186	195	207	188	209	225	225
Female	219	240	273	257	292	287	310	348

Note: Data are for postsecondary institutions participating in Title IV federal financial aid programs.

NA = Not available.

[1]Includes geology/earth science, general; geochemistry; geophysics; paleontology; hydrology; oceanography; and geological and earth sciences, other.
[2]Includes physics, general; atomic/molecular physics; elementary particle physics; nuclear physics; optics; acoustics; theoretical physics; and physics, other.

Table A-37. Degrees Conferred by Post-Secondary Institutions, by Level of Degree and Sex of Student, 1970–1971 through 2017–2018—Continued

(Number.)

Degree conferred, level of degree, and sex of student (when available)	2010–11	2011–12	2012–13	2013–14	2014–15	2015–16	2016–17	2017–18
Agriculture and Natural Resources								
Bachelor's degrees, total	28,630	30,972	33,592	35,125	36,278	36,995	37,734	39,314
Male	14,678	15,485	16,618	17,254	17,585	17,617	17,823	18,202
Female	13,952	15,487	16,974	17,871	18,693	19,378	19,911	21,112
Master's degrees, total	5,766	6,390	6,336	6,544	6,426	6,702	6,843	6,967
Male	2,746	3,026	2,912	2,966	2,904	2,965	3,037	2,997
Female	3,020	3,364	3,424	3,578	3,522	3,737	3,806	3,970
Doctor's degrees, total	1,246	1,333	1,411	1,407	1,561	1,526	1,561	1,496
Male	675	721	767	739	811	827	805	798
Female	571	612	644	668	750	699	756	698
Architecture and Related Services								
Bachelor's degrees, total	9,831	9,727	9,757	9,149	9,090	8,825	8,579	8,464
Male	5,698	5,566	5,581	5,174	5,116	4,853	4,588	4,474
Female	4,133	4,161	4,176	3,975	3,974	3,972	3,991	3,990
Master's degrees, total	7,788	8,448	8,095	8,048	8,006	7,991	7,883	7,317
Male	4,265	4,504	4,261	4,122	4,147	4,165	4,009	3,516
Female	3,523	3,944	3,834	3,926	3,859	3,826	3,874	3,801
Doctor's degrees, total	205	255	247	247	272	245	291	250
Male	110	147	134	134	145	128	146	136
Female	95	108	113	113	127	117	145	114
Biological and Biomedical Sciences								
Bachelor's degrees, total	89,984	95,850	100,397	104,657	109,904	113,794	116,768	118,663
Male	36,888	39,542	41,556	43,440	45,104	45,613	45,514	44,852
Female	53,096	56,308	58,841	61,217	64,800	68,181	71,254	73,811
Master's degrees, total	11,324	12,419	13,300	13,964	14,655	15,717	16,282	17,180
Male	4,869	5,378	5,783	6,073	6,252	6,707	6,839	7,028
Female	6,455	7,041	7,517	7,891	8,403	9,010	9,443	10,152
Doctor's degrees, total	7,693	7,935	7,939	8,302	8,053	7,939	8,087	8,222
Male	3,648	3,708	3,689	3,884	3,763	3,733	3,852	3,829
Female	4,045	4,227	4,250	4,418	4,290	4,206	4,235	4,393
Biology, Microbiology, and Zoology								
Biology, general								
Bachelor's degree	61,236	64,616	66,692	69,425	71,622	73,044	74,055	73,983
Master's degree	3,283	3,494	3,479	3,465	3,432	3,448	3,437	3,579
Doctor's degree	935	964	1,003	1,053	976	948	1,020	1,036
Microbiology								
Bachelor's degree	2,466	2,532	2,582	2,572	2,567	2,637	2,745	2,690
Master's degree	337	395	402	465	510	524	491	585
Doctor's degree	739	687	704	674	688	643	649	622
Zoology								
Bachelor's degree	2,062	2,174	2,246	2,269	2,250	2,311	2,315	2,388
Master's degree	338	346	416	464	421	501	398	306
Doctor's degree	230	258	231	217	230	271	233	237
Business								
Bachelor's degrees, total	365,133	367,235	360,887	358,132	363,741	371,690	381,109	386,201
Male	187,116	190,180	187,843	188,468	191,288	196,309	201,724	204,839
Female	178,017	177,055	173,044	169,664	172,453	175,381	179,385	181,362
Master's degrees, total	187,178	191,606	188,617	189,364	185,236	186,835	187,412	192,184
Male	101,440	103,250	101,599	101,061	98,593	99,488	98,775	99,860
Female	85,738	88,356	87,018	88,303	86,643	87,347	88,637	92,324
Doctor's degrees, total	2,286	2,538	2,828	3,039	3,116	3,325	3,328	3,338
Male	1,357	1,461	1,605	1,722	1,716	1,933	1,853	1,926
Female	929	1,077	1,223	1,317	1,400	1,392	1,475	1,412
Communication, Journalism, and Related Programs in Communication Technologies								
Bachelor's degrees, total	88,089	88,754	89,805	92,603	95,793	97,375	98,409	96,521
Male	33,018	33,525	33,670	34,393	35,220	35,540	35,359	34,187
Female	55,071	55,229	56,135	58,210	60,573	61,835	63,050	62,334
Master's degrees, total	8,804	9,502	9,337	9,930	10,135	10,167	10,658	10,772
Male	2,819	3,068	3,021	3,131	3,111	3,104	3,215	3,187
Female	5,985	6,434	6,316	6,799	7,024	7,063	7,443	7,585
Doctor's degrees, total	578	567	612	614	644	633	615	666
Male	207	242	246	267	259	258	208	252
Female	371	325	366	347	385	375	407	414

Note: Data are for postsecondary institutions participating in Title IV federal financial aid programs.

NA = Not available.

[1]Includes geology/earth science, general; geochemistry; geophysics; paleontology; hydrology; oceanography; and geological and earth sciences, other.

[2]Includes physics, general; atomic/molecular physics; elementary particle physics; nuclear physics; optics; acoustics; theoretical physics; and physics, other.

Table A-37. Degrees Conferred by Post-Secondary Institutions, by Level of Degree and Sex of Student, 1970–1971 through 2017–2018—*Continued*

(Number.)

Degree conferred, level of degree, and sex of student (when available)	1970–71	1971–72	1972–73	1973–74	1974–75	1975–76	1976–77	1977–78
Computer and Information Sciences								
Bachelor's degrees, total	2,388	3,402	4,304	4,756	5,033	5,652	6,407	7,201
Male	2,064	2,941	3,664	3,976	4,080	4,534	4,876	5,349
Female	324	461	640	780	953	1,118	1,531	1,852
Master's degrees, total	1,588	1,977	2,113	2,276	2,299	2,603	2,798	3,038
Male	1,424	1,752	1,888	1,983	1,961	2,226	2,332	2,471
Female	164	225	225	293	338	377	466	567
Doctor's degrees, total	128	167	196	198	213	244	216	196
Male	125	155	181	189	199	221	197	181
Female	3	12	15	9	14	23	19	15
Education								
Bachelor's degrees, total	176,307	190,880	193,984	184,907	166,758	154,437	143,234	135,821
Male	44,896	49,344	51,300	48,997	44,463	42,004	39,867	37,410
Female	131,411	141,536	142,684	135,910	122,295	112,433	103,367	98,411
Master's degrees, total	87,666	96,668	103,777	110,402	117,841	126,061	124,267	116,916
Male	38,365	41,141	43,298	44,112	44,430	44,831	42,308	37,662
Female	49,301	55,527	60,479	66,290	73,411	81,230	81,959	79,254
Doctor's degrees, total	6,041	6,648	6,857	6,757	6,975	7,202	7,338	7,018
Male	4,771	5,104	5,191	4,974	4,856	4,826	4,832	4,281
Female	1,270	1,544	1,666	1,783	2,119	2,376	2,506	2,737
Engineering and Engineering Technologies								
Bachelor's degrees, total	50,182	51,258	51,384	50,412	47,131	46,676	49,402	56,150
Male	49,775	50,726	50,766	49,611	46,105	45,184	47,238	52,353
Female	407	532	618	801	1,026	1,492	2,244	3,797
Master's degrees, total	16,947	17,299	16,988	15,851	15,837	16,800	16,659	16,887
Male	16,734	17,009	16,694	15,470	15,426	16,174	15,891	15,940
Female	213	290	294	381	411	626	768	947
Doctor's degrees, total	3,688	3,708	3,513	3,374	3,181	2,874	2,622	2,483
Male	3,663	3,685	3,459	3,318	3,113	2,805	2,547	2,424
Female	25	23	54	56	68	69	75	59
Chemical, Civil, Electrical, and Mechanical Engineering								
Chemical engineering								
Bachelor's degree	3,579	3,625	3,578	3,399	3,070	3,140	3,524	4,569
Master's degree	1,100	1,154	1,051	1,044	990	1,031	1,086	1,235
Doctor's degree	406	394	397	400	346	308	291	259
Civil engineering								
Bachelor's degree	6,526	6,803	7,390	8,017	7,651	7,923	8,228	9,135
Master's degree	2,425	2,487	2,627	2,652	2,769	2,999	2,964	2,685
Doctor's degree	446	415	397	368	356	370	309	277
Electrical, electronics, and communications engineering								
Bachelor's degree	12,198	12,101	12,313	11,316	10,161	9,791	9,936	11,133
Master's degree	4,282	4,206	3,895	3,499	3,469	3,774	3,788	3,740
Doctor's degree	879	824	791	705	701	649	566	503
Mechanical engineering								
Bachelor's degree	8,858	8,530	8,523	7,677	6,890	6,800	7,703	8,875
Master's degree	2,237	2,282	2,141	1,843	1,858	1,907	1,952	1,942
Doctor's degree	438	411	370	385	340	305	283	279
English Language and Literature/Letters								
Bachelor's degrees, total	63,914	63,707	60,607	54,190	47,062	41,452	37,343	34,799
Male	22,005	22,580	22,022	20,082	17,689	15,898	14,135	12,972
Female	41,909	41,127	38,585	34,108	29,373	25,554	23,208	21,827
Master's degrees, total	10,441	10,412	10,035	9,573	9,178	8,599	7,824	7,444
Male	4,126	4,066	3,988	3,824	3,463	3,290	2,907	2,623
Female	6,315	6,346	6,047	5,749	5,715	5,309	4,917	4,821
Doctor's degrees, total	1,554	1,734	1,817	1,755	1,595	1,514	1,373	1,272
Male	1,107	1,173	1,189	1,142	974	895	768	698
Female	447	561	628	613	621	619	605	574
Foreign Languages and Literatures								
Bachelor's degrees, total	20,988	19,890	20,170	20,197	19,103	17,068	15,496	14,334
Male	5,508	5,196	5,119	5,063	4,723	4,270	3,965	3,684
Female	15,480	14,694	15,051	15,134	14,380	12,798	11,531	10,650
Master's degrees, total	5,480	5,283	5,068	4,851	4,721	4,432	4,056	3,624
Male	1,961	1,919	1,909	1,788	1,672	1,581	1,365	1,194
Female	3,519	3,364	3,159	3,063	3,049	2,851	2,691	2,430
Doctor's degrees, total	1,084	1,134	1,347	1,248	1,220	1,245	1,103	1,002
Male	714	742	829	703	665	643	574	490
Female	370	392	518	545	555	602	529	512

Note: Data are for postsecondary institutions participating in Title IV federal financial aid programs.

NA = Not available.

[1] Includes geology/earth science, general; geochemistry; geophysics; paleontology; hydrology; oceanography; and geological and earth sciences, other.

[2] Includes physics, general; atomic/molecular physics; elementary particle physics; nuclear physics; optics; acoustics; theoretical physics; and physics, other.

Table A-37.   Degrees Conferred by Post-Secondary Institutions, by Level of Degree and Sex of Student, 1970–1971 through 2017–2018—*Continued*

(Number.)

Degree conferred, level of degree, and sex of student (when available)	1978–79	1979–80	1980–81	1981–82	1982–83	1983–84	1984–85	1985–86
Computer and Information Sciences								
Bachelor's degrees, total	8,719	11,154	15,121	20,267	24,565	32,439	39,121	42,337
Male	6,272	7,782	10,202	13,218	15,641	20,416	24,737	27,208
Female	2,447	3,372	4,919	7,049	8,924	12,023	14,384	15,129
Master's degrees, total	3,055	3,647	4,218	4,935	5,321	6,190	7,101	8,070
Male	2,480	2,883	3,247	3,625	3,813	4,379	5,064	5,658
Female	575	764	971	1,310	1,508	1,811	2,037	2,412
Doctor's degrees, total	236	240	252	251	262	251	248	344
Male	206	213	227	230	228	225	223	299
Female	30	27	25	21	34	26	25	45
Education								
Bachelor's degrees, total	125,873	118,038	108,074	100,932	97,908	92,310	88,078	87,147
Male	33,743	30,901	27,039	24,380	23,651	22,200	21,254	20,982
Female	92,130	87,137	81,035	76,552	74,257	70,110	66,824	66,165
Master's degrees, total	109,866	101,819	96,713	91,601	83,254	75,700	74,667	74,816
Male	34,410	30,300	27,548	25,339	22,824	21,164	20,539	20,302
Female	75,456	71,519	69,165	66,262	60,430	54,536	54,128	54,514
Doctor's degrees, total	7,170	7,314	7,279	6,999	7,063	6,914	6,614	6,610
Male	4,174	4,100	3,843	3,612	3,550	3,448	3,174	3,088
Female	2,996	3,214	3,436	3,387	3,513	3,466	3,440	3,522
Engineering and Engineering Technologies								
Bachelor's degrees, total	62,898	69,387	75,355	80,632	89,811	95,295	97,099	97,122
Male	57,603	62,877	67,573	71,305	78,673	82,841	83,991	84,050
Female	5,295	6,510	7,782	9,327	11,138	12,454	13,108	13,072
Master's degrees, total	16,012	16,765	17,216	18,475	19,949	21,197	22,124	22,146
Male	14,971	15,535	15,761	16,747	18,038	18,916	19,688	19,545
Female	1,041	1,230	1,455	1,728	1,911	2,281	2,436	2,601
Doctor's degrees, total	2,545	2,546	2,608	2,676	2,871	3,032	3,269	3,456
Male	2,459	2,447	2,499	2,532	2,742	2,864	3,055	3,220
Female	86	99	109	144	129	168	214	236
Chemical, Civil, Electrical, and Mechanical Engineering								
Chemical engineering								
Bachelor's degree	5,568	6,320	6,527	6,740	7,185	7,475	7,146	5,877
Master's degree	1,149	1,270	1,267	1,285	1,368	1,514	1,544	1,361
Doctor's degree	304	284	300	311	319	330	418	446
Civil engineering								
Bachelor's degree	9,809	10,326	10,678	10,524	9,989	9,693	9,162	8,679
Master's degree	2,646	2,683	2,891	2,995	3,074	3,146	3,172	2,926
Doctor's degree	253	270	325	329	340	369	377	395
Electrical, electronics, and communications engineering								
Bachelor's degree	12,338	13,821	14,938	16,455	18,049	19,943	21,691	23,742
Master's degree	3,591	3,836	3,901	4,462	4,531	5,078	5,153	5,534
Doctor's degree	586	525	535	526	550	585	660	722
Mechanical engineering								
Bachelor's degree	10,107	11,808	13,329	13,922	15,675	16,629	16,794	16,194
Master's degree	1,877	2,060	2,291	2,399	2,511	2,797	3,053	3,075
Doctor's degree	271	281	276	333	299	319	409	426
English Language and Literature/Letters								
Bachelor's degrees, total	33,218	32,187	31,922	33,078	31,327	32,296	32,686	34,083
Male	12,085	11,237	11,082	11,300	10,699	11,007	11,195	11,657
Female	21,133	20,950	20,840	21,778	20,628	21,289	21,491	22,426
Master's degrees, total	6,503	6,026	5,742	5,593	4,866	4,814	4,987	5,335
Male	2,307	2,181	2,026	1,916	1,653	1,681	1,723	1,811
Female	4,196	3,845	3,716	3,677	3,213	3,133	3,264	3,524
Doctor's degrees, total	1,186	1,196	1,040	986	877	899	915	895
Male	639	635	497	467	419	413	414	390
Female	547	561	543	519	458	486	501	505
Foreign Languages and Literatures								
Bachelor's degrees, total	13,211	12,480	11,638	11,175	11,170	10,985	11,436	11,550
Male	3,391	3,226	3,013	2,919	3,048	3,098	3,186	3,374
Female	9,820	9,254	8,625	8,256	8,122	7,887	8,250	8,176
Master's degrees, total	3,248	3,067	2,934	2,892	2,706	2,814	2,708	2,690
Male	1,092	1,026	1,039	997	1,001	984	932	878
Female	2,156	2,041	1,895	1,895	1,705	1,830	1,776	1,812
Doctor's degrees, total	960	857	931	869	790	779	761	768
Male	471	412	460	407	362	353	342	338
Female	489	445	471	462	428	426	419	430

Note: Data are for postsecondary institutions participating in Title IV federal financial aid programs.

NA = Not available.

[1]Includes geology/earth science, general; geochemistry; geophysics; paleontology; hydrology; oceanography; and geological and earth sciences, other.

[2]Includes physics, general; atomic/molecular physics; elementary particle physics; nuclear physics; optics; acoustics; theoretical physics; and physics, other.

Table A-37. Degrees Conferred by Post-Secondary Institutions, by Level of Degree and Sex of Student, 1970–1971 through 2017–2018—*Continued*

(Number.)

Degree conferred, level of degree, and sex of student (when available)	1986–87	1987–88	1988–89	1989–90	1990–91	1991–92	1992–93	1993–94
Computer and Information Sciences								
Bachelor's degrees, total	39,767	34,651	30,560	27,347	25,159	24,821	24,519	24,527
Male	25,962	23,414	21,143	19,159	17,771	17,685	17,606	17,528
Female	13,805	11,237	9,417	8,188	7,388	7,136	6,913	6,999
Master's degrees, total	8,481	9,197	9,414	9,677	9,324	9,655	10,353	10,568
Male	5,985	6,726	6,775	6,960	6,563	6,980	7,557	7,836
Female	2,496	2,471	2,639	2,717	2,761	2,675	2,796	2,732
Doctor's degrees, total	374	428	551	627	676	772	805	810
Male	322	380	466	534	584	669	689	685
Female	52	48	85	93	92	103	116	125
Education								
Bachelor's degrees, total	86,788	90,928	96,740	105,112	110,807	107,836	107,578	107,440
Male	20,705	20,947	21,643	23,007	23,417	22,655	23,199	24,424
Female	66,083	69,981	75,097	82,105	87,390	85,181	84,379	83,016
Master's degrees, total	72,619	75,270	79,793	84,890	87,352	91,225	94,497	97,427
Male	18,955	18,777	19,616	20,469	20,448	20,897	21,857	22,656
Female	53,664	56,493	60,177	64,421	66,904	70,328	72,640	74,771
Doctor's degrees, total	5,905	5,568	5,884	6,503	6,189	6,423	6,581	6,450
Male	2,745	2,530	2,522	2,776	2,614	2,652	2,712	2,555
Female	3,160	3,038	3,362	3,727	3,575	3,771	3,869	3,895
Engineering and Engineering Technologies								
Bachelor's degrees, total	93,560	89,406	85,982	82,480	79,751	78,036	78,619	78,580
Male	80,543	76,886	74,020	70,859	68,482	67,086	67,214	66,867
Female	13,017	12,520	11,962	11,621	11,269	10,950	11,405	11,713
Master's degrees, total	23,101	23,839	25,066	25,294	25,450	26,373	29,103	30,102
Male	20,137	20,815	21,731	21,753	21,780	22,397	24,721	25,394
Female	2,964	3,024	3,335	3,541	3,670	3,976	4,382	4,708
Doctor's degrees, total	3,854	4,237	4,572	5,030	5,330	5,499	5,870	5,954
Male	3,585	3,941	4,160	4,576	4,834	4,967	5,300	5,288
Female	269	296	412	454	496	532	570	666
Chemical, Civil, Electrical, and Mechanical Engineering								
Chemical engineering								
Bachelor's degree	4,991	3,917	3,663	3,430	3,444	3,754	4,459	5,163
Master's degree	1,184	1,088	1,093	1,035	903	956	990	1,032
Doctor's degree	497	579	602	562	611	590	595	604
Civil engineering								
Bachelor's degree	8,147	7,488	7,312	7,252	7,314	8,034	8,868	9,479
Master's degree	2,901	2,836	2,903	2,812	2,927	3,113	3,610	3,873
Doctor's degree	451	481	505	516	536	540	577	651
Electrical, electronics, and communications engineering								
Bachelor's degree	24,547	23,597	21,908	20,711	19,320	17,958	17,281	15,823
Master's degree	6,183	6,688	7,028	7,225	7,095	7,360	7,870	7,791
Doctor's degree	724	860	998	1,162	1,220	1,282	1,413	1,470
Mechanical engineering								
Bachelor's degree	15,450	14,900	14,843	14,336	13,977	14,067	14,464	15,030
Master's degree	3,198	3,329	3,498	3,424	3,516	3,653	3,982	4,099
Doctor's degree	528	596	633	742	757	851	871	887
English Language and Literature/Letters								
Bachelor's degrees, total	35,667	38,106	41,786	46,803	51,064	54,250	55,289	53,150
Male	12,133	12,687	13,729	15,437	16,891	18,314	19,007	18,214
Female	23,534	25,419	28,057	31,366	34,173	35,936	36,282	34,936
Master's degrees, total	5,298	5,366	5,716	6,317	6,784	7,215	7,537	7,611
Male	1,819	1,796	1,930	2,125	2,203	2,441	2,570	2,620
Female	3,479	3,570	3,786	4,192	4,581	4,774	4,967	4,991
Doctor's degrees, total	853	858	929	986	1,056	1,142	1,201	1,205
Male	367	380	405	444	469	484	495	512
Female	486	478	524	542	587	658	706	693
Foreign Languages and Literatures								
Bachelor's degrees, total	11,706	11,515	12,403	13,133	13,937	14,634	15,305	15,242
Male	3,374	3,223	3,432	3,625	4,008	4,225	4,435	4,573
Female	8,332	8,292	8,971	9,508	9,929	10,409	10,870	10,669
Master's degrees, total	2,574	2,680	2,837	3,018	3,049	3,229	3,513	3,612
Male	847	931	955	987	1,018	1,074	1,182	1,199
Female	1,727	1,749	1,882	2,031	2,031	2,155	2,331	2,413
Doctor's degrees, total	769	725	727	816	889	984	977	1,033
Male	332	330	317	348	396	434	417	418
Female	437	395	410	468	493	550	560	615

Note: Data are for postsecondary institutions participating in Title IV federal financial aid programs.
NA = Not available.
[1]Includes geology/earth science, general; geochemistry; geophysics; paleontology; hydrology; oceanography; and geological and earth sciences, other.
[2]Includes physics, general; atomic/molecular physics; elementary particle physics; nuclear physics; optics; acoustics; theoretical physics; and physics, other.

Table A-37. Degrees Conferred by Post-Secondary Institutions, by Level of Degree and Sex of Student, 1970–1971 through 2017–2018—*Continued*

(Number.)

Degree conferred, level of degree, and sex of student (when available)	1994–95	1995–96	1996–97	1997–98	1998–99	1999–2000	2000–01	2001–02
Computer and Information Sciences								
Bachelor's degrees, total	24,737	24,506	25,422	27,829	30,552	37,788	44,142	50,365
Male	17,684	17,757	18,527	20,372	22,289	27,185	31,923	36,462
Female	7,053	6,749	6,895	7,457	8,263	10,603	12,219	13,903
Master's degrees, total	10,595	10,579	10,513	11,765	12,843	14,990	16,911	17,173
Male	7,805	7,729	7,526	8,343	8,866	9,978	11,195	11,447
Female	2,790	2,850	2,987	3,422	3,977	5,012	5,716	5,726
Doctor's degrees, total	887	869	857	858	806	779	768	752
Male	726	743	721	718	656	648	632	581
Female	161	126	136	140	150	131	136	171
Education								
Bachelor's degrees, total	105,929	105,384	105,116	105,833	107,372	108,034	105,458	106,295
Male	25,619	26,214	26,242	26,285	26,321	26,103	24,580	24,049
Female	80,310	79,170	78,874	79,548	81,051	81,931	80,878	82,246
Master's degrees, total	99,835	104,936	108,720	113,374	118,226	123,045	127,829	135,189
Male	23,511	24,955	25,518	26,814	28,077	29,081	29,997	31,907
Female	76,324	79,981	83,202	86,560	90,149	93,964	97,832	103,282
Doctor's degrees, total	6,475	6,246	6,297	6,261	6,471	6,409	6,284	6,549
Male	2,490	2,404	2,367	2,334	2,297	2,295	2,237	2,211
Female	3,985	3,842	3,930	3,927	4,174	4,114	4,047	4,338
Engineering and Engineering Technologies								
Bachelor's degrees, total	78,483	77,997	75,659	74,557	72,796	73,323	72,869	74,588
Male	66,157	65,362	62,994	61,880	59,859	59,668	59,489	60,417
Female	12,326	12,635	12,665	12,677	12,937	13,655	13,380	14,171
Master's degrees, total	29,949	28,843	27,016	27,244	26,689	26,648	27,187	26,987
Male	25,028	23,840	22,047	21,800	21,348	21,047	21,341	21,212
Female	4,921	5,003	4,969	5,444	5,341	5,601	5,846	5,775
Doctor's degrees, total	6,108	6,354	6,166	5,966	5,413	5,367	5,547	5,181
Male	5,378	5,559	5,408	5,230	4,643	4,539	4,630	4,285
Female	730	795	758	736	770	828	917	896
Chemical, Civil, Electrical, and Mechanical Engineering								
Chemical engineering								
Bachelor's degree	5,901	6,319	6,564	6,319	6,038	5,807	5,611	5,462
Master's degree	1,085	1,176	1,131	1,128	1,130	1,078	1,083	973
Doctor's degree	571	670	650	652	575	590	610	605
Civil engineering								
Bachelor's degree	9,927	10,607	10,437	9,926	9,178	8,136	7,588	7,665
Master's degree	4,077	3,905	3,833	3,795	3,656	3,433	3,310	3,295
Doctor's degree	625	616	640	610	534	543	571	574
Electrical, electronics, and communications engineering								
Bachelor's degree	14,929	13,900	13,336	12,995	12,606	12,930	13,091	13,056
Master's degree	7,693	7,103	6,393	6,737	6,708	6,926	6,815	6,587
Doctor's degree	1,543	1,591	1,512	1,458	1,309	1,392	1,417	1,235
Mechanical engineering								
Bachelor's degree	14,794	14,177	13,493	13,071	12,753	12,807	12,817	13,058
Master's degree	4,213	3,881	3,608	3,441	3,268	3,273	3,371	3,391
Doctor's degree	890	940	913	933	788	776	849	772
English Language and Literature/Letters								
Bachelor's degrees, total	51,170	49,928	48,641	49,016	49,877	50,106	50,569	52,375
Male	17,581	17,007	16,325	16,280	16,332	16,124	15,997	16,457
Female	33,589	32,921	32,316	32,736	33,545	33,982	34,572	35,918
Master's degrees, total	7,612	7,657	7,487	7,587	7,326	7,022	6,763	7,097
Male	2,672	2,727	2,650	2,568	2,452	2,315	2,160	2,270
Female	4,940	4,930	4,837	5,019	4,874	4,707	4,603	4,827
Doctor's degrees, total	1,393	1,395	1,431	1,489	1,412	1,470	1,330	1,291
Male	589	535	610	611	554	611	533	532
Female	804	860	821	878	858	859	797	759
Foreign Languages and Literatures								
Bachelor's degrees, total	14,558	14,832	14,487	15,279	15,835	15,886	16,128	16,258
Male	4,496	4,514	4,388	4,585	4,738	4,616	4,695	4,685
Female	10,062	10,318	10,099	10,694	11,097	11,270	11,433	11,573
Master's degrees, total	3,439	3,443	3,361	3,181	3,109	3,037	3,035	3,075
Male	1,124	1,141	1,104	1,033	976	944	969	958
Female	2,315	2,302	2,257	2,148	2,133	2,093	2,066	2,117
Doctor's degrees, total	1,081	1,020	1,064	1,118	1,049	1,086	1,078	1,003
Male	479	446	450	473	443	446	420	418
Female	602	574	614	645	606	640	658	585

Note: Data are for postsecondary institutions participating in Title IV federal financial aid programs.
NA = Not available.
[1]Includes geology/earth science, general; geochemistry; geophysics; paleontology; hydrology; oceanography; and geological and earth sciences, other.
[2]Includes physics, general; atomic/molecular physics; elementary particle physics; nuclear physics; optics; acoustics; theoretical physics; and physics, other.

Table A-37. Degrees Conferred by Post-Secondary Institutions, by Level of Degree and Sex of Student, 1970–1971 through 2017–2018—*Continued*

(Number.)

Degree conferred, level of degree, and sex of student (when available)	2002–03	2003–04	2004–05	2005–06	2006–07	2007–08	2008–09	2009–10
Computer and Information Sciences								
Bachelor's degrees, total	57,433	59,488	54,111	47,480	42,170	38,476	37,992	39,593
Male	41,950	44,585	42,125	37,705	34,342	31,694	31,213	32,414
Female	15,483	14,903	11,986	9,775	7,828	6,782	6,779	7,179
Master's degrees, total	19,509	20,143	18,416	17,055	16,232	17,087	17,907	17,955
Male	13,267	13,868	13,136	12,470	11,985	12,513	13,063	13,019
Female	6,242	6,275	5,280	4,585	4,247	4,574	4,844	4,936
Doctor's degrees, total	816	909	1,119	1,416	1,595	1,698	1,580	1,599
Male	648	709	905	1,109	1,267	1,323	1,226	1,250
Female	168	200	214	307	328	375	354	349
Education								
Bachelor's degrees, total	105,845	106,278	105,451	107,238	105,641	102,582	101,716	101,287
Male	22,604	22,802	22,513	22,448	22,516	21,828	21,163	20,739
Female	83,241	83,476	82,938	84,790	83,125	80,754	80,553	80,548
Master's degrees, total	147,883	162,345	167,490	174,620	176,572	175,880	178,538	182,165
Male	34,033	37,843	38,863	40,700	40,164	40,055	40,312	41,284
Female	113,850	124,502	128,627	133,920	136,408	135,825	138,226	140,881
Doctor's degrees, total	6,832	7,088	7,681	7,584	8,261	8,491	9,028	9,237
Male	2,314	2,403	2,557	2,664	2,681	2,773	2,956	3,023
Female	4,518	4,685	5,124	4,920	5,580	5,718	6,072	6,214
Engineering and Engineering Technologies								
Bachelor's degrees, total	77,231	78,079	79,544	81,406	81,854	83,608	84,404	88,735
Male	62,821	63,401	65,033	66,866	68,081	69,540	70,504	73,838
Female	14,410	14,678	14,511	14,540	13,773	14,068	13,900	14,897
Master's degrees, total	30,583	35,053	34,988	33,389	31,989	34,430	38,008	39,391
Male	24,097	27,561	27,049	25,568	24,746	26,461	29,458	30,554
Female	6,486	7,492	7,939	7,821	7,243	7,969	8,550	8,837
Doctor's degrees, total	5,252	5,859	6,467	7,318	7,928	7,977	7,803	7,773
Male	4,353	4,821	5,263	5,848	6,285	6,263	6,123	5,986
Female	899	1,038	1,204	1,470	1,643	1,714	1,680	1,787
Chemical, Civil, Electrical, and Mechanical Engineering								
Chemical engineering								
Bachelor's degree	5,109	4,742	4,397	4,326	4,492	4,795	5,036	5,740
Master's degree	1,065	1,165	1,183	1,116	957	933	994	1,043
Doctor's degree	542	623	773	819	835	853	789	830
Civil engineering								
Bachelor's degree	7,836	7,827	8,186	9,090	9,671	10,455	10,785	11,335
Master's degree	3,596	3,790	3,834	3,768	3,482	3,595	3,794	4,079
Doctor's degree	599	636	713	750	805	752	763	717
Electrical, electronics, and communications engineering								
Bachelor's degree	13,627	14,123	14,171	13,966	13,089	12,375	11,620	11,450
Master's degree	7,621	9,511	9,054	8,123	7,777	8,631	9,178	9,052
Doctor's degree	1,256	1,440	1,566	1,860	2,042	1,996	1,812	1,869
Mechanical engineering								
Bachelor's degree	13,693	14,050	14,609	15,850	16,601	17,367	17,352	18,498
Master's degree	3,695	4,420	4,637	4,443	4,294	4,497	4,620	4,818
Doctor's degree	747	787	915	1,096	1,106	1,109	1,142	996
English Language and Literature/Letters								
Bachelor's degrees, total	53,699	53,984	54,379	55,096	55,122	55,038	55,465	53,229
Male	16,738	16,792	17,154	17,316	17,475	17,681	17,973	17,050
Female	36,961	37,192	37,225	37,780	37,647	37,357	37,492	36,179
Master's degrees, total	7,428	7,956	8,468	8,845	8,742	9,161	9,262	9,202
Male	2,433	2,459	2,615	2,860	2,867	3,027	3,000	3,006
Female	4,995	5,497	5,853	5,985	5,875	6,134	6,262	6,196
Doctor's degrees, total	1,246	1,207	1,212	1,254	1,178	1,262	1,271	1,334
Male	492	479	494	510	478	453	464	523
Female	754	728	718	744	700	809	807	811
Foreign Languages and Literatures								
Bachelor's degrees, total	16,912	17,754	18,386	19,410	20,275	20,977	21,169	21,507
Male	4,996	5,215	5,370	5,842	6,173	6,254	6,305	6,607
Female	11,916	12,539	13,016	13,568	14,102	14,723	14,864	14,900
Master's degrees, total	3,049	3,124	3,407	3,539	3,443	3,565	3,592	3,756
Male	874	957	1,056	1,049	1,058	1,128	1,211	1,254
Female	2,175	2,167	2,351	2,490	2,385	2,437	2,381	2,502
Doctor's degrees, total	1,042	1,031	1,027	1,074	1,059	1,078	1,111	1,091
Male	424	410	410	436	437	431	426	446
Female	618	621	617	638	622	647	685	645

Note: Data are for postsecondary institutions participating in Title IV federal financial aid programs.
NA = Not available.
[1]Includes geology/earth science, general; geochemistry; geophysics; paleontology; hydrology; oceanography; and geological and earth sciences, other.
[2]Includes physics, general; atomic/molecular physics; elementary particle physics; nuclear physics; optics; acoustics; theoretical physics; and physics, other.

Table A-37. Degrees Conferred by Post-Secondary Institutions, by Level of Degree and Sex of Student, 1970–1971 through 2017–2018—*Continued*

(Number.)

Degree conferred, level of degree, and sex of student (when available)	2010–11	2011–12	2012–13	2013–14	2014–15	2015–16	2016–17	2017–18
Computer and Information Sciences								
Bachelor's degrees, total	43,066	47,406	50,961	55,271	59,586	64,402	71,416	79,598
Male	35,477	38,796	41,874	45,320	48,844	52,330	57,763	63,704
Female	7,589	8,610	9,087	9,951	10,742	12,072	13,653	15,894
Master's degrees, total	19,516	20,925	22,782	24,514	31,475	40,130	46,553	46,468
Male	14,010	15,132	16,539	17,472	21,893	27,788	32,172	31,397
Female	5,506	5,793	6,243	7,042	9,582	12,342	14,381	15,071
Doctor's degrees, total	1,588	1,698	1,834	1,982	1,998	1,989	1,982	2,017
Male	1,267	1,332	1,480	1,566	1,548	1,591	1,538	1,580
Female	321	366	354	416	450	398	444	437
Education								
Bachelor's degrees, total	104,008	105,656	104,698	98,838	91,596	87,221	85,130	82,621
Male	21,206	21,714	21,824	20,357	18,467	17,429	16,067	15,167
Female	82,802	83,942	82,874	78,481	73,129	69,792	69,063	67,454
Master's degrees, total	185,127	179,047	164,652	154,655	146,581	145,792	145,624	146,367
Male	42,043	41,364	37,816	35,974	33,963	33,791	33,163	32,871
Female	143,084	137,683	126,836	118,681	112,618	112,001	112,461	113,496
Doctor's degrees, total	9,642	10,118	10,572	10,929	11,772	11,838	12,692	12,780
Male	3,070	3,262	3,418	3,464	3,838	3,693	4,015	4,112
Female	6,572	6,856	7,154	7,465	7,934	8,145	8,677	8,668
Engineering and Engineering Technologies								
Bachelor's degrees, total	93,097	98,654	102,997	108,976	115,105	123,948	133,790	140,683
Male	77,080	81,364	84,645	88,941	93,541	99,568	106,559	111,171
Female	16,017	17,290	18,352	20,035	21,564	24,380	27,231	29,512
Master's degrees, total	43,179	45,116	45,328	47,343	51,441	57,713	60,229	58,968
Male	33,372	34,712	34,496	35,791	38,453	43,198	45,206	43,627
Female	9,807	10,404	10,832	11,552	12,988	14,515	15,023	15,341
Doctor's degrees, total	8,425	8,856	9,467	10,117	10,362	10,398	10,523	11,029
Male	6,548	6,838	7,305	7,820	7,958	7,960	8,027	8,331
Female	1,877	2,018	2,162	2,297	2,404	2,438	2,496	2,698
Chemical, Civil, Electrical, and Mechanical Engineering								
Chemical engineering								
Bachelor's degree	6,311	7,027	7,529	8,104	8,980	9,917	10,915	11,542
Master's degree	1,283	1,389	1,450	1,518	1,626	1,699	1,797	1,920
Doctor's degree	831	823	835	992	1,015	1,009	989	1,010
Civil engineering								
Bachelor's degree	12,557	12,808	13,262	12,995	12,673	13,244	13,596	14,039
Master's degree	4,860	5,359	5,353	5,501	5,365	5,626	5,677	5,796
Doctor's degree	751	787	868	972	1,031	1,015	1,077	1,056
Electrical, electronics, and communications engineering								
Bachelor's degree	11,575	12,110	12,835	13,856	14,599	15,680	16,921	16,901
Master's degree	9,691	9,696	9,485	9,829	11,917	13,782	12,792	11,514
Doctor's degree	2,037	2,119	2,118	2,301	2,320	2,258	2,290	2,327
Mechanical engineering								
Bachelor's degree	19,171	20,541	21,990	24,301	26,394	29,216	32,308	35,182
Master's degree	5,802	5,840	5,872	6,182	6,841	7,558	8,278	8,150
Doctor's degree	1,106	1,213	1,321	1,387	1,526	1,470	1,450	1,586
English Language and Literature/Letters								
Bachelor's degrees, total	52,754	53,765	52,401	50,464	45,851	42,797	41,314	40,002
Male	16,917	16,976	16,508	15,831	14,055	12,777	12,243	11,680
Female	35,837	36,789	35,893	34,633	31,796	30,020	29,071	28,322
Master's degrees, total	9,475	9,938	9,755	9,294	8,928	8,581	8,244	8,300
Male	3,137	3,403	3,213	3,115	3,052	2,884	2,738	2,640
Female	6,338	6,535	6,542	6,179	5,876	5,697	5,506	5,660
Doctor's degrees, total	1,344	1,427	1,377	1,393	1,418	1,402	1,347	1,295
Male	529	548	554	557	554	522	519	512
Female	815	879	823	836	864	880	828	783
Foreign Languages and Literatures								
Bachelor's degrees, total	21,705	21,756	21,647	20,332	19,493	18,436	17,643	16,958
Male	6,719	6,629	6,842	6,266	6,066	5,755	5,560	5,288
Female	14,986	15,127	14,805	14,066	13,427	12,681	12,083	11,670
Master's degrees, total	3,727	3,827	3,708	3,482	3,566	3,407	3,271	3,261
Male	1,256	1,280	1,235	1,222	1,241	1,174	1,170	1,084
Female	2,471	2,547	2,473	2,260	2,325	2,233	2,101	2,177
Doctor's degrees, total	1,158	1,231	1,304	1,230	1,243	1,278	1,168	1,213
Male	477	497	531	498	532	514	479	507
Female	681	734	773	732	711	764	689	706

Note: Data are for postsecondary institutions participating in Title IV federal financial aid programs.

NA = Not available.

[1]Includes geology/earth science, general; geochemistry; geophysics; paleontology; hydrology; oceanography; and geological and earth sciences, other.

[2]Includes physics, general; atomic/molecular physics; elementary particle physics; nuclear physics; optics; acoustics; theoretical physics; and physics, other.

Table A-37. Degrees Conferred by Post-Secondary Institutions, by Level of Degree and Sex of Student, 1970–1971 through 2017–2018—*Continued*

(Number.)

Degree conferred, level of degree, and sex of student (when available)	1970–71	1971–72	1972–73	1973–74	1974–75	1975–76	1976–77	1977–78
French, German, Italian, and Spanish Language and Literature								
French								
Bachelor's degree	7,306	6,822	6,705	6,263	5,745	4,783	4,228	3,708
Master's degree	1,437	1,421	1,277	1,195	1,077	914	875	692
Doctor's degree	192	193	203	213	200	190	177	155
German								
Bachelor's degree	2,601	2,477	2,520	2,425	2,289	1,983	1,820	1,647
Master's degree	690	608	598	550	480	471	394	357
Doctor's degree	144	167	176	149	147	164	126	101
Italian								
Bachelor's degree	201	287	313	292	329	342	325	301
Master's degree	87	104	78	81	100	85	89	58
Doctor's degree	10	19	27	19	13	19	16	19
Spanish								
Bachelor's degree	7,068	6,847	7,209	7,250	6,719	5,984	5,359	4,832
Master's degree	1,456	1,421	1,298	1,217	1,228	1,080	930	822
Doctor's degree	168	152	206	203	202	176	153	113
Arabic, Chinese, Korean, and Russian Language and Literature								
Arabic								
Bachelor's degree	15	10	12	20	13	10	7	8
Master's degree	6	4	3	5	11	7	15	3
Doctor's degree	4	0	1	1	2	2	1	1
Chinese								
Bachelor's degree	89	103	98	121	141	150	112	116
Master's degree	22	20	29	37	26	23	32	23
Doctor's degree	8	11	13	5	12	6	6	4
Korean								
Bachelor's degree	NA	NA	NA	NA	NA	NA	NA	NA
Master's degree	NA	NA	NA	NA	NA	NA	NA	NA
Doctor's degree	NA	NA	NA	NA	NA	NA	NA	NA
Russian								
Bachelor's degree	715	658	622	624	598	531	528	442
Master's degree	110	150	120	100	106	81	66	50
Doctor's degree	14	15	27	27	20	13	19	12
Health Professions and Related Programs								
Bachelor's degrees, total	25,223	28,611	33,562	41,421	49,002	53,885	57,222	59,445
Male	5,785	7,005	7,752	9,347	10,844	11,386	11,896	11,600
Female	19,438	21,606	25,810	32,074	38,158	42,499	45,326	47,845
Master's degrees, total	5,330	6,811	7,978	9,232	10,277	12,164	12,627	14,027
Male	2,165	2,749	3,189	3,444	3,686	3,837	3,865	3,972
Female	3,165	4,062	4,789	5,788	6,591	8,327	8,762	10,055
Doctor's degrees, total	15,988	16,538	18,215	20,094	22,191	25,267	24,972	26,516
Male	14,863	15,373	16,870	18,287	19,808	21,980	21,022	21,622
Female	1,125	1,165	1,345	1,807	2,383	3,287	3,950	4,894
Mathematics and Statistics								
Bachelor's degrees, total	24,801	23,713	23,067	21,635	18,181	15,984	14,196	12,569
Male	15,369	14,454	13,796	12,791	10,586	9,475	8,303	7,398
Female	9,432	9,259	9,271	8,844	7,595	6,509	5,893	5,171
Master's degrees, total	5,191	5,198	5,028	4,834	4,327	3,857	3,695	3,373
Male	3,673	3,655	3,525	3,337	2,905	2,547	2,396	2,228
Female	1,518	1,543	1,503	1,497	1,422	1,310	1,299	1,145
Doctor's degrees, total	1,199	1,128	1,068	1,031	975	856	823	805
Male	1,106	1,039	966	931	865	762	714	681
Female	93	89	102	100	110	94	109	124
Physical Sciences and Science Technologies								
Bachelor's degrees, total	21,410	20,743	20,692	21,170	20,770	21,458	22,482	22,975
Male	18,457	17,661	17,622	17,669	16,986	17,349	17,985	18,083
Female	2,953	3,082	3,070	3,501	3,784	4,109	4,497	4,892
Master's degrees, total	6,336	6,268	6,230	6,019	5,782	5,428	5,281	5,507
Male	5,495	5,390	5,388	5,157	4,949	4,622	4,411	4,583
Female	841	878	842	862	833	806	870	924
Doctor's degrees, total	4,324	4,075	3,961	3,558	3,577	3,388	3,295	3,073
Male	4,082	3,805	3,698	3,312	3,284	3,097	2,981	2,763
Female	242	270	263	246	293	291	314	310

Note: Data are for postsecondary institutions participating in Title IV federal financial aid programs.

NA = Not available.

[1]Includes geology/earth science, general; geochemistry; geophysics; paleontology; hydrology; oceanography; and geological and earth sciences, other.

[2]Includes physics, general; atomic/molecular physics; elementary particle physics; nuclear physics; optics; acoustics; theoretical physics; and physics, other.

Table A-37. Degrees Conferred by Post-Secondary Institutions, by Level of Degree and Sex of Student, 1970–1971 through 2017–2018—*Continued*

(Number.)

Degree conferred, level of degree, and sex of student (when available)	1978–79	1979–80	1980–81	1981–82	1982–83	1983–84	1984–85	1985–86
French, German, Italian, and Spanish Language and Literature								
French								
Bachelor's degree..	3,558	3,285	3,178	3,054	2,871	2,876	2,991	3,015
Master's degree..	576	513	460	485	360	418	385	409
Doctor's degree...	143	128	115	92	106	86	74	86
German								
Bachelor's degree..	1,524	1,466	1,286	1,327	1,367	1,292	1,411	1,396
Master's degree..	344	309	294	324	281	241	240	249
Doctor's degree...	106	94	79	76	68	63	58	73
Italian								
Bachelor's degree..	236	272	205	208	224	206	190	240
Master's degree..	60	49	65	55	45	41	44	42
Doctor's degree...	14	9	13	14	18	13	9	10
Spanish								
Bachelor's degree..	4,563	4,331	3,870	3,633	3,349	3,254	3,415	3,385
Master's degree..	720	685	592	568	506	537	505	521
Doctor's degree...	118	103	131	140	129	102	115	95
Arabic, Chinese, Korean, and Russian Language and Literature								
Arabic								
Bachelor's degree..	4	13	6	15	12	6	9	5
Master's degree..	4	2	7	4	4	2	4	4
Doctor's degree...	5	5	0	4	1	0	0	0
Chinese								
Bachelor's degree..	91	79	73	68	92	115	97	87
Master's degree..	22	33	20	14	15	14	21	23
Doctor's degree...	12	7	6	10	7	10	3	11
Korean								
Bachelor's degree..	NA	NA	NA	NA	NA	NA	NA	NA
Master's degree..	NA	NA	NA	NA	NA	NA	NA	NA
Doctor's degree...	NA	NA	NA	NA	NA	NA	NA	NA
Russian								
Bachelor's degree..	465	402	409	324	342	340	432	493
Master's degree..	51	60	68	49	33	39	47	33
Doctor's degree...	9	6	8	7	5	3	6	3
Health Professions and Related Programs								
Bachelor's degrees, total...	62,095	63,848	63,665	63,660	65,642	65,305	65,331	65,309
Male...	11,214	11,330	10,531	10,110	10,247	10,068	9,741	9,629
Female..	50,881	52,518	53,134	53,550	55,395	55,237	55,590	55,680
Master's degrees, total..	15,110	15,374	16,176	16,212	16,941	17,351	17,442	18,603
Male...	4,155	4,060	4,024	3,743	4,138	4,124	4,046	4,355
Female..	10,955	11,314	12,152	12,469	12,803	13,227	13,396	14,248
Doctor's degrees, total...	27,766	28,190	29,595	30,096	30,800	31,655	31,493	31,922
Male...	22,194	22,157	22,792	22,968	22,920	22,851	22,045	22,069
Female..	5,572	6,033	6,803	7,128	7,880	8,804	9,448	9,853
Mathematics and Statistics								
Bachelor's degrees, total...	11,806	11,378	11,078	11,599	12,294	13,087	15,009	16,122
Male...	6,899	6,562	6,342	6,593	6,888	7,290	8,080	8,623
Female..	4,907	4,816	4,736	5,006	5,406	5,797	6,929	7,499
Master's degrees, total..	3,036	2,860	2,567	2,727	2,810	2,723	2,859	3,131
Male...	1,985	1,828	1,692	1,821	1,838	1,773	1,858	2,028
Female..	1,051	1,032	875	906	972	950	1,001	1,103
Doctor's degrees, total...	730	724	728	681	697	695	699	742
Male...	608	624	614	587	581	569	590	618
Female..	122	100	114	94	116	126	109	124
Physical Sciences and Science Technologies								
Bachelor's degrees, total...	23,197	23,407	23,936	24,045	23,374	23,645	23,694	21,711
Male...	17,976	17,861	18,052	17,861	16,988	17,112	17,065	15,750
Female..	5,221	5,546	5,884	6,184	6,386	6,533	6,629	5,961
Master's degrees, total..	5,418	5,167	5,246	5,446	5,250	5,541	5,752	5,860
Male...	4,438	4,210	4,172	4,274	4,131	4,249	4,425	4,443
Female..	980	957	1,074	1,172	1,119	1,292	1,327	1,417
Doctor's degrees, total...	3,061	3,044	3,105	3,246	3,214	3,269	3,349	3,521
Male...	2,717	2,669	2,733	2,804	2,767	2,789	2,808	2,946
Female..	344	375	372	442	447	480	541	575

Note: Data are for postsecondary institutions participating in Title IV federal financial aid programs.
NA = Not available.
[1]Includes geology/earth science, general; geochemistry; geophysics; paleontology; hydrology; oceanography; and geological and earth sciences, other.
[2]Includes physics, general; atomic/molecular physics; elementary particle physics; nuclear physics; optics; acoustics; theoretical physics; and physics, other.

Table A-37. Degrees Conferred by Post-Secondary Institutions, by Level of Degree and Sex of Student, 1970–1971 through 2017–2018—*Continued*

(Number.)

Degree conferred, level of degree, and sex of student (when available)	1986–87	1987–88	1988–89	1989–90	1990–91	1991–92	1992–93	1993–94
French, German, Italian, and Spanish Language and Literature								
French								
Bachelor's degree................................	3,062	3,082	3,297	3,259	3,355	3,371	3,280	3,094
Master's degree..................................	421	437	444	478	480	465	513	479
Doctor's degree..................................	85	89	83	115	98	112	98	104
German								
Bachelor's degree................................	1,366	1,350	1,428	1,437	1,543	1,616	1,572	1,580
Master's degree..................................	234	244	263	253	242	273	317	298
Doctor's degree..................................	70	71	59	67	58	85	86	61
Italian								
Bachelor's degree................................	219	224	239	247	253	238	274	264
Master's degree..................................	53	45	45	38	36	55	50	47
Doctor's degree..................................	17	7	17	19	21	18	13	24
Spanish								
Bachelor's degree................................	3,450	3,416	3,748	4,176	4,480	4,768	5,233	5,505
Master's degree..................................	504	553	552	573	609	647	667	691
Doctor's degree..................................	104	93	101	108	125	143	145	160
Arabic, Chinese, Korean, and Russian Language and Literature								
Arabic								
Bachelor's degree................................	8	9	6	4	9	13	8	8
Master's degree..................................	1	4	2	0	0	0	3	2
Doctor's degree..................................	1	0	1	1	1	0	2	0
Chinese								
Bachelor's degree................................	110	103	138	144	150	183	129	112
Master's degree..................................	16	31	27	33	24	36	54	48
Doctor's degree..................................	10	9	8	8	9	14	8	18
Korean								
Bachelor's degree................................	NA	NA	NA	NA	NA	NA	NA	NA
Master's degree..................................	NA	NA	NA	NA	NA	NA	NA	NA
Doctor's degree..................................	NA	NA	NA	NA	NA	NA	NA	NA
Russian								
Bachelor's degree................................	502	472	469	549	593	629	612	611
Master's degree..................................	54	54	55	52	70	68	68	71
Doctor's degree..................................	8	8	6	5	6	7	4	3
Health Professions and Related Programs								
Bachelor's degrees, total............................	63,963	61,614	59,850	58,983	59,875	62,779	68,434	75,890
Male.......................................	9,137	8,955	8,878	9,075	9,619	10,330	11,605	13,377
Female.....................................	54,826	52,659	50,972	49,908	50,256	52,449	56,829	62,513
Master's degrees, total............................	18,442	18,774	19,493	20,406	21,354	23,671	26,190	28,442
Male.......................................	3,818	4,004	4,197	4,486	4,423	4,794	5,249	5,813
Female.....................................	14,624	14,770	15,296	15,920	16,931	18,877	20,941	22,629
Doctor's degrees, total............................	29,500	30,060	30,546	30,101	29,842	31,479	31,089	30,959
Male.......................................	19,686	19,853	19,893	19,118	18,492	19,362	18,446	17,988
Female.....................................	9,814	10,207	10,653	10,983	11,350	12,117	12,643	12,971
Mathematics and Statistics								
Bachelor's degrees, total............................	16,257	15,712	15,017	14,276	14,393	14,468	14,384	14,171
Male.......................................	8,673	8,408	8,081	7,674	7,580	7,668	7,566	7,594
Female.....................................	7,584	7,304	6,936	6,602	6,813	6,800	6,818	6,577
Master's degrees, total............................	3,283	3,413	3,405	3,624	3,549	3,558	3,644	3,682
Male.......................................	1,995	2,052	2,061	2,172	2,096	2,151	2,151	2,237
Female.....................................	1,288	1,361	1,344	1,452	1,453	1,407	1,493	1,445
Doctor's degrees, total............................	723	750	866	917	978	1,048	1,138	1,125
Male.......................................	598	625	700	754	790	825	867	880
Female.....................................	125	125	166	163	188	223	271	245
Physical Sciences and Science Technologies								
Bachelor's degrees, total............................	20,060	17,797	17,179	16,056	16,334	16,970	17,577	18,474
Male.......................................	14,365	12,385	12,071	11,026	11,170	11,443	11,853	12,271
Female.....................................	5,695	5,412	5,108	5,030	5,164	5,527	5,724	6,203
Master's degrees, total............................	5,586	5,696	5,691	5,410	5,281	5,397	5,392	5,718
Male.......................................	4,193	4,300	4,180	3,996	3,823	3,935	3,840	4,069
Female.....................................	1,393	1,396	1,511	1,414	1,458	1,462	1,552	1,649
Doctor's degrees, total............................	3,629	3,758	3,795	4,116	4,248	4,378	4,372	4,652
Male.......................................	3,004	3,085	3,046	3,328	3,417	3,433	3,426	3,657
Female.....................................	625	673	749	788	831	945	946	995

Note: Data are for postsecondary institutions participating in Title IV federal financial aid programs.
NA = Not available.
[1]Includes geology/earth science, general; geochemistry; geophysics; paleontology; hydrology; oceanography; and geological and earth sciences, other.
[2]Includes physics, general; atomic/molecular physics; elementary particle physics; nuclear physics; optics; acoustics; theoretical physics; and physics, other.

Table A-37. Degrees Conferred by Post-Secondary Institutions, by Level of Degree and Sex of Student, 1970–1971 through 2017–2018—*Continued*

(Number.)

Degree conferred, level of degree, and sex of student (when available)	1994–95	1995–96	1996–97	1997–98	1998–99	1999–2000	2000–01	2001–02
French, German, Italian, and Spanish Language and Literature								
French								
Bachelor's degree	2,764	2,655	2,468	2,530	2,565	2,514	2,371	2,396
Master's degree	470	446	414	389	365	343	376	356
Doctor's degree	118	113	119	104	115	129	115	89
German								
Bachelor's degree	1,352	1,290	1,214	1,181	1,237	1,125	1,143	1,092
Master's degree	278	305	281	209	242	184	242	208
Doctor's degree	83	75	80	94	78	76	73	64
Italian								
Bachelor's degree	271	232	234	252	257	237	286	263
Master's degree	69	44	49	60	41	48	42	46
Doctor's degree	31	22	18	25	12	13	11	15
Spanish								
Bachelor's degree	5,602	5,995	6,161	6,595	6,992	7,031	7,164	7,243
Master's degree	709	769	677	781	697	718	716	792
Doctor's degree	161	151	175	160	153	175	185	193
Arabic, Chinese, Korean, and Russian Language and Literature								
Arabic								
Bachelor's degree	10	8	9	16	13	6	7	13
Master's degree	1	3	3	2	3	4	2	2
Doctor's degree	1	2	0	1	1	5	3	2
Chinese								
Bachelor's degree	107	136	152	161	178	183	183	189
Master's degree	63	42	31	21	20	18	13	16
Doctor's degree	16	19	15	13	14	15	7	12
Korean								
Bachelor's degree	NA	NA	NA	NA	NA	NA	NA	NA
Master's degree	NA	NA	NA	NA	NA	NA	NA	NA
Doctor's degree	NA	NA	NA	NA	NA	NA	NA	NA
Russian								
Bachelor's degree	572	494	455	383	398	340	335	277
Master's degree	66	58	46	49	29	33	24	34
Doctor's degree	3	7	9	9	4	10	7	5
Health Professions and Related Programs								
Bachelor's degrees, total	81,596	86,087	87,997	86,843	84,989	80,863	75,933	72,887
Male	14,812	15,942	16,440	15,700	15,191	13,342	12,514	10,869
Female	66,784	70,145	71,557	71,143	69,798	67,521	63,419	62,018
Master's degrees, total	31,770	33,920	36,162	39,567	40,628	42,593	43,623	43,560
Male	6,718	7,017	7,536	8,644	9,152	9,500	9,711	9,588
Female	25,052	26,903	28,626	30,923	31,476	33,093	33,912	33,972
Doctor's degrees, total	32,124	32,678	34,971	35,369	35,939	37,829	39,019	39,435
Male	18,463	18,495	19,619	19,370	19,673	19,984	20,260	19,760
Female	13,661	14,183	15,352	15,999	16,266	17,845	18,759	19,675
Mathematics and Statistics								
Bachelor's degrees, total	13,494	12,713	12,401	11,795	12,011	11,418	11,171	11,950
Male	7,154	6,847	6,649	6,247	6,206	5,955	5,791	6,333
Female	6,340	5,866	5,752	5,548	5,805	5,463	5,380	5,617
Master's degrees, total	3,820	3,651	3,504	3,409	3,304	3,208	3,209	3,350
Male	2,289	2,178	2,055	1,985	1,912	1,749	1,857	1,913
Female	1,531	1,473	1,449	1,424	1,392	1,459	1,352	1,437
Doctor's degrees, total	1,181	1,158	1,134	1,215	1,107	1,075	997	923
Male	919	919	861	903	812	803	715	658
Female	262	239	273	312	295	272	282	265
Physical Sciences and Science Technologies								
Bachelor's degrees, total	19,247	19,716	19,594	19,454	18,448	18,427	18,025	17,890
Male	12,556	12,634	12,285	11,999	11,119	11,019	10,628	10,349
Female	6,691	7,082	7,309	7,455	7,329	7,408	7,397	7,541
Master's degrees, total	5,798	5,910	5,616	5,411	5,241	4,888	5,134	5,082
Male	4,058	4,031	3,799	3,484	3,454	3,167	3,276	3,186
Female	1,740	1,879	1,817	1,927	1,787	1,721	1,858	1,896
Doctor's degrees, total	4,486	4,589	4,501	4,592	4,229	4,017	3,968	3,824
Male	3,443	3,543	3,479	3,451	3,206	3,002	2,914	2,766
Female	1,043	1,046	1,022	1,141	1,023	1,015	1,054	1,058

Note: Data are for postsecondary institutions participating in Title IV federal financial aid programs.

NA = Not available.

[1]Includes geology/earth science, general; geochemistry; geophysics; paleontology; hydrology; oceanography; and geological and earth sciences, other.

[2]Includes physics, general; atomic/molecular physics; elementary particle physics; nuclear physics; optics; acoustics; theoretical physics; and physics, other.

Table A-37. Degrees Conferred by Post-Secondary Institutions, by Level of Degree and Sex of Student, 1970–1971 through 2017–2018—*Continued*

(Number.)

Degree conferred, level of degree, and sex of student (when available)	2002–03	2003–04	2004–05	2005–06	2006–07	2007–08	2008–09	2009–10
French, German, Italian, and Spanish Language and Literature								
French								
Bachelor's degree	2,294	2,362	2,394	2,410	2,462	2,432	2,450	2,488
Master's degree	348	361	356	395	364	359	386	391
Doctor's degree	75	85	80	84	95	102	86	87
German								
Bachelor's degree	1,097	1,031	1,103	1,106	1,055	1,085	1,058	1,028
Master's degree	188	153	180	172	158	173	163	143
Doctor's degree	77	30	56	48	56	51	47	46
Italian								
Bachelor's degree	307	279	277	321	280	359	341	336
Master's degree	54	49	70	94	97	88	76	73
Doctor's degree	20	31	12	17	20	25	34	23
Spanish								
Bachelor's degree	7,619	7,991	8,304	8,690	9,013	9,278	9,333	9,138
Master's degree	791	833	919	981	982	990	878	962
Doctor's degree	190	199	190	192	195	193	218	199
Arabic, Chinese, Korean, and Russian Language and Literature								
Arabic								
Bachelor's degree	13	13	21	26	68	57	85	121
Master's degree	3	3	5	4	2	8	14	10
Doctor's degree	0	1	0	2	0	1	1	6
Chinese								
Bachelor's degree	190	186	208	241	261	289	384	456
Master's degree	12	15	21	20	30	35	45	51
Doctor's degree	9	5	8	10	2	5	11	12
Korean								
Bachelor's degree	5	9	8	17	13	15	24	27
Master's degree	0	2	0	4	0	4	2	19
Doctor's degree	0	1	0	3	0	1	1	1
Russian								
Bachelor's degree	271	301	298	279	311	294	325	356
Master's degree	16	21	18	28	18	20	21	19
Doctor's degree	6	3	0	7	4	1	1	1
Health Professions and Related Programs								
Bachelor's degrees, total	71,261	73,934	80,685	91,973	101,810	111,478	120,420	129,623
Male	10,096	10,017	10,858	12,914	14,325	16,286	17,776	19,309
Female	61,165	63,917	69,827	79,059	87,485	95,192	102,644	110,314
Master's degrees, total	42,748	44,939	46,703	51,380	54,531	58,120	62,642	69,112
Male	9,280	9,670	9,816	10,630	10,636	11,010	11,848	12,874
Female	33,468	35,269	36,887	40,750	43,895	47,110	50,794	56,238
Doctor's degrees, total	39,799	41,861	44,201	45,677	48,943	51,675	54,846	57,750
Male	19,493	19,587	19,697	19,640	20,522	21,616	22,678	23,946
Female	20,306	22,274	24,504	26,037	28,421	30,059	32,168	33,804
Mathematics and Statistics								
Bachelor's degrees, total	12,505	13,327	14,351	14,770	14,954	15,192	15,507	16,029
Male	6,784	7,203	7,937	8,115	8,360	8,490	8,801	9,087
Female	5,721	6,124	6,414	6,655	6,594	6,702	6,706	6,942
Master's degrees, total	3,620	4,191	4,477	4,730	4,884	4,980	5,211	5,639
Male	1,996	2,302	2,525	2,712	2,859	2,860	3,064	3,378
Female	1,624	1,889	1,952	2,018	2,025	2,120	2,147	2,261
Doctor's degrees, total	1,007	1,060	1,176	1,293	1,351	1,360	1,535	1,596
Male	734	762	841	911	949	938	1,059	1,118
Female	273	298	335	382	402	422	476	478
Physical Sciences and Science Technologies								
Bachelor's degrees, total	18,038	18,131	19,104	20,522	21,291	22,179	22,691	23,381
Male	10,625	10,577	11,065	11,978	12,604	13,143	13,465	13,866
Female	7,413	7,554	8,039	8,544	8,687	9,036	9,226	9,515
Master's degrees, total	5,196	5,714	5,823	6,063	6,012	6,061	5,862	6,066
Male	3,284	3,470	3,569	3,666	3,675	3,762	3,576	3,654
Female	1,912	2,244	2,254	2,397	2,337	2,299	2,286	2,412
Doctor's degrees, total	3,939	3,937	4,248	4,642	5,041	4,994	5,237	5,065
Male	2,854	2,855	3,071	3,258	3,454	3,513	3,554	3,406
Female	1,085	1,082	1,177	1,384	1,587	1,481	1,683	1,659

Note: Data are for postsecondary institutions participating in Title IV federal financial aid programs.
NA = Not available.
[1]Includes geology/earth science, general; geochemistry; geophysics; paleontology; hydrology; oceanography; and geological and earth sciences, other.
[2]Includes physics, general; atomic/molecular physics; elementary particle physics; nuclear physics; optics; acoustics; theoretical physics; and physics, other.

Table A-37. Degrees Conferred by Post-Secondary Institutions, by Level of Degree and Sex of Student, 1970–1971 through 2017–2018—*Continued*

(Number.)

Degree conferred, level of degree, and sex of student (when available)	2010–11	2011–12	2012–13	2013–14	2014–15	2015–16	2016–17	2017–18
French, German, Italian, and Spanish Language and Literature								
French								
Bachelor's degree	2,490	2,358	2,278	2,043	1,916	1,750	1,625	1,438
Master's degree	366	341	332	308	270	306	265	277
Doctor's degree	81	96	115	107	110	95	85	86
German								
Bachelor's degree	1,019	1,001	931	878	828	809	753	697
Master's degree	156	130	102	123	115	88	96	77
Doctor's degree	43	67	52	44	52	64	49	42
Italian								
Bachelor's degree	313	332	284	271	231	191	183	145
Master's degree	83	72	73	58	55	34	56	36
Doctor's degree	28	35	27	29	23	27	35	22
Spanish								
Bachelor's degree	8,920	8,714	8,419	8,034	7,508	6,875	6,421	6,011
Master's degree	955	991	928	832	830	747	737	731
Doctor's degree	179	189	205	192	198	197	171	209
Arabic, Chinese, Korean, and Russian Language and Literature								
Arabic								
Bachelor's degree	141	143	167	165	169	155	160	153
Master's degree	5	8	12	6	4	18	8	6
Doctor's degree	1	7	1	0	2	1	2	2
Chinese								
Bachelor's degree	449	496	510	497	509	482	450	466
Master's degree	51	46	61	46	48	44	51	46
Doctor's degree	8	9	12	3	6	7	14	11
Korean								
Bachelor's degree	28	38	43	32	43	54	67	55
Master's degree	10	8	14	10	8	6	5	6
Doctor's degree	3	3	0	8	2	2	2	2
Russian								
Bachelor's degree	340	392	392	371	339	304	296	296
Master's degree	11	17	11	14	15	13	13	10
Doctor's degree	3	2	5	1	4	0	4	3
Health Professions and Related Programs								
Bachelor's degrees, total	143,463	163,675	181,149	198,777	216,228	228,907	237,979	244,909
Male	21,540	24,905	28,208	30,932	33,658	36,262	37,746	38,022
Female	121,923	138,770	152,941	167,845	182,570	192,645	200,233	206,887
Master's degrees, total	75,571	84,355	90,933	97,416	103,052	110,350	119,242	125,216
Male	14,034	15,675	16,747	17,751	18,793	20,424	21,984	22,768
Female	61,537	68,680	74,186	79,665	84,259	89,926	97,258	102,448
Doctor's degrees, total	60,221	62,097	64,192	67,447	71,004	73,687	77,693	80,305
Male	25,386	26,074	26,852	28,082	29,427	30,387	31,845	32,494
Female	34,835	36,023	37,340	39,365	41,577	43,300	45,848	47,811
Mathematics and Statistics								
Bachelor's degrees, total	17,182	18,841	20,449	20,987	21,854	22,778	24,075	25,256
Male	9,782	10,722	11,599	11,970	12,462	13,090	14,003	14,541
Female	7,400	8,119	8,850	9,017	9,392	9,688	10,072	10,715
Master's degrees, total	5,866	6,246	6,957	7,273	7,589	8,451	9,082	10,443
Male	3,459	3,695	4,178	4,256	4,508	4,924	5,113	5,959
Female	2,407	2,551	2,779	3,017	3,081	3,527	3,969	4,484
Doctor's degrees, total	1,586	1,669	1,823	1,863	1,801	1,855	1,925	2,010
Male	1,132	1,198	1,292	1,325	1,298	1,324	1,403	1,448
Female	454	471	531	538	503	531	522	562
Physical Sciences and Science Technologies								
Bachelor's degrees, total	24,705	26,664	28,053	29,307	30,042	30,483	31,272	31,542
Male	14,778	15,972	17,142	17,804	18,480	18,671	18,863	18,938
Female	9,927	10,692	10,911	11,503	11,562	11,812	12,409	12,604
Master's degrees, total	6,386	6,911	7,014	6,984	7,100	7,131	7,136	7,196
Male	3,907	4,299	4,377	4,312	4,438	4,435	4,416	4,492
Female	2,479	2,612	2,637	2,672	2,662	2,696	2,720	2,704
Doctor's degrees, total	5,295	5,370	5,514	5,806	5,823	6,057	6,027	6,181
Male	3,608	3,609	3,646	3,873	3,826	4,102	4,072	4,074
Female	1,687	1,761	1,868	1,933	1,997	1,955	1,955	2,107

Note: Data are for postsecondary institutions participating in Title IV federal financial aid programs.

NA = Not available.

[1]Includes geology/earth science, general; geochemistry; geophysics; paleontology; hydrology; oceanography; and geological and earth sciences, other.

[2]Includes physics, general; atomic/molecular physics; elementary particle physics; nuclear physics; optics; acoustics; theoretical physics; and physics, other.

Table A-37. Degrees Conferred by Post-Secondary Institutions, by Level of Degree and Sex of Student, 1970–1971 through 2017–2018—*Continued*

(Number.)

Degree conferred, level of degree, and sex of student (when available)	1970–71	1971–72	1972–73	1973–74	1974–75	1975–76	1976–77	1977–78
Chemistry, Geology and Earth Science, and Physics								
Chemistry								
Bachelor's degree	11,061	10,588	10,124	10,430	10,541	11,015	11,200	11,304
Master's degree	2,244	2,229	2,198	2,082	1,961	1,745	1,717	1,832
Doctor's degree[1]	2,093	1,943	1,827	1,755	1,773	1,578	1,522	1,461
Geology and earth science[1]								
Bachelor's degree	3,312	3,766	4,117	4,526	4,566	4,677	5,280	5,648
Master's degree	1,074	1,233	1,296	1,479	1,320	1,384	1,446	1,633
Doctor's degree	408	433	430	416	433	445	480	419
Physics[2]								
Bachelor's degree	5,071	4,634	4,259	3,952	3,706	3,544	3,420	3,330
Master's degree	2,188	2,033	1,747	1,655	1,574	1,451	1,319	1,294
Doctor's degree	1,482	1,344	1,338	1,115	1,080	997	945	873
Psychology								
Bachelor's degrees, total	38,187	43,433	47,940	52,139	51,245	50,278	47,861	44,879
Male	21,227	23,352	25,117	25,868	24,284	22,898	20,627	18,422
Female	16,960	20,081	22,823	26,271	26,961	27,380	27,234	26,457
Master's degrees, total	5,717	6,764	7,619	8,796	9,394	10,167	10,859	10,282
Male	3,395	3,934	4,325	4,983	5,035	5,136	5,293	4,670
Female	2,322	2,830	3,294	3,813	4,359	5,031	5,566	5,612
Doctor's degrees, total	2,144	2,277	2,550	2,872	2,913	3,157	3,386	3,164
Male	1,629	1,694	1,797	1,987	1,979	2,115	2,127	1,974
Female	515	583	753	885	934	1,042	1,259	1,190
Public Administration and Social Services								
Bachelor's degrees, total	5,466	7,508	10,690	11,966	13,661	15,440	16,136	16,607
Male	1,726	2,588	3,998	4,266	4,630	5,706	5,544	5,096
Female	3,740	4,920	6,692	7,700	9,031	9,734	10,592	11,511
Master's degrees, total	7,785	8,756	10,068	11,415	13,617	15,209	17,026	17,337
Male	3,893	4,537	5,271	6,028	7,200	7,969	8,810	8,513
Female	3,892	4,219	4,797	5,387	6,417	7,240	8,216	8,824
Doctor's degrees, total	174	193	198	201	257	292	292	357
Male	132	150	160	154	192	192	197	237
Female	42	43	38	47	65	100	95	120
Social Sciences and History								
Bachelor's degrees, total	155,324	158,060	155,970	150,320	135,190	126,396	117,040	112,952
Male	98,173	100,895	99,735	95,650	84,826	78,691	71,128	67,217
Female	57,151	57,165	56,235	54,670	50,364	47,705	45,912	45,735
Master's degrees, total	16,539	17,445	17,477	17,293	16,977	15,953	15,533	14,718
Male	11,833	12,540	12,605	12,321	11,875	10,918	10,413	9,845
Female	4,706	4,905	4,872	4,972	5,102	5,035	5,120	4,873
Doctor's degrees, total	3,660	4,081	4,234	4,124	4,212	4,157	3,802	3,594
Male	3,153	3,483	3,573	3,383	3,334	3,262	2,957	2,722
Female	507	598	661	741	878	895	845	872
Economics, History, Political Science and Government, and Sociology								
Economics								
Bachelor's degree	15,758	15,231	14,770	14,285	14,046	14,741	15,296	15,661
Master's degree	1,995	2,224	2,225	2,141	2,127	2,087	2,158	1,995
Doctor's degree	721	794	845	788	815	763	758	706
History								
Bachelor's degree	44,663	43,695	40,943	37,049	31,470	28,400	25,433	23,004
Master's degree	5,157	5,217	5,030	4,533	4,226	3,658	3,393	3,033
Doctor's degree	991	1,133	1,140	1,114	1,117	1,014	921	813
Political science and government								
Bachelor's degree	27,482	28,135	30,100	30,744	29,126	28,302	26,411	26,069
Master's degree	2,318	2,451	2,398	2,448	2,333	2,191	2,222	2,069
Doctor's degree	700	758	747	766	680	723	641	636
Sociology								
Bachelor's degree	33,263	35,216	35,436	35,491	31,488	27,634	24,713	22,750
Master's degree	1,808	1,944	1,923	2,196	2,112	2,009	1,830	1,611
Doctor's degree	574	636	583	632	693	729	714	599

Note: Data are for postsecondary institutions participating in Title IV federal financial aid programs.

NA = Not available.

[1]Includes geology/earth science, general; geochemistry; geophysics; paleontology; hydrology; oceanography; and geological and earth sciences, other.

[2]Includes physics, general; atomic/molecular physics; elementary particle physics; nuclear physics; optics; acoustics; theoretical physics; and physics, other.

Table A-37. Degrees Conferred by Post-Secondary Institutions, by Level of Degree and Sex of Student, 1970–1971 through 2017–2018—*Continued*

(Number.)

Degree conferred, level of degree, and sex of student (when available)	1978–79	1979–80	1980–81	1981–82	1982–83	1983–84	1984–85	1985–86
Chemistry, Geology and Earth Science, and Physics								
Chemistry								
Bachelor's degree	11,499	11,229	11,331	11,058	10,789	10,698	10,472	10,110
Master's degree	1,724	1,671	1,616	1,683	1,582	1,632	1,675	1,712
Doctor's degree	1,475	1,500	1,586	1,682	1,691	1,707	1,735	1,878
Geology and earth science[1]								
Bachelor's degree	5,753	5,785	6,332	6,650	6,981	7,524	7,194	5,760
Master's degree	1,596	1,623	1,702	1,848	1,784	1,747	1,927	2,036
Doctor's degree	414	440	404	452	406	408	401	395
Physics[2]								
Bachelor's degree	3,337	3,396	3,441	3,472	3,793	3,907	4,097	4,180
Master's degree	1,319	1,192	1,294	1,284	1,369	1,532	1,523	1,501
Doctor's degree	918	830	866	873	873	953	951	1,010
Psychology								
Bachelor's degrees, total	42,697	42,093	41,068	41,212	40,460	39,955	39,900	40,628
Male	16,540	15,440	14,332	13,645	13,131	12,812	12,706	12,605
Female	26,157	26,653	26,736	27,567	27,329	27,143	27,194	28,023
Master's degrees, total	10,132	9,938	10,223	9,947	9,981	9,525	9,891	9,845
Male	4,405	4,096	4,066	3,823	3,647	3,400	3,452	3,347
Female	5,727	5,842	6,157	6,124	6,334	6,125	6,439	6,498
Doctor's degrees, total	3,228	3,395	3,576	3,461	3,602	3,535	3,447	3,593
Male	1,895	1,921	2,002	1,856	1,838	1,774	1,739	1,724
Female	1,333	1,474	1,574	1,605	1,764	1,761	1,708	1,869
Public Administration and Social Services								
Bachelor's degrees, total	17,328	16,644	16,707	16,495	14,414	12,570	11,754	11,887
Male	4,938	4,451	4,248	4,176	3,343	2,998	2,829	2,966
Female	12,390	12,193	12,459	12,319	11,071	9,572	8,925	8,921
Master's degrees, total	17,306	17,560	17,803	17,416	16,046	15,060	15,575	15,692
Male	8,051	7,866	7,460	6,975	5,961	5,634	5,573	5,594
Female	9,255	9,694	10,343	10,441	10,085	9,426	10,002	10,098
Doctor's degrees, total	315	342	362	372	347	420	431	382
Male	215	216	212	205	184	230	213	171
Female	100	126	150	167	163	190	218	211
Social Sciences and History								
Bachelor's degrees, total	108,059	103,662	100,513	99,705	95,228	93,323	91,570	93,840
Male	62,852	58,511	56,131	55,196	52,771	52,154	51,226	52,724
Female	45,207	45,151	44,382	44,509	42,457	41,169	40,344	41,116
Master's degrees, total	12,963	12,176	11,945	12,002	11,205	10,577	10,503	10,564
Male	8,395	7,794	7,457	7,468	6,974	6,551	6,475	6,419
Female	4,568	4,382	4,488	4,534	4,231	4,026	4,028	4,145
Doctor's degrees, total	3,371	3,230	3,122	3,061	2,931	2,911	2,851	2,955
Male	2,501	2,357	2,274	2,237	2,042	2,030	1,933	1,970
Female	870	873	848	824	889	881	918	985
Economics, History, Political Science and Government, and Sociology								
Economics								
Bachelor's degree	16,409	17,863	18,753	19,876	20,517	20,719	20,711	21,602
Master's degree	1,955	1,821	1,911	1,964	1,972	1,891	1,992	1,937
Doctor's degree	712	677	727	677	734	729	749	789
History								
Bachelor's degree	21,019	19,301	18,301	17,146	16,467	16,643	16,049	16,415
Master's degree	2,536	2,367	2,237	2,210	2,041	1,940	1,921	1,961
Doctor's degree	756	712	643	636	575	561	468	497
Political science and government								
Bachelor's degree	25,628	25,457	24,977	25,658	25,791	25,719	25,834	26,439
Master's degree	2,037	1,938	1,875	1,954	1,829	1,769	1,500	1,704
Doctor's degree	563	535	484	513	435	457	441	439
Sociology								
Bachelor's degree	20,285	18,881	17,272	16,042	14,105	13,145	11,968	12,271
Master's degree	1,415	1,341	1,240	1,145	1,112	1,008	1,022	965
Doctor's degree	612	583	610	558	522	520	480	504

Note: Data are for postsecondary institutions participating in Title IV federal financial aid programs.

NA = Not available.

[1]Includes geology/earth science, general; geochemistry; geophysics; paleontology; hydrology; oceanography; and geological and earth sciences, other.

[2]Includes physics, general; atomic/molecular physics; elementary particle physics; nuclear physics; optics; acoustics; theoretical physics; and physics, other.

Table A-37.   Degrees Conferred by Post-Secondary Institutions, by Level of Degree and Sex of Student, 1970–1971 through 2017–2018—*Continued*

(Number.)

Degree conferred, level of degree, and sex of student (when available)	1986–87	1987–88	1988–89	1989–90	1990–91	1991–92	1992–93	1993–94
Chemistry, Geology and Earth Science, and Physics								
Chemistry								
Bachelor's degree	9,660	9,043	8,618	8,122	8,311	8,629	8,903	9,417
Master's degree	1,695	1,671	1,742	1,643	1,637	1,746	1,822	1,968
Doctor's degree	1,932	1,944	1,974	2,135	2,196	2,233	2,216	2,298
Geology and earth science[1]								
Bachelor's degree	3,943	3,204	2,847	2,372	2,367	2,784	3,123	3,456
Master's degree	1,835	1,722	1,609	1,399	1,336	1,245	1,195	1,221
Doctor's degree	399	462	492	562	600	549	626	577
Physics[2]								
Bachelor's degree	4,318	4,100	4,352	4,155	4,236	4,098	4,063	4,001
Master's degree	1,543	1,675	1,736	1,831	1,725	1,834	1,777	1,945
Doctor's degree	1,074	1,093	1,112	1,192	1,209	1,337	1,277	1,465
Psychology								
Bachelor's degrees, total	43,152	45,371	49,083	53,952	58,655	63,683	66,931	69,419
Male	13,395	13,579	14,265	15,336	16,067	17,062	17,942	18,668
Female	29,757	31,792	34,818	38,616	42,588	46,621	48,989	50,751
Master's degrees, total	11,000	10,488	11,329	10,730	11,349	11,659	12,518	13,723
Male	3,516	3,256	3,465	3,377	3,329	3,335	3,380	3,763
Female	7,484	7,232	7,864	7,353	8,020	8,324	9,138	9,960
Doctor's degrees, total	4,062	3,973	4,143	3,811	3,932	3,814	4,100	4,021
Male	1,801	1,783	1,773	1,566	1,520	1,490	1,570	1,497
Female	2,261	2,190	2,370	2,245	2,412	2,324	2,530	2,524
Public Administration and Social Services								
Bachelor's degrees, total	12,328	12,385	13,162	13,908	14,350	15,987	16,775	17,815
Male	2,993	2,923	3,214	3,334	3,215	3,479	3,801	3,919
Female	9,335	9,462	9,948	10,574	11,135	12,508	12,974	13,896
Master's degrees, total	16,432	16,424	17,020	17,399	17,905	19,243	20,634	21,833
Male	5,673	5,631	5,615	5,634	5,679	5,769	6,105	6,406
Female	10,759	10,793	11,405	11,765	12,226	13,474	14,529	15,427
Doctor's degrees, total	398	470	428	508	430	432	459	519
Male	216	238	210	235	190	204	215	238
Female	182	232	218	273	240	228	244	281
Social Sciences and History								
Bachelor's degrees, total	96,342	100,460	108,151	118,083	125,107	133,974	135,703	133,680
Male	53,949	56,377	60,121	65,887	68,701	73,001	73,589	72,006
Female	42,393	44,083	48,030	52,196	56,406	60,973	62,114	61,674
Master's degrees, total	10,506	10,412	11,023	11,634	12,233	12,702	13,471	14,561
Male	6,373	6,310	6,599	6,898	7,016	7,237	7,671	8,152
Female	4,133	4,102	4,424	4,736	5,217	5,465	5,800	6,409
Doctor's degrees, total	2,916	2,781	2,885	3,010	3,012	3,218	3,460	3,627
Male	2,026	1,849	1,949	2,019	1,956	2,126	2,203	2,317
Female	890	932	936	991	1,056	1,092	1,257	1,310
Economics, History, Political Science and Government, and Sociology								
Economics								
Bachelor's degree	22,378	22,911	23,454	23,923	23,488	23,423	21,321	19,496
Master's degree	1,855	1,847	1,886	1,950	1,951	2,106	2,292	2,521
Doctor's degree	750	770	827	806	802	866	879	869
History								
Bachelor's degree	16,997	18,207	20,159	22,476	24,541	26,966	27,774	27,503
Master's degree	2,021	2,093	2,121	2,369	2,591	2,754	2,952	3,009
Doctor's degree	534	517	487	570	606	644	690	752
Political science and government								
Bachelor's degree	26,817	27,207	30,450	33,560	35,737	37,805	37,931	36,097
Master's degree	1,618	1,579	1,598	1,580	1,772	1,908	1,943	2,147
Doctor's degree	435	391	452	480	468	535	529	616
Sociology								
Bachelor's degree	12,239	13,024	14,435	16,035	17,550	19,568	20,896	22,368
Master's degree	950	984	1,135	1,198	1,260	1,347	1,521	1,639
Doctor's degree	451	452	451	432	465	501	536	530

Note: Data are for postsecondary institutions participating in Title IV federal financial aid programs.
NA = Not available.
[1] Includes geology/earth science, general; geochemistry; geophysics; paleontology; hydrology; oceanography; and geological and earth sciences, other.
[2] Includes physics, general; atomic/molecular physics; elementary particle physics; nuclear physics; optics; acoustics; theoretical physics; and physics, other.

Table A-37. Degrees Conferred by Post-Secondary Institutions, by Level of Degree and Sex of Student, 1970–1971 through 2017–2018—*Continued*

(Number.)

Degree conferred, level of degree, and sex of student (when available)	1994–95	1995–96	1996–97	1997–98	1998–99	1999–2000	2000–01	2001–02
Chemistry, Geology and Earth Science, and Physics								
Chemistry								
Bachelor's degree............................	9,706	10,395	10,609	10,528	10,109	9,989	9,466	9,084
Master's degree............................	2,062	2,214	2,203	2,108	2,019	1,857	1,952	1,823
Doctor's degree............................	2,211	2,228	2,202	2,291	2,175	2,028	2,056	1,984
Geology and earth science[1]								
Bachelor's degree............................	4,032	4,019	4,023	3,866	3,570	3,516	3,495	3,449
Master's degree............................	1,280	1,288	1,258	1,227	1,196	1,186	1,220	1,263
Doctor's degree............................	539	555	564	588	533	492	472	494
Physics[2]								
Bachelor's degree............................	3,823	3,679	3,376	3,441	3,200	3,342	3,418	3,627
Master's degree............................	1,817	1,678	1,496	1,371	1,326	1,232	1,365	1,344
Doctor's degree............................	1,424	1,462	1,410	1,393	1,257	1,208	1,169	1,096
Psychology								
Bachelor's degrees, total.........................	72,233	73,416	74,308	74,107	73,747	74,194	73,645	76,775
Male............................	19,570	19,836	19,408	18,976	18,376	17,451	16,585	17,284
Female............................	52,663	53,580	54,900	55,131	55,371	56,743	57,060	59,491
Master's degrees, total............................	15,378	15,152	15,769	15,142	15,560	15,740	16,539	16,357
Male............................	4,210	4,090	4,155	3,978	3,959	3,821	3,892	3,814
Female............................	11,168	11,062	11,614	11,164	11,601	11,919	12,647	12,543
Doctor's degrees, total............................	4,252	4,141	4,507	4,541	4,678	4,731	5,091	4,759
Male............................	1,562	1,380	1,495	1,470	1,528	1,529	1,598	1,503
Female............................	2,690	2,761	3,012	3,071	3,150	3,202	3,493	3,256
Public Administration and Social Services								
Bachelor's degrees, total............................	18,586	19,849	20,649	20,408	20,323	20,185	19,447	19,392
Male............................	3,935	4,205	4,177	3,881	3,799	3,816	3,670	3,706
Female............................	14,651	15,644	16,472	16,527	16,524	16,369	15,777	15,686
Master's degrees, total............................	23,501	24,229	24,781	25,144	25,038	25,594	25,268	25,448
Male............................	6,870	6,927	6,957	7,025	6,621	6,808	6,544	6,505
Female............................	16,631	17,302	17,824	18,119	18,417	18,786	18,724	18,943
Doctor's degrees, total............................	556	499	518	499	534	537	574	571
Male............................	274	220	243	223	240	227	263	250
Female............................	282	279	275	276	294	310	311	321
Social Sciences and History								
Bachelor's degrees, total............................	128,154	126,479	124,891	125,040	124,815	127,101	128,036	132,874
Male............................	68,139	65,872	64,115	63,537	61,843	62,062	61,749	64,170
Female............................	60,015	60,607	60,776	61,503	62,972	65,039	66,287	68,704
Master's degrees, total............................	14,845	15,012	14,787	14,938	14,396	14,066	13,791	14,112
Male............................	8,207	8,093	7,830	7,960	7,440	7,024	6,816	6,941
Female............................	6,638	6,919	6,957	6,978	6,956	7,042	6,975	7,171
Doctor's degrees, total............................	3,725	3,760	3,989	4,127	3,873	4,095	3,930	3,902
Male............................	2,319	2,339	2,479	2,445	2,290	2,407	2,302	2,219
Female............................	1,406	1,421	1,510	1,682	1,583	1,688	1,628	1,683
Economics, History, Political Science and Government, and Sociology								
Economics								
Bachelor's degree............................	17,673	16,674	16,539	17,074	17,577	18,441	19,437	20,927
Master's degree............................	2,400	2,533	2,433	2,435	2,332	2,168	2,139	2,330
Doctor's degree............................	910	916	968	928	819	851	851	826
History								
Bachelor's degree............................	26,598	26,005	25,214	25,726	24,742	25,247	25,090	26,001
Master's degree............................	3,091	2,898	2,901	2,895	2,618	2,573	2,365	2,420
Doctor's degree............................	816	805	873	937	931	984	931	924
Political science and government								
Bachelor's degree............................	33,013	30,775	28,969	28,044	27,476	27,635	27,792	29,354
Master's degree............................	2,019	2,024	1,909	1,957	1,667	1,627	1,596	1,641
Doctor's degree............................	637	634	686	705	694	693	688	625
Sociology								
Bachelor's degree............................	22,886	24,071	24,672	24,806	24,979	25,598	25,268	25,202
Master's degree............................	1,748	1,772	1,731	1,737	1,940	1,996	1,845	1,928
Doctor's degree............................	546	527	591	596	521	595	546	534

Note: Data are for postsecondary institutions participating in Title IV federal financial aid programs.

NA = Not available.

[1]Includes geology/earth science, general; geochemistry; geophysics; paleontology; hydrology; oceanography; and geological and earth sciences, other.

[2]Includes physics, general; atomic/molecular physics; elementary particle physics; nuclear physics; optics; acoustics; theoretical physics; and physics, other.

Table A-37. Degrees Conferred by Post-Secondary Institutions, by Level of Degree and Sex of Student, 1970–1971 through 2017–2018—*Continued*

(Number.)

Degree conferred, level of degree, and sex of student (when available)	2002–03	2003–04	2004–05	2005–06	2006–07	2007–08	2008–09	2009–10
Chemistry, Geology and Earth Science, and Physics								
Chemistry								
Bachelor's degree	9,013	9,016	9,664	10,606	10,994	11,568	11,852	12,107
Master's degree	1,777	2,009	1,879	2,044	2,097	2,194	2,085	2,123
Doctor's degree	2,092	2,033	2,148	2,403	2,514	2,410	2,556	2,470
Geology and earth science[1]								
Bachelor's degree	3,381	3,312	3,276	3,322	3,319	3,561	3,809	4,093
Master's degree	1,323	1,389	1,420	1,476	1,437	1,350	1,352	1,447
Doctor's degree	466	463	476	505	640	577	614	613
Physics[2]								
Bachelor's degree	3,900	4,118	4,182	4,541	4,843	4,862	4,824	4,984
Master's degree	1,438	1,625	1,785	1,846	1,777	1,791	1,653	1,793
Doctor's degree	1,089	1,119	1,254	1,341	1,442	1,507	1,580	1,571
Psychology								
Bachelor's degrees, total	78,650	82,098	85,614	88,134	90,039	92,587	94,273	97,215
Male	17,514	18,193	19,000	19,865	20,343	21,202	21,490	22,262
Female	61,136	63,905	66,614	68,269	69,696	71,385	72,783	74,953
Master's degrees, total	17,161	17,898	18,830	19,770	21,037	21,431	23,415	23,763
Male	3,839	3,789	3,900	4,079	4,265	4,356	4,789	4,799
Female	13,322	14,109	14,930	15,691	16,772	17,075	18,626	18,964
Doctor's degrees, total	4,835	4,827	5,106	4,921	5,153	5,296	5,477	5,540
Male	1,483	1,496	1,466	1,347	1,382	1,440	1,478	1,478
Female	3,352	3,331	3,640	3,574	3,771	3,856	3,999	4,062
Public Administration and Social Services								
Bachelor's degrees, total	19,900	20,552	21,769	21,986	23,147	23,493	23,852	25,421
Male	3,726	3,793	4,209	4,126	4,354	4,202	4,373	4,578
Female	16,174	16,759	17,560	17,860	18,793	19,291	19,479	20,843
Master's degrees, total	25,903	28,250	29,552	30,510	31,131	33,029	33,934	35,740
Male	6,391	7,001	7,370	7,572	7,758	8,140	8,346	8,868
Female	19,512	21,249	22,182	22,938	23,373	24,889	25,588	26,872
Doctor's degrees, total	599	649	673	704	726	760	812	838
Male	265	275	272	285	253	269	306	323
Female	334	374	401	419	473	491	506	515
Social Sciences and History								
Bachelor's degrees, total	143,256	150,357	156,892	161,485	164,183	167,363	168,517	172,782
Male	69,517	73,834	77,702	80,799	82,417	84,868	85,202	87,404
Female	73,739	76,523	79,190	80,686	81,766	82,495	83,315	85,378
Master's degrees, total	14,630	16,110	16,952	17,369	17,665	18,495	19,241	20,234
Male	7,202	7,810	8,256	8,415	8,577	9,349	9,605	9,967
Female	7,428	8,300	8,696	8,954	9,088	9,146	9,636	10,267
Doctor's degrees, total	3,850	3,811	3,819	3,914	3,844	4,059	4,234	4,238
Male	2,196	2,188	2,184	2,218	2,110	2,194	2,353	2,292
Female	1,654	1,623	1,635	1,696	1,734	1,865	1,881	1,946
Economics, History, Political Science and Government, and Sociology								
Economics								
Bachelor's degree	23,007	24,069	24,217	23,807	23,916	25,278	26,301	27,623
Master's degree	2,582	2,824	3,092	2,941	2,962	3,187	3,233	3,358
Doctor's degree	836	849	973	930	941	1,025	1,015	983
History								
Bachelor's degree	27,757	29,808	31,398	33,153	34,446	34,441	34,713	35,191
Master's degree	2,521	2,522	2,893	2,992	3,144	3,403	3,543	3,858
Doctor's degree	861	855	819	852	807	860	918	888
Political science and government								
Bachelor's degree	33,205	35,581	38,107	39,409	39,899	40,259	39,202	39,462
Master's degree	1,664	1,869	1,983	2,054	2,102	2,156	2,171	2,252
Doctor's degree	671	618	636	649	614	639	709	745
Sociology								
Bachelor's degree	26,095	26,939	28,473	28,467	28,960	28,815	28,735	28,650
Master's degree	1,897	2,009	1,499	1,547	1,545	1,560	1,580	1,428
Doctor's degree	591	558	527	562	569	585	628	603

Note: Data are for postsecondary institutions participating in Title IV federal financial aid programs.

NA = Not available.

[1]Includes geology/earth science, general; geochemistry; geophysics; paleontology; hydrology; oceanography; and geological and earth sciences, other.

[2]Includes physics, general; atomic/molecular physics; elementary particle physics; nuclear physics; optics; acoustics; theoretical physics; and physics, other.

Table A-37. Degrees Conferred by Post-Secondary Institutions, by Level of Degree and Sex of Student, 1970–1971 through 2017–2018—*Continued*

(Number.)

Degree conferred, level of degree, and sex of student (when available)	2010–11	2011–12	2012–13	2013–14	2014–15	2015–16	2016–17	2017–18
Chemistry, Geology and Earth Science, and Physics								
Chemistry								
Bachelor's degree....................	12,656	13,473	13,814	14,443	14,447	14,483	14,954	14,737
Master's degree....................	2,272	2,435	2,396	2,357	2,425	2,455	2,489	2,388
Doctor's degree....................	2,599	2,537	2,617	2,796	2,792	2,894	2,887	2,951
Geology and earth science[1]								
Bachelor's degree....................	4,611	5,111	5,539	5,959	6,405	6,552	6,616	6,702
Master's degree....................	1,568	1,807	1,845	1,933	1,955	1,912	1,940	1,813
Doctor's degree....................	567	612	657	735	681	771	737	759
Physics[2]								
Bachelor's degree....................	5,199	5,531	6,082	6,263	6,658	6,948	7,112	7,515
Master's degree....................	1,769	1,873	1,975	1,866	1,926	1,956	1,849	2,149
Doctor's degree....................	1,670	1,752	1,740	1,768	1,840	1,845	1,826	1,879
Psychology								
Bachelor's degrees, total....................	100,906	109,099	114,446	117,312	117,573	117,447	116,859	116,432
Male....................	23,230	25,420	26,814	27,306	26,803	26,277	25,520	24,578
Female....................	77,676	83,679	87,632	90,006	90,770	91,170	91,339	91,854
Master's degrees, total....................	25,062	27,052	27,787	27,926	26,772	27,645	27,539	27,841
Male....................	5,127	5,482	5,715	5,729	5,538	5,571	5,586	5,526
Female....................	19,935	21,570	22,072	22,197	21,234	22,074	21,953	22,315
Doctor's degrees, total....................	5,851	5,936	6,326	6,634	6,583	6,540	6,702	6,275
Male....................	1,481	1,525	1,628	1,680	1,624	1,658	1,691	1,649
Female....................	4,370	4,411	4,698	4,954	4,959	4,882	5,011	4,626
Public Administration and Social Services								
Bachelor's degrees, total....................	26,799	29,695	31,950	33,483	34,364	34,433	35,461	35,629
Male....................	4,913	5,386	5,664	5,916	6,146	6,023	6,238	6,127
Female....................	21,886	24,309	26,286	27,567	28,218	28,410	29,223	29,502
Master's degrees, total....................	38,614	41,737	43,591	44,508	45,948	46,754	45,361	46,294
Male....................	9,791	10,494	10,864	10,834	11,181	11,184	10,794	10,692
Female....................	28,823	31,243	32,727	33,674	34,767	35,570	34,567	35,602
Doctor's degrees, total....................	851	890	979	1,047	1,123	1,066	1,116	1,157
Male....................	327	343	351	346	374	354	381	399
Female....................	524	547	628	701	749	712	735	758
Social Sciences and History								
Bachelor's degrees, total....................	177,169	178,534	177,767	173,132	166,971	161,211	159,097	159,967
Male....................	89,809	90,628	90,143	88,254	85,484	81,292	79,565	79,628
Female....................	87,360	87,906	87,624	84,878	81,487	79,919	79,532	80,339
Master's degrees, total....................	21,085	21,891	21,591	21,497	20,533	19,861	20,004	19,884
Male....................	10,578	10,987	10,811	10,764	10,318	10,010	9,905	9,832
Female....................	10,507	10,904	10,780	10,733	10,215	9,851	10,099	10,052
Doctor's degrees, total....................	4,390	4,597	4,610	4,724	4,828	4,706	4,706	4,676
Male....................	2,331	2,464	2,461	2,494	2,589	2,594	2,572	2,475
Female....................	2,059	2,133	2,149	2,230	2,239	2,112	2,134	2,201
Economics, History, Political Science and Government, and Sociology								
Economics								
Bachelor's degree....................	28,517	27,994	28,449	29,999	32,683	33,474	34,056	35,327
Master's degree....................	3,731	3,890	3,872	4,115	3,993	3,953	4,044	4,098
Doctor's degree....................	1,018	1,130	1,076	1,059	1,128	1,162	1,150	1,195
History								
Bachelor's degree....................	35,008	35,122	34,188	31,122	28,038	25,589	24,054	23,382
Master's degree....................	4,003	4,155	4,083	3,955	3,703	3,465	3,435	3,272
Doctor's degree....................	908	969	1,003	1,040	986	980	925	911
Political science and government								
Bachelor's degree....................	40,133	39,792	38,466	37,360	35,442	33,955	34,196	34,968
Master's degree....................	2,488	2,510	2,332	2,294	2,082	1,983	1,842	1,854
Doctor's degree....................	722	746	821	792	844	793	796	789
Sociology								
Bachelor's degree....................	29,281	30,136	30,531	30,070	29,000	28,001	27,433	27,294
Master's degree....................	1,559	1,696	1,603	1,611	1,447	1,363	1,391	1,411
Doctor's degree....................	656	626	615	674	722	646	682	687

Note: Data are for postsecondary institutions participating in Title IV federal financial aid programs.

NA = Not available.

[1]Includes geology/earth science, general; geochemistry; geophysics; paleontology; hydrology; oceanography; and geological and earth sciences, other.

[2]Includes physics, general; atomic/molecular physics; elementary particle physics; nuclear physics; optics; acoustics; theoretical physics; and physics, other.

Table A-37. Degrees Conferred by Post-Secondary Institutions, by Level of Degree and Sex of Student, 1970–1971 through 2017–2018—*Continued*

(Number.)

Degree conferred, level of degree, and sex of student (when available)	1970–71	1971–72	1972–73	1973–74	1974–75	1975–76	1976–77	1977–78
Visual and Performing Arts								
Bachelor's degrees, total	30,394	33,831	36,017	39,730	40,782	42,138	41,793	40,951
Male	12,256	13,580	14,267	15,821	15,532	16,491	16,166	15,572
Female	18,138	20,251	21,750	23,909	25,250	25,647	25,627	25,379
Master's degrees, total	6,675	7,537	7,254	8,001	8,362	8,817	8,636	9,036
Male	3,510	4,049	4,005	4,325	4,448	4,507	4,211	4,327
Female	3,165	3,488	3,249	3,676	3,914	4,310	4,425	4,709
Doctor's degrees, total	621	572	616	585	649	620	662	708
Male	483	428	449	440	446	447	447	448
Female	138	144	167	145	203	173	215	260

Note: Data are for postsecondary institutions participating in Title IV federal financial aid programs.

NA = Not available.

[1]Includes geology/earth science, general; geochemistry; geophysics; paleontology; hydrology; oceanography; and geological and earth sciences, other.

[2]Includes physics, general; atomic/molecular physics; elementary particle physics; nuclear physics; optics; acoustics; theoretical physics; and physics, other.

Table A-37. Degrees Conferred by Post-Secondary Institutions, by Level of Degree and Sex of Student, 1970–1971 through 2017–2018—*Continued*

(Number.)

Degree conferred, level of degree, and sex of student (when available)	1978–79	1979–80	1980–81	1981–82	1982–83	1983–84	1984–85	1985–86
Visual and Performing Arts								
Bachelor's degrees, total	40,969	40,892	40,479	40,422	39,804	40,131	38,285	37,241
Male	15,380	15,065	14,798	14,819	14,695	15,089	14,518	14,236
Female	25,589	25,827	25,681	25,603	25,109	25,042	23,767	23,005
Master's degrees, total	8,524	8,708	8,629	8,746	8,763	8,526	8,720	8,420
Male	3,933	4,067	4,056	3,866	4,013	3,897	3,896	3,775
Female	4,591	4,641	4,573	4,880	4,750	4,629	4,824	4,645
Doctor's degrees, total	700	655	654	670	692	730	696	722
Male	454	413	396	380	404	406	407	396
Female	246	242	258	290	288	324	289	326

Note: Data are for postsecondary institutions participating in Title IV federal financial aid programs.

NA = Not available.

[1]Includes geology/earth science, general; geochemistry; geophysics; paleontology; hydrology; oceanography; and geological and earth sciences, other.

[2]Includes physics, general; atomic/molecular physics; elementary particle physics; nuclear physics; optics; acoustics; theoretical physics; and physics, other.

Table A-37. Degrees Conferred by Post-Secondary Institutions, by Level of Degree and Sex of Student, 1970–1971 through 2017–2018—*Continued*

(Number.)

Degree conferred, level of degree, and sex of student (when available)	1986–87	1987–88	1988–89	1989–90	1990–91	1991–92	1992–93	1993–94
Visual and Performing Arts								
Bachelor's degrees, total	36,873	37,150	38,420	39,934	42,186	46,522	47,761	49,053
Male	13,980	14,225	14,698	15,189	15,761	17,616	18,610	19,538
Female	22,893	22,925	23,722	24,745	26,425	28,906	29,151	29,515
Master's degrees, total	8,508	7,939	8,267	8,481	8,657	9,353	9,440	9,925
Male	3,756	3,442	3,611	3,706	3,830	4,078	4,099	4,229
Female	4,752	4,497	4,656	4,775	4,827	5,275	5,341	5,696
Doctor's degrees, total	793	727	753	849	838	906	882	1,054
Male	447	424	446	472	466	504	478	585
Female	346	303	307	377	372	402	404	469

Note: Data are for postsecondary institutions participating in Title IV federal financial aid programs.
NA = Not available.
[1]Includes geology/earth science, general; geochemistry; geophysics; paleontology; hydrology; oceanography; and geological and earth sciences, other.
[2]Includes physics, general; atomic/molecular physics; elementary particle physics; nuclear physics; optics; acoustics; theoretical physics; and physics, other.

Table A-37. Degrees Conferred by Post-Secondary Institutions, by Level of Degree and Sex of Student, 1970–1971 through 2017–2018—*Continued*

(Number.)

Degree conferred, level of degree, and sex of student (when available)	1994–95	1995–96	1996–97	1997–98	1998–99	1999–2000	2000–01	2001–02
Visual and Performing Arts								
Bachelor's degrees, total	48,690	49,296	50,083	52,077	54,446	58,791	61,148	66,773
Male	19,781	20,126	20,729	21,483	22,270	24,003	24,967	27,130
Female	28,909	29,170	29,354	30,594	32,176	34,788	36,181	39,643
Master's degrees, total	10,277	10,280	10,627	11,145	10,762	10,918	11,404	11,595
Male	4,374	4,361	4,470	4,596	4,544	4,672	4,788	4,912
Female	5,903	5,919	6,157	6,549	6,218	6,246	6,616	6,683
Doctor's degrees, total	1,080	1,067	1,060	1,163	1,117	1,127	1,167	1,114
Male	545	524	525	566	567	537	568	490
Female	535	543	535	597	550	590	599	624

Note: Data are for postsecondary institutions participating in Title IV federal financial aid programs.

NA = Not available.

[1]Includes geology/earth science, general; geochemistry; geophysics; paleontology; hydrology; oceanography; and geological and earth sciences, other.

[2]Includes physics, general; atomic/molecular physics; elementary particle physics; nuclear physics; optics; acoustics; theoretical physics; and physics, other.

Table A-37.   Degrees Conferred by Post-Secondary Institutions, by Level of Degree and Sex of Student, 1970–1971 through 2017–2018—*Continued*

(Number.)

Degree conferred, level of degree, and sex of student (when available)	2002–03	2003–04	2004–05	2005–06	2006–07	2007–08	2008–09	2009–10
Visual and Performing Arts								
Bachelor's degrees, total	71,482	77,181	80,955	83,297	85,186	87,703	89,143	91,798
Male	27,922	30,037	31,355	32,117	32,729	33,862	35,055	35,768
Female	43,560	47,144	49,600	51,180	52,457	53,841	54,088	56,030
Master's degrees, total	11,982	12,906	13,183	13,530	13,767	14,164	14,918	15,562
Male	4,975	5,531	5,646	5,801	5,910	5,998	6,325	6,531
Female	7,007	7,375	7,537	7,729	7,857	8,166	8,593	9,031
Doctor's degrees, total	1,293	1,282	1,278	1,383	1,364	1,453	1,569	1,599
Male	613	572	594	639	625	675	726	700
Female	680	710	684	744	739	778	843	899

Note: Data are for postsecondary institutions participating in Title IV federal financial aid programs.

NA = Not available.

[1]Includes geology/earth science, general; geochemistry; geophysics; paleontology; hydrology; oceanography; and geological and earth sciences, other.

[2]Includes physics, general; atomic/molecular physics; elementary particle physics; nuclear physics; optics; acoustics; theoretical physics; and physics, other.

Table A-37. Degrees Conferred by Post-Secondary Institutions, by Level of Degree and Sex of Student, 1970–1971 through 2017–2018—*Continued*

(Number.)

Degree conferred, level of degree, and sex of student (when available)	2010–11	2011–12	2012–13	2013–14	2014–15	2015–16	2016–17	2017–18
Visual and Performing Arts								
Bachelor's degrees, total	93,939	95,806	97,799	97,414	95,840	92,979	91,291	88,582
Male	36,342	37,164	38,063	38,177	38,024	36,712	35,304	34,202
Female	57,597	58,642	59,736	59,237	57,816	56,267	55,987	54,380
Master's degrees, total	16,277	17,307	17,869	17,869	17,756	18,052	17,516	17,686
Male	6,881	7,320	7,610	7,712	7,643	7,679	7,561	7,399
Female	9,396	9,987	10,259	10,157	10,113	10,373	9,955	10,287
Doctor's degrees, total	1,646	1,728	1,814	1,778	1,793	1,809	1,774	1,759
Male	770	790	850	869	837	853	812	852
Female	876	938	964	909	956	956	962	907

Note: Data are for postsecondary institutions participating in Title IV federal financial aid programs.

NA = Not available.

[1]Includes geology/earth science, general; geochemistry; geophysics; paleontology; hydrology; oceanography; and geological and earth sciences, other.

[2]Includes physics, general; atomic/molecular physics; elementary particle physics; nuclear physics; optics; acoustics; theoretical physics; and physics, other.

NOTES AND DEFINITIONS: NATIONAL EDUCATION STATISTICS

ENROLLMENT TABLES A-1 through A-8 and A-10 THROUGH A-17

Source: U.S. Census Bureau. School Enrollment in the United States. *Current Population Survey (CPS) Report.* https://www.census.gov/data/tables/2019/demo/school-enrollment/2019-cps.html and https://www.census.gov/data/tables/time-series/demo/school-enrollment/cps-historical-time-series.html

ENROLLMENT TABLES A-9 AND A-18 THROUGH A-23

Source: U.S. Department of Education, National Center for Education Statistics, Institute of Education Sciences, *Digest of Education Statistics, 2018 and 2019.* https://nces.ed.gov/programs/digest/current_tables.asp

ATTAINMENT TABLES A-24 THROUGH A-35

Source: U.S. Census Bureau, Educational Attainment in the United States. *Current Population Survey (CPS) Report.* https://www.census.gov/data/tables/2019/demo/educational-attainment/cps-detailed-tables.html and https://www.census.gov/data/tables/time-series/demo/educational-attainment/cps-historical-time-series.html.

ATTAINMENT TABLES A-36 AND A-37

Source: U.S. Department of Education, National Center for Education Statistics, Institute of Education Sciences, *Digest of Education Statistics, 2018 and 2019.* https://nces.ed.gov/programs/digest/current_tables.asp

SCHOOL ENROLLMENT AND EDUCATIONAL ATTAINMENT TABLES

The School Enrollment and Educational Attainment tables in Part A are derived from the Current Population Survey (CPS).

The Census Bureau disseminated comparable tables in the P-20 series of *Current Population Reports* (CPR) for most years between 1947 and 1994. Since then, these tables have not been available in printed form. However, they can be found on the Census Bureau website at www.census.gov. In the historical series, data before 1992 are not strictly comparable to data after 1992. Before 1992, the CPS did not ask questions about degrees received; educational attainment was gauged only by years of school completed.

Age. Age classification is based on the age of the person at his or her last birthday.

Citizenship status. There are five categories of citizenship status: (1) born in the United States; (2) born in Puerto Rico or another outlying area of the United States; (3) born abroad to U.S. citizen parents; (4) naturalized citizens; and (5) non-citizens. Place of birth was asked for every household member and for the parents of every household member in the CPS sample. People born in the United States or its outlying areas, or whose parents were born in the United States or its outlying areas, were not asked citizenship questions. Citizenship statuses (1), (2), and (3) were assigned during the editing phase of data preparation, based on the place of birth of the household member or the place of birth of the household member's parents. People born outside the United States and its outlying areas, whose parents were born outside the United States and its outlying areas, were asked, "Are you a citizen of the United States?" 'Yes' answers were assigned to the "naturalized citizen" category (4), and 'No' answers were assigned to the "not a citizen" category (5) during the editing process. People for whom no birthplace was provided were also assigned a citizenship status during the editing process; for example, the citizenship status of a child might have been assigned based on the citizenship status of the child's mother.

Dropouts. See School, Dropout rate, annual high school.

Earnings. See Income.

Educational attainment. Data on educational attainment are derived from a single question that asks, "What is the highest grade of school . . . completed, or the highest degree . . . received?"

The single educational attainment question now in use was introduced into the CPS in January 1992. It is similar to the question used in the 1990 Decennial Census of Population and Housing. Consequently, data on educational attainment from the 1992 CPS are not directly comparable to CPS data from earlier years. The new question replaces the previous two-part question used in the CPS, which asked respondents to report the highest grade they attended and whether or not they completed that grade.

The question concerning educational attainment applies only to progress in "regular" schools. Such schools include graded public, private, and parochial elementary and high schools (both junior and senior high schools), colleges, universities, and professional schools, and both day schools and night schools. Thus, regular schooling is that which may advance a person toward an elementary school certificate, a high school diploma, or a college, university, or professional school degree. Non-regular schooling was counted only if the credits obtained were regarded as transferable to a school within the regular school system.

Family. A family is a group of two people or more residing together (including the householder) related by birth, marriage, or adoption; all such people (including related subfamily members) are considered members of one family. Beginning with the 1980 Current Population Survey, unrelated subfamilies (formerly referred to as secondary families) are no longer included in the count of families, nor are members of unrelated subfamilies included in the count of family members. The number of families is equal to the number of family households; however, the count of family members differs from the count of family household members, as family household members include any non-relatives living in the household.

Family household. A family household is a household maintained by a householder within a family (as defined above). It includes any unrelated people (unrelated subfamily members and/or secondary individuals) residing in the household. The number of family households is equal to the number of families; however, the count of family household members differs from the count of family members. Family household members include all people living in the household, whereas family members include only the householder and his or her relatives. (See Family for more information.)

Hispanic origin. People of Hispanic origin were identified by a question that asked respondents to self-identify their origin or descent. Respondents were asked to select their origin (and the origin of other household members) from a "flash card" listing different ethnicities. People of Hispanic origin were those who indicated that their descent was of Mexican, Puerto Rican, Cuban, Central or South American, or some other Hispanic origin. It should be noted that people of Hispanic origin may be of any race.

People who were of non-Hispanic White origin were identified by crossing the responses to two self-identification questions: (1) origin or descent; and (2) race. Respondents were asked to select their race (and the race of other household members) from a "flash card" listing racial groups. There are six racial categories CPS respondents can select from: White; Black; American Indian, or Alaska Native; Asian; Native Hawaiian or Pacific Islander; and Other. The other category includes any race other than the six indicated races. Respondents who reported more than one race are included in the Two or More Races category. Respondents who identified their race as White and did not select one of the Hispanic origin subgroups (Mexican, Puerto Rican, Cuban, Central or South American) were classified as non-Hispanic White.

Household. A household consists of all the people who occupy a housing unit. A house, apartment, group of rooms, or single room is regarded as a housing unit when it is occupied or intended for occupancy as separate living quarters (meaning that occupants do not live and eat with any other persons in the structure and have direct access to their dwelling from outside or through a common hall). A household includes related family members and all unrelated people—such as lodgers, foster children, wards, or employees—who share the housing unit. A person living alone in a housing unit, or a group of unrelated people sharing a dwelling (such as partners or roomers), are also counted as a household. The count of households excludes group quarters. There are two major categories of households: "family" and "nonfamily." (See Family household and Nonfamily household for more information.)

Householder. The householder is the person (or one of the people) in whose name the housing unit is owned or rented (maintained). If there is no such person, any adult member of the household—excluding roomers, boarders, and paid employees—can be counted as the householder. If a married couple jointly owns or rents the housing unit, the householder may be either the husband or the wife. The person designated as the householder is the "reference person" to whom the relationship of all other household members, if any, is recorded.

The number of householders is equal to the number of households. The number of family householders is also equal to the number of families.

INCOME. Definitions of income and the types of income are found below.

Income, Official definition of. For each person age 15 years and over in the sample, the CPS asks questions about the amount of money income received during the preceding calendar year from each of the following sources: earnings; unemployment compensation; workers' compensation; Social Security; Supplemental Security Income; public assistance or welfare payments; veterans' payments; survivor benefits; disability benefits; pension or retirement income; interest, dividends, rents, royalties, and estates and trusts; educational assistance; child support; alimony; financial assistance from outside the household; and other income.

Although the income statistics refer to receipts during the preceding calendar year, demographic characteristics such as age, labor force status, and family or household composition are as of the survey date. The income of the family/household does not include amounts received by members who were members of the family/household during all or part of the income year if these people no longer resided in the family/household at the time of interview. However, the CPS collects income data for people who are current residents, but who did not reside in the household during the income year.

Data on consumer income collected in the CPS by the Census Bureau cover money income (exclusive of certain money receipts, such as capital gains) received before payments for personal income taxes, Social Security, union dues, Medicare deductions, and so on. Therefore, money income does not reflect the fact that some families receive part of their income in the form of noncash benefits, such as food stamps, health benefits, rent-free housing, and goods produced and consumed on the farm. Money income also does not reflect the fact that noncash benefits are also received by some nonfarm residents. These benefits often take the form of the use of business transportation and facilities, full or partial payments by business for retirement programs, medical and educational expenses, and so on. Data users should consider these elements when comparing income levels. Moreover, readers should be aware that respondents in household surveys tend to underreport their income for many different reasons. Based on an analysis of independently derived income estimates, the Census Bureau determined that respondents report income earned from wages or salaries much more accurately than income earned from other sources of income, and that the reported wage and salary income is nearly equal to independent estimates of aggregate income.

The Census Bureau collects data for the following income sources:

Alimony. Alimony includes all periodic payments received from ex-spouses. It excludes one-time property settlements.

Child support. Child support includes all periodic payments received from an absent parent for the support of his or her children, even if these payments are made through a state or local government office.

Disability benefits. Disability benefits include payments people received due to a health problem or disability (other than those received from Social Security). Respondents can report payments from 10 sources, including workers' compensation, companies or unions, federal government (civil service), military, state or local governments, railroad retirement, accident or disability insurance, Black Lung payments, state temporary sickness, or other disability payments.

Dividends. Dividends include income received from stock holdings and mutual fund shares. The CPS does not include capital gains from the sale of stock holdings as income.

Earnings. The Census Bureau classifies earnings from respondents' longest job (or self-employment) and other employment earnings into three types:

- Money wage or salary income, is the total income people receive for work performed as an employee during the income year. This category includes wages, salary, armed forces pay, commissions, tips, piece-rate payments, and cash bonuses earned, before deductions are made for items such as taxes, bonds, pensions, and union dues.

- Net income from nonfarm self-employment is the net money income (gross receipts minus expenses) from a respondent's own business, professional enterprise, or partnership. Gross receipts include the value of all goods sold and all services rendered. Expenses include items such as the costs of goods purchased; rent, heat, power, and depreciation charges; wages and salaries paid; and business taxes (but not personal income taxes). In general, the Census Bureau considers inventory changes in determining net income from nonfarm self-employment; replies based on income tax returns or other official records reflect inventory changes. However, when respondents do not report values of inventory changes, interviewers will accept net income figures exclusive of inventory changes. The Census Bureau does not include the value of saleable merchandise consumed by the proprietors of retail stores as part of net income.

- Net income from farm self-employment is the net money income (gross receipts minus operating expenses) from the operation of a farm by a person acting on their own account as owner, renter, or sharecropper. Gross receipts include the value of all products sold, payments from government farm programs, money received from renting farm equipment to others, rent received from farm property if payment is based on the percentage of crops produced, and incidental receipts from the sale of items such as wood, sand, and gravel.

- Operating expenses include items such as the cost of feed, fertilizer, seed, and other farming supplies; cash wages paid to farmhands; depreciation charges; cash rent; interest on farm mortgages; farm building repairs; and farm taxes (not state and federal personal income taxes). The Census Bureau does not include the value of fuel, food, or other farm products used for family living as part of net income, and only considers inventory changes in determining net income when they are accounted for in income tax returns or other official records. Otherwise, the Census Bureau does not take inventory changes into account.

Educational assistance. Educational assistance includes Pell Grants, other government educational assistance, scholarships or grants, and any financial assistance received from employers, friends, or relatives not residing in the student's household.

Financial assistance from outside the household. Financial assistance from outside the household includes periodic payments received from nonhousehold members. This type of assistance excludes gifts and sporadic assistance.

Government transfers. Government transfers include payments received from the following sources: unemployment compensation, state workers' compensation, Social Security, Supplemental Security Income (SSI), public assistance, veterans' payments, government survivor benefits, government disability benefits, government pensions, and government educational assistance.

Interest income. Interest income includes payments received or credited to accounts from bonds, treasury notes, individual retirement accounts (IRAs), certificates of deposit, interest-bearing savings and checking accounts, and all other interest-paying investments.

Other income. Other income includes any other unclassified payments received regularly. Some examples are state programs such as foster child payments, military family allotments, and income received from foreign government pensions.

Pension or retirement income. Pension or retirement income includes payments received from eight sources, including companies or unions; federal government (civil service); military; state or local governments; railroad retirement; annuities or paid-up insurance policies; IRAs, Keogh, or 401(k) payments; or other retirement income.

Public assistance or welfare payments. Public assistance or welfare payments include cash payments to low-income persons, including payments given under programs such as Aid to Families with Dependent Children (AFDC, ADC) and Temporary Assistance to Needy Families (TANF), emergency assistance, and other general assistance.

Rents, royalties, and estates and trusts. Rents, royalties, and estates and trusts include net income received from the rental of a house, a store, or other property; receipts from boarders or lodgers; net royalty income; and periodic payments from estate or trust funds.

Social Security. Social Security includes pensions, survivors' benefits, and permanent disability insurance payments made by the Social Security Administration prior to medical insurance deductions. The Census Bureau does not include Medicare reimbursements for health services as Social Security benefits.

Supplemental Security Income. Supplemental Security Income includes federal, state, and local welfare agency payments to low-income people age 65 years and over and to blind or disabled people of any age.

Survivor benefits. Survivor benefits include payments received from survivors' or widows' pensions, estates, trusts, annuities, or any other types of survivors' benefits. Respondents can report payments from 10 different sources, including private companies or unions, federal government (civil service), military, state or local governments, railroad retirement, workers' compensation, Black Lung payments, estates and trusts, annuities or paid-up insurance policies, and other survivor payments.

Unemployment compensation. Unemployment compensation includes payments made to the respondent from government unemployment agencies or private companies during periods of unemployment. It also accounts for any strike benefits the respondent received from union funds.

Veterans' payments. Veterans' payments include periodic payments from the Department of Veterans Affairs to disabled members of the armed forces or survivors of deceased veterans for education and on-the-job training. These payments also include means-tested assistance to veterans.

Workers' compensation. Workers' compensation includes periodic payments from public or private insurance companies for work-related injuries.

The Census Bureau does not count the following receipts as income: (1) capital gains (or losses) from the sale of property, including stocks, bonds, houses, or cars (unless the person was engaged in the business of selling such property, in which case the CPS counts the net proceeds as income from self-employment); (2) withdrawals of bank deposits; (3) money borrowed; (4) tax refunds; (5) gifts; and (6) lump-sum inheritances or insurance payments.

The Census Bureau combines all sources of income into two major types:

Total money earnings. Total money earnings is the algebraic sum of money wages, salary, and net income from farm and nonfarm self-employment.

Income other than earnings. Income other than earnings is the algebraic sum of all sources of money income, except wages and salaries and income from self-employment.

Mean (average) income. Mean (average) income is the amount obtained by dividing the total aggregate income of a group by the number of units in that group. The means for households, families, and unrelated individuals are based respectively on all households, all families, and all unrelated individuals. The means (averages) for people are based on people age 15 years and over with income.

Median income. Median income is the amount that divides the income distribution into two equal groups. Half of all people have incomes above the median, and half of all people have incomes below the median. The medians for households, families, and unrelated individuals are respectively based on all households, all families, and all unrelated individuals. The medians for people are based on people age 15 years and over with income.

LABOR FORCE STATUS. Definitions of labor force characteristics are found below:

Civilian labor force. Consists of people classified as employed or unemployed. Excluded are institutionalized people and people on active duty in the United States Armed Forces. The entire labor force consists of people classified as employed or unemployed and people in the armed forces.

Current job (basic data). A worker's current job is the job held during the reference week (the week before the survey). A person holding two or more jobs is classified as being in the job at which he or she spent the most hours during the reference week. The unemployed are classified according to their most recent full-time job of two weeks or more, or by the job (either the full-time or part-time job) from which they were laid off. The occupation/industry classification system for the 1990 Decennial Census of Population was first used to code CPS data for the January 1992 file. The occupation/industry classification system for the 2000 Decennial Census of Population was first used to code CPS data for the January 2003 file.

Employed. Employed persons include all civilians who, during the survey week, did any work at all (for at least one hour) as paid employees or in their own business or profession, or on their own farm, or who worked 15 hours or more as unpaid workers on a farm or a business operated by a member of the family; and all people who had jobs but were not working due to illness, bad weather, vacation, labor-management dispute, or personal reasons, whether or not they were seeking other jobs. Each employed person is counted only once. People who held two or more jobs are counted as working in the job at which they worked the greatest number of hours during the survey week. If a person worked an equal number of hours at two or more jobs, he or she is counted as working at the job that they have held the longest.

Labor force. Workers are classified as being in the labor force if they are employed, unemployed, or in the armed forces during the survey week. The "civilian labor force" includes all civilians classified as employed or unemployed. The file includes labor force data for civilians age 15 years and over. However, the official definition of the civilian labor force consists of workers age 16 years and over.

Not in labor force. All civilians age 15 years and over who are not classified as employed or unemployed are considered not to be in the labor force. These people are further classified as being engaged in a major activity such as keeping house, going to school, unable to work because of long-term physical or mental illness, and "other," which is mostly composed of retired persons. Those who report doing unpaid work on a family-owned farm or in a family-owned business for less than 15 hours are also classified as not in the labor force.

For persons not in the labor force, questions about previous work experience, intentions to seek work again, current desire for a job, and reasons for not seeking work are only asked of households in the fourth and eighth months of the sample. These are the "outgoing" groups—those that were in the sample for three previous months and would not be in it for the subsequent month.

Finally, it should be noted that the unemployment rate represents the number of unemployed persons as a percentage of the civilian labor force age 16 years and over. This measure can be computed for groups within the labor force by sex, age, marital status, race, and so on. The job loser, job leaver, reentrant, and new entrant rates are each calculated as a percentage of the civilian labor force age 16 years and over; the sum of the rates for the four groups thus equals the total unemployment rate.

Unemployed. Unemployed persons are civilians who, during the survey week, had no employment but were available for work and had engaged in any specific job-seeking activity within the past four previous weeks, such as registering at a public or private employment office, meeting with prospective employers, checking with friends or relatives, placing and answering advertisements, writing letters of application, or being on a union or professional register. Others in this category were waiting to be called back to a job from which they had been laid off or were within 30 days of starting a new wage or salary job. This category consists of job leavers, job losers, new job entrants, and job reentrants.

Work experience. A person with work experience is one who did any work for pay or profit or worked without pay on a family-operated farm or business at any time during the preceding calendar year, on a part-time or full-time basis. A full-time worker is a worker who worked 35 hours or more per week during a majority of the weeks in the preceding calendar year. A year-round worker is a worker who worked for 50 weeks or more during the preceding calendar year. A full-time, year-round worker is a person who worked full-time (35 or more hours per week) for 50 or more weeks during the previous calendar year.

Level of school completed. The statistics on level of school completed indicate the number of persons enrolled at each of five levels: nursery school, kindergarten, elementary school (first to eighth grades), high school (ninth to twelfth grades), and college or professional school. The last group includes graduate students at colleges and universities. Those enrolled in elementary school, middle school, intermediate school, or junior high through eighth grade are classified as being in elementary school. All persons enrolled in ninth through twelfth grade are classified as being in high school.

Modal grade. See School, Modal grade.

Nativity. There are two major categories of nativity, native born and foreign born. A person who is native is a citizen at birth. All people with the following citizenship status are native born: (1) born in the United States; (2) born in Puerto Rico or an outlying area of the United States; and (3) born abroad of American parents. (See Citizenship status for more information.) All other people are classified as foreign born.

Nonfamily household. A nonfamily household consists of a householder living alone (a one-person household) or a household shared exclusively by unrelated people.

Population coverage. The sample for the CPS includes the civilian noninstitutional population of the United States, along with members of the armed forces in the United States living off post or with their families on post. It excludes all other members of the armed forces. The information on the Hispanic population from the CPS was collected in the 50 states and the District of Columbia and does not include residents of outlying areas or of U.S. territories such as Guam, Puerto Rico, and the U.S. Virgin Islands.

Race. The race of individuals was identified through a question requiring self-identification of the person's race. Respondents were asked to select their race from a "flash card" listing racial groups. Since March 1989, the population has been divided into five groups on the basis of race: White; Black; American Indian, Eskimo or Aleut; Asian or Pacific Islander; and Other races. The last category includes any other race except the five mentioned. In most of the published tables, "Other races" are included in the total population data line but are not shown individually.

Reference person. The reference person serves as the central point for determining relationships within the household. The household reference person is the person listed as the householder. (See Householder for more information.) The subfamily reference person is either the single parent or the husband or wife in a married-couple situation.

Rounding. Percentages are rounded to the nearest 10th of a percent; therefore, the percentages in a distribution do not always sum to exactly 100 percent.

School, Dropout rate, annual high school. The annual high school dropout rate is an estimate of the proportion of students who drop out of school in a single year. This section briefly explains how the annual dropout rate is calculated; for further explanation and details of its derivation, see *Current Population Report (Series P-20, No. 413): "School Enrollment—Social and Economic Characteristics of Students: October 1983."*

Annual dropout rates for a single grade (X) are estimated as the ratio between the number of people enrolled in grade (X) in the year preceding the survey who did not complete grade (X) and are not currently enrolled in grade (X) at the start of the year preceding this survey. People reported as enrolled last year but not currently enrolled are presented by the highest grade completed in Table 8 of the *Current Population Report* on school enrollment. They are presumed to have dropped out of the succeeding grade (except for those who graduated this year). Thus, individuals counted as 10th grade dropouts are those whose highest grade completed is the 9th grade, but who are not currently enrolled in school. (The dropout classification also includes those people who finished the 9th grade in the spring preceding the survey and were not enrolled on the survey date.) These estimates form the numerator of the annual grade-specific dropout rate.

People currently enrolled in high school are presumed to have been enrolled in and have successfully completed the preceding grade during the preceding year. For example, those who have successfully completed the 10th grade would be enrolled in the 11th grade. Along with the people who dropped out of that grade, they comprise the denominator of the estimate of the annual grade-specific dropout rate:

$$\text{Dropout from Grade n} = \frac{\text{Not enrolled and highest grade completed} = n-1}{\left(\begin{array}{c}\text{Enrolled in } n+1 + \text{ Not enrolled and} \\ \text{highest grade completed} = n-1\end{array}\right)}$$

It cannot be presumed that all 12th grade graduates will enroll in college. The estimate of the number of people enrolled in the 12th grade one year before the survey is constructed as the sum of the number of people reported to have graduated from high school "this year" (whether or not they are currently enrolled in college) and those not currently enrolled who were enrolled last year and whose highest grade completed is the 11th grade (dropouts). The annual dropout rate for all grades during one year can be obtained by summing the components of the rates for the individual grades—the sum of all people previously enrolled in the 10th, 11th, or 12th grade last year, but who are not currently enrolled and do not have a high school diploma.

In addition to the annual rate, two other estimates of dropouts are frequently used. The annual dropout rate is different from a "pool" (or status) measure, such as the proportion of high school dropouts within an age group. A third measure of dropouts is the "cohort measure," most commonly from a longitudinal study, in which the proportion of a specific group of people enrolled in a specific year is calculated. These people did not receive diplomas (and are no longer in school) some years later. For example, the proportion of a cohort enrolled in 9th grade in year X, who were not enrolled and had not received a diploma by year X equals 4.

School enrollment. The school enrollment statistics from the CPS are based on replies to inquiries concerning current regular school enrollment. Those counted as enrolled had attended a public, parochial, or other private school in the regular school system at any time during the current or previous school year. Such schools include nursery schools, kindergartens, elementary schools, high schools, colleges, universities, and professional schools. Attendance could have been on either a full-time or part-time basis during the day or night. Regular schooling is that which advances a person toward an elementary or high school diploma or toward a college, university, or professional school degree. Children enrolled in nursery schools and kindergarten are included in the enrollment figures for regular schools and are shown separately.

Enrollment in schools not in the regular school system, such as trade schools, business colleges, and schools for the mentally handicapped is not included, as these schools do not advance students toward regular school degrees.

People enrolled in classes not requiring their physical presence in school, such as correspondence courses or other courses of independent study, and those enrolled in training courses given directly on the job, are also excluded from the count of those enrolled in school, unless such courses are being counted for credit at a regular school.

School enrollment in the year preceding current survey. All respondents were asked to state their school enrollment status as of October of the preceding year. Before 1988, this question was only asked of people not currently attending regular school and people who were enrolled in college. In the tabulations of previous year's secondary school enrollment, those currently enrolled in high school were assumed to have been enrolled the previous year.

Comparability of enrollment data in previous years. Changes in the edit and tabulation packages used to process the October CPS school enrollment supplement caused some minor revisions to the estimates. The current edit and tabulation package began with 1987 data. The 1986 data published in the *Current Population Report (Series P-20 No. 429)* were reprocessed with the rewritten programs in order to clarify comparability. Time series tables usually show only the revised estimates for 1986. The previous edit and tabulation package was used from 1967 to 1986.

Major changes in the data caused by the 1987 edit revisions were: (1) Among 14- and 15-year-olds, an edit improvement allowed people with unreported enrollment data, who were previously imputed as "not enrolled," to be enrolled; (2) Revisions in the tabulation of enrollment in the previous year simplified the calculation of an annual high school dropout rate; (3) Edit improvements caused increases in college enrollment estimates, most notably above the age of 24. This age group was largely ignored in earlier edits; (4) Type of college is fully allocated (discussed earlier in the section); (5) Tabulations of type of college (2-year and 4-year colleges) were made available by race; (6) Dependent family members became consistently defined; (7) New tabulations of employment status, vocational course enrollment, college retention and re-entry, and families with children enrolled in public and private school became available beginning in 1987.

In the series of reports on school enrollment for 1987 to 1992, race and Hispanic origin were erroneously tabulated for a small percentage of children age 3 to 14 years. Race and Hispanic origin of an adult in the household were attributed to the child, rather than using the child's reported characteristics. In the vast majority of cases, these characteristics were the same for family members, but for a small percentage of children, they were different. The correction made the following proportional changes in the numbers of children in each group: White (-0.5 percent), Black (+3.1 percent), and Hispanic (-4.6 percent).

Published data on enrollment from the October CPS for 1981 to 1993 used population controls based on the 1980 census. Beginning in 1994, estimates used 1990 census–based population controls, including adjustment for undercount. Time series tables show two sets of data for 1993; the data labeled "1993r" were processed using population controls based on the 1990 census with adjustments for undercount. The change in 1994 from a paper-and-pencil survey to a computer-assisted survey had some affect on the data. Most notably, the enrollment question for children age 3 to 5 years was different from the question for older children—it included a reference to nursery school. In 1994, reported nursery school enrollment was significantly higher than in earlier years.

Attendance, full-time and part-time. College students are classified according to their attendance status. A student is categorized as attending college full-time if he or she was taking 12 or more hours of classes during the average school week, and part-time if he or she was taking less than 12 hours of classes per average school week.

College enrollment. The college enrollment statistics are based on reports of school enrollment, including the grade in which the respondent was enrolled. Students enrolled in college at any time during the current term or school year were counted as enrolled, except those who had left for the remainder of the term. Thus, regular college enrollment includes those attending two-year or four-year colleges, universities, or professional schools (such as medical or law schools) in courses that advance students

toward a recognized college or university degree (such as a B.A. or an M.A.). Attendance may be full-time or part-time during the day or night. The college student need not be working toward a degree, but he or she must be enrolled in a class for which credit would be applied toward a degree. (See school enrollment for more information.) Students are classified by year of college, based on the academic year (not calendar year). The undergraduate years are the first through fourth year, or freshman through senior years. Graduate or professional school years include the fifth year and higher.

Two-year and four-year colleges. College students were asked if their school was a two-year college (junior or community college) or a four-year college or university. Students enrolled in the first four years of college (undergraduates) were classified by the type of school that they attended. Graduate students are shown as a separate group.

Vocational school enrollment. Vocational school enrollment includes enrollment in business, vocational, technical, secretarial, trade, or correspondence courses that are not counted as regular school enrollment. This category excludes recreation or adult education classes. Courses that counted as college enrollment are also excluded.

School, Modal grade. Enrolled people are classified according to their relative progress in school and whether the grade or year in which they were enrolled was below, at, or above the modal (or typical) grade for students of their age at the time of the survey. The modal grade is the year of school in which the largest proportion of students of a given age were enrolled.

School, Nursery. A nursery school is defined as a group or class that has been organized to provide educational experiences for children during the year or years preceding kindergarten. It includes instruction as an important and integral phase of its childcare program. Private homes, in which essentially custodial care is provided, are not considered nursery schools. Children attending nursery school are classified as attending for part of the day or for the full day. Part-day attendance refers to those who attend either in the morning or in the afternoon. Full-day attendance refers to those who attend in the morning and in the afternoon. Children enrolled in Head Start programs or similar local agency-sponsored programs that provide preschool education to young children are counted as being enrolled in nursery school.

School, Public or private. A public school is defined as any educational institution operated by publicly elected or appointed school officials and supported by public funds. Private schools include educational institutions established and operated by religious bodies, as well as those that are under other private controls. In cases in which a school or college was both publicly and privately controlled or supported, enrollment was counted according to whether the school was primarily public or private.

Undocumented immigrants or illegal aliens. Since all residents of the United States living in households are represented in the sample of households interviewed by the CPS, undocumented immigrants or illegal aliens are probably included in CPS data. Because the CPS makes no attempt to ascertain the legal status of any person interviewed, these individuals cannot be identified from CPS data.

POSTSECONDARY EDUCATION TABLES

Tables A-9 and A-18 through A-23 were adapted from the most current published tables from the National Center for Education Statistics' *Digest of Education Statistics.*

Consumer Price Index. This price index measures the average change in the cost of a fixed market basket of goods and services purchased by consumers.

Control of institution describes whether an institution is operated by publicly elected or appointed officials (public control) or by privately elected or appointed officials and derives its major source of funds from private sources (private not-for-profit or private for-profit control). There are nine institutional categories resulting from dividing the universe according to control and level. Control categories are public, private not-for-profit, and private for-profit. Level categories are 4-year and higher (4 year), 2-but-less-than 4-year (2 year), and less than 2-year. For example: Public, 4-year is one of the institution sectors.

Fall enrollment. IPEDS collects data on the number of students enrolled in the fall at postsecondary institutions. Students reported are those enrolled in courses creditable toward a degree or other formal award; students enrolled in courses that are part of a vocational or occupational program, including those enrolled in off-campus or extension centers; and high school students taking regular college courses for credit. Institutions report annually the number of full- and part-time students, by gender, race/ethnicity, and level (undergraduate, graduate, first-professional); the total number of undergraduate entering students (first-time, full- and part-time students, transfer-ins, and nondegree students); and retention rates. In even-numbered years, data are collected for state of residence of first-time students and for the number of those students who graduated from high school or received high school equivalent certificates in the past 12 months. Also in even-numbered years, 4-year institutions are required to provide enrollment data by gender, race/ethnicity, and level for selected fields of study. In odd-numbered years, data are collected for enrollment by age category by student level and gender.

Data through 1995 are for institutions of higher education, while later data are for degree-granting institutions. Degree-granting institutions grant associate's or higher degrees and participate in Title IV federal financial aid programs. The degree-granting classification is very similar to the earlier higher education classification, but it includes more 2-year colleges and excludes a few higher education institutions that did not grant degrees.

Nonresident alien is a person who is not a citizen or national of the United States and who is in this country on a visa or temporary basis and does not have the right to remain indefinitely.

A **Postbaccalaureate student** is a student with a bachelor's degree who is enrolled in graduate-level or first-professional courses.

Price of attendance includes tuition and required fees, books and supplies, room and board charges, and other expenses. Amounts are institutional averages as reported by the institution, not average amounts paid by students (for example, charges are not weighted by enrollment). Out-of-state average tuition and required fees were used for private institutions that reported varying tuitions by residency. The 2,578 institutions with academic calendars that differ by program or allow continuous enrollment are not included. U.S. service academies are not included. All amounts from 2011–2012 were converted to 2013–2014 dollars using the average Consumer Price Index values for the 12-month periods ending in October 2011 and October 2013. On-campus average price is based on those institutions that offer on-campus housing and/or meal service. Off-campus average price is based on

those institutions that do not require full-time, first-time students to live on campus. For public institutions, "in district" refers to the charges paid by a student who lives in the locality surrounding the institution, such as a county.

Race/ethnicity categories were developed in 1997 by the Office of Management and Budget (OMB) and are used to describe groups to which individuals belong, identify with, or belong in the eyes of the community. The categories do not denote scientific definitions of anthropological origins. The designations are used to categorize U.S. citizens, resident aliens, and other eligible non-citizens. Individuals are asked to first designate ethnicity as Hispanic/Latino or not Hispanic/Latino. Hispanic/Latino refers to a person of Cuban, Mexican, Puerto Rican, South or Central American, or other Spanish culture or origin, regardless of race. Second, individuals are asked to indicate all races that apply among the following:

American Indian or Alaska Native A person having origins in any of the original peoples of North and South America (including Central America) who maintains cultural identification through tribal affiliation or community attachment.

Asian A person having origins in any of the original peoples of the Far East, Southeast Asia, or the Indian Subcontinent, including, for example, Cambodia, China, India, Japan, Korea, Malaysia, Pakistan, the Philippine Islands, Thailand, and Vietnam.

Black or African American A person having origins in any of the black racial groups of Africa.

Native Hawaiian or Other Pacific Islander A person having origins in any of the original peoples of Hawaii, Guam, Samoa, or other Pacific Islands.

White A person having origins in any of the original peoples of Europe, the Middle East, or North Africa.

Before 1997, slightly different race/ethnicity categories were used and persons could identify with only one racial category.

Tuition and required fees is the amount of tuition and required fees covering a full academic year most frequently charged to students. These values represent what a typical student would be charged and may not be the same for all students at an institution. If tuition is charged on a per-credit-hour basis, the average full-time credit hour load for an entire academic year is used to estimate average tuition. Required fees include all fixed sum charges that are required of such a large proportion of all students that the student who does not pay the charges is an exception.

PART B

REGION AND STATE
EDUCATION STATISTICS

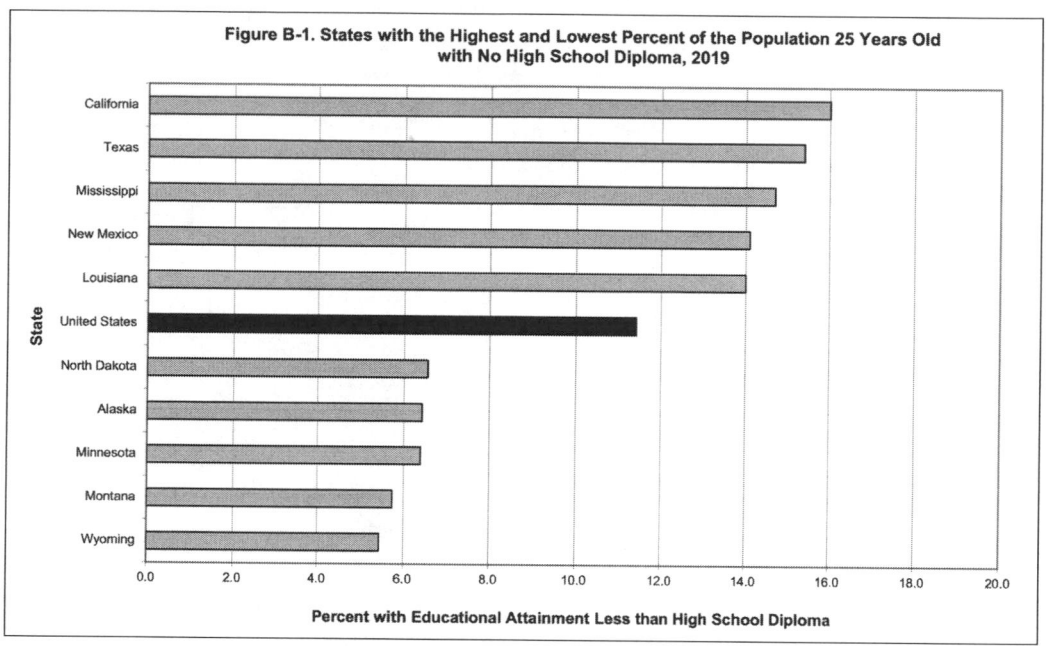

Figure B-1. States with the Highest and Lowest Percent of the Population 25 Years Old with No High School Diploma, 2019

In 2019, 88.6 percent of the U.S. population 25 years old and over had graduated from high school and/or a higher education establishment. The West region had the lowest average high-school attainment rate of 87.3 percent, followed by the South (87.5 percent), the Northeast (89.8 percent) and the Midwest (91.2 percent). All states had high-school attainment levels of more than 84 percent. California had the lowest level at 84.0 percent. Wyoming had the highest high-school graduation rate at 94.5 percent. (Table B-2)

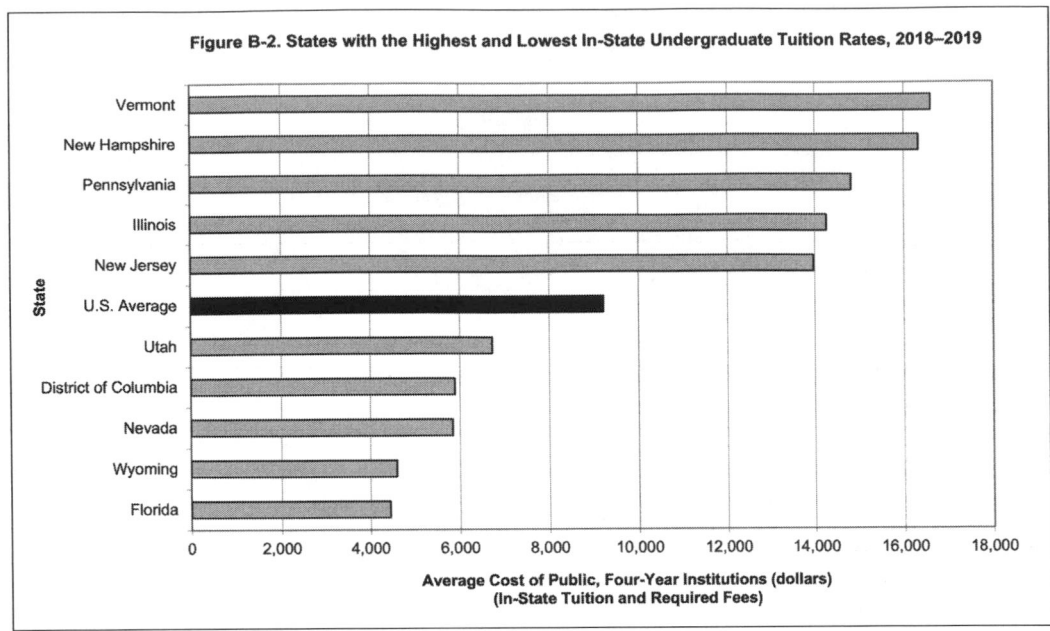

Figure B-2. States with the Highest and Lowest In-State Undergraduate Tuition Rates, 2018–2019

The average cost of in-state tuition and fees at public, 4-year colleges during the 2018-2019 school year was $9,212. Out-of-state tuition at public, 4-year colleges averaged $26,382, and the average tuition and fees at private, 4-year colleges was $31,875. Vermont was the state with the highest in-state tuition and fees ($16,604), and Florida was the state with the lowest average in-state tuition and fees ($4,443). Vermont also had the most expensive out-of-state tuition and fees at a cost of $39,947 per year. The District of Columbia had the lowest out-of-state cost with a tuition rate of $12,416 for non-residents. South Dakota had the smallest margin between in-state and out-of-state tuition, with its out-of-state tuition rate ($12,465) being just $3,694 more than the in-state rate ($8,772). (Table B-15)

There are several ways to measure high school dropouts. "Event dropout rates" provide the state's estimate of students who have left their schools with no documented reason (for example, transfer, move, or illness). In 2018, 5.3 percent of the population 16 to 24 years old were estimated to have dropped out of school before graduation because they are no longer enrolled in school and are not high school graduates. Of the states, North Dakota had the lowest percentage of these dropouts (2.7 percent) and New Mexico had the highest percentage of dropouts (10.3 percent). (Table B-11)

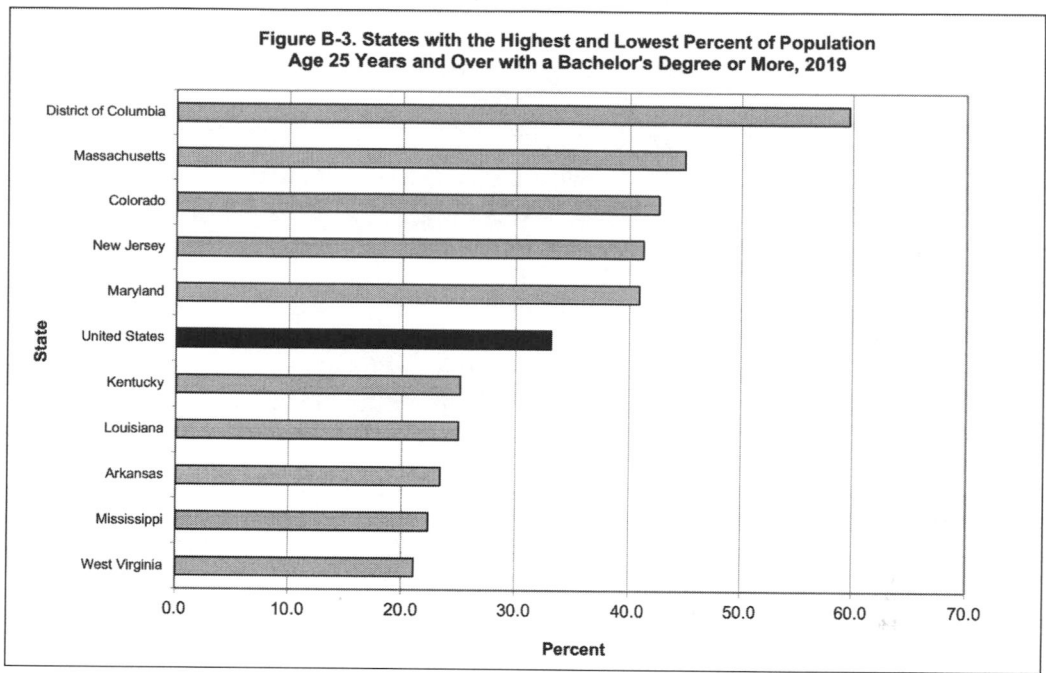

Figure B-3. States with the Highest and Lowest Percent of Population Age 25 Years and Over with a Bachelor's Degree or More, 2019

The proportion of the U.S. population with a bachelor's degree or more was 33.1 percent for the population age 25 and over in 2019. In the District of Columbia, 59.7 percent of residents held a bachelor's degree or more, the highest rate in the nation. Among the states, 14 had proportions of college graduates exceeding 35 percent. West Virginia had the lowest college attainment level of 21.1 percent. The Northeast region had the highest college attainment rate (37.9 percent), followed by the West (34.4 percent), the Midwest (31.6 percent), and the South (30.9 percent). (Table B-2)

Among people age 25 years old and older, people who self-identified as Asian had the highest college attainment (55.6 percent), followed by White (34.4 percent), Black (22.5 percent), and Hispanic (17.6 percent) individuals. The District of Columbia had the highest percent of White, Asian, and Hispanic individuals with bachelor's degrees or more (89.3 percent, 80.3 percent, and 52.0 percent respectively). Wyoming was the state with the highest percent of Black individuals with bachelor's degrees or more (46.5 percent). (Table B-2)

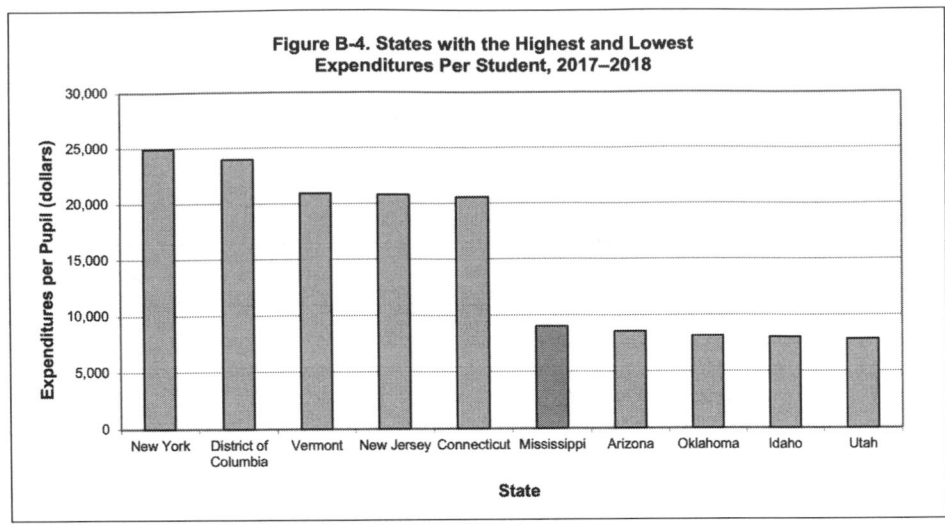

Figure B-4. States with the Highest and Lowest Expenditures Per Student, 2017–2018

Nationally, education expenditures for 2017-2018 were 60.7 percent for instruction, 35.3 percent for support services, and 4.0 percent for non-instruction related expenses. New York had the highest proportion of instruction-related expenditures, with 69.2 percent of the state's total expenditures for elementary and secondary programs used for this purpose. Alaska had the lowest, with 53.6 percent of expenditures going toward instruction. The state with the largest expenditure per student was New York, where the expenditure per pupil was $24,919. Utah, the state with the smallest expenditure per student spent $7,847 per pupil. (Table B-10)

Schools can be divided into four locales: city, suburban, town, or rural. The majority of charter schools in the nation in fall 2017 were in cities (56.1 percent) compared to suburbs (26.3 percent), rural areas (11.5 percent), and towns (6.1 percent). Of traditional schools, the highest percent were in suburbs (32.1 percent), followed by rural areas (29.1 percent), cities (24.9 percent), and towns (13.9 percent). (Table B-4)

Hawaii was the state with the highest percent of students enrolled in private schools for all grade levels. Among lower elementary students (grades 1 to 4), 17.4 percent attended private schools. Of the upper elementary students (grades 5 to 8), 18.8 percent attended private schools, and 23.3 percent of high-school students (grades 9 to 12) attended private schools. (Table B-5)

Nationally, the student-teacher ratio was 16.0 in Fall 2017. Arizona and California had the highest student-teacher ratios, with an average of 23.2 students per teacher. Vermont had the lowest student-teacher ratio (10.6 students per teacher). (Table B-9)

During the 2017–2018 school year, 52.6 percent of students nationwide were eligible for free or reduced-price lunch. The District of Columbia had the highest percent of students eligible for free or reduced-price lunch (76.4 percent), followed by Mississippi (74.5 percent), and New Mexico (73.6 percent). The states with the highest percent of students with IEPs during the 2018-2019 school year were New York (19.5 percent), Maine (19.2 percent), and Pennsylvania (19.1 percent). (Table B-7)

Table B-1. Educational Attainment of the Population 18 Years and Over, by Region, Age, and Sex, 2019

(Number; percent.)

Characteristic	United States Number	United States Percent	Northeast Number	Northeast Percent	Midwest Number	Midwest Percent	South Number	South Percent	West Number	West Percent
Total......................................	255,271,738	100.0	44,491,642	100.0	53,001,257	100.0	97,129,283	100.0	60,649,556	100.0
18 to 24 years..................................	30,373,170	11.9	5,097,235	11.5	6,386,198	12.0	11,633,544	12.0	7,256,193	12.0
Less than 9th grade	430,596	1.4	68,674	1.3	95,777	1.5	175,026	1.5	91,119	1.3
9th to 12th grade, no diploma.......	3,231,484	10.6	460,408	9.0	670,804	10.5	1,353,533	11.6	746,739	10.3
High school graduate (includes equivalency).............................	9,921,331	32.7	1,539,374	30.2	2,067,788	32.4	3,923,225	33.7	2,390,944	33.0
Some college, no degree..............	11,482,480	37.8	1,922,255	37.7	2,426,118	38.0	4,307,240	37.0	2,826,867	39.0
Associate's degree	1,685,800	5.6	245,721	4.8	352,812	5.5	670,518	5.8	416,749	5.7
Bachelor's degree........................	3,352,406	11.0	788,028	15.5	720,358	11.3	1,112,264	9.6	731,756	10.1
Graduate or professional degree...	269,073	0.9	72,775	1.4	52,541	0.8	91,738	0.8	52,019	0.7
25 to 34 years..................................	45,578,475	17.9	7,715,613	17.3	9,075,588	17.1	17,125,244	17.6	11,662,030	19.2
Less than 9th grade	1,182,302	2.6	188,140	2.4	193,117	2.1	478,917	2.8	322,128	2.8
9th to 12th grade, no diploma.......	2,606,207	5.7	338,012	4.4	433,702	4.8	1,124,671	6.6	709,822	6.1
High school graduate (includes equivalency).............................	11,140,748	24.4	1,730,258	22.4	2,206,394	24.3	4,504,294	26.3	2,699,802	23.2
Some college, no degree..............	9,778,564	21.5	1,292,468	16.8	1,987,736	21.9	3,782,456	22.1	2,715,904	23.3
Associate's degree	4,033,109	8.8	624,977	8.1	895,463	9.9	1,535,067	9.0	977,602	8.4
Bachelor's degree........................	11,770,702	25.8	2,342,621	30.4	2,379,751	26.2	3,999,686	23.4	3,048,644	26.1
Graduate or professional degree...	5,066,843	11.1	1,199,137	15.5	979,425	10.8	1,700,153	9.9	1,188,128	10.2
35 to 44 years..................................	41,914,845	16.4	6,878,858	15.5	8,446,830	15.9	16,149,341	16.6	10,439,816	17.2
Less than 9th grade	1,878,547	4.5	253,559	3.7	267,071	3.2	773,308	4.8	584,609	5.6
9th to 12th grade, no diploma.......	2,725,778	6.5	352,805	5.1	445,304	5.3	1,173,505	7.3	754,164	7.2
High school graduate (includes equivalency).............................	9,731,105	23.2	1,576,498	22.9	1,991,710	23.6	4,007,078	24.8	2,155,819	20.6
Some college, no degree..............	7,975,203	19.0	1,054,256	15.3	1,679,695	19.9	3,139,845	19.4	2,101,407	20.1
Associate's degree	3,915,980	9.3	595,521	8.7	913,415	10.8	1,494,633	9.3	912,411	8.7
Bachelor's degree........................	9,374,311	22.4	1,700,843	24.7	1,928,014	22.8	3,344,446	20.7	2,401,008	23.0
Graduate or professional degree...	6,313,921	15.1	1,345,376	19.6	1,221,621	14.5	2,216,526	13.7	1,530,398	14.7
45 to 64 years..................................	83,331,220	32.6	14,987,869	33.7	17,535,679	33.1	31,675,473	32.6	19,132,199	31.5
Less than 9th grade	4,043,215	4.9	604,042	4.0	509,874	2.9	1,508,115	4.8	1,421,184	7.4
9th to 12th grade, no diploma.......	5,467,719	6.6	843,809	5.6	964,421	5.5	2,373,434	7.5	1,286,055	6.7
High school graduate (includes equivalency).............................	23,030,202	27.6	4,430,715	29.6	5,281,239	30.1	9,075,875	28.7	4,242,373	22.2
Some college, no degree..............	16,521,361	19.8	2,359,869	15.7	3,673,476	20.9	6,306,385	19.9	4,181,631	21.9
Associate's degree	7,745,212	9.3	1,371,936	9.2	1,815,936	10.4	2,835,229	9.0	1,722,111	9.0
Bachelor's degree........................	16,093,480	19.3	3,100,219	20.7	3,314,558	18.9	5,845,519	18.5	3,833,184	20.0
Graduate or professional degree...	10,430,031	12.5	2,277,279	15.2	1,976,175	11.3	3,730,916	11.8	2,445,661	12.8
65 years and over	54,074,028	21.2	9,812,067	22.1	11,556,962	21.8	20,545,681	21.2	12,159,318	20.0
Less than 9th grade	3,770,621	7.0	701,495	7.1	507,372	4.4	1,538,094	7.5	1,023,660	8.4
9th to 12th grade, no diploma.......	3,944,152	7.3	720,650	7.3	790,183	6.8	1,733,528	8.4	699,791	5.8
High school graduate (includes equivalency).............................	16,580,298	30.7	3,310,264	33.7	4,209,402	36.4	6,291,606	30.6	2,769,026	22.8
Some college, no degree..............	10,638,958	19.7	1,466,756	14.9	2,356,464	20.4	4,054,364	19.7	2,761,374	22.7
Associate's degree	3,687,636	6.8	636,918	6.5	755,511	6.5	1,335,813	6.5	959,394	7.9
Bachelor's degree........................	8,491,986	15.7	1,505,999	15.3	1,649,801	14.3	3,108,326	15.1	2,227,860	18.3
Graduate or professional degree...	6,960,377	12.9	1,469,985	15.0	1,288,229	11.1	2,483,950	12.1	1,718,213	14.1
Male	124,267,346	48.7	21,426,582	48.2	25,870,856	48.8	46,946,758	48.3	30,023,150	49.5
18 to 24 years..................................	15,556,254	12.5	2,574,089	12.0	3,263,180	12.6	5,966,720	12.7	3,752,265	12.5
Less than 9th grade	253,626	1.6	40,027	1.6	52,019	1.6	108,456	1.8	53,124	1.4
9th to 12th grade, no diploma.......	1,873,139	12.0	265,702	10.3	383,847	11.8	786,516	13.2	437,074	11.6
High school graduate (includes equivalency).............................	5,613,801	36.1	863,864	33.6	1,174,413	36.0	2,229,606	37.4	1,345,918	35.9
Some college, no degree..............	5,543,981	35.6	926,530	36.0	1,164,656	35.7	2,053,207	34.4	1,399,588	37.3
Associate's degree	754,294	4.8	110,788	4.3	165,746	5.1	291,758	4.9	186,002	5.0
Bachelor's degree........................	1,416,531	9.1	342,314	13.3	302,092	9.3	463,547	7.8	308,578	8.2
Graduate or professional degree...	100,882	0.6	24,864	1.0	20,407	0.6	33,630	0.6	21,981	0.6
25 to 34 years..................................	23,099,299	18.6	3,900,264	18.2	4,600,279	17.8	8,578,806	18.3	6,019,950	20.1
Less than 9th grade	682,687	3.0	107,320	2.8	103,942	2.3	282,332	3.3	189,093	3.1
9th to 12th grade, no diploma.......	1,499,692	6.5	189,751	4.9	256,318	5.6	643,403	7.5	410,220	6.8
High school graduate (includes equivalency).............................	6,464,769	28.0	1,013,042	26.0	1,301,637	28.3	2,576,187	30.0	1,573,903	26.1
Some college, no degree..............	4,994,460	21.6	683,601	17.5	1,007,867	21.9	1,888,722	22.0	1,414,270	23.5
Associate's degree	1,857,056	8.0	295,580	7.6	415,951	9.0	678,032	7.9	467,493	7.8
Bachelor's degree........................	5,520,794	23.9	1,134,543	29.1	1,120,386	24.4	1,822,889	21.2	1,442,976	24.0
Graduate or professional degree...	2,079,841	9.0	476,427	12.2	394,178	8.6	687,241	8.0	521,995	8.7
35 to 44 years..................................	20,920,715	16.8	3,408,611	15.9	4,231,629	16.4	7,985,711	17.0	5,294,764	17.6
Less than 9th grade	1,015,410	4.9	138,228	4.1	139,411	3.3	429,465	5.4	308,306	5.8
9th to 12th grade, no diploma.......	1,546,874	7.4	198,906	5.8	257,382	6.1	670,393	8.4	420,193	7.9
High school graduate (includes equivalency).............................	5,573,933	26.6	898,862	26.4	1,184,740	28.0	2,275,189	28.5	1,215,142	22.9
Some college, no degree..............	4,000,639	19.1	542,318	15.9	840,812	19.9	1,532,664	19.2	1,084,845	20.5

Table B-1. Educational Attainment of the Population 18 Years and Over, by Region, Age, and Sex, 2019—*Continued*

(Number; percent.)

Characteristic	United States		Northeast		Midwest		South		West	
	Number	Percent	Number	Percent	Number	Percent	Number	Percent	Number	Percent
Associate's degree	1,732,527	8.3	267,493	7.8	398,260	9.4	640,877	8.0	425,897	8.0
Bachelor's degree	4,350,263	20.8	800,536	23.5	897,071	21.2	1,512,747	18.9	1,139,909	21.5
Graduate or professional degree ...	2,701,069	12.9	562,268	16.5	513,953	12.1	924,376	11.6	700,472	13.2
45 to 64 years	40,646,797	32.7	7,267,421	33.9	8,627,366	33.3	15,311,600	32.6	9,440,410	31.4
Less than 9th grade	2,088,875	5.1	309,345	4.3	267,749	3.1	811,681	5.3	700,100	7.4
9th to 12th grade, no diploma	2,981,479	7.3	452,220	6.2	539,105	6.2	1,289,898	8.4	700,256	7.4
High school graduate (includes equivalency)	12,002,869	29.5	2,310,913	31.8	2,801,461	32.5	4,671,654	30.5	2,218,841	23.5
Some college, no degree	7,890,025	19.4	1,146,132	15.8	1,781,468	20.6	2,946,611	19.2	2,015,814	21.4
Associate's degree	3,227,173	7.9	549,395	7.6	763,140	8.8	1,157,835	7.6	756,803	8.0
Bachelor's degree	7,519,558	18.5	1,452,981	20.0	1,548,304	17.9	2,684,911	17.5	1,833,362	19.4
Graduate or professional degree ...	4,936,818	12.1	1,046,435	14.4	926,139	10.7	1,749,010	11.4	1,215,234	12.9
65 years and over	24,044,281	19.3	4,276,197	20.0	5,148,402	19.9	9,103,921	19.4	5,515,761	18.4
Less than 9th grade	1,614,697	6.7	289,146	6.8	226,838	4.4	684,108	7.5	414,605	7.5
9th to 12th grade, no diploma	1,657,216	6.9	307,890	7.2	340,015	6.6	719,020	7.9	290,291	5.3
High school graduate (includes equivalency)	6,510,243	27.1	1,272,791	29.8	1,695,794	32.9	2,446,393	26.9	1,095,265	19.9
Some college, no degree	4,693,401	19.5	652,440	15.3	1,054,807	20.5	1,763,070	19.4	1,223,084	22.2
Associate's degree	1,574,653	6.5	256,990	6.0	320,523	6.2	563,129	6.2	434,011	7.9
Bachelor's degree	4,255,044	17.7	744,277	17.4	826,674	16.1	1,587,631	17.4	1,096,462	19.9
Graduate or professional degree ...	3,739,027	15.6	752,663	17.6	683,751	13.3	1,340,570	14.7	962,043	17.4
Female	131,004,392	51.3	23,065,060	51.8	27,130,401	51.2	50,182,525	51.7	30,626,406	50.5
18 to 24 years	14,816,916	11.3	2,523,146	10.9	3,123,018	11.5	5,666,824	11.3	3,503,928	11.4
Less than 9th grade	176,970	1.2	28,647	1.1	43,758	1.4	66,570	1.2	37,995	1.1
9th to 12th grade, no diploma	1,358,345	9.2	194,706	7.7	286,957	9.2	567,017	10.0	309,665	8.8
High school graduate (includes equivalency)	4,307,530	29.1	675,510	26.8	893,375	28.6	1,693,619	29.9	1,045,026	29.8
Some college, no degree	5,938,499	40.1	995,725	39.5	1,261,462	40.4	2,264,033	39.8	1,427,279	40.7
Associate's degree	931,506	6.3	134,933	5.3	187,066	6.0	378,760	6.7	230,747	6.6
Bachelor's degree	1,935,875	13.1	445,714	17.7	418,266	13.4	648,717	11.4	423,178	12.1
Graduate or professional degree ...	168,191	1.1	47,911	1.9	32,134	1.0	58,108	1.0	30,038	0.9
25 to 34 years	22,479,176	17.2	3,815,349	16.5	4,475,309	16.5	8,546,438	17.0	5,642,080	18.4
Less than 9th grade	499,615	2.2	80,820	2.1	89,175	2.0	196,585	2.3	133,035	2.4
9th to 12th grade, no diploma	1,106,515	4.9	148,261	3.9	177,384	4.0	481,268	5.6	299,602	5.3
High school graduate (includes equivalency)	4,675,979	20.8	717,216	18.8	904,757	20.2	1,928,107	22.6	1,125,899	20.0
Some college, no degree	4,784,104	21.3	608,867	16.0	979,869	21.9	1,893,734	22.2	1,301,634	23.1
Associate's degree	2,176,053	9.7	329,397	8.6	479,512	10.7	857,035	10.0	510,109	9.0
Bachelor's degree	6,249,908	27.8	1,208,078	31.7	1,259,365	28.1	2,176,797	25.5	1,605,668	28.5
Graduate or professional degree ...	2,987,002	13.3	722,710	18.9	585,247	13.1	1,012,912	11.9	666,133	11.8
35 to 44 years	20,994,130	16.0	3,470,247	15.0	4,215,201	15.5	8,163,630	16.3	5,145,052	16.8
Less than 9th grade	863,137	4.1	115,331	3.3	127,660	3.0	343,843	4.2	276,303	5.4
9th to 12th grade, no diploma	1,178,904	5.6	153,899	4.4	187,922	4.5	503,112	6.2	333,971	6.5
High school graduate (includes equivalency)	4,157,172	19.8	677,636	19.5	806,970	19.1	1,731,889	21.2	940,677	18.3
Some college, no degree	3,974,564	18.9	511,938	14.8	838,883	19.9	1,607,181	19.7	1,016,562	19.8
Associate's degree	2,183,453	10.4	328,028	9.5	515,155	12.2	853,756	10.5	486,514	9.5
Bachelor's degree	5,024,048	23.9	900,307	25.9	1,030,943	24.5	1,831,699	22.4	1,261,099	24.5
Graduate or professional degree ...	3,612,852	17.2	783,108	22.6	707,668	16.8	1,292,150	15.8	829,926	16.1
45 to 64 years	42,684,423	32.6	7,720,448	33.5	8,908,313	32.8	16,363,873	32.6	9,691,789	31.6
Less than 9th grade	1,954,340	4.6	294,697	3.8	242,125	2.7	696,434	4.3	721,084	7.4
9th to 12th grade, no diploma	2,486,240	5.8	391,589	5.1	425,316	4.8	1,083,536	6.6	585,799	6.0
High school graduate (includes equivalency)	11,027,333	25.8	2,119,802	27.5	2,479,778	27.8	4,404,221	26.9	2,023,532	20.9
Some college, no degree	8,631,336	20.2	1,213,737	15.7	1,892,008	21.2	3,359,774	20.5	2,165,817	22.3
Associate's degree	4,518,039	10.6	822,541	10.7	1,052,796	11.8	1,677,394	10.3	965,308	10.0
Bachelor's degree	8,573,922	20.1	1,647,238	21.3	1,766,254	19.8	3,160,608	19.3	1,999,822	20.6
Graduate or professional degree ...	5,493,213	12.9	1,230,844	15.9	1,050,036	11.8	1,981,906	12.1	1,230,427	12.7
65 years and over	30,029,747	22.9	5,535,870	24.0	6,408,560	23.6	11,441,760	22.8	6,643,557	21.7
Less than 9th grade	2,155,924	7.2	412,349	7.4	280,534	4.4	853,986	7.5	609,055	9.2
9th to 12th grade, no diploma	2,286,936	7.6	412,760	7.5	450,168	7.0	1,014,508	8.9	409,500	6.2
High school graduate (includes equivalency)	10,070,055	33.5	2,037,473	36.8	2,513,608	39.2	3,845,213	33.6	1,673,761	25.2
Some college, no degree	5,945,557	19.8	814,316	14.7	1,301,657	20.3	2,291,294	20.0	1,538,290	23.2
Associate's degree	2,112,983	7.0	379,928	6.9	434,988	6.8	772,684	6.8	525,383	7.9
Bachelor's degree	4,236,942	14.1	761,722	13.8	823,127	12.8	1,520,695	13.3	1,131,398	17.0
Graduate or professional degree ...	3,221,350	10.7	717,322	13.0	604,478	9.4	1,143,380	10.0	756,170	11.4

Table B-2. Educational Attainment of the Population 25 Years Old and Over, by Sex, Race, Hispanic Origin, and Region or State, 2019

(Number; percent.)

Region or State	Population	Less than 9th grade	9th to 12th grade, no diploma	High school graduate (includes equivalency)	Some college, no degree	Associate degree	Bachelor's degree	Graduate or professional degree	High school graduate or higher (percent)	Bachelor's degree or higher (percent)
United States	224,898,568	10,874,685	14,743,856	60,482,353	44,914,086	19,381,937	45,730,479	28,771,172	88.6	33.1
Northeast Region	39,394,407	1,747,236	2,255,276	11,047,735	6,173,349	3,229,352	8,649,682	6,291,777	89.8	37.9
Midwest Region	46,615,059	1,477,434	2,633,610	13,688,745	9,697,371	4,380,325	9,272,124	5,465,450	91.2	31.6
South Region	85,495,739	4,298,434	6,405,138	23,878,853	17,283,050	7,200,742	16,297,977	10,131,545	87.5	30.9
West Region..................	53,393,363	3,351,581	3,449,832	11,867,020	11,760,316	4,571,518	11,510,696	6,882,400	87.3	34.4
Alabama......................	3,360,058	130,320	302,753	1,039,241	700,473	301,914	547,975	337,382	87.1	26.3
Alaska	484,058	10,424	20,666	139,156	124,261	43,394	89,583	56,574	93.6	30.2
Arizona.......................	4,944,540	252,459	360,539	1,170,685	1,236,845	431,854	931,038	561,120	87.6	30.2
Arkansas	2,036,456	94,376	160,617	710,306	444,052	151,738	307,185	168,182	87.5	23.3
California......................	26,937,872	2,346,235	1,955,278	5,546,711	5,542,372	2,118,792	5,889,724	3,538,760	84.0	35.0
Colorado......................	3,974,943	127,702	174,518	836,590	805,570	334,961	1,057,825	637,777	92.4	42.7
Connecticut..................	2,496,420	99,132	132,707	668,361	410,972	190,700	549,166	445,382	90.7	39.8
Delaware......................	687,311	23,925	42,597	207,642	128,063	56,885	134,287	93,912	90.3	33.2
District of Columbia	505,145	16,459	24,709	79,881	65,745	16,922	129,825	171,604	91.9	59.7
Florida........................	15,484,502	712,764	1,081,871	4,396,122	3,001,381	1,538,727	2,982,643	1,770,994	88.4	30.7
Georgia	7,080,222	319,929	536,096	1,939,945	1,414,554	568,130	1,410,395	891,173	87.9	32.5
Hawaii........................	996,668	36,278	39,700	273,421	205,964	106,096	219,979	115,230	92.4	33.6
Idaho..........................	1,170,997	34,969	64,937	305,274	304,578	124,584	220,189	116,466	91.5	28.7
Illinois........................	8,694,694	388,348	494,289	2,255,611	1,737,416	710,058	1,886,240	1,222,732	89.8	35.8
Indiana........................	4,502,015	162,057	306,026	1,526,825	896,654	397,627	777,771	435,055	89.6	26.9
Iowa..........................	2,123,004	57,894	98,587	658,822	433,870	251,578	420,199	202,054	92.6	29.3
Kansas........................	1,918,081	63,799	93,958	504,035	430,549	173,251	414,851	237,638	91.8	34.0
Kentucky	3,048,442	154,759	235,894	1,012,643	619,035	260,188	453,040	312,883	87.2	25.1
Louisiana	3,140,201	138,644	302,200	1,066,026	646,746	202,310	503,947	280,328	86.0	25.0
Maine..........................	991,152	20,783	46,531	311,108	184,723	99,008	205,722	123,277	93.2	33.2
Maryland......................	4,183,858	168,321	233,831	1,030,636	753,547	287,293	911,781	798,449	90.4	40.9
Massachusetts..............	4,850,576	203,412	217,529	1,158,066	729,016	360,810	1,197,208	984,535	91.3	45.0
Michigan......................	6,894,627	186,035	410,252	2,005,981	1,572,770	648,794	1,252,685	818,110	91.4	30.0
Minnesota....................	3,847,212	103,730	141,960	939,997	785,721	442,578	942,830	490,396	93.6	37.3
Mississippi...................	1,979,664	91,377	199,540	598,609	440,939	207,448	270,712	171,039	85.3	22.3
Missouri......................	4,206,162	122,379	269,436	1,308,859	900,486	333,721	775,808	495,473	90.7	30.2
Montana......................	741,950	12,087	30,595	211,079	169,641	69,400	171,309	77,839	94.2	33.6
Nebraska.....................	1,271,770	43,627	57,645	326,389	280,333	141,189	277,159	145,428	92.0	33.2
Nevada.......................	2,136,466	109,903	171,012	593,417	525,746	187,469	355,837	193,082	86.9	25.7
New Hampshire.............	979,750	19,331	46,341	275,105	174,078	96,658	224,636	143,601	93.3	37.6
New Jersey	6,191,229	287,999	311,620	1,666,321	974,540	398,984	1,555,781	995,984	90.3	41.2
New Mexico	1,425,988	82,436	118,892	376,390	324,141	129,531	221,281	173,317	85.9	27.7
New York.....................	13,664,734	795,539	898,691	3,524,192	2,075,506	1,204,588	2,898,440	2,267,778	87.6	37.8
North Carolina..............	7,187,077	299,154	519,770	1,839,042	1,480,044	727,882	1,471,420	849,765	88.6	32.3
North Dakota................	504,375	13,284	19,735	134,432	112,811	70,716	108,527	44,870	93.5	30.4
Ohio..........................	8,049,805	221,017	519,830	2,627,758	1,622,014	702,601	1,464,945	891,640	90.8	29.3
Oklahoma....................	2,619,244	100,954	202,312	825,284	596,289	207,896	447,888	238,621	88.4	26.2
Oregon........................	2,988,118	98,217	160,182	687,243	741,058	269,102	627,911	404,405	91.4	34.5
Pennsylvania................	9,028,036	273,775	538,057	3,103,046	1,420,062	775,694	1,761,627	1,155,775	91.0	32.3
Rhode Island................	746,952	37,697	42,510	212,282	129,984	64,204	156,087	104,188	89.3	34.8
South Carolina	3,563,204	132,646	283,032	1,015,260	725,158	352,549	656,496	398,063	88.3	29.6
South Dakota	588,029	16,462	29,832	176,644	120,476	69,831	121,231	53,553	92.1	29.7
Tennessee	4,693,962	202,493	360,324	1,480,753	953,282	348,886	845,100	503,124	88.0	28.7
Texas..........................	18,772,550	1,436,483	1,445,905	4,734,422	3,976,607	1,402,600	3,750,797	2,025,736	84.6	30.8
Utah	1,911,592	46,767	86,293	442,206	486,888	184,777	448,109	216,552	93.0	34.8
Vermont......................	445,558	9,568	21,290	129,254	74,468	38,706	101,015	71,257	93.1	38.7
Virginia.......................	5,872,757	222,224	362,488	1,387,610	1,107,258	468,107	1,312,800	1,012,270	90.0	39.6
Washington..................	5,290,324	187,558	252,516	1,167,347	1,199,747	527,524	1,204,728	750,904	91.7	37.0
West Virginia................	1,281,086	53,606	111,199	515,431	229,877	101,267	161,686	108,020	87.1	21.1
Wisconsin	4,015,285	98,802	192,060	1,223,392	804,271	438,381	829,878	428,501	92.8	31.3
Wyoming	389,847	6,546	14,704	117,501	93,505	44,034	73,183	40,374	94.5	29.1

[1] May be of any race.

... = Not available

Table B-2. Educational Attainment of the Population 25 Years Old and Over, by Sex, Race, Hispanic Origin, and Region or State, 2019—*Continued*

(Number; percent.)

Region or State	Population	Less than 9th grade	9th to 12th grade, no diploma	High school graduate (includes equivalency)	Some college, no degree	Associate degree	Bachelor's degree	Graduate or professional degree	High school graduate or higher (percent)	Bachelor's degree or higher (percent)
United States	108,711,092	5,401,669	7,685,261	30,551,814	21,578,525	8,391,409	21,645,659	13,456,755	88.0	32.3
Northeast Region	18,852,493	844,039	1,148,767	5,495,608	3,024,491	1,369,458	4,132,337	2,837,793	89.4	37.0
Midwest Region	22,607,676	737,940	1,392,820	6,983,632	4,684,954	1,897,874	4,392,435	2,518,021	90.6	30.6
South Region	40,980,038	2,207,586	3,322,714	11,969,423	8,131,067	3,039,873	7,608,178	4,701,197	86.5	30.0
West Region	26,270,885	1,612,104	1,820,960	6,103,151	5,738,013	2,084,204	5,512,709	3,399,744	86.9	33.9
Alabama	1,586,206	71,215	152,700	512,181	319,537	124,955	255,317	150,301	85.9	25.6
Alaska	248,666	5,845	10,642	78,101	66,261	21,997	40,480	25,340	93.4	26.5
Arizona	2,423,466	125,602	188,217	593,553	592,821	199,184	446,041	278,048	87.1	29.9
Arkansas	975,517	49,841	81,100	362,841	209,719	56,732	138,501	76,783	86.6	22.1
California	13,208,824	1,111,415	1,030,198	2,845,945	2,709,335	951,967	2,806,332	1,753,632	83.8	34.5
Colorado	1,982,756	66,925	90,936	438,996	406,110	150,857	519,763	309,169	92.0	41.8
Connecticut	1,195,271	50,027	70,183	329,406	198,237	80,368	261,219	205,831	89.9	39.1
Delaware	325,736	11,488	24,067	98,750	61,608	23,579	62,719	43,525	89.1	32.6
District of Columbia	236,952	8,124	13,386	36,627	26,972	8,169	62,428	81,246	90.9	60.6
Florida	7,435,836	349,619	571,380	2,167,938	1,429,199	649,865	1,410,262	857,573	87.6	30.5
Georgia	3,352,785	168,720	277,058	967,909	653,765	244,460	654,577	386,296	86.7	31.0
Hawaii	488,577	14,584	17,956	145,966	105,146	52,976	99,134	52,815	93.3	31.1
Idaho	579,656	17,143	35,945	162,883	141,396	57,615	102,458	62,216	90.8	28.4
Illinois	4,192,414	189,100	263,650	1,133,810	830,315	310,574	900,767	564,198	89.2	34.9
Indiana	2,174,011	83,764	157,183	777,020	417,779	168,165	370,748	199,352	88.9	26.2
Iowa	1,040,234	30,675	52,520	347,951	210,828	109,952	194,498	93,810	92.0	27.7
Kansas	935,217	32,307	49,880	260,089	207,452	79,778	195,407	110,304	91.2	32.7
Kentucky	1,468,976	82,751	124,901	525,573	288,595	97,986	220,641	128,529	85.9	23.8
Louisiana	1,491,097	78,344	157,650	536,578	297,354	80,509	222,046	118,616	84.2	22.8
Maine	475,676	10,868	25,626	162,607	87,021	44,415	92,083	53,056	92.3	30.5
Maryland	1,979,022	88,195	118,798	516,202	354,630	115,779	417,359	368,059	89.5	39.7
Massachusetts	2,312,900	99,740	107,288	590,020	348,014	145,579	572,590	449,669	91.0	44.2
Michigan	3,338,285	90,930	213,705	1,009,979	771,368	270,111	596,013	386,179	90.9	29.4
Minnesota	1,893,200	47,551	78,903	497,978	386,797	205,669	451,563	224,739	93.3	35.7
Mississippi	928,666	50,314	104,916	305,725	200,942	81,174	117,492	68,103	83.3	20.0
Missouri	2,021,577	63,474	138,581	667,680	425,150	138,553	368,603	219,536	90.0	29.1
Montana	367,446	6,666	16,809	109,837	83,427	30,358	82,825	37,524	93.6	32.8
Nebraska	624,305	22,385	31,517	167,659	134,082	71,378	130,034	67,250	91.4	31.6
Nevada	1,061,616	53,331	86,608	303,515	267,456	87,320	167,519	95,867	86.8	24.8
New Hampshire	479,211	9,928	27,571	144,178	83,519	42,564	107,286	64,165	92.2	35.8
New Jersey	2,966,074	140,880	158,039	804,887	483,983	164,457	726,690	487,138	89.9	40.9
New Mexico	691,222	38,868	61,306	196,679	154,835	59,854	101,314	78,366	85.5	26.0
New York	6,500,180	370,237	451,796	1,748,881	1,035,209	520,358	1,395,801	978,526	87.4	36.5
North Carolina	3,398,408	158,893	279,143	927,213	686,315	295,114	674,417	377,313	87.1	30.9
North Dakota	254,515	6,525	11,648	72,697	60,565	34,542	48,572	19,966	92.9	26.9
Ohio	3,870,968	112,360	268,705	1,324,274	785,690	274,437	693,201	412,301	90.2	28.6
Oklahoma	1,269,169	51,961	102,749	419,818	283,759	91,780	207,982	111,120	87.8	25.1
Oregon	1,459,257	51,478	89,416	346,700	353,440	129,143	298,995	190,085	90.3	33.5
Pennsylvania	4,346,893	138,184	274,609	1,539,562	689,364	327,733	854,109	523,332	90.5	31.7
Rhode Island	357,935	19,346	20,242	105,478	63,923	26,856	75,811	46,279	88.9	34.1
South Carolina	1,678,161	71,741	148,500	496,169	328,559	150,629	313,518	169,045	86.9	28.8
South Dakota	293,272	9,316	16,728	93,409	57,884	32,441	59,698	23,796	91.1	28.5
Tennessee	2,238,460	104,982	189,922	735,374	451,148	144,599	387,959	224,476	86.8	27.4
Texas	9,165,437	724,394	733,467	2,382,325	1,903,611	637,094	1,781,441	1,003,105	84.1	30.4
Utah	949,043	24,164	44,780	216,579	232,133	81,110	222,158	128,119	92.7	36.9
Vermont	217,725	4,829	13,413	70,589	35,221	17,128	46,748	29,797	91.6	35.2
Virginia	2,825,457	108,758	187,372	708,896	527,730	197,146	606,292	489,263	89.5	38.8
Washington	2,612,977	92,016	140,490	598,117	581,291	241,293	591,069	368,701	91.1	36.7
West Virginia	624,153	28,246	55,605	269,304	107,624	40,303	75,227	47,844	86.6	19.7
Wisconsin	1,969,678	49,553	109,800	631,086	397,044	202,274	383,331	196,590	91.9	29.4
Wyoming	197,379	4,067	7,657	66,280	44,362	20,530	34,621	19,862	94.1	27.6

Note: Male, age 25 years and over

[1]May be of any race.
... = Not available

Table B-2. Educational Attainment of the Population 25 Years Old and Over, by Sex, Race, Hispanic Origin, and Region or State, 2019—*Continued*

(Number; percent.)

Region or State	Population	Less than 9th grade	9th to 12th grade, no diploma	High school graduate (includes equivalency)	Some college, no degree	Associate degree	Bachelor's degree	Graduate or professional degree	High school graduate or higher (percent)	Bachelor's degree or higher (percent)
				Female, age 25 years and over						
United States	116,187,476	5,473,016	7,058,595	29,930,539	23,335,561	10,990,528	24,084,820	15,314,417	89.2	33.9
Northeast Region	20,541,914	903,197	1,106,509	5,552,127	3,148,858	1,859,894	4,517,345	3,453,984	90.2	38.8
Midwest Region	24,007,383	739,494	1,240,790	6,705,113	5,012,417	2,482,451	4,879,689	2,947,429	91.8	32.6
South Region	44,515,701	2,090,848	3,082,424	11,909,430	9,151,983	4,160,869	8,689,799	5,430,348	88.4	31.7
West Region.................	27,122,478	1,739,477	1,628,872	5,763,869	6,022,303	2,487,314	5,997,987	3,482,656	87.6	35.0
Alabama......................	1,773,852	59,105	150,053	527,060	380,936	176,959	292,658	187,081	88.2	27.0
Alaska	235,392	4,579	10,024	61,055	58,000	21,397	49,103	31,234	93.8	34.1
Arizona.......................	2,521,074	126,857	172,322	577,132	644,024	232,670	484,997	283,072	88.1	30.5
Arkansas	1,060,939	44,535	79,517	347,465	234,333	95,006	168,684	91,399	88.3	24.5
California.....................	13,729,048	1,234,820	925,080	2,700,766	2,833,037	1,166,825	3,083,392	1,785,128	84.3	35.5
Colorado	1,992,187	60,777	83,582	397,594	399,460	184,104	538,062	328,608	92.8	43.5
Connecticut..................	1,301,149	49,105	62,524	338,955	212,735	110,332	287,947	239,551	91.4	40.5
Delaware	361,575	12,437	18,530	108,892	66,455	33,306	71,568	50,387	91.4	33.7
District of Columbia	268,193	8,335	11,323	43,254	38,773	8,753	67,397	90,358	92.7	58.8
Florida.........................	8,048,666	363,145	510,491	2,228,184	1,572,182	888,862	1,572,381	913,421	89.1	30.9
Georgia	3,727,437	151,209	259,038	972,036	760,789	323,670	755,818	504,877	89.0	33.8
Hawaii	508,091	21,694	21,744	127,455	100,818	53,120	120,845	62,415	91.5	36.1
Idaho..........................	591,341	17,826	28,992	142,391	163,182	66,969	117,731	54,250	92.1	29.1
Illinois	4,502,280	199,248	230,639	1,121,801	907,101	399,484	985,473	658,534	90.5	36.5
Indiana	2,328,004	78,293	148,843	749,805	478,875	229,462	407,023	235,703	90.2	27.6
Iowa...........................	1,082,770	27,219	46,067	310,871	223,042	141,626	225,701	108,244	93.2	30.8
Kansas	982,864	31,492	44,078	243,946	223,097	93,473	219,444	127,334	92.3	35.3
Kentucky.....................	1,579,466	72,008	110,993	487,070	330,440	162,202	232,399	184,354	88.4	26.4
Louisiana	1,649,104	60,300	144,550	529,448	349,392	121,801	281,901	161,712	87.6	26.9
Maine	515,476	9,915	20,905	148,501	97,702	54,593	113,639	70,221	94.0	35.7
Maryland......................	2,204,836	80,126	115,033	514,434	398,917	171,514	494,422	430,390	91.1	41.9
Massachusetts	2,537,676	103,672	110,241	568,046	381,002	215,231	624,618	534,866	91.6	45.7
Michigan	3,556,342	95,105	196,547	996,002	801,402	378,683	656,672	431,931	91.8	30.6
Minnesota	1,954,012	56,179	63,057	442,019	398,924	236,909	491,267	265,657	93.9	38.7
Mississippi..................	1,050,998	41,063	94,624	292,884	239,997	126,274	153,220	102,936	87.1	24.4
Missouri......................	2,184,585	58,905	130,855	641,179	475,336	195,168	407,205	275,937	91.3	31.3
Montana......................	374,504	5,421	13,786	101,242	86,214	39,042	88,484	40,315	94.9	34.4
Nebraska.....................	647,465	21,242	26,128	158,730	146,251	69,811	147,125	78,178	92.7	34.8
Nevada	1,074,850	56,572	84,404	289,902	258,290	100,149	188,318	97,215	86.9	26.6
New Hampshire.............	500,539	9,403	18,770	130,927	90,559	54,094	117,350	79,436	94.4	39.3
New Jersey	3,225,155	147,119	153,581	861,434	490,557	234,527	829,091	508,846	90.7	41.5
New Mexico	734,766	43,568	57,586	179,711	169,306	69,677	119,967	94,951	86.2	29.2
New York.....................	7,163,926	425,302	446,895	1,775,311	1,040,297	684,230	1,502,639	1,289,252	87.8	39.0
North Carolina..............	3,788,669	140,261	240,627	911,829	793,729	432,768	797,003	472,452	89.9	33.5
North Dakota................	249,860	6,759	8,087	61,735	52,246	36,174	59,955	24,904	94.1	34.0
Ohio	4,178,837	108,657	251,125	1,303,484	836,324	428,164	771,744	479,339	91.4	29.9
Oklahoma....................	1,350,075	48,993	99,563	405,466	312,530	116,116	239,906	127,501	89.0	27.2
Oregon........................	1,528,861	46,739	70,766	340,543	387,618	139,959	328,916	214,320	92.3	35.5
Pennsylvania................	4,681,143	135,591	263,448	1,563,484	730,698	447,961	907,518	632,443	91.5	32.9
Rhode Island................	389,017	18,351	22,268	106,804	66,061	37,348	80,276	57,909	89.6	35.5
South Carolina	1,885,043	60,905	134,532	519,091	396,599	201,920	342,978	229,018	89.6	30.3
South Dakota	294,757	7,146	13,104	83,235	62,592	37,390	61,533	29,757	93.1	31.0
Tennessee	2,455,502	97,511	170,402	745,379	502,134	204,287	457,141	278,648	89.1	30.0
Texas..........................	9,607,113	712,089	712,438	2,352,097	2,072,996	765,506	1,969,356	1,022,631	85.2	31.1
Utah...........................	962,549	22,603	41,513	225,627	254,755	103,667	225,951	88,433	93.3	32.7
Vermont.......................	227,833	4,739	7,877	58,665	39,247	21,578	54,267	41,460	94.5	42.0
Virginia........................	3,047,300	113,466	175,116	678,714	579,528	270,961	706,508	523,007	90.5	40.3
Washington..................	2,677,347	95,542	112,026	569,230	618,456	286,231	613,659	382,203	92.2	37.2
West Virginia................	656,933	25,360	55,594	246,127	122,253	60,964	86,459	60,176	87.7	22.3
Wisconsin	2,045,607	49,249	82,260	592,306	407,227	236,107	446,547	231,911	93.6	33.2
Wyoming	192,468	2,479	7,047	51,221	49,143	23,504	38,562	20,512	95.1	30.7

[1]May be of any race.
... = Not available

Table B-2. Educational Attainment of the Population 25 Years Old and Over, by Sex, Race, Hispanic Origin, and Region or State, 2019—*Continued*

(Number; percent.)

Region or State		White alone, age 25 years and over					
	Population	Less than a high school diploma	High school graduate (includes equivalency)	Some college or associate's degree	Bachelor's degree or higher	High school graduate or higher (percent)	Bachelor's degree or higher (percent)
United States	167,334,031	16,059,994	45,168,415	48,491,383	57,614,239	90.4	34.4
Northeast Region	38,601,748	2,896,840	11,465,389	11,687,362	12,552,157	92.5	32.5
Midwest Region	29,349,798	2,236,666	8,283,638	7,097,576	11,731,918	92.4	40.0
South Region	61,935,787	7,028,785	17,092,273	17,718,528	20,096,201	88.7	32.4
West Region	37,446,698	3,897,703	8,327,115	11,987,917	13,233,963	89.6	35.3
Alabama	2,363,674	272,567	703,265	713,276	674,566	88.5	28.5
Alaska	336,103	13,623	81,493	120,929	120,058	95.9	35.7
Arizona	4,002,380	448,909	941,141	1,365,801	1,246,529	88.8	31.1
Arkansas	1,625,302	186,131	568,025	475,900	395,246	88.5	24.3
California	16,461,029	2,238,619	3,397,327	4,968,577	5,856,506	86.4	35.6
Colorado	3,406,342	225,301	696,900	974,174	1,509,967	93.4	44.3
Connecticut	1,939,577	138,595	502,622	471,592	826,768	92.9	42.6
Delaware	490,907	45,086	141,737	133,986	170,098	90.8	34.6
District of Columbia	230,095	4,171	5,954	14,441	205,529	98.2	89.3
Florida	12,023,439	1,226,998	3,351,605	3,535,800	3,909,036	89.8	32.5
Georgia	4,279,288	454,537	1,143,892	1,163,492	1,517,367	89.4	35.5
Hawaii	259,996	8,020	54,114	82,106	115,756	96.9	44.5
Idaho	1,066,998	76,803	278,728	400,381	311,086	92.8	29.2
Illinois	6,414,127	521,595	1,696,106	1,806,561	2,389,865	91.9	37.3
Indiana	3,843,248	361,425	1,320,287	1,110,926	1,050,610	90.6	27.3
Iowa	1,950,864	124,635	613,165	636,931	576,133	93.6	29.5
Kansas	1,653,103	112,454	432,480	524,360	583,809	93.2	35.3
Kentucky	2,705,849	340,994	912,080	771,660	681,115	87.4	25.2
Louisiana	2,036,883	240,316	673,801	545,036	577,730	88.2	28.4
Maine	944,133	61,368	299,158	271,270	312,337	93.5	33.1
Maryland	2,385,477	170,392	560,188	569,372	1,085,525	92.9	45.5
Massachusetts	3,865,466	253,367	929,572	885,108	1,797,419	93.4	46.5
Michigan	5,564,561	429,437	1,621,596	1,795,493	1,718,035	92.3	30.9
Minnesota	3,298,386	146,084	810,479	1,072,726	1,269,097	95.6	38.5
Mississippi	1,217,710	142,140	352,718	408,637	314,215	88.3	25.8
Missouri	3,537,955	306,371	1,096,454	1,036,719	1,098,411	91.3	31.0
Montana	672,576	34,911	191,045	215,758	230,862	94.8	34.3
Nebraska	1,130,659	73,333	288,192	381,342	387,792	93.5	34.3
Nevada	1,444,872	157,059	404,891	494,792	388,130	89.1	26.9
New Hampshire	919,746	59,123	261,232	258,655	340,736	93.6	37.0
New Jersey	4,294,038	344,820	1,177,377	967,461	1,804,380	92.0	42.0
New Mexico	1,081,586	135,725	275,119	338,636	332,106	87.5	30.7
New York	8,910,770	736,141	2,220,857	2,180,692	3,773,080	91.7	42.3
North Carolina	5,103,713	473,626	1,260,967	1,578,199	1,790,921	90.7	35.1
North Dakota	446,532	25,686	119,472	160,036	141,338	94.2	31.7
Ohio	6,706,983	552,138	2,233,581	1,892,540	2,028,724	91.8	30.2
Oklahoma	1,999,360	209,490	628,435	605,729	555,706	89.5	27.8
Oregon	2,568,427	190,706	596,786	890,928	890,007	92.6	34.7
Pennsylvania	7,439,802	560,718	2,594,017	1,797,244	2,487,823	92.5	33.4
Rhode Island	613,613	56,378	174,628	157,371	225,236	90.8	36.7
South Carolina	2,483,427	226,996	644,376	768,318	843,737	90.9	34.0
South Dakota	516,050	31,260	152,996	169,427	162,367	93.9	31.5
Tennessee	3,744,336	423,484	1,192,130	1,015,133	1,113,589	88.7	29.7
Texas	13,971,984	2,122,808	3,520,467	4,028,221	4,300,488	84.8	30.8
Utah	1,694,118	93,524	386,159	608,502	605,933	94.5	35.8
Vermont	422,653	26,156	124,175	108,183	164,139	93.8	38.8
Virginia	4,069,698	331,618	943,952	1,084,707	1,709,421	91.9	42.0
Washington	4,090,653	255,875	918,040	1,397,625	1,519,113	93.7	37.1
West Virginia	1,204,645	157,431	488,681	306,621	251,912	86.9	20.9
Wisconsin	3,539,280	212,422	1,080,581	1,100,301	1,145,976	94.0	32.4
Wyoming	361,618	18,628	105,372	129,708	107,910	94.8	29.8

¹May be of any race.
... = Not available

Table B-2. Educational Attainment of the Population 25 Years Old and Over, by Sex, Race, Hispanic Origin, and Region or State, 2019—*Continued*

(Number; percent.)

Region or State	Black or African American alone, age 25 years and over						
	Population	Less than a high school diploma	High school graduate (includes equivalency)	Some college or associate's degree	Bachelor's degree or higher	High school graduate or higher (percent)	Bachelor's degree or higher (percent)
United States	27,336,967	3,537,086	8,732,838	8,902,977	6,164,066	87.1	22.5
Northeast Region	4,533,097	600,591	1,465,877	1,583,761	882,868	86.8	19.5
Midwest Region	4,531,148	611,562	1,522,838	1,312,078	1,084,670	86.5	23.9
South Region	15,792,403	2,090,887	5,117,279	5,040,528	3,543,709	86.8	22.4
West Region.................	2,480,319	234,046	626,844	966,610	652,819	90.6	26.3
Alabama.......................	855,485	127,765	308,132	255,223	164,365	85.1	19.2
Alaska	15,832	1,672	5,155	5,478	3,527	89.4	22.3
Arizona........................	214,990	21,719	47,591	87,000	58,680	89.9	27.3
Arkansas......................	292,048	38,272	109,869	94,224	49,683	86.9	17.0
California......................	1,573,950	148,975	390,803	607,546	426,626	90.5	27.1
Colorado	155,881	11,920	41,503	59,381	43,077	92.4	27.6
Connecticut..................	257,234	35,115	89,391	76,819	55,909	86.3	21.7
Delaware	145,150	13,656	54,418	41,415	35,661	90.6	24.6
District of Columbia	220,748	29,868	67,667	61,193	62,020	86.5	28.1
Florida.........................	2,216,463	347,859	753,382	687,258	427,964	84.3	19.3
Georgia	2,186,956	264,883	681,361	698,653	542,059	87.9	24.8
Hawaii	18,397	301	2,900	9,486	5,710	98.4	31.0
Idaho...........................	5,607	399	1,587	2,872	749	92.9	13.4
Illinois.........................	1,177,578	158,421	335,514	416,955	266,688	86.5	22.6
Indiana	395,797	48,698	145,196	125,408	76,495	87.7	19.3
Iowa............................	72,382	12,304	24,106	25,208	10,764	83.0	14.9
Kansas	101,769	12,844	31,364	36,299	21,262	87.4	20.9
Kentucky	232,582	27,500	76,855	83,355	44,872	88.2	19.3
Louisiana	948,531	169,833	350,550	266,370	161,778	82.1	17.1
Maine...........................	11,899	1,487	2,891	2,990	4,531	87.5	38.1
Maryland......................	1,241,353	118,381	366,446	374,099	382,427	90.5	30.8
Massachusetts..............	350,938	50,202	98,502	104,131	98,103	85.7	28.0
Michigan	889,006	107,297	296,454	324,928	160,327	87.9	18.0
Minnesota	207,288	37,079	58,214	66,928	45,067	82.1	21.7
Mississippi...................	702,026	134,501	231,659	223,889	111,977	80.8	16.0
Missouri.......................	450,283	55,057	162,033	145,379	87,814	87.8	19.5
Montana.......................	2,977	462	525	729	1,261	84.5	42.4
Nebraska......................	54,590	8,006	17,309	17,451	11,824	85.3	21.7
Nevada.........................	192,799	18,597	60,059	79,129	35,014	90.4	18.2
New Hampshire.............	13,726	1,929	4,118	2,608	5,071	85.9	36.9
New Jersey	813,816	91,364	274,402	241,873	206,177	88.8	25.3
New Mexico	29,349	3,803	5,690	11,528	8,328	87.0	28.4
New York......................	2,097,135	313,601	675,424	594,039	514,071	85.0	24.5
North Carolina..............	1,486,857	201,584	453,900	498,246	333,127	86.4	22.4
North Dakota................	13,471	915	4,246	5,380	2,930	93.2	21.8
Ohio	939,875	123,826	310,698	341,268	164,083	86.8	17.5
Oklahoma.....................	180,859	19,076	60,497	65,552	35,734	89.5	19.8
Oregon.........................	51,503	4,929	13,336	17,545	15,693	90.4	30.5
Pennsylvania................	931,454	112,507	359,066	272,083	187,798	87.9	20.2
Rhode Island................	49,190	4,375	17,398	15,919	11,498	91.1	23.4
South Carolina	899,954	144,896	330,356	267,131	157,571	83.9	17.5
South Dakota	11,679	2,670	2,743	4,060	2,206	77.1	18.9
Tennessee	737,044	94,424	244,728	237,845	160,047	87.2	21.7
Texas...........................	2,289,499	201,619	677,732	822,016	588,132	91.2	25.7
Utah	19,937	2,741	4,856	8,863	3,477	86.3	17.4
Vermont.......................	5,756	982	1,646	1,616	1,512	82.9	26.3
Virginia........................	1,110,132	153,100	329,908	347,254	279,870	86.2	25.2
Washington..................	195,806	18,489	52,064	76,107	49,146	90.6	25.1
West Virginia................	46,716	3,670	19,819	16,805	6,422	92.1	13.7
Wisconsin	219,379	33,474	78,000	74,497	33,408	84.7	15.2
Wyoming	3,291	39	775	946	1,531	98.8	46.5

[1]May be of any race.
... = Not available

Table B-2. Educational Attainment of the Population 25 Years Old and Over, by Sex, Race, Hispanic Origin, and Region or State, 2019—*Continued*

(Number; percent.)

Region or State	Population	Less than a high school diploma	High school graduate (includes equivalency)	Some college or associate's degree	Bachelor's degree or higher	High school graduate or higher (percent)	Bachelor's degree or higher (percent)
					Asian alone, age 25 years and over		
United States	13,381,406	1,634,327	1,931,625	2,380,606	7,434,848	87.8	55.6
Northeast Region	1,540,588	196,028	203,814	230,224	910,522	87.3	59.1
Midwest Region	2,646,189	394,903	395,484	340,941	1,514,861	85.1	57.2
South Region	3,112,253	360,094	443,740	501,878	1,806,541	88.4	58.0
West Region.................	6,082,376	683,302	888,587	1,307,563	3,202,924	88.8	52.7
Alabama......................	47,226	5,856	6,987	8,005	26,378	87.6	55.9
Alaska	30,918	2,063	10,169	9,851	8,835	93.3	28.6
Arizona.......................	172,708	19,271	21,063	29,535	102,839	88.8	59.5
Arkansas	29,658	2,792	6,308	4,045	16,513	90.6	55.7
California.....................	4,363,485	499,622	588,567	904,888	2,370,408	88.5	54.3
Colorado	134,942	13,429	22,524	26,952	72,037	90.0	53.4
Connecticut..................	114,306	10,713	15,012	13,985	74,596	90.6	65.3
Delaware	25,875	1,443	3,037	4,337	17,058	94.4	65.9
District of Columbia	22,230	1,031	1,940	1,414	17,845	95.4	80.3
Florida........................	441,665	56,578	80,337	81,402	223,348	87.2	50.6
Georgia	302,385	40,051	45,576	43,402	173,356	86.8	57.3
Hawaii	434,234	45,903	106,929	129,323	152,079	89.4	35.0
Idaho..........................	18,301	2,476	3,440	3,600	8,785	86.5	48.0
Illinois.........................	513,285	48,798	56,928	73,922	333,637	90.5	65.0
Indiana.......................	101,424	15,659	13,889	11,969	59,907	84.6	59.1
Iowa...........................	48,872	9,893	6,790	7,255	24,934	79.8	51.0
Kansas	56,876	8,319	10,704	9,506	28,347	85.4	49.8
Kentucky	47,711	6,633	6,791	6,969	27,318	86.1	57.3
Louisiana	54,463	9,041	11,847	8,623	24,952	83.4	45.8
Maine.........................	10,990	2,005	2,257	1,699	5,029	81.8	45.8
Maryland.....................	277,535	29,587	33,792	38,559	175,597	89.3	63.3
Massachusetts.............	326,204	44,719	41,762	33,450	206,273	86.3	63.2
Michigan	218,309	22,170	25,327	29,441	141,371	89.8	64.8
Minnesota	180,643	33,366	28,560	35,435	83,282	81.5	46.1
Mississippi..................	20,681	3,283	3,806	5,034	8,558	84.1	41.4
Missouri......................	87,803	9,380	10,779	13,796	53,848	89.3	61.3
Montana......................	6,867	471	1,092	2,011	3,293	93.1	48.0
Nebraska.....................	30,283	6,814	4,145	5,047	14,277	77.5	47.1
Nevada........................	198,870	18,475	37,640	57,344	85,411	90.7	42.9
New Hampshire.............	25,955	2,180	4,148	2,908	16,719	91.6	64.4
New Jersey	613,693	43,574	62,969	67,794	439,356	92.9	71.6
New Mexico	27,650	3,007	4,977	5,948	13,718	89.1	49.6
New York......................	1,213,907	240,608	221,328	172,013	579,958	80.2	47.8
North Carolina..............	213,997	27,313	26,504	34,954	125,226	87.2	58.5
North Dakota................	7,164	1,368	871	2,019	2,906	80.9	40.6
Ohio	185,785	24,537	24,447	20,655	116,146	86.8	62.5
Oklahoma....................	58,425	10,829	11,184	11,197	25,215	81.5	43.2
Oregon	136,123	16,383	17,305	28,945	73,490	88.0	54.0
Pennsylvania................	309,518	46,918	42,608	43,509	176,483	84.8	57.0
Rhode Island................	25,461	3,146	4,597	4,307	13,411	87.6	52.7
South Carolina	58,659	7,112	9,852	11,559	30,136	87.9	51.4
South Dakota	7,098	1,341	1,421	1,307	3,029	81.1	42.7
Tennessee	87,030	12,267	13,988	15,337	45,438	85.9	52.2
Texas..........................	1,008,252	106,876	132,693	157,980	610,703	89.4	60.6
Utah	52,276	5,075	8,388	10,077	28,736	90.3	55.0
Vermont......................	6,155	1,040	803	1,276	3,036	83.1	49.3
Virginia.......................	405,441	38,101	48,109	67,628	251,603	90.6	62.1
Washington..................	502,312	57,058	65,319	98,361	281,574	88.6	56.1
West Virginia................	11,020	1,301	989	1,433	7,297	88.2	66.2
Wisconsin	103,046	14,383	19,953	19,872	48,838	86.0	47.4
Wyoming	3,690	69	1,174	728	1,719	98.1	46.6

[1]May be of any race.
... = Not available

Table B-2. Educational Attainment of the Population 25 Years Old and Over, by Sex, Race, Hispanic Origin, and Region or State, 2019—*Continued*

(Number; percent.)

Region or State	Population	Less than a high school diploma	High school graduate (includes equivalency)	Some college or associate's degree	Bachelor's degree or higher	High school graduate or higher (percent)	Bachelor's degree or higher (percent)
United States	34,949,077	10,325,431	9,853,963	8,605,585	6,164,098	70.5	17.6
Northeast Region	2,942,446	824,597	876,321	723,116	518,412	72.0	17.6
Midwest Region	5,018,519	1,330,243	1,530,638	1,140,200	1,017,438	73.5	20.3
South Region	13,370,478	3,873,183	3,721,131	3,156,543	2,619,621	71.0	19.6
West Region	13,617,634	4,297,408	3,725,873	3,585,726	2,008,627	68.4	14.8
Alabama	104,045	40,287	24,236	22,443	17,079	61.3	16.4
Alaska	28,365	3,964	6,647	12,113	5,641	86.0	19.9
Arizona........................	1,292,262	373,731	363,031	376,059	179,441	71.1	13.9
Arkansas	117,900	48,702	39,034	18,558	11,606	58.7	9.8
California.....................	9,150,608	3,074,068	2,419,795	2,340,965	1,315,780	66.4	14.4
Colorado	712,267	176,630	218,631	185,275	131,731	75.2	18.5
Connecticut..................	347,589	90,676	117,998	76,961	61,954	73.9	17.8
Delaware	49,372	18,634	13,470	10,396	6,872	62.3	13.9
District of Columbia	50,141	9,642	6,734	7,701	26,064	80.8	52.0
Florida.........................	3,773,205	770,993	1,064,287	968,352	969,573	79.6	25.7
Georgia	546,665	194,898	138,200	108,632	104,935	64.3	19.2
Hawaii	77,881	6,875	25,901	27,175	17,930	91.2	23.0
Idaho...........................	115,826	36,180	33,709	31,262	14,675	68.8	12.7
Illinois	1,256,316	360,905	385,576	298,932	210,903	71.3	16.8
Indiana........................	247,337	74,430	79,467	54,829	38,611	69.9	15.6
Iowa............................	94,822	30,787	27,233	23,705	13,097	67.5	13.8
Kansas	177,719	56,166	51,450	45,017	25,086	68.4	14.1
Kentucky	84,517	25,124	24,454	18,249	16,690	70.3	19.7
Louisiana	145,024	38,258	47,126	34,386	25,254	73.6	17.4
Maine	13,580	1,367	3,380	3,694	5,139	89.9	37.8
Maryland......................	358,740	117,737	96,019	66,228	78,756	67.2	22.0
Massachusetts	486,528	130,369	144,111	110,814	101,234	73.2	20.8
Michigan	273,449	66,817	78,141	69,482	59,009	75.6	21.6
Minnesota	158,254	39,548	41,971	40,678	36,057	75.0	22.8
Mississippi...................	46,120	14,857	14,605	11,205	5,453	67.8	11.8
Missouri.......................	138,178	30,709	36,010	39,864	31,595	77.8	22.9
Montana.......................	22,102	3,388	5,602	7,189	5,923	84.7	26.8
Nebraska......................	106,780	39,253	30,335	22,848	14,344	63.2	13.4
Nevada.........................	512,330	168,839	164,850	124,168	54,473	67.0	10.6
New Hampshire.............	29,638	6,320	8,226	7,696	7,396	78.7	25.0
New Jersey	1,134,354	279,191	365,774	250,526	238,863	75.4	21.1
New Mexico	630,721	138,751	197,711	190,338	103,921	78.0	16.5
New York......................	2,359,532	645,991	677,529	538,927	497,085	72.6	21.1
North Carolina..............	513,662	190,987	128,902	106,515	87,258	62.8	17.0
North Dakota.................	15,357	2,444	5,659	4,593	2,661	84.1	17.3
Ohio	247,310	59,143	73,630	64,487	50,050	76.1	20.2
Oklahoma.....................	215,930	79,509	63,753	46,687	25,981	63.2	12.0
Oregon.........................	301,623	93,795	77,826	81,871	48,131	68.9	16.0
Pennsylvania.................	544,225	147,380	180,810	126,097	89,938	72.9	16.5
Rhode Island.................	97,435	28,307	31,756	23,387	13,985	70.9	14.4
South Carolina	157,206	53,773	39,975	35,132	28,326	65.8	18.0
South Dakota	16,720	3,211	4,524	4,714	4,271	80.8	25.5
Tennessee	188,951	69,768	49,533	34,661	34,989	63.1	18.5
Texas...........................	6,538,918	2,073,793	1,856,044	1,553,994	1,055,087	68.3	16.1
Utah	233,666	58,972	69,971	68,166	36,557	74.8	15.6
Vermont........................	5,638	642	1,054	2,098	1,844	88.6	32.7
Virginia........................	465,976	124,310	110,526	108,622	122,518	73.3	26.3
Washington...................	509,771	156,560	130,605	131,600	91,006	69.3	17.9
West Virginia.................	14,106	1,911	4,233	4,782	3,180	86.5	22.5
Wisconsin	210,204	61,184	62,325	53,967	32,728	70.9	15.6
Wyoming	30,212	5,655	11,594	9,545	3,418	81.3	11.3

[1]May be of any race.
... = Not available

Table B-3. Selected Characteristics of Children and the School-Age Population, by Region and State, 2019

(Number; dollars; percent.)

| Region or State | Population in households | | | Median family income for families with own children (in 2019 inflation-adjusted dollars) | Poverty status | |
	Children under 18 years old	6 to 17 years old	6 to 17 years old (percent)		Total children under 18 years old for whom poverty status is determined	Children under 18 years old in poverty (percent)
UNITED STATES	72,745,745	61,506,085	90.5	$78,001	71,590,037	16.7
Northeast Region	11,437,397	9,643,156	91.9	$90,776	11,256,040	15.3
Midwest Region	15,281,154	12,903,194	90.1	$78,549	15,020,036	15.5
South Region	28,376,674	24,011,409	90.1	$70,599	27,943,403	19.0
West Region.........................	17,650,520	14,948,326	90.4	$82,305	17,370,558	14.9
Alabama..............................	1,083,213	919,104	89.1	$62,404	1,068,092	21.3
Alaska	179,431	148,921	88.3	$83,674	175,667	13.0
Arizona................................	1,636,292	1,396,660	88.6	$70,158	1,612,007	19.1
Arkansas..............................	696,686	593,337	90.1	$57,294	685,202	22.1
California.............................	8,865,747	7,497,077	91.3	$85,332	8,723,097	15.6
Colorado..............................	1,252,814	1,063,904	91.3	$92,511	1,237,733	10.9
Connecticut..........................	725,502	621,839	93.8	$98,318	715,813	14.1
Delaware	203,258	171,859	91.0	$77,223	197,070	16.4
District of Columbia	127,038	100,752	94.9	$106,667	125,914	18.7
Florida.................................	4,220,331	3,569,089	91.0	$65,772	4,154,036	17.7
Georgia	2,498,168	2,135,332	91.1	$70,797	2,460,644	18.7
Hawaii.................................	300,059	248,427	90.0	$93,338	295,051	12.4
Idaho...................................	448,429	382,469	87.6	$72,539	441,454	13.2
Illinois.................................	2,807,337	2,374,681	91.8	$86,620	2,769,855	15.7
Indiana................................	1,562,432	1,319,521	88.4	$71,089	1,521,907	15.1
Iowa....................................	719,154	610,384	90.0	$77,936	709,251	12.9
Kansas................................	697,561	590,731	90.4	$75,707	685,834	14.7
Kentucky..............................	997,664	840,945	87.5	$65,141	975,947	21.7
Louisiana	1,083,189	918,439	90.4	$61,275	1,067,551	27.0
Maine..................................	245,139	210,650	89.8	$75,579	236,619	13.8
Maryland..............................	1,329,368	1,125,566	90.3	$103,580	1,306,322	12.0
Massachusetts......................	1,346,208	1,135,164	92.6	$111,761	1,327,816	11.6
Michigan..............................	2,137,075	1,807,192	90.4	$73,725	2,105,240	17.6
Minnesota............................	1,296,658	1,090,187	90.7	$97,217	1,277,035	11.2
Mississippi...........................	696,280	589,651	91.6	$53,104	684,941	28.1
Missouri...............................	1,366,575	1,149,676	89.6	$72,072	1,338,880	17.1
Montana...............................	224,592	190,062	87.9	$71,554	220,055	14.8
Nebraska..............................	473,014	395,160	89.8	$80,271	462,231	10.9
Nevada................................	689,095	585,950	87.9	$69,315	677,821	16.9
New Hampshire.....................	255,376	219,327	91.9	$102,407	249,589	7.0
New Jersey	1,930,842	1,634,223	93.9	$108,421	1,912,898	12.3
New Mexico	472,626	403,423	90.0	$53,394	464,914	24.9
New York.............................	3,997,775	3,341,059	92.1	$83,592	3,924,862	18.1
North Carolina......................	2,288,227	1,947,393	89.8	$68,891	2,252,616	19.5
North Dakota........................	176,182	145,570	85.6	$87,595	173,882	10.2
Ohio	2,569,038	2,168,011	89.6	$72,098	2,526,100	18.4
Oklahoma.............................	949,748	802,874	90.4	$62,212	934,343	19.9
Oregon	859,908	732,703	89.3	$81,203	842,121	13.0
Pennsylvania........................	2,620,256	2,213,550	89.5	$80,661	2,577,223	16.8
Rhode Island........................	203,394	172,161	90.5	$82,251	200,063	14.0
South Carolina	1,108,364	936,065	90.0	$66,670	1,087,106	19.7
South Dakota	214,036	179,080	88.1	$75,085	209,635	14.9
Tennessee	1,507,432	1,264,907	89.4	$66,371	1,478,299	19.7
Texas...................................	7,377,862	6,236,556	89.5	$72,065	7,293,514	19.1
Utah	926,646	786,519	90.4	$87,271	919,415	9.8
Vermont...............................	112,905	95,183	93.2	$82,202	111,157	10.2
Virginia................................	1,852,313	1,556,854	90.8	$94,463	1,824,325	13.4
Washington..........................	1,661,272	1,397,569	89.8	$91,467	1,630,792	12.0
West Virginia........................	357,533	302,686	87.5	$58,467	347,481	20.1
Wisconsin	1,262,092	1,073,001	90.2	$82,043	1,240,186	13.5
Wyoming	133,609	114,642	89.3	$80,008	130,431	11.6

- = Zero or rounds to zero.

Table B-3. Selected Characteristics of Children and the School-Age Population, by Region and State, 2019—*Continued*

(Number; dollars; percent.)

Region or State	Child's relationship to householder				Race and ethnicity of children under 18 years old		
	Own child (biological, step or adopted)	Grandchild	Other relatives	Foster child or other unrelated child	Total, children under 18 years old in households	White (percent)	Black or African American (percent)
UNITED STATES	87.0	8.5	2.5	2.0	72,745,745	66.6	13.9
Northeast Region	88.3	7.4	2.4	1.9	11,437,397	65.7	13.7
Midwest Region	89.5	6.7	1.7	2.1	15,281,154	74.3	12.1
South Region	85.7	9.8	2.7	1.9	28,376,674	64.5	20.8
West Region........................	86.3	8.7	3.1	1.9	17,650,520	64.0	4.7
Alabama...............................	83.6	11.8	2.9	1.7	1,083,213	62.5	29.4
Alaska	86.6	8.7	2.1	2.5	179,431	53.7	2.2
Arizona................................	84.6	10.2	3.2	1.9	1,636,292	72.9	5.4
Arkansas	85.4	10.5	2.0	2.1	696,686	70.5	17.1
California.............................	85.1	9.4	3.6	1.9	8,865,747	56.0	5.3
Colorado..............................	89.3	6.9	2.3	1.5	1,252,814	79.1	4.6
Connecticut..........................	89.8	6.2	2.3	1.7	725,502	66.3	12.8
Delaware..............................	85.4	8.6	2.5	3.4	203,258	58.0	25.4
District of Columbia	81.4	14.6	3.1	1.0	127,038	28.4	54.9
Florida.................................	85.0	9.9	3.1	2.0	4,220,331	66.0	20.2
Georgia	85.3	9.8	3.0	1.8	2,498,168	52.0	33.5
Hawaii	77.0	16.1	4.8	2.1	300,059	17.0	1.7
Idaho...................................	88.6	7.2	2.3	1.8	448,429	86.1	1.1
Illinois.................................	89.0	7.4	2.0	1.6	2,807,337	66.1	14.9
Indiana................................	87.6	7.4	2.0	3.0	1,562,432	77.3	11.2
Iowa....................................	92.0	4.8	1.5	1.7	719,154	85.6	5.7
Kansas	90.4	5.8	1.6	2.2	697,561	78.8	6.0
Kentucky	84.7	9.8	2.8	2.7	997,664	82.1	8.8
Louisiana	84.3	11.6	2.4	1.7	1,083,189	55.7	36.3
Maine..................................	88.9	6.3	0.9	4.0	245,139	90.4	3.0
Maryland..............................	86.3	8.2	3.4	2.1	1,329,368	48.2	31.1
Massachusetts	89.8	6.7	1.8	1.7	1,346,208	69.5	9.8
Michigan..............................	89.4	7.0	1.7	1.9	2,137,075	72.4	15.7
Minnesota............................	92.0	4.4	1.7	1.9	1,296,658	73.3	9.5
Mississippi...........................	80.6	15.0	2.5	1.9	696,280	51.4	42.0
Missouri..............................	87.7	8.4	1.4	2.6	1,366,575	76.5	13.2
Montana...............................	88.0	7.5	2.1	2.4	224,592	81.0	1.4
Nebraska..............................	90.6	5.3	1.3	2.8	473,014	80.8	6.0
Nevada................................	85.6	8.7	3.7	2.0	689,095	57.4	10.8
New Hampshire.....................	87.8	8.2	1.5	2.4	255,376	88.8	2.0
New Jersey	89.3	7.0	2.5	1.2	1,930,842	61.7	13.9
New Mexico	83.6	11.0	3.5	1.8	472,626	69.6	2.5
New York..............................	86.9	8.0	2.9	2.2	3,997,775	58.0	17.0
North Carolina......................	87.7	8.1	2.3	1.9	2,288,227	61.3	22.9
North Dakota........................	93.1	5.0	0.5	1.5	176,182	79.9	3.1
Ohio	88.5	7.5	1.8	2.1	2,569,038	74.9	14.6
Oklahoma............................	86.5	9.1	2.4	2.0	949,748	64.5	7.7
Oregon................................	88.1	6.8	2.5	2.5	859,908	78.1	2.0
Pennsylvania........................	88.1	7.8	2.1	2.0	2,620,256	72.4	13.9
Rhode Island........................	89.9	7.2	1.1	1.8	203,394	68.8	8.7
South Carolina	84.1	11.4	2.2	2.3	1,108,364	59.4	28.5
South Dakota	88.2	7.5	1.8	2.5	214,036	76.2	3.1
Tennessee	85.1	10.0	2.6	2.3	1,507,432	71.3	18.5
Texas..................................	86.5	9.4	2.7	1.4	7,377,862	71.3	12.1
Utah	91.7	5.2	1.8	1.2	926,646	86.0	1.3
Vermont...............................	89.8	6.3	1.9	2.0	112,905	91.3	1.9
Virginia................................	87.7	8.1	2.2	2.0	1,852,313	61.3	20.4
Washington..........................	89.5	6.4	1.8	2.2	1,661,272	67.1	4.5
West Virginia........................	82.7	11.6	2.3	3.5	357,533	90.7	3.1
Wisconsin	91.6	4.9	1.4	2.1	1,262,092	77.6	8.7
Wyoming	90.0	5.7	1.3	3.0	133,609	86.8	1.7

- = Zero or rounds to zero.

Table B-3. Selected Characteristics of Children and the School-Age Population, by Region and State, 2019—*Continued*

(Number; dollars; percent.)

Region or State	Race and ethnicity of children under 18 years old					
	Hispanic or Latino origin (may be of any race) (percent)	Asian (percent)	Native Hawaiian and Other Pacific Islander (percent)	American Indian, Alaska Native (percent)	Some other race (percent)	Two or more races (percent)
UNITED STATES	25.5	4.8	0.2	1.0	6.5	6.9
Northeast Region	20.9	6.3	-	0.3	7.5	6.5
Midwest Region	12.4	3.2	0.1	0.8	3.3	6.2
South Region	24.9	3.2	0.1	0.7	4.7	5.9
West Region..........................	40.9	7.9	0.6	2.1	11.4	9.4
Alabama...............................	8.2	1.3	0.1	0.4	2.7	3.7
Alaska	9.6	4.9	1.7	20.9	2.1	14.6
Arizona.................................	44.5	2.7	0.2	5.8	5.5	7.5
Arkansas...............................	12.2	1.6	0.9	0.4	3.7	5.8
California..............................	52.1	11.5	0.4	0.8	16.8	9.3
Colorado	31.4	2.8	0.1	1.0	4.5	8.0
Connecticut..........................	25.3	4.6	0.1	0.4	7.8	8.0
Delaware	16.5	3.8	-	0.5	4.5	7.8
District of Columbia	17.0	1.8	-	0.1	9.0	5.8
Florida..................................	32.1	2.5	0.1	0.3	4.4	6.6
Georgia	14.9	3.8	0.1	0.4	4.4	5.8
Hawaii..................................	18.5	25.9	13.4	0.5	1.7	39.9
Idaho....................................	18.3	1.2	0.2	1.3	4.2	5.9
Illinois..................................	24.8	4.9	-	0.3	7.9	5.9
Indiana.................................	11.4	2.6	0.1	0.2	3.0	5.5
Iowa.....................................	10.2	2.4	0.1	0.4	1.4	4.5
Kansas	18.6	2.8	0.1	0.6	4.4	7.3
Kentucky	6.3	1.9	0.1	0.2	1.4	5.5
Louisiana	7.4	1.8	0.1	0.7	1.7	3.7
Maine	2.6	0.9	-	0.8	0.7	4.2
Maryland...............................	16.4	5.7	-	0.3	7.8	6.9
Massachusetts......................	19.2	6.6	-	0.2	5.9	7.9
Michigan	8.5	3.1	-	0.6	1.7	6.5
Minnesota.............................	9.0	5.8	-	1.3	2.7	7.3
Mississippi...........................	4.5	1.1	-	0.6	1.7	3.2
Missouri...............................	6.8	1.7	0.3	0.4	1.8	6.1
Montana...............................	5.3	0.5	-	10.3	0.5	6.3
Nebraska..............................	17.9	2.3	0.1	1.4	3.5	5.9
Nevada.................................	41.4	6.3	0.8	1.5	14.1	9.0
New Hampshire......................	6.7	2.5	0.1	0.2	1.3	5.1
New Jersey	27.8	9.1	-	0.2	8.7	6.4
New Mexico	60.6	1.4	-	11.3	9.0	6.2
New York...............................	25.0	7.7	-	0.4	10.7	6.2
North Carolina.......................	16.7	2.9	0.1	1.3	5.3	6.2
North Dakota.........................	5.6	0.8	0.4	8.1	0.7	6.9
Ohio	6.4	2.2	-	0.2	1.4	6.6
Oklahoma.............................	17.7	2.0	0.2	9.6	3.2	12.9
Oregon	22.2	3.9	0.4	1.4	5.2	9.1
Pennsylvania.........................	12.7	3.5	0.1	0.3	3.9	6.1
Rhode Island.........................	26.4	3.1	-	0.1	9.4	9.8
South Carolina	9.5	1.8	0.3	0.3	3.7	6.0
South Dakota	5.9	1.0	0.3	13.0	0.8	5.7
Tennessee	10.2	1.7	0.1	0.3	2.9	5.2
Texas....................................	49.5	4.3	0.1	0.4	6.7	5.1
Utah	18.0	1.3	1.0	1.0	3.8	5.5
Vermont................................	2.8	1.2	-	0.4	0.4	4.9
Virginia.................................	14.1	6.1	-	0.3	4.1	7.8
Washington...........................	21.6	7.1	0.7	1.6	7.3	11.6
West Virginia.........................	2.6	0.6	-	0.2	0.8	4.5
Wisconsin	12.0	3.3	0.1	1.2	3.2	5.8
Wyoming	14.6	0.3	0.2	2.9	2.0	6.2

- = Zero or rounds to zero.

Table B-4. Percentage Distribution of Public Traditional and Charter Schools, by School Locale and State, Fall 2017

(Number; percent.)

State	Traditional schools				Charter schools			
	City	Suburban	Town	Rural	City	Suburban	Town	Rural
UNITED STATES	24.9	32.1	13.9	29.1	56.1	26.3	6.1	11.5
Alabama..	22.7	17.5	14.6	45.1	100.0	-	-	-
Alaska..	18.5	2.5	16.5	62.5	34.5	10.3	41.4	13.8
Arizona...	41.3	23.9	15.9	18.8	58.7	24.8	7.4	9.2
Arkansas.......................................	20.6	10.8	21.6	47.0	48.8	17.1	14.6	19.5
California......................................	37.9	41.7	8.8	11.7	52.6	29.0	7.0	11.4
Colorado.......................................	31.8	30.7	12.4	25.1	51.6	29.2	4.8	14.4
Connecticut...................................	28.0	53.5	3.5	15.0	83.3	8.3	8.3	-
Delaware.......................................	13.8	52.7	16.7	16.7	41.7	41.7	4.2	12.5
District of Columbia	99.1	-	-	0.9	100.0	-	-	-
Florida..	27.1	51.4	7.9	13.6	29.2	56.9	2.4	11.5
Georgia...	17.4	37.6	12.1	32.9	37.6	40.9	7.5	14.0
Hawaii..	24.6	39.5	25.0	10.9	16.7	19.4	16.7	47.2
Idaho..	17.7	17.9	23.6	40.8	18.6	30.5	27.1	23.7
Illinois..	22.8	42.7	13.6	20.8	93.7	5.6	-	0.7
Indiana...	25.3	21.6	16.5	36.6	75.8	15.2	3.0	6.1
Iowa...	17.8	8.4	23.7	50.0	33.3	-	33.3	33.3
Kansas..	19.2	11.5	23.7	45.7	10.0	-	20.0	70.0
Kentucky.......................................	18.7	13.9	25.6	41.7	NA	NA	NA	NA
Louisiana	21.9	26.2	17.4	34.5	76.7	10.7	2.7	10.0
Maine..	8.3	11.6	13.9	66.2	27.3	-	27.3	45.5
Maryland.......................................	21.4	57.9	4.0	16.7	68.0	30.0	-	2.0
Massachusetts...............................	17.2	68.9	2.2	11.6	46.3	48.8	-	5.0
Michigan.......................................	19.3	37.2	14.9	28.7	49.5	32.5	3.6	14.5
Minnesota.....................................	17.4	28.5	22.7	31.5	47.5	24.9	8.6	19.0
Mississippi....................................	11.0	8.9	30.5	49.7	100.0	-	-	-
Missouri..	15.0	23.5	19.8	41.7	100.0	-	-	-
Montana..	8.3	1.3	16.1	74.3	NA	NA	NA	NA
Nebraska.......................................	23.5	7.9	18.9	49.8	NA	NA	NA	NA
Nevada..	40.9	27.8	12.3	19.1	72.2	19.4	4.2	4.2
New Hampshire..............................	8.9	26.8	13.7	50.5	29.0	32.3	19.4	19.4
New Jersey	8.0	79.9	2.6	9.4	49.4	46.1	1.1	3.4
New Mexico...................................	23.1	10.8	27.6	38.5	54.6	11.3	18.6	15.5
New York.......................................	41.4	33.5	8.0	17.1	95.7	3.9	-	0.4
North Carolina...............................	25.7	19.3	12.9	42.1	42.2	22.0	9.2	26.6
North Dakota.................................	13.2	5.2	15.3	66.3	NA	NA	NA	NA
Ohio..	16.7	38.8	14.5	30.0	76.5	16.5	5.6	1.5
Oklahoma......................................	13.9	12.4	21.8	52.0	67.2	10.3	5.2	17.2
Oregon..	28.3	20.9	24.9	25.8	18.9	20.5	18.1	42.5
Pennsylvania.................................	16.4	47.2	10.5	25.9	66.5	26.3	2.2	5.0
Rhode Island.................................	22.7	65.0	-	12.2	41.9	48.4	-	9.7
South Carolina	17.1	28.5	12.4	41.9	30.0	35.7	10.0	24.3
South Dakota	9.5	0.9	16.2	73.5	NA	NA	NA	NA
Tennessee.....................................	29.1	16.6	17.2	37.1	91.8	6.4	-	1.8
Texas..	35.2	25.5	13.2	26.0	67.9	20.8	3.4	7.9
Utah..	17.2	50.3	13.8	18.7	18.3	61.1	6.9	13.7
Vermont..	4.8	6.1	19.3	69.8	NA	NA	NA	NA
Virginia...	23.8	36.6	8.7	30.9	62.5	-	-	37.5
Washington...................................	30.4	34.0	14.2	21.4	90.0	10.0	-	-
West Virginia.................................	12.3	18.6	19.6	49.5	NA	NA	NA	NA
Wisconsin......................................	22.8	21.3	19.5	36.4	37.8	15.9	18.9	27.5
Wyoming	14.6	1.4	32.7	51.4	40.0	-	20.0	40.0

- = Zero or rounds to zero.
NA = Not applicable; no charter schools in state.

Table B-5. Population 3 Years and Over Enrolled in Public or Private School, by Selected Grade Levels and Region or State, 2019

(Number; percent.)

Region or State	Total enrolled population	Nursery school			Kindergarten		
		Total enrolled	Percent in public school	Percent in private school	Total enrolled	Percent in public school	Percent in private school
UNITED STATES	80,465,620	5,044,389	59.7	40.3	4,011,764	87.6	12.4
Northeast Region..............................	13,228,363	860,223	56.7	43.3	635,168	86.1	13.9
Midwest Region.................................	16,589,013	1,080,657	63.3	36.7	841,504	86.4	13.6
South Region....................................	30,869,765	1,924,186	60.1	39.9	1,549,252	88.0	12.0
West Region......................................	19,778,479	1,179,323	58.0	42.0	985,840	89.1	10.9
Alabama...	1,164,195	65,500	64.4	35.6	60,362	86.7	13.3
Alaska..	180,074	11,471	63.1	36.9	11,916	92.6	7.4
Arizona..	1,773,809	91,621	65.4	34.6	85,086	89.3	10.7
Arkansas..	738,272	50,302	72.6	27.4	38,926	90.2	9.8
California...	10,305,759	604,513	58.5	41.5	501,476	89.9	10.1
Colorado..	1,406,414	94,038	61.0	39.0	69,622	93.0	7.0
Connecticut......................................	882,104	52,328	57.3	42.7	42,818	94.8	5.2
Delaware..	227,551	14,393	55.9	44.1	10,699	86.6	13.4
District of Columbia	169,418	17,354	75.5	24.5	9,221	90.8	9.2
Florida...	4,795,224	314,700	54.4	45.6	221,192	84.8	15.2
Georgia..	2,771,807	181,271	62.8	37.2	142,208	90.2	9.8
Hawaii..	317,419	24,827	35.4	64.6	16,663	80.9	19.1
Idaho...	457,955	23,531	48.5	51.5	25,700	86.6	13.4
Illinois...	3,123,418	220,385	60.0	40.0	143,711	84.5	15.5
Indiana..	1,646,376	97,833	61.7	38.3	79,674	86.8	13.2
Iowa..	783,468	54,923	72.6	27.4	43,862	89.6	10.4
Kansas...	753,423	51,104	67.4	32.6	39,216	86.8	13.2
Kentucky..	1,025,269	63,759	65.4	34.6	51,113	87.9	12.1
Louisiana...	1,149,360	80,394	64.6	35.4	62,180	81.9	18.1
Maine...	275,036	16,400	61.0	39.0	12,779	86.7	13.3
Maryland..	1,509,619	100,085	50.9	49.1	67,143	84.1	15.9
Massachusetts..................................	1,691,491	104,969	50.6	49.4	75,037	89.6	10.4
Michigan..	2,387,441	144,796	66.2	33.8	118,974	87.4	12.6
Minnesota..	1,386,106	98,330	67.3	32.7	70,167	89.9	10.1
Mississippi.......................................	754,558	52,404	63.6	36.4	38,624	86.4	13.6
Missouri...	1,444,801	96,538	58.6	41.4	74,263	85.8	14.2
Montana...	242,758	12,710	54.4	45.6	12,297	89.1	10.9
Nebraska..	507,156	33,488	61.8	38.2	26,660	81.0	19.0
Nevada...	707,075	37,463	67.2	32.8	34,608	92.3	7.7
New Hampshire.................................	298,926	20,615	49.7	50.3	13,508	90.6	9.4
New Jersey	2,192,217	166,380	58.0	42.0	117,651	87.2	12.8
New Mexico......................................	516,495	27,671	68.6	31.4	24,362	88.4	11.6
New York..	4,594,259	293,750	61.2	38.8	220,364	82.7	17.3
North Carolina..................................	2,556,961	152,450	51.8	48.2	120,219	88.8	11.2
North Dakota....................................	187,040	9,991	73.2	26.8	8,251	94.8	5.2
Ohio...	2,771,284	184,171	59.9	40.1	141,535	84.6	15.4
Oklahoma...	999,896	64,349	76.1	23.9	55,802	90.0	10.0
Oregon...	947,627	58,703	50.0	50.0	48,408	84.1	15.9
Pennsylvania....................................	2,896,469	182,378	51.3	48.7	135,543	84.5	15.5
Rhode Island....................................	253,795	14,013	57.7	42.3	11,170	92.7	7.3
South Carolina	1,180,396	59,581	59.6	40.4	62,015	86.0	14.0
South Dakota	214,461	15,523	64.6	35.4	13,452	92.6	7.4
Tennessee..	1,572,331	88,895	58.0	42.0	82,161	86.6	13.4
Texas...	7,763,174	466,305	64.3	35.7	414,867	90.7	9.3
Utah..	1,012,792	62,386	58.4	41.6	53,254	89.0	11.0
Vermont..	144,066	9,390	71.3	28.7	6,298	92.1	7.9
Virginia..	2,118,036	132,600	47.8	52.2	93,308	85.7	14.3
Washington.......................................	1,764,122	122,229	51.4	48.6	95,733	85.1	14.9
West Virginia....................................	373,698	19,844	78.8	21.2	19,212	96.7	3.3
Wisconsin...	1,384,039	73,575	68.4	31.6	81,739	86.6	13.4
Wyoming..	146,180	8,160	71.8	28.2	6,715	91.2	8.8

Table B-5. Population 3 Years and Over Enrolled in Public or Private School, by Selected Grade Levels and Region or State, 2019—*Continued*

(Number; percent.)

Region or State	Elementary: grades 1-4			Elementary: grades 5-8			High school: grades 9-12		
	Total enrolled	Percent in public school	Percent in private school	Total enrolled	Percent in public school	Percent in private school	Total enrolled	Percent in public school	Percent in private school
UNITED STATES	15,728,625	89.4	10.6	16,918,899	89.2	10.8	16,932,635	89.8	10.2
Northeast Region.............................	2,441,779	88.0	12.0	2,653,119	88.0	12.0	2,746,045	86.8	13.2
Midwest Region...............................	3,293,995	87.8	12.2	3,522,079	88.2	11.8	3,535,649	90.0	10.0
South Region...................................	6,191,696	89.7	10.3	6,672,733	89.0	11.0	6,512,212	89.8	10.2
West Region.....................................	3,801,155	91.2	8.8	4,070,968	91.4	8.6	4,138,729	91.8	8.2
Alabama...	236,267	89.9	10.1	252,866	87.6	12.4	248,164	86.9	13.1
Alaska..	40,280	91.0	9.0	37,128	92.8	7.2	37,219	91.1	8.9
Arizona..	354,299	90.9	9.1	390,888	91.9	8.1	386,787	92.8	7.2
Arkansas..	157,360	90.5	9.5	155,462	92.7	7.3	159,614	92.9	7.1
California...	1,895,898	91.9	8.1	2,026,836	91.5	8.5	2,133,603	91.6	8.4
Colorado..	272,713	92.0	8.0	294,975	91.3	8.7	290,150	91.4	8.6
Connecticut......................................	159,068	91.5	8.5	167,795	90.7	9.3	194,410	88.8	11.2
Delaware..	44,633	87.6	12.4	45,858	86.6	13.4	49,508	89.9	10.1
District of Columbia.........................	28,171	89.1	10.9	24,894	84.1	15.9	19,289	83.5	16.5
Florida...	912,157	86.1	13.9	1,006,115	85.8	14.2	993,773	88.1	11.9
Georgia..	551,927	91.9	8.1	592,959	89.1	10.9	584,349	90.1	9.9
Hawaii..	62,403	82.6	17.4	63,415	81.2	18.8	64,938	76.7	23.3
Idaho..	93,130	86.6	13.4	103,563	91.1	8.9	103,810	90.8	9.2
Illinois...	603,415	89.1	10.9	657,517	88.4	11.6	665,932	90.7	9.3
Indiana...	331,380	87.4	12.6	370,786	87.6	12.4	357,591	90.2	9.8
Iowa...	159,087	89.5	10.5	161,203	91.2	8.8	158,248	92.1	7.9
Kansas...	154,320	88.8	11.2	161,322	90.1	9.9	157,106	90.1	9.9
Kentucky..	202,152	89.4	10.6	234,784	87.4	12.6	219,823	87.0	13.0
Louisiana...	241,830	83.0	17.0	250,964	83.2	16.8	242,881	83.8	16.2
Maine...	52,633	89.2	10.8	56,952	90.7	9.3	60,658	86.3	13.7
Maryland..	288,002	87.5	12.5	312,651	85.4	14.6	305,148	85.1	14.9
Massachusetts..................................	286,604	92.5	7.5	312,906	91.0	9.0	336,422	88.4	11.6
Michigan..	454,261	89.0	11.0	487,248	89.5	10.5	522,075	90.8	9.2
Minnesota..	286,475	89.0	11.0	294,778	90.5	9.5	297,824	92.8	7.2
Mississippi.......................................	158,750	90.2	9.8	164,833	86.9	13.1	155,686	86.8	13.2
Missouri...	299,032	86.6	13.4	313,618	86.6	13.4	307,608	88.4	11.6
Montana...	50,610	86.9	13.1	50,974	89.0	11.0	52,301	89.4	10.6
Nebraska..	102,276	84.2	15.8	106,058	86.9	13.1	103,156	87.7	12.3
Nevada...	148,317	91.6	8.4	161,318	93.1	6.9	158,269	94.1	5.9
New Hampshire.................................	52,642	91.5	8.5	62,669	90.5	9.5	63,598	89.1	10.9
New Jersey	417,139	89.8	10.2	452,205	90.2	9.8	455,654	87.7	12.3
New Mexico......................................	105,805	93.0	7.0	118,347	91.9	8.1	106,957	93.3	6.7
New York..	846,114	85.7	14.3	916,532	85.7	14.3	944,207	85.2	14.8
North Carolina..................................	494,853	89.3	10.7	543,387	87.9	12.1	540,099	90.9	9.1
North Dakota....................................	37,767	90.0	10.0	39,491	91.9	8.1	35,207	91.1	8.9
Ohio...	550,585	86.4	13.6	585,566	86.6	13.4	589,542	87.4	12.6
Oklahoma...	214,627	90.3	9.7	223,196	90.9	9.1	209,546	89.7	10.3
Oregon...	186,728	88.9	11.1	199,267	90.9	9.1	194,947	90.7	9.3
Pennsylvania....................................	562,342	86.2	13.8	609,802	86.8	13.2	614,072	86.5	13.5
Rhode Island....................................	40,148	89.6	10.4	49,617	89.9	10.1	48,449	89.9	10.1
South Carolina	248,733	90.0	10.0	264,830	88.9	11.1	253,806	91.1	8.9
South Dakota	45,213	90.0	10.0	49,641	88.2	11.8	43,382	88.6	11.4
Tennessee..	321,487	86.0	14.0	356,534	86.7	13.3	342,101	86.1	13.9
Texas...	1,605,125	92.9	7.1	1,735,884	93.0	7.0	1,668,907	93.4	6.6
Utah...	206,069	92.4	7.6	215,431	94.0	6.0	210,717	94.0	6.0
Vermont..	25,089	93.1	6.9	24,641	94.9	5.1	28,575	89.2	10.8
Virginia..	409,466	89.9	10.1	425,920	89.3	10.7	435,600	89.6	10.4
Washington.......................................	351,490	89.7	10.3	377,519	89.7	10.3	370,024	92.9	7.1
West Virginia....................................	76,156	92.7	7.3	81,596	90.9	9.1	83,918	91.8	8.2
Wisconsin...	270,184	85.4	14.6	294,851	85.7	14.3	297,978	90.4	9.6
Wyoming...	33,413	92.9	7.1	31,307	92.8	7.2	29,007	92.4	7.6

Table B-5. Population 3 Years and Over Enrolled in Public or Private School, by Selected Grade Levels and Region or State, 2019—*Continued*

(Number; percent.)

Region or State	College, undergraduate			Graduate, professional school		
	Total enrolled	Percent in public school	Percent in private school	Total enrolled	Percent in public school	Percent in private school
UNITED STATES	17,507,427	78.9	21.1	4,321,881	60.0	40.0
Northeast Region	3,031,096	63.1	36.9	860,933	42.1	57.9
Midwest Region	3,448,619	78.8	21.2	866,510	64.7	35.3
South Region	6,436,449	82.3	17.7	1,583,237	65.7	34.3
West Region	4,591,263	84.7	15.3	1,011,201	62.4	37.6
Alabama	245,959	87.5	12.5	55,077	78.1	21.9
Alaska	32,585	83.1	16.9	9,475	75.7	24.3
Arizona	379,433	86.6	13.4	85,695	66.5	33.5
Arkansas	144,756	82.6	17.4	31,852	81.2	18.8
California	2,602,279	85.6	14.4	541,154	56.9	43.1
Colorado	300,591	86.9	13.1	84,325	68.0	32.0
Connecticut	208,462	68.5	31.5	57,223	50.7	49.3
Delaware	49,071	84.2	15.8	13,389	64.6	35.4
District of Columbia	46,376	25.2	74.8	24,113	30.4	69.6
Florida	1,092,451	80.2	19.8	254,836	60.6	39.4
Georgia	570,395	82.7	17.3	148,698	65.8	34.2
Hawaii	68,224	80.0	20.0	16,949	63.0	37.0
Idaho	90,843	73.7	26.3	17,378	70.8	29.2
Illinois	640,069	72.6	27.4	192,389	51.0	49.0
Indiana	336,963	78.6	21.4	72,149	70.7	29.3
Iowa	167,931	77.0	23.0	38,214	60.9	39.1
Kansas	154,872	85.0	15.0	35,483	78.6	21.4
Kentucky	204,507	82.3	17.7	49,131	70.1	29.9
Louisiana	222,438	84.2	15.8	48,673	66.6	33.4
Maine	62,332	69.8	30.2	13,282	61.2	38.8
Maryland	321,720	81.6	18.4	114,870	57.1	42.9
Massachusetts	430,747	52.5	47.5	144,806	30.4	69.6
Michigan	535,091	85.7	14.3	124,996	77.9	22.1
Minnesota	266,465	78.0	22.0	72,067	63.6	36.4
Mississippi	154,486	89.1	10.9	29,775	71.1	28.9
Missouri	273,925	74.0	26.0	79,817	59.4	40.6
Montana	50,132	90.8	9.2	13,734	77.1	22.9
Nebraska	104,516	80.8	19.2	31,002	68.5	31.5
Nevada	134,114	81.6	18.4	32,986	66.2	33.8
New Hampshire	69,266	65.5	34.5	16,628	46.7	53.3
New Jersey	451,251	73.2	26.8	131,937	48.9	51.1
New Mexico	105,715	88.9	11.1	27,638	83.7	16.3
New York	1,071,424	62.6	37.4	301,868	40.1	59.9
North Carolina	578,192	80.9	19.1	127,761	63.5	36.5
North Dakota	46,309	91.5	8.5	10,024	75.9	24.1
Ohio	581,547	76.9	23.1	138,338	68.0	32.0
Oklahoma	192,580	86.9	13.1	39,796	75.2	24.8
Oregon	209,253	82.8	17.2	50,321	65.2	34.8
Pennsylvania	621,464	61.5	38.5	170,868	44.6	55.4
Rhode Island	74,656	57.8	42.2	15,742	44.5	55.5
South Carolina	236,545	80.0	20.0	54,886	67.8	32.2
South Dakota	39,996	86.5	13.5	7,254	70.9	29.1
Tennessee	303,160	76.9	23.1	77,993	61.3	38.7
Texas	1,522,926	85.7	14.3	349,160	71.9	28.1
Utah	223,677	73.6	26.4	41,258	70.5	29.5
Vermont	41,494	70.3	29.7	8,579	59.0	41.0
Virginia	476,758	79.6	20.4	144,384	59.6	40.4
Washington	364,428	84.9	15.1	82,699	66.4	33.6
West Virginia	74,129	87.0	13.0	18,843	81.7	18.3
Wisconsin	300,935	82.4	17.6	64,777	65.2	34.8
Wyoming	29,989	92.3	7.7	7,589	79.0	21.0

Table B-6. Number of Operating Public Schools and Districts, Student Membership, Teachers, and Pupil/Teacher Ratio, by State, 2018–2019

(Number; percent.)

Region or state	Number of operating schools	Number of operating school districts	State level		
			Student membership	Number of teachers	Pupil/Teacher ratio
UNITED STATES	98,780	19,289	50,694,061	3,169,762	16.0
Alabama...	1,528	177	739,716	42,114	17.6
Alaska...	507	54	130963	7,657	17.1
Arizona..	2,344	704	1,141,511	48,510	23.5
Arkansas..	1,079	294	495,291	38,019	13.0
California..	10,434	2,170	6,272,734	271,805	23.1
Colorado..	1915	270	911,536	53,147	17.2
Connecticut.......................................	1022	204	526,634	42,828	12.3
Delaware..	225	46	138405	9,624	14.4
District of Columbia	228	68	88493	7,312	12.1
Florida...	4,181	76	2,846,444	164,399	17.3
Georgia	2309	232	1,767,202	117,159	15.1
Hawaii...	292	1	181,278	12,132	14.9
Idaho..	746	168	310522	16,745	18.5
Illinois...	4345	1056	1982327	132,423	15.0
Indiana..	1916	431	1,055,706	61,155	17.3
Iowa...	1316	339	514,833	35,618	14.5
Kansas..	1314	311	497,733	36,724	13.6
Kentucky..	1534	186	677,821	41,827	16.2
Louisiana...	1383	204	711,783	38,913	18.3
Maine..	599	276	180,461	15,034	12.0
Maryland..	1418	25	896827	60,699	14.8
Massachusetts....................................	1852	432	962297	73,868	13.0
Michigan..	3728	893	1,504,194	85,015	17.7
Minnesota...	2540	564	889,304	57,698	15.4
Mississippi..	1054	155	471,298	31,963	14.7
Missouri...	2427	564	913,441	68,498	13.3
Montana...	823	487	148844	10,575	14.1
Nebraska..	1081	279	326,392	23,912	13.6
Nevada..	722	21	492640	23,240	21.2
New Hampshire...................................	494	308	178,515	14,644	12.2
New Jersey	2573	688	1400069	116,189	12.0
New Mexico	882	146	333537	21,139	15.8
New York..	4796	1024	2700833	212,157	12.7
North Carolina....................................	2657	330	1,552,497	100,220	15.5
North Dakota.....................................	523	221	113845	9,470	12.0
Ohio...	3566	1,043	1,695,762	101,739	16.7
Oklahoma...	1807	597	698,891	42,448	16.5
Oregon..	1256	222	609507	30,152	20.2
Pennsylvania......................................	2969	789	1,730,757	123,350	14.0
Rhode Island......................................	320	64	143,436	10,749	13.3
South Carolina	1265	102	780,882	52,730	14.8
South Dakota.....................................	697	166	138,975	9,865	14.1
Tennessee...	1,862	147	1007624	64,116	15.7
Texas..	8979	1226	5433471	359,576	15.1
Utah...	1061	161	677,031	29,753	22.8
Vermont...	312	235	87074	8,317	10.5
Virginia..	2115	215	1,289,367	86,974	14.8
Washington.......................................	2445	336	1,123,736	61,837	18.2
West Virginia......................................	721	57	267906	18,912	14.2
Wisconsin...	2255	463	859333	59,484	14.4
Wyoming	363	62	94,313	7,327	12.9

Table B-7. Participation in Public School Services, by State

(Number; percent.)

State	Enrollment in public elementary and secondary schools (2017–18)	Percent of students eligible for free or reduced-price lunch (2017–18)	Percent of students with IEP (2018–19)	Percent English language learner students (Fall 2017)	Percent homeless students (2016–17)
UNITED STATES	50,044,716	52.6	14.1	10.1	2.7
Alabama...................................	742,437	56.0	12.7	3.5	2.1
Alaska.....................................	132,820	54.3	14.6	12.1	3.0
Arizona....................................	977,571	55.1	13.0	8.1	2.3
Arkansas..................................	495,773	63.6	15.1	8.3	2.7
California..................................	6,195,446	60.1	12.5	19.2	4.2
Colorado	910,050	41.8	11.5	11.9	2.3
Connecticut...............................	519,710	36.3	15.7	7.4	0.8
Delaware	136,041	35.0	17.8	9.1	2.2
District of Columbia	86,360	76.4	16.2	10.9	7.5
Florida.....................................	2,832,766	57.3	14.2	10.1	2.7
Georgia....................................	1,768,562	60.9	12.4	6.6	2.2
Hawaii.....................................	180,837	47.1	10.8	8.2	1.6
Idaho.......................................	301,118	44.0	11.3	6.0	2.5
Illinois.....................................	1,992,111	49.4	14.9	11.3	2.5
Indiana....................................	1,053,841	49.9	16.9	5.4	1.8
Iowa..	502,877	40.1	13.3	6.1	1.3
Kansas....................................	490,629	47.6	15.3	10.3	1.9
Kentucky..................................	680,860	59.7	15.6	3.9	3.9
Louisiana.................................	715,096	54.1	12.2	3.6	4.3
Maine......................................	175,304	44.8	19.2	3.3	1.4
Maryland..................................	893,679	46.5	12.3	9.2	1.9
Massachusetts...........................	953,645	39.9	18.3	10.0	2.2
Michigan..................................	1,471,209	50.3	13.3	6.6	2.4
Minnesota................................	884,397	37.2	15.9	8.5	2.0
Mississippi...............................	478,124	74.5	14.7	2.7	2.1
Missouri...................................	910,283	52.6	14.5	3.8	3.7
Montana...................................	146,550	44.3	12.9	2.2	2.5
Nebraska..................................	323,728	45.9	16.0	7.6	1.1
Nevada....................................	481,005	58.8	12.2	17.1	3.5
New Hampshire..........................	178,306	26.5	16.8	2.8	2.2
New Jersey	1,370,584	37.9	17.2	5.9	0.8
New Mexico...............................	333,879	73.6	16.3	16.3	3.5
New York..................................	2,697,327	54.8	19.5	9.2	5.4
North Carolina...........................	1,553,494	55.9	13.0	6.9	1.9
North Dakota.............................	109,688	30.1	14.3	3.4	2.0
Ohio..	1,701,472	46.0	16.0	3.2	1.8
Oklahoma.................................	694,932	62.3	16.5	8.0	3.9
Oregon.....................................	553,257	49.3	14.6	8.8	4.0
Pennsylvania.............................	1,601,823	49.6	19.1	3.6	1.5
Rhode Island.............................	141,448	46.8	16.9	9.0	0.9
South Carolina...........................	777,254	66.2	13.7	6.1	1.5
South Dakota	137,251	37.5	15.6	4.1	1.5
Tennessee................................	994,568	58.8	13.0	4.6	1.7
Texas......................................	5,400,720	58.7	9.8	18.0	2.1
Utah..	666,841	34.1	12.8	7.1	2.3
Vermont...................................	84,334	38.1	17.1	2.2	1.2
Virginia....................................	1,278,044	43.8	13.6	9.1	1.6
Washington...............................	1,110,163	43.0	13.2	11.7	3.7
West Virginia.............................	272,253	55.6	17.5	0.8	3.3
Wisconsin.................................	860,067	37.1	14.1	6.2	2.2
Wyoming..................................	94,182	37.1	16.5	3.0	2.0

Table B-8. Number of Private Schools, Students, Teachers, High School Graduates, and Percent Change in Enrollment, by State, Fall 2017

State	Private schools				
	Number of private schools, Fall 2017	Total teachers, Fall 2017	High school graduates, 2016–2017	Enrollment in Pre-K to 12th grade, Fall 2017	Enrollment percent change, Fall 2007 to Fall 2017
UNITED STATES	32,460	482,320	348,230	5,719,990	-3.2
Alabama.................................	370	5,890	4,580	70,840	-15.5
Alaska	50	410	*	4,470	-10.4
Arizona...................................	330	4,300	3,570	56,800	-12.5
Arkansas.................................	230	2,460	1,680	30,530	-23.9
California.................................	3,340	51,490	41,310	643,010	-8.6
Colorado.................................	410	5,070	2,960	56,420	-12.9
Connecticut.............................	370	7,840	5,950	62,680	-26.4
Delaware.................................	160	2,530	1,390	28,130	-13.5
District of Columbia	60	1,700	1,060	14,280	-27.3
Florida.....................................	2,870	37,960	26,900	471,580	20.4
Georgia	840	14,990	10,100	166,310	5.6
Hawaii.....................................	130	3,570	3,510	40,840	9.5
Idaho.......................................	280	1,820	890	26,040	5.4
Illinois.....................................	1,350	19,200	14450	258,280	-17.3
Indiana....................................	910	10,370	6,610	144,780	20.7
Iowa..	320	4,030	2,810	51,040	6.7
Kansas....................................	200	3,350	2,870	43,660	-8.6
Kentucky.................................	420	7,300	7,260	86,880	14.1
Louisiana	530	10,940	8,700	146,100	6.3
Maine......................................	140	1,990	2,530	18,340	-13.7
Maryland..................................	750	14,050	9,830	157,180	-5.2
Massachusetts.........................	660	14,540	10,700	121,040	-20.2
Michigan..................................	840	10,940	7,930	147,650	-7.2
Minnesota................................	810	9,640	6,260	128,690	26.5
Mississippi..............................	200	3,800	3,030	47,450	-14.1
Missouri..................................	780	10,100	8,250	132,030	5.1
Montana..................................	120	1,040	530	10,390	-30.9
Nebraska.................................	270	4,420	3,900	50,940	26.3
Nevada....................................	140	1,830	1330	26,330	-11.7
New Hampshire........................	350	3,460	2,840	32,490	5.1
New Jersey	1,100	18,990	15070	214,840	-15.2
New Mexico	*	*	1,080	*	-100.0
New York.................................	1,690	43,290	31,020	469,720	-9.5
North Carolina.........................	640	11,730	6,820	122,060	0.3
North Dakota............................	50	790	*	9,260	24.6
Ohio..	1,430	18,190	14,640	247,790	3.5
Oklahoma................................	150	2,790	1,770	31,550	-21.8
Oregon....................................	400	4,410	3260	52,960	-20.1
Pennsylvania............................	2,500	23,630	18,060	282,330	-12.9
Rhode Island............................	110	1,750	1,780	18,770	-33.6
South Carolina	390	5,620	3,260	65,200	-8.7
South Dakota	80	1,000	690	12,170	-0.9
Tennessee................................	490	9,200	7,790	99,110	-15.7
Texas......................................	2,090	31,300	17,390	347,430	17.2
Utah	150	1,820	1,690	22,650	8.6
Vermont...................................	100	1,120	870	9,090	-27.9
Virginia....................................	820	11,710	7,440	131,290	-8.3
Washington..............................	620	7,870	4,330	99,620	-4.3
West Virginia............................	120	1,280	860	14,310	-4.5
Wisconsin................................	910	11,280	6,160	151,990	9.9
Wyoming	40	220	*	2,320	-20.8

* = Reporting standards not met.

Table B-9. Staff Employed by Public Elementary and Secondary School Systems, Fall 2017

State	Total staff	Student/ Teacher Ratio	Student/ Staff Ratio	School staff							
				Principals and assistant principals		School and library support staff		Teachers		Instructional aides	
				Number	Percent	Number	Percent	Number	Percent	Number	Percent
UNITED STATES	6,544,767	16.0	7.7	189,155	2.9	284,192	4.3	3,169,750	48.4	824,051	12.6
Alabama................................	91,778	17.8	8.1	3,930	4.3	3,289	3.6	41,802	45.5	7,028	7.7
Alaska...................................	17,154	17.2	7.7	646	3.8	1,165	6.8	7,743	45.1	2,608	15.2
Arizona.................................	103,508	23.2	10.7	2,452	2.4	3,851	3.7	47,868	46.2	15,694	15.2
Arkansas..............................	73,587	13.9	6.7	1,880	2.6	3,088	4.2	35,800	48.6	9,128	12.4
California..............................	604,248	23.2	10.4	17,719	2.9	35,181	5.8	271,523	44.9	81,898	13.6
Colorado	113,320	17.4	8.0	3,629	3.2	6,078	5.4	52,373	46.2	17,199	15.2
Connecticut..........................	97,989	11.8	5.4	2,311	2.4	3,451	3.5	45,081	46.0	16,039	16.4
Delaware	18,398	14.5	7.4	505	2.7	402	2.2	9,399	51.1	2,572	14.0
District of Columbia	14,171	13.1	6.2	561	4.0	739	5.2	6,659	47.0	1,983	14.0
Florida..................................	352,746	15.2	8.0	8,826	2.5	16,780	4.8	186,128	52.8	33,375	9.5
Georgia	231,644	15.2	7.6	6,590	2.8	10,325	4.5	116,022	50.1	25,882	11.2
Hawaii..................................	23,141	15.0	7.8	712	3.1	1,020	4.4	12,033	52.0	2,626	11.3
Idaho....................................	28,860	18.2	10.4	728	2.5	1,245	4.3	16,592	57.5	3,164	11.0
Illinois..................................	248,682	15.6	8.1	6,818	2.7	10,130	4.1	128,204	51.6	28,848	11.6
Indiana.................................	142,014	17.3	7.4	3,504	2.5	7,489	5.3	61,018	43.0	16,541	11.6
Iowa.....................................	75,694	14.4	6.8	1,744	2.3	2,685	3.5	35,553	47.0	12,868	17.0
Kansas	69,442	13.7	7.2	1,899	2.7	2,657	3.8	36,387	52.4	8,969	12.9
Kentucky	98,363	16.2	6.9	3,522	3.6	5,610	5.7	42,064	42.8	13,134	13.4
Louisiana	81,650	17.8	8.8	3,282	4.0	3,589	4.4	40,281	49.3	11,617	14.2
Maine...................................	35,983	12.2	5.0	956	2.7	1,737	4.8	14,760	41.0	6,171	17.1
Maryland..............................	118,384	14.9	7.5	3,612	3.1	5,997	5.1	60,175	50.8	11,434	9.7
Massachusetts.....................	132,727	13.1	7.3	5,051	3.8	6,761	5.1	73,381	55.3	26,065	19.6
Michigan	184,986	18.0	8.2	6,741	3.6	11,786	6.4	84,473	45.7	20,410	11.0
Minnesota	121,035	15.5	7.3	2,572	2.1	4,576	3.8	57,260	47.3	19,975	16.5
Mississippi...........................	67,521	15.1	7.1	2,044	3.0	2,568	3.8	31,625	46.8	8,265	12.2
Missouri...............................	125,779	13.4	7.3	3,379	2.7	329	0.3	68,496	54.5	14,305	11.4
Montana...............................	21,223	14.2	7.0	527	2.5	734	3.5	10,515	49.5	2,717	12.8
Nebraska..............................	48,012	13.6	6.7	1,094	2.3	1,910	4.0	23,771	49.5	6,544	13.6
Nevada.................................	35,848	20.5	13.6	1,194	3.3	1,822	5.1	23,709	66.1	6,196	17
New Hampshire.....................	31,618	12.3	5.7	527	1.7	777	2.5	14,589	46.1	7,143	22.6
New Jersey	238,785	12.2	5.9	5,215	2.2	9,587	4.0	115,496	48.4	39,356	16.5
New Mexico	36,473	15.9	9.2	1,125	3.1	2,052	5.6	21,092	57.8	5,818	16.0
New York..............................	425,292	12.8	6.4	13,075	3.1	11,450	2.7	213,159	50.1	67,567	15.9
North Carolina......................	193,798	15.5	8.0	5,933	3.1	7,252	3.7	100,401	51.8	22,366	11.5
North Dakota........................	18,599	12.1	6.0	498	2.7	770	4.1	9,284	49.9	2,849	15.3
Ohio.....................................	323,566	17.2	5.3	5,458	1.7	13,965	4.3	98,912	30.6	23,002	7.1
Oklahoma.............................	85,021	16.7	8.2	2,273	2.7	4,455	5.2	41,597	48.9	10,232	12.0
Oregon.................................	68,520	20.3	8.9	1,741	2.5	4,838	7.1	29,909	43.7	11,516	16.8
Pennsylvania........................	244,015	14.2	7.1	5,319	2.2	10,645	4.4	121,918	50.0	31,419	12.9
Rhode Island........................	20,376	13.4	7.0	549	2.7	747	3.7	10,687	52.4	2,662	13.1
South Carolina	88,410	14.8	8.8	3,336	3.8	3,000	3.4	52,467	59.3	11,835	13.4
South Dakota	19,787	14.0	7.0	459	2.3	611	3.1	9,833	49.7	2,877	14.5
Tennessee	131,312	15.7	7.6	3,860	2.9	5,385	4.1	64,019	48.8	17,396	13.2
Texas....................................	713,764	15.1	7.6	27,347	3.8	28,622	4.0	356,877	50.0	72,123	10.1
Utah.....................................	60,086	22.9	11.1	1,545	2.6	2,709	4.5	29,212	48.6	10,061	16.7
Vermont................................	18,268	10.6	4.8	497	2.7	860	4.7	8,313	45.5	4,043	22.1
Virginia.................................	183,485	15.0	7.0	4,333	2.4	8,640	4.7	85,936	46.8	19,676	10.7
Washington...........................	99,520	18.4	11.2	3,499	3.5	4,956	5.0	60,183	60.5	12,883	12.9
West Virginia........................	37,603	14.2	7.2	1,119	3.0	465	1.2	19,239	51.2	3,612	9.6
Wisconsin	112,001	14.7	7.7	2,640	2.4	4,458	4.0	58,598	52.3	9,938	8.9
Wyoming	16,580	12.9	5.7	381	2.3	952	5.7	7,335	44.2	2,424	14.6

- = Zero or rounds to zero.
NA = Not available.

Table B-9. Staff Employed by Public Elementary and Secondary School Systems, Fall 2017—*Continued*

| | School staff | | | | School district staff | | | | | | Student support staff | | Other support services staff | |
| | Guidance counselors | | Librarians | | Officials and administrators | | Administrative support staff | | Instruction coordinators | | | | | |
State	Number	Percent	Number	Percent	Number	Percent	Number	Percent	Number	Percent	Number	Percent	Number	Percent
UNITED STATES	114,703	1.8	42,605	0.7	74,411	1.1	194,312	3.0	95,746	1.5	356,959	5.5	1,198,883	18.3
Alabama	1,796	2.0	1,323	1.4	1,789	1.9	1,895	2.1	122	0.1	8,004	8.7	20,801	22.7
Alaska	312	1.8	136	0.8	707	4.1	813	4.7	0	-	688	4.0	2,337	13.6
Arizona...................................	1,201	1.2	419	0.4	1,409	1.4	4,093	4.0	629	0.6	11,812	11.4	14,080	13.6
Arkansas	1,288	1.7	954	1.3	643	0.9	2,587	3.5	986	1.3	7,461	10.1	9,772	13.3
California	9,794	1.6	93	-	3,821	0.6	21,873	3.6	25,495	4.2	20,544	3.4	116,308	19.2
Colorado	2,598	2.3	551	0.5	1,400	1.2	4,707	4.2	3,325	2.9	7,429	6.6	14,031	12.4
Connecticut............................	1,204	1.2	768	0.8	2,052	2.1	1,572	1.6	5,119	5.2	2,931	3.0	17,460	17.8
Delaware	344	1.9	114	0.6	469	2.5	340	1.8	336	1.8	841	4.6	3,076	16.7
District of Columbia	156	1.1	118	0.8	663	4.7	930	6.6	85	0.6	1,465	10.3	811	5.7
Florida....................................	5,931	1.7	1,972	0.6	2,318	0.7	15,597	4.4	759	0.2	12,049	3.4	69,012	19.6
Georgia	3,854	1.7	2,075	0.9	2,711	1.2	2,683	1.2	3,882	1.7	8,841	3.8	48,780	21.1
Hawaii	653	2.8	143	0.6	324	1.4	735	3.2	613	2.6	1,748	7.6	2,534	10.9
Idaho......................................	572	2.0	47	0.2	143	0.5	713	2.5	238	0.8	550	1.9	4,868	16.9
Illinois	2,963	1.2	1,475	0.6	3,475	1.4	6,379	2.6	1,513	0.6	31,020	12.5	27,856	11.2
Indiana	2,140	1.5	643	0.5	604	0.4	749	0.5	4,832	3.4	8,680	6.1	35,815	25.2
Iowa.......................................	1,296	1.7	407	0.5	1,898	2.5	1,931	2.6	2,527	3.3	4,595	6.1	10,191	13.5
Kansas	1,068	1.5	567	0.8	450	0.6	1,392	2.0	1,056	1.5	4,566	6.6	10,432	15.0
Kentucky	1,592	1.6	1,053	1.1	961	1.0	2,314	2.4	1,661	1.7	3,255	3.3	23,197	23.6
Louisiana	1,567	1.9	984	1.2	95	0.1	427	0.5	1,376	1.7	3,887	4.8	14,547	17.8
Maine......................................	566	1.6	195	0.5	639	1.8	714	2.0	515	1.4	4,249	11.8	5,482	15.2
Maryland................................	2,415	2.0	1,162	1.0	3,740	3.2	1,969	1.7	1,998	1.7	6,550	5.5	19,333	16.3
Massachusetts	2,377	1.8	644	0.5	2,640	2.0	2,880	2.2	469	0.4	10,648	8.0	1,809	1.4
Michigan	2,092	1.1	437	0.2	4,232	2.3	1,149	0.6	1,289	0.7	14,653	7.9	37,725	20.4
Minnesota	1,323	1.1	537	0.4	2,451	2.0	2,084	1.7	2,934	2.4	14,402	11.9	12,920	10.7
Mississippi.............................	1,072	1.6	766	1.1	1,012	1.5	2,077	3.1	670	1.0	3,225	4.8	14,198	21.0
Missouri.................................	2,706	2.2	1,383	1.1	898	0.7	6,200	4.9	1,449	1.2	5,725	4.6	20,909	16.6
Montana.................................	478	2.3	375	1.8	483	2.3	687	3.2	208	1.0	749	3.5	3,749	17.7
Nebraska................................	842	1.8	540	1.1	673	1.4	1,302	2.7	767	1.6	1,633	3.4	8,936	18.6
Nevada...................................	1,016	2.8	298	0.8	38	0.1	79	-	36	-	369	1.0	1,092	3.0
New Hampshire......................	825	2.6	323	1.0	758	2.4	763	2.4	271	0.9	687	2.2	4,957	15.7
New Jersey	3,810	1.6	1,333	0.6	1,455	0.6	5,503	2.3	3,836	1.6	13,452	5.6	39,742	16.6
New Mexico	690	1.9	217	0.6	206	0.6	32	0.1	360	1.0	1,345	3.7	3,536	9.7
New York................................	9,347	2.2	2,593	0.6	4,384	1.0	21,058	5.0	2,671	0.6	15,116	3.6	64,872	15.3
North Carolina.......................	4,300	2.2	2,127	1.1	1,711	0.9	5,688	2.9	1,209	0.6	11,420	5.9	31,390	16.2
North Dakota..........................	369	2.0	190	1.0	516	2.8	287	1.5	202	1.1	942	5.1	2,691	14.5
Ohio.......................................	3,844	1.2	803	0.2	2,610	0.8	14,785	4.6	2,374	0.7	27,170	8.4	130,643	40.4
Oklahoma...............................	1,604	1.9	900	1.1	833	1.0	3,088	3.6	334	0.4	4,771	5.6	14,933	17.6
Oregon...................................	1,255	1.9	159	0.2	481	0.7	2,575	3.8	553	0.8	3,063	4.5	12,431	18.1
Pennsylvania..........................	4,550	1.9	1,633	0.7	2,447	1.0	7,256	3.0	1,738	0.7	9,633	3.9	47,456	19.4
Rhode Island..........................	340	1.7	202	1.0	297	1.5	540	2.6	212	1.0	2,130	10.5	2,011	9.9
South Carolina	2,205	2.5	1,113	1.3	864	1.0	2,585	2.9	1,533	1.7	2,926	3.3	6,547	7.4
South Dakota	354	1.8	96	0.5	710	3.6	353	1.8	141	0.7	1,010	5.1	3,343	16.9
Tennessee	3,045	2.3	1,536	1.2	401	0.3	1,494	1.1	974	0.7	4,152	3.2	29,051	22.1
Texas.....................................	12,546	1.8	4,626	0.6	7,232	1.0	22,770	3.2	4,245	0.6	25,990	3.6	151,385	21.2
Utah	1,032	1.7	229	0.4	925	1.5	1,671	2.8	2,199	3.7	2,086	3.5	8,417	14.0
Vermont.................................	449	2.5	204	1.1	132	0.7	488	2.7	281	1.5	1,030	5.6	1,971	10.8
Virginia..................................	3,576	1.9	1,782	1.0	1,876	1.0	4,411	2.4	2,082	1.1	12,436	6.8	38,736	21.1
Washington............................	2,285	2.3	1,067	1.1	1,456	1.5	3,368	3.4	3,734	3.8	3,648	3.7	2,441	2.5
West Virginia..........................	726	1.9	243	0.6	872	2.3	1,355	3.6	373	1.0	1,154	3.1	8,445	22.5
Wisconsin	2,050	1.8	960	0.9	1,132	1.0	2,907	2.6	1,289	1.2	9,332	8.3	18,697	16.7
Wyoming	282	1.7	88	0.5	376	2.3	466	2.8	247	1.5	896	5.4	3,133	18.9

- = Zero or rounds to zero.
NA = Not available.

Table B-10. Revenues and Expenditures for Public Elementary and Secondary Schools, by State, 2017–2018

(Dollars in thousands except as noted; percent.)

| State | Revenues for public elementary and secondary schools, by source | | | | Current expenditures for public elementary and secondary schools, by function | | | | |
| | Total revenue (thousands of dollars) | Percent from: | | | Total current expenditures (thousands of dollars) | Current expenditure per pupil (dollars) | Percent for: | | |
		Federal government	State government	Local government			Instruction	Support services	Non-instruction
UNITED STATES	734,244,219	7.8	46.8	45.3	639,951,946	NA	60.7	35.3	4.0
Alabama	8,012,258	11.1	55.3	33.6	7,214,075	9,544	56.9	36.4	6.7
Alaska	2,529,601	15.9	62.4	21.7	2,355,261	18,903	53.6	42.8	3.7
Arizona	10,634,430	12.4	47.1	40.4	9,182,464	8,534	53.9	40.9	5.2
Arkansas	5,750,621	10.8	51.9	37.3	5,044,098	10,517	56.3	38.4	5.3
California	91,630,317	8.4	56.5	35.1	79,838,726	12,867	59.1	37.0	3.9
Colorado	11,208,343	6.3	41.7	52.0	9,319,502	10,616	55.7	40.5	3.8
Connecticut	11,518,273	4.3	39.8	55.9	10,703,917	20,572	62.0	35.1	2.9
Delaware	2,221,082	8.2	60.5	31.3	2,082,803	15,799	62.1	34.0	3.9
District of Columbia	2,550,537	8.2	†	91.8	2,021,822	23,972	55.3	41.2	3.6
Florida	30,117,218	11.4	39.2	49.4	27,371,046	9,422	61.9	33.2	4.9
Georgia	21,484,070	8.8	46.8	44.4	19,030,988	10,673	60.9	33.6	5.4
Hawaii	3,272,179	8.3	89.9	1.9	2,756,317	15,763	59.4	35.6	5.1
Idaho	2,730,604	9.6	66.7	23.7	2,363,037	8,023	59.3	36.0	4.7
Illinois	37,297,193	6.2	40.2	53.6	31,848,886	17,074	62.0	35.6	2.5
Indiana	13,274,778	7.7	62.5	29.9	10,576,789	10,149	57.4	37.9	4.7
Iowa	7,049,052	7.2	53.2	39.5	6,000,945	12,073	60.2	35.4	4.4
Kansas	6,726,852	7.8	64.7	27.5	5,515,083	11,450	59.5	35.9	4.6
Kentucky	8,458,983	10.9	56.3	32.9	7,546,109	12,072	58.7	34.9	6.4
Louisiana	9,133,401	12.6	43.1	44.2	8,321,373	11,896	56.1	38.7	5.2
Maine	2,891,163	6.6	39.4	54.0	2,719,621	16,101	58.6	37.5	3.9
Maryland	15,984,598	5.3	42.3	52.4	13,543,614	16,064	63.5	33.7	2.9
Massachusetts	18,325,196	4.9	38.7	56.4	17,682,658	18,832	64.1	33.0	2.8
Michigan	20,921,364	8.4	60.3	31.3	17,723,898	12,380	57.3	39.1	3.6
Minnesota	13,644,405	5.5	66.6	28.0	11,424,355	13,205	64.8	30.7	4.5
Mississippi	4,775,374	13.8	50.4	35.8	4,261,381	8,985	56.5	37.5	6.0
Missouri	11,808,339	8.0	32.3	59.7	10,101,337	11,269	59.3	36.2	4.6
Montana	1,929,334	12.7	43.4	43.9	1,720,717	11,883	58.8	36.7	4.6
Nebraska	4,632,500	7.4	32.4	60.2	4,148,386	13,550	64.3	28.9	6.8
Nevada	5,208,133	8.5	35.6	55.9	4,391,673	9,175	58.6	37.5	3.9
New Hampshire	3,195,008	5.3	31.3	63.4	2,976,514	16,478	63.7	33.9	2.3
New Jersey	31,478,321	4.1	43.3	52.6	28,607,598	20,775	59.4	37.5	3.1
New Mexico	4,035,432	13.4	68.4	18.2	3,330,970	9,449	56.5	38.5	5.0
New York	72,370,750	4.3	39.6	56.1	62,984,846	24,919	69.2	28.9	1.9
North Carolina	15,106,896	10.9	62.1	27.0	14,412,683	9,484	62.5	32.3	5.2
North Dakota	1,802,784	9.5	56.2	34.3	1,542,633	13,380	59.5	33.0	7.4
Ohio	25,419,736	7.2	42.1	50.7	21,975,446	12,648	59.3	37.5	3.2
Oklahoma	6,572,438	10.8	46.9	42.3	5,681,424	8,106	55.4	37.2	7.4
Oregon	8,489,845	6.8	52.8	40.4	6,911,762	12,486	58.5	38.1	3.4
Pennsylvania	32,332,500	6.9	38.1	54.9	28,279,577	16,850	62.0	34.3	3.7
Rhode Island	2,620,838	7.1	43.0	49.9	2,423,529	17,629	60.4	36.9	2.7
South Carolina	10,497,277	8.7	49.0	42.3	8,322,870	11,264	54.8	39.9	5.3
South Dakota	1,655,437	13.8	34.5	51.7	1,414,542	10,211	59.1	35.3	5.6
Tennessee	10,579,176	11.0	46.8	42.2	9,618,295	9,605	60.7	34.0	5.3
Texas	63,244,529	10.5	37.4	52.1	52,233,513	9,936	58.4	36.1	5.5
Utah	6,075,051	7.5	56.0	36.5	5,062,984	7,847	63.2	32.2	4.5
Vermont	1,779,236	6.4	89.9	3.7	1,773,661	20,930	63.2	34.0	2.8
Virginia	17,041,255	6.5	39.9	53.7	15,786,284	12,381	61.1	35.1	3.8
Washington	17,043,420	6.2	64.2	29.6	14,418,081	13,658	58.1	38.2	3.8
West Virginia	3,521,580	10.9	55.3	33.8	3,150,576	12,211	57.3	36.3	6.4
Wisconsin	11,841,411	7.0	46.8	46.2	10,712,520	12,625	58.4	38.1	3.6
Wyoming	1,821,103	6.4	56.8	36.8	1,520,759	17,153	59.5	37.5	3.0

NA = Not available.

Table B-11. Percentage of High School Dropouts Among Persons 16 to 24 Years Old, by Race/Ethnicity and State, 2018

(Percent.)

State	Total	White	Black	Hispanic	Asian	Pacific Islander	American Indian/ Alaska Native	Two or more races
UNITED STATES	5.3	4.2	6.4	8.0	1.9	8.1	9.5	5.2
Alabama...............................	5.4	4.5	5.7	10.7	NA	NA	NA	7.9
Alaska..................................	4.4	2.7	NA	NA	NA	NA	9.0	NA
Arizona................................	7.7	6.0	8.1	9.6	1.4	NA	9.6	6.9
Arkansas..............................	5.6	4.8	4.4	10.1	NA	NA	NA	10.0
California..............................	4.3	2.3	6.1	6.0	1.5	4.8	5.6	2.7
Colorado..............................	4.7	3.3	3.8	8.6	2.3	NA	NA	NA
Connecticut..........................	3.9	2.4	2.5	10.0	NA	NA	NA	NA
Delaware..............................	5.0	6.0	4.5	5.0	NA	NA	NA	NA
District of Columbia	4.5	NA	7.3	NA	NA	NA	NA	NA
Florida.................................	6.5	5.5	7.8	7.9	NA	NA	21.9	6.4
Georgia................................	6.2	6.2	4.8	11.9	2.1	NA	NA	5.5
Hawaii..................................	5.5	NA	NA	5.2	7.4	9.7	NA	4.6
Idaho...................................	7.4	6.2	NA	10.5	NA	NA	12.3	14.9
Illinois.................................	4.6	3.6	7.1	6.2	1.6	NA	NA	4.6
Indiana................................	7.4	7.5	8.3	6.6	3.2	NA	NA	9.0
Iowa....................................	4.7	3.9	12.7	10.5	NA	NA	NA	NA
Kansas	5.2	4.2	5.5	11.0	NA	NA	NA	NA
Kentucky..............................	5.6	5.1	6.9	13.4	NA	NA	NA	5.5
Louisiana	7.8	4.9	10.9	11.6	NA	NA	NA	11.4
Maine...................................	4.3	4.3	NA	NA	NA	NA	NA	NA
Maryland..............................	3.9	2.9	4.7	7.6	NA	NA	NA	4.6
Massachusetts......................	3.8	2.7	6.7	8.7	1.0	NA	NA	2.6
Michigan..............................	5.3	4.8	8.1	5.3	3.7	NA	4.1	3.7
Minnesota	4.2	3.1	5.4	7.3	4.3	NA	31.8	7.6
Mississippi...........................	6.2	5.6	5.5	29.7	NA	NA	NA	NA
Missouri...............................	6.0	5.8	7.0	8.4	5.9	NA	NA	3.7
Montana...............................	6.5	6.1	NA	NA	NA	NA	9.0	NA
Nebraska..............................	4.3	3.3	NA	11.2	NA	NA	NA	NA
Nevada................................	7.9	6.1	9.6	9.6	5.7	NA	NA	7.2
New Hampshire......................	4.1	3.8	NA	NA	NA	NA	NA	12.8
New Jersey	3.6	1.8	5.5	7.0	1.2	NA	NA	3.3
New Mexico	10.3	8.5	NA	12.2	NA	NA	8.3	NA
New York...............................	4.8	3.2	5.3	8.8	1.6	NA	NA	7.0
North Carolina......................	5.7	4.3	6.5	9.1	6.6	NA	7.6	8.0
North Dakota.........................	2.7	2.2	NA	NA	NA	NA	12.9	NA
Ohio	5.2	4.4	7.5	10.7	NA	NA	NA	6.2
Oklahoma.............................	7.2	6.1	8.2	10.4	NA	NA	9.7	7.5
Oregon.................................	6.1	4.9	NA	12.6	NA	NA	15.8	3.4
Pennsylvania.........................	5.4	5.1	5.6	8.9	2.8	NA	NA	3.7
Rhode Island.........................	4.0	5.3	NA	2.0	NA	NA	NA	NA
South Carolina	6.4	4.9	8.6	9.7	NA	NA	NA	7.0
South Dakota	8.1	5.9	NA	NA	NA	NA	20.7	NA
Tennessee	5.4	4.2	7.9	10.9	NA	NA	NA	3.0
Texas...................................	6.0	3.8	4.5	8.3	2.0	NA	NA	6.0
Utah.....................................	3.9	3.1	NA	7.0	NA	NA	NA	NA
Vermont................................	4.1	4.4	NA	NA	NA	NA	NA	NA
Virginia.................................	3.4	2.3	3.6	9.2	NA	NA	NA	3.4
Washington...........................	6.0	5.1	4.6	11.6	1.2	15.5	11.5	3.9
West Virginia.........................	6.4	6.2	10.1	NA	NA	NA	NA	NA
Wisconsin	4.4	2.7	15.5	9.6	2.7	NA	NA	6.1
Wyoming...............................	2.8	3.0	NA	NA	NA	NA	NA	NA

NA = Not available. Reporting standards not met.
NOTE: Status dropouts are 16- to 24-year-olds who are not enrolled in school and who have not completed a high school program, regardless of when they left school. People who have received equivalency credentials, such as the GED, are counted as high school completers. Data are based on sample surveys of the entire population residing within the United States, including both noninstitutionalized persons (e.g., those living in households, college housing, or military housing located within the United States) and institutionalized persons (e.g., those living in prisons, nursing facilities, or other healthcare facilities). Totals include other racial/ethnic groups not separately shown. Race categories exclude persons of Hispanic ethnicity.

Table B-12. Total Fall Enrollment in Degree-Granting Postsecondary Institutions, by Level and Control of School, and State, 2018

(Number.)

	Public				Private							
	Undergraduate				Undergraduate					Postbaccalaureate		
State	Total	4-year	2-year	Post-baccalaureate	Total	Nonprofit 4-year	For-profit 4-year	Nonprofit 2-year	For-profit 2-year	Total	Nonprofit 4-year	For-profit 4-year
UNITED STATES ...	13,049,326	7,502,622	5,546,704	1,479,938	3,560,909	2,776,499	585,906	45,154	153,350	1,555,745	1,312,591	243,154
Alabama	217,610	137,380	80,230	37,477	37,784	21,155	16,523	NA	106	11,311	5,106	6,205
Alaska	22,659	22,659	NA	1,990	842	346	NA	81	415	201	201	NA
Arizona	331,864	153,026	178,838	35,334	151,152	5,496	136,052	NA	9,604	63,632	5,427	58,205
Arkansas	124,058	80,394	43,664	18,324	15,178	13,504	292	1,326	56	2,178	2,102	76
California	2,131,013	897,291	1,233,722	119,206	279,221	167,358	87,204	1,260	23,399	182,980	142,955	40,025
Colorado	240,200	199,657	40,543	39,295	59,442	20,933	29,992	130	8,387	21,600	12,817	8,783
Connecticut	101,145	53,236	47,909	13,384	59,394	50,262	9,132	NA	NA	23,557	22,761	796
Delaware	38,059	38,059	NA	4,542	11,420	11,010	292	118	NA	6,679	6,620	59
District of Columbia	3,867	3,867	NA	633	48,230	40,395	7,487	NA	348	45,046	40,996	4,050
Florida	730,278	707,095	23,183	70,173	213,533	130,141	46,487	20,444	16,461	54,079	49,744	4,335
Georgia	383,200	265,868	117,332	52,544	80,023	57,441	15,311	1,931	5,340	27,676	21,729	5,947
Hawaii	45,731	22,004	23,727	5,332	9,628	8,624	313	NA	691	1,164	1,071	93
Idaho	69,427	45,686	23,741	7,706	45,618	45,190	NA	NA	428	736	736	NA
Illinois	416,652	133,237	283,415	48,577	169,947	127,625	38,998	411	2,913	103,272	85,416	17,856
Indiana	254,093	182,087	72,006	42,136	74,266	70,602	597	415	2,652	17,853	17,782	71
Iowa	176,979	87,557	89,422	22,252	41,090	38,244	2,770	NA	76	13,737	13,223	514
Kansas	157,337	78,674	78,663	22,263	27,277	18,804	7,663	NA	810	5,860	4,508	1,352
Kentucky	176,907	99,233	77,674	22,841	36,008	29,190	5,835	NA	983	27,205	26,314	891
Louisiana	184,973	119,985	64,988	25,723	23,027	19,148	75	492	3,312	7,678	7,678	NA
Maine	44,050	27,438	16,612	4,282	18,011	17,743	NA	61	207	5,430	5,430	NA
Maryland	259,256	143,509	115,747	42,703	29,367	25,512	2,565	NA	1,290	30,116	29,500	616
Massachusetts	180,511	97,191	83,320	27,256	176,610	173,512	1,753	1,212	133	115,392	115,208	184
Michigan	402,635	258,761	143,874	64,171	58,143	56,503	392	NA	1,248	16,147	16,128	19
Minnesota	220,809	104,391	116,418	24,355	72,480	49,757	22,392	106	225	91,139	21,327	69,812
Mississippi	136,456	64,431	72,025	14,127	12,997	11,862	442	NA	693	5,780	5,714	66
Missouri	206,021	120,353	85,668	26,019	92,343	88,415	2,664	183	1,081	50,041	49,820	221
Montana	39,639	31,691	7,948	5,286	4,168	3,820	NA	305	43	270	270	NA
Nebraska	86,113	45,884	40,229	14,481	23,200	23,032	107	15	46	11,144	11,144	NA
Nevada	99,950	99,950	NA	8,708	6,049	1,118	1,763	97	3,071	3,091	3,018	73
New Hampshire	34,762	22,977	11,785	3,973	95,337	95,225	NA	112	NA	26,671	26,671	NA
New Jersey	290,369	150,871	139,498	38,668	60,770	50,006	6,530	159	4,075	24,609	24,248	361
New Mexico	107,982	43,597	64,385	12,311	2,196	736	473	NA	987	808	762	46
New York	620,840	334,678	286,162	69,257	383,982	346,439	24,678	2,705	10,160	176,208	173,206	3,002
North Carolina	409,025	190,357	218,668	47,103	79,715	69,937	7,059	594	2,125	27,867	26,591	1,276
North Dakota	40,348	33,021	7,327	6,183	5,225	4,612	613	NA	NA	1,530	1,528	2
Ohio	435,996	274,388	161,608	59,616	120,552	105,503	4,742	1,164	9,143	28,798	28,636	162
Oklahoma	150,793	96,081	54,712	20,186	20,371	17,378	1,088	578	1,327	4,593	4,593	NA
Oregon	173,373	84,805	88,568	18,570	22,901	20,723	1,366	45	767	13,296	13,041	255
Pennsylvania	342,616	221,101	121,515	50,155	213,074	195,317	3,627	4,692	9,438	94,484	94,028	456
Rhode Island	36,001	21,462	14,539	4,081	33,393	33,393	NA	NA	NA	7,393	7,393	NA
South Carolina	175,543	94,704	80,839	20,982	38,244	31,696	2,929	869	2,750	5,764	4,385	1,379
South Dakota	38,327	31,490	6,837	5,544	7,914	6,069	1,845	NA	NA	1,580	1,336	244
Tennessee	200,939	112,838	88,101	24,342	72,783	60,524	6,200	709	5,350	24,051	22,741	1,310
Texas	1,317,560	634,490	683,070	151,027	133,000	99,810	15,879	1,610	15,701	41,955	40,333	1,622
Utah	170,354	141,198	29,156	13,595	138,414	133,169	2,769	1,996	480	37,409	36,479	930
Vermont	22,521	17,143	5,378	2,676	13,948	13,875	73	NA	NA	3,769	3,769	NA
Virginia	338,130	174,068	164,062	46,749	113,428	86,041	23,787	393	3,207	53,734	50,681	3,053
Washington	293,919	261,380	32,539	25,458	35,880	29,694	3,943	941	1,302	11,799	11,632	167
West Virginia	70,170	53,686	16,484	11,435	48,512	6,983	39,214	NA	2,315	9,986	1,385	8,601
Wisconsin	252,742	162,191	90,551	24,436	44,784	42,627	1,990	NA	167	14,447	14,408	39
Wyoming	30,020	9,998	20,022	2,452	38	NA	NA	NA	38	NA	NA	NA

NA = Not applicable.
NOTE: Degree-granting institutions grant associate's or higher degrees and participate in Title IV federal financial aid programs.

Table B-13. Degrees Conferred by Institutions of Higher Education, by State, 2018–2019

(Number.)

State	Total degrees	Associate's degrees				Bachelor's degrees			
		Total	Public	Private not-for-profit	Private for-profit	Total	Public	Private not-for-profit	Private for-profit
UNITED STATES	4,070,790	1,036,662	915,011	54,432	67,219	2,012,854	1,340,147	575,586	97,121
Alabama	62,371	13,198	10,759	220	2,219	33,068	25,928	3,688	3,452
Alaska	3,772	1,197	1,149	12	36	1,922	1,863	59	0
Arizona	120,649	26,875	19,275	149	7,451	60,301	33,258	907	26,136
Arkansas	33,632	10,060	9,619	412	29	16,746	14,188	2,540	18
California	519,889	197,152	185,168	1,660	10,324	219,511	164,747	40,163	14,601
Colorado	68,202	12,961	10,014	428	2,519	36,814	27,777	3,902	5,135
Connecticut	43,916	6,614	5,388	943	283	23,785	11,854	10,910	1,021
Delaware	13,249	2,037	1,945	79	13	7,274	5,021	2,222	31
District of Columbia	27,620	759	195	226	338	10,220	386	9,151	683
Florida	246,438	94,671	76,670	12,305	5,696	108,197	78,990	22,463	6,744
Georgia	97,580	18,553	16,470	898	1,185	54,036	41,025	10,631	2,380
Hawaii	12,171	4,015	3,755	204	56	6,365	4,681	1,562	122
Idaho	20,542	5,193	3,479	1,585	129	12,955	6,895	6,060	0
Illinois	160,311	35,642	32,914	829	1,899	72,735	32,455	30,641	9,639
Indiana	88,852	14,656	12,714	1,486	456	51,271	36,911	14,243	117
Iowa	44,161	11,293	10,750	344	199	24,153	14,319	9,130	704
Kansas	40,576	10,958	9,902	276	780	20,359	16,008	3,679	672
Kentucky	51,290	12,049	10,547	281	1,221	24,522	18,985	4,875	662
Louisiana	40,978	6,804	5,956	300	548	23,093	19,532	3,561	0
Maine	12,820	2,572	2,344	115	113	7,337	4,127	3,210	0
Maryland	75,468	16,890	16,624	21	245	34,586	28,545	5,752	289
Massachusetts	124,565	12,198	10,819	1,275	104	61,699	21,838	39,755	106
Michigan	111,861	25,444	23,480	1,766	198	59,782	47,805	11,848	129
Minnesota	86,022	17,088	14,982	782	1,324	37,024	21,456	10,786	4,782
Mississippi	36,987	13,632	13,566	55	11	16,608	14,274	2,321	13
Missouri	80,854	15,322	12,306	2,640	376	40,610	23,036	17,149	425
Montana	10,480	2,409	2,336	54	19	6,242	5,438	804	0
Nebraska	26,621	5,007	4,807	164	36	14,445	9,134	5,290	21
Nevada	19,280	6,209	5,759	0	450	9,702	8,943	503	256
New Hampshire	33,553	4,566	2,097	2,469	0	19,005	5,397	13,608	0
New Jersey	87,911	22,647	20,773	241	1,633	44,690	33,705	10,057	928
New Mexico	22,254	9,670	9,491	0	179	8,560	8,284	174	102
New York	299,217	64,521	51,197	7,239	6,085	143,790	68,457	71,868	3,465
North Carolina	116,110	34,326	32,925	853	548	56,892	41,884	14,474	534
North Dakota	11,435	2,323	1,970	164	189	6,623	5,926	687	10
Ohio	134,058	31,330	25,982	3,025	2,323	72,250	50,892	20,974	384
Oklahoma	41,125	11,240	10,708	191	341	21,574	17,752	3,791	31
Oregon	48,089	13,538	13,181	29	328	24,107	18,720	5,380	7
Pennsylvania	164,242	23,031	17,214	3,234	2,583	91,190	48,358	42,295	537
Rhode Island	19,761	3,311	1,988	1,323	0	12,345	4,808	7,537	0
South Carolina	45,686	10,322	9,689	329	304	26,761	20,178	6,301	282
South Dakota	11,090	2,433	2,167	34	232	6,170	4,734	1,077	359
Tennessee	65,208	14,090	11,949	938	1,203	34,960	22,388	12,171	401
Texas	304,221	97,018	91,062	1,469	4,487	141,280	118,027	21,333	1,920
Utah	80,752	13,939	12,007	1,261	671	46,121	17,697	28,080	344
Vermont	10,139	941	796	122	23	6,481	3,605	2,842	34
Virginia	113,788	23,251	18,129	1,458	3,664	59,752	38,997	17,466	3,289
Washington	79,712	30,855	30,197	147	511	35,690	28,308	7,099	283
West Virginia	30,635	6,718	3,382	141	3,195	16,841	9,470	1,358	6,013
Wisconsin	61,464	12,459	11,740	256	463	36,626	27,357	9,209	60
Wyoming	5,625	2,675	2,675	0	0	2,228	2,228	0	0

[1]Includes Ph.D., Ed.D., and comparable degrees at the doctoral level. Includes most degrees formerly classified as first-professional prior to 2010-11, such as M.D., D.D.S., and law degrees.

NOTE: Data are for postsecondary institutions participating in Title IV federal financial aid programs.

Table B-13. Degrees Conferred by Institutions of Higher Education, by State, 2018–2019— *Continued*

(Number.)

State	Master's degrees				Doctoral degrees[1]			
	Total	Public	Private not-for-profit	Private for-profit	Total	Public	Private not-for-profit	Private for-profit
UNITED STATES	833,706	386,166	380,885	66,655	187,568	94,563	85,706	7,299
Alabama.................................	13,418	10,467	865	2,086	2,687	1,973	690	24
Alaska....................................	605	558	47	0	48	43	5	0
Arizona..................................	29,583	10,497	675	18,411	3,890	2,171	862	857
Arkansas...............................	5,766	5,253	495	18	1,060	971	89	0
California...............................	83,342	33,317	41,245	8,780	19,884	7,198	10,920	1,766
Colorado	15,447	9,343	3,866	2,238	2,980	1,906	563	511
Connecticut............................	11,322	3,318	7,716	288	2,195	779	1,416	0
Delaware	3,480	1,118	2,350	12	458	331	127	0
District of Columbia	13,226	133	12,035	1,058	3,415	65	3,350	0
Florida...................................	34,375	18,582	13,929	1,864	9,195	5,179	3,941	75
Georgia	20,136	12,676	5,193	2,267	4,855	2,686	1,890	279
Hawaii	1,312	868	407	37	479	479	0	0
Idaho.....................................	2,008	1,782	226	0	386	372	14	0
Illinois	42,953	12,706	25,112	5,135	8,981	3,131	5,563	287
Indiana	18,865	13,400	5,429	36	4,060	2,844	1,216	0
Iowa	5,865	2,859	2,848	158	2,850	1,443	1,407	0
Kansas	7,570	5,658	1,406	506	1,689	1,495	194	0
Kentucky	12,207	5,511	6,418	278	2,512	1,821	607	84
Louisiana	8,645	6,410	2,235	0	2,436	1,627	809	0
Maine	2,195	811	1,384	0	716	156	560	0
Maryland................................	21,045	11,258	9,535	252	2,947	2,109	838	0
Massachusetts........................	42,146	6,871	35,275	0	8,522	920	7,602	0
Michigan................................	20,919	17,063	3,856	0	5,716	4,650	1,066	0
Minnesota..............................	26,203	5,514	5,822	14,867	5,707	1,816	1,165	2,726
Mississippi.............................	5,216	3,399	1,808	9	1,531	1,199	332	0
Missouri.................................	19,721	6,614	13,023	84	5,201	1,768	3,433	0
Montana.................................	1,309	1,166	143	0	520	520	0	0
Nebraska................................	5,390	2,970	2,420	0	1,779	890	889	0
Nevada..................................	2,296	1,804	445	47	1,073	564	509	0
New Hampshire.......................	9,465	1,100	8,365	0	517	170	347	0
New Jersey	17,236	9,992	7,111	133	3,338	2,348	990	0
New Mexico	3,341	3,037	281	23	683	682	1	0
New York................................	76,229	19,747	55,067	1,415	14,677	3,204	11,472	1
North Carolina........................	19,722	12,550	6,785	387	5,170	2,872	2,283	15
North Dakota..........................	1,876	1,421	454	1	613	494	119	0
Ohio	24,153	15,639	8,446	68	6,325	4,750	1,575	0
Oklahoma...............................	6,671	5,213	1,458	0	1,640	1,352	288	0
Oregon	8,152	4,400	3,680	72	2,292	1,074	1,218	0
Pennsylvania..........................	39,367	13,123	26,098	146	10,654	3,432	7,222	0
Rhode Island..........................	3,328	869	2,459	0	777	262	515	0
South Carolina	6,516	5,038	1,248	230	2,087	1,642	212	233
South Dakota	2,024	1,388	393	243	463	407	16	40
Tennessee	11,974	5,697	6,003	274	4,184	1,916	2,103	165
Texas.....................................	54,215	42,640	11,086	489	11,708	8,956	2,722	30
Utah	19,343	4,035	15,192	116	1,349	953	230	166
Vermont.................................	2,335	645	1,690	0	382	262	120	0
Virginia..................................	24,971	11,803	11,420	1,748	5,814	3,448	2,333	33
Washington............................	10,282	6,642	3,582	58	2,885	2,101	777	7
West Virginia..........................	5,937	2,737	391	2,809	1,139	1,009	130	0
Wisconsin	9,518	6,038	3,468	12	2,861	1,885	976	0
Wyoming	484	484	0	0	238	238	0	0

[1]Includes Ph.D., Ed.D., and comparable degrees at the doctoral level. Includes most degrees formerly classified as first-professional prior to 2010-11, such as M.D., D.D.S., and law degrees.

NOTE: Data are for postsecondary institutions participating in Title IV federal financial aid programs.

Table B-14. Race/Ethnicity of Students Enrolled in Institutions of Higher Education, Fall 2018

(Number; percent.)

State	Total enrolled	Percent of U.S. resident students							Nonresident alien total
		White (percent)	Black (percent)	Hispanic or Latino (may be of any race) (percent)	Asian (percent)	Pacific Islander (percent)	American Indian/ Alaska Native (percent)	Two or more races (percent)	
UNITED STATES	19,645,918	55.2	13.4	19.5	7.0	0.3	0.7	3.9	992,055
Alabama...................................	304,182	64.2	26.3	4.0	2.1	0.1	0.7	2.7	9,025
Alaska......................................	25,692	59.6	3.2	8.6	5.7	1.6	11.0	10.4	523
Arizona....................................	581,982	50.3	12.6	26.0	4.1	0.5	2.4	4.1	19,964
Arkansas..................................	159,738	70.7	15.8	7.0	1.9	0.1	0.7	3.9	5,099
California..................................	2,712,420	28.8	6.5	43.3	15.7	0.5	0.4	4.8	147,918
Colorado..................................	360,537	63.5	7.8	18.7	3.9	0.2	1.0	4.7	12,141
Connecticut..............................	197,480	59.6	14.0	16.6	6.0	0.1	0.3	3.3	11,172
Delaware..................................	60,700	59.7	23.2	9.2	4.0	0.1	0.5	3.3	4,830
District of Columbia..................	97,776	49.0	28.0	11.0	8.0	0.2	0.3	3.6	11,037
Florida.....................................	1,068,063	44.6	18.5	29.2	3.8	0.2	0.3	3.4	46,328
Georgia....................................	543,443	49.7	31.9	8.7	5.9	0.1	0.3	3.3	24,421
Hawaii......................................	61,855	17.4	2.1	12.8	33.0	6.2	0.2	28.3	4,002
Idaho.......................................	123,487	80.1	1.2	10.6	1.8	0.5	0.9	5.0	8,619
Illinois.....................................	738,448	55.3	13.3	20.4	7.5	0.1	0.2	3.0	41,518
Indiana.....................................	388,348	75.2	9.7	7.3	3.7	0.1	0.2	3.8	24,283
Iowa..	254,058	76.3	8.7	8.2	3.1	0.2	0.5	2.9	11,380
Kansas.....................................	212,737	71.3	8.7	11.3	3.1	0.2	1.3	4.2	13,095
Kentucky..................................	262,961	81.4	8.8	4.1	2.0	0.1	0.2	3.3	16,730
Louisiana.................................	241,401	55.9	31.5	5.8	2.7	0.5	0.7	2.9	7,196
Maine.......................................	71,773	85.6	4.3	3.5	2.8	0.1	1.0	2.7	1,531
Maryland..................................	361,442	47.0	29.6	10.2	8.3	0.2	0.3	4.4	22,200
Massachusetts..........................	499,769	63.1	10.1	13.3	9.6	0.1	0.2	3.6	61,698
Michigan..................................	541,096	73.0	12.2	5.8	4.6	0.1	0.6	3.8	29,645
Minnesota................................	408,783	67.6	15.5	6.2	6.0	0.2	0.8	3.7	15,397
Mississippi...............................	169,360	56.7	36.9	2.7	1.3	0.1	0.5	1.9	3,138
Missouri...................................	374,424	74.1	12.1	5.9	3.6	0.2	0.5	3.7	16,745
Montana...................................	49,363	82.0	1.0	4.1	1.7	0.2	7.0	4.0	1,380
Nebraska..................................	134,938	75.8	5.7	10.8	3.3	0.2	0.7	3.5	5,353
Nevada.....................................	117,798	42.9	7.9	29.1	11.2	1.1	0.7	7.0	2,280
New Hampshire.........................	160,743	72.5	13.0	8.7	2.8	0.3	0.6	2.2	2,987
New Jersey...............................	414,416	49.2	14.6	23.1	10.2	0.2	0.2	2.4	21,153
New Mexico..............................	123,297	33.0	3.0	49.7	2.2	0.2	9.5	2.4	3,321
New York..................................	1,250,287	51.0	14.7	19.9	10.9	0.2	0.4	2.8	108,425
North Carolina..........................	563,710	59.7	22.8	8.9	3.9	0.1	1.1	3.4	19,585
North Dakota............................	53,286	83.0	3.6	4.1	1.5	0.1	4.3	3.4	2,383
Ohio..	644,962	75.8	12.1	4.8	3.2	0.1	0.3	3.7	31,566
Oklahoma................................	195,943	60.2	8.3	10.6	3.3	0.2	7.3	10.2	9,499
Oregon....................................	228,140	67.5	3.2	14.6	6.3	0.7	1.1	6.7	11,118
Pennsylvania............................	700,329	70.1	11.6	8.1	6.4	0.1	0.2	3.4	47,041
Rhode Island............................	80,868	67.9	7.9	14.6	5.1	0.1	0.3	4.0	4,614
South Carolina.........................	240,533	64.5	24.5	5.3	1.9	0.1	0.4	3.4	5,302
South Dakota...........................	53,365	82.8	3.9	3.7	1.4	0.2	5.4	2.6	1,816
Tennessee................................	322,115	69.7	18.7	5.1	2.8	0.1	0.3	3.2	8,578
Texas.......................................	1,643,542	37.0	12.9	40.1	6.6	0.1	0.4	2.9	67,160
Utah..	359,772	76.0	5.1	10.7	2.9	0.7	0.7	3.9	7,158
Vermont...................................	42,914	82.1	4.0	6.0	3.0	0.1	0.4	4.5	1,699
Virginia....................................	552,041	58.5	19.9	9.4	7.0	0.2	0.4	4.5	19,599
Washington..............................	367,056	60.1	4.9	14.5	10.5	0.7	1.1	8.2	22,944
West Virginia............................	140,103	76.9	10.1	6.8	1.8	0.4	0.4	3.5	3,913
Wisconsin................................	336,409	78.4	5.7	7.7	4.3	0.1	0.7	3.1	12,425
Wyoming..................................	32,510	83.1	1.3	9.5	1.0	0.2	1.4	3.6	914

NA = Not available.

[1]NOTE: Includes special education, vocational/technical education, and alternative schools. Tabulation includes schools that offer kindergarten or higher grade. Includes enrollment of students in prekindergarten through grade 12 in schools that offer kindergarten or higher grade. Detail may not sum to totals because of rounding.

* Not applicable. Some states/jurisdictions do not have charter school authorization and some states/jurisdictions do not designate magnet schools.

‡ Reporting standards not met. Data missing for more than 80 percent of schools in the state or jurisdiction.

Table B-15. Average Undergraduate Tuition, Fees, and Room and Board Rates for Full-Time College Students, by State, 2018–2019

(Dollars.)

State	Public 4-year					Private 4-year				Public 2-year, tuition and required fees	
	In-state				Out-of-state tuition and required fees						
	Total	Tuition and required fees	Room	Board		Total	Tuition and required fees	Room	Board	In-state	Out-of-state
UNITED STATES	20,598	9,212	6,459	4,927	26,382	44,662	31,875	7,179	5,608	3,313	7,917
Alabama..................................	19,982	10,138	5,543	4,301	25,782	26,195	16,119	5,005	5,071	4,770	9,612
Alaska....................................	19,563	8,396	6,226	4,941	24,454	26,788	19,315	3,720	3,753	NA	NA
Arizona..................................	23,105	10,666	7,199	5,240	26,383	22,419	12,711	5,330	4,378	2,161	8,516
Arkansas...............................	17,977	8,391	5,310	4,276	20,825	31,564	23,179	4,255	4,130	3,291	4,698
California...............................	22,664	8,118	8,147	6,399	31,423	49,860	35,524	7,976	6,360	1,271	7,849
Colorado	21,867	9,394	6,323	6,149	30,140	36,285	23,560	7,482	5,243	3,655	7,967
Connecticut...........................	26,203	12,959	7,254	5,990	33,709	56,549	41,807	8,527	6,215	4,434	13,202
Delaware...............................	23,447	10,607	7,661	5,179	30,405	26,709	14,758	6,032	5,920	NA	NA
District of Columbia	NA	5,888	NA	NA	12,416	59,233	43,143	10,844	5,246	NA	NA
Florida...................................	15,059	4,443	6,173	4,443	18,456	38,438	26,317	6,918	5,203	2,506	9,111
Georgia	18,003	7,319	6,346	4,337	22,751	41,520	28,839	6,955	5,726	2,916	8,038
Hawaii	21,865	9,952	6,046	5,868	31,581	29,781	17,098	5,870	6,813	3,140	8,277
Idaho.....................................	16,134	7,586	4,061	4,487	23,850	13,157	6,139	2,436	4,583	3,345	7,971
Illinois...................................	25,469	14,259	6,087	5,122	28,522	46,552	33,454	7,530	5,568	3,966	11,480
Indiana..................................	19,755	9,225	5,553	4,977	29,092	45,382	33,402	6,204	5,775	4,368	8,402
Iowa......................................	20,122	9,966	5,709	4,448	24,521	43,364	33,821	4,687	4,855	5,137	6,449
Kansas	18,618	8,941	5,062	4,616	23,302	31,701	22,571	4,406	4,723	3,435	4,491
Kentucky	21,313	10,674	6,038	4,601	25,430	37,081	27,648	4,661	4,773	4,274	14,418
Louisiana...............................	19,206	9,358	5,704	4,144	22,208	51,025	37,830	7,315	5,880	4,143	8,034
Maine.....................................	20,195	9,930	5,119	5,146	27,735	52,527	38,972	6,772	6,783	3,753	6,614
Maryland................................	21,895	9,521	7,057	5,317	26,883	57,222	43,141	8,180	5,901	4,225	9,990
Massachusetts......................	26,787	13,286	8,337	5,164	30,966	61,747	46,016	9,177	6,555	5,192	10,606
Michigan................................	23,376	12,888	5,262	5,226	35,844	38,074	27,936	5,096	5,043	3,582	6,372
Minnesota..............................	20,860	11,381	5,194	4,286	22,780	43,677	33,212	5,616	4,850	5,389	5,947
Mississippi............................	18,391	8,340	5,887	4,164	19,942	26,352	17,953	4,352	4,046	3,262	5,709
Missouri.................................	18,121	8,554	5,612	3,956	19,914	35,803	25,417	6,021	4,366	3,358	6,558
Montana.................................	16,604	6,972	4,481	5,150	24,481	34,988	25,918	4,291	4,779	3,756	8,394
Nebraska...............................	19,551	8,467	6,239	4,845	21,516	34,626	25,075	5,502	4,049	3,174	3,985
Nevada..................................	17,503	5,845	6,039	5,619	21,125	38,130	24,423	6,711	6,996	NA	NA
New Hampshire......................	28,145	16,329	7,258	4,558	29,447	46,952	33,364	8,690	4,898	7,599	16,429
New Jersey	27,481	13,963	8,343	5,175	28,669	51,045	37,329	7,963	5,753	4,715	8,257
New Mexico	16,256	6,902	4,764	4,590	18,350	40,206	30,137	5,645	4,424	1,705	6,698
New York................................	23,053	8,184	9,746	5,123	22,083	55,741	40,527	9,115	6,098	5,367	9,197
North Carolina.......................	17,302	7,174	5,766	4,362	22,968	46,268	33,990	6,350	5,928	2,504	8,655
North Dakota..........................	16,668	8,091	3,733	4,844	15,565	22,856	15,206	3,099	4,551	4,895	9,293
Ohio	22,153	10,068	6,597	5,488	24,454	44,035	32,597	5,942	5,496	4,082	7,300
Oklahoma..............................	16,732	7,866	4,738	4,128	21,526	37,447	27,694	4,872	4,882	4,112	9,393
Oregon	22,585	10,286	7,204	5,095	30,929	53,036	40,597	6,536	5,903	4,709	8,779
Pennsylvania.........................	26,287	14,812	6,893	4,582	28,527	55,248	41,703	7,434	6,111	5,284	14,111
Rhode Island.........................	24,827	12,576	7,666	4,585	29,998	57,176	42,108	8,981	6,088	4,564	12,156
South Carolina	23,113	13,013	6,241	3,859	32,174	35,174	25,621	4,811	4,743	4,728	9,874
South Dakota	16,847	8,772	3,917	4,159	12,465	31,359	23,252	4,002	4,105	6,170	5,839
Tennessee	19,713	9,789	5,205	4,719	26,068	38,571	28,080	5,885	4,607	4,287	16,582
Texas.....................................	18,779	8,678	5,553	4,548	25,031	46,268	34,476	6,580	5,213	2,259	5,920
Utah	14,389	6,731	3,554	4,104	21,557	15,804	7,852	4,002	3,950	3,843	12,206
Vermont.................................	28,681	16,604	7,646	4,431	39,947	58,137	44,068	7,683	6,387	7,120	14,090
Virginia..................................	24,492	13,413	6,242	4,838	34,890	34,470	23,380	5,890	5,199	5,241	11,455
Washington............................	19,272	7,036	6,517	5,719	29,228	50,873	38,754	6,381	5,739	4,169	5,691
West Virginia.........................	18,461	8,016	5,603	4,842	21,996	21,892	12,513	4,505	4,874	4,276	9,834
Wisconsin..............................	17,172	8,697	5,407	3,068	25,063	45,269	34,424	6,183	4,663	4,411	6,408
Wyoming	14,639	4,596	4,493	5,550	14,268	NA	NA	NA	NA	3,219	7,752

NA = Not applicable.

NOTES AND DEFINITIONS: REGION AND STATE EDUCATION STATISTICS

TABLES B-1, B-2, B-3 AND B-5

Source: U.S. Census Bureau. *American Community Survey, 2019*, Tables B15001, C15002, C15002A, C15002B, C15002D, C15002I, S0901, and C14002. (ACS 1-Year Estimates) https://data.census.gov.

Tables B-1, B-2, B-3, and B-5 are from the American Community Survey (ACS), the sample survey that has replaced the long form of the decennial census. The sample data are estimates of the actual figures that would have been obtained from a complete count. Estimates derived from a sample are expected to be different from the 100-percent figures because they are subject to sampling and nonsampling errors. Sampling error in data arises from the selection of people and housing units included in the sample. Nonsampling error affects both sample and 100-percent data. It is introduced as a result of errors that may occur during the data collection and processing phases of the census. Conclusions should not be based on small numbers or small differences and users should consult the ACS website to determine the appropriate margins of error. The ACS is ongoing and data are released on an annual basis for all regions and states.

For additional information about the American Community Survey, see https://www.census.gov/programs-surveys/acs/.

Educational Attainment. In the ACS, respondents are classified according to the highest degree or the highest level of school completed. Statistics for educational attainment only include persons 25 years old and over. The question includes instructions for people currently enrolled in school to report the level of the previous grade attended or the highest degree received.

High school graduate or higher. This category includes persons who have received a high school diploma or its equivalent (for example, GED), and those who reported any level higher than a high school diploma.

Bachelor's degree or higher. This category includes persons who have received bachelor's degrees, master's degrees, professional school degrees (such as law school or medical school degrees), and doctoral degrees.

Geographic Definitions

Data are presented for the four major regions of the United States. These groups of states are as follows:

Northeast: Connecticut, Maine, Massachusetts, New Hampshire, New Jersey, New York, Pennsylvania, Rhode Island, and Vermont

Midwest: Illinois, Indiana, Iowa, Kansas, Michigan, Minnesota, Missouri, Nebraska, North Dakota, Ohio, South Dakota, and Wisconsin

South: Alabama, Arkansas, Delaware, District of Columbia, Florida, Georgia, Kentucky, Louisiana, Maryland, Mississippi, North Carolina, Oklahoma, South Carolina, Tennessee, Texas, Virginia, and West Virginia

West: Alaska, Arizona, California, Colorado, Hawaii, Idaho, Montana, Nevada, New Mexico, Oregon, Utah, Washington, and Wyoming

Income and Poverty. The Census Bureau reports income from several major household surveys and programs. The Census Bureau recommends using the ACS for single-year estimates of income and poverty at the state level.

Total income is the sum of the amounts reported separately for wages, salary, commissions, bonuses, or tips; self-employment income from own nonfarm or farm businesses, including proprietorships and partnerships; interest, dividends, net rental income, royalty income, or income from estates and trusts; Social Security or Railroad Retirement income; Supplemental Security Income (SSI); any public assistance or welfare payments from the state or local welfare office; retirement, survivor, or disability pensions; and any other sources of income received regularly such as Veterans' (VA) payments, unemployment compensation, child support, or alimony. Receipts not counted as income include various "lump sum" payments, such as capital gains or inheritances. The total represents the amount of income received before deductions for personal income taxes, Social Security, bond purchases, union dues, Medicare deductions, and the like.

Poverty status is based on the definition prescribed by the U.S. Office of Management and Budget as the standard to be used by federal agencies for statistical purposes.

School enrollment is enrollment in a regular school, either public or private, including nursery schools, kindergarten, and elementary schools, as well as schooling that leads to a high school diploma or college degree. Schools supported and controlled primarily by the federal, state, or local government are defined as public schools (including tribal schools). Schools primarily supported and controlled by religious organizations or other private groups are considered private schools.

TABLES B-4 AND B-6 THROUGH B-15

Sources: U.S. Department of Education, National Center for Education Statistics, Institute of Education Sciences, *Digest of Education Statistics, 2018 and 2019.* https:// nces.ed.gov/programs/digest/current_tables. asp

U.S. Department of Education, National Center for Education Statistics (NCES), Common Core of Data (CCD), Table 2. https://nces.ed.gov/ccd/tables/201819_summary_2.asp.

The locales of "city," "suburban," "town," and "rural" are a collapse of the 12 category, urban-centric locale code.

A **charter school** is a school that provides free public elementary and/or secondary education to eligible students under a specific charter granted by the state legislature or other appropriate authority; the school must have also been designated as a charter school by these authorities. Charter schools can be administered by regular school districts, State Education Agencies (SEAs), or chartering organizations.

A **Title I eligible** school is a school designated under appropriate state and federal regulations as being high poverty and eligible for participation in programs (such as remedial reading or remedial math) authorized by Title I of P.L. 107–110. A Title I school is one in which the percentage of children from low-income families is at least as high as the percentage of children from low-income families served by the LEA as a whole, or a school designated by the LEA as Title I eligible because 35 percent or more of the children are from low-income families. A Title I schoolwide school is a school in which all the students are designated under appropriate state and federal regulations as eligible for participation in Title I programs authorized by Title I of P.L. 107–110. The number of students who received Title I services is from the Public School Data File of the Schools and Staffing Survey.

STUDENTS WHO ARE ELIGIBLE FOR FREE OR REDUCED-PRICE LUNCH
The Free and Reduced-Price Lunch Program is a program under the National School Lunch Act that provides cash subsidies for free or reduced-price meals to students based on family size and income criteria. Participation in the Free and Reduced-Price Lunch Program depends on income, and eligibility is often used to estimate student needs.

STUDENTS WITH INDIVIDUAL EDUCATION PROGRAM

An Individualized Education Program (IEP) is a written instructional plan for students with disabilities who are designated as special education students under IDEA (Individuals with Disabilities Education Act). An IEP includes a statement of present levels of educational performance of a child; a statement of annual goals, including short-term instructional objectives; a statement of specific educational services to be provided and the extent to which the child will be able to participate in regular educational programs; a projected date for initiation and the anticipated duration of services; appropriate objectives, criteria, and evaluation procedures; and schedules for determining, on at least an annual basis, whether instructional objectives are being achieved.

STUDENTS WHO ARE ENGLISH-LANGUAGE LEARNERS

This category includes the number of students who are served in appropriate programs of language assistance (e.g., English as a Second Language, High Intensity Language Training, and bilingual education). This designation changed from Limited-English Proficient (LEP) to English-Language Learners (ELL) in the 2001–2002 school year.

PRIVATE SCHOOLS

Since 1989, the Census Bureau has conducted the biennial Private School Universe Survey (PSS) for NCES. The PSS is designed to generate biennial data on the total number of private schools, students, and teachers and to build a universe of private schools in all of the states and the District of Columbia to serve as a sampling frame of private schools for NCES sample surveys. The target population for the PSS is every school in all of the states and the District of Columbia that are not primarily supported by public funds, provide instruction for one or more grades between kindergarten and grade 12 (or comparable ungraded levels), and have one or more teachers. Organizations or institutions that provide support for home schooling, but do not provide classroom instruction, are not included. Although the PSS has begun to collect limited data on the many private schools for which kindergarten is the highest grade, the data in this volume are for (traditional) schools that include at least one grade between grades 1 and 12.

A private school is controlled by an individual or agency other than a state, a subdivision of a state, or the federal government; is usually supported primarily by nonpublic funds; and the operation of its program does not rest with publicly elected or appointed officials. Private schools include both nonprofit and proprietary institutions.

Data for private schools in Arkansas, Colorado, Washington, D.C., Idaho, Indiana, and Nebraska, should be interpreted with caution. The coefficient of variation for these estimates is larger than 25 percent.

PUBLIC SCHOOL STAFF

The number of teachers represents full-time equivalent teachers employed within the state. Instructional aides directly assist teachers in providing instruction. Instructional coordinators help teachers through curriculum development and in-service training. Support staff includes those involved with food, health, library, maintenance, transportation, security, and other services in public schools. School administrators are principals and assistant principals. School district administrators include the Local Education Agency (LEA) superintendents, deputies, assistant superintendents, and other persons with district-wide responsibilities.

REVENUES

The state data include adjustments made by NCES. Values that were missing and not reported elsewhere in the survey were imputed based on corresponding proportions in reporting states. Other adjustments were made when a single value was reported that included two or more categories. NCES distributed portions of the single reported value to the missing items. In Nebraska and Wyoming, the fiscal data do not include prekindergarten. In Illinois and Wisconsin, revenues for charter schools are not included. In addition to these adjustments, the NPEFS may also include state-run education programs. Consequently, these numbers may differ from the state totals in Table C, which are derived from a different survey.

Revenues from federal sources include direct grants-in-aid from the federal government, federal grants-in-aid through the state or an intermediate agency, and other revenue in lieu of taxes to compensate a school district for nontaxable federal institutions within a district's boundaries.

State revenues include revenues that can be used without restriction, revenues for categorical purposes, and revenues in lieu of taxation. Also included are revenues from payments made by a state for the benefit of the Local Education Agency (LEA) or contributions of equipment or supplies. Such revenues include the payment of a pension fund by the state on behalf of an LEA employee for services rendered and contributions of fixed assets (property, plant, or equipment), such as school buses and textbooks.

Revenues from local sources include local property and non-property tax revenues, taxes levied or assessed by an LEA, revenues from a local government to the LEA, tuition received, transportation fees, earnings on investments from LEA holdings, net revenues from food services (gross receipts less gross expenditures), net revenues from student activities (gross receipts less gross expenditures), and other revenues (textbook sales, donations, and property rentals). Intermediate revenues were included in local revenue totals. Intermediate revenues are derived from sources other than Local or State Education Agencies; these sources operate at an intermediate level between Local and State Education Agencies and possess independent fundraising capabilities (such as county or municipal agencies).

EXPENDITURES

The state data include adjustments made by NCES. Values that were missing and not reported elsewhere in the survey were imputed based on proportions in reporting states. Other adjustments were made when a single value was reported that included two or more categories. NCES distributed portions of the single reported value to the missing items. In Nebraska and Wyoming, the fiscal data do not include prekindergarten. In Illinois and Wisconsin, expenditures for charter schools are not included. In addition to these adjustments, the NPEFS may include state-run education programs. Consequently, these numbers may differ from the state totals in Table C, which come from a different survey.

Current expenditures consist of expenditures for the categories of instruction, support services, and non-instructional services for salaries; employee benefits; purchased services and supplies; and payments by the state made for or on behalf of school systems. These expenditures do not include expenditures for debt service, capital outlay, and property (e.g., equipment), or direct costs (e.g., Head Start, adult education, community colleges, etc.) and community services expenditures.

Instruction and instruction-related expenses comprise current expenditures for activities that deal directly with the interaction between students and teachers. These expenditures include teacher salaries and benefits, supplies (such as textbooks), instructional staff support (for example, salaries for librarians and instructional specialists), and purchased instructional services.

Support services expenditures consist of current expenditures for activities supporting instruction. These services include operation and maintenance of buildings, school administration, student support services (e.g., nurses, therapists, and guidance counselors), student transportation, school district administration, business services, research, and data processing.

Non-instruction expenditures are mostly for food service, but also consist of expenditures for enterprise operations, such as bookstores and interscholastic athletics.

DROPOUTS
"Status" dropouts are 16- to 24-year-olds who are not enrolled in school and who have not completed a high school program, regardless of when they left school. People who have received GED credentials are counted as high school completers. Data are based on sample surveys of the entire population in the given age range residing within the United States, including both noninstitutionalized persons (e.g., those living in households, college housing, or military housing located within the United States) and institutionalized persons (e.g., those living in prisons, nursing facilities, or other healthcare facilities). Totals include other racial/ethnic groups not separately shown. Race categories exclude persons of Hispanic ethnicity.

HIGHER EDUCATION
The Integrated Postsecondary Education Data System (IPEDS) surveys approximately 10,000 postsecondary institutions, including universities, colleges, and institutions offering technical and vocational education beyond the high school level. This survey, which began in 1986, replaced the Higher Education General Information Survey (HEGIS). IPEDS is made up of eight integrated components that obtain information on who provides postsecondary education (institutions), who participates in it and completes it (students), what programs are offered and which ones are completed, and the specific human and financial resources involved in the provision of institutionally based postsecondary education. These components are organized into the following categories: Institutional Characteristics, including instructional activity; Fall Enrollment, including age and residence; Enrollment in Occupationally Specific Programs; Completions; Finance; Staff; Salaries of Full-Time Instructional Faculty; and Academic Libraries.

Institutions of higher education include those with courses leading to an associate's degree or higher, or those with courses accepted for credit toward such degrees. A public institution is controlled and operated by publicly elected or appointed officials and derives its primary support from public funds. A private institution is controlled by an individual or agency other than a state, a subdivision of a state, or the federal government; it is usually primarily supported by nonpublic funds, and the operation of its program does not rest with publicly elected or appointed officials. Private institutions comprise both not-for-profit and proprietary institutions.

Full-time students include undergraduate students enrolled for 12 or more semester credits, 12 or more quarter credits, or 24 or more contact hours a week each term; graduate students enrolled for 9 or more semester credits or 9 or more quarter credits, or students involved in thesis or dissertation preparation who are considered full time students by the institution; and first-professional students (as defined by the institution).

Types of institutions include the following:

• Degree-granting institutions, which offer associate's, bachelor's, master's, doctoral and/or first-professional degrees.

- Level categories include four-year and higher (four-year) institutions, at least two but less than four-year (two-year) institutions, and less than two-year institutions.
  - A four-year institution is a postsecondary institution that offers programs of at least four years' duration or programs at or above the baccalaureate level. This category includes schools that only offer post-baccalaureate certificates and those that only offer graduate programs. Also included are freestanding medical, law, and other first-professional schools.
  - A two-year institution is a postsecondary institution that offers programs of at least two years' duration but less than four years' duration. This category includes occupational and vocational schools with programs of at least 1,800 hours and academic institutions with programs of less than four years' duration. It does not include bachelor's degree–granting institutions where the baccalaureate program can be completed in three years.

Control categories are public, private not-for-profit, and private for-profit.

Undergraduate students are registered at an institution of higher education and are working in a program leading to a baccalaureate degree or other formal award below the baccalaureate, such as an associate degree.

Postbaccalaureate students are working towards master's or doctor's degree or are enrolled in graduate-level classes, but not enrolled in degree programs.

Race/ethnicity categories are categories used to describe groups to which individuals belong, identify with, or belong to in the eyes of the community. A person may be counted in only one group. Classification is based on self-identification. Race categories exclude persons of Hispanic ethnicity.

A nonresident alien is a person who is not a citizen or national of the United States, and who is in this country on a visa or temporary basis; a nonresident alien does not have the right to remain in the United States indefinitely.

Migration refers to the movement of students from their home state of residence to another state to attend a postsecondary institution. The percentages in columns 123 and 124 refer to all first-time postsecondary students enrolled in degree granting institutions in fall 2012.

An associate's degree is a degree granted for the successful completion of a sub-baccalaureate program of studies, and usually requires at least two years (or the equivalent) of full-time college-level study. This category also includes degrees granted in a cooperative or work-study program.

A bachelor's degree is a degree granted for the successful completion of a baccalaureate program of studies, and usually requires at least four years (or the equivalent) of full-time college-level study. This category includes degrees granted in a cooperative or work-study program.

A master's degree is awarded for successful completion of a program generally requiring 1 or 2 years of full-time, college-level study beyond the bachelor's degree. One type of master's degree, including the master of arts degree (M.A.), and the master of science degree (M.S.), is awarded in the liberal arts and sciences for advanced scholarship in a subject field or discipline and demonstrated ability to perform scholarly research. A second type of master's degree is awarded for the completion of a professionally oriented program. These include master's degrees in education (M.Ed.), business administration (M.B.A.), fine arts (M.F.A.), music (M.M.), social work (M.S.W.), and public administration (M.P.A.) A third type of master's degree is awarded in professional fields for study beyond the first-professional degree, such as the master of laws (LL.M.) and the masters of science in various medical specializations. Some master's degrees—such as divinity degrees (M.Div. or M.H.L./Rav), which were formerly classified as "first-professional"—may require more than 2 years of full-time study beyond the bachelor's degree.

A doctor's degree is an earned degree that generally carries the title of Doctor. The Doctor of Philosophy degree (Ph.D.) is the highest academic degree and requires mastery within a field of knowledge and demonstrated ability to perform scholarly research. Other doctor's degrees are awarded for fulfilling specialized requirements in professional fields, such as education (Ed.D.), musical arts (D.M.A.), business administration (D.B.A.), and engineering (D.Eng. or D.E.S.). Many doctor's degrees in academic and professional fields require an earned master's degree as a prerequisite. The doctor's degree classification includes most degrees that NCES formerly classified as first-professional degrees. Such degrees are awarded in the fields of dentistry (D.D.S. or D.M.D.), medicine (M.D.), optometry (O.D.), osteopathic medicine (D.O.), pharmacy (Pharm.D.), podiatry (D.P.M., Pod.D., or D.P.), veterinary medicine (D.V.M.), chiropractic (D.C. or D.C.M.), and law (L.L.B. or J.D.).

Tuition and required fees are payments or charges for instruction or compensation for services, privileges, or the use of equipment, books, or other goods. Data are for the entire academic year and are average charges. In-state tuition and fees were weighted by the number of full-time-equivalent undergraduates but were not adjusted to reflect student residency. Out-of-state tuition and fees were weighted by the number of first-time freshmen attending the institution in fall 2018 from out of state.

PART C

COUNTY EDUCATION STATISTICS

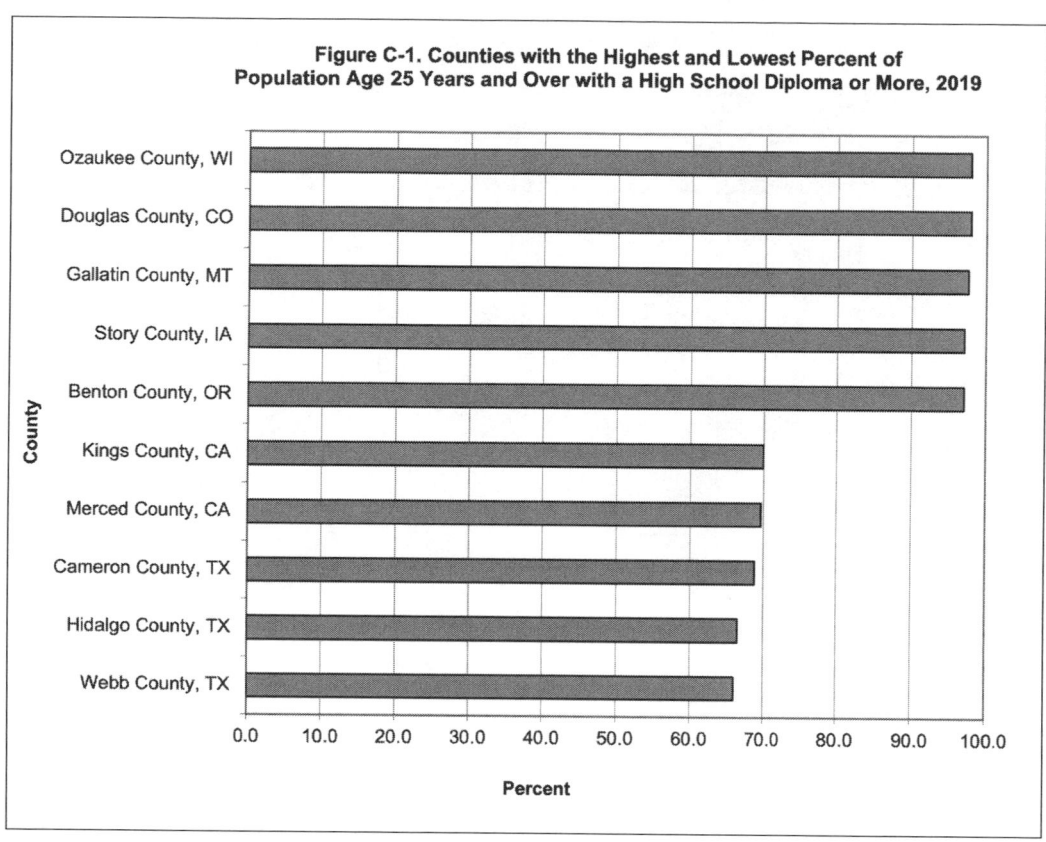

Figure C-1. Counties with the Highest and Lowest Percent of Population Age 25 Years and Over with a High School Diploma or More, 2019

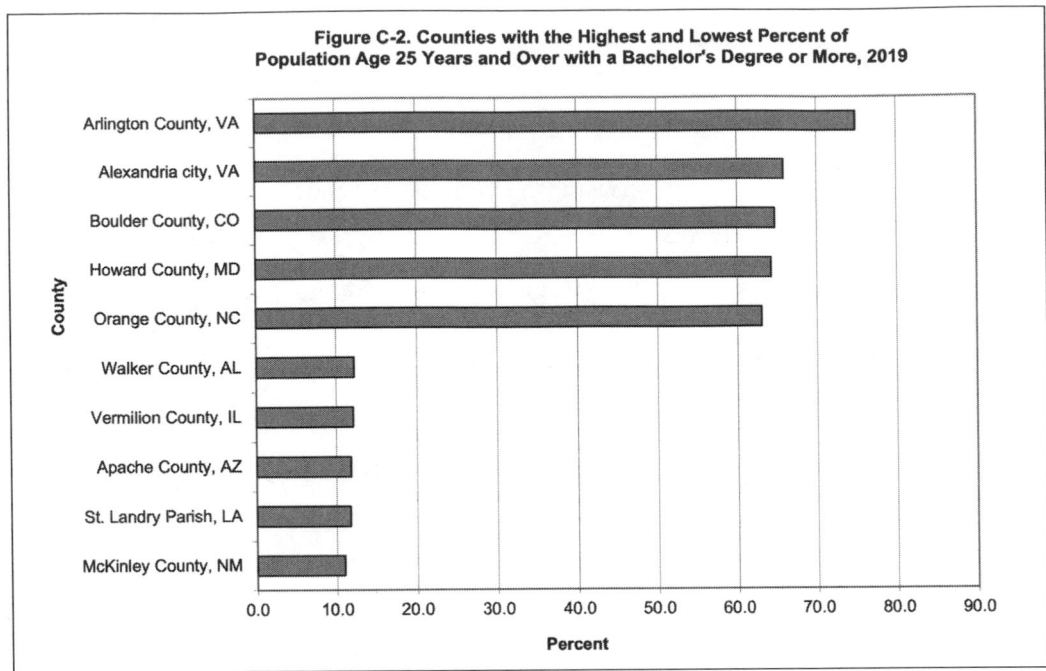

Figure C-2. Counties with the Highest and Lowest Percent of Population Age 25 Years and Over with a Bachelor's Degree or More, 2019

In 2019, there were 6 counties where more than 97 percent of the population age 25 years old and over had graduated from high school. The highest proportion was 98.5 percent of the population in Ozaukee County, Wisconsin. Four U.S. counties had high school attainment levels of less than 70 percent: Merced County, California; Cameron County, Texas; Hidalgo County, Texas; and Webb County, Texas. (Table C-2)

In 2019, 11 counties had 60 percent or more of the population with a bachelor's degree or more. Arlington County, Virginia (which is near Washington, DC), led the way with 74.9 percent of population age 25 years and over having bachelor's degrees or more. Five of the top ten counties were in the Washington, DC, metropolitan area. The others were Boulder County, Colorado (64.8 percent with bachelor's degrees or higher), Orange County, North Carolina (63.1 percent), Hamilton County, Indiana (63.0 percent), New York County, New York (62.0 percent), and Williamson County, Tennessee (61.8 percent). McKinley County, New Mexico, had the lowest college attainment rate, with 11.0 percent of the population having a bachelor's degree or more. (Table C-2)

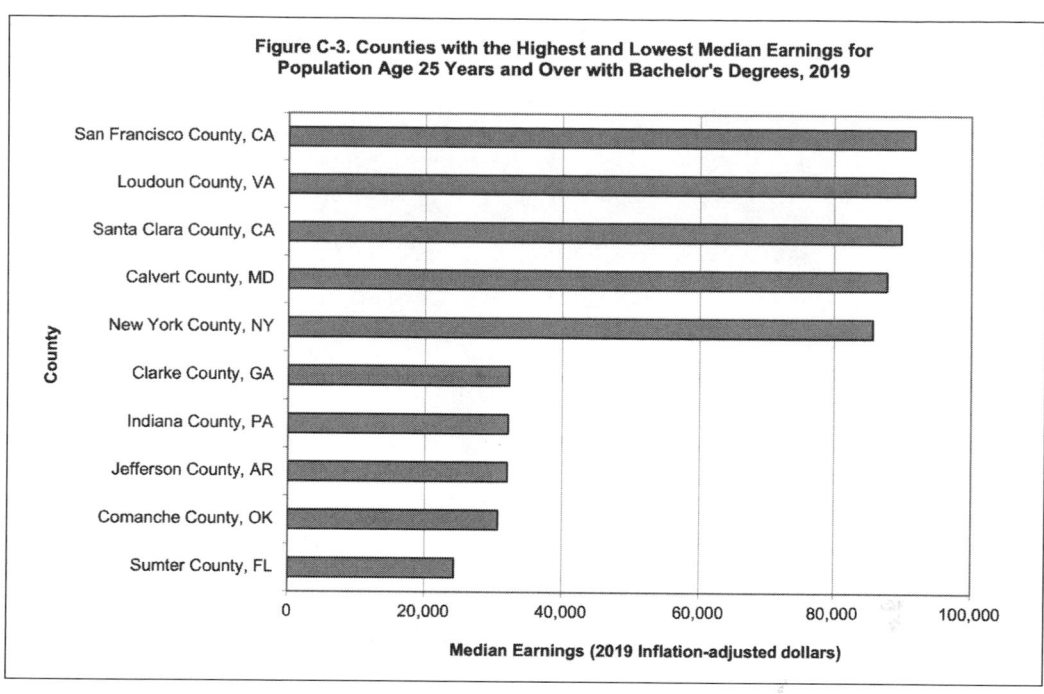

Figure C-3. Counties with the Highest and Lowest Median Earnings for Population Age 25 Years and Over with Bachelor's Degrees, 2019

Arlington County was the county with the highest median earnings for 2019 at $80,929. Six counties had median earnings over $70,000. Sumter County, Florida, had the lowest median earnings: $23,864. Fourteen counties had median earnings less than $30,000. (Table C-2)

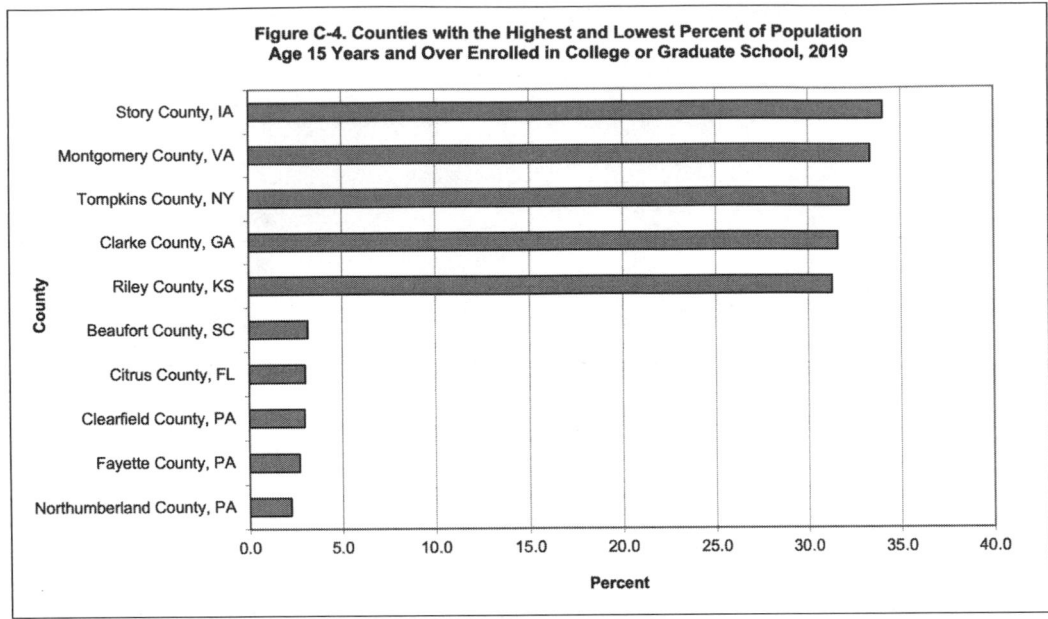

Figure C-4. Counties with the Highest and Lowest Percent of Population Age 15 Years and Over Enrolled in College or Graduate School, 2019

Nationwide, 8.2 percent of the population age 15 years and over was enrolled in college or graduate school in 2019. The counties with the highest percent of population enrolled in college or graduate school in 2019 were: Story County, Iowa, where Iowa State is located (34.0 percent), Montgomery County, Virginia, which is the home of Virginia Tech (33.4 percent), and Tompkins County, New York, home to Cornell University (32.2 percent). (Table C-3)

Table C-1. Population and Poverty Characteristics, by Selected Counties, 2019

(Number; percent.)

State/County	Population		Children under 18 years old in poverty (percent)	Under 19 years old with no health insurance (percent)
	Total under 18 years old for whom poverty status is determined	Percent under 18 years old		
UNITED STATES	71,633,453	22.4	16.8	5.7
ALABAMA	1,068,804	22.4	21.4	3.5
Baldwin County, Alabama...........................	45,702	20.8	11.5	2.7
Calhoun County, Alabama...........................	23,946	21.7	25.1	3.6
Cullman County, Alabama...........................	18,693	22.6	13.9	1.7
DeKalb County, Alabama............................	17,382	24.6	34.5	2.5
Elmore County, Alabama............................	17,919	23.4	20.7	4.9
Etowah County, Alabama............................	21,197	21.1	29.5	9.6
Houston County, Alabama...........................	23,704	22.7	29.5	2.9
Jefferson County, Alabama.........................	147,879	22.9	23.1	3.1
Lauderdale County, Alabama........................	18,255	20.0	20.6	8.5
Lee County, Alabama...............................	34,650	21.8	6.8	1.9
Limestone County, Alabama.........................	21,935	23.0	20.8	5.4
Madison County, Alabama...........................	80,390	22.1	18.0	3.0
Marshall County, Alabama..........................	24,047	25.2	20.2	1.1
Mobile County, Alabama............................	95,251	23.4	26.2	2.2
Montgomery County, Alabama........................	50,802	23.3	20.9	2.8
Morgan County, Alabama............................	26,152	22.4	18.5	6.9
St. Clair County, Alabama.........................	20,024	23.0	12.1	0.8
Shelby County, Alabama	50,206	23.4	5.6	2.1
Talladega County, Alabama.........................	16,510	21.7	24.0	4.0
Tuscaloosa County, Alabama........................	43,373	21.8	19.0	4.0
Walker County, Alabama	13,290	21.4	25.8	23.7
ALASKA..	175,678	24.6	13.0	9.4
Anchorage Municipality, Alaska....................	67,890	24.1	11.9	7.1
Fairbanks North Star Borough, Alaska	22,272	24.1	4.3	5.1
Matanuska-Susitna Borough, Alaska.................	27,913	26.4	15.2	14.7
ARIZONA	1,612,619	22.7	19.1	9.2
Apache County, Arizona	18,863	26.7	47.8	36.6
Cochise County, Arizona	26,565	22.2	26.4	7.6
Coconino County, Arizona	27,446	21.2	11.6	10.6
Maricopa County, Arizona	1,037,006	23.4	17.3	9.1
Mohave County, Arizona	35,166	16.9	29.0	5.3
Navajo County, Arizona	28,985	26.7	34.9	20.7
Pima County, Arizona	211,410	20.8	18.4	7.3
Pinal County, Arizona	100,796	23.2	16.6	9.5
Yavapai County, Arizona	35,623	15.5	14.0	9.8
Yuma County, Arizona	52,352	25.3	34.1	9.2
ARKANSAS...	685,484	23.4	22.1	5.9
Benton County, Arkansas	72,049	26.2	13.4	6.3
Craighead County, Arkansas	25,770	24.2	30.6	5.4
Faulkner County, Arkansas.........................	28,498	23.6	17.4	2.8
Garland County, Arkansas	19,289	19.7	24.0	10.2
Jefferson County, Arkansas........................	14,245	23.6	35.1	7.5
Lonoke County, Arkansas...........................	18,411	25.4	16.6	4.2
Pulaski County, Arkansas..........................	88,885	23.1	19.5	5.0
Saline County, Arkansas...........................	28,110	23.2	20.1	6.2
Sebastian County, Arkansas........................	30,047	23.9	21.7	6.3
Washington County, Arkansas	56,391	24.5	15.9	9.2
White County, Arkansas	17,887	23.9	19.7	4.1
CALIFORNIA	8,728,833	22.5	15.6	3.6
Alameda County, California	333,545	20.3	9.7	2.3
Butte County, California...........................	43,130	20.2	13.2	2.9
Contra Costa County, California	255,420	22.3	10.4	3.2
El Dorado County, California	36,496	19.2	10.1	3.9
Fresno County, California	277,653	28.3	29.7	3.7
Humboldt County, California	25,051	18.9	19.5	4.6
Imperial County, California........................	50,729	29.8	35.4	3.5
Kern County, California	254,085	29.1	26.7	2.9
Kings County, California...........................	40,912	29.6	23.9	2.9
Lake County, California............................	13,236	20.8	24.9	1.6
Los Angeles County, California.....................	2,106,428	21.3	18.4	4.0
Madera County, California..........................	42,683	28.8	27.4	3.0
Marin County, California...........................	50,812	20.0	7.5	2.6
Mendocino County, California	17,976	21.1	17.6	2.1
Merced County, California	79,245	29.3	22.7	5.4
Monterey County, California........................	111,270	26.7	19.6	2.1

Table C-1. Population and Poverty Characteristics, by Selected Counties, 2019—*Continued*

(Number; percent.)

State/County	Population		Children under 18 years old in poverty (percent)	Under 19 years old with no health insurance (percent)
	Total under 18 years old for whom poverty status is determined	Percent under 18 years old		
CALIFORNIA—(*Continued*)				
Napa County, California...............................	27,218	20.2	7.0	3.9
Nevada County, California	16,735	16.9	14.3	3.9
Orange County, California	680,184	21.7	12.5	4.0
Placer County, California	87,372	22.1	9.4	3.7
Riverside County, California	600,891	24.8	14.0	3.8
Sacramento County, California.....................	356,825	23.3	15.9	3.1
San Bernardino County, California	560,441	26.3	18.4	4.4
San Diego County, California........................	702,953	21.6	12.7	3.9
San Francisco County, California...................	114,772	13.2	7.3	0.9
San Joaquin County, California	199,762	26.9	18.7	3.2
San Luis Obispo County, California	48,010	17.9	11.3	4.9
San Mateo County, California.......................	153,217	20.1	6.2	2.5
Santa Barbara County, California..................	94,130	22.2	12.5	3.4
Santa Clara County, California......................	407,695	21.5	5.1	2.0
Santa Cruz County, California.......................	50,750	19.4	7.1	2.0
Shasta County, California	37,907	21.4	13.1	3.5
Solano County, California.............................	96,391	22.1	11.2	2.4
Sonoma County, California...........................	92,336	19.0	6.4	4.5
Stanislaus County, California.......................	146,474	26.8	16.8	3.4
Sutter County, California.............................	24,788	25.8	15.9	2.6
Tehama County, California...........................	14,808	23.1	29.4	0.6
Tulare County, California.............................	139,914	30.4	26.0	1.8
Ventura County, California...........................	186,184	22.4	11.3	4.1
Yolo County, California................................	43,379	20.5	14.0	1.7
Yuba County, California...............................	20,811	27.1	14.4	6.4
COLORADO..	1,238,626	22.0	10.9	5.5
Adams County, Colorado.............................	133,883	26.1	11.9	5.1
Arapahoe County, Colorado.........................	149,331	23.0	8.2	7.0
Boulder County, Colorado	60,791	19.4	7.9	4.7
Broomfield County, Colorado	15,209	21.8	4.8	2.8
Denver County, Colorado	136,914	19.2	14.9	4.8
Douglas County, Colorado...........................	88,453	25.3	1.7	1.8
El Paso County, Colorado............................	168,495	24.0	9.6	5.4
Jefferson County, Colorado.........................	111,927	19.5	10.4	6.5
Larimer County, Colorado	67,233	19.4	8.2	3.0
Mesa County, Colorado...............................	32,004	21.2	13.1	7.6
Pueblo County, Colorado.............................	36,913	22.4	26.3	2.1
Weld County, Colorado................................	83,150	26.2	9.3	6.2
CONNECTICUT	716,121	20.7	14.1	3.5
Fairfield County, Connecticut......................	207,672	22.4	12.4	6.6
Hartford County, Connecticut......................	182,690	21.0	14.4	1.7
Litchfield County, Connecticut.....................	31,647	17.8	11.7	3.8
Middlesex County, Connecticut....................	27,760	17.6	8.8	1.9
New Haven County, Connecticut	168,392	20.3	19.3	2.6
New London County, Connecticut	49,684	19.6	11.7	2.0
Tolland County, Connecticut........................	25,509	18.8	6.5	2.1
Windham County, Connecticut.....................	22,767	20.4	12.8	2.1
DELAWARE...	197,150	20.9	16.4	4.8
Kent County, Delaware	38,983	22.4	18.0	9.9
New Castle County, Delaware......................	116,669	21.6	12.4	3.0
Sussex County, Delaware............................	41,498	18.1	25.9	5.0
DISTRICT OF COLUMBIA...........................	126,313	18.8	18.9	2.0
District of Columbia, District of Columbia............	126,313	18.8	18.9	2.0
FLORIDA..	4,155,155	19.7	17.7	7.6
Alachua County, Florida..............................	47,610	18.6	15.6	5.7
Bay County, Florida	35,682	20.7	12.2	8.3
Brevard County, Florida..............................	107,234	18.0	10.1	5.8
Broward County, Florida..............................	404,721	20.9	16.3	10.6
Charlotte County, Florida............................	21,437	11.6	22.9	9.5
Citrus County, Florida.................................	21,118	14.4	25.2	10.5
Clay County, Florida	49,056	22.6	12.5	5.7
Collier County, Florida................................	64,046	16.8	11.5	7.7
Columbia County, Florida............................	14,950	22.5	15.4	7.9
Duval County, Florida.................................	212,366	22.7	19.4	6.5
Escambia County, Florida............................	64,345	21.5	24.7	6.8
Flagler County, Florida................................	18,889	16.5	15.7	17.6
Hernando County, Florida............................	34,134	17.9	18.5	8.1

Table C-1. Population and Poverty Characteristics, by Selected Counties, 2019—*Continued*

(Number; percent.)

State/County	Population			Under 19 years old with no health insurance (percent)
	Total under 18 years old for whom poverty status is determined	Percent under 18 years old	Children under 18 years old in poverty (percent)	
FLORIDA—(*Continued*)				
Highlands County, Florida	18,227	17.4	22.2	8.3
Hillsborough County, Florida	322,404	22.2	18.4	6.4
Indian River County, Florida	25,677	16.2	25.0	3.6
Lake County, Florida	67,661	18.7	21.0	5.4
Lee County, Florida	133,121	17.5	19.1	9.0
Leon County, Florida	53,443	19.1	24.3	6.4
Manatee County, Florida	71,109	17.8	21.2	4.8
Marion County, Florida	65,255	18.4	26.6	6.5
Martin County, Florida	25,581	16.2	7.1	3.9
Miami-Dade County, Florida	544,596	20.3	20.5	7.3
Monroe County, Florida	10,508	14.4	6.5	14.6
Nassau County, Florida	17,177	19.6	13.9	3.1
Okaloosa County, Florida	45,096	22.2	18.2	8.2
Orange County, Florida	299,661	22.0	18.1	7.0
Osceola County, Florida	89,325	23.9	19.3	8.2
Palm Beach County, Florida	278,383	18.9	15.9	8.8
Pasco County, Florida	109,885	20.1	16.7	7.1
Pinellas County, Florida	151,235	15.8	13.1	6.5
Polk County, Florida	155,311	21.9	21.2	7.4
Putnam County, Florida	15,034	20.6	36.2	4.7
St. Johns County, Florida	56,053	21.4	6.1	8.0
St. Lucie County, Florida	63,467	19.5	10.0	11.5
Santa Rosa County, Florida	38,765	21.9	11.7	6.9
Sarasota County, Florida	59,362	13.9	6.8	6.7
Seminole County, Florida	97,674	20.9	11.3	4.8
Sumter County, Florida	8,674	7.1	6.8	23.6
Volusia County, Florida	94,944	17.5	19.9	9.3
Walton County, Florida	14,837	20.5	11.3	7.9
GEORGIA	2,462,583	23.8	18.7	7.4
Barrow County, Georgia	21,001	25.4	12.7	5.2
Bartow County, Georgia	25,116	23.7	15.2	10.9
Bibb County, Georgia	35,915	24.5	39.0	3.6
Bulloch County, Georgia	14,731	20.6	17.8	4.3
Carroll County, Georgia	27,818	23.9	25.3	4.1
Catoosa County, Georgia	15,421	23.0	11.9	5.1
Chatham County, Georgia	59,605	21.5	19.9	7.7
Cherokee County, Georgia	61,643	24.0	8.4	5.3
Clarke County, Georgia	21,718	18.7	29.3	7.1
Clayton County, Georgia	79,913	27.9	23.1	12.4
Cobb County, Georgia	172,757	23.1	11.4	7.7
Columbia County, Georgia	38,610	24.8	5.0	3.4
Coweta County, Georgia	36,039	24.4	9.8	2.4
DeKalb County, Georgia	170,537	22.9	17.3	6.6
Dougherty County, Georgia	20,184	24.0	39.3	6.4
Douglas County, Georgia	36,389	25.2	14.3	9.2
Fayette County, Georgia	25,569	22.6	5.4	7.3
Floyd County, Georgia	22,209	23.6	25.7	6.7
Forsyth County, Georgia	65,178	26.8	5.4	5.4
Fulton County, Georgia	226,200	22.0	22.3	4.0
Glynn County, Georgia	17,972	21.4	28.3	7.1
Gwinnett County, Georgia	247,999	26.7	13.2	11.1
Hall County, Georgia	49,999	24.7	25.7	11.8
Henry County, Georgia	59,017	25.3	12.9	6.8
Houston County, Georgia	39,666	25.5	12.3	11.2
Jackson County, Georgia	18,586	25.8	10.9	11.1
Lowndes County, Georgia	27,819	24.7	30.4	7.3
Muscogee County, Georgia	47,793	25.2	24.8	3.2
Newton County, Georgia	28,398	25.8	9.7	10.4
Paulding County, Georgia	43,678	26.0	6.0	7.2
Richmond County, Georgia	45,080	23.5	35.6	6.0
Rockdale County, Georgia	21,771	24.2	13.0	15.1
Spalding County, Georgia	15,075	23.2	28.0	8.7
Troup County, Georgia	15,684	23.2	33.8	4.8
Walker County, Georgia	14,698	21.7	14.5	12.0
Walton County, Georgia	22,482	24.1	19.2	11.5
Whitfield County, Georgia	26,427	25.7	18.8	7.4
HAWAII	295,071	21.4	12.4	2.8
Hawaii County, Hawaii	42,761	21.5	19.4	2.3
Honolulu County, Hawaii	201,291	21.3	9.9	2.4

Table C-1. Population and Poverty Characteristics, by Selected Counties, 2019—*Continued*

(Number; percent.)

State/County	Population		Children under 18 years old in poverty (percent)	Under 19 years old with no health insurance (percent)
	Total under 18 years old for whom poverty status is determined	Percent under 18 years old		
HAWAII—(*Continued*)				
Kauai County, Hawaii	15,589	21.8	13.2	4.4
Maui County, Hawaii	35,430	21.4	17.6	5.3
IDAHO	441,454	25.2	13.2	5.0
Ada County, Idaho	109,680	23.3	11.8	4.4
Bannock County, Idaho	21,725	25.5	15.6	3.6
Bonneville County, Idaho	36,147	30.6	8.4	3.6
Canyon County, Idaho	62,802	27.8	10.3	6.2
Kootenai County, Idaho	36,926	22.6	15.9	5.4
Twin Falls County, Idaho	24,458	28.4	9.1	2.8
ILLINOIS	2,771,838	22.4	15.7	4.0
Adams County, Illinois	13,941	21.9	23.2	4.4
Champaign County, Illinois	38,516	19.8	21.4	1.3
Cook County, Illinois	1,098,427	21.7	18.3	4.6
DeKalb County, Illinois	22,225	22.1	11.3	3.0
DuPage County, Illinois	205,898	22.6	7.8	3.6
Kane County, Illinois	129,779	24.7	14.1	3.0
Kankakee County, Illinois	23,527	22.4	19.6	0.9
Kendall County, Illinois	35,980	28.0	4.1	7.2
Lake County, Illinois	164,963	24.3	10.6	4.1
LaSalle County, Illinois	22,183	21.2	21.3	1.6
McHenry County, Illinois	70,100	23.0	6.6	5.1
McLean County, Illinois	35,981	22.3	8.4	5.1
Macon County, Illinois	22,414	22.4	19.6	4.5
Madison County, Illinois	56,681	22.0	14.3	2.4
Peoria County, Illinois	41,600	23.9	21.9	5.7
Rock Island County, Illinois	31,071	22.7	22.6	5.6
St. Clair County, Illinois	58,892	23.1	19.3	5.6
Sangamon County, Illinois	41,674	21.9	19.1	1.8
Tazewell County, Illinois	29,791	23.1	7.3	3.5
Vermilion County, Illinois	17,390	23.9	27.3	1.4
Will County, Illinois	167,126	24.6	9.2	2.3
Williamson County, Illinois	13,876	21.7	16.2	5.9
Winnebago County, Illinois	63,902	23.0	29.9	2.0
INDIANA	1,522,694	23.4	15.2	7.1
Allen County, Indiana	95,455	25.6	12.0	4.4
Bartholomew County, Indiana	19,621	23.8	25.2	3.3
Boone County, Indiana	17,251	25.9	11.4	3.3
Clark County, Indiana	26,155	22.4	12.0	2.3
Delaware County, Indiana	19,569	18.4	27.2	6.5
Elkhart County, Indiana	54,768	27.2	9.9	18.8
Floyd County, Indiana	17,615	23.0	16.9	5.7
Grant County, Indiana	13,150	22.0	23.2	2.1
Hamilton County, Indiana	88,483	26.4	5.3	3.7
Hancock County, Indiana	17,163	22.2	1.2	0.7
Hendricks County, Indiana	38,907	23.5	4.5	6.3
Howard County, Indiana	18,430	22.8	16.4	12.1
Johnson County, Indiana	36,953	23.9	4.6	4.5
Kosciusko County, Indiana	18,812	24.1	11.5	7.1
Lake County, Indiana	111,170	23.2	20.7	5.5
LaPorte County, Indiana	22,882	22.5	29.4	4.4
Madison County, Indiana	26,612	21.6	18.5	8.1
Marion County, Indiana	228,343	24.2	19.6	7.0
Monroe County, Indiana	21,772	16.5	17.5	2.7
Morgan County, Indiana	15,388	22.3	16.0	7.0
Porter County, Indiana	36,716	22.0	6.8	4.6
St. Joseph County, Indiana	61,821	23.9	23.6	6.1
Tippecanoe County, Indiana	39,897	22.3	14.9	5.1
Vanderburgh County, Indiana	38,209	21.9	21.0	3.0
Vigo County, Indiana	20,483	20.8	28.5	2.7
Wayne County, Indiana	14,314	22.8	26.0	14.2
IOWA	709,897	23.2	13.0	2.9
Black Hawk County, Iowa	27,727	21.9	15.2	1.5
Dallas County, Iowa	24,876	26.8	2.1	3.7
Dubuque County, Iowa	21,849	23.3	12.0	2.5
Johnson County, Iowa	29,666	20.6	10.0	7.5
Linn County, Iowa	50,985	23.1	16.8	1.3
Polk County, Iowa	119,571	24.8	12.2	1.8

Table C-1. Population and Poverty Characteristics, by Selected Counties, 2019—*Continued*

(Number; percent.)

State/County	Population			Under 19 years old with no health insurance (percent)
	Total under 18 years old for whom poverty status is determined	Percent under 18 years old	Children under 18 years old in poverty (percent)	
IOWA—(*Continued*)				
Pottawattamie County, Iowa	21,194	23.3	10.2	2.1
Scott County, Iowa	40,164	23.7	14.0	3.8
Story County, Iowa	14,779	17.3	7.5	1.9
Woodbury County, Iowa	26,029	26.0	15.3	0.9
KANSAS	686,510	24.3	14.7	5.8
Butler County, Kansas	16,677	26.3	8.9	9.4
Douglas County, Kansas	22,241	19.5	14.9	4.7
Johnson County, Kansas	142,513	23.9	6.1	3.9
Leavenworth County, Kansas	18,383	24.2	6.4	5.4
Riley County, Kansas	11,762	18.4	14.0	1.0
Sedgwick County, Kansas	128,730	25.3	17.1	5.4
Shawnee County, Kansas	39,544	23.0	11.4	2.9
Wyandotte County, Kansas	45,247	27.6	33.4	13.4
KENTUCKY	976,902	22.6	21.7	4.3
Boone County, Kentucky	32,701	24.9	9.9	4.4
Bullitt County, Kentucky	17,364	21.4	6.9	1.2
Campbell County, Kentucky	19,285	21.3	12.5	1.7
Christian County, Kentucky	18,992	29.7	22.5	10.6
Daviess County, Kentucky	24,240	24.6	23.1	7.3
Fayette County, Kentucky	65,817	21.2	17.6	4.1
Hardin County, Kentucky	25,116	23.5	7.1	2.1
Jefferson County, Kentucky	165,296	22.0	20.3	4.4
Kenton County, Kentucky	39,214	23.7	17.7	2.2
McCracken County, Kentucky	14,673	22.9	24.9	7.0
Madison County, Kentucky	18,924	22.0	20.1	2.6
Oldham County, Kentucky	16,379	25.9	6.6	4.6
Warren County, Kentucky	29,831	23.8	21.5	1.8
LOUISIANA	1,068,098	23.7	27.0	4.4
Ascension Parish, Louisiana	33,276	26.5	11.8	6.5
Bossier Parish, Louisiana	30,085	24.3	31.4	14.3
Caddo Parish, Louisiana	55,476	23.6	37.5	3.9
Calcasieu Parish, Louisiana	50,992	25.5	28.7	3.9
East Baton Rouge Parish, Louisiana	99,286	23.0	24.1	7.9
Iberia Parish, Louisiana	17,452	25.3	30.2	5.7
Jefferson Parish, Louisiana	93,920	21.9	22.3	4.7
Lafayette Parish, Louisiana	56,866	23.8	25.2	2.1
Lafourche Parish, Louisiana	21,675	22.9	32.1	5.8
Livingston Parish, Louisiana	35,399	25.4	14.9	2.2
Orleans Parish, Louisiana	75,934	20.0	33.1	4.0
Ouachita Parish, Louisiana	37,620	25.8	39.9	6.2
Rapides Parish, Louisiana	31,812	25.2	26.0	5.4
St. Landry Parish, Louisiana	20,236	25.2	29.0	2.8
St. Tammany Parish, Louisiana	61,074	23.7	17.4	2.9
Tangipahoa Parish, Louisiana	32,447	24.7	35.3	3.2
Terrebonne Parish, Louisiana	26,864	24.8	30.9	1.7
MAINE	236,723	18.2	13.8	5.6
Androscoggin County, Maine	22,611	21.5	11.4	6.6
Aroostook County, Maine	11,484	17.8	25.0	3.7
Cumberland County, Maine	51,906	18.1	9.6	2.9
Kennebec County, Maine	21,811	18.5	13.2	9.7
Penobscot County, Maine	25,571	17.6	13.0	7.2
York County, Maine	37,212	18.2	9.7	3.2
MARYLAND	1,306,674	22.2	12.0	3.4
Allegany County, Maryland	11,454	18.6	19.7	4.1
Anne Arundel County, Maryland	127,491	22.7	7.4	1.8
Baltimore County, Maryland	176,762	21.9	10.6	3.8
Calvert County, Maryland	20,994	22.9	9.4	3.4
Carroll County, Maryland	35,333	21.5	5.0	2.9
Cecil County, Maryland	21,534	21.3	14.3	1.9
Charles County, Maryland	37,810	23.5	8.8	4.7
Frederick County, Maryland	59,027	23.2	5.5	1.2
Harford County, Maryland	55,901	22.0	9.4	2.0
Howard County, Maryland	78,572	24.3	4.4	3.2
Montgomery County, Maryland	236,663	22.8	9.4	3.1
Prince George's County, Maryland	196,762	22.2	12.6	5.7
St. Mary's County, Maryland	26,740	24.2	11.1	1.2

Table C-1. Population and Poverty Characteristics, by Selected Counties, 2019—*Continued*

(Number; percent.)

State/County	Population		Children under 18 years old in poverty (percent)	Under 19 years old with no health insurance (percent)
	Total under 18 years old for whom poverty status is determined	Percent under 18 years old		
MARYLAND—(*Continued*)				
Washington County, Maryland	31,712	22.3	18.1	3.2
Wicomico County, Maryland	21,068	21.4	28.0	3.1
Baltimore city, Maryland	117,310	20.5	30.5	4.1
MASSACHUSETTS	1,328,584	20.0	11.6	1.5
Barnstable County, Massachusetts	30,993	14.7	7.9	2.1
Berkshire County, Massachusetts	19,733	16.6	15.5	1.4
Bristol County, Massachusetts	114,245	20.7	16.5	2.3
Essex County, Massachusetts	163,259	21.2	11.4	1.9
Franklin County, Massachusetts	11,620	16.8	7.3	0.5
Hampden County, Massachusetts	98,499	21.7	18.7	1.8
Hampshire County, Massachusetts	22,437	16.3	10.1	3.7
Middlesex County, Massachusetts	311,328	20.0	6.8	1.2
Norfolk County, Massachusetts	145,318	21.1	5.1	0.7
Plymouth County, Massachusetts	109,001	21.4	10.1	1.2
Suffolk County, Massachusetts	126,754	16.7	24.1	2.0
Worcester County, Massachusetts	170,135	21.2	11.6	1.0
MICHIGAN	2,105,855	21.5	17.6	3.4
Allegan County, Michigan	27,638	23.7	21.2	4.4
Bay County, Michigan	20,555	20.1	23.2	2.8
Berrien County, Michigan	32,218	21.4	24.1	7.3
Calhoun County, Michigan	29,453	22.5	20.3	4.3
Clinton County, Michigan	17,307	22.0	7.2	3.9
Eaton County, Michigan	22,715	20.9	9.0	3.6
Genesee County, Michigan	88,516	22.1	21.7	2.0
Grand Traverse County, Michigan	17,910	19.5	8.1	3.3
Ingham County, Michigan	55,811	20.5	16.8	2.5
Isabella County, Michigan	11,277	17.7	28.8	6.9
Jackson County, Michigan	33,390	22.4	16.5	2.3
Kalamazoo County, Michigan	55,453	21.5	11.9	2.0
Kent County, Michigan	154,185	23.9	15.5	2.9
Lapeer County, Michigan	17,127	20.0	14.8	5.2
Lenawee County, Michigan	19,696	21.2	16.8	3.6
Livingston County, Michigan	39,563	20.7	3.1	1.1
Macomb County, Michigan	179,816	20.8	11.2	3.3
Marquette County, Michigan	11,407	18.1	10.2	1.4
Midland County, Michigan	18,118	22.1	9.6	2.5
Monroe County, Michigan	30,920	20.8	17.3	3.2
Muskegon County, Michigan	37,909	22.7	14.6	2.3
Oakland County, Michigan	258,037	20.7	9.3	3.5
Ottawa County, Michigan	68,250	24.2	8.0	2.9
Saginaw County, Michigan	39,809	21.6	31.8	2.2
St. Clair County, Michigan	31,791	20.2	12.1	0.8
Shiawassee County, Michigan	13,896	20.7	14.8	1.4
Van Buren County, Michigan	17,308	23.1	15.6	5.2
Washtenaw County, Michigan	66,677	19.2	13.5	1.8
Wayne County, Michigan	406,859	23.5	29.4	3.2
MINNESOTA	1,277,682	23.2	11.2	3.1
Anoka County, Minnesota	82,991	23.5	8.2	2.0
Blue Earth County, Minnesota	12,834	20.1	15.6	4.0
Carver County, Minnesota	27,031	26.1	5.2	1.6
Crow Wing County, Minnesota	13,940	21.7	14.9	0.9
Dakota County, Minnesota	102,700	24.1	8.8	2.2
Hennepin County, Minnesota	271,672	21.8	12.1	1.7
Olmsted County, Minnesota	38,067	24.4	6.4	2.6
Ramsey County, Minnesota	125,721	23.4	17.5	3.8
Rice County, Minnesota	14,092	24.1	5.8	6.6
St. Louis County, Minnesota	35,858	18.8	12.3	1.3
Scott County, Minnesota	40,046	27.2	4.2	3.3
Sherburne County, Minnesota	24,074	25.7	6.6	2.3
Stearns County, Minnesota	37,125	24.0	17.0	2.4
Washington County, Minnesota	62,310	24.1	5.8	1.3
Wright County, Minnesota	37,847	27.6	6.4	5.2
MISSISSIPPI	685,080	23.8	28.1	6.1
DeSoto County, Mississippi	45,858	25.1	14.1	6.0
Forrest County, Mississippi	16,777	23.3	26.7	3.1
Harrison County, Mississippi	48,657	24.0	27.3	8.2

Table C-1. Population and Poverty Characteristics, by Selected Counties, 2019—*Continued*

(Number; percent.)

State/County	Population			Under 19 years old with no health insurance (percent)
	Total under 18 years old for whom poverty status is determined	Percent under 18 years old	Children under 18 years old in poverty (percent)	
MISSISSIPPI—(*Continued*)				
Hinds County, Mississippi	53,879	24.1	28.6	6.2
Jackson County, Mississippi	31,818	22.6	21.4	5.5
Jones County, Mississippi	16,722	25.2	45.3	6.6
Lauderdale County, Mississippi	16,961	24.1	31.5	1.9
Lee County, Mississippi	20,952	24.9	25.9	8.9
Madison County, Mississippi	26,212	25.0	15.0	1.5
Rankin County, Mississippi	35,243	23.4	15.5	4.7
MISSOURI	1,339,545	22.5	17.1	6.5
Boone County, Missouri	36,091	21.0	16.3	5.3
Buchanan County, Missouri	18,831	22.7	22.5	6.2
Cape Girardeau County, Missouri	16,279	21.5	22.8	2.3
Cass County, Missouri	24,903	23.8	15.8	6.6
Christian County, Missouri	21,645	24.7	17.0	2.9
Clay County, Missouri	59,315	23.9	17.3	4.1
Cole County, Missouri	16,335	23.1	15.5	6.0
Franklin County, Missouri	22,803	22.3	12.3	6.4
Greene County, Missouri	57,974	20.7	9.5	13.8
Jackson County, Missouri	160,708	23.3	20.3	8.4
Jasper County, Missouri	29,340	24.7	32.5	8.5
Jefferson County, Missouri	50,191	22.6	11.3	3.6
Platte County, Missouri	24,151	23.4	4.6	3.8
St. Charles County, Missouri	91,068	23.1	5.0	3.7
St. Francois County, Missouri	13,244	21.9	13.7	1.4
St. Louis County, Missouri	212,324	21.8	12.5	2.5
St. Louis city, Missouri	55,053	18.9	24.1	6.8
MONTANA	220,375	21.1	14.9	6.2
Cascade County, Montana	17,325	22.0	23.0	6.1
Flathead County, Montana	22,096	21.5	8.3	4.4
Gallatin County, Montana	21,548	19.6	8.8	8.3
Lewis and Clark County, Montana	13,301	19.7	13.4	1.8
Missoula County, Montana	21,984	18.8	5.8	2.3
Yellowstone County, Montana	36,031	22.9	18.7	1.5
NEBRASKA	462,947	24.7	11.0	5.7
Douglas County, Nebraska	143,638	25.7	12.4	5.8
Lancaster County, Nebraska	70,629	23.1	10.8	5.8
Sarpy County, Nebraska	50,221	27.1	7.5	3.3
NEVADA	678,509	22.3	16.9	8.0
Clark County, Nevada	511,339	22.8	17.7	8.1
Washoe County, Nevada	99,038	21.3	11.1	7.6
NEW HAMPSHIRE	249,612	19.0	7.1	3.7
Cheshire County, New Hampshire	13,716	19.2	10.5	1.8
Grafton County, New Hampshire	14,148	16.9	6.8	3.5
Hillsborough County, New Hampshire	82,241	20.1	7.5	4.4
Merrimack County, New Hampshire	28,473	19.6	3.6	4.1
Rockingham County, New Hampshire	57,800	18.9	4.6	2.9
Strafford County, New Hampshire	22,200	18.4	4.6	3.9
NEW JERSEY	1,913,827	22.0	12.3	4.3
Atlantic County, New Jersey	55,074	21.3	13.4	2.9
Bergen County, New Jersey	194,566	21.1	5.1	3.0
Burlington County, New Jersey	90,627	20.9	7.4	2.9
Camden County, New Jersey	112,044	22.5	15.5	2.5
Cape May County, New Jersey	15,941	17.6	11.1	1.9
Cumberland County, New Jersey	35,332	25.5	17.1	2.5
Essex County, New Jersey	187,567	24.1	18.6	5.8
Gloucester County, New Jersey	62,575	21.7	7.0	5.2
Hudson County, New Jersey	133,967	20.2	20.5	5.0
Hunterdon County, New Jersey	22,811	18.9	1.0	1.5
Mercer County, New Jersey	77,168	22.1	14.1	4.6
Middlesex County, New Jersey	177,149	22.1	11.9	5.1
Monmouth County, New Jersey	128,254	20.9	6.2	3.7
Morris County, New Jersey	101,925	21.0	6.9	3.9
Ocean County, New Jersey	144,748	24.1	13.8	2.7
Passaic County, New Jersey	117,568	23.8	21.0	7.4
Salem County, New Jersey	12,827	21.0	20.2	2.2

Table C-1. Population and Poverty Characteristics, by Selected Counties, 2019—*Continued*

(Number; percent.)

| State/County | Population | | Children under 18 years old in poverty (percent) | Under 19 years old with no health insurance (percent) |
	Total under 18 years old for whom poverty status is determined	Percent under 18 years old		
NEW JERSEY—(*Continued*)				
Somerset County, New Jersey	69,861	21.5	8.8	6.3
Sussex County, New Jersey	27,043	19.4	6.8	1.4
Union County, New Jersey	127,538	23.3	12.0	6.4
Warren County, New Jersey	19,242	18.7	9.9	1.5
NEW MEXICO	465,341	22.7	24.9	5.7
Bernalillo County, New Mexico	142,420	21.3	22.5	4.1
Chaves County, New Mexico	16,535	26.4	23.0	4.4
Doña Ana County, New Mexico	52,337	24.6	34.4	6.6
Lea County, New Mexico	20,262	29.9	21.3	5.3
McKinley County, New Mexico	19,760	28.0	42.5	18.4
Otero County, New Mexico	15,480	24.4	28.2	1.3
Sandoval County, New Mexico	33,057	22.6	13.8	2.2
San Juan County, New Mexico	32,040	26.2	30.5	6.6
Santa Fe County, New Mexico	25,407	17.2	17.4	10.7
Valencia County, New Mexico	15,838	21.3	27.5	7.1
NEW YORK	3,928,154	20.7	18.1	2.4
Albany County, New York	54,690	18.9	17.4	0.6
Bronx County, New York	337,430	24.4	37.1	2.3
Broome County, New York	35,561	19.7	28.4	2.7
Cattaraugus County, New York	16,366	22.1	20.3	11.0
Cayuga County, New York	14,079	19.5	23.9	1.9
Chautauqua County, New York	24,289	20.0	25.3	4.9
Chemung County, New York	16,860	21.3	18.9	3.5
Clinton County, New York	13,313	18.3	20.8	2.4
Dutchess County, New York	52,795	19.0	8.5	4.7
Erie County, New York	181,903	20.4	19.5	1.3
Jefferson County, New York	24,750	24.1	23.1	2.0
Kings County, New York	570,597	22.5	24.5	1.5
Livingston County, New York	11,177	19.4	22.1	0.8
Madison County, New York	13,421	20.5	8.6	1.6
Monroe County, New York	150,101	21.0	19.4	1.1
Nassau County, New York	284,797	21.3	6.2	3.1
New York County, New York	229,274	14.5	15.8	2.0
Niagara County, New York	40,233	19.6	16.4	1.0
Oneida County, New York	47,632	21.9	17.6	5.6
Onondaga County, New York	94,807	21.5	19.1	1.4
Ontario County, New York	20,656	19.5	7.6	0.9
Orange County, New York	96,511	25.7	18.6	1.9
Oswego County, New York	23,328	20.9	30.2	3.6
Putnam County, New York	18,342	19.0	1.6	2.0
Queens County, New York	436,609	19.7	13.4	2.5
Rensselaer County, New York	29,842	19.5	15.5	0.8
Richmond County, New York	102,664	21.8	12.5	1.9
Rockland County, New York	91,877	28.6	22.2	1.9
St. Lawrence County, New York	20,460	21.2	32.8	15.1
Saratoga County, New York	44,956	19.8	5.4	0.7
Schenectady County, New York	33,248	22.0	20.9	2.4
Steuben County, New York	19,961	21.2	23.2	5.6
Suffolk County, New York	300,276	20.7	9.2	2.6
Sullivan County, New York	15,600	21.4	27.1	0.5
Tompkins County, New York	13,732	15.4	13.9	1.8
Ulster County, New York	30,164	17.8	16.7	1.5
Warren County, New York	11,076	17.5	11.2	0.3
Wayne County, New York	18,656	21.0	18.8	1.3
Westchester County, New York	206,178	21.8	9.6	1.5
NORTH CAROLINA	2,253,959	22.1	19.5	5.8
Alamance County, North Carolina	37,103	22.4	25.2	3.2
Brunswick County, North Carolina	20,650	14.5	21.2	4.4
Buncombe County, North Carolina	46,770	18.4	17.1	8.6
Burke County, North Carolina	16,418	18.6	40.0	3.2
Cabarrus County, North Carolina	54,374	25.3	8.3	5.9
Caldwell County, North Carolina	16,096	19.8	12.5	5.9
Carteret County, North Carolina	11,700	17.1	12.3	7.1
Catawba County, North Carolina	34,488	22.0	20.7	16.9
Chatham County, North Carolina	14,321	19.5	10.9	3.9
Cleveland County, North Carolina	20,828	21.7	37.9	4.1
Craven County, North Carolina	20,910	21.7	19.0	7.5
Cumberland County, North Carolina	81,150	25.5	25.9	4.4
Davidson County, North Carolina	34,729	21.0	27.7	5.2

Table C-1. Population and Poverty Characteristics, by Selected Counties, 2019—*Continued*

(Number; percent.)

State/County	Population		Children under 18 years old in poverty (percent)	Under 19 years old with no health insurance (percent)
	Total under 18 years old for whom poverty status is determined	Percent under 18 years old		
NORTH CAROLINA—(*Continued*)				
Durham County, North Carolina	65,569	21.4	20.8	7.5
Forsyth County, North Carolina	86,219	23.2	23.2	4.5
Franklin County, North Carolina	15,256	22.3	9.2	6.6
Gaston County, North Carolina	48,261	21.9	13.5	5.1
Guilford County, North Carolina	116,661	22.6	24.0	4.5
Harnett County, North Carolina	34,500	26.1	22.8	5.1
Henderson County, North Carolina	21,849	18.8	22.6	7.2
Iredell County, North Carolina	40,434	22.4	9.8	5.3
Johnston County, North Carolina	52,078	25.1	22.4	6.5
Lincoln County, North Carolina	17,828	20.9	7.3	5.4
Mecklenburg County, North Carolina	255,184	23.3	13.2	7.0
Moore County, North Carolina	20,566	20.7	20.1	8.8
Nash County, North Carolina	20,197	21.9	21.0	5.9
New Hanover County, North Carolina	42,548	18.7	15.2	5.5
Onslow County, North Carolina	47,710	26.7	15.9	3.1
Orange County, North Carolina	28,038	20.6	17.2	3.6
Pitt County, North Carolina	37,865	21.9	24.2	4.5
Randolph County, North Carolina	31,197	22.0	18.4	6.5
Robeson County, North Carolina	31,923	25.1	49.4	3.2
Rockingham County, North Carolina	17,604	19.8	28.5	5.2
Rowan County, North Carolina	30,298	22.0	19.1	3.9
Rutherford County, North Carolina	13,372	20.3	34.3	5.2
Surry County, North Carolina	14,675	20.7	23.7	4.1
Union County, North Carolina	62,445	26.4	7.9	5.1
Wake County, North Carolina	258,239	23.7	9.3	5.6
Wayne County, North Carolina	29,014	24.0	33.2	4.0
Wilkes County, North Carolina	12,727	18.9	20.6	5.0
Wilson County, North Carolina	18,181	22.7	38.6	3.2
NORTH DAKOTA	173,950	23.5	10.2	7.8
Burleigh County, North Dakota	21,505	23.2	4.0	3.8
Cass County, North Dakota	39,915	22.5	11.4	5.9
Grand Forks County, North Dakota	14,223	21.7	12.3	4.5
Ward County, North Dakota	15,605	23.7	6.9	3.1
OHIO	2,527,306	22.2	18.4	4.8
Allen County, Ohio	22,554	23.0	19.7	5.0
Ashtabula County, Ohio	20,910	22.2	32.4	12.9
Athens County, Ohio	9,925	17.8	29.2	2.3
Belmont County, Ohio	12,528	19.8	10.7	2.8
Butler County, Ohio	87,512	23.6	14.7	3.3
Clark County, Ohio	29,413	22.4	20.1	4.3
Clermont County, Ohio	45,934	22.5	12.2	3.4
Columbiana County, Ohio	20,226	20.7	14.8	1.1
Cuyahoga County, Ohio	250,292	20.7	23.3	2.9
Delaware County, Ohio	53,696	26.0	7.8	4.0
Erie County, Ohio	15,060	20.5	22.2	4.5
Fairfield County, Ohio	36,856	23.9	13.2	3.9
Franklin County, Ohio	300,484	23.4	18.4	4.3
Geauga County, Ohio	21,416	23.1	2.4	14.2
Greene County, Ohio	34,356	21.5	15.8	2.2
Hamilton County, Ohio	184,324	23.1	20.8	4.5
Hancock County, Ohio	16,182	22.1	10.4	1.3
Jefferson County, Ohio	12,343	19.5	28.7	3.6
Lake County, Ohio	44,630	19.7	11.7	4.3
Licking County, Ohio	39,296	22.8	11.7	5.1
Lorain County, Ohio	66,362	22.1	21.2	3.9
Lucas County, Ohio	96,416	23.0	26.8	4.1
Mahoning County, Ohio	45,019	20.3	27.8	1.1
Marion County, Ohio	13,201	22.3	19.4	1.8
Medina County, Ohio	39,013	21.9	6.5	4.6
Miami County, Ohio	24,228	22.9	11.6	4.7
Montgomery County, Ohio	114,072	22.2	23.1	6.1
Muskingum County, Ohio	16,836	20.4	23.6	6.8
Portage County, Ohio	29,259	18.9	14.2	3.1
Richland County, Ohio	25,510	22.4	19.8	6.4
Ross County, Ohio	16,338	23.0	17.0	5.6
Scioto County, Ohio	16,166	22.5	32.8	1.9
Stark County, Ohio	76,231	21.2	19.4	4.3
Summit County, Ohio	109,754	20.7	22.2	2.0
Trumbull County, Ohio	39,819	20.5	25.6	7.4
Tuscarawas County, Ohio	20,394	22.5	18.9	14.1

Table C-1. Population and Poverty Characteristics, by Selected Counties, 2019—*Continued*

(Number; percent.)

State/County	Population		Children under 18 years old in poverty (percent)	Under 19 years old with no health insurance (percent)
	Total under 18 years old for whom poverty status is determined	Percent under 18 years old		
OHIO—(*Continued*)				
Warren County, Ohio	56,249	24.9	3.6	2.1
Wayne County, Ohio	27,368	24.5	13.6	24.2
Wood County, Ohio	25,884	20.9	11.2	1.4
OKLAHOMA	935,016	24.3	19.9	8.6
Canadian County, Oklahoma	37,790	26.0	14.3	3.7
Cleveland County, Oklahoma	59,309	21.7	9.0	5.3
Comanche County, Oklahoma	27,022	24.2	25.2	5.1
Creek County, Oklahoma	16,465	23.4	17.9	3.7
Muskogee County, Oklahoma	16,443	25.6	36.1	5.9
Oklahoma County, Oklahoma	200,240	25.6	19.1	7.9
Payne County, Oklahoma	15,073	20.7	27.5	11.8
Pottawatomie County, Oklahoma	16,837	24.2	13.2	8.9
Rogers County, Oklahoma	21,080	23.2	19.0	9.5
Tulsa County, Oklahoma	160,685	25.1	20.2	8.3
Wagoner County, Oklahoma	19,055	23.6	7.9	8.3
OREGON	842,982	20.4	13.1	4.1
Benton County, Oregon	14,710	16.8	13.3	3.3
Clackamas County, Oregon	87,276	21.0	5.9	7.4
Deschutes County, Oregon	37,806	19.3	12.9	2.5
Douglas County, Oregon	21,067	19.1	12.3	1.7
Jackson County, Oregon	43,674	20.0	19.6	3.5
Josephine County, Oregon	14,784	17.4	23.8	10.4
Klamath County, Oregon	14,350	21.2	19.5	0.1
Lane County, Oregon	67,968	18.1	12.6	4.2
Linn County, Oregon	27,014	21.2	19.0	5.7
Marion County, Oregon	82,495	24.3	13.0	4.3
Multnomah County, Oregon	147,106	18.4	14.6	3.2
Polk County, Oregon	19,202	22.7	10.3	3.3
Umatilla County, Oregon	19,330	26.3	17.9	3.4
Washington County, Oregon	132,079	22.2	10.0	3.3
Yamhill County, Oregon	22,825	22.4	14.9	5.6
PENNSYLVANIA	2,578,279	20.8	16.9	4.6
Adams County, Pennsylvania	19,640	19.9	9.0	7.4
Allegheny County, Pennsylvania	222,244	18.8	14.1	2.1
Armstrong County, Pennsylvania	12,294	19.2	13.1	3.4
Beaver County, Pennsylvania	30,977	19.2	21.1	1.5
Berks County, Pennsylvania	91,519	22.5	16.8	4.8
Blair County, Pennsylvania	24,040	20.2	24.8	4.4
Bucks County, Pennsylvania	124,465	20.1	7.3	1.7
Butler County, Pennsylvania	36,412	20.0	6.6	1.1
Cambria County, Pennsylvania	24,126	19.5	26.8	2.2
Carbon County, Pennsylvania	11,255	17.9	6.7	0.7
Centre County, Pennsylvania	23,178	16.1	4.9	13.2
Chester County, Pennsylvania	116,869	22.8	6.1	4.0
Clearfield County, Pennsylvania	14,117	19.3	18.3	5.9
Columbia County, Pennsylvania	11,239	18.5	20.0	3.7
Crawford County, Pennsylvania	16,920	20.9	17.1	11.1
Cumberland County, Pennsylvania	50,579	21.1	9.2	7.7
Dauphin County, Pennsylvania	61,806	22.6	18.2	5.8
Delaware County, Pennsylvania	122,545	22.4	14.4	2.2
Erie County, Pennsylvania	55,194	21.5	26.2	1.1
Fayette County, Pennsylvania	23,157	18.6	30.1	1.6
Franklin County, Pennsylvania	33,689	22.0	10.1	7.3
Indiana County, Pennsylvania	14,925	19.0	17.9	14.7
Lackawanna County, Pennsylvania	41,965	20.8	19.9	3.3
Lancaster County, Pennsylvania	125,193	23.5	15.5	15.6
Lawrence County, Pennsylvania	16,604	19.9	16.3	3.8
Lebanon County, Pennsylvania	31,190	22.5	19.8	7.5
Lehigh County, Pennsylvania	81,891	22.9	19.3	2.9
Luzerne County, Pennsylvania	61,347	20.1	26.5	3.1
Lycoming County, Pennsylvania	22,197	20.8	19.5	3.7
Mercer County, Pennsylvania	19,405	19.0	17.7	7.0
Monroe County, Pennsylvania	32,729	19.5	20.3	5.1
Montgomery County, Pennsylvania	176,425	21.8	6.9	2.6
Northampton County, Pennsylvania	59,266	20.1	8.8	1.3
Northumberland County, Pennsylvania	16,798	19.5	22.9	4.3
Philadelphia County, Pennsylvania	333,485	21.7	32.1	4.4
Schuylkill County, Pennsylvania	27,141	20.3	13.9	4.0
Somerset County, Pennsylvania	13,065	19.2	20.1	4.4

Table C-1. Population and Poverty Characteristics, by Selected Counties, 2019—*Continued*

(Number; percent.)

State/County	Population			Under 19 years old with no health insurance (percent)
	Total under 18 years old for whom poverty status is determined	Percent under 18 years old	Children under 18 years old in poverty (percent)	
PENNSYLVANIA—(*Continued*)				
Washington County, Pennsylvania	39,332	19.6	12.0	1.8
Westmoreland County, Pennsylvania	62,892	18.4	14.8	2.6
York County, Pennsylvania	95,766	21.8	13.1	2.5
RHODE ISLAND	200,063	19.6	14.0	1.9
Kent County, Rhode Island	29,272	18.0	7.7	1.3
Newport County, Rhode Island	12,732	16.2	5.4	2.2
Providence County, Rhode Island	128,549	21.0	18.5	2.2
Washington County, Rhode Island	20,379	16.9	5.0	1.8
SOUTH CAROLINA	1,087,523	21.7	19.7	5.8
Aiken County, South Carolina	36,321	21.6	16.2	3.8
Anderson County, South Carolina	44,379	22.3	19.6	10.5
Beaufort County, South Carolina	34,569	18.4	21.7	8.1
Berkeley County, South Carolina	53,202	23.8	14.2	6.6
Charleston County, South Carolina	79,389	19.9	14.2	9.8
Darlington County, South Carolina	14,613	22.3	33.4	3.5
Dorchester County, South Carolina	37,785	23.7	11.5	10.0
Florence County, South Carolina	31,657	23.4	21.3	2.7
Greenville County, South Carolina	117,933	23.1	15.1	5.0
Greenwood County, South Carolina	15,096	22.3	28.4	3.2
Horry County, South Carolina	60,906	17.5	20.6	5.8
Kershaw County, South Carolina	15,350	23.1	25.8	4.7
Lancaster County, South Carolina	19,197	20.4	11.0	4.6
Laurens County, South Carolina	14,480	22.2	26.2	18.7
Lexington County, South Carolina	67,250	22.8	19.4	5.6
Oconee County, South Carolina	15,856	20.1	19.2	2.9
Orangeburg County, South Carolina	19,064	22.9	48.5	1.8
Pickens County, South Carolina	23,388	19.4	13.6	4.4
Richland County, South Carolina	86,384	22.5	22.2	4.7
Spartanburg County, South Carolina	72,051	23.2	18.5	6.7
Sumter County, South Carolina	25,301	24.2	23.6	2.3
York County, South Carolina	65,903	23.9	9.5	3.8
SOUTH DAKOTA	209,778	24.5	15.0	7.8
Minnehaha County, South Dakota	47,567	25.3	9.4	8.4
Pennington County, South Dakota	25,333	22.9	15.7	5.7
TENNESSEE	1,478,841	22.2	19.7	5.0
Anderson County, Tennessee	15,258	20.3	25.5	6.4
Blount County, Tennessee	26,485	20.3	12.4	8.8
Bradley County, Tennessee	22,867	21.9	17.0	1.9
Davidson County, Tennessee	139,697	20.8	17.5	6.8
Greene County, Tennessee	13,028	19.5	28.8	5.5
Hamilton County, Tennessee	75,498	21.1	19.4	6.2
Knox County, Tennessee	97,214	21.2	16.2	4.6
Madison County, Tennessee	21,235	22.6	33.6	3.6
Maury County, Tennessee	22,362	23.5	7.2	4.3
Montgomery County, Tennessee	54,397	26.7	17.3	3.9
Putnam County, Tennessee	15,549	20.3	22.1	2.4
Robertson County, Tennessee	16,728	23.6	15.7	2.7
Rutherford County, Tennessee	80,126	24.5	16.1	5.4
Sevier County, Tennessee	19,316	20.0	22.2	2.8
Shelby County, Tennessee	228,384	24.8	25.9	6.2
Sullivan County, Tennessee	29,496	18.9	27.0	1.9
Sumner County, Tennessee	43,924	23.2	12.0	5.4
Washington County, Tennessee	23,527	18.9	21.6	3.6
Williamson County, Tennessee	61,993	26.3	4.4	2.4
Wilson County, Tennessee	33,743	23.6	12.1	3.5
TEXAS	7,300,287	25.7	19.2	12.7
Angelina County, Texas	22,045	26.0	18.5	11.2
Bastrop County, Texas	22,079	25.6	36.8	17.7
Bell County, Texas	98,398	28.1	17.7	9.3
Bexar County, Texas	499,190	25.3	23.0	9.0
Bowie County, Texas	21,919	25.2	20.6	4.5
Brazoria County, Texas	97,246	26.8	9.4	10.0
Brazos County, Texas	46,517	21.8	20.9	8.4
Cameron County, Texas	126,190	30.0	37.1	17.6
Collin County, Texas	263,236	25.6	7.1	8.0
Comal County, Texas	34,380	22.2	3.6	7.9
Coryell County, Texas	16,684	27.5	11.8	5.1
Dallas County, Texas	674,318	25.9	21.3	17.0

Table C-1. Population and Poverty Characteristics, by Selected Counties, 2019—*Continued*

(Number; percent.)

State/County	Population		Children under 18 years old in poverty (percent)	Under 19 years old with no health insurance (percent)
	Total under 18 years old for whom poverty status is determined	Percent under 18 years old		
TEXAS—(*Continued*)				
Denton County, Texas..............................	211,623	24.2	7.0	9.7
Ector County, Texas.................................	49,622	30.2	16.0	20.1
Ellis County, Texas	47,951	26.3	13.7	12.4
El Paso County, Texas..............................	222,211	27.0	26.6	12.5
Fort Bend County, Texas...........................	220,235	27.4	6.1	9.1
Galveston County, Texas	81,783	24.3	15.4	11.1
Grayson County, Texas.............................	31,024	23.3	17.1	15.2
Gregg County, Texas	31,398	26.3	27.0	15.7
Guadalupe County, Texas	40,410	24.6	8.7	11.6
Harris County, Texas	1,233,379	26.4	21.7	15.0
Harrison County, Texas	16,028	24.7	38.0	10.3
Hays County, Texas	50,457	22.8	13.2	10.5
Henderson County, Texas	16,674	20.5	37.4	14.2
Hidalgo County, Texas..............................	277,590	32.3	38.3	16.7
Hunt County, Texas	23,271	24.3	22.0	8.9
Jefferson County, Texas	57,115	24.4	25.5	11.8
Johnson County, Texas	45,510	26.3	18.4	14.3
Kaufman County, Texas............................	37,160	27.7	14.9	9.8
Liberty County, Texas	23,801	29.3	14.0	18.0
Lubbock County, Texas	72,574	24.3	24.1	9.3
McLennan County, Texas	61,943	25.1	23.7	7.5
Midland County, Texas	50,759	29.0	11.5	20.9
Montgomery County, Texas.......................	157,472	26.1	14.1	9.1
Nacogdoches County, Texas......................	14,768	24.8	24.7	4.7
Nueces County, Texas	87,187	24.6	22.5	9.3
Orange County, Texas..............................	20,322	24.7	16.0	12.9
Parker County, Texas	34,838	24.9	8.7	9.2
Potter County, Texas	31,689	28.6	25.6	19.2
Randall County, Texas	31,961	23.8	14.2	6.0
Rockwall County, Texas............................	27,896	26.8	5.9	11.9
San Patricio County, Texas.......................	17,256	26.3	14.8	6.6
Smith County, Texas................................	55,821	24.6	14.1	13.0
Tarrant County, Texas..............................	539,704	26.0	13.9	11.6
Taylor County, Texas	33,453	25.4	18.2	11.9
Tom Green County, Texas.........................	27,784	24.6	16.2	5.1
Travis County, Texas................................	266,216	21.4	14.1	12.2
Victoria County, Texas	22,198	24.6	24.2	20.1
Walker County, Texas	10,607	18.2	20.6	12.0
Webb County, Texas	88,656	32.4	28.5	17.4
Wichita County, Texas	29,083	24.4	13.9	12.7
Williamson County, Texas	147,662	25.2	6.1	6.6
Wise County, Texas.................................	17,230	25.0	6.6	15.4
UTAH	920,337	29.1	9.9	8.3
Cache County, Utah..................................	38,200	30.5	17.1	3.4
Davis County, Utah..................................	111,945	31.7	6.4	6.2
Salt Lake County, Utah	305,384	26.6	11.1	8.7
Tooele County, Utah	23,101	32.2	1.2	7.9
Utah County, Utah	207,184	33.4	9.2	7.1
Washington County, Utah..........................	43,700	25.0	14.8	16.3
Weber County, Utah	71,693	27.9	5.6	8.0
VERMONT	111,164	18.6	10.2	2.1
Chittenden County, Vermont	28,036	18.2	11.2	2.7
VIRGINIA	1,825,458	22.0	13.4	4.9
Albemarle County, Virginia........................	21,154	20.7	3.7	1.6
Arlington County, Virginia	42,749	18.3	11.7	2.4
Augusta County, Virginia	12,517	17.8	9.2	5.3
Bedford County, Virginia	15,563	19.9	6.8	0.6
Chesterfield County, Virginia.....................	80,973	23.3	9.4	5.5
Fairfax County, Virginia	263,679	23.2	8.4	5.6
Fauquier County, Virginia	16,451	23.2	8.2	7.2
Frederick County, Virginia	19,915	22.7	7.5	4.4
Hanover County, Virginia..........................	22,867	21.6	5.3	2.5
Henrico County, Virginia	73,578	22.4	14.3	3.0
James City County, Virginia	14,970	19.7	5.3	1.7
Loudoun County, Virginia..........................	113,964	27.7	2.6	2.4
Montgomery County, Virginia	13,712	15.4	15.1	0.9
Prince William County, Virginia..................	123,421	26.6	8.5	7.3
Roanoke County, Virginia..........................	18,355	20.0	7.0	7.1
Rockingham County, Virginia.....................	17,707	22.1	11.3	8.4
Spotsylvania County, Virginia....................	33,127	24.5	7.4	5.6

Table C-1. Population and Poverty Characteristics, by Selected Counties, 2019—*Continued*

(Number; percent.)

State/County	Population			Under 19 years old with no health insurance (percent)
	Total under 18 years old for whom poverty status is determined	Percent under 18 years old	Children under 18 years old in poverty (percent)	
VIRGINIA—(*Continued*)				
Stafford County, Virginia	38,920	26.2	7.8	5.7
York County, Virginia	15,929	24.0	5.0	3.3
Alexandria city, Virginia	27,860	17.7	14.2	2.8
Chesapeake city, Virginia	57,841	24.2	12.9	5.6
Hampton city, Virginia	27,286	21.1	21.0	2.9
Lynchburg city, Virginia	15,363	21.2	12.1	7.8
Newport News city, Virginia	41,307	24.2	23.3	6.3
Norfolk city, Virginia	46,594	21.4	28.9	3.8
Portsmouth city, Virginia	21,218	23.5	29.4	4.8
Richmond city, Virginia	38,308	17.4	24.1	8.8
Roanoke city, Virginia	21,198	21.8	32.6	1.4
Suffolk city, Virginia	21,788	23.8	13.8	4.7
Virginia Beach city, Virginia	98,110	22.3	8.8	3.3
WASHINGTON	1,631,276	21.8	12.0	3.1
Benton County, Washington	52,968	26.2	19.2	2.7
Chelan County, Washington	17,915	23.5	22.8	2.4
Clallam County, Washington	12,301	16.2	11.7	4.8
Clark County, Washington	112,886	23.3	12.8	1.8
Cowlitz County, Washington	24,360	22.4	16.4	2.6
Franklin County, Washington	30,972	33.4	21.8	10.0
Grant County, Washington	28,108	29.2	22.3	1.6
Grays Harbor County, Washington	15,044	20.9	12.8	2.7
Island County, Washington	15,139	18.4	5.0	4.8
King County, Washington	446,104	20.1	7.4	2.6
Kitsap County, Washington	53,433	20.4	8.2	3.4
Lewis County, Washington	16,624	20.9	12.0	1.8
Mason County, Washington	12,891	19.6	23.2	4.9
Pierce County, Washington	205,761	23.2	11.6	2.7
Skagit County, Washington	25,577	20.3	21.5	3.6
Snohomish County, Washington	181,274	22.4	7.8	3.4
Spokane County, Washington	111,742	22.0	12.5	2.1
Thurston County, Washington	60,231	21.0	13.7	2.2
Whatcom County, Washington	42,727	19.1	8.5	4.5
Yakima County, Washington	72,331	29.3	26.1	6.5
WEST VIRGINIA	347,481	20.0	20.1	3.5
Berkeley County, West Virginia	23,959	20.7	17.7	5.0
Cabell County, West Virginia	17,915	20.3	21.2	5.0
Harrison County, West Virginia	14,023	21.2	5.5	3.0
Kanawha County, West Virginia	34,703	19.8	21.5	3.2
Monongalia County, West Virginia	17,127	17.2	18.2	3.8
Raleigh County, West Virginia	15,020	21.3	23.3	1.8
Wood County, West Virginia	17,091	20.7	16.4	1.2
WISCONSIN	1,240,584	21.9	13.5	3.8
Brown County, Wisconsin	61,910	24.0	13.8	4.2
Dane County, Wisconsin	108,780	20.4	5.5	1.6
Dodge County, Wisconsin	18,323	21.7	8.2	2.4
Eau Claire County, Wisconsin	20,124	20.1	8.7	5.6
Fond du Lac County, Wisconsin	20,831	20.8	8.3	2.5
Jefferson County, Wisconsin	17,599	21.6	4.7	0.4
Kenosha County, Wisconsin	38,292	23.1	9.9	3.3
La Crosse County, Wisconsin	22,909	20.2	7.1	3.6
Manitowoc County, Wisconsin	15,941	20.4	11.9	4.7
Marathon County, Wisconsin	30,861	23.0	11.1	5.4
Milwaukee County, Wisconsin	220,169	23.8	23.7	3.0
Outagamie County, Wisconsin	42,948	23.3	10.8	6.9
Ozaukee County, Wisconsin	18,934	21.7	6.6	0.2
Portage County, Wisconsin	12,240	18.3	11.6	2.0
Racine County, Wisconsin	44,204	23.2	16.9	2.0
Rock County, Wisconsin	35,103	22.1	21.3	2.6
St. Croix County, Wisconsin	22,236	24.7	10.7	2.1
Sheboygan County, Wisconsin	24,949	22.2	14.0	3.5
Walworth County, Wisconsin	20,920	20.7	5.5	2.1
Washington County, Wisconsin	28,719	21.3	6.2	5.4
Waukesha County, Wisconsin	85,107	21.3	6.5	1.3
Winnebago County, Wisconsin	34,685.0	21.1	13.5	5.2
Wood County, Wisconsin	15,552.0	21.5	20.2	1.3
WYOMING	130,431.0	23.1	11.6	10.6
Laramie County, Wyoming	22,021.0	22.8	12.1	6.1
Natrona County, Wyoming	18,914.0	24.2	12.3	8.0

Table C-2. Educational Attainment of the Population, by Selected Counties, 2019

(Number; percent; dollars.)

State/County	Population 18 to 24 years				
	Total	Less than high school graduate (percent)	High school graduate (includes equivalency) (percent)	Some college or associate's degree (percent)	Bachelor's degree or higher (percent)
UNITED STATES	30,373,170	12.1	32.7	43.4	11.9
ALABAMA	457,530	12.3	34.7	45.3	7.6
Baldwin County, Alabama................................	16,614	13.9	44.5	32.2	9.3
Calhoun County, Alabama...............................	10,047	8.9	20.9	64.8	5.4
Cullman County, Alabama...............................	6,160	11.9	30.4	50.5	7.3
DeKalb County, Alabama................................	7,072	17.5	34.5	44.1	3.8
Elmore County, Alabama................................	5,605	18.8	34.4	38.9	7.9
Etowah County, Alabama...............................	8,535	14.3	24.9	58.4	2.4
Houston County, Alabama..............................	8,142	11.8	46.5	39.2	2.5
Jefferson County, Alabama	57,373	10.9	33.2	42.2	13.8
Lauderdale County, Alabama..........................	10,176	9.3	27.5	54.9	8.3
Lee County, Alabama...................................	28,496	5.4	25.4	59.4	9.7
Limestone County, Alabama...........................	8,067	12.1	43.9	34.5	9.5
Madison County, Alabama.............................	35,057	9.6	29.8	49.3	11.3
Marshall County, Alabama.............................	7,683	20.7	38.5	35.5	5.2
Mobile County, Alabama	36,415	15.2	36.5	42.0	6.3
Montgomery County, Alabama........................	22,175	8.9	32.6	48.4	10.1
Morgan County, Alabama..............................	10,235	12.1	50.9	35.0	2.0
St. Clair County, Alabama..............................	6,475	19.3	30.6	39.3	10.9
Shelby County, Alabama...............................	18,232	10.9	32.4	42.4	14.3
Talladega County, Alabama...........................	7,442	7.5	51.2	41.3	0.0
Tuscaloosa County, Alabama.........................	33,771	9.5	32.0	51.1	7.3
Walker County, Alabama	4,753	17.1	44.3	35.6	3.0
ALASKA...	67,738	12.5	40.1	42.8	4.6
Anchorage Municipality, Alaska........................	28,342	9.0	41.8	43.7	5.5
Fairbanks North Star Borough, Alaska	12,565	6.6	22.6	66.1	4.6
Matanuska-Susitna Borough, Alaska...................	9,305	19.7	42.8	34.2	3.3
ARIZONA	694,529	14.5	35.5	39.9	10.1
Apache County, Arizona	6,532	16.1	32.6	48.8	2.5
Cochise County, Arizona	10,486	20.9	29.6	48.8	0.7
Coconino County, Arizona	30,789	4.2	27.9	61.6	6.3
Maricopa County, Arizona	415,899	14.1	36.0	37.4	12.4
Mohave County, Arizona...............................	13,365	20.8	46.5	29.0	3.7
Navajo County, Arizona................................	8,316	22.4	44.8	30.8	2.0
Pima County, Arizona..................................	121,224	12.3	33.5	44.2	10.0
Pinal County, Arizona..................................	36,198	25.4	40.4	29.2	5.0
Yavapai County, Arizona...............................	15,991	20.8	31.2	45.8	2.2
Yuma County, Arizona.................................	23,129	13.9	32.0	50.6	3.6
ARKANSAS...	282,336	11.8	34.5	44.7	9.0
Benton County, Arkansas	22,680	10.8	32.3	39.8	17.1
Craighead County, Arkansas...........................	12,383	5.3	23.0	64.3	7.4
Faulkner County, Arkansas............................	20,754	6.3	16.3	65.6	11.8
Garland County, Arkansas.............................	7,282	4.1	64.3	26.7	4.9
Jefferson County, Arkansas............................	6,583	6.8	42.2	44.1	6.9
Lonoke County, Arkansas..............................	5,391	8.6	54.3	27.5	9.6
Pulaski County, Arkansas..............................	32,978	11.5	30.9	36.9	20.7
Saline County, Arkansas...............................	9,376	23.3	39.5	32.6	4.6
Sebastian County, Arkansas...........................	11,776	13.4	31.5	50.5	4.6
Washington County, Arkansas	35,778	9.4	27.2	55.3	8.1
White County, Arkansas...............................	9,032	16.1	26.5	50.7	6.8
CALIFORNIA	3,683,287	10.0	31.3	47.2	11.6
Alameda County, California	136,124	8.7	27.4	46.8	17.1
Butte County, California................................	30,915	9.1	23.7	56.7	10.5
Contra Costa County, California	91,955	11.2	32.6	43.2	13.1
El Dorado County, California	12,404	9.9	43.4	35.8	10.8
Fresno County, California	96,278	11.3	35.1	46.6	7.1
Humboldt County, California	16,845	6.6	26.7	61.7	5.0
Imperial County, California.............................	17,862	17.6	28.1	50.8	3.5
Kern County, California	89,126	18.2	39.6	37.9	4.3
Kings County, California................................	16,514	13.4	41.2	41.3	4.0
Lake County, California................................	3,768	32.9	25.2	41.9	0.0
Los Angeles County, California........................	932,944	10.6	27.8	48.6	13.0
Madera County, California.............................	14,795	24.0	29.4	43.2	3.4
Marin County, California...............................	18,717	9.9	34.7	38.7	16.7

Table C-2. Educational Attainment of the Population, by Selected Counties, 2019—*Continued*

(Number; percent; dollars.)

State/County	Population 25 years and over							
	Total	Less than 9th grade (percent)	9th to 12th grade, no diploma (percent)	High school graduate (includes equivalency) (percent)	Some college, no degree (percent)	Associate's degree (percent)	Bachelor's degree (percent)	Graduate or professional degree (percent)
UNITED STATES	224,898,568	4.8	6.6	26.9	20.0	8.6	20.3	12.8
ALABAMA	3,360,058	3.9	9.0	30.9	20.8	9.0	16.3	10.0
Baldwin County, Alabama..........................	159,717	1.9	7.6	26.2	21.9	10.1	20.5	11.7
Calhoun County, Alabama..........................	79,084	4.2	11.2	34.5	21.8	9.0	11.5	7.8
Cullman County, Alabama..........................	58,795	4.5	14.2	30.5	23.5	11.5	10.1	5.6
DeKalb County, Alabama............................	47,007	9.9	11.4	38.0	18.4	9.4	7.9	4.9
Elmore County, Alabama............................	57,553	3.6	6.7	34.7	20.0	10.1	16.4	8.5
Etowah County, Alabama...........................	71,744	3.8	12.0	32.1	25.5	9.3	10.5	6.8
Houston County, Alabama..........................	73,454	5.1	9.9	30.4	22.6	9.4	14.2	8.5
Jefferson County, Alabama	451,818	2.2	6.6	26.9	21.0	8.6	20.4	14.3
Lauderdale County, Alabama......................	64,267	4.8	10.2	34.2	20.8	7.7	13.2	9.0
Lee County, Alabama.................................	101,326	3.0	5.0	22.0	19.0	9.5	21.0	20.4
Limestone County, Alabama.......................	68,441	3.1	9.5	33.5	18.9	9.5	18.6	7.0
Madison County, Alabama..........................	257,136	2.2	4.9	19.5	20.3	9.0	26.6	17.4
Marshall County, Alabama.........................	64,756	6.8	11.1	32.8	20.2	9.0	15.0	5.1
Mobile County, Alabama	280,453	3.3	9.3	36.1	20.3	8.2	14.9	8.0
Montgomery County, Alabama....................	151,310	3.2	7.3	24.9	21.3	8.0	20.2	15.2
Morgan County, Alabama...........................	82,462	5.8	8.3	35.2	19.5	7.8	15.4	8.0
St. Clair County, Alabama..........................	62,861	5.3	9.2	35.7	24.1	12.2	8.7	4.9
Shelby County, Alabama............................	149,221	2.6	3.9	20.1	21.0	7.9	29.2	15.3
Talladega County, Alabama........................	55,521	5.2	14.5	35.3	21.0	8.7	9.1	6.3
Tuscaloosa County, Alabama......................	131,589	2.9	8.0	30.7	19.2	7.6	19.1	12.5
Walker County, Alabama............................	44,577	4.6	13.1	35.3	24.3	10.6	8.8	3.4
ALASKA..	484,058	2.2	4.3	28.7	25.7	9.0	18.5	11.7
Anchorage Municipality, Alaska..................	190,461	1.7	3.2	25.2	24.2	9.3	22.2	14.1
Fairbanks North Star Borough, Alaska	61,280	2.3	2.1	20.8	33.0	8.7	16.7	16.6
Matanuska-Susitna Borough, Alaska............	70,425	1.7	4.3	33.4	25.6	10.7	17.1	7.3
ARIZONA	4,944,540	5.1	7.3	23.7	25.0	8.7	18.8	11.3
Apache County, Arizona	46,255	9.0	9.3	31.3	29.8	8.9	6.1	5.7
Cochise County, Arizona	88,433	4.5	6.8	26.8	25.2	11.6	15.1	9.9
Coconino County, Arizona..........................	84,682	2.3	4.3	20.4	25.1	8.4	22.0	17.6
Maricopa County, Arizona..........................	3,017,076	5.2	6.6	22.3	23.6	8.8	21.3	12.3
Mohave County, Arizona............................	163,211	2.5	10.5	33.8	30.7	8.9	8.6	4.9
Navajo County, Arizona.............................	73,486	4.9	11.5	28.5	33.1	8.8	7.1	6.1
Pima County, Arizona................................	710,449	4.7	7.2	22.0	25.3	8.2	18.9	13.7
Pinal County, Arizona................................	324,018	4.9	8.3	30.0	28.7	8.6	14.0	5.4
Yavapai County, Arizona............................	181,941	1.6	6.6	26.0	29.0	8.3	15.6	12.9
Yuma County, Arizona...............................	137,087	13.8	12.0	26.0	25.5	8.5	9.1	5.1
ARKANSAS...	2,036,456	4.6	7.9	34.9	21.8	7.5	15.1	8.3
Benton County, Arkansas	183,203	5.0	5.5	29.0	18.7	6.8	22.5	12.5
Craighead County, Arkansas......................	71,813	4.8	5.8	32.9	22.1	8.9	15.6	9.8
Faulkner County, Arkansas........................	76,684	2.5	3.7	32.5	22.6	9.3	20.9	8.5
Garland County, Arkansas	72,565	2.9	5.9	28.8	25.5	8.3	18.4	10.1
Jefferson County, Arkansas........................	45,719	3.4	9.8	39.4	22.2	6.8	12.0	6.4
Lonoke County, Arkansas...........................	49,301	3.8	7.1	40.8	20.3	8.9	12.5	6.5
Pulaski County, Arkansas..........................	268,684	2.8	5.6	26.2	22.4	8.2	20.9	14.0
Saline County, Arkansas...........................	84,730	1.8	8.6	34.6	20.3	8.2	17.7	8.9
Sebastian County, Arkansas.......................	85,379	4.9	10.6	28.6	23.9	6.9	16.6	8.5
Washington County, Arkansas	145,660	7.4	8.3	27.3	19.1	6.0	19.2	12.7
White County, Arkansas............................	51,446	5.7	12.9	42.7	12.6	9.8	10.0	6.4
CALIFORNIA	26,937,872	8.7	7.3	20.6	20.6	7.9	21.9	13.1
Alameda County, California........................	1,195,107	5.2	5.2	17.3	15.5	6.2	29.3	21.3
Butte County, California.............................	143,815	3.7	7.9	21.7	26.5	9.8	20.6	9.8
Contra Costa County, California	802,187	5.2	5.7	17.9	20.1	8.1	25.8	17.2
El Dorado County, California.......................	142,068	2.8	4.2	22.3	24.3	11.1	24.6	10.8
Fresno County, California...........................	621,440	12.7	10.6	22.0	23.2	9.4	14.7	7.3
Humboldt County, California	93,098	2.1	7.0	20.7	28.0	11.8	20.5	9.9
Imperial County, California.........................	111,755	12.0	16.4	23.3	23.6	6.4	13.9	4.5
Kern County, California..............................	551,956	13.0	10.6	28.1	22.7	8.4	11.7	5.3
Kings County, California.............................	95,083	13.5	15.0	22.6	24.6	6.7	12.0	5.6
Lake County, California..............................	47,186	4.6	9.5	30.4	32.0	8.1	9.9	5.5
Los Angeles County, California....................	6,961,614	11.8	8.4	20.7	18.5	6.9	22.3	11.5
Madera County, California..........................	99,392	15.1	12.0	25.2	25.6	8.0	10.2	3.9
Marin County, California............................	188,509	4.5	3.0	11.2	15.8	5.9	36.3	23.4

Table C-2. Educational Attainment of the Population, by Selected Counties, 2019—*Continued*

(Number; percent; dollars.)

State/County		Population 18 to 24 years			
	Total	Less than high school graduate (percent)	High school graduate (includes equivalency) (percent)	Some college or associate's degree (percent)	Bachelor's degree or higher (percent)
CALIFORNIA—*(Continued)*					
Mendocino County, California	6,869	13.8	34.6	48.5	3.1
Merced County, California	29,440	10.5	28.4	57.4	3.7
Monterey County, California	42,946	14.1	28.3	52.2	5.4
Napa County, California	12,155	5.4	44.5	42.9	7.2
Nevada County, California	5,916	10.0	56.7	29.5	3.8
Orange County, California	285,538	9.3	28.6	48.0	14.2
Placer County, California	28,650	10.5	31.2	44.6	13.7
Riverside County, California	235,474	9.9	37.5	46.1	6.6
Sacramento County, California	130,401	9.3	36.6	44.9	9.3
San Bernardino County, California	219,659	10.8	37.6	44.4	7.3
San Diego County, California	336,060	7.4	33.3	47.9	11.3
San Francisco County, California	62,024	3.7	20.2	42.1	34.0
San Joaquin County, California	73,677	11.2	39.3	44.0	5.5
San Luis Obispo County, California	42,827	3.2	25.1	60.6	11.1
San Mateo County, California	55,801	9.3	29.6	35.3	25.8
Santa Barbara County, California	69,881	8.0	24.0	57.4	10.6
Santa Clara County, California	161,254	9.0	24.2	45.8	21.1
Santa Cruz County, California	40,243	7.0	27.5	51.5	14.1
Shasta County, California	13,758	11.6	43.1	36.2	9.2
Solano County, California	38,051	12.6	29.7	50.8	7.0
Sonoma County, California	39,735	11.1	32.9	45.9	10.2
Stanislaus County, California	53,308	9.7	40.4	45.8	4.0
Sutter County, California	9,110	12.3	30.5	50.0	7.2
Tehama County, California	3,906	27.7	38.5	29.2	4.6
Tulare County, California	46,486	11.8	40.8	44.4	2.9
Ventura County, California	78,461	8.7	32.5	49.6	9.2
Yolo County, California	44,853	4.4	25.2	55.6	14.8
Yuba County, California	6,314	15.1	30.3	48.6	6.1
COLORADO	527,473	12.4	31.8	42.0	13.7
Adams County, Colorado	45,363	20.1	42.0	29.8	8.1
Arapahoe County, Colorado	52,627	16.4	34.5	32.0	17.1
Boulder County, Colorado	46,943	6.3	23.5	53.6	16.6
Broomfield County, Colorado	5,380	12.9	32.8	36.8	17.5
Denver County, Colorado	58,044	12.0	29.0	35.4	23.6
Douglas County, Colorado	27,202	8.5	35.9	39.8	15.8
El Paso County, Colorado	77,821	10.3	32.0	48.8	8.9
Jefferson County, Colorado	43,778	10.8	31.9	42.0	15.4
Larimer County, Colorado	49,663	4.4	24.2	53.5	18.0
Mesa County, Colorado	14,127	15.7	33.4	44.6	6.4
Pueblo County, Colorado	14,633	18.6	27.2	48.6	5.6
Weld County, Colorado	29,580	15.6	36.3	40.6	7.5
CONNECTICUT	341,435	10.3	29.9	43.2	16.5
Fairfield County, Connecticut	86,006	11.0	25.9	42.2	20.9
Hartford County, Connecticut	79,746	10.6	29.2	40.7	19.5
Litchfield County, Connecticut	12,655	19.8	36.7	29.2	14.3
Middlesex County, Connecticut	14,818	8.4	24.5	42.2	24.9
New Haven County, Connecticut	83,454	10.3	35.7	41.3	12.7
New London County, Connecticut	26,131	9.7	37.1	39.1	14.1
Tolland County, Connecticut	26,424	1.5	22.4	67.9	8.1
Windham County, Connecticut	12,201	15.9	24.4	52.0	7.6
DELAWARE	82,507	11.2	32.6	46.3	10.0
Kent County, Delaware	17,628	11.6	29.8	48.1	10.5
New Castle County, Delaware	50,741	9.7	33.6	46.8	9.9
Sussex County, Delaware	14,138	15.9	32.2	42.1	9.8
DISTRICT OF COLUMBIA	72,703	4.4	26.2	46.3	23.1
District of Columbia, District of Columbia	72,703	4.4	26.2	46.3	23.1
FLORIDA	1,761,280	14.3	32.1	42.9	10.6
Alachua County, Florida	54,783	6.0	20.2	55.4	18.4
Bay County, Florida	12,727	11.4	45.3	28.3	15.0
Brevard County, Florida	41,797	19.4	33.5	40.7	6.4
Broward County, Florida	150,776	16.1	31.8	41.9	10.3
Charlotte County, Florida	7,969	18.1	44.6	29.6	7.7
Citrus County, Florida	7,713	24.0	37.7	36.3	2.0

Table C-2. Educational Attainment of the Population, by Selected Counties, 2019—*Continued*

(Number; percent; dollars.)

State/County	Total	Less than 9th grade (percent)	9th to 12th grade, no diploma (percent)	High school graduate (includes equivalency) (percent)	Some college, no degree (percent)	Associate's degree (percent)	Bachelor's degree (percent)	Graduate or professional degree (percent)
CALIFORNIA—*(Continued)*								
Mendocino County, California	61,561	7.2	9.2	22.4	28.7	9.2	14.6	8.7
Merced County, California	167,460	19.1	11.8	24.3	23.0	7.4	10.2	4.3
Monterey County, California	277,924	19.6	8.3	20.5	17.3	8.6	15.0	10.7
Napa County, California	97,666	8.0	6.5	18.4	22.6	8.3	22.1	14.1
Nevada County, California	77,008	1.7	3.0	22.2	26.6	10.7	22.5	13.3
Orange County, California	2,200,478	7.3	6.6	17.8	19.6	7.7	25.8	15.2
Placer County, California	281,521	2.5	3.4	18.0	23.2	11.0	27.8	14.1
Riverside County, California	1,620,917	8.6	8.3	26.3	25.1	8.3	15.0	8.5
Sacramento County, California	1,058,536	5.2	5.9	23.3	24.7	9.7	20.8	10.4
San Bernardino County, California	1,390,788	8.2	11.0	25.8	24.4	8.1	14.6	7.9
San Diego County, California	2,287,472	6.3	5.7	18.2	21.8	8.3	24.5	15.4
San Francisco County, California	701,279	6.8	4.8	11.9	12.4	4.9	35.1	24.1
San Joaquin County, California	484,712	11.7	8.7	29.1	22.1	8.4	14.1	5.9
San Luis Obispo County, California	191,183	3.4	5.8	19.4	24.9	9.2	22.8	14.4
San Mateo County, California	555,980	5.6	3.9	15.3	15.4	7.4	28.8	23.6
Santa Barbara County, California	278,334	12.6	6.1	18.2	20.9	7.7	20.6	13.9
Santa Clara County, California	1,350,681	6.5	4.5	13.8	14.7	6.9	28.0	25.7
Santa Cruz County, California	181,121	8.6	3.9	15.4	19.6	8.6	25.3	18.5
Shasta County, California	127,504	1.4	5.4	24.9	33.1	13.5	15.3	6.5
Solano County, California	310,707	5.5	5.3	23.6	26.6	10.1	19.1	9.8
Sonoma County, California	359,124	5.4	4.9	19.0	23.8	9.5	23.4	14.1
Stanislaus County, California	349,579	11.4	8.2	30.6	25.3	7.1	12.4	4.9
Sutter County, California	62,991	10.4	10.1	23.1	25.1	10.3	12.4	8.6
Tehama County, California	45,751	5.7	11.1	32.4	24.7	9.8	9.7	6.6
Tulare County, California	277,457	16.2	9.7	25.6	24.3	10.6	9.1	4.6
Ventura County, California	577,254	8.4	5.2	20.9	21.5	9.2	21.9	12.9
Yolo County, California	131,248	6.4	4.9	20.0	19.2	9.7	22.2	17.7
Yuba County, California	50,675	6.7	12.4	25.6	27.6	10.0	13.1	4.8
COLORADO	3,974,943	3.2	4.4	21.0	20.3	8.4	26.6	16.0
Adams County, Colorado	336,931	6.1	9.0	29.8	21.0	8.6	17.1	8.3
Arapahoe County, Colorado	451,535	3.4	4.0	19.9	20.2	8.6	26.9	16.9
Boulder County, Colorado	217,746	2.9	2.7	10.1	13.2	6.3	35.6	29.2
Broomfield County, Colorado	49,543	1.7	2.0	13.4	17.0	9.0	33.0	23.9
Denver County, Colorado	530,543	4.2	4.6	17.0	16.0	5.0	32.6	20.5
Douglas County, Colorado	235,325	0.5	1.6	12.5	19.4	7.9	36.2	21.9
El Paso County, Colorado	471,313	1.9	3.1	20.8	23.4	11.7	24.5	14.5
Jefferson County, Colorado	425,906	2.0	3.4	19.9	19.4	7.7	30.9	16.8
Larimer County, Colorado	238,189	0.8	2.7	18.0	20.1	9.3	30.1	18.9
Mesa County, Colorado	107,348	2.5	6.4	27.5	25.7	8.2	19.7	10.1
Pueblo County, Colorado	116,378	2.9	5.8	29.2	26.3	12.4	15.4	8.0
Weld County, Colorado	210,630	6.6	5.7	25.0	22.6	10.1	18.2	11.6
CONNECTICUT	2,496,420	4.0	5.3	26.8	16.5	7.6	22.0	17.8
Fairfield County, Connecticut	647,664	5.4	4.4	21.9	12.7	6.5	27.5	21.5
Hartford County, Connecticut	625,639	4.1	5.7	25.6	17.2	8.5	21.2	17.8
Litchfield County, Connecticut	135,306	1.8	4.4	30.7	17.1	9.8	21.3	14.7
Middlesex County, Connecticut	119,565	1.5	5.1	26.7	15.9	8.1	24.1	18.7
New Haven County, Connecticut	600,678	4.4	6.2	30.6	16.8	6.9	18.7	16.5
New London County, Connecticut	188,179	2.0	4.7	28.4	23.5	8.1	18.1	15.2
Tolland County, Connecticut	97,922	1.8	4.0	27.5	16.8	9.0	22.8	18.0
Windham County, Connecticut	81,467	2.8	8.1	35.2	21.2	9.0	14.8	8.9
DELAWARE	687,311	3.5	6.2	30.2	18.6	8.3	19.5	13.7
Kent County, Delaware	121,855	3.8	7.5	31.9	22.9	9.4	15.7	8.8
New Castle County, Delaware	388,655	3.0	5.5	29.7	17.6	7.4	21.5	15.3
Sussex County, Delaware	176,801	4.3	6.8	30.1	17.9	9.5	17.9	13.4
DISTRICT OF COLUMBIA	505,145	3.3	4.9	15.8	13.0	3.3	25.7	34.0
District of Columbia, District of Columbia	505,145	3.3	4.9	15.8	13.0	3.3	25.7	34.0
FLORIDA	15,484,502	4.6	7.0	28.4	19.4	9.9	19.3	11.4
Alachua County, Florida	165,792	1.8	4.4	19.9	16.3	11.7	23.4	22.5
Bay County, Florida	126,060	2.2	6.8	28.6	25.0	11.0	16.2	10.2
Brevard County, Florida	450,772	1.7	5.8	27.8	21.7	12.6	18.8	11.6
Broward County, Florida	1,392,064	4.7	5.9	28.3	18.3	9.8	20.7	12.2
Charlotte County, Florida	158,584	2.6	6.9	35.6	23.6	9.3	14.0	8.1
Citrus County, Florida	120,131	2.8	9.3	31.3	24.8	9.3	12.7	9.9

Table C-2. Educational Attainment of the Population, by Selected Counties, 2019—*Continued*

(Number; percent; dollars.)

State/County		Population 18 to 24 years			
	Total	Less than high school graduate (percent)	High school graduate (includes equivalency) (percent)	Some college or associate's degree (percent)	Bachelor's degree or higher (percent)
FLORIDA—(*Continued*)					
Clay County, Florida	17,678	11.2	54.5	29.2	5.1
Collier County, Florida	26,653	16.2	34.4	40.8	8.7
Columbia County, Florida	7,673	25.2	46.9	25.6	2.3
Duval County, Florida	83,390	11.2	40.8	40.0	8.0
Escambia County, Florida	35,160	9.2	30.3	43.6	16.8
Flagler County, Florida	7,620	18.5	46.1	29.5	5.9
Hernando County, Florida	13,468	16.7	39.6	38.2	5.5
Highlands County, Florida	7,281	16.6	57.1	20.4	5.9
Hillsborough County, Florida	129,467	12.9	31.2	43.9	12.0
Indian River County, Florida	9,503	26.6	37.9	28.6	7.0
Lake County, Florida	24,350	18.0	47.5	26.5	8.0
Lee County, Florida	52,353	17.5	32.5	41.1	8.9
Leon County, Florida	63,034	8.8	17.7	59.0	14.4
Manatee County, Florida	28,040	26.0	29.9	36.0	8.1
Marion County, Florida	24,472	16.8	42.7	37.0	3.5
Martin County, Florida	9,905	8.9	31.3	51.0	8.8
Miami-Dade County, Florida	225,335	12.7	28.6	47.2	11.6
Monroe County, Florida	5,342	17.1	36.8	39.7	6.4
Nassau County, Florida	4,305	9.2	48.5	28.2	14.1
Okaloosa County, Florida	18,815	16.8	31.9	33.7	17.6
Orange County, Florida	143,238	10.9	27.6	48.6	12.9
Osceola County, Florida	36,545	8.3	28.4	54.8	8.4
Palm Beach County, Florida	111,830	17.3	26.0	42.2	14.5
Pasco County, Florida	39,792	13.7	36.0	41.0	9.4
Pinellas County, Florida	64,853	12.5	35.2	43.2	9.1
Polk County, Florida	61,355	18.0	39.1	36.3	6.5
Putnam County, Florida	5,139	25.8	46.1	27.1	1.0
St. Johns County, Florida	20,086	15.8	32.8	39.0	12.4
St. Lucie County, Florida	23,944	17.3	40.7	36.5	5.5
Santa Rosa County, Florida	14,991	12.1	36.1	36.8	14.9
Sarasota County, Florida	26,246	17.7	36.5	38.4	7.4
Seminole County, Florida	38,569	9.9	20.9	52.9	16.3
Sumter County, Florida	4,934	28.9	51.6	11.0	8.5
Volusia County, Florida	43,681	14.5	32.0	45.2	8.2
Walton County, Florida	4,362	5.9	31.0	56.6	6.5
GEORGIA	1,034,172	15.0	34.4	40.6	10.0
Barrow County, Georgia	6,369	19.1	35.0	35.0	10.9
Bartow County, Georgia	9,942	13.9	49.4	31.4	5.3
Bibb County, Georgia	15,624	13.7	27.3	53.8	5.2
Bulloch County, Georgia	20,043	5.0	17.0	73.7	4.3
Carroll County, Georgia	14,244	12.4	37.0	49.2	1.4
Catoosa County, Georgia	5,434	17.2	39.8	40.3	2.7
Chatham County, Georgia	31,835	13.4	34.3	33.8	18.4
Cherokee County, Georgia	20,126	21.3	30.6	35.9	12.2
Clarke County, Georgia	34,556	1.9	21.0	66.3	10.8
Clayton County, Georgia	29,946	23.9	35.7	34.5	5.8
Cobb County, Georgia	67,654	12.1	29.0	43.2	15.7
Columbia County, Georgia	13,754	15.3	28.2	44.7	11.8
Coweta County, Georgia	11,311	9.9	28.4	49.0	12.8
DeKalb County, Georgia	63,632	10.5	32.6	38.8	18.1
Dougherty County, Georgia	11,541	20.4	44.1	30.8	4.8
Douglas County, Georgia	16,508	22.7	35.4	33.3	8.7
Fayette County, Georgia	8,114	6.7	47.5	32.0	13.8
Floyd County, Georgia	9,726	10.9	36.0	46.9	6.2
Forsyth County, Georgia	18,402	16.7	35.9	35.3	12.1
Fulton County, Georgia	107,102	13.4	22.5	44.3	19.8
Glynn County, Georgia	6,820	18.0	44.4	33.8	3.8
Gwinnett County, Georgia	85,632	14.0	34.2	41.3	10.5
Hall County, Georgia	18,735	26.5	30.4	34.2	8.9
Henry County, Georgia	22,707	23.7	24.9	39.3	12.1
Houston County, Georgia	16,227	9.7	26.8	58.6	5.0
Jackson County, Georgia	4,140	20.7	37.4	36.0	5.9
Lowndes County, Georgia	19,256	15.6	31.8	39.7	12.8
Muscogee County, Georgia	19,872	15.1	35.2	44.1	5.6
Newton County, Georgia	10,655	19.9	41.9	32.7	5.6
Paulding County, Georgia	14,406	13.3	41.1	38.9	6.8
Richmond County, Georgia	22,867	16.2	45.8	33.5	4.4

Table C-2. Educational Attainment of the Population, by Selected Counties, 2019—*Continued*

(Number; percent; dollars.)

State/County	Total	Less than 9th grade (percent)	9th to 12th grade, no diploma (percent)	High school graduate (includes equivalency) (percent)	Some college, no degree (percent)	Associate's degree (percent)	Bachelor's degree (percent)	Graduate or professional degree (percent)
FLORIDA—(*Continued*)								
Clay County, Florida	151,268	1.8	3.4	27.9	24.1	14.3	18.7	9.9
Collier County, Florida	293,211	5.7	5.3	27.1	17.3	8.7	20.8	14.9
Columbia County, Florida	48,523	2.5	10.9	42.2	21.8	7.2	10.2	5.2
Duval County, Florida	658,820	3.2	6.5	28.6	21.1	10.1	20.3	10.3
Escambia County, Florida	216,927	3.4	7.9	30.0	24.1	10.7	14.8	9.1
Flagler County, Florida	88,396	2.6	6.2	35.0	21.4	8.4	17.6	9.0
Hernando County, Florida	144,676	2.8	8.2	33.1	25.9	10.2	13.2	6.5
Highlands County, Florida	80,665	4.8	10.0	35.8	23.7	8.9	11.1	5.6
Hillsborough County, Florida	1,017,078	5.0	6.3	26.9	17.4	9.7	21.7	13.0
Indian River County, Florida	124,448	3.5	5.6	29.0	21.0	9.7	20.7	10.6
Lake County, Florida	273,207	3.6	7.0	30.0	22.7	11.3	15.8	9.5
Lee County, Florida	584,326	4.7	6.2	31.0	19.6	9.4	18.1	10.9
Leon County, Florida	175,914	2.2	5.4	18.2	19.4	8.0	25.8	21.0
Manatee County, Florida	302,893	3.1	6.6	29.9	20.1	9.7	18.3	12.4
Marion County, Florida	273,855	3.2	7.9	36.6	21.2	10.6	12.6	8.0
Martin County, Florida	125,010	2.4	6.4	24.6	22.4	8.7	21.5	14.0
Miami-Dade County, Florida	1,941,926	9.5	10.1	26.1	14.6	8.9	19.3	11.4
Monroe County, Florida	58,378	3.3	3.7	27.5	20.7	10.4	20.8	13.7
Nassau County, Florida	66,706	4.3	7.1	30.6	20.6	7.8	18.8	10.8
Okaloosa County, Florida	144,638	1.9	5.3	27.7	23.3	10.2	20.6	11.0
Orange County, Florida	944,200	4.5	7.2	25.1	17.5	10.4	23.3	11.9
Osceola County, Florida	248,607	5.6	8.8	29.3	20.2	11.8	15.9	8.4
Palm Beach County, Florida	1,101,068	5.9	5.1	23.7	18.3	9.3	22.7	15.0
Pasco County, Florida	402,199	2.8	6.9	33.0	21.0	10.9	16.8	8.6
Pinellas County, Florida	754,705	2.8	6.2	27.4	20.7	9.9	21.6	11.4
Polk County, Florida	504,283	4.8	8.6	34.2	21.2	10.5	13.7	7.0
Putnam County, Florida	53,584	4.4	13.2	39.0	21.6	9.4	7.6	4.8
St. Johns County, Florida	187,354	1.2	3.2	22.2	19.0	8.5	28.6	17.4
St. Lucie County, Florida	240,303	4.6	8.7	33.1	21.5	10.4	14.0	7.6
Santa Rosa County, Florida	129,127	2.7	6.3	28.3	24.6	11.3	17.9	8.8
Sarasota County, Florida	346,738	2.2	4.1	28.0	20.2	9.2	20.7	15.7
Seminole County, Florida	334,286	2.3	4.1	21.4	19.2	11.9	26.6	14.6
Sumter County, Florida	118,386	1.2	4.3	31.9	20.8	8.6	20.6	12.6
Volusia County, Florida	412,871	2.9	5.9	33.1	21.8	12.2	15.2	8.8
Walton County, Florida	54,627	1.9	7.5	28.0	21.9	10.9	21.0	8.9
GEORGIA	7,080,222	4.5	7.6	27.4	20.0	8.0	19.9	12.6
Barrow County, Georgia	55,286	4.3	10.9	31.6	21.3	8.8	15.0	8.1
Bartow County, Georgia	72,076	5.5	10.7	34.9	25.0	6.2	13.0	4.8
Bibb County, Georgia	100,417	4.0	9.0	30.6	24.3	7.1	13.6	11.3
Bulloch County, Georgia	44,070	1.1	9.0	31.7	21.7	9.8	16.0	10.7
Carroll County, Georgia	77,477	4.6	12.4	35.5	22.3	6.3	11.3	7.6
Catoosa County, Georgia	46,682	1.7	8.0	32.4	24.0	10.5	16.6	6.8
Chatham County, Georgia	197,156	3.0	7.4	24.7	25.4	5.5	21.3	12.8
Cherokee County, Georgia	176,477	3.8	5.4	23.0	21.8	7.8	26.7	11.4
Clarke County, Georgia	71,774	2.2	6.6	16.1	17.2	9.8	24.4	23.7
Clayton County, Georgia	181,688	6.3	10.0	35.4	20.8	8.7	12.6	6.2
Cobb County, Georgia	515,943	4.6	3.3	18.1	18.6	7.3	30.4	17.6
Columbia County, Georgia	103,621	2.0	4.8	21.6	19.3	11.4	26.5	14.3
Coweta County, Georgia	101,159	4.1	6.3	26.8	25.5	10.6	16.7	10.1
DeKalb County, Georgia	521,555	4.0	6.0	21.4	16.0	7.7	25.5	19.4
Dougherty County, Georgia	56,078	4.6	13.1	28.0	23.8	10.0	9.4	11.0
Douglas County, Georgia	92,396	3.6	5.7	31.2	19.6	8.1	19.9	11.9
Fayette County, Georgia	79,987	1.2	2.8	21.1	20.1	9.7	29.7	15.3
Floyd County, Georgia	66,042	6.1	8.4	37.2	18.1	7.3	11.9	10.9
Forsyth County, Georgia	160,296	2.8	3.7	14.3	16.4	6.8	36.3	19.7
Fulton County, Georgia	729,041	1.8	4.3	15.4	15.1	5.8	33.7	23.9
Glynn County, Georgia	60,245	3.3	6.7	28.0	25.4	8.5	14.4	13.8
Gwinnett County, Georgia	601,285	6.2	5.9	21.1	17.8	9.7	25.6	13.6
Hall County, Georgia	135,110	11.8	8.6	26.9	19.9	7.3	15.5	9.9
Henry County, Georgia	152,577	3.1	5.3	33.9	22.7	8.8	18.0	8.3
Houston County, Georgia	101,387	2.6	4.6	31.2	19.8	13.9	16.3	11.6
Jackson County, Georgia	50,045	5.4	9.5	33.4	16.9	9.8	18.5	6.5
Lowndes County, Georgia	69,672	3.2	6.2	32.4	21.3	11.8	17.5	7.7
Muscogee County, Georgia	127,592	3.8	7.4	26.3	26.8	11.0	13.0	11.7
Newton County, Georgia	72,226	4.5	9.7	34.1	26.5	7.4	10.5	7.4
Paulding County, Georgia	110,398	3.3	8.9	30.8	27.1	7.9	13.8	8.3
Richmond County, Georgia	133,688	4.2	9.0	35.1	23.1	8.6	12.3	7.7

Table C-2. Educational Attainment of the Population, by Selected Counties, 2019—*Continued*

(Number; percent; dollars.)

State/County	Population 18 to 24 years				
	Total	Less than high school graduate (percent)	High school graduate (includes equivalency) (percent)	Some college or associate's degree (percent)	Bachelor's degree or higher (percent)
GEORGIA—(*Continued*)					
Rockdale County, Georgia	8,709	12.0	39.0	37.4	11.6
Spalding County, Georgia	5,582	20.5	47.7	29.1	2.7
Troup County, Georgia	6,524	18.2	42.3	39.1	0.4
Walker County, Georgia	5,616	16.8	48.3	31.1	3.8
Walton County, Georgia	6,376	9.0	65.0	21.5	4.5
Whitfield County, Georgia	10,170	14.7	34.0	48.7	2.7
HAWAII	119,017	7.4	43.2	41.2	8.2
Hawaii County, Hawaii	14,257	10.4	38.2	45.4	6.0
Honolulu County, Hawaii	88,983	6.5	43.9	40.8	8.7
Kauai County, Hawaii	5,120	10.2	45.0	42.4	2.3
Maui County, Hawaii	10,657	9.3	43.3	37.8	9.6
IDAHO	166,713	12.0	37.5	42.8	7.7
Ada County, Idaho	40,520	9.9	27.8	50.5	11.8
Bannock County, Idaho	8,882	7.5	39.1	47.6	5.9
Bonneville County, Idaho	9,920	17.8	36.8	35.8	9.7
Canyon County, Idaho	21,875	12.5	45.7	34.4	7.5
Kootenai County, Idaho	12,319	22.1	37.9	37.5	2.5
Twin Falls County, Idaho	7,764	10.2	57.5	31.2	1.2
ILLINOIS	1,162,448	11.7	29.5	44.1	14.7
Adams County, Illinois	4,856	7.2	29.7	32.8	30.3
Champaign County, Illinois	48,517	8.0	16.4	52.8	22.8
Cook County, Illinois	447,152	11.9	27.6	42.3	18.2
DeKalb County, Illinois	20,898	3.2	15.2	68.2	13.4
DuPage County, Illinois	78,374	10.4	24.0	44.1	21.5
Kane County, Illinois	47,937	13.2	32.0	42.8	12.0
Kankakee County, Illinois	13,308	11.0	44.0	38.4	6.7
Kendall County, Illinois	10,050	5.9	38.4	43.4	12.3
Lake County, Illinois	70,627	9.8	37.7	40.6	11.9
LaSalle County, Illinois	8,113	12.3	32.2	49.7	5.9
McHenry County, Illinois	25,468	10.1	36.1	41.7	12.2
McLean County, Illinois	30,523	8.7	16.6	64.7	10.0
Macon County, Illinois	8,759	18.7	35.5	40.8	4.9
Madison County, Illinois	20,971	8.7	27.0	55.9	8.4
Peoria County, Illinois	16,208	11.6	26.2	49.6	12.6
Rock Island County, Illinois	12,718	8.9	43.7	38.4	9.1
St. Clair County, Illinois	20,514	14.8	36.0	41.5	7.7
Sangamon County, Illinois	15,163	16.2	27.6	45.4	10.8
Tazewell County, Illinois	9,284	14.1	32.6	41.4	12.0
Vermilion County, Illinois	6,163	20.2	45.3	31.8	2.7
Will County, Illinois	62,635	11.9	31.8	41.5	14.8
Williamson County, Illinois	4,787	16.0	30.9	46.8	6.4
Winnebago County, Illinois	24,017	19.6	34.8	37.1	8.4
INDIANA	662,783	14.2	35.5	39.6	10.7
Allen County, Indiana	34,496	14.4	31.9	40.8	12.9
Bartholomew County, Indiana	6,370	11.1	43.1	26.9	18.9
Boone County, Indiana	5,001	5.9	40.5	20.1	33.5
Clark County, Indiana	9,807	20.9	43.9	30.1	5.0
Delaware County, Indiana	22,034	4.1	21.4	68.3	6.2
Elkhart County, Indiana	18,595	22.4	35.0	31.8	10.8
Floyd County, Indiana	6,740	24.0	24.1	31.3	20.6
Grant County, Indiana	8,322	6.8	32.4	52.9	7.9
Hamilton County, Indiana	26,361	14.4	34.3	24.9	26.4
Hancock County, Indiana	6,229	28.3	29.8	41.4	0.5
Hendricks County, Indiana	13,017	17.6	26.2	43.3	12.9
Howard County, Indiana	5,873	10.9	31.3	52.5	5.3
Johnson County, Indiana	14,008	22.9	35.0	31.1	11.0
Kosciusko County, Indiana	6,632	13.0	38.2	40.4	8.3
Lake County, Indiana	41,143	17.5	43.5	29.1	9.9
LaPorte County, Indiana	9,195	14.8	54.1	24.4	6.7
Madison County, Indiana	11,059	16.3	43.6	30.6	9.4
Marion County, Indiana	90,395	13.4	36.7	35.9	14.0
Monroe County, Indiana	40,630	3.1	21.1	64.2	11.6
Morgan County, Indiana	5,680	28.3	39.8	25.5	6.5

Table C-2. Educational Attainment of the Population, by Selected Counties, 2019—*Continued*

(Number; percent; dollars.)

State/County	Population 25 years and over							
	Total	Less than 9th grade (percent)	9th to 12th grade, no diploma (percent)	High school graduate (includes equivalency) (percent)	Some college, no degree (percent)	Associate's degree (percent)	Bachelor's degree (percent)	Graduate or professional degree (percent)
GEORGIA—*(Continued)*								
Rockdale County, Georgia	60,224	3.1	8.9	29.2	26.1	9.2	15.8	7.8
Spalding County, Georgia	45,479	4.7	10.5	42.3	15.5	9.3	10.3	7.4
Troup County, Georgia	46,785	3.8	7.3	40.3	20.8	8.1	13.4	6.4
Walker County, Georgia	49,130	6.7	13.0	35.4	21.7	6.4	10.3	6.4
Walton County, Georgia	65,348	3.6	10.7	32.2	23.5	6.5	15.4	8.1
Whitfield County, Georgia	67,441	16.9	11.3	29.4	19.0	6.9	9.7	6.8
HAWAII	996,668	3.6	4.0	27.4	20.7	10.6	22.1	11.6
Hawaii County, Hawaii	143,872	3.7	3.7	31.1	22.2	9.3	19.7	10.3
Honolulu County, Hawaii	680,706	3.5	3.9	25.8	19.9	11.0	23.4	12.4
Kauai County, Hawaii	51,455	3.3	3.9	30.4	21.3	12.6	18.7	9.9
Maui County, Hawaii	120,620	4.7	4.7	30.7	22.8	9.4	18.9	8.8
IDAHO	1,170,997	3.0	5.5	26.1	26.0	10.6	18.8	9.9
Ada County, Idaho	329,339	1.4	3.8	19.8	24.9	10.4	25.4	14.3
Bannock County, Idaho	56,426	1.3	4.7	24.6	32.2	7.7	19.8	9.7
Bonneville County, Idaho	72,956	2.9	4.1	25.8	23.4	11.1	22.9	9.8
Canyon County, Idaho	143,774	6.3	6.8	30.0	25.9	10.6	14.6	5.9
Kootenai County, Idaho	115,561	1.2	5.2	25.6	30.9	12.5	15.5	9.1
Twin Falls County, Idaho	54,509	7.3	7.2	26.7	28.1	9.3	12.4	9.0
ILLINOIS	8,694,694	4.5	5.7	25.9	20.0	8.2	21.7	14.1
Adams County, Illinois	46,146	1.9	7.0	37.2	20.8	9.2	15.9	8.0
Champaign County, Illinois	121,881	2.7	3.9	22.8	15.6	8.8	20.4	25.9
Cook County, Illinois	3,590,364	6.1	6.0	22.8	17.9	6.7	23.8	16.8
DeKalb County, Illinois	61,531	2.8	4.5	24.0	23.1	9.7	23.3	12.6
DuPage County, Illinois	636,969	3.0	3.1	18.8	17.5	6.9	30.5	20.2
Kane County, Illinois	351,487	7.0	7.1	24.1	20.8	7.9	21.7	11.4
Kankakee County, Illinois	72,229	3.5	6.1	37.7	23.4	9.7	11.9	7.7
Kendall County, Illinois	82,912	3.7	3.6	21.8	19.0	12.5	22.6	16.9
Lake County, Illinois	459,783	5.0	4.7	20.3	18.7	6.3	27.1	17.9
LaSalle County, Illinois	77,631	2.4	8.2	37.4	24.9	10.9	10.6	5.7
McHenry County, Illinois	210,880	2.5	4.0	26.8	21.9	9.8	24.0	10.9
McLean County, Illinois	104,545	2.0	3.5	22.2	18.3	8.2	30.7	15.1
Macon County, Illinois	72,287	1.7	4.9	39.8	24.9	7.1	14.4	7.2
Madison County, Illinois	184,866	1.4	5.2	28.7	23.4	11.0	18.9	11.3
Peoria County, Illinois	120,735	1.7	5.1	29.8	21.5	9.5	19.4	13.0
Rock Island County, Illinois	97,621	3.8	7.6	30.3	23.9	10.4	14.3	9.7
St. Clair County, Illinois	178,605	2.6	5.9	27.3	26.3	10.4	16.1	11.5
Sangamon County, Illinois	136,578	2.1	4.9	28.0	22.2	8.7	21.9	12.2
Tazewell County, Illinois	92,059	1.5	4.2	32.4	23.9	10.7	19.2	8.1
Vermilion County, Illinois	51,836	2.4	8.0	44.5	21.8	11.2	7.9	4.2
Will County, Illinois	459,279	3.8	4.8	27.4	20.2	8.6	22.8	12.4
Williamson County, Illinois	47,356	2.1	4.6	30.7	22.8	10.4	18.8	10.6
Winnebago County, Illinois	192,880	4.0	7.2	30.5	23.4	10.1	16.0	8.8
INDIANA	4,502,015	3.6	6.8	33.9	19.9	8.8	17.3	9.7
Allen County, Indiana	247,992	4.4	6.1	27.5	21.6	11.4	19.6	9.3
Bartholomew County, Indiana	57,421	4.5	4.6	29.3	17.2	8.0	21.6	14.9
Boone County, Indiana	45,007	2.5	5.2	16.8	19.4	9.6	27.9	18.6
Clark County, Indiana	82,101	1.6	7.6	33.8	22.4	12.2	15.1	7.3
Delaware County, Indiana	71,731	0.6	7.2	36.6	20.7	12.2	11.7	10.9
Elkhart County, Indiana	131,077	9.1	8.4	37.2	18.9	6.4	14.0	5.9
Floyd County, Indiana	53,589	1.2	6.8	32.3	21.9	9.2	18.1	10.6
Grant County, Indiana	43,982	4.7	6.5	39.0	21.6	7.0	12.8	8.4
Hamilton County, Indiana	221,657	0.9	1.9	13.6	13.8	6.7	38.6	24.4
Hancock County, Indiana	54,474	3.4	7.1	30.3	21.1	8.8	21.0	8.4
Hendricks County, Indiana	115,132	1.2	3.6	29.6	20.1	8.5	25.6	11.4
Howard County, Indiana	57,393	4.4	5.8	34.4	28.7	8.6	11.9	6.3
Johnson County, Indiana	105,736	2.7	4.8	32.5	20.5	8.3	21.8	9.4
Kosciusko County, Indiana	53,973	4.8	8.7	34.9	17.9	6.6	17.0	10.2
Lake County, Indiana	331,902	4.3	6.0	36.1	23.1	7.9	14.9	7.7
LaPorte County, Indiana	77,292	2.4	9.0	39.3	20.4	10.9	12.4	5.5
Madison County, Indiana	90,782	3.4	8.1	38.7	21.7	9.5	12.1	6.5
Marion County, Indiana	637,578	4.2	8.6	29.8	18.5	7.8	20.0	11.1
Monroe County, Indiana	84,605	1.2	3.5	24.4	18.2	6.5	23.6	22.6
Morgan County, Indiana	49,000	2.2	7.3	38.5	26.6	8.0	11.7	5.6

Table C-2. Educational Attainment of the Population, by Selected Counties, 2019—*Continued*

(Number; percent; dollars.)

State/County	Population 18 to 24 years				
	Total	Less than high school graduate (percent)	High school graduate (includes equivalency) (percent)	Some college or associate's degree (percent)	Bachelor's degree or higher (percent)
INDIANA—(*Continued*)					
Porter County, Indiana	16,196	14.1	42.7	34.8	8.4
St. Joseph County, Indiana	29,865	7.7	31.3	48.3	12.7
Tippecanoe County, Indiana	46,802	4.4	33.8	50.6	11.2
Vanderburgh County, Indiana	17,988	11.2	38.9	40.3	9.7
Vigo County, Indiana	15,921	7.7	28.3	56.4	7.6
Wayne County, Indiana	5,896	18.6	52.6	25.1	3.7
IOWA	310,236	10.4	29.4	50.1	10.1
Black Hawk County, Iowa	19,233	9.5	22.3	61.7	6.6
Dallas County, Iowa	7,378	6.2	32.9	42.0	18.9
Dubuque County, Iowa	10,173	8.2	23.5	56.3	11.9
Johnson County, Iowa	31,976	10.5	18.2	53.2	18.2
Linn County, Iowa	20,497	7.6	27.6	52.7	12.1
Polk County, Iowa	42,390	12.4	31.4	42.5	13.7
Pottawattamie County, Iowa	7,667	8.8	54.0	32.9	4.2
Scott County, Iowa	14,050	13.7	34.3	40.2	11.8
Story County, Iowa	26,940	0.9	14.8	77.6	6.7
Woodbury County, Iowa	9,512	7.3	30.1	54.9	7.6
KANSAS	294,932	11.5	31.3	46.5	10.7
Butler County, Kansas	5,452	9.1	42.5	40.4	8.1
Douglas County, Kansas	27,168	1.4	23.1	59.4	16.1
Johnson County, Kansas	48,150	9.8	29.8	41.1	19.4
Leavenworth County, Kansas	7,904	7.8	46.0	44.4	1.7
Riley County, Kansas	25,117	3.1	20.9	68.1	7.9
Sedgwick County, Kansas	47,005	12.8	36.5	42.8	7.9
Shawnee County, Kansas	15,421	11.2	39.4	35.3	14.1
Wyandotte County, Kansas	14,053	19.4	38.3	27.7	14.7
KENTUCKY	417,406	12.2	37.0	41.2	9.7
Boone County, Kentucky	11,637	15.6	34.6	37.5	12.2
Bullitt County, Kentucky	6,166	6.7	50.4	40.6	2.3
Campbell County, Kentucky	9,342	2.7	37.8	41.9	17.6
Christian County, Kentucky	10,208	12.9	42.8	41.6	2.7
Daviess County, Kentucky	7,872	8.8	36.4	44.5	10.3
Fayette County, Kentucky	44,233	6.0	21.2	54.8	18.0
Hardin County, Kentucky	9,527	17.3	48.7	28.7	5.3
Jefferson County, Kentucky	65,212	11.1	36.5	36.9	15.5
Kenton County, Kentucky	14,456	8.8	45.2	30.0	16.0
McCracken County, Kentucky	5,124	5.3	41.6	48.3	4.8
Madison County, Kentucky	16,684	8.0	30.5	52.2	9.3
Oldham County, Kentucky	5,387	14.9	26.7	46.4	11.9
Warren County, Kentucky	21,372	6.6	30.7	52.1	10.6
LOUISIANA	423,707	15.8	35.1	40.6	8.5
Ascension Parish, Louisiana	10,303	14.6	45.2	33.4	6.8
Bossier Parish, Louisiana	10,876	17.7	32.5	44.0	5.7
Caddo Parish, Louisiana	20,748	20.1	29.7	39.3	10.8
Calcasieu Parish, Louisiana	17,854	20.7	28.6	45.8	4.8
East Baton Rouge Parish, Louisiana	58,609	9.6	25.8	51.5	13.0
Iberia Parish, Louisiana	5,462	25.1	41.6	31.8	1.6
Jefferson Parish, Louisiana	32,164	16.0	36.0	34.3	13.7
Lafayette Parish, Louisiana	22,852	9.6	29.6	49.3	11.5
Lafourche Parish, Louisiana	8,422	17.2	44.8	35.4	2.6
Livingston Parish, Louisiana	12,009	12.5	40.2	37.8	9.5
Orleans Parish, Louisiana	33,605	12.8	25.6	51.6	10.0
Ouachita Parish, Louisiana	14,638	16.7	19.8	50.3	13.2
Rapides Parish, Louisiana	11,271	12.4	46.5	37.9	3.2
St. Landry Parish, Louisiana	6,754	29.1	49.7	18.4	2.9
St. Tammany Parish, Louisiana	19,550	21.7	39.3	31.7	7.3
Tangipahoa Parish, Louisiana	14,685	19.3	26.8	50.0	4.0
Terrebonne Parish, Louisiana	7,724	11.0	34.4	33.9	20.7
MAINE	106,707	10.8	34.6	41.7	12.8
Androscoggin County, Maine	9,169	6.2	38.1	39.4	16.2
Aroostook County, Maine	4,632	16.2	38.8	42.4	2.6
Cumberland County, Maine	25,058	9.0	27.9	38.8	24.3
Kennebec County, Maine	10,046	11.7	31.6	45.6	11.2

Table C-2. Educational Attainment of the Population, by Selected Counties, 2019—*Continued*

(Number; percent; dollars.)

State/County	Total	Population 25 years and over						
		Less than 9th grade (percent)	9th to 12th grade, no diploma (percent)	High school graduate (includes equivalency) (percent)	Some college, no degree (percent)	Associate's degree (percent)	Bachelor's degree (percent)	Graduate or professional degree (percent)
INDIANA—(*Continued*)								
Porter County, Indiana	117,121	1.7	3.4	38.0	19.4	9.9	17.7	10.0
St. Joseph County, Indiana	178,476	2.4	7.3	32.1	19.6	8.4	18.0	12.1
Tippecanoe County, Indiana	108,603	3.2	6.2	27.2	16.8	7.2	21.3	18.1
Vanderburgh County, Indiana	124,267	2.2	7.1	34.3	19.4	9.5	19.0	8.6
Vigo County, Indiana	69,630	1.6	6.2	34.4	22.5	9.5	14.9	10.8
Wayne County, Indiana	45,134	4.4	7.6	35.9	23.1	11.3	10.8	7.0
IOWA	2,123,004	2.7	4.6	31.0	20.4	11.9	19.8	9.5
Black Hawk County, Iowa	83,655	2.2	4.9	32.7	19.4	10.5	19.9	10.3
Dallas County, Iowa	61,134	1.4	1.8	17.1	13.9	11.6	38.2	15.9
Dubuque County, Iowa	65,072	1.9	3.7	34.4	15.7	11.6	21.8	10.8
Johnson County, Iowa	89,161	2.3	3.5	15.9	16.4	8.1	28.6	25.3
Linn County, Iowa	153,872	1.8	4.1	28.0	19.2	13.9	22.6	10.4
Polk County, Iowa	326,674	3.7	4.1	23.9	21.1	9.7	26.4	11.1
Pottawattamie County, Iowa	63,895	2.8	6.2	31.7	23.3	12.8	16.3	6.9
Scott County, Iowa	118,176	2.4	4.8	27.7	21.8	11.4	20.0	11.9
Story County, Iowa	54,858	0.9	1.7	16.9	18.7	10.4	29.1	22.4
Woodbury County, Iowa	66,887	7.5	6.5	32.6	21.9	9.7	14.6	7.2
KANSAS	1,918,081	3.3	4.9	26.3	22.4	9.0	21.6	12.4
Butler County, Kansas	44,092	1.7	5.2	26.5	27.3	8.3	19.5	11.4
Douglas County, Kansas	72,338	1.6	3.3	20.9	18.1	8.9	29.7	17.4
Johnson County, Kansas	409,324	1.6	2.3	15.0	17.9	7.2	34.6	21.4
Leavenworth County, Kansas	54,599	2.7	4.6	28.5	24.8	7.6	19.9	11.8
Riley County, Kansas	37,327	0.7	2.4	17.8	25.2	8.8	25.1	20.0
Sedgwick County, Kansas	337,752	3.6	6.1	26.4	23.8	8.7	20.3	11.1
Shawnee County, Kansas	120,718	1.8	4.5	30.6	23.5	8.2	20.6	10.7
Wyandotte County, Kansas	105,645	9.8	9.6	33.3	19.1	8.4	12.5	7.4
KENTUCKY	3,048,442	5.1	7.7	33.2	20.3	8.5	14.9	10.3
Boone County, Kentucky	87,428	3.5	4.3	26.5	24.2	9.6	20.8	11.1
Bullitt County, Kentucky	57,989	3.2	8.4	40.4	21.5	11.0	10.8	4.8
Campbell County, Kentucky	64,791	3.2	5.3	26.8	17.5	7.1	26.2	13.9
Christian County, Kentucky	41,216	6.1	8.6	28.3	24.2	11.8	15.4	5.5
Daviess County, Kentucky	68,986	5.0	7.9	31.1	21.1	10.1	15.3	9.5
Fayette County, Kentucky	211,577	3.1	4.4	21.2	19.2	7.1	24.7	20.3
Hardin County, Kentucky	74,583	2.3	6.1	31.1	24.6	12.1	15.0	8.8
Jefferson County, Kentucky	532,991	2.7	5.8	26.7	21.5	8.2	21.1	14.0
Kenton County, Kentucky	113,122	3.5	5.5	29.1	19.8	9.3	20.2	12.6
McCracken County, Kentucky	45,495	3.4	7.3	33.3	22.3	9.1	14.3	10.3
Madison County, Kentucky	57,084	2.4	6.5	30.5	19.8	7.9	18.7	14.1
Oldham County, Kentucky	44,929	1.4	4.8	23.7	20.8	8.1	26.0	15.3
Warren County, Kentucky	81,148	6.0	4.5	25.7	18.9	9.5	21.3	14.1
LOUISIANA	3,140,201	4.4	9.6	33.9	20.6	6.4	16.0	8.9
Ascension Parish, Louisiana	82,678	1.5	6.3	34.2	22.3	10.1	17.1	8.6
Bossier Parish, Louisiana	84,723	4.2	5.2	33.3	26.7	8.3	13.8	8.5
Caddo Parish, Louisiana	163,212	3.0	10.4	34.1	21.9	6.9	14.5	9.2
Calcasieu Parish, Louisiana	134,238	3.5	10.4	35.4	19.2	8.5	14.5	8.4
East Baton Rouge Parish, Louisiana	281,377	2.4	6.6	28.2	22.3	5.6	22.0	12.9
Iberia Parish, Louisiana	46,888	6.3	9.2	47.5	13.3	7.5	12.4	3.7
Jefferson Parish, Louisiana	305,032	4.9	7.5	30.4	22.3	6.9	18.0	9.9
Lafayette Parish, Louisiana	163,888	4.1	5.9	29.3	20.1	5.7	24.6	10.3
Lafourche Parish, Louisiana	66,430	8.7	13.1	40.0	16.4	5.1	11.4	5.2
Livingston Parish, Louisiana	92,898	4.2	13.6	35.6	19.1	6.1	16.8	4.5
Orleans Parish, Louisiana	279,405	2.9	9.4	23.1	21.0	3.9	21.7	18.0
Ouachita Parish, Louisiana	100,705	3.5	9.6	32.5	22.3	6.1	16.6	9.4
Rapides Parish, Louisiana	86,467	4.2	9.7	36.4	23.3	7.0	13.5	5.9
St. Landry Parish, Louisiana	54,195	8.4	14.6	42.8	17.3	5.1	8.0	3.7
St. Tammany Parish, Louisiana	179,016	2.5	6.3	26.9	23.1	5.1	23.0	13.1
Tangipahoa Parish, Louisiana	87,255	6.3	9.1	35.7	18.2	6.0	15.5	9.3
Terrebonne Parish, Louisiana	75,048	7.7	11.6	38.7	18.5	7.6	10.2	5.7
MAINE	991,152	2.1	4.7	31.4	18.6	10.0	20.8	12.4
Androscoggin County, Maine	75,837	3.3	5.6	34.1	18.1	13.8	16.7	8.4
Aroostook County, Maine	50,069	4.2	4.8	40.5	19.2	12.4	12.5	6.5
Cumberland County, Maine	216,410	1.8	3.4	21.2	15.8	7.7	31.4	18.7
Kennebec County, Maine	89,536	2.3	4.4	32.9	21.9	9.7	16.7	12.1

Table C-2. Educational Attainment of the Population, by Selected Counties, 2019—*Continued*

(Number; percent; dollars.)

State/County	Population 18 to 24 years				
	Total	Less than high school graduate (percent)	High school graduate (includes equivalency) (percent)	Some college or associate's degree (percent)	Bachelor's degree or higher (percent)
MAINE—*(Continued)*					
Penobscot County, Maine	16,023	7.6	33.0	51.9	7.6
York County, Maine	14,929	12.3	45.3	32.5	9.9
MARYLAND	529,535	11.8	30.6	41.5	16.0
Allegany County, Maryland	8,929	12.2	39.0	46.5	2.4
Anne Arundel County, Maryland........................	50,545	9.8	33.5	38.1	18.6
Baltimore County, Maryland..............................	72,386	10.3	33.2	43.6	12.9
Calvert County, Maryland	6,844	5.4	42.0	31.6	21.0
Carroll County, Maryland..................................	14,844	5.4	31.7	44.4	18.4
Cecil County, Maryland	8,783	10.9	31.9	51.9	5.3
Charles County, Maryland	14,201	7.6	42.6	37.4	12.4
Frederick County, Maryland..............................	21,625	19.0	28.7	38.3	14.1
Harford County, Maryland.................................	19,961	12.6	32.2	40.4	14.8
Howard County, Maryland.................................	26,063	10.4	26.3	37.7	25.6
Montgomery County, Maryland..........................	81,523	14.9	25.0	33.4	26.7
Prince George's County, Maryland	85,570	11.3	30.9	46.2	11.5
St. Mary's County, Maryland	11,408	9.3	40.6	37.1	12.9
Washington County, Maryland	12,084	19.0	37.2	34.6	9.2
Wicomico County, Maryland	15,490	11.7	20.1	61.3	6.9
Baltimore city, Maryland	56,373	12.7	28.3	42.0	17.1
MASSACHUSETTS	690,150	9.2	27.1	44.2	19.5
Barnstable County, Massachusetts	13,751	15.0	29.0	38.0	18.0
Berkshire County, Massachusetts	11,852	10.7	28.6	54.6	6.1
Bristol County, Massachusetts..........................	50,198	10.7	37.0	38.3	14.0
Essex County, Massachusetts...........................	70,580	13.5	31.4	38.5	16.7
Franklin County, Massachusetts	4,967	3.7	46.5	38.8	11.0
Hampden County, Massachusetts......................	46,744	11.7	33.6	44.9	9.8
Hampshire County, Massachusetts....................	37,056	3.8	10.5	77.9	7.9
Middlesex County, Massachusetts.....................	158,706	7.9	24.6	40.2	27.2
Norfolk County, Massachusetts	61,868	6.7	27.8	36.6	28.9
Plymouth County, Massachusetts	44,446	10.9	35.2	40.5	13.4
Suffolk County, Massachusetts	108,552	7.2	17.4	51.3	24.1
Worcester County, Massachusetts......................	79,818	10.3	31.9	43.7	14.0
MICHIGAN...	949,408	12.7	32.4	43.3	11.6
Allegan County, Michigan.................................	8,826	14.8	52.2	25.0	8.0
Bay County, Michigan	7,594	19.5	26.6	43.1	10.8
Berrien County, Michigan	12,858	18.8	30.6	45.1	5.4
Calhoun County, Michigan	12,265	12.7	40.4	40.4	6.6
Clinton County, Michigan	7,070	10.5	35.0	46.0	8.6
Eaton County, Michigan	9,651	12.8	28.0	50.3	8.9
Genesee County, Michigan...............................	34,308	14.6	37.6	40.8	7.0
Grand Traverse County, Michigan	7,166	13.1	31.1	41.1	14.8
Ingham County, Michigan	55,276	6.0	25.1	58.5	10.5
Isabella County, Michigan	17,764	4.6	28.9	59.5	7.0
Jackson County, Michigan	13,533	16.5	31.6	49.4	2.5
Kalamazoo County, Michigan	41,971	9.4	27.4	48.4	14.8
Kent County, Michigan	61,729	11.7	34.3	39.6	14.4
Lapeer County, Michigan..................................	7,521	27.2	33.3	35.4	4.0
Lenawee County, Michigan	8,841	14.9	43.3	37.8	4.0
Livingston County, Michigan	15,176	16.9	32.1	37.4	13.5
Macomb County, Michigan	69,918	9.8	35.5	41.7	13.0
Marquette County, Michigan.............................	9,961	12.3	27.1	48.5	12.2
Midland County, Michigan................................	6,432	9.3	21.6	50.4	18.8
Monroe County, Michigan	11,835	15.7	33.7	43.9	6.7
Muskegon County, Michigan.............................	15,363	14.6	39.8	40.3	5.3
Oakland County, Michigan................................	101,508	11.2	29.0	40.9	19.0
Ottawa County, Michigan.................................	38,783	11.0	30.9	48.4	9.8
Saginaw County, Michigan................................	17,361	18.0	34.2	41.2	6.7
St. Clair County, Michigan................................	13,034	15.9	44.3	30.9	9.0
Shiawassee County, Michigan...........................	5,449	14.5	42.1	40.1	3.3
Van Buren County, Michigan.............................	5,501	11.6	32.9	50.0	5.4
Washtenaw County, Michigan	67,177	7.3	14.1	57.4	21.2
Wayne County, Michigan..................................	149,384	15.0	36.2	38.1	10.7
MINNESOTA...	489,751	12.1	29.6	43.2	15.1
Anoka County, Minnesota	26,767	12.7	33.7	41.9	11.7
Blue Earth County, Minnesota...........................	14,968	2.5	27.4	60.3	9.7

Table C-2. Educational Attainment of the Population, by Selected Counties, 2019—*Continued*

(Number; percent; dollars.)

State/County	Total	Population 25 years and over						
		Less than 9th grade (percent)	9th to 12th grade, no diploma (percent)	High school graduate (includes equivalency) (percent)	Some college, no degree (percent)	Associate's degree (percent)	Bachelor's degree (percent)	Graduate or professional degree (percent)
MAINE—(*Continued*)								
Penobscot County, Maine	109,291	2.4	4.5	32.8	20.1	10.7	19.5	10.0
York County, Maine	154,666	1.3	5.1	30.8	19.3	10.9	19.6	13.0
MARYLAND	4,183,858	4.0	5.6	24.6	18.0	6.9	21.8	19.1
Allegany County, Maryland	49,440	2.6	7.5	43.2	16.1	9.6	13.3	7.9
Anne Arundel County, Maryland	400,105	2.1	4.9	23.4	18.5	7.2	24.7	19.2
Baltimore County, Maryland	575,977	2.7	5.2	25.5	18.2	7.6	23.3	17.5
Calvert County, Maryland	64,371	0.9	3.3	32.0	23.1	9.0	16.2	15.4
Carroll County, Maryland	117,243	1.4	3.8	28.5	18.9	10.2	21.6	15.6
Cecil County, Maryland	71,592	1.3	7.6	35.6	20.7	9.6	16.3	8.8
Charles County, Maryland	110,194	3.2	4.0	31.9	24.3	8.0	16.7	12.0
Frederick County, Maryland	177,932	4.2	3.4	24.2	18.9	7.4	23.6	18.3
Harford County, Maryland	179,036	2.3	3.9	25.2	22.1	9.5	21.0	16.0
Howard County, Maryland	220,678	1.7	3.1	13.3	12.5	4.9	32.1	32.2
Montgomery County, Maryland	727,128	5.7	4.1	14.4	12.7	5.4	26.4	31.4
Prince George's County, Maryland	622,295	7.2	6.2	25.9	20.5	6.7	19.2	14.4
St. Mary's County, Maryland	75,021	3.0	6.6	33.6	15.9	10.1	19.0	11.6
Washington County, Maryland	106,200	3.5	8.6	37.2	21.9	6.3	12.4	10.1
Wicomico County, Maryland	65,728	5.7	8.9	31.5	17.7	5.9	16.6	13.6
Baltimore city, Maryland	417,550	4.5	9.8	28.3	19.3	4.8	17.6	15.7
MASSACHUSETTS	4,850,576	4.2	4.5	23.9	15.0	7.4	24.7	20.3
Barnstable County, Massachusetts	167,562	1.1	2.4	20.2	19.4	9.8	26.2	20.9
Berkshire County, Massachusetts	92,243	2.2	5.6	29.6	18.4	10.4	17.5	16.4
Bristol County, Massachusetts	399,297	7.4	6.3	30.0	17.5	8.8	20.0	10.0
Essex County, Massachusetts	552,144	5.6	5.1	24.3	15.8	7.8	24.6	16.8
Franklin County, Massachusetts	53,376	2.3	5.6	27.2	16.1	11.5	20.4	16.9
Hampden County, Massachusetts	319,983	5.3	7.9	33.4	16.7	8.8	16.7	11.2
Hampshire County, Massachusetts	100,574	1.4	3.8	18.6	15.2	8.4	25.4	27.3
Middlesex County, Massachusetts	1,137,894	2.9	3.2	19.0	11.9	5.8	28.2	29.0
Norfolk County, Massachusetts	497,759	2.9	3.2	18.8	13.1	6.8	28.7	26.4
Plymouth County, Massachusetts	366,337	3.6	3.4	28.4	17.7	8.7	24.5	13.7
Suffolk County, Massachusetts	564,188	7.3	4.8	21.5	13.1	5.2	25.7	22.4
Worcester County, Massachusetts	577,452	2.9	5.2	28.2	17.8	9.0	22.0	15.0
MICHIGAN	6,894,627	2.7	6.0	29.1	22.8	9.4	18.2	11.9
Allegan County, Michigan	81,159	2.2	5.6	41.5	19.5	7.4	17.6	6.1
Bay County, Michigan	74,917	1.5	5.6	34.3	25.9	11.1	14.8	6.8
Berrien County, Michigan	107,341	2.1	7.6	27.2	25.4	10.7	15.9	11.1
Calhoun County, Michigan	91,740	2.2	7.2	37.6	22.9	9.9	13.2	7.1
Clinton County, Michigan	54,934	2.3	2.6	26.5	24.2	10.6	19.8	14.1
Eaton County, Michigan	77,708	1.4	3.3	29.0	25.5	11.4	18.9	10.5
Genesee County, Michigan	280,937	2.2	7.4	30.7	27.4	10.8	13.5	8.0
Grand Traverse County, Michigan	67,821	1.0	4.2	22.3	24.6	8.7	25.1	14.0
Ingham County, Michigan	179,605	2.8	3.5	21.3	23.3	8.6	22.5	18.0
Isabella County, Michigan	39,986	3.0	5.9	33.8	22.1	8.1	14.1	13.0
Jackson County, Michigan	111,444	3.0	6.8	35.8	22.5	9.0	15.3	7.7
Kalamazoo County, Michigan	166,083	3.1	4.5	22.9	22.7	8.6	22.8	15.5
Kent County, Michigan	438,160	3.8	4.6	23.7	22.9	8.8	23.8	12.4
Lapeer County, Michigan	62,672	2.1	6.5	34.7	28.2	9.3	12.8	6.4
Lenawee County, Michigan	69,088	2.5	7.3	35.4	23.2	10.4	13.7	7.6
Livingston County, Michigan	136,805	1.0	4.1	26.8	22.9	9.5	24.0	11.7
Macomb County, Michigan	622,199	3.6	5.7	30.5	24.1	10.7	16.0	9.3
Marquette County, Michigan	44,541	1.2	3.6	30.4	20.2	9.4	24.1	11.1
Midland County, Michigan	58,581	1.7	4.0	28.8	18.3	10.9	22.0	14.3
Monroe County, Michigan	107,063	2.3	6.8	32.1	22.5	11.8	16.5	8.0
Muskegon County, Michigan	118,945	2.6	5.3	34.2	24.4	12.7	14.2	6.6
Oakland County, Michigan	896,196	1.8	3.3	18.9	19.2	8.0	27.8	21.1
Ottawa County, Michigan	183,870	2.4	4.8	28.0	20.3	8.9	23.9	11.7
Saginaw County, Michigan	132,466	2.6	7.7	33.1	23.6	11.2	14.0	7.9
St. Clair County, Michigan	113,904	1.6	6.8	31.8	25.8	12.4	14.1	7.6
Shiawassee County, Michigan	48,493	2.2	6.0	39.6	24.0	10.2	12.4	5.6
Van Buren County, Michigan	52,769	4.8	6.9	31.7	23.5	10.0	14.4	8.7
Washtenaw County, Michigan	232,925	1.2	3.4	14.2	18.0	7.2	25.8	30.0
Wayne County, Michigan	1,187,569	3.6	8.7	31.3	23.3	8.2	14.6	10.4
MINNESOTA	3,847,212	2.7	3.7	24.4	20.4	11.5	24.5	12.7
Anoka County, Minnesota	245,395	1.9	3.8	27.1	22.2	12.7	23.8	8.5
Blue Earth County, Minnesota	39,211	0.9	2.9	26.5	22.3	10.8	25.2	11.3

Table C-2. Educational Attainment of the Population, by Selected Counties, 2019—*Continued*

(Number; percent; dollars.)

State/County	Total	Population 18 to 24 years			
		Less than high school graduate (percent)	High school graduate (includes equivalency) (percent)	Some college or associate's degree (percent)	Bachelor's degree or higher (percent)
MINNESOTA—(*Continued*)					
Carver County, Minnesota	8,211	11.4	25.0	48.5	15.1
Crow Wing County, Minnesota	3,967	15.2	32.8	44.6	7.3
Dakota County, Minnesota	34,406	13.6	31.9	38.5	16.0
Hennepin County, Minnesota	107,423	10.1	26.8	37.9	25.2
Olmsted County, Minnesota	11,356	16.4	40.5	23.4	19.7
Ramsey County, Minnesota	52,342	12.8	25.7	45.9	15.6
Rice County, Minnesota	10,237	10.3	14.8	70.2	4.7
St. Louis County, Minnesota	23,689	6.1	25.5	51.5	16.9
Scott County, Minnesota	11,463	20.2	25.6	31.7	22.6
Sherburne County, Minnesota	8,093	19.3	30.2	44.2	6.2
Stearns County, Minnesota	23,597	7.4	25.8	58.3	8.4
Washington County, Minnesota	19,589	11.2	31.6	39.3	17.9
Wright County, Minnesota	9,704	13.7	35.3	37.0	14.0
MISSISSIPPI	298,065	15.0	28.4	49.8	6.8
DeSoto County, Mississippi	16,284	20.2	28.2	45.4	6.2
Forrest County, Mississippi	10,834	8.0	16.6	68.4	7.1
Harrison County, Mississippi	21,929	11.7	27.3	55.0	6.0
Hinds County, Mississippi	25,474	11.4	31.1	49.5	8.0
Jackson County, Mississippi	11,464	11.3	41.0	38.5	9.3
Jones County, Mississippi	6,443	16.8	26.7	48.0	8.5
Lauderdale County, Mississippi	5,803	14.3	37.9	44.4	3.4
Lee County, Mississippi	8,540	19.2	11.3	59.8	9.7
Madison County, Mississippi	9,332	6.1	19.2	60.0	14.8
Rankin County, Mississippi	12,672	15.8	27.4	39.8	17.0
MISSOURI	558.571	11.3	33.8	43.2	11.7
Boone County, Missouri	34,590	2.3	17.3	69.9	10.5
Buchanan County, Missouri	7,459	17.1	21.2	49.5	12.2
Cape Girardeau County, Missouri	10,698	2.1	31.1	57.9	8.9
Cass County, Missouri	8,225	9.8	50.8	30.3	9.1
Christian County, Missouri	6,347	9.8	25.9	55.7	8.6
Clay County, Missouri	20,496	11.4	34.1	46.2	8.2
Cole County, Missouri	5,461	5.0	39.4	26.2	29.4
Franklin County, Missouri	7,676	21.6	28.6	42.2	7.6
Greene County, Missouri	40,298	11.2	21.7	53.4	13.6
Jackson County, Missouri	58,068	12.8	39.6	34.2	13.4
Jasper County, Missouri	11,462	20.1	33.2	38.2	8.5
Jefferson County, Missouri	16,627	11.2	41.8	40.0	7.1
Platte County, Missouri	8,062	16.4	26.4	39.5	17.7
St. Charles County, Missouri	33,272	11.4	27.7	48.0	12.8
St. Francois County, Missouri	5,033	11.8	32.9	55.3	0.0
St. Louis County, Missouri	83,082	9.4	33.2	38.5	19.0
St. Louis city, Missouri	26,301	5.5	28.5	42.4	23.6
MONTANA	100,304	14.0	35.2	41.3	9.5
Cascade County, Montana	8,510	7.1	39.8	47.0	6.1
Flathead County, Montana	6,724	11.3	47.9	36.5	4.4
Gallatin County, Montana	18,919	9.6	23.4	51.5	15.5
Lewis and Clark County, Montana	6,192	22.3	33.5	36.1	8.1
Missoula County, Montana	15,418	5.4	30.3	50.7	13.6
Yellowstone County, Montana	11,908	11.1	44.7	37.8	6.5
NEBRASKA	187,542	9.2	29.1	47.4	14.4
Douglas County, Nebraska	51,616	7.6	31.1	44.0	17.2
Lancaster County, Nebraska	48,453	6.0	19.7	58.0	16.3
Sarpy County, Nebraska	15,585	6.2	29.7	47.2	16.8
NEVADA	252,953	13.6	42.2	37.7	6.5
Clark County, Nevada	184,971	14.3	44.2	35.5	6.1
Washoe County, Nevada	42,837	8.9	33.1	48.9	9.1
NEW HAMPSHIRE	123,941	11.3	32.1	44.2	12.5
Cheshire County, New Hampshire	8,565	2.3	26.0	66.0	5.6
Grafton County, New Hampshire	11,242	5.8	25.3	60.1	8.9
Hillsborough County, New Hampshire	35,154	13.3	33.3	38.2	15.2
Merrimack County, New Hampshire	13,842	20.7	33.0	39.4	6.9

Table C-2. Educational Attainment of the Population, by Selected Counties, 2019—*Continued*

(Number; percent; dollars.)

State/County	Population 25 years and over							
	Total	Less than 9th grade (percent)	9th to 12th grade, no diploma (percent)	High school graduate (includes equivalency) (percent)	Some college, no degree (percent)	Associate's degree (percent)	Bachelor's degree (percent)	Graduate or professional degree (percent)
MINNESOTA—(*Continued*)								
Carver County, Minnesota	69,175	3.0	3.2	15.1	17.3	9.4	35.9	16.1
Crow Wing County, Minnesota	46,894	0.5	4.4	30.4	24.8	14.5	16.0	9.4
Dakota County, Minnesota	290,701	2.0	2.4	21.2	20.3	11.4	28.7	13.9
Hennepin County, Minnesota	882,398	3.1	2.8	16.5	18.0	8.9	32.4	18.4
Olmsted County, Minnesota	108,246	3.3	2.0	20.7	15.4	11.5	24.5	22.5
Ramsey County, Minnesota	370,025	4.5	4.2	21.8	17.5	8.8	26.9	16.3
Rice County, Minnesota	42,197	1.4	5.0	30.7	18.4	12.9	18.9	12.7
St. Louis County, Minnesota	137,764	1.6	3.5	26.4	25.5	13.0	19.5	10.5
Scott County, Minnesota	97,194	1.8	3.9	20.6	19.6	12.6	28.9	12.5
Sherburne County, Minnesota	63,742	1.4	3.6	30.7	24.7	13.0	18.8	7.8
Stearns County, Minnesota	100,173	5.8	3.7	29.3	21.8	12.3	18.9	8.3
Washington County, Minnesota	179,294	1.3	2.3	21.1	19.9	9.7	29.3	16.6
Wright County, Minnesota	90,127	1.2	2.5	29.1	21.2	12.2	22.8	11.0
MISSISSIPPI	1,979,664	4.6	10.1	30.2	22.3	10.5	13.7	8.6
DeSoto County, Mississippi	121,767	2.3	7.5	27.8	23.8	10.4	17.2	10.9
Forrest County, Mississippi	47,190	3.1	8.1	29.6	22.5	11.6	15.1	9.9
Harrison County, Mississippi	136,815	3.1	7.5	30.3	24.5	11.1	15.1	8.2
Hinds County, Mississippi	151,101	3.7	8.2	24.5	26.2	8.4	16.4	12.5
Jackson County, Mississippi	98,981	3.1	6.8	30.1	25.3	10.9	16.2	7.6
Jones County, Mississippi	44,623	5.6	8.1	35.2	19.9	12.5	11.5	7.2
Lauderdale County, Mississippi	51,061	4.6	14.7	25.0	23.1	13.8	12.4	6.3
Lee County, Mississippi	55,589	4.5	11.9	26.7	20.6	11.2	16.7	8.5
Madison County, Mississippi	70,657	3.2	5.5	20.4	15.6	6.5	31.0	17.7
Rankin County, Mississippi	107,148	2.6	7.6	25.5	23.2	10.8	20.2	9.9
MISSOURI	4,206,162	2.9	6.4	31.1	21.4	7.9	18.4	11.8
Boone County, Missouri	109,405	2.5	3.9	20.1	19.2	7.3	25.7	21.2
Buchanan County, Missouri	60,706	4.4	6.0	42.4	21.0	6.6	14.5	5.1
Cape Girardeau County, Missouri	51,517	2.1	7.0	28.8	22.5	5.4	21.2	13.2
Cass County, Missouri	72,252	2.0	4.4	37.8	22.9	7.1	15.8	9.9
Christian County, Missouri	59,930	2.4	7.3	28.7	22.5	9.9	18.6	10.6
Clay County, Missouri	169,514	2.2	3.6	29.2	23.1	9.6	22.5	9.7
Cole County, Missouri	54,710	2.4	5.6	29.0	20.6	9.5	21.8	11.1
Franklin County, Missouri	72,871	4.0	6.6	32.7	25.3	11.7	13.0	6.8
Greene County, Missouri	192,520	3.5	4.9	29.0	25.4	7.0	19.4	10.8
Jackson County, Missouri	480,715	2.4	6.1	29.6	22.1	7.3	20.4	12.2
Jasper County, Missouri	79,894	5.5	9.2	32.8	23.4	5.4	16.8	6.9
Jefferson County, Missouri	157,026	2.5	7.9	32.1	24.1	13.6	12.6	7.1
Platte County, Missouri	71,879	1.4	2.6	23.7	20.0	8.2	27.0	17.1
St. Charles County, Missouri	276,339	1.5	4.2	23.4	21.5	9.0	25.8	14.6
St. Francois County, Missouri	48,484	4.8	8.7	36.9	27.7	7.8	6.5	7.7
St. Louis County, Missouri	693,434	1.5	4.5	21.4	19.8	7.2	25.4	20.2
St. Louis city, Missouri	218,004	3.4	7.1	24.7	20.8	5.5	20.4	18.1
MONTANA	741,950	1.6	4.1	28.4	22.9	9.4	23.1	10.5
Cascade County, Montana	54,619	2.4	4.8	33.7	24.6	8.8	17.6	8.0
Flathead County, Montana	74,553	0.8	3.2	27.6	23.0	9.8	26.3	9.3
Gallatin County, Montana	73,589	0.9	1.3	18.0	20.3	6.8	35.2	17.5
Lewis and Clark County, Montana	49,458	0.6	2.7	23.6	19.5	9.1	28.3	16.3
Missoula County, Montana	81,796	1.4	2.8	22.1	20.1	9.1	30.0	14.4
Yellowstone County, Montana	112,005	1.8	4.6	31.2	21.0	8.5	22.1	10.9
NEBRASKA	1,271,770	3.4	4.5	25.7	22.0	11.1	21.8	11.4
Douglas County, Nebraska	374,023	4.1	4.4	21.6	20.9	7.4	26.5	15.0
Lancaster County, Nebraska	198,449	2.8	4.1	20.4	19.7	12.8	25.6	14.7
Sarpy County, Nebraska	120,539	1.4	2.1	23.3	22.9	10.9	26.2	13.1
NEVADA	2,136,466	5.1	8.0	27.8	24.6	8.8	16.7	9.0
Clark County, Nevada	1,560,947	5.5	8.2	28.2	24.0	8.5	16.8	8.8
Washoe County, Nevada	328,153	4.7	6.6	22.5	25.3	9.3	19.3	12.2
NEW HAMPSHIRE	979,750	2.0	4.7	28.1	17.8	9.9	22.9	14.7
Cheshire County, New Hampshire	53,697	2.7	3.1	30.6	20.7	9.0	21.1	12.8
Grafton County, New Hampshire	64,180	2.3	6.4	23.8	17.3	8.8	20.3	21.1
Hillsborough County, New Hampshire	297,602	2.7	5.0	26.3	18.1	10.1	24.4	13.4
Merrimack County, New Hampshire	108,510	2.0	6.0	29.1	16.9	10.3	21.3	14.4

Table C-2. Educational Attainment of the Population, by Selected Counties, 2019—*Continued*

(Number; percent; dollars.)

State/County	Total	Population 18 to 24 years			
		Less than high school graduate (percent)	High school graduate (includes equivalency) (percent)	Some college or associate's degree (percent)	Bachelor's degree or higher (percent)
NEW HAMPSHIRE—(*Continued*)					
Rockingham County, New Hampshire..................	22,217	9.3	40.6	30.1	19.9
Strafford County, New Hampshire........................	20,533	5.2	20.6	61.3	13.0
NEW JERSEY	752,937	9.5	29.3	42.5	18.7
Atlantic County, New Jersey................................	24,683	10.9	28.6	45.9	14.6
Bergen County, New Jersey	74,163	8.1	23.9	41.8	26.1
Burlington County, New Jersey	36,899	9.1	35.5	37.6	17.7
Camden County, New Jersey................................	41,040	12.6	33.2	39.5	14.7
Cape May County, New Jersey	6,132	8.1	47.3	33.1	11.5
Cumberland County, New Jersey	11,270	17.1	38.8	34.1	9.9
Essex County, New Jersey	69,333	11.6	34.6	39.9	13.9
Gloucester County, New Jersey...........................	25,981	3.6	29.3	51.7	15.3
Hudson County, New Jersey	52,068	9.5	25.8	41.6	23.1
Hunterdon County, New Jersey	9,882	10.2	35.1	29.2	25.5
Mercer County, New Jersey.................................	41,153	8.6	23.1	58.9	9.4
Middlesex County, New Jersey............................	76,973	8.6	25.9	50.0	15.5
Monmouth County, New Jersey	49,925	8.0	26.5	40.4	25.1
Morris County, New Jersey	41,892	9.4	26.7	36.6	27.2
Ocean County, New Jersey..................................	43,993	6.4	30.0	43.2	20.4
Passaic County, New Jersey................................	48,205	13.4	40.6	32.1	13.8
Salem County, New Jersey	5,015	4.2	28.2	53.0	14.5
Somerset County, New Jersey	27,734	10.4	23.5	39.1	27.1
Sussex County, New Jersey	11,404	10.4	31.6	43.9	14.1
Union County, New Jersey	46,439	10.2	27.4	45.3	17.1
Warren County, New Jersey	8,753	6.7	27.7	44.5	21.1
NEW MEXICO	196,991	15.5	36.5	40.4	7.7
Bernalillo County, New Mexico...........................	60,061	11.9	33.5	43.4	11.2
Chaves County, New Mexico	5,918	11.1	66.8	22.1	0.0
Doña Ana County, New Mexico	30,938	10.7	29.2	51.2	8.9
Lea County, New Mexico....................................	7,453	25.7	34.5	32.2	7.6
McKinley County, New Mexico	6,572	22.1	34.8	42.9	0.2
Otero County, New Mexico	6,601	16.0	38.0	39.9	6.1
Sandoval County, New Mexico............................	11,127	11.4	36.2	47.0	5.4
San Juan County, New Mexico............................	10,423	25.9	28.6	44.4	1.1
Santa Fe County, New Mexico............................	11,288	17.2	42.8	33.1	6.8
Valencia County, New Mexico	9,341	18.8	42.8	27.8	10.6
NEW YORK	1,766,731	10.3	28.2	43.2	18.4
Albany County, New York...................................	43,901	4.8	33.6	41.2	20.5
Bronx County, New York	137,331	19.4	27.3	42.5	10.8
Broome County, New York	27,051	6.2	33.6	44.6	15.6
Cattaraugus County, New York............................	6,604	13.7	37.2	42.5	6.6
Cayuga County, New York..................................	5,798	20.7	28.6	41.7	9.0
Chautauqua County, New York............................	12,402	15.8	36.1	43.7	4.4
Chemung County, New York................................	6,596	16.6	33.6	44.7	5.1
Clinton County, New York...................................	10,675	4.5	30.6	57.8	7.1
Dutchess County, New York	31,325	11.7	29.0	49.2	10.1
Erie County, New York..	83,447	7.6	31.0	45.3	16.1
Jefferson County, New York................................	13,874	8.7	53.1	32.3	5.9
Kings County, New York.....................................	202,230	11.1	30.1	38.2	20.6
Livingston County, New York	9,687	7.1	31.7	56.4	4.8
Madison County, New York	9,235	5.8	26.7	61.6	5.9
Monroe County, New York	71,906	7.6	28.4	48.3	15.7
Nassau County, New York..................................	116,989	8.8	24.8	41.8	24.7
New York County, New York...............................	145,284	7.1	20.1	38.7	34.1
Niagara County, New York..................................	16,439	9.7	30.0	42.2	18.2
Oneida County, New York...................................	21,322	12.7	28.5	46.6	12.2
Onondaga County, New York...............................	47,488	7.9	25.0	48.8	18.3
Ontario County, New York	9,967	3.1	40.1	34.8	22.0
Orange County, New York	40,814	10.7	34.8	41.3	13.2
Oswego County, New York..................................	12,628	10.0	27.8	55.2	7.0
Putnam County, New York..................................	7,290	7.3	24.5	48.1	20.1
Queens County, New York..................................	168,832	10.3	26.2	45.3	18.2
Rensselaer County, New York	16,456	7.7	39.2	37.4	15.6
Richmond County, New York	38,961	10.2	26.5	41.7	21.6
Rockland County, New York................................	29,647	16.3	29.3	33.1	21.4
St. Lawrence County, New York	14,624	9.4	25.4	60.8	4.4

Table C-2. Educational Attainment of the Population, by Selected Counties, 2019—*Continued*

(Number; percent; dollars.)

State/County	Total	Population 25 years and over						
		Less than 9th grade (percent)	9th to 12th grade, no diploma (percent)	High school graduate (includes equivalency) (percent)	Some college, no degree (percent)	Associate's degree (percent)	Bachelor's degree (percent)	Graduate or professional degree (percent)
NEW HAMPSHIRE—*(Continued)*								
Rockingham County, New Hampshire	227,909	1.1	2.9	27.8	16.8	8.8	25.8	16.7
Strafford County, New Hampshire	86,617	1.9	4.4	27.1	19.4	11.1	21.1	15.0
NEW JERSEY	6,191,229	4.7	5.0	26.9	15.7	6.4	25.1	16.1
Atlantic County, New Jersey	183,492	4.8	7.5	33.8	19.2	6.4	19.1	9.1
Bergen County, New Jersey	661,729	3.6	3.5	20.9	14.0	6.0	31.7	20.3
Burlington County, New Jersey	316,291	1.8	4.1	27.3	18.8	8.4	25.0	14.6
Camden County, New Jersey	351,426	4.6	5.8	30.0	18.4	7.7	21.2	12.4
Cape May County, New Jersey	69,957	2.4	4.1	34.9	19.3	7.2	18.2	13.9
Cumberland County, New Jersey	102,701	6.1	12.7	40.4	17.6	7.1	10.4	5.7
Essex County, New Jersey	540,264	6.7	6.5	29.8	16.0	5.2	21.9	13.8
Gloucester County, New Jersey	202,556	2.5	4.5	32.0	18.2	8.8	22.2	11.7
Hudson County, New Jersey	483,796	9.0	5.3	23.2	12.4	4.9	26.8	18.5
Hunterdon County, New Jersey	90,777	1.8	4.0	19.2	15.0	6.0	32.0	22.1
Mercer County, New Jersey	248,215	4.7	6.5	23.3	14.2	6.8	23.0	21.5
Middlesex County, New Jersey	569,641	4.9	6.2	24.5	14.8	5.7	26.0	17.9
Monmouth County, New Jersey	439,267	1.8	3.5	22.9	16.1	7.6	29.1	19.1
Morris County, New Jersey	347,474	2.5	2.7	19.5	13.2	5.6	33.7	22.8
Ocean County, New Jersey	416,503	2.3	4.8	34.6	18.2	7.8	21.4	10.9
Passaic County, New Jersey	334,603	8.9	5.8	35.5	15.4	5.3	19.6	9.5
Salem County, New Jersey	44,241	4.4	7.9	37.5	19.4	10.8	12.0	8.1
Somerset County, New Jersey	230,443	3.3	2.2	20.5	12.1	6.0	31.2	24.8
Sussex County, New Jersey	101,838	1.6	4.0	26.8	20.5	8.9	23.9	14.2
Union County, New Jersey	379,853	8.3	5.4	29.0	14.9	5.3	22.9	14.3
Warren County, New Jersey	76,162	1.6	5.0	29.8	21.7	8.0	25.1	8.8
NEW MEXICO	1,425,988	5.8	8.3	26.4	22.7	9.1	15.5	12.2
Bernalillo County, New Mexico	473,995	3.8	7.3	23.9	20.8	9.1	19.5	15.6
Chaves County, New Mexico	41,909	10.1	13.3	25.2	26.2	7.7	11.0	6.4
Doña Ana County, New Mexico	134,579	13.6	8.4	20.8	20.2	9.7	15.3	11.9
Lea County, New Mexico	42,477	11.7	12.6	27.8	24.4	10.4	7.3	5.7
McKinley County, New Mexico	44,710	6.8	14.3	36.9	24.8	6.2	5.6	5.4
Otero County, New Mexico	45,409	8.4	6.7	32.3	29.5	8.9	8.6	5.7
Sandoval County, New Mexico	102,218	2.7	4.5	26.4	22.8	10.7	19.0	13.9
San Juan County, New Mexico	81,169	3.4	10.9	30.4	25.2	15.6	8.2	6.2
Santa Fe County, New Mexico	112,842	5.8	6.0	19.3	21.6	7.1	21.5	18.6
Valencia County, New Mexico	50,276	4.0	8.8	32.8	24.5	10.0	9.8	10.0
NEW YORK	13,664,734	5.8	6.6	25.8	15.2	8.8	21.2	16.6
Albany County, New York	205,840	2.7	5.3	21.3	14.6	12.5	23.3	20.3
Bronx County, New York	932,813	11.5	14.1	29.1	17.1	7.8	12.7	7.7
Broome County, New York	126,674	3.0	6.6	30.9	18.9	13.4	13.8	13.4
Cattaraugus County, New York	52,903	3.3	6.1	39.1	18.1	12.2	11.4	9.9
Cayuga County, New York	56,060	4.5	8.3	33.3	18.7	12.1	14.8	8.4
Chautauqua County, New York	89,055	3.5	6.6	33.5	16.9	13.4	14.6	11.3
Chemung County, New York	59,575	1.6	6.3	32.2	20.7	14.0	13.7	11.6
Clinton County, New York	56,005	4.3	8.5	35.9	15.7	10.1	14.3	11.2
Dutchess County, New York	208,001	2.8	5.0	27.5	18.7	10.8	19.1	16.1
Erie County, New York	649,982	2.5	4.5	28.0	18.4	12.7	19.2	14.7
Jefferson County, New York	70,019	2.7	6.6	36.2	20.5	11.7	13.5	8.9
Kings County, New York	1,777,543	8.5	7.8	26.6	12.2	5.8	23.6	15.6
Livingston County, New York	41,954	2.6	6.1	34.6	16.8	14.6	13.5	11.7
Madison County, New York	48,107	1.1	5.4	37.6	16.7	15.0	13.7	10.5
Monroe County, New York	516,914	3.3	6.0	22.1	16.2	11.7	23.0	17.7
Nassau County, New York	948,980	4.7	3.4	21.9	15.0	7.9	26.3	20.9
New York County, New York	1,251,551	6.4	5.9	12.7	9.6	3.4	32.2	29.8
Niagara County, New York	151,144	2.1	6.1	31.1	19.7	12.9	17.4	10.7
Oneida County, New York	158,832	4.0	7.3	30.3	18.5	11.6	16.0	12.2
Onondaga County, New York	315,947	3.1	5.4	26.2	16.9	12.0	20.0	16.4
Ontario County, New York	78,035	2.4	4.0	26.5	15.1	12.6	20.9	18.5
Orange County, New York	246,320	3.6	6.8	27.6	20.0	10.5	17.2	14.4
Oswego County, New York	79,882	2.9	8.5	35.7	18.6	12.2	13.0	9.2
Putnam County, New York	72,210	3.2	4.6	26.4	20.8	7.0	21.1	17.0
Queens County, New York	1,633,699	10.1	6.9	27.3	14.5	8.0	20.5	12.7
Rensselaer County, New York	111,620	2.5	5.9	28.3	14.7	13.5	18.7	16.3
Richmond County, New York	333,496	4.9	6.1	29.2	16.3	7.3	21.6	14.7
Rockland County, New York	203,574	4.7	6.4	21.3	17.1	8.2	22.8	19.4
St. Lawrence County, New York	72,234	5.1	7.7	35.4	16.7	12.4	12.0	10.7

Table C-2. Educational Attainment of the Population, by Selected Counties, 2019—*Continued*

(Number; percent; dollars.)

State/County	Population 18 to 24 years				
	Total	Less than high school graduate (percent)	High school graduate (includes equivalency) (percent)	Some college or associate's degree (percent)	Bachelor's degree or higher (percent)
NEW YORK —*(Continued)*					
Saratoga County, New York..................................	18,930	9.7	28.1	44.7	17.5
Schenectady County, New York...........................	12,868	5.8	41.3	40.6	12.3
Steuben County, New York..................................	7,294	20.6	33.6	34.3	11.4
Suffolk County, New York...................................	131,886	9.8	28.0	43.2	19.0
Sullivan County, New York.................................	5,226	8.3	37.2	42.4	12.1
Tompkins County, New York	28,029	0.7	10.0	65.8	23.5
Ulster County, New York	16,616	10.5	22.2	50.4	16.9
Warren County, New York	4,425	8.7	23.3	51.4	16.6
Wayne County, New York	6,304	13.0	36.9	39.7	10.3
Westchester County, New York	83,974	9.1	24.9	42.0	24.0
NORTH CAROLINA	1,007,035	12.0	31.8	45.3	10.8
Alamance County, North Carolina..........................	18,021	12.5	29.1	53.7	4.7
Brunswick County, North Carolina	7,258	7.1	36.8	48.4	7.7
Buncombe County, North Carolina	19,693	13.2	42.0	36.2	8.6
Burke County, North Carolina.............................	6,680	11.6	44.0	34.8	9.6
Cabarrus County, North Carolina........................	18,508	10.7	43.1	34.5	11.7
Caldwell County, North Carolina.........................	6,499	19.3	49.0	25.2	6.5
Carteret County, North Carolina	5,242	16.3	30.4	49.3	4.0
Catawba County, North Carolina.........................	13,464	8.3	33.8	47.7	10.2
Chatham County, North Carolina.........................	4,618	18.0	34.2	37.9	9.9
Cleveland County, North Carolina........................	10,263	8.3	29.7	56.4	5.6
Craven County, North Carolina............................	12,507	7.4	60.4	26.8	5.4
Cumberland County, North Carolina.....................	43,859	9.9	37.3	47.5	5.3
Davidson County, North Carolina	11,780	13.3	27.3	48.6	10.8
Durham County, North Carolina	32,206	10.2	20.1	50.7	19.0
Forsyth County, North Carolina	37,025	17.7	31.8	40.2	10.3
Franklin County, North Carolina	5,782	19.5	32.2	42.5	5.8
Gaston County, North Carolina...........................	17,531	13.4	35.9	38.9	11.8
Guilford County, North Carolina	58,963	10.0	22.5	56.8	10.7
Harnett County, North Carolina	13,194	12.4	48.4	29.3	9.8
Henderson County, North Carolina.......................	6,743	12.8	28.1	57.2	2.0
Iredell County, North Carolina............................	14,648	12.4	47.5	30.5	9.5
Johnston County, North Carolina	17,708	17.6	29.6	48.8	4.0
Lincoln County, North Carolina...........................	5,876	7.9	42.3	39.6	10.2
Mecklenburg County, North Carolina	100,094	12.2	23.2	47.8	16.8
Moore County, North Carolina............................	6,051	11.8	33.3	44.9	10.1
Nash County, North Carolina..............................	8,576	27.3	27.9	35.8	9.0
New Hanover County, North Carolina....................	29,481	8.7	22.2	54.5	14.6
Onslow County, North Carolina	40,952	6.5	49.8	40.9	2.8
Orange County, North Carolina...........................	26,283	4.1	17.0	59.1	19.7
Pitt County, North Carolina................................	30,208	6.9	31.6	47.8	13.7
Randolph County, North Carolina........................	11,780	18.2	36.6	40.0	5.2
Robeson County, North Carolina.........................	13,369	16.6	34.5	45.3	3.5
Rockingham County, North Carolina	6,620	18.4	28.1	49.5	4.1
Rowan County, North Carolina............................	12,648	11.1	26.7	49.1	13.2
Rutherford County, North Carolina.......................	5,210	10.7	38.5	36.6	14.2
Surry County, North Carolina.............................	5,751	16.1	31.3	47.2	5.4
Union County, North Carolina.............................	22,433	18.4	35.3	40.4	5.8
Wake County, North Carolina.............................	101,240	8.8	26.1	44.2	20.8
Wayne County, North Carolina............................	13,622	14.2	31.9	48.6	5.3
Wilkes County, North Carolina	6,020	3.4	59.8	36.8	0.0
Wilson County, North Carolina............................	7,245	23.6	38.9	27.2	10.3
NORTH DAKOTA	80,981	9.2	26.5	51.5	12.8
Burleigh County, North Dakota............................	9,671	6.5	41.0	43.7	8.8
Cass County, North Dakota	24,132	6.4	17.6	56.1	19.9
Grand Forks County, North Dakota.......................	13,533	7.0	14.8	65.1	13.0
Ward County, North Dakota................................	8,848	7.5	37.0	48.2	7.3
OHIO	1,064,448	12.8	35.7	41.4	10.1
Allen County, Ohio...	9,673	12.9	41.6	40.0	5.5
Ashtabula County, Ohio.....................................	7,656	15.6	51.7	29.2	3.5
Athens County, Ohio	17,953	5.2	20.6	66.2	7.9
Belmont County, Ohio	5,116	24.2	52.1	23.2	0.5
Butler County, Ohio..	48,126	9.9	42.7	41.0	6.4
Clark County, Ohio...	12,491	11.2	41.5	41.9	5.5

Table C-2. Educational Attainment of the Population, by Selected Counties, 2019—*Continued*

(Number; percent; dollars.)

State/County	Total	Less than 9th grade (percent)	9th to 12th grade, no diploma (percent)	High school graduate (includes equivalency) (percent)	Some college, no degree (percent)	Associate's degree (percent)	Bachelor's degree (percent)	Graduate or professional degree (percent)
NEW YORK —(*Continued*)								
Saratoga County, New York	165,720	1.3	4.9	24.6	15.6	11.0	24.2	18.3
Schenectady County, New York	108,994	2.6	4.6	28.8	16.7	12.2	20.8	14.3
Steuben County, New York	67,762	2.7	5.9	36.3	17.1	13.6	11.9	12.5
Suffolk County, New York	1,035,815	4.1	5.0	26.2	16.5	9.8	20.7	17.6
Sullivan County, New York	54,336	5.5	6.8	35.2	18.1	8.5	14.8	11.0
Tompkins County, New York	59,698	1.9	2.7	17.1	12.3	9.2	23.8	33.1
Ulster County, New York	129,942	3.0	6.2	28.6	17.2	12.1	16.5	16.4
Warren County, New York	48,358	4.4	4.9	27.6	16.6	13.0	18.7	14.8
Wayne County, New York	64,603	2.9	7.3	33.6	19.2	13.0	13.9	10.0
Westchester County, New York	673,174	5.0	5.1	19.2	13.0	6.3	25.4	25.9
NORTH CAROLINA	7,187,077	4.2	7.2	25.6	20.6	10.1	20.5	11.8
Alamance County, North Carolina	114,122	5.2	7.5	30.3	20.6	11.0	17.8	7.5
Brunswick County, North Carolina	114,779	1.7	5.0	26.4	22.1	11.9	21.0	12.0
Buncombe County, North Carolina	193,633	3.2	4.8	23.8	17.1	10.7	24.9	15.6
Burke County, North Carolina	67,177	7.3	10.4	32.9	18.6	12.2	10.7	7.8
Cabarrus County, North Carolina	142,955	3.5	5.6	26.2	20.6	9.8	22.6	11.8
Caldwell County, North Carolina	59,342	6.4	14.8	29.1	21.2	11.7	12.8	4.1
Carteret County, North Carolina	52,454	2.0	7.1	26.3	25.9	8.1	18.3	12.4
Catawba County, North Carolina	111,167	4.6	8.9	28.8	21.6	12.7	16.6	6.8
Chatham County, North Carolina	55,042	6.4	6.4	21.5	13.4	8.3	21.6	22.4
Cleveland County, North Carolina	66,240	6.0	9.0	35.5	18.8	11.8	12.2	6.6
Craven County, North Carolina	67,879	3.2	6.6	27.3	25.5	15.6	13.5	8.4
Cumberland County, North Carolina	208,611	2.7	6.3	27.1	28.2	10.9	15.8	9.1
Davidson County, North Carolina	120,125	5.8	8.6	35.3	22.1	9.3	13.1	5.8
Durham County, North Carolina	223,247	5.8	4.9	18.6	14.6	6.7	24.1	25.2
Forsyth County, North Carolina	258,434	4.6	6.6	26.4	20.2	9.0	20.3	12.9
Franklin County, North Carolina	48,608	2.9	7.7	30.7	22.3	14.3	16.5	5.6
Gaston County, North Carolina	157,145	4.3	10.4	29.7	22.9	9.2	16.6	6.9
Guilford County, North Carolina	359,317	4.1	7.5	22.5	19.3	9.6	23.9	13.2
Harnett County, North Carolina	87,796	3.2	7.8	30.4	22.2	12.3	16.7	7.5
Henderson County, North Carolina	88,613	2.8	6.7	24.3	25.3	10.9	18.8	11.2
Iredell County, North Carolina	126,121	2.8	7.0	27.9	20.8	10.6	21.2	9.7
Johnston County, North Carolina	138,897	4.8	7.7	24.9	22.3	16.3	18.1	5.9
Lincoln County, North Carolina	62,105	2.1	5.8	32.5	21.3	12.3	17.2	8.8
Mecklenburg County, North Carolina	752,114	4.9	4.7	16.2	19.9	8.6	29.8	15.9
Moore County, North Carolina	73,523	3.8	5.0	21.5	20.9	9.5	25.8	13.4
Nash County, North Carolina	65,190	4.4	9.7	37.3	20.2	10.7	13.8	4.0
New Hanover County, North Carolina	162,287	2.1	4.9	19.1	20.9	9.9	28.0	15.0
Onslow County, North Carolina	108,676	2.4	5.9	29.7	24.5	12.8	17.5	7.1
Orange County, North Carolina	93,642	1.8	3.7	13.1	12.2	6.0	28.9	34.2
Pitt County, North Carolina	112,043	3.6	8.1	25.6	17.8	12.8	19.3	12.8
Randolph County, North Carolina	100,084	6.5	12.0	34.7	21.3	10.6	10.1	4.9
Robeson County, North Carolina	85,215	6.4	15.5	34.6	18.8	9.9	10.0	4.9
Rockingham County, North Carolina	66,036	4.7	12.6	41.3	18.6	8.6	9.6	4.7
Rowan County, North Carolina	98,238	5.3	8.4	30.5	24.6	12.9	11.4	6.9
Rutherford County, North Carolina	48,325	3.5	9.5	31.4	26.3	9.5	14.7	5.0
Surry County, North Carolina	51,205	6.2	11.6	27.1	23.0	13.9	13.2	5.1
Union County, North Carolina	154,095	3.5	5.7	23.5	21.3	8.6	25.4	12.1
Wake County, North Carolina	747,815	2.7	4.0	15.2	16.3	7.7	32.9	21.2
Wayne County, North Carolina	80,491	7.8	6.5	31.9	21.8	13.9	11.8	6.3
Wilkes County, North Carolina	49,347	5.9	11.5	35.3	21.0	9.6	13.0	3.8
Wilson County, North Carolina	55,881	7.2	11.3	32.2	20.5	9.8	12.6	6.4
NORTH DAKOTA	504,375	2.6	3.9	26.7	22.4	14.0	21.5	8.9
Burleigh County, North Dakota	64,200	3.2	2.5	24.0	19.2	15.2	25.4	10.5
Cass County, North Dakota	117,528	2.0	2.7	22.1	20.7	11.0	28.3	13.2
Grand Forks County, North Dakota	41,481	1.2	2.4	19.3	23.0	16.4	21.5	16.1
Ward County, North Dakota	43,064	0.9	2.5	28.9	22.8	16.0	20.3	8.5
OHIO	8,049,805	2.7	6.5	32.6	20.1	8.7	18.2	11.1
Allen County, Ohio	69,051	1.9	7.2	41.9	21.7	7.9	13.3	6.1
Ashtabula County, Ohio	68,336	3.8	8.1	45.5	21.7	7.2	10.0	3.7
Athens County, Ohio	37,297	2.0	5.2	31.0	16.4	9.1	17.2	19.0
Belmont County, Ohio	49,321	2.7	6.7	45.7	16.7	11.4	11.0	5.9
Butler County, Ohio	245,864	1.8	6.6	33.8	17.6	8.1	21.0	11.1
Clark County, Ohio	91,882	1.7	7.9	41.8	22.5	9.9	9.3	6.9

Table C-2. Educational Attainment of the Population, by Selected Counties, 2019—*Continued*

(Number; percent; dollars.)

State/County	Population 18 to 24 years				
	Total	Less than high school graduate (percent)	High school graduate (includes equivalency) (percent)	Some college or associate's degree (percent)	Bachelor's degree or higher (percent)
OHIO—(*Continued*)					
Clermont County, Ohio	15,793	11.4	45.7	29.7	13.2
Columbiana County, Ohio	7,424	14.2	47.8	31.8	6.1
Cuyahoga County, Ohio	106,237	12.1	31.7	41.4	14.8
Delaware County, Ohio	16,386	10.8	33.5	43.0	12.7
Erie County, Ohio	5,376	9.1	48.6	38.4	4.0
Fairfield County, Ohio	12,530	11.7	41.5	37.8	9.0
Franklin County, Ohio	127,248	12.1	29.8	42.7	15.3
Geauga County, Ohio	7,883	26.5	28.0	32.4	13.1
Greene County, Ohio	19,824	5.8	23.9	56.4	14.0
Hamilton County, Ohio	76,960	9.5	36.2	39.5	14.8
Hancock County, Ohio	6,732	4.1	36.8	44.6	14.5
Jefferson County, Ohio	6,177	10.0	40.7	42.8	6.5
Lake County, Ohio	18,153	14.2	33.6	41.2	11.0
Licking County, Ohio	16,699	13.3	33.2	46.4	7.1
Lorain County, Ohio	25,896	16.6	32.3	44.1	7.1
Lucas County, Ohio	36,854	15.2	33.7	41.5	9.6
Mahoning County, Ohio	21,149	17.5	33.6	39.7	9.2
Marion County, Ohio	4,782	8.4	54.7	32.2	4.7
Medina County, Ohio	12,867	16.8	34.1	40.8	8.3
Miami County, Ohio	8,275	12.6	46.7	39.3	1.4
Montgomery County, Ohio	49,533	11.0	32.3	47.3	9.3
Muskingum County, Ohio	8,510	11.2	47.3	38.6	2.9
Portage County, Ohio	26,304	5.8	22.6	61.7	9.9
Richland County, Ohio	9,656	18.8	35.6	40.7	4.9
Ross County, Ohio	5,654	10.1	67.2	15.7	7.0
Scioto County, Ohio	6,314	15.0	38.0	38.9	8.1
Stark County, Ohio	30,785	10.8	42.5	39.1	7.6
Summit County, Ohio	46,046	11.1	33.9	42.3	12.8
Trumbull County, Ohio	15,393	21.0	42.4	30.5	6.2
Tuscarawas County, Ohio	7,019	15.6	41.7	35.6	7.1
Warren County, Ohio	18,029	14.7	38.4	36.4	10.5
Wayne County, Ohio	12,186	21.5	37.8	34.5	6.3
Wood County, Ohio	22,799	4.0	23.5	63.0	9.5
OKLAHOMA	385,498	14.4	35.4	41.7	8.5
Canadian County, Oklahoma	12,512	16.3	40.6	36.3	6.8
Cleveland County, Oklahoma	43,395	8.1	19.3	60.0	12.6
Comanche County, Oklahoma	14,845	10.4	45.4	39.5	4.7
Creek County, Oklahoma	5,627	20.6	53.1	22.1	4.2
Muskogee County, Oklahoma	5,871	23.7	38.2	30.6	7.6
Oklahoma County, Oklahoma	72,124	12.9	33.9	41.9	11.3
Payne County, Oklahoma	21,055	5.3	22.6	65.1	7.0
Pottawatomie County, Oklahoma	7,239	22.4	28.2	43.6	5.7
Rogers County, Oklahoma	7,958	15.7	38.4	39.4	6.5
Tulsa County, Oklahoma	57,477	13.7	34.1	41.7	10.5
Wagoner County, Oklahoma	6,299	14.6	44.4	32.8	8.3
OREGON	366,803	13.3	31.2	44.8	10.7
Benton County, Oregon	21,018	1.7	17.2	66.0	15.0
Clackamas County, Oregon	31,689	12.9	38.0	39.2	10.0
Deschutes County, Oregon	13,603	15.1	37.7	42.8	4.4
Douglas County, Oregon	7,075	21.2	36.0	39.4	3.5
Jackson County, Oregon	16,827	11.1	39.4	45.5	4.0
Josephine County, Oregon	5,297	30.0	26.1	40.9	3.0
Klamath County, Oregon	5,070	8.1	27.6	53.1	11.1
Lane County, Oregon	47,635	9.5	27.0	50.7	12.8
Linn County, Oregon	10,238	16.8	31.0	45.9	6.3
Marion County, Oregon	32,246	15.8	35.6	40.5	8.1
Multnomah County, Oregon	63,723	12.1	22.7	49.8	15.4
Polk County, Oregon	11,384	5.1	34.1	48.6	12.2
Umatilla County, Oregon	6,415	21.0	47.2	25.9	5.9
Washington County, Oregon	49,155	15.5	28.4	41.0	15.2
Yamhill County, Oregon	10,515	7.5	37.5	48.8	6.2
PENNSYLVANIA	1,141,628	12.0	34.9	39.7	13.5
Adams County, Pennsylvania	10,239	6.5	48.7	37.1	7.7
Allegheny County, Pennsylvania	105,078	8.9	29.8	41.0	20.3
Armstrong County, Pennsylvania	4,227	8.4	55.6	24.9	11.0

Table C-2. Educational Attainment of the Population, by Selected Counties, 2019—*Continued*

(Number; percent; dollars.)

State/County	Total	Less than 9th grade (percent)	9th to 12th grade, no diploma (percent)	High school graduate (includes equivalency) (percent)	Some college, no degree (percent)	Associate's degree (percent)	Bachelor's degree (percent)	Graduate or professional degree (percent)
OHIO—*(Continued)*								
Clermont County, Ohio	143,749	2.5	6.8	32.0	21.7	7.8	19.8	9.4
Columbiana County, Ohio	73,872	2.6	5.7	46.4	19.4	10.4	10.4	5.2
Cuyahoga County, Ohio	874,679	3.0	6.7	26.9	21.4	8.3	19.8	13.9
Delaware County, Ohio	138,636	0.5	3.1	18.4	19.0	6.8	31.5	20.6
Erie County, Ohio	53,808	2.0	5.5	37.0	21.1	10.1	15.4	8.8
Fairfield County, Ohio	107,394	1.8	4.5	33.6	22.0	8.7	19.7	9.7
Franklin County, Ohio	884,103	3.1	5.6	23.5	19.3	6.7	26.2	15.6
Geauga County, Ohio	64,228	7.8	3.1	26.3	17.4	9.5	23.1	13.0
Greene County, Ohio	114,206	0.8	3.9	23.5	22.7	8.2	23.5	17.5
Hamilton County, Ohio	553,480	2.2	5.9	25.9	17.2	8.4	23.6	16.8
Hancock County, Ohio	52,463	2.0	6.2	34.9	21.7	8.5	14.3	12.4
Jefferson County, Ohio	46,725	1.6	5.3	45.4	17.7	11.0	12.6	6.4
Lake County, Ohio	166,562	2.0	5.7	31.0	24.7	10.4	17.6	8.7
Licking County, Ohio	119,819	1.7	7.0	33.2	20.4	10.7	17.7	9.2
Lorain County, Ohio	216,161	2.6	7.9	31.5	21.6	11.5	15.1	9.8
Lucas County, Ohio	293,502	2.8	8.1	29.1	22.9	10.2	16.8	10.2
Mahoning County, Ohio	161,985	2.5	6.9	36.2	21.2	7.8	16.8	8.7
Marion County, Ohio	46,591	1.9	9.4	43.4	24.4	7.4	8.3	5.2
Medina County, Ohio	127,164	0.5	4.1	30.4	21.0	9.2	22.2	12.5
Miami County, Ohio	74,110	2.6	5.8	36.5	23.1	10.2	12.8	9.0
Montgomery County, Ohio	365,816	2.7	7.0	26.9	25.4	9.4	17.4	11.1
Muskingum County, Ohio	59,137	3.1	10.2	41.4	18.2	8.7	10.7	7.7
Portage County, Ohio	106,424	2.5	5.6	38.3	17.6	7.4	17.2	11.5
Richland County, Ohio	85,392	3.6	7.7	40.2	18.4	11.3	11.2	7.6
Ross County, Ohio	54,460	2.7	7.0	45.7	19.9	8.9	11.0	4.9
Scioto County, Ohio	52,701	4.0	10.6	37.9	19.0	9.2	13.0	6.3
Stark County, Ohio	260,893	2.0	6.5	39.8	19.9	9.8	14.7	7.3
Summit County, Ohio	382,817	2.2	5.3	30.5	21.6	7.7	20.8	11.8
Trumbull County, Ohio	142,450	3.4	8.0	42.7	18.7	7.8	13.2	6.3
Tuscarawas County, Ohio	64,032	6.6	9.0	44.2	15.1	6.9	13.1	5.3
Warren County, Ohio	159,843	1.1	3.7	27.3	16.0	7.0	27.5	17.4
Wayne County, Ohio	75,847	9.5	5.3	37.5	18.8	6.8	13.1	9.1
Wood County, Ohio	81,457	1.3	3.6	30.0	18.1	10.0	22.8	14.2
OKLAHOMA	2,619,244	3.9	7.7	31.5	22.8	7.9	17.1	9.1
Canadian County, Oklahoma	97,242	3.4	8.1	31.8	21.8	7.5	18.8	8.6
Cleveland County, Oklahoma	180,400	2.7	4.9	24.0	24.2	8.5	21.9	13.7
Comanche County, Oklahoma	77,989	1.8	7.4	34.1	28.6	7.3	12.4	8.4
Creek County, Oklahoma	49,128	2.2	9.3	40.2	22.1	8.6	12.5	5.1
Muskogee County, Oklahoma	45,522	4.2	9.5	30.9	22.5	11.5	15.3	6.1
Oklahoma County, Oklahoma	522,715	5.1	7.1	26.0	22.3	7.0	20.2	12.4
Payne County, Oklahoma	45,198	1.9	4.2	27.8	20.0	6.9	21.0	18.1
Pottawatomie County, Oklahoma	48,262	2.4	8.9	37.0	23.2	8.5	13.3	6.7
Rogers County, Oklahoma	63,129	3.0	6.1	30.4	25.0	11.8	16.7	7.0
Tulsa County, Oklahoma	430,396	3.6	6.6	25.2	22.2	8.8	22.2	11.3
Wagoner County, Oklahoma	55,510	3.2	5.7	33.2	25.6	9.5	16.0	6.9
OREGON	2,988,118	3.3	5.4	23.0	24.8	9.0	21.0	13.5
Benton County, Oregon	57,153	0.9	1.8	13.0	18.0	8.5	30.6	27.3
Clackamas County, Oregon	298,137	1.8	4.6	22.4	24.9	9.2	23.9	13.2
Deschutes County, Oregon	145,040	2.2	4.6	18.9	24.4	11.1	23.6	15.1
Douglas County, Oregon	82,538	1.4	6.3	34.3	32.6	9.7	9.5	6.2
Jackson County, Oregon	159,402	2.8	6.6	28.3	26.0	8.7	16.0	11.6
Josephine County, Oregon	65,400	0.8	10.0	33.2	30.5	8.7	10.7	6.1
Klamath County, Oregon	48,479	3.4	6.7	33.1	24.4	10.8	13.3	8.4
Lane County, Oregon	264,861	2.0	5.2	23.2	28.5	8.8	19.2	13.1
Linn County, Oregon	90,726	3.3	9.0	26.7	32.6	9.5	12.2	6.6
Marion County, Oregon	230,945	7.8	6.7	24.2	26.2	9.7	16.8	8.5
Multnomah County, Oregon	599,465	3.7	4.3	17.0	20.0	7.2	28.5	19.3
Polk County, Oregon	55,301	2.6	4.0	22.1	28.2	10.8	19.6	12.6
Umatilla County, Oregon	52,110	3.8	9.6	29.0	27.0	11.7	11.8	7.1
Washington County, Oregon	417,283	3.4	3.0	19.3	21.7	8.5	26.2	17.9
Yamhill County, Oregon	73,372	3.4	8.6	24.1	29.0	9.9	16.2	8.8
PENNSYLVANIA	9,028,036	3.0	6.0	34.4	15.7	8.6	19.5	12.8
Adams County, Pennsylvania	72,723	3.6	7.3	42.6	17.1	7.9	12.0	9.6
Allegheny County, Pennsylvania	884,569	1.5	3.2	26.2	16.1	10.0	24.8	18.1
Armstrong County, Pennsylvania	48,151	2.7	5.0	51.7	16.1	8.9	11.0	4.6

Table C-2. Educational Attainment of the Population, by Selected Counties, 2019—*Continued*

(Number; percent; dollars.)

State/County	Total	Population 18 to 24 years			
		Less than high school graduate (percent)	High school graduate (includes equivalency) (percent)	Some college or associate's degree (percent)	Bachelor's degree or higher (percent)
PENNSYLVANIA—*(Continued)*					
Beaver County, Pennsylvania	11,457	10.2	36.9	44.1	8.7
Berks County, Pennsylvania	40,120	14.2	37.7	38.1	10.0
Blair County, Pennsylvania	9,208	14.7	44.2	29.3	11.9
Bucks County, Pennsylvania	47,973	11.5	30.5	35.3	22.7
Butler County, Pennsylvania	15,765	7.2	37.7	40.5	14.7
Cambria County, Pennsylvania	11,522	6.7	37.6	49.5	6.2
Carbon County, Pennsylvania	4,099	22.3	44.6	23.8	9.3
Centre County, Pennsylvania	38,136	4.1	28.6	56.9	10.4
Chester County, Pennsylvania	47,846	13.0	27.2	38.3	21.5
Clearfield County, Pennsylvania	5,404	17.0	54.6	23.9	4.5
Columbia County, Pennsylvania	9,367	8.6	29.7	55.9	5.8
Crawford County, Pennsylvania	7,796	20.4	33.8	38.7	7.0
Cumberland County, Pennsylvania	24,151	11.0	25.8	52.8	10.4
Dauphin County, Pennsylvania	22,009	13.3	45.0	30.6	11.1
Delaware County, Pennsylvania	55,825	10.0	34.7	40.9	14.4
Erie County, Pennsylvania	26,112	12.5	36.9	38.8	11.8
Fayette County, Pennsylvania	9,230	6.7	57.4	22.3	13.6
Franklin County, Pennsylvania	11,303	21.3	43.6	30.8	4.3
Indiana County, Pennsylvania	12,104	11.5	23.6	59.8	5.0
Lackawanna County, Pennsylvania	16,800	8.2	25.8	49.5	16.5
Lancaster County, Pennsylvania	48,229	24.7	35.5	29.1	10.7
Lawrence County, Pennsylvania	6,895	11.3	42.4	39.7	6.6
Lebanon County, Pennsylvania	12,055	9.5	55.7	25.3	9.5
Lehigh County, Pennsylvania	33,469	11.6	33.2	45.3	9.9
Luzerne County, Pennsylvania	27,113	13.1	32.6	47.4	6.9
Lycoming County, Pennsylvania	9,590	9.3	43.8	40.6	6.2
Mercer County, Pennsylvania	10,393	10.6	48.1	33.0	8.3
Monroe County, Pennsylvania	17,910	15.2	37.5	36.5	10.9
Montgomery County, Pennsylvania	65,786	9.5	28.9	42.3	19.3
Northampton County, Pennsylvania	30,181	12.1	30.2	46.2	11.5
Northumberland County, Pennsylvania	6,155	23.6	49.5	22.0	4.8
Philadelphia County, Pennsylvania	153,369	10.7	33.2	39.0	17.1
Schuylkill County, Pennsylvania	9,510	21.7	42.7	31.9	3.7
Somerset County, Pennsylvania	4,951	17.0	52.0	22.3	8.8
Washington County, Pennsylvania	17,848	8.8	37.8	41.9	11.5
Westmoreland County, Pennsylvania	25,559	8.3	32.6	46.3	12.8
York County, Pennsylvania	35,896	12.6	38.4	39.1	9.9
RHODE ISLAND	108,834	9.3	32.3	45.9	12.5
Kent County, Rhode Island	11,848	11.5	37.2	34.4	16.9
Newport County, Rhode Island	8,005	9.8	26.1	40.6	23.6
Providence County, Rhode Island	66,343	10.8	32.9	47.8	8.4
Washington County, Rhode Island	16,461	4.1	32.3	47.2	16.5
SOUTH CAROLINA	473,210	12.6	35.1	42.8	9.4
Aiken County, South Carolina	14,017	11.8	32.9	51.0	4.3
Anderson County, South Carolina	17,417	15.1	46.6	32.2	6.1
Beaufort County, South Carolina	18,116	17.9	48.3	30.2	3.7
Berkeley County, South Carolina	20,731	13.6	38.6	36.9	10.8
Charleston County, South Carolina	36,300	11.0	20.5	47.4	21.2
Darlington County, South Carolina	6,867	22.2	29.0	34.9	14.0
Dorchester County, South Carolina	12,118	12.5	52.0	31.9	3.6
Florence County, South Carolina	11,923	14.6	37.9	35.0	12.5
Greenville County, South Carolina	44,869	13.9	35.8	36.8	13.5
Greenwood County, South Carolina	6,358	3.0	30.2	57.7	9.1
Horry County, South Carolina	25,310	7.1	39.8	48.6	4.5
Kershaw County, South Carolina	4,674	17.6	48.4	26.5	7.5
Lancaster County, South Carolina	6,464	12.0	37.0	40.2	10.8
Laurens County, South Carolina	5,797	18.4	35.5	40.8	5.4
Lexington County, South Carolina	22,500	13.0	35.8	40.6	10.6
Oconee County, South Carolina	5,437	19.3	43.0	24.6	13.0
Orangeburg County, South Carolina	8,499	8.8	31.1	54.0	6.1
Pickens County, South Carolina	22,818	6.7	24.5	52.4	16.3
Richland County, South Carolina	63,170	8.4	29.8	53.7	8.0
Spartanburg County, South Carolina	28,942	9.3	38.7	42.2	9.8
Sumter County, South Carolina	10,188	17.2	32.0	41.9	8.9
York County, South Carolina	22,146	12.6	32.6	48.3	6.5

Table C-2. Educational Attainment of the Population, by Selected Counties, 2019—*Continued*

(Number; percent; dollars.)

State/County	Total	Less than 9th grade (percent)	9th to 12th grade, no diploma (percent)	High school graduate (includes equivalency) (percent)	Some college, no degree (percent)	Associate's degree (percent)	Bachelor's degree (percent)	Graduate or professional degree (percent)
PENNSYLVANIA—*(Continued)*								
Beaver County, Pennsylvania	121,056	1.7	5.8	33.0	20.3	12.4	17.5	9.4
Berks County, Pennsylvania	287,425	5.2	7.6	37.4	15.4	8.9	16.3	9.1
Blair County, Pennsylvania	88,001	2.6	5.8	44.1	15.0	9.3	14.9	8.2
Bucks County, Pennsylvania	453,452	2.0	4.0	27.2	16.1	8.4	24.9	17.3
Butler County, Pennsylvania	134,990	0.7	3.8	32.0	15.7	10.3	24.4	13.1
Cambria County, Pennsylvania	93,957	1.4	4.7	46.4	14.8	12.0	13.2	7.4
Carbon County, Pennsylvania	48,384	3.3	7.2	46.3	15.4	9.3	11.8	6.7
Centre County, Pennsylvania	100,886	2.0	4.9	28.4	14.1	6.7	21.6	22.2
Chester County, Pennsylvania	359,177	2.8	3.3	20.3	12.6	6.4	32.0	22.7
Clearfield County, Pennsylvania	59,496	3.2	8.7	51.0	12.3	8.7	10.4	5.8
Columbia County, Pennsylvania	44,205	2.5	7.0	42.1	13.7	9.9	15.8	9.1
Crawford County, Pennsylvania	59,674	5.1	6.0	45.6	14.7	7.1	13.5	8.0
Cumberland County, Pennsylvania	177,952	2.6	5.0	30.5	15.0	8.5	23.6	14.7
Dauphin County, Pennsylvania	193,469	3.6	6.7	33.8	14.3	10.2	19.6	11.8
Delaware County, Pennsylvania	386,376	1.9	5.1	29.2	16.1	7.0	23.6	17.1
Erie County, Pennsylvania	186,755	2.4	6.8	36.5	14.8	10.0	18.7	10.8
Fayette County, Pennsylvania	95,435	2.4	9.7	46.8	15.0	8.3	11.7	6.1
Franklin County, Pennsylvania	109,489	3.6	8.3	44.3	14.4	7.4	13.3	8.7
Indiana County, Pennsylvania	56,900	3.5	5.8	43.4	16.2	7.7	14.0	9.4
Lackawanna County, Pennsylvania	149,972	2.6	6.0	37.8	15.6	8.8	18.2	10.9
Lancaster County, Pennsylvania	369,623	7.0	7.3	34.8	14.6	8.0	18.4	9.8
Lawrence County, Pennsylvania	61,638	1.8	5.7	44.5	14.9	10.3	14.6	8.3
Lebanon County, Pennsylvania	98,178	4.8	8.5	44.2	13.9	7.7	13.7	7.2
Lehigh County, Pennsylvania	252,649	4.1	5.9	35.2	16.4	8.8	18.7	10.8
Luzerne County, Pennsylvania	227,307	3.0	5.6	39.9	19.9	10.1	12.8	8.9
Lycoming County, Pennsylvania	80,491	2.7	7.7	39.5	15.8	10.2	15.4	8.9
Mercer County, Pennsylvania	78,317	3.7	7.1	41.7	13.5	10.6	14.6	8.8
Monroe County, Pennsylvania	119,245	2.1	6.7	35.2	20.7	9.3	17.0	9.0
Montgomery County, Pennsylvania	586,787	1.8	3.3	22.8	14.3	7.8	28.5	21.6
Northampton County, Pennsylvania	215,118	2.9	5.7	35.2	16.1	9.2	19.3	11.5
Northumberland County, Pennsylvania	66,938	3.4	8.0	51.9	14.3	6.4	11.4	4.7
Philadelphia County, Pennsylvania	1,088,441	5.0	9.0	32.5	16.5	5.9	18.0	13.0
Schuylkill County, Pennsylvania	104,188	2.1	7.4	47.0	16.9	9.9	11.5	5.1
Somerset County, Pennsylvania	54,894	3.7	7.6	48.0	13.2	9.8	11.5	6.2
Washington County, Pennsylvania	148,862	2.2	4.9	34.7	17.0	10.3	20.3	10.7
Westmoreland County, Pennsylvania	259,586	1.5	4.0	37.1	16.7	11.4	19.1	10.2
York County, Pennsylvania	314,523	3.0	7.0	38.0	16.1	9.5	17.3	9.1
RHODE ISLAND	746,952	5.0	5.7	28.4	17.4	8.6	20.9	13.9
Kent County, Rhode Island	122,379	2.4	5.7	29.2	20.4	9.8	20.8	11.7
Newport County, Rhode Island	61,095	2.0	3.9	23.7	15.2	7.7	27.4	20.0
Providence County, Rhode Island	441,579	7.2	6.6	30.0	17.8	8.6	18.3	11.5
Washington County, Rhode Island	88,728	1.0	3.6	23.8	14.1	8.6	28.4	20.4
SOUTH CAROLINA	3,563,204	3.7	7.9	28.5	20.4	9.9	18.4	11.2
Aiken County, South Carolina	119,990	3.2	6.7	30.9	20.2	9.8	19.4	9.9
Anderson County, South Carolina	139,550	2.9	9.7	31.7	19.2	11.7	15.7	9.0
Beaufort County, South Carolina	138,686	2.7	4.4	21.4	21.7	8.8	23.5	17.5
Berkeley County, South Carolina	153,104	3.1	6.6	29.9	22.4	10.5	17.2	10.3
Charleston County, South Carolina	294,309	2.6	5.4	20.4	17.0	8.4	28.4	17.8
Darlington County, South Carolina	45,089	5.1	11.6	36.7	17.7	9.2	12.8	7.0
Dorchester County, South Carolina	111,372	4.0	7.6	25.3	24.1	10.9	19.4	8.8
Florence County, South Carolina	94,107	3.7	8.1	34.5	20.9	8.0	14.9	9.8
Greenville County, South Carolina	358,605	3.6	7.9	22.9	19.2	10.0	23.5	13.0
Greenwood County, South Carolina	48,788	3.4	7.4	31.1	20.4	12.0	15.4	10.3
Horry County, South Carolina	265,998	3.9	7.1	32.5	21.6	10.5	15.3	9.0
Kershaw County, South Carolina	46,523	2.8	9.3	32.0	21.4	10.3	15.5	8.5
Lancaster County, South Carolina	70,463	5.9	7.3	27.9	22.4	13.5	15.5	7.4
Laurens County, South Carolina	46,889	4.5	10.2	34.2	20.3	11.1	12.9	6.8
Lexington County, South Carolina	207,409	3.9	7.7	26.4	21.1	10.9	19.3	10.7
Oconee County, South Carolina	57,928	5.8	9.1	31.0	18.1	9.5	14.9	11.6
Orangeburg County, South Carolina	58,454	3.1	11.2	31.8	21.1	11.8	10.8	10.1
Pickens County, South Carolina	80,497	3.5	9.2	29.5	19.8	11.3	14.9	11.8
Richland County, South Carolina	263,496	2.3	6.5	21.5	19.2	8.2	24.8	17.5
Spartanburg County, South Carolina	217,131	4.2	9.2	28.6	22.0	9.8	15.9	10.4
Sumter County, South Carolina	71,171	4.7	7.2	30.2	24.9	11.3	13.7	8.0
York County, South Carolina	191,318	2.3	4.9	23.9	23.8	10.1	22.5	12.6

Table C-2. Educational Attainment of the Population, by Selected Counties, 2019—*Continued*

(Number; percent; dollars.)

State/County	Population 18 to 24 years				
	Total	Less than high school graduate (percent)	High school graduate (includes equivalency) (percent)	Some college or associate's degree (percent)	Bachelor's degree or higher (percent)
SOUTH DAKOTA	81,361	13.8	34.3	41.5	10.5
Minnehaha County, South Dakota	15,832	13.9	29.9	41.8	14.4
Pennington County, South Dakota	9,274	11.7	42.5	38.5	7.2
TENNESSEE	624,460	10.9	34.7	43.0	11.4
Anderson County, Tennessee	5,639	2.6	67.1	29.3	1.0
Blount County, Tennessee...................................	10,095	11.0	39.8	43.5	5.7
Bradley County, Tennessee..................................	9,103	14.7	26.8	51.1	7.3
Davidson County, Tennessee...............................	67,195	6.4	27.3	43.8	22.6
Greene County, Tennessee..................................	5,390	3.0	45.3	49.3	2.4
Hamilton County, Tennessee	32,173	10.0	26.3	54.0	9.8
Knox County, Tennessee	54,893	6.6	27.6	48.1	17.7
Madison County, Tennessee................................	10,727	10.0	34.0	52.1	3.9
Maury County, Tennessee	7,196	7.7	51.2	36.3	4.8
Montgomery County, Tennessee..........................	23,296	10.5	34.3	48.2	6.9
Putnam County, Tennessee	10,968	6.4	20.6	64.3	8.8
Robertson County, Tennessee.............................	5,214	11.7	51.6	31.6	5.1
Rutherford County, Tennessee	42,577	10.7	30.0	47.7	11.6
Sevier County, Tennessee...................................	7,605	9.6	35.8	43.9	10.7
Shelby County, Tennessee..................................	84,794	11.4	30.9	44.6	13.1
Sullivan County, Tennessee................................	11,998	6.6	45.6	39.0	8.8
Sumner County, Tennessee.................................	14,940	7.0	32.4	49.9	10.7
Washington County, Tennessee...........................	16,288	5.7	39.2	36.6	18.5
Williamson County, Tennessee............................	18,518	16.6	32.5	26.7	24.1
Wilson County, Tennessee	10,259	18.2	35.0	36.3	10.5
TEXAS...	2,826,700	13.9	34.6	42.1	9.5
Angelina County, Texas	7,540	15.8	48.1	32.9	3.2
Bastrop County, Texas.......................................	9,554	5.5	58.8	29.3	6.4
Bell County, Texas	40,652	12.0	42.7	38.2	7.1
Bexar County, Texas...	204,553	15.3	37.1	40.4	7.2
Bowie County, Texas	8,256	21.0	23.1	49.3	6.6
Brazoria County, Texas......................................	30,953	12.2	35.8	38.7	13.3
Brazos County, Texas	57,845	2.9	20.5	62.1	14.5
Cameron County, Texas.....................................	44,882	18.1	38.0	40.6	3.3
Collin County, Texas	85,315	10.3	33.5	42.5	13.7
Comal County, Texas...	11,978	12.5	46.1	35.7	5.7
Coryell County, Texas..	10,051	6.6	56.5	35.3	1.6
Dallas County, Texas...	250,631	14.9	32.4	39.3	13.3
Denton County, Texas..	82,498	8.7	26.7	49.3	15.2
Ector County, Texas..	15,216	19.5	38.9	35.8	5.8
Ellis County, Texas...	17,072	17.2	38.4	40.1	4.3
El Paso County, Texas.......................................	94,688	11.1	35.3	45.8	7.8
Fort Bend County, Texas.....................................	67,050	13.5	29.8	42.9	13.9
Galveston County, Texas....................................	28,711	11.2	36.6	45.5	6.7
Grayson County, Texas......................................	12,387	21.4	39.0	36.8	2.7
Gregg County, Texas	10,916	6.9	40.3	47.4	5.3
Guadalupe County, Texas	14,454	9.1	52.9	32.2	5.8
Harris County, Texas...	434,396	15.5	34.1	40.2	10.2
Harrison County, Texas	5,558	14.7	46.3	31.3	7.6
Hays County, Texas	38,047	9.1	31.9	50.1	8.8
Henderson County, Texas...................................	6,607	13.1	49.3	32.9	4.7
Hidalgo County, Texas.......................................	96,873	16.5	29.3	49.2	5.0
Hunt County, Texas	9,831	8.5	36.4	48.1	7.0
Jefferson County, Texas.....................................	23,505	14.8	33.1	45.4	6.6
Johnson County, Texas	15,458	15.7	50.2	27.6	6.6
Kaufman County, Texas.....................................	12,386	20.8	34.5	32.6	12.1
Liberty County, Texas..	7,089	17.4	48.0	32.3	2.3
Lubbock County, Texas	51,251	7.8	27.2	52.7	12.3
McLennan County, Texas	37,096	10.6	30.5	52.8	6.1
Midland County, Texas	14,543	21.5	27.7	39.8	11.0
Montgomery County, Texas.................................	50,337	14.7	31.9	43.0	10.5
Nacogdoches County, Texas...............................	11,219	9.3	26.1	53.7	10.9
Nueces County, Texas.......................................	35,532	14.6	34.9	46.6	3.9
Orange County, Texas..	6,117	10.3	46.2	37.3	6.2
Parker County, Texas..	11,521	15.6	37.2	41.1	6.1
Potter County, Texas...	11,076	12.3	50.3	33.0	4.5
Randall County, Texas.......................................	14,100	7.9	31.9	45.2	15.0

Table C-2. Educational Attainment of the Population, by Selected Counties, 2019—*Continued*

(Number; percent; dollars.)

State/County	Total	Less than 9th grade (percent)	9th to 12th grade, no diploma (percent)	High school graduate (includes equivalency) (percent)	Some college, no degree (percent)	Associate's degree (percent)	Bachelor's degree (percent)	Graduate or professional degree (percent)
SOUTH DAKOTA	588,029	2.8	5.1	30.0	20.5	11.9	20.6	9.1
Minnehaha County, South Dakota	128,596	3.8	3.8	25.2	20.3	11.7	25.5	9.7
Pennington County, South Dakota	78,460	0.9	5.2	27.4	24.6	10.2	20.9	10.9
TENNESSEE	4,693,962	4.3	7.7	31.5	20.3	7.4	18.0	10.7
Anderson County, Tennessee	55,758	3.3	7.9	36.5	21.0	10.1	12.3	9.0
Blount County, Tennessee	96,046	4.3	7.6	36.3	22.6	6.0	14.7	8.6
Bradley County, Tennessee	75,366	5.2	10.3	33.6	21.3	7.1	16.3	6.3
Davidson County, Tennessee	483,895	4.1	6.4	19.8	17.8	6.3	28.3	17.3
Greene County, Tennessee	50,371	6.0	9.6	41.6	17.4	6.3	11.2	7.8
Hamilton County, Tennessee	259,208	3.8	6.9	24.1	21.1	9.0	22.4	12.7
Knox County, Tennessee	316,983	2.9	5.4	25.5	19.7	8.8	22.4	15.2
Madison County, Tennessee	65,367	3.1	7.2	34.0	21.4	7.1	16.8	10.3
Maury County, Tennessee	66,799	3.3	7.6	34.0	19.6	10.4	18.1	7.0
Montgomery County, Tennessee	129,477	1.9	4.4	27.3	22.5	13.1	19.1	11.7
Putnam County, Tennessee	52,987	6.6	6.3	32.6	20.3	5.9	18.9	9.5
Robertson County, Tennessee	49,804	5.6	9.6	36.0	22.0	5.6	16.2	5.0
Rutherford County, Tennessee	208,175	2.7	4.9	27.3	25.5	8.8	20.5	10.3
Sevier County, Tennessee	70,573	5.2	10.2	38.0	20.8	6.9	13.8	5.2
Shelby County, Tennessee	620,000	3.8	7.9	28.1	22.6	6.0	18.9	12.8
Sullivan County, Tennessee	116,476	4.1	7.3	33.3	21.0	7.9	16.3	10.1
Sumner County, Tennessee	131,695	4.1	6.1	30.7	20.3	8.2	20.8	9.8
Washington County, Tennessee	89,010	3.1	7.5	30.8	18.2	8.6	18.0	13.8
Williamson County, Tennessee	155,962	1.3	3.3	13.5	14.4	5.8	38.9	22.9
Wilson County, Tennessee	100,464	2.7	4.3	29.6	20.4	7.9	22.8	12.2
TEXAS	18,772,550	7.7	7.7	25.2	21.2	7.5	20.0	10.8
Angelina County, Texas	57,118	6.7	7.1	32.5	28.9	6.1	10.5	8.0
Bastrop County, Texas	56,957	9.5	8.5	35.3	25.4	4.8	10.6	5.8
Bell County, Texas	222,526	2.9	6.6	25.7	27.9	11.6	15.4	9.9
Bexar County, Texas	1,292,560	7.4	7.9	25.6	22.6	8.3	17.8	10.3
Bowie County, Texas	62,896	4.9	8.6	33.2	27.5	6.7	12.1	7.0
Brazoria County, Texas	245,811	4.9	6.5	27.3	24.3	7.6	20.0	9.4
Brazos County, Texas	124,081	4.9	6.7	21.9	19.4	4.7	23.8	18.6
Cameron County, Texas	251,660	18.2	13.5	26.2	17.6	7.4	11.8	5.4
Collin County, Texas	684,124	3.3	2.6	16.2	17.9	7.5	32.5	20.1
Comal County, Texas	109,243	2.5	4.1	23.5	20.6	9.5	25.9	13.9
Coryell County, Texas	48,826	3.3	8.7	29.1	30.9	11.0	11.4	5.6
Dallas County, Texas	1,704,727	10.4	8.8	23.6	19.1	5.6	20.2	12.2
Denton County, Texas	589,252	2.7	4.9	17.5	21.5	7.2	30.6	15.5
Ector County, Texas	100,671	10.6	13.2	30.1	23.5	7.5	10.0	5.2
Ellis County, Texas	119,062	4.7	7.4	27.8	25.7	8.4	17.7	8.4
El Paso County, Texas	520,251	11.4	8.8	25.5	21.4	9.6	16.4	6.9
Fort Bend County, Texas	522,896	5.1	4.1	17.6	19.1	7.8	27.9	18.3
Galveston County, Texas	231,134	4.0	5.4	26.3	24.5	9.1	19.8	10.8
Grayson County, Texas	91,846	4.8	5.5	31.1	26.6	10.3	14.5	7.3
Gregg County, Texas	81,223	4.7	8.6	27.9	26.4	10.3	15.0	7.1
Guadalupe County, Texas	111,089	3.2	7.9	29.3	19.6	10.7	19.5	9.8
Harris County, Texas	3,033,489	9.7	8.1	23.7	19.0	7.4	20.4	11.8
Harrison County, Texas	44,410	4.7	9.7	31.7	26.9	7.3	13.2	6.5
Hays County, Texas	139,245	3.1	6.3	25.6	21.8	6.7	24.7	11.8
Henderson County, Texas	59,318	4.4	14.0	35.0	23.2	7.7	10.8	5.0
Hidalgo County, Texas	493,247	19.5	13.0	24.5	18.8	5.2	13.5	5.5
Hunt County, Texas	65,064	6.5	9.4	34.0	24.7	5.3	12.5	7.7
Jefferson County, Texas	167,653	7.4	8.5	30.3	24.1	8.7	13.9	7.0
Johnson County, Texas	114,824	4.8	9.5	39.8	21.0	6.0	13.5	5.4
Kaufman County, Texas	85,762	4.6	10.1	31.5	26.4	8.5	14.0	5.0
Liberty County, Texas	57,272	8.8	11.4	36.4	24.8	6.2	8.4	3.9
Lubbock County, Texas	185,987	6.6	6.7	25.3	24.0	5.3	19.4	12.6
McLennan County, Texas	156,625	5.0	8.2	26.4	22.5	12.1	16.4	9.4
Midland County, Texas	110,966	6.5	7.7	22.9	26.5	7.1	19.9	9.4
Montgomery County, Texas	398,614	5.0	6.8	23.2	24.4	6.7	23.0	10.9
Nacogdoches County, Texas	38,985	7.7	7.5	31.2	25.1	4.9	14.6	9.0
Nueces County, Texas	238,820	6.7	8.8	31.1	21.6	8.1	14.8	8.8
Orange County, Texas	56,626	4.3	8.3	31.1	24.6	12.9	16.1	2.7
Parker County, Texas	95,222	4.1	8.1	27.6	21.7	13.5	16.6	8.4
Potter County, Texas	74,335	9.9	13.1	31.5	23.4	8.8	9.0	4.4
Randall County, Texas	90,495	3.0	3.6	24.8	24.6	8.8	23.5	11.7

Table C-2. Educational Attainment of the Population, by Selected Counties, 2019—*Continued*

(Number; percent; dollars.)

State/County	Population 18 to 24 years				
	Total	Less than high school graduate (percent)	High school graduate (includes equivalency) (percent)	Some college or associate's degree (percent)	Bachelor's degree or higher (percent)
TEXAS—(*Continued*)					
Rockwall County, Texas	7,662	7.0	34.8	47.4	10.9
San Patricio County, Texas	6,090	25.9	36.0	27.5	10.6
Smith County, Texas	23,428	6.2	32.9	55.8	5.1
Tarrant County, Texas	197,127	12.6	34.9	42.4	10.1
Taylor County, Texas	18,911	7.0	38.4	44.1	10.5
Tom Green County, Texas	14,727	8.1	33.3	47.0	11.6
Travis County, Texas	115,382	9.1	26.8	46.4	17.7
Victoria County, Texas	9,799	17.2	46.4	32.4	4.0
Walker County, Texas	15,514	6.2	13.8	68.4	11.7
Webb County, Texas	31,528	17.3	30.7	46.9	5.1
Wichita County, Texas	17,556	8.0	39.0	45.1	7.9
Williamson County, Texas	46,552	12.2	37.3	40.4	10.1
Wise County, Texas	5,717	15.1	49.7	32.7	2.5
UTAH	364,058	10.7	33.0	49.3	7.0
Cache County, Utah	23,066	8.4	19.2	64.0	8.4
Davis County, Utah	33,522	13.5	39.7	43.3	3.5
Salt Lake County, Utah	110,813	11.8	35.6	42.7	9.9
Tooele County, Utah	5,838	11.5	41.4	44.0	3.0
Utah County, Utah	106,163	6.9	27.3	58.7	7.1
Washington County, Utah	16,483	9.3	40.2	44.7	5.8
Weber County, Utah	25,530	12.5	37.7	46.7	3.1
VERMONT	64,872	8.0	32.8	47.2	12.1
Chittenden County, Vermont	24,391	4.4	22.3	55.9	17.4
VIRGINIA	805,157	9.7	34.0	43.1	13.1
Albemarle County, Virginia	13,700	9.0	32.0	44.1	14.8
Arlington County, Virginia	18,825	4.7	11.8	23.9	59.6
Augusta County, Virginia	5,279	8.4	51.3	20.8	19.5
Bedford County, Virginia	6,531	6.2	46.0	38.6	9.1
Chesterfield County, Virginia	30,727	13.2	37.0	42.1	7.7
Fairfax County, Virginia	95,471	12.7	25.5	37.9	23.9
Fauquier County, Virginia	5,446	7.1	35.1	51.2	6.7
Frederick County, Virginia	6,326	17.7	35.6	33.0	13.7
Hanover County, Virginia	9,612	14.7	40.0	33.8	11.5
Henrico County, Virginia	25,069	15.7	40.3	35.4	8.6
James City County, Virginia	4,830	10.5	24.3	46.5	18.7
Loudoun County, Virginia	31,476	16.3	20.7	40.3	22.7
Montgomery County, Virginia	28,014	1.9	21.1	67.4	9.6
Prince William County, Virginia	41,188	9.9	31.0	51.3	7.8
Roanoke County, Virginia	7,673	17.9	43.3	31.7	7.1
Rockingham County, Virginia	7,246	6.9	36.4	48.0	8.8
Spotsylvania County, Virginia	11,577	12.0	48.2	33.5	6.3
Stafford County, Virginia	14,635	7.0	48.3	36.7	8.0
York County, Virginia	5,654	4.1	41.7	43.0	11.2
Alexandria city, Virginia	8,200	8.8	36.3	29.7	25.2
Chesapeake city, Virginia	20,919	16.3	32.2	40.8	10.7
Hampton city, Virginia	15,223	5.7	25.6	62.6	6.2
Lynchburg city, Virginia	19,573	4.8	27.8	50.9	16.5
Newport News city, Virginia	20,261	9.8	43.7	41.3	5.1
Norfolk city, Virginia	43,719	5.5	48.4	40.4	5.7
Portsmouth city, Virginia	9,302	16.5	27.3	49.4	6.8
Richmond city, Virginia	27,817	5.6	29.0	44.8	20.6
Roanoke city, Virginia	8,704	8.3	48.7	30.6	12.4
Suffolk city, Virginia	7,177	13.3	34.0	49.5	3.1
Virginia Beach city, Virginia	40,495	6.5	37.6	44.6	11.3
WASHINGTON	661,604	14.2	32.8	41.3	11.7
Benton County, Washington	16,907	20.6	32.3	36.7	10.4
Chelan County, Washington	5,946	23.6	38.4	37.0	1.1
Clallam County, Washington	4,142	15.6	39.0	40.7	4.7
Clark County, Washington	39,877	17.8	38.4	35.0	8.8
Cowlitz County, Washington	7,921	15.7	41.1	40.7	2.4
Franklin County, Washington	9,062	26.4	26.3	40.9	6.3
Grant County, Washington	8,751	24.8	45.9	22.4	7.0
Grays Harbor County, Washington	4,855	25.6	41.4	30.2	2.8
Island County, Washington	8,139	18.2	35.4	42.3	4.1

Table C-2. Educational Attainment of the Population, by Selected Counties, 2019—*Continued*

(Number; percent; dollars.)

State/County	Population 25 years and over							
	Total	Less than 9th grade (percent)	9th to 12th grade, no diploma (percent)	High school graduate (includes equivalency) (percent)	Some college, no degree (percent)	Associate's degree (percent)	Bachelor's degree (percent)	Graduate or professional degree (percent)
TEXAS—(*Continued*)								
Rockwall County, Texas	69,312	3.3	2.5	17.7	24.5	11.9	23.6	16.5
San Patricio County, Texas	42,954	10.4	7.9	36.3	24.0	6.2	11.2	4.0
Smith County, Texas	152,733	6.1	6.7	23.8	26.4	9.7	18.4	9.0
Tarrant County, Texas	1,358,155	5.9	6.8	24.4	21.1	7.6	23.1	11.0
Taylor County, Texas	84,874	3.4	5.3	31.1	25.1	8.4	17.4	9.4
Tom Green County, Texas	76,497	6.0	6.6	29.8	27.2	6.4	13.6	10.5
Travis County, Texas	888,630	5.9	4.2	15.8	15.7	5.7	32.6	20.0
Victoria County, Texas	59,261	6.8	8.3	31.7	22.8	11.3	12.0	7.1
Walker County, Texas	46,727	6.4	7.0	40.1	19.9	7.1	13.1	6.3
Webb County, Texas	156,048	18.3	15.7	19.8	17.9	8.1	15.0	5.2
Wichita County, Texas	85,011	3.5	8.5	34.9	23.2	7.7	13.2	9.1
Williamson County, Texas	394,429	3.1	3.3	21.1	22.5	8.4	28.4	13.3
Wise County, Texas	46,688	6.8	7.5	36.4	25.6	6.4	12.8	4.5
UTAH	1,911,592	2.4	4.5	23.1	25.5	9.7	23.4	11.3
Cache County, Utah	66,833	1.8	5.7	21.6	28.0	6.6	23.1	13.2
Davis County, Utah	209,151	1.3	2.4	20.9	27.9	11.0	25.1	11.4
Salt Lake County, Utah	740,478	3.2	5.2	22.7	22.7	8.9	24.5	12.8
Tooele County, Utah	43,188	0.5	5.6	32.7	29.3	9.0	16.2	6.7
Utah County, Utah	320,787	1.7	2.6	17.8	26.6	10.2	29.0	12.1
Washington County, Utah	116,046	1.7	4.6	21.9	31.0	13.5	16.8	10.5
Weber County, Utah	162,187	2.8	5.3	28.8	26.3	9.7	19.5	7.6
VERMONT	445,558	2.1	4.8	29.0	16.7	8.7	22.7	16.0
Chittenden County, Vermont	110,844	3.1	3.6	18.5	14.9	8.5	29.2	22.2
VIRGINIA	5,872,757	3.8	6.2	23.6	18.9	8.0	22.4	17.2
Albemarle County, Virginia	74,077	2.1	2.7	15.3	15.2	4.1	30.1	30.4
Arlington County, Virginia	175,033	3.3	2.2	7.2	7.8	4.6	34.8	40.1
Augusta County, Virginia	57,274	4.0	8.5	40.3	20.9	7.0	13.8	5.5
Bedford County, Virginia	56,485	3.9	6.6	25.6	25.1	7.2	19.2	12.5
Chesterfield County, Virginia	238,956	2.9	4.7	24.1	20.0	8.1	24.9	15.4
Fairfax County, Virginia	785,130	4.2	3.1	12.0	12.2	6.1	31.5	30.9
Fauquier County, Virginia	49,325	3.0	5.4	25.9	22.0	8.3	22.5	13.0
Frederick County, Virginia	62,677	3.6	7.2	32.3	20.6	8.4	15.6	12.3
Hanover County, Virginia	74,806	1.5	4.7	26.1	19.7	7.7	24.7	15.6
Henrico County, Virginia	231,548	2.6	5.9	21.9	20.2	6.7	25.2	17.6
James City County, Virginia	56,634	2.0	2.5	19.1	16.7	7.8	26.3	25.5
Loudoun County, Virginia	266,796	2.7	2.9	12.2	13.6	6.3	36.9	25.4
Montgomery County, Virginia	56,445	1.8	2.9	27.2	17.2	5.3	21.5	24.1
Prince William County, Virginia	302,837	6.6	4.7	18.1	19.4	8.2	25.6	17.4
Roanoke County, Virginia	67,995	1.4	7.1	24.5	17.7	10.9	24.3	14.1
Rockingham County, Virginia	56,875	6.3	9.4	35.3	16.3	6.5	15.0	11.3
Spotsylvania County, Virginia	90,746	3.2	5.4	28.6	21.6	9.5	20.0	11.6
Stafford County, Virginia	98,469	3.3	3.4	25.1	21.0	7.2	24.3	15.6
York County, Virginia	46,576	2.8	2.8	18.5	17.0	7.8	26.4	24.7
Alexandria city, Virginia	122,536	3.1	3.9	10.4	11.1	5.5	31.7	34.2
Chesapeake city, Virginia	164,745	2.2	7.0	24.7	23.2	10.9	19.6	12.5
Hampton city, Virginia	91,041	2.2	6.1	30.1	25.5	9.8	15.9	10.3
Lynchburg city, Virginia	46,645	2.5	10.0	23.4	20.7	6.2	23.1	14.1
Newport News city, Virginia	117,211	2.4	6.7	30.4	22.6	11.7	15.5	10.8
Norfolk city, Virginia	152,165	3.3	8.4	25.9	23.2	8.6	18.9	11.7
Portsmouth city, Virginia	63,624	2.2	10.0	29.3	27.2	9.8	14.2	7.3
Richmond city, Virginia	163,388	4.8	10.6	21.7	18.8	4.8	23.7	15.6
Roanoke city, Virginia	68,745	4.7	7.1	35.5	20.3	8.6	13.8	10.0
Suffolk city, Virginia	62,892	2.3	6.6	25.1	25.1	10.1	19.5	11.4
Virginia Beach city, Virginia	310,431	1.7	4.2	18.7	24.9	12.2	22.9	15.3
WASHINGTON	5,290,324	3.5	4.8	22.1	22.7	10.0	22.8	14.2
Benton County, Washington	133,790	5.2	4.2	24.0	23.2	11.3	20.3	11.8
Chelan County, Washington	52,950	8.2	9.3	25.0	21.1	11.0	17.7	7.6
Clallam County, Washington	60,272	1.3	6.9	26.4	26.9	10.0	15.3	13.2
Clark County, Washington	333,679	1.8	4.7	26.3	25.1	10.6	20.7	10.8
Cowlitz County, Washington	77,474	3.3	6.8	29.4	32.8	12.4	10.3	5.0
Franklin County, Washington	54,970	16.0	11.4	27.4	18.0	10.2	11.5	5.5
Grant County, Washington	60,165	12.0	10.7	29.5	18.2	11.6	14.3	3.7
Grays Harbor County, Washington	54,932	3.6	4.4	36.8	23.9	11.9	11.5	7.9
Island County, Washington	61,817	1.1	3.8	20.1	27.8	12.6	20.1	14.5

Table C-2. Educational Attainment of the Population, by Selected Counties, 2019—*Continued*

(Number; percent; dollars.)

State/County	Total	Population 18 to 24 years			
		Less than high school graduate (percent)	High school graduate (includes equivalency) (percent)	Some college or associate's degree (percent)	Bachelor's degree or higher (percent)
WASHINGTON—(*Continued*)					
King County, Washington	180,726	11.4	23.7	41.5	23.4
Kitsap County, Washington	25,718	12.9	37.2	41.5	8.4
Lewis County, Washington	5,918	19.3	41.6	35.9	3.2
Mason County, Washington	4,580	22.5	61.9	15.6	0.0
Pierce County, Washington	81,962	13.4	38.4	40.7	7.4
Skagit County, Washington	9,455	11.9	41.1	43.2	3.7
Snohomish County, Washington	62,348	16.4	36.5	37.9	9.2
Spokane County, Washington	49,080	11.1	34.1	46.6	8.2
Thurston County, Washington	23,714	15.6	38.8	37.8	7.9
Whatcom County, Washington	32,247	9.2	28.6	52.6	9.6
Yakima County, Washington	23,383	18.1	45.1	31.7	5.1
WEST VIRGINIA	152,243	12.3	39.0	38.8	10.0
Berkeley County, West Virginia	8,992	15.7	33.3	32.3	18.7
Cabell County, West Virginia	11,702	11.1	35.7	39.8	13.4
Harrison County, West Virginia	4,761	26.6	39.4	26.2	7.8
Kanawha County, West Virginia	11,934	16.0	42.1	33.7	8.3
Monongalia County, West Virginia	21,545	3.5	19.9	59.6	17.0
Raleigh County, West Virginia	5,577	2.0	41.1	34.7	22.2
Wood County, West Virginia	6,358	15.0	56.3	20.2	8.6
WISCONSIN	543,737	10.3	33.4	44.5	11.8
Brown County, Wisconsin	24,513	10.5	29.8	43.7	16.0
Dane County, Wisconsin	72,512	4.0	22.3	48.8	25.0
Dodge County, Wisconsin	5,929	10.5	45.4	35.3	8.8
Eau Claire County, Wisconsin	16,829	6.7	29.5	56.5	7.3
Fond du Lac County, Wisconsin	9,486	8.2	31.5	54.8	5.4
Jefferson County, Wisconsin	7,384	6.9	42.6	48.6	1.9
Kenosha County, Wisconsin	16,485	14.0	41.9	38.8	5.3
La Crosse County, Wisconsin	18,096	2.3	25.4	63.7	8.6
Manitowoc County, Wisconsin	5,662	5.8	51.0	33.8	9.4
Marathon County, Wisconsin	9,837	13.1	40.6	39.2	7.1
Milwaukee County, Wisconsin	89,483	14.3	30.8	43.4	11.5
Outagamie County, Wisconsin	15,310	10.2	36.4	41.2	12.2
Ozaukee County, Wisconsin	7,502	4.8	28.6	40.5	26.2
Portage County, Wisconsin	11,604	8.6	33.4	52.3	5.7
Racine County, Wisconsin	16,508	16.0	43.2	31.3	9.5
Rock County, Wisconsin	15,018	11.1	38.4	46.6	4.0
St. Croix County, Wisconsin	6,647	4.4	54.5	30.9	10.2
Sheboygan County, Wisconsin	9,473	6.4	45.6	34.4	13.5
Walworth County, Wisconsin	13,256	9.4	29.8	52.7	8.2
Washington County, Wisconsin	9,861	6.9	33.3	45.7	14.1
Waukesha County, Wisconsin	31,054	12.5	34.2	38.2	15.2
Winnebago County, Wisconsin	18,999	7.9	33.1	48.9	10.2
Wood County, Wisconsin	4,689	10.2	41.0	37.7	11.2
WYOMING	54,723	11.4	33.7	46.0	8.9
Laramie County, Wyoming	8,742	10.5	50.7	30.5	8.3
Natrona County, Wyoming	6,222	6.5	27.5	59.2	6.8

Table C-2. Educational Attainment of the Population, by Selected Counties, 2019—*Continued*

(Number; percent; dollars.)

State/County	Population 25 years and over							
	Total	Less than 9th grade (percent)	9th to 12th grade, no diploma (percent)	High school graduate (includes equivalency) (percent)	Some college, no degree (percent)	Associate's degree (percent)	Bachelor's degree (percent)	Graduate or professional degree (percent)
WASHINGTON—*(Continued)*								
King County, Washington	1,620,440	3.5	3.4	14.4	17.2	7.3	31.7	22.4
Kitsap County, Washington	190,817	1.4	2.4	22.2	28.7	10.5	23.0	11.8
Lewis County, Washington	57,583	3.5	10.4	28.1	28.2	10.9	12.1	6.9
Mason County, Washington	49,157	3.4	6.0	30.0	28.7	11.0	12.4	8.6
Pierce County, Washington	612,563	2.6	5.4	27.8	24.5	11.6	18.6	9.5
Skagit County, Washington	91,972	3.7	6.2	25.4	27.8	9.9	17.6	9.4
Snohomish County, Washington	575,484	2.9	4.3	23.2	25.4	11.2	21.9	11.1
Spokane County, Washington	358,868	1.7	4.6	22.6	26.9	13.3	19.5	11.5
Thurston County, Washington	205,115	1.8	4.8	22.6	25.5	10.9	20.0	14.3
Whatcom County, Washington	152,930	1.3	4.5	24.0	23.5	10.9	22.6	13.2
Yakima County, Washington	153,801	16.0	9.4	27.8	21.3	8.2	11.1	6.2
WEST VIRGINIA	1,281,086	4.2	8.7	40.2	17.9	7.9	12.6	8.4
Berkeley County, West Virginia	82,743	3.4	8.6	37.8	18.7	8.4	14.2	9.0
Cabell County, West Virginia	62,154	4.7	9.0	33.0	16.2	7.9	17.9	11.2
Harrison County, West Virginia	48,151	1.7	8.1	39.7	15.3	9.6	16.0	9.7
Kanawha County, West Virginia	130,820	2.7	7.1	38.6	18.7	7.2	14.9	10.9
Monongalia County, West Virginia	66,795	2.4	6.6	23.6	15.3	7.3	20.2	24.6
Raleigh County, West Virginia	52,700	5.3	6.2	40.7	21.5	6.7	11.7	7.9
Wood County, West Virginia	59,703	3.0	8.2	33.1	24.3	11.1	12.8	7.6
WISCONSIN	4,015,285	2.5	4.8	30.5	20.0	10.9	20.7	10.7
Brown County, Wisconsin	177,809	4.0	3.7	30.1	19.9	12.1	21.6	8.7
Dane County, Wisconsin	363,916	1.3	2.7	16.7	15.8	9.4	31.9	22.2
Dodge County, Wisconsin	63,466	2.8	7.5	39.5	20.5	12.2	13.5	4.0
Eau Claire County, Wisconsin	66,896	1.7	2.7	25.7	21.8	15.3	20.9	12.0
Fond du Lac County, Wisconsin	72,712	1.7	5.3	36.1	20.8	12.5	15.4	8.2
Jefferson County, Wisconsin	59,478	2.8	4.3	34.3	19.3	12.3	19.2	7.8
Kenosha County, Wisconsin	114,483	2.9	5.6	28.9	22.3	10.6	17.9	11.7
La Crosse County, Wisconsin	76,786	1.7	2.5	27.2	20.5	13.0	22.3	12.8
Manitowoc County, Wisconsin	57,164	1.8	4.5	39.0	21.1	11.8	14.7	7.2
Marathon County, Wisconsin	94,762	2.5	5.2	34.9	19.9	12.8	17.0	7.6
Milwaukee County, Wisconsin	630,822	4.4	6.5	28.9	20.1	8.4	20.7	11.0
Outagamie County, Wisconsin	128,752	1.7	4.2	31.9	20.1	12.1	20.9	9.0
Ozaukee County, Wisconsin	62,768	0.4	1.0	23.1	17.5	9.7	30.6	17.6
Portage County, Wisconsin	45,971	1.5	3.6	33.6	15.6	10.2	24.8	10.7
Racine County, Wisconsin	134,721	2.1	8.3	30.3	22.6	10.7	17.0	9.1
Rock County, Wisconsin	110,935	2.0	6.2	37.3	20.4	11.0	15.5	7.7
St. Croix County, Wisconsin	61,770	0.8	3.8	24.6	19.1	13.2	26.9	11.6
Sheboygan County, Wisconsin	80,744	1.6	3.5	34.8	20.9	11.3	20.5	7.4
Walworth County, Wisconsin	69,576	2.5	5.9	31.2	21.8	7.7	20.5	10.3
Washington County, Wisconsin	97,023	0.6	4.4	30.3	21.3	12.3	23.1	8.0
Waukesha County, Wisconsin	287,092	1.3	2.3	21.4	19.5	9.6	30.2	15.9
Winnebago County, Wisconsin	117,903	2.1	5.6	32.3	18.8	10.1	22.2	8.9
Wood County, Wisconsin	52,656	2.8	6.1	39.0	19.6	12.8	12.7	7.0
WYOMING	389,847	1.7	3.8	30.1	24.0	11.3	18.8	10.4
Laramie County, Wyoming	67,775	2.4	3.2	28.0	24.9	11.5	17.8	12.3
Natrona County, Wyoming	54,280	1.5	5.6	34.4	25.9	12.1	14.1	6.6

Table C-2. Educational Attainment of the Population, by Selected Counties, 2019—*Continued*

(Number; percent; dollars.)

State/County	Population 25 to 34 years			Population 35 to 44 years		
	Total	High school graduate or more (percent)	Bachelor's degree or more (percent)	Total	High school graduate or more (percent)	Bachelor's degree or more (percent)
UNITED STATES	45,578,475	91.7	36.9	41,914,845	89.0	37.4
ALABAMA	637,403	89.3	27.5	605,739	87.8	29.6
Baldwin County, Alabama...................................	24,401	90.3	27.0	28,477	90.6	39.6
Calhoun County, Alabama	14,981	88.7	13.7	14,394	83.9	21.9
Cullman County, Alabama.................................	10,588	88.0	16.9	10,281	85.4	24.8
DeKalb County, Alabama..................................	8,436	83.5	15.9	9,017	69.1	16.8
Elmore County, Alabama..................................	13,121	89.2	22.6	10,084	97.0	24.3
Etowah County, Alabama..................................	12,286	83.2	8.9	11,934	85.0	28.8
Houston County, Alabama.................................	13,868	87.9	19.3	13,214	87.1	23.7
Jefferson County, Alabama...............................	95,477	93.9	40.8	84,192	88.8	40.0
Lauderdale County, Alabama.............................	10,833	87.8	19.8	10,597	83.5	18.9
Lee County, Alabama..	22,519	92.1	47.8	22,401	94.4	45.0
Limestone County, Alabama..............................	12,286	86.0	26.6	13,100	90.9	28.9
Madison County, Alabama.................................	52,680	91.1	45.3	46,056	92.7	42.9
Marshall County, Alabama................................	12,099	78.9	21.1	11,407	80.9	17.8
Mobile County, Alabama...................................	58,515	90.5	23.1	49,290	88.7	25.4
Montgomery County, Alabama............................	32,904	92.8	35.0	28,653	89.1	36.5
Morgan County, Alabama..................................	11,759	90.3	14.0	15,336	84.1	27.4
St. Clair County, Alabama.................................	12,436	86.1	12.2	11,304	85.3	20.0
Shelby County, Alabama...................................	27,287	93.1	42.2	29,919	96.3	49.1
Talladega County, Alabama...............................	9,499	76.4	8.3	9,636	81.7	16.1
Tuscaloosa County, Alabama.............................	30,237	94.8	37.2	25,141	87.8	32.9
Walker County, Alabama...................................	7,059	78.6	4.4	7,176	87.6	14.0
ALASKA...	117,978	92.4	25.9	93,035	95.1	35.0
Anchorage Municipality, Alaska.........................	49,731	93.0	34.0	37,828	96.8	42.7
Fairbanks North Star Borough, Alaska	16,186	98.4	24.8	12,659	97.1	39.2
Matanuska-Susitna Borough, Alaska....................	14,699	93.3	17.6	14,137	91.6	25.6
ARIZONA	1,001,594	88.7	28.2	898,533	86.6	32.2
Apache County, Arizona	9,316	86.1	9.2	7,153	93.4	11.2
Cochise County, Arizona	15,467	86.9	23.5	14,188	86.2	24.7
Coconino County, Arizona.................................	19,997	95.9	38.7	15,283	93.1	45.6
Maricopa County, Arizona.................................	658,682	89.9	32.7	583,814	86.0	34.8
Mohave County, Arizona...................................	20,109	82.0	7.3	19,281	90.1	18.9
Navajo County, Arizona....................................	12,793	81.5	4.3	13,028	85.4	21.2
Pima County, Arizona.......................................	135,885	88.5	27.5	120,304	87.9	36.2
Pinal County, Arizona.......................................	60,718	83.2	9.3	60,986	89.0	18.8
Yavapai County, Arizona...................................	19,717	89.3	16.9	20,965	90.9	21.2
Yuma County, Arizona......................................	30,027	80.8	9.4	22,967	81.2	19.9
ARKANSAS	386,602	91.0	25.6	377,184	89.3	27.3
Benton County, Arkansas	41,123	92.7	42.5	40,324	91.8	38.4
Craighead County, Arkansas	16,407	84.2	23.9	15,686	91.0	26.6
Faulkner County, Arkansas...............................	16,493	96.4	31.3	16,977	99.0	35.6
Garland County, Arkansas................................	10,991	94.6	18.3	11,839	88.5	35.1
Jefferson County, Arkansas..............................	8,910	94.3	17.3	7,692	90.0	9.6
Lonoke County, Arkansas.................................	10,179	92.7	18.3	10,433	93.8	21.1
Pulaski County, Arkansas.................................	57,542	92.6	35.2	50,979	90.2	40.0
Saline County, Arkansas..................................	14,903	92.0	34.3	16,077	92.9	30.9
Sebastian County, Arkansas.............................	17,072	86.0	30.8	15,520	85.8	27.8
Washington County, Arkansas	33,619	85.4	38.7	32,640	83.6	33.2
White County, Arkansas	9,766	84.5	23.8	8,721	88.8	16.7
CALIFORNIA	6,036,052	90.4	38.2	5,298,911	84.5	38.2
Alameda County, California	278,792	94.1	58.5	255,680	91.3	58.6
Butte County, California....................................	29,152	92.0	24.2	24,949	84.4	31.3
Contra Costa County, California	146,499	89.8	35.0	156,803	86.7	46.9
El Dorado County, California	19,605	90.2	29.1	23,073	94.0	41.3
Fresno County, California	154,601	84.9	22.9	129,486	75.1	22.7
Humboldt County, California	18,419	93.9	23.6	17,407	88.8	30.1
Imperial County, California................................	27,562	77.3	17.3	22,000	81.2	33.7
Kern County, California	141,225	84.6	18.0	115,848	76.4	17.8
Kings County, California	26,301	79.1	15.2	20,966	71.9	17.2
Lake County, California	7,711	89.2	11.8	7,634	79.7	16.8
Los Angeles County, California..........................	1,636,784	89.8	40.0	1,375,634	81.8	37.1
Madera County, California.................................	21,339	78.4	14.4	20,918	70.7	12.7

Table C-2. Educational Attainment of the Population, by Selected Counties, 2019—*Continued*

(Number; percent; dollars.)

State/County	Population 45 to 64 years			Population 65 years and over		
	Total	High school graduate or more (percent)	Bachelor's degree or more (percent)	Total	High school graduate or more (percent)	Bachelor's degree or more (percent)
UNITED STATES	83,331,220	88.6	31.8	54,074,028	85.7	28.6
ALABAMA	1,262,604	87.9	26.4	854,312	83.8	23.2
Baldwin County, Alabama.............................	59,151	91.3	31.8	47,688	89.6	31.0
Calhoun County, Alabama............................	29,153	85.6	18.9	20,556	80.5	22.1
Cullman County, Alabama............................	22,503	80.9	13.1	15,423	74.4	12.7
DeKalb County, Alabama.............................	17,616	82.0	10.3	11,938	77.5	11.1
Elmore County, Alabama.............................	21,587	88.6	25.8	12,761	86.3	26.1
Etowah County, Alabama.............................	27,530	86.1	17.4	19,994	81.5	15.3
Houston County, Alabama............................	27,351	85.2	23.5	19,021	81.2	23.3
Jefferson County, Alabama...........................	163,853	92.6	32.3	108,296	88.6	28.4
Lauderdale County, Alabama........................	23,613	86.3	24.8	19,224	82.6	22.3
Lee County, Alabama..................................	35,661	93.1	37.2	20,745	87.2	37.9
Limestone County, Alabama.........................	26,775	88.0	24.4	16,280	84.7	23.9
Madison County, Alabama............................	100,510	94.4	45.8	57,890	92.1	40.7
Marshall County, Alabama...........................	24,513	83.8	22.2	16,737	82.7	17.8
Mobile County, Alabama..............................	104,639	87.1	23.2	68,009	84.6	20.5
Montgomery County, Alabama......................	54,147	89.1	38.5	35,606	87.5	30.1
Morgan County, Alabama.............................	33,691	86.7	27.5	21,676	83.4	19.3
St. Clair County, Alabama............................	24,702	86.1	11.4	14,419	84.4	13.4
Shelby County, Alabama..............................	56,777	93.8	47.4	35,238	90.9	37.7
Talladega County, Alabama..........................	21,775	80.7	18.8	14,611	81.3	14.2
Tuscaloosa County, Alabama........................	47,358	88.3	30.8	28,853	85.7	25.9
Walker County, Alabama.............................	18,330	84.0	15.4	12,012	78.8	10.7
ALASKA..	182,457	94.1	30.2	90,588	92.5	30.8
Anchorage Municipality, Alaska.....................	70,086	95.6	35.1	32,816	95.1	35.1
Fairbanks North Star Borough, Alaska	21,485	96.7	36.2	10,950	87.9	33.2
Matanuska-Susitna Borough, Alaska..................	27,992	94.5	26.8	13,597	96.6	25.1
ARIZONA	1,737,172	87.0	29.6	1,307,241	88.3	31.0
Apache County, Arizona	18,183	85.0	11.7	11,603	65.9	14.5
Cochise County, Arizona.............................	29,839	89.5	22.3	28,939	89.9	28.7
Coconino County, Arizona............................	30,816	94.3	35.2	18,586	89.9	42.9
Maricopa County, Arizona............................	1,078,113	87.4	33.1	696,467	89.4	33.8
Mohave County, Arizona..............................	57,994	89.0	13.7	65,827	85.8	13.5
Navajo County, Arizona	27,105	83.8	11.5	20,560	83.2	15.7
Pima County, Arizona.................................	241,664	87.0	30.3	212,596	89.3	36.6
Pinal County, Arizona.................................	106,648	85.9	19.9	95,666	88.6	25.8
Yavapai County, Arizona..............................	64,129	91.1	30.9	77,130	93.3	31.5
Yuma County, Arizona................................	43,285	69.3	14.5	40,808	70.7	14.1
ARKANSAS..	748,433	87.7	22.2	524,237	83.3	20.5
Benton County, Arkansas.............................	63,571	87.2	31.3	38,185	87.3	29.4
Craighead County, Arkansas	24,839	92.3	27.8	14,881	88.6	22.0
Faulkner County, Arkansas...........................	27,104	92.5	25.3	16,110	87.7	27.8
Garland County, Arkansas............................	25,936	92.6	29.8	23,799	89.6	28.8
Jefferson County, Arkansas..........................	17,103	87.7	22.3	12,014	77.9	19.2
Lonoke County, Arkansas.............................	18,286	86.3	20.1	10,403	85.6	15.7
Pulaski County, Arkansas.............................	96,189	93.6	32.7	63,974	89.0	33.9
Saline County, Arkansas..............................	31,152	89.9	20.7	22,598	85.5	26.3
Sebastian County, Arkansas..........................	31,118	86.7	21.3	21,669	79.3	24.0
Washington County, Arkansas	50,243	84.6	30.7	29,158	83.1	24.7
White County, Arkansas..............................	19,744	82.2	12.6	13,215	73.1	16.1
CALIFORNIA	9,767,911	81.6	32.9	5,834,998	81.1	32.3
Alameda County, California	422,358	89.6	47.2	238,277	82.6	38.9
Butte County, California...............................	49,155	88.3	32.0	40,559	88.6	32.6
Contra Costa County, California	311,991	89.1	44.3	186,894	90.4	43.7
El Dorado County, California	57,301	94.4	39.6	42,089	91.7	29.0
Fresno County, California.............................	211,617	73.0	20.5	125,736	74.0	22.8
Humboldt County, California..........................	32,246	91.2	28.9	25,026	89.6	37.5
Imperial County, California...........................	38,510	67.9	15.0	23,683	62.5	10.9
Kern County, California	193,223	71.0	14.8	101,660	75.1	19.3
Kings County, California	31,709	67.2	20.1	16,107	67.3	17.2
Lake County, California	17,475	83.7	15.4	14,366	90.2	16.7
Los Angeles County, California.......................	2,535,441	76.0	30.4	1,413,755	73.2	29.4
Madera County, California	34,288	67.0	12.1	22,847	78.9	18.2

Table C-2. Educational Attainment of the Population, by Selected Counties, 2019—*Continued*

(Number; percent; dollars.)

	Population 25 to 34 years			Population 35 to 44 years		
State/County	Total	High school graduate or more (percent)	Bachelor's degree or more (percent)	Total	High school graduate or more (percent)	Bachelor's degree or more (percent)
CALIFORNIA—(*Continued*)						
Marin County, California	21,341	86.8	52.5	28,975	88.0	61.2
Mendocino County, California	8,430	77.3	29.8	10,799	84.4	16.3
Merced County, California	41,053	79.7	15.0	36,588	74.3	16.0
Monterey County, California	61,159	78.3	22.5	57,771	63.7	19.3
Napa County, California	17,125	90.5	33.4	16,887	86.3	34.9
Nevada County, California	10,144	97.9	28.4	11,883	99.2	38.5
Orange County, California	457,902	92.3	45.5	410,729	85.5	46.0
Placer County, California	42,356	91.2	42.7	53,144	95.2	49.8
Riverside County, California	345,381	89.5	21.8	320,798	83.4	23.9
Sacramento County, California	244,536	91.9	33.4	211,156	90.4	31.5
San Bernardino County, California	336,303	88.0	24.2	283,746	80.7	25.0
San Diego County, California	549,118	93.8	40.9	452,635	90.0	45.1
San Francisco County, California	204,061	97.2	79.8	141,927	94.0	65.4
San Joaquin County, California	106,728	84.7	18.1	101,242	77.9	22.4
San Luis Obispo County, California	31,779	93.3	33.9	32,080	87.2	36.8
San Mateo County, California	114,318	93.7	59.5	111,071	91.1	63.1
Santa Barbara County, California	59,846	83.6	35.9	50,654	73.5	29.5
Santa Clara County, California	315,114	94.7	63.1	278,958	90.2	59.7
Santa Cruz County, California	33,165	89.8	42.9	31,799	86.9	41.3
Shasta County, California	22,996	93.7	21.0	20,956	97.2	28.2
Solano County, California	65,438	91.3	26.8	57,782	87.5	28.2
Sonoma County, California	61,535	92.6	31.7	61,553	83.6	32.5
Stanislaus County, California	78,774	88.4	16.7	70,383	83.4	19.4
Sutter County, California	12,894	81.8	16.2	11,722	73.3	24.0
Tehama County, California	8,096	86.9	13.6	9,099	74.7	18.1
Tulare County, California	66,710	86.3	12.0	59,012	73.4	14.0
Ventura County, California	113,309	90.0	29.0	104,866	85.7	34.7
Yolo County, California	29,946	93.5	44.0	27,437	86.1	39.0
Yuba County, California	13,130	88.6	19.4	9,176	80.8	21.2
COLORADO	907,627	93.8	44.4	805,306	91.3	45.7
Adams County, Colorado	85,655	87.9	28.0	76,461	83.1	31.0
Arapahoe County, Colorado	104,474	93.5	43.1	95,130	92.2	45.7
Boulder County, Colorado	46,369	95.6	64.3	40,746	92.2	74.7
Broomfield County, Colorado	10,735	98.1	61.0	10,405	96.3	59.1
Denver County, Colorado	172,142	95.2	62.0	117,716	91.8	54.9
Douglas County, Colorado	39,301	97.1	54.1	51,904	96.8	63.2
El Paso County, Colorado	116,485	96.1	34.2	92,583	93.4	41.4
Jefferson County, Colorado	88,288	94.4	52.3	82,233	95.9	55.5
Larimer County, Colorado	53,029	98.8	49.5	44,701	92.9	49.2
Mesa County, Colorado	19,179	93.8	27.9	19,894	90.7	28.1
Pueblo County, Colorado	21,977	90.1	20.6	20,773	91.1	22.0
Weld County, Colorado	49,494	91.5	31.8	44,463	86.5	31.0
CONNECTICUT	444,509	93.4	44.4	426,967	91.5	45.2
Fairfield County, Connecticut	108,198	92.1	52.3	117,338	90.8	52.4
Hartford County, Connecticut	119,057	92.8	44.3	111,539	90.7	46.3
Litchfield County, Connecticut	20,500	97.3	46.7	18,662	94.3	35.2
Middlesex County, Connecticut	17,810	94.5	48.1	17,894	91.5	55.1
New Haven County, Connecticut	114,713	93.8	41.3	101,405	90.5	40.9
New London County, Connecticut	33,911	94.0	33.9	30,493	95.3	31.1
Tolland County, Connecticut	16,002	95.8	47.7	16,105	97.4	52.3
Windham County, Connecticut	14,318	93.6	25.4	13,531	93.7	28.7
DELAWARE	128,412	91.2	32.8	113,704	87.6	37.8
Kent County, Delaware	24,919	90.9	25.8	20,856	91.9	36.9
New Castle County, Delaware	81,002	91.5	37.4	69,737	88.7	39.4
Sussex County, Delaware	22,491	90.5	24.1	23,111	80.6	33.6
DISTRICT OF COLUMBIA	164,375	95.1	73.4	108,905	93.0	66.0
District of Columbia, District of Columbia	164,375	95.1	73.4	108,905	93.0	66.0
FLORIDA	2,768,060	90.7	31.0	2,612,250	88.9	33.9
Alachua County, Florida	40,540	94.9	48.2	30,979	92.5	51.4
Bay County, Florida	23,211	93.1	27.7	21,012	92.1	35.3
Brevard County, Florida	70,135	92.9	30.3	63,155	96.0	33.6
Broward County, Florida	261,831	93.0	34.0	260,809	91.1	35.7
Charlotte County, Florida	14,987	86.9	14.9	14,661	84.8	16.7

Table C-2. Educational Attainment of the Population, by Selected Counties, 2019—*Continued*

(Number; percent; dollars.)

State/County	Population 45 to 64 years			Population 65 years and over		
	Total	High school graduate or more (percent)	Bachelor's degree or more (percent)	Total	High school graduate or more (percent)	Bachelor's degree or more (percent)
CALIFORNIA—(*Continued*)						
Marin County, California	78,635	93.5	62.1	59,558	95.5	58.3
Mendocino County, California	22,031	81.3	16.5	20,301	88.3	31.8
Merced County, California	58,109	59.7	11.9	31,710	66.3	16.5
Monterey County, California	98,327	69.1	26.1	60,667	78.7	34.4
Napa County, California	36,628	78.5	37.2	27,026	91.2	37.4
Nevada County, California	27,255	92.0	36.5	27,726	95.9	36.7
Orange County, California	846,551	83.9	38.6	485,296	84.7	36.9
Placer County, California	106,876	95.8	42.1	79,145	92.7	35.9
Riverside County, California	588,523	80.1	22.2	366,215	81.6	26.9
Sacramento County, California	378,915	87.7	30.7	223,929	86.4	29.6
San Bernardino County, California	509,927	77.5	21.0	260,812	77.7	20.4
San Diego County, California	801,247	85.3	38.0	484,472	84.5	37.1
San Francisco County, California	213,827	85.0	48.6	141,464	75.2	39.3
San Joaquin County, California	177,332	79.5	19.9	99,410	76.0	19.7
San Luis Obispo County, California	67,700	88.2	35.3	59,624	94.2	41.3
San Mateo County, California	203,955	90.9	49.9	126,636	86.7	40.4
Santa Barbara County, California	97,504	78.9	33.0	70,330	88.1	39.1
Santa Clara County, California	489,784	87.8	49.9	266,825	83.1	43.4
Santa Cruz County, California	68,074	84.6	43.7	48,083	90.3	46.4
Shasta County, California	45,557	92.0	20.7	37,995	92.4	20.1
Solano County, California	114,873	89.3	28.6	72,614	88.6	32.0
Sonoma County, California	133,934	89.6	38.0	102,102	91.6	43.1
Stanislaus County, California	126,827	77.3	16.2	73,595	73.9	18.0
Sutter County, California	23,253	82.4	22.4	15,122	77.9	20.5
Tehama County, California	15,303	86.7	16.2	13,253	82.9	16.7
Tulare County, California	97,954	69.1	13.5	53,781	68.9	15.6
Ventura County, California	222,456	85.5	36.5	136,623	85.8	37.1
Yolo County, California	45,370	88.4	36.0	28,495	86.8	42.5
Yuba County, California	18,094	75.1	16.3	10,275	81.8	15.7
COLORADO	1,416,632	92.5	41.9	845,378	91.8	39.2
Adams County, Colorado	119,191	83.4	21.1	55,624	85.7	23.0
Arapahoe County, Colorado	163,562	92.3	43.0	88,369	92.1	44.0
Boulder County, Colorado	83,085	94.4	63.9	47,546	95.2	58.4
Broomfield County, Colorado	18,728	94.9	57.7	9,675	96.9	48.3
Denver County, Colorado	153,933	89.3	46.7	86,752	85.9	44.4
Douglas County, Colorado	99,929	98.5	60.6	44,191	98.5	50.0
El Paso County, Colorado	166,917	95.5	41.3	95,328	94.3	38.8
Jefferson County, Colorado	156,296	94.6	46.4	99,089	93.7	38.8
Larimer County, Colorado	82,630	96.9	50.0	57,829	96.4	47.0
Mesa County, Colorado	37,153	89.8	29.9	31,122	91.3	31.9
Pueblo County, Colorado	41,949	92.8	25.1	31,679	90.3	24.1
Weld County, Colorado	75,818	86.8	29.2	40,855	85.8	27.6
CONNECTICUT	995,912	91.6	39.0	629,032	86.8	34.2
Fairfield County, Connecticut	268,330	91.6	51.4	153,798	85.8	40.2
Hartford County, Connecticut	239,527	91.8	38.1	155,516	85.6	31.0
Litchfield County, Connecticut	56,471	93.6	33.7	39,673	91.8	34.4
Middlesex County, Connecticut	50,164	95.3	36.5	33,697	91.0	42.8
New Haven County, Connecticut	231,846	89.6	31.7	152,714	85.2	31.9
New London County, Connecticut	74,005	94.5	34.6	49,770	90.1	32.2
Tolland County, Connecticut	41,261	94.1	39.0	24,554	91.1	32.1
Windham County, Connecticut	34,308	87.6	20.8	19,310	85.2	24.1
DELAWARE	255,557	91.5	33.9	189,638	89.7	29.7
Kent County, Delaware	44,087	87.4	22.6	31,993	86.6	18.0
New Castle County, Delaware	148,067	93.4	38.0	89,849	90.6	32.1
Sussex County, Delaware	63,403	90.1	32.2	67,796	90.1	32.1
DISTRICT OF COLUMBIA	144,328	90.8	47.8	87,537	86.0	45.5
District of Columbia, District of Columbia	144,328	90.8	47.8	87,537	86.0	45.5
FLORIDA	5,605,994	89.0	30.2	4,498,198	86.0	29.2
Alachua County, Florida	54,909	94.8	46.3	39,364	92.3	38.6
Bay County, Florida	49,552	91.0	23.4	32,285	89.0	24.2
Brevard County, Florida	171,708	92.4	30.8	145,774	90.8	28.5
Broward County, Florida	534,818	89.8	33.8	334,606	84.3	28.7
Charlotte County, Florida	51,021	91.1	23.3	77,915	92.0	23.7

Table C-2. Educational Attainment of the Population, by Selected Counties, 2019—*Continued*

(Number; percent; dollars.)

	Population 25 to 34 years			Population 35 to 44 years		
State/County	Total	High school graduate or more (percent)	Bachelor's degree or more (percent)	Total	High school graduate or more (percent)	Bachelor's degree or more (percent)
FLORIDA—(*Continued*)						
Citrus County, Florida	12,271	79.0	12.6	11,902	86.9	24.4
Clay County, Florida	25,534	97.0	27.4	28,635	96.9	27.7
Collier County, Florida	34,396	90.0	23.9	36,537	84.8	30.2
Columbia County, Florida	8,068	78.5	12.0	7,876	89.9	26.2
Duval County, Florida	157,115	91.7	29.6	124,092	91.0	34.3
Escambia County, Florida	48,724	90.9	27.3	34,710	87.8	23.9
Flagler County, Florida	10,247	91.0	25.3	11,208	93.4	21.4
Hernando County, Florida	19,730	89.0	16.9	19,739	94.2	21.9
Highlands County, Florida	7,347	81.9	12.1	9,707	92.5	21.9
Hillsborough County, Florida	225,612	90.6	38.7	203,737	89.7	39.2
Indian River County, Florida	15,260	91.0	25.8	14,865	86.1	26.4
Lake County, Florida	39,087	89.7	23.9	40,964	91.1	33.6
Lee County, Florida	82,852	87.2	25.7	80,572	86.6	25.5
Leon County, Florida	41,652	94.7	51.4	31,772	93.3	54.1
Manatee County, Florida	41,082	89.5	26.2	41,161	88.0	31.3
Marion County, Florida	39,613	90.1	14.5	36,615	86.1	22.1
Martin County, Florida	15,650	92.7	20.9	13,484	90.2	43.8
Miami-Dade County, Florida	383,209	90.4	35.8	369,126	85.5	36.1
Monroe County, Florida	9,103	91.5	34.7	8,660	90.1	33.5
Nassau County, Florida	10,988	91.2	18.8	9,136	89.2	27.2
Okaloosa County, Florida	33,147	94.0	30.4	25,965	89.2	30.8
Orange County, Florida	234,299	90.8	38.3	200,209	89.2	38.4
Osceola County, Florida	52,744	88.5	26.6	57,948	89.0	27.0
Palm Beach County, Florida	177,743	88.5	32.2	171,872	86.4	40.9
Pasco County, Florida	60,791	91.3	22.8	69,910	92.7	35.5
Pinellas County, Florida	116,999	92.4	36.5	107,171	91.7	37.6
Polk County, Florida	95,470	89.7	17.3	86,569	84.3	21.5
Putnam County, Florida	7,138	84.4	8.2	8,097	81.2	5.6
St. Johns County, Florida	23,330	93.5	35.9	34,893	98.2	55.8
St. Lucie County, Florida	36,644	89.6	23.9	38,835	82.1	24.1
Santa Rosa County, Florida	24,795	89.9	21.3	23,082	94.6	33.6
Sarasota County, Florida	35,235	96.1	26.0	35,800	90.3	34.1
Seminole County, Florida	68,314	94.9	43.1	65,968	94.3	44.9
Sumter County, Florida	6,013	85.1	8.7	8,714	84.8	20.9
Volusia County, Florida	65,058	92.9	20.9	58,550	89.9	24.1
Walton County, Florida	8,817	93.4	25.5	10,036	95.1	34.5
GEORGIA	1,458,596	90.6	34.7	1,401,934	87.5	35.6
Barrow County, Georgia	12,111	88.0	23.2	12,425	85.1	30.0
Bartow County, Georgia	13,990	90.1	20.8	13,537	85.0	18.9
Bibb County, Georgia	21,039	88.8	26.0	17,841	88.7	24.1
Bulloch County, Georgia	11,379	97.5	26.2	7,938	86.7	24.8
Carroll County, Georgia	16,176	89.7	21.1	17,267	75.2	11.3
Catoosa County, Georgia	8,421	98.1	9.3	8,046	87.5	29.7
Chatham County, Georgia	47,343	92.7	37.5	35,838	86.1	39.3
Cherokee County, Georgia	32,323	92.9	39.9	36,436	94.2	43.0
Clarke County, Georgia	19,852	93.0	54.9	12,251	93.9	52.5
Clayton County, Georgia	44,728	88.6	21.8	39,843	79.3	19.1
Cobb County, Georgia	112,173	94.9	49.0	106,681	89.6	51.4
Columbia County, Georgia	20,936	90.6	41.6	22,083	94.5	29.9
Coweta County, Georgia	19,247	91.0	26.1	19,050	85.9	36.8
DeKalb County, Georgia	127,742	90.1	48.1	108,290	89.2	49.2
Dougherty County, Georgia	10,740	89.3	23.5	10,335	85.5	18.2
Douglas County, Georgia	15,786	94.9	44.6	20,488	89.1	37.2
Fayette County, Georgia	10,407	93.2	33.2	14,764	97.6	55.8
Floyd County, Georgia	12,670	83.8	20.4	10,601	87.8	32.8
Forsyth County, Georgia	22,546	92.5	55.7	39,945	90.8	64.2
Fulton County, Georgia	183,771	96.5	62.4	150,614	93.9	63.0
Glynn County, Georgia	10,859	87.2	18.8	9,650	87.6	29.0
Gwinnett County, Georgia	123,579	88.9	42.0	133,177	87.2	38.2
Hall County, Georgia	25,534	81.6	22.3	24,598	71.0	22.7
Henry County, Georgia	28,384	96.0	31.9	30,816	92.2	28.6
Houston County, Georgia	21,061	90.4	30.0	20,865	94.9	29.1
Jackson County, Georgia	10,529	89.3	27.9	10,027	82.8	24.3
Lowndes County, Georgia	18,698	92.5	17.8	14,121	91.9	31.7
Muscogee County, Georgia	29,951	93.8	25.0	25,336	91.1	23.1
Newton County, Georgia	15,216	90.8	15.4	13,838	86.4	19.2
Paulding County, Georgia	20,199	90.2	26.7	26,085	83.4	26.0

Table C-2. Educational Attainment of the Population, by Selected Counties, 2019—*Continued*

(Number; percent; dollars.)

State/County	Population 45 to 64 years			Population 65 years and over		
	Total	High school graduate or more (percent)	Bachelor's degree or more (percent)	Total	High school graduate or more (percent)	Bachelor's degree or more (percent)
FLORIDA—(*Continued*)						
Citrus County, Florida	40,568	89.6	22.5	55,390	88.9	24.5
Clay County, Florida	61,642	94.4	29.3	35,457	92.4	29.1
Collier County, Florida	95,751	88.9	31.4	126,527	89.9	43.9
Columbia County, Florida	19,283	85.6	11.9	13,296	90.7	16.1
Duval County, Florida	239,237	90.9	30.2	138,376	87.3	29.0
Escambia County, Florida	78,934	88.5	21.3	54,559	87.8	24.8
Flagler County, Florida	31,117	92.6	27.6	35,824	89.5	27.6
Hernando County, Florida	51,939	90.3	19.9	53,268	85.9	19.8
Highlands County, Florida	26,089	80.7	12.9	37,522	86.9	18.9
Hillsborough County, Florida	373,654	89.0	34.0	214,075	85.2	27.7
Indian River County, Florida	39,596	90.8	30.2	54,727	92.2	35.0
Lake County, Florida	94,252	89.5	22.0	98,904	88.5	25.7
Lee County, Florida	196,239	89.0	27.9	224,663	90.5	32.4
Leon County, Florida	61,821	89.5	41.5	40,669	93.7	44.7
Manatee County, Florida	106,680	90.4	27.1	113,970	91.5	35.4
Marion County, Florida	90,677	89.3	21.2	106,950	89.3	21.8
Martin County, Florida	44,441	91.9	38.3	51,435	90.4	35.3
Miami-Dade County, Florida	737,544	82.1	30.5	452,047	64.8	22.0
Monroe County, Florida	22,991	95.2	31.1	17,624	92.3	39.3
Nassau County, Florida	25,885	86.6	28.1	20,697	89.5	38.1
Okaloosa County, Florida	51,116	94.2	31.5	34,410	92.6	33.5
Orange County, Florida	338,695	88.7	34.6	170,997	82.8	28.5
Osceola County, Florida	87,134	87.1	23.4	50,781	76.5	20.5
Palm Beach County, Florida	386,894	89.7	38.1	364,559	89.7	38.4
Pasco County, Florida	146,092	90.6	26.1	125,406	88.2	20.2
Pinellas County, Florida	282,899	91.8	33.8	247,636	89.1	28.4
Polk County, Florida	173,219	88.4	20.1	149,025	84.0	23.3
Putnam County, Florida	20,854	83.0	12.4	17,495	81.4	17.2
St. Johns County, Florida	73,889	95.3	44.7	55,242	95.4	45.5
St. Lucie County, Florida	83,691	89.8	18.3	81,133	84.2	22.5
Santa Rosa County, Florida	50,002	93.1	26.3	31,248	85.9	26.7
Sarasota County, Florida	114,109	93.0	33.4	161,594	94.5	41.3
Seminole County, Florida	124,889	93.6	41.2	75,115	92.1	36.3
Sumter County, Florida	24,875	95.6	26.8	78,784	95.9	38.4
Volusia County, Florida	152,067	92.0	24.1	137,196	89.9	25.5
Walton County, Florida	20,845	94.0	27.7	14,929	81.3	32.5
GEORGIA	2,696,500	88.6	32.9	1,523,192	84.4	26.8
Barrow County, Georgia	20,372	85.2	21.9	10,378	80.1	17.0
Bartow County, Georgia	28,338	85.1	19.7	16,211	75.4	10.6
Bibb County, Georgia	37,051	88.5	24.7	24,486	81.7	24.9
Bulloch County, Georgia	15,698	87.6	31.5	9,055	87.0	20.4
Carroll County, Georgia	27,419	85.9	23.0	16,615	79.6	17.8
Catoosa County, Georgia	18,321	89.5	31.1	11,894	87.8	17.2
Chatham County, Georgia	67,395	90.0	31.5	46,580	88.7	30.2
Cherokee County, Georgia	69,371	90.3	40.9	38,347	86.7	27.1
Clarke County, Georgia	25,192	87.2	38.6	14,479	93.1	51.5
Clayton County, Georgia	69,058	85.4	18.2	28,059	78.1	15.2
Cobb County, Georgia	200,672	92.0	49.3	96,417	91.5	40.4
Columbia County, Georgia	38,532	95.9	48.9	22,070	89.7	37.1
Coweta County, Georgia	41,296	91.5	25.5	21,566	88.1	20.9
DeKalb County, Georgia	187,824	91.3	43.0	97,699	88.5	39.7
Dougherty County, Georgia	20,306	81.3	20.5	14,697	76.1	19.6
Douglas County, Georgia	38,563	92.6	31.0	17,559	85.0	16.1
Fayette County, Georgia	32,903	96.2	50.7	21,913	96.0	35.0
Floyd County, Georgia	25,758	83.9	17.6	17,013	87.9	26.5
Forsyth County, Georgia	67,330	95.4	57.5	30,475	93.6	42.2
Fulton County, Georgia	266,900	93.9	56.5	127,756	90.1	46.4
Glynn County, Georgia	21,890	89.3	28.8	17,846	94.0	32.6
Gwinnett County, Georgia	246,085	88.6	41.3	98,444	85.5	31.6
Hall County, Georgia	53,916	81.2	25.0	31,062	81.9	30.6
Henry County, Georgia	65,367	92.1	26.5	28,010	85.4	17.1
Houston County, Georgia	39,263	95.6	27.5	20,198	87.7	25.1
Jackson County, Georgia	18,628	84.6	23.7	10,861	84.0	24.8
Lowndes County, Georgia	22,176	91.8	29.7	14,677	85.4	21.9
Muscogee County, Georgia	45,506	88.3	25.1	26,799	82.1	25.2
Newton County, Georgia	28,465	86.7	21.5	14,707	78.3	12.2
Paulding County, Georgia	46,231	90.3	21.6	17,883	85.3	12.7

Table C-2. Educational Attainment of the Population, by Selected Counties, 2019—*Continued*

(Number; percent; dollars.)

State/County	Population 25 to 34 years			Population 35 to 44 years		
	Total	High school graduate or more (percent)	Bachelor's degree or more (percent)	Total	High school graduate or more (percent)	Bachelor's degree or more (percent)
GEORGIA—*(Continued)*						
Richmond County, Georgia	32,969	90.6	22.9	23,274	86.8	25.3
Rockdale County, Georgia	10,012	84.7	21.5	11,748	87.0	24.1
Spalding County, Georgia	7,968	96.8	11.9	7,166	82.2	16.8
Troup County, Georgia	11,580	93.2	14.4	7,949	82.1	20.1
Walker County, Georgia	8,305	86.4	15.7	8,988	82.1	25.4
Walton County, Georgia	13,431	87.5	23.8	11,122	88.0	32.7
Whitfield County, Georgia	12,745	90.7	17.4	15,106	60.6	12.3
HAWAII	195,781	96.2	33.3	185,133	94.8	38.2
Hawaii County, Hawaii	21,122	95.7	23.3	25,683	92.5	32.2
Honolulu County, Hawaii	146,382	96.5	36.5	125,615	96.3	42.9
Kauai County, Hawaii	8,035	94.5	25.2	9,940	93.3	26.8
Maui County, Hawaii	20,242	95.2	24.2	23,890	89.7	25.1
IDAHO	234,800	92.7	27.5	225,804	91.6	33.1
Ada County, Idaho	70,119	94.2	37.9	68,200	95.5	44.3
Bannock County, Idaho	13,297	96.9	30.6	11,003	95.9	39.2
Bonneville County, Idaho	17,084	95.0	36.0	14,791	95.1	40.6
Canyon County, Idaho	31,419	88.5	15.4	28,987	85.0	26.7
Kootenai County, Idaho	20,618	97.3	17.6	20,385	90.8	18.1
Twin Falls County, Idaho	11,422	81.3	19.3	10,528	91.0	23.9
ILLINOIS	1,748,323	93.3	43.1	1,641,179	90.2	41.9
Adams County, Illinois	7,879	90.5	25.8	8,160	92.5	34.3
Champaign County, Illinois	28,867	93.0	56.1	22,799	93.6	50.3
Cook County, Illinois	841,725	93.7	51.8	700,021	89.7	46.6
DeKalb County, Illinois	12,550	94.0	46.8	11,822	94.2	36.2
DuPage County, Illinois	116,204	95.8	54.2	120,994	93.6	55.5
Kane County, Illinois	63,003	91.3	36.2	70,405	80.2	35.4
Kankakee County, Illinois	12,314	88.0	28.1	13,231	93.6	20.7
Kendall County, Illinois	17,166	95.7	38.8	19,095	95.4	52.0
Lake County, Illinois	78,325	92.7	38.8	87,089	87.8	50.0
LaSalle County, Illinois	13,300	89.5	13.4	13,463	88.6	22.8
McHenry County, Illinois	35,131	94.4	37.6	39,177	94.5	38.6
McLean County, Illinois	21,096	95.2	49.5	21,561	94.6	56.5
Macon County, Illinois	13,199	96.3	24.3	12,029	91.7	20.4
Madison County, Illinois	34,824	94.3	32.7	31,619	92.9	44.3
Peoria County, Illinois	23,609	95.6	39.5	21,694	93.1	41.9
Rock Island County, Illinois	16,552	91.5	23.9	17,204	84.0	26.3
St. Clair County, Illinois	34,978	94.5	22.9	32,573	94.0	34.5
Sangamon County, Illinois	24,672	91.2	33.2	23,985	93.5	40.2
Tazewell County, Illinois	15,173	94.4	33.0	16,838	93.9	31.3
Vermilion County, Illinois	9,020	89.5	11.9	8,435	87.8	11.9
Will County, Illinois	82,925	93.6	35.5	92,931	89.1	42.3
Williamson County, Illinois	8,654	95.2	31.1	8,901	96.7	35.3
Winnebago County, Illinois	34,366	88.3	24.8	34,265	85.9	27.5
INDIANA	886,319	90.6	30.8	825,768	89.6	31.9
Allen County, Indiana	52,113	91.9	32.6	48,086	89.0	32.0
Bartholomew County, Indiana	12,579	85.3	49.8	10,847	93.6	44.5
Boone County, Indiana	7,606	91.4	42.5	10,105	86.7	47.3
Clark County, Indiana	15,720	97.9	28.3	16,730	83.9	19.1
Delaware County, Indiana	12,949	95.4	24.2	10,993	91.9	20.6
Elkhart County, Indiana	26,657	85.7	16.2	23,446	75.9	24.6
Floyd County, Indiana	9,820	95.0	35.2	9,861	93.0	31.5
Grant County, Indiana	7,845	93.4	23.4	6,327	92.2	21.7
Hamilton County, Indiana	38,248	98.7	68.9	50,345	97.4	71.0
Hancock County, Indiana	10,368	98.6	29.7	9,516	98.0	46.8
Hendricks County, Indiana	22,787	94.9	33.3	23,510	93.9	47.8
Howard County, Indiana	10,446	89.5	12.3	9,369	86.2	18.9
Johnson County, Indiana	20,453	94.7	34.6	20,217	93.6	43.0
Kosciusko County, Indiana	10,870	89.4	36.6	8,899	93.5	26.2
Lake County, Indiana	60,112	91.8	22.4	61,329	91.9	26.8
LaPorte County, Indiana	13,758	84.7	19.5	13,416	84.0	19.2
Madison County, Indiana	16,463	83.5	21.2	15,102	91.9	23.8
Marion County, Indiana	164,580	87.7	37.3	124,692	88.8	33.6
Monroe County, Indiana	19,957	97.3	49.1	15,701	96.8	60.3

Table C-2. Educational Attainment of the Population, by Selected Counties, 2019—*Continued*

(Number; percent; dollars.)

State/County	Population 45 to 64 years			Population 65 years and over		
	Total	High school graduate or more (percent)	Bachelor's degree or more (percent)	Total	High school graduate or more (percent)	Bachelor's degree or more (percent)
GEORGIA—(*Continued*)						
Richmond County, Georgia	47,743	88.3	17.3	29,702	80.3	16.7
Rockdale County, Georgia	24,663	92.5	25.4	13,801	83.5	21.6
Spalding County, Georgia	18,021	82.3	18.0	12,324	82.2	21.6
Troup County, Georgia	16,609	88.5	22.3	10,647	90.0	21.2
Walker County, Georgia	18,853	77.5	13.1	12,984	79.3	16.4
Walton County, Georgia	25,685	88.2	23.5	15,110	78.2	16.4
Whitfield County, Georgia	24,640	68.8	13.4	14,950	72.0	25.5
HAWAII	346,284	93.3	32.8	269,470	86.8	31.8
Hawaii County, Hawaii	53,042	93.6	27.7	44,025	90.0	34.7
Honolulu County, Hawaii	230,853	93.4	35.6	177,856	85.8	30.7
Kauai County, Hawaii	18,213	95.2	31.0	15,267	88.7	28.7
Maui County, Hawaii	44,168	91.6	25.5	32,320	87.2	34.8
IDAHO	421,776	90.8	27.6	288,617	91.3	28.0
Ada County, Idaho	119,486	94.3	40.2	71,534	95.2	36.3
Bannock County, Idaho	19,792	91.6	23.7	12,334	93.3	29.0
Bonneville County, Idaho	25,488	89.3	27.4	15,593	94.8	30.4
Canyon County, Idaho	50,716	86.5	19.7	32,652	87.6	21.0
Kootenai County, Idaho	42,476	94.4	26.7	32,082	91.7	30.2
Twin Falls County, Idaho	18,565	86.2	20.1	13,994	83.8	22.8
ILLINOIS	3,259,831	89.7	33.9	2,045,361	86.8	27.5
Adams County, Illinois	16,795	91.7	21.3	13,312	89.9	19.6
Champaign County, Illinois	42,330	93.7	42.7	27,885	93.4	38.0
Cook County, Illinois	1,272,487	86.5	36.3	776,131	82.2	29.8
DeKalb County, Illinois	23,460	91.2	34.6	13,699	93.1	28.2
DuPage County, Illinois	250,875	93.9	51.8	148,896	92.6	42.2
Kane County, Illinois	142,139	86.4	32.4	75,940	86.1	29.9
Kankakee County, Illinois	27,968	92.9	18.2	18,716	85.9	15.1
Kendall County, Illinois	31,914	92.6	38.3	14,737	86.0	26.8
Lake County, Illinois	191,042	91.0	47.4	103,327	89.5	41.1
LaSalle County, Illinois	29,586	88.1	15.7	21,282	91.4	14.7
McHenry County, Illinois	89,925	94.3	36.7	46,647	90.5	26.4
McLean County, Illinois	38,444	95.2	44.2	23,444	92.5	35.2
Macon County, Illinois	25,884	94.0	21.4	21,175	91.8	20.6
Madison County, Illinois	72,024	93.5	29.0	46,399	93.0	20.7
Peoria County, Illinois	43,812	93.8	30.5	31,620	90.7	23.4
Rock Island County, Illinois	36,224	88.6	22.8	27,641	89.6	24.0
St. Clair County, Illinois	69,052	90.8	30.1	42,002	88.4	21.9
Sangamon County, Illinois	51,870	94.4	33.1	36,051	91.9	32.2
Tazewell County, Illinois	33,996	94.3	25.4	26,052	94.5	24.1
Vermilion County, Illinois	19,774	89.3	11.7	14,607	91.4	13.0
Will County, Illinois	189,970	92.1	36.0	93,453	90.3	26.2
Williamson County, Illinois	16,623	93.6	29.6	13,178	89.2	23.8
Winnebago County, Illinois	73,618	90.7	23.0	50,631	88.5	25.5
INDIANA	1,705,456	90.1	25.8	1,084,472	88.0	21.7
Allen County, Indiana	91,031	87.3	28.1	56,762	91.3	24.2
Bartholomew County, Indiana	20,069	92.0	31.5	13,926	92.6	25.3
Boone County, Indiana	17,880	94.4	52.4	9,416	95.1	37.7
Clark County, Indiana	30,050	92.2	24.7	19,601	88.4	16.8
Delaware County, Indiana	27,484	91.0	21.4	20,305	92.1	24.3
Elkhart County, Indiana	49,488	83.1	19.0	31,486	83.4	21.0
Floyd County, Indiana	20,945	91.9	29.6	12,963	89.2	19.9
Grant County, Indiana	17,197	89.0	26.2	12,613	84.1	12.9
Hamilton County, Indiana	88,414	97.8	64.0	44,650	94.6	47.3
Hancock County, Indiana	21,263	87.7	31.7	13,327	79.2	13.0
Hendricks County, Indiana	44,356	96.7	38.4	24,479	93.9	27.3
Howard County, Indiana	21,881	89.7	17.1	15,697	92.4	23.2
Johnson County, Indiana	41,346	91.9	29.5	23,720	90.7	21.0
Kosciusko County, Indiana	20,681	83.4	22.6	13,523	84.5	27.0
Lake County, Indiana	128,067	90.5	22.5	82,394	85.4	19.8
LaPorte County, Indiana	30,430	92.0	15.9	19,688	89.1	19.2
Madison County, Indiana	34,608	89.8	16.6	24,609	88.0	16.4
Marion County, Indiana	224,265	86.3	28.2	124,041	86.4	25.2
Monroe County, Indiana	29,166	95.1	39.7	19,781	92.3	41.7

Table C-2. Educational Attainment of the Population, by Selected Counties, 2019—*Continued*

(Number; percent; dollars.)

State/County	Population 25 to 34 years			Population 35 to 44 years		
	Total	High school graduate or more (percent)	Bachelor's degree or more (percent)	Total	High school graduate or more (percent)	Bachelor's degree or more (percent)
INDIANA—(*Continued*)						
Morgan County, Indiana	7,958	95.5	10.4	8,707	91.6	14.4
Porter County, Indiana	20,423	94.2	25.7	22,705	95.8	31.9
St. Joseph County, Indiana	36,641	92.1	35.7	30,967	89.3	38.1
Tippecanoe County, Indiana	27,971	91.3	48.0	20,848	88.7	40.9
Vanderburgh County, Indiana	25,155	90.1	31.4	22,247	91.3	32.7
Vigo County, Indiana	14,001	89.3	24.7	11,703	91.9	30.2
Wayne County, Indiana	7,374	90.3	19.4	7,587	90.5	19.7
IOWA	400,299	94.3	36.1	392,097	92.3	35.1
Black Hawk County, Iowa	16,730	94.4	35.7	15,205	93.5	47.6
Dallas County, Iowa	13,700	98.7	65.3	15,777	97.0	66.0
Dubuque County, Iowa	11,724	97.7	46.6	10,739	96.2	39.3
Johnson County, Iowa	21,757	94.6	63.4	18,323	95.6	56.6
Linn County, Iowa	31,159	95.9	37.2	28,206	96.1	36.3
Polk County, Iowa	74,289	95.1	46.5	69,208	91.2	40.3
Pottawattamie County, Iowa	10,881	94.9	24.4	11,729	91.3	28.9
Scott County, Iowa	22,407	94.9	34.1	22,621	96.2	38.5
Story County, Iowa	15,877	98.9	57.9	9,638	97.0	58.2
Woodbury County, Iowa	13,711	88.7	16.8	13,577	74.7	21.5
KANSAS	377,373	93.0	37.3	362,905	90.2	37.7
Butler County, Kansas	7,131	92.8	38.6	9,689	90.5	35.5
Douglas County, Kansas	17,335	97.4	47.7	14,236	92.7	51.5
Johnson County, Kansas	82,070	95.7	58.5	85,318	95.5	60.7
Leavenworth County, Kansas	10,301	95.1	22.2	11,014	94.0	46.2
Riley County, Kansas	12,610	98.7	49.7	7,011	97.2	52.4
Sedgwick County, Kansas	73,745	92.0	34.3	64,319	89.2	33.4
Shawnee County, Kansas	21,735	96.5	33.5	20,383	87.9	29.3
Wyandotte County, Kansas	25,313	86.9	28.8	22,197	73.9	18.7
KENTUCKY	576,692	91.8	30.1	556,896	89.7	29.3
Boone County, Kentucky	15,520	95.2	34.9	18,609	91.0	42.1
Bullitt County, Kentucky	10,543	100.0	23.4	11,319	93.4	25.1
Campbell County, Kentucky	13,347	96.0	59.2	11,450	92.2	41.0
Christian County, Kentucky	12,527	90.4	16.5	6,883	87.9	25.1
Daviess County, Kentucky	12,949	86.2	30.6	13,095	87.1	33.9
Fayette County, Kentucky	49,777	93.4	48.3	43,578	92.2	48.4
Hardin County, Kentucky	15,126	95.4	22.3	14,568	91.4	29.4
Jefferson County, Kentucky	113,270	96.1	45.9	96,390	91.0	38.4
Kenton County, Kentucky	24,473	89.0	40.6	21,679	93.6	39.4
McCracken County, Kentucky	7,255	86.9	18.0	7,801	88.9	36.0
Madison County, Kentucky	11,633	89.7	43.9	11,145	92.8	37.6
Oldham County, Kentucky	6,720	89.9	36.9	9,100	96.3	45.8
Warren County, Kentucky	17,869	91.4	39.9	16,961	85.5	28.1
LOUISIANA	643,422	87.8	28.3	606,785	87.2	27.9
Ascension Parish, Louisiana	18,463	90.9	27.2	18,336	97.8	30.0
Bossier Parish, Louisiana	17,804	91.5	19.0	18,176	83.9	22.9
Caddo Parish, Louisiana	32,347	85.1	21.8	29,268	87.1	22.3
Calcasieu Parish, Louisiana	28,579	80.8	16.9	26,020	89.0	27.6
East Baton Rouge Parish, Louisiana	64,420	91.5	41.3	54,403	88.6	37.3
Iberia Parish, Louisiana	9,388	85.3	18.1	8,403	91.1	19.8
Jefferson Parish, Louisiana	61,606	91.8	32.6	54,288	90.2	31.0
Lafayette Parish, Louisiana	38,773	94.0	45.3	33,205	90.3	35.5
Lafourche Parish, Louisiana	14,110	81.8	23.3	11,587	89.5	16.7
Livingston Parish, Louisiana	20,688	79.3	27.8	19,528	81.1	30.7
Orleans Parish, Louisiana	66,383	91.2	47.1	55,768	88.7	43.7
Ouachita Parish, Louisiana	21,516	88.7	29.1	19,275	90.3	29.0
Rapides Parish, Louisiana	16,419	87.6	17.5	16,324	82.2	19.9
St. Landry Parish, Louisiana	10,354	74.4	8.9	9,484	79.8	14.3
St. Tammany Parish, Louisiana	28,744	91.1	42.3	34,802	90.7	45.2
Tangipahoa Parish, Louisiana	17,356	89.4	21.5	17,294	85.6	31.4
Terrebonne Parish, Louisiana	17,381	88.1	23.8	13,885	80.9	11.7
MAINE	164,231	94.9	35.5	153,615	96.3	37.4
Androscoggin County, Maine	12,846	98.7	25.8	13,432	92.3	30.5
Aroostook County, Maine	6,660	97.0	20.9	7,042	98.3	21.1
Cumberland County, Maine	41,032	96.0	55.6	36,867	98.1	58.2

Table C-2. Educational Attainment of the Population, by Selected Counties, 2019—*Continued*

(Number; percent; dollars.)

State/County	Population 45 to 64 years			Population 65 years and over		
	Total	High school graduate or more (percent)	Bachelor's degree or more (percent)	Total	High school graduate or more (percent)	Bachelor's degree or more (percent)
INDIANA—(*Continued*)						
Morgan County, Indiana	20,390	90.3	21.0	11,945	86.6	17.9
Porter County, Indiana	45,512	96.7	29.9	28,481	92.0	22.3
St. Joseph County, Indiana	67,423	90.2	26.0	43,445	89.7	26.4
Tippecanoe County, Indiana	37,314	90.2	35.7	22,470	92.2	33.3
Vanderburgh County, Indiana	45,451	92.9	27.1	31,414	87.6	21.6
Vigo County, Indiana	26,013	93.9	22.8	17,913	92.1	28.0
Wayne County, Indiana	17,452	87.8	17.2	12,721	85.4	16.4
IOWA	777,033	93.1	27.0	553,575	91.0	23.6
Black Hawk County, Iowa	29,510	91.1	20.7	22,210	93.7	27.0
Dallas County, Iowa	20,348	95.6	46.7	11,309	96.1	37.5
Dubuque County, Iowa	24,788	95.3	28.7	17,821	89.7	24.9
Johnson County, Iowa	30,698	93.5	48.6	18,383	93.7	48.5
Linn County, Iowa	57,978	94.6	34.4	36,529	90.3	24.7
Polk County, Iowa	116,484	91.6	33.2	66,693	91.1	32.2
Pottawattamie County, Iowa	24,567	89.3	23.2	16,718	90.5	18.6
Scott County, Iowa	44,743	93.4	30.5	28,405	87.4	27.1
Story County, Iowa	16,888	97.7	48.6	12,455	95.4	41.9
Woodbury County, Iowa	24,138	89.4	25.7	15,461	88.0	20.4
KANSAS	699,807	91.9	33.0	477,996	91.7	30.1
Butler County, Kansas	16,541	95.2	30.1	10,731	92.3	23.0
Douglas County, Kansas	24,651	96.0	47.7	16,116	93.0	41.6
Johnson County, Kansas	151,458	96.6	57.9	90,478	96.3	46.2
Leavenworth County, Kansas	21,286	90.8	28.0	11,998	92.7	33.0
Riley County, Kansas	10,556	95.7	33.8	7,150	95.2	46.7
Sedgwick County, Kansas	122,810	89.9	30.0	76,878	90.3	29.0
Shawnee County, Kansas	45,331	93.2	30.5	33,269	96.2	32.3
Wyandotte County, Kansas	37,466	82.1	16.6	20,669	77.3	15.9
KENTUCKY	1,160,295	87.5	23.5	754,559	81.4	20.8
Boone County, Kentucky	34,819	91.7	28.5	18,480	92.0	25.5
Bullitt County, Kentucky	22,532	89.4	12.8	13,595	73.8	6.3
Campbell County, Kentucky	24,555	94.7	36.4	15,439	81.9	28.6
Christian County, Kentucky	12,534	79.6	16.1	9,272	83.8	30.5
Daviess County, Kentucky	25,496	88.7	20.1	17,446	85.5	20.3
Fayette County, Kentucky	73,996	92.6	43.3	44,226	91.3	40.6
Hardin County, Kentucky	28,500	92.0	23.2	16,389	87.7	21.3
Jefferson County, Kentucky	195,467	90.6	31.7	127,864	89.1	28.2
Kenton County, Kentucky	42,201	92.2	29.5	24,769	88.8	24.8
McCracken County, Kentucky	17,755	91.1	27.4	12,684	88.3	17.5
Madison County, Kentucky	21,151	93.4	28.7	13,155	87.0	25.8
Oldham County, Kentucky	19,088	96.5	41.9	10,021	89.3	39.0
Warren County, Kentucky	29,455	90.0	36.5	16,863	90.8	35.9
LOUISIANA	1,147,800	86.3	23.1	742,194	82.9	22.7
Ascension Parish, Louisiana	29,479	91.8	27.8	16,400	88.2	15.3
Bossier Parish, Louisiana	30,230	92.5	26.0	18,513	93.4	18.8
Caddo Parish, Louisiana	58,647	87.0	22.8	42,950	86.9	27.4
Calcasieu Parish, Louisiana	48,780	89.3	24.4	30,859	83.7	22.4
East Baton Rouge Parish, Louisiana	98,906	92.0	31.8	63,648	90.9	31.0
Iberia Parish, Louisiana	17,944	82.6	14.8	11,153	81.7	13.8
Jefferson Parish, Louisiana	112,047	86.3	25.9	77,091	84.2	24.8
Lafayette Parish, Louisiana	58,733	90.1	30.7	33,177	84.5	29.4
Lafourche Parish, Louisiana	24,554	78.3	14.9	16,179	66.7	13.5
Livingston Parish, Louisiana	33,745	83.9	16.9	18,937	83.3	12.3
Orleans Parish, Louisiana	96,670	86.8	35.1	60,584	83.9	35.0
Ouachita Parish, Louisiana	36,374	85.4	21.4	23,540	84.4	27.6
Rapides Parish, Louisiana	32,109	88.9	17.6	21,615	83.6	22.9
St. Landry Parish, Louisiana	20,464	85.8	12.7	13,893	63.8	10.4
St. Tammany Parish, Louisiana	70,421	92.0	32.2	45,049	90.3	31.3
Tangipahoa Parish, Louisiana	32,509	85.4	21.5	20,096	78.4	27.1
Terrebonne Parish, Louisiana	27,262	81.8	16.8	16,520	71.2	9.7
MAINE	387,328	94.0	31.4	285,978	89.6	32.0
Androscoggin County, Maine	30,038	92.3	25.1	19,521	83.6	21.0
Aroostook County, Maine	19,629	93.5	21.7	16,738	82.5	14.0
Cumberland County, Maine	82,154	95.2	49.4	56,357	91.4	42.0

Table C-2. Educational Attainment of the Population, by Selected Counties, 2019—*Continued*

(Number; percent; dollars.)

State/County	Population 25 to 34 years			Population 35 to 44 years		
	Total	High school graduate or more (percent)	Bachelor's degree or more (percent)	Total	High school graduate or more (percent)	Bachelor's degree or more (percent)
MAINE—(*Continued*)						
Kennebec County, Maine	14,652	93.2	30.8	13,543	98.0	32.3
Penobscot County, Maine	20,402	93.9	38.6	16,739	96.0	31.3
York County, Maine	26,507	94.6	29.3	23,414	96.1	36.0
MARYLAND	820,575	93.2	43.3	786,924	89.8	45.4
Allegany County, Maryland	8,474	91.3	21.1	8,040	91.0	22.8
Anne Arundel County, Maryland	80,901	94.4	45.2	78,156	92.9	50.4
Baltimore County, Maryland	112,414	96.1	41.6	102,514	91.4	47.5
Calvert County, Maryland	10,840	96.0	21.9	12,128	97.9	45.0
Carroll County, Maryland	18,775	96.8	37.0	19,097	97.3	55.1
Cecil County, Maryland	13,039	94.0	30.7	12,196	95.1	36.6
Charles County, Maryland	20,003	94.7	28.8	21,957	94.1	32.5
Frederick County, Maryland	32,755	95.0	46.6	36,349	88.8	47.3
Harford County, Maryland	31,957	95.0	40.4	32,228	94.6	46.1
Howard County, Maryland	39,117	96.7	66.6	46,325	94.9	67.1
Montgomery County, Maryland	131,637	91.4	53.4	144,468	88.4	58.2
Prince George's County, Maryland	132,059	90.3	38.0	121,793	82.6	34.0
St. Mary's County, Maryland	14,973	94.8	34.2	14,409	92.4	30.0
Washington County, Maryland	19,772	91.8	27.5	19,253	87.5	25.4
Wicomico County, Maryland	11,366	87.4	33.2	12,370	89.2	30.0
Baltimore city, Maryland	112,273	92.5	47.5	77,086	88.1	38.0
MASSACHUSETTS	992,607	94.4	54.3	849,654	93.0	51.2
Barnstable County, Massachusetts	19,619	97.0	39.6	19,425	91.5	44.0
Berkshire County, Massachusetts	12,954	95.2	35.3	13,456	89.9	42.8
Bristol County, Massachusetts	73,643	93.0	38.5	69,349	90.7	33.0
Essex County, Massachusetts	99,576	92.3	40.5	95,478	88.3	45.8
Franklin County, Massachusetts	8,158	91.9	44.2	8,560	93.7	40.6
Hampden County, Massachusetts	62,850	86.2	29.1	55,090	90.7	31.6
Hampshire County, Massachusetts	16,201	96.6	62.4	15,192	95.6	58.4
Middlesex County, Massachusetts	250,181	96.5	67.4	214,315	95.8	66.0
Norfolk County, Massachusetts	91,608	96.3	66.8	89,756	94.3	64.5
Plymouth County, Massachusetts	57,432	94.8	38.9	58,999	94.2	45.0
Suffolk County, Massachusetts	188,441	95.1	66.7	104,922	91.1	52.1
Worcester County, Massachusetts	108,696	94.0	42.8	100,582	94.0	41.7
MICHIGAN	1,302,017	92.8	34.0	1,174,029	91.4	34.9
Allegan County, Michigan	14,433	95.3	27.2	14,604	91.4	23.2
Bay County, Michigan	12,189	94.9	23.9	12,164	91.7	28.4
Berrien County, Michigan	18,354	91.8	26.3	17,242	93.0	27.1
Calhoun County, Michigan	16,572	91.5	21.8	16,100	88.5	21.9
Clinton County, Michigan	9,518	95.5	37.7	9,411	96.6	44.7
Eaton County, Michigan	14,496	94.4	35.3	12,675	95.0	30.3
Genesee County, Michigan	50,664	92.3	22.5	46,993	89.7	24.2
Grand Traverse County, Michigan	12,064	99.1	46.1	10,647	91.8	38.4
Ingham County, Michigan	41,508	95.3	44.7	34,268	91.5	44.5
Isabella County, Michigan	9,127	91.4	26.8	6,870	90.0	30.2
Jackson County, Michigan	20,163	92.7	29.8	18,814	91.4	24.3
Kalamazoo County, Michigan	34,127	93.7	41.0	32,551	91.6	43.5
Kent County, Michigan	104,524	93.2	41.9	83,776	92.4	38.9
Lapeer County, Michigan	9,677	91.9	22.5	9,567	87.5	23.3
Lenawee County, Michigan	10,879	90.3	14.8	12,184	87.7	25.9
Livingston County, Michigan	21,397	97.7	38.1	22,589	95.1	49.0
Macomb County, Michigan	119,593	92.2	30.4	104,359	91.8	29.3
Marquette County, Michigan	7,623	96.7	41.8	7,554	97.3	39.4
Midland County, Michigan	10,131	96.1	47.3	10,533	96.1	41.7
Monroe County, Michigan	17,660	92.5	24.0	17,673	96.3	29.7
Muskegon County, Michigan	22,270	91.5	17.8	20,035	95.1	25.3
Oakland County, Michigan	168,474	97.1	56.4	156,835	95.9	57.9
Ottawa County, Michigan	34,465	96.5	41.8	36,769	90.8	38.3
Saginaw County, Michigan	24,168	86.0	24.4	20,400	90.0	32.8
St. Clair County, Michigan	18,212	94.7	23.6	17,156	91.4	31.0
Shiawassee County, Michigan	8,055	88.8	19.5	7,782	91.3	28.5
Van Buren County, Michigan	8,817	94.6	24.5	8,639	82.2	26.3
Washtenaw County, Michigan	52,674	96.9	62.6	44,329	94.6	59.0
Wayne County, Michigan	253,346	90.0	26.6	204,189	87.7	28.2
MINNESOTA	765,578	94.7	43.1	730,399	94.1	43.4
Anoka County, Minnesota	47,577	96.1	39.1	49,136	94.2	37.7

Table C-2. Educational Attainment of the Population, by Selected Counties, 2019—*Continued*

(Number; percent; dollars.)

State/County	Population 45 to 64 years			Population 65 years and over		
	Total	High school graduate or more (percent)	Bachelor's degree or more (percent)	Total	High school graduate or more (percent)	Bachelor's degree or more (percent)
MAINE—*(Continued)*						
Kennebec County, Maine..................................	36,144	92.9	28.4	25,197	91.4	26.4
Penobscot County, Maine	42,724	95.4	27.2	29,426	87.2	25.2
York County, Maine..	60,900	94.3	29.6	43,845	90.5	36.9
MARYLAND	1,616,472	91.6	40.5	959,887	86.5	35.7
Allegany County, Maryland..............................	18,386	94.6	22.7	14,540	82.6	18.2
Anne Arundel County, Maryland........................	154,221	94.3	44.7	86,827	89.3	35.5
Baltimore County, Maryland.............................	216,090	94.0	41.4	144,959	86.5	34.5
Calvert County, Maryland................................	27,226	95.1	31.4	14,177	94.9	28.3
Carroll County, Maryland................................	50,193	95.9	35.8	29,178	89.9	28.0
Cecil County, Maryland...................................	29,704	91.1	20.0	16,653	85.8	21.4
Charles County, Maryland	47,629	93.4	28.8	20,605	88.2	24.4
Frederick County, Maryland.............................	69,534	95.3	41.7	39,294	88.3	33.2
Harford County, Maryland...............................	72,565	96.0	35.2	42,286	88.3	30.5
Howard County, Maryland...............................	88,608	95.9	65.3	46,628	92.6	58.1
Montgomery County, Maryland.........................	281,979	91.0	59.6	169,044	89.7	57.7
Prince George's County, Maryland	242,190	88.0	33.7	126,253	83.8	28.3
St. Mary's County, Maryland...........................	30,259	90.9	33.2	15,380	82.9	22.8
Washington County, Maryland	40,805	89.0	21.9	26,370	83.5	17.5
Wicomico County, Maryland	25,266	82.2	30.3	16,726	86.0	28.2
Baltimore city, Maryland	141,926	85.4	25.3	86,265	75.3	23.7
MASSACHUSETTS	1,836,022	91.7	43.2	1,172,293	86.9	35.4
Barnstable County, Massachusetts	61,357	97.2	47.0	67,161	97.2	50.3
Berkshire County, Massachusetts	35,760	92.8	30.6	30,073	91.3	33.2
Bristol County, Massachusetts.........................	158,247	87.4	30.1	98,058	76.4	21.6
Essex County, Massachusetts..........................	218,388	89.9	43.9	138,702	86.9	35.0
Franklin County, Massachusetts.......................	20,350	92.4	30.9	16,308	90.9	40.0
Hampden County, Massachusetts	120,977	88.6	30.0	81,066	81.9	21.2
Hampshire County, Massachusetts	39,819	96.9	51.5	29,362	90.7	45.9
Middlesex County, Massachusetts	420,714	94.1	54.7	252,684	89.5	43.9
Norfolk County, Massachusetts........................	194,431	94.9	54.8	121,964	90.0	39.9
Plymouth County, Massachusetts......................	152,625	92.9	38.0	97,281	91.3	33.9
Suffolk County, Massachusetts.........................	171,842	84.4	35.9	98,983	76.8	30.1
Worcester County, Massachusetts	234,361	93.0	36.9	133,813	86.8	28.7
MICHIGAN..	2,652,172	92.1	29.0	1,766,409	89.1	25.5
Allegan County, Michigan................................	31,855	91.1	24.1	20,267	92.0	20.9
Bay County, Michigan	29,177	94.6	17.1	21,387	90.3	22.5
Berrien County, Michigan................................	40,781	90.5	25.1	30,964	87.9	29.9
Calhoun County, Michigan	34,574	92.9	20.8	24,494	88.1	17.3
Clinton County, Michigan	22,044	95.1	33.6	13,961	93.9	24.3
Eaton County, Michigan	29,179	96.6	30.2	21,358	94.5	23.9
Genesee County, Michigan	110,071	91.9	22.8	73,209	87.2	17.2
Grand Traverse County, Michigan	25,616	96.3	36.5	19,494	91.8	38.6
Ingham County, Michigan	63,382	94.9	36.4	40,447	92.0	39.0
Isabella County, Michigan	14,693	90.1	26.2	9,296	93.3	26.7
Jackson County, Michigan	43,340	90.2	19.5	29,127	87.8	22.5
Kalamazoo County, Michigan...........................	58,972	92.6	36.3	40,433	91.8	34.5
Kent County, Michigan....................................	157,154	91.8	34.1	92,706	88.7	31.3
Lapeer County, Michigan................................	26,996	92.8	19.1	16,432	91.0	15.1
Lenawee County, Michigan	26,734	91.1	21.0	19,291	90.5	22.4
Livingston County, Michigan	58,484	96.5	35.1	34,335	90.2	26.5
Macomb County, Michigan	245,938	90.9	25.5	152,309	88.3	18.3
Marquette County, Michigan............................	16,267	93.4	30.8	13,097	95.4	34.3
Midland County, Michigan...............................	22,448	93.9	36.5	15,469	92.5	25.3
Monroe County, Michigan...............................	43,353	92.4	26.6	28,377	84.5	18.6
Muskegon County, Michigan............................	46,249	92.1	19.7	30,391	90.6	21.9
Oakland County, Michigan...............................	353,397	95.6	47.5	217,490	91.3	38.8
Ottawa County, Michigan................................	67,106	94.1	36.4	45,530	89.9	27.6
Saginaw County, Michigan..............................	50,744	92.6	19.7	37,154	88.2	17.0
St. Clair County, Michigan..............................	47,544	90.3	17.8	30,992	92.0	21.3
Shiawassee County, Michigan..........................	19,595	94.0	16.7	13,061	90.4	12.7
Van Buren County, Michigan............................	20,838	90.2	21.6	14,475	85.2	22.4
Washtenaw County, Michigan..........................	82,670	96.4	53.8	53,252	92.7	49.8
Wayne County, Michigan................................	453,398	88.6	25.2	276,636	84.3	21.0
MINNESOTA..	1,429,744	94.2	35.8	921,491	91.4	29.8
Anoka County, Minnesota	96,952	95.2	32.6	51,730	91.0	20.1

Table C-2. Educational Attainment of the Population, by Selected Counties, 2019—*Continued*

(Number; percent; dollars.)

	Population 25 to 34 years			Population 35 to 44 years		
State/County	Total	High school graduate or more (percent)	Bachelor's degree or more (percent)	Total	High school graduate or more (percent)	Bachelor's degree or more (percent)
MINNESOTA—(*Continued*)						
Blue Earth County, Minnesota	8,801	96.7	39.1	7,506	97.4	48.9
Carver County, Minnesota	11,399	93.9	53.9	15,204	94.5	59.7
Crow Wing County, Minnesota	7,054	96.8	24.0	7,312	96.5	28.5
Dakota County, Minnesota	54,344	94.9	44.3	59,586	94.3	47.5
Hennepin County, Minnesota	213,168	95.4	58.3	175,820	94.1	56.7
Olmsted County, Minnesota	24,136	93.9	56.6	19,132	98.1	62.7
Ramsey County, Minnesota	92,000	94.6	47.9	70,355	91.2	46.2
Rice County, Minnesota	7,375	98.9	30.7	7,906	86.7	30.5
St. Louis County, Minnesota	23,225	95.5	33.7	23,528	96.7	34.5
Scott County, Minnesota	18,603	95.5	35.5	22,386	94.8	51.7
Sherburne County, Minnesota	12,520	95.6	20.2	14,026	94.8	28.6
Stearns County, Minnesota	18,913	93.5	31.3	18,991	92.6	30.8
Washington County, Minnesota	30,151	97.3	45.5	36,438	97.0	52.2
Wright County, Minnesota	16,380	98.1	38.9	19,461	97.0	46.2
MISSISSIPPI	368,227	88.5	22.8	379,610	87.5	23.3
DeSoto County, Mississippi	24,222	92.7	30.9	26,139	90.5	33.3
Forrest County, Mississippi	10,535	94.9	25.2	9,217	81.4	18.6
Harrison County, Mississippi	26,102	93.7	22.9	26,382	92.4	18.2
Hinds County, Mississippi	33,303	92.4	34.8	27,897	87.3	28.5
Jackson County, Mississippi	17,585	91.9	23.0	18,809	92.9	25.4
Jones County, Mississippi	8,846	86.7	12.8	8,300	81.2	17.5
Lauderdale County, Mississippi	9,931	75.5	26.8	8,985	81.0	16.4
Lee County, Mississippi	9,246	87.7	29.3	12,116	85.9	34.2
Madison County, Mississippi	13,136	93.0	54.3	15,858	89.8	47.6
Rankin County, Mississippi	22,437	89.9	21.5	21,975	86.7	37.4
MISSOURI	823,722	93.2	35.5	756,709	92.0	35.5
Boone County, Missouri	27,796	94.0	50.3	21,286	97.9	49.1
Buchanan County, Missouri	12,193	89.9	19.5	10,851	92.4	22.7
Cape Girardeau County, Missouri	10,191	96.8	39.0	8,496	89.5	43.3
Cass County, Missouri	13,075	93.2	28.8	13,138	90.8	26.2
Christian County, Missouri	11,900	94.4	27.6	12,347	86.6	36.3
Clay County, Missouri	35,481	96.2	35.0	34,011	94.4	35.8
Cole County, Missouri	10,130	92.1	32.6	10,040	87.3	34.9
Franklin County, Missouri	12,523	92.8	19.3	11,998	93.8	20.6
Greene County, Missouri	41,705	92.7	31.2	33,812	91.5	35.2
Jackson County, Missouri	109,697	92.8	39.4	89,807	92.1	37.0
Jasper County, Missouri	17,395	92.3	24.2	14,992	86.0	30.7
Jefferson County, Missouri	27,721	93.9	26.1	30,441	93.9	24.1
Platte County, Missouri	13,579	99.3	46.6	14,708	95.6	48.5
St. Charles County, Missouri	51,308	96.8	51.2	54,927	93.5	47.2
St. Francois County, Missouri	10,799	92.1	12.5	9,383	84.4	15.8
St. Louis County, Missouri	128,856	96.5	48.5	120,691	95.9	53.1
St. Louis city, Missouri	61,329	94.8	54.6	39,963	93.4	47.3
MONTANA	133,119	94.1	37.5	132,472	95.1	39.5
Cascade County, Montana	10,975	93.8	27.3	9,443	95.3	38.4
Flathead County, Montana	12,378	94.5	51.9	13,517	97.0	40.0
Gallatin County, Montana	19,041	97.9	55.5	14,983	96.7	57.3
Lewis and Clark County, Montana	8,716	98.5	43.0	8,300	96.3	54.5
Missoula County, Montana	18,717	95.7	38.5	16,379	90.3	51.3
Yellowstone County, Montana	21,717	91.9	39.4	21,738	98.6	33.9
NEBRASKA	257,931	93.4	39.4	243,052	92.4	41.5
Douglas County, Nebraska	87,633	92.4	46.5	77,929	90.6	50.4
Lancaster County, Nebraska	43,126	96.7	48.2	40,761	92.0	45.1
Sarpy County, Nebraska	27,109	98.0	37.7	25,989	97.5	50.8
NEVADA	449,055	88.7	24.2	410,321	84.3	26.9
Clark County, Nevada	337,397	88.5	23.8	313,092	84.1	26.6
Washoe County, Nevada	70,847	91.1	31.5	59,214	83.5	34.0
NEW HAMPSHIRE	170,730	94.9	40.4	158,985	94.4	44.5
Cheshire County, New Hampshire	9,137	92.4	34.2	7,739	95.3	38.2
Grafton County, New Hampshire	11,119	94.1	48.3	9,754	96.9	45.0
Hillsborough County, New Hampshire	57,502	93.6	41.2	52,499	93.4	46.5

Table C-2. Educational Attainment of the Population, by Selected Counties, 2019—*Continued*

(Number; percent; dollars.)

State/County	Population 45 to 64 years			Population 65 years and over		
	Total	High school graduate or more (percent)	Bachelor's degree or more (percent)	Total	High school graduate or more (percent)	Bachelor's degree or more (percent)
MINNESOTA—(*Continued*)						
Blue Earth County, Minnesota	13,321	95.9	32.6	9,583	95.0	29.9
Carver County, Minnesota	29,692	95.2	53.4	12,880	90.0	37.7
Crow Wing County, Minnesota	17,551	94.7	24.5	14,977	94.0	25.5
Dakota County, Minnesota	113,626	96.6	42.6	63,145	95.3	36.7
Hennepin County, Minnesota	309,675	93.6	47.1	183,735	93.5	42.6
Olmsted County, Minnesota	39,348	95.2	41.0	25,630	92.3	35.8
Ramsey County, Minnesota	125,718	89.4	41.2	81,952	90.5	38.0
Rice County, Minnesota	16,301	93.4	32.1	10,615	95.4	32.4
St. Louis County, Minnesota	51,086	95.3	28.8	39,925	92.8	26.6
Scott County, Minnesota	39,470	95.6	44.4	16,735	88.9	27.1
Sherburne County, Minnesota	25,875	96.0	27.9	11,321	92.5	28.5
Stearns County, Minnesota	36,553	92.6	27.9	25,716	83.9	20.5
Washington County, Minnesota	72,565	96.6	47.1	40,140	94.9	37.8
Wright County, Minnesota	35,763	96.0	30.1	18,523	94.7	23.3
MISSISSIPPI	745,023	86.4	22.1	486,804	79.5	21.6
DeSoto County, Mississippi	46,998	90.0	27.9	24,408	87.7	20.4
Forrest County, Mississippi	16,971	90.9	26.9	10,467	85.4	27.2
Harrison County, Mississippi	52,503	87.5	26.5	31,828	86.2	22.9
Hinds County, Mississippi	55,788	91.8	25.5	34,113	78.4	29.1
Jackson County, Mississippi	38,445	90.8	22.1	24,142	85.7	25.9
Jones County, Mississippi	15,146	88.1	22.7	12,331	87.2	18.8
Lauderdale County, Mississippi	19,230	82.7	17.9	12,915	81.3	15.3
Lee County, Mississippi	21,281	82.4	19.4	12,946	80.7	23.4
Madison County, Mississippi	27,244	95.3	49.3	14,419	84.0	44.0
Rankin County, Mississippi	38,415	92.8	30.9	24,321	87.5	30.5
MISSOURI	1,567,788	90.8	29.1	1,057,943	87.6	24.0
Boone County, Missouri	37,948	92.0	45.1	22,375	91.6	43.8
Buchanan County, Missouri	23,475	88.9	21.2	14,187	88.5	14.5
Cape Girardeau County, Missouri	19,801	91.4	32.0	13,029	86.9	28.4
Cass County, Missouri	27,873	94.6	25.8	18,166	94.2	23.0
Christian County, Missouri	21,891	91.1	33.7	13,792	88.9	17.1
Clay County, Missouri	63,952	95.4	32.3	36,070	89.5	26.0
Cole County, Missouri	20,908	95.7	34.9	13,632	89.7	28.7
Franklin County, Missouri	29,760	89.2	21.6	18,590	84.6	16.7
Greene County, Missouri	68,211	91.9	29.4	48,792	90.3	26.7
Jackson County, Missouri	173,239	91.0	29.5	107,972	90.5	26.7
Jasper County, Missouri	28,182	84.2	23.2	19,325	80.3	18.5
Jefferson County, Missouri	64,352	89.7	18.1	34,512	82.2	14.1
Platte County, Missouri	28,121	94.2	44.1	15,471	96.5	37.6
St. Charles County, Missouri	106,797	94.5	38.4	63,307	92.5	28.9
St. Francois County, Missouri	17,027	85.1	15.2	11,275	85.2	12.8
St. Louis County, Missouri	259,512	93.5	46.5	184,375	91.7	37.3
St. Louis city, Missouri	73,444	87.9	27.3	43,268	81.4	26.9
MONTANA	268,450	95.3	31.3	207,909	92.4	30.2
Cascade County, Montana	18,823	92.7	21.2	15,378	90.4	21.8
Flathead County, Montana	27,730	98.2	27.5	20,928	93.2	33.7
Gallatin County, Montana	24,064	99.3	49.3	15,501	96.4	50.3
Lewis and Clark County, Montana	18,750	96.7	43.4	13,692	95.9	41.1
Missoula County, Montana	27,182	98.5	45.8	19,518	96.3	42.5
Yellowstone County, Montana	40,157	93.9	31.8	28,393	90.8	28.7
NEBRASKA	458,492	91.4	30.7	312,295	91.5	25.4
Douglas County, Nebraska	131,607	90.9	38.4	76,854	92.8	32.3
Lancaster County, Nebraska	69,089	91.8	37.1	45,473	92.9	33.2
Sarpy County, Nebraska	44,702	96.0	40.7	22,739	94.3	25.7
NEVADA	778,871	86.0	24.9	498,219	88.5	27.3
Clark County, Nevada	567,799	85.4	25.0	342,659	87.8	27.6
Washoe County, Nevada	118,529	88.4	29.8	79,563	90.9	32.1
NEW HAMPSHIRE	396,888	93.6	35.4	253,147	90.9	34.7
Cheshire County, New Hampshire	21,062	96.1	31.5	15,759	92.2	35.0
Grafton County, New Hampshire	24,395	91.1	38.7	18,912	87.1	39.0
Hillsborough County, New Hampshire	120,458	92.4	35.1	67,143	90.1	32.9

Table C-2. Educational Attainment of the Population, by Selected Counties, 2019—*Continued*

(Number; percent; dollars.)

State/County	Population 25 to 34 years			Population 35 to 44 years		
	Total	High school graduate or more (percent)	Bachelor's degree or more (percent)	Total	High school graduate or more (percent)	Bachelor's degree or more (percent)
NEW HAMPSHIRE—(*Continued*)						
Merrimack County, New Hampshire	18,504	95.2	38.1	17,547	93.6	46.7
Rockingham County, New Hampshire	37,790	96.5	49.1	36,416	97.4	50.0
Strafford County, New Hampshire	16,863	96.9	39.5	15,395	95.6	38.5
NEW JERSEY	1,148,458	94.0	47.8	1,144,104	90.8	48.3
Atlantic County, New Jersey	30,123	91.9	30.3	31,483	88.3	31.3
Bergen County, New Jersey	108,207	95.3	59.1	123,814	94.3	63.3
Burlington County, New Jersey	56,063	96.2	45.0	55,312	94.1	46.7
Camden County, New Jersey	70,845	94.8	39.5	64,658	92.7	39.0
Cape May County, New Jersey	9,238	97.2	28.0	8,845	91.7	29.9
Cumberland County, New Jersey	22,023	82.9	11.8	19,775	78.0	15.2
Essex County, New Jersey	110,494	92.3	37.2	110,820	87.9	40.8
Gloucester County, New Jersey	34,872	97.7	43.4	37,169	94.5	42.2
Hudson County, New Jersey	141,570	95.9	66.5	107,686	89.3	53.4
Hunterdon County, New Jersey	12,105	91.6	58.2	14,168	91.1	59.7
Mercer County, New Jersey	45,746	90.2	48.5	46,358	90.3	50.2
Middlesex County, New Jersey	109,141	94.0	51.3	113,602	89.1	52.7
Monmouth County, New Jersey	68,193	96.8	51.9	71,431	92.5	57.2
Morris County, New Jersey	54,285	97.9	63.5	59,988	92.6	63.9
Ocean County, New Jersey	66,955	94.5	41.3	61,538	94.7	38.2
Passaic County, New Jersey	67,982	89.0	33.2	62,606	86.0	31.5
Salem County, New Jersey	6,725	92.9	17.8	7,624	86.3	23.7
Somerset County, New Jersey	35,806	95.4	60.4	42,156	96.6	65.8
Sussex County, New Jersey	15,139	93.9	40.9	16,800	95.0	49.9
Union County, New Jersey	70,617	91.3	39.5	76,781	85.6	42.4
Warren County, New Jersey	12,329	96.3	40.6	11,490	96.5	38.8
NEW MEXICO	278,627	89.1	24.1	261,847	85.0	26.9
Bernalillo County, New Mexico	100,450	89.8	31.8	91,043	88.8	37.3
Chaves County, New Mexico	8,545	76.9	16.7	7,892	74.5	17.6
Doña Ana County, New Mexico	29,722	93.3	31.0	23,907	74.7	22.5
Lea County, New Mexico	8,418	86.3	13.7	10,222	82.9	15.8
McKinley County, New Mexico	11,163	84.9	14.4	8,185	88.2	10.1
Otero County, New Mexico	9,017	90.3	8.9	8,522	77.2	13.5
Sandoval County, New Mexico	18,580	96.9	24.6	18,641	87.0	36.5
San Juan County, New Mexico	16,896	85.9	6.5	15,231	85.2	14.6
Santa Fe County, New Mexico	16,860	89.0	23.5	17,160	85.4	28.8
Valencia County, New Mexico	7,445	85.0	11.1	9,039	85.6	18.7
NEW YORK	2,865,401	92.3	47.2	2,430,106	89.4	43.9
Albany County, New York	40,729	92.3	48.9	35,917	93.2	50.5
Bronx County, New York	227,113	83.7	25.5	180,518	77.8	22.3
Broome County, New York	21,728	94.1	36.4	20,066	87.1	30.3
Cattaraugus County, New York	8,514	92.3	18.2	8,235	90.5	26.1
Cayuga County, New York	8,981	90.4	29.1	9,510	82.5	19.0
Chautauqua County, New York	14,645	89.7	22.3	13,667	88.5	39.9
Chemung County, New York	10,759	89.3	33.2	9,182	90.7	22.5
Clinton County, New York	10,240	92.3	28.0	9,973	89.9	33.2
Dutchess County, New York	34,121	93.3	37.5	35,168	96.8	35.9
Erie County, New York	131,885	94.9	42.7	105,466	94.3	42.2
Jefferson County, New York	18,457	93.1	25.7	12,724	91.7	29.3
Kings County, New York	470,688	91.4	53.1	357,558	89.0	48.1
Livingston County, New York	6,470	93.2	29.3	6,810	94.2	30.1
Madison County, New York	7,364	94.9	17.5	7,342	98.0	26.5
Monroe County, New York	105,912	92.9	47.5	85,563	90.6	45.6
Nassau County, New York	159,711	94.2	54.0	163,814	93.1	55.7
New York County, New York	361,731	96.8	77.0	234,018	93.2	69.5
Niagara County, New York	27,332	92.7	37.9	23,192	95.3	31.7
Oneida County, New York	29,204	91.2	34.3	25,337	88.7	37.6
Onondaga County, New York	60,866	93.3	42.7	52,852	89.9	39.7
Ontario County, New York	12,951	93.7	40.5	11,578	94.3	51.4
Orange County, New York	45,085	95.1	33.6	45,637	91.4	37.9
Oswego County, New York	14,422	85.0	27.0	12,664	93.0	28.6
Putnam County, New York	12,458	91.6	39.1	11,648	89.5	43.3
Queens County, New York	360,026	92.7	47.0	306,325	86.1	38.1
Rensselaer County, New York	22,532	94.8	47.1	18,651	86.7	45.8
Richmond County, New York	63,991	93.4	47.4	59,901	91.2	43.4
Rockland County, New York	37,319	87.8	32.9	37,240	85.9	38.4

Table C-2. Educational Attainment of the Population, by Selected Counties, 2019—*Continued*

(Number; percent; dollars.)

State/County	Population 45 to 64 years			Population 65 years and over		
	Total	High school graduate or more (percent)	Bachelor's degree or more (percent)	Total	High school graduate or more (percent)	Bachelor's degree or more (percent)
NEW HAMPSHIRE—(*Continued*)						
Merrimack County, New Hampshire	44,363	91.6	33.3	28,096	89.4	30.6
Rockingham County, New Hampshire	95,969	96.3	40.1	57,734	94.2	37.5
Strafford County, New Hampshire	33,764	94.6	35.9	20,595	88.0	32.0
NEW JERSEY	2,423,592	91.3	40.2	1,475,075	85.5	32.2
Atlantic County, New Jersey	72,771	89.3	29.2	49,115	82.1	23.6
Bergen County, New Jersey	265,097	94.5	51.6	164,611	87.9	39.4
Burlington County, New Jersey	127,552	95.2	39.4	77,364	90.8	30.7
Camden County, New Jersey	134,264	88.4	31.5	81,659	84.9	27.8
Cape May County, New Jersey	27,053	93.8	35.0	24,821	92.5	31.3
Cumberland County, New Jersey	37,399	83.9	15.7	23,504	78.2	21.5
Essex County, New Jersey	207,875	87.9	34.5	111,075	78.3	31.6
Gloucester County, New Jersey	83,191	93.3	32.4	47,324	87.8	23.3
Hudson County, New Jersey	152,380	83.9	32.2	82,160	66.9	22.1
Hunterdon County, New Jersey	40,195	96.4	56.6	24,309	93.8	44.5
Mercer County, New Jersey	98,624	88.5	43.4	57,487	86.7	38.6
Middlesex County, New Jersey	219,136	89.0	41.7	127,762	84.1	33.2
Monmouth County, New Jersey	187,259	96.8	49.4	112,384	91.5	38.0
Morris County, New Jersey	146,989	95.6	56.8	86,212	93.1	46.5
Ocean County, New Jersey	149,681	93.3	31.1	138,329	91.0	26.7
Passaic County, New Jersey	128,836	87.1	28.9	75,179	78.5	24.0
Salem County, New Jersey	17,543	89.1	20.0	12,349	83.8	19.1
Somerset County, New Jersey	99,294	94.6	56.7	53,187	91.9	43.9
Sussex County, New Jersey	45,280	95.2	37.0	24,619	92.8	30.5
Union County, New Jersey	150,692	88.8	37.1	81,763	78.0	30.4
Warren County, New Jersey	32,481	94.2	37.2	19,862	88.4	21.6
NEW MEXICO	507,784	86.3	27.1	377,730	83.5	31.6
Bernalillo County, New Mexico	167,601	89.6	34.4	114,901	87.3	37.4
Chaves County, New Mexico	15,153	74.7	17.4	10,319	80.8	18.1
Doña Ana County, New Mexico	45,776	77.6	26.9	35,174	67.6	27.7
Lea County, New Mexico	16,141	70.9	13.0	7,696	64.1	8.7
McKinley County, New Mexico	15,287	79.0	7.0	10,075	64.4	14.0
Otero County, New Mexico	16,065	85.8	16.7	11,805	85.2	15.6
Sandoval County, New Mexico	37,946	93.6	32.1	27,051	93.0	37.4
San Juan County, New Mexico	29,789	89.9	16.6	19,253	79.2	18.0
Santa Fe County, New Mexico	40,886	85.4	40.9	37,936	92.1	51.9
Valencia County, New Mexico	19,695	94.9	23.9	14,097	78.5	19.5
NEW YORK	5,073,259	87.7	34.7	3,295,968	82.1	30.0
Albany County, New York	75,697	92.2	41.9	53,497	90.8	37.5
Bronx County, New York	335,730	73.3	18.0	189,452	62.1	16.7
Broome County, New York	47,834	88.0	24.4	37,046	93.1	23.4
Cattaraugus County, New York	20,692	90.0	21.5	15,462	90.7	20.2
Cayuga County, New York	22,526	88.4	25.1	15,043	86.6	19.3
Chautauqua County, New York	34,728	90.0	23.6	26,015	90.4	23.8
Chemung County, New York	23,619	93.7	24.3	16,015	92.5	22.9
Clinton County, New York	21,739	86.3	22.0	14,053	82.9	23.5
Dutchess County, New York	85,817	93.0	36.5	52,895	87.1	31.2
Erie County, New York	243,624	94.0	31.2	169,007	89.4	25.8
Jefferson County, New York	23,213	92.2	17.6	15,625	85.1	19.8
Kings County, New York	581,919	81.3	31.1	367,378	72.6	25.6
Livingston County, New York	17,072	92.0	25.2	11,602	87.4	20.1
Madison County, New York	19,866	93.1	25.3	13,535	90.8	24.8
Monroe County, New York	192,916	91.9	40.2	132,523	87.5	32.9
Nassau County, New York	378,787	92.4	47.2	246,668	88.9	37.3
New York County, New York	379,199	84.4	52.9	276,603	76.0	48.4
Niagara County, New York	59,543	92.4	26.5	41,077	88.6	21.9
Oneida County, New York	60,586	88.6	25.5	43,705	87.0	22.5
Onondaga County, New York	122,147	92.0	35.3	80,082	90.6	31.0
Ontario County, New York	30,968	93.6	36.8	22,538	93.1	35.9
Orange County, New York	100,304	90.5	31.0	55,294	82.0	25.8
Oswego County, New York	33,190	89.9	20.2	19,606	86.5	17.8
Putnam County, New York	30,819	95.1	41.2	17,285	89.3	28.3
Queens County, New York	598,888	82.2	28.5	368,460	72.2	23.2
Rensselaer County, New York	42,253	93.6	30.9	28,184	89.3	24.5
Richmond County, New York	130,303	90.1	33.3	79,301	82.0	26.7
Rockland County, New York	77,246	91.0	47.6	51,769	88.5	43.7

Table C-2. Educational Attainment of the Population, by Selected Counties, 2019—*Continued*

(Number; percent; dollars.)

State/County	Population 25 to 34 years			Population 35 to 44 years		
	Total	High school graduate or more (percent)	Bachelor's degree or more (percent)	Total	High school graduate or more (percent)	Bachelor's degree or more (percent)
NEW YORK —(*Continued*)						
St. Lawrence County, New York.............	12,736	85.0	26.0	11,678	87.1	27.8
Saratoga County, New York..................	27,893	95.3	43.3	28,041	95.4	56.3
Schenectady County, New York............	22,283	94.7	32.7	19,194	92.3	44.4
Steuben County, New York..................	11,362	90.3	27.1	11,010	95.0	29.7
Suffolk County, New York....................	177,876	93.0	44.0	172,326	87.9	40.4
Sullivan County, New York..................	8,817	95.9	25.8	7,751	90.6	27.0
Tompkins County, New York	12,901	97.1	74.0	10,239	97.7	61.4
Ulster County, New York....................	21,170	90.1	32.2	21,518	91.8	37.9
Warren County, New York...................	7,884	92.1	36.6	6,593	93.6	38.2
Wayne County, New York...................	10,441	93.2	29.1	9,890	95.8	26.6
Westchester County, New York	112,485	91.7	50.9	123,477	89.8	57.7
NORTH CAROLINA	1,401,663	90.5	35.6	1,312,661	88.2	36.6
Alamance County, North Carolina.........	21,436	87.6	29.1	20,590	88.4	24.8
Brunswick County, North Carolina........	14,711	82.8	24.2	13,978	94.7	31.0
Buncombe County, North Carolina........	37,500	92.9	42.8	34,448	92.7	46.5
Burke County, North Carolina.............	10,655	87.2	17.3	10,696	71.9	14.9
Cabarrus County, North Carolina.........	29,190	97.1	43.1	28,102	92.3	41.3
Caldwell County, North Carolina..........	9,521	88.1	18.4	8,132	83.0	25.3
Carteret County, North Carolina	6,321	90.2	42.4	7,298	89.2	26.2
Catawba County, North Carolina.........	19,700	94.5	25.6	17,994	90.7	25.3
Chatham County, North Carolina.........	8,219	85.9	41.8	7,343	77.0	41.9
Cleveland County, North Carolina........	10,348	87.5	17.4	11,710	82.4	19.1
Craven County, North Carolina...........	13,653	92.5	18.8	10,440	87.8	18.2
Cumberland County, North Carolina.....	56,877	92.8	22.3	40,268	92.7	28.7
Davidson County, North Carolina	20,577	94.9	18.5	16,947	88.3	28.6
Durham County, North Carolina	58,885	91.8	57.5	45,968	83.9	49.8
Forsyth County, North Carolina	50,895	89.6	33.6	46,024	86.2	35.7
Franklin County, North Carolina	8,303	91.9	26.0	8,957	89.3	22.5
Gaston County, North Carolina...........	30,771	89.4	27.0	27,731	92.7	27.6
Guilford County, North Carolina	74,284	89.4	38.9	64,923	86.8	40.5
Harnett County, North Carolina	20,277	91.8	30.7	17,116	89.6	25.9
Henderson County, North Carolina.......	12,295	92.6	24.4	13,516	86.6	23.5
Iredell County, North Carolina............	21,523	91.7	35.9	22,956	91.1	39.2
Johnston County, North Carolina.........	24,528	90.6	30.9	29,156	84.3	30.0
Lincoln County, North Carolina	9,722	91.3	20.2	10,177	91.1	38.2
Mecklenburg County, North Carolina	190,917	92.1	50.6	163,146	89.3	50.5
Moore County, North Carolina............	12,885	92.8	48.0	11,363	87.4	37.9
Nash County, North Carolina..............	11,231	84.1	18.2	10,682	91.6	19.9
New Hanover County, North Carolina....	31,268	92.2	44.3	30,060	91.8	41.0
Onslow County, North Carolina...........	34,669	92.9	24.6	21,798	92.2	29.6
Orange County, North Carolina...........	19,193	95.6	66.4	16,654	95.9	67.9
Pitt County, North Carolina...............	25,655	88.4	31.7	20,706	87.2	42.9
Randolph County, North Carolina........	17,664	89.3	14.4	16,377	76.7	12.5
Robeson County, North Carolina..........	16,593	83.3	12.3	15,493	71.8	11.5
Rockingham County, North Carolina	9,496	82.0	17.8	10,584	90.3	18.0
Rowan County, North Carolina...........	17,290	88.4	16.6	16,904	86.9	22.8
Rutherford County, North Carolina.......	7,488	95.4	11.9	6,718	88.8	18.1
Surry County, North Carolina	8,136	86.7	23.0	7,659	89.6	18.5
Union County, North Carolina............	22,847	90.3	33.9	33,879	86.8	46.4
Wake County, North Carolina............	163,904	93.3	59.0	165,078	93.2	59.4
Wayne County, North Carolina	15,139	85.4	17.5	13,128	82.7	20.5
Wilkes County, North Carolina	6,621	82.0	13.8	8,315	84.1	16.9
Wilson County, North Carolina............	8,102	71.8	15.7	11,302	84.2	19.4
NORTH DAKOTA	117,574	94.6	33.4	96,037	95.3	38.1
Burleigh County, North Dakota...........	12,696	98.6	41.9	12,564	96.6	37.3
Cass County, North Dakota...............	32,569	96.0	44.5	24,795	94.5	51.5
Grand Forks County, North Dakota......	11,639	95.6	34.2	7,039	95.0	48.1
Ward County, North Dakota...............	11,984	98.3	30.5	8,446	95.9	38.6
OHIO	1,544,717	92.6	34.2	1,404,148	91.9	34.7
Allen County, Ohio........................	12,641	88.4	20.1	12,730	89.4	27.1
Ashtabula County, Ohio...................	11,691	91.0	14.2	10,771	88.6	17.9
Athens County, Ohio	8,239	96.4	50.3	6,609	94.6	35.8
Belmont County, Ohio	7,979	90.8	17.1	8,595	96.3	19.6
Butler County, Ohio.......................	43,989	94.5	35.3	46,862	90.3	38.2

Table C-2. Educational Attainment of the Population, by Selected Counties, 2019—*Continued*

(Number; percent; dollars.)

State/County	Population 45 to 64 years			Population 65 years and over		
	Total	High school graduate or more (percent)	Bachelor's degree or more (percent)	Total	High school graduate or more (percent)	Bachelor's degree or more (percent)
NEW YORK —(*Continued*)						
St. Lawrence County, New York	28,298	91.0	21.8	19,522	83.2	18.9
Saratoga County, New York	66,782	93.8	43.6	43,004	91.6	31.4
Schenectady County, New York	40,168	92.3	34.6	27,349	92.3	31.0
Steuben County, New York	26,382	92.3	23.7	19,008	88.8	20.7
Suffolk County, New York	429,856	91.9	38.0	255,757	89.6	33.3
Sullivan County, New York	23,030	83.3	23.0	14,738	87.9	29.6
Tompkins County, New York	21,169	94.7	51.8	15,389	93.7	46.5
Ulster County, New York	51,278	93.6	31.1	35,976	86.5	32.8
Warren County, New York	18,454	90.8	28.6	15,427	88.6	35.8
Wayne County, New York	26,782	89.6	21.9	17,490	84.8	22.4
Westchester County, New York	268,813	92.3	54.0	168,399	84.8	42.6
NORTH CAROLINA	2,721,818	89.5	31.9	1,750,935	86.0	27.2
Alamance County, North Carolina	43,036	87.3	26.0	29,060	86.2	22.1
Brunswick County, North Carolina	39,355	93.8	29.4	46,735	95.8	39.3
Buncombe County, North Carolina	67,569	92.0	38.4	54,116	90.8	37.5
Burke County, North Carolina	27,117	81.8	20.0	18,709	86.1	19.4
Cabarrus County, North Carolina	55,144	89.8	35.4	30,519	85.8	18.0
Caldwell County, North Carolina	25,419	74.4	13.9	16,270	78.3	16.2
Carteret County, North Carolina	20,969	90.5	29.5	17,866	92.5	29.9
Catawba County, North Carolina	44,165	83.5	22.3	29,308	83.1	22.4
Chatham County, North Carolina	20,572	89.6	48.3	18,908	89.2	41.1
Cleveland County, North Carolina	25,575	87.2	19.6	18,607	82.1	18.3
Craven County, North Carolina	23,664	91.7	22.7	20,122	88.4	25.1
Cumberland County, North Carolina	70,818	91.4	25.4	40,648	86.3	23.7
Davidson County, North Carolina	51,234	85.0	18.1	31,367	79.1	15.4
Durham County, North Carolina	73,664	90.7	47.3	44,730	88.9	41.2
Forsyth County, North Carolina	99,921	89.1	34.5	61,594	89.5	29.1
Franklin County, North Carolina	19,552	88.8	22.0	11,796	89.0	19.5
Gaston County, North Carolina	60,898	83.9	22.9	37,745	78.7	18.3
Guilford County, North Carolina	137,178	90.0	38.3	82,932	86.2	30.6
Harnett County, North Carolina	33,268	91.0	24.8	17,135	81.6	13.5
Henderson County, North Carolina	31,877	89.1	29.6	30,925	92.7	35.4
Iredell County, North Carolina	53,088	90.6	30.7	28,554	87.7	20.8
Johnston County, North Carolina	57,550	88.3	22.5	27,663	86.5	15.1
Lincoln County, North Carolina	27,139	92.3	24.3	15,067	93.1	24.4
Mecklenburg County, North Carolina	270,759	90.7	44.3	127,292	88.0	35.1
Moore County, North Carolina	24,636	92.6	35.8	24,639	90.7	38.5
Nash County, North Carolina	25,499	88.4	16.2	17,778	80.2	18.6
New Hanover County, North Carolina	58,527	96.3	46.7	42,432	90.1	38.7
Onslow County, North Carolina	33,473	92.1	23.7	18,736	88.1	20.5
Orange County, North Carolina	35,868	93.8	63.0	21,927	93.4	56.7
Pitt County, North Carolina	40,960	89.7	30.0	24,722	87.0	26.9
Randolph County, North Carolina	39,242	83.1	13.0	26,801	76.9	19.6
Robeson County, North Carolina	32,636	81.9	16.3	20,493	72.7	17.1
Rockingham County, North Carolina	27,217	83.8	10.5	18,739	77.4	15.8
Rowan County, North Carolina	38,865	88.7	19.5	25,179	80.7	14.7
Rutherford County, North Carolina	18,665	83.8	22.9	15,454	85.9	20.3
Surry County, North Carolina	20,108	81.9	18.5	15,302	76.6	15.1
Union County, North Carolina	66,716	93.8	38.9	30,653	89.1	27.3
Wake County, North Carolina	285,169	94.6	54.2	133,664	90.9	41.2
Wayne County, North Carolina	31,425	85.7	16.9	20,799	88.1	18.9
Wilkes County, North Carolina	18,962	84.6	16.2	15,449	79.7	18.7
Wilson County, North Carolina	21,410	85.9	20.1	15,067	78.5	18.9
NORTH DAKOTA	170,587	95.5	28.7	120,177	88.0	23.8
Burleigh County, North Dakota	22,784	97.5	35.9	16,156	84.5	30.1
Cass County, North Dakota	37,440	96.0	37.1	22,724	94.0	33.6
Grand Forks County, North Dakota	13,419	98.4	38.1	9,384	95.5	33.5
Ward County, North Dakota	13,992	95.7	26.7	8,642	96.3	20.3
OHIO	3,057,392	91.7	28.1	2,043,548	87.4	23.6
Allen County, Ohio	25,316	93.3	15.4	18,364	90.4	19.0
Ashtabula County, Ohio	26,640	90.7	14.3	19,234	82.4	9.9
Athens County, Ohio	13,640	89.8	30.1	8,809	92.3	33.0
Belmont County, Ohio	18,679	91.5	14.6	14,068	85.9	18.2
Butler County, Ohio	97,874	93.8	32.5	57,139	86.3	23.6

Table C-2. Educational Attainment of the Population, by Selected Counties, 2019—*Continued*

(Number; percent; dollars.)

State/County	Population 25 to 34 years			Population 35 to 44 years		
	Total	High school graduate or more (percent)	Bachelor's degree or more (percent)	Total	High school graduate or more (percent)	Bachelor's degree or more (percent)
OHIO—(*Continued*)						
Clark County, Ohio	15,030	90.1	11.6	14,679	89.3	18.3
Clermont County, Ohio	25,812	90.5	27.4	25,161	94.9	42.2
Columbiana County, Ohio	11,341	95.7	19.9	11,233	94.1	22.2
Cuyahoga County, Ohio	177,166	92.5	40.6	143,793	92.4	40.1
Delaware County, Ohio	20,062	98.2	49.6	32,356	98.5	68.4
Erie County, Ohio	9,220	94.9	32.1	7,364	89.2	22.9
Fairfield County, Ohio	17,255	97.9	29.9	22,351	94.5	40.6
Franklin County, Ohio	240,165	94.8	50.0	178,176	91.4	44.2
Geauga County, Ohio	8,296	81.3	29.3	9,653	90.1	36.4
Greene County, Ohio	23,944	96.5	45.8	19,005	97.0	40.5
Hamilton County, Ohio	124,750	94.3	46.7	98,687	94.3	47.1
Hancock County, Ohio	10,590	92.8	38.0	8,723	91.6	28.3
Jefferson County, Ohio	7,355	92.6	26.2	6,489	96.5	27.6
Lake County, Ohio	27,947	96.2	30.4	26,400	91.7	28.2
Licking County, Ohio	19,189	93.1	25.5	22,245	94.4	32.8
Lorain County, Ohio	34,305	91.6	25.6	38,196	88.3	26.4
Lucas County, Ohio	62,740	89.9	31.8	48,757	90.7	27.5
Mahoning County, Ohio	26,018	91.9	29.5	25,619	92.3	32.2
Marion County, Ohio	8,332	91.3	15.0	8,037	89.3	21.4
Medina County, Ohio	19,731	96.7	33.4	22,623	95.2	45.0
Miami County, Ohio	12,081	95.0	22.0	13,447	89.6	26.6
Montgomery County, Ohio	73,220	92.8	30.5	60,958	89.9	27.0
Muskingum County, Ohio	9,782	83.2	18.0	9,643	87.6	21.8
Portage County, Ohio	19,221	94.5	33.6	17,097	93.5	35.5
Richland County, Ohio	15,873	89.7	19.4	13,312	92.7	22.3
Ross County, Ohio	10,008	91.8	14.3	9,893	94.8	24.0
Scioto County, Ohio	10,036	87.0	15.0	8,706	91.5	25.3
Stark County, Ohio	43,780	93.5	23.0	43,452	92.4	23.7
Summit County, Ohio	72,374	93.6	33.5	63,979	93.1	38.1
Trumbull County, Ohio	22,668	88.2	22.6	21,655	89.1	23.7
Tuscarawas County, Ohio	10,624	76.6	17.7	10,777	87.2	20.3
Warren County, Ohio	27,007	94.4	43.3	31,861	97.9	51.3
Wayne County, Ohio	13,182	85.1	25.8	12,652	83.4	29.1
Wood County, Ohio	16,444	95.3	43.4	13,648	97.0	41.8
OKLAHOMA	536,999	89.9	25.7	501,516	87.9	29.2
Canadian County, Oklahoma	20,645	93.2	29.7	22,759	82.0	30.1
Cleveland County, Oklahoma	40,032	94.5	40.7	36,695	92.9	40.5
Comanche County, Oklahoma	20,938	90.1	16.5	15,568	94.6	19.8
Creek County, Oklahoma	8,441	90.0	17.4	8,365	86.1	23.2
Muskogee County, Oklahoma	8,885	88.3	16.4	8,638	86.1	22.0
Oklahoma County, Oklahoma	123,419	89.4	34.2	104,521	86.0	36.3
Payne County, Oklahoma	11,731	96.7	43.9	8,248	95.6	43.7
Pottawatomie County, Oklahoma	8,639	94.1	17.8	9,580	87.0	27.1
Rogers County, Oklahoma	11,665	90.4	23.4	11,135	90.7	22.8
Tulsa County, Oklahoma	95,358	90.6	30.3	84,832	88.1	36.3
Wagoner County, Oklahoma	10,497	93.9	19.8	10,693	91.3	24.8
OREGON	594,585	92.8	35.1	578,846	90.2	39.9
Benton County, Oregon	11,360	99.6	43.7	11,142	94.4	61.1
Clackamas County, Oregon	49,935	95.2	34.2	58,826	92.8	43.5
Deschutes County, Oregon	24,463	98.2	36.3	26,366	87.3	36.7
Douglas County, Oregon	12,133	98.3	15.2	12,297	86.5	25.1
Jackson County, Oregon	25,544	89.8	22.2	26,685	86.7	31.3
Josephine County, Oregon	9,990	86.1	9.9	9,196	92.5	15.3
Klamath County, Oregon	8,672	84.9	19.0	7,826	91.2	31.7
Lane County, Oregon	49,618	92.4	31.1	48,154	93.8	36.4
Linn County, Oregon	17,570	89.3	28.1	15,406	85.2	15.7
Marion County, Oregon	48,617	88.6	21.7	44,447	81.0	29.0
Multnomah County, Oregon	152,197	94.4	50.1	136,684	93.1	53.7
Polk County, Oregon	9,448	98.2	28.7	10,173	95.6	39.1
Umatilla County, Oregon	12,317	85.6	14.1	9,081	93.5	17.4
Washington County, Oregon	95,084	95.6	46.1	90,676	91.9	48.2
Yamhill County, Oregon	14,868	78.4	19.1	13,431	90.4	33.8
PENNSYLVANIA	1,704,848	93.1	40.0	1,520,179	92.2	38.9
Adams County, Pennsylvania	11,030	90.8	24.0	10,892	89.1	27.2
Allegheny County, Pennsylvania	188,156	95.7	56.8	147,350	96.4	53.8

Table C-2. Educational Attainment of the Population, by Selected Counties, 2019—*Continued*

(Number; percent; dollars.)

State/County	Population 45 to 64 years			Population 65 years and over		
	Total	High school graduate or more (percent)	Bachelor's degree or more (percent)	Total	High school graduate or more (percent)	Bachelor's degree or more (percent)
OHIO—(*Continued*)						
Clark County, Ohio	36,096	91.5	16.4	26,077	89.8	17.5
Clermont County, Ohio	58,303	93.3	29.3	34,473	83.3	21.0
Columbiana County, Ohio	29,548	92.0	13.9	21,750	87.9	12.0
Cuyahoga County, Ohio	323,660	90.3	31.4	230,060	87.1	27.4
Delaware County, Ohio	56,854	96.1	52.0	29,364	93.2	36.3
Erie County, Ohio	21,186	93.1	23.6	16,038	91.6	20.9
Fairfield County, Ohio	42,445	94.6	29.1	25,343	88.8	19.8
Franklin County, Ohio	303,036	91.0	38.6	162,726	86.6	33.0
Geauga County, Ohio	26,782	89.5	43.7	19,497	91.7	28.2
Greene County, Ohio	41,302	96.3	43.6	29,955	91.8	33.6
Hamilton County, Ohio	200,995	92.0	37.9	129,048	87.5	32.7
Hancock County, Ohio	19,720	91.8	26.3	13,430	91.1	17.4
Jefferson County, Ohio	18,340	95.0	17.3	14,541	89.3	13.6
Lake County, Ohio	64,743	93.2	27.3	47,472	89.4	21.4
Licking County, Ohio	49,176	90.4	28.5	29,209	89.4	20.8
Lorain County, Ohio	84,439	91.3	24.5	59,221	86.6	24.2
Lucas County, Ohio	110,620	88.9	25.6	71,385	87.5	24.3
Mahoning County, Ohio	61,591	91.1	24.0	48,757	88.6	21.7
Marion County, Ohio	18,512	90.4	10.8	11,710	83.7	11.1
Medina County, Ohio	51,623	96.9	37.9	33,187	92.2	23.7
Miami County, Ohio	27,814	95.3	21.1	20,768	86.0	19.5
Montgomery County, Ohio	134,016	91.3	29.3	97,622	87.1	27.0
Muskingum County, Ohio	23,850	89.3	19.4	15,862	84.6	15.3
Portage County, Ohio	42,192	91.1	26.3	27,914	90.7	24.8
Richland County, Ohio	32,678	88.7	16.6	23,529	85.7	19.4
Ross County, Ohio	21,628	87.7	13.3	12,931	90.2	15.0
Scioto County, Ohio	20,113	88.2	20.5	13,846	76.7	17.1
Stark County, Ohio	100,255	92.7	22.4	73,406	88.2	19.8
Summit County, Ohio	146,557	92.8	32.5	99,907	90.8	28.7
Trumbull County, Ohio	54,643	90.7	19.7	43,484	86.0	15.5
Tuscarawas County, Ohio	23,975	86.7	19.3	18,656	84.5	16.3
Warren County, Ohio	66,332	96.6	46.7	34,643	90.5	36.6
Wayne County, Ohio	28,717	87.0	19.8	21,296	83.9	19.0
Wood County, Ohio	31,180	96.4	35.9	20,185	91.7	30.3
OKLAHOMA	945,507	88.7	25.8	635,222	87.2	24.8
Canadian County, Oklahoma	34,100	90.8	26.7	19,738	87.1	23.1
Cleveland County, Oklahoma	64,176	93.6	33.4	39,497	87.7	29.4
Comanche County, Oklahoma	26,805	93.1	20.5	14,678	83.4	28.5
Creek County, Oklahoma	19,086	90.3	17.8	13,236	86.5	13.9
Muskogee County, Oklahoma	16,424	87.5	20.5	11,575	83.2	26.2
Oklahoma County, Oklahoma	182,812	86.8	30.0	111,963	89.6	31.8
Payne County, Oklahoma	13,875	90.3	35.6	11,344	94.1	35.3
Pottawatomie County, Oklahoma	18,109	87.5	20.5	11,934	88.0	15.2
Rogers County, Oklahoma	24,857	92.9	25.2	15,472	87.9	21.7
Tulsa County, Oklahoma	153,754	90.2	34.8	96,452	89.5	32.3
Wagoner County, Oklahoma	20,682	90.2	24.2	13,638	90.3	21.8
OREGON	1,047,191	90.6	32.8	767,496	92.1	32.5
Benton County, Oregon	19,646	97.2	65.0	15,005	98.2	57.2
Clackamas County, Oregon	110,965	93.2	36.6	78,411	93.7	34.9
Deschutes County, Oregon	53,541	93.6	41.1	40,670	93.4	38.4
Douglas County, Oregon	28,619	92.5	13.9	29,489	92.1	13.8
Jackson County, Oregon	55,719	91.1	26.5	51,454	92.6	29.7
Josephine County, Oregon	23,202	86.6	17.4	23,012	91.9	19.8
Klamath County, Oregon	17,211	93.4	20.7	14,770	88.0	19.0
Lane County, Oregon	91,057	91.0	28.9	76,032	94.5	34.6
Linn County, Oregon	32,911	89.4	14.4	24,839	86.0	20.0
Marion County, Oregon	81,513	83.7	23.8	56,368	88.7	27.4
Multnomah County, Oregon	197,449	89.3	44.1	113,135	91.7	44.2
Polk County, Oregon	19,949	92.8	33.2	15,731	89.6	28.5
Umatilla County, Oregon	18,123	87.1	21.8	12,589	82.1	20.6
Washington County, Oregon	147,952	92.6	41.7	83,571	94.6	41.5
Yamhill County, Oregon	26,272	88.6	23.2	18,801	92.9	25.7
PENNSYLVANIA	3,414,791	91.7	30.5	2,388,218	87.8	25.2
Adams County, Pennsylvania	29,103	89.4	18.5	21,698	87.8	21.6
Allegheny County, Pennsylvania	313,579	96.2	38.8	235,484	92.9	30.5

Table C-2. Educational Attainment of the Population, by Selected Counties, 2019—*Continued*

(Number; percent; dollars.)

	Population 25 to 34 years			Population 35 to 44 years		
State/County	Total	High school graduate or more (percent)	Bachelor's degree or more (percent)	Total	High school graduate or more (percent)	Bachelor's degree or more (percent)
PENNSYLVANIA—(*Continued*)						
Armstrong County, Pennsylvania	7,240	91.9	19.7	7,068	94.7	26.7
Beaver County, Pennsylvania	20,386	95.5	33.0	18,177	95.4	38.8
Berks County, Pennsylvania	52,567	91.1	25.7	48,799	87.3	28.5
Blair County, Pennsylvania	15,336	91.7	26.0	13,637	92.4	37.3
Bucks County, Pennsylvania	69,604	95.5	50.0	76,973	94.8	47.2
Butler County, Pennsylvania	21,837	97.3	42.1	21,579	97.9	53.4
Cambria County, Pennsylvania	13,387	95.3	26.0	13,821	98.1	30.0
Carbon County, Pennsylvania	7,286	95.7	18.7	7,214	95.1	23.1
Centre County, Pennsylvania	22,280	92.8	57.5	17,174	94.0	47.5
Chester County, Pennsylvania	60,414	93.5	56.8	65,560	92.1	61.9
Clearfield County, Pennsylvania	9,695	85.3	25.1	9,466	90.2	18.9
Columbia County, Pennsylvania	6,999	96.3	38.5	7,014	92.9	19.5
Crawford County, Pennsylvania	9,290	87.3	28.3	8,936	87.2	28.0
Cumberland County, Pennsylvania	32,580	90.5	42.4	30,555	93.7	42.2
Dauphin County, Pennsylvania	38,363	92.4	39.8	33,120	88.7	35.2
Delaware County, Pennsylvania	73,056	95.6	43.7	69,595	90.5	48.8
Erie County, Pennsylvania	34,675	94.1	39.1	31,593	91.3	32.8
Fayette County, Pennsylvania	15,846	92.0	18.3	14,213	88.9	25.8
Franklin County, Pennsylvania	17,790	90.2	24.3	19,379	89.4	27.9
Indiana County, Pennsylvania	10,635	89.8	30.3	8,356	92.8	34.4
Lackawanna County, Pennsylvania	26,980	92.5	35.3	24,589	92.7	29.5
Lancaster County, Pennsylvania	72,220	85.0	31.9	63,869	87.9	35.6
Lawrence County, Pennsylvania	9,614	92.7	23.8	9,121	94.5	31.7
Lebanon County, Pennsylvania	17,218	85.3	28.1	16,213	91.4	29.4
Lehigh County, Pennsylvania	48,117	95.2	31.8	47,166	93.1	35.9
Luzerne County, Pennsylvania	40,091	93.0	19.0	37,911	91.6	25.3
Lycoming County, Pennsylvania	14,697	92.1	25.8	13,223	87.9	27.3
Mercer County, Pennsylvania	11,679	89.4	25.4	11,128	91.7	30.1
Monroe County, Pennsylvania	19,507	91.7	28.5	18,500	93.1	20.6
Montgomery County, Pennsylvania	103,927	97.9	56.5	106,310	95.1	57.4
Northampton County, Pennsylvania	37,466	97.1	39.8	35,066	94.6	35.9
Northumberland County, Pennsylvania	12,302	88.7	18.8	9,948	92.2	25.4
Philadelphia County, Pennsylvania	304,816	92.2	44.8	201,727	88.6	35.0
Schuylkill County, Pennsylvania	17,007	93.2	22.9	17,006	90.3	19.3
Somerset County, Pennsylvania	8,211	94.8	22.2	8,234	90.7	25.2
Washington County, Pennsylvania	22,788	96.3	37.4	24,053	95.3	45.0
Westmoreland County, Pennsylvania	37,573	94.1	35.9	38,213	95.4	36.2
York County, Pennsylvania	56,108	92.0	32.7	54,456	91.9	32.7
RHODE ISLAND	148,180	92.8	42.6	124,433	92.1	38.3
Kent County, Rhode Island	21,669	94.7	42.6	19,328	93.7	36.3
Newport County, Rhode Island	10,494	98.2	54.9	8,771	94.6	58.6
Providence County, Rhode Island	99,832	91.1	39.6	79,149	90.3	32.0
Washington County, Rhode Island	12,383	97.3	54.1	11,843	95.9	53.8
SOUTH CAROLINA	670,757	90.2	31.8	628,604	89.3	32.4
Aiken County, South Carolina	22,696	92.2	33.5	19,546	89.8	26.4
Anderson County, South Carolina	24,362	93.7	28.3	24,418	84.4	27.3
Beaufort County, South Carolina	20,499	92.4	28.1	17,757	91.7	30.9
Berkeley County, South Carolina	34,458	90.0	32.5	29,628	90.2	25.6
Charleston County, South Carolina	67,794	92.3	51.9	55,864	94.8	56.5
Darlington County, South Carolina	7,604	90.1	20.5	6,945	87.6	18.7
Dorchester County, South Carolina	22,772	86.1	25.1	23,370	87.1	40.8
Florence County, South Carolina	18,393	94.5	27.8	16,258	92.3	26.6
Greenville County, South Carolina	73,809	88.4	40.4	66,973	89.1	40.8
Greenwood County, South Carolina	9,287	94.3	25.5	8,853	93.4	18.0
Horry County, South Carolina	39,591	87.4	20.6	39,068	84.1	25.1
Kershaw County, South Carolina	7,488	88.3	25.1	8,544	92.2	28.8
Lancaster County, South Carolina	10,855	89.7	22.9	13,290	90.1	28.6
Laurens County, South Carolina	8,483	90.8	21.7	7,562	88.9	21.7
Lexington County, South Carolina	39,983	90.3	36.6	38,586	87.1	29.3
Oconee County, South Carolina	9,374	90.0	35.1	7,323	82.9	26.7
Orangeburg County, South Carolina	10,013	85.9	17.6	8,714	89.9	17.8
Pickens County, South Carolina	15,649	89.1	30.0	13,058	95.5	29.4
Richland County, South Carolina	60,812	91.7	43.6	51,893	90.8	46.5
Spartanburg County, South Carolina	43,317	91.4	25.7	39,336	87.8	24.6
Sumter County, South Carolina	14,734	95.4	17.2	12,785	88.7	26.3
York County, South Carolina	35,852	92.9	36.5	39,348	93.0	40.6

Table C-2. Educational Attainment of the Population, by Selected Counties, 2019—*Continued*

(Number; percent; dollars.)

State/County	Population 45 to 64 years			Population 65 years and over		
	Total	High school graduate or more (percent)	Bachelor's degree or more (percent)	Total	High school graduate or more (percent)	Bachelor's degree or more (percent)
PENNSYLVANIA—*(Continued)*						
Armstrong County, Pennsylvania	19,192	93.9	13.3	14,651	89.2	11.3
Beaver County, Pennsylvania	46,234	92.2	24.0	36,259	89.8	21.2
Berks County, Pennsylvania	111,846	87.0	26.0	74,213	84.7	22.1
Blair County, Pennsylvania	33,051	94.3	20.4	25,977	87.7	17.5
Bucks County, Pennsylvania	186,217	95.5	41.4	120,658	90.3	35.7
Butler County, Pennsylvania	55,433	95.8	36.8	36,141	92.3	26.2
Cambria County, Pennsylvania	36,334	95.0	19.9	30,415	90.0	14.9
Carbon County, Pennsylvania	20,005	90.0	21.1	13,879	82.9	12.6
Centre County, Pennsylvania	37,236	92.8	41.7	24,196	93.1	31.8
Chester County, Pennsylvania	145,849	95.7	57.3	87,354	92.9	43.5
Clearfield County, Pennsylvania	23,473	89.9	16.1	16,862	86.0	9.4
Columbia County, Pennsylvania	17,199	89.2	27.6	12,993	87.7	16.8
Crawford County, Pennsylvania	23,388	92.6	21.9	18,060	85.9	14.2
Cumberland County, Pennsylvania	67,067	94.8	40.0	47,750	89.7	30.7
Dauphin County, Pennsylvania	73,908	89.6	30.9	48,078	88.7	23.2
Delaware County, Pennsylvania	149,108	94.2	39.5	94,617	91.0	34.3
Erie County, Pennsylvania	70,692	90.3	27.0	49,795	89.0	24.2
Fayette County, Pennsylvania	37,754	89.2	16.9	27,622	83.4	14.6
Franklin County, Pennsylvania	41,109	87.1	20.1	31,211	87.6	19.6
Indiana County, Pennsylvania	21,240	94.3	19.7	16,669	85.7	18.1
Lackawanna County, Pennsylvania	55,694	91.9	30.4	42,709	89.2	23.4
Lancaster County, Pennsylvania	133,188	87.0	26.7	100,346	83.0	23.0
Lawrence County, Pennsylvania	23,834	93.3	21.3	19,069	90.5	20.2
Lebanon County, Pennsylvania	37,402	86.2	18.4	27,345	85.5	14.9
Lehigh County, Pennsylvania	94,368	89.9	29.5	62,998	83.8	23.3
Luzerne County, Pennsylvania	86,441	92.3	23.7	62,864	89.4	18.1
Lycoming County, Pennsylvania	29,886	91.1	22.5	22,685	87.2	23.9
Mercer County, Pennsylvania	30,764	90.0	23.8	24,746	86.8	18.7
Monroe County, Pennsylvania	51,296	90.6	28.7	29,942	90.8	23.1
Montgomery County, Pennsylvania	225,519	95.3	50.8	151,031	92.2	39.4
Northampton County, Pennsylvania	82,831	92.3	29.8	59,755	84.3	23.5
Northumberland County, Pennsylvania	25,119	90.8	14.5	19,569	84.1	11.7
Philadelphia County, Pennsylvania	360,548	83.8	22.6	221,350	78.2	22.2
Schuylkill County, Pennsylvania	40,761	92.3	15.4	29,414	86.4	12.9
Somerset County, Pennsylvania	21,583	91.3	18.1	16,866	81.3	11.3
Washington County, Pennsylvania	58,359	92.6	25.8	43,662	89.9	26.7
Westmoreland County, Pennsylvania	102,746	95.7	28.5	81,054	92.6	24.1
York County, Pennsylvania	123,001	91.4	24.1	80,958	85.3	21.2
RHODE ISLAND	287,184	89.4	33.0	187,155	84.4	29.4
Kent County, Rhode Island	49,649	93.6	31.6	31,733	86.1	24.7
Newport County, Rhode Island	22,960	95.5	45.3	18,870	89.9	40.6
Providence County, Rhode Island	162,894	84.9	26.5	99,704	80.0	23.5
Washington County, Rhode Island	37,566	96.2	48.5	26,936	92.9	44.6
SOUTH CAROLINA	1,328,305	88.9	28.2	935,538	85.6	28.1
Aiken County, South Carolina	44,266	92.1	26.5	33,482	86.5	31.5
Anderson County, South Carolina	53,418	87.2	23.6	37,352	85.4	22.3
Beaufort County, South Carolina	46,664	91.5	37.9	53,766	94.6	51.8
Berkeley County, South Carolina	57,216	91.2	25.5	31,802	89.1	27.3
Charleston County, South Carolina	101,377	92.3	40.9	69,274	89.2	40.4
Darlington County, South Carolina	17,550	88.0	20.9	12,990	71.0	18.6
Dorchester County, South Carolina	41,336	91.1	25.7	23,894	87.2	23.0
Florence County, South Carolina	35,405	89.2	23.0	24,051	78.8	23.6
Greenville County, South Carolina	133,481	89.6	34.2	84,342	86.4	33.2
Greenwood County, South Carolina	16,377	85.8	27.4	14,271	87.3	28.8
Horry County, South Carolina	98,851	90.3	23.1	88,488	90.3	27.1
Kershaw County, South Carolina	18,053	88.4	23.1	12,438	83.6	21.5
Lancaster County, South Carolina	25,564	84.6	19.0	20,754	85.6	24.1
Laurens County, South Carolina	18,374	83.7	17.8	12,470	82.0	20.0
Lexington County, South Carolina	80,503	90.0	31.6	48,337	85.1	22.4
Oconee County, South Carolina	22,226	80.3	23.9	19,005	89.2	25.2
Orangeburg County, South Carolina	22,401	88.2	21.9	17,326	80.2	22.9
Pickens County, South Carolina	30,118	84.1	25.7	21,672	85.5	24.0
Richland County, South Carolina	95,148	92.2	41.9	55,643	89.1	37.6
Spartanburg County, South Carolina	82,590	87.7	28.6	51,888	80.1	24.5
Sumter County, South Carolina	25,472	88.7	23.4	18,180	81.0	19.6
York County, South Carolina	74,061	93.3	35.2	42,057	91.6	28.6

Table C-2. Educational Attainment of the Population, by Selected Counties, 2019—*Continued*

(Number; percent; dollars.)

State/County	Population 25 to 34 years			Population 35 to 44 years		
	Total	High school graduate or more (percent)	Bachelor's degree or more (percent)	Total	High school graduate or more (percent)	Bachelor's degree or more (percent)
SOUTH DAKOTA	114,420	92.3	35.0	106,071	93.2	32.6
Minnehaha County, South Dakota	28,841	94.7	41.6	25,716	95.8	38.3
Pennington County, South Dakota	14,411	92.0	30.6	12,788	93.3	35.0
TENNESSEE	934,878	92.3	33.6	849,159	89.4	32.8
Anderson County, Tennessee	9,459	92.9	19.5	8,540	91.1	19.1
Blount County, Tennessee	16,319	87.4	22.4	14,374	91.0	29.4
Bradley County, Tennessee	14,674	87.2	26.4	13,963	90.5	27.8
Davidson County, Tennessee................................	143,001	93.5	59.2	95,473	89.0	48.6
Greene County, Tennessee	7,719	93.0	20.7	8,099	79.2	19.2
Hamilton County, Tennessee	53,464	94.3	39.3	46,304	87.2	42.1
Knox County, Tennessee	65,315	93.5	37.4	59,474	92.7	42.3
Madison County, Tennessee.................................	11,330	89.7	28.5	11,361	94.5	29.5
Maury County, Tennessee	13,831	88.3	30.1	11,305	92.1	29.0
Montgomery County, Tennessee	37,377	95.9	28.9	29,751	95.2	37.3
Putnam County, Tennessee	10,602	92.3	22.5	9,119	91.7	45.2
Robertson County, Tennessee	9,629	90.7	28.0	9,414	90.6	24.8
Rutherford County, Tennessee	46,301	95.7	34.8	46,709	93.7	32.7
Sevier County, Tennessee....................................	11,866	95.1	18.3	11,096	87.1	25.0
Shelby County, Tennessee...................................	141,059	91.0	32.1	116,569	87.4	34.7
Sullivan County, Tennessee.................................	18,855	97.1	31.4	17,429	90.2	25.7
Sumner County, Tennessee..................................	23,312	92.4	30.3	25,727	86.9	34.9
Washington County, Tennessee............................	17,525	94.4	39.9	13,831	90.3	35.2
Williamson County, Tennessee.............................	20,472	98.2	66.4	37,607	93.1	62.4
Wilson County, Tennessee	18,189	95.0	46.2	20,583	92.1	40.8
TEXAS..	4,242,661	89.6	32.8	3,959,419	85.0	33.5
Angelina County, Texas	11,218	93.6	20.3	11,724	87.6	12.3
Bastrop County, Texas..	10,768	81.9	8.0	10,852	75.7	18.0
Bell County, Texas	60,395	92.1	22.5	47,895	91.2	28.3
Bexar County, Texas..	320,679	90.8	27.7	275,076	86.0	32.4
Bowie County, Texas..	11,935	84.9	13.1	10,722	86.7	15.3
Brazoria County, Texas.......................................	50,522	92.5	29.0	56,179	92.2	40.5
Brazos County, Texas	34,708	90.8	48.8	27,245	92.2	41.5
Cameron County, Texas.......................................	53,297	83.0	17.2	50,695	73.2	18.8
Collin County, Texas..	132,326	95.1	50.5	164,365	93.4	60.0
Comal County, Texas..	18,346	95.4	34.5	18,684	96.0	51.8
Coryell County, Texas..	14,311	90.7	17.4	10,017	84.3	10.8
Dallas County, Texas..	438,125	87.5	38.4	360,295	78.1	32.0
Denton County, Texas...	131,152	94.6	46.7	135,797	90.8	51.8
Ector County, Texas...	28,829	87.5	20.5	22,636	84.8	15.5
Ellis County, Texas..	22,799	93.6	25.9	25,009	87.3	31.0
El Paso County, Texas..	127,347	91.7	27.0	103,617	88.3	25.9
Fort Bend County, Texas.....................................	95,950	93.6	42.1	123,841	94.4	56.0
Galveston County, Texas	46,730	91.8	34.5	43,763	91.0	33.4
Grayson County, Texas.......................................	15,013	92.9	18.2	17,245	87.6	14.8
Gregg County, Texas..	17,275	87.5	16.5	16,068	85.5	21.9
Guadalupe County, Texas	21,605	90.2	24.0	24,010	90.1	33.1
Harris County, Texas..	753,587	87.9	35.7	675,273	81.3	33.1
Harrison County, Texas	8,111	81.3	12.0	7,707	95.2	31.5
Hays County, Texas...	31,916	91.2	36.4	31,874	88.1	37.7
Henderson County, Texas....................................	9,972	66.5	12.5	8,585	87.9	13.1
Hidalgo County, Texas..	116,661	85.1	22.3	108,441	73.4	21.0
Hunt County, Texas..	11,527	91.2	26.7	11,735	79.8	16.1
Jefferson County, Texas	36,064	88.4	26.1	32,516	78.2	20.3
Johnson County, Texas	22,064	91.0	19.0	22,980	82.7	17.5
Kaufman County, Texas......................................	17,474	86.8	21.1	20,348	87.9	25.1
Liberty County, Texas...	13,088	92.1	13.6	11,441	79.3	15.0
Lubbock County, Texas.......................................	46,036	93.3	36.8	37,173	89.1	38.3
McLennan County, Texas	32,274	91.8	26.2	30,589	85.3	26.8
Midland County, Texas	30,621	88.8	30.8	26,628	90.7	31.2
Montgomery County, Texas..................................	75,709	91.1	31.0	85,303	83.4	35.3
Nacogdoches County, Texas.................................	8,211	87.4	14.3	7,123	90.4	38.9
Nueces County, Texas	52,031	90.8	24.7	47,815	84.5	20.4
Orange County, Texas...	12,198	90.5	16.8	9,397	91.8	17.4
Parker County, Texas..	15,643	85.0	23.9	18,265	90.7	25.2
Potter County, Texas..	16,904	76.4	9.6	15,425	76.7	14.3
Randall County, Texas..	18,919	94.8	36.8	19,038	94.7	37.7

Table C-2. Educational Attainment of the Population, by Selected Counties, 2019—*Continued*

(Number; percent; dollars.)

State/County	Population 45 to 64 years			Population 65 years and over		
	Total	High school graduate or more (percent)	Bachelor's degree or more (percent)	Total	High school graduate or more (percent)	Bachelor's degree or more (percent)
SOUTH DAKOTA	213,739	92.9	29.0	153,799	90.1	24.8
Minnehaha County, South Dakota	47,755	90.4	33.1	26,284	90.4	29.0
Pennington County, South Dakota	29,529	94.4	29.9	21,732	94.8	33.2
TENNESSEE	1,770,960	88.3	27.8	1,138,965	82.9	23.1
Anderson County, Tennessee	21,623	86.8	20.7	16,136	88.0	24.5
Blount County, Tennessee	37,293	89.9	23.4	28,060	84.7	20.4
Bradley County, Tennessee..................	28,190	82.4	20.7	18,539	81.3	18.3
Davidson County, Tennessee................	158,522	87.5	37.8	86,899	87.2	34.4
Greene County, Tennessee	19,504	85.1	22.9	15,049	81.5	13.1
Hamilton County, Tennessee	93,920	91.5	33.5	65,520	83.6	29.1
Knox County, Tennessee	116,419	91.7	38.6	75,775	89.1	32.9
Madison County, Tennessee.................	25,420	91.3	28.7	17,256	83.9	22.5
Maury County, Tennessee	25,893	89.6	21.6	15,770	86.7	23.8
Montgomery County, Tennessee............	42,142	93.1	29.6	20,207	89.1	27.5
Putnam County, Tennessee..................	19,674	87.7	29.4	13,592	79.3	20.1
Robertson County, Tennessee..............	19,559	86.6	22.2	11,202	71.9	10.4
Rutherford County, Tennessee	79,410	92.7	30.5	35,755	86.0	23.7
Sevier County, Tennessee...................	27,613	82.8	15.9	19,998	79.5	20.3
Shelby County, Tennessee..................	231,219	89.5	32.5	131,153	84.4	27.3
Sullivan County, Tennessee.................	45,131	86.5	23.4	35,061	85.7	27.7
Sumner County, Tennessee.................	51,817	92.3	33.3	30,839	86.1	22.6
Washington County, Tennessee............	34,112	93.1	30.8	23,542	79.5	24.9
Williamson County, Tennessee.............	65,675	97.2	65.4	32,208	92.8	50.6
Wilson County, Tennessee	38,454	94.3	32.0	23,238	89.9	26.3
TEXAS......................................	6,831,743	83.6	29.8	3,738,727	80.5	27.4
Angelina County, Texas	19,356	85.4	21.2	14,820	80.5	18.9
Bastrop County, Texas.......................	21,493	87.4	17.8	13,844	78.8	19.6
Bell County, Texas	73,886	91.0	26.0	40,350	86.5	24.8
Bexar County, Texas	448,977	83.0	27.1	247,828	78.3	25.7
Bowie County, Texas	24,556	86.2	19.8	15,683	88.2	24.9
Brazoria County, Texas	94,403	86.6	27.1	44,707	84.2	20.9
Brazos County, Texas	40,476	84.2	37.0	21,652	87.3	43.2
Cameron County, Texas......................	88,970	67.9	16.9	58,698	51.4	16.1
Collin County, Texas	270,858	95.3	53.0	116,575	91.2	43.3
Comal County, Texas.........................	43,939	93.5	39.7	28,274	90.0	35.6
Coryell County, Texas........................	16,401	85.8	19.2	8,097	92.2	19.6
Dallas County, Texas.........................	614,563	77.7	29.0	291,744	80.4	31.0
Denton County, Texas........................	228,227	93.1	46.1	94,076	89.8	37.2
Ector County, Texas..........................	33,337	64.9	12.2	15,869	67.1	10.9
Ellis County, Texas	47,985	86.7	26.2	23,269	85.7	20.9
El Paso County, Texas	183,950	79.1	24.1	105,337	58.2	15.0
Fort Bend County, Texas.....................	208,906	89.4	46.2	94,199	86.0	37.9
Galveston County, Texas.....................	89,459	91.4	29.5	51,182	87.5	26.8
Grayson County, Texas.......................	34,351	89.5	22.9	25,237	89.6	26.9
Gregg County, Texas.........................	28,146	83.6	25.9	19,734	91.5	22.0
Guadalupe County, Texas	42,292	90.1	32.2	23,182	84.4	25.1
Harris County, Texas	1,090,713	80.4	30.0	513,916	79.3	30.6
Harrison County, Texas......................	16,562	81.5	15.7	12,030	87.9	23.0
Hays County, Texas..........................	49,798	91.0	37.1	25,657	92.3	33.9
Henderson County, Texas....................	21,192	82.0	17.5	19,569	86.2	16.7
Hidalgo County, Texas.......................	169,365	62.5	17.7	98,780	48.9	15.4
Hunt County, Texas	26,489	83.5	18.4	15,313	83.2	21.3
Jefferson County, Texas.....................	62,731	83.1	18.6	36,342	86.7	20.2
Johnson County, Texas	44,773	84.0	17.1	25,007	86.8	23.5
Kaufman County, Texas......................	31,096	84.5	17.1	16,844	82.2	13.0
Liberty County, Texas........................	20,162	75.6	11.4	12,581	74.2	10.2
Lubbock County, Texas	63,943	84.0	27.5	38,835	81.1	27.7
McLennan County, Texas	55,919	85.8	24.1	37,843	85.2	27.5
Midland County, Texas.......................	35,418	84.9	27.2	18,299	75.5	28.0
Montgomery County, Texas..................	156,291	90.0	37.4	81,311	87.0	28.2
Nacogdoches County, Texas.................	13,990	79.9	23.1	9,661	85.4	20.8
Nueces County, Texas........................	84,616	86.0	26.2	54,358	75.9	21.3
Orange County, Texas........................	21,512	86.5	21.6	13,519	83.0	17.3
Parker County, Texas.........................	38,875	88.0	25.4	22,439	87.1	25.2
Potter County, Texas.........................	26,234	75.9	13.7	15,772	80.0	16.0
Randall County, Texas........................	30,795	92.1	31.0	21,743	93.1	37.8

Table C-2. Educational Attainment of the Population, by Selected Counties, 2019—*Continued*

(Number; percent; dollars.)

State/County	Population 25 to 34 years			Population 35 to 44 years		
	Total	High school graduate or more (percent)	Bachelor's degree or more (percent)	Total	High school graduate or more (percent)	Bachelor's degree or more (percent)
TEXAS—(*Continued*)						
Rockwall County, Texas	11,625	96.1	39.0	16,699	90.1	40.1
San Patricio County, Texas	8,090	95.6	5.6	9,162	85.5	19.2
Smith County, Texas	32,324	92.3	24.4	27,463	84.7	23.7
Tarrant County, Texas	313,443	90.6	35.3	289,070	87.1	35.8
Taylor County, Texas	20,023	93.6	24.8	16,682	90.3	27.5
Tom Green County, Texas	17,037	95.6	23.4	15,341	95.0	26.0
Travis County, Texas	257,251	93.6	58.6	205,707	87.6	52.7
Victoria County, Texas	10,941	94.3	21.7	11,077	87.5	16.1
Walker County, Texas	8,488	92.2	22.5	9,505	92.6	15.8
Webb County, Texas	38,011	79.0	21.2	35,438	69.8	27.0
Wichita County, Texas	19,284	93.4	18.5	15,371	88.9	25.5
Williamson County, Texas	82,727	96.2	40.0	97,023	94.7	46.7
Wise County, Texas	8,433	96.2	19.1	9,156	82.4	27.9
UTAH	472,153	94.2	35.0	443,692	93.8	38.1
Cache County, Utah	18,773	96.1	32.4	15,531	95.5	44.9
Davis County, Utah	49,580	98.5	37.4	53,145	95.8	40.8
Salt Lake County, Utah	191,572	92.8	38.6	172,233	93.6	39.8
Tooele County, Utah	10,788	95.3	17.1	10,122	95.1	25.3
Utah County, Utah	92,775	97.0	41.0	80,685	94.9	44.7
Washington County, Utah	20,411	93.7	26.6	20,474	90.5	26.5
Weber County, Utah	40,417	91.5	26.4	36,595	93.4	30.3
VERMONT	76,649	93.7	42.2	70,815	93.9	44.5
Chittenden County, Vermont	24,324	94.0	56.2	20,094	92.7	62.4
VIRGINIA	1,174,655	93.4	42.4	1,128,152	91.3	44.7
Albemarle County, Virginia	13,401	96.3	58.3	12,398	96.0	65.1
Arlington County, Virginia	56,528	98.6	84.9	39,677	93.2	75.2
Augusta County, Virginia	8,941	93.4	17.4	9,843	84.7	28.3
Bedford County, Virginia	7,784	91.5	31.6	8,256	93.1	52.3
Chesterfield County, Virginia	42,956	94.7	32.6	47,669	90.4	43.5
Fairfax County, Virginia	151,762	94.6	63.7	165,764	92.0	66.4
Fauquier County, Virginia	8,262	85.0	28.2	8,749	93.4	45.0
Frederick County, Virginia	11,018	89.2	33.7	10,261	90.6	37.7
Hanover County, Virginia	10,583	94.9	40.1	13,850	94.3	56.0
Henrico County, Virginia	48,370	94.6	46.4	44,321	92.1	44.8
James City County, Virginia	8,287	91.2	39.5	8,518	98.8	41.7
Loudoun County, Virginia	47,142	95.5	58.0	70,394	94.1	70.5
Montgomery County, Virginia	13,116	98.0	51.9	10,228	97.0	43.2
Prince William County, Virginia	62,432	92.1	38.5	70,935	88.7	46.9
Roanoke County, Virginia	10,676	85.6	36.4	11,341	97.5	40.5
Rockingham County, Virginia	9,441	94.6	34.9	9,779	77.1	28.7
Spotsylvania County, Virginia	15,613	92.6	36.6	18,973	91.6	38.5
Stafford County, Virginia	18,846	93.1	38.3	23,614	91.6	37.9
York County, Virginia	7,500	100.0	44.6	9,085	94.3	56.0
Alexandria city, Virginia	34,911	95.7	65.9	30,343	91.9	70.9
Chesapeake city, Virginia	31,442	91.2	29.0	35,640	91.8	35.0
Hampton city, Virginia	21,901	94.6	31.0	15,773	87.9	21.7
Lynchburg city, Virginia	13,066	97.8	49.7	7,447	89.8	28.7
Newport News city, Virginia	31,523	91.1	27.1	21,751	95.7	28.5
Norfolk city, Virginia	45,947	93.1	34.0	28,126	90.6	34.3
Portsmouth city, Virginia	14,669	96.5	34.8	12,699	93.1	21.3
Richmond city, Virginia	50,970	91.9	48.3	28,750	82.4	41.9
Roanoke city, Virginia	14,690	92.9	30.8	12,317	92.5	25.5
Suffolk city, Virginia	12,232	96.1	34.3	12,290	93.1	28.7
Virginia Beach city, Virginia	72,683	95.2	38.0	61,209	95.1	41.0
WASHINGTON	1,164,010	92.9	39.8	1,032,245	90.8	40.2
Benton County, Washington	27,601	91.8	29.1	28,218	88.8	32.3
Chelan County, Washington	9,356	86.0	27.2	9,843	79.2	26.3
Clallam County, Washington	8,469	87.9	23.7	8,196	90.9	25.6
Clark County, Washington	65,991	92.6	31.1	64,122	92.0	29.6
Cowlitz County, Washington	14,615	88.5	15.8	13,288	81.1	15.1
Franklin County, Washington	13,711	73.1	18.5	13,317	72.1	19.8
Grant County, Washington	13,459	81.0	20.1	11,788	74.5	12.4
Grays Harbor County, Washington	8,591	94.8	15.8	8,168	94.3	21.0
Island County, Washington	11,414	97.1	23.3	9,419	93.0	30.2

Table C-2. Educational Attainment of the Population, by Selected Counties, 2019—*Continued*

(Number; percent; dollars.)

State/County	Population 45 to 64 years			Population 65 years and over		
	Total	High school graduate or more (percent)	Bachelor's degree or more (percent)	Total	High school graduate or more (percent)	Bachelor's degree or more (percent)
TEXAS—*(Continued)*						
Rockwall County, Texas..........................	28,134	95.1	41.2	12,854	95.9	38.4
San Patricio County, Texas.....................	15,382	82.9	19.4	10,320	65.4	12.9
Smith County, Texas.............................	53,728	85.1	28.4	39,218	88.0	31.0
Tarrant County, Texas...........................	510,964	86.0	33.2	244,678	85.7	32.1
Taylor County, Texas............................	27,766	91.4	28.0	20,403	90.2	26.2
Tom Green County, Texas.......................	25,837	82.2	23.2	18,282	80.9	24.6
Travis County, Texas............................	296,234	88.6	50.2	129,438	88.8	45.9
Victoria County, Texas..........................	22,329	85.0	18.8	14,914	76.2	20.0
Walker County, Texas...........................	18,900	80.5	18.1	9,834	87.5	22.6
Webb County, Texas.............................	55,372	63.4	17.5	27,227	48.6	15.8
Wichita County, Texas...........................	30,636	86.7	20.6	19,720	84.5	26.3
Williamson County, Texas	141,466	93.1	40.0	73,213	90.5	40.4
Wise County, Texas	19,133	82.8	12.3	9,966	85.8	15.9
UTAH..	630,549	91.6	33.8	365,198	93.0	32.1
Cache County, Utah..............................	19,980	88.8	38.0	12,549	89.3	28.6
Davis County, Utah...............................	69,835	94.8	35.1	36,591	96.8	31.7
Salt Lake County, Utah	246,070	89.1	35.7	130,603	91.8	35.1
Tooele County, Utah	15,603	94.0	24.7	6,675	89.9	24.2
Utah County, Utah	97,042	95.6	40.7	50,285	94.7	36.3
Washington County, Utah........................	35,926	94.1	25.3	39,235	95.0	29.8
Weber County, Utah..............................	54,680	91.0	26.2	30,495	92.2	25.4
VERMONT	172,893	93.4	36.7	125,201	91.7	35.9
Chittenden County, Vermont	40,201	94.3	49.1	26,225	91.6	42.2
VIRGINIA	2,211,614	90.4	39.5	1,358,336	85.6	33.2
Albemarle County, Virginia......................	27,267	94.4	62.6	21,011	95.1	56.6
Arlington County, Virginia.......................	52,806	93.1	71.2	26,022	90.6	60.1
Augusta County, Virginia........................	21,653	88.0	16.1	16,837	85.4	19.4
Bedford County, Virginia........................	23,230	93.0	31.6	17,215	82.3	22.0
Chesterfield County, Virginia....................	94,104	93.0	44.3	54,227	91.5	36.4
Fairfax County, Virginia	306,975	92.8	62.4	160,629	91.4	57.0
Fauquier County, Virginia	20,259	93.9	37.5	12,055	90.9	30.0
Frederick County, Virginia	25,433	90.7	21.9	15,965	85.7	27.0
Hanover County, Virginia........................	30,863	94.5	42.4	19,510	91.6	25.9
Henrico County, Virginia	85,073	90.2	41.9	53,784	90.6	39.3
James City County, Virginia	19,812	97.8	53.5	20,017	93.4	59.3
Loudoun County, Virginia........................	109,110	95.8	64.8	40,150	90.1	46.5
Montgomery County, Virginia	20,283	95.5	47.5	12,818	91.0	38.0
Prince William County, Virginia.................	120,728	87.8	43.9	48,742	86.9	40.5
Roanoke County, Virginia.......................	25,159	95.2	44.8	20,819	86.8	30.6
Rockingham County, Virginia....................	21,629	87.0	22.6	16,026	79.1	24.5
Spotsylvania County, Virginia...................	36,260	92.3	30.7	19,900	88.4	22.7
Stafford County, Virginia........................	39,694	95.6	42.8	16,315	90.4	37.8
York County, Virginia............................	18,933	93.9	59.2	11,058	91.5	37.4
Alexandria city, Virginia.........................	38,964	90.5	63.9	18,318	94.2	62.0
Chesapeake city, Virginia.......................	64,149	92.0	34.5	33,514	87.4	27.5
Hampton city, Virginia...........................	32,083	95.2	27.6	21,284	86.3	22.6
Lynchburg city, Virginia.........................	14,377	82.2	35.0	11,755	81.3	31.5
Newport News city, Virginia	39,705	90.4	24.3	24,232	87.0	26.3
Norfolk city, Virginia.............................	49,838	85.9	27.8	28,254	82.4	26.6
Portsmouth city, Virginia........................	21,968	85.9	14.9	14,288	77.1	18.6
Richmond city, Virginia..........................	52,012	83.6	33.4	31,656	76.6	32.3
Roanoke city, Virginia	25,081	86.5	20.6	16,657	83.2	21.0
Suffolk city, Virginia.............................	24,552	91.8	31.8	13,818	83.6	28.3
Virginia Beach city, Virginia....................	110,280	93.3	38.5	66,259	93.4	35.3
WASHINGTON	1,886,384	91.6	35.1	1,207,685	91.5	34.4
Benton County, Washington.....................	46,948	90.8	33.1	31,023	91.1	33.3
Chelan County, Washington	19,108	76.7	19.2	14,643	90.1	31.4
Clallam County, Washington	20,008	91.4	26.2	23,599	93.7	33.0
Clark County, Washington.......................	125,192	94.3	32.8	78,374	94.0	31.4
Cowlitz County, Washington.....................	28,559	93.5	13.1	21,012	91.5	18.0
Franklin County, Washington	19,122	70.7	11.7	8,820	76.3	21.9
Grant County, Washington	21,490	74.8	19.6	13,428	80.1	18.2
Grays Harbor County, Washington.............	21,313	91.5	19.3	16,860	90.2	20.6
Island County, Washington	20,404	92.1	31.8	20,580	98.0	45.9

Table C-2. Educational Attainment of the Population, by Selected Counties, 2019—*Continued*

(Number; percent; dollars.)

State/County	Population 25 to 34 years			Population 35 to 44 years		
	Total	High school graduate or more (percent)	Bachelor's degree or more (percent)	Total	High school graduate or more (percent)	Bachelor's degree or more (percent)
WASHINGTON—(*Continued*)						
King County, Washington	416,655	95.9	61.3	342,732	92.9	59.7
Kitsap County, Washington	39,866	96.4	23.2	34,074	96.2	36.9
Lewis County, Washington	10,043	82.2	15.1	9,216	85.5	20.1
Mason County, Washington	8,025	89.9	10.8	7,766	83.6	10.7
Pierce County, Washington	141,209	91.3	25.8	121,601	91.8	30.3
Skagit County, Washington	16,558	88.9	22.0	15,537	87.0	32.7
Snohomish County, Washington	123,322	94.6	35.9	119,234	91.0	37.4
Spokane County, Washington	78,107	93.2	30.7	65,597	94.3	31.8
Thurston County, Washington	39,829	92.1	29.6	39,598	94.8	34.8
Whatcom County, Washington	29,325	95.3	31.6	28,365	91.1	37.4
Yakima County, Washington	35,135	79.2	15.4	29,453	71.3	20.4
WEST VIRGINIA	211,267	91.8	24.5	219,899	91.3	27.0
Berkeley County, West Virginia	16,432	92.8	19.8	16,258	89.6	24.8
Cabell County, West Virginia	11,420	90.9	38.3	10,836	95.0	40.0
Harrison County, West Virginia	7,739	90.6	24.9	8,802	93.2	35.0
Kanawha County, West Virginia	23,198	96.3	30.1	21,672	89.3	29.1
Monongalia County, West Virginia	17,087	86.1	49.7	13,777	97.4	53.5
Raleigh County, West Virginia	8,701	94.6	21.5	9,364	97.8	28.0
Wood County, West Virginia	9,068	88.6	20.6	10,127	89.3	28.2
WISCONSIN	737,315	94.6	37.2	714,436	92.9	37.6
Brown County, Wisconsin	34,724	95.8	36.6	33,391	91.5	33.8
Dane County, Wisconsin	85,318	97.1	64.7	74,512	96.1	63.0
Dodge County, Wisconsin	10,482	96.7	20.9	10,754	89.6	20.0
Eau Claire County, Wisconsin	14,385	96.0	39.3	12,007	96.0	36.8
Fond du Lac County, Wisconsin	11,896	95.7	29.5	12,214	88.7	33.3
Jefferson County, Wisconsin	9,802	94.8	27.6	10,786	96.2	39.0
Kenosha County, Wisconsin	22,812	93.6	27.7	21,965	90.7	39.5
La Crosse County, Wisconsin	15,455	95.5	36.2	13,937	99.6	47.1
Manitowoc County, Wisconsin	8,655	94.4	27.0	8,615	96.2	17.2
Marathon County, Wisconsin	15,971	94.9	29.4	16,961	91.6	29.2
Milwaukee County, Wisconsin	155,678	93.6	38.9	122,128	89.2	34.6
Outagamie County, Wisconsin	26,655	93.1	33.7	24,969	95.3	34.9
Ozaukee County, Wisconsin	9,052	99.3	43.1	9,949	99.1	57.9
Portage County, Wisconsin	8,092	97.4	44.9	8,042	93.4	42.6
Racine County, Wisconsin	22,020	86.4	26.2	24,650	86.2	26.5
Rock County, Wisconsin	19,554	92.9	27.5	19,454	92.3	28.1
St. Croix County, Wisconsin	10,059	98.6	45.9	13,233	92.5	37.3
Sheboygan County, Wisconsin	14,438	95.0	35.2	13,052	95.0	32.4
Walworth County, Wisconsin	10,395	92.2	27.5	11,595	91.4	33.9
Washington County, Wisconsin	13,999	99.5	38.0	16,624	96.7	36.5
Waukesha County, Wisconsin	42,515	96.7	48.8	50,118	97.9	64.5
Winnebago County, Wisconsin	23,601	92.6	31.0	21,014	90.3	36.9
Wood County, Wisconsin	8,354	98.4	19.4	8,096	92.1	26.6
WYOMING	76,649	93.8	26.4	73,671	94.9	33.5
Laramie County, Wyoming	14,095	95.5	26.2	12,167	94.3	33.9
Natrona County, Wyoming	11,124	91.0	15.1	11,009	93.6	26.5

Table C-2. Educational Attainment of the Population, by Selected Counties, 2019—*Continued*

(Number; percent; dollars.)

State/County	Population 45 to 64 years			Population 65 years and over		
	Total	High school graduate or more (percent)	Bachelor's degree or more (percent)	Total	High school graduate or more (percent)	Bachelor's degree or more (percent)
WASHINGTON—(*Continued*)						
King County, Washington....................	556,995	92.5	50.0	304,058	90.4	45.6
Kitsap County, Washington..................	66,970	97.3	39.5	49,907	94.6	36.2
Lewis County, Washington...................	21,017	86.6	16.6	17,307	88.2	23.4
Mason County, Washington	17,493	87.7	25.5	15,873	97.9	26.3
Pierce County, Washington..................	221,502	92.5	27.8	128,251	92.1	29.3
Skagit County, Washington..................	31,960	90.3	21.9	27,917	92.3	32.6
Snohomish County, Washington...........	218,361	93.3	31.7	114,567	91.8	27.8
Spokane County, Washington..............	128,644	93.7	28.8	86,520	93.7	33.5
Thurston County, Washington..............	74,437	93.6	35.7	51,251	93.0	35.8
Whatcom County, Washington.............	53,344	95.1	36.4	41,896	94.1	36.7
Yakima County, Washington................	53,818	70.6	16.9	35,395	78.7	16.9
WEST VIRGINIA	482,520	88.0	19.6	367,400	80.8	17.4
Berkeley County, West Virginia	32,257	87.4	24.9	17,796	83.5	21.5
Cabell County, West Virginia	22,421	85.5	24.9	17,477	78.9	21.8
Harrison County, West Virginia	18,458	91.7	24.1	13,152	85.8	22.1
Kanawha County, West Virginia...........	48,193	92.1	24.5	37,757	84.7	22.8
Monongalia County, West Virginia	21,678	96.2	41.5	14,253	82.7	35.5
Raleigh County, West Virginia	19,034	91.2	18.3	15,601	76.4	15.2
Wood County, West Virginia	23,247	88.4	18.0	17,261	89.2	19.0
WISCONSIN	1,543,638	93.1	29.7	1,019,896	90.9	25.3
Brown County, Wisconsin	68,291	91.8	29.7	41,403	91.1	23.1
Dane County, Wisconsin......................	126,701	95.5	47.6	77,385	95.8	44.6
Dodge County, Wisconsin....................	25,906	89.5	17.3	16,324	85.5	14.4
Eau Claire County, Wisconsin.............	23,863	97.2	33.5	16,641	92.9	23.6
Fond du Lac County, Wisconsin...........	29,024	95.3	22.3	19,578	90.7	15.9
Jefferson County, Wisconsin...............	23,902	92.7	24.1	14,988	89.4	22.5
Kenosha County, Wisconsin................	45,070	93.8	32.4	24,636	86.1	17.5
La Crosse County, Wisconsin..............	27,090	96.9	32.5	20,304	92.0	29.4
Manitowoc County, Wisconsin.............	22,924	94.5	23.5	16,970	91.0	19.4
Marathon County, Wisconsin...............	37,025	93.9	23.3	24,805	88.7	20.5
Milwaukee County, Wisconsin.............	220,768	87.5	27.4	132,248	86.2	27.6
Outagamie County, Wisconsin	48,626	96.3	30.0	28,502	90.2	21.9
Ozaukee County, Wisconsin................	25,908	99.0	53.7	17,859	97.3	37.6
Portage County, Wisconsin.................	17,659	94.6	31.8	12,178	94.6	29.9
Racine County, Wisconsin...................	54,472	91.1	26.8	33,579	92.0	24.5
Rock County, Wisconsin......................	44,457	91.1	22.6	27,470	92.1	17.7
St. Croix County, Wisconsin...............	25,181	97.3	37.0	13,297	92.4	37.2
Sheboygan County, Wisconsin............	32,222	96.7	26.3	21,032	92.0	22.4
Walworth County, Wisconsin...............	28,347	90.4	28.2	19,239	92.9	34.5
Washington County, Wisconsin	40,668	94.8	32.2	25,732	91.6	22.1
Waukesha County, Wisconsin	116,614	96.2	46.1	77,845	95.7	32.4
Winnebago County, Wisconsin............	44,294	94.2	33.8	28,994	90.8	23.0
Wood County, Wisconsin.....................	20,717	90.0	18.8	15,489	88.0	17.4
WYOMING..	140,738	95.2	26.9	98,789	94.0	31.2
Laramie County, Wyoming..................	24,692	96.4	29.4	16,821	90.7	31.5
Natrona County, Wyoming..................	19,474	94.3	17.5	12,673	92.1	25.3

Table C-2. Educational Attainment of the Population, by Selected Counties, 2019—*Continued*

(Number; percent; dollars.)

	Educational attainment by race/ethnicity, 25 years and over								
	White alone			White alone, not Hispanic			Black alone		
State/County	Total	High school graduate or more (percent)	Bachelor's degree or more (percent)	Total	High school graduate or more (percent)	Bachelor's degree or more (percent)	Total	High school graduate or more (percent)	Bachelor's degree or more (percent)
UNITED STATES	167,334,031	90.4	34.4	144,203,068	93.3	36.9	27,336,967	87.1	22.5
ALABAMA	2,363,674	88.5	28.5	2,299,781	89.1	28.8	855,485	85.1	19.2
Baldwin County, Alabama............................	138,720	92.2	33.1	136,823	92.2	33.1	12,416	83.0	31.4
Calhoun County, Alabama............................	59,838	86.3	21.2	58,922	86.7	21.4	15,807	86.1	15.3
Cullman County, Alabama	56,181	81.2	15.3	54,705	81.5	14.9	N	N	N
DeKalb County, Alabama.............................	42,647	82.9	13.2	41,434	83.4	13.4	N	N	N
Elmore County, Alabama.............................	44,102	90.6	26.2	42,835	91.6	26.8	12,100	86.8	16.5
Etowah County, Alabama.............................	58,563	86.0	18.4	57,912	85.9	18.3	10,262	79.9	9.3
Houston County, Alabama...........................	52,019	89.0	26.6	50,363	90.3	27.0	18,892	75.0	11.5
Jefferson County, Alabama.........................	245,394	92.9	43.8	237,302	93.7	44.7	187,778	89.8	22.0
Lauderdale County, Alabama.......................	56,566	85.6	22.3	55,952	85.6	22.5	6,498	87.6	25.6
Lee County, Alabama..................................	70,441	92.4	42.4	68,498	93.0	42.9	23,399	90.9	29.6
Limestone County, Alabama........................	55,187	88.6	26.9	54,279	88.8	27.2	9,815	82.7	16.4
Madison County, Alabama...........................	182,039	94.9	46.3	175,158	95.5	46.5	58,456	88.4	35.4
Marshall County, Alabama...........................	60,689	82.4	19.9	55,808	85.6	21.1	N	N	N
Mobile County, Alabama	172,134	88.0	25.6	167,606	88.3	25.7	95,432	88.8	17.3
Montgomery County, Alabama.....................	58,347	95.0	46.4	56,067	96.2	47.0	84,797	85.8	26.0
Morgan County, Alabama............................	69,641	86.3	26.4	65,834	88.8	27.4	9,636	82.6	6.9
St. Clair County, Alabama...........................	55,115	86.4	14.3	54,592	86.4	14.4	6,643	78.3	6.2
Shelby County, Alabama.............................	122,844	95.2	46.4	119,199	95.6	46.5	18,139	87.3	31.9
Talladega County, Alabama.........................	36,989	83.1	18.0	36,718	83.4	18.0	17,289	76.3	10.8
Tuscaloosa County, Alabama.......................	86,959	90.6	37.0	84,076	91.2	37.6	41,397	86.6	20.5
Walker County, Alabama	40,840	81.6	12.6	40,542	82.0	12.7	N	N	N
ALASKA..	336,103	95.9	35.7	316,918	96.5	36.7	15,832	89.4	22.3
Anchorage Municipality, Alaska...................	130,180	96.8	43.0	120,340	97.4	45.1	10,906	90.9	22.9
Fairbanks North Star Borough, Alaska	48,559	96.8	34.2	45,291	96.7	35.5	N	N	N
Matanuska-Susitna Borough, Alaska...........	60,697	94.9	25.3	58,608	95.1	25.0	N	N	N
ARIZONA	4,002,380	88.8	31.1	3,010,564	94.6	36.6	214,990	89.9	27.3
Apache County, Arizona	11,619	88.6	18.0	10,128	91.9	20.0	N	N	N
Cochise County, Arizona.............................	77,300	89.0	25.1	54,097	94.1	29.5	3,383	97.4	38.0
Coconino County, Arizona...........................	55,879	97.6	52.4	49,360	98.2	54.5	N	N	N
Maricopa County, Arizona...........................	2,454,787	88.9	33.8	1,847,462	95.2	40.1	163,517	90.1	28.7
Mohave County, Arizona.............................	148,684	87.4	13.4	132,505	89.0	14.6	N	N	N
Navajo County, Arizona..............................	37,327	91.9	19.8	34,297	94.3	21.4	N	N	N
Pima County, Arizona.................................	564,919	90.6	35.4	414,154	95.6	41.4	24,397	84.2	23.8
Pinal County, Arizona.................................	265,817	87.7	20.7	201,967	92.8	23.9	14,625	94.6	14.7
Yavapai County, Arizona.............................	166,082	93.2	28.8	154,171	94.3	29.6	N	N	N
Yuma County, Arizona................................	121,701	74.2	14.1	51,661	91.6	20.6	N	N	N
ARKANSAS......................................	1,625,302	88.5	24.3	1,550,578	89.9	24.9	292,048	86.9	17.0
Benton County, Arkansas...........................	162,642	89.9	33.3	141,585	93.4	36.6	2,722	94.3	55.9
Craighead County, Arkansas	61,026	89.0	25.9	57,644	92.8	26.6	8,013	93.0	18.6
Faulkner County, Arkansas.........................	66,806	94.0	29.6	65,284	94.1	29.9	8,238	91.7	28.2
Garland County, Arkansas..........................	63,966	92.1	30.5	62,089	92.9	31.0	5,699	91.8	11.5
Jefferson County, Arkansas........................	20,525	84.7	14.8	20,465	85.0	14.8	23,672	87.8	21.8
Lonoke County, Arkansas...........................	44,628	90.4	20.4	42,849	91.3	20.4	3,166	75.4	4.8
Pulaski County, Arkansas...........................	160,700	92.9	39.3	152,977	94.2	40.5	92,739	90.1	25.2
Saline County, Arkansas.............................	76,299	89.6	27.4	73,922	90.4	28.1	5,599	92.9	17.1
Sebastian County, Arkansas.......................	66,627	88.0	26.5	63,688	88.4	26.8	5,488	79.0	22.6
Washington County, Arkansas	122,132	88.4	34.7	110,842	93.0	37.7	4,341	84.1	16.5
White County, Arkansas	47,961	81.6	16.4	46,918	81.8	16.8	N	N	N
CALIFORNIA	16,461,029	86.4	35.6	11,075,547	95.3	45.3	1,573,950	90.5	27.1
Alameda County, California	489,465	94.0	55.8	402,674	96.4	61.1	128,093	92.8	30.6
Butte County, California..............................	120,306	90.2	32.5	108,903	92.1	34.0	2,553	87.0	17.0
Contra Costa County, California	448,337	93.1	46.7	377,291	96.6	50.9	70,180	94.9	33.0
El Dorado County, California	125,356	93.6	34.8	114,212	94.9	36.3	N	N	N
Fresno County, California	404,313	78.9	23.7	215,743	91.8	33.9	29,298	89.9	20.1
Humboldt County, California	76,827	92.7	32.8	73,784	92.9	32.6	N	N	N
Imperial County, California..........................	74,480	75.9	18.1	14,194	95.0	28.5	N	N	N
Kern County, California	399,382	78.0	17.0	216,434	90.2	23.7	28,074	88.9	15.6
Kings County, California	69,985	71.7	17.2	34,548	91.2	27.2	7,175	80.4	24.0
Lake County, California...............................	38,241	88.0	16.0	35,079	91.4	17.0	N	N	N
Los Angeles County, California....................	3,710,088	81.5	36.1	2,062,021	95.4	52.9	581,836	90.1	27.9

Table C-2. Educational Attainment of the Population, by Selected Counties, 2019—*Continued*

(Number; percent; dollars.)

State/County	Educational attainment by race/ethnicity, 25 years and over								
	American Indian or Alaska Native alone			Asian alone			Native Hawaiian or Other Pacific Islander alone		
	Total	High school graduate or more (percent)	Bachelor's degree or more (percent)	Total	High school graduate or more (percent)	Bachelor's degree or more (percent)	Total	High school graduate or more (percent)	Bachelor's degree or more (percent)
UNITED STATES	1,802,438	81.5	16.1	13,381,406	87.8	55.6	395,310	86.3	18.1
ALABAMA	16,782	78.9	18.7	47,226	87.6	55.9	N	N	N
Baldwin County, Alabama............................	N	N	N	N	N	N	N	N	N
Calhoun County, Alabama............................	N	N	N	N	N	N	N	N	N
Cullman County, Alabama............................	N	N	N	N	N	N	N	N	N
DeKalb County, Alabama.............................	N	N	N	N	N	N	N	N	N
Elmore County, Alabama.............................	N	N	N	N	N	N	N	N	N
Etowah County, Alabama.............................	N	N	N	N	N	N	N	N	N
Houston County, Alabama............................	N	N	N	662	71.3	36.4	N	N	N
Jefferson County, Alabama	N	N	N	8,220	89.1	61.5	N	N	N
Lauderdale County, Alabama........................	N	N	N	N	N	N	N	N	N
Lee County, Alabama..................................	N	N	N	N	N	N	N	N	N
Limestone County, Alabama.........................	N	N	N	N	N	N	N	N	N
Madison County, Alabama............................	N	N	N	7,658	97.6	64.8	N	N	N
Marshall County, Alabama...........................	N	N	N	N	N	N	N	N	N
Mobile County, Alabama..............................	N	N	N	5,172	68.4	36.9	N	N	N
Montgomery County, Alabama......................	N	N	N	5,158	94.5	64.4	N	N	N
Morgan County, Alabama.............................	N	N	N	N	N	N	N	N	N
St. Clair County, Alabama............................	N	N	N	N	N	N	N	N	N
Shelby County, Alabama	N	N	N	N	N	N	N	N	N
Talladega County, Alabama..........................	N	N	N	N	N	N	N	N	N
Tuscaloosa County, Alabama........................	N	N	N	2,173	81.9	30.6	N	N	N
Walker County, Alabama	N	N	N	N	N	N	N	N	N
ALASKA...	66,228	83.5	9.0	30,918	93.3	28.6	N	N	N
Anchorage Municipality, Alaska....................	15,468	85.0	10.8	17,343	97.0	28.8	N	N	N
Fairbanks North Star Borough, Alaska	4,575	90.5	33.8	N	N	N	N	N	N
Matanuska-Susitna Borough, Alaska............	4,450	82.9	9.5	N	N	N	N	N	N
ARIZONA	198,701	79.5	11.2	172,708	88.8	59.5	9,550	87.7	10.2
Apache County, Arizona	32,395	80.2	8.8	N	N	N	N	N	N
Cochise County, Arizona.............................	N	N	N	N	N	N	N	N	N
Coconino County, Arizona...........................	21,423	82.3	8.2	N	N	N	N	N	N
Maricopa County, Arizona...........................	56,284	84.3	19.2	136,878	90.0	62.6	6,573	85.2	13.0
Mohave County, Arizona.............................	2,756	84.7	8.9	N	N	N	N	N	N
Navajo County, Arizona	30,397	75.1	6.2	N	N	N	N	N	N
Pima County, Arizona.................................	23,309	71.9	9.4	20,859	87.5	54.1	N	N	N
Pinal County, Arizona.................................	15,087	77.7	7.0	5,122	76.1	31.3	N	N	N
Yavapai County, Arizona.............................	3,300	75.5	21.6	N	N	N	N	N	N
Yuma County, Arizona................................	2,014	59.9	16.5	N	N	N	N	N	N
ARKANSAS.......................................	12,779	83.3	15.3	29,658	90.6	55.7	4,386	44.3	11.8
Benton County, Arkansas............................	2,926	81.7	12.0	7,890	96.4	78.4	N	N	N
Craighead County, Arkansas	N	N	N	N	N	N	N	N	N
Faulkner County, Arkansas..........................	N	N	N	N	N	N	N	N	N
Garland County, Arkansas...........................	N	N	N	N	N	N	N	N	N
Jefferson County, Arkansas.........................	N	N	N	N	N	N	N	N	N
Lonoke County, Arkansas............................	N	N	N	N	N	N	N	N	N
Pulaski County, Arkansas............................	N	N	N	6,224	98.2	71.4	N	N	N
Saline County, Arkansas.............................	N	N	N	N	N	N	N	N	N
Sebastian County, Arkansas........................	N	N	N	3,538	89.7	44.7	N	N	N
Washington County, Arkansas	N	N	N	3,196	79.5	46.4	N	N	N
White County, Arkansas	N	N	N	N	N	N	N	N	N
CALIFORNIA	218,013	78.4	16.8	4,363,485	88.5	54.3	106,486	86.5	20.7
Alameda County, California	8,131	81.7	27.0	387,062	88.6	61.5	9,799	89.3	22.5
Butte County, California..............................	N	N	N	5,766	88.1	33.4	N	N	N
Contra Costa County, California	4,473	76.1	20.5	150,242	91.1	59.0	N	N	N
El Dorado County, California	N	N	N	7,619	94.0	50.9	N	N	N
Fresno County, California	8,850	83.6	8.2	69,077	79.9	30.8	N	N	N
Humboldt County, California........................	4,065	87.6	11.4	N	N	N	N	N	N
Imperial County, California..........................	N	N	N	1,855	79.4	44.2	N	N	N
Kern County, California	6,193	68.5	4.7	30,367	83.3	43.4	N	N	N
Kings County, California..............................	N	N	N	4,078	94.0	37.1	N	N	N
Lake County, California	N	N	N	N	N	N	N	N	N
Los Angeles County, California....................	56,226	68.5	15.9	1,142,812	89.1	53.6	18,109	87.6	22.9

Table C-2. Educational Attainment of the Population, by Selected Counties, 2019—*Continued*

(Number; percent; dollars.)

	Educational attainment by race/ethnicity, 25 years and over								
	White alone			White alone, not Hispanic			Black alone		
State/County	Total	High school graduate or more (percent)	Bachelor's degree or more (percent)	Total	High school graduate or more (percent)	Bachelor's degree or more (percent)	Total	High school graduate or more (percent)	Bachelor's degree or more (percent)
CALIFORNIA—(*Continued*)									
Madera County, California............	69,646	81.0	16.5	40,600	93.7	21.2	3,111	82.7	4.6
Marin County, California...............	155,734	95.6	64.0	143,270	97.9	66.7	3,760	87.2	20.1
Mendocino County, California	54,423	85.8	24.1	44,372	91.6	26.9	N	N	N
Merced County, California............	92,120	77.0	17.2	53,972	87.9	23.1	6,484	84.1	13.0
Monterey County, California.........	141,048	86.5	38.4	100,127	95.9	47.4	8,766	90.1	18.7
Napa County, California...............	74,245	89.2	39.9	57,548	96.0	47.3	N	N	N
Nevada County, California	72,777	96.0	35.1	68,089	97.0	36.3	N	N	N
Orange County, California............	1,342,307	89.8	40.8	974,398	96.8	49.2	38,360	92.3	33.6
Placer County, California.............	238,360	94.5	40.4	211,515	96.2	42.3	5,344	99.3	46.5
Riverside County, California	1,028,768	86.5	24.7	650,253	94.7	31.1	109,723	92.0	24.8
Sacramento County, California.....	625,484	92.2	32.2	516,330	95.0	34.7	98,867	92.0	24.8
San Bernardino County, California	886,106	81.2	20.7	444,396	92.5	29.0	115,703	88.5	24.5
San Diego County, California........	1,653,225	88.4	40.2	1,134,118	96.2	49.9	108,728	91.4	25.4
San Francisco County, California...	332,778	96.9	74.9	297,090	98.5	78.5	35,155	85.3	35.0
San Joaquin County, California.....	285,583	80.4	18.1	174,975	92.6	24.3	35,953	86.7	16.7
San Luis Obispo County, California	167,684	92.0	38.6	139,836	95.5	42.2	3,195	90.5	6.5
San Mateo County, California.......	286,281	93.1	54.9	229,266	97.3	61.4	13,724	95.1	37.5
Santa Barbara County, California...	219,017	82.7	35.6	141,498	97.0	48.9	6,806	88.5	39.1
Santa Clara County, California......	624,654	90.6	51.6	454,730	97.1	62.3	33,240	91.7	38.7
Santa Cruz County, California.......	146,553	90.6	46.9	115,677	97.8	53.8	N	N	N
Shasta County, California............	112,754	93.7	21.9	105,803	94.3	21.9	N	N	N
Solano County, California.............	172,413	89.7	27.9	129,137	95.2	31.6	44,030	92.8	26.1
Sonoma County, California...........	280,178	94.4	42.2	248,671	96.5	44.6	5,793	84.8	27.5
Stanislaus County, California.......	282,823	80.7	16.2	164,814	90.6	20.9	8,616	83.0	12.6
Sutter County, California	44,105	81.6	20.4	31,920	92.2	25.2	N	N	N
Tehama County, California............	39,649	84.2	17.1	32,929	90.4	20.6	N	N	N
Tulare County, California..............	187,119	77.0	15.3	95,595	91.2	23.9	3,482	92.7	24.4
Ventura County, California............	469,448	86.4	34.0	291,180	97.1	45.6	10,854	95.4	40.2
Yolo County, California.................	99,532	88.9	37.8	68,360	95.9	48.0	3,370	94.7	25.3
Yuba County, California................	40,810	80.3	17.3	29,981	88.4	18.5	N	N	N
COLORADO..................	3,406,342	93.4	44.3	2,877,914	96.8	49.0	155,881	92.4	27.6
Adams County, Colorado...........	274,908	86.1	26.1	188,011	94.8	33.7	10,871	93.2	23.7
Arapahoe County, Colorado........	334,982	94.3	47.8	292,549	97.0	51.7	47,670	95.6	29.3
Boulder County, Colorado...........	198,162	95.2	65.8	177,031	98.3	70.1	N	N	N
Broomfield County, Colorado	43,216	97.8	58.3	39,176	99.1	60.7	N	N	N
Denver County, Colorado	421,739	92.1	57.4	325,238	97.9	67.9	43,287	89.6	26.6
Douglas County, Colorado..........	209,457	98.1	58.6	195,387	98.3	59.3	3,866	89.5	34.0
El Paso County, Colorado...........	387,839	96.1	41.2	345,451	97.2	43.6	28,532	97.3	29.4
Jefferson County, Colorado.........	390,228	94.8	48.0	345,195	96.9	51.3	4,278	82.5	47.1
Larimer County, Colorado	221,645	96.8	49.2	203,904	97.3	50.6	N	N	N
Mesa County, Colorado..............	102,008	91.4	30.3	91,340	92.4	32.9	N	N	N
Pueblo County, Colorado.............	97,095	93.2	25.1	66,396	96.3	29.5	N	N	N
Weld County, Colorado...............	188,251	89.3	30.9	148,702	95.6	36.0	2,223	81.4	9.2
CONNECTICUT.................	1,939,577	92.9	42.6	1,748,083	94.6	44.9	257,234	86.3	21.7
Fairfield County, Connecticut......	482,513	93.3	54.7	415,114	96.1	59.6	74,730	83.1	22.1
Hartford County, Connecticut......	451,295	92.9	42.3	403,824	94.5	44.7	81,380	88.7	22.6
Litchfield County, Connecticut.....	126,914	94.0	35.7	120,984	94.9	35.7	N	N	N
Middlesex County, Connecticut....	105,819	94.7	43.8	103,161	94.7	43.6	6,176	80.9	34.0
New Haven County, Connecticut ...	452,916	91.2	37.7	401,579	93.4	40.5	77,215	87.0	20.3
New London County, Connecticut ...	156,675	94.7	35.3	148,644	95.7	36.2	10,529	89.3	15.6
Tolland County, Connecticut........	87,471	94.4	40.6	83,809	95.3	40.9	N	N	N
Windham County, Connecticut.....	75,974	89.9	24.7	70,968	90.4	25.6	N	N	N
DELAWARE..................	490,907	90.8	34.6	457,913	93.0	36.1	145,150	90.6	24.6
Kent County, Delaware	85,086	88.2	25.4	79,163	89.0	26.3	29,995	89.1	23.6
New Castle County, Delaware......	255,419	92.0	38.5	235,157	94.7	40.4	96,651	92.8	26.8
Sussex County, Delaware...........	150,402	90.3	33.3	143,593	92.3	34.3	18,504	81.2	14.5
DISTRICT OF COLUMBIA..........	230,095	98.2	89.3	204,162	99.5	92.1	220,748	86.5	28.1
District of Columbia, District of Columbia....	230,095	98.2	89.3	204,162	99.5	92.1	220,748	86.5	28.1
FLORIDA..................	12,023,439	89.8	32.5	8,887,273	93.1	34.5	2,216,463	84.3	19.3
Alachua County, Florida..............	116,724	95.3	50.8	105,617	95.6	49.8	31,765	88.9	21.4
Bay County, Florida....................	105,268	92.0	28.1	99,625	92.0	28.2	11,866	89.0	12.1
Brevard County, Florida...............	380,949	93.0	31.2	348,481	93.1	31.2	38,487	86.9	20.9

Table C-2. Educational Attainment of the Population, by Selected Counties, 2019—*Continued*

(Number; percent; dollars.)

State/County	American Indian or Alaska Native alone			Asian alone			Native Hawaiian or Other Pacific Islander alone		
	Total	High school graduate or more (percent)	Bachelor's degree or more (percent)	Total	High school graduate or more (percent)	Bachelor's degree or more (percent)	Total	High school graduate or more (percent)	Bachelor's degree or more (percent)
CALIFORNIA—(*Continued*)									
Madera County, California	N	N	N	3,005	54.8	16.7	N	N	N
Marin County, California	N	N	N	12,554	92.7	60.3	N	N	N
Mendocino County, California	2,205	65.3	6.9	N	N	N	N	N	N
Merced County, California	1,957	94.1	8.9	13,532	82.5	34.7	N	N	N
Monterey County, California	N	N	N	20,321	89.3	36.7	N	N	N
Napa County, California	N	N	N	7,606	87.2	37.8	N	N	N
Nevada County, California	N	N	N	N	N	N	N	N	N
Orange County, California	8,987	80.0	28.8	495,753	89.1	56.4	6,563	90.9	26.0
Placer County, California	N	N	N	22,536	92.5	67.6	N	N	N
Riverside County, California	14,067	85.1	19.2	121,797	89.2	47.1	5,807	85.3	21.0
Sacramento County, California	6,839	87.8	18.9	176,710	84.3	41.9	13,042	79.8	13.9
San Bernardino County, California	10,667	85.6	14.3	115,812	92.6	56.6	5,816	92.0	12.5
San Diego County, California	16,619	88.6	15.2	298,565	90.1	52.4	9,429	87.2	30.6
San Francisco County, California	N	N	N	252,800	79.3	48.8	N	N	N
San Joaquin County, California	3,424	76.1	16.8	82,367	81.7	35.5	3,636	94.9	25.0
San Luis Obispo County, California	2,483	76.3	31.4	6,733	84.8	52.2	N	N	N
San Mateo County, California	2,703	71.3	20.7	178,711	93.4	60.9	6,169	77.7	18.6
Santa Barbara County, California	3,201	77.9	20.5	14,547	92.3	55.5	N	N	N
Santa Clara County, California	5,442	76.4	18.3	536,745	90.9	65.6	4,661	97.3	14.4
Santa Cruz County, California	N	N	N	8,034	96.7	54.3	N	N	N
Shasta County, California	N	N	N	3,940	85.5	41.6	N	N	N
Solano County, California	N	N	N	53,144	91.1	40.2	2,843	88.1	14.0
Sonoma County, California	N	N	N	15,083	86.8	46.7	N	N	N
Stanislaus County, California	2,432	87.7	29.9	22,160	83.3	37.9	N	N	N
Sutter County, California	N	N	N	10,839	66.6	25.5	N	N	N
Tehama County, California	N	N	N	N	N	N	N	N	N
Tulare County, California	5,690	78.7	22.8	11,383	71.5	27.7	N	N	N
Ventura County, California	3,295	65.5	9.0	48,430	95.8	57.4	N	N	N
Yolo County, California	N	N	N	15,798	92.2	64.5	N	N	N
Yuba County, California	N	N	N	2,718	77.9	21.7	N	N	N
COLORADO	38,549	84.1	22.0	134,942	90.0	53.4	5,685	60.5	16.9
Adams County, Colorado	3,426	67.1	18.6	14,213	84.0	35.6	N	N	N
Arapahoe County, Colorado	3,609	81.9	16.4	29,326	86.2	50.0	N	N	N
Boulder County, Colorado	N	N	N	10,233	95.7	70.3	N	N	N
Broomfield County, Colorado	N	N	N	3,618	92.1	59.2	N	N	N
Denver County, Colorado	3,466	97.5	31.2	21,027	88.8	60.2	N	N	N
Douglas County, Colorado	N	N	N	12,831	97.1	69.8	N	N	N
El Paso County, Colorado	4,921	79.3	26.1	14,216	92.5	42.9	N	N	N
Jefferson County, Colorado	3,074	100.0	29.9	12,172	91.6	50.5	N	N	N
Larimer County, Colorado	N	N	N	4,385	90.9	61.8	N	N	N
Mesa County, Colorado	N	N	N	N	N	N	N	N	N
Pueblo County, Colorado	4,250	70.4	9.6	N	N	N	N	N	N
Weld County, Colorado	N	N	N	3,407	93.8	51.3	N	N	N
CONNECTICUT	5,100	90.3	24.7	114,306	90.6	65.3	N	N	N
Fairfield County, Connecticut	N	N	N	36,479	91.1	68.4	N	N	N
Hartford County, Connecticut	N	N	N	35,336	90.6	70.0	N	N	N
Litchfield County, Connecticut	N	N	N	2,734	91.9	53.8	N	N	N
Middlesex County, Connecticut	N	N	N	3,687	86.8	41.2	N	N	N
New Haven County, Connecticut	N	N	N	23,443	91.1	65.6	N	N	N
New London County, Connecticut	N	N	N	7,919	88.2	46.4	N	N	N
Tolland County, Connecticut	N	N	N	N	N	N	N	N	N
Windham County, Connecticut	N	N	N	N	N	N	N	N	N
DELAWARE	3,160	83.2	11.8	25,875	94.4	65.9	N	N	N
Kent County, Delaware	N	N	N	2,401	99.2	25.2	N	N	N
New Castle County, Delaware	N	N	N	21,266	94.0	70.5	N	N	N
Sussex County, Delaware	N	N	N	N	N	N	N	N	N
DISTRICT OF COLUMBIA	N	N	N	22,230	95.4	80.3	N	N	N
District of Columbia, District of Columbia	N	N	N	22,230	95.4	80.3	N	N	N
FLORIDA	41,021	81.3	23.9	441,665	87.2	50.6	9,935	80.8	33.3
Alachua County, Florida	N	N	N	9,632	94.4	72.9	N	N	N
Bay County, Florida	N	N	N	2,809	75.0	23.6	N	N	N
Brevard County, Florida	N	N	N	11,488	90.9	44.0	N	N	N

Table C-2. Educational Attainment of the Population, by Selected Counties, 2019—*Continued*

(Number; percent; dollars.)

State/County	Educational attainment by race/ethnicity, 25 years and over								
	White alone			White alone, not Hispanic			Black alone		
	Total	High school graduate or more (percent)	Bachelor's degree or more (percent)	Total	High school graduate or more (percent)	Bachelor's degree or more (percent)	Total	High school graduate or more (percent)	Bachelor's degree or more (percent)
FLORIDA—(*Continued*)									
Broward County, Florida	889,455	91.3	37.5	536,155	94.0	40.2	366,215	87.0	21.5
Charlotte County, Florida	142,991	91.9	22.7	136,326	92.6	23.1	8,105	71.3	9.8
Citrus County, Florida	112,031	88.0	21.9	107,162	88.2	22.3	3,229	75.8	12.4
Clay County, Florida	121,563	95.5	28.2	113,350	95.4	28.4	16,938	91.1	32.2
Collier County, Florida	269,097	90.6	37.2	205,100	95.4	43.3	15,627	71.4	16.2
Columbia County, Florida	38,751	86.2	16.6	37,143	86.3	15.2	7,797	88.4	5.2
Duval County, Florida	411,812	91.7	35.0	370,917	92.7	35.8	179,621	87.6	18.7
Escambia County, Florida	154,716	90.6	27.2	147,302	91.2	27.1	43,830	82.2	10.8
Flagler County, Florida	75,232	90.8	26.2	68,995	91.3	27.4	7,463	95.0	15.9
Hernando County, Florida	131,142	90.5	20.6	116,316	91.3	21.0	6,627	76.8	7.6
Highlands County, Florida	69,994	87.3	17.6	58,610	88.8	17.7	7,285	78.7	9.2
Hillsborough County, Florida	737,540	90.4	36.7	524,197	93.3	41.2	158,830	88.0	23.1
Indian River County, Florida	112,357	92.4	32.4	100,092	94.6	34.6	8,789	78.7	17.3
Lake County, Florida	230,763	90.4	25.6	198,890	91.8	26.7	25,237	84.7	27.6
Lee County, Florida	507,946	90.5	30.2	422,602	94.1	33.3	40,114	85.7	15.1
Leon County, Florida	113,695	95.3	52.3	106,950	96.0	53.8	50,062	85.2	30.9
Manatee County, Florida	268,603	91.2	31.4	234,076	94.6	34.4	20,857	89.7	17.9
Marion County, Florida	232,354	90.0	21.7	203,366	91.1	21.5	30,583	84.6	12.2
Martin County, Florida	113,894	92.4	36.6	103,741	93.8	38.1	5,614	72.5	21.2
Miami-Dade County, Florida	1,501,054	80.4	33.1	242,940	94.7	52.8	303,913	80.0	17.4
Monroe County, Florida	51,082	92.7	36.1	40,438	97.8	41.1	4,512	98.4	18.3
Nassau County, Florida	60,234	88.3	30.5	58,816	89.0	31.0	4,577	93.0	24.7
Okaloosa County, Florida	116,567	94.4	34.0	111,532	94.6	34.2	12,172	87.9	17.3
Orange County, Florida	623,508	91.1	37.9	398,863	94.8	44.9	186,981	83.0	24.9
Osceola County, Florida	181,052	88.1	26.2	83,116	91.1	28.8	29,577	79.8	15.4
Palm Beach County, Florida	835,371	91.8	42.0	649,778	95.8	46.3	182,483	81.0	19.3
Pasco County, Florida	354,923	90.6	24.0	308,089	91.4	24.5	21,714	89.0	33.1
Pinellas County, Florida	636,600	91.7	34.2	588,280	92.3	34.6	66,468	88.1	17.3
Polk County, Florida	392,948	88.4	21.7	315,307	90.7	22.9	69,973	82.3	13.4
Putnam County, Florida	44,006	82.2	12.9	40,470	86.4	13.9	7,959	86.0	11.6
St. Johns County, Florida	169,361	96.1	46.9	158,620	96.3	47.1	9,630	91.0	26.4
St. Lucie County, Florida	182,106	88.4	21.9	148,838	90.6	22.1	42,145	81.4	15.0
Santa Rosa County, Florida	113,457	92.4	27.6	108,920	92.3	27.7	6,973	84.1	14.7
Sarasota County, Florida	321,591	94.2	37.1	300,770	94.8	37.8	12,041	89.7	16.7
Seminole County, Florida	248,475	95.4	43.3	207,011	96.6	46.3	38,420	89.1	23.2
Sumter County, Florida	107,602	95.2	33.6	103,609	95.8	33.9	7,155	85.2	15.3
Volusia County, Florida	339,418	92.1	25.2	311,105	92.9	25.9	37,348	89.7	17.2
Walton County, Florida	48,591	91.0	30.9	47,024	91.3	31.2	N	N	N
GEORGIA	4,279,288	89.4	35.5	3,947,682	91.2	36.5	2,186,956	87.9	24.8
Barrow County, Georgia	44,249	85.9	23.1	40,286	86.7	23.0	6,562	81.1	20.2
Bartow County, Georgia	62,129	83.7	19.5	58,851	85.0	19.7	6,945	88.9	1.1
Bibb County, Georgia	43,954	90.8	36.4	42,345	91.8	37.1	51,744	84.3	13.5
Bulloch County, Georgia	30,778	90.3	30.6	29,963	90.0	29.6	11,969	92.2	17.1
Carroll County, Georgia	59,599	84.0	21.5	56,739	86.2	21.6	14,125	85.2	9.0
Catoosa County, Georgia	44,909	90.5	23.8	43,396	90.4	24.6	N	N	N
Chatham County, Georgia	110,132	94.6	41.8	104,199	95.0	42.3	74,272	85.0	24.4
Cherokee County, Georgia	152,500	92.2	38.3	141,689	94.0	39.6	12,136	92.6	33.9
Clarke County, Georgia	45,125	96.3	60.2	40,176	96.6	64.3	21,318	82.4	20.4
Clayton County, Georgia	32,234	75.1	12.5	21,370	80.0	12.5	129,070	88.6	20.7
Cobb County, Georgia	305,657	94.0	53.0	283,623	95.6	54.8	139,766	96.1	40.3
Columbia County, Georgia	78,207	93.1	43.3	72,802	94.8	43.8	18,665	95.3	27.8
Coweta County, Georgia	78,089	91.7	28.5	73,457	92.5	29.5	17,679	84.9	22.7
DeKalb County, Georgia	188,911	94.1	68.8	169,667	98.0	73.1	277,415	89.9	28.7
Dougherty County, Georgia	16,869	86.6	31.4	16,330	86.1	30.2	37,909	80.6	15.5
Douglas County, Georgia	46,018	89.0	23.8	40,460	91.7	25.6	41,512	94.9	41.3
Fayette County, Georgia	53,401	97.1	48.9	49,660	97.6	50.6	19,759	92.6	31.8
Floyd County, Georgia	52,551	87.9	24.7	49,465	89.4	26.0	9,212	83.4	17.8
Forsyth County, Georgia	121,333	95.4	51.4	113,853	96.7	52.2	7,018	95.6	64.3
Fulton County, Georgia	341,131	97.5	74.1	312,101	98.3	75.7	309,945	90.3	35.4
Glynn County, Georgia	42,772	93.9	33.3	41,352	93.8	33.6	14,509	84.4	13.9
Gwinnett County, Georgia	291,085	90.4	42.4	237,645	95.2	46.9	165,471	94.5	39.3
Hall County, Georgia	118,239	79.4	26.2	91,122	88.6	30.4	9,993	90.9	21.7
Henry County, Georgia	72,763	89.3	21.3	66,483	93.3	22.1	71,969	95.5	31.5
Houston County, Georgia	64,284	94.2	28.8	61,258	94.9	29.2	30,080	92.1	25.4
Jackson County, Georgia	42,848	86.8	26.2	40,447	87.6	25.8	4,007	85.8	19.9
Lowndes County, Georgia	41,028	94.2	31.9	39,563	95.3	32.7	24,771	85.7	12.1

Table C-2. Educational Attainment of the Population, by Selected Counties, 2019—*Continued*

(Number; percent; dollars.)

State/County	Educational attainment by race/ethnicity, 25 years and over								
	American Indian or Alaska Native alone			Asian alone			Native Hawaiian or Other Pacific Islander alone		
	Total	High school graduate or more (percent)	Bachelor's degree or more (percent)	Total	High school graduate or more (percent)	Bachelor's degree or more (percent)	Total	High school graduate or more (percent)	Bachelor's degree or more (percent)
FLORIDA—*(Continued)*									
Broward County, Florida	3,382	82.4	33.0	53,960	85.9	48.6	N	N	N
Charlotte County, Florida	N	N	N	2,172	74.4	30.3	N	N	N
Citrus County, Florida	N	N	N	N	N	N	N	N	N
Clay County, Florida	N	N	N	5,324	92.5	31.8	N	N	N
Collier County, Florida	N	N	N	3,700	62.2	39.9	N	N	N
Columbia County, Florida	N	N	N	N	N	N	N	N	N
Duval County, Florida	N	N	N	32,463	94.0	43.6	N	N	N
Escambia County, Florida	N	N	N	6,328	86.7	32.5	N	N	N
Flagler County, Florida	N	N	N	N	N	N	N	N	N
Hernando County, Florida	N	N	N	N	N	N	N	N	N
Highlands County, Florida	N	N	N	N	N	N	N	N	N
Hillsborough County, Florida	N	N	N	43,953	84.9	62.2	N	N	N
Indian River County, Florida	N	N	N	N	N	N	N	N	N
Lake County, Florida	N	N	N	5,502	93.6	24.4	N	N	N
Lee County, Florida	N	N	N	9,671	90.8	49.7	N	N	N
Leon County, Florida	N	N	N	N	N	N	N	N	N
Manatee County, Florida	N	N	N	7,018	73.1	48.8	N	N	N
Marion County, Florida	N	N	N	3,361	82.8	23.2	N	N	N
Martin County, Florida	N	N	N	N	N	N	N	N	N
Miami-Dade County, Florida	N	N	N	32,711	91.5	58.7	N	N	N
Monroe County, Florida	N	N	N	N	N	N	N	N	N
Nassau County, Florida	N	N	N	N	N	N	N	N	N
Okaloosa County, Florida	N	N	N	4,442	90.3	32.1	N	N	N
Orange County, Florida	N	N	N	55,368	85.9	50.6	N	N	N
Osceola County, Florida	N	N	N	6,816	90.7	49.7	N	N	N
Palm Beach County, Florida	N	N	N	31,586	89.1	51.6	N	N	N
Pasco County, Florida	N	N	N	10,794	91.6	55.0	N	N	N
Pinellas County, Florida	N	N	N	25,718	82.5	42.7	N	N	N
Polk County, Florida	N	N	N	9,912	79.0	42.6	N	N	N
Putnam County, Florida	N	N	N	N	N	N	N	N	N
St. Johns County, Florida	N	N	N	4,797	97.4	63.0	N	N	N
St. Lucie County, Florida	N	N	N	5,645	70.2	44.7	N	N	N
Santa Rosa County, Florida	N	N	N	N	N	N	N	N	N
Sarasota County, Florida	N	N	N	5,162	84.5	54.2	N	N	N
Seminole County, Florida	N	N	N	16,392	90.0	69.3	N	N	N
Sumter County, Florida	N	N	N	N	N	N	N	N	N
Volusia County, Florida	N	N	N	7,710	88.6	33.6	N	N	N
Walton County, Florida	N	N	N	N	N	N	N	N	N
GEORGIA	24,821	67.3	13.8	302,385	86.8	57.3	3,675	85.0	31.8
Barrow County, Georgia	N	N	N	N	N	N	N	N	N
Bartow County, Georgia	N	N	N	N	N	N	N	N	N
Bibb County, Georgia	N	N	N	2,288	78.8	60.6	N	N	N
Bulloch County, Georgia	N	N	N	N	N	N	N	N	N
Carroll County, Georgia	N	N	N	N	N	N	N	N	N
Catoosa County, Georgia	N	N	N	N	N	N	N	N	N
Chatham County, Georgia	N	N	N	5,932	64.2	21.1	N	N	N
Cherokee County, Georgia	N	N	N	N	N	N	N	N	N
Clarke County, Georgia	N	N	N	N	N	N	N	N	N
Clayton County, Georgia	N	N	N	9,552	67.2	19.8	N	N	N
Cobb County, Georgia	N	N	N	29,254	93.1	69.3	N	N	N
Columbia County, Georgia	N	N	N	3,827	87.2	52.1	N	N	N
Coweta County, Georgia	N	N	N	N	N	N	N	N	N
DeKalb County, Georgia	5,957	64.8	6.8	32,532	81.0	56.2	N	N	N
Dougherty County, Georgia	N	N	N	N	N	N	N	N	N
Douglas County, Georgia	N	N	N	N	N	N	N	N	N
Fayette County, Georgia	N	N	N	N	N	N	N	N	N
Floyd County, Georgia	N	N	N	N	N	N	N	N	N
Forsyth County, Georgia	N	N	N	23,311	95.8	86.5	N	N	N
Fulton County, Georgia	N	N	N	53,697	96.8	85.9	N	N	N
Glynn County, Georgia	N	N	N	N	N	N	N	N	N
Gwinnett County, Georgia	N	N	N	79,887	84.6	44.8	N	N	N
Hall County, Georgia	N	N	N	2,434	66.7	24.6	N	N	N
Henry County, Georgia	N	N	N	5,308	73.7	22.7	N	N	N
Houston County, Georgia	N	N	N	N	N	N	N	N	N
Jackson County, Georgia	N	N	N	N	N	N	N	N	N
Lowndes County, Georgia	N	N	N	N	N	N	N	N	N

Table C-2. Educational Attainment of the Population, by Selected Counties, 2019—*Continued*

(Number; percent; dollars.)

State/County	Educational attainment by race/ethnicity, 25 years and over								
	White alone			White alone, not Hispanic			Black alone		
	Total	High school graduate or more (percent)	Bachelor's degree or more (percent)	Total	High school graduate or more (percent)	Bachelor's degree or more (percent)	Total	High school graduate or more (percent)	Bachelor's degree or more (percent)
GEORGIA—*(Continued)*									
Muscogee County, Georgia	57,911	90.3	30.7	54,685	90.2	31.0	59,575	88.2	18.8
Newton County, Georgia	38,259	81.9	17.9	34,770	86.2	19.6	33,342	90.1	17.9
Paulding County, Georgia	84,856	86.2	20.9	78,946	87.7	21.2	21,097	94.7	26.9
Richmond County, Georgia	51,272	86.2	26.9	49,059	86.0	26.3	73,615	86.6	12.6
Rockdale County, Georgia	24,712	85.7	17.9	20,804	87.0	19.6	31,488	91.3	28.3
Spalding County, Georgia	29,690	85.3	19.2	27,728	86.6	19.5	15,090	83.2	14.9
Troup County, Georgia	28,103	91.7	28.1	27,350	91.8	28.7	16,343	86.3	3.8
Walker County, Georgia	45,629	80.3	16.5	45,408	80.2	16.5	N	N	N
Walton County, Georgia	50,895	88.9	25.0	48,783	88.9	25.0	12,050	71.3	14.6
Whitfield County, Georgia	60,736	71.8	16.5	43,750	83.9	21.5	2,891	91.3	21.3
HAWAII	259,996	96.9	44.5	237,027	97.3	46.3	18,397	98.4	31.0
Hawaii County, Hawaii	55,759	97.0	41.6	51,790	97.4	43.9	N	N	N
Honolulu County, Hawaii	138,786	97.6	48.6	125,726	97.8	49.9	16,895	98.8	29.7
Kauai County, Hawaii	18,129	96.8	40.1	17,239	97.1	40.5	N	N	N
Maui County, Hawaii	47,317	94.9	37.6	42,272	96.0	40.6	N	N	N
IDAHO	1,066,998	92.8	29.2	998,524	94.2	30.1	5,607	92.9	13.4
Ada County, Idaho	301,205	95.3	39.6	285,028	96.1	40.5	N	N	N
Bannock County, Idaho	50,031	95.3	28.8	48,218	95.2	28.8	N	N	N
Bonneville County, Idaho	67,028	93.9	33.3	62,584	95.3	34.2	N	N	N
Canyon County, Idaho	118,379	91.9	22.2	108,803	93.2	23.2	N	N	N
Kootenai County, Idaho	110,242	94.0	24.6	106,894	94.0	25.1	N	N	N
Twin Falls County, Idaho	52,351	85.4	21.3	46,005	90.2	23.2	N	N	N
ILLINOIS	6,414,127	91.9	37.3	5,640,997	94.6	39.9	1,177,578	86.5	22.6
Adams County, Illinois	43,399	91.3	24.1	42,787	91.1	23.7	N	N	N
Champaign County, Illinois	92,924	95.1	46.9	88,714	96.4	47.5	14,313	82.9	16.0
Cook County, Illinois	2,121,092	90.4	47.2	1,661,656	95.1	55.1	812,165	87.1	23.7
DeKalb County, Illinois	53,726	93.3	34.0	51,325	94.5	34.4	N	N	N
DuPage County, Illinois	497,249	95.1	49.8	444,385	97.1	53.0	28,250	89.3	33.4
Kane County, Illinois	273,150	89.0	36.0	220,923	96.3	41.5	19,425	90.7	23.5
Kankakee County, Illinois	60,432	91.5	20.1	55,659	93.3	20.9	9,479	85.6	10.4
Kendall County, Illinois	68,358	93.8	39.6	58,606	96.4	42.4	6,171	92.6	40.3
Lake County, Illinois	353,407	92.0	47.1	302,496	96.6	52.8	28,756	87.4	20.3
LaSalle County, Illinois	71,979	90.9	17.0	67,982	92.1	17.6	N	N	N
McHenry County, Illinois	196,680	94.3	34.6	177,300	96.3	36.4	3,012	95.6	49.5
McLean County, Illinois	90,167	95.6	45.6	86,804	95.8	46.0	7,253	88.3	29.1
Macon County, Illinois	58,620	94.5	23.5	57,978	94.6	23.4	11,179	88.4	10.4
Madison County, Illinois	165,749	94.6	31.1	162,240	94.9	31.1	14,046	80.6	21.1
Peoria County, Illinois	93,516	95.1	33.4	90,987	95.3	33.7	19,121	87.4	15.2
Rock Island County, Illinois	81,247	91.0	25.7	75,569	92.6	26.7	9,083	74.1	6.3
St. Clair County, Illinois	121,006	93.4	30.4	116,736	93.7	30.5	50,435	88.1	19.9
Sangamon County, Illinois	117,117	94.4	35.5	114,600	94.6	35.8	14,162	83.3	17.7
Tazewell County, Illinois	89,539	94.6	27.5	88,067	94.6	27.0	N	N	N
Vermilion County, Illinois	44,376	91.2	13.4	43,040	92.5	13.3	6,128	82.4	2.0
Will County, Illinois	346,975	93.0	35.6	305,833	95.7	38.5	52,321	92.1	31.7
Williamson County, Illinois	43,758	93.4	30.0	43,438	93.6	30.3	N	N	N
Winnebago County, Illinois	159,606	89.8	25.2	143,908	93.0	27.0	22,265	85.7	13.5
INDIANA	3,843,248	90.6	27.3	3,692,360	91.3	27.7	395,797	87.7	19.3
Allen County, Indiana	201,712	92.4	30.7	192,723	93.6	31.4	26,346	88.0	18.4
Bartholomew County, Indiana	49,686	90.9	32.1	47,210	91.7	31.7	N	N	N
Boone County, Indiana	42,238	92.9	47.2	40,935	92.7	46.2	N	N	N
Clark County, Indiana	73,848	90.8	21.6	71,018	92.5	21.2	N	N	N
Delaware County, Indiana	65,076	93.1	22.9	63,717	93.0	23.4	4,775	80.0	5.7
Elkhart County, Indiana	113,189	83.9	21.0	105,225	85.3	21.8	6,939	83.2	13.1
Floyd County, Indiana	50,058	92.4	29.6	49,042	93.3	30.1	2,169	92.6	6.7
Grant County, Indiana	39,252	88.8	22.2	38,240	88.7	22.3	2,455	91.2	9.7
Hamilton County, Indiana	194,341	97.9	62.8	187,931	98.2	63.5	10,072	100.0	59.6
Hancock County, Indiana	50,511	90.2	29.3	50,121	90.2	29.3	N	N	N
Hendricks County, Indiana	99,651	95.1	36.0	96,959	95.0	36.2	8,133	99.5	40.4
Howard County, Indiana	50,893	90.2	19.0	50,329	90.3	19.2	5,225	84.1	11.3
Johnson County, Indiana	96,996	93.8	31.9	95,019	94.0	32.5	N	N	N
Kosciusko County, Indiana	50,091	86.4	27.0	48,317	88.2	27.5	N	N	N
Lake County, Indiana	221,501	92.6	25.8	193,950	93.8	27.3	73,100	88.1	15.3
LaPorte County, Indiana	67,179	90.0	19.3	64,140	90.8	20.0	7,787	76.9	7.7

Table C-2. Educational Attainment of the Population, by Selected Counties, 2019—*Continued*

(Number; percent; dollars.)

| | Educational attainment by race/ethnicity, 25 years and over | | | | | | | | |
| | American Indian or Alaska Native alone | | | Asian alone | | | Native Hawaiian or Other Pacific Islander alone | | |
State/County	Total	High school graduate or more (percent)	Bachelor's degree or more (percent)	Total	High school graduate or more (percent)	Bachelor's degree or more (percent)	Total	High school graduate or more (percent)	Bachelor's degree or more (percent)
GEORGIA—(*Continued*)									
Muscogee County, Georgia	N	N	N	3,730	88.1	32.0	N	N	N
Newton County, Georgia	N	N	N	N	N	N	N	N	N
Paulding County, Georgia	N	N	N	N	N	N	N	N	N
Richmond County, Georgia	N	N	N	2,074	71.8	34.7	N	N	N
Rockdale County, Georgia	N	N	N	N	N	N	N	N	N
Spalding County, Georgia	N	N	N	N	N	N	N	N	N
Troup County, Georgia	N	N	N	N	N	N	N	N	N
Walker County, Georgia	N	N	N	N	N	N	N	N	N
Walton County, Georgia	N	N	N	N	N	N	N	N	N
Whitfield County, Georgia	N	N	N	1,201	90.1	36.8	N	N	N
HAWAII	3,815	70.0	28.6	434,234	89.4	35.0	98,477	89.1	12.2
Hawaii County, Hawaii	N	N	N	37,978	90.9	32.6	15,750	89.1	10.4
Honolulu County, Hawaii	N	N	N	339,406	89.7	36.9	65,315	90.0	13.2
Kauai County, Hawaii	N	N	N	17,840	89.5	27.7	5,322	86.5	9.2
Maui County, Hawaii	N	N	N	39,008	85.6	24.8	12,082	85.6	10.0
IDAHO	14,880	82.3	19.9	18,301	86.5	48.0	N	N	N
Ada County, Idaho	2,615	87.1	29.7	9,073	85.6	49.2	N	N	N
Bannock County, Idaho	N	N	N	N	N	N	N	N	N
Bonneville County, Idaho	N	N	N	N	N	N	N	N	N
Canyon County, Idaho	N	N	N	N	N	N	N	N	N
Kootenai County, Idaho	N	N	N	N	N	N	N	N	N
Twin Falls County, Idaho	N	N	N	N	N	N	N	N	N
ILLINOIS	20,287	74.0	23.6	513,285	90.5	65.0	2,792	93.4	34.1
Adams County, Illinois	N	N	N	N	N	N	N	N	N
Champaign County, Illinois	N	N	N	10,617	93.0	77.8	N	N	N
Cook County, Illinois	10,328	71.1	24.9	292,621	89.5	63.1	N	N	N
DeKalb County, Illinois	N	N	N	N	N	N	N	N	N
DuPage County, Illinois	N	N	N	80,606	93.6	73.4	N	N	N
Kane County, Illinois	N	N	N	15,047	85.0	53.0	N	N	N
Kankakee County, Illinois	N	N	N	N	N	N	N	N	N
Kendall County, Illinois	N	N	N	N	N	N	N	N	N
Lake County, Illinois	N	N	N	39,009	96.7	75.4	N	N	N
LaSalle County, Illinois	N	N	N	N	N	N	N	N	N
McHenry County, Illinois	N	N	N	6,244	78.9	49.0	N	N	N
McLean County, Illinois	N	N	N	5,160	86.6	74.7	N	N	N
Macon County, Illinois	N	N	N	N	N	N	N	N	N
Madison County, Illinois	N	N	N	1,967	89.4	37.0	N	N	N
Peoria County, Illinois	N	N	N	N	N	N	N	N	N
Rock Island County, Illinois	N	N	N	1,644	88.2	61.8	N	N	N
St. Clair County, Illinois	N	N	N	2,614	79.0	33.3	N	N	N
Sangamon County, Illinois	N	N	N	N	N	N	N	N	N
Tazewell County, Illinois	N	N	N	N	N	N	N	N	N
Vermilion County, Illinois	N	N	N	N	N	N	N	N	N
Will County, Illinois	N	N	N	27,967	92.1	58.0	N	N	N
Williamson County, Illinois	N	N	N	N	N	N	N	N	N
Winnebago County, Illinois	N	N	N	5,204	84.3	63.5	N	N	N
INDIANA	13,195	81.2	11.0	101,424	84.6	59.1	N	N	N
Allen County, Indiana	N	N	N	9,297	49.2	32.5	N	N	N
Bartholomew County, Indiana	N	N	N	N	N	N	N	N	N
Boone County, Indiana	N	N	N	N	N	N	N	N	N
Clark County, Indiana	N	N	N	N	N	N	N	N	N
Delaware County, Indiana	N	N	N	N	N	N	N	N	N
Elkhart County, Indiana	N	N	N	N	N	N	N	N	N
Floyd County, Indiana	N	N	N	N	N	N	N	N	N
Grant County, Indiana	N	N	N	N	N	N	N	N	N
Hamilton County, Indiana	N	N	N	13,552	89.2	74.5	N	N	N
Hancock County, Indiana	N	N	N	N	N	N	N	N	N
Hendricks County, Indiana	N	N	N	N	N	N	N	N	N
Howard County, Indiana	N	N	N	N	N	N	N	N	N
Johnson County, Indiana	N	N	N	3,291	59.4	37.5	N	N	N
Kosciusko County, Indiana	N	N	N	N	N	N	N	N	N
Lake County, Indiana	N	N	N	6,021	85.1	50.3	N	N	N
LaPorte County, Indiana	N	N	N	N	N	N	N	N	N

Table C-2. Educational Attainment of the Population, by Selected Counties, 2019—*Continued*

(Number; percent; dollars.)

State/County	Educational attainment by race/ethnicity, 25 years and over								
	White alone			White alone, not Hispanic			Black alone		
	Total	High school graduate or more (percent)	Bachelor's degree or more (percent)	Total	High school graduate or more (percent)	Bachelor's degree or more (percent)	Total	High school graduate or more (percent)	Bachelor's degree or more (percent)
INDIANA—(*Continued*)									
Madison County, Indiana..............	81,336	88.9	18.6	79,371	89.5	18.2	7,183	86.4	14.1
Marion County, Indiana................	415,725	89.0	35.1	383,033	90.8	36.6	169,458	87.3	20.4
Monroe County, Indiana...............	75,962	95.1	44.2	74,865	95.2	44.5	N	N	N
Morgan County, Indiana...............	47,744	90.9	17.7	47,453	90.9	17.7	N	N	N
Porter County, Indiana	108,846	95.0	27.6	100,406	95.3	27.8	3,848	94.5	11.0
St. Joseph County, Indiana	144,639	91.6	31.7	137,287	92.6	31.6	19,583	86.1	17.0
Tippecanoe County, Indiana	92,129	92.4	38.1	87,365	92.7	38.7	5,248	93.2	34.1
Vanderburgh County, Indiana......	109,364	91.3	28.7	108,179	91.4	28.8	9,559	84.3	13.3
Vigo County, Indiana..................	61,357	92.6	25.8	60,512	92.8	25.6	4,938	90.6	18.3
Wayne County, Indiana...............	41,309	88.5	17.4	41,125	88.5	17.5	N	N	N
IOWA...........................	1,950,864	93.6	29.5	1,877,984	94.6	30.2	72,382	83.0	14.9
Black Hawk County, Iowa............	72,602	93.6	31.0	70,794	93.7	31.2	7,135	86.5	17.9
Dallas County, Iowa...................	55,483	97.3	53.6	53,024	97.9	54.2	N	N	N
Dubuque County, Iowa...............	61,354	95.3	33.3	61,033	95.3	33.1	N	N	N
Johnson County, Iowa................	75,631	95.3	56.1	73,280	95.6	56.6	N	N	N
Linn County, Iowa.....................	139,066	95.5	33.2	135,887	95.7	33.5	6,961	74.2	10.9
Polk County, Iowa	284,275	94.5	39.3	268,257	96.3	41.0	19,926	84.1	20.1
Pottawattamie County, Iowa.......	60,348	91.6	23.5	57,731	92.5	23.4	N	N	N
Scott County, Iowa....................	104,425	94.3	33.3	99,028	94.6	33.7	7,925	86.4	9.4
Story County, Iowa....................	44,962	97.7	49.7	44,809	97.7	49.6	N	N	N
Woodbury County, Iowa..............	58,747	88.8	23.9	51,485	94.4	26.7	N	N	N
KANSAS	1,653,103	93.2	35.3	1,530,789	95.1	36.9	101,769	87.4	20.9
Butler County, Kansas...............	41,264	93.4	31.1	40,009	93.7	31.0	N	N	N
Douglas County, Kansas	61,552	95.7	48.8	58,840	96.2	48.9	N	N	N
Johnson County, Kansas.............	354,763	96.8	57.0	337,396	98.0	58.6	17,439	91.6	39.1
Leavenworth County, Kansas	47,626	94.7	33.1	45,261	94.8	34.4	4,151	82.4	23.8
Riley County, Kansas..................	31,297	97.0	46.3	29,775	98.0	47.8	N	N	N
Sedgwick County, Kansas	273,842	92.0	34.0	246,914	94.7	35.8	27,753	88.7	16.8
Shawnee County, Kansas	101,268	95.7	34.4	95,261	96.2	35.9	9,340	81.7	8.6
Wyandotte County, Kansas	63,709	83.8	21.7	49,685	91.3	25.9	23,362	85.1	15.8
KENTUCKY	2,705,849	87.4	25.2	2,648,824	87.7	25.2	232,582	88.2	19.3
Boone County, Kentucky	81,940	93.4	31.9	78,870	94.7	33.0	N	N	N
Bullitt County, Kentucky.............	55,770	88.9	15.6	55,047	88.8	15.8	N	N	N
Campbell County, Kentucky.........	62,098	92.0	40.6	61,344	92.0	40.5	N	N	N
Christian County, Kentucky	29,666	83.1	22.7	28,158	83.8	23.5	9,238	91.7	12.6
Daviess County, Kentucky	63,145	88.9	25.3	62,274	89.0	25.4	1,595	93.0	42.0
Fayette County, Kentucky	162,526	94.1	48.8	157,326	95.3	49.8	29,208	89.5	23.1
Hardin County, Kentucky.............	60,226	91.4	21.9	57,950	91.2	21.4	9,127	91.3	26.3
Jefferson County, Kentucky.........	399,770	92.3	37.3	378,915	92.9	37.8	107,576	88.6	21.6
Kenton County, Kentucky	105,182	91.8	33.5	103,746	92.2	33.4	4,417	84.5	15.2
McCracken County, Kentucky.......	40,088	89.9	25.6	39,849	90.1	25.5	4,111	81.8	9.4
Madison County, Kentucky..........	53,361	91.2	32.3	52,706	91.4	32.2	N	N	N
Oldham County, Kentucky...........	40,882	94.3	41.8	39,583	94.4	42.2	3,050	86.1	39.0
Warren County, Kentucky...........	67,989	92.1	36.9	65,887	92.8	37.2	7,089	82.6	18.4
LOUISIANA......................	2,036,883	88.2	28.4	1,938,051	88.9	28.9	948,531	82.1	17.1
Ascension Parish, Louisiana	59,802	93.9	28.7	58,095	93.8	28.9	19,041	90.9	16.0
Bossier Parish, Louisiana	62,764	90.9	26.0	58,749	93.6	27.5	18,001	89.0	9.3
Caddo Parish, Louisiana	81,640	91.1	31.6	79,724	91.2	31.9	75,742	81.7	15.4
Calcasieu Parish, Louisiana........	97,989	87.9	24.5	94,751	88.8	24.7	30,816	80.4	15.5
East Baton Rouge Parish, Louisiana	139,443	95.6	46.3	134,728	95.8	46.7	123,220	86.9	21.7
Iberia Parish, Louisiana..............	30,198	87.8	20.3	29,664	88.3	20.4	13,750	76.9	6.4
Jefferson Parish, Louisiana.........	203,006	89.2	30.1	172,440	90.8	32.8	75,032	86.5	20.8
Lafayette Parish, Louisiana.........	118,902	91.6	38.7	113,903	93.0	39.9	39,311	85.7	21.6
Lafourche Parish, Louisiana........	56,204	78.3	17.2	54,053	78.8	17.8	7,366	79.7	16.5
Livingston Parish, Louisiana.......	84,587	83.4	19.3	83,289	83.6	19.3	5,429	81.1	51.4
Orleans Parish, Louisiana...........	104,672	95.6	64.7	96,147	96.9	66.2	157,313	82.5	22.7
Ouachita Parish, Louisiana.........	62,465	88.9	31.9	61,917	88.8	32.0	34,209	84.5	15.4
Rapides Parish, Louisiana...........	57,519	90.3	22.1	55,983	91.3	21.7	25,305	77.6	13.2
St. Landry Parish, Louisiana........	32,249	80.3	15.4	31,014	80.2	16.0	21,257	71.5	6.3
St. Tammany Parish, Louisiana....	151,829	92.9	38.0	143,997	93.4	38.1	20,617	81.9	22.0
Tangipahoa Parish, Louisiana......	62,867	85.6	25.3	60,321	86.6	26.1	22,621	80.7	22.3
Terrebonne Parish, Louisiana......	54,536	80.3	16.5	52,318	80.3	17.2	13,456	79.6	10.0

Table C-2. Educational Attainment of the Population, by Selected Counties, 2019—*Continued*

(Number; percent; dollars.)

| | Educational attainment by race/ethnicity, 25 years and over | | | | | | | | |
| | American Indian or Alaska Native alone | | | Asian alone | | | Native Hawaiian or Other Pacific Islander alone | | |
State/County	Total	High school graduate or more (percent)	Bachelor's degree or more (percent)	Total	High school graduate or more (percent)	Bachelor's degree or more (percent)	Total	High school graduate or more (percent)	Bachelor's degree or more (percent)
INDIANA—*(Continued)*									
Madison County, Indiana	N	N	N	N	N	N	N	N	N
Marion County, Indiana	N	N	N	22,741	82.8	53.7	N	N	N
Monroe County, Indiana	N	N	N	N	N	N	N	N	N
Morgan County, Indiana	N	N	N	N	N	N	N	N	N
Porter County, Indiana	N	N	N	N	N	N	N	N	N
St. Joseph County, Indiana	N	N	N	4,336	95.2	67.9	N	N	N
Tippecanoe County, Indiana	N	N	N	6,845	95.0	74.5	N	N	N
Vanderburgh County, Indiana	N	N	N	N	N	N	N	N	N
Vigo County, Indiana	N	N	N	N	N	N	N	N	N
Wayne County, Indiana	N	N	N	N	N	N	N	N	N
IOWA	7,678	82.0	8.3	48,872	79.8	51.0	N	N	N
Black Hawk County, Iowa	N	N	N	N	N	N	N	N	N
Dallas County, Iowa	N	N	N	N	N	N	N	N	N
Dubuque County, Iowa	N	N	N	N	N	N	N	N	N
Johnson County, Iowa	N	N	N	N	N	N	N	N	N
Linn County, Iowa	N	N	N	N	N	N	N	N	N
Polk County, Iowa	N	N	N	14,889	68.5	35.1	N	N	N
Pottawattamie County, Iowa	N	N	N	N	N	N	N	N	N
Scott County, Iowa	N	N	N	3,706	68.9	45.7	N	N	N
Story County, Iowa	N	N	N	N	N	N	N	N	N
Woodbury County, Iowa	N	N	N	1,955	68.7	2.6	N	N	N
KANSAS	16,317	86.9	14.8	56,876	85.4	49.8	N	N	N
Butler County, Kansas	N	N	N	N	N	N	N	N	N
Douglas County, Kansas	N	N	N	N	N	N	N	N	N
Johnson County, Kansas	N	N	N	21,822	93.9	69.0	N	N	N
Leavenworth County, Kansas	N	N	N	N	N	N	N	N	N
Riley County, Kansas	N	N	N	N	N	N	N	N	N
Sedgwick County, Kansas	N	N	N	15,022	79.1	28.3	N	N	N
Shawnee County, Kansas	N	N	N	N	N	N	N	N	N
Wyandotte County, Kansas	N	N	N	5,511	65.4	30.8	N	N	N
KENTUCKY	5,539	76.0	17.0	47,711	86.1	57.3	N	N	N
Boone County, Kentucky	N	N	N	2,369	67.1	27.2	N	N	N
Bullitt County, Kentucky	N	N	N	N	N	N	N	N	N
Campbell County, Kentucky	N	N	N	N	N	N	N	N	N
Christian County, Kentucky	N	N	N	N	N	N	N	N	N
Daviess County, Kentucky	N	N	N	N	N	N	N	N	N
Fayette County, Kentucky	N	N	N	9,263	93.6	72.8	N	N	N
Hardin County, Kentucky	N	N	N	N	N	N	N	N	N
Jefferson County, Kentucky	N	N	N	15,482	91.9	71.9	N	N	N
Kenton County, Kentucky	N	N	N	N	N	N	N	N	N
McCracken County, Kentucky	N	N	N	N	N	N	N	N	N
Madison County, Kentucky	N	N	N	N	N	N	N	N	N
Oldham County, Kentucky	N	N	N	724	100.0	32.5	N	N	N
Warren County, Kentucky	N	N	N	N	N	N	N	N	N
LOUISIANA	18,751	78.7	16.6	54,463	83.4	45.8	N	N	N
Ascension Parish, Louisiana	N	N	N	N	N	N	N	N	N
Bossier Parish, Louisiana	N	N	N	N	N	N	N	N	N
Caddo Parish, Louisiana	N	N	N	N	N	N	N	N	N
Calcasieu Parish, Louisiana	N	N	N	2,016	86.1	57.8	N	N	N
East Baton Rouge Parish, Louisiana	N	N	N	9,312	86.1	44.9	N	N	N
Iberia Parish, Louisiana	N	N	N	N	N	N	N	N	N
Jefferson Parish, Louisiana	N	N	N	13,120	79.1	43.5	N	N	N
Lafayette Parish, Louisiana	N	N	N	2,354	85.5	52.5	N	N	N
Lafourche Parish, Louisiana	N	N	N	N	N	N	N	N	N
Livingston Parish, Louisiana	N	N	N	N	N	N	N	N	N
Orleans Parish, Louisiana	N	N	N	8,207	84.6	53.7	N	N	N
Ouachita Parish, Louisiana	N	N	N	N	N	N	N	N	N
Rapides Parish, Louisiana	N	N	N	N	N	N	N	N	N
St. Landry Parish, Louisiana	N	N	N	N	N	N	N	N	N
St. Tammany Parish, Louisiana	N	N	N	N	N	N	N	N	N
Tangipahoa Parish, Louisiana	N	N	N	N	N	N	N	N	N
Terrebonne Parish, Louisiana	N	N	N	N	N	N	N	N	N

Table C-2. Educational Attainment of the Population, by Selected Counties, 2019—*Continued*

(Number; percent; dollars.)

	Educational attainment by race/ethnicity, 25 years and over								
	White alone			White alone, not Hispanic			Black alone		
State/County	Total	High school graduate or more (percent)	Bachelor's degree or more (percent)	Total	High school graduate or more (percent)	Bachelor's degree or more (percent)	Total	High school graduate or more (percent)	Bachelor's degree or more (percent)
MAINE	944,133	93.5	33.1	935,086	93.5	33.0	11,899	87.5	38.1
Androscoggin County, Maine	71,572	92.1	24.6	70,984	92.3	24.8	N	N	N
Aroostook County, Maine	47,915	90.9	18.0	47,641	91.1	18.1	N	N	N
Cumberland County, Maine	201,763	95.6	50.9	199,053	95.6	50.8	5,716	91.7	36.9
Kennebec County, Maine	85,845	93.4	27.7	85,161	93.3	27.4	N	N	N
Penobscot County, Maine	104,150	93.3	29.1	103,148	93.5	29.2	N	N	N
York County, Maine	148,236	93.7	32.7	146,750	93.6	32.6	N	N	N
MARYLAND	2,385,477	92.9	45.5	2,223,960	94.1	46.5	1,241,353	90.5	30.8
Allegany County, Maryland	44,161	90.5	21.9	43,871	90.8	22.0	N	N	N
Anne Arundel County, Maryland	296,490	93.8	44.7	279,471	94.4	45.4	68,576	91.7	40.8
Baltimore County, Maryland	357,976	92.9	43.4	345,288	93.4	43.8	160,997	92.2	33.3
Calvert County, Maryland	52,554	96.3	34.3	50,674	96.4	34.4	9,002	94.1	15.2
Carroll County, Maryland	109,129	94.9	36.9	106,511	95.0	37.1	3,827	94.5	29.2
Cecil County, Maryland	64,151	91.1	24.6	62,736	91.2	24.4	5,717	89.9	26.5
Charles County, Maryland	48,443	92.4	30.2	45,123	92.9	30.9	53,993	93.9	27.2
Frederick County, Maryland	145,945	92.6	42.8	134,411	95.3	44.4	16,706	97.2	31.0
Harford County, Maryland	144,496	94.1	37.9	139,391	94.4	38.2	23,838	91.5	26.6
Howard County, Maryland	127,155	96.0	65.8	118,802	97.4	67.4	42,185	95.6	52.9
Montgomery County, Maryland	390,858	94.7	67.6	336,070	97.8	72.9	130,457	92.3	42.1
Prince George's County, Maryland	103,617	87.4	41.7	82,695	93.4	47.5	401,366	93.2	34.9
St. Mary's County, Maryland	59,968	91.1	33.0	57,431	91.5	33.9	10,174	84.2	13.2
Washington County, Maryland	89,202	88.5	22.5	86,434	88.9	23.1	11,709	85.1	11.5
Wicomico County, Maryland	44,967	87.6	34.7	43,154	88.7	35.6	16,367	88.0	18.7
Baltimore city, Maryland	137,930	91.2	60.3	128,143	92.0	60.8	254,060	83.1	17.0
MASSACHUSETTS	3,865,466	93.4	46.5	3,601,315	94.8	48.2	350,938	85.7	28.0
Barnstable County, Massachusetts	156,082	96.7	48.6	152,320	97.8	49.2	4,412	97.9	26.2
Berkshire County, Massachusetts	85,466	93.1	34.3	84,633	93.1	34.4	2,265	89.8	21.3
Bristol County, Massachusetts	347,162	87.2	30.1	336,613	87.3	30.4	17,600	82.4	24.8
Essex County, Massachusetts	446,558	93.1	45.5	406,589	95.3	48.0	21,766	85.2	32.3
Franklin County, Massachusetts	50,312	92.2	36.3	49,503	92.4	36.3	N	N	N
Hampden County, Massachusetts	264,426	87.5	28.5	216,672	91.9	32.5	26,884	89.4	24.2
Hampshire County, Massachusetts	90,807	94.9	51.7	88,492	95.5	51.8	N	N	N
Middlesex County, Massachusetts	883,783	95.6	57.6	838,642	96.3	58.6	55,729	89.6	36.1
Norfolk County, Massachusetts	388,015	96.7	56.9	376,633	96.8	56.9	34,266	89.1	36.7
Plymouth County, Massachusetts	309,340	96.0	41.0	303,354	96.5	41.4	37,128	76.2	19.2
Suffolk County, Massachusetts	328,341	92.6	60.1	274,476	96.0	67.5	119,200	84.1	22.7
Worcester County, Massachusetts	496,764	92.7	36.2	455,386	94.5	38.1	26,243	90.3	36.7
MICHIGAN	5,564,561	92.3	30.9	5,377,567	92.8	31.1	889,006	87.9	18.0
Allegan County, Michigan	76,977	92.4	23.7	73,674	93.8	24.4	N	N	N
Bay County, Michigan	71,553	92.8	21.3	68,929	93.2	21.8	N	N	N
Berrien County, Michigan	89,527	91.7	28.9	85,861	92.1	28.8	12,721	79.8	11.1
Calhoun County, Michigan	76,835	91.4	21.6	74,146	91.5	22.1	8,625	85.4	9.7
Clinton County, Michigan	52,172	95.1	33.9	50,922	95.6	34.1	N	N	N
Eaton County, Michigan	68,849	95.5	28.3	66,291	95.5	28.6	4,551	94.2	36.5
Genesee County, Michigan	218,107	91.2	23.1	213,201	91.3	23.1	52,133	88.4	13.2
Grand Traverse County, Michigan	64,975	94.9	39.2	63,843	94.8	39.2	N	N	N
Ingham County, Michigan	141,587	94.9	39.2	132,016	95.5	40.3	20,749	89.0	34.8
Isabella County, Michigan	35,882	91.8	25.7	34,719	91.6	25.2	N	N	N
Jackson County, Michigan	99,390	91.2	24.2	97,254	91.3	24.1	8,056	82.4	9.8
Kalamazoo County, Michigan	139,399	94.2	39.6	136,523	94.2	39.4	15,932	80.2	25.1
Kent County, Michigan	364,366	93.5	38.8	344,094	95.3	39.9	37,292	90.2	15.9
Lapeer County, Michigan	60,483	92.2	19.3	58,946	93.0	19.8	N	N	N
Lenawee County, Michigan	65,503	90.1	21.8	61,402	91.6	22.1	N	N	N
Livingston County, Michigan	132,280	95.3	35.7	129,727	95.3	35.6	N	N	N
Macomb County, Michigan	514,205	91.1	25.5	504,390	91.4	25.7	66,977	91.2	16.6
Marquette County, Michigan	41,887	95.4	35.8	41,569	95.5	36.1	N	N	N
Midland County, Michigan	55,188	94.5	35.1	54,526	94.5	35.0	N	N	N
Monroe County, Michigan	101,992	90.7	24.3	99,541	90.5	24.1	N	N	N
Muskegon County, Michigan	100,687	93.7	22.8	96,758	94.4	23.2	13,640	84.9	7.0
Oakland County, Michigan	684,014	95.0	48.4	660,458	95.2	48.6	119,331	94.1	33.7
Ottawa County, Michigan	168,558	94.8	37.4	159,962	95.9	38.6	N	N	N
Saginaw County, Michigan	104,311	90.9	24.1	97,070	91.8	24.1	22,056	84.5	10.1
St. Clair County, Michigan	108,152	91.8	21.6	106,221	92.2	21.7	N	N	N
Shiawassee County, Michigan	47,273	91.9	18.4	46,019	91.9	18.1	N	N	N

Table C-2. Educational Attainment of the Population, by Selected Counties, 2019—*Continued*

(Number; percent; dollars.)

State/County	Educational attainment by race/ethnicity, 25 years and over								
	American Indian or Alaska Native alone			Asian alone			Native Hawaiian or Other Pacific Islander alone		
	Total	High school graduate or more (percent)	Bachelor's degree or more (percent)	Total	High school graduate or more (percent)	Bachelor's degree or more (percent)	Total	High school graduate or more (percent)	Bachelor's degree or more (percent)
MAINE	6,426	94.1	24.8	10,990	81.8	45.8	N	N	N
Androscoggin County, Maine	N	N	N	N	N	N	N	N	N
Aroostook County, Maine...........................	N	N	N	N	N	N	N	N	N
Cumberland County, Maine........................	N	N	N	4,808	78.8	46.0	N	N	N
Kennebec County, Maine............................	N	N	N	N	N	N	N	N	N
Penobscot County, Maine	986	96.7	41.5	N	N	N	N	N	N
York County, Maine	N	N	N	N	N	N	N	N	N
MARYLAND	14,328	79.2	26.1	277,535	89.3	63.3	N	N	N
Allegany County, Maryland.........................	N	N	N	N	N	N	N	N	N
Anne Arundel County, Maryland..................	N	N	N	15,556	88.2	50.0	N	N	N
Baltimore County, Maryland.......................	N	N	N	34,746	86.0	54.5	N	N	N
Calvert County, Maryland...........................	N	N	N	N	N	N	N	N	N
Carroll County, Maryland...........................	N	N	N	2,140	87.6	50.7	N	N	N
Cecil County, Maryland	N	N	N	N	N	N	N	N	N
Charles County, Maryland	N	N	N	3,820	88.3	44.0	N	N	N
Frederick County, Maryland........................	N	N	N	8,820	90.8	58.6	N	N	N
Harford County, Maryland..........................	N	N	N	5,511	91.2	64.1	N	N	N
Howard County, Maryland..........................	N	N	N	41,754	93.3	74.0	N	N	N
Montgomery County, Maryland	N	N	N	117,968	89.7	66.9	N	N	N
Prince George's County, Maryland	N	N	N	27,146	86.0	54.3	N	N	N
St. Mary's County, Maryland	N	N	N	N	N	N	N	N	N
Washington County, Maryland	N	N	N	N	N	N	N	N	N
Wicomico County, Maryland	N	N	N	N	N	N	N	N	N
Baltimore city, Maryland	N	N	N	10,629	91.2	68.2	N	N	N
MASSACHUSETTS	12,808	73.1	20.4	326,204	86.3	63.2	N	N	N
Barnstable County, Massachusetts	N	N	N	N	N	N	N	N	N
Berkshire County, Massachusetts	N	N	N	N	N	N	N	N	N
Bristol County, Massachusetts....................	N	N	N	8,758	89.8	70.7	N	N	N
Essex County, Massachusetts......................	N	N	N	19,389	79.8	46.7	N	N	N
Franklin County, Massachusetts..................	N	N	N	N	N	N	N	N	N
Hampden County, Massachusetts................	N	N	N	8,144	76.9	40.1	N	N	N
Hampshire County, Massachusetts..............	N	N	N	N	N	N	N	N	N
Middlesex County, Massachusetts...............	N	N	N	139,701	92.1	73.1	N	N	N
Norfolk County, Massachusetts	N	N	N	57,877	79.0	54.7	N	N	N
Plymouth County, Massachusetts................	N	N	N	5,656	84.2	47.8	N	N	N
Suffolk County, Massachusetts...................	N	N	N	50,666	81.6	55.8	N	N	N
Worcester County, Massachusetts...............	N	N	N	29,282	85.2	63.2	N	N	N
MICHIGAN......................................	38,741	87.6	11.7	218,309	89.8	64.8	N	N	N
Allegan County, Michigan...........................	N	N	N	N	N	N	N	N	N
Bay County, Michigan	N	N	N	N	N	N	N	N	N
Berrien County, Michigan...........................	N	N	N	N	N	N	N	N	N
Calhoun County, Michigan	N	N	N	N	N	N	N	N	N
Clinton County, Michigan	N	N	N	N	N	N	N	N	N
Eaton County, Michigan	N	N	N	N	N	N	N	N	N
Genesee County, Michigan.........................	N	N	N	2,777	75.5	60.2	N	N	N
Grand Traverse County, Michigan	N	N	N	N	N	N	N	N	N
Ingham County, Michigan	N	N	N	11,125	88.8	70.6	N	N	N
Isabella County, Michigan..........................	1,430	73.1	17.0	N	N	N	N	N	N
Jackson County, Michigan	N	N	N	N	N	N	N	N	N
Kalamazoo County, Michigan......................	N	N	N	3,988	83.5	52.2	N	N	N
Kent County, Michigan...............................	N	N	N	13,323	77.0	49.9	N	N	N
Lapeer County, Michigan............................	N	N	N	N	N	N	N	N	N
Lenawee County, Michigan.........................	N	N	N	N	N	N	N	N	N
Livingston County, Michigan......................	N	N	N	1,486	84.3	33.0	N	N	N
Macomb County, Michigan	N	N	N	25,461	84.6	44.5	N	N	N
Marquette County, Michigan	N	N	N	N	N	N	N	N	N
Midland County, Michigan..........................	N	N	N	N	N	N	N	N	N
Monroe County, Michigan..........................	N	N	N	N	N	N	N	N	N
Muskegon County, Michigan......................	N	N	N	N	N	N	N	N	N
Oakland County, Michigan..........................	2,267	88.4	12.7	71,796	95.8	79.6	N	N	N
Ottawa County, Michigan	N	N	N	5,297	73.4	18.5	N	N	N
Saginaw County, Michigan.........................	N	N	N	N	N	N	N	N	N
St. Clair County, Michigan..........................	N	N	N	N	N	N	N	N	N
Shiawassee County, Michigan.....................	N	N	N	N	N	N	N	N	N

Table C-2. Educational Attainment of the Population, by Selected Counties, 2019—*Continued*

(Number; percent; dollars.)

| | Educational attainment by race/ethnicity, 25 years and over | | | | | | | | |
| | White alone | | | White alone, not Hispanic | | | Black alone | | |
State/County	Total	High school graduate or more (percent)	Bachelor's degree or more (percent)	Total	High school graduate or more (percent)	Bachelor's degree or more (percent)	Total	High school graduate or more (percent)	Bachelor's degree or more (percent)
MICHIGAN—*(Continued)*									
Van Buren County, Michigan	48,184	88.3	24.1	44,680	90.2	25.5	N	N	N
Washtenaw County, Michigan	178,638	96.0	57.3	171,194	96.3	58.0	27,074	89.2	28.3
Wayne County, Michigan	659,129	89.6	30.3	626,612	90.6	30.9	442,805	86.5	14.8
MINNESOTA	3,298,386	95.6	38.5	3,208,417	96.0	38.8	207,288	82.1	21.7
Anoka County, Minnesota	210,697	95.5	33.1	205,975	95.9	33.3	13,706	91.7	27.7
Blue Earth County, Minnesota	36,625	96.1	35.2	36,108	96.3	35.5	N	N	N
Carver County, Minnesota	64,038	95.4	52.5	62,365	96.7	53.5	N	N	N
Crow Wing County, Minnesota	45,268	95.0	25.3	45,016	95.0	25.3	N	N	N
Dakota County, Minnesota	246,925	97.6	44.1	237,504	98.1	44.9	16,530	90.2	27.9
Hennepin County, Minnesota	678,281	97.6	56.4	657,463	98.1	56.8	96,210	79.7	17.4
Olmsted County, Minnesota	93,056	96.4	47.2	89,309	97.3	48.0	5,030	70.4	23.3
Ramsey County, Minnesota	268,511	95.7	48.0	254,253	96.5	49.4	38,952	86.9	26.0
Rice County, Minnesota	37,893	95.6	34.5	36,673	96.1	34.8	N	N	N
St. Louis County, Minnesota	128,715	95.7	30.6	127,533	95.9	30.5	N	N	N
Scott County, Minnesota	83,486	95.2	42.2	80,461	95.6	41.9	N	N	N
Sherburne County, Minnesota	59,679	96.1	26.9	59,144	96.2	27.1	1,626	78.8	23.6
Stearns County, Minnesota	90,564	94.3	28.7	89,406	94.6	28.9	N	N	N
Washington County, Minnesota	154,527	97.3	46.7	151,088	97.6	46.8	8,176	90.7	23.6
Wright County, Minnesota	84,860	96.3	33.4	83,872	96.4	33.8	N	N	N
MISSISSIPPI	1,217,710	88.3	25.8	1,190,544	88.7	26.1	702,026	80.8	16.0
DeSoto County, Mississippi	82,889	90.6	27.1	79,807	90.8	27.4	34,528	89.1	28.6
Forrest County, Mississippi	29,545	92.2	34.6	28,389	92.7	35.7	16,930	82.2	6.5
Harrison County, Mississippi	98,455	90.4	26.0	93,745	90.4	26.5	30,307	89.2	15.3
Hinds County, Mississippi	41,941	93.1	44.9	41,188	93.8	45.5	106,460	86.2	22.5
Jackson County, Mississippi	73,662	91.3	25.3	69,824	91.8	25.8	19,643	90.1	14.8
Jones County, Mississippi	31,497	87.7	23.0	30,162	90.4	23.9	12,707	82.7	8.7
Lauderdale County, Mississippi	29,081	90.3	27.8	28,305	90.8	28.6	21,437	67.8	6.5
Lee County, Mississippi	38,930	86.7	29.1	38,447	86.7	29.0	14,942	77.8	14.5
Madison County, Mississippi	42,182	96.7	60.7	41,325	97.5	61.6	25,455	84.7	31.2
Rankin County, Mississippi	81,895	92.2	28.9	80,881	92.7	29.1	21,442	84.3	32.2
MISSOURI	3,537,955	91.3	31.0	3,449,298	91.6	31.2	450,283	87.8	19.5
Boone County, Missouri	91,725	93.7	47.8	89,644	93.7	48.2	8,213	90.7	29.4
Buchanan County, Missouri	53,109	91.3	20.8	51,473	91.1	20.7	3,451	93.0	8.9
Cape Girardeau County, Missouri	46,333	91.1	34.0	45,663	91.0	34.3	3,269	86.4	9.5
Cass County, Missouri	66,910	93.4	25.3	65,171	93.3	25.0	3,857	93.6	24.8
Christian County, Missouri	57,880	90.0	28.4	56,530	91.3	29.0	N	N	N
Clay County, Missouri	146,810	95.1	33.8	141,997	95.4	34.2	9,754	91.6	20.9
Cole County, Missouri	46,424	93.8	34.4	45,281	93.9	34.4	6,331	85.7	27.0
Franklin County, Missouri	70,110	89.5	20.0	69,813	89.5	20.1	N	N	N
Greene County, Missouri	175,813	92.4	30.5	172,764	92.4	30.4	5,437	76.0	17.1
Jackson County, Missouri	342,744	93.0	37.1	322,972	93.9	37.9	102,781	90.0	18.4
Jasper County, Missouri	74,241	84.9	23.5	70,266	87.3	24.5	N	N	N
Jefferson County, Missouri	152,141	89.6	20.0	149,617	89.7	20.3	N	N	N
Platte County, Missouri	62,530	96.7	45.4	59,441	96.8	45.1	4,643	89.7	40.0
St. Charles County, Missouri	249,681	94.6	39.6	244,705	94.5	39.6	14,049	94.9	47.2
St. Francois County, Missouri	44,431	87.0	14.6	43,970	87.5	14.7	N	N	N
St. Louis County, Missouri	488,998	95.7	51.9	479,339	95.7	51.8	154,279	89.2	20.3
St. Louis city, Missouri	113,110	94.4	54.7	108,102	95.3	54.9	90,905	84.4	16.5
MONTANA	672,576	94.8	34.3	658,762	95.0	34.5	2,977	84.5	42.4
Cascade County, Montana	50,305	93.0	25.4	49,352	93.1	25.4	N	N	N
Flathead County, Montana	70,342	96.2	34.8	69,777	96.2	34.9	N	N	N
Gallatin County, Montana	69,405	98.5	53.5	68,401	98.5	54.1	N	N	N
Lewis and Clark County, Montana	46,264	97.5	44.2	45,672	97.5	44.3	N	N	N
Missoula County, Montana	75,615	95.6	45.1	73,880	95.8	44.6	N	N	N
Yellowstone County, Montana	102,859	93.6	33.8	99,641	94.2	34.4	N	N	N
NEBRASKA	1,130,659	93.5	34.3	1,055,888	95.7	35.7	54,590	85.3	21.7
Douglas County, Nebraska	307,695	93.2	43.9	279,647	96.5	47.0	37,206	84.5	21.2
Lancaster County, Nebraska	176,064	94.9	41.9	168,316	96.5	43.0	7,082	85.9	20.5
Sarpy County, Nebraska	107,178	97.3	41.4	100,533	98.2	42.4	4,243	92.0	23.0

Table C-2. Educational Attainment of the Population, by Selected Counties, 2019—*Continued*

(Number; percent; dollars.)

	Educational attainment by race/ethnicity, 25 years and over								
	American Indian or Alaska Native alone			Asian alone			Native Hawaiian or Other Pacific Islander alone		
State/County	Total	High school graduate or more (percent)	Bachelor's degree or more (percent)	Total	High school graduate or more (percent)	Bachelor's degree or more (percent)	Total	High school graduate or more (percent)	Bachelor's degree or more (percent)
MICHIGAN—(*Continued*)									
Van Buren County, Michigan	N	N	N	N	N	N	N	N	N
Washtenaw County, Michigan	N	N	N	19,756	97.5	84.8	N	N	N
Wayne County, Michigan	4,148	87.5	11.5	41,182	86.7	58.4	N	N	N
MINNESOTA	34,650	83.6	14.8	180,643	81.5	46.1	N	N	N
Anoka County, Minnesota	N	N	N	11,349	86.6	31.9	N	N	N
Blue Earth County, Minnesota	N	N	N	N	N	N	N	N	N
Carver County, Minnesota	N	N	N	3,591	67.9	45.1	N	N	N
Crow Wing County, Minnesota	N	N	N	N	N	N	N	N	N
Dakota County, Minnesota	N	N	N	14,824	89.3	53.5	N	N	N
Hennepin County, Minnesota	4,864	85.0	24.6	61,732	88.3	58.1	N	N	N
Olmsted County, Minnesota	N	N	N	7,164	87.2	66.2	N	N	N
Ramsey County, Minnesota	1,893	78.5	29.1	47,208	70.9	32.9	N	N	N
Rice County, Minnesota	N	N	N	N	N	N	N	N	N
St. Louis County, Minnesota	2,620	72.4	16.5	N	N	N	N	N	N
Scott County, Minnesota	N	N	N	5,543	84.9	45.4	N	N	N
Sherburne County, Minnesota	N	N	N	N	N	N	N	N	N
Stearns County, Minnesota	N	N	N	N	N	N	N	N	N
Washington County, Minnesota	N	N	N	10,535	90.8	58.6	N	N	N
Wright County, Minnesota	N	N	N	N	N	N	N	N	N
MISSISSIPPI	8,424	75.8	9.2	20,681	84.1	41.4	N	N	N
DeSoto County, Mississippi	N	N	N	N	N	N	N	N	N
Forrest County, Mississippi	N	N	N	N	N	N	N	N	N
Harrison County, Mississippi	N	N	N	3,643	67.1	21.1	N	N	N
Hinds County, Mississippi	N	N	N	N	N	N	N	N	N
Jackson County, Mississippi	N	N	N	2,542	75.0	41.1	N	N	N
Jones County, Mississippi	N	N	N	N	N	N	N	N	N
Lauderdale County, Mississippi	N	N	N	N	N	N	N	N	N
Lee County, Mississippi	N	N	N	N	N	N	N	N	N
Madison County, Mississippi	N	N	N	2,180	86.7	32.4	N	N	N
Rankin County, Mississippi	N	N	N	N	N	N	N	N	N
MISSOURI	18,101	88.3	15.4	87,803	89.3	61.3	4,114	79.2	16.9
Boone County, Missouri	N	N	N	N	N	N	N	N	N
Buchanan County, Missouri	N	N	N	N	N	N	N	N	N
Cape Girardeau County, Missouri	N	N	N	N	N	N	N	N	N
Cass County, Missouri	N	N	N	N	N	N	N	N	N
Christian County, Missouri	N	N	N	N	N	N	N	N	N
Clay County, Missouri	N	N	N	3,489	85.4	44.4	N	N	N
Cole County, Missouri	N	N	N	N	N	N	N	N	N
Franklin County, Missouri	N	N	N	N	N	N	N	N	N
Greene County, Missouri	N	N	N	N	N	N	N	N	N
Jackson County, Missouri	1,695	87.3	33.3	8,847	85.0	49.1	N	N	N
Jasper County, Missouri	N	N	N	N	N	N	N	N	N
Jefferson County, Missouri	N	N	N	N	N	N	N	N	N
Platte County, Missouri	N	N	N	N	N	N	N	N	N
St. Charles County, Missouri	N	N	N	7,547	82.5	51.8	N	N	N
St. Francois County, Missouri	N	N	N	N	N	N	N	N	N
St. Louis County, Missouri	N	N	N	31,359	96.0	78.1	N	N	N
St. Louis city, Missouri	N	N	N	7,500	81.2	59.7	N	N	N
MONTANA	37,153	87.5	15.2	6,867	93.1	48.0	N	N	N
Cascade County, Montana	N	N	N	N	N	N	N	N	N
Flathead County, Montana	N	N	N	N	N	N	N	N	N
Gallatin County, Montana	N	N	N	N	N	N	N	N	N
Lewis and Clark County, Montana	N	N	N	N	N	N	N	N	N
Missoula County, Montana	N	N	N	N	N	N	N	N	N
Yellowstone County, Montana	4,607	95.9	14.8	N	N	N	N	N	N
NEBRASKA	10,910	83.4	10.6	30,283	77.5	47.1	N	N	N
Douglas County, Nebraska	2,424	77.1	6.0	14,618	79.0	57.9	N	N	N
Lancaster County, Nebraska	N	N	N	8,794	73.3	38.8	N	N	N
Sarpy County, Nebraska	N	N	N	3,259	86.7	32.8	N	N	N

Table C-2. Educational Attainment of the Population, by Selected Counties, 2019—*Continued*

(Number; percent; dollars.)

State/County		Educational attainment by race/ethnicity, 25 years and over							
	White alone			White alone, not Hispanic			Black alone		
	Total	High school graduate or more (percent)	Bachelor's degree or more (percent)	Total	High school graduate or more (percent)	Bachelor's degree or more (percent)	Total	High school graduate or more (percent)	Bachelor's degree or more (percent)
NEVADA	1,444,872	89.1	26.9	1,148,711	94.2	30.7	192,799	90.4	18.2
Clark County, Nevada	974,939	88.3	26.9	736,197	94.3	31.7	181,932	90.6	17.8
Washoe County, Nevada	259,281	92.3	33.1	225,038	95.9	36.1	6,849	92.8	29.0
NEW HAMPSHIRE	919,746	93.6	37.0	897,818	93.9	37.3	13,726	85.9	36.9
Cheshire County, New Hampshire	52,122	94.8	34.0	51,619	94.8	34.0	N	N	N
Grafton County, New Hampshire	59,954	91.3	40.0	59,090	91.2	39.7	N	N	N
Hillsborough County, New Hampshire	269,875	92.9	37.3	257,549	94.2	38.5	6,801	78.0	29.4
Merrimack County, New Hampshire	103,286	92.0	34.9	102,411	92.1	35.0	N	N	N
Rockingham County, New Hampshire	217,518	96.0	42.1	212,422	96.1	41.9	2,101	93.8	35.2
Strafford County, New Hampshire	80,983	94.0	35.7	79,499	93.9	35.8	N	N	N
NEW JERSEY	4,294,038	92.0	42.0	3,577,879	94.8	45.8	813,816	88.8	25.3
Atlantic County, New Jersey	125,763	90.9	31.5	112,954	93.3	33.2	23,540	84.9	12.4
Bergen County, New Jersey	476,078	93.2	49.7	376,322	95.6	53.7	37,821	91.8	45.4
Burlington County, New Jersey	233,720	95.0	41.0	219,431	95.5	42.2	52,177	91.5	30.5
Camden County, New Jersey	235,502	93.1	37.5	212,882	94.9	39.4	64,502	89.8	21.0
Cape May County, New Jersey	65,010	94.7	33.6	61,621	95.0	34.6	2,690	76.0	9.2
Cumberland County, New Jersey	70,451	83.4	19.7	52,840	93.1	23.0	20,381	80.6	8.5
Essex County, New Jersey	246,698	88.8	46.2	176,034	94.2	57.7	213,736	87.1	21.7
Gloucester County, New Jersey	169,251	93.8	33.3	163,370	94.7	33.5	21,069	90.6	33.8
Hudson County, New Jersey	281,098	85.5	42.7	152,458	93.6	59.1	57,670	86.2	30.4
Hunterdon County, New Jersey	82,438	95.9	53.8	78,403	97.0	54.9	N	N	N
Mercer County, New Jersey	155,999	91.4	47.3	130,090	95.3	52.3	49,779	84.5	18.7
Middlesex County, New Jersey	330,778	89.2	36.3	261,364	92.2	41.1	57,544	91.7	31.2
Monmouth County, New Jersey	369,000	95.6	49.8	341,740	96.5	51.6	32,144	92.6	24.6
Morris County, New Jersey	286,606	95.5	55.5	252,306	97.4	58.5	12,159	95.3	37.4
Ocean County, New Jersey	384,892	93.2	32.1	359,422	93.7	33.1	13,043	93.9	27.7
Passaic County, New Jersey	230,099	86.8	33.3	148,201	93.9	42.1	37,329	89.0	16.3
Salem County, New Jersey	36,224	89.4	21.6	34,361	89.6	22.4	5,665	81.0	8.5
Somerset County, New Jersey	148,299	95.2	53.9	133,381	97.3	56.9	22,475	93.9	39.8
Sussex County, New Jersey	95,716	94.5	37.2	88,793	95.2	37.6	N	N	N
Union County, New Jersey	201,938	89.7	44.8	158,476	93.5	50.8	82,879	90.8	26.5
Warren County, New Jersey	68,478	93.8	33.2	63,430	94.0	33.5	3,359	95.1	31.0
NEW MEXICO	1,081,586	87.5	30.7	606,478	94.4	41.2	29,349	87.0	28.4
Bernalillo County, New Mexico	361,788	90.7	38.2	207,510	96.4	49.8	12,801	86.1	34.8
Chaves County, New Mexico	37,466	76.6	17.9	18,737	88.1	23.3	N	N	N
Doña Ana County, New Mexico	108,752	78.8	27.3	42,840	94.2	45.0	N	N	N
Lea County, New Mexico	38,041	76.0	12.5	17,373	87.9	17.5	1,556	87.8	2.4
McKinley County, New Mexico	6,613	92.8	35.5	4,848	92.7	41.3	N	N	N
Otero County, New Mexico	36,630	85.6	15.1	24,352	92.7	18.9	N	N	N
Sandoval County, New Mexico	76,240	94.9	36.5	49,190	96.7	41.5	N	N	N
San Juan County, New Mexico	44,787	89.0	19.5	34,662	90.5	21.9	N	N	N
Santa Fe County, New Mexico	95,930	89.2	43.5	56,415	97.7	62.5	N	N	N
Valencia County, New Mexico	43,127	86.9	20.5	19,292	90.9	27.6	N	N	N
NEW YORK	8,910,770	91.7	42.3	7,894,691	93.7	44.5	2,097,135	85.0	24.5
Albany County, New York	162,395	94.9	45.6	156,059	95.3	46.0	21,291	83.0	29.6
Bronx County, New York	227,750	74.2	24.9	94,201	84.8	39.2	359,027	78.9	19.5
Broome County, New York	112,851	91.6	28.0	111,248	91.7	28.1	6,311	85.8	14.7
Cattaraugus County, New York	49,306	90.9	21.6	48,947	90.9	21.6	N	N	N
Cayuga County, New York	51,536	89.0	24.5	50,892	89.5	24.4	N	N	N
Chautauqua County, New York	83,145	91.3	26.1	80,613	91.4	26.0	N	N	N
Chemung County, New York	53,528	93.2	26.1	52,234	93.7	25.6	3,746	79.5	10.1
Clinton County, New York	51,693	88.2	26.3	50,729	88.2	26.6	N	N	N
Dutchess County, New York	165,478	93.1	37.5	153,747	93.6	38.4	22,381	91.8	20.0
Erie County, New York	527,571	95.1	36.2	515,388	95.3	36.4	77,194	86.5	17.7
Jefferson County, New York	62,861	91.0	22.4	60,035	91.0	22.5	3,103	90.5	21.8
Kings County, New York	783,732	90.2	55.2	659,773	93.0	61.0	574,467	86.3	24.2
Livingston County, New York	39,416	92.2	25.9	39,095	92.3	26.0	N	N	N
Madison County, New York	46,700	93.9	24.3	46,268	93.9	24.4	N	N	N
Monroe County, New York	409,987	93.6	44.6	387,435	94.9	45.9	70,855	81.1	18.2
Nassau County, New York	656,805	93.8	50.0	580,032	95.9	52.3	109,459	92.7	33.7
New York County, New York	732,236	94.6	77.4	618,310	98.0	84.0	170,988	83.8	31.0
Niagara County, New York	134,853	92.1	28.6	133,201	92.0	28.5	8,486	88.9	19.2

Table C-2. Educational Attainment of the Population, by Selected Counties, 2019—*Continued*

(Number; percent; dollars.)

State/County	Educational attainment by race/ethnicity, 25 years and over								
	American Indian or Alaska Native alone			Asian alone			Native Hawaiian or Other Pacific Islander alone		
	Total	High school graduate or more (percent)	Bachelor's degree or more (percent)	Total	High school graduate or more (percent)	Bachelor's degree or more (percent)	Total	High school graduate or more (percent)	Bachelor's degree or more (percent)
NEVADA	28,056	75.8	14.8	198,870	90.7	42.9	14,368	88.0	19.6
Clark County, Nevada	14,528	66.7	15.9	173,741	90.2	42.3	11,411	87.9	19.0
Washoe County, Nevada	4,966	84.3	17.2	18,760	94.9	52.4	N	N	N
NEW HAMPSHIRE	N	N	N	25,955	91.6	64.4	N	N	N
Cheshire County, New Hampshire	N	N	N	N	N	N	N	N	N
Grafton County, New Hampshire	N	N	N	N	N	N	N	N	N
Hillsborough County, New Hampshire	N	N	N	12,070	89.1	59.6	N	N	N
Merrimack County, New Hampshire	N	N	N	N	N	N	N	N	N
Rockingham County, New Hampshire	N	N	N	5,144	95.9	59.6	N	N	N
Strafford County, New Hampshire	N	N	N	N	N	N	N	N	N
NEW JERSEY	12,055	75.7	28.4	613,693	92.9	71.6	N	N	N
Atlantic County, New Jersey	N	N	N	14,228	81.1	36.2	N	N	N
Bergen County, New Jersey	N	N	N	113,462	95.7	70.3	N	N	N
Burlington County, New Jersey	N	N	N	15,819	88.1	56.4	N	N	N
Camden County, New Jersey	N	N	N	20,701	83.5	60.0	N	N	N
Cape May County, New Jersey	N	N	N	N	N	N	N	N	N
Cumberland County, New Jersey	N	N	N	1,491	93.6	35.8	N	N	N
Essex County, New Jersey	N	N	N	32,122	95.6	72.4	N	N	N
Gloucester County, New Jersey	N	N	N	5,985	92.8	61.9	N	N	N
Hudson County, New Jersey	N	N	N	82,498	94.2	78.4	N	N	N
Hunterdon County, New Jersey	N	N	N	N	N	N	N	N	N
Mercer County, New Jersey	N	N	N	28,679	93.8	83.7	N	N	N
Middlesex County, New Jersey	N	N	N	137,340	91.1	73.9	N	N	N
Monmouth County, New Jersey	N	N	N	24,093	91.3	68.6	N	N	N
Morris County, New Jersey	N	N	N	37,438	93.5	75.5	N	N	N
Ocean County, New Jersey	N	N	N	8,288	90.3	56.7	N	N	N
Passaic County, New Jersey	N	N	N	18,273	91.1	47.8	N	N	N
Salem County, New Jersey	N	N	N	N	N	N	N	N	N
Somerset County, New Jersey	N	N	N	42,036	95.8	84.1	N	N	N
Sussex County, New Jersey	N	N	N	2,231	100.0	53.0	N	N	N
Union County, New Jersey	N	N	N	22,118	95.4	70.7	N	N	N
Warren County, New Jersey	N	N	N	N	N	N	N	N	N
NEW MEXICO	125,785	81.8	11.8	27,650	89.1	49.6	N	N	N
Bernalillo County, New Mexico	22,745	91.6	26.8	14,159	85.7	46.0	N	N	N
Chaves County, New Mexico	N	N	N	672	81.5	38.2	N	N	N
Doña Ana County, New Mexico	N	N	N	N	N	N	N	N	N
Lea County, New Mexico	N	N	N	N	N	N	N	N	N
McKinley County, New Mexico	33,253	75.1	5.0	N	N	N	N	N	N
Otero County, New Mexico	3,196	82.2	12.3	N	N	N	N	N	N
Sandoval County, New Mexico	11,391	81.9	14.4	N	N	N	N	N	N
San Juan County, New Mexico	31,164	80.5	6.9	N	N	N	N	N	N
Santa Fe County, New Mexico	3,896	90.5	8.5	N	N	N	N	N	N
Valencia County, New Mexico	N	N	N	N	N	N	N	N	N
NEW YORK	50,556	76.0	18.5	1,213,907	80.2	47.8	5,020	82.3	18.9
Albany County, New York	N	N	N	12,606	84.5	56.9	N	N	N
Bronx County, New York	5,868	75.3	10.5	38,188	78.8	40.1	N	N	N
Broome County, New York	N	N	N	3,732	70.4	32.0	N	N	N
Cattaraugus County, New York	1,637	90.9	10.5	N	N	N	N	N	N
Cayuga County, New York	N	N	N	N	N	N	N	N	N
Chautauqua County, New York	N	N	N	N	N	N	N	N	N
Chemung County, New York	N	N	N	N	N	N	N	N	N
Clinton County, New York	N	N	N	N	N	N	N	N	N
Dutchess County, New York	N	N	N	6,500	91.2	52.8	N	N	N
Erie County, New York	3,757	89.0	18.4	19,942	80.9	50.3	N	N	N
Jefferson County, New York	N	N	N	N	N	N	N	N	N
Kings County, New York	4,556	66.1	25.9	222,754	69.2	36.0	N	N	N
Livingston County, New York	N	N	N	N	N	N	N	N	N
Madison County, New York	N	N	N	N	N	N	N	N	N
Monroe County, New York	N	N	N	16,297	77.0	55.8	N	N	N
Nassau County, New York	N	N	N	98,194	93.2	64.5	N	N	N
New York County, New York	N	N	N	161,631	81.5	67.4	N	N	N
Niagara County, New York	N	N	N	N	N	N	N	N	N

Table C-2. Educational Attainment of the Population, by Selected Counties, 2019—*Continued*

(Number; percent; dollars.)

| State/County | \multicolumn{9}{c}{Educational attainment by race/ethnicity, 25 years and over} |
| | White alone | | | White alone, not Hispanic | | | Black alone | | |
	Total	High school graduate or more (percent)	Bachelor's degree or more (percent)	Total	High school graduate or more (percent)	Bachelor's degree or more (percent)	Total	High school graduate or more (percent)	Bachelor's degree or more (percent)
NEW YORK —(*Continued*)									
Oneida County, New York	140,513	91.2	29.9	136,245	91.9	30.5	7,974	68.0	10.3
Onondaga County, New York	263,608	94.6	38.6	257,713	94.9	38.6	30,477	82.0	21.2
Ontario County, New York	73,292	94.1	40.3	71,933	94.3	40.8	N	N	N
Orange County, New York	188,906	91.0	33.4	161,850	92.4	34.3	27,037	88.6	24.8
Oswego County, New York	77,695	88.6	21.9	77,048	88.8	21.8	N	N	N
Putnam County, New York	63,050	93.3	38.8	56,539	94.0	39.0	N	N	N
Queens County, New York	620,068	87.4	39.1	434,282	92.1	47.0	297,663	87.5	25.7
Rensselaer County, New York	99,411	92.8	36.1	97,110	92.8	36.2	7,054	80.4	10.8
Richmond County, New York	249,372	90.4	36.6	210,270	93.2	39.3	30,478	90.3	27.2
Rockland County, New York	141,057	92.7	46.4	126,423	92.9	47.7	26,787	82.8	25.8
St. Lawrence County, New York	67,429	88.2	23.0	66,936	88.5	23.1	N	N	N
Saratoga County, New York	155,605	93.8	41.3	152,342	94.0	41.3	N	N	N
Schenectady County, New York	85,465	94.6	37.6	82,915	95.1	38.1	10,377	93.3	18.9
Steuben County, New York	64,436	91.6	23.5	64,154	91.7	23.5	1,409	94.5	20.6
Suffolk County, New York	849,278	92.8	39.9	732,730	95.1	43.2	74,835	87.1	29.2
Sullivan County, New York	42,250	92.9	28.0	40,103	93.3	28.6	3,870	83.8	22.4
Tompkins County, New York	51,825	96.2	56.7	50,493	96.2	55.9	N	N	N
Ulster County, New York	113,413	91.8	34.4	106,699	92.4	34.9	7,201	85.7	16.2
Warren County, New York	46,010	91.6	33.1	45,285	92.8	33.4	N	N	N
Wayne County, New York	60,341	90.9	24.8	59,120	91.5	25.4	N	N	N
Westchester County, New York	441,300	92.8	57.9	373,262	95.3	61.9	103,448	87.8	34.5
NORTH CAROLINA	5,103,713	90.7	35.1	4,805,279	92.2	36.0	1,486,857	86.4	22.4
Alamance County, North Carolina	82,533	88.3	27.6	77,050	91.3	28.7	23,449	88.8	16.6
Brunswick County, North Carolina	99,868	93.1	34.2	97,628	93.7	34.8	8,900	92.0	23.6
Buncombe County, North Carolina	175,276	92.6	42.1	168,012	93.5	43.1	11,717	90.7	18.4
Burke County, North Carolina	57,475	86.3	21.0	56,771	86.4	21.3	2,848	84.8	3.8
Cabarrus County, North Carolina	104,276	92.9	34.9	97,893	93.8	34.8	25,671	88.0	25.2
Caldwell County, North Carolina	54,250	78.9	17.5	53,435	79.1	17.5	N	N	N
Carteret County, North Carolina	48,502	91.3	31.0	47,282	91.4	30.9	2,327	82.9	20.9
Catawba County, North Carolina	93,123	88.1	24.2	89,048	89.2	24.5	8,935	83.4	16.0
Chatham County, North Carolina	43,804	89.0	45.2	41,276	89.7	46.9	6,172	94.7	53.7
Cleveland County, North Carolina	51,181	86.5	21.0	50,320	86.8	20.9	13,009	83.4	12.7
Craven County, North Carolina	50,582	92.6	25.8	47,692	93.3	26.9	14,340	87.7	8.9
Cumberland County, North Carolina	105,954	92.3	26.8	93,633	93.4	27.7	78,666	90.3	22.2
Davidson County, North Carolina	104,453	86.9	19.8	98,362	87.3	20.0	11,733	87.4	13.3
Durham County, North Carolina	124,835	89.9	56.0	108,280	97.1	62.5	77,037	90.0	35.3
Forsyth County, North Carolina	176,854	91.0	37.0	160,460	94.6	39.1	65,687	86.6	21.6
Franklin County, North Carolina	34,119	91.6	25.9	31,909	94.3	27.3	11,957	86.3	13.7
Gaston County, North Carolina	123,461	85.6	23.2	117,254	85.7	23.7	25,309	84.8	22.5
Guilford County, North Carolina	208,431	92.1	44.3	196,173	93.2	45.1	115,237	85.8	24.8
Harnett County, North Carolina	62,554	90.7	25.6	57,864	91.9	25.3	19,097	88.6	18.8
Henderson County, North Carolina	82,569	91.0	30.7	76,876	92.3	32.3	2,961	87.7	13.9
Iredell County, North Carolina	103,091	92.2	32.4	99,321	92.8	33.0	13,682	82.6	15.3
Johnston County, North Carolina	107,932	89.5	24.9	99,962	91.9	26.1	22,125	90.6	25.1
Lincoln County, North Carolina	57,201	92.2	26.9	53,864	93.5	27.2	3,902	89.6	10.1
Mecklenburg County, North Carolina	418,619	93.9	55.7	379,872	96.7	58.6	231,274	91.6	31.4
Moore County, North Carolina	60,822	95.0	40.9	58,928	94.9	40.7	8,562	76.4	31.5
Nash County, North Carolina	34,824	91.4	23.2	34,544	91.6	23.2	26,074	84.7	12.6
New Hanover County, North Carolina	134,928	94.9	46.9	130,493	95.3	47.4	19,357	84.9	19.9
Onslow County, North Carolina	83,575	93.2	24.1	74,684	94.3	24.6	16,980	85.1	25.0
Orange County, North Carolina	72,735	96.0	68.6	67,127	96.8	69.7	11,836	86.5	29.1
Pitt County, North Carolina	63,658	94.6	42.1	62,563	95.2	42.6	39,228	79.7	17.1
Randolph County, North Carolina	87,945	82.5	14.2	83,349	85.0	14.8	5,534	84.0	18.4
Robeson County, North Carolina	25,531	83.2	18.0	24,269	85.0	18.7	19,905	80.0	12.7
Rockingham County, North Carolina	50,715	85.4	14.3	49,563	85.5	14.7	12,906	74.2	10.9
Rowan County, North Carolina	78,969	87.6	18.6	74,899	89.3	18.5	13,966	87.5	18.7
Rutherford County, North Carolina	42,437	87.8	21.2	41,487	88.9	20.8	4,829	81.0	5.5
Surry County, North Carolina	47,510	82.2	18.4	44,745	83.8	19.2	N	N	N
Union County, North Carolina	125,272	91.5	38.4	115,078	94.1	40.2	17,649	92.4	28.3
Wake County, North Carolina	501,390	96.5	59.7	471,820	97.7	61.8	149,263	90.1	34.8
Wayne County, North Carolina	52,793	86.1	20.3	47,033	92.3	21.3	24,658	88.1	11.1
Wilkes County, North Carolina	45,470	83.8	17.6	43,444	85.1	18.0	N	N	N
Wilson County, North Carolina	29,956	86.9	27.3	28,859	87.5	27.2	21,754	81.9	9.9
NORTH DAKOTA	446,532	94.2	31.7	438,065	94.5	31.7	13,471	93.2	21.8
Burleigh County, North Dakota	59,771	94.7	36.2	59,189	94.7	36.5	N	N	N

Table C-2. Educational Attainment of the Population, by Selected Counties, 2019—*Continued*

(Number; percent; dollars.)

	American Indian or Alaska Native alone			Asian alone			Native Hawaiian or Other Pacific Islander alone		
State/County	Total	High school graduate or more (percent)	Bachelor's degree or more (percent)	Total	High school graduate or more (percent)	Bachelor's degree or more (percent)	Total	High school graduate or more (percent)	Bachelor's degree or more (percent)
NEW YORK —(*Continued*)									
Oneida County, New York...............	N	N	N	4,634	53.0	24.1	N	N	N
Onondaga County, New York............	N	N	N	8,484	68.0	46.3	N	N	N
Ontario County, New York...............	N	N	N	N	N	N	N	N	N
Orange County, New York...............	N	N	N	7,319	90.6	54.6	N	N	N
Oswego County, New York...............	N	N	N	N	N	N	N	N	N
Putnam County, New York...............	N	N	N	N	N	N	N	N	N
Queens County, New York...............	8,536	74.5	17.7	440,933	79.2	38.4	N	N	N
Rensselaer County, New York..........	N	N	N	N	N	N	N	N	N
Richmond County, New York...........	N	N	N	37,222	82.2	44.1	N	N	N
Rockland County, New York............	N	N	N	14,166	92.8	70.0	N	N	N
St. Lawrence County, New York.......	N	N	N	N	N	N	N	N	N
Saratoga County, New York............	N	N	N	N	N	N	N	N	N
Schenectady County, New York.......	N	N	N	5,354	87.1	46.1	N	N	N
Steuben County, New York.............	N	N	N	N	N	N	N	N	N
Suffolk County, New York...............	3,755	72.9	9.2	39,634	89.2	57.5	N	N	N
Sullivan County, New York..............	N	N	N	N	N	N	N	N	N
Tompkins County, New York............	N	N	N	N	N	N	N	N	N
Ulster County, New York.................	N	N	N	1,922	85.3	49.0	N	N	N
Warren County, New York...............	N	N	N	N	N	N	N	N	N
Wayne County, New York................	N	N	N	N	N	N	N	N	N
Westchester County, New York........	2,254	86.0	26.0	43,827	94.1	74.5	N	N	N
NORTH CAROLINA	81,694	77.4	14.7	213,997	87.2	58.5	4,374	88.7	34.3
Alamance County, North Carolina.......	N	N	N	N	N	N	N	N	N
Brunswick County, North Carolina	N	N	N	N	N	N	N	N	N
Buncombe County, North Carolina......	N	N	N	N	N	N	N	N	N
Burke County, North Carolina...........	N	N	N	2,096	66.3	7.0	N	N	N
Cabarrus County, North Carolina.......	N	N	N	5,974	94.8	64.8	N	N	N
Caldwell County, North Carolina........	N	N	N	N	N	N	N	N	N
Carteret County, North Carolina	N	N	N	N	N	N	N	N	N
Catawba County, North Carolina.......	N	N	N	4,083	88.3	34.1	N	N	N
Chatham County, North Carolina.......	N	N	N	N	N	N	N	N	N
Cleveland County, North Carolina......	N	N	N	N	N	N	N	N	N
Craven County, North Carolina.........	N	N	N	N	N	N	N	N	N
Cumberland County, North Carolina.....	3,134	82.9	4.4	6,507	85.0	37.6	N	N	N
Davidson County, North Carolina.......	N	N	N	N	N	N	N	N	N
Durham County, North Carolina	N	N	N	10,615	86.5	74.1	N	N	N
Forsyth County, North Carolina.........	N	N	N	6,168	92.1	72.8	N	N	N
Franklin County, North Carolina........	N	N	N	N	N	N	N	N	N
Gaston County, North Carolina.........	N	N	N	N	N	N	N	N	N
Guilford County, North Carolina........	N	N	N	17,861	75.0	46.4	N	N	N
Harnett County, North Carolina	N	N	N	N	N	N	N	N	N
Henderson County, North Carolina.....	N	N	N	N	N	N	N	N	N
Iredell County, North Carolina..........	N	N	N	3,558	93.9	55.3	N	N	N
Johnston County, North Carolina.......	N	N	N	N	N	N	N	N	N
Lincoln County, North Carolina.........	N	N	N	N	N	N	N	N	N
Mecklenburg County, North Carolina.....	N	N	N	44,959	86.1	60.0	N	N	N
Moore County, North Carolina..........	N	N	N	N	N	N	N	N	N
Nash County, North Carolina...........	N	N	N	N	N	N	N	N	N
New Hanover County, North Carolina...	N	N	N	N	N	N	N	N	N
Onslow County, North Carolina........	N	N	N	2,547	80.2	21.1	N	N	N
Orange County, North Carolina........	N	N	N	7,228	91.9	62.6	N	N	N
Pitt County, North Carolina.............	N	N	N	N	N	N	N	N	N
Randolph County, North Carolina......	N	N	N	N	N	N	N	N	N
Robeson County, North Carolina........	34,413	76.6	14.0	N	N	N	N	N	N
Rockingham County, North Carolina.....	N	N	N	N	N	N	N	N	N
Rowan County, North Carolina.........	N	N	N	N	N	N	N	N	N
Rutherford County, North Carolina......	N	N	N	N	N	N	N	N	N
Surry County, North Carolina	N	N	N	N	N	N	N	N	N
Union County, North Carolina..........	N	N	N	5,186	93.6	65.1	N	N	N
Wake County, North Carolina	N	N	N	56,986	93.1	74.7	N	N	N
Wayne County, North Carolina.........	N	N	N	N	N	N	N	N	N
Wilkes County, North Carolina.........	N	N	N	N	N	N	N	N	N
Wilson County, North Carolina.........	N	N	N	N	N	N	N	N	N
NORTH DAKOTA	21,476	84.5	17.6	7,164	80.9	40.6	N	N	N
Burleigh County, North Dakota.........	N	N	N	N	N	N	N	N	N

Table C-2. Educational Attainment of the Population, by Selected Counties, 2019—*Continued*

(Number; percent; dollars.)

	Educational attainment by race/ethnicity, 25 years and over								
	White alone			White alone, not Hispanic			Black alone		
State/County	Total	High school graduate or more (percent)	Bachelor's degree or more (percent)	Total	High school graduate or more (percent)	Bachelor's degree or more (percent)	Total	High school graduate or more (percent)	Bachelor's degree or more (percent)
NORTH DAKOTA—(*Continued*)									
Cass County, North Dakota	102,519	96.8	45.0	101,194	96.8	45.0	6,896	94.3	17.5
Grand Forks County, North Dakota	36,350	96.2	36.6	35,614	96.2	36.4	N	N	N
Ward County, North Dakota	38,093	97.5	29.6	37,234	97.5	29.9	N	N	N
OHIO	6,706,983	91.8	30.2	6,552,807	92.1	30.4	939,875	86.8	17.5
Allen County, Ohio	58,791	92.2	20.2	57,640	92.2	20.2	7,372	89.1	12.5
Ashtabula County, Ohio	64,210	87.7	14.3	62,553	87.6	13.7	N	N	N
Athens County, Ohio	35,049	92.4	33.9	34,606	92.5	34.1	N	N	N
Belmont County, Ohio	46,727	91.0	17.4	46,458	91.0	17.5	N	N	N
Butler County, Ohio	211,463	92.4	31.6	205,102	93.3	31.8	20,886	90.6	29.9
Clark County, Ohio	81,639	90.7	16.5	80,179	90.9	16.3	7,740	91.1	10.1
Clermont County, Ohio	137,546	90.9	29.4	135,639	91.0	29.3	N	N	N
Columbiana County, Ohio	70,566	91.6	16.0	70,045	91.7	16.1	N	N	N
Cuyahoga County, Ohio	573,660	92.9	41.0	548,470	93.7	42.0	242,929	85.8	14.3
Delaware County, Ohio	120,543	96.6	50.4	118,295	96.6	50.4	4,774	88.3	30.8
Erie County, Ohio	47,601	93.5	25.7	46,244	93.9	26.3	4,323	86.8	8.1
Fairfield County, Ohio	94,724	94.2	29.2	93,667	94.2	29.3	7,899	91.1	31.7
Franklin County, Ohio	611,985	93.2	46.8	590,286	93.8	47.3	185,059	88.3	22.3
Geauga County, Ohio	62,717	89.1	36.7	62,365	89.0	36.4	N	N	N
Greene County, Ohio	100,876	95.3	39.9	99,148	95.2	40.0	6,440	96.6	48.8
Hamilton County, Ohio	390,342	93.8	47.0	381,291	94.4	47.4	133,644	86.5	18.2
Hancock County, Ohio	48,940	92.5	25.8	47,570	93.0	26.2	N	N	N
Jefferson County, Ohio	43,273	93.0	18.7	43,097	93.1	18.5	2,431	95.6	18.3
Lake County, Ohio	155,163	92.9	26.9	150,616	93.6	27.3	6,775	91.3	11.2
Licking County, Ohio	111,209	91.8	27.1	109,804	91.8	27.2	4,817	89.2	28.5
Lorain County, Ohio	190,472	90.5	26.0	176,870	91.9	27.3	14,717	80.9	12.4
Lucas County, Ohio	223,255	91.9	30.1	214,477	92.1	30.6	51,264	80.6	10.6
Mahoning County, Ohio	135,278	92.2	27.6	129,509	93.4	28.3	20,770	84.9	12.1
Marion County, Ohio	41,849	89.5	13.4	41,284	89.7	13.6	N	N	N
Medina County, Ohio	121,632	95.3	35.0	119,998	95.5	35.1	N	N	N
Miami County, Ohio	70,638	92.0	21.5	69,790	92.5	21.5	N	N	N
Montgomery County, Ohio	273,654	91.2	29.7	269,496	91.5	29.9	70,888	88.2	21.4
Muskingum County, Ohio	54,901	87.4	18.1	54,901	87.4	18.1	N	N	N
Portage County, Ohio	99,383	91.9	29.2	97,880	91.9	29.2	3,844	90.9	18.0
Richland County, Ohio	74,889	89.7	20.1	74,122	89.5	20.3	7,969	78.8	6.3
Ross County, Ohio	49,656	90.7	16.6	49,278	90.7	16.4	3,181	81.7	4.6
Scioto County, Ohio	49,764	85.8	19.2	49,556	85.7	18.9	N	N	N
Stark County, Ohio	234,159	92.1	23.0	231,839	92.2	22.9	18,568	88.7	7.7
Summit County, Ohio	311,433	94.4	35.5	306,395	94.5	35.5	50,265	90.6	15.0
Trumbull County, Ohio	128,630	88.3	19.5	127,086	88.2	19.5	11,585	91.9	16.5
Tuscarawas County, Ohio	62,185	85.0	18.7	61,240	85.0	18.3	N	N	N
Warren County, Ohio	139,774	95.5	42.4	137,652	95.4	42.7	6,502	89.2	34.8
Wayne County, Ohio	73,238	85.7	22.5	72,755	85.7	22.6	N	N	N
Wood County, Ohio	77,034	95.7	36.4	74,161	96.2	36.7	N	N	N
OKLAHOMA	1,999,360	89.5	27.8	1,851,190	91.6	29.0	180,859	89.5	19.8
Canadian County, Oklahoma	83,222	90.4	28.6	77,674	93.1	29.3	N	N	N
Cleveland County, Oklahoma	147,677	92.9	36.6	137,361	94.0	37.4	7,309	89.6	34.4
Comanche County, Oklahoma	51,212	92.1	24.1	46,669	91.7	24.3	12,147	93.6	18.0
Creek County, Oklahoma	40,645	88.7	17.9	39,168	89.2	18.4	N	N	N
Muskogee County, Oklahoma	29,240	86.9	22.1	28,356	86.7	22.7	4,504	92.7	18.5
Oklahoma County, Oklahoma	376,046	88.7	35.6	324,029	94.1	39.2	75,697	89.9	20.6
Payne County, Oklahoma	36,633	94.3	40.1	35,943	94.6	40.2	N	N	N
Pottawatomie County, Oklahoma	38,741	89.3	21.2	37,393	89.8	21.7	1,453	88.9	22.3
Rogers County, Oklahoma	49,657	91.4	25.1	48,029	92.3	25.5	N	N	N
Tulsa County, Oklahoma	320,263	91.4	36.3	290,880	93.8	38.7	40,082	89.9	21.0
Wagoner County, Oklahoma	43,923	91.6	23.9	42,102	92.4	24.7	1,969	99.3	27.9
OREGON	2,568,427	92.6	34.7	2,376,419	94.4	36.1	51,503	90.4	30.5
Benton County, Oregon	49,407	98.3	58.1	47,994	98.6	58.5	N	N	N
Clackamas County, Oregon	263,913	94.1	36.3	252,089	95.3	37.2	3,227	91.4	36.1
Deschutes County, Oregon	135,619	93.5	39.8	129,998	94.0	41.0	N	N	N
Douglas County, Oregon	77,381	92.5	16.1	74,065	92.9	16.3	N	N	N
Jackson County, Oregon	146,607	90.8	27.5	134,737	93.2	28.2	N	N	N
Josephine County, Oregon	61,022	89.3	17.2	57,869	90.2	17.5	N	N	N
Klamath County, Oregon	43,136	90.2	20.6	39,321	91.3	21.3	N	N	N
Lane County, Oregon	235,930	93.4	32.6	226,876	93.7	32.8	2,912	100.0	37.2

Table C-2. Educational Attainment of the Population, by Selected Counties, 2019—*Continued*

(Number; percent; dollars.)

State/County	American Indian or Alaska Native alone			Asian alone			Native Hawaiian or Other Pacific Islander alone		
	Total	High school graduate or more (percent)	Bachelor's degree or more (percent)	Total	High school graduate or more (percent)	Bachelor's degree or more (percent)	Total	High school graduate or more (percent)	Bachelor's degree or more (percent)
NORTH DAKOTA—*(Continued)*									
Cass County, North Dakota	N	N	N	N	N	N	N	N	N
Grand Forks County, North Dakota	N	N	N	N	N	N	N	N	N
Ward County, North Dakota	N	N	N	N	N	N	N	N	N
OHIO	15,473	79.2	17.7	185,785	86.8	62.5	3,809	70.8	38.9
Allen County, Ohio	N	N	N	N	N	N	N	N	N
Ashtabula County, Ohio	N	N	N	N	N	N	N	N	N
Athens County, Ohio	N	N	N	N	N	N	N	N	N
Belmont County, Ohio	N	N	N	N	N	N	N	N	N
Butler County, Ohio	N	N	N	8,314	76.3	51.1	N	N	N
Clark County, Ohio	N	N	N	N	N	N	N	N	N
Clermont County, Ohio	N	N	N	N	N	N	N	N	N
Columbiana County, Ohio	N	N	N	N	N	N	N	N	N
Cuyahoga County, Ohio	2,372	61.9	14.5	29,151	85.6	63.3	N	N	N
Delaware County, Ohio	N	N	N	10,425	96.0	81.4	N	N	N
Erie County, Ohio	N	N	N	N	N	N	N	N	N
Fairfield County, Ohio	N	N	N	2,087	80.5	35.8	N	N	N
Franklin County, Ohio	N	N	N	48,523	87.3	63.0	N	N	N
Geauga County, Ohio	N	N	N	N	N	N	N	N	N
Greene County, Ohio	N	N	N	N	N	N	N	N	N
Hamilton County, Ohio	N	N	N	15,379	91.7	70.5	N	N	N
Hancock County, Ohio	N	N	N	N	N	N	N	N	N
Jefferson County, Ohio	N	N	N	N	N	N	N	N	N
Lake County, Ohio	N	N	N	2,144	85.5	36.9	N	N	N
Licking County, Ohio	N	N	N	N	N	N	N	N	N
Lorain County, Ohio	N	N	N	2,711	85.5	38.3	N	N	N
Lucas County, Ohio	N	N	N	5,761	90.6	65.9	N	N	N
Mahoning County, Ohio	N	N	N	N	N	N	N	N	N
Marion County, Ohio	N	N	N	N	N	N	N	N	N
Medina County, Ohio	N	N	N	N	N	N	N	N	N
Miami County, Ohio	N	N	N	N	N	N	N	N	N
Montgomery County, Ohio	N	N	N	7,768	92.8	75.5	N	N	N
Muskingum County, Ohio	N	N	N	N	N	N	N	N	N
Portage County, Ohio	N	N	N	N	N	N	N	N	N
Richland County, Ohio	N	N	N	N	N	N	N	N	N
Ross County, Ohio	N	N	N	N	N	N	N	N	N
Scioto County, Ohio	N	N	N	N	N	N	N	N	N
Stark County, Ohio	N	N	N	2,877	89.1	51.9	N	N	N
Summit County, Ohio	N	N	N	12,258	60.7	38.5	N	N	N
Trumbull County, Ohio	N	N	N	N	N	N	N	N	N
Tuscarawas County, Ohio	N	N	N	N	N	N	N	N	N
Warren County, Ohio	N	N	N	10,665	96.8	78.4	N	N	N
Wayne County, Ohio	N	N	N	N	N	N	N	N	N
Wood County, Ohio	N	N	N	N	N	N	N	N	N
OKLAHOMA	187,385	86.4	17.6	58,425	81.5	43.2	2,691	82.3	10.6
Canadian County, Oklahoma	3,643	83.5	28.2	3,005	62.9	28.8	N	N	N
Cleveland County, Oklahoma	7,467	90.9	15.3	7,110	87.8	45.5	N	N	N
Comanche County, Oklahoma	3,595	92.9	14.8	2,707	85.6	29.1	N	N	N
Creek County, Oklahoma	5,181	89.2	17.2	N	N	N	N	N	N
Muskogee County, Oklahoma	6,999	85.7	19.5	N	N	N	N	N	N
Oklahoma County, Oklahoma	16,877	86.6	22.8	19,791	83.9	48.6	N	N	N
Payne County, Oklahoma	1,564	85.6	18.3	N	N	N	N	N	N
Pottawatomie County, Oklahoma	6,164	83.4	12.3	N	N	N	N	N	N
Rogers County, Oklahoma	6,781	88.5	16.9	N	N	N	N	N	N
Tulsa County, Oklahoma	22,731	86.4	26.3	14,757	81.2	40.6	N	N	N
Wagoner County, Oklahoma	4,839	87.6	15.6	571	69.2	6.5	N	N	N
OREGON	34,708	85.9	20.2	136,123	88.0	54.0	8,893	93.1	20.3
Benton County, Oregon	N	N	N	N	N	N	N	N	N
Clackamas County, Oregon	N	N	N	14,218	94.0	64.2	N	N	N
Deschutes County, Oregon	N	N	N	N	N	N	N	N	N
Douglas County, Oregon	N	N	N	N	N	N	N	N	N
Jackson County, Oregon	N	N	N	2,353	89.4	39.3	N	N	N
Josephine County, Oregon	N	N	N	N	N	N	N	N	N
Klamath County, Oregon	N	N	N	N	N	N	N	N	N
Lane County, Oregon	2,823	88.1	16.0	5,501	92.1	45.7	N	N	N

Table C-2. Educational Attainment of the Population, by Selected Counties, 2019—*Continued*

(Number; percent; dollars.)

State/County	Educational attainment by race/ethnicity, 25 years and over								
	White alone			White alone, not Hispanic			Black alone		
	Total	High school graduate or more (percent)	Bachelor's degree or more (percent)	Total	High school graduate or more (percent)	Bachelor's degree or more (percent)	Total	High school graduate or more (percent)	Bachelor's degree or more (percent)
OREGON—(*Continued*)									
Linn County, Oregon	82,747	88.8	18.7	79,741	89.4	18.8	N	N	N
Marion County, Oregon	193,423	88.9	26.5	166,986	92.5	29.0	N	N	N
Multnomah County, Oregon	480,767	94.2	50.9	441,000	96.5	53.3	28,744	88.8	24.9
Polk County, Oregon	50,078	93.6	32.3	46,168	95.5	32.7	N	N	N
Umatilla County, Oregon	44,552	88.7	19.6	36,807	91.5	20.7	N	N	N
Washington County, Oregon	321,458	95.0	43.0	289,226	97.2	46.2	8,374	92.4	45.1
Yamhill County, Oregon	65,275	91.0	25.7	59,203	93.6	26.8	N	N	N
PENNSYLVANIA	7,439,802	92.5	33.4	7,155,025	93.0	33.9	931,454	87.9	20.2
Adams County, Pennsylvania	69,477	89.8	22.1	67,125	90.4	22.8	N	N	N
Allegheny County, Pennsylvania	731,811	96.3	44.6	720,819	96.3	44.5	101,419	91.8	23.1
Armstrong County, Pennsylvania	47,073	92.2	15.8	46,944	92.3	15.8	N	N	N
Beaver County, Pennsylvania	111,814	92.9	27.3	110,546	93.3	27.4	7,210	85.9	15.6
Berks County, Pennsylvania	243,448	89.2	26.4	220,730	90.6	27.5	15,090	82.9	14.9
Blair County, Pennsylvania	85,180	91.5	22.7	84,556	91.8	22.8	N	N	N
Bucks County, Pennsylvania	399,402	94.9	42.2	387,426	95.3	42.8	16,545	95.7	28.6
Butler County, Pennsylvania	131,070	95.5	36.9	129,095	95.5	36.9	N	N	N
Cambria County, Pennsylvania	89,646	93.9	21.2	88,600	93.9	21.3	2,776	93.5	7.5
Carbon County, Pennsylvania	45,362	91.0	18.9	44,276	91.0	18.6	N	N	N
Centre County, Pennsylvania	90,893	93.9	43.1	88,871	94.0	42.5	3,917	68.1	14.8
Chester County, Pennsylvania	305,090	95.4	55.5	294,426	96.2	56.0	18,672	91.9	31.9
Clearfield County, Pennsylvania	55,233	89.9	16.3	54,620	90.1	16.5	N	N	N
Columbia County, Pennsylvania	42,586	90.6	24.2	41,632	90.5	24.8	N	N	N
Crawford County, Pennsylvania	57,618	89.1	21.4	57,338	89.1	21.4	N	N	N
Cumberland County, Pennsylvania	159,120	93.0	38.3	154,986	93.2	38.7	5,962	80.7	20.4
Dauphin County, Pennsylvania	142,034	92.7	32.7	136,425	93.0	32.9	32,999	88.4	26.7
Delaware County, Pennsylvania	276,158	94.6	44.0	269,581	94.7	44.3	76,843	90.6	25.0
Erie County, Pennsylvania	166,612	92.7	30.6	164,180	92.8	30.6	11,107	81.8	14.1
Fayette County, Pennsylvania	89,136	88.4	18.5	88,830	88.5	18.5	3,882	78.1	2.1
Franklin County, Pennsylvania	102,383	88.5	22.3	99,011	88.4	22.5	N	N	N
Indiana County, Pennsylvania	54,691	90.8	23.0	54,325	90.8	23.0	N	N	N
Lackawanna County, Pennsylvania	137,425	92.2	29.3	130,973	92.7	30.0	4,183	88.6	25.6
Lancaster County, Pennsylvania	330,685	86.7	29.1	313,244	87.4	29.9	14,687	85.6	20.0
Lawrence County, Pennsylvania	58,315	93.1	22.9	57,994	93.1	22.8	N	N	N
Lebanon County, Pennsylvania	86,723	88.6	22.1	83,516	89.1	22.3	N	N	N
Lehigh County, Pennsylvania	212,453	91.4	31.2	174,136	93.7	35.1	17,154	84.4	12.9
Luzerne County, Pennsylvania	200,222	93.0	22.6	193,058	94.0	22.9	11,972	87.8	10.9
Lycoming County, Pennsylvania	75,738	89.5	24.4	74,472	89.4	24.2	3,618	91.8	11.7
Mercer County, Pennsylvania	72,741	89.7	23.7	72,067	90.0	24.0	4,278	78.2	11.2
Monroe County, Pennsylvania	95,623	91.3	25.5	82,216	92.6	26.4	16,088	92.5	27.3
Montgomery County, Pennsylvania	475,563	95.9	50.4	456,742	96.5	51.1	52,579	90.3	34.1
Northampton County, Pennsylvania	186,094	92.7	31.2	171,857	93.2	32.7	11,192	89.2	23.2
Northumberland County, Pennsylvania	64,312	88.9	15.9	62,506	89.7	16.4	N	N	N
Philadelphia County, Pennsylvania	467,047	91.1	45.5	422,814	92.7	48.0	432,647	86.9	17.6
Schuylkill County, Pennsylvania	97,897	90.9	16.9	95,227	91.7	17.1	N	N	N
Somerset County, Pennsylvania	52,543	89.0	17.9	52,154	89.2	18.0	N	N	N
Washington County, Pennsylvania	141,696	93.0	31.3	140,041	93.2	31.4	4,245	90.3	17.1
Westmoreland County, Pennsylvania	248,823	94.8	29.3	247,108	94.8	29.2	5,714	88.0	10.6
York County, Pennsylvania	282,021	91.1	27.5	271,667	92.1	28.3	16,387	87.0	12.7
RHODE ISLAND	613,613	90.8	36.7	565,077	92.3	38.5	49,190	91.1	23.4
Kent County, Rhode Island	110,960	92.4	32.4	108,829	92.5	32.5	2,852	84.6	36.5
Newport County, Rhode Island	56,664	94.3	47.5	54,139	94.0	48.7	N	N	N
Providence County, Rhode Island	331,498	87.9	32.1	289,880	90.6	34.7	43,362	91.8	21.6
Washington County, Rhode Island	83,068	95.7	48.5	81,501	95.7	48.6	N	N	N
SOUTH CAROLINA	2,483,427	90.9	34.0	2,396,696	91.5	34.4	899,954	83.9	17.5
Aiken County, South Carolina	88,278	92.6	31.5	84,312	93.1	32.4	28,874	83.2	20.2
Anderson County, South Carolina	113,598	88.8	27.7	111,800	89.2	27.9	20,321	83.2	7.8
Beaufort County, South Carolina	109,888	95.7	48.4	103,990	96.9	49.9	20,292	84.8	8.9
Berkeley County, South Carolina	102,204	92.2	31.8	100,216	92.3	32.1	36,349	88.3	19.5
Charleston County, South Carolina	206,605	96.6	56.3	202,084	96.8	56.6	70,743	83.3	18.4
Darlington County, South Carolina	27,598	89.4	27.9	26,711	90.4	28.8	16,795	74.0	6.2
Dorchester County, South Carolina	76,702	92.2	30.7	74,256	92.7	30.4	26,396	86.2	24.7
Florence County, South Carolina	52,736	90.0	30.8	51,605	90.8	31.3	38,594	85.7	15.5
Greenville County, South Carolina	270,325	91.6	42.1	255,974	92.1	43.1	60,050	82.9	14.6

Table C-2. Educational Attainment of the Population, by Selected Counties, 2019—*Continued*

(Number; percent; dollars.)

| | Educational attainment by race/ethnicity, 25 years and over | | | | | | | | |
| | American Indian or Alaska Native alone | | | Asian alone | | | Native Hawaiian or Other Pacific Islander alone | | |
State/County	Total	High school graduate or more (percent)	Bachelor's degree or more (percent)	Total	High school graduate or more (percent)	Bachelor's degree or more (percent)	Total	High school graduate or more (percent)	Bachelor's degree or more (percent)
OREGON—*(Continued)*									
Linn County, Oregon	N	N	N	N	N	N	N	N	N
Marion County, Oregon	3,684	68.6	6.7	6,417	91.0	33.2	N	N	N
Multnomah County, Oregon	4,502	84.2	39.3	44,954	77.0	43.0	4,213	94.5	17.3
Polk County, Oregon	N	N	N	N	N	N	N	N	N
Umatilla County, Oregon	1,503	86.7	12.9	N	N	N	N	N	N
Washington County, Oregon	N	N	N	49,833	94.3	66.5	N	N	N
Yamhill County, Oregon	N	N	N	N	N	N	N	N	N
PENNSYLVANIA	17,215	77.5	20.5	309,518	84.8	57.0	2,139	78.1	33.0
Adams County, Pennsylvania	N	N	N	608	100.0	42.9	N	N	N
Allegheny County, Pennsylvania	N	N	N	31,307	87.6	70.9	N	N	N
Armstrong County, Pennsylvania	N	N	N	N	N	N	N	N	N
Beaver County, Pennsylvania	N	N	N	N	N	N	N	N	N
Berks County, Pennsylvania	N	N	N	4,332	89.5	49.1	N	N	N
Blair County, Pennsylvania	N	N	N	N	N	N	N	N	N
Bucks County, Pennsylvania	N	N	N	23,534	90.6	65.2	N	N	N
Butler County, Pennsylvania	N	N	N	N	N	N	N	N	N
Cambria County, Pennsylvania	N	N	N	N	N	N	N	N	N
Carbon County, Pennsylvania	N	N	N	N	N	N	N	N	N
Centre County, Pennsylvania	N	N	N	N	N	N	N	N	N
Chester County, Pennsylvania	N	N	N	20,833	93.3	80.0	N	N	N
Clearfield County, Pennsylvania	N	N	N	N	N	N	N	N	N
Columbia County, Pennsylvania	N	N	N	N	N	N	N	N	N
Crawford County, Pennsylvania	N	N	N	N	N	N	N	N	N
Cumberland County, Pennsylvania	N	N	N	7,247	90.7	68.4	N	N	N
Dauphin County, Pennsylvania	N	N	N	9,705	65.6	42.8	N	N	N
Delaware County, Pennsylvania	N	N	N	22,569	87.8	59.5	N	N	N
Erie County, Pennsylvania	N	N	N	2,474	72.9	53.3	N	N	N
Fayette County, Pennsylvania	N	N	N	N	N	N	N	N	N
Franklin County, Pennsylvania	N	N	N	N	N	N	N	N	N
Indiana County, Pennsylvania	N	N	N	N	N	N	N	N	N
Lackawanna County, Pennsylvania	N	N	N	4,583	85.3	46.3	N	N	N
Lancaster County, Pennsylvania	N	N	N	7,659	74.5	37.8	N	N	N
Lawrence County, Pennsylvania	N	N	N	N	N	N	N	N	N
Lebanon County, Pennsylvania	N	N	N	N	N	N	N	N	N
Lehigh County, Pennsylvania	N	N	N	8,304	82.3	47.6	N	N	N
Luzerne County, Pennsylvania	N	N	N	2,288	89.2	48.1	N	N	N
Lycoming County, Pennsylvania	N	N	N	N	N	N	N	N	N
Mercer County, Pennsylvania	N	N	N	N	N	N	N	N	N
Monroe County, Pennsylvania	N	N	N	2,424	91.5	33.9	N	N	N
Montgomery County, Pennsylvania	N	N	N	45,512	92.3	69.3	N	N	N
Northampton County, Pennsylvania	N	N	N	5,814	93.3	54.9	N	N	N
Northumberland County, Pennsylvania	N	N	N	N	N	N	N	N	N
Philadelphia County, Pennsylvania	3,945	71.8	9.9	83,466	75.8	42.3	N	N	N
Schuylkill County, Pennsylvania	N	N	N	N	N	N	N	N	N
Somerset County, Pennsylvania	N	N	N	N	N	N	N	N	N
Washington County, Pennsylvania	N	N	N	1,396	83.3	54.9	N	N	N
Westmoreland County, Pennsylvania	N	N	N	N	N	N	N	N	N
York County, Pennsylvania	N	N	N	4,711	80.3	41.5	N	N	N
RHODE ISLAND	N	N	N	25,461	87.6	52.7	N	N	N
Kent County, Rhode Island	N	N	N	N	N	N	N	N	N
Newport County, Rhode Island	N	N	N	N	N	N	N	N	N
Providence County, Rhode Island	N	N	N	18,050	84.3	47.7	N	N	N
Washington County, Rhode Island	N	N	N	N	N	N	N	N	N
SOUTH CAROLINA	13,884	77.3	18.9	58,659	87.9	51.4	N	N	N
Aiken County, South Carolina	N	N	N	N	N	N	N	N	N
Anderson County, South Carolina	N	N	N	N	N	N	N	N	N
Beaufort County, South Carolina	N	N	N	N	N	N	N	N	N
Berkeley County, South Carolina	N	N	N	4,077	86.8	22.1	N	N	N
Charleston County, South Carolina	N	N	N	N	N	N	N	N	N
Darlington County, South Carolina	N	N	N	N	N	N	N	N	N
Dorchester County, South Carolina	N	N	N	N	N	N	N	N	N
Florence County, South Carolina	N	N	N	N	N	N	N	N	N
Greenville County, South Carolina	N	N	N	9,307	88.7	51.4	N	N	N

Table C-2. Educational Attainment of the Population, by Selected Counties, 2019—*Continued*

(Number; percent; dollars.)

	Educational attainment by race/ethnicity, 25 years and over								
	White alone			White alone, not Hispanic			Black alone		
State/County	Total	High school graduate or more (percent)	Bachelor's degree or more (percent)	Total	High school graduate or more (percent)	Bachelor's degree or more (percent)	Total	High school graduate or more (percent)	Bachelor's degree or more (percent)
SOUTH CAROLINA—(*Continued*)									
Greenwood County, South Carolina	32,514	90.0	31.5	30,913	90.1	30.2	15,727	87.7	12.6
Horry County, South Carolina	225,972	91.0	26.2	218,020	92.1	26.5	30,035	81.4	9.2
Kershaw County, South Carolina	33,072	87.8	26.0	32,806	88.0	25.8	12,041	86.8	14.9
Lancaster County, South Carolina	54,364	90.1	25.5	51,691	91.3	26.7	14,548	75.0	10.6
Laurens County, South Carolina	33,086	85.5	18.9	32,373	85.8	18.4	10,968	85.7	20.3
Lexington County, South Carolina	167,799	89.2	30.8	161,222	90.6	31.7	29,068	87.4	24.8
Oconee County, South Carolina	52,156	86.8	27.7	50,538	87.0	27.5	4,180	81.7	13.9
Orangeburg County, South Carolina	22,035	86.4	21.2	21,746	86.8	21.5	35,235	85.6	21.0
Pickens County, South Carolina	71,401	87.4	27.1	70,149	87.5	26.9	5,843	81.4	10.8
Richland County, South Carolina	120,366	94.4	52.1	115,822	94.9	52.4	125,840	89.8	32.5
Spartanburg County, South Carolina	163,046	88.7	29.5	154,779	90.2	30.2	42,796	79.9	16.3
Sumter County, South Carolina	34,858	91.6	26.3	33,799	92.1	27.1	32,408	84.7	18.0
York County, South Carolina	146,234	93.8	36.9	139,091	94.3	37.5	34,141	90.2	23.6
SOUTH DAKOTA	516,050	93.9	31.5	505,241	94.2	31.6	11,679	77.1	18.9
Minnehaha County, South Dakota	115,022	94.6	37.7	110,586	95.1	38.0	6,231	71.4	13.7
Pennington County, South Dakota	68,725	94.5	33.9	67,240	94.9	34.3	N	N	N
TENNESSEE	3,744,336	88.7	29.7	3,613,025	89.6	30.1	737,044	87.2	21.7
Anderson County, Tennessee	50,566	89.4	20.9	49,952	89.8	20.9	N	N	N
Blount County, Tennessee	91,712	88.6	23.5	89,082	89.7	24.1	N	N	N
Bradley County, Tennessee	67,149	86.8	23.9	65,600	86.9	23.9	4,186	79.1	14.4
Davidson County, Tennessee	323,611	91.1	52.1	297,060	94.5	55.3	120,156	88.7	29.6
Greene County, Tennessee	48,069	84.6	19.3	47,634	84.9	19.4	N	N	N
Hamilton County, Tennessee	201,513	91.0	38.4	194,179	92.0	38.9	44,937	84.6	16.9
Knox County, Tennessee	277,336	92.0	38.7	268,405	92.9	39.2	23,888	93.2	21.1
Madison County, Tennessee	40,627	92.1	32.8	39,823	92.5	33.2	21,779	86.7	18.3
Maury County, Tennessee	57,836	89.1	24.9	54,765	92.1	26.2	7,488	88.8	27.4
Montgomery County, Tennessee	92,889	94.4	31.6	85,813	94.3	32.0	25,143	93.9	25.7
Putnam County, Tennessee	49,290	86.2	28.4	47,391	87.4	27.9	N	N	N
Robertson County, Tennessee	43,674	85.7	21.9	42,363	86.1	21.9	3,906	78.5	14.4
Rutherford County, Tennessee	163,192	92.9	31.5	153,742	94.0	31.5	30,778	94.4	33.3
Sevier County, Tennessee	67,334	84.3	18.8	65,190	85.2	19.3	N	N	N
Shelby County, Tennessee	261,651	92.7	45.4	244,870	94.9	47.5	321,714	86.7	19.9
Sullivan County, Tennessee	111,165	89.0	26.4	110,241	89.0	26.4	2,394	90.6	14.7
Sumner County, Tennessee	115,565	91.0	29.7	113,262	91.4	29.7	9,378	93.1	43.8
Washington County, Tennessee	82,776	89.4	31.5	81,039	89.2	31.8	3,432	100.0	37.0
Williamson County, Tennessee	138,724	95.3	60.8	133,015	95.5	62.3	6,713	95.9	53.3
Wilson County, Tennessee	88,604	93.0	34.5	86,300	94.1	34.7	7,603	94.3	41.2
TEXAS	13,971,984	84.8	30.8	8,669,915	94.4	39.4	2,289,499	91.2	25.7
Angelina County, Texas	47,380	85.5	20.6	37,454	92.2	21.7	8,611	92.9	7.9
Bastrop County, Texas	41,449	86.1	21.5	34,539	90.3	21.8	N	N	N
Bell County, Texas	144,030	91.1	27.7	109,523	94.7	29.0	54,025	89.6	19.9
Bexar County, Texas	1,012,592	84.5	27.9	394,623	96.5	43.1	98,128	93.4	28.4
Bowie County, Texas	45,412	86.6	23.9	42,456	88.3	25.2	14,650	84.9	5.4
Brazoria County, Texas	179,384	88.2	26.4	121,481	93.3	31.8	36,507	96.4	35.0
Brazos County, Texas	98,185	87.6	44.1	70,652	95.2	55.5	14,497	89.9	17.1
Cameron County, Texas	235,383	68.7	17.4	29,303	88.7	34.7	N	N	N
Collin County, Texas	473,818	94.1	48.6	400,079	97.6	52.6	68,389	95.9	46.0
Comal County, Texas	100,384	93.6	40.3	77,327	95.6	40.6	N	N	N
Coryell County, Texas	36,800	88.9	18.0	29,851	91.8	18.8	5,970	86.3	14.2
Dallas County, Texas	1,036,971	78.7	33.8	581,608	95.4	51.3	393,341	90.9	25.8
Denton County, Texas	445,177	92.8	44.1	363,596	96.7	47.4	58,608	93.9	43.8
Ector County, Texas	79,457	76.6	15.4	36,119	90.0	22.8	6,610	90.6	16.5
Ellis County, Texas	97,873	88.8	26.0	76,686	94.0	30.6	12,482	93.6	29.6
El Paso County, Texas	420,109	80.5	24.4	67,844	94.5	41.0	18,611	98.3	28.1
Fort Bend County, Texas	269,878	90.1	44.2	178,607	97.2	52.9	107,005	96.1	42.7
Galveston County, Texas	186,057	91.3	30.5	140,809	95.7	35.6	28,111	89.3	27.4
Grayson County, Texas	81,460	90.4	22.7	73,833	93.8	24.2	4,661	89.8	1.3
Gregg County, Texas	61,974	86.1	24.5	50,700	91.2	27.8	15,907	87.9	11.6
Guadalupe County, Texas	92,520	89.1	30.4	58,738	96.6	37.4	9,800	96.9	28.9
Harris County, Texas	1,871,684	81.7	33.9	1,003,744	96.2	49.7	580,351	91.6	26.0
Harrison County, Texas	33,589	87.3	21.8	30,012	90.3	24.1	7,692	83.4	13.1
Hays County, Texas	125,447	90.6	37.7	80,299	97.3	48.9	4,692	90.9	12.7
Henderson County, Texas	53,457	83.6	16.4	48,222	86.3	17.6	N	N	N
Hidalgo County, Texas	411,078	69.3	18.9	38,545	92.4	35.6	3,608	78.8	28.8

Table C-2. Educational Attainment of the Population, by Selected Counties, 2019—*Continued*

(Number; percent; dollars.)

| | Educational attainment by race/ethnicity, 25 years and over | | | | | | | | |
| | American Indian or Alaska Native alone | | | Asian alone | | | Native Hawaiian or Other Pacific Islander alone | | |
State/County	Total	High school graduate or more (percent)	Bachelor's degree or more (percent)	Total	High school graduate or more (percent)	Bachelor's degree or more (percent)	Total	High school graduate or more (percent)	Bachelor's degree or more (percent)
SOUTH CAROLINA—*(Continued)*									
Greenwood County, South Carolina	N	N	N	N	N	N	N	N	N
Horry County, South Carolina	N	N	N	3,174	88.0	47.4	N	N	N
Kershaw County, South Carolina	N	N	N	N	N	N	N	N	N
Lancaster County, South Carolina	N	N	N	N	N	N	N	N	N
Laurens County, South Carolina	N	N	N	N	N	N	N	N	N
Lexington County, South Carolina	N	N	N	4,419	89.2	61.3	N	N	N
Oconee County, South Carolina	N	N	N	N	N	N	N	N	N
Orangeburg County, South Carolina	N	N	N	N	N	N	N	N	N
Pickens County, South Carolina	N	N	N	N	N	N	N	N	N
Richland County, South Carolina	N	N	N	7,558	84.9	68.6	N	N	N
Spartanburg County, South Carolina	N	N	N	5,628	86.5	20.3	N	N	N
Sumter County, South Carolina	N	N	N	N	N	N	N	N	N
York County, South Carolina	1,629	83.9	10.0	5,026	90.6	71.9	N	N	N
SOUTH DAKOTA	38,100	80.0	8.8	7,098	81.1	42.7	N	N	N
Minnehaha County, South Dakota	N	N	N	2,652	67.0	17.5	N	N	N
Pennington County, South Dakota	4,890	85.4	6.5	N	N	N	N	N	N
TENNESSEE	14,977	78.0	15.5	87,030	85.9	52.2	N	N	N
Anderson County, Tennessee	N	N	N	N	N	N	N	N	N
Blount County, Tennessee	N	N	N	N	N	N	N	N	N
Bradley County, Tennessee	N	N	N	N	N	N	N	N	N
Davidson County, Tennessee	N	N	N	18,256	83.4	55.8	N	N	N
Greene County, Tennessee	N	N	N	N	N	N	N	N	N
Hamilton County, Tennessee	N	N	N	N	N	N	N	N	N
Knox County, Tennessee	N	N	N	7,615	87.0	64.9	N	N	N
Madison County, Tennessee	N	N	N	N	N	N	N	N	N
Maury County, Tennessee	N	N	N	N	N	N	N	N	N
Montgomery County, Tennessee	N	N	N	N	N	N	N	N	N
Putnam County, Tennessee	N	N	N	N	N	N	N	N	N
Robertson County, Tennessee	N	N	N	N	N	N	N	N	N
Rutherford County, Tennessee	N	N	N	8,213	84.5	15.6	N	N	N
Sevier County, Tennessee	N	N	N	N	N	N	N	N	N
Shelby County, Tennessee	N	N	N	17,848	81.5	52.2	N	N	N
Sullivan County, Tennessee	N	N	N	N	N	N	N	N	N
Sumner County, Tennessee	N	N	N	2,477	72.2	44.0	N	N	N
Washington County, Tennessee	N	N	N	N	N	N	N	N	N
Williamson County, Tennessee	N	N	N	N	N	N	N	N	N
Wilson County, Tennessee	N	N	N	N	N	N	N	N	N
TEXAS	98,802	84.3	24.0	1,008,252	89.4	60.6	16,349	88.9	22.2
Angelina County, Texas	N	N	N	N	N	N	N	N	N
Bastrop County, Texas	N	N	N	N	N	N	N	N	N
Bell County, Texas	N	N	N	8,175	85.9	29.2	N	N	N
Bexar County, Texas	11,492	81.9	16.7	42,011	92.2	54.3	N	N	N
Bowie County, Texas	N	N	N	N	N	N	N	N	N
Brazoria County, Texas	N	N	N	18,516	89.0	60.1	N	N	N
Brazos County, Texas	N	N	N	7,458	94.0	73.2	N	N	N
Cameron County, Texas	N	N	N	N	N	N	N	N	N
Collin County, Texas	2,249	90.6	42.4	112,941	94.6	76.6	N	N	N
Comal County, Texas	N	N	N	N	N	N	N	N	N
Coryell County, Texas	N	N	N	N	N	N	N	N	N
Dallas County, Texas	8,119	80.0	16.2	121,268	89.7	62.0	N	N	N
Denton County, Texas	N	N	N	57,481	93.5	71.7	N	N	N
Ector County, Texas	N	N	N	N	N	N	N	N	N
Ellis County, Texas	N	N	N	N	N	N	N	N	N
El Paso County, Texas	3,455	89.3	16.8	6,687	85.5	42.5	N	N	N
Fort Bend County, Texas	N	N	N	112,532	92.4	60.4	N	N	N
Galveston County, Texas	N	N	N	9,042	87.5	50.0	N	N	N
Grayson County, Texas	N	N	N	N	N	N	N	N	N
Gregg County, Texas	N	N	N	N	N	N	N	N	N
Guadalupe County, Texas	N	N	N	N	N	N	N	N	N
Harris County, Texas	14,016	81.0	23.1	242,381	86.5	54.0	N	N	N
Harrison County, Texas	N	N	N	N	N	N	N	N	N
Hays County, Texas	N	N	N	N	N	N	N	N	N
Henderson County, Texas	N	N	N	N	N	N	N	N	N
Hidalgo County, Texas	N	N	N	5,586	79.5	55.3	N	N	N

Table C-2. Educational Attainment of the Population, by Selected Counties, 2019—*Continued*

(Number; percent; dollars.)

State/County	Educational attainment by race/ethnicity, 25 years and over								
	White alone			White alone, not Hispanic			Black alone		
	Total	High school graduate or more (percent)	Bachelor's degree or more (percent)	Total	High school graduate or more (percent)	Bachelor's degree or more (percent)	Total	High school graduate or more (percent)	Bachelor's degree or more (percent)
TEXAS—(*Continued*)									
Hunt County, Texas	55,092	86.3	21.9	49,808	90.1	23.4	5,539	79.9	16.2
Jefferson County, Texas	101,373	83.6	23.8	74,532	93.9	30.5	54,112	89.2	13.4
Johnson County, Texas	104,937	85.7	18.2	86,470	90.4	20.5	4,704	91.1	20.6
Kaufman County, Texas	69,478	85.0	18.6	56,757	89.1	20.0	11,853	93.4	18.7
Liberty County, Texas	46,701	80.8	12.4	37,780	86.2	13.8	5,617	92.0	16.8
Lubbock County, Texas	150,397	87.6	34.1	104,496	94.5	42.6	13,269	90.3	16.0
McLennan County, Texas	128,259	87.2	27.3	95,963	93.8	32.9	20,460	87.6	12.3
Midland County, Texas	81,810	88.1	31.9	54,946	95.1	40.3	8,109	91.0	22.1
Montgomery County, Texas	348,537	87.9	33.0	277,338	94.1	36.8	20,175	92.3	29.5
Nacogdoches County, Texas	30,099	85.0	27.1	24,812	92.0	30.6	7,649	84.4	8.1
Nueces County, Texas	215,292	83.7	22.6	77,778	94.0	31.9	9,133	90.1	16.1
Orange County, Texas	49,507	87.4	18.5	46,526	88.3	18.4	5,353	87.9	17.7
Parker County, Texas	90,416	88.5	24.6	82,862	90.7	25.4	N	N	N
Potter County, Texas	59,549	80.5	15.4	37,579	89.9	20.8	7,979	75.6	2.2
Randall County, Texas	82,266	93.4	34.5	68,430	95.9	36.8	N	N	N
Rockwall County, Texas	57,961	95.5	42.7	49,638	96.7	45.0	5,530	98.9	26.1
San Patricio County, Texas	39,649	82.2	15.5	18,003	95.3	22.8	N	N	N
Smith County, Texas	119,402	87.0	29.2	99,817	93.8	33.2	25,486	91.7	21.4
Tarrant County, Texas	926,680	88.9	35.9	692,576	95.2	41.5	224,439	92.5	29.5
Taylor County, Texas	70,790	91.6	27.6	57,177	94.3	30.2	6,888	97.6	19.5
Tom Green County, Texas	68,630	88.2	23.9	43,902	94.7	29.9	N	N	N
Travis County, Texas	664,211	91.9	56.6	478,444	98.1	66.3	72,632	91.4	29.1
Victoria County, Texas	52,308	84.7	20.1	29,940	94.8	27.6	4,617	95.1	11.8
Walker County, Texas	34,600	87.0	19.6	28,303	94.6	23.5	10,712	84.4	19.3
Webb County, Texas	148,439	65.1	19.2	7,136	88.5	39.8	N	N	N
Wichita County, Texas	70,978	89.8	24.0	59,152	93.4	26.7	8,227	82.3	4.6
Williamson County, Texas	318,872	93.5	40.3	245,142	96.8	45.1	26,594	98.6	29.6
Wise County, Texas	44,865	85.5	17.1	38,024	92.1	18.8	N	N	N
UTAH	1,694,118	94.5	35.8	1,540,298	96.1	37.6	19,937	86.3	17.4
Cache County, Utah	61,157	94.9	37.4	55,932	96.7	39.9	N	N	N
Davis County, Utah	191,739	96.5	37.0	178,195	97.7	38.7	N	N	N
Salt Lake County, Utah	612,072	94.0	39.2	551,237	95.6	41.3	12,337	84.9	18.8
Tooele County, Utah	40,685	93.9	23.9	35,891	94.9	25.4	N	N	N
Utah County, Utah	295,622	95.9	41.4	266,376	97.6	43.7	N	N	N
Washington County, Utah	108,503	94.8	27.7	101,671	95.6	28.7	N	N	N
Weber County, Utah	149,448	92.5	27.6	129,084	95.2	29.7	N	N	N
VERMONT	422,653	93.8	38.8	418,747	93.8	38.9	5,756	82.9	26.3
Chittenden County, Vermont	100,159	95.9	52.9	98,481	95.8	53.1	2,953	85.0	30.3
VIRGINIA	4,069,698	91.9	42.0	3,782,506	93.0	43.0	1,110,132	86.2	25.2
Albemarle County, Virginia	62,997	95.5	62.6	60,291	96.2	63.5	6,081	90.5	27.3
Arlington County, Virginia	128,545	95.5	80.5	110,399	99.0	86.2	16,165	93.7	50.4
Augusta County, Virginia	52,952	88.0	20.3	51,192	89.3	20.5	3,428	76.3	4.4
Bedford County, Virginia	52,029	91.5	32.7	51,361	91.7	32.8	3,029	62.5	7.6
Chesterfield County, Virginia	162,019	93.7	43.4	154,505	94.6	44.4	51,939	94.0	34.3
Fairfax County, Virginia	482,723	94.8	67.0	413,083	98.0	73.0	76,656	94.9	50.1
Fauquier County, Virginia	43,192	92.4	36.5	40,105	95.3	38.4	4,190	86.2	25.4
Frederick County, Virginia	57,487	88.6	28.7	53,448	89.8	30.4	N	N	N
Hanover County, Virginia	64,739	95.6	41.2	63,666	95.6	41.3	7,130	81.3	30.3
Henrico County, Virginia	133,192	94.8	50.5	128,198	94.9	50.7	68,144	88.2	20.2
James City County, Virginia	46,905	96.5	55.8	44,191	97.4	56.3	6,810	85.9	21.0
Loudoun County, Virginia	171,118	96.7	62.9	151,642	97.9	66.1	21,063	93.2	46.3
Montgomery County, Virginia	49,652	95.1	44.0	49,123	95.1	43.9	N	N	N
Prince William County, Virginia	177,908	90.4	45.0	135,788	96.3	52.0	64,896	95.1	42.8
Roanoke County, Virginia	61,443	91.3	37.7	59,807	91.6	37.8	N	N	N
Rockingham County, Virginia	53,455	85.5	27.4	51,461	86.6	27.9	N	N	N
Spotsylvania County, Virginia	66,486	93.9	33.9	63,994	94.5	34.0	14,931	93.3	18.6
Stafford County, Virginia	66,492	95.1	42.3	61,552	95.7	43.3	19,584	96.7	38.0
York County, Virginia	34,482	94.9	50.7	33,534	94.8	50.8	7,180	96.2	49.8
Alexandria city, Virginia	78,749	94.9	75.6	67,513	97.8	79.5	25,648	91.5	44.1
Chesapeake city, Virginia	102,317	94.7	34.1	97,674	94.8	33.5	48,994	84.6	26.7
Hampton city, Virginia	39,734	93.1	25.8	37,291	93.7	27.0	45,195	92.1	27.3
Lynchburg city, Virginia	30,328	90.1	43.6	29,562	90.0	43.1	13,877	82.3	16.9
Newport News city, Virginia	59,299	92.0	30.8	53,563	93.7	32.8	47,189	89.4	19.6
Norfolk city, Virginia	76,323	92.7	39.6	72,056	93.3	40.1	61,985	83.0	18.4

Table C-2. Educational Attainment of the Population, by Selected Counties, 2019—*Continued*

(Number; percent; dollars.)

State/County	Educational attainment by race/ethnicity, 25 years and over								
	American Indian or Alaska Native alone			Asian alone			Native Hawaiian or Other Pacific Islander alone		
	Total	High school graduate or more (percent)	Bachelor's degree or more (percent)	Total	High school graduate or more (percent)	Bachelor's degree or more (percent)	Total	High school graduate or more (percent)	Bachelor's degree or more (percent)
TEXAS—(*Continued*)									
Hunt County, Texas	N	N	N	N	N	N	N	N	N
Jefferson County, Texas	N	N	N	6,484	69.2	39.5	N	N	N
Johnson County, Texas	N	N	N	N	N	N	N	N	N
Kaufman County, Texas	N	N	N	N	N	N	N	N	N
Liberty County, Texas	N	N	N	N	N	N	N	N	N
Lubbock County, Texas	N	N	N	4,596	92.4	68.4	N	N	N
McLennan County, Texas	N	N	N	N	N	N	N	N	N
Midland County, Texas	N	N	N	N	N	N	N	N	N
Montgomery County, Texas	N	N	N	13,169	97.9	67.6	N	N	N
Nacogdoches County, Texas	N	N	N	N	N	N	N	N	N
Nueces County, Texas	N	N	N	N	N	N	N	N	N
Orange County, Texas	N	N	N	N	N	N	N	N	N
Parker County, Texas	N	N	N	N	N	N	N	N	N
Potter County, Texas	N	N	N	N	N	N	N	N	N
Randall County, Texas	N	N	N	N	N	N	N	N	N
Rockwall County, Texas	N	N	N	2,633	86.9	41.4	N	N	N
San Patricio County, Texas	N	N	N	N	N	N	N	N	N
Smith County, Texas	N	N	N	N	N	N	N	N	N
Tarrant County, Texas	7,468	85.2	33.3	81,340	86.3	52.8	N	N	N
Taylor County, Texas	N	N	N	N	N	N	N	N	N
Tom Green County, Texas	N	N	N	N	N	N	N	N	N
Travis County, Texas	7,529	82.0	42.0	62,967	91.5	76.5	N	N	N
Victoria County, Texas	N	N	N	N	N	N	N	N	N
Walker County, Texas	N	N	N	N	N	N	N	N	N
Webb County, Texas	N	N	N	N	N	N	N	N	N
Wichita County, Texas	N	N	N	1,824	85.5	52.4	N	N	N
Williamson County, Texas	N	N	N	30,843	92.1	71.6	N	N	N
Wise County, Texas	N	N	N	N	N	N	N	N	N
UTAH	20,630	81.9	11.7	52,276	90.3	55.0	16,930	90.9	15.4
Cache County, Utah	N	N	N	2,080	80.3	42.1	N	N	N
Davis County, Utah	N	N	N	4,897	93.4	46.7	N	N	N
Salt Lake County, Utah	6,129	89.4	19.4	34,599	89.4	59.4	10,016	88.1	10.2
Tooele County, Utah	N	N	N	N	N	N	N	N	N
Utah County, Utah	N	N	N	4,814	90.8	62.0	2,961	94.7	29.6
Washington County, Utah	N	N	N	N	N	N	N	N	N
Weber County, Utah	N	N	N	2,771	96.9	41.2	N	N	N
VERMONT	2,033	71.9	15.5	6,155	83.1	49.3	N	N	N
Chittenden County, Vermont	N	N	N	3,388	69.3	41.3	N	N	N
VIRGINIA	15,850	82.8	29.9	405,441	90.6	62.1	3,029	93.5	39.2
Albemarle County, Virginia	N	N	N	N	N	N	N	N	N
Arlington County, Virginia	N	N	N	17,844	94.0	70.5	N	N	N
Augusta County, Virginia	N	N	N	N	N	N	N	N	N
Bedford County, Virginia	N	N	N	N	N	N	N	N	N
Chesterfield County, Virginia	N	N	N	9,236	91.4	60.2	N	N	N
Fairfax County, Virginia	N	N	N	164,313	91.4	64.3	N	N	N
Fauquier County, Virginia	N	N	N	N	N	N	N	N	N
Frederick County, Virginia	N	N	N	N	N	N	N	N	N
Hanover County, Virginia	N	N	N	N	N	N	N	N	N
Henrico County, Virginia	N	N	N	19,806	87.2	73.9	N	N	N
James City County, Virginia	N	N	N	N	N	N	N	N	N
Loudoun County, Virginia	1,238	77.1	37.6	55,413	94.2	76.0	N	N	N
Montgomery County, Virginia	N	N	N	N	N	N	N	N	N
Prince William County, Virginia	N	N	N	29,701	87.3	52.9	N	N	N
Roanoke County, Virginia	N	N	N	N	N	N	N	N	N
Rockingham County, Virginia	N	N	N	N	N	N	N	N	N
Spotsylvania County, Virginia	N	N	N	2,390	91.1	55.7	N	N	N
Stafford County, Virginia	N	N	N	3,749	89.1	46.9	N	N	N
York County, Virginia	N	N	N	3,137	84.0	60.9	N	N	N
Alexandria city, Virginia	N	N	N	8,603	91.4	70.1	N	N	N
Chesapeake city, Virginia	N	N	N	7,577	87.3	46.3	N	N	N
Hampton city, Virginia	N	N	N	2,436	67.4	32.8	N	N	N
Lynchburg city, Virginia	N	N	N	N	N	N	N	N	N
Newport News city, Virginia	N	N	N	4,898	94.6	46.4	N	N	N
Norfolk city, Virginia	N	N	N	6,198	92.4	52.9	N	N	N

Table C-2. Educational Attainment of the Population, by Selected Counties, 2019—*Continued*

(Number; percent; dollars.)

State/County	Educational attainment by race/ethnicity, 25 years and over								
	White alone			White alone, not Hispanic			Black alone		
	Total	High school graduate or more (percent)	Bachelor's degree or more (percent)	Total	High school graduate or more (percent)	Bachelor's degree or more (percent)	Total	High school graduate or more (percent)	Bachelor's degree or more (percent)
VIRGINIA—*(Continued)*									
Portsmouth city, Virginia....................	27,529	90.3	22.9	26,361	90.2	23.1	33,781	85.9	20.4
Richmond city, Virginia....................	79,665	93.1	64.9	76,190	94.7	66.3	70,843	78.6	12.9
Roanoke city, Virginia	45,988	88.9	26.3	44,181	89.2	26.9	19,346	85.2	9.9
Suffolk city, Virginia	33,881	95.9	36.4	32,777	96.4	36.9	25,058	84.3	22.4
Virginia Beach city, Virginia....................	211,504	96.4	41.5	199,124	96.5	42.0	55,967	91.5	30.4
WASHINGTON	4,090,653	93.7	37.1	3,821,704	95.2	38.2	195,806	90.6	25.1
Benton County, Washington...................	113,729	94.2	33.4	100,832	95.6	35.6	N	N	N
Chelan County, Washington	43,334	90.0	29.2	40,245	91.7	30.2	N	N	N
Clallam County, Washington	54,574	92.5	29.3	52,235	92.7	29.4	N	N	N
Clark County, Washington...................	288,385	94.8	31.6	272,404	95.7	32.3	6,833	93.9	30.2
Cowlitz County, Washington...................	69,798	89.8	15.9	67,319	90.6	16.0	N	N	N
Franklin County, Washington	39,786	80.3	19.8	26,831	94.4	26.0	N	N	N
Grant County, Washington	45,580	82.9	21.2	37,536	91.1	22.8	N	N	N
Grays Harbor County, Washington..............	49,436	91.9	18.8	45,967	93.4	20.0	N	N	N
Island County, Washington	53,741	95.6	36.8	51,745	95.4	37.0	N	N	N
King County, Washington....................	1,063,074	96.4	57.1	1,005,529	97.3	58.2	97,278	86.6	27.4
Kitsap County, Washington	159,463	96.8	36.2	152,662	97.2	36.9	5,249	98.6	23.1
Lewis County, Washington...................	52,085	88.4	20.4	50,075	89.7	20.9	N	N	N
Mason County, Washington	43,465	92.5	21.1	41,803	93.1	21.8	N	N	N
Pierce County, Washington	460,774	93.2	29.3	433,465	93.9	29.7	41,819	95.4	23.0
Skagit County, Washington	79,190	91.8	28.6	74,100	94.5	29.8	N	N	N
Snohomish County, Washington.................	437,984	94.3	31.6	414,541	95.1	31.8	17,926	91.0	20.8
Spokane County, Washington...................	324,551	94.1	31.3	313,782	94.3	31.5	5,927	93.9	12.6
Thurston County, Washington...................	172,205	94.4	34.9	160,954	95.4	35.5	6,464	94.5	32.2
Whatcom County, Washington...................	131,828	95.0	36.7	126,970	95.7	36.7	N	N	N
Yakima County, Washington...................	119,433	78.0	18.5	79,979	92.2	25.1	N	N	N
WEST VIRGINIA	1,204,645	86.9	20.9	1,194,674	86.9	20.9	46,716	92.1	13.7
Berkeley County, West Virginia	73,323	88.2	24.6	71,059	88.4	24.8	6,689	86.5	10.8
Cabell County, West Virginia	57,320	85.7	28.1	56,803	85.8	28.1	3,104	90.4	24.6
Harrison County, West Virginia...................	45,877	90.6	25.7	45,711	90.5	25.8	N	N	N
Kanawha County, West Virginia....................	117,144	90.1	25.5	116,086	90.0	25.4	9,299	91.3	16.5
Monongalia County, West Virginia	60,681	91.0	44.1	59,884	90.8	43.8	2,313	100.0	25.4
Raleigh County, West Virginia	47,391	87.4	19.3	46,677	87.5	18.9	3,989	98.2	11.1
Wood County, West Virginia	58,036	88.7	20.7	57,758	88.7	20.8	N	N	N
WISCONSIN	3,539,280	94.0	32.4	3,408,152	94.8	33.0	219,379	84.7	15.2
Brown County, Wisconsin	157,698	94.2	30.9	152,212	95.3	31.7	3,854	77.4	22.1
Dane County, Wisconsin	316,898	97.0	54.8	303,587	97.9	55.9	16,334	91.0	34.5
Dodge County, Wisconsin	60,794	89.6	18.2	58,517	90.3	18.6	N	N	N
Eau Claire County, Wisconsin...................	62,882	95.7	33.4	61,686	96.2	33.6	N	N	N
Fond du Lac County, Wisconsin...................	68,611	93.1	22.6	67,058	93.8	22.9	N	N	N
Jefferson County, Wisconsin...................	56,495	93.1	27.6	54,920	93.6	27.7	N	N	N
Kenosha County, Wisconsin...................	102,694	92.0	30.0	93,042	92.8	31.7	6,892	87.9	23.5
La Crosse County, Wisconsin...................	71,020	96.1	35.1	70,312	96.3	35.1	N	N	N
Manitowoc County, Wisconsin...................	54,195	94.3	22.2	53,201	94.6	22.2	N	N	N
Marathon County, Wisconsin...................	88,030	92.9	24.6	86,921	93.4	24.8	N	N	N
Milwaukee County, Wisconsin...................	409,132	92.7	39.3	366,060	95.4	42.2	147,046	84.7	13.1
Outagamie County, Wisconsin...................	118,124	95.3	30.5	115,836	95.5	30.6	N	N	N
Ozaukee County, Wisconsin...................	59,230	98.6	48.7	58,060	98.6	48.8	N	N	N
Portage County, Wisconsin...................	43,583	95.7	34.8	43,078	95.8	35.0	N	N	N
Racine County, Wisconsin...................	113,883	92.0	29.0	104,480	94.1	30.4	12,921	74.8	6.2
Rock County, Wisconsin...................	99,667	93.3	24.0	97,802	93.4	24.0	4,691	92.5	13.2
St. Croix County, Wisconsin...................	59,882	95.6	38.0	58,808	96.4	38.4	N	N	N
Sheboygan County, Wisconsin...................	73,143	95.5	28.2	71,155	96.1	28.4	N	N	N
Walworth County, Wisconsin...................	65,671	92.3	31.7	61,885	94.7	33.1	N	N	N
Washington County, Wisconsin	92,752	95.0	31.1	91,442	95.3	31.2	N	N	N
Waukesha County, Wisconsin...................	268,121	96.9	45.5	259,704	97.5	46.2	3,765	92	31
Winnebago County, Wisconsin...................	108,489	95.0	32.5	106,166	95.2	33.0	2,211	68	7
Wood County, Wisconsin...................	50,416	92.1	19.5	49,257	92.2	19.7	N	N	N
WYOMING	361,618	94.8	29.8	340,863	95.7	30.8	3,291	99	47
Laramie County, Wyoming...................	60,989	94.6	31.7	55,827	96.0	33.4	N	N	N
Natrona County, Wyoming	51,454	93.0	21.2	48,479	94.7	22.1	N	N	N

Table C-2. Educational Attainment of the Population, by Selected Counties, 2019—*Continued*

(Number; percent; dollars.)

	Educational attainment by race/ethnicity, 25 years and over								
	American Indian or Alaska Native alone			Asian alone			Native Hawaiian or Other Pacific Islander alone		
State/County	Total	High school graduate or more (percent)	Bachelor's degree or more (percent)	Total	High school graduate or more (percent)	Bachelor's degree or more (percent)	Total	High school graduate or more (percent)	Bachelor's degree or more (percent)
VIRGINIA—(*Continued*)									
Portsmouth city, Virginia..........................	N	N	N	N	N	N	N	N	N
Richmond city, Virginia..............................	N	N	N	N	N	N	N	N	N
Roanoke city, Virginia	N	N	N	N	N	N	N	N	N
Suffolk city, Virginia	N	N	N	N	N	N	N	N	N
Virginia Beach city, Virginia.......................	N	N	N	25,248	85.7	38.2	N	N	N
WASHINGTON	66,153	82.3	15.7	502,312	88.6	56.1	31,931	88.0	10.5
Benton County, Washington........................	N	N	N	3,402	80.0	65.3	N	N	N
Chelan County, Washington	N	N	N	N	N	N	N	N	N
Clallam County, Washington	2,817	84.2	14.6	N	N	N	N	N	N
Clark County, Washington...........................	1,890	90.8	31.3	16,261	90.1	43.4	2,253	76.3	22.2
Cowlitz County, Washington........................	N	N	N	N	N	N	N	N	N
Franklin County, Washington	N	N	N	N	N	N	N	N	N
Grant County, Washington	N	N	N	N	N	N	N	N	N
Grays Harbor County, Washington..............	N	N	N	N	N	N	N	N	N
Island County, Washington	N	N	N	2,966	82.1	22.3	N	N	N
King County, Washington............................	10,074	79.8	27.4	313,217	89.4	63.6	10,939	84.6	10.8
Kitsap County, Washington.........................	2,526	89.0	19.2	10,864	91.8	36.6	N	N	N
Lewis County, Washington..........................	N	N	N	N	N	N	N	N	N
Mason County, Washington	1,258	75.7	20.5	N	N	N	N	N	N
Pierce County, Washington	7,578	82.6	14.0	43,081	87.0	33.9	7,767	87.0	7.7
Skagit County, Washington	2,378	80.7	8.6	1,921	80.1	36.5	N	N	N
Snohomish County, Washington..................	5,911	84.2	18.1	71,849	88.8	50.6	N	N	N
Spokane County, Washington	4,969	83.2	13.8	7,805	82.1	43.5	N	N	N
Thurston County, Washington.....................	N	N	N	11,751	85.0	39.6	N	N	N
Whatcom County, Washington.....................	3,427	91.1	19.1	5,479	90.1	53.5	N	N	N
Yakima County, Washington........................	6,275	70.3	2.3	2,093	86.5	50.7	N	N	N
WEST VIRGINIA	2,261	84.4	20.4	11,020	88.2	66.2	N	N	N
Berkeley County, West Virginia	N	N	N	N	N	N	N	N	N
Cabell County, West Virginia	N	N	N	N	N	N	N	N	N
Harrison County, West Virginia	N	N	N	N	N	N	N	N	N
Kanawha County, West Virginia...................	N	N	N	N	N	N	N	N	N
Monongalia County, West Virginia	N	N	N	N	N	N	N	N	N
Raleigh County, West Virginia	N	N	N	N	N	N	N	N	N
Wood County, West Virginia	N	N	N	N	N	N	N	N	N
WISCONSIN	34,006	90.8	14.5	103,046	86.0	47.4	N	N	N
Brown County, Wisconsin	3,909	90.9	8.6	5,477	88.4	55.0	N	N	N
Dane County, Wisconsin	N	N	N	19,944	91.4	67.5	N	N	N
Dodge County, Wisconsin	N	N	N	N	N	N	N	N	N
Eau Claire County, Wisconsin......................	N	N	N	N	N	N	N	N	N
Fond du Lac County, Wisconsin...................	N	N	N	N	N	N	N	N	N
Jefferson County, Wisconsin.......................	N	N	N	N	N	N	N	N	N
Kenosha County, Wisconsin........................	N	N	N	N	N	N	N	N	N
La Crosse County, Wisconsin......................	N	N	N	3,232	89.0	34.5	N	N	N
Manitowoc County, Wisconsin.....................	N	N	N	N	N	N	N	N	N
Marathon County, Wisconsin.......................	N	N	N	4,364	92.7	36.6	N	N	N
Milwaukee County, Wisconsin.....................	3,423	94.1	20.0	25,802	77.9	37.9	N	N	N
Outagamie County, Wisconsin	1,914	90.1	13.0	3,949	80.9	31.5	N	N	N
Ozaukee County, Wisconsin........................	N	N	N	N	N	N	N	N	N
Portage County, Wisconsin	N	N	N	N	N	N	N	N	N
Racine County, Wisconsin...........................	N	N	N	1,725	81.1	25.8	N	N	N
Rock County, Wisconsin	N	N	N	N	N	N	N	N	N
St. Croix County, Wisconsin........................	N	N	N	N	N	N	N	N	N
Sheboygan County, Wisconsin.....................	N	N	N	4,124	83.7	28.6	N	N	N
Walworth County, Wisconsin.......................	N	N	N	N	N	N	N	N	N
Washington County, Wisconsin	N	N	N	N	N	N	N	N	N
Waukesha County, Wisconsin......................	N	N	N	10,408	96	70	N	N	N
Winnebago County, Wisconsin	N	N	N	3,301	77	29	N	N	N
Wood County, Wisconsin.............................	N	N	N	N	N	N	N	N	N
WYOMING..	8,656	92	11	3,690	98	47	N	N	N
Laramie County, Wyoming..........................	N	N	N	N	N	N	N	N	N
Natrona County, Wyoming	N	N	N	N	N	N	N	N	N

Table C-2. Educational Attainment of the Population, by Selected Counties, 2019—*Continued*

(Number; percent; dollars.)

| | Educational attainment by race/ethnicity, 25 years and over | | | | | | | | |
| | Some other race alone | | | Two or more races | | | Hispanic or Latino (of any race) | | |
State/County	Total	High school graduate or more (percent)	Bachelor's degree or more (percent)	Total	High school graduate or more (percent)	Bachelor's degree or more (percent)	Total	High school graduate or more (percent)	Bachelor's degree or more (percent)
UNITED STATES	9,752,522	64.4	13.3	4,895,894	89.2	33.4	34,949,077	70.5	17.6
ALABAMA	36,540	51.7	10.8	39,473	86.2	32.8	104,045	61.3	16.4
Baldwin County, Alabama	N	N	N	N	N	N	5,145	82.0	24.5
Calhoun County, Alabama	N	N	N	N	N	N	N	N	N
Cullman County, Alabama	N	N	N	N	N	N	N	N	N
DeKalb County, Alabama	N	N	N	N	N	N	4,516	33.4	1.4
Elmore County, Alabama	N	N	N	N	N	N	N	N	N
Etowah County, Alabama	N	N	N	N	N	N	N	N	N
Houston County, Alabama	N	N	N	686	78.9	24.8	1,984	53.9	14.0
Jefferson County, Alabama	4,361	61.7	16.9	4,569	94.3	37.1	12,770	66.8	14.6
Lauderdale County, Alabama	N	N	N	N	N	N	N	N	N
Lee County, Alabama	N	N	N	N	N	N	N	N	N
Limestone County, Alabama	N	N	N	N	N	N	N	N	N
Madison County, Alabama	N	N	N	4,488	89.1	52.3	9,836	71.8	34.3
Marshall County, Alabama	N	N	N	N	N	N	5,595	48.3	6.3
Mobile County, Alabama	N	N	N	4,071	80.9	30.8	7,365	70.1	16.4
Montgomery County, Alabama	N	N	N	N	N	N	3,490	64.4	27.0
Morgan County, Alabama	N	N	N	N	N	N	4,743	46.6	7.5
St. Clair County, Alabama	N	N	N	N	N	N	N	N	N
Shelby County, Alabama	N	N	N	N	N	N	6,009	74.6	32.1
Talladega County, Alabama	N	N	N	N	N	N	N	N	N
Tuscaloosa County, Alabama	N	N	N	N	N	N	3,162	70.7	19.4
Walker County, Alabama	N	N	N	N	N	N	N	N	N
ALASKA	6,790	84.4	17.3	22,413	96.2	29.2	28,365	86.0	19.9
Anchorage Municipality, Alaska	2,880	85.8	22.4	8,985	97.6	38.5	14,289	88.6	20.2
Fairbanks North Star Borough, Alaska	N	N	N	N	N	N	N	N	N
Matanuska-Susitna Borough, Alaska	N	N	N	2,896	93.2	21.5	2,938	88.9	28.1
ARIZONA	223,940	70.1	11.2	122,271	88.4	29.3	1,292,262	71.1	13.9
Apache County, Arizona	N	N	N	N	N	N	N	N	N
Cochise County, Arizona	N	N	N	3,143	90.2	22.2	26,825	76.5	15.2
Coconino County, Arizona	N	N	N	2,399	100.0	27.9	10,087	92.6	30.8
Maricopa County, Arizona	128,517	68.2	12.4	70,520	91.4	32.4	771,974	69.9	14.0
Mohave County, Arizona	4,518	58.5	3.3	3,968	100.0	13.9	21,617	71.4	5.7
Navajo County, Arizona	3,131	70.7	0.3	N	N	N	8,096	69.0	0.9
Pima County, Arizona	50,754	73.4	11.4	25,316	80.7	26.2	225,759	75.1	16.5
Pinal County, Arizona	14,306	78.1	7.4	7,924	81.6	24.5	83,208	72.2	9.7
Yavapai County, Arizona	6,900	72.8	5.0	N	N	N	19,297	75.1	14.1
Yuma County, Arizona	5,919	67.6	8.3	3,154	81.0	16.5	78,069	62.5	9.6
ARKANSAS	38,425	52.1	7.5	33,858	85.7	25.3	117,900	58.7	9.8
Benton County, Arkansas	3,112	62.2	8.9	3,291	98.4	49.3	24,903	66.6	11.6
Craighead County, Arkansas	N	N	N	N	N	N	N	N	N
Faulkner County, Arkansas	N	N	N	N	N	N	N	N	N
Garland County, Arkansas	N	N	N	N	N	N	2,436	67.4	11.3
Jefferson County, Arkansas	N	N	N	N	N	N	N	N	N
Lonoke County, Arkansas	N	N	N	N	N	N	N	N	N
Pulaski County, Arkansas	N	N	N	3,416	89.8	46.0	12,597	68.8	16.8
Saline County, Arkansas	N	N	N	N	N	N	2,893	66.4	10.5
Sebastian County, Arkansas	N	N	N	N	N	N	9,442	55.2	10.4
Washington County, Arkansas	8,566	38.9	5.6	N	N	N	19,950	39.9	4.4
White County, Arkansas	N	N	N	N	N	N	N	N	N
CALIFORNIA	3,279,489	61.9	11.5	935,420	89.1	36.4	9,150,608	66.4	14.4
Alameda County, California	119,770	71.0	18.2	52,787	92.6	53.8	225,685	77.0	24.5
Butte County, California	6,429	60.4	4.4	6,525	91.4	29.9	19,864	67.6	12.8
Contra Costa County, California	90,966	61.3	10.0	34,103	90.2	37.3	175,906	68.7	16.1
El Dorado County, California	2,626	52.6	16.2	2,746	94.4	43.0	15,142	75.9	19.1
Fresno County, California	91,393	58.2	9.4	16,556	80.5	25.4	294,209	63.0	11.3
Humboldt County, California	N	N	N	4,677	94.5	23.1	7,714	80.6	24.7
Imperial County, California	27,384	57.2	17.4	2,615	90.1	28.9	90,978	67.7	16.8
Kern County, California	70,495	56.9	7.7	16,919	87.6	17.8	262,914	62.4	8.6
Kings County, California	9,258	50.3	6.1	N	N	N	46,738	53.2	7.5
Lake County, California	N	N	N	N	N	N	8,056	63.0	4.4
Los Angeles County, California	1,239,114	60.6	11.2	213,429	87.4	39.6	3,021,478	63.0	13.6

Table C-2. Educational Attainment of the Population, by Selected Counties, 2019—*Continued*

(Number; percent; dollars.)

State/County	Median earnings in the past 12 months (2019 inflation-adjusted dollars)					
	Population 25 years and over with earnings					
	Total	Less than high school graduate	High school graduate (includes equivalency)	Some college or associate's degree	Bachelor's degree	Graduate or professional degree
UNITED STATES	41,801	25,876	31,956	38,125	56,344	75,495
ALABAMA	37,217	22,395	30,845	35,107	50,643	60,922
Baldwin County, Alabama.............................	39,627	20,711	30,500	37,139	42,839	57,366
Calhoun County, Alabama	35,441	20,589	30,086	35,269	45,331	57,117
Cullman County, Alabama	32,905	28,829	31,475	31,382	43,046	50,848
DeKalb County, Alabama	31,528	21,683	31,694	35,365	40,858	46,667
Elmore County, Alabama	37,103	30,395	30,994	39,240	44,428	68,117
Etowah County, Alabama.............................	30,599	21,492	26,228	31,654	38,125	78,270
Houston County, Alabama............................	35,563	25,898	30,033	31,862	54,427	54,674
Jefferson County, Alabama	40,400	21,568	30,479	32,427	52,963	65,627
Lauderdale County, Alabama........................	36,531	21,810	34,040	39,218	38,671	55,773
Lee County, Alabama..................................	40,537	10,696	33,650	34,332	42,033	58,852
Limestone County, Alabama.........................	41,336	15,945	29,960	40,111	56,830	61,614
Madison County, Alabama...........................	45,347	20,278	32,492	36,548	55,957	85,150
Marshall County, Alabama...........................	32,180	22,021	30,702	32,363	51,977	52,097
Mobile County, Alabama.............................	36,324	24,479	31,210	34,003	47,645	55,361
Montgomery County, Alabama......................	35,966	21,504	26,676	31,225	45,522	59,526
Morgan County, Alabama............................	36,950	20,384	32,124	37,261	53,394	75,768
St. Clair County, Alabama............................	41,308	22,425	37,499	41,286	58,782	67,643
Shelby County, Alabama.............................	51,047	29,220	36,765	45,041	62,167	64,390
Talladega County, Alabama..........................	34,399	21,111	31,129	33,235	52,733	51,920
Tuscaloosa County, Alabama........................	37,660	24,566	30,852	31,993	51,321	54,425
Walker County, Alabama	38,318	36,181	32,297	36,451	60,434	65,661
ALASKA..	47,809	23,264	36,522	47,878	53,033	71,947
Anchorage Municipality, Alaska....................	50,012	23,602	36,048	50,156	54,890	75,795
Fairbanks North Star Borough, Alaska	55,940	26,449	44,595	55,651	42,178	70,742
Matanuska-Susitna Borough, Alaska.................	49,859	25,387	40,355	48,724	61,264	70,790
ARIZONA	39,956	25,701	31,371	37,016	52,077	69,902
Apache County, Arizona	35,292	22,319	30,949	35,598	37,844	55,496
Cochise County, Arizona	35,373	24,518	24,627	35,071	49,681	80,634
Coconino County, Arizona...........................	38,699	23,734	32,312	35,530	42,903	60,201
Maricopa County, Arizona...........................	41,740	26,707	31,955	39,876	55,942	73,588
Mohave County, Arizona	31,097	22,939	30,906	29,827	47,912	52,108
Navajo County, Arizona	30,478	24,020	23,258	30,724	42,582	60,719
Pima County, Arizona	35,198	22,273	29,299	32,336	47,053	62,202
Pinal County, Arizona	39,148	26,156	36,561	40,162	45,664	52,243
Yavapai County, Arizona.............................	31,322	23,616	27,459	29,168	39,668	60,438
Yuma County, Arizona	30,075	19,517	27,129	32,077	41,924	70,396
ARKANSAS..	35,215	25,695	30,057	31,778	46,964	62,027
Benton County, Arkansas	41,914	30,014	34,203	39,074	56,930	80,000
Craighead County, Arkansas	36,222	24,225	30,203	33,132	50,157	63,538
Faulkner County, Arkansas..........................	40,734	24,827	34,563	35,297	51,552	56,370
Garland County, Arkansas...........................	27,470	23,111	20,936	25,470	47,057	60,269
Jefferson County, Arkansas.........................	30,454	19,543	25,922	26,006	32,022	48,250
Lonoke County, Arkansas............................	40,376	38,386	32,752	40,685	50,130	64,554
Pulaski County, Arkansas............................	37,106	22,065	30,229	31,720	48,167	61,033
Saline County, Arkansas.............................	44,047	29,409	35,858	39,036	54,410	69,589
Sebastian County, Arkansas........................	31,041	26,388	24,613	30,233	46,168	70,585
Washington County, Arkansas	35,900	24,781	31,052	34,434	46,521	64,567
White County, Arkansas	32,574	19,930	31,099	27,195	45,870	54,389
CALIFORNIA	45,095	25,949	33,494	41,090	65,078	92,334
Alameda County, California	61,748	30,469	42,417	50,583	78,633	101,945
Butte County, California..............................	38,191	29,059	31,269	32,742	48,789	81,437
Contra Costa County, California	57,962	29,960	41,682	50,188	78,426	101,368
El Dorado County, California	50,688	26,253	39,151	48,282	66,633	93,268
Fresno County, California	36,279	23,458	31,243	36,649	54,504	80,299
Humboldt County, California........................	36,069	36,108	26,250	35,268	41,719	56,356
Imperial County, California..........................	32,476	17,322	36,205	32,315	44,681	65,855
Kern County, California	35,265	22,748	27,865	38,141	61,372	90,536
Kings County, California	36,783	22,616	37,399	39,022	60,251	92,095
Lake County, California	31,630	26,006	30,526	31,815	59,462	31,233
Los Angeles County, California......................	40,677	25,043	31,705	38,782	60,216	81,800

Table C-2. Educational Attainment of the Population, by Selected Counties, 2019—*Continued*

(Number; percent; dollars.)

	Educational attainment by race/ethnicity, 25 years and over								
	Some other race alone			Two or more races			Hispanic or Latino (of any race)		
State/County	Total	High school graduate or more (percent)	Bachelor's degree or more (percent)	Total	High school graduate or more (percent)	Bachelor's degree or more (percent)	Total	High school graduate or more (percent)	Bachelor's degree or more (percent)
CALIFORNIA—(*Continued*)									
Madera County, California	19,634	44.4	5.5	2,496	80.1	8.5	50,007	56.1	8.2
Marin County, California	10,277	45.2	16.5	5,445	98.4	52.2	24,146	60.1	24.9
Mendocino County, California	N	N	N	N	N	N	12,353	58.7	11.3
Merced County, California	49,451	47.0	4.1	3,882	77.0	15.2	90,187	54.0	6.4
Monterey County, California	96,937	44.5	5.3	8,358	91.3	34.9	142,746	51.2	8.9
Napa County, California	9,470	52.9	9.6	3,746	90.0	39.3	27,738	62.3	12.9
Nevada County, California	N	N	N	N	N	N	5,143	82.3	19.3
Orange County, California	245,863	58.1	11.9	62,645	90.3	45.7	637,379	66.3	16.4
Placer County, California	4,044	79.8	22.1	8,932	92.1	27.7	33,620	81.9	25.3
Riverside County, California	296,277	64.6	9.2	44,478	89.6	26.2	707,430	69.7	11.9
Sacramento County, California	81,293	69.4	13.7	56,301	92.1	29.2	208,400	76.2	18.1
San Bernardino County, California	205,589	65.2	9.8	51,095	87.0	25.6	679,754	69.0	11.8
San Diego County, California	116,734	72.5	20.2	84,172	92.9	40.7	674,835	72.5	19.4
San Francisco County, California	49,602	77.5	23.4	26,308	95.0	67.6	94,366	80.4	32.6
San Joaquin County, California	34,109	63.7	9.0	39,640	75.2	13.0	174,695	63.4	8.7
San Luis Obispo County, California	6,895	68.5	13.5	3,986	98.8	21.1	35,999	73.0	19.9
San Mateo County, California	50,927	67.4	17.8	17,465	91.4	51.3	114,643	72.6	24.6
Santa Barbara County, California	27,176	59.4	13.0	7,324	92.0	43.6	110,034	58.2	11.6
Santa Clara County, California	100,478	65.1	14.7	45,461	94.5	47.6	285,423	71.1	20.0
Santa Cruz County, California	16,331	52.4	16.3	6,153	97.0	49.3	50,521	61.7	20.0
Shasta County, California	2,687	93.0	18.9	3,905	91.2	14.2	10,396	88.2	19.7
Solano County, California	20,805	68.8	16.2	15,446	94.2	29.4	69,969	72.8	16.3
Sonoma County, California	39,937	59.7	7.4	13,413	87.5	28.5	77,534	68.1	15.4
Stanislaus County, California	18,854	66.2	9.5	12,291	85.4	19.8	142,839	67.4	9.8
Sutter County, California	2,861	69.7	12.4	3,098	93.8	10.7	16,616	60.4	7.5
Tehama County, California	N	N	N	N	N	N	9,834	62.2	5.3
Tulare County, California	58,909	63.7	3.9	10,460	74.4	14.6	161,362	63.2	6.0
Ventura County, California	27,326	67.5	11.0	16,976	90.0	35.0	214,781	69.0	14.8
Yolo County, California	5,602	77.0	15.3	4,424	90.1	58.9	38,184	74.2	16.9
Yuba County, California	N	N	N	3,362	83.7	25.6	12,161	59.1	13.1
COLORADO	128,870	73.4	16.0	104,674	91.5	38.7	712,267	75.2	18.5
Adams County, Colorado	19,143	72.7	12.2	13,925	75.2	22.9	115,568	68.1	10.3
Arapahoe County, Colorado	21,693	73.4	14.9	12,814	91.8	38.4	70,699	75.1	18.4
Boulder County, Colorado	N	N	N	4,714	85.9	56.5	24,032	68.8	28.0
Broomfield County, Colorado	N	N	N	N	N	N	5,451	78.5	30.2
Denver County, Colorado	23,538	78.4	21.8	17,201	94.2	54.0	126,448	74.2	22.5
Douglas County, Colorado	4,068	94.2	27.7	N	N	N	19,074	95.1	43.5
El Paso County, Colorado	17,493	74.9	15.2	16,963	95.6	31.5	68,183	84.3	20.2
Jefferson County, Colorado	6,564	89.5	20.7	9,442	96.0	50.8	55,422	80.9	24.1
Larimer County, Colorado	3,066	83.8	14.6	4,340	94.0	57.9	22,435	90.6	32.2
Mesa County, Colorado	N	N	N	N	N	N	11,989	80.7	9.9
Pueblo County, Colorado	7,121	76.6	10.0	3,756	92.8	26.3	44,478	83.6	14.5
Weld County, Colorado	9,543	56.0	14.8	4,824	84.6	17.2	52,790	64.4	12.3
CONNECTICUT	121,383	69.2	14.3	58,085	83.7	31.0	347,589	73.9	17.8
Fairfield County, Connecticut	38,882	64.1	14.4	14,233	89.7	43.0	116,112	72.1	20.2
Hartford County, Connecticut	39,730	68.7	13.3	16,560	76.9	23.9	96,294	73.2	15.7
Litchfield County, Connecticut	N	N	N	N	N	N	7,889	77.5	32.5
Middlesex County, Connecticut	N	N	N	N	N	N	5,843	84.6	29.2
New Haven County, Connecticut	30,889	71.0	14.2	15,232	85.2	30.0	92,479	73.7	15.3
New London County, Connecticut	5,504	85.8	15.2	5,603	74.6	15.3	16,124	80.8	15.4
Tolland County, Connecticut	N	N	N	N	N	N	5,618	80.5	31.5
Windham County, Connecticut	N	N	N	N	N	N	7,230	81.0	9.1
DELAWARE	12,058	59.4	13.5	9,900	90.7	34.1	49,372	62.3	13.9
Kent County, Delaware	N	N	N	N	N	N	7,342	80.6	12.2
New Castle County, Delaware	7,786	54.8	14.2	5,987	86.6	39.7	31,851	61.2	14.8
Sussex County, Delaware	3,149	59.3	10.4	1,792	93.5	38.8	10,179	52.3	12.5
DISTRICT OF COLUMBIA	17,430	69.3	33.9	13,127	94.3	74.9	50,141	80.8	52.0
District of Columbia, District of Columbia	17,430	69.3	33.9	13,127	94.3	74.9	50,141	80.8	52.0
FLORIDA	468,004	75.0	19.7	283,975	87.2	31.0	3,773,205	79.6	25.7
Alachua County, Florida	N	N	N	3,807	85.9	43.9	15,081	88.6	54.7
Bay County, Florida	N	N	N	N	N	N	6,898	88.6	26.8
Brevard County, Florida	7,154	91.5	17.4	10,895	96.6	26.1	41,962	90.4	28.7

Table C-2. Educational Attainment of the Population, by Selected Counties, 2019—*Continued*

(Number; percent; dollars.)

State/County	Median earnings in the past 12 months (2019 inflation-adjusted dollars)					
	Population 25 years and over with earnings					
	Total	Less than high school graduate	High school graduate (includes equivalency)	Some college or associate's degree	Bachelor's degree	Graduate or professional degree
CALIFORNIA—(*Continued*)						
Madera County, California	29,746	22,631	32,069	26,098	48,202	56,300
Marin County, California	63,972	26,135	41,677	49,122	76,824	126,720
Mendocino County, California	35,887	18,150	43,032	33,785	47,812	42,614
Merced County, California	33,675	29,593	31,659	37,726	47,344	70,650
Monterey County, California	35,726	24,061	31,494	40,698	59,846	85,392
Napa County, California	50,622	27,402	41,000	43,695	76,863	90,405
Nevada County, California	39,216	19,292	35,709	35,432	60,089	54,911
Orange County, California	49,152	26,393	32,231	43,740	66,608	91,837
Placer County, California	59,365	26,581	37,255	48,805	80,951	97,961
Riverside County, California	40,364	26,443	33,903	41,081	52,262	78,518
Sacramento County, California	43,744	27,743	33,839	40,646	60,744	85,029
San Bernardino County, California	39,246	26,664	32,295	38,974	54,230	75,805
San Diego County, California	46,395	26,200	31,552	40,417	62,806	89,813
San Francisco County, California	74,175	25,309	34,872	47,412	91,809	121,346
San Joaquin County, California	40,462	29,968	35,753	41,455	57,071	80,754
San Luis Obispo County, California	41,806	29,334	35,707	39,270	55,404	75,351
San Mateo County, California	67,707	30,977	38,774	51,234	82,635	131,461
Santa Barbara County, California	40,820	25,481	31,732	41,682	61,180	86,061
Santa Clara County, California	69,611	32,006	39,851	49,640	89,859	131,480
Santa Cruz County, California	45,945	26,373	36,192	40,535	65,443	84,758
Shasta County, California	38,650	35,600	31,209	33,471	60,729	66,044
Solano County, California	49,777	31,055	41,739	49,042	64,080	72,903
Sonoma County, California	46,272	29,779	36,612	46,351	61,631	70,952
Stanislaus County, California	40,814	30,057	34,432	42,469	62,802	86,962
Sutter County, California	35,512	17,955	33,331	40,289	45,023	67,196
Tehama County, California	35,827	26,661	30,670	34,574	58,915	56,950
Tulare County, California	32,217	22,063	31,625	33,752	60,196	83,816
Ventura County, California	45,349	25,970	32,470	44,676	62,685	92,472
Yolo County, California	47,377	27,424	39,923	46,925	50,243	85,477
Yuba County, California	40,281	25,371	35,701	43,963	60,433	66,880
COLORADO	46,887	30,968	35,537	40,819	58,229	71,616
Adams County, Colorado	41,871	32,479	34,880	41,844	58,852	66,229
Arapahoe County, Colorado	47,988	31,687	36,780	43,249	60,409	69,083
Boulder County, Colorado	51,446	31,213	35,446	37,760	57,394	75,887
Broomfield County, Colorado	65,381	36,832	46,503	46,496	75,007	83,802
Denver County, Colorado	51,532	31,345	31,889	43,521	61,887	75,214
Douglas County, Colorado	66,061	46,747	38,879	49,030	76,366	86,486
El Paso County, Colorado	42,343	27,652	35,662	36,453	51,965	76,070
Jefferson County, Colorado	52,590	33,837	38,867	43,417	66,412	75,597
Larimer County, Colorado	46,348	16,864	32,392	41,331	51,327	65,254
Mesa County, Colorado	35,020	21,760	32,514	31,478	46,402	46,997
Pueblo County, Colorado	35,972	17,500	28,516	34,601	49,229	55,266
Weld County, Colorado	44,686	36,576	39,935	42,063	54,687	66,343
CONNECTICUT	50,788	24,426	37,017	42,884	64,143	85,175
Fairfield County, Connecticut	55,628	24,146	35,274	42,688	71,493	100,982
Hartford County, Connecticut	51,156	23,444	35,532	45,721	65,129	82,399
Litchfield County, Connecticut	48,268	26,304	45,228	41,255	57,496	66,918
Middlesex County, Connecticut	52,355	11,389	39,699	43,584	66,967	77,364
New Haven County, Connecticut	47,066	25,127	36,292	42,451	60,008	77,755
New London County, Connecticut	45,611	31,856	38,275	38,994	51,632	81,359
Tolland County, Connecticut	60,956	28,537	47,074	51,303	67,253	90,122
Windham County, Connecticut	41,797	27,879	37,253	42,942	51,403	64,894
DELAWARE	43,164	31,024	33,671	38,048	56,603	70,579
Kent County, Delaware	37,174	28,333	32,918	35,140	44,175	66,535
New Castle County, Delaware	48,948	30,547	36,245	41,865	61,801	74,775
Sussex County, Delaware	37,978	32,355	30,006	35,437	53,313	61,640
DISTRICT OF COLUMBIA	71,361	30,883	31,768	44,248	75,222	101,956
District of Columbia, District of Columbia	71,361	30,883	31,768	44,248	75,222	101,956
FLORIDA	36,021	23,292	30,064	34,752	47,810	62,425
Alachua County, Florida	40,906	14,830	31,937	35,874	46,871	61,175
Bay County, Florida	35,540	24,127	27,745	36,666	41,027	81,305
Brevard County, Florida	36,798	20,816	28,019	34,815	50,218	70,727

Table C-2. Educational Attainment of the Population, by Selected Counties, 2019—*Continued*

(Number; percent; dollars.)

| | Educational attainment by race/ethnicity, 25 years and over | | | | | | | | |
| | Some other race alone | | | Two or more races | | | Hispanic or Latino (of any race) | | |
State/County	Total	High school graduate or more (percent)	Bachelor's degree or more (percent)	Total	High school graduate or more (percent)	Bachelor's degree or more (percent)	Total	High school graduate or more (percent)	Bachelor's degree or more (percent)
FLORIDA—*(Continued)*									
Broward County, Florida	43,356	80.0	19.0	34,532	82.0	30.1	417,459	86.0	31.3
Charlotte County, Florida	N	N	N	N	N	N	10,177	83.6	15.0
Citrus County, Florida	N	N	N	N	N	N	6,013	84.2	15.2
Clay County, Florida	N	N	N	N	N	N	13,526	95.6	26.4
Collier County, Florida	2,775	62.5	1.0	N	N	N	67,575	75.0	17.7
Columbia County, Florida	N	N	N	N	N	N	2,248	76.5	45.9
Duval County, Florida	17,345	83.8	28.2	14,782	84.3	25.0	61,043	82.4	25.8
Escambia County, Florida	N	N	N	7,943	96.6	24.1	11,164	76.3	22.9
Flagler County, Florida	N	N	N	N	N	N	7,796	83.0	11.7
Hernando County, Florida	N	N	N	N	N	N	18,391	83.8	16.6
Highlands County, Florida	N	N	N	N	N	N	13,650	73.9	14.1
Hillsborough County, Florida	46,513	67.9	18.0	27,060	90.3	35.1	276,482	80.4	24.7
Indian River County, Florida	N	N	N	N	N	N	13,185	75.2	14.3
Lake County, Florida	7,141	77.5	14.6	N	N	N	38,665	82.9	20.4
Lee County, Florida	19,272	57.3	13.7	5,521	87.5	39.1	106,564	69.7	14.8
Leon County, Florida	N	N	N	N	N	N	9,237	87.4	30.6
Manatee County, Florida	N	N	N	2,874	94.4	27.5	38,290	67.7	11.0
Marion County, Florida	N	N	N	3,376	79.1	28.1	32,853	81.5	22.1
Martin County, Florida	N	N	N	N	N	N	12,469	76.9	18.2
Miami-Dade County, Florida	70,114	73.0	22.6	30,874	85.9	29.5	1,377,363	77.4	28.7
Monroe County, Florida	N	N	N	N	N	N	12,778	76.8	16.6
Nassau County, Florida	N	N	N	N	N	N	2,445	70.3	5.8
Okaloosa County, Florida	4,880	66.9	11.9	5,840	95.2	28.3	11,902	80.1	22.1
Orange County, Florida	50,705	75.3	21.2	24,039	88.6	43.5	291,498	82.7	25.4
Osceola County, Florida	24,059	72.9	14.5	6,821	85.6	22.8	131,843	82.2	21.5
Palm Beach County, Florida	29,699	64.5	20.1	17,755	88.7	34.8	225,343	75.0	25.9
Pasco County, Florida	6,559	75.2	14.3	6,642	89.3	41.2	57,066	84.7	20.2
Pinellas County, Florida	9,658	89.3	36.5	14,133	89.0	34.2	64,065	85.6	29.6
Polk County, Florida	23,197	75.4	15.6	6,523	79.6	34.0	103,924	78.2	16.1
Putnam County, Florida	N	N	N	N	N	N	3,950	35.8	0.7
St. Johns County, Florida	N	N	N	N	N	N	12,591	92.9	42.5
St. Lucie County, Florida	N	N	N	N	N	N	41,716	80.2	21.4
Santa Rosa County, Florida	N	N	N	2,875	85.5	33.5	6,894	90.6	18.0
Sarasota County, Florida	2,831	81.2	20.8	4,776	91.9	31.9	25,531	86.4	24.9
Seminole County, Florida	23,785	87.3	32.0	5,864	91.0	36.4	69,291	88.0	27.9
Sumter County, Florida	N	N	N	N	N	N	5,260	79.4	26.0
Volusia County, Florida	21,473	80.9	12.6	5,985	85.7	24.9	52,105	82.3	15.9
Walton County, Florida	N	N	N	N	N	N	2,458	86.0	26.8
GEORGIA	174,770	57.6	14.1	108,327	87.2	36.5	546,665	64.3	19.2
Barrow County, Georgia	N	N	N	N	N	N	5,915	72.6	21.1
Bartow County, Georgia	N	N	N	N	N	N	N	N	N
Bibb County, Georgia	N	N	N	N	N	N	2,718	60.9	10.1
Bulloch County, Georgia	N	N	N	N	N	N	N	N	N
Carroll County, Georgia	N	N	N	N	N	N	N	N	N
Catoosa County, Georgia	N	N	N	N	N	N	N	N	N
Chatham County, Georgia	N	N	N	2,049	79.2	48.5	10,502	85.6	22.8
Cherokee County, Georgia	N	N	N	N	N	N	15,694	63.5	18.0
Clarke County, Georgia	N	N	N	N	N	N	6,453	93.9	33.6
Clayton County, Georgia	6,120	57.0	6.1	N	N	N	18,154	64.1	9.9
Cobb County, Georgia	27,955	51.5	12.8	10,445	95.0	50.6	53,492	61.3	20.1
Columbia County, Georgia	N	N	N	N	N	N	6,356	72.9	34.6
Coweta County, Georgia	N	N	N	N	N	N	6,505	69.0	11.2
DeKalb County, Georgia	7,786	62.0	13.0	8,770	83.7	54.8	32,973	57.5	22.9
Dougherty County, Georgia	N	N	N	N	N	N	N	N	N
Douglas County, Georgia	N	N	N	N	N	N	7,513	65.4	13.5
Fayette County, Georgia	N	N	N	N	N	N	5,360	92.9	23.9
Floyd County, Georgia	N	N	N	N	N	N	5,608	56.5	5.0
Forsyth County, Georgia	5,013	45.8	21.1	N	N	N	12,854	60.1	29.0
Fulton County, Georgia	11,131	67.8	30.8	11,261	94.4	62.3	43,744	83.8	47.7
Glynn County, Georgia	N	N	N	N	N	N	N	N	N
Gwinnett County, Georgia	48,275	55.6	11.6	14,516	85.6	36.7	108,404	63.6	17.6
Hall County, Georgia	N	N	N	N	N	N	30,123	48.8	12.0
Henry County, Georgia	N	N	N	N	N	N	8,705	57.4	20.1
Houston County, Georgia	N	N	N	N	N	N	4,811	78.8	15.5
Jackson County, Georgia	N	N	N	N	N	N	N	N	N
Lowndes County, Georgia	N	N	N	N	N	N	2,944	69.8	12.7

Table C-2. Educational Attainment of the Population, by Selected Counties, 2019—*Continued*

(Number; percent; dollars.)

State/County	Median earnings in the past 12 months (2019 inflation-adjusted dollars)					
	Population 25 years and over with earnings					
	Total	Less than high school graduate	High school graduate (includes equivalency)	Some college or associate's degree	Bachelor's degree	Graduate or professional degree
FLORIDA—*(Continued)*						
Broward County, Florida..............................	37,078	21,938	31,397	36,083	48,139	71,146
Charlotte County, Florida.............................	31,326	24,588	25,344	31,015	45,580	61,774
Citrus County, Florida.................................	31,077	25,804	28,173	29,542	45,623	48,217
Clay County, Florida	39,148	26,197	32,256	36,751	42,992	69,835
Collier County, Florida................................	36,057	22,483	31,255	37,184	51,407	64,551
Columbia County, Florida............................	31,947	30,142	25,861	31,025	52,783	57,272
Duval County, Florida	38,125	22,451	31,273	34,999	54,386	70,053
Escambia County, Florida	35,049	20,071	28,890	35,293	46,548	50,774
Flagler County, Florida................................	36,162	13,981	29,272	36,377	54,424	50,661
Hernando County, Florida............................	32,322	19,310	30,338	31,257	41,646	62,021
Highlands County, Florida	30,464	20,426	26,854	30,852	42,086	51,280
Hillsborough County, Florida........................	39,378	24,773	30,330	36,893	51,289	72,048
Indian River County, Florida........................	31,562	22,753	28,390	31,318	44,552	71,814
Lake County, Florida..................................	32,661	21,947	27,418	32,485	46,957	51,373
Lee County, Florida	35,354	26,831	31,312	33,389	45,790	55,494
Leon County, Florida..................................	39,146	24,397	25,763	31,612	47,353	55,701
Manatee County, Florida.............................	35,568	25,382	26,936	35,287	53,152	67,299
Marion County, Florida...............................	32,368	28,914	30,543	30,229	41,447	61,995
Martin County, Florida................................	38,791	22,027	25,255	35,362	62,734	63,158
Miami-Dade County, Florida.........................	32,598	22,589	27,662	32,830	45,195	61,161
Monroe County, Florida	37,400	26,327	31,067	34,417	51,096	60,898
Nassau County, Florida	38,519	30,934	36,856	39,146	41,475	57,581
Okaloosa County, Florida............................	36,172	17,057	27,230	38,395	40,259	76,406
Orange County, Florida...............................	35,941	22,048	27,120	32,546	46,477	61,141
Osceola County, Florida..............................	31,562	25,421	25,943	32,056	39,964	51,533
Palm Beach County, Florida	37,485	23,792	27,874	35,757	50,076	66,795
Pasco County, Florida	39,682	26,141	31,555	38,217	52,652	62,913
Pinellas County, Florida..............................	39,006	22,931	30,406	36,241	49,771	63,089
Polk County, Florida	31,855	22,106	30,123	31,978	42,719	51,613
Putnam County, Florida..............................	31,115	25,933	27,096	32,186	41,342	46,624
St. Johns County, Florida............................	48,349	23,887	34,957	40,514	60,796	70,481
St. Lucie County, Florida	33,767	24,446	30,913	35,200	44,306	47,172
Santa Rosa County, Florida	37,758	23,488	26,969	38,644	42,104	67,411
Sarasota County, Florida	36,080	20,865	32,799	32,752	43,502	61,225
Seminole County, Florida	41,402	24,400	31,039	33,968	52,905	66,751
Sumter County, Florida	23,864	18,855	22,112	35,491	24,263	14,548
Volusia County, Florida...............................	32,403	30,128	30,696	31,869	41,946	52,241
Walton County, Florida...............................	35,617	29,728	26,415	35,489	45,193	67,156
GEORGIA	40,312	25,479	31,184	35,846	53,662	70,027
Barrow County, Georgia..............................	41,298	29,199	36,346	41,421	47,404	61,662
Bartow County, Georgia..............................	40,536	35,195	36,359	40,075	47,362	65,642
Bibb County, Georgia	32,809	20,826	30,675	32,161	42,143	58,533
Bulloch County, Georgia.............................	34,291	30,115	36,038	23,127	35,480	56,000
Carroll County, Georgia..............................	37,840	27,248	29,039	37,375	43,966	58,563
Catoosa County, Georgia............................	39,630	32,232	31,157	37,072	48,842	60,635
Chatham County, Georgia............................	35,287	23,101	31,309	29,132	46,491	61,680
Cherokee County, Georgia...........................	50,008	25,279	35,944	45,141	62,055	76,244
Clarke County, Georgia...............................	31,118	32,891	25,044	23,169	32,296	47,468
Clayton County, Georgia.............................	33,223	27,870	30,046	37,325	36,908	44,015
Cobb County, Georgia	47,929	26,292	32,996	40,403	60,822	75,646
Columbia County, Georgia...........................	50,925	27,068	36,010	44,368	61,418	71,208
Coweta County, Georgia.............................	45,924	34,426	41,439	43,350	51,609	65,531
DeKalb County, Georgia..............................	41,673	21,911	28,213	34,988	55,615	79,814
Dougherty County, Georgia	32,122	22,081	27,141	31,178	40,897	47,469
Douglas County, Georgia............................	40,948	30,251	32,992	38,474	47,408	59,662
Fayette County, Georgia.............................	51,973	25,047	41,105	42,038	73,500	65,502
Floyd County, Georgia................................	31,397	17,727	27,194	30,761	41,444	62,075
Forsyth County, Georgia.............................	61,098	25,941	41,091	42,274	77,336	87,233
Fulton County, Georgia...............................	54,376	21,710	29,628	36,148	66,932	86,548
Glynn County, Georgia	36,915	25,702	31,668	37,059	51,316	63,056
Gwinnett County, Georgia	41,209	27,193	31,552	37,311	52,162	66,561
Hall County, Georgia..................................	36,258	23,485	34,458	40,357	55,859	62,076
Henry County, Georgia...............................	43,036	31,481	33,909	49,677	49,973	66,094
Houston County, Georgia............................	41,088	32,162	36,477	38,287	60,405	71,949
Jackson County, Georgia............................	41,442	19,152	33,602	51,338	48,472	67,715
Lowndes County, Georgia...........................	31,451	21,427	30,426	29,840	42,542	62,303

Table C-2. Educational Attainment of the Population, by Selected Counties, 2019—*Continued*

(Number; percent; dollars.)

State/County	Educational attainment by race/ethnicity, 25 years and over								
	Some other race alone			Two or more races			Hispanic or Latino (of any race)		
	Total	High school graduate or more (percent)	Bachelor's degree or more (percent)	Total	High school graduate or more (percent)	Bachelor's degree or more (percent)	Total	High school graduate or more (percent)	Bachelor's degree or more (percent)
GEORGIA—*(Continued)*									
Muscogee County, Georgia	N	N	N	N	N	N	7,752	82.5	23.4
Newton County, Georgia	N	N	N	N	N	N	N	N	N
Paulding County, Georgia	N	N	N	N	N	N	6,760	61.8	15.0
Richmond County, Georgia	N	N	N	N	N	N	5,359	90.0	28.0
Rockdale County, Georgia	N	N	N	N	N	N	4,984	75.1	10.0
Spalding County, Georgia	N	N	N	N	N	N	N	N	N
Troup County, Georgia	N	N	N	N	N	N	N	N	N
Walker County, Georgia	N	N	N	N	N	N	N	N	N
Walton County, Georgia	N	N	N	N	N	N	2,718	91.9	20.0
Whitfield County, Georgia	N	N	N	N	N	N	19,153	39.9	3.7
HAWAII	15,453	86.8	24.9	166,296	95.3	26.9	77,881	91.2	23.0
Hawaii County, Hawaii	N	N	N	30,697	94.0	17.2	12,754	78.3	13.2
Honolulu County, Hawaii	10,356	96.0	30.4	108,435	95.7	31.4	49,676	95.6	28.4
Kauai County, Hawaii	N	N	N	9,246	95.7	18.9	4,397	90.8	16.8
Maui County, Hawaii	N	N	N	17,918	94.2	20.7	11,049	86.4	12.6
IDAHO	37,977	60.3	7.5	25,837	90.3	38.9	115,826	68.8	12.7
Ada County, Idaho	4,799	79.1	21.3	8,295	97.4	61.3	22,659	81.5	22.1
Bannock County, Idaho	N	N	N	N	N	N	4,063	85.0	21.1
Bonneville County, Idaho	N	N	N	N	N	N	7,828	74.2	16.9
Canyon County, Idaho	17,007	54.4	5.8	5,005	74.4	13.7	29,144	61.8	8.1
Kootenai County, Idaho	N	N	N	N	N	N	4,136	91.4	9.0
Twin Falls County, Idaho	N	N	N	N	N	N	7,600	55.6	8.3
ILLINOIS	422,033	68.1	13.4	144,592	90.6	39.0	1,256,316	71.3	16.8
Adams County, Illinois	N	N	N	N	N	N	N	N	N
Champaign County, Illinois	N	N	N	N	N	N	5,538	73.4	40.9
Cook County, Illinois	282,874	68.8	14.8	69,718	91.7	45.1	778,104	72.3	17.7
DeKalb County, Illinois	N	N	N	N	N	N	5,645	77.0	24.7
DuPage County, Illinois	17,762	66.6	7.2	12,705	95.7	41.0	74,577	76.6	19.4
Kane County, Illinois	34,561	62.0	7.8	7,945	80.8	33.0	93,030	60.9	13.0
Kankakee County, Illinois	N	N	N	N	N	N	5,670	72.9	11.1
Kendall County, Illinois	N	N	N	N	N	N	14,652	80.8	21.9
Lake County, Illinois	28,447	64.4	4.2	8,530	92.4	43.4	82,402	65.2	10.5
LaSalle County, Illinois	1,819	51.6	0.1	N	N	N	5,915	64.6	5.4
McHenry County, Illinois	2,439	64.4	19.8	N	N	N	22,641	75.4	17.2
McLean County, Illinois	N	N	N	N	N	N	3,902	85.7	31.2
Macon County, Illinois	N	N	N	N	N	N	1,106	83.5	24.7
Madison County, Illinois	N	N	N	N	N	N	4,737	81.6	25.1
Peoria County, Illinois	N	N	N	N	N	N	4,270	72.8	20.8
Rock Island County, Illinois	3,127	67.7	5.6	2,109	85.2	27.4	9,984	71.6	12.0
St. Clair County, Illinois	N	N	N	2,593	98.7	32.6	6,238	80.0	27.9
Sangamon County, Illinois	N	N	N	N	N	N	2,700	84.0	23.8
Tazewell County, Illinois	N	N	N	N	N	N	N	N	N
Vermilion County, Illinois	N	N	N	N	N	N	1,765	52.8	12.1
Will County, Illinois	22,598	68.3	12.3	8,395	83.3	27.9	67,858	72.2	14.1
Williamson County, Illinois	N	N	N	N	N	N	N	N	N
Winnebago County, Illinois	2,688	69.4	29.5	2,774	87.2	11.8	19,124	61.9	10.1
INDIANA	85,178	61.8	9.3	61,423	88.4	26.7	247,337	69.9	15.6
Allen County, Indiana	5,479	61.5	9.6	4,178	89.0	30.9	14,515	65.2	12.4
Bartholomew County, Indiana	N	N	N	N	N	N	2,964	72.4	37.4
Boone County, Indiana	N	N	N	N	N	N	N	N	N
Clark County, Indiana	N	N	N	N	N	N	3,463	57.8	33.8
Delaware County, Indiana	N	N	N	N	N	N	N	N	N
Elkhart County, Indiana	7,398	60.7	4.6	N	N	N	15,685	64.0	7.9
Floyd County, Indiana	N	N	N	N	N	N	N	N	N
Grant County, Indiana	N	N	N	N	N	N	N	N	N
Hamilton County, Indiana	N	N	N	N	N	N	8,038	83.1	38.3
Hancock County, Indiana	N	N	N	N	N	N	N	N	N
Hendricks County, Indiana	N	N	N	N	N	N	N	N	N
Howard County, Indiana	N	N	N	N	N	N	N	N	N
Johnson County, Indiana	N	N	N	N	N	N	N	N	N
Kosciusko County, Indiana	N	N	N	N	N	N	3,373	55.2	6.4
Lake County, Indiana	24,331	71.1	6.3	5,112	86.2	36.5	55,383	78.1	11.6
LaPorte County, Indiana	N	N	N	N	N	N	4,040	77.1	6.2

Table C-2. Educational Attainment of the Population, by Selected Counties, 2019—*Continued*

(Number; percent; dollars.)

State/County	Median earnings in the past 12 months (2019 inflation-adjusted dollars)					
	Population 25 years and over with earnings					
	Total	Less than high school graduate	High school graduate (includes equivalency)	Some college or associate's degree	Bachelor's degree	Graduate or professional degree
GEORGIA—(*Continued*)						
Muscogee County, Georgia	35,133	21,035	27,175	34,187	47,511	57,459
Newton County, Georgia	31,860	19,966	25,704	29,949	44,606	57,106
Paulding County, Georgia	43,848	30,886	41,132	42,224	50,023	67,004
Richmond County, Georgia	30,819	21,950	27,266	27,495	44,703	63,744
Rockdale County, Georgia	40,117	18,341	38,460	40,026	46,202	51,306
Spalding County, Georgia	33,390	24,790	30,894	36,254	37,470	46,717
Troup County, Georgia	35,027	31,653	23,983	32,450	51,145	47,180
Walker County, Georgia	31,032	23,802	31,296	30,790	43,581	48,727
Walton County, Georgia	39,449	26,992	32,579	38,411	51,527	72,974
Whitfield County, Georgia	31,970	30,134	31,675	31,057	49,291	64,217
HAWAII	44,557	31,620	35,573	41,842	52,183	72,035
Hawaii County, Hawaii	36,621	33,041	31,542	34,762	44,980	65,607
Honolulu County, Hawaii	47,223	31,092	35,300	44,436	55,489	75,908
Kauai County, Hawaii	41,827	32,208	40,531	41,762	44,572	55,788
Maui County, Hawaii	41,209	31,219	38,466	41,077	52,090	66,884
IDAHO	36,445	27,667	31,395	33,984	46,364	60,816
Ada County, Idaho	41,047	23,792	32,311	36,120	51,257	65,374
Bannock County, Idaho	32,479	26,824	27,169	31,199	38,432	65,048
Bonneville County, Idaho	36,013	26,631	27,725	31,807	48,123	90,672
Canyon County, Idaho	35,144	26,575	31,636	34,686	43,236	49,239
Kootenai County, Idaho	35,362	25,398	31,351	32,075	49,063	52,385
Twin Falls County, Idaho	40,393	38,884	37,341	31,002	45,664	52,135
ILLINOIS	45,015	27,186	32,304	39,400	60,357	76,363
Adams County, Illinois	36,494	30,016	32,303	31,998	42,437	61,658
Champaign County, Illinois	41,140	31,151	28,615	41,206	44,617	54,744
Cook County, Illinois	46,504	27,450	31,617	38,815	61,648	77,279
DeKalb County, Illinois	43,663	33,370	37,383	47,599	48,680	56,948
DuPage County, Illinois	53,538	30,809	36,360	42,165	65,172	87,291
Kane County, Illinois	43,715	29,854	35,905	41,187	64,923	78,569
Kankakee County, Illinois	40,840	21,969	32,411	39,405	55,405	68,841
Kendall County, Illinois	51,014	19,625	47,659	41,443	55,714	81,874
Lake County, Illinois	51,125	27,091	33,817	40,790	72,910	100,567
LaSalle County, Illinois	36,830	22,577	32,267	40,076	44,723	60,798
McHenry County, Illinois	49,783	32,425	40,810	42,291	65,286	71,450
McLean County, Illinois	47,426	20,324	35,143	40,989	55,386	61,505
Macon County, Illinois	40,140	24,524	32,357	40,022	47,125	53,442
Madison County, Illinois	43,205	21,794	31,020	40,619	54,274	76,476
Peoria County, Illinois	40,253	26,425	26,523	31,400	53,035	76,043
Rock Island County, Illinois	40,490	26,269	34,049	36,826	51,416	69,730
St. Clair County, Illinois	39,206	22,983	28,482	36,714	60,836	66,280
Sangamon County, Illinois	45,032	20,273	33,960	38,034	58,124	71,088
Tazewell County, Illinois	41,701	17,689	31,652	42,768	52,347	68,935
Vermilion County, Illinois	34,119	30,526	31,194	34,511	54,870	50,860
Will County, Illinois	50,731	27,960	37,814	45,611	61,838	81,761
Williamson County, Illinois	37,589	18,953	26,079	37,162	42,202	82,050
Winnebago County, Illinois	37,222	26,198	30,298	36,435	46,929	70,390
INDIANA	39,833	27,765	32,101	37,154	50,630	65,941
Allen County, Indiana	39,812	28,315	31,071	36,828	49,728	69,413
Bartholomew County, Indiana	41,656	21,870	35,777	30,435	57,207	67,750
Boone County, Indiana	50,680	24,932	34,434	46,027	72,496	98,951
Clark County, Indiana	37,200	25,522	31,715	35,941	47,324	51,714
Delaware County, Indiana	34,514	33,180	27,053	34,818	40,981	55,898
Elkhart County, Indiana	35,691	31,946	33,656	31,431	50,571	51,095
Floyd County, Indiana	41,044	31,800	30,872	38,568	53,542	66,920
Grant County, Indiana	33,777	20,970	33,652	31,566	43,142	49,464
Hamilton County, Indiana	61,265	36,748	35,036	47,411	63,627	95,318
Hancock County, Indiana	50,221	50,853	38,365	45,762	60,586	75,635
Hendricks County, Indiana	49,774	28,239	39,463	47,695	57,118	78,431
Howard County, Indiana	34,116	18,790	33,722	31,703	45,636	56,583
Johnson County, Indiana	45,938	25,891	35,361	41,407	58,705	65,837
Kosciusko County, Indiana	39,915	31,190	27,104	41,838	50,996	57,064
Lake County, Indiana	40,584	25,662	32,472	36,818	55,213	72,420
LaPorte County, Indiana	36,000	20,140	31,619	39,000	55,389	64,063

Table C-2. Educational Attainment of the Population, by Selected Counties, 2019—*Continued*

(Number; percent; dollars.)

State/County	Some other race alone			Two or more races			Hispanic or Latino (of any race)		
	Total	High school graduate or more (percent)	Bachelor's degree or more (percent)	Total	High school graduate or more (percent)	Bachelor's degree or more (percent)	Total	High school graduate or more (percent)	Bachelor's degree or more (percent)
INDIANA—(*Continued*)									
Madison County, Indiana	N	N	N	N	N	N	2,773	66.6	32.5
Marion County, Indiana	14,768	43.1	11.4	12,414	86.9	28.2	49,960	60.1	15.9
Monroe County, Indiana	N	N	N	N	N	N	N	N	N
Morgan County, Indiana	N	N	N	N	N	N	N	N	N
Porter County, Indiana	N	N	N	N	N	N	10,163	91.2	23.4
St. Joseph County, Indiana	4,829	62.9	18.3	4,176	92.6	18.8	11,794	70.3	26.0
Tippecanoe County, Indiana	N	N	N	N	N	N	7,716	62.1	18.9
Vanderburgh County, Indiana	N	N	N	N	N	N	2,530	83.3	12.0
Vigo County, Indiana	N	N	N	N	N	N	N	N	N
Wayne County, Indiana	N	N	N	N	N	N	N	N	N
IOWA	17,543	64.6	14.1	24,563	92.5	29.0	94,822	67.5	13.8
Black Hawk County, Iowa	N	N	N	N	N	N	2,757	83.4	28.5
Dallas County, Iowa	N	N	N	N	N	N	2,755	81.5	40.0
Dubuque County, Iowa	N	N	N	N	N	N	N	N	N
Johnson County, Iowa	N	N	N	N	N	N	4,181	80.1	31.2
Linn County, Iowa	N	N	N	N	N	N	3,896	86.7	20.5
Polk County, Iowa	2,907	50.3	4.6	3,738	88.0	39.0	20,189	63.2	9.4
Pottawattamie County, Iowa	N	N	N	N	N	N	3,273	68.5	23.2
Scott County, Iowa	N	N	N	N	N	N	6,291	85.5	24.2
Story County, Iowa	N	N	N	N	N	N	N	N	N
Woodbury County, Iowa	N	N	N	N	N	N	8,362	51.2	4.9
KANSAS	46,958	61.0	10.0	41,525	91.1	27.5	177,719	68.4	14.1
Butler County, Kansas	N	N	N	N	N	N	N	N	N
Douglas County, Kansas	N	N	N	N	N	N	3,723	75.5	40.1
Johnson County, Kansas	7,131	80.7	17.3	7,263	94.5	52.1	25,509	77.8	24.4
Leavenworth County, Kansas	N	N	N	N	N	N	3,155	79.3	9.0
Riley County, Kansas	N	N	N	N	N	N	N	N	N
Sedgwick County, Kansas	8,019	59.6	13.5	9,437	91.7	24.9	37,715	67.2	16.6
Shawnee County, Kansas	4,751	76.3	12.8	2,610	88.5	19.0	11,208	84.9	12.6
Wyandotte County, Kansas	9,896	54.4	8.9	2,470	90.5	24.9	24,716	57.2	8.2
KENTUCKY	21,419	56.3	11.3	32,799	86.5	26.8	84,517	70.3	19.7
Boone County, Kentucky	N	N	N	N	N	N	N	N	N
Bullitt County, Kentucky	N	N	N	N	N	N	N	N	N
Campbell County, Kentucky	N	N	N	N	N	N	N	N	N
Christian County, Kentucky	N	N	N	N	N	N	2,175	67.0	4.7
Daviess County, Kentucky	N	N	N	N	N	N	N	N	N
Fayette County, Kentucky	5,164	66.8	15.2	5,009	83.4	27.0	11,966	60.6	18.1
Hardin County, Kentucky	N	N	N	N	N	N	3,515	95.3	29.6
Jefferson County, Kentucky	2,241	70.4	32.5	6,360	96.5	37.1	25,232	82.4	29.1
Kenton County, Kentucky	N	N	N	N	N	N	2,394	49.2	24.2
McCracken County, Kentucky	N	N	N	N	N	N	N	N	N
Madison County, Kentucky	N	N	N	N	N	N	N	N	N
Oldham County, Kentucky	N	N	N	N	N	N	N	N	N
Warren County, Kentucky	N	N	N	N	N	N	3,663	55.3	18.0
LOUISIANA	39,604	68.8	13.6	41,559	87.2	26.7	145,024	73.6	17.4
Ascension Parish, Louisiana	N	N	N	N	N	N	N	N	N
Bossier Parish, Louisiana	N	N	N	N	N	N	5,024	60.3	7.6
Caddo Parish, Louisiana	N	N	N	2,509	93.2	19.0	3,106	84.3	25.9
Calcasieu Parish, Louisiana	N	N	N	N	N	N	4,680	67.3	20.9
East Baton Rouge Parish, Louisiana	4,747	68.6	15.9	N	N	N	9,908	78.5	23.5
Iberia Parish, Louisiana	N	N	N	N	N	N	N	N	N
Jefferson Parish, Louisiana	7,722	76.2	14.5	4,516	79.4	26.6	39,830	79.0	14.6
Lafayette Parish, Louisiana	N	N	N	N	N	N	6,309	57.7	14.0
Lafourche Parish, Louisiana	N	N	N	N	N	N	N	N	N
Livingston Parish, Louisiana	N	N	N	N	N	N	N	N	N
Orleans Parish, Louisiana	4,196	76.2	21.1	3,999	96.2	44.8	13,079	79.8	38.1
Ouachita Parish, Louisiana	N	N	N	N	N	N	2,015	69.5	12.2
Rapides Parish, Louisiana	N	N	N	N	N	N	N	N	N
St. Landry Parish, Louisiana	N	N	N	N	N	N	N	N	N
St. Tammany Parish, Louisiana	N	N	N	N	N	N	9,566	81.1	31.4
Tangipahoa Parish, Louisiana	N	N	N	N	N	N	N	N	N
Terrebonne Parish, Louisiana	N	N	N	N	N	N	N	N	N

Table C-2. Educational Attainment of the Population, by Selected Counties, 2019—*Continued*

(Number; percent; dollars.)

State/County	Median earnings in the past 12 months (2019 inflation-adjusted dollars)					
	Population 25 years and over with earnings					
	Total	Less than high school graduate	High school graduate (includes equivalency)	Some college or associate's degree	Bachelor's degree	Graduate or professional degree
INDIANA—(*Continued*)						
Madison County, Indiana	36,488	22,407	31,040	39,458	49,848	65,486
Marion County, Indiana	37,350	26,380	30,881	35,653	47,691	60,630
Monroe County, Indiana	36,450	30,863	28,668	32,014	36,584	57,105
Morgan County, Indiana	40,037	22,572	38,477	36,365	65,065	112,411
Porter County, Indiana	46,739	27,141	44,025	42,079	55,986	70,099
St. Joseph County, Indiana	36,920	26,780	31,869	31,984	42,987	59,942
Tippecanoe County, Indiana	37,527	26,312	30,560	37,872	43,656	52,092
Vanderburgh County, Indiana	36,246	20,774	30,896	31,801	48,262	61,645
Vigo County, Indiana	35,336	27,168	27,449	34,384	40,262	70,519
Wayne County, Indiana	31,358	30,984	28,233	31,168	39,087	53,859
IOWA	41,268	30,381	33,066	39,073	51,751	66,887
Black Hawk County, Iowa	39,558	31,138	31,605	38,476	49,888	70,171
Dallas County, Iowa	58,603	33,489	32,743	48,891	63,416	76,384
Dubuque County, Iowa	40,111	22,565	35,234	36,990	46,451	62,170
Johnson County, Iowa	46,590	22,466	32,136	37,858	51,097	66,510
Linn County, Iowa	45,102	23,221	35,503	41,211	56,029	74,108
Polk County, Iowa	45,499	29,514	33,743	40,722	60,022	71,578
Pottawattamie County, Iowa	40,008	35,102	31,506	36,594	46,235	60,682
Scott County, Iowa	44,852	24,097	35,127	39,593	55,300	75,403
Story County, Iowa	41,548	31,692	29,007	35,276	49,779	55,978
Woodbury County, Iowa	36,921	33,376	27,944	39,349	46,698	78,036
KANSAS	41,181	26,549	32,106	36,994	51,678	62,008
Butler County, Kansas	43,587	46,862	33,232	39,300	49,848	56,143
Douglas County, Kansas	41,294	22,574	30,627	36,243	46,222	58,816
Johnson County, Kansas	54,343	30,547	35,426	44,719	62,650	75,347
Leavenworth County, Kansas	45,111	31,265	30,530	45,129	60,072	61,864
Riley County, Kansas	36,812	17,329	27,898	33,612	45,271	50,213
Sedgwick County, Kansas	40,035	24,571	31,800	35,885	50,560	63,571
Shawnee County, Kansas	41,074	27,573	34,364	38,870	50,247	60,817
Wyandotte County, Kansas	32,557	24,632	33,853	31,684	49,071	56,013
KENTUCKY	37,674	24,631	31,313	35,326	50,711	60,270
Boone County, Kentucky	45,969	40,232	36,805	41,419	57,339	74,312
Bullitt County, Kentucky	43,649	31,194	37,813	42,170	60,510	59,903
Campbell County, Kentucky	45,701	35,093	36,992	36,127	51,131	62,057
Christian County, Kentucky	35,716	32,009	28,230	32,390	52,287	58,771
Daviess County, Kentucky	38,092	26,472	30,841	34,161	51,083	59,563
Fayette County, Kentucky	40,962	21,459	28,309	33,847	46,171	64,253
Hardin County, Kentucky	41,231	21,579	32,240	40,371	55,157	59,364
Jefferson County, Kentucky	40,715	23,787	31,319	36,819	51,068	64,295
Kenton County, Kentucky	43,694	25,935	35,296	44,573	54,593	63,259
McCracken County, Kentucky	33,769	33,859	30,205	27,191	49,235	57,706
Madison County, Kentucky	37,291	20,339	27,034	31,720	41,285	55,048
Oldham County, Kentucky	51,278	7,417	40,090	42,623	64,402	81,930
Warren County, Kentucky	36,400	25,307	26,686	34,338	48,991	55,218
LOUISIANA	37,599	22,913	30,786	35,064	50,699	60,992
Ascension Parish, Louisiana	51,732	27,058	36,278	47,779	77,417	59,959
Bossier Parish, Louisiana	34,217	19,656	27,637	35,058	47,082	60,428
Caddo Parish, Louisiana	36,238	16,304	29,938	31,556	47,307	58,165
Calcasieu Parish, Louisiana	39,457	27,782	34,667	35,963	46,207	65,522
East Baton Rouge Parish, Louisiana	41,113	26,164	29,267	35,834	52,271	64,074
Iberia Parish, Louisiana	35,972	26,763	32,051	33,943	52,219	43,723
Jefferson Parish, Louisiana	36,852	20,446	31,548	34,060	50,031	56,972
Lafayette Parish, Louisiana	41,377	20,612	30,605	39,552	50,840	70,834
Lafourche Parish, Louisiana	37,281	27,326	31,560	32,303	50,030	55,606
Livingston Parish, Louisiana	45,007	31,619	41,700	46,543	55,341	65,165
Orleans Parish, Louisiana	37,190	20,811	23,578	29,727	46,386	66,851
Ouachita Parish, Louisiana	34,186	22,532	25,011	35,951	45,386	66,261
Rapides Parish, Louisiana	36,737	20,366	34,986	33,893	50,771	66,738
St. Landry Parish, Louisiana	34,418	24,755	35,114	30,898	46,358	42,159
St. Tammany Parish, Louisiana	42,056	24,739	33,274	37,635	55,591	82,748
Tangipahoa Parish, Louisiana	34,217	13,427	29,274	31,876	56,469	50,691
Terrebonne Parish, Louisiana	35,819	49,261	31,510	31,140	38,737	41,341

Table C-2. Educational Attainment of the Population, by Selected Counties, 2019—*Continued*

(Number; percent; dollars.)

	Educational attainment by race/ethnicity, 25 years and over								
	Some other race alone			Two or more races			Hispanic or Latino (of any race)		
State/County	Total	High school graduate or more (percent)	Bachelor's degree or more (percent)	Total	High school graduate or more (percent)	Bachelor's degree or more (percent)	Total	High school graduate or more (percent)	Bachelor's degree or more (percent)
MAINE	3,042	85.8	28.2	14,470	88.7	31.7	13,580	89.9	37.8
Androscoggin County, Maine	N	N	N	1,526	77.0	14.8	N	N	N
Aroostook County, Maine	N	N	N	N	N	N	N	N	N
Cumberland County, Maine	N	N	N	2,930	83.9	45.7	3,538	84.6	54.9
Kennebec County, Maine	N	N	N	N	N	N	N	N	N
Penobscot County, Maine	N	N	N	N	N	N	N	N	N
York County, Maine	N	N	N	N	N	N	N	N	N
MARYLAND	172,165	56.9	12.8	91,388	93.3	44.0	358,740	67.2	22.0
Allegany County, Maryland	N	N	N	N	N	N	N	N	N
Anne Arundel County, Maryland	6,928	79.2	33.7	11,473	93.5	41.3	25,573	81.2	31.5
Baltimore County, Maryland	9,801	71.6	21.5	10,780	98.9	40.6	25,411	76.8	25.9
Calvert County, Maryland	N	N	N	N	N	N	N	N	N
Carroll County, Maryland	N	N	N	N	N	N	3,523	95.0	33.3
Cecil County, Maryland	N	N	N	N	N	N	N	N	N
Charles County, Maryland	N	N	N	2,737	97.6	19.0	5,482	83.4	22.5
Frederick County, Maryland	2,026	61.5	14.0	3,395	86.1	39.3	15,062	63.2	23.4
Harford County, Maryland	N	N	N	3,002	100.0	28.2	7,524	89.4	29.9
Howard County, Maryland	2,672	98.6	48.9	5,620	88.8	57.0	12,811	78.6	37.5
Montgomery County, Maryland	63,011	57.4	12.8	21,430	93.9	58.1	124,170	67.3	23.4
Prince George's County, Maryland	72,512	48.8	5.7	14,886	93.8	41.5	98,075	53.4	9.8
St. Mary's County, Maryland	N	N	N	N	N	N	3,677	81.0	18.5
Washington County, Maryland	N	N	N	N	N	N	4,532	73.3	7.4
Wicomico County, Maryland	N	N	N	N	N	N	N	N	N
Baltimore city, Maryland	6,608	62.5	33.8	6,281	87.7	45.2	18,255	76.6	44.5
MASSACHUSETTS	180,134	71.8	17.0	113,285	83.8	40.5	486,528	73.2	20.8
Barnstable County, Massachusetts	N	N	N	N	N	N	4,560	60.1	25.6
Berkshire County, Massachusetts	N	N	N	1,761	89.2	32.0	2,984	75.2	22.1
Bristol County, Massachusetts	17,985	67.8	10.9	6,380	94.3	39.0	24,628	73.2	14.7
Essex County, Massachusetts	51,510	63.9	8.6	11,095	81.1	38.6	99,239	66.7	14.1
Franklin County, Massachusetts	N	N	N	N	N	N	N	N	N
Hampden County, Massachusetts	13,089	74.7	20.5	6,442	88.6	18.6	67,506	69.8	12.1
Hampshire County, Massachusetts	N	N	N	N	N	N	4,123	72.0	35.8
Middlesex County, Massachusetts	32,755	69.6	19.6	22,778	89.4	55.9	77,511	76.7	32.0
Norfolk County, Massachusetts	7,724	82.8	41.0	8,784	93.2	63.8	20,524	93.0	45.3
Plymouth County, Massachusetts	7,774	68.3	15.5	5,481	83.8	29.8	12,325	76.3	20.8
Suffolk County, Massachusetts	29,161	82.0	23.8	35,123	70.2	32.6	115,020	73.9	22.8
Worcester County, Massachusetts	15,007	84.1	19.4	8,266	92.2	28.7	56,072	75.6	15.0
MICHIGAN	64,422	68.1	16.5	118,032	90.1	30.0	273,449	75.6	21.6
Allegan County, Michigan	N	N	N	N	N	N	4,586	64.2	10.8
Bay County, Michigan	N	N	N	N	N	N	3,347	87.2	13.9
Berrien County, Michigan	N	N	N	N	N	N	4,958	83.1	28.8
Calhoun County, Michigan	N	N	N	2,588	92.2	25.2	4,104	85.6	8.7
Clinton County, Michigan	N	N	N	N	N	N	2,047	83.2	17.6
Eaton County, Michigan	N	N	N	N	N	N	3,438	96.2	15.9
Genesee County, Michigan	N	N	N	5,496	90.4	20.2	7,750	84.1	20.0
Grand Traverse County, Michigan	N	N	N	N	N	N	N	N	N
Ingham County, Michigan	N	N	N	3,755	87.3	36.1	12,360	88.7	28.4
Isabella County, Michigan	N	N	N	N	N	N	N	N	N
Jackson County, Michigan	N	N	N	1,779	88.1	15.2	2,822	88.9	30.3
Kalamazoo County, Michigan	N	N	N	4,441	90.9	31.4	5,860	78.3	37.2
Kent County, Michigan	11,265	54.0	14.1	10,711	93.1	30.8	35,050	61.5	19.9
Lapeer County, Michigan	N	N	N	N	N	N	2,131	56.8	3.5
Lenawee County, Michigan	N	N	N	N	N	N	4,395	69.2	17.0
Livingston County, Michigan	N	N	N	N	N	N	N	N	N
Macomb County, Michigan	2,956	70.8	15.3	10,094	90.6	33.8	13,558	74.6	15.5
Marquette County, Michigan	N	N	N	N	N	N	N	N	N
Midland County, Michigan	N	N	N	N	N	N	N	N	N
Monroe County, Michigan	N	N	N	N	N	N	3,105	94.7	28.7
Muskegon County, Michigan	N	N	N	N	N	N	5,175	79.5	11.0
Oakland County, Michigan	5,071	87.1	49.1	13,545	95.0	52.9	30,386	88.1	42.4
Ottawa County, Michigan	4,633	54.9	6.9	N	N	N	14,466	69.3	13.4
Saginaw County, Michigan	N	N	N	2,420	88.8	15.7	9,234	80.2	19.8
St. Clair County, Michigan	N	N	N	N	N	N	2,456	75.0	10.8
Shiawassee County, Michigan	N	N	N	N	N	N	N	N	N

Table C-2. Educational Attainment of the Population, by Selected Counties, 2019—*Continued*

(Number; percent; dollars.)

State/County	Total	Less than high school graduate	High school graduate (includes equivalency)	Some college or associate's degree	Bachelor's degree	Graduate or professional degree
MAINE	39,550	25,504	31,798	36,274	47,375	60,347
Androscoggin County, Maine	40,346	22,177	32,408	37,697	52,346	71,716
Aroostook County, Maine	33,660	20,009	27,310	33,180	45,518	51,820
Cumberland County, Maine	47,304	27,997	35,494	40,495	54,336	66,338
Kennebec County, Maine	39,374	29,941	35,198	35,926	46,239	65,043
Penobscot County, Maine	37,010	23,922	31,280	36,035	42,131	56,911
York County, Maine	41,290	40,292	34,565	37,367	50,999	51,638
MARYLAND	52,011	30,300	36,700	44,022	65,193	89,066
Allegany County, Maryland..................................	35,134	14,714	27,189	30,125	49,358	57,767
Anne Arundel County, Maryland..........................	60,638	35,396	43,113	50,650	70,835	92,115
Baltimore County, Maryland...............................	50,507	26,578	36,317	45,240	58,410	78,562
Calvert County, Maryland...................................	63,310	47,091	50,162	57,074	87,748	95,601
Carroll County, Maryland....................................	57,490	25,562	40,587	50,535	76,376	81,558
Cecil County, Maryland	50,057	15,348	37,437	55,425	52,037	77,871
Charles County, Maryland	62,154	34,393	42,178	59,758	83,135	89,936
Frederick County, Maryland................................	56,037	32,253	37,207	48,117	69,072	83,903
Harford County, Maryland	57,973	38,736	42,249	50,120	67,511	89,391
Howard County, Maryland...................................	72,512	30,761	41,019	46,924	76,448	102,249
Montgomery County, Maryland............................	60,143	26,314	31,987	40,741	70,639	101,682
Prince George's County, Maryland	50,115	34,076	37,743	44,790	65,063	84,382
St. Mary's County, Maryland	57,070	36,934	40,236	52,104	71,646	91,192
Washington County, Maryland	41,775	31,964	35,278	41,000	46,744	73,205
Wicomico County, Maryland	40,787	24,047	31,127	35,031	57,404	61,945
Baltimore city, Maryland	41,309	23,443	31,660	35,595	55,264	70,996
MASSACHUSETTS	52,470	30,693	39,463	42,066	65,373	85,717
Barnstable County, Massachusetts	46,841	31,304	41,056	40,459	50,594	67,826
Berkshire County, Massachusetts	40,666	24,133	36,565	36,280	42,775	61,968
Bristol County, Massachusetts............................	48,058	31,407	40,968	41,919	61,187	78,251
Essex County, Massachusetts.............................	51,540	32,000	40,026	41,474	65,948	85,526
Franklin County, Massachusetts..........................	37,038	25,779	31,149	36,246	42,500	62,511
Hampden County, Massachusetts........................	42,192	24,072	35,908	41,481	55,515	69,659
Hampshire County, Massachusetts......................	50,966	32,430	44,822	36,532	46,524	67,558
Middlesex County, Massachusetts.......................	62,709	32,758	40,478	45,065	73,844	94,156
Norfolk County, Massachusetts	62,169	30,048	41,883	46,605	70,655	93,477
Plymouth County, Massachusetts........................	52,048	31,860	41,613	46,914	65,359	86,336
Suffolk County, Massachusetts...........................	52,039	30,219	34,634	38,265	65,113	84,452
Worcester County, Massachusetts	50,804	30,308	39,710	42,336	63,145	82,073
MICHIGAN...	40,450	23,192	31,028	36,272	54,634	71,623
Allegan County, Michigan...................................	39,365	32,447	31,635	37,536	55,701	80,978
Bay County, Michigan	38,565	20,732	30,287	41,834	53,250	68,914
Berrien County, Michigan	36,802	17,118	28,937	36,909	51,060	56,178
Calhoun County, Michigan	36,148	26,401	32,472	36,345	43,871	61,381
Clinton County, Michigan	45,640	21,662	32,646	42,216	59,432	74,958
Eaton County, Michigan	43,849	17,721	32,468	41,823	53,790	66,497
Genesee County, Michigan.................................	36,623	19,091	29,898	35,631	53,288	71,997
Grand Traverse County, Michigan	38,404	21,418	32,426	33,383	46,656	66,757
Ingham County, Michigan	37,697	24,194	29,666	32,028	47,291	67,020
Isabella County, Michigan	32,983	20,405	31,222	26,894	41,392	71,250
Jackson County, Michigan	40,155	19,931	33,414	37,393	55,706	66,800
Kalamazoo County, Michigan	38,532	26,608	31,052	35,146	40,773	71,460
Kent County, Michigan	40,619	24,965	31,833	36,176	49,976	67,176
Lapeer County, Michigan....................................	39,678	23,930	31,753	41,679	62,931	72,413
Lenawee County, Michigan	35,302	27,007	30,608	32,910	50,102	61,053
Livingston County, Michigan...............................	51,567	21,608	37,087	42,494	72,289	81,307
Macomb County, Michigan	41,269	23,783	31,461	40,398	57,332	74,625
Marquette County, Michigan...............................	35,366	41,060	27,281	30,801	37,171	58,013
Midland County, Michigan..................................	43,815	20,925	29,716	39,127	60,727	72,110
Monroe County, Michigan...................................	46,554	17,121	37,211	41,376	60,981	65,618
Muskegon County, Michigan...............................	35,424	22,486	31,812	32,263	50,817	60,838
Oakland County, Michigan..................................	51,786	25,244	31,801	37,278	66,654	86,140
Ottawa County, Michigan	41,890	30,223	31,268	39,537	54,667	67,426
Saginaw County, Michigan.................................	33,792	20,547	27,956	30,999	47,446	66,296
St. Clair County, Michigan..................................	39,859	21,515	31,718	40,063	50,471	70,660
Shiawassee County, Michigan.............................	37,732	25,467	31,637	38,031	51,553	60,049

Table C-2. Educational Attainment of the Population, by Selected Counties, 2019—*Continued*

(Number; percent; dollars.)

State/County	Educational attainment by race/ethnicity, 25 years and over								
	Some other race alone			Two or more races			Hispanic or Latino (of any race)		
	Total	High school graduate or more (percent)	Bachelor's degree or more (percent)	Total	High school graduate or more (percent)	Bachelor's degree or more (percent)	Total	High school graduate or more (percent)	Bachelor's degree or more (percent)
MICHIGAN—(*Continued*)									
Van Buren County, Michigan	N	N	N	N	N	N	4,429	68.3	6.6
Washtenaw County, Michigan	N	N	N	5,106	94.7	41.3	9,307	89.5	44.4
Wayne County, Michigan	20,630	60.7	8.9	19,565	85.4	30.1	56,703	66.7	14.2
MINNESOTA	57,270	66.2	16.8	67,207	94.2	31.2	158,254	75.0	22.8
Anoka County, Minnesota	3,455	54.4	7.4	4,352	98.0	34.6	8,742	67.1	21.0
Blue Earth County, Minnesota	N	N	N	N	N	N	N	N	N
Carver County, Minnesota	N	N	N	N	N	N	2,088	54.7	13.6
Crow Wing County, Minnesota	N	N	N	N	N	N	N	N	N
Dakota County, Minnesota	5,798	40.5	15.4	5,590	94.6	24.4	16,568	70.1	18.2
Hennepin County, Minnesota	21,525	68.0	18.0	19,283	92.6	41.0	45,966	75.9	29.7
Olmsted County, Minnesota	N	N	N	N	N	N	4,677	81.0	35.8
Ramsey County, Minnesota	5,266	78.6	31.7	8,065	95.4	33.6	21,541	80.8	24.0
Rice County, Minnesota	N	N	N	N	N	N	N	N	N
St. Louis County, Minnesota	N	N	N	2,649	97.3	21.7	2,062	76.5	41.7
Scott County, Minnesota	N	N	N	3,043	99.7	30.1	3,864	83.4	41.7
Sherburne County, Minnesota	N	N	N	N	N	N	N	N	N
Stearns County, Minnesota	N	N	N	N	N	N	2,247	81.2	15.4
Washington County, Minnesota	1,733	81.0	40.1	3,795	95.4	31.8	6,067	84.9	35.2
Wright County, Minnesota	N	N	N	N	N	N	N	N	N
MISSISSIPPI	14,862	53.4	12.4	15,831	87.2	27.7	46,120	67.8	11.8
DeSoto County, Mississippi	N	N	N	N	N	N	5,058	84.6	20.1
Forrest County, Mississippi	N	N	N	N	N	N	N	N	N
Harrison County, Mississippi	N	N	N	N	N	N	5,676	86.8	12.3
Hinds County, Mississippi	N	N	N	N	N	N	N	N	N
Jackson County, Mississippi	N	N	N	N	N	N	5,470	74.0	18.6
Jones County, Mississippi	N	N	N	N	N	N	N	N	N
Lauderdale County, Mississippi	N	N	N	N	N	N	N	N	N
Lee County, Mississippi	N	N	N	N	N	N	N	N	N
Madison County, Mississippi	N	N	N	N	N	N	N	N	N
Rankin County, Mississippi	N	N	N	N	N	N	N	N	N
MISSOURI	41,151	73.3	17.6	66,755	89.5	30.7	138,178	77.8	22.9
Boone County, Missouri	N	N	N	2,895	94.3	32.6	2,734	93.2	28.9
Buchanan County, Missouri	N	N	N	N	N	N	3,373	68.0	18.1
Cape Girardeau County, Missouri	N	N	N	N	N	N	N	N	N
Cass County, Missouri	N	N	N	N	N	N	N	N	N
Christian County, Missouri	N	N	N	N	N	N	N	N	N
Clay County, Missouri	4,636	78.2	6.7	3,872	87.2	25.9	10,070	81.9	16.8
Cole County, Missouri	N	N	N	N	N	N	1,687	85.6	22.7
Franklin County, Missouri	N	N	N	N	N	N	N	N	N
Greene County, Missouri	N	N	N	4,261	96.5	23.2	5,356	80.3	28.8
Jackson County, Missouri	14,135	70.4	15.5	9,363	91.6	31.8	33,795	74.1	21.2
Jasper County, Missouri	N	N	N	N	N	N	4,580	46.1	3.9
Jefferson County, Missouri	N	N	N	N	N	N	2,605	80.8	3.8
Platte County, Missouri	N	N	N	N	N	N	4,083	92.4	47.2
St. Charles County, Missouri	N	N	N	2,543	100.0	41.5	7,206	94.5	39.2
St. Francois County, Missouri	N	N	N	N	N	N	N	N	N
St. Louis County, Missouri	6,829	82.6	29.2	10,604	88.7	42.6	16,316	88.5	41.8
St. Louis city, Missouri	N	N	N	3,715	97.6	59.2	7,598	74.3	36.3
MONTANA	5,369	78.2	27.6	16,804	94.3	39.3	22,102	84.7	26.8
Cascade County, Montana	N	N	N	N	N	N	N	N	N
Flathead County, Montana	N	N	N	N	N	N	N	N	N
Gallatin County, Montana	N	N	N	N	N	N	N	N	N
Lewis and Clark County, Montana	N	N	N	N	N	N	N	N	N
Missoula County, Montana	N	N	N	N	N	N	N	N	N
Yellowstone County, Montana	N	N	N	N	N	N	4,811	78.0	13.8
NEBRASKA	26,006	60.7	7.7	18,136	94.8	30.4	106,780	63.2	13.4
Douglas County, Nebraska	4,738	79.0	11.6	7,286	96.8	44.9	34,976	63.5	13.9
Lancaster County, Nebraska	2,618	77.9	18.1	N	N	N	10,584	63.4	18.9
Sarpy County, Nebraska	N	N	N	N	N	N	9,536	82.3	20.6

Table C-2. Educational Attainment of the Population, by Selected Counties, 2019—*Continued*

(Number; percent; dollars.)

State/County	Median earnings in the past 12 months (2019 inflation-adjusted dollars)					
	Population 25 years and over with earnings					
	Total	Less than high school graduate	High school graduate (includes equivalency)	Some college or associate's degree	Bachelor's degree	Graduate or professional degree
MICHIGAN—(*Continued*)						
Van Buren County, Michigan	33,513	20,686	26,964	35,876	45,537	53,173
Washtenaw County, Michigan	50,444	15,879	31,396	36,306	56,316	71,793
Wayne County, Michigan	37,691	22,174	30,362	35,536	55,763	70,566
MINNESOTA	47,050	28,327	35,337	41,858	60,316	75,925
Anoka County, Minnesota	50,556	31,934	37,397	47,143	63,900	80,181
Blue Earth County, Minnesota	41,792	40,273	33,995	40,362	50,723	66,493
Carver County, Minnesota	59,722	32,027	41,591	48,073	75,114	89,466
Crow Wing County, Minnesota	38,610	24,569	30,665	41,294	45,313	67,013
Dakota County, Minnesota	51,544	21,838	36,548	45,146	65,828	82,084
Hennepin County, Minnesota	51,750	26,297	34,849	41,625	65,579	81,627
Olmsted County, Minnesota	51,812	25,830	36,425	41,362	61,884	77,306
Ramsey County, Minnesota	43,927	27,420	31,459	40,183	54,110	71,395
Rice County, Minnesota	45,219	33,510	39,579	40,566	51,908	75,507
St. Louis County, Minnesota	41,198	23,958	33,895	37,226	50,601	64,505
Scott County, Minnesota	56,227	40,921	41,870	50,767	74,527	81,269
Sherburne County, Minnesota	50,865	31,270	45,876	44,763	70,456	81,022
Stearns County, Minnesota	42,334	14,923	36,933	42,036	52,235	64,674
Washington County, Minnesota	54,748	30,678	35,119	46,882	66,759	90,640
Wright County, Minnesota	55,154	26,580	41,094	52,156	65,776	72,066
MISSISSIPPI	32,574	20,764	27,158	31,459	44,148	56,208
DeSoto County, Mississippi	43,277	22,897	35,472	40,830	56,358	61,295
Forrest County, Mississippi	27,052	18,791	25,199	26,466	34,697	51,282
Harrison County, Mississippi	36,350	25,747	30,764	30,288	49,168	55,247
Hinds County, Mississippi	31,230	20,481	25,648	27,102	40,354	51,934
Jackson County, Mississippi	37,883	30,322	27,700	37,223	44,059	82,319
Jones County, Mississippi	27,734	18,342	21,888	28,216	36,872	48,150
Lauderdale County, Mississippi	27,776	15,615	20,401	31,264	41,358	49,699
Lee County, Mississippi	36,645	22,230	28,529	36,309	46,476	81,955
Madison County, Mississippi	43,301	18,615	29,050	32,949	54,180	63,926
Rankin County, Mississippi	40,701	25,102	31,813	39,120	50,502	59,428
MISSOURI	40,078	24,831	31,297	36,127	51,217	63,368
Boone County, Missouri	42,396	23,226	30,691	36,504	47,381	61,623
Buchanan County, Missouri	35,638	17,017	30,875	34,434	42,391	62,740
Cape Girardeau County, Missouri	38,237	12,338	31,464	37,047	41,992	49,635
Cass County, Missouri	43,363	30,962	36,869	41,684	65,632	57,857
Christian County, Missouri	40,453	30,457	32,999	36,965	50,890	48,049
Clay County, Missouri	44,613	31,310	35,480	40,481	55,064	69,660
Cole County, Missouri	37,707	23,231	31,296	35,873	47,380	49,270
Franklin County, Missouri	39,752	26,382	29,921	41,458	50,249	71,857
Greene County, Missouri	37,270	23,001	32,293	31,298	42,996	51,774
Jackson County, Missouri	41,373	25,393	31,821	37,569	52,986	63,526
Jasper County, Missouri	29,870	18,190	25,708	29,539	38,657	49,012
Jefferson County, Missouri	41,346	24,761	35,260	42,272	53,689	61,279
Platte County, Missouri	51,115	19,019	33,940	41,866	60,517	72,435
St. Charles County, Missouri	51,237	29,415	36,302	43,826	64,165	76,557
St. Francois County, Missouri	28,524	16,517	19,834	30,398	41,296	57,762
St. Louis County, Missouri	47,224	25,691	30,159	38,280	59,940	77,471
St. Louis city, Missouri	40,796	26,286	31,454	32,632	51,423	59,000
MONTANA	36,953	27,804	30,843	33,040	42,150	58,287
Cascade County, Montana	35,077	35,179	27,266	30,583	44,731	71,473
Flathead County, Montana	36,814	22,672	35,302	32,408	40,590	55,850
Gallatin County, Montana	41,987	35,833	31,967	44,045	42,353	52,397
Lewis and Clark County, Montana	40,362	38,761	27,026	32,031	47,293	59,255
Missoula County, Montana	36,935	33,661	32,498	35,145	37,523	61,840
Yellowstone County, Montana	40,433	22,273	32,477	32,933	54,245	65,868
NEBRASKA	41,488	30,298	32,174	38,209	50,779	61,853
Douglas County, Nebraska	45,443	27,048	31,284	41,784	54,256	62,937
Lancaster County, Nebraska	41,297	29,100	31,521	37,024	48,366	56,931
Sarpy County, Nebraska	50,082	35,528	38,893	42,824	60,855	75,743

Table C-2. Educational Attainment of the Population, by Selected Counties, 2019—*Continued*

(Number; percent; dollars.)

State/County	Some other race alone Total	Some other race alone High school graduate or more (percent)	Some other race alone Bachelor's degree or more (percent)	Two or more races Total	Two or more races High school graduate or more (percent)	Two or more races Bachelor's degree or more (percent)	Hispanic or Latino (of any race) Total	Hispanic or Latino (of any race) High school graduate or more (percent)	Hispanic or Latino (of any race) Bachelor's degree or more (percent)
NEVADA	190,619	62.8	8.8	66,882	89.1	24.9	512,330	67.0	10.6
Clark County, Nevada	151,382	65.1	9.4	53,014	89.3	26.0	411,068	68.0	11.0
Washoe County, Nevada	27,808	50.8	7.0	8,426	90.1	27.2	64,837	60.8	10.4
NEW HAMPSHIRE	5,977	86.1	18.2	12,804	88.8	32.1	29,638	78.7	25.0
Cheshire County, New Hampshire	N	N	N	N	N	N	N	N	N
Grafton County, New Hampshire	N	N	N	N	N	N	N	N	N
Hillsborough County, New Hampshire	3,651	87.4	21.4	4,691	88.6	32.6	16,809	69.3	16.1
Merrimack County, New Hampshire	N	N	N	N	N	N	N	N	N
Rockingham County, New Hampshire	N	N	N	N	N	N	6,314	88.9	41.0
Strafford County, New Hampshire	N	N	N	N	N	N	1,829	100.0	31.2
NEW JERSEY	342,229	69.4	15.4	112,926	89.4	39.7	1,134,354	75.4	21.1
Atlantic County, New Jersey	14,096	67.6	18.0	4,785	93.7	27.1	29,073	70.5	19.0
Bergen County, New Jersey	19,044	72.9	20.0	13,730	89.0	43.9	126,560	83.5	33.2
Burlington County, New Jersey	5,576	90.0	24.7	8,292	98.2	31.9	22,491	89.3	24.1
Camden County, New Jersey	24,372	61.2	8.5	5,650	90.6	31.3	49,555	67.9	12.7
Cape May County, New Jersey	N	N	N	N	N	N	4,426	78.6	12.5
Cumberland County, New Jersey	6,511	60.2	1.4	N	N	N	26,449	56.8	7.3
Essex County, New Jersey	36,161	62.0	13.1	10,452	92.4	40.9	116,163	71.6	16.9
Gloucester County, New Jersey	3,505	71.0	21.8	2,601	89.9	36.7	10,568	71.3	25.6
Hudson County, New Jersey	43,824	72.5	20.1	15,694	88.8	46.6	192,070	74.7	22.3
Hunterdon County, New Jersey	N	N	N	N	N	N	5,344	67.4	28.3
Mercer County, New Jersey	9,752	50.9	15.1	3,434	94.8	41.4	38,579	67.2	20.5
Middlesex County, New Jersey	31,556	74.3	16.4	11,025	81.9	45.4	107,788	76.3	17.5
Monmouth County, New Jersey	8,424	83.4	14.3	5,369	86.0	38.1	38,875	84.7	23.8
Morris County, New Jersey	6,758	74.2	30.1	4,253	95.7	58.0	43,341	80.6	32.0
Ocean County, New Jersey	5,979	74.7	23.1	3,786	92.6	29.7	32,219	84.4	17.4
Passaic County, New Jersey	42,389	71.7	10.3	5,888	85.9	25.7	130,214	73.9	15.5
Salem County, New Jersey	N	N	N	N	N	N	3,084	77.2	8.9
Somerset County, New Jersey	14,395	84.1	17.8	N	N	N	30,197	79.7	25.5
Sussex County, New Jersey	N	N	N	N	N	N	7,867	83.7	29.9
Union County, New Jersey	65,627	66.8	14.8	6,763	89.6	43.1	113,075	71.3	19.8
Warren County, New Jersey	N	N	N	N	N	N	6,416	90.5	30.3
NEW MEXICO	126,817	74.0	12.8	33,989	91.5	26.5	630,721	78.0	16.5
Bernalillo County, New Mexico	47,327	74.5	14.3	14,788	91.7	28.8	213,180	81.4	20.6
Chaves County, New Mexico	2,279	63.1	0.3	N	N	N	21,400	65.2	12.0
Doña Ana County, New Mexico	17,782	68.6	20.0	1,275	88.8	38.0	85,137	68.7	16.5
Lea County, New Mexico	N	N	N	N	N	N	22,744	64.6	9.5
McKinley County, New Mexico	N	N	N	N	N	N	5,479	86.0	15.5
Otero County, New Mexico	2,868	69.5	4.7	N	N	N	15,634	72.6	7.9
Sandoval County, New Mexico	6,680	91.7	16.5	3,289	96.3	27.0	36,580	90.9	25.6
San Juan County, New Mexico	N	N	N	N	N	N	13,933	83.3	9.0
Santa Fe County, New Mexico	7,747	70.1	9.4	2,730	93.8	37.8	50,306	76.6	15.7
Valencia County, New Mexico	N	N	N	N	N	N	27,830	84.2	14.7
NEW YORK	1,060,782	68.0	16.2	326,564	84.3	35.7	2,359,532	72.6	21.1
Albany County, New York	2,609	81.0	25.0	6,732	70.1	23.7	9,731	82.1	32.8
Bronx County, New York	265,986	67.9	14.7	35,446	74.7	22.8	502,485	68.3	14.9
Broome County, New York	N	N	N	N	N	N	3,540	79.0	16.5
Cattaraugus County, New York	N	N	N	N	N	N	N	N	N
Cayuga County, New York	N	N	N	N	N	N	N	N	N
Chautauqua County, New York	N	N	N	N	N	N	4,678	71.7	23.6
Chemung County, New York	N	N	N	N	N	N	1,718	82.3	40.6
Clinton County, New York	N	N	N	N	N	N	N	N	N
Dutchess County, New York	7,267	67.5	16.7	5,731	100.0	31.6	22,786	81.7	24.7
Erie County, New York	13,279	70.2	14.9	7,952	88.0	40.8	28,216	78.8	22.5
Jefferson County, New York	N	N	N	2,140	99.4	22.1	3,808	88.0	18.0
Kings County, New York	142,179	60.3	14.5	49,168	87.0	46.4	314,231	69.4	20.1
Livingston County, New York	N	N	N	N	N	N	N	N	N
Madison County, New York	N	N	N	N	N	N	N	N	N
Monroe County, New York	8,880	66.1	17.8	9,413	86.2	41.6	37,193	72.6	21.2
Nassau County, New York	59,204	71.7	18.4	22,375	80.2	34.7	145,253	75.2	26.1
New York County, New York	140,031	66.6	17.7	41,805	82.4	51.5	297,113	71.2	27.7
Niagara County, New York	N	N	N	3,573	85.3	22.2	3,750	95.3	29.2

Table C-2. Educational Attainment of the Population, by Selected Counties, 2019—*Continued*

(Number; percent; dollars.)

| State/County | Median earnings in the past 12 months (2019 inflation-adjusted dollars) | | | | | |
| | Population 25 years and over with earnings | | | | | |
	Total	Less than high school graduate	High school graduate (includes equivalency)	Some college or associate's degree	Bachelor's degree	Graduate or professional degree
NEVADA	39,505	29,609	32,879	40,057	50,293	66,105
Clark County, Nevada..............................	38,216	29,167	32,075	39,621	50,232	65,657
Washoe County, Nevada...........................	41,585	28,897	36,887	41,158	50,635	68,116
NEW HAMPSHIRE...................................	47,392	30,119	37,820	42,368	60,544	71,884
Cheshire County, New Hampshire........................	41,138	30,959	40,870	35,598	51,528	51,542
Grafton County, New Hampshire........................	40,281	30,056	28,311	35,669	41,706	72,030
Hillsborough County, New Hampshire	49,540	26,952	38,624	44,435	60,063	71,632
Merrimack County, New Hampshire.....................	46,597	30,775	41,903	42,072	54,403	63,018
Rockingham County, New Hampshire..................	55,922	34,783	40,902	48,866	74,226	85,050
Strafford County, New Hampshire........................	45,900	26,872	31,838	45,800	62,113	67,538
NEW JERSEY	51,786	28,427	35,048	44,983	67,038	92,098
Atlantic County, New Jersey	40,128	29,371	32,302	36,228	57,090	77,039
Bergen County, New Jersey	61,970	30,380	37,194	51,463	71,627	100,653
Burlington County, New Jersey	54,053	24,986	38,510	45,596	69,192	86,785
Camden County, New Jersey	46,213	26,291	32,358	41,412	61,203	81,387
Cape May County, New Jersey	48,220	28,389	35,924	41,744	65,512	80,192
Cumberland County, New Jersey	32,949	25,298	27,817	43,342	60,278	56,051
Essex County, New Jersey	44,677	26,550	31,470	41,175	62,418	94,029
Gloucester County, New Jersey.............................	52,124	29,842	37,859	46,528	65,748	80,701
Hudson County, New Jersey	51,675	27,394	30,436	41,495	69,494	100,364
Hunterdon County, New Jersey	63,745	27,001	41,363	43,867	80,907	97,478
Mercer County, New Jersey..................................	51,410	31,497	31,788	43,734	66,587	84,405
Middlesex County, New Jersey.............................	53,238	28,744	36,363	46,779	68,460	92,222
Monmouth County, New Jersey	57,731	26,953	40,145	45,245	69,573	90,871
Morris County, New Jersey...................................	66,846	30,255	35,966	50,626	77,228	102,277
Ocean County, New Jersey...................................	49,150	31,975	36,932	46,113	59,485	70,808
Passaic County, New Jersey.................................	42,461	29,398	31,275	45,857	60,756	86,149
Salem County, New Jersey...................................	41,434	25,417	30,395	41,622	60,324	80,216
Somerset County, New Jersey	66,329	26,864	40,530	54,946	71,910	103,214
Sussex County, New Jersey..................................	57,646	39,405	43,797	50,933	74,750	91,257
Union County, New Jersey	48,091	27,410	35,785	41,551	61,960	93,171
Warren County, New Jersey	52,293	31,543	39,652	48,773	69,085	67,292
NEW MEXICO	35,284	21,016	29,002	32,187	45,109	62,501
Bernalillo County, New Mexico...........................	38,597	21,033	30,296	34,133	47,625	67,398
Chaves County, New Mexico	33,309	22,363	30,106	26,361	50,013	65,510
Doña Ana County, New Mexico	29,557	15,555	24,658	27,187	37,665	58,442
Lea County, New Mexico......................................	49,283	36,698	52,083	46,857	60,811	70,299
McKinley County, New Mexico	27,443	16,965	21,845	30,862	49,366	55,820
Otero County, New Mexico	26,096	12,964	18,681	29,390	40,356	77,133
Sandoval County, New Mexico	39,853	22,003	31,602	34,359	47,879	65,098
San Juan County, New Mexico.............................	31,355	21,913	30,181	31,843	41,620	50,550
Santa Fe County, New Mexico	34,213	26,171	30,004	30,126	46,063	60,758
Valencia County, New Mexico	40,023	12,330	40,480	35,065	55,609	50,410
NEW YORK	47,645	26,036	33,491	41,421	62,699	81,041
Albany County, New York......................................	51,157	18,438	32,164	44,678	61,481	71,722
Bronx County, New York	33,473	23,139	30,012	35,787	50,367	65,642
Broome County, New York	38,107	25,169	31,480	35,309	56,265	61,727
Cattaraugus County, New York.............................	36,483	35,032	29,215	34,506	56,326	54,309
Cayuga County, New York.....................................	40,814	37,961	30,277	41,812	48,360	71,769
Chautauqua County, New York..............................	37,649	32,719	31,118	35,306	45,767	61,206
Chemung County, New York.................................	40,914	21,899	31,988	35,281	43,727	70,310
Clinton County, New York.....................................	41,623	30,490	35,583	39,519	51,423	61,115
Dutchess County, New York.................................	50,542	24,833	31,877	44,541	60,206	89,567
Erie County, New York..	42,404	21,432	33,646	38,867	52,476	65,006
Jefferson County, New York..................................	40,033	20,225	32,122	36,306	50,086	64,464
Kings County, New York.......................................	47,345	24,669	32,597	41,214	67,050	80,260
Livingston County, New York	41,775	32,216	35,866	38,713	57,949	65,340
Madison County, New York	39,862	31,444	32,091	40,878	51,850	70,656
Monroe County, New York	43,241	25,759	31,222	36,659	51,988	65,298
Nassau County, New York.....................................	60,958	29,086	40,537	47,815	74,254	96,852
New York County, New York................................	72,404	22,839	31,618	39,545	85,699	110,007
Niagara County, New York....................................	41,783	30,454	32,375	41,377	50,766	66,084

Table C-2. Educational Attainment of the Population, by Selected Counties, 2019—*Continued*

(Number; percent; dollars.)

| | Educational attainment by race/ethnicity, 25 years and over | | | | | | | | |
| | Some other race alone | | | Two or more races | | | Hispanic or Latino (of any race) | | |
State/County	Total	High school graduate or more (percent)	Bachelor's degree or more (percent)	Total	High school graduate or more (percent)	Bachelor's degree or more (percent)	Total	High school graduate or more (percent)	Bachelor's degree or more (percent)
NEW YORK —(*Continued*)									
Oneida County, New York	1,828	81.8	5.2	3,458	87.9	18.4	7,209	74.7	12.9
Onondaga County, New York	3,788	63.9	14.5	7,529	68.3	21.0	12,681	74.2	25.4
Ontario County, New York	N	N	N	N	N	N	2,934	74.8	20.2
Orange County, New York	14,695	77.0	14.7	7,275	85.8	22.6	46,978	80.5	22.9
Oswego County, New York	N	N	N	N	N	N	N	N	N
Putnam County, New York	4,098	70.8	21.6	N	N	N	11,021	81.4	31.9
Queens County, New York	214,700	71.5	16.2	50,866	85.9	34.0	420,903	74.5	19.5
Rensselaer County, New York	N	N	N	N	N	N	4,076	79.0	22.3
Richmond County, New York	11,092	73.7	27.2	4,529	99.2	30.5	52,903	75.5	23.3
Rockland County, New York	17,139	64.4	12.6	4,194	86.6	35.4	34,765	76.5	25.1
St. Lawrence County, New York	N	N	N	N	N	N	N	N	N
Saratoga County, New York	N	N	N	N	N	N	4,016	86.3	37.6
Schenectady County, New York	4,373	66.5	15.8	3,162	89.0	21.6	6,985	83.2	19.6
Steuben County, New York	N	N	N	N	N	N	N	N	N
Suffolk County, New York	52,093	68.9	14.1	15,874	89.6	33.9	174,444	74.9	17.7
Sullivan County, New York	N	N	N	N	N	N	7,475	60.6	9.7
Tompkins County, New York	N	N	N	N	N	N	N	N	N
Ulster County, New York	3,632	71.2	21.3	3,442	93.3	21.8	10,760	75.9	20.3
Warren County, New York	N	N	N	N	N	N	N	N	N
Wayne County, New York	N	N	N	N	N	N	N	N	N
Westchester County, New York	69,452	72.2	22.0	12,828	87.0	45.0	152,938	76.5	29.2
NORTH CAROLINA	185,783	53.6	11.4	110,659	89.9	33.6	513,662	62.8	17.0
Alamance County, North Carolina	4,039	59.7	7.9	N	N	N	10,622	52.1	10.3
Brunswick County, North Carolina	N	N	N	N	N	N	N	N	N
Buncombe County, North Carolina	N	N	N	N	N	N	9,446	70.7	19.9
Burke County, North Carolina	N	N	N	N	N	N	N	N	N
Cabarrus County, North Carolina	N	N	N	N	N	N	10,969	67.5	26.3
Caldwell County, North Carolina	N	N	N	N	N	N	2,005	74.7	12.8
Carteret County, North Carolina	N	N	N	N	N	N	N	N	N
Catawba County, North Carolina	N	N	N	N	N	N	8,263	58.5	15.1
Chatham County, North Carolina	N	N	N	N	N	N	4,196	62.5	11.5
Cleveland County, North Carolina	N	N	N	N	N	N	N	N	N
Craven County, North Carolina	N	N	N	N	N	N	N	N	N
Cumberland County, North Carolina	6,104	82.7	20.7	7,461	96.9	26.5	20,869	85.5	19.9
Davidson County, North Carolina	N	N	N	N	N	N	6,551	75.2	16.4
Durham County, North Carolina	5,272	64.9	31.5	N	N	N	22,150	48.3	16.9
Forsyth County, North Carolina	5,190	45.3	7.6	3,335	84.1	37.6	23,734	55.4	14.0
Franklin County, North Carolina	N	N	N	N	N	N	N	N	N
Gaston County, North Carolina	2,809	75.5	4.2	2,025	79.5	24.7	9,045	79.9	11.6
Guilford County, North Carolina	9,333	65.1	14.8	6,861	88.3	27.9	21,994	71.4	24.6
Harnett County, North Carolina	2,434	68.2	5.3	N	N	N	8,400	72.9	27.3
Henderson County, North Carolina	N	N	N	N	N	N	6,954	68.7	7.7
Iredell County, North Carolina	2,941	60.9	8.4	2,661	83.8	43.8	7,719	73.6	19.2
Johnston County, North Carolina	5,147	35.4	5.2	N	N	N	13,536	51.4	8.7
Lincoln County, North Carolina	N	N	N	N	N	N	3,863	75.2	22.5
Mecklenburg County, North Carolina	39,130	51.2	11.1	15,402	86.9	41.5	81,524	59.1	18.4
Moore County, North Carolina	N	N	N	N	N	N	3,403	60.0	30.1
Nash County, North Carolina	N	N	N	N	N	N	3,748	44.0	8.0
New Hanover County, North Carolina	N	N	N	N	N	N	6,659	81.8	26.6
Onslow County, North Carolina	N	N	N	N	N	N	11,394	85.4	27.6
Orange County, North Carolina	N	N	N	N	N	N	6,435	86.2	55.1
Pitt County, North Carolina	4,647	71.8	10.8	N	N	N	6,005	71.0	12.4
Randolph County, North Carolina	N	N	N	N	N	N	8,500	42.8	4.8
Robeson County, North Carolina	3,603	35.0	4.3	N	N	N	4,768	37.6	2.6
Rockingham County, North Carolina	N	N	N	N	N	N	N	N	N
Rowan County, North Carolina	N	N	N	N	N	N	6,858	50.5	12.7
Rutherford County, North Carolina	N	N	N	N	N	N	N	N	N
Surry County, North Carolina	N	N	N	N	N	N	3,847	61.9	10.3
Union County, North Carolina	N	N	N	N	N	N	13,423	61.0	17.3
Wake County, North Carolina	26,058	56.0	14.9	10,702	92.1	50.0	60,563	69.7	21.8
Wayne County, North Carolina	N	N	N	N	N	N	6,453	36.2	12.9
Wilkes County, North Carolina	N	N	N	N	N	N	N	N	N
Wilson County, North Carolina	N	N	N	N	N	N	N	N	N
NORTH DAKOTA	4,140	85.1	3.8	10,065	92.4	16.9	15,357	84.1	17.3
Burleigh County, North Dakota	N	N	N	N	N	N	N	N	N

Table C-2. Educational Attainment of the Population, by Selected Counties, 2019—*Continued*

(Number; percent; dollars.)

| State/County | Median earnings in the past 12 months (2019 inflation-adjusted dollars) | | | | | |
| | Population 25 years and over with earnings | | | | | |
	Total	Less than high school graduate	High school graduate (includes equivalency)	Some college or associate's degree	Bachelor's degree	Graduate or professional degree
NEW YORK —(*Continued*)						
Oneida County, New York	41,846	25,754	35,359	39,578	51,985	56,535
Onondaga County, New York	43,673	24,610	31,838	40,313	52,253	66,879
Ontario County, New York	42,085	23,952	33,965	37,427	50,288	62,390
Orange County, New York	51,067	29,937	38,008	47,632	67,378	87,299
Oswego County, New York	40,186	30,425	32,486	36,874	51,568	60,851
Putnam County, New York	54,251	25,274	42,166	50,786	65,633	76,520
Queens County, New York	42,761	26,782	32,255	41,640	59,902	74,378
Rensselaer County, New York	46,681	26,115	31,697	46,525	59,101	70,093
Richmond County, New York	54,122	25,746	40,015	51,518	66,196	79,025
Rockland County, New York	52,136	25,822	40,210	48,655	65,921	83,130
St. Lawrence County, New York	38,426	21,877	30,165	37,276	55,369	60,697
Saratoga County, New York	53,879	26,415	39,262	42,140	62,444	83,683
Schenectady County, New York	42,156	35,233	30,374	40,666	58,910	75,823
Steuben County, New York	39,138	30,864	31,240	35,179	53,906	62,868
Suffolk County, New York	55,461	33,801	42,949	50,956	66,572	90,966
Sullivan County, New York	40,377	20,903	32,306	40,237	49,230	70,686
Tompkins County, New York	41,304	26,250	31,891	36,654	34,485	57,917
Ulster County, New York	42,745	24,612	37,240	36,932	48,972	70,101
Warren County, New York	46,251	31,156	38,264	42,460	50,766	66,228
Wayne County, New York	36,742	31,873	30,204	37,670	52,505	57,184
Westchester County, New York	61,702	28,886	36,973	46,380	76,994	101,664
NORTH CAROLINA	38,534	23,976	30,369	34,861	50,977	65,620
Alamance County, North Carolina	37,891	23,865	31,155	35,181	51,156	63,154
Brunswick County, North Carolina	33,535	18,871	25,646	31,289	46,421	55,483
Buncombe County, North Carolina	36,479	19,154	28,078	31,946	41,222	53,522
Burke County, North Carolina	31,996	21,441	32,745	29,095	42,183	50,574
Cabarrus County, North Carolina	41,287	36,077	28,871	35,827	55,031	72,092
Caldwell County, North Carolina	32,154	26,834	31,582	31,037	39,137	51,661
Carteret County, North Carolina	33,971	22,695	29,855	31,872	45,990	55,283
Catawba County, North Carolina	34,781	26,671	31,973	35,366	42,350	47,262
Chatham County, North Carolina	41,697	30,136	25,827	40,129	55,360	64,773
Cleveland County, North Carolina	30,970	25,489	26,947	31,963	44,993	58,996
Craven County, North Carolina	34,296	22,289	28,779	41,268	53,468	55,640
Cumberland County, North Carolina	32,114	22,293	26,753	30,801	41,872	61,644
Davidson County, North Carolina	36,920	22,420	35,025	35,069	50,246	60,572
Durham County, North Carolina	41,862	24,138	26,121	31,963	50,817	67,793
Forsyth County, North Carolina	36,899	22,341	28,413	32,352	49,400	61,678
Franklin County, North Carolina	37,209	24,626	32,068	35,038	66,526	51,712
Gaston County, North Carolina	37,759	24,015	29,384	37,036	54,583	56,507
Guilford County, North Carolina	37,276	22,459	28,721	32,101	47,884	60,768
Harnett County, North Carolina	36,230	24,215	27,938	35,711	49,930	62,296
Henderson County, North Carolina	36,027	25,581	31,471	36,221	41,394	53,288
Iredell County, North Carolina	40,084	30,113	35,522	36,294	57,891	61,252
Johnston County, North Carolina	41,952	26,836	40,346	41,675	50,441	57,077
Lincoln County, North Carolina	44,334	31,964	32,429	41,277	65,845	71,275
Mecklenburg County, North Carolina	43,387	24,627	30,170	36,397	58,669	75,772
Moore County, North Carolina	38,721	21,328	31,378	31,709	50,308	71,993
Nash County, North Carolina	35,974	38,320	34,573	30,330	48,015	30,629
New Hanover County, North Carolina	38,179	20,531	26,337	34,000	46,158	61,778
Onslow County, North Carolina	32,969	21,473	30,112	31,461	45,082	57,101
Orange County, North Carolina	46,099	26,613	29,242	35,101	46,549	71,603
Pitt County, North Carolina	37,242	17,167	28,925	35,268	52,013	58,514
Randolph County, North Carolina	33,473	22,013	31,188	38,144	41,789	47,388
Robeson County, North Carolina	30,782	28,452	28,271	26,831	45,499	53,113
Rockingham County, North Carolina	31,756	23,203	28,015	39,858	49,547	37,211
Rowan County, North Carolina	36,568	19,268	34,581	38,567	41,724	64,346
Rutherford County, North Carolina	33,694	30,870	26,241	31,004	51,049	65,293
Surry County, North Carolina	34,665	23,527	26,234	36,642	45,072	49,715
Union County, North Carolina	46,995	30,683	35,394	41,715	56,023	99,665
Wake County, North Carolina	50,840	21,995	30,868	40,158	64,951	77,743
Wayne County, North Carolina	31,944	19,343	30,229	32,429	37,840	56,165
Wilkes County, North Carolina	31,963	21,052	30,459	31,163	52,157	64,275
Wilson County, North Carolina	35,097	31,493	39,842	25,913	41,658	61,458
NORTH DAKOTA	43,865	28,756	34,343	41,818	51,854	61,288
Burleigh County, North Dakota	48,743	30,972	36,539	42,274	52,983	81,190

Table C-2. Educational Attainment of the Population, by Selected Counties, 2019—*Continued*

(Number; percent; dollars.)

State/County	Some other race alone			Two or more races			Hispanic or Latino (of any race)		
	Total	High school graduate or more (percent)	Bachelor's degree or more (percent)	Total	High school graduate or more (percent)	Bachelor's degree or more (percent)	Total	High school graduate or more (percent)	Bachelor's degree or more (percent)
NORTH DAKOTA—(*Continued*)									
Cass County, North Dakota	N	N	N	N	N	N	2,495	100.0	29.5
Grand Forks County, North Dakota	N	N	N	N	N	N	N	N	N
Ward County, North Dakota	N	N	N	N	N	N	N	N	N
OHIO	71,858	70.2	16.2	126,022	88.4	25.2	247,310	76.1	20.2
Allen County, Ohio	N	N	N	N	N	N	1,789	76.9	15.0
Ashtabula County, Ohio	N	N	N	N	N	N	N	N	N
Athens County, Ohio	N	N	N	N	N	N	N	N	N
Belmont County, Ohio	N	N	N	N	N	N	N	N	N
Butler County, Ohio	N	N	N	2,952	90.8	36.6	8,306	66.5	21.5
Clark County, Ohio	N	N	N	N	N	N	1,868	77.7	25.7
Clermont County, Ohio	N	N	N	N	N	N	2,157	83.8	36.1
Columbiana County, Ohio	N	N	N	N	N	N	N	N	N
Cuyahoga County, Ohio	12,963	69.4	14.0	13,076	91.1	27.4	44,421	73.4	16.9
Delaware County, Ohio	N	N	N	N	N	N	3,194	98.9	51.3
Erie County, Ohio	N	N	N	N	N	N	N	N	N
Fairfield County, Ohio	N	N	N	N	N	N	N	N	N
Franklin County, Ohio	15,672	67.9	16.6	20,445	90.9	40.2	37,985	73.7	27.7
Geauga County, Ohio	N	N	N	N	N	N	N	N	N
Greene County, Ohio	N	N	N	N	N	N	2,815	100.0	30.2
Hamilton County, Ohio	3,823	89.6	34.7	9,342	88.9	33.0	13,884	78.5	31.9
Hancock County, Ohio	N	N	N	N	N	N	2,275	71.4	10.0
Jefferson County, Ohio	N	N	N	N	N	N	N	N	N
Lake County, Ohio	N	N	N	N	N	N	5,167	64.6	10.9
Licking County, Ohio	N	N	N	N	N	N	N	N	N
Lorain County, Ohio	N	N	N	4,624	89.8	13.7	18,159	72.7	12.6
Lucas County, Ohio	4,676	58.0	13.8	6,916	77.9	14.1	16,281	79.7	14.9
Mahoning County, Ohio	N	N	N	2,782	85.0	12.4	8,402	64.9	10.5
Marion County, Ohio	N	N	N	N	N	N	N	N	N
Medina County, Ohio	N	N	N	N	N	N	2,209	83.9	29.7
Miami County, Ohio	N	N	N	N	N	N	N	N	N
Montgomery County, Ohio	4,324	68.8	14.0	7,834	86.1	17.8	8,553	65.8	15.3
Muskingum County, Ohio	N	N	N	N	N	N	N	N	N
Portage County, Ohio	N	N	N	N	N	N	N	N	N
Richland County, Ohio	N	N	N	N	N	N	N	N	N
Ross County, Ohio	N	N	N	1,386	95.7	10.4	N	N	N
Scioto County, Ohio	N	N	N	N	N	N	N	N	N
Stark County, Ohio	N	N	N	4,104	79.9	13.9	4,415	78.3	30.9
Summit County, Ohio	N	N	N	6,533	82.4	25.3	6,593	83.0	31.0
Trumbull County, Ohio	N	N	N	N	N	N	1,838	93.5	19.9
Tuscarawas County, Ohio	N	N	N	N	N	N	N	N	N
Warren County, Ohio	N	N	N	N	N	N	3,864	90.1	40.6
Wayne County, Ohio	N	N	N	N	N	N	N	N	N
Wood County, Ohio	N	N	N	N	N	N	3,803	77.4	25.5
OKLAHOMA	51,498	55.4	8.3	139,026	89.3	23.3	215,930	63.2	12.0
Canadian County, Oklahoma	N	N	N	3,102	83.9	20.8	7,515	50.0	15.1
Cleveland County, Oklahoma	N	N	N	8,054	94.5	30.5	13,586	78.5	27.8
Comanche County, Oklahoma	N	N	N	6,365	80.4	4.5	8,706	91.4	17.7
Creek County, Oklahoma	N	N	N	2,101	88.6	12.9	1,861	78.3	3.2
Muskogee County, Oklahoma	N	N	N	3,420	85.0	26.4	2,432	72.0	8.1
Oklahoma County, Oklahoma	13,369	53.3	6.7	20,338	92.7	33.1	68,273	55.4	11.9
Payne County, Oklahoma	N	N	N	2,071	91.5	22.4	N	N	N
Pottawatomie County, Oklahoma	N	N	N	1,383	97.3	16.8	1,839	80.2	9.6
Rogers County, Oklahoma	N	N	N	4,614	94.8	22.6	2,397	74.3	20.4
Tulsa County, Oklahoma	9,773	55.5	9.9	22,380	90.2	31.0	42,020	65.8	12.0
Wagoner County, Oklahoma	N	N	N	3,371	92.9	20.1	2,901	72.6	10.3
OREGON	85,411	62.5	12.5	103,053	91.4	32.6	301,623	68.9	16.0
Benton County, Oregon	N	N	N	N	N	N	3,223	78.2	34.4
Clackamas County, Oregon	6,641	72.0	18.3	7,879	93.7	37.0	20,450	70.8	17.3
Deschutes County, Oregon	N	N	N	3,311	100.0	23.3	8,788	79.0	18.6
Douglas County, Oregon	N	N	N	3,366	87.9	3.5	3,757	83.9	13.8
Jackson County, Oregon	N	N	N	N	N	N	15,139	65.8	19.0
Josephine County, Oregon	N	N	N	N	N	N	3,808	73.3	11.0
Klamath County, Oregon	N	N	N	N	N	N	4,981	76.0	12.2
Lane County, Oregon	7,579	69.5	12.0	9,603	94.5	38.4	18,720	81.5	20.0

Table C-2. Educational Attainment of the Population, by Selected Counties, 2019—*Continued*

(Number; percent; dollars.)

State/County	Median earnings in the past 12 months (2019 inflation-adjusted dollars)					
	Population 25 years and over with earnings					
	Total	Less than high school graduate	High school graduate (includes equivalency)	Some college or associate's degree	Bachelor's degree	Graduate or professional degree
NORTH DAKOTA—(*Continued*)						
Cass County, North Dakota	42,886	22,929	27,631	39,653	53,592	55,753
Grand Forks County, North Dakota	44,516	87,905	32,848	42,449	50,192	57,830
Ward County, North Dakota	46,545	17,361	40,388	42,862	50,361	71,536
OHIO	40,586	24,836	31,514	36,821	53,680	71,180
Allen County, Ohio	37,012	26,123	30,039	41,131	43,810	69,223
Ashtabula County, Ohio	31,872	31,610	26,511	34,978	48,163	69,847
Athens County, Ohio	37,683	30,177	30,985	34,697	35,982	70,868
Belmont County, Ohio	30,820	14,764	27,068	34,375	50,148	54,909
Butler County, Ohio	46,153	22,791	36,841	40,299	61,760	76,352
Clark County, Ohio	34,627	22,497	30,091	35,944	50,948	65,441
Clermont County, Ohio	43,594	30,735	39,425	38,405	57,115	73,797
Columbiana County, Ohio	33,635	30,875	29,063	31,473	46,017	53,339
Cuyahoga County, Ohio	40,833	22,151	29,783	35,697	55,167	72,195
Delaware County, Ohio	60,417	23,578	31,222	48,750	81,231	89,118
Erie County, Ohio	34,291	17,646	31,502	34,238	43,568	47,845
Fairfield County, Ohio	42,343	20,167	31,938	41,724	51,653	76,261
Franklin County, Ohio	42,185	23,467	30,300	36,591	53,623	72,582
Geauga County, Ohio	46,392	41,367	30,875	40,922	60,009	81,676
Greene County, Ohio	42,469	17,170	33,236	35,149	50,659	82,158
Hamilton County, Ohio	42,359	24,016	31,302	36,605	54,891	76,541
Hancock County, Ohio	42,919	22,400	36,863	36,988	55,790	74,093
Jefferson County, Ohio	36,181	18,848	30,983	35,164	46,005	52,184
Lake County, Ohio	41,973	26,826	31,667	40,958	59,189	70,475
Licking County, Ohio	42,100	30,163	34,367	40,158	58,060	70,929
Lorain County, Ohio	41,403	21,661	31,486	41,361	60,290	57,374
Lucas County, Ohio	36,709	20,573	30,360	35,014	50,447	67,366
Mahoning County, Ohio	36,223	23,416	29,639	34,545	48,199	64,835
Marion County, Ohio	33,013	19,340	26,241	36,036	47,248	72,891
Medina County, Ohio	51,094	38,699	32,488	47,448	65,632	81,330
Miami County, Ohio	39,149	30,731	34,290	35,099	57,475	73,513
Montgomery County, Ohio	37,269	21,954	31,076	32,235	52,262	72,538
Muskingum County, Ohio	32,397	25,540	25,158	31,937	55,920	45,915
Portage County, Ohio	39,307	28,760	31,376	39,001	45,848	61,015
Richland County, Ohio	33,847	21,646	30,678	31,964	45,536	56,149
Ross County, Ohio	36,745	29,811	31,098	36,039	48,299	55,236
Scioto County, Ohio	40,067	27,160	31,907	35,896	55,554	61,115
Stark County, Ohio	37,030	26,095	31,676	34,314	52,568	72,671
Summit County, Ohio	39,075	25,867	31,105	34,973	56,021	66,905
Trumbull County, Ohio	36,154	24,664	31,233	35,715	42,299	60,998
Tuscarawas County, Ohio	35,559	40,115	31,745	28,100	52,575	61,405
Warren County, Ohio	54,825	32,050	35,110	50,094	67,400	88,781
Wayne County, Ohio	36,410	38,445	30,796	35,571	41,276	64,138
Wood County, Ohio	43,207	20,692	32,468	40,579	51,998	68,103
OKLAHOMA	38,088	24,760	31,766	35,955	47,828	61,092
Canadian County, Oklahoma	41,984	20,479	37,103	42,069	53,024	56,344
Cleveland County, Oklahoma	43,873	23,280	36,472	41,184	48,881	62,058
Comanche County, Oklahoma	31,262	16,559	28,205	32,165	30,639	41,582
Creek County, Oklahoma	37,012	29,726	34,455	35,546	42,510	59,900
Muskogee County, Oklahoma	35,436	26,842	30,632	30,905	41,678	56,356
Oklahoma County, Oklahoma	39,867	23,162	31,112	36,008	51,239	75,360
Payne County, Oklahoma	31,076	21,775	26,767	22,310	46,604	31,267
Pottawatomie County, Oklahoma	37,545	27,888	36,314	35,795	41,878	54,247
Rogers County, Oklahoma	41,547	34,375	36,379	41,643	44,521	62,287
Tulsa County, Oklahoma	40,223	25,504	32,074	35,708	50,557	64,958
Wagoner County, Oklahoma	42,936	37,885	36,672	42,310	50,910	60,595
OREGON	40,774	27,408	31,451	36,817	52,498	70,854
Benton County, Oregon	42,203	25,651	31,797	35,004	44,131	62,347
Clackamas County, Oregon	46,863	31,819	35,803	45,032	63,440	76,233
Deschutes County, Oregon	37,262	25,530	30,988	34,361	46,929	65,654
Douglas County, Oregon	31,578	27,687	28,160	30,778	49,616	55,133
Jackson County, Oregon	33,544	25,671	30,539	31,739	49,722	60,697
Josephine County, Oregon	30,097	30,089	21,942	29,392	38,506	73,322
Klamath County, Oregon	34,915	21,756	30,738	30,588	53,508	50,500
Lane County, Oregon	36,380	22,316	31,599	33,815	45,910	57,813

Table C-2. Educational Attainment of the Population, by Selected Counties, 2019—*Continued*

(Number; percent; dollars.)

	Educational attainment by race/ethnicity, 25 years and over								
	Some other race alone			Two or more races			Hispanic or Latino (of any race)		
State/County	Total	High school graduate or more (percent)	Bachelor's degree or more (percent)	Total	High school graduate or more (percent)	Bachelor's degree or more (percent)	Total	High school graduate or more (percent)	Bachelor's degree or more (percent)
OREGON—(*Continued*)									
Linn County, Oregon	N	N	N	3,836	73.5	19.2	6,314	66.8	12.0
Marion County, Oregon	15,533	44.9	10.5	10,173	84.0	27.4	47,637	61.2	11.5
Multnomah County, Oregon	12,769	61.8	18.1	23,516	96.2	45.2	56,205	67.6	24.7
Polk County, Oregon	N	N	N	N	N	N	5,897	80.6	26.3
Umatilla County, Oregon	N	N	N	1,765	94.2	16.3	11,167	71.2	11.5
Washington County, Oregon	20,176	72.9	12.0	13,547	91.2	43.0	55,160	73.5	13.2
Yamhill County, Oregon	N	N	N	N	N	N	10,132	56.9	11.2
PENNSYLVANIA	196,555	63.1	10.8	131,353	88.7	30.4	544,225	72.9	16.5
Adams County, Pennsylvania	N	N	N	N	N	N	3,528	60.9	1.7
Allegheny County, Pennsylvania	4,596	81.2	31.5	14,129	90.4	39.8	16,434	88.0	46.6
Armstrong County, Pennsylvania	N	N	N	N	N	N	N	N	N
Beaver County, Pennsylvania	N	N	N	N	N	N	1,845	71.8	17.5
Berks County, Pennsylvania	20,103	69.0	18.8	3,685	73.7	15.1	49,004	71.8	15.8
Blair County, Pennsylvania	N	N	N	N	N	N	N	N	N
Bucks County, Pennsylvania	7,674	54.0	9.2	6,001	94.7	32.1	21,018	72.1	17.5
Butler County, Pennsylvania	N	N	N	N	N	N	N	N	N
Cambria County, Pennsylvania	N	N	N	N	N	N	N	N	N
Carbon County, Pennsylvania	N	N	N	N	N	N	2,009	80.5	22.6
Centre County, Pennsylvania	N	N	N	N	N	N	2,891	90.7	66.7
Chester County, Pennsylvania	8,396	47.4	16.4	5,687	97.5	48.5	20,540	62.8	28.6
Clearfield County, Pennsylvania	N	N	N	N	N	N	N	N	N
Columbia County, Pennsylvania	N	N	N	N	N	N	N	N	N
Crawford County, Pennsylvania	N	N	N	N	N	N	N	N	N
Cumberland County, Pennsylvania	N	N	N	3,485	93.7	22.6	6,121	87.2	24.0
Dauphin County, Pennsylvania	N	N	N	3,383	95.3	29.3	13,499	77.0	18.1
Delaware County, Pennsylvania	4,543	63.8	20.7	5,508	95.8	34.4	12,208	76.8	24.0
Erie County, Pennsylvania	N	N	N	3,437	77.1	23.2	6,040	59.2	19.8
Fayette County, Pennsylvania	N	N	N	N	N	N	N	N	N
Franklin County, Pennsylvania	N	N	N	N	N	N	5,051	80.3	13.2
Indiana County, Pennsylvania	N	N	N	N	N	N	N	N	N
Lackawanna County, Pennsylvania	N	N	N	N	N	N	9,144	76.8	10.9
Lancaster County, Pennsylvania	9,615	65.0	4.6	6,762	77.9	26.6	32,346	72.5	12.0
Lawrence County, Pennsylvania	N	N	N	N	N	N	N	N	N
Lebanon County, Pennsylvania	5,409	61.3	4.7	N	N	N	10,334	64.2	8.0
Lehigh County, Pennsylvania	9,720	75.3	12.0	4,464	87.6	24.4	52,780	79.1	11.8
Luzerne County, Pennsylvania	9,983	65.3	9.4	2,552	90.5	22.6	22,314	70.9	9.3
Lycoming County, Pennsylvania	N	N	N	N	N	N	N	N	N
Mercer County, Pennsylvania	N	N	N	N	N	N	N	N	N
Monroe County, Pennsylvania	N	N	N	N	N	N	17,076	84.4	21.4
Montgomery County, Pennsylvania	5,183	72.5	16.4	7,209	97.2	50.9	24,592	79.6	29.4
Northampton County, Pennsylvania	7,781	60.7	6.8	3,790	89.9	42.3	24,292	77.9	15.2
Northumberland County, Pennsylvania	N	N	N	N	N	N	2,092	66.6	1.5
Philadelphia County, Pennsylvania	75,690	59.5	6.6	25,128	87.7	31.3	135,692	66.9	13.1
Schuylkill County, Pennsylvania	N	N	N	N	N	N	3,871	64.1	11.8
Somerset County, Pennsylvania	N	N	N	N	N	N	N	N	N
Washington County, Pennsylvania	N	N	N	N	N	N	N	N	N
Westmoreland County, Pennsylvania	N	N	N	N	N	N	2,403	81.9	31.8
York County, Pennsylvania	5,656	59.3	9.4	4,875	87.1	18.2	18,494	64.0	6.6
RHODE ISLAND	36,544	66.2	10.5	18,859	81.8	30.6	97,435	70.9	14.4
Kent County, Rhode Island	N	N	N	N	N	N	5,362	69.3	18.3
Newport County, Rhode Island	N	N	N	N	N	N	N	N	N
Providence County, Rhode Island	32,347	64.8	9.0	14,240	78.9	26.3	85,822	69.2	12.5
Washington County, Rhode Island	N	N	N	N	N	N	N	N	N
SOUTH CAROLINA	60,585	53.4	12.3	42,843	89.5	29.5	157,206	65.8	18.0
Aiken County, South Carolina	N	N	N	N	N	N	N	N	N
Anderson County, South Carolina	N	N	N	N	N	N	4,123	66.5	8.9
Beaufort County, South Carolina	N	N	N	N	N	N	11,079	69.3	14.0
Berkeley County, South Carolina	6,321	70.6	7.3	3,265	93.9	32.6	8,295	78.2	17.4
Charleston County, South Carolina	6,721	44.3	11.4	4,440	95.6	46.6	11,547	62.2	25.2
Darlington County, South Carolina	N	N	N	N	N	N	N	N	N
Dorchester County, South Carolina	N	N	N	N	N	N	5,526	47.7	20.7
Florence County, South Carolina	N	N	N	N	N	N	N	N	N
Greenville County, South Carolina	10,823	48.1	12.8	4,983	76.2	29.1	27,064	67.1	18.8

Table C-2. Educational Attainment of the Population, by Selected Counties, 2019—*Continued*

(Number; percent; dollars.)

State/County	Median earnings in the past 12 months (2019 inflation-adjusted dollars)					
	Population 25 years and over with earnings					
	Total	Less than high school graduate	High school graduate (includes equivalency)	Some college or associate's degree	Bachelor's degree	Graduate or professional degree
OREGON—*(Continued)*						
Linn County, Oregon	36,617	36,875	31,210	40,432	35,547	53,144
Marion County, Oregon	36,479	30,186	27,162	36,317	46,955	66,867
Multnomah County, Oregon	44,774	25,963	30,649	38,351	56,185	72,163
Polk County, Oregon	47,578	34,280	41,280	48,131	42,216	67,855
Umatilla County, Oregon	35,009	30,906	31,398	36,381	35,384	67,022
Washington County, Oregon	50,470	30,087	33,974	41,452	62,431	92,322
Yamhill County, Oregon	41,587	29,099	34,451	40,854	60,415	70,653
PENNSYLVANIA	42,229	26,343	32,567	39,075	55,326	73,805
Adams County, Pennsylvania	38,664	30,944	32,124	40,076	46,494	75,982
Allegheny County, Pennsylvania	47,309	22,066	32,366	39,998	56,870	73,404
Armstrong County, Pennsylvania	38,686	22,006	33,125	38,189	51,644	71,607
Beaver County, Pennsylvania	40,788	21,266	33,497	37,755	52,491	65,452
Berks County, Pennsylvania	41,642	31,090	36,526	40,274	53,943	67,762
Blair County, Pennsylvania	36,169	26,198	30,868	36,385	46,075	71,344
Bucks County, Pennsylvania	54,742	40,270	40,514	48,300	65,776	85,210
Butler County, Pennsylvania	46,945	25,534	35,693	41,397	62,342	80,328
Cambria County, Pennsylvania	36,635	22,197	30,307	36,005	47,254	62,677
Carbon County, Pennsylvania	38,280	12,743	38,497	36,525	45,957	71,331
Centre County, Pennsylvania	41,638	27,389	31,173	35,066	46,842	63,963
Chester County, Pennsylvania	60,112	31,022	37,073	45,623	74,874	100,597
Clearfield County, Pennsylvania	33,901	19,207	28,971	35,762	41,488	56,923
Columbia County, Pennsylvania	37,498	20,333	29,852	36,561	52,206	75,634
Crawford County, Pennsylvania	36,218	26,958	30,354	36,641	47,939	65,304
Cumberland County, Pennsylvania	48,681	31,104	35,961	41,344	61,082	74,262
Dauphin County, Pennsylvania	41,439	27,049	31,059	40,355	53,413	66,067
Delaware County, Pennsylvania	49,038	22,290	35,143	41,870	59,643	86,197
Erie County, Pennsylvania	36,145	18,268	30,790	31,961	45,989	59,256
Fayette County, Pennsylvania	37,192	19,983	32,189	37,080	51,052	71,158
Franklin County, Pennsylvania	39,827	35,175	35,000	40,982	45,791	61,785
Indiana County, Pennsylvania	36,603	33,840	34,053	37,529	32,157	52,243
Lackawanna County, Pennsylvania	37,485	20,867	30,878	31,936	49,180	62,105
Lancaster County, Pennsylvania	41,166	38,135	35,716	37,550	50,465	65,144
Lawrence County, Pennsylvania	37,178	20,654	30,080	36,455	51,589	64,225
Lebanon County, Pennsylvania	40,352	21,148	39,825	36,909	53,126	67,685
Lehigh County, Pennsylvania	39,142	25,371	33,720	35,500	56,976	81,558
Luzerne County, Pennsylvania	37,275	27,870	30,690	37,882	52,097	70,319
Lycoming County, Pennsylvania	35,823	26,548	31,378	34,079	42,542	67,044
Mercer County, Pennsylvania	37,875	25,249	31,250	35,064	53,420	63,669
Monroe County, Pennsylvania	40,822	31,551	37,313	37,307	46,186	74,820
Montgomery County, Pennsylvania	55,858	27,412	37,119	45,616	66,658	85,272
Northampton County, Pennsylvania	44,202	26,998	36,054	42,141	55,263	77,426
Northumberland County, Pennsylvania	35,941	30,486	30,753	35,527	52,004	58,969
Philadelphia County, Pennsylvania	37,417	22,981	28,214	33,318	50,803	68,897
Schuylkill County, Pennsylvania	40,153	27,289	36,019	36,798	51,380	66,549
Somerset County, Pennsylvania	36,254	20,617	34,774	32,435	52,368	47,798
Washington County, Pennsylvania	43,723	19,629	35,701	38,826	58,895	68,582
Westmoreland County, Pennsylvania	41,467	20,279	31,741	39,441	52,239	66,895
York County, Pennsylvania	44,329	23,852	36,667	42,427	59,943	72,119
RHODE ISLAND	46,060	31,893	36,883	40,363	57,398	76,827
Kent County, Rhode Island	48,861	37,543	37,200	45,507	60,289	77,072
Newport County, Rhode Island	49,528	31,702	35,713	36,748	61,084	81,230
Providence County, Rhode Island	42,421	31,869	36,635	40,002	54,150	71,118
Washington County, Rhode Island	51,243	30,801	38,960	36,781	60,927	84,862
SOUTH CAROLINA	37,727	23,085	30,592	35,994	50,734	60,788
Aiken County, South Carolina	38,396	20,226	31,929	37,843	45,853	76,167
Anderson County, South Carolina	35,251	25,175	31,298	33,390	40,836	72,240
Beaufort County, South Carolina	37,925	23,150	30,084	35,164	50,913	66,560
Berkeley County, South Carolina	41,525	30,220	36,838	40,796	52,102	59,563
Charleston County, South Carolina	47,671	18,115	31,278	41,226	58,547	73,768
Darlington County, South Carolina	33,974	23,019	31,190	32,373	60,075	47,549
Dorchester County, South Carolina	41,375	27,571	36,767	39,962	50,962	66,462
Florence County, South Carolina	35,775	21,040	30,176	30,710	55,656	60,079
Greenville County, South Carolina	41,166	22,214	30,517	39,275	53,726	66,498

Table C-2. Educational Attainment of the Population, by Selected Counties, 2019—*Continued*

(Number; percent; dollars.)

State/County	Educational attainment by race/ethnicity, 25 years and over								
	Some other race alone			Two or more races			Hispanic or Latino (of any race)		
	Total	High school graduate or more (percent)	Bachelor's degree or more (percent)	Total	High school graduate or more (percent)	Bachelor's degree or more (percent)	Total	High school graduate or more (percent)	Bachelor's degree or more (percent)
SOUTH CAROLINA—(*Continued*)									
Greenwood County, South Carolina	N	N	N	N	N	N	N	N	N
Horry County, South Carolina	N	N	N	2,732	97.5	37.4	11,815	50.2	12.3
Kershaw County, South Carolina	N	N	N	N	N	N	N	N	N
Lancaster County, South Carolina	N	N	N	N	N	N	N	N	N
Laurens County, South Carolina	N	N	N	N	N	N	N	N	N
Lexington County, South Carolina	N	N	N	2,140	84.3	9.2	9,805	55.2	11.4
Oconee County, South Carolina	N	N	N	N	N	N	2,713	58.8	23.5
Orangeburg County, South Carolina	N	N	N	N	N	N	N	N	N
Pickens County, South Carolina	N	N	N	N	N	N	2,524	91.6	39.9
Richland County, South Carolina	4,690	56.7	17.4	4,241	88.4	37.3	10,841	71.1	26.3
Spartanburg County, South Carolina	2,515	64.5	4.4	2,468	86.5	26.0	11,509	64.3	14.7
Sumter County, South Carolina	N	N	N	N	N	N	N	N	N
York County, South Carolina	N	N	N	N	N	N	9,713	81.7	22.7
SOUTH DAKOTA	3,771	71.1	34.0	9,997	88.5	24.2	16,720	80.8	25.5
Minnehaha County, South Dakota	N	N	N	2,200	89.8	16.0	5,213	81.0	27.5
Pennington County, South Dakota	N	N	N	N	N	N	N	N	N
TENNESSEE	52,512	56.8	16.6	56,291	88.3	31.2	188,951	63.1	18.5
Anderson County, Tennessee	N	N	N	N	N	N	N	N	N
Blount County, Tennessee	N	N	N	N	N	N	2,693	50.8	3.9
Bradley County, Tennessee	N	N	N	N	N	N	3,929	60.3	8.4
Davidson County, Tennessee	12,108	59.5	23.5	7,587	94.5	48.5	36,785	52.4	16.2
Greene County, Tennessee	N	N	N	N	N	N	N	N	N
Hamilton County, Tennessee	N	N	N	N	N	N	10,611	66.8	30.4
Knox County, Tennessee	N	N	N	4,384	94.9	28.3	10,828	63.0	22.1
Madison County, Tennessee	N	N	N	N	N	N	N	N	N
Maury County, Tennessee	N	N	N	N	N	N	N	N	N
Montgomery County, Tennessee	N	N	N	5,341	94.4	33.4	10,672	89.9	23.0
Putnam County, Tennessee	N	N	N	N	N	N	N	N	N
Robertson County, Tennessee	N	N	N	N	N	N	2,649	75.5	19.0
Rutherford County, Tennessee	N	N	N	N	N	N	13,629	74.7	27.4
Sevier County, Tennessee	N	N	N	N	N	N	N	N	N
Shelby County, Tennessee	10,554	45.6	16.8	7,211	82.3	31.7	28,935	55.1	15.7
Sullivan County, Tennessee	N	N	N	N	N	N	1,758	65.3	26.9
Sumner County, Tennessee	N	N	N	N	N	N	5,182	60.1	21.8
Washington County, Tennessee	N	N	N	N	N	N	N	N	N
Williamson County, Tennessee	N	N	N	N	N	N	6,564	90.1	29.7
Wilson County, Tennessee	N	N	N	N	N	N	N	N	N
TEXAS	1,030,092	62.0	12.7	357,572	88.3	33.4	6,538,918	68.3	16.1
Angelina County, Texas	N	N	N	N	N	N	10,259	60.6	15.8
Bastrop County, Texas	10,203	58.6	2.1	N	N	N	18,249	62.6	9.1
Bell County, Texas	6,606	81.4	19.2	6,875	98.2	19.9	49,184	81.1	21.4
Bexar County, Texas	88,402	71.4	16.2	37,674	88.2	34.1	737,436	76.4	18.0
Bowie County, Texas	N	N	N	N	N	N	4,002	65.9	4.2
Brazoria County, Texas	7,469	56.9	6.0	N	N	N	67,173	75.4	14.8
Brazos County, Texas	N	N	N	N	N	N	29,544	69.3	14.5
Cameron County, Texas	9,705	53.4	7.5	2,404	60.6	6.5	218,424	65.2	14.6
Collin County, Texas	14,664	82.9	25.5	11,488	96.1	54.0	89,714	75.9	27.2
Comal County, Texas	N	N	N	N	N	N	25,948	86.0	37.9
Coryell County, Texas	N	N	N	4,330	80.8	5.6	8,156	77.8	14.5
Dallas County, Texas	111,295	51.7	10.0	32,644	90.9	38.0	582,360	56.9	11.5
Denton County, Texas	11,318	68.9	21.6	13,642	87.2	41.0	97,389	74.7	27.7
Ector County, Texas	10,273	67.1	2.8	N	N	N	56,724	65.6	9.0
Ellis County, Texas	4,925	55.6	8.0	N	N	N	26,715	67.5	8.9
El Paso County, Texas	61,286	67.0	13.5	10,034	87.2	17.7	423,740	76.4	20.0
Fort Bend County, Texas	21,054	61.5	17.7	9,802	94.7	48.1	117,309	74.3	25.6
Galveston County, Texas	3,493	70.9	13.6	3,804	89.9	31.0	50,408	77.1	14.9
Grayson County, Texas	N	N	N	N	N	N	9,182	59.3	8.6
Gregg County, Texas	N	N	N	N	N	N	12,015	63.6	10.2
Guadalupe County, Texas	3,626	80.3	4.3	N	N	N	38,537	76.9	16.9
Harris County, Texas	263,937	59.9	13.1	59,692	90.9	37.2	1,168,898	64.3	15.3
Harrison County, Texas	N	N	N	N	N	N	4,124	58.3	2.6
Hays County, Texas	4,030	88.9	8.6	N	N	N	50,600	80.3	17.0
Henderson County, Texas	N	N	N	N	N	N	5,609	59.9	5.2
Hidalgo County, Texas	66,058	54.9	16.4	6,308	65.0	20.2	444,385	65.1	17.1

Table C-2. Educational Attainment of the Population, by Selected Counties, 2019—*Continued*

(Number; percent; dollars.)

State/County	Median earnings in the past 12 months (2019 inflation-adjusted dollars)					
	Population 25 years and over with earnings					
	Total	Less than high school graduate	High school graduate (includes equivalency)	Some college or associate's degree	Bachelor's degree	Graduate or professional degree
SOUTH CAROLINA—(*Continued*)						
Greenwood County, South Carolina	31,296	17,358	27,808	32,363	38,622	45,849
Horry County, South Carolina	31,495	20,575	26,234	33,407	40,576	51,198
Kershaw County, South Carolina	40,016	29,010	35,708	35,584	47,957	55,973
Lancaster County, South Carolina	39,221	28,741	30,476	36,607	68,602	65,095
Laurens County, South Carolina	34,515	27,897	31,202	40,151	43,817	47,385
Lexington County, South Carolina	41,330	27,870	31,811	39,782	55,268	61,097
Oconee County, South Carolina	32,916	27,752	29,444	30,189	39,743	66,183
Orangeburg County, South Carolina	30,600	16,393	29,468	26,877	36,345	50,339
Pickens County, South Carolina	36,554	24,399	31,262	35,068	45,308	50,952
Richland County, South Carolina	39,536	17,349	26,986	32,232	46,698	57,106
Spartanburg County, South Carolina	37,404	28,618	31,903	36,253	50,523	55,117
Sumter County, South Carolina	35,355	23,687	31,885	32,065	50,203	52,634
York County, South Carolina	42,777	25,479	31,772	38,518	59,541	70,211
SOUTH DAKOTA	38,646	22,131	31,306	36,732	47,630	57,244
Minnehaha County, South Dakota	41,616	19,373	31,877	40,612	51,315	59,952
Pennington County, South Dakota	32,422	20,968	30,170	35,214	36,069	62,931
TENNESSEE	37,610	25,365	30,596	35,518	50,633	62,832
Anderson County, Tennessee	32,595	26,555	30,492	31,977	42,600	56,330
Blount County, Tennessee	38,238	24,110	34,179	36,655	51,808	49,530
Bradley County, Tennessee	34,014	24,951	28,461	32,528	47,871	61,417
Davidson County, Tennessee	42,293	26,731	29,168	36,924	52,211	63,017
Greene County, Tennessee	32,848	21,934	28,701	32,017	35,122	65,247
Hamilton County, Tennessee	38,230	25,085	26,129	34,137	52,356	62,633
Knox County, Tennessee	41,264	24,946	29,676	36,791	50,782	63,506
Madison County, Tennessee	36,294	27,516	30,660	36,493	47,764	51,372
Maury County, Tennessee	40,296	22,867	35,068	39,005	52,097	54,916
Montgomery County, Tennessee	39,079	13,574	33,597	36,155	41,419	64,435
Putnam County, Tennessee	34,158	20,935	29,768	33,866	41,042	60,096
Robertson County, Tennessee	40,050	36,044	32,388	37,362	49,203	70,359
Rutherford County, Tennessee	40,254	30,668	32,265	39,678	43,400	61,092
Sevier County, Tennessee	30,861	21,482	28,683	30,414	36,101	61,888
Shelby County, Tennessee	37,249	22,547	28,434	32,152	50,847	72,327
Sullivan County, Tennessee	35,078	22,019	27,535	32,610	46,629	61,321
Sumner County, Tennessee	41,933	28,795	36,747	39,491	56,032	65,479
Washington County, Tennessee	36,786	28,102	27,205	36,001	45,111	75,405
Williamson County, Tennessee	62,369	24,954	36,803	37,446	76,242	90,794
Wilson County, Tennessee	44,667	31,085	33,523	41,675	52,075	61,372
TEXAS	40,895	25,282	31,234	38,121	56,853	72,195
Angelina County, Texas	31,923	20,532	24,342	27,407	46,237	65,939
Bastrop County, Texas	32,468	21,823	30,818	34,962	45,350	52,310
Bell County, Texas	37,350	22,279	30,257	35,393	51,254	66,985
Bexar County, Texas	36,408	23,458	30,116	34,745	54,516	66,759
Bowie County, Texas	38,240	22,179	34,105	40,221	46,068	59,219
Brazoria County, Texas	56,331	31,577	42,178	50,987	71,627	86,146
Brazos County, Texas	39,408	24,274	32,392	32,516	47,606	65,999
Cameron County, Texas	26,953	17,834	26,405	28,040	46,324	61,143
Collin County, Texas	57,676	27,029	32,498	46,454	70,192	91,222
Comal County, Texas	51,229	23,315	35,348	49,204	63,666	60,418
Coryell County, Texas	32,357	22,643	31,062	32,849	39,338	62,213
Dallas County, Texas	40,190	27,069	30,001	38,386	60,265	74,212
Denton County, Texas	52,065	30,121	35,222	47,134	62,997	80,442
Ector County, Texas	45,199	29,139	46,905	42,463	52,286	65,322
Ellis County, Texas	42,319	29,182	38,415	45,240	56,072	71,662
El Paso County, Texas	31,720	16,872	26,133	30,514	48,339	60,270
Fort Bend County, Texas	51,711	29,714	32,308	41,290	70,017	100,713
Galveston County, Texas	50,284	29,674	32,125	45,227	61,059	71,434
Grayson County, Texas	35,465	21,210	30,299	40,039	49,643	56,369
Gregg County, Texas	36,463	22,295	32,647	36,334	47,497	57,468
Guadalupe County, Texas	39,285	24,984	30,500	40,817	57,289	60,413
Harris County, Texas	40,668	26,176	30,816	37,118	58,758	75,616
Harrison County, Texas	42,312	21,659	34,361	51,140	60,289	75,654
Hays County, Texas	41,585	28,976	37,274	35,444	55,273	60,303
Henderson County, Texas	31,909	28,053	30,465	39,835	38,643	52,329
Hidalgo County, Texas	26,683	18,186	22,172	29,903	42,751	58,895

Table C-2. Educational Attainment of the Population, by Selected Counties, 2019—*Continued*

(Number; percent; dollars.)

	Educational attainment by race/ethnicity, 25 years and over								
	Some other race alone			Two or more races			Hispanic or Latino (of any race)		
State/County	Total	High school graduate or more (percent)	Bachelor's degree or more (percent)	Total	High school graduate or more (percent)	Bachelor's degree or more (percent)	Total	High school graduate or more (percent)	Bachelor's degree or more (percent)
TEXAS—*(Continued)*									
Hunt County, Texas	N	N	N	N	N	N	7,869	56.0	5.1
Jefferson County, Texas	N	N	N	N	N	N	30,344	53.1	5.2
Johnson County, Texas	N	N	N	N	N	N	21,184	64.6	8.7
Kaufman County, Texas	2,154	41.1	0.0	N	N	N	15,311	63.5	10.3
Liberty County, Texas	N	N	N	N	N	N	12,172	51.5	4.6
Lubbock County, Texas	12,491	69.8	10.4	4,109	87.2	27.7	60,688	72.0	13.7
McLennan County, Texas	2,122	79.1	37.3	3,048	72.1	20.9	35,442	67.2	12.5
Midland County, Texas	16,297	71.7	13.5	N	N	N	45,278	74.2	13.8
Montgomery County, Texas	8,329	72.6	25.8	7,238	89.2	34.1	81,802	64.8	19.3
Nacogdoches County, Texas	N	N	N	N	N	N	5,872	53.3	10.8
Nueces County, Texas	5,404	83.7	12.7	N	N	N	144,259	78.2	17.0
Orange County, Texas	N	N	N	N	N	N	3,889	76.9	21.3
Parker County, Texas	N	N	N	N	N	N	9,343	61.4	18.5
Potter County, Texas	N	N	N	N	N	N	24,840	63.9	5.9
Randall County, Texas	N	N	N	N	N	N	16,843	82.7	22.9
Rockwall County, Texas	N	N	N	N	N	N	10,970	79.8	22.1
San Patricio County, Texas	N	N	N	N	N	N	23,312	72.1	9.3
Smith County, Texas	3,505	57.3	7.8	N	N	N	23,538	54.3	9.0
Tarrant County, Texas	91,818	58.6	10.7	23,568	90.8	34.2	334,745	67.1	17.0
Taylor County, Texas	4,405	82.2	15.1	N	N	N	18,171	80.7	16.0
Tom Green County, Texas	N	N	N	N	N	N	28,094	75.8	14.0
Travis County, Texas	56,198	64.7	12.8	24,842	85.4	47.2	257,335	73.4	28.0
Victoria County, Texas	N	N	N	N	N	N	24,152	71.8	9.4
Walker County, Texas	N	N	N	N	N	N	6,805	54.9	1.9
Webb County, Texas	3,685	76.8	31.3	N	N	N	146,733	64.5	18.7
Wichita County, Texas	N	N	N	N	N	N	13,874	68.9	9.9
Williamson County, Texas	6,703	92.4	21.2	8,890	92.9	44.0	84,792	83.5	24.8
Wise County, Texas	N	N	N	N	N	N	7,089	48.4	7.7
UTAH	70,693	65.9	12.0	37,008	93.7	35.2	233,666	74.8	15.6
Cache County, Utah	N	N	N	N	N	N	6,709	70.9	9.8
Davis County, Utah	3,356	90.0	18.2	3,688	98.4	38.1	17,706	81.8	16.9
Salt Lake County, Utah	48,477	63.8	10.8	16,848	95.1	35.5	114,281	73.1	16.1
Tooele County, Utah	N	N	N	N	N	N	5,449	85.5	13.2
Utah County, Utah	6,123	85.1	13.6	8,428	97.9	50.6	36,516	82.4	20.2
Washington County, Utah	N	N	N	N	N	N	9,754	78.3	11.8
Weber County, Utah	3,095	60.1	12.5	2,670	94.1	24.0	24,876	73.9	14.0
VERMONT	N	N	N	7,602	75.7	33.2	5,638	88.6	32.7
Chittenden County, Vermont	N	N	N	N	N	N	2,355	96.3	40.3
VIRGINIA	141,159	65.4	19.7	127,448	92.1	39.6	465,976	73.3	26.3
Albemarle County, Virginia	N	N	N	N	N	N	3,002	79.5	39.9
Arlington County, Virginia	5,662	70.0	25.4	6,180	100.0	80.6	24,880	73.8	42.3
Augusta County, Virginia	N	N	N	N	N	N	N	N	N
Bedford County, Virginia	N	N	N	N	N	N	N	N	N
Chesterfield County, Virginia	10,791	66.1	7.9	4,188	100.0	33.7	18,215	69.5	16.3
Fairfax County, Virginia	38,008	66.1	23.8	20,666	95.6	57.4	111,624	72.5	28.9
Fauquier County, Virginia	N	N	N	N	N	N	3,714	61.5	14.0
Frederick County, Virginia	N	N	N	N	N	N	4,618	74.1	9.3
Hanover County, Virginia	N	N	N	N	N	N	1,828	84.4	29.6
Henrico County, Virginia	N	N	N	6,773	94.1	43.7	10,792	76.1	26.3
James City County, Virginia	N	N	N	N	N	N	N	N	N
Loudoun County, Virginia	9,042	60.8	17.2	8,682	93.3	54.4	32,321	79.7	33.4
Montgomery County, Virginia	N	N	N	N	N	N	N	N	N
Prince William County, Virginia	18,325	51.5	10.9	9,982	87.6	40.7	64,797	66.9	19.7
Roanoke County, Virginia	N	N	N	N	N	N	N	N	N
Rockingham County, Virginia	N	N	N	N	N	N	3,267	65.9	10.9
Spotsylvania County, Virginia	4,286	52.7	21.6	2,505	82.4	43.0	7,864	63.1	23.7
Stafford County, Virginia	6,153	63.8	13.1	2,275	96.9	49.3	11,602	75.4	21.3
York County, Virginia	N	N	N	N	N	N	N	N	N
Alexandria city, Virginia	N	N	N	4,937	97.8	46.7	16,640	74.6	48.2
Chesapeake city, Virginia	N	N	N	N	N	N	8,648	82.0	31.1
Hampton city, Virginia	N	N	N	N	N	N	4,577	86.1	14.3
Lynchburg city, Virginia	N	N	N	N	N	N	N	N	N
Newport News city, Virginia	N	N	N	3,347	92.9	13.0	9,236	78.3	13.4
Norfolk city, Virginia	3,121	64.7	19.0	3,856	98.0	22.1	9,634	80.0	26.4

Table C-2. Educational Attainment of the Population, by Selected Counties, 2019—*Continued*

(Number; percent; dollars.)

State/County	Median earnings in the past 12 months (2019 inflation-adjusted dollars)					
	Population 25 years and over with earnings					
	Total	Less than high school graduate	High school graduate (includes equivalency)	Some college or associate's degree	Bachelor's degree	Graduate or professional degree
TEXAS—*(Continued)*						
Hunt County, Texas	40,637	27,762	30,679	45,647	51,418	71,505
Jefferson County, Texas	40,123	33,010	30,919	36,730	52,382	65,501
Johnson County, Texas	40,156	32,969	36,724	38,356	57,029	70,095
Kaufman County, Texas	43,707	31,081	37,130	49,729	51,760	60,473
Liberty County, Texas	38,934	22,986	36,901	36,338	56,376	67,203
Lubbock County, Texas	35,590	25,196	30,155	34,084	46,653	58,014
McLennan County, Texas	37,148	23,470	32,570	35,167	47,809	69,473
Midland County, Texas	47,944	20,883	40,672	44,764	55,322	65,433
Montgomery County, Texas	50,975	27,653	39,386	45,483	63,859	103,652
Nacogdoches County, Texas	35,157	25,490	27,077	31,941	39,572	62,936
Nueces County, Texas	36,551	25,159	30,814	36,593	51,845	61,938
Orange County, Texas	50,420	35,259	44,338	42,168	80,302	62,447
Parker County, Texas	42,072	27,488	36,542	41,675	60,865	82,277
Potter County, Texas	29,283	24,579	23,315	35,677	52,053	54,253
Randall County, Texas	43,722	25,622	36,376	36,589	51,762	68,683
Rockwall County, Texas	60,528	26,470	39,559	61,961	59,685	82,371
San Patricio County, Texas	36,074	22,306	29,595	37,936	51,266	50,247
Smith County, Texas	37,141	24,784	31,066	36,828	47,251	68,212
Tarrant County, Texas	44,209	28,808	32,651	41,095	58,421	75,465
Taylor County, Texas	32,994	25,275	26,885	32,158	47,458	60,609
Tom Green County, Texas	36,410	26,190	28,314	40,688	47,580	59,007
Travis County, Texas	49,891	24,257	30,836	41,850	60,241	75,785
Victoria County, Texas	37,753	15,821	34,362	40,524	51,074	60,235
Walker County, Texas	36,202	29,219	34,487	36,417	35,662	60,711
Webb County, Texas	31,866	20,111	31,143	31,533	56,976	66,974
Wichita County, Texas	32,577	23,681	29,001	31,325	46,972	59,226
Williamson County, Texas	48,119	24,493	32,795	46,511	60,211	81,444
Wise County, Texas	41,511	24,360	33,328	45,342	76,226	91,994
UTAH	41,679	28,028	34,667	37,247	51,611	76,099
Cache County, Utah	35,580	28,364	32,007	30,828	38,308	67,388
Davis County, Utah	46,616	22,396	35,801	38,393	57,531	86,548
Salt Lake County, Utah	42,350	28,523	34,787	38,925	53,617	73,832
Tooele County, Utah	50,643	30,916	49,427	45,910	51,534	76,806
Utah County, Utah	42,456	31,618	31,803	37,042	50,965	81,448
Washington County, Utah	36,873	26,549	31,299	34,638	44,223	65,375
Weber County, Utah	41,490	35,507	37,982	38,680	49,089	80,288
VERMONT	41,496	27,052	32,425	39,882	47,170	61,617
Chittenden County, Vermont	50,393	27,892	36,480	42,339	51,814	75,556
VIRGINIA	46,873	23,892	32,366	40,071	61,529	85,582
Albemarle County, Virginia	52,346	22,206	36,325	42,559	61,852	72,240
Arlington County, Virginia	80,929	22,278	30,220	50,335	82,029	105,244
Augusta County, Virginia	40,762	23,770	36,154	40,305	53,493	69,236
Bedford County, Virginia	43,089	19,685	40,777	40,156	55,698	62,042
Chesterfield County, Virginia	46,989	31,004	32,323	41,421	57,228	67,020
Fairfax County, Virginia	66,110	22,671	36,033	43,752	74,060	106,509
Fauquier County, Virginia	56,253	30,269	35,082	55,197	75,665	71,250
Frederick County, Virginia	46,068	17,354	31,970	48,402	61,434	71,135
Hanover County, Virginia	50,707	16,898	36,641	39,244	65,013	75,107
Henrico County, Virginia	43,689	25,002	32,272	37,423	60,114	71,375
James City County, Virginia	47,478	29,167	31,079	45,523	60,284	71,460
Loudoun County, Virginia	78,844	30,459	41,162	51,639	91,802	110,917
Montgomery County, Virginia	41,894	20,360	32,434	35,139	41,635	60,809
Prince William County, Virginia	52,301	26,576	38,421	48,810	69,920	90,940
Roanoke County, Virginia	47,145	21,822	35,508	42,269	57,036	71,411
Rockingham County, Virginia	38,296	27,002	33,233	40,590	47,542	57,276
Spotsylvania County, Virginia	49,291	23,850	35,834	48,709	65,264	76,061
Stafford County, Virginia	53,538	26,697	41,602	47,084	57,495	96,483
York County, Virginia	55,325	34,203	30,654	51,595	60,229	82,163
Alexandria city, Virginia	69,273	28,263	27,652	35,403	72,005	102,278
Chesapeake city, Virginia	44,290	21,101	35,967	41,195	55,410	74,792
Hampton city, Virginia	38,388	21,507	30,782	39,242	48,439	56,189
Lynchburg city, Virginia	36,160	31,930	30,440	34,124	40,974	45,178
Newport News city, Virginia	37,752	24,795	32,776	36,886	48,391	62,072
Norfolk city, Virginia	35,567	23,070	30,898	31,901	44,606	59,419

Table C-2. Educational Attainment of the Population, by Selected Counties, 2019—*Continued*

(Number; percent; dollars.)

	Educational attainment by race/ethnicity, 25 years and over								
	Some other race alone			Two or more races			Hispanic or Latino (of any race)		
State/County	Total	High school graduate or more (percent)	Bachelor's degree or more (percent)	Total	High school graduate or more (percent)	Bachelor's degree or more (percent)	Total	High school graduate or more (percent)	Bachelor's degree or more (percent)
VIRGINIA—(*Continued*)									
Portsmouth city, Virginia	N	N	N	N	N	N	N	N	N
Richmond city, Virginia	5,357	32.7	6.2	N	N	N	8,868	41.4	15.4
Roanoke city, Virginia	N	N	N	N	N	N	N	N	N
Suffolk city, Virginia	N	N	N	N	N	N	2,380	86.7	22.9
Virginia Beach city, Virginia	5,876	85.3	31.7	10,376	90.0	21.1	22,081	90.0	31.3
WASHINGTON	197,368	61.5	11.9	206,101	91.7	33.3	509,771	69.3	17.9
Benton County, Washington	8,800	48.6	3.1	3,594	95.2	56.8	22,282	70.0	11.2
Chelan County, Washington	7,627	35.8	3.6	N	N	N	11,091	46.9	7.6
Clallam County, Washington	N	N	N	N	N	N	3,103	84.5	26.5
Clark County, Washington	6,432	65.5	7.7	11,625	83.8	28.8	24,339	76.3	17.3
Cowlitz County, Washington	N	N	N	N	N	N	4,975	78.3	10.8
Franklin County, Washington	10,852	43.5	4.9	N	N	N	24,854	48.4	6.1
Grant County, Washington	11,561	50.3	3.4	N	N	N	19,953	48.9	8.8
Grays Harbor County, Washington	N	N	N	N	N	N	4,064	72.1	4.1
Island County, Washington	N	N	N	N	N	N	3,106	100.0	24.9
King County, Washington	57,114	64.4	16.9	68,744	94.0	44.7	126,288	73.5	28.1
Kitsap County, Washington	3,505	92.4	17.3	7,492	92.5	27.2	12,016	89.9	19.4
Lewis County, Washington	N	N	N	4,059	60.7	2.4	4,006	46.0	7.8
Mason County, Washington	N	N	N	N	N	N	3,320	62.0	2.8
Pierce County, Washington	19,088	74.3	16.5	32,456	91.7	26.5	52,006	79.2	19.1
Skagit County, Washington	5,438	70.8	0.7	2,028	91.3	23.5	11,796	63.9	8.4
Snohomish County, Washington	16,432	75.8	16.6	22,453	92.9	32.1	45,431	78.3	22.8
Spokane County, Washington	3,552	92.1	33.4	10,747	94.5	30.0	17,075	91.3	26.9
Thurston County, Washington	2,369	68.5	23.3	7,609	93.6	35.5	14,535	79.1	24.7
Whatcom County, Washington	N	N	N	6,095	94.5	29.9	10,871	78.2	28.9
Yakima County, Washington	19,445	48.7	8.9	4,071	83.5	24.0	61,804	49.5	5.6
WEST VIRGINIA	3,128	83.3	14.6	13,045	88.3	23.9	14,106	86.5	22.5
Berkeley County, West Virginia	N	N	N	N	N	N	N	N	N
Cabell County, West Virginia	N	N	N	N	N	N	N	N	N
Harrison County, West Virginia	N	N	N	N	N	N	N	N	N
Kanawha County, West Virginia	N	N	N	N	N	N	N	N	N
Monongalia County, West Virginia	N	N	N	N	N	N	N	N	N
Raleigh County, West Virginia	N	N	N	N	N	N	N	N	N
Wood County, West Virginia	N	N	N	N	N	N	N	N	N
WISCONSIN	69,021	65.0	13.4	48,265	94.0	31.5	210,204	70.9	15.6
Brown County, Wisconsin	3,839	44.8	6.0	3,032	84.1	24.2	10,824	61.7	10.1
Dane County, Wisconsin	4,356	69.8	23.4	4,775	94.4	57.4	18,006	73.4	28.4
Dodge County, Wisconsin	N	N	N	N	N	N	2,603	73.4	7.6
Eau Claire County, Wisconsin	N	N	N	N	N	N	N	N	N
Fond du Lac County, Wisconsin	N	N	N	N	N	N	N	N	N
Jefferson County, Wisconsin	N	N	N	N	N	N	3,172	77.6	15.3
Kenosha County, Wisconsin	N	N	N	N	N	N	11,730	83.8	12.0
La Crosse County, Wisconsin	N	N	N	N	N	N	N	N	N
Manitowoc County, Wisconsin	N	N	N	N	N	N	N	N	N
Marathon County, Wisconsin	N	N	N	N	N	N	2,076	49.5	3.1
Milwaukee County, Wisconsin	32,712	68.7	12.8	12,624	95.6	41.4	77,687	69.7	13.7
Outagamie County, Wisconsin	N	N	N	N	N	N	4,604	71.6	26.4
Ozaukee County, Wisconsin	N	N	N	N	N	N	N	N	N
Portage County, Wisconsin	N	N	N	N	N	N	N	N	N
Racine County, Wisconsin	N	N	N	N	N	N	13,667	69.5	12.2
Rock County, Wisconsin	4,413	68.2	12.1	N	N	N	6,472	74.8	16.1
St. Croix County, Wisconsin	N	N	N	N	N	N	N	N	N
Sheboygan County, Wisconsin	N	N	N	N	N	N	3,515	85.7	21.9
Walworth County, Wisconsin	N	N	N	N	N	N	5,557	60.0	8.8
Washington County, Wisconsin	N	N	N	N	N	N	2,262	76.4	19.0
Waukesha County, Wisconsin	N	N	N	N	N	N	10,815	73.9	20.3
Winnebago County, Wisconsin	N	N	N	N	N	N	4,130	50.8	4.5
Wood County, Wisconsin	N	N	N	N	N	N	N	N	N
WYOMING	6,722	82	4	5,495	91	20	30,212	81.3	11.3
Laramie County, Wyoming	N	N	N	N	N	N	8,178	84.1	10.6
Natrona County, Wyoming	N	N	N	N	N	N	3,679	66.6	5.8

Table C-2. Educational Attainment of the Population, by Selected Counties, 2019—*Continued*

(Number; percent; dollars.)

State/County	Median earnings in the past 12 months (2019 inflation-adjusted dollars)					
	Population 25 years and over with earnings					
	Total	Less than high school graduate	High school graduate (includes equivalency)	Some college or associate's degree	Bachelor's degree	Graduate or professional degree
VIRGINIA—(*Continued*)						
Portsmouth city, Virginia	40,619	29,500	27,262	41,382	45,162	53,841
Richmond city, Virginia	36,183	19,216	22,482	31,454	50,716	65,211
Roanoke city, Virginia	34,179	19,454	22,239	35,590	50,210	57,174
Suffolk city, Virginia	45,885	29,175	40,168	40,983	51,421	80,831
Virginia Beach city, Virginia	45,290	19,431	32,399	39,846	55,072	66,439
WASHINGTON	48,567	30,627	36,441	42,030	62,447	86,167
Benton County, Washington	44,352	27,094	31,527	41,164	65,829	82,076
Chelan County, Washington	35,159	28,541	26,559	39,395	49,782	63,393
Clallam County, Washington	33,857	23,203	26,910	31,392	42,197	61,818
Clark County, Washington	46,225	31,271	36,770	41,845	60,399	75,119
Cowlitz County, Washington	39,160	32,352	30,500	41,808	50,309	59,639
Franklin County, Washington	35,855	26,479	36,536	42,952	66,275	71,997
Grant County, Washington	36,681	28,030	27,352	43,101	47,581	77,956
Grays Harbor County, Washington	35,738	29,875	31,323	35,402	50,578	71,426
Island County, Washington	41,878	30,656	36,928	41,718	37,418	62,098
King County, Washington	60,869	32,780	37,227	45,677	73,663	100,926
Kitsap County, Washington	47,331	31,165	35,856	44,819	61,218	78,595
Lewis County, Washington	40,209	22,319	32,455	41,320	45,321	80,878
Mason County, Washington	39,415	30,084	31,049	46,701	39,917	46,746
Pierce County, Washington	47,288	35,295	40,271	45,650	57,490	77,296
Skagit County, Washington	41,172	30,314	40,136	39,684	56,003	66,955
Snohomish County, Washington	52,059	36,870	42,621	46,134	69,638	90,718
Spokane County, Washington	40,344	26,739	31,574	36,810	51,032	67,385
Thurston County, Washington	45,452	22,313	31,969	40,796	53,592	79,087
Whatcom County, Washington	44,676	41,066	37,155	40,117	46,618	70,008
Yakima County, Washington	32,466	25,661	32,251	36,100	56,042	77,523
WEST VIRGINIA	35,440	20,200	30,573	32,380	45,304	58,802
Berkeley County, West Virginia	37,906	22,278	33,609	39,062	47,870	81,597
Cabell County, West Virginia	31,532	11,724	30,322	26,159	50,234	50,311
Harrison County, West Virginia	41,021	25,507	34,007	32,056	52,282	52,162
Kanawha County, West Virginia	35,260	24,023	26,540	32,725	47,088	64,238
Monongalia County, West Virginia	37,320	11,631	29,329	30,051	37,855	73,534
Raleigh County, West Virginia	32,684	9,120	27,718	31,928	37,826	46,358
Wood County, West Virginia	31,326	19,019	27,674	29,878	38,134	52,587
WISCONSIN	42,222	29,561	33,547	40,482	52,425	67,112
Brown County, Wisconsin	42,212	26,717	31,856	40,736	51,709	65,267
Dane County, Wisconsin	50,756	26,394	37,155	41,606	56,753	69,193
Dodge County, Wisconsin	41,913	36,871	37,203	41,709	50,474	68,211
Eau Claire County, Wisconsin	40,424	26,298	31,994	35,459	43,816	61,948
Fond du Lac County, Wisconsin	43,150	38,989	37,488	41,596	49,228	66,359
Jefferson County, Wisconsin	43,166	32,090	31,664	45,941	51,679	65,886
Kenosha County, Wisconsin	41,800	26,053	31,648	40,901	54,454	60,288
La Crosse County, Wisconsin	38,851	21,932	31,541	36,687	45,143	65,415
Manitowoc County, Wisconsin	40,302	24,138	33,045	39,121	56,092	63,259
Marathon County, Wisconsin	38,953	29,043	32,716	37,369	47,416	61,326
Milwaukee County, Wisconsin	41,274	25,757	31,127	40,214	51,935	67,381
Outagamie County, Wisconsin	42,069	23,478	38,691	38,674	48,185	68,567
Ozaukee County, Wisconsin	50,266	45,972	37,663	41,940	56,107	85,644
Portage County, Wisconsin	40,682	21,215	33,860	39,046	47,513	55,741
Racine County, Wisconsin	43,546	30,729	33,867	42,142	60,344	71,980
Rock County, Wisconsin	40,840	30,400	32,814	40,492	49,031	63,652
St. Croix County, Wisconsin	49,744	38,774	36,381	48,257	51,944	70,524
Sheboygan County, Wisconsin	41,485	32,761	36,928	37,104	56,501	63,385
Walworth County, Wisconsin	41,791	29,262	37,045	40,491	52,313	66,902
Washington County, Wisconsin	49,007	35,794	40,257	45,789	61,554	77,161
Waukesha County, Wisconsin	52,709	37,959	37,950	42,426	68,443	79,261
Winnebago County, Wisconsin	41,426	35,498	33,240	40,290	52,126	64,065
Wood County, Wisconsin	37,512	31,803	29,553	38,185	50,508	70,348
WYOMING	40,800	29,982	36,929	36,885	47,962	61,288
Laramie County, Wyoming	44,790	27,802	35,226	36,920	53,679	71,789
Natrona County, Wyoming	41,863	38,106	35,761	39,909	51,825	68,478

Table C-3. College Enrollment of the Population 15 Years Old and Over, by Selected Counties, 2019

(Number.)

State/County	Total population age 15 years and over	Population enrolled in college or graduate school	Male			Female		
			Total population	Enrolled in public college or graduate school	Enrolled in private college or graduate school	Total population	Enrolled in public college or graduate school	Enrolled in private college or graduate school
UNITED STATES	267,720,772	21,829,308	130,629,205	7,358,207	2,343,938	137,091,567	9,053,070	3,074,093
ALABAMA	4,004,468	301,036	1,909,410	108,871	18,106	2,095,058	149,489	24,570
Baldwin County, Alabama..................................	185,419	10,027	88,707	3,330	831	96,712	4,642	1,224
Calhoun County, Alabama.................................	93,598	8,020	44,302	2,400	275	49,296	4,895	450
Elmore County, Alabama..................................	66,487	3,221	31,766	986	682	34,721	1,321	232
Etowah County, Alabama..................................	83,268	5,248	39,464	1,987	198	43,804	2,560	503
Houston County, Alabama................................	85,853	5,506	40,303	2,318	402	45,550	2,290	496
Jefferson County, Alabama..............................	533,235	41,553	247,054	13,180	2,587	286,181	20,386	5,400
Lauderdale County, Alabama...........................	78,194	7,234	37,453	2,926	61	40,741	4,146	101
Lee County, Alabama......................................	135,865	29,663	66,155	12,610	1,282	69,710	14,648	1,123
Limestone County, Alabama............................	81,082	3,440	40,018	1,313	66	41,064	1,911	150
Madison County, Alabama...............................	305,060	28,680	147,377	12,063	2,233	157,683	11,520	2,864
Marshall County, Alabama..............................	77,146	4,025	37,487	1,426	36	39,659	2,479	84
Mobile County, Alabama	332,920	20,237	156,240	6,340	1,124	176,680	10,031	2,742
Montgomery County, Alabama.........................	182,066	17,426	83,721	6,766	1,661	98,345	7,407	1,592
Morgan County, Alabama................................	98,625	4,414	47,645	1,845	31	50,980	2,315	223
Shelby County, Alabama	176,544	13,021	84,342	4,228	998	92,202	5,643	2,152
Tuscaloosa County, Alabama..........................	173,211	26,246	82,695	10,917	551	90,516	14,132	646
ALASKA............................	578,225	42,060	301,975	15,228	4,093	276,250	19,023	3,716
Anchorage Municipality, Alaska.......................	228,797	19,668	115,780	7,832	1,919	113,017	8,333	1,584
Fairbanks North Star Borough, Alaska	77,107	8,798	42,322	4,014	392	34,785	4,155	237
Matanuska-Susitna Borough, Alaska..................	84,408	4,966	43,741	1,204	590	40,667	2,444	728
ARIZONA	5,919,085	465,128	2,926,106	182,940	34,661	2,992,979	202,759	44,768
Cochise County, Arizona	103,679	7,401	52,783	3,534	266	50,896	3,331	270
Coconino County, Arizona	120,198	28,128	58,951	12,265	130	61,247	15,179	554
Maricopa County, Arizona	3,613,221	278,471	1,772,506	106,849	23,289	1,840,715	116,601	31,732
Mohave County, Arizona	182,766	7,348	91,920	2,759	491	90,846	3,325	773
Navajo County, Arizona	86,345	3,275	42,887	978	361	43,458	1,647	289
Pima County, Arizona	868,253	84,982	424,663	35,852	4,928	443,590	39,148	5,054
Pinal County, Arizona	377,276	19,949	198,100	8,333	1,365	179,176	7,977	2,274
Yavapai County, Arizona.................................	204,834	14,812	99,866	3,385	3,566	104,968	5,033	2,828
Yuma County, Arizona.....................................	168,840	11,708	87,291	5,394	265	81,549	5,795	254
ARKANSAS........................	2,439,812	176,608	1,181,259	62,500	13,595	1,258,553	82,877	17,636
Benton County, Arkansas	218,425	14,426	107,437	4,966	2,388	110,988	4,339	2,733
Craighead County, Arkansas	88,261	10,175	42,197	3,633	392	46,064	5,057	1,093
Faulkner County, Arkansas.............................	102,305	13,168	48,565	4,684	476	53,740	6,514	1,494
Garland County, Arkansas	83,789	3,704	38,902	1,200	269	44,887	1,930	305
Jefferson County, Arkansas............................	54,852	4,743	26,853	1,084	1,008	27,999	1,266	1,385
Lonoke County, Arkansas...............................	58,067	2,920	27,618	893	95	30,449	1,605	327
Pulaski County, Arkansas...............................	316,083	25,962	148,113	8,263	1,954	167,970	12,575	3,170
Saline County, Arkansas.................................	99,587	4,291	48,305	1,079	661	51,282	2,033	518
Sebastian County, Arkansas...........................	102,782	7,928	48,896	3,146	482	53,886	3,980	320
Washington County, Arkansas	190,585	28,779	94,732	12,055	804	95,853	14,931	989
White County, Arkansas	63,386	5,962	30,488	998	2,197	32,898	753	2,014
CALIFORNIA	32,124,112	3,143,433	15,865,087	1,170,878	270,132	16,259,025	1,365,060	337,363
Alameda County, California	1,386,582	139,002	677,435	54,346	8,177	709,147	63,151	13,328
Butte County, California..................................	182,007	25,851	89,676	10,980	787	92,331	12,612	1,472
Contra Costa County, California	941,049	74,593	455,491	27,550	5,188	485,558	32,913	8,942
El Dorado County, California	161,523	9,319	79,776	4,572	165	81,747	3,714	868
Fresno County, California................................	762,545	75,046	378,110	29,561	4,556	384,435	35,664	5,265
Humboldt County, California	113,703	15,118	55,457	6,666	882	58,246	7,096	474
Imperial County, California..............................	138,048	10,802	70,908	3,353	135	67,140	7,167	147
Kern County, California...................................	683,174	56,190	350,479	18,664	7,318	332,695	23,761	6,447
Kings County, California..................................	117,603	11,514	66,668	3,629	2,162	50,935	4,657	1,066
Los Angeles County, California........................	8,257,074	834,000	4,036,279	286,654	89,471	4,220,795	352,806	105,069
Madera County, California...............................	121,413	11,782	58,416	3,414	540	62,997	5,420	2,408
Marin County, California..................................	217,645	14,742	106,423	4,727	1,038	111,222	6,543	2,434
Mendocino County, California	71,254	5,387	34,608	1,673	105	36,646	2,636	973
Merced County, California	210,908	21,013	106,396	8,742	663	104,512	11,114	494
Monterey County, California	339,438	29,996	172,212	12,266	1,012	167,226	15,421	1,297
Napa County, California..................................	115,159	8,254	56,834	2,727	1,187	58,325	3,214	1,126
Nevada County, California	85,898	3,404	41,428	1,233	122	44,470	1,533	516
Orange County, California	2,607,309	273,985	1,276,611	115,122	20,741	1,330,698	115,370	22,752

Table C-3. College Enrollment of the Population 15 Years Old and Over, by Selected Counties, 2019—*Continued*

(Number.)

State/County	Total population age 15 years and over	Population enrolled in college or graduate school	Male			Female		
			Total population	Enrolled in public college or graduate school	Enrolled in private college or graduate school	Total population	Enrolled in public college or graduate school	Enrolled in private college or graduate school
CALIFORNIA—(*Continued*)								
Placer County, California	326,077	17,418	157,925	7,447	671	168,152	6,999	2,301
Riverside County, California	1,963,549	182,776	972,606	64,966	14,420	990,943	82,689	20,701
Sacramento County, California	1,249,003	118,969	604,273	47,567	5,091	644,730	55,736	10,575
San Bernardino County, California	1,705,866	167,689	843,289	60,771	14,523	862,577	73,179	19,216
San Diego County, California	2,738,830	292,453	1,373,575	111,878	28,595	1,365,255	121,196	30,784
San Francisco County, California	780,127	73,347	396,761	23,834	10,500	383,366	28,132	10,881
San Joaquin County, California	593,462	56,901	294,215	19,178	5,903	299,247	24,918	6,902
San Luis Obispo County, California	242,491	34,626	121,463	16,368	352	121,028	17,190	716
San Mateo County, California	638,311	48,940	312,924	17,577	5,591	325,387	19,270	6,502
Santa Barbara County, California	363,975	58,378	181,546	25,920	1,797	182,429	27,704	2,957
Santa Clara County, California	1,582,921	154,936	799,440	55,755	18,644	783,481	58,142	22,395
Santa Cruz County, California	230,666	37,176	113,747	16,655	1,033	116,919	18,075	1,413
Shasta County, California	148,240	10,717	72,469	3,274	910	75,771	4,694	1,839
Solano County, California	365,135	31,143	179,829	10,917	3,464	185,306	13,438	3,324
Sonoma County, California	416,679	33,777	201,101	13,735	2,679	215,578	14,252	3,111
Stanislaus County, California	428,124	34,325	209,810	12,909	2,022	218,314	17,034	2,360
Sutter County, California	76,168	6,059	38,259	2,571	201	37,909	3,024	263
Tehama County, California	52,507	3,717	25,652	1,687	112	26,855	1,235	683
Tulare County, California	347,265	29,130	171,844	11,881	1,217	175,421	12,887	3,145
Ventura County, California	690,217	58,144	338,281	21,228	5,085	351,936	24,655	7,176
Yolo County, California	183,923	44,795	88,487	18,824	941	95,436	24,144	886
Yuba County, California	59,665	6,269	30,558	1,992	579	29,107	2,592	1,106
COLORADO	4,720,810	384,916	2,372,402	150,548	29,707	2,348,408	168,038	36,623
Adams County, Colorado	405,343	23,725	204,731	9,184	2,407	200,612	9,668	2,466
Arapahoe County, Colorado	530,645	36,472	262,169	12,659	3,677	268,476	15,250	4,886
Boulder County, Colorado	276,608	43,603	138,786	19,460	2,182	137,822	20,042	1,919
Broomfield County, Colorado	58,047	3,456	29,321	955	172	28,726	2,036	293
Denver County, Colorado	608,905	47,968	304,548	14,616	5,263	304,357	18,581	9,508
Douglas County, Colorado	280,305	18,628	138,748	7,376	1,692	141,557	7,243	2,317
El Paso County, Colorado	577,626	58,334	291,572	23,579	6,257	286,054	23,343	5,155
Jefferson County, Colorado	490,331	34,895	243,332	14,654	2,469	246,999	14,472	3,300
Larimer County, Colorado	299,971	43,220	149,847	20,905	1,215	150,124	19,751	1,349
Mesa County, Colorado	127,048	8,707	61,697	2,595	119	65,351	5,502	491
Pueblo County, Colorado	137,908	9,702	67,151	4,071	212	70,757	4,961	458
Weld County, Colorado	254,364	21,555	128,098	7,647	1,574	126,266	11,519	815
CONNECTICUT	2,975,029	265,685	1,441,236	75,553	40,478	1,533,793	96,159	53,495
Fairfield County, Connecticut	773,101	64,687	372,785	18,824	10,319	400,316	19,874	15,670
Hartford County, Connecticut	739,383	63,502	355,995	21,864	6,759	383,388	24,264	10,615
Litchfield County, Connecticut	154,521	8,796	75,747	2,042	1,274	78,774	4,393	1,087
Middlesex County, Connecticut	140,501	12,005	68,894	1,710	3,031	71,607	4,218	3,046
New Haven County, Connecticut	715,827	70,013	341,169	13,808	15,961	374,658	21,538	18,706
New London County, Connecticut	223,903	15,411	112,041	3,224	2,389	111,862	6,360	3,438
Tolland County, Connecticut	129,698	23,232	65,263	9,594	552	64,435	12,404	682
Windham County, Connecticut	98,095	8,039	49,342	4,487	193	48,753	3,108	251
DELAWARE	805,442	62,460	385,178	20,716	5,518	420,264	29,235	6,991
Kent County, Delaware	146,439	13,106	69,081	4,473	1,335	77,358	5,707	1,591
New Castle County, Delaware	460,611	39,192	220,868	13,063	3,001	239,743	18,884	4,244
Sussex County, Delaware	198,392	10,162	95,229	3,180	1,182	103,163	4,644	1,156
DISTRICT OF COLUMBIA	593,107	70,489	277,264	8,715	20,564	315,843	10,315	30,895
District of Columbia, District of Columbia	593,107	70,489	277,264	8,715	20,564	315,843	10,315	30,895
FLORIDA	17,964,694	1,347,287	8,699,523	443,725	133,396	9,265,171	586,659	183,507
Alachua County, Florida	228,094	54,056	107,898	22,776	1,094	120,196	29,488	698
Bay County, Florida	145,416	10,056	70,628	3,831	704	74,788	4,819	702
Brevard County, Florida	512,477	33,516	248,283	9,654	5,318	264,194	13,536	5,008
Broward County, Florida	1,611,631	127,196	777,708	40,946	15,233	833,923	50,027	20,990
Charlotte County, Florida	170,307	6,516	81,692	1,757	365	88,615	3,760	634
Citrus County, Florida	131,452	3,934	63,174	1,539	41	68,278	1,517	837
Clay County, Florida	178,760	12,444	87,040	3,173	949	91,720	5,645	2,677
Collier County, Florida	331,631	15,368	162,434	2,958	3,335	169,197	5,229	3,846
Columbia County, Florida	59,254	2,561	30,583	706	0	28,671	1,541	314

Table C-3. College Enrollment of the Population 15 Years Old and Over, by Selected Counties, 2019—*Continued*

(Number.)

State/County	Total population age 15 years and over	Population enrolled in college or graduate school	Male			Female		
			Total population	Enrolled in public college or graduate school	Enrolled in private college or graduate school	Total population	Enrolled in public college or graduate school	Enrolled in private college or graduate school
FLORIDA—(*Continued*)								
Duval County, Florida	773,281	58,247	370,033	19,283	4,891	403,248	26,459	7,614
Escambia County, Florida	262,451	23,637	128,413	7,283	2,640	134,038	8,656	5,058
Flagler County, Florida	98,954	5,314	47,294	1,782	695	51,660	1,748	1,089
Hernando County, Florida	164,163	8,963	78,864	2,714	944	85,299	4,023	1,282
Hillsborough County, Florida	1,200,440	98,045	580,470	29,676	10,672	619,970	44,388	13,309
Indian River County, Florida	139,818	4,828	66,818	1,815	401	73,000	2,206	406
Lake County, Florida	310,134	12,443	148,481	3,692	1,126	161,653	5,364	2,261
Lee County, Florida	659,973	34,003	321,387	11,920	3,003	338,586	15,505	3,575
Leon County, Florida	247,801	56,418	115,650	22,960	1,235	132,151	30,428	1,795
Manatee County, Florida	343,982	15,236	165,890	4,207	1,324	178,092	7,264	2,441
Marion County, Florida	309,957	15,481	146,288	3,823	2,038	163,669	6,558	3,062
Martin County, Florida	139,744	7,679	70,121	2,516	1,262	69,623	3,337	564
Miami-Dade County, Florida	2,258,491	210,801	1,085,613	72,470	23,635	1,172,878	84,522	30,174
Monroe County, Florida	65,073	2,296	33,812	659	253	31,261	1,095	289
Okaloosa County, Florida	171,062	9,462	86,982	3,860	710	84,080	3,937	955
Orange County, Florida	1,138,784	121,382	552,716	41,147	10,945	586,068	54,098	15,192
Osceola County, Florida	301,414	27,654	147,131	9,053	2,498	154,283	11,053	5,050
Palm Beach County, Florida	1,262,139	88,433	605,863	29,239	6,881	656,276	38,702	13,611
Pasco County, Florida	461,649	24,868	222,243	5,778	2,633	239,406	11,699	4,758
Pinellas County, Florida	846,576	57,004	402,355	19,953	4,315	444,221	25,121	7,615
Polk County, Florida	593,006	40,643	287,909	11,661	5,187	305,097	16,998	6,797
Putnam County, Florida	61,292	2,589	29,820	534	350	31,472	1,417	288
St. Johns County, Florida	217,875	14,042	104,535	4,044	1,194	113,340	6,794	2,010
St. Lucie County, Florida	275,076	15,790	132,665	4,006	1,649	142,411	7,725	2,410
Santa Rosa County, Florida	150,363	9,441	76,561	3,786	722	73,802	4,631	302
Sarasota County, Florida	384,389	17,946	180,907	5,660	1,594	203,482	8,634	2,058
Seminole County, Florida	390,335	36,417	186,244	14,453	4,086	204,091	13,968	3,970
Volusia County, Florida	472,977	29,687	229,332	8,314	5,346	243,645	9,944	6,083
GEORGIA	8,540,772	719,093	4,102,634	236,808	54,823	4,438,138	332,526	94,936
Barrow County, Georgia	65,308	3,866	32,554	1,625	424	32,754	1,475	342
Bartow County, Georgia	86,090	6,279	41,612	2,048	575	44,478	2,667	989
Bibb County, Georgia	121,831	13,351	55,684	2,375	2,033	66,147	5,681	3,262
Bulloch County, Georgia	66,601	18,129	32,686	8,891	0	33,915	9,046	192
Carroll County, Georgia	96,402	8,288	45,975	3,774	448	50,427	3,773	293
Catoosa County, Georgia	54,848	3,296	25,823	1,073	275	29,025	1,429	519
Chatham County, Georgia	238,908	25,287	112,776	7,652	3,137	126,132	7,104	7,394
Cherokee County, Georgia	207,694	13,898	100,589	4,278	1,265	107,105	6,103	2,252
Clarke County, Georgia	108,105	34,184	50,132	14,824	752	57,973	18,174	434
Clayton County, Georgia	224,412	19,548	101,721	5,430	2,205	122,691	8,885	3,028
Cobb County, Georgia	615,028	53,436	295,923	19,760	2,577	319,105	26,425	4,674
Columbia County, Georgia	125,213	10,482	60,792	3,720	1,051	64,421	5,024	687
Coweta County, Georgia	118,921	7,443	57,695	1,772	1,492	61,226	3,115	1,064
DeKalb County, Georgia	611,488	57,230	282,803	17,709	6,447	328,685	21,987	11,087
Dougherty County, Georgia	70,642	7,936	31,492	2,470	68	39,150	5,034	364
Douglas County, Georgia	115,940	12,630	52,812	3,237	155	63,128	7,932	1,306
Fayette County, Georgia	93,879	5,316	44,402	1,855	550	49,477	2,198	713
Floyd County, Georgia	80,057	6,639	37,691	803	989	42,366	3,404	1,443
Forsyth County, Georgia	190,990	13,576	93,873	5,282	1,159	97,117	6,147	988
Fulton County, Georgia	875,395	90,293	419,191	29,368	9,000	456,204	36,218	15,707
Gwinnett County, Georgia	733,002	62,622	354,188	20,189	6,811	378,814	26,001	9,621
Hall County, Georgia	162,997	9,822	80,123	2,871	727	82,874	4,443	1,781
Henry County, Georgia	186,533	14,420	88,345	4,706	1,096	98,188	7,064	1,554
Houston County, Georgia	124,171	14,392	60,053	5,339	559	64,118	6,085	2,409
Jackson County, Georgia	57,220	3,766	27,683	1,211	158	29,537	1,907	490
Lowndes County, Georgia	92,864	11,289	44,237	4,053	773	48,627	5,594	869
Muscogee County, Georgia	154,722	15,095	73,750	4,951	711	80,972	7,316	2,117
Newton County, Georgia	85,672	8,286	39,337	1,476	423	46,335	5,441	946
Paulding County, Georgia	133,276	10,737	64,083	2,826	1,117	69,193	5,122	1,672
Richmond County, Georgia	164,292	12,359	78,180	4,216	495	86,112	6,471	1,177
Rockdale County, Georgia	73,008	5,353	34,035	2,145	186	38,973	2,120	902
Troup County, Georgia	56,085	3,350	25,777	402	446	30,308	2,017	485
Walton County, Georgia	75,825	3,974	36,464	1,321	379	39,361	2,061	213
HAWAII	1,163,465	85,173	578,494	30,463	8,945	584,971	34,795	10,970
Hawaii County, Hawaii	165,270	8,453	81,439	3,300	386	83,831	4,501	266
Honolulu County, Hawaii	801,814	67,938	400,810	23,818	8,159	401,004	26,711	9,250

Table C-3. College Enrollment of the Population 15 Years Old and Over, by Selected Counties, 2019—*Continued*

(Number.)

State/County	Total population age 15 years and over	Population enrolled in college or graduate school	Male			Female		
			Total population	Enrolled in public college or graduate school	Enrolled in private college or graduate school	Total population	Enrolled in public college or graduate school	Enrolled in private college or graduate school
HAWAII—*(Continued)*								
Kauai County, Hawaii	59,065	3,282	29,078	1,080	74	29,987	1,509	619
Maui County, Hawaii	137,301	5,500	67,162	2,265	326	70,139	2,074	835
IDAHO	1,416,602	108,221	708,387	38,975	15,410	708,215	40,310	13,526
Ada County, Idaho	390,495	35,515	195,934	15,655	2,462	194,561	14,237	3,161
Bannock County, Idaho	69,144	7,808	34,758	3,687	215	34,386	3,488	418
Bonneville County, Idaho	88,833	6,003	44,556	2,308	914	44,277	1,835	946
Canyon County, Idaho	176,669	10,021	87,621	3,297	1,258	89,048	3,972	1,494
Kootenai County, Idaho	134,554	6,511	65,610	2,002	628	68,944	2,805	1,076
Twin Falls County, Idaho	65,870	3,425	32,404	1,420	339	33,466	1,273	393
ILLINOIS	10,353,312	832,458	5,033,953	250,887	120,211	5,319,359	311,527	149,833
Adams County, Illinois	53,105	3,291	25,738	828	748	27,367	1,140	575
Champaign County, Illinois	176,859	45,470	86,806	21,770	1,443	90,053	20,972	1,285
Cook County, Illinois	4,222,966	350,258	2,028,521	85,925	69,725	2,194,445	114,251	80,357
DeKalb County, Illinois	86,107	15,811	42,215	6,992	723	43,892	7,350	746
DuPage County, Illinois	753,277	63,782	367,392	19,232	10,031	385,885	19,118	15,401
Kane County, Illinois	424,549	34,107	209,836	10,779	3,939	214,713	13,867	5,522
Kankakee County, Illinois	89,589	6,928	44,210	1,500	1,199	45,379	2,272	1,957
Kendall County, Illinois	99,944	7,591	47,529	2,837	491	52,415	3,187	1,076
Lake County, Illinois	562,545	43,342	280,225	13,108	6,285	282,320	16,292	7,657
LaSalle County, Illinois	90,068	3,935	45,257	1,675	117	44,811	1,544	599
McHenry County, Illinois	249,912	16,061	123,968	5,351	1,393	125,944	7,645	1,672
McLean County, Illinois	141,348	27,762	67,156	12,589	1,208	74,192	12,905	1,060
Macon County, Illinois	84,875	4,245	39,628	385	1,092	45,247	1,297	1,471
Madison County, Illinois	215,826	17,213	103,787	6,997	1,157	112,039	8,023	1,036
Peoria County, Illinois	143,693	11,192	68,347	2,047	3,156	75,346	2,604	3,385
Rock Island County, Illinois	115,827	7,546	56,037	1,217	1,708	59,790	2,960	1,661
St. Clair County, Illinois	209,667	13,187	99,206	4,851	947	110,461	5,555	1,834
Sangamon County, Illinois	159,316	10,784	75,290	3,747	646	84,026	6,002	389
Tazewell County, Illinois	107,255	5,694	52,670	2,802	468	54,585	1,716	708
Vermilion County, Illinois	60,631	2,823	29,635	872	45	30,996	1,702	204
Will County, Illinois	554,816	39,958	273,616	12,997	4,516	281,200	14,281	8,164
Winnebago County, Illinois	228,335	13,579	110,104	2,763	2,087	118,231	5,703	3,026
INDIANA	5,434,807	409,112	2,654,430	137,970	42,535	2,780,377	177,995	50,612
Allen County, Indiana	298,307	20,778	144,021	6,635	1,818	154,286	9,624	2,701
Bartholomew County, Indiana	67,670	3,346	33,171	923	579	34,499	1,198	646
Boone County, Indiana	53,099	3,009	25,364	1,223	394	27,735	1,013	379
Clark County, Indiana	95,877	4,226	45,461	1,138	890	50,416	1,951	247
Delaware County, Indiana	97,780	17,635	46,964	7,779	332	50,816	9,464	60
Elkhart County, Indiana	159,808	6,780	78,169	921	734	81,639	3,656	1,469
Floyd County, Indiana	63,053	4,947	30,470	1,623	158	32,583	2,282	884
Grant County, Indiana	54,510	7,110	25,788	725	1,230	28,722	1,291	3,864
Hamilton County, Indiana	264,229	14,513	127,262	4,941	1,608	136,967	6,080	1,884
Hendricks County, Indiana	134,892	8,587	66,618	2,985	1,074	68,274	3,442	1,086
Howard County, Indiana	66,955	3,274	32,535	1,254	0	34,420	2,020	0
Johnson County, Indiana	126,480	6,714	62,040	1,945	909	64,440	2,699	1,161
Kosciusko County, Indiana	63,483	3,294	31,639	1,057	701	31,844	757	779
Lake County, Indiana	393,644	23,456	187,799	6,523	1,765	205,845	11,816	3,352
LaPorte County, Indiana	91,184	2,960	47,554	1,089	124	43,630	1,624	123
Madison County, Indiana	106,473	5,978	53,075	1,916	561	53,398	2,366	1,135
Marion County, Indiana	764,542	54,250	363,185	16,418	5,956	401,357	24,242	7,634
Monroe County, Indiana	129,152	39,991	64,016	20,271	229	65,136	18,955	536
Morgan County, Indiana	57,858	2,955	28,457	1,168	451	29,401	1,248	88
Porter County, Indiana	140,415	10,231	68,817	1,870	2,143	71,598	3,350	2,868
St. Joseph County, Indiana	219,347	26,194	105,374	4,865	7,528	113,973	6,713	7,088
Tippecanoe County, Indiana	161,700	41,416	83,332	22,315	576	78,368	18,042	483
Vanderburgh County, Indiana	148,324	9,860	70,556	2,603	1,376	77,768	5,025	856
Vigo County, Indiana	89,334	12,059	45,238	4,358	1,389	44,096	5,990	322
Wayne County, Indiana	53,594	2,798	25,497	631	430	28,097	983	754
IOWA	2,554,896	206,145	1,262,984	67,782	21,799	1,291,912	84,869	31,695
Black Hawk County, Iowa	107,483	13,422	52,171	4,751	593	55,312	7,208	870
Dallas County, Iowa	72,430	3,579	35,248	1,330	263	37,182	1,509	477
Dubuque County, Iowa	79,432	6,720	39,643	644	1,927	39,789	2,373	1,776

Table C-3. College Enrollment of the Population 15 Years Old and Over, by Selected Counties, 2019—*Continued*

(Number.)

			Male			Female		
State/County	Total population age 15 years and over	Population enrolled in college or graduate school	Total population	Enrolled in public college or graduate school	Enrolled in private college or graduate school	Total population	Enrolled in public college or graduate school	Enrolled in private college or graduate school
IOWA—(*Continued*)								
Johnson County, Iowa..........................	125,939	32,094	61,704	13,615	715	64,235	16,416	1,348
Linn County, Iowa	183,007	14,419	88,870	3,571	1,924	94,137	6,194	2,730
Polk County, Iowa	388,723	26,824	190,127	7,177	4,658	198,596	7,954	7,035
Pottawattamie County, Iowa..............	75,246	3,740	36,545	1,511	264	38,701	1,577	388
Scott County, Iowa............................	138,692	7,725	67,785	1,373	913	70,907	2,732	2,707
Story County, Iowa	84,137	28,646	44,542	14,659	905	39,595	12,681	401
Woodbury County, Iowa.....................	80,695	6,195	40,164	1,705	1,181	40,531	1,897	1,412
KANSAS	2,329,808	190,355	1,149,861	73,435	15,103	1,179,947	86,032	15,785
Douglas County, Kansas	103,407	23,248	50,460	11,363	404	52,947	10,552	929
Johnson County, Kansas....................	482,935	34,163	234,574	11,591	3,318	248,361	15,106	4,148
Leavenworth County, Kansas	65,447	5,061	35,394	1,630	1,251	30,053	1,713	467
Riley County, Kansas.........................	63,931	20,017	34,091	10,360	140	29,840	9,355	162
Sedgwick County, Kansas	406,397	32,661	199,069	11,103	2,819	207,328	14,227	4,512
Shawnee County, Kansas	143,061	7,199	68,756	2,420	547	74,305	3,820	412
Wyandotte County, Kansas	126,502	6,518	61,843	2,691	427	64,659	2,620	780
KENTUCKY	3,637,530	253,638	1,770,359	86,342	20,004	1,867,171	116,408	30,884
Boone County, Kentucky	105,553	7,196	51,544	2,999	907	54,009	2,739	551
Bullitt County, Kentucky	67,331	3,470	33,455	809	190	33,876	1,749	722
Campbell County, Kentucky................	77,364	7,328	37,619	2,981	431	39,745	3,148	768
Daviess County, Kentucky	80,553	4,476	38,714	832	489	41,839	2,187	968
Fayette County, Kentucky	266,529	37,929	129,198	15,698	1,492	137,331	18,137	2,602
Hardin County, Kentucky	88,914	5,601	43,426	1,482	317	45,488	2,542	1,260
Jefferson County, Kentucky...............	625,918	46,441	297,834	14,012	5,346	328,084	18,545	8,538
Kenton County, Kentucky...................	133,874	7,906	65,488	3,023	609	68,386	2,894	1,380
Madison County, Kentucky.................	76,895	14,215	37,117	5,734	749	39,778	7,064	668
Oldham County, Kentucky..................	53,525	3,713	27,839	920	336	25,686	1,351	1,106
Warren County, Kentucky...................	107,884	15,104	52,022	6,250	446	55,862	7,913	495
LOUISIANA	3,740,573	271,111	1,802,230	87,125	20,773	1,938,343	132,544	30,669
Bossier Parish, Louisiana..................	101,271	9,060	49,851	3,365	256	51,420	4,962	477
Caddo Parish, Louisiana	193,006	13,052	89,946	5,309	299	103,060	6,019	1,425
Calcasieu Parish, Louisiana..............	160,309	9,122	76,962	2,828	370	83,347	5,440	484
East Baton Rouge Parish, Louisiana ...	356,790	47,313	167,849	17,862	1,624	188,941	26,116	1,711
Jefferson Parish, Louisiana...............	351,968	22,565	168,120	6,495	3,109	183,848	8,199	4,762
Lafayette Parish, Louisiana...............	195,842	16,227	93,220	4,487	564	102,622	10,541	635
Lafourche Parish, Louisiana..............	77,830	4,433	37,910	1,387	285	39,920	2,571	190
Orleans Parish, Louisiana.................	324,816	35,662	151,149	5,733	6,948	173,667	11,813	11,168
Ouachita Parish, Louisiana...............	121,776	7,491	57,273	3,159	494	64,503	3,361	477
Rapides Parish, Louisiana.................	103,083	6,504	48,770	1,210	810	54,313	3,267	1,217
St. Tammany Parish, Louisiana..........	209,531	9,978	99,545	4,110	663	109,986	4,719	486
Tangipahoa Parish, Louisiana...........	106,908	9,821	51,464	2,920	0	55,444	5,813	1,088
MAINE	1,143,655	75,614	554,012	23,159	9,191	589,643	28,448	14,816
Androscoggin County, Maine..............	88,877	6,039	43,204	1,840	1,003	45,673	1,959	1,237
Aroostook County, Maine...................	56,789	3,515	28,046	863	316	28,743	2,079	257
Cumberland County, Maine................	251,359	19,427	120,541	5,436	2,912	130,818	6,582	4,497
Kennebec County, Maine...................	103,780	6,803	49,506	1,513	914	54,274	1,752	2,624
Penobscot County, Maine	130,894	13,423	64,523	6,287	915	66,371	5,129	1,092
York County, Maine...........................	176,857	8,187	84,897	1,757	1,424	91,960	2,892	2,114
MARYLAND	4,937,192	436,590	2,362,338	143,709	46,236	2,574,854	184,581	62,064
Allegany County, Maryland................	60,339	6,344	31,826	2,865	58	28,513	3,104	317
Anne Arundel County, Maryland.........	471,540	35,166	231,675	12,485	3,654	239,865	14,715	4,312
Baltimore County, Maryland..............	678,240	67,203	316,840	20,800	6,561	361,400	31,199	8,643
Calvert County, Maryland..................	75,167	4,824	36,880	1,526	242	38,287	2,538	518
Carroll County, Maryland..................	139,180	11,128	67,872	3,397	2,311	71,308	4,040	1,380
Cecil County, Maryland	83,802	6,237	41,389	2,296	498	42,413	2,604	839
Charles County, Maryland.................	131,463	11,716	62,218	3,518	941	69,245	6,131	1,126
Frederick County, Maryland...............	209,787	17,245	102,350	4,519	2,813	107,437	6,700	3,213
Harford County, Maryland.................	208,740	16,988	101,279	6,495	1,705	107,461	7,060	1,728
Howard County, Maryland.................	261,276	21,945	125,978	8,379	1,886	135,298	8,370	3,310
Montgomery County, Maryland..........	850,224	65,491	405,006	21,186	8,156	445,218	25,830	10,319
Prince George's County, Maryland	739,372	80,330	350,194	29,839	5,295	389,178	34,537	10,659
St. Mary's County, Maryland.............	91,643	7,592	45,906	2,649	461	45,737	3,516	966

Table C-3. College Enrollment of the Population 15 Years Old and Over, by Selected Counties, 2019—Continued

(Number.)

State/County	Total population age 15 years and over	Population enrolled in college or graduate school	Male			Female		
			Total population	Enrolled in public college or graduate school	Enrolled in private college or graduate school	Total population	Enrolled in public college or graduate school	Enrolled in private college or graduate school
MARYLAND—(Continued)								
Washington County, Maryland	123,529	5,979	62,749	2,134	233	60,780	3,026	586
Wicomico County, Maryland	85,528	12,848	39,155	4,723	180	46,373	7,450	495
Baltimore city, Maryland	491,535	48,655	226,505	10,830	9,954	265,030	16,429	11,442
MASSACHUSETTS	5,786,309	575,553	2,780,028	121,735	135,951	3,006,281	148,411	169,456
Barnstable County, Massachusetts	187,972	8,058	89,461	2,432	1,401	98,511	3,017	1,208
Berkshire County, Massachusetts	108,755	8,568	52,299	1,862	2,407	56,456	2,222	2,077
Bristol County, Massachusetts	470,746	32,630	225,270	10,168	4,263	245,476	12,776	5,423
Essex County, Massachusetts	652,972	48,123	310,940	12,065	7,862	342,032	16,117	12,079
Franklin County, Massachusetts	60,729	3,496	28,891	985	353	31,838	1,745	413
Hampden County, Massachusetts	384,933	33,189	183,015	10,943	3,388	201,918	13,365	5,493
Hampshire County, Massachusetts	142,457	36,105	64,831	11,051	2,867	77,626	14,753	7,434
Middlesex County, Massachusetts	1,352,001	146,093	657,737	28,242	43,626	694,264	26,791	47,434
Norfolk County, Massachusetts	587,239	48,797	279,076	7,743	13,935	308,163	9,732	17,387
Plymouth County, Massachusetts	431,850	32,959	208,098	9,786	3,883	223,752	14,152	5,138
Suffolk County, Massachusetts	693,672	111,146	331,979	10,207	38,076	361,693	15,436	47,427
Worcester County, Massachusetts	689,195	65,451	336,321	16,202	13,718	352,874	17,908	17,623
MICHIGAN	8,222,619	660,087	4,014,963	249,791	46,256	4,207,656	306,092	57,948
Allegan County, Michigan	94,850	3,574	47,010	1,227	167	47,840	1,054	1,126
Bay County, Michigan	86,489	4,353	42,633	1,761	156	43,856	2,181	255
Berrien County, Michigan	125,695	9,130	60,826	2,260	1,306	64,869	3,854	1,710
Calhoun County, Michigan	109,365	6,527	53,192	2,169	800	56,173	2,789	769
Clinton County, Michigan	65,193	6,218	32,053	2,253	242	33,140	3,280	443
Eaton County, Michigan	91,517	6,421	44,552	1,963	1,072	46,965	2,145	1,241
Genesee County, Michigan	331,391	20,004	157,353	7,077	2,359	174,038	9,512	1,056
Grand Traverse County, Michigan	78,262	6,820	37,747	2,601	319	40,515	3,550	350
Ingham County, Michigan	244,634	56,030	118,293	24,414	907	126,341	29,149	1,560
Isabella County, Michigan	59,880	16,573	28,886	6,552	210	30,994	9,551	260
Jackson County, Michigan	130,971	8,516	66,379	2,862	470	64,592	4,038	1,146
Kalamazoo County, Michigan	217,375	29,983	105,192	12,957	1,637	112,183	13,754	1,635
Kent County, Michigan	526,174	36,621	256,588	11,610	4,684	269,586	14,151	6,176
Lapeer County, Michigan	73,748	2,526	37,500	608	148	36,248	1,495	275
Lenawee County, Michigan	81,651	4,793	41,549	649	951	40,102	1,721	1,472
Livingston County, Michigan	159,752	10,930	79,025	4,550	847	80,727	4,626	907
Macomb County, Michigan	725,060	51,539	349,547	18,594	2,960	375,513	24,863	5,122
Marquette County, Michigan	56,308	6,438	27,947	3,169	167	28,361	2,840	262
Midland County, Michigan	68,204	4,768	33,064	1,280	616	35,140	1,982	890
Monroe County, Michigan	124,458	7,885	60,736	2,627	793	63,722	3,795	670
Muskegon County, Michigan	140,928	6,957	69,313	1,768	453	71,615	3,336	1,400
Oakland County, Michigan	1,045,792	79,244	508,390	31,242	5,966	537,402	33,783	8,253
Ottawa County, Michigan	234,398	26,124	115,167	9,624	2,815	119,231	10,503	3,182
Saginaw County, Michigan	156,947	11,744	75,916	4,522	636	81,031	6,429	157
St. Clair County, Michigan	133,265	6,673	65,906	2,742	806	67,359	2,511	614
Shiawassee County, Michigan	56,874	2,099	27,730	926	248	29,144	803	122
Van Buren County, Michigan	61,070	3,557	30,474	1,486	21	30,596	1,723	327
Washtenaw County, Michigan	312,323	63,662	153,926	29,378	1,963	158,397	31,114	1,207
Wayne County, Michigan	1,406,491	102,038	666,986	34,920	7,785	739,505	49,580	9,753
MINNESOTA	4,555,944	338,532	2,252,132	112,932	31,249	2,303,812	140,821	53,530
Anoka County, Minnesota	287,025	18,318	142,383	5,965	1,571	144,642	7,841	2,941
Blue Earth County, Minnesota	56,091	11,494	27,798	5,020	293	28,293	5,195	986
Carver County, Minnesota	82,735	5,761	40,632	1,869	444	42,103	2,428	1,020
Crow Wing County, Minnesota	53,220	1,897	26,195	702	89	27,025	858	248
Dakota County, Minnesota	342,818	22,103	167,414	7,872	1,848	175,404	8,525	3,858
Hennepin County, Minnesota	1,033,693	87,533	508,634	32,233	8,806	525,059	34,829	11,665
Olmsted County, Minnesota	126,614	7,470	61,248	2,118	479	65,366	3,431	1,442
Ramsey County, Minnesota	442,191	42,623	213,480	11,025	5,973	228,711	15,503	10,122
Rice County, Minnesota	54,768	7,563	28,219	708	2,997	26,549	801	3,057
St. Louis County, Minnesota	167,977	18,545	83,860	7,223	1,198	84,117	7,449	2,675
Scott County, Minnesota	115,172	8,084	57,547	2,435	579	57,625	4,163	907
Stearns County, Minnesota	129,709	14,296	64,741	5,482	1,493	64,968	5,442	1,879
Washington County, Minnesota	210,174	12,713	102,976	4,830	982	107,198	5,492	1,409
Wright County, Minnesota	107,110	5,211	54,629	1,571	380	52,481	2,060	1,200
MISSISSIPPI	2,395,111	184,261	1,142,814	67,563	9,084	1,252,297	91,269	16,345
DeSoto County, Mississippi	146,674	9,799	70,036	2,978	743	76,638	5,360	718
Forrest County, Mississippi	60,242	7,920	27,975	3,680	47	32,267	3,441	752

Table C-3. College Enrollment of the Population 15 Years Old and Over, by Selected Counties, 2019—*Continued*

(Number.)

State/County	Total population age 15 years and over	Population enrolled in college or graduate school	Male			Female		
			Total population	Enrolled in public college or graduate school	Enrolled in private college or graduate school	Total population	Enrolled in public college or graduate school	Enrolled in private college or graduate school
MISSISSIPPI—(*Continued*)								
Harrison County, Mississippi	166,662	13,541	79,865	3,668	237	86,797	8,715	921
Hinds County, Mississippi	186,011	17,134	84,635	5,712	1,232	101,376	7,554	2,636
Jackson County, Mississippi	116,315	8,040	56,513	2,623	224	59,802	3,729	1,464
Lee County, Mississippi	67,571	4,422	31,619	1,016	686	35,952	2,495	225
Madison County, Mississippi	84,548	8,588	39,292	2,472	458	45,256	3,248	2,410
Rankin County, Mississippi	125,461	7,748	59,627	2,419	791	65,834	3,588	950
MISSOURI	4,999,389	353,742	2,424,912	111,036	45,743	2,574,477	139,071	57,892
Boone County, Missouri	149,660	34,092	71,131	14,252	1,481	78,529	17,096	1,263
Buchanan County, Missouri	71,313	5,084	35,778	1,757	181	35,535	2,905	241
Cape Girardeau County, Missouri	65,081	6,905	31,179	2,721	387	33,902	3,553	244
Christian County, Missouri	69,806	4,423	34,187	1,823	268	35,619	1,948	384
Clay County, Missouri	200,977	12,446	96,582	3,974	607	104,395	5,512	2,353
Cole County, Missouri	62,865	3,481	32,381	1,513	533	30,484	1,269	166
Franklin County, Missouri	84,734	2,779	42,027	910	174	42,707	980	715
Greene County, Missouri	242,815	30,124	116,626	11,594	2,177	126,189	13,923	2,430
Jackson County, Missouri	565,929	34,344	270,424	9,676	3,916	295,505	15,801	4,951
Jasper County, Missouri	96,592	5,532	46,550	2,146	441	50,042	1,826	1,119
Jefferson County, Missouri	183,671	10,266	90,590	3,226	469	93,081	5,207	1,364
Platte County, Missouri	84,187	5,383	40,585	1,322	728	43,602	2,316	1,017
St. Charles County, Missouri	325,429	23,745	158,469	6,965	4,391	166,960	6,284	6,105
St. Francois County, Missouri	55,845	3,318	30,669	1,467	333	25,176	873	645
St. Louis County, Missouri	814,428	61,812	380,094	13,812	14,607	434,334	16,939	16,454
St. Louis city, Missouri	253,045	22,490	120,774	3,166	6,432	132,271	4,274	8,618
MONTANA	880,322	63,866	440,051	26,368	3,726	440,271	29,733	4,039
Cascade County, Montana	65,918	4,542	33,066	2,122	239	32,852	1,918	263
Gallatin County, Montana	96,279	16,054	50,868	7,598	346	45,411	7,388	722
Lewis and Clark County, Montana	58,003	4,127	28,264	528	704	29,739	2,120	775
Missoula County, Montana	100,814	12,616	49,723	5,206	11	51,091	7,193	206
Yellowstone County, Montana	129,822	7,685	63,755	2,605	1,298	66,067	3,198	584
NEBRASKA	1,536,162	135,518	761,033	50,171	12,641	775,129	55,568	17,138
Douglas County, Nebraska	448,868	41,601	219,280	13,302	5,115	229,588	15,301	7,883
Lancaster County, Nebraska	257,552	39,446	128,679	17,060	2,625	128,873	16,570	3,191
Sarpy County, Nebraska	144,734	13,525	71,376	5,666	1,013	73,358	5,103	1,743
NEVADA	2,503,983	167,100	1,249,424	58,930	13,844	1,254,559	72,339	21,987
Clark County, Nevada	1,832,525	118,155	908,369	39,914	10,547	924,156	50,658	17,036
Washoe County, Nevada	387,554	35,047	194,750	14,395	2,570	192,804	15,018	3,064
NEW HAMPSHIRE	1,151,800	85,894	567,125	21,592	14,369	584,675	31,523	18,410
Cheshire County, New Hampshire	64,600	7,708	31,418	2,148	687	33,182	3,610	1,263
Grafton County, New Hampshire	78,203	9,594	38,754	1,928	3,088	39,449	2,382	2,196
Hillsborough County, New Hampshire	348,352	21,942	172,296	3,997	4,932	176,056	6,296	6,717
Merrimack County, New Hampshire	127,978	8,677	62,802	1,917	1,923	65,176	2,312	2,525
Rockingham County, New Hampshire	262,086	14,322	128,753	2,907	2,346	133,333	5,932	3,137
Strafford County, New Hampshire	111,014	16,783	53,979	6,508	374	57,035	8,692	1,209
NEW JERSEY	7,282,469	583,188	3,525,209	176,015	88,791	3,757,260	218,724	99,658
Atlantic County, New Jersey	217,722	17,304	104,683	4,913	1,257	113,039	9,554	1,580
Bergen County, New Jersey	772,148	61,156	371,143	19,480	10,613	401,005	20,669	10,394
Burlington County, New Jersey	370,243	28,024	180,963	8,200	3,200	189,280	10,410	6,214
Camden County, New Jersey	412,140	28,635	196,363	8,503	3,148	215,777	12,340	4,644
Cape May County, New Jersey	78,793	2,734	37,689	672	557	41,104	823	682
Cumberland County, New Jersey	119,639	6,657	61,994	1,833	1,234	57,645	2,635	955
Essex County, New Jersey	640,444	50,750	303,445	12,859	7,723	336,999	20,978	9,190
Gloucester County, New Jersey	240,131	20,215	115,624	6,694	2,504	124,507	8,396	2,621
Hudson County, New Jersey	554,857	45,355	274,837	13,708	9,078	280,020	13,778	8,791
Hunterdon County, New Jersey	105,925	6,815	52,274	2,746	560	53,651	2,148	1,361
Mercer County, New Jersey	303,103	38,647	145,813	9,590	8,395	157,290	13,433	7,229
Middlesex County, New Jersey	677,903	67,541	332,792	25,129	7,035	345,111	26,582	8,795
Monmouth County, New Jersey	514,709	38,627	248,400	11,329	6,738	266,309	11,628	8,932
Morris County, New Jersey	409,760	31,479	199,727	8,158	6,220	210,033	11,317	5,784
Ocean County, New Jersey	483,101	37,376	229,495	10,519	7,744	253,606	12,731	6,382
Passaic County, New Jersey	402,588	30,258	194,177	9,990	2,640	208,411	13,561	4,067
Salem County, New Jersey	51,865	3,430	25,181	1,072	133	26,684	1,676	549
Somerset County, New Jersey	271,994	19,704	132,110	5,763	3,132	139,884	7,337	3,472

Table C-3. College Enrollment of the Population 15 Years Old and Over, by Selected Counties, 2019—*Continued*

(Number.)

State/County	Total population age 15 years and over	Population enrolled in college or graduate school	Male			Female		
			Total population	Enrolled in public college or graduate school	Enrolled in private college or graduate school	Total population	Enrolled in public college or graduate school	Enrolled in private college or graduate school
NEW JERSEY—(*Continued*)								
Sussex County, New Jersey	118,669	8,611	58,482	2,442	976	60,187	3,897	1,296
Union County, New Jersey	447,945	32,538	216,691	10,238	5,240	231,254	12,680	4,380
Warren County, New Jersey	88,790	7,332	43,326	2,177	664	45,464	2,151	2,340
NEW MEXICO	1,702,893	133,353	836,630	52,320	6,421	866,263	64,777	9,835
Bernalillo County, New Mexico	559,719	51,533	271,360	19,449	2,467	288,359	25,645	3,972
Chaves County, New Mexico	50,280	3,838	25,054	1,174	1,102	25,226	1,087	475
Doña Ana County, New Mexico	174,545	22,301	85,030	11,382	262	89,515	10,093	564
Lea County, New Mexico	52,698	2,405	27,596	1,075	192	25,102	932	206
McKinley County, New Mexico	54,056	3,483	25,516	1,413	106	28,540	1,733	231
Otero County, New Mexico	54,165	2,932	28,552	1,225	27	25,613	1,582	98
Sandoval County, New Mexico	119,346	8,967	57,618	3,364	744	61,728	3,925	934
San Juan County, New Mexico	97,171	7,101	47,736	1,858	465	49,435	4,380	398
Santa Fe County, New Mexico	128,948	6,129	61,709	1,992	427	67,239	2,558	1,152
Valencia County, New Mexico	62,711	4,312	31,337	1,405	0	31,374	2,595	312
NEW YORK	16,117,350	1,373,292	7,740,453	361,471	245,778	8,376,897	429,970	336,073
Albany County, New York	259,549	34,513	123,683	9,042	4,187	135,866	14,500	6,784
Bronx County, New York	1,126,224	103,505	520,406	27,663	12,773	605,818	43,290	19,779
Broome County, New York	160,099	22,709	78,426	11,029	1,007	81,673	9,405	1,268
Cattaraugus County, New York	62,534	3,821	31,182	1,083	901	31,352	1,048	789
Cayuga County, New York	64,404	3,012	32,896	667	393	31,508	1,416	536
Chautauqua County, New York	106,284	6,579	51,317	2,939	378	54,967	2,876	386
Chemung County, New York	69,472	3,302	34,399	793	389	35,073	1,319	801
Clinton County, New York	68,946	7,270	35,639	2,420	254	33,307	4,376	220
Dutchess County, New York	249,950	22,745	123,657	4,294	4,702	126,293	6,756	6,993
Erie County, New York	766,241	63,077	366,860	25,644	5,690	399,381	23,616	8,127
Jefferson County, New York	88,088	5,289	46,738	2,074	587	41,350	2,118	510
Kings County, New York	2,065,951	159,976	959,833	40,574	29,708	1,106,118	48,574	41,120
Madison County, New York	59,903	7,579	29,486	2,094	1,517	30,417	1,839	2,129
Monroe County, New York	615,692	55,646	293,429	11,177	15,128	322,263	13,603	15,738
Nassau County, New York	1,118,617	92,088	539,814	24,216	17,690	578,803	24,294	25,888
New York County, New York	1,430,466	137,219	670,919	19,109	37,807	759,547	23,381	56,922
Niagara County, New York	174,614	11,452	85,205	2,733	1,597	89,409	4,105	3,017
Oneida County, New York	188,633	14,030	93,266	3,716	3,525	95,367	3,340	3,449
Onondaga County, New York	380,621	42,025	180,727	7,743	10,642	199,894	9,349	14,291
Ontario County, New York	91,815	6,003	44,221	984	1,628	47,594	1,794	1,597
Orange County, New York	304,414	28,742	151,568	9,781	4,107	152,846	9,482	5,372
Oswego County, New York	96,938	7,995	48,396	3,937	417	48,542	3,356	285
Putnam County, New York	83,326	5,475	41,593	767	1,494	41,733	2,549	665
Queens County, New York	1,873,771	155,139	899,328	47,026	21,080	974,443	53,743	33,290
Rensselaer County, New York	133,685	12,284	65,807	1,842	4,783	67,878	2,518	3,141
Richmond County, New York	391,032	32,801	187,177	10,620	4,663	203,855	10,236	7,282
Rockland County, New York	248,604	17,955	121,086	3,300	4,988	127,518	4,139	5,528
St. Lawrence County, New York	90,653	11,751	45,820	2,532	3,307	44,833	3,399	2,513
Saratoga County, New York	193,412	11,178	94,922	3,221	1,542	98,490	2,857	3,558
Schenectady County, New York	126,817	7,887	60,836	1,838	1,757	65,981	2,767	1,525
Steuben County, New York	78,652	2,751	38,502	934	143	40,150	1,072	602
Suffolk County, New York	1,226,112	102,245	599,668	33,468	12,522	626,444	39,329	16,926
Tompkins County, New York	90,772	29,262	45,056	2,591	12,011	45,716	2,592	12,068
Ulster County, New York	152,631	12,322	75,133	3,953	820	77,498	5,692	1,857
Wayne County, New York	74,606	3,719	36,945	1,107	384	37,661	1,122	1,106
Westchester County, New York	796,296	64,893	380,454	15,812	13,248	415,842	16,268	19,565
NORTH CAROLINA	8,589,271	705,953	4,123,129	230,968	72,171	4,466,142	318,056	84,758
Alamance County, North Carolina	138,572	11,394	63,621	2,433	1,758	74,951	3,933	3,270
Brunswick County, North Carolina	125,910	4,550	60,145	1,498	317	65,765	2,210	525
Buncombe County, North Carolina	221,984	13,244	104,945	4,546	778	117,039	6,314	1,606
Burke County, North Carolina	76,830	3,696	37,931	1,829	134	38,899	1,202	531
Cabarrus County, North Carolina	171,106	11,529	82,436	4,967	471	88,670	4,855	1,236
Carteret County, North Carolina	60,107	3,947	28,685	1,306	286	31,422	1,519	836
Catawba County, North Carolina	131,609	7,055	63,850	1,844	1,026	67,759	2,474	1,711
Cleveland County, North Carolina	80,138	6,594	37,643	2,058	1,360	42,495	1,234	1,942
Craven County, North Carolina	83,475	6,073	40,922	2,129	293	42,553	2,985	666
Cumberland County, North Carolina	265,200	29,692	130,418	9,334	4,288	134,782	12,392	3,678
Davidson County, North Carolina	137,941	5,820	66,403	2,014	327	71,538	2,009	1,470
Durham County, North Carolina	265,789	29,657	125,707	4,744	7,633	140,082	8,882	8,398
Forsyth County, North Carolina	310,507	26,579	144,726	6,012	5,062	165,781	10,290	5,215

Table C-3. College Enrollment of the Population 15 Years Old and Over, by Selected Counties, 2019—*Continued*

(Number.)

State/County	Total population age 15 years and over	Population enrolled in college or graduate school	Male			Female		
			Total population	Enrolled in public college or graduate school	Enrolled in private college or graduate school	Total population	Enrolled in public college or graduate school	Enrolled in private college or graduate school
NORTH CAROLINA—(*Continued*)								
Gaston County, North Carolina	183,220	10,119	87,323	2,963	1,345	95,897	4,768	1,043
Guilford County, North Carolina	438,740	47,002	203,959	14,817	4,284	234,781	22,633	5,268
Harnett County, North Carolina	107,377	10,639	52,907	2,752	2,158	54,470	3,220	2,509
Henderson County, North Carolina	99,653	4,598	47,604	1,871	491	52,049	1,639	597
Iredell County, North Carolina	148,861	8,821	73,392	2,845	517	75,469	4,095	1,364
Johnston County, North Carolina	165,992	14,770	80,886	5,200	1,511	85,106	7,553	506
Mecklenburg County, North Carolina	894,524	76,362	423,775	23,851	9,014	470,749	32,480	11,017
Moore County, North Carolina	83,307	6,357	39,745	1,976	1,154	43,562	2,965	262
Nash County, North Carolina	77,498	5,316	37,231	1,454	940	40,267	2,055	867
New Hanover County, North Carolina	199,117	23,909	91,930	9,037	1,021	107,187	13,063	788
Onslow County, North Carolina	156,693	18,435	87,415	7,590	1,245	69,278	8,597	1,003
Orange County, North Carolina	125,276	27,966	59,157	11,127	368	66,119	15,891	580
Pitt County, North Carolina	148,497	23,390	67,997	9,593	437	80,500	12,960	400
Randolph County, North Carolina	117,167	5,003	57,883	1,611	68	59,284	3,149	175
Robeson County, North Carolina	103,869	7,737	49,435	2,942	546	54,434	3,454	795
Rowan County, North Carolina	116,197	10,343	56,532	2,668	1,879	59,665	3,861	1,935
Rutherford County, North Carolina	55,820	3,957	25,910	1,218	911	29,910	1,403	425
Surry County, North Carolina	59,813	2,854	29,219	1,201	185	30,594	1,278	190
Union County, North Carolina	189,245	13,562	92,322	4,133	1,294	96,923	6,274	1,861
Wake County, North Carolina	894,963	85,248	430,874	30,856	6,821	464,089	38,587	8,984
Wayne County, North Carolina	98,699	7,870	46,966	2,662	1,093	51,733	3,226	889
Wilson County, North Carolina	65,754	4,838	30,311	1,217	583	35,443	3,022	16
NORTH DAKOTA	612,127	56,333	310,800	24,766	2,646	301,327	25,226	3,695
Burleigh County, North Dakota	77,176	6,263	38,167	2,451	649	39,009	2,361	802
Cass County, North Dakota	147,423	20,124	74,100	9,485	362	73,323	9,371	906
Grand Forks County, North Dakota	57,060	11,283	29,448	5,671	151	27,612	5,266	195
Ward County, North Dakota	54,103	4,567	27,947	1,505	122	26,156	2,699	241
OHIO	9,559,851	719,885	4,639,358	242,436	72,679	4,920,493	298,755	106,015
Allen County, Ohio	82,974	5,577	41,515	1,749	1,633	41,459	1,755	440
Ashtabula County, Ohio	79,729	4,191	40,063	1,156	364	39,666	2,400	271
Athens County, Ohio	57,466	16,830	28,285	7,966	127	29,181	8,543	194
Butler County, Ohio	309,553	32,953	149,959	12,267	1,644	159,594	15,575	3,467
Clark County, Ohio	110,025	7,086	52,306	2,521	432	57,719	2,041	2,092
Clermont County, Ohio	167,915	7,967	81,708	2,430	505	86,207	3,794	1,238
Columbiana County, Ohio	84,863	3,976	42,743	1,253	293	42,120	1,952	478
Cuyahoga County, Ohio	1,024,661	82,551	481,648	22,155	13,472	543,013	29,962	16,962
Delaware County, Ohio	164,761	11,408	81,298	4,032	1,230	83,463	4,650	1,496
Fairfield County, Ohio	126,576	6,310	62,230	2,499	499	64,346	2,239	1,073
Franklin County, Ohio	1,057,041	110,648	510,722	42,789	6,156	546,319	48,924	12,779
Greene County, Ohio	139,952	19,542	67,975	5,890	2,936	71,977	7,488	3,228
Hamilton County, Ohio	660,763	59,973	315,429	20,787	5,183	345,334	25,850	8,153
Hancock County, Ohio	62,003	3,592	30,640	580	618	31,363	660	1,734
Jefferson County, Ohio	55,038	3,356	26,531	847	529	28,507	631	1,349
Lake County, Ohio	192,994	12,903	93,211	3,789	1,596	99,783	5,594	1,924
Licking County, Ohio	143,798	11,189	68,936	3,119	1,024	74,862	4,171	2,875
Lorain County, Ohio	254,237	18,518	124,147	5,795	2,202	130,090	6,970	3,551
Lucas County, Ohio	346,402	25,927	165,252	11,243	1,296	181,150	10,894	2,494
Mahoning County, Ohio	191,493	13,445	93,059	4,977	1,000	98,434	6,967	501
Marion County, Ohio	54,049	2,592	28,724	924	55	25,325	1,480	133
Medina County, Ohio	147,585	8,709	72,132	3,661	777	75,453	3,485	786
Miami County, Ohio	87,026	5,372	42,620	2,306	381	44,406	2,129	556
Montgomery County, Ohio	434,847	38,107	206,595	9,821	8,007	228,252	10,736	9,543
Muskingum County, Ohio	70,647	4,235	34,569	348	1,360	36,078	1,728	799
Portage County, Ohio	138,484	19,965	67,375	7,319	981	71,109	10,435	1,230
Richland County, Ohio	99,160	5,016	50,497	1,035	669	48,663	2,512	800
Stark County, Ohio	305,706	15,675	147,319	4,772	2,534	158,387	5,009	3,360
Summit County, Ohio	448,070	30,527	215,499	12,984	1,846	232,571	13,099	2,598
Trumbull County, Ohio	164,849	8,128	79,486	2,758	377	85,363	3,891	1,102
Tuscarawas County, Ohio	74,470	2,981	36,741	670	370	37,729	1,517	424
Warren County, Ohio	189,422	11,046	95,312	3,607	1,111	94,110	5,052	1,276
Wayne County, Ohio	93,007	5,863	45,910	1,225	1,620	47,097	1,365	1,653
Wood County, Ohio	109,449	18,216	53,544	8,034	583	55,905	9,176	423
OKLAHOMA	3,162,944	232,376	1,551,528	87,517	13,865	1,611,416	109,824	21,170
Canadian County, Oklahoma	116,561	6,911	56,847	1,865	528	59,714	3,338	1,180
Cleveland County, Oklahoma	234,645	37,091	116,737	16,988	743	117,908	18,273	1,087

Table C-3. College Enrollment of the Population 15 Years Old and Over, by Selected Counties, 2019—*Continued*

(Number.)

State/County	Total population age 15 years and over	Population enrolled in college or graduate school	Male			Female		
			Total population	Enrolled in public college or graduate school	Enrolled in private college or graduate school	Total population	Enrolled in public college or graduate school	Enrolled in private college or graduate school
OKLAHOMA—(*Continued*)								
Comanche County, Oklahoma	97,262	6,854	51,093	3,293	258	46,169	2,939	364
Creek County, Oklahoma	57,685	2,260	27,959	700	66	29,726	1,300	194
Muskogee County, Oklahoma	54,126	3,309	26,178	1,541	51	27,948	1,342	375
Oklahoma County, Oklahoma	626,466	47,707	303,051	15,653	4,114	323,415	22,001	5,939
Payne County, Oklahoma	68,853	20,101	34,026	10,578	241	34,827	8,940	342
Pottawatomie County, Oklahoma	58,313	4,634	27,654	1,228	166	30,659	1,703	1,537
Rogers County, Oklahoma	74,797	3,145	36,972	895	200	37,825	1,651	399
Tulsa County, Oklahoma	514,476	38,174	247,853	11,608	4,870	266,623	16,035	5,661
Wagoner County, Oklahoma	65,332	2,968	32,009	1,094	325	33,323	1,398	151
OREGON	3,504,094	259,574	1,722,666	93,067	19,348	1,781,428	113,117	34,042
Benton County, Oregon	81,083	20,918	40,174	10,781	154	40,909	9,546	437
Clackamas County, Oregon	345,940	21,108	169,858	9,001	691	176,082	8,366	3,050
Deschutes County, Oregon	166,622	8,536	81,768	3,502	407	84,854	3,892	735
Douglas County, Oregon	93,186	4,068	45,104	1,248	100	48,082	1,803	917
Jackson County, Oregon	183,298	10,213	88,019	2,700	278	95,279	6,402	833
Klamath County, Oregon	55,726	3,614	27,320	1,724	0	28,406	1,819	71
Lane County, Oregon	324,577	35,253	157,333	14,573	1,251	167,244	17,917	1,512
Linn County, Oregon	106,979	6,868	52,674	3,134	251	54,305	2,780	703
Marion County, Oregon	278,280	17,130	136,918	5,203	2,522	141,362	6,054	3,351
Multnomah County, Oregon	686,724	60,559	338,498	18,392	6,479	348,226	25,281	10,407
Polk County, Oregon	70,271	7,792	34,360	2,742	395	35,911	4,333	322
Umatilla County, Oregon	61,573	3,709	32,114	1,830	268	29,459	1,396	215
Washington County, Oregon	489,736	34,610	240,520	10,280	3,934	249,216	13,361	7,035
Yamhill County, Oregon	88,250	7,019	43,651	1,257	1,651	44,599	1,659	2,452
PENNSYLVANIA	10,628,076	792,332	5,159,722	206,601	143,005	5,468,354	251,589	191,137
Adams County, Pennsylvania	86,908	6,656	42,245	1,270	1,544	44,663	1,476	2,366
Allegheny County, Pennsylvania	1,027,809	86,884	492,183	24,512	15,286	535,626	27,838	19,248
Beaver County, Pennsylvania	138,074	5,989	66,005	1,609	961	72,069	1,587	1,832
Berks County, Pennsylvania	344,080	26,982	167,798	6,446	3,489	176,282	12,193	4,854
Blair County, Pennsylvania	101,369	4,931	49,067	1,835	369	52,302	2,090	637
Bucks County, Pennsylvania	525,900	32,896	256,224	11,217	3,996	269,676	10,415	7,268
Butler County, Pennsylvania	157,342	10,951	76,770	3,342	944	80,572	5,525	1,140
Cambria County, Pennsylvania	110,370	6,646	53,690	1,619	1,129	56,680	2,350	1,548
Centre County, Pennsylvania	143,113	38,601	74,899	20,443	892	68,214	15,935	1,331
Chester County, Pennsylvania	429,012	34,636	210,497	10,598	4,565	218,515	12,730	6,743
Clearfield County, Pennsylvania	67,613	1,999	36,054	727	98	31,559	737	437
Columbia County, Pennsylvania	55,537	7,188	26,661	2,361	539	28,876	4,010	278
Crawford County, Pennsylvania	70,506	3,812	33,808	551	931	36,698	958	1,372
Cumberland County, Pennsylvania	210,236	18,361	103,714	4,974	2,890	106,522	6,236	4,261
Dauphin County, Pennsylvania	226,510	14,663	109,050	5,419	1,278	117,460	5,934	2,032
Delaware County, Pennsylvania	463,746	43,033	220,339	8,464	10,044	243,407	10,237	14,288
Erie County, Pennsylvania	222,829	16,612	108,382	4,994	3,195	114,447	3,965	4,458
Fayette County, Pennsylvania	109,263	2,907	53,780	1,014	194	55,483	1,581	118
Franklin County, Pennsylvania	126,361	5,463	61,583	1,362	518	64,778	2,175	1,408
Indiana County, Pennsylvania	71,638	9,162	35,716	4,262	235	35,922	3,927	738
Lackawanna County, Pennsylvania	174,040	12,717	83,292	1,328	4,911	90,748	2,263	4,215
Lancaster County, Pennsylvania	438,922	25,121	212,114	6,294	5,425	226,808	8,505	4,897
Lawrence County, Pennsylvania	71,590	3,530	34,686	888	622	36,904	1,252	768
Lebanon County, Pennsylvania	115,277	6,003	56,049	1,348	1,448	59,228	1,860	1,347
Lehigh County, Pennsylvania	300,902	22,003	145,520	4,531	4,247	155,382	7,537	5,688
Luzerne County, Pennsylvania	265,911	19,620	130,268	4,701	4,253	135,643	4,788	5,878
Lycoming County, Pennsylvania	94,005	6,094	45,950	2,586	846	48,055	2,038	624
Mercer County, Pennsylvania	92,461	5,821	44,879	877	1,819	47,582	1,529	1,596
Monroe County, Pennsylvania	143,425	9,506	71,127	2,552	764	72,298	5,169	1,021
Montgomery County, Pennsylvania	684,301	49,061	329,126	12,264	9,167	355,175	13,515	14,115
Northampton County, Pennsylvania	256,319	23,041	124,824	4,875	5,412	131,495	5,664	7,090
Northumberland County, Pennsylvania	75,978	1,673	38,434	458	150	37,544	807	258
Philadelphia County, Pennsylvania	1,292,929	131,556	600,920	22,360	32,664	692,009	30,953	45,579
Schuylkill County, Pennsylvania	118,733	3,922	61,071	946	584	57,662	1,746	646
Washington County, Pennsylvania	173,753	10,784	84,440	3,504	1,424	89,313	3,928	1,928
Westmoreland County, Pennsylvania	297,364	16,275	144,670	3,904	3,049	152,694	5,171	4,151
York County, Pennsylvania	368,035	22,944	180,729	5,613	4,998	187,306	7,307	5,026
RHODE ISLAND	892,832	90,398	432,431	23,591	17,684	460,401	26,564	22,559
Kent County, Rhode Island	139,905	8,997	67,316	2,334	1,874	72,589	3,194	1,595
Newport County, Rhode Island	71,333	5,853	34,452	1,803	1,121	36,881	1,226	1,703

Table C-3. College Enrollment of the Population 15 Years Old and Over, by Selected Counties, 2019—*Continued*

(Number.)

State/County	Total population age 15 years and over	Population enrolled in college or graduate school	Male			Female		
			Total population	Enrolled in public college or graduate school	Enrolled in private college or graduate school	Total population	Enrolled in public college or graduate school	Enrolled in private college or graduate school
RHODE ISLAND—(*Continued*)								
Providence County, Rhode Island	530,805	55,500	257,551	12,846	12,101	273,254	14,812	15,741
Washington County, Rhode Island	109,456	14,547	53,125	5,437	1,104	56,331	6,623	1,383
SOUTH CAROLINA	4,224,180	291,431	2,015,500	95,522	25,322	2,208,680	130,924	39,663
Aiken County, South Carolina	139,615	7,808	65,150	2,580	940	74,465	3,421	867
Anderson County, South Carolina	166,004	9,347	78,685	2,368	1,444	87,319	3,520	2,015
Beaufort County, South Carolina	162,921	5,105	79,041	1,347	223	83,880	2,818	717
Berkeley County, South Carolina	183,487	12,949	90,267	5,155	1,574	93,220	4,779	1,441
Charleston County, South Carolina	342,842	26,498	164,098	10,346	2,944	178,744	9,841	3,367
Darlington County, South Carolina	54,662	3,603	25,328	953	249	29,334	2,203	198
Dorchester County, South Carolina	130,223	9,822	62,410	2,844	297	67,813	5,441	1,240
Florence County, South Carolina	111,634	7,462	51,928	1,851	829	59,706	4,039	743
Greenville County, South Carolina	423,087	29,564	202,438	6,387	4,818	220,649	11,509	6,850
Greenwood County, South Carolina	57,766	4,491	26,282	1,918	172	31,484	2,338	63
Horry County, South Carolina	301,546	16,603	143,026	5,641	1,113	158,520	7,798	2,051
Lexington County, South Carolina	241,350	15,672	115,069	5,367	411	126,281	8,188	1,706
Oconee County, South Carolina	66,146	3,037	32,213	624	0	33,933	1,909	504
Orangeburg County, South Carolina	70,237	6,155	32,253	1,955	745	37,984	2,297	1,158
Pickens County, South Carolina	107,119	18,156	52,845	8,874	341	54,274	8,192	749
Richland County, South Carolina	342,294	43,231	162,533	16,542	2,034	179,761	19,276	5,379
Spartanburg County, South Carolina	258,380	17,566	123,483	5,179	2,593	134,897	6,270	3,524
Sumter County, South Carolina	85,579	7,418	40,669	1,840	614	44,910	3,969	995
York County, South Carolina	224,594	12,624	106,751	3,659	723	117,843	7,818	424
SOUTH DAKOTA	703,693	47,250	353,022	18,136	2,562	350,671	21,604	4,948
Minnehaha County, South Dakota	152,306	10,092	77,114	3,116	1,272	75,192	3,959	1,745
Pennington County, South Dakota	92,229	6,970	46,329	3,291	239	45,900	2,874	566
TENNESSEE	5,572,864	381,153	2,688,514	123,435	41,119	2,884,350	157,546	59,053
Anderson County, Tennessee	64,228	3,858	31,130	1,399	426	33,098	1,460	573
Blount County, Tennessee	110,981	5,632	53,217	1,612	365	57,764	2,411	1,244
Bradley County, Tennessee	89,585	6,368	43,009	1,126	1,400	46,576	1,512	2,330
Davidson County, Tennessee	571,294	50,368	272,276	9,844	9,778	299,018	13,199	17,547
Greene County, Tennessee	58,140	2,398	28,753	511	223	29,387	904	760
Hamilton County, Tennessee	304,394	24,622	144,895	7,416	2,822	159,499	11,052	3,332
Knox County, Tennessee	388,729	36,396	185,221	15,029	2,665	203,508	16,302	2,400
Madison County, Tennessee	78,572	6,667	35,793	1,052	1,140	42,779	2,260	2,215
Montgomery County, Tennessee	160,704	15,677	79,096	5,798	1,961	81,608	7,095	823
Putnam County, Tennessee	66,458	9,793	32,671	5,291	15	33,787	4,393	94
Robertson County, Tennessee	57,803	2,466	28,298	667	351	29,505	1,122	326
Rutherford County, Tennessee	264,360	27,481	129,000	12,373	992	135,360	12,226	1,890
Shelby County, Tennessee	741,794	58,651	346,245	17,837	6,348	395,549	26,525	7,941
Sullivan County, Tennessee	133,729	5,889	64,127	2,205	582	69,602	2,507	595
Sumner County, Tennessee	154,190	9,755	74,306	2,727	768	79,884	5,054	1,206
Washington County, Tennessee	109,300	11,665	53,343	4,663	553	55,957	5,429	1,020
Williamson County, Tennessee	187,139	8,322	90,246	3,282	932	96,893	2,277	1,831
Wilson County, Tennessee	115,778	5,717	56,024	1,960	215	59,754	1,952	1,590
TEXAS	22,833,954	1,872,086	11,246,327	704,216	150,108	11,587,627	851,967	165,795
Bell County, Texas	278,402	29,806	138,080	11,039	2,638	140,322	11,844	4,285
Bexar County, Texas	1,581,145	143,326	774,378	48,549	17,828	806,767	56,837	20,112
Bowie County, Texas	74,841	3,700	37,540	1,316	276	37,301	1,974	134
Brazoria County, Texas	292,841	21,294	146,765	8,194	1,111	146,076	11,163	826
Brazos County, Texas	188,922	53,493	94,824	27,266	904	94,098	23,840	1,483
Cameron County, Texas	318,865	21,014	153,324	8,590	523	165,541	11,269	632
Collin County, Texas	818,033	63,583	399,356	22,288	5,079	418,677	30,848	5,368
Comal County, Texas	127,394	7,703	62,190	3,943	293	65,204	2,956	511
Coryell County, Texas	61,147	5,850	30,613	2,910	389	30,534	2,457	94
Dallas County, Texas	2,064,970	149,472	1,009,061	52,544	15,430	1,055,909	65,914	15,584
Denton County, Texas	710,565	75,025	344,169	29,847	7,173	366,396	32,857	5,148
Ector County, Texas	123,265	8,353	62,868	3,934	0	60,397	4,419	0
Ellis County, Texas	144,682	10,525	71,258	4,214	598	73,424	3,653	2,060
El Paso County, Texas	652,364	70,571	319,515	29,175	5,494	332,849	32,008	3,894
Fort Bend County, Texas	629,479	51,687	305,130	20,348	3,397	324,349	21,325	6,617
Galveston County, Texas	274,579	22,796	133,747	8,181	1,148	140,832	12,726	741
Grayson County, Texas	109,181	6,465	52,423	1,839	816	56,758	2,854	956
Gregg County, Texas	97,761	6,797	46,852	1,422	1,674	50,909	2,795	906
Guadalupe County, Texas	132,528	10,853	65,405	3,586	1,315	67,123	4,481	1,471

Table C-3. College Enrollment of the Population 15 Years Old and Over, by Selected Counties, 2019—*Continued*

(Number.)

State/County	Total population age 15 years and over	Population enrolled in college or graduate school	Male			Female		
			Total population	Enrolled in public college or graduate school	Enrolled in private college or graduate school	Total population	Enrolled in public college or graduate school	Enrolled in private college or graduate school
TEXAS—*(Continued)*								
Harris County, Texas	3,670,686	297,498	1,809,337	110,157	24,074	1,861,349	138,795	24,472
Hays County, Texas	186,126	31,172	91,565	11,524	568	94,561	18,023	1,057
Hidalgo County, Texas	636,599	55,549	308,029	20,869	2,840	328,570	28,105	3,735
Hunt County, Texas	78,919	6,084	38,357	2,810	264	40,562	2,820	190
Jefferson County, Texas	200,530	12,411	102,314	4,850	536	98,216	6,316	709
Johnson County, Texas	138,330	6,627	68,943	1,753	712	69,387	3,312	850
Kaufman County, Texas	104,663	10,910	51,718	5,234	517	52,945	4,474	685
Lubbock County, Texas	249,137	39,456	121,976	17,740	1,092	127,161	19,506	1,118
McLennan County, Texas	204,353	29,098	98,116	7,052	6,116	106,237	7,828	8,102
Midland County, Texas	132,749	11,071	66,379	5,215	628	66,370	4,952	276
Montgomery County, Texas	475,362	26,369	232,346	10,076	2,126	243,016	12,830	1,337
Nacogdoches County, Texas	52,649	9,956	25,625	4,166	55	27,024	5,705	30
Nueces County, Texas	289,525	20,892	141,520	7,455	966	148,005	11,552	919
Orange County, Texas	66,708	3,170	32,830	1,237	290	33,878	1,208	435
Potter County, Texas	90,574	4,889	46,431	1,587	61	44,143	3,235	6
Randall County, Texas	109,927	10,834	53,682	3,706	360	56,245	6,679	89
Rockwall County, Texas	82,032	6,958	39,759	2,258	1,022	42,273	3,118	560
San Patricio County, Texas	52,030	2,890	26,041	1,143	53	25,989	1,554	140
Smith County, Texas	185,415	14,164	87,496	4,951	806	97,919	7,854	553
Tarrant County, Texas	1,649,036	141,123	797,109	47,912	14,359	851,927	62,152	16,700
Taylor County, Texas	109,424	12,643	52,505	2,712	2,906	56,919	3,019	4,006
Tom Green County, Texas	95,940	10,773	46,444	5,646	77	49,496	4,741	309
Travis County, Texas	1,047,191	99,336	526,509	42,106	7,059	520,682	42,739	7,432
Victoria County, Texas	73,072	4,494	35,726	1,911	66	37,346	2,405	112
Walker County, Texas	63,724	13,582	38,267	7,092	38	25,457	6,097	355
Webb County, Texas	202,272	17,175	97,818	7,184	338	104,454	9,264	389
Wichita County, Texas	106,946	9,490	55,557	4,179	464	51,389	4,576	271
Williamson County, Texas	466,923	33,951	227,068	13,124	2,333	239,855	13,734	4,760
Wise County, Texas	55,400	2,322	28,063	955	114	27,337	751	502
UTAH	2,434,424	264,935	1,214,886	96,084	36,548	1,219,538	97,655	34,648
Cache County, Utah	96,287	19,807	47,633	8,558	703	48,654	9,571	975
Davis County, Utah	261,645	23,747	130,186	9,791	1,386	131,459	9,914	2,656
Salt Lake County, Utah	904,193	82,182	450,982	35,664	6,651	453,211	32,124	7,743
Utah County, Utah	461,033	84,437	231,358	22,856	23,053	229,675	20,177	18,351
Washington County, Utah	140,407	9,097	68,495	2,790	1,115	71,912	3,843	1,349
Weber County, Utah	199,985	18,081	100,082	6,887	1,367	99,903	8,453	1,374
VERMONT	531,842	50,073	261,751	14,489	6,681	270,091	19,742	9,161
Chittenden County, Vermont	140,729	22,999	68,351	7,681	1,727	72,378	10,638	2,953
VIRGINIA	6,988,054	621,142	3,405,420	216,357	69,762	3,582,634	249,341	85,682
Albemarle County, Virginia	91,847	13,127	44,182	6,026	373	47,665	6,153	575
Arlington County, Virginia	199,459	17,690	98,958	4,841	3,709	100,501	4,928	4,212
Bedford County, Virginia	66,013	3,873	32,112	1,231	605	33,901	832	1,205
Chesterfield County, Virginia	284,722	21,370	135,271	8,187	1,147	149,451	9,802	2,234
Fairfax County, Virginia	926,315	81,312	456,008	30,736	9,784	470,307	32,066	8,726
Fauquier County, Virginia	57,721	3,728	27,661	1,512	406	30,060	1,650	160
Hanover County, Virginia	88,732	6,578	42,500	1,983	1,004	46,232	2,235	1,356
Henrico County, Virginia	269,486	18,902	125,624	6,518	1,368	143,862	8,621	2,395
James City County, Virginia	64,383	3,787	29,999	1,944	384	34,384	1,232	227
Loudoun County, Virginia	318,169	26,633	156,893	9,409	2,702	161,276	11,197	3,325
Montgomery County, Virginia	86,714	28,947	44,602	16,092	520	42,112	12,260	75
Prince William County, Virginia	365,031	37,456	180,585	14,471	3,432	184,446	13,560	5,993
Roanoke County, Virginia	79,121	3,962	37,737	1,375	102	41,384	1,734	751
Rockingham County, Virginia	67,356	5,079	32,793	1,420	754	34,563	1,561	1,344
Spotsylvania County, Virginia	108,249	6,992	53,160	2,484	914	55,089	3,256	338
Stafford County, Virginia	120,305	10,159	60,164	3,257	606	60,141	4,293	2,003
York County, Virginia	54,593	4,355	26,002	1,585	935	28,591	1,362	473
Alexandria city, Virginia	134,053	10,033	63,895	2,884	1,364	70,158	3,859	1,926
Chesapeake city, Virginia	195,814	16,770	94,172	5,391	1,137	101,642	8,199	2,043
Hampton city, Virginia	110,746	13,290	52,642	4,082	2,683	58,104	3,293	3,232
Lynchburg city, Virginia	68,356	16,887	32,044	1,857	6,613	36,312	1,923	6,494
Newport News city, Virginia	143,459	13,719	68,346	4,203	1,641	75,113	6,131	1,744
Norfolk city, Virginia	201,932	27,694	106,005	10,052	2,372	95,927	13,017	2,253
Portsmouth city, Virginia	75,905	6,397	35,938	2,313	804	39,967	2,178	1,102
Richmond city, Virginia	196,570	26,001	92,551	8,034	2,315	104,019	11,449	4,203

Table C-3. College Enrollment of the Population 15 Years Old and Over, by Selected Counties, 2019—*Continued*

(Number.)

State/County	Total population age 15 years and over	Population enrolled in college or graduate school	Male Total population	Male Enrolled in public college or graduate school	Male Enrolled in private college or graduate school	Female Total population	Female Enrolled in public college or graduate school	Female Enrolled in private college or graduate school
VIRGINIA—(*Continued*)								
Roanoke city, Virginia	80,875	4,290	38,078	2,029	392	42,797	1,562	307
Suffolk city, Virginia	73,736	5,571	35,305	1,961	611	38,431	1,887	1,112
Virginia Beach city, Virginia	367,049	33,522	178,665	11,046	5,952	188,384	12,255	4,269
WASHINGTON	6,225,423	447,127	3,095,428	169,822	35,772	3,129,995	194,464	47,069
Benton County, Washington	160,197	8,307	79,556	1,725	821	80,641	5,083	678
Chelan County, Washington	61,978	4,151	31,233	1,001	452	30,745	2,357	341
Clallam County, Washington	66,526	2,311	32,649	1,038	220	33,877	816	237
Clark County, Washington	393,960	21,641	192,998	7,664	1,097	200,962	10,800	2,080
Cowlitz County, Washington	89,879	4,861	44,250	1,628	225	45,629	2,546	462
Franklin County, Washington	69,048	4,817	35,754	2,143	455	33,294	2,150	69
Island County, Washington	72,076	3,239	36,748	1,269	164	35,328	1,392	414
King County, Washington	1,872,673	155,728	937,565	60,468	12,515	935,108	63,559	19,186
Kitsap County, Washington	225,534	13,107	114,495	5,066	653	111,039	5,900	1,488
Lewis County, Washington	66,581	3,229	33,392	1,223	144	33,189	1,431	431
Pierce County, Washington	727,543	51,960	361,082	19,881	3,964	366,461	22,450	5,665
Skagit County, Washington	105,878	5,454	51,386	1,676	459	54,492	3,017	302
Snohomish County, Washington	667,627	41,665	332,655	16,374	2,995	334,972	18,692	3,604
Spokane County, Washington	427,021	36,247	209,922	12,186	6,067	217,099	13,002	4,992
Thurston County, Washington	239,582	15,818	116,209	5,466	1,506	123,373	6,287	2,559
Whatcom County, Washington	192,188	21,163	93,645	8,147	1,016	98,543	11,706	294
Yakima County, Washington	189,355	10,472	94,178	3,879	883	95,177	3,856	1,854
WEST VIRGINIA	1,497,185	92,972	734,220	35,920	4,940	762,965	43,933	8,179
Berkeley County, West Virginia	96,366	5,473	47,182	1,325	292	49,184	3,033	823
Cabell County, West Virginia	76,950	8,843	37,340	3,878	565	39,610	4,245	155
Kanawha County, West Virginia	148,811	7,211	70,898	2,627	225	77,913	2,871	1,488
Monongalia County, West Virginia	91,078	21,677	46,550	11,316	257	44,528	9,810	294
Raleigh County, West Virginia	60,718	3,857	30,059	890	331	30,659	1,906	730
Wood County, West Virginia	69,236	2,782	33,361	594	329	35,875	1,367	492
WISCONSIN	4,781,987	365,712	2,363,075	133,489	28,948	2,418,912	156,670	46,605
Brown County, Wisconsin	212,871	16,845	104,782	4,964	2,521	108,089	6,189	3,171
Dane County, Wisconsin	454,661	64,488	224,773	29,175	1,882	229,888	29,646	3,785
Dodge County, Wisconsin	73,092	3,350	37,861	1,158	155	35,231	1,843	194
Eau Claire County, Wisconsin	87,248	12,929	42,782	4,477	1,628	44,466	6,634	190
Fond du Lac County, Wisconsin	85,853	6,950	41,580	1,604	869	44,273	2,455	2,022
Jefferson County, Wisconsin	70,226	5,252	34,723	1,602	786	35,503	2,111	753
Kenosha County, Wisconsin	137,924	9,631	67,416	2,824	1,050	70,508	3,675	2,082
La Crosse County, Wisconsin	98,614	15,526	47,610	6,226	646	51,004	7,301	1,353
Manitowoc County, Wisconsin	66,137	2,285	32,942	1,123	144	33,195	856	162
Marathon County, Wisconsin	109,853	5,287	55,405	1,506	386	54,448	2,873	522
Milwaukee County, Wisconsin	755,872	63,407	360,936	20,038	8,153	394,936	20,859	14,357
Outagamie County, Wisconsin	151,268	11,877	74,894	4,035	881	76,374	4,773	2,188
Ozaukee County, Wisconsin	73,871	6,086	36,259	1,700	1,299	37,612	1,295	1,792
Portage County, Wisconsin	59,723	7,963	29,580	2,902	86	30,143	4,768	207
Racine County, Wisconsin	159,305	7,766	79,032	2,898	170	80,273	3,786	912
Rock County, Wisconsin	133,285	9,247	64,135	2,912	1,082	69,150	4,197	1,056
St. Croix County, Wisconsin	72,302	3,597	35,692	1,222	87	36,610	1,973	315
Sheboygan County, Wisconsin	94,132	4,952	47,527	1,133	989	46,605	1,632	1,198
Walworth County, Wisconsin	87,160	9,042	43,717	3,944	388	43,443	4,129	581
Washington County, Wisconsin	112,765	6,538	56,022	2,899	295	56,743	2,608	736
Waukesha County, Wisconsin	334,841	18,498	163,943	5,717	2,268	170,898	6,901	3,612
Winnebago County, Wisconsin	143,063	12,851	71,700	4,529	162	71,363	7,181	979
Wood County, Wisconsin	59,998	2,238	29,354	809	117	30,644	1,244	68
WYOMING	466,224	37,578	237,532	15,538	1,645	228,692	18,146	2,249
Laramie County, Wyoming	80,320	5,280	40,789	1,476	463	39,531	2,389	952
Natrona County, Wyoming	63,887	3,452	31,493	1,458	361	32,394	1,572	61

Table C-4. Primary and Secondary School Enrollment, by Sex and Selected Counties, 2019

(Number.)

State/County	Population 3 years and over	Male					Female				
		Enrolled in school					Enrolled in school				
		Nursery school, Pre-school	Kindergarten	Grades 1 to 4	Grades 5 to 8	Grades 9 to 12	Nursery school, Pre-school	Kindergarten	Grades 1 to 4	Grades 5 to 8	Grades 9 to 12
UNITED STATES	316,992,457	2,596,823	2,060,683	8,046,670	8,688,749	8,673,511	2,447,566	1,951,081	7,681,955	8,230,150	8,259,124
ALABAMA	4,739,065	34,089	32,164	121,022	134,513	126,289	31,411	28,198	115,245	118,353	121,875
Baldwin County, Alabama	216,753	1,020	1,859	3,127	8,056	5,584	804	1,153	5,951	3,953	6,049
Calhoun County, Alabama	108,929	692	608	2,564	3,049	2,751	626	582	2,936	2,745	1,536
Cullman County, Alabama	81,399	716	703	2,191	2,082	2,044	708	396	1,604	2,898	1,813
Elmore County, Alabama	78,142	651	702	2,386	2,005	2,448	77	451	2,386	1,092	2,259
Etowah County, Alabama	99,818	735	1,204	1,946	3,353	2,311	542	214	2,159	2,947	2,232
Houston County, Alabama	102,402	927	685	2,575	3,296	2,515	1,025	573	2,515	2,516	3,218
Jefferson County, Alabama	633,528	5,005	4,204	15,955	18,043	16,409	5,154	3,305	15,372	16,178	15,950
Lauderdale County, Alabama	90,763	125	251	2,081	2,639	2,961	684	230	1,634	2,937	2,688
Lee County, Alabama	159,453	2,024	1,191	6,823	2,315	4,516	1,522	2,006	2,139	3,148	3,766
Limestone County, Alabama	96,320	648	526	2,163	2,920	3,001	865	431	2,308	2,639	2,816
Madison County, Alabama	360,091	2,194	2,927	8,467	9,904	8,357	3,062	1,714	8,034	9,389	9,665
Marshall County, Alabama	93,005	638	611	2,762	2,317	2,876	836	1,280	2,224	2,556	3,666
Mobile County, Alabama	396,526	2,314	3,142	8,727	11,587	11,373	1,972	2,875	9,855	11,013	9,709
Montgomery County, Alabama	218,943	2,218	1,087	6,408	6,716	6,057	2,712	1,805	6,014	5,321	5,183
Morgan County, Alabama	114,628	827	883	3,161	4,079	2,336	456	425	2,625	2,760	3,460
Shelby County, Alabama	210,898	1,722	1,132	6,025	6,711	6,023	1,870	531	5,929	6,111	6,224
Tuscaloosa County, Alabama	201,549	2,233	763	3,279	6,245	6,302	723	1,499	6,045	2,936	3,936
ALASKA	700,993	5,444	7,164	21,218	18,523	21,380	6,027	4,752	19,062	18,605	15,839
Anchorage Municipality, Alaska	276,008	2,161	3,864	7,797	5,881	8,239	2,722	1,559	7,457	7,530	5,576
Fairbanks North Star Borough, Alaska	92,916	814	353	3,368	2,604	3,085	922	596	2,444	2,101	1,270
Matanuska-Susitna Borough, Alaska	104,303	855	880	3,490	2,819	3,687	582	905	3,109	3,024	2,956
ARIZONA	7,039,085	43,464	41,717	180,479	202,531	199,917	48,157	43,369	173,820	188,357	186,870
Cochise County, Arizona	121,949	995	505	3,725	2,949	3,325	946	1,147	2,461	3,236	3,106
Coconino County, Arizona	139,384	993	1,074	3,374	3,064	3,235	1,371	472	2,894	3,800	2,707
Maricopa County, Arizona	4,328,828	27,894	28,334	112,079	129,217	126,217	28,839	27,358	109,447	120,641	120,743
Mohave County, Arizona	206,587	404	1,071	4,263	5,012	3,385	1,322	1,119	3,274	5,039	3,850
Navajo County, Arizona	106,805	356	771	3,469	3,207	3,932	751	1,008	3,022	3,401	3,733
Pima County, Arizona	1,015,663	6,574	4,655	23,697	27,253	25,540	7,482	6,059	24,983	22,555	25,464
Pinal County, Arizona	449,319	2,507	1,398	11,305	14,475	13,808	2,157	2,226	12,857	11,226	10,824
Yavapai County, Arizona	230,383	1,225	326	5,571	4,492	5,865	1,916	1,051	3,116	5,272	3,819
Yuma County, Arizona	205,968	1,220	1,853	6,396	5,428	6,730	1,741	1,089	6,424	6,384	5,637
ARKANSAS	2,914,455	26,735	19,792	79,746	80,765	82,319	23,567	19,134	77,614	74,697	77,295
Benton County, Arkansas	269,756	2,509	1,767	10,339	6,770	8,295	1,781	1,774	8,909	8,296	7,251
Craighead County, Arkansas	107,112	2,458	605	2,497	2,559	2,959	1,083	1,125	2,476	3,249	2,162
Faulkner County, Arkansas	122,595	1,200	482	3,849	4,111	3,376	885	884	3,434	2,868	2,979
Garland County, Arkansas	96,793	1,094	457	2,226	2,175	1,785	219	717	1,944	2,191	1,968
Jefferson County, Arkansas	64,401	566	345	2,503	726	2,482	164	273	1,407	1,719	1,124
Lonoke County, Arkansas	70,563	320	479	2,197	1,691	2,496	763	0	1,827	2,206	2,644
Pulaski County, Arkansas	378,179	4,741	2,689	9,735	10,568	10,105	3,880	3,103	10,450	8,694	8,930
Saline County, Arkansas	118,673	526	970	3,203	2,584	3,332	1,164	736	2,466	3,685	3,882
Sebastian County, Arkansas	123,114	1,091	968	2,943	4,341	3,557	977	1,029	3,795	2,821	3,171
Washington County, Arkansas	230,260	1,617	1,943	6,616	6,886	7,155	3,099	1,312	6,620	5,041	6,356
CALIFORNIA	38,142,157	309,297	253,153	974,965	1,036,089	1,098,456	295,216	248,323	920,933	990,747	1,035,147
Alameda County, California	1,613,494	12,523	10,503	37,020	37,737	40,565	14,159	10,471	32,703	38,375	37,341
Butte County, California	210,574	726	1,511	5,403	4,270	5,946	1,310	912	5,192	5,495	4,113
Contra Costa County, California	1,116,596	9,186	8,194	29,199	28,413	35,269	10,225	6,074	29,925	26,290	33,765
El Dorado County, California	188,120	2,006	1,820	3,321	4,880	4,365	1,181	1,302	3,596	5,379	4,511
Fresno County, California	956,284	7,933	8,016	31,956	33,009	34,422	5,678	9,017	30,989	33,625	31,288
Humboldt County, California	132,071	1,595	789	2,549	3,559	2,070	385	1,736	2,805	2,583	2,187
Imperial County, California	173,145	3,041	1,570	5,699	6,048	8,906	1,543	1,778	4,689	6,061	5,623
Kern County, California	861,611	6,480	10,019	27,869	28,499	34,266	7,957	9,102	25,922	31,729	30,424
Kings County, California	145,568	1,463	1,461	2,506	5,779	6,966	709	1,041	4,286	5,297	4,598
Los Angeles County, California	9,704,924	76,748	61,260	231,811	252,800	263,242	74,855	58,761	219,925	237,845	249,703
Madera County, California	151,013	627	442	6,286	3,562	7,180	788	2,656	4,439	3,815	5,694
Marin County, California	252,415	1,609	2,147	4,869	6,330	6,845	1,280	2,272	4,257	5,351	8,362
Mendocino County, California	84,527	423	119	1,936	2,867	1,698	788	486	2,461	2,141	2,096
Merced County, California	264,673	1,300	2,677	8,815	10,637	9,061	1,932	2,648	8,166	9,020	8,905
Monterey County, California	416,354	4,133	2,916	13,754	11,511	15,369	3,085	3,855	10,935	12,708	14,859
Napa County, California	133,940	882	815	2,567	3,676	3,721	852	709	2,438	3,657	3,810
Nevada County, California	96,420	743	527	1,644	1,420	1,975	536	76	1,710	2,154	1,957

Table C-4. Primary and Secondary School Enrollment, by Sex and Selected Counties, 2019—*Continued*

(Number.)

		Male					Female				
		Enrolled in school					Enrolled in school				
State/County	Population 3 years and over	Nursery school, Pre-school	Kindergarten	Grades 1 to 4	Grades 5 to 8	Grades 9 to 12	Nursery school, Pre-school	Kindergarten	Grades 1 to 4	Grades 5 to 8	Grades 9 to 12
CALIFORNIA—(*Continued*)											
Orange County, California	3,068,735	31,495	17,673	77,048	80,151	85,114	26,717	18,379	71,755	73,385	81,147
Placer County, California	386,631	2,943	3,201	9,802	10,393	11,069	3,243	2,331	9,259	9,477	11,078
Riverside County, California	2,381,437	14,270	18,166	63,788	80,333	76,741	14,105	13,441	65,150	73,163	73,033
Sacramento County, California	1,496,545	12,212	10,158	42,682	39,558	42,840	12,146	12,130	38,258	39,043	39,745
San Bernardino County, California	2,093,445	18,435	15,356	64,020	64,785	71,386	14,921	12,577	62,300	61,494	66,613
San Diego County, California	3,220,151	25,644	20,733	76,211	79,640	85,404	23,086	19,060	74,998	75,841	78,875
San Francisco County, California...	857,412	5,377	2,419	13,849	12,786	10,907	7,150	3,559	11,918	11,095	11,706
San Joaquin County, California	732,515	6,558	3,868	24,499	25,024	26,226	5,302	4,887	22,541	24,037	23,046
San Luis Obispo County, California..............................	276,020	1,583	1,559	4,940	6,986	5,510	1,813	1,047	5,053	6,407	5,609
San Mateo County, California	741,869	6,693	5,658	17,305	16,910	17,547	6,110	5,426	15,207	17,447	18,301
Santa Barbara County, California...	430,641	3,051	2,265	12,590	10,122	10,703	2,650	2,428	10,134	11,168	11,660
Santa Clara County, California	1,865,801	18,384	9,516	43,923	50,471	51,131	20,583	13,460	40,202	45,791	49,229
Santa Cruz County, California........	265,824	3,052	906	6,991	4,328	7,333	1,955	926	5,857	6,128	5,571
Shasta County, California	173,667	1,414	1,487	4,701	3,999	4,147	678	1,625	3,981	3,867	4,283
Solano County, California	433,041	2,722	3,136	11,817	10,733	11,632	3,167	3,070	10,147	11,736	10,043
Sonoma County, California	481,921	3,548	3,297	11,407	9,074	12,403	3,724	2,835	8,575	10,337	14,575
Stanislaus County, California........	527,815	4,344	2,585	15,472	19,015	17,267	4,674	3,625	16,781	15,592	17,199
Tulare County, California	442,657	2,938	5,715	13,656	17,689	17,769	3,783	2,728	15,920	17,459	14,523
Ventura County, California.............	821,038	6,681	4,651	19,968	24,925	23,807	6,087	3,869	17,973	23,089	25,439
Yolo County, California..................	213,531	1,810	780	5,311	4,944	5,693	1,168	2,105	4,879	3,496	6,729
Yuba County, California..................	75,239	383	458	2,630	1,851	2,084	1,443	1,266	2,718	1,489	1,310
COLORADO.........................	5,569,826	51,287	37,149	136,710	154,897	150,370	42,751	32,473	136,003	140,078	139,780
Adams County, Colorado..............	496,190	5,269	4,779	17,309	15,208	15,397	3,291	2,744	16,027	13,245	15,217
Arapahoe County, Colorado..........	634,053	5,705	4,862	14,905	19,953	18,430	5,476	6,184	14,430	17,295	16,901
Boulder County, Colorado	318,092	2,794	1,731	6,615	8,017	8,264	2,626	1,501	5,901	8,436	8,180
Broomfield County, Colorado	68,504	748	471	1,444	2,229	2,473	606	295	1,721	1,782	1,480
Denver County, Colorado	703,027	7,780	4,208	13,247	16,339	13,334	6,006	3,119	15,371	14,658	13,222
Douglas County, Colorado............	340,104	4,045	2,083	9,208	12,264	12,601	2,631	1,767	9,066	10,973	12,387
El Paso County, Colorado.............	695,155	5,404	4,387	19,590	20,389	19,183	5,023	5,710	20,174	16,338	18,480
Jefferson County, Colorado...........	565,688	5,079	2,791	11,825	15,018	13,375	4,146	2,842	12,500	12,565	11,978
Larimer County, Colorado	346,918	2,797	2,446	7,256	8,641	8,133	3,408	1,076	5,755	9,488	8,168
Mesa County, Colorado.................	148,563	1,414	757	3,339	4,411	4,297	382	908	4,173	3,802	2,913
Pueblo County, Colorado..............	162,627	1,235	972	4,229	4,985	4,374	749	658	4,601	4,297	4,266
Weld County, Colorado.................	311,188	3,973	3,256	8,630	9,589	10,026	2,618	2,387	9,203	8,953	9,223
CONNECTICUT......................	3,461,616	26,130	21,559	81,022	84,065	105,513	26,198	21,259	78,046	83,730	88,897
Fairfield County, Connecticut........	913,479	8,345	7,176	23,011	25,580	29,660	7,513	5,119	22,682	26,355	25,912
Hartford County, Connecticut.......	864,473	6,611	5,119	22,110	19,698	27,355	6,638	6,430	19,936	21,029	22,289
Litchfield County, Connecticut......	176,418	1,489	1,227	3,739	2,953	5,246	971	254	2,880	4,907	4,121
Middlesex County, Connecticut.....	159,240	972	558	3,226	4,204	4,557	470	1,086	3,305	3,290	3,318
New Haven County, Connecticut ...	829,140	5,701	4,985	18,975	19,242	23,985	6,721	5,082	19,393	17,235	21,204
New London County, Connecticut.	257,489	1,739	1,455	3,832	6,838	8,058	1,855	1,390	5,149	5,448	6,842
Tolland County, Connecticut.........	147,053	823	557	3,612	2,813	3,370	1,335	919	2,336	3,272	2,398
Windham County, Connecticut......	114,324	450	482	2,517	2,737	3,282	695	979	2,365	2,194	2,813
DELAWARE..........................	942,365	6,295	5,387	22,854	22,909	24,745	8,098	5,312	21,779	22,949	24,763
Kent County, Delaware	174,833	776	1,648	4,504	4,928	4,039	1,233	1,333	4,036	3,837	4,946
New Castle County, Delaware........	540,405	4,172	2,669	13,561	12,846	15,059	4,988	2,972	12,681	14,327	14,123
Sussex County, Delaware..............	227,127	1,347	1,070	4,789	5,135	5,647	1,877	1,007	5,062	4,785	5,694
DISTRICT OF COLUMBIA.........	679,463	8,928	4,856	13,912	12,681	9,904	8,426	4,365	14,259	12,213	9,385
District of Columbia, District of Columbia.................................	679,463	8,928	4,856	13,912	12,681	9,904	8,426	4,365	14,259	12,213	9,385
FLORIDA.............................	20,825,863	160,858	118,227	458,634	529,646	502,099	153,842	102,965	453,523	476,469	491,674
Alachua County, Florida................	261,145	2,375	524	4,516	7,174	4,018	2,423	1,021	4,510	5,814	5,646
Bay County, Florida	168,733	1,267	361	4,447	5,526	3,100	824	1,339	4,074	3,157	5,377
Brevard County, Florida.................	586,100	3,728	1,716	11,639	15,086	14,128	3,719	2,886	9,548	15,462	14,314
Broward County, Florida...............	1,891,595	20,627	11,426	42,465	51,318	48,872	18,332	9,802	46,253	45,875	46,192
Charlotte County, Florida..............	186,996	545	674	2,648	2,595	2,576	116	1,314	2,650	2,889	2,599
Clay County, Florida	211,858	1,221	1,454	7,134	4,778	6,099	1,520	1,120	4,561	6,445	6,961
Collier County, Florida...................	374,681	2,468	1,675	6,088	7,556	9,252	1,640	734	7,278	7,190	8,359
Duval County, Florida	921,592	7,647	5,174	22,636	28,166	19,546	7,068	6,819	23,537	22,474	19,886
Escambia County, Florida..............	306,487	2,668	1,374	9,123	5,766	7,381	1,901	1,050	8,938	7,404	5,592

Table C-4. Primary and Secondary School Enrollment, by Sex and Selected Counties, 2019—*Continued*

(Number.)

| | | Male | | | | | Female | | | | |
| | | Enrolled in school | | | | | Enrolled in school | | | | |
State/County	Population 3 years and over	Nursery school, Pre-school	Kindergarten	Grades 1 to 4	Grades 5 to 8	Grades 9 to 12	Nursery school, Pre-school	Kindergarten	Grades 1 to 4	Grades 5 to 8	Grades 9 to 12
FLORIDA—(*Continued*)											
Flagler County, Florida	111,825	251	257	2,354	2,011	2,233	553	593	2,559	2,995	3,019
Hernando County, Florida	189,190	680	1,301	3,808	4,379	3,979	790	1,157	3,743	5,213	3,910
Hillsborough County, Florida	1,415,420	11,691	10,277	34,820	40,888	35,907	10,040	8,598	31,182	35,771	37,461
Indian River County, Florida	156,364	813	1,118	3,024	3,533	4,626	1,082	285	3,343	1,667	3,314
Lake County, Florida	357,647	1,879	2,374	6,239	11,314	6,928	2,913	1,312	8,870	6,429	9,184
Lee County, Florida	751,249	4,822	3,829	14,997	17,108	17,650	6,369	3,332	14,353	13,486	15,765
Leon County, Florida	284,237	2,188	1,732	6,066	6,398	6,767	1,774	791	7,437	5,222	5,763
Manatee County, Florida	394,216	3,885	1,173	9,149	9,286	10,272	1,759	1,001	8,209	9,282	6,230
Marion County, Florida	354,538	2,384	2,968	7,111	8,647	7,779	914	1,073	7,023	7,991	8,857
Martin County, Florida	157,938	1,353	578	3,889	3,633	3,228	595	498	2,199	3,649	2,912
Miami-Dade County, Florida	2,625,481	22,853	16,561	58,663	68,357	66,648	25,945	13,557	56,163	65,223	67,916
Nassau County, Florida	86,043	362	449	2,382	1,479	2,101	566	324	2,080	2,212	1,599
Okaloosa County, Florida	203,041	1,881	1,140	5,847	5,472	4,741	1,344	1,713	4,438	5,257	5,288
Orange County, Florida	1,344,148	12,193	8,865	33,375	34,136	36,052	13,745	7,101	35,731	31,859	33,282
Osceola County, Florida	364,145	2,107	3,408	7,334	14,719	9,994	2,715	1,539	10,111	9,994	10,507
Palm Beach County, Florida	1,453,797	12,243	8,454	31,846	34,981	36,756	10,714	5,712	29,423	31,627	35,166
Pasco County, Florida	536,999	4,952	3,466	13,146	12,141	13,824	2,660	1,599	12,322	12,630	12,641
Pinellas County, Florida	953,409	7,536	3,875	19,134	18,131	16,654	6,197	4,166	15,369	17,755	17,620
Polk County, Florida	700,870	4,090	3,799	14,356	20,694	19,255	4,679	5,157	16,878	16,119	20,164
St. Johns County, Florida	257,653	1,314	1,257	5,708	7,950	7,127	2,329	2,025	5,357	6,906	7,650
St. Lucie County, Florida	317,557	1,631	1,633	6,198	8,825	7,420	2,604	1,379	5,347	9,557	6,624
Santa Rosa County, Florida	178,223	1,113	1,030	3,889	6,072	4,819	744	1,152	3,777	4,291	4,556
Sarasota County, Florida	426,388	1,720	1,422	5,309	9,468	8,978	1,501	960	7,287	7,500	7,568
Seminole County, Florida	457,184	3,858	2,945	11,900	10,205	11,853	3,172	2,881	12,949	9,545	11,951
Volusia County, Florida	536,833	2,413	3,688	10,233	10,264	13,246	2,246	3,379	11,927	9,092	11,530
GEORGIA	10,254,587	93,440	73,575	281,934	302,611	305,763	87,831	68,633	269,993	290,348	278,586
Barrow County, Georgia	80,179	856	674	1,701	3,089	3,500	527	842	2,420	2,878	1,293
Bartow County, Georgia	104,983	635	171	3,874	2,807	1,925	595	694	3,135	3,680	2,792
Bibb County, Georgia	147,075	824	1,066	5,110	4,346	3,579	1,064	1,120	3,727	4,352	4,155
Carroll County, Georgia	115,559	1,376	419	2,210	3,611	3,115	1,151	953	3,630	2,443	3,181
Catoosa County, Georgia	65,623	811	747	2,147	1,209	2,237	700	331	2,618	1,048	1,435
Chatham County, Georgia	280,321	2,430	1,573	8,206	9,131	5,306	2,392	1,893	5,594	6,848	6,513
Cherokee County, Georgia	250,746	3,216	1,414	8,033	6,719	7,986	2,224	1,366	6,104	8,777	7,692
Clarke County, Georgia	123,341	375	2,004	2,433	2,488	1,139	816	737	2,145	1,859	2,280
Clayton County, Georgia	278,603	532	3,488	8,298	9,416	9,235	1,529	2,953	7,542	11,895	8,495
Cobb County, Georgia	733,541	8,392	4,514	18,909	20,640	21,470	7,459	6,163	18,687	17,986	19,898
Columbia County, Georgia	151,778	372	1,646	5,647	5,032	4,346	889	855	3,980	3,795	5,086
Coweta County, Georgia	143,524	597	2,047	4,512	3,696	4,856	1,147	1,027	3,450	5,009	3,219
DeKalb County, Georgia	728,208	7,602	4,281	19,204	19,539	18,659	7,259	4,952	18,669	18,713	17,957
Dougherty County, Georgia	84,431	952	1,065	1,926	2,765	1,741	1,542	236	2,468	1,805	2,613
Douglas County, Georgia	141,397	906	533	3,582	5,804	4,896	998	659	3,153	4,589	6,575
Fayette County, Georgia	110,999	1,264	583	2,888	3,239	3,464	634	592	3,240	3,667	3,561
Floyd County, Georgia	95,522	606	934	2,945	1,998	2,449	631	548	2,740	1,471	2,137
Forsyth County, Georgia	237,227	3,319	1,944	7,907	8,380	8,499	2,917	1,244	7,647	8,252	8,856
Fulton County, Georgia	1,029,958	10,903	6,507	23,558	25,042	30,157	13,529	5,384	26,269	23,809	26,895
Glynn County, Georgia	83,160	828	1,079	2,308	1,785	1,751	511	189	2,531	2,432	2,015
Gwinnett County, Georgia	903,457	7,276	6,927	28,101	30,032	31,422	7,774	6,465	26,031	29,178	30,318
Hall County, Georgia	197,132	1,245	1,628	3,891	6,504	6,254	1,135	1,996	4,539	6,784	5,603
Henry County, Georgia	228,559	2,421	1,893	6,911	6,816	10,587	1,680	1,731	6,802	6,433	7,046
Houston County, Georgia	152,779	1,530	1,527	3,923	5,532	5,736	686	862	5,379	5,257	3,459
Jackson County, Georgia	70,270	528	247	2,515	1,849	1,988	818	431	2,649	1,951	2,027
Lowndes County, Georgia	112,247	1,639	1,040	2,987	3,513	2,937	470	1,040	3,884	2,935	2,454
Muscogee County, Georgia	188,586	2,446	1,760	6,353	4,213	5,515	1,688	2,120	6,075	4,778	5,022
Newton County, Georgia	106,625	1,590	868	2,213	3,555	2,905	881	591	5,321	3,789	1,677
Paulding County, Georgia	163,718	2,150	194	4,624	6,668	6,043	747	1,008	5,156	5,276	4,375
Richmond County, Georgia	194,133	1,900	1,059	5,759	3,708	5,659	823	519	4,105	6,021	5,662
Rockdale County, Georgia	88,436	1,138	540	3,004	2,061	3,736	539	27	1,895	3,525	2,610
Walton County, Georgia	91,350	908	403	3,221	2,642	2,405	1,196	605	2,557	2,032	3,261
Whitfield County, Georgia	100,371	1,431	1,845	2,163	2,873	3,535	1,041	980	2,840	2,065	3,655
HAWAII	1,364,240	12,856	7,898	32,206	32,145	33,860	11,971	8,765	30,197	31,270	31,078
Hawaii County, Hawaii	194,886	1,712	1,232	4,867	4,919	5,289	1,411	1,146	4,753	4,895	4,473
Honolulu County, Hawaii	938,178	9,845	5,460	21,273	21,749	22,735	8,443	5,441	20,501	21,097	21,178
Kauai County, Hawaii	69,549	354	282	1,575	1,732	1,968	596	689	1,837	2,239	1,200
Maui County, Hawaii	161,612	945	924	4,491	3,745	3,868	1,521	1,489	3,106	3,039	4,227

Table C-4. Primary and Secondary School Enrollment, by Sex and Selected Counties, 2019—*Continued*

(Number.)

State/County	Population 3 years and over	Male — Nursery school, Pre-school	Male — Kindergarten	Male — Grades 1 to 4	Male — Grades 5 to 8	Male — Grades 9 to 12	Female — Nursery school, Pre-school	Female — Kindergarten	Female — Grades 1 to 4	Female — Grades 5 to 8	Female — Grades 9 to 12
IDAHO..............................	1,721,105	11,770	14,272	47,232	53,151	53,640	11,761	11,428	45,898	50,412	50,170
Ada County, Idaho......................	466,745	3,960	3,384	9,643	14,954	14,059	2,993	2,067	10,482	14,585	13,133
Bannock County, Idaho	84,320	1,072	663	1,919	2,970	2,199	700	912	1,776	2,095	2,009
Bonneville County, Idaho..............	113,885	1,243	1,100	4,567	4,283	3,617	1,263	731	3,709	4,019	3,939
Canyon County, Idaho..................	222,360	1,179	2,049	7,083	6,881	8,067	949	2,279	6,763	6,587	7,704
Kootenai County, Idaho................	158,833	499	1,117	5,792	4,562	4,120	807	1,391	3,996	3,417	4,383
Twin Falls County, Idaho	82,857	414	898	2,321	2,190	2,213	872	692	3,729	3,080	2,305
ILLINOIS...........................	12,238,923	113,919	77,034	307,575	333,083	334,405	106,466	66,677	295,840	324,434	331,527
Adams County, Illinois	63,622	471	593	1,426	1,574	1,535	823	643	1,634	1,380	1,109
Champaign County, Illinois	203,416	1,143	1,417	4,849	4,808	4,837	1,743	830	3,656	5,002	5,284
Cook County, Illinois	4,964,366	47,054	29,978	121,657	129,388	123,918	42,542	26,201	118,352	127,750	125,888
DeKalb County, Illinois	101,605	959	583	2,512	2,892	3,098	534	262	1,442	3,158	2,908
DuPage County, Illinois	890,944	10,381	6,151	22,376	23,913	27,453	7,308	5,502	21,087	22,929	25,220
Kane County, Illinois	512,358	5,032	5,049	11,921	17,556	17,431	3,332	3,382	11,150	16,428	16,708
Kankakee County, Illinois	105,633	670	920	2,616	1,888	2,891	382	448	3,239	3,149	2,365
Kendall County, Illinois................	124,438	1,929	566	4,781	3,817	2,831	1,014	584	5,789	4,284	5,569
Lake County, Illinois...................	674,910	5,295	4,863	19,078	18,691	23,735	4,465	4,643	17,538	19,351	21,819
LaSalle County, Illinois................	105,409	1,023	628	2,533	2,802	3,015	969	680	2,682	1,803	2,473
McHenry County, Illinois..............	298,380	2,717	2,097	7,983	8,568	9,436	3,459	1,927	8,086	7,137	8,503
McLean County, Illinois................	166,354	1,443	1,011	4,413	4,925	2,971	1,751	1,189	3,889	4,832	4,281
Macon County, Illinois.................	100,641	851	278	3,618	3,029	2,707	609	517	2,630	2,490	3,206
Madison County, Illinois...............	254,987	2,974	1,529	6,274	7,294	5,917	2,874	998	6,401	6,634	5,409
Peoria County, Illinois	172,176	937	696	4,720	4,683	5,207	2,009	1,558	5,001	4,013	4,671
Rock Island County, Illinois..........	137,180	959	926	2,687	3,734	3,465	1,524	589	3,372	4,014	3,403
St. Clair County, Illinois...............	251,908	3,893	2,134	5,158	7,477	7,890	3,341	1,258	5,403	8,068	6,535
Sangamon County, Illinois	188,077	2,225	1,227	5,189	4,010	5,242	1,717	889	4,595	5,749	4,637
Tazewell County, Illinois	128,365	723	707	3,343	3,536	3,789	1,628	281	3,983	3,070	3,505
Vermilion County, Illinois	71,885	828	795	1,496	1,800	1,634	447	466	1,899	2,298	2,058
Will County, Illinois	668,280	4,912	3,736	17,769	21,809	22,756	5,594	2,841	17,385	20,928	22,002
Williamson County, Illinois...........	64,304	524	406	1,833	1,602	1,681	933	111	1,589	1,655	1,460
Winnebago County, Illinois	272,179	2,549	1,250	6,908	9,204	8,081	1,960	1,623	7,517	7,168	8,020
INDIANA	6,489,206	54,132	41,050	170,478	188,464	185,763	43,701	38,624	160,902	182,322	171,828
Allen County, Indiana	363,710	3,582	2,941	10,650	11,119	9,806	2,233	2,627	10,996	10,375	9,982
Bartholomew County, Indiana	81,119	907	267	2,265	2,987	2,409	864	190	1,894	2,508	2,428
Boone County, Indiana	65,664	328	886	2,060	2,724	1,758	163	336	1,188	2,869	1,750
Clark County, Indiana	113,006	270	656	2,597	2,756	3,939	1,973	1,205	2,764	2,791	3,005
Delaware County, Indiana.............	110,568	726	465	2,295	2,178	2,753	210	546	2,200	1,901	2,021
Elkhart County, Indiana	196,273	1,025	1,523	5,713	6,780	7,002	617	1,228	5,319	7,378	6,261
Floyd County, Indiana..................	75,718	534	293	2,263	2,442	2,350	669	416	1,914	1,728	2,375
Grant County, Indiana	64,080	762	115	1,966	2,007	1,281	330	311	1,253	1,133	1,375
Hamilton County, Indiana.............	327,282	3,903	1,955	9,777	13,439	10,807	3,526	1,976	10,064	10,516	11,821
Hendricks County, Indiana	165,599	747	1,210	4,375	6,252	5,453	1,202	1,359	5,715	4,754	4,701
Johnson County, Indiana..............	151,926	1,446	650	4,855	3,956	5,345	918	530	3,653	5,236	3,526
Kosciusko County, Indiana...........	76,310	460	322	1,527	2,932	2,245	1,030	720	1,665	2,124	1,959
Lake County, Indiana...................	469,266	4,237	2,610	11,982	14,097	15,108	3,671	2,897	10,502	13,477	14,921
LaPorte County, Indiana...............	105,798	450	959	2,299	2,563	3,467	595	824	2,598	2,051	2,168
Madison County, Indiana..............	126,181	702	1,197	2,626	3,742	3,313	930	404	2,446	3,098	3,199
Marion County, Indiana................	922,637	11,201	5,365	25,156	25,486	25,883	4,237	5,579	26,181	25,898	22,523
Monroe County, Indiana...............	145,384	1,336	891	2,923	2,370	2,577	1,159	773	2,202	2,350	3,059
Porter County, Indiana	165,801	1,092	1,229	3,347	4,608	4,847	1,246	1,169	2,973	4,902	4,592
St. Joseph County, Indiana	261,892	3,080	1,683	7,138	7,605	6,956	1,592	1,393	6,141	8,024	6,316
Tippecanoe County, Indiana	189,104	1,466	1,046	5,076	3,428	4,997	1,313	700	4,317	4,812	4,163
Vanderburgh County, Indiana.......	174,678	1,134	694	4,805	4,705	3,415	806	833	3,873	5,987	4,333
Vigo County, Indiana...................	103,154	671	799	2,160	2,298	2,880	483	798	2,250	1,969	1,960
Wayne County, Indiana................	63,138	514	277	1,767	1,471	1,281	663	476	1,849	1,575	1,227
IOWA...............................	3,046,300	30,544	23,685	82,926	78,373	82,865	24,379	20,177	76,161	82,830	75,383
Black Hawk County, Iowa.............	126,825	1,426	1,145	3,385	2,486	3,031	788	1,199	2,757	3,013	2,898
Dallas County, Iowa....................	89,776	1,095	1,011	2,444	2,359	2,168	1,657	439	2,828	2,810	3,220
Dubuque County, Iowa.................	93,707	1,116	397	2,576	2,519	3,191	600	585	1,796	3,181	2,007
Johnson County, Iowa..................	146,113	966	1,307	3,423	3,208	3,641	1,750	671	2,475	3,527	2,754
Linn County, Iowa	219,200	2,443	2,410	5,142	5,809	5,615	1,813	1,768	5,768	6,361	4,929
Polk County, Iowa	469,535	6,498	2,527	15,151	11,998	13,426	3,582	3,225	14,093	11,847	12,955

Table C-4. Primary and Secondary School Enrollment, by Sex and Selected Counties, 2019—*Continued*

(Number.)

State/County	Population 3 years and over	Male					Female				
		Enrolled in school					Enrolled in school				
		Nursery school, Pre-school	Kindergarten	Grades 1 to 4	Grades 5 to 8	Grades 9 to 12	Nursery school, Pre-school	Kindergarten	Grades 1 to 4	Grades 5 to 8	Grades 9 to 12
IOWA—*(Continued)*											
Pottawattamie County, Iowa..........	90,192	935	394	3,457	1,639	2,462	889	331	1,934	2,169	1,891
Scott County, Iowa.......................	167,225	1,527	1,484	4,892	4,859	4,423	1,642	1,757	4,146	4,739	4,002
Story County, Iowa......................	94,815	1,251	629	1,518	1,253	1,473	392	354	1,587	2,159	1,227
Woodbury County, Iowa...............	99,646	1,396	767	2,860	3,440	2,541	1,026	429	2,854	3,692	2,545
KANSAS	2,806,484	25,813	18,940	78,837	82,081	79,803	25,291	20,276	75,483	79,241	77,303
Butler County, Kansas..................	65,433	659	500	2,521	1,710	1,780	577	638	1,860	1,890	2,296
Douglas County, Kansas	119,489	706	360	2,411	2,694	2,120	625	1,358	3,913	1,516	2,488
Johnson County, Kansas..............	581,664	6,116	3,106	15,184	18,172	17,891	6,113	3,995	14,937	16,812	16,969
Leavenworth County, Kansas	78,373	972	379	2,436	2,122	1,731	770	447	1,674	2,043	1,918
Sedgwick County, Kansas	495,089	4,431	2,901	13,704	14,967	15,952	4,603	2,554	13,441	16,726	14,592
Shawnee County, Kansas	171,432	1,327	2,554	4,308	4,306	3,983	755	2,082	4,964	3,712	3,848
Wyandotte County, Kansas	157,142	1,912	1,198	4,967	5,229	4,536	797	1,341	6,024	3,968	4,763
KENTUCKY	4,310,912	33,425	25,921	104,353	120,284	110,780	30,334	25,192	97,799	114,500	109,043
Boone County, Kentucky	127,483	1,291	820	3,284	4,895	3,365	1,245	428	3,168	3,513	4,967
Bullitt County, Kentucky...............	79,366	777	242	2,083	2,641	1,994	540	717	1,679	1,981	2,032
Campbell County, Kentucky..........	89,887	795	357	2,047	2,216	1,988	809	389	2,013	2,430	1,963
Christian County, Kentucky	66,862	188	365	2,909	971	1,386	550	498	1,262	1,951	3,186
Daviess County, Kentucky	97,830	1,118	784	3,489	1,838	2,322	1,389	851	1,537	3,696	2,337
Fayette County, Kentucky	311,906	2,817	1,848	6,924	7,543	7,291	2,189	2,455	6,480	6,792	6,621
Hardin County, Kentucky..............	106,428	785	656	2,610	3,952	3,380	1,135	401	3,378	2,193	2,916
Jefferson County, Kentucky..........	737,882	4,923	4,589	17,346	20,015	17,371	4,690	3,823	15,822	20,669	17,672
Kenton County, Kentucky	160,719	1,844	1,091	4,508	4,132	3,891	1,531	1,191	3,206	4,748	4,393
Madison County, Kentucky...........	89,222	287	251	1,667	2,224	2,285	310	472	1,670	1,977	2,176
Oldham County, Kentucky............	65,120	421	308	1,217	2,763	2,428	1,005	671	1,875	2,144	1,846
Warren County, Kentucky..............	128,934	779	1,214	2,592	4,194	3,177	848	676	3,198	3,339	3,752
LOUISIANA	4,484,044	37,167	32,142	124,868	129,210	127,344	43,227	30,038	116,962	121,754	115,537
Bossier Parish, Louisiana..............	123,508	1,373	996	3,212	4,179	4,372	1,475	963	3,862	2,465	2,640
Caddo Parish, Louisiana...............	232,094	1,289	1,296	7,124	6,601	5,869	3,017	1,781	7,621	5,079	6,735
Calcasieu Parish, Louisiana..........	194,847	1,151	2,411	6,616	4,532	5,979	1,855	2,090	5,524	5,392	5,019
East Baton Rouge Parish, Louisiana	424,112	3,777	3,168	10,678	12,932	10,466	4,086	2,957	9,811	10,890	10,819
Iberia Parish, Louisiana...............	66,949	535	447	2,101	1,785	2,717	758	384	2,140	1,907	1,964
Jefferson Parish, Louisiana..........	416,764	4,744	3,424	12,206	7,727	10,025	4,387	3,850	10,303	10,680	10,649
Lafayette Parish, Louisiana	237,433	2,208	1,932	5,989	6,767	6,452	2,230	1,867	6,647	5,801	5,864
Lafourche Parish, Louisiana..........	94,783	996	389	2,500	2,795	2,110	670	460	2,311	2,382	1,170
Livingston Parish, Louisiana........	135,111	522	929	2,642	5,271	4,223	1,464	239	2,842	5,806	4,106
Orleans Parish, Louisiana	376,397	2,511	1,784	8,091	9,819	9,379	3,697	1,821	7,262	9,777	8,580
Ouachita Parish, Louisiana...........	147,578	1,274	709	4,722	4,307	4,596	1,361	1,665	4,275	3,898	4,601
Rapides Parish, Louisiana............	124,615	734	1,224	4,124	3,101	3,997	797	882	2,754	3,093	5,066
St. Landry Parish, Louisiana.........	78,750	868	694	2,452	2,026	3,542	737	1,211	1,596	2,719	1,474
St. Tammany Parish, Louisiana.....	251,015	2,586	1,387	7,074	9,291	6,550	2,796	1,089	7,518	7,021	7,261
Tangipahoa Parish, Louisiana.......	128,941	1,143	486	3,970	5,130	3,469	1,651	638	3,236	3,874	2,602
Terrebonne Parish, Louisiana.......	105,838	493	308	2,641	2,749	2,624	1,331	780	3,073	3,147	3,458
MAINE	1,309,618	9,102	5,644	27,043	29,412	30,709	7,298	7,135	25,590	27,540	29,949
Androscoggin County, Maine	104,480	700	243	2,448	3,311	2,582	508	1,244	2,411	2,109	2,472
Aroostook County, Maine.............	65,669	594	494	1,514	1,223	1,651	168	285	1,645	1,153	1,103
Cumberland County, Maine	288,181	2,170	1,278	5,975	5,470	6,765	2,409	1,128	5,433	6,048	6,950
Kennebec County, Maine..............	119,136	927	686	1,790	3,156	2,821	423	1,046	1,313	4,025	2,669
Penobscot County, Maine	148,112	858	544	2,699	3,446	3,585	404	744	2,469	3,194	3,608
York County, Maine......................	201,428	1,486	822	4,516	3,994	4,681	1,117	1,179	4,479	3,802	4,471
MARYLAND	5,841,878	49,519	35,316	148,278	157,395	153,700	50,566	31,827	139,724	155,256	151,448
Allegany County, Maryland...........	68,679	481	192	1,876	1,172	1,889	620	130	880	1,591	1,122
Anne Arundel County, Maryland....	559,817	5,972	4,513	15,153	13,132	14,111	6,636	3,331	13,268	14,735	13,265
Baltimore County, Maryland..........	800,083	7,343	4,450	19,461	21,286	20,914	6,361	4,538	17,822	22,562	16,501
Calvert County, Maryland	89,710	470	598	2,590	2,665	2,647	576	261	2,382	2,402	2,331
Carroll County, Maryland..............	164,738	1,457	1,563	3,722	4,621	4,835	1,756	1,208	3,921	3,115	4,648
Cecil County, Maryland	99,969	721	282	3,122	2,988	2,555	759	594	1,577	2,526	2,697
Charles County, Maryland	158,333	736	645	4,959	5,197	4,242	1,253	776	4,406	5,255	4,668
Frederick County, Maryland..........	249,799	1,820	1,060	7,495	7,396	6,772	1,963	1,162	6,643	7,316	8,488
Harford County, Maryland............	247,878	3,021	1,365	4,860	8,734	6,069	2,305	1,301	5,571	7,763	6,964

Table C-4. Primary and Secondary School Enrollment, by Sex and Selected Counties, 2019—*Continued*

(Number.)

State/County	Population 3 years and over	Male					Female				
		Enrolled in school					Enrolled in school				
		Nursery school, Pre-school	Kindergarten	Grades 1 to 4	Grades 5 to 8	Grades 9 to 12	Nursery school, Pre-school	Kindergarten	Grades 1 to 4	Grades 5 to 8	Grades 9 to 12
MARYLAND—(*Continued*)											
Howard County, Maryland.............	314,157	2,046	1,400	9,153	9,599	9,505	2,469	1,736	7,958	9,252	10,546
Montgomery County, Maryland.....	1,014,125	9,524	6,315	26,839	29,090	31,127	10,716	5,135	26,089	27,029	28,776
Prince George's County, Maryland	874,989	6,853	5,108	22,913	22,013	19,640	6,334	4,298	19,880	23,699	22,103
St. Mary's County, Maryland	109,118	711	467	1,972	3,376	3,719	360	434	3,055	4,063	3,200
Washington County, Maryland	146,584	1,277	988	3,235	3,922	4,112	628	1,523	4,123	3,628	3,705
Wicomico County, Maryland	101,012	807	1,176	1,992	2,898	2,645	1,082	1,143	2,286	2,007	3,008
Baltimore city, Maryland	570,658	4,361	3,586	12,581	12,767	12,649	5,052	2,014	14,471	12,652	12,697
MASSACHUSETTS	6,681,257	54,613	39,628	142,750	163,840	170,353	50,356	35,409	143,854	149,066	166,069
Barnstable County, Massachusetts	208,954	1,565	432	3,165	4,669	5,382	1,168	706	3,532	3,432	3,991
Berkshire County, Massachusetts .	121,778	779	613	2,024	3,071	2,880	890	299	2,077	2,018	2,952
Bristol County, Massachusetts......	548,054	3,186	2,725	11,882	13,564	14,614	3,259	2,794	11,071	13,292	14,958
Essex County, Massachusetts	763,454	5,947	3,704	18,896	20,374	22,833	6,976	4,506	15,744	19,583	19,009
Franklin County, Massachusetts....	68,671	546	354	1,083	1,814	1,348	350	372	1,518	1,299	1,377
Hampden County, Massachusetts .	451,502	4,042	2,995	10,658	12,133	12,890	3,521	2,905	11,243	8,708	13,035
Hampshire County, Massachusetts.........................	158,127	941	645	2,362	3,690	3,074	1,240	516	2,240	2,488	3,218
Middlesex County, Massachusetts	1,561,447	16,108	9,855	35,347	35,198	37,198	11,958	9,093	34,724	34,040	36,167
Norfolk County, Massachusetts	685,035	5,972	4,675	14,830	18,974	18,035	7,196	3,042	17,187	16,740	18,309
Plymouth County, Massachusetts..	505,132	4,462	3,418	9,940	15,675	14,404	3,926	2,011	12,057	12,778	14,761
Suffolk County, Massachusetts	778,068	5,013	4,172	13,306	15,252	14,618	5,002	5,333	12,917	13,328	15,721
Worcester County, Massachusetts	803,479	6,052	6,040	19,096	18,768	22,688	4,870	3,701	18,895	19,967	22,025
MICHIGAN..........................	9,656,927	71,788	61,533	235,810	248,565	266,786	73,008	57,441	218,451	238,683	255,289
Allegan County, Michigan.............	113,797	547	836	3,571	2,850	3,217	853	684	2,741	3,728	2,980
Bay County, Michigan	99,714	324	328	2,149	1,977	3,473	568	704	1,777	2,604	2,401
Berrien County, Michigan..............	148,999	1,648	957	3,260	3,966	4,650	1,961	1,158	4,197	3,062	3,371
Calhoun County, Michigan	129,651	1,025	770	3,466	3,657	4,150	1,091	716	3,226	2,945	3,291
Clinton County, Michigan	76,927	571	373	2,277	1,862	2,099	266	459	1,529	1,961	1,731
Eaton County, Michigan	106,547	761	1,053	2,193	2,846	3,082	331	526	2,781	2,467	2,369
Genesee County, Michigan............	391,039	2,460	2,707	10,856	8,581	11,390	2,483	2,316	8,300	11,131	11,459
Grand Traverse County, Michigan .	90,740	838	398	1,716	2,284	2,203	533	173	2,157	2,099	1,821
Ingham County, Michigan	282,125	1,715	1,010	7,998	5,989	6,917	2,147	1,712	5,606	7,000	6,228
Isabella County, Michigan	68,201	576	535	1,128	1,478	1,561	347	340	1,028	1,349	1,032
Jackson County, Michigan	153,084	1,446	1,238	3,997	4,132	4,241	803	585	3,553	3,718	4,062
Kalamazoo County, Michigan	254,945	1,486	1,710	5,824	8,115	5,777	2,012	1,443	5,621	6,673	6,474
Kent County, Michigan	630,663	4,181	6,307	17,193	17,096	18,915	5,875	4,466	16,007	15,990	17,743
Lapeer County, Michigan...............	85,023	414	463	1,735	2,186	2,988	727	245	1,735	2,193	2,039
Lenawee County, Michigan	94,815	519	518	2,120	2,117	2,431	633	834	1,900	2,307	3,046
Livingston County, Michigan.........	186,113	1,565	1,503	3,255	5,179	5,643	1,494	628	4,374	4,180	5,610
Macomb County, Michigan	846,270	6,297	4,589	19,558	20,675	21,756	6,756	4,834	19,120	20,471	20,148
Marquette County, Michigan	64,637	287	588	1,840	1,137	1,116	372	436	1,390	1,288	1,463
Midland County, Michigan.............	80,379	461	419	2,361	2,420	2,280	793	264	1,689	2,038	2,114
Monroe County, Michigan..............	145,516	1,135	1,053	2,871	3,653	3,700	767	1,059	3,007	4,247	3,644
Muskegon County, Michigan........	168,144	797	1,584	4,639	4,190	4,612	2,020	1,643	4,938	3,594	3,714
Oakland County, Michigan.............	1,219,098	11,043	7,321	27,373	30,875	34,179	10,073	6,438	26,330	28,981	34,214
Ottawa County, Michigan	283,068	3,291	2,312	7,788	7,845	7,848	2,244	2,440	7,551	7,208	8,940
Saginaw County, Michigan............	184,116	1,465	1,201	4,642	4,503	5,578	1,297	1,141	4,525	4,310	4,555
St. Clair County, Michigan.............	155,157	1,425	1,262	2,702	4,249	4,550	997	482	3,251	4,019	4,447
Shiawassee County, Michigan.......	66,106	236	325	1,737	1,656	1,949	465	508	1,872	1,231	2,180
Van Buren County, Michigan	72,663	180	631	1,734	2,330	2,220	224	358	1,759	2,127	1,807
Washtenaw County, Michigan	358,196	3,228	1,783	6,737	8,081	9,607	3,114	1,750	6,107	8,380	10,444
Wayne County, Michigan...............	1,682,852	12,938	10,036	45,586	48,272	47,830	13,666	11,187	41,860	44,637	47,347
MINNESOTA........................	5,432,866	51,533	35,708	148,799	148,098	150,410	46,797	34,459	137,676	146,680	147,414
Anoka County, Minnesota	344,104	2,577	2,407	7,318	11,675	9,985	2,273	2,528	7,892	10,251	10,768
Blue Earth County, Minnesota	64,802	498	631	1,637	1,140	1,220	657	189	1,498	1,452	1,115
Carver County, Minnesota.............	101,073	1,096	721	3,164	3,394	3,584	1,003	787	2,620	3,397	3,941
Crow Wing County, Minnesota	62,697	478	328	1,488	1,826	1,433	650	413	1,532	1,687	1,487
Dakota County, Minnesota	414,058	5,085	2,336	11,774	12,236	14,192	3,183	2,291	11,479	12,458	12,204
Hennepin County, Minnesota	1,216,089	12,518	6,620	33,863	28,509	29,857	12,134	9,132	26,855	29,595	30,793
Olmsted County, Minnesota	151,138	2,986	1,017	3,808	3,859	4,679	1,012	855	4,504	2,822	4,186
Ramsey County, Minnesota..........	528,629	4,156	3,474	15,829	14,252	13,498	4,378	3,299	14,119	13,164	13,104
Rice County, Minnesota	64,694	625	571	1,554	1,554	1,766	695	400	1,451	1,558	1,938
St. Louis County, Minnesota	193,048	1,439	914	4,279	4,491	4,710	1,136	784	3,456	4,252	4,410
Scott County, Minnesota	143,115	1,232	1,166	5,251	4,717	5,100	1,346	1,440	4,712	5,169	3,638
Sherburne County, Minnesota.......	93,653	879	1,142	3,318	2,271	2,957	244	594	3,670	2,106	2,833

Table C-4. Primary and Secondary School Enrollment, by Sex and Selected Counties, 2019—*Continued*

(Number.)

State/County	Population 3 years and over	Male					Female				
		Enrolled in school					Enrolled in school				
		Nursery school, Pre-school	Kindergarten	Grades 1 to 4	Grades 5 to 8	Grades 9 to 12	Nursery school, Pre-school	Kindergarten	Grades 1 to 4	Grades 5 to 8	Grades 9 to 12
MINNESOTA—(*Continued*)											
Stearns County, Minnesota	155,855	1,210	1,190	4,544	4,428	3,543	1,407	970	4,611	4,130	4,361
Washington County, Minnesota	254,289	2,068	2,072	7,000	7,303	7,565	2,429	1,330	7,299	7,091	7,886
Wright County, Minnesota............	133,730	1,705	721	4,333	3,817	5,556	977	1,198	3,995	4,447	4,548
MISSISSIPPI.......................	2,869,520	28,205	16,599	80,434	84,681	77,676	24,199	22,025	78,316	80,152	78,010
DeSoto County, Mississippi	178,763	1,570	1,163	5,610	6,014	6,313	2,164	1,118	6,003	4,783	4,597
Forrest County, Mississippi..........	73,243	815	164	2,345	1,910	1,315	159	1,507	1,904	2,530	1,366
Harrison County, Mississippi	199,236	2,141	922	5,307	6,367	6,547	1,237	519	4,586	5,883	5,288
Hinds County, Mississippi............	222,737	3,453	1,906	5,566	6,262	5,265	2,734	1,575	5,452	6,247	6,409
Jackson County, Mississippi........	139,537	1,503	188	4,381	4,589	3,557	1,384	647	2,894	5,268	3,717
Madison County, Mississippi	102,012	1,629	832	2,722	3,043	2,505	1,043	360	3,556	3,662	2,607
Rankin County, Mississippi...........	149,873	2,029	898	4,587	3,194	3,650	1,033	1,413	4,467	4,077	2,944
MISSOURI.........................	5,920,529	48,986	37,680	158,286	160,869	157,867	47,552	36,583	140,746	152,749	149,741
Boone County, Missouri...............	173,635	1,613	987	3,659	4,409	3,120	1,110	1,428	3,316	3,700	3,883
Buchanan County, Missouri	82,358	371	768	1,986	1,950	1,941	290	438	1,805	2,013	1,767
Cape Girardeau County, Missouri..	75,980	350	710	2,306	1,586	1,533	472	214	1,787	2,074	1,621
Cass County, Missouri	100,590	355	276	2,818	3,697	2,673	368	1,208	2,533	2,289	2,774
Christian County, Missouri...........	84,804	561	988	2,941	2,159	2,624	741	905	2,110	1,872	1,836
Clay County, Missouri	240,368	2,440	1,732	5,874	7,086	6,946	1,722	1,158	7,137	7,145	7,464
Cole County, Missouri	74,397	1,117	456	2,515	1,459	1,937	190	343	1,897	1,628	1,778
Franklin County, Missouri	100,300	961	511	2,664	3,711	2,602	929	682	2,207	2,517	2,648
Greene County, Missouri..............	284,027	1,705	1,339	6,827	7,724	5,801	2,213	992	6,497	5,248	5,240
Jackson County, Missouri............	677,676	5,254	4,958	17,815	19,542	16,831	5,106	4,754	16,051	20,748	16,389
Jasper County, Missouri...............	116,917	1,190	1,661	3,608	3,157	3,947	1,061	1,024	3,924	2,389	3,227
Jefferson County, Missouri..........	217,874	1,408	1,241	6,166	6,734	6,546	2,768	1,845	5,648	5,449	5,934
Platte County, Missouri................	101,348	1,093	315	2,375	3,237	2,869	756	1,095	2,323	2,591	3,499
St. Charles County, Missouri........	387,927	3,001	2,640	10,517	11,032	11,525	2,683	2,751	10,292	10,969	10,945
St. Louis County, Missouri...........	961,562	11,732	7,087	25,242	23,432	27,174	9,882	4,652	21,177	26,418	25,455
St. Louis city, Missouri	290,301	2,495	1,539	6,388	6,533	5,245	2,998	1,349	6,155	4,809	5,377
MONTANA..........................	1,034,193	6,852	6,934	26,274	25,487	26,213	5,858	5,363	24,336	25,487	26,088
Cascade County, Montana............	77,720	718	713	1,855	1,730	1,503	70	173	2,297	1,125	2,175
Flathead County, Montana............	100,663	562	674	3,682	2,098	2,329	240	545	2,705	2,056	2,438
Gallatin County, Montana.............	111,536	752	719	2,281	2,624	2,683	389	995	2,130	2,448	2,341
Lewis and Clark County, Montana.	66,772	500	410	1,137	2,082	2,139	506	152	1,261	1,907	1,400
Missoula County, Montana............	116,161	584	825	2,320	2,428	2,204	820	484	1,836	3,364	2,688
Yellowstone County, Montana.......	155,357	1,370	717	5,554	4,055	4,060	837	1,090	4,515	3,631	4,190
NEBRASKA..........................	1,856,531	16,964	13,569	52,452	54,101	53,926	16,524	13,091	49,824	51,957	49,230
Douglas County, Nebraska	545,227	4,569	3,202	15,977	16,021	17,361	5,133	4,933	15,945	13,989	15,256
Lancaster County, Nebraska.........	307,525	2,544	2,630	7,668	9,251	7,362	1,803	1,608	7,771	8,875	7,034
Sarpy County, Nebraska...............	179,954	2,251	1,759	5,540	5,425	5,690	1,946	1,341	5,276	5,659	5,639
NEVADA	2,977,011	19,758	18,543	75,988	83,474	79,301	17,705	16,065	72,329	77,844	78,968
Clark County, Nevada	2,189,686	14,702	13,679	55,268	63,729	61,103	12,611	12,512	54,143	59,178	59,781
Washoe County, Nevada...............	455,823	2,623	2,252	12,876	12,042	10,483	2,150	2,242	9,810	11,824	11,493
NEW HAMPSHIRE..................	1,323,662	11,796	7,171	28,323	31,622	30,703	8,819	6,337	24,319	31,047	32,895
Cheshire County, New Hampshire.	74,533	847	352	1,260	1,884	1,337	571	256	1,790	1,456	1,481
Grafton County, New Hampshire...	87,742	622	435	1,694	1,773	1,561	637	525	1,285	1,581	1,489
Hillsborough County, New Hampshire	404,083	3,363	2,751	8,748	11,206	10,462	2,860	1,903	7,623	10,165	10,759
Merrimack County, New Hampshire	147,336	1,802	1,062	3,309	3,194	3,508	968	661	3,048	3,816	3,586
Rockingham County, New Hampshire	302,022	2,832	688	7,994	5,157	8,254	2,503	1,467	5,195	7,308	8,379
Strafford County, New Hampshire.	126,885	785	1,128	2,314	3,879	1,609	460	492	2,098	3,325	2,588
NEW JERSEY	8,584,773	81,519	61,617	216,521	225,784	235,095	84,861	56,034	200,618	226,421	220,559
Atlantic County, New Jersey..........	256,564	2,285	1,741	6,348	7,019	7,178	2,637	1,210	6,852	6,956	5,280
Bergen County, New Jersey	902,644	8,683	4,319	22,178	25,174	23,885	8,631	5,466	20,783	21,721	24,004
Burlington County, New Jersey	432,164	4,348	2,615	10,202	11,398	11,033	3,374	2,679	9,343	10,477	12,524
Camden County, New Jersey.........	489,033	4,798	2,840	13,842	13,152	12,777	5,588	3,786	12,285	13,625	12,390
Cape May County, New Jersey	89,875	574	512	2,145	1,940	1,563	401	1,032	1,616	1,810	1,471
Cumberland County, New Jersey ..	145,236	523	1,568	3,809	4,817	6,175	3,393	325	3,285	5,081	2,511
Essex County, New Jersey	769,773	8,096	6,315	20,269	21,893	22,505	7,811	5,571	19,238	22,801	20,669

Table C-4. Primary and Secondary School Enrollment, by Sex and Selected Counties, 2019—*Continued*

(Number.)

		Male					Female				
		Enrolled in school					Enrolled in school				
State/County	Population 3 years and over	Nursery school, Pre-school	Kindergarten	Grades 1 to 4	Grades 5 to 8	Grades 9 to 12	Nursery school, Pre-school	Kindergarten	Grades 1 to 4	Grades 5 to 8	Grades 9 to 12
NEW JERSEY—*(Continued)*											
Gloucester County, New Jersey.....	281,388	2,214	2,265	6,442	8,001	7,125	1,764	2,010	6,454	7,179	7,511
Hudson County, New Jersey	644,310	5,986	6,172	13,950	14,260	11,796	7,486	5,702	14,533	13,672	12,680
Hunterdon County, New Jersey.....	120,726	434	964	2,384	3,118	3,608	700	617	2,805	2,610	3,708
Mercer County, New Jersey..........	357,628	3,776	3,945	8,273	7,887	9,675	3,877	2,286	6,477	9,725	9,863
Middlesex County, New Jersey......	796,864	7,617	5,497	19,193	20,999	22,534	7,067	5,535	18,325	21,081	18,803
Monmouth County, New Jersey	600,808	4,965	3,990	16,466	13,086	17,746	6,401	3,029	15,263	13,775	16,413
Morris County, New Jersey	477,568	4,117	2,712	12,313	12,532	13,506	4,582	2,257	13,225	13,225	12,834
Ocean County, New Jersey..........	580,575	5,470	4,720	17,455	16,136	15,437	4,930	4,099	14,200	16,936	16,203
Passaic County, New Jersey.........	482,734	4,767	3,483	11,892	14,207	15,178	4,776	3,448	12,861	13,932	12,980
Salem County, New Jersey...........	61,022	436	417	1,012	1,679	1,585	875	193	1,647	1,183	1,400
Somerset County, New Jersey	320,854	2,946	1,682	8,463	7,917	11,514	2,951	2,630	7,224	8,318	8,426
Sussex County, New Jersey	137,207	1,276	563	3,179	3,945	3,814	633	897	2,627	3,659	3,449
Union County, New Jersey...........	536,253	7,165	4,597	14,339	15,058	13,518	6,285	2,962	13,143	15,768	14,923
Warren County, New Jersey	101,557	1,043	700	2,367	1,566	2,943	699	300	1,819	2,887	2,517
NEW MEXICO	2,027,626	13,610	13,422	53,982	59,144	55,604	14,061	10,940	51,823	59,203	51,353
Bernalillo County, New Mexico......	657,475	3,685	3,292	16,596	18,027	16,236	4,215	2,071	15,765	18,280	15,796
Chaves County, New Mexico	62,532	501	637	1,854	2,449	1,329	922	155	2,472	2,444	1,293
Doña Ana County, New Mexico	210,229	1,989	1,242	6,142	6,524	7,073	1,176	958	5,130	6,695	6,812
McKinley County, New Mexico......	68,892	384	1,025	2,042	1,884	2,093	457	1,129	2,313	2,681	2,600
Sandoval County, New Mexico	141,706	783	1,331	2,529	4,865	4,398	1,150	1,059	3,982	3,540	3,875
San Juan County, New Mexico......	119,107	703	652	4,478	4,346	3,060	695	1,256	2,365	4,350	3,352
Santa Fe County, New Mexico	147,250	1,347	1,021	1,984	3,500	3,507	672	156	3,563	2,783	2,471
NEW YORK	18,794,281	150,237	113,039	437,808	472,085	485,113	143,513	107,325	408,306	444,447	459,094
Albany County, New York..............	296,944	2,059	2,355	5,132	7,307	6,602	1,918	1,104	5,506	7,065	7,103
Bronx County, New York	1,359,850	13,873	10,141	35,366	43,964	39,993	13,307	9,526	35,026	38,763	40,217
Broome County, New York	183,370	783	1,054	3,508	4,660	4,560	1,094	1,464	2,974	3,915	4,160
Cattaraugus County, New York......	73,701	421	419	1,991	1,555	2,238	340	468	1,674	1,854	1,792
Cayuga County, New York	74,439	616	412	1,371	2,057	1,820	413	657	1,389	2,085	1,764
Chautauqua County, New York	123,132	483	501	3,645	2,336	2,520	1,315	888	2,191	2,965	3,266
Chemung County, New York.........	80,297	503	257	1,913	1,905	2,181	391	399	2,244	2,223	1,345
Dutchess County, New York.........	287,621	2,557	780	5,535	8,416	8,006	1,554	2,009	5,532	5,343	7,629
Erie County, New York.................	887,965	7,370	4,346	20,606	21,735	22,043	4,537	5,071	19,926	21,435	21,562
Jefferson County, New York.........	105,475	928	914	3,041	2,528	2,788	1,119	792	2,960	2,317	2,391
Kings County, New York...............	2,449,839	24,564	16,887	64,655	64,479	60,683	21,944	20,775	58,288	61,341	61,315
Livingston County, New York	61,337	445	305	970	1,553	2,231	239	149	1,412	1,050	1,464
Madison County, New York	69,112	590	572	1,509	1,011	1,622	258	303	1,249	1,715	1,225
Monroe County, New York	718,701	4,710	3,538	15,572	19,267	18,241	5,829	3,902	15,273	18,297	16,879
Nassau County, New York	1,311,691	11,225	7,370	31,228	34,310	37,831	10,783	6,245	31,812	31,678	35,082
New York County, New York.........	1,580,096	9,848	8,161	26,554	21,988	24,285	8,685	7,193	21,328	25,516	23,265
Niagara County, New York............	202,072	1,630	1,091	3,379	5,549	5,411	1,868	960	4,504	3,862	5,427
Oneida County, New York.............	221,820	1,454	1,968	5,564	6,041	5,460	1,371	931	5,310	5,822	5,338
Onondaga County, New York........	445,375	3,410	3,190	8,783	13,024	13,097	3,685	2,262	10,334	10,115	11,075
Ontario County, New York	107,287	1,305	636	2,564	3,330	2,269	632	265	2,151	2,127	3,161
Orange County, New York	370,160	2,661	3,537	9,514	13,922	11,949	3,043	2,397	11,149	9,650	10,865
Oswego County, New York...........	112,881	423	173	2,274	3,400	3,776	1,039	454	2,547	2,785	2,649
Queens County, New York............	2,174,748	16,442	13,558	50,160	48,135	53,267	16,502	11,360	46,046	49,251	47,958
Rensselaer County, New York	153,871	1,252	867	3,215	3,545	3,437	993	598	3,924	2,585	4,040
Richmond County, New York	461,503	3,784	2,697	11,827	11,921	12,982	4,534	2,506	11,837	9,795	12,804
Rockland County, New York	309,670	3,235	2,880	9,152	12,178	11,187	3,134	2,344	10,055	10,474	10,900
St. Lawrence County, New York	104,936	324	603	2,274	2,673	2,517	377	483	1,697	2,483	2,387
Saratoga County, New York	223,232	2,064	1,030	6,116	5,023	6,256	992	964	4,765	4,804	5,606
Schenectady County, New York.....	150,647	801	1,060	3,555	5,009	3,277	907	782	4,459	3,112	3,102
Steuben County, New York...........	92,432	590	471	2,312	2,530	2,341	687	674	1,889	2,253	2,372
Suffolk County, New York.............	1,430,645	10,484	8,497	36,278	35,011	41,052	11,782	7,333	29,999	35,781	37,621
Sullivan County, New York	72,603	595	399	1,816	1,716	2,540	572	313	1,733	1,312	1,447
Tompkins County, New York	100,380	996	397	996	2,237	2,008	776	120	1,471	1,853	998
Ulster County, New York	173,286	759	963	3,549	3,505	3,909	830	1,242	2,961	4,024	3,948
Wayne County, New York	87,131	538	679	2,430	1,907	2,489	620	302	2,245	2,327	1,941
Westchester County, New York	938,723	10,278	5,055	24,059	23,303	28,898	8,694	5,428	18,395	24,549	27,161
NORTH CAROLINA	10,147,231	80,312	60,903	255,313	277,046	270,082	72,138	59,316	239,540	266,341	270,017
Alamance County, North Carolina..	162,700	803	1,035	4,883	2,980	4,785	1,438	445	4,316	4,224	4,147
Brunswick County, North Carolina	139,523	357	937	2,800	2,306	2,453	624	477	1,892	1,672	2,348
Buncombe County, North Carolina	256,070	1,766	1,298	4,092	5,410	6,623	1,838	1,568	4,850	5,154	6,260
Burke County, North Carolina........	87,764	461	220	2,266	1,711	2,059	375	339	1,255	2,462	2,696

Table C-4. Primary and Secondary School Enrollment, by Sex and Selected Counties, 2019—*Continued*

(Number.)

State/County	Population 3 years and over	Male — Enrolled in school					Female — Enrolled in school				
		Nursery school, Pre-school	Kindergarten	Grades 1 to 4	Grades 5 to 8	Grades 9 to 12	Nursery school, Pre-school	Kindergarten	Grades 1 to 4	Grades 5 to 8	Grades 9 to 12
NORTH CAROLINA—*(Continued)*											
Cabarrus County, North Carolina...	209,671	2,586	840	6,687	6,394	7,275	2,404	1,254	4,537	5,975	8,073
Carteret County, North Carolina	68,278	844	419	1,140	1,048	1,941	486	519	1,308	1,480	1,837
Catawba County, North Carolina....	155,254	741	844	3,450	4,994	4,508	409	1,151	2,915	4,559	3,311
Cleveland County, North Carolina..	94,633	310	403	2,345	3,144	1,614	316	847	2,794	2,116	2,893
Craven County, North Carolina.....	98,539	1,112	1,024	2,372	1,826	1,589	1,039	365	2,576	2,489	2,405
Cumberland County, North Carolina...................	320,622	2,892	3,072	8,748	8,421	7,899	3,154	2,661	8,969	9,338	7,991
Davidson County, North Carolina ..	162,807	813	830	4,395	3,747	4,100	737	1,124	3,944	4,447	4,584
Durham County, North Carolina	311,307	3,133	1,738	8,433	6,366	6,789	3,464	1,975	6,500	6,648	6,970
Forsyth County, North Carolina.....	370,477	2,648	3,316	9,807	9,396	11,172	2,385	2,865	9,704	9,497	10,212
Gaston County, North Carolina.....	217,143	1,582	937	5,481	6,977	6,381	1,366	1,311	5,825	4,633	5,013
Guilford County, North Carolina	519,281	3,035	3,487	13,490	14,280	13,697	3,748	2,075	9,787	16,168	14,774
Harnett County, North Carolina	130,186	1,132	1,563	3,248	3,140	5,024	1,112	640	3,234	4,585	3,669
Henderson County, North Carolina...................	114,697	581	187	3,579	2,542	2,928	733	581	1,863	2,556	2,607
Iredell County, North Carolina.......	176,039	1,649	1,164	4,870	4,569	6,017	897	778	4,212	4,798	4,755
Johnston County, North Carolina ...	201,758	1,824	901	5,193	6,991	6,884	1,104	1,149	5,308	6,738	5,369
Lincoln County, North Carolina	82,962	1,030	754	1,381	2,678	2,213	398	820	2,049	1,415	1,994
Mecklenburg County, North Carolina...................	1,067,990	11,202	7,112	26,231	32,462	28,083	9,700	5,832	25,339	32,119	27,621
Moore County, North Carolina.......	97,182	1,082	369	1,551	2,883	2,735	808	429	1,997	2,064	2,233
Nash County, North Carolina........	90,351	483	477	2,639	2,415	1,895	339	749	1,945	2,360	2,714
New Hanover County, North Carolina...................	227,879	1,671	1,011	4,967	5,784	4,008	1,641	940	4,481	4,586	5,955
Onslow County, North Carolina	188,941	1,389	1,430	4,605	8,113	4,628	1,389	1,290	4,984	4,362	4,184
Orange County, North Carolina.....	145,038	1,126	1,225	3,373	2,646	4,045	1,225	873	2,997	4,190	3,213
Pitt County, North Carolina...........	175,933	1,040	1,106	3,619	4,867	3,928	1,521	1,551	4,692	4,494	3,778
Randolph County, North Carolina..	140,044	1,082	554	4,025	3,867	3,800	607	1,002	3,225	3,898	3,306
Robeson County, North Carolina...	125,043	574	480	4,345	3,056	3,622	401	835	3,225	4,298	3,624
Rowan County, North Carolina.....	136,527	1,183	177	3,853	3,909	3,770	1,519	1,259	2,627	3,811	3,538
Rutherford County, North Carolina	64,748	401	808	1,745	1,209	668	121	353	1,759	1,328	1,686
Union County, North Carolina.......	233,293	2,558	1,499	6,250	9,815	9,039	1,995	1,798	6,573	7,927	8,735
Wake County, North Carolina	1,072,539	10,634	7,738	27,733	32,060	29,780	10,942	7,755	27,242	29,617	32,608
Wayne County, North Carolina	119,118	392	461	3,000	4,160	3,636	518	652	3,056	3,376	3,587
NORTH DAKOTA	731,445	6,042	4,827	18,119	20,777	16,997	3,949	3,424	19,648	18,714	18,210
Burleigh County, North Dakota......	92,379	558	589	2,183	3,294	2,203	829	497	1,683	2,963	2,054
Cass County, North Dakota	174,538	1,571	1,052	3,810	5,913	3,046	661	521	4,683	4,709	4,388
Grand Forks County, North Dakota...................	67,211	696	281	1,694	1,421	1,379	178	719	1,726	895	1,389
Ward County, North Dakota..........	64,365	447	612	1,549	2,241	1,026	155	380	2,165	1,275	1,717
OHIO	11,288,040	98,899	75,459	277,847	297,519	304,002	85,272	66,076	272,738	288,047	285,540
Allen County, Ohio........................	99,229	1,096	119	3,192	3,280	3,172	460	355	2,257	2,933	3,096
Ashtabula County, Ohio................	94,642	435	654	2,189	2,825	2,475	641	202	2,662	2,105	1,995
Belmont County, Ohio	64,668	225	268	1,103	2,170	1,963	309	189	1,613	1,313	1,996
Butler County, Ohio	370,453	2,191	2,375	10,247	10,904	11,003	2,678	2,036	9,478	10,781	9,837
Clark County, Ohio	129,546	878	848	3,570	3,442	2,953	929	1,052	2,420	3,716	3,833
Clermont County, Ohio.................	199,785	1,525	1,498	4,346	5,944	5,791	1,324	648	5,049	6,849	5,354
Columbiana County, Ohio.............	99,203	975	557	2,484	2,350	2,311	604	1,045	2,358	1,747	2,272
Cuyahoga County, Ohio................	1,193,911	10,393	5,424	26,572	31,348	31,824	8,179	6,997	27,997	27,061	31,856
Delaware County, Ohio.................	201,742	1,786	1,762	6,292	6,731	7,250	2,098	1,068	5,289	6,946	6,106
Erie County, Ohio.........................	71,915	552	438	1,492	1,472	1,819	558	577	1,218	2,002	1,827
Fairfield County, Ohio	152,107	2,071	1,135	4,221	4,247	4,854	1,391	812	3,423	4,451	4,109
Franklin County, Ohio	1,261,357	13,039	10,686	31,915	31,935	31,842	9,146	8,790	32,585	32,621	30,359
Geauga County, Ohio...................	90,783	828	1,069	2,083	2,894	2,352	693	190	2,398	2,144	2,621
Greene County, Ohio	163,188	2,574	904	3,436	3,230	4,302	967	859	3,961	3,279	3,334
Hamilton County, Ohio..................	785,006	6,336	5,747	20,615	18,171	21,709	7,702	5,348	20,590	19,471	19,210
Hancock County, Ohio..................	72,843	470	396	2,164	2,123	1,744	240	385	1,857	1,919	1,425
Jefferson County, Ohio.................	63,492	513	343	872	1,914	1,387	566	363	1,264	1,445	1,345
Lake County, Ohio	223,431	2,079	1,447	5,886	4,297	5,774	1,481	1,567	5,084	5,862	5,391
Licking County, Ohio	169,613	826	747	4,296	5,291	4,814	1,023	709	4,826	4,491	4,535
Lorain County, Ohio	299,290	2,655	1,730	6,955	8,108	9,597	2,289	1,812	7,820	6,296	7,512
Lucas County, Ohio	411,404	2,847	3,336	10,425	10,966	10,522	3,363	1,776	10,436	11,503	10,117
Mahoning County, Ohio.................	222,672	2,163	952	5,424	5,448	5,755	2,304	1,568	4,752	5,008	4,928
Medina County, Ohio....................	174,148	1,726	1,319	4,944	4,121	5,194	1,491	1,002	3,651	5,300	4,716
Miami County, Ohio......................	103,270	1,199	435	2,185	3,219	3,586	741	480	2,438	3,093	2,552

Table C-4. Primary and Secondary School Enrollment, by Sex and Selected Counties, 2019—*Continued*

(Number.)

State/County	Population 3 years and over	Male					Female				
		Enrolled in school					Enrolled in school				
		Nursery school, Pre-school	Kindergarten	Grades 1 to 4	Grades 5 to 8	Grades 9 to 12	Nursery school, Pre-school	Kindergarten	Grades 1 to 4	Grades 5 to 8	Grades 9 to 12
OHIO—(*Continued*)											
Montgomery County, Ohio	512,215	4,282	3,721	11,691	14,314	12,251	4,160	3,325	11,343	13,592	11,206
Muskingum County, Ohio	83,865	394	588	2,029	2,805	2,289	532	382	1,599	2,833	2,077
Portage County, Ohio	158,246	946	852	2,601	2,867	3,826	1,021	808	2,723	4,248	3,380
Richland County, Ohio	117,054	977	237	3,091	4,005	2,805	566	611	3,261	2,965	2,530
Ross County, Ohio	74,188	724	587	1,722	2,472	1,823	791	775	1,252	1,524	1,981
Stark County, Ohio	358,928	3,778	2,124	7,831	9,299	9,839	3,175	2,068	8,479	7,577	9,408
Summit County, Ohio	524,979	5,249	4,052	13,107	12,695	12,007	2,870	2,804	12,606	11,969	12,510
Trumbull County, Ohio	192,100	605	1,270	4,109	4,679	4,986	729	1,101	3,930	4,538	4,356
Tuscarawas County, Ohio	88,049	408	916	2,648	2,338	2,085	265	419	2,079	1,958	1,745
Warren County, Ohio	228,464	3,069	1,780	6,028	6,131	7,547	2,216	1,283	6,257	7,063	6,682
Wayne County, Ohio	112,269	1,144	627	3,297	3,053	2,355	886	525	2,465	3,201	2,539
Wood County, Ohio	127,371	1,286	800	2,615	3,390	3,652	1,518	529	3,063	2,651	2,958
OKLAHOMA	3,810,097	33,085	29,119	114,602	114,496	106,508	31,264	26,683	100,025	108,700	103,038
Canadian County, Oklahoma	141,996	806	1,082	4,182	5,480	4,435	870	1,084	3,861	4,524	4,389
Cleveland County, Oklahoma	275,218	1,474	1,415	7,362	7,818	7,229	1,554	1,225	5,582	8,670	6,285
Comanche County, Oklahoma	116,288	1,110	749	4,352	2,272	3,341	1,191	1,120	3,255	2,066	4,102
Creek County, Oklahoma	69,109	561	298	2,105	2,234	1,801	346	610	2,033	1,620	1,866
Muskogee County, Oklahoma	65,205	270	359	2,399	1,829	1,848	641	274	2,196	1,605	1,636
Oklahoma County, Oklahoma	762,846	5,601	6,715	23,462	24,229	20,162	7,677	6,073	20,269	22,618	20,338
Payne County, Oklahoma	79,480	1,007	613	1,679	2,113	1,370	415	359	1,839	1,650	1,740
Pottawatomie County, Oklahoma	70,352	1,124	228	1,796	2,633	1,969	615	414	1,673	1,932	1,873
Rogers County, Oklahoma	88,435	259	608	2,532	2,977	2,234	223	495	2,062	2,825	2,211
Tulsa County, Oklahoma	625,047	5,854	4,821	19,448	18,071	17,656	5,550	4,796	17,057	18,244	17,017
Wagoner County, Oklahoma	78,831	842	610	1,880	2,782	2,524	639	618	2,555	1,701	2,038
OREGON	4,090,528	29,098	25,828	98,510	102,380	98,969	29,605	22,580	88,218	96,887	95,978
Benton County, Oregon	91,183	785	558	1,373	1,389	1,761	417	283	1,405	2,362	1,908
Clackamas County, Oregon	405,021	2,186	3,595	9,841	10,394	10,780	3,278	1,860	10,288	8,987	10,157
Deschutes County, Oregon	193,189	1,644	1,408	6,571	3,618	4,686	1,541	1,350	3,232	3,986	5,412
Douglas County, Oregon	109,112	976	654	2,020	3,176	2,168	1,167	989	1,302	3,080	2,785
Jackson County, Oregon	214,645	1,502	1,880	4,953	4,623	4,699	2,043	1,692	4,588	4,278	3,837
Klamath County, Oregon	65,420	708	466	1,984	1,492	1,201	78	679	1,620	1,162	1,490
Lane County, Oregon	373,081	2,082	1,345	7,610	8,881	7,133	2,358	1,705	6,870	7,612	8,577
Linn County, Oregon	126,091	1,266	515	2,496	4,398	3,070	245	603	3,101	3,143	3,151
Marion County, Oregon	334,568	1,144	3,018	9,802	10,623	9,988	2,334	2,054	8,822	8,680	10,078
Multnomah County, Oregon	788,337	6,352	3,956	18,424	15,322	16,990	6,356	4,200	14,897	17,049	14,132
Polk County, Oregon	83,564	965	372	2,607	2,035	1,945	438	387	1,989	2,578	2,043
Umatilla County, Oregon	75,359	1,084	57	1,380	4,023	1,933	839	477	2,480	2,206	2,464
Washington County, Oregon	581,231	4,344	3,695	14,338	17,397	16,481	5,169	2,980	13,831	15,764	15,517
Yamhill County, Oregon	103,588	449	611	2,222	3,410	2,568	838	509	2,132	3,230	2,914
PENNSYLVANIA	12,394,896	95,912	65,748	287,311	316,377	314,304	86,466	69,795	275,031	293,425	299,768
Adams County, Pennsylvania	100,133	767	689	2,264	2,180	2,841	443	222	1,738	2,728	2,627
Allegheny County, Pennsylvania	1,177,943	8,305	5,883	23,733	27,180	27,813	8,801	7,560	24,313	21,631	25,809
Armstrong County, Pennsylvania	62,477	416	363	1,815	1,015	1,212	245	205	1,517	1,007	1,389
Beaver County, Pennsylvania	159,537	1,168	963	3,612	3,529	3,567	1,562	1,150	2,923	3,318	3,593
Berks County, Pennsylvania	407,276	2,624	2,613	9,606	12,656	11,590	4,731	2,439	9,557	10,531	10,513
Blair County, Pennsylvania	118,027	1,102	282	3,635	2,950	3,080	814	462	2,565	3,014	2,559
Bucks County, Pennsylvania	610,164	4,888	3,928	13,817	14,992	17,182	4,381	2,614	13,230	15,759	16,447
Butler County, Pennsylvania	182,041	1,309	1,069	3,786	4,615	4,651	898	1,546	3,921	3,415	4,174
Cambria County, Pennsylvania	126,718	770	903	2,233	3,051	3,332	503	948	2,861	2,193	3,186
Carbon County, Pennsylvania	62,585	721	232	996	1,749	1,439	357	508	1,029	1,481	1,496
Centre County, Pennsylvania	159,255	916	225	2,471	2,969	2,298	622	562	2,544	2,454	4,182
Chester County, Pennsylvania	508,715	5,180	1,851	13,373	14,536	15,705	3,843	3,298	12,380	14,470	14,711
Clearfield County, Pennsylvania	77,037	827	447	1,225	1,817	1,830	425	174	1,855	1,229	1,695
Columbia County, Pennsylvania	63,626	412	196	1,531	1,425	1,252	329	265	830	1,311	1,361
Crawford County, Pennsylvania	81,952	618	354	2,370	2,014	1,763	280	513	1,585	1,751	1,912
Cumberland County, Pennsylvania	245,128	1,818	928	5,711	5,814	6,016	1,916	937	5,496	6,088	5,554
Dauphin County, Pennsylvania	268,250	3,273	1,546	6,019	7,228	7,629	2,771	1,667	5,374	8,010	5,858
Delaware County, Pennsylvania	547,403	5,345	2,697	12,208	15,841	14,831	4,375	2,912	14,302	14,183	12,967
Erie County, Pennsylvania	261,545	2,503	1,550	6,070	6,129	6,734	1,979	1,044	6,516	5,707	7,600
Fayette County, Pennsylvania	125,980	767	524	3,109	2,577	2,914	957	893	3,100	2,140	3,160
Franklin County, Pennsylvania	149,492	782	867	3,971	3,897	4,381	419	869	3,066	4,048	3,857
Indiana County, Pennsylvania	82,110	254	482	1,552	1,883	1,758	313	416	1,954	1,441	1,470
Lackawanna County, Pennsylvania	204,404	2,171	792	5,084	5,686	4,330	1,889	1,132	4,306	5,168	5,019
Lancaster County, Pennsylvania	525,366	4,668	2,701	13,842	14,635	13,490	2,806	3,299	12,735	14,666	13,786
Lawrence County, Pennsylvania	82,893	576	391	1,965	1,910	2,019	445	426	1,440	2,314	1,639
Lebanon County, Pennsylvania	136,981	685	419	3,933	4,317	2,854	647	978	3,647	3,696	3,320

Table C-4. Primary and Secondary School Enrollment, by Sex and Selected Counties, 2019—*Continued*

(Number.)

State/County	Population 3 years and over	Male					Female				
		Enrolled in school					Enrolled in school				
		Nursery school, Pre-school	Kindergarten	Grades 1 to 4	Grades 5 to 8	Grades 9 to 12	Nursery school, Pre-school	Kindergarten	Grades 1 to 4	Grades 5 to 8	Grades 9 to 12
PENNSYLVANIA—(*Continued*)											
Lehigh County, Pennsylvania	355,796	2,451	2,491	8,245	10,908	9,685	1,869	1,905	9,503	9,400	8,993
Luzerne County, Pennsylvania.......	308,880	1,897	1,930	8,542	4,899	7,058	1,837	1,647	6,508	6,598	8,204
Lycoming County, Pennsylvania....	109,813	836	358	2,991	2,238	2,780	276	846	2,559	2,946	2,366
Mercer County, Pennsylvania........	105,551	442	464	2,036	2,490	2,747	865	720	1,854	1,995	1,958
Monroe County, Pennsylvania.......	166,294	490	2,083	2,603	3,919	5,292	651	1,377	3,653	3,719	3,768
Montgomery County, Pennsylvania............................	803,680	7,377	3,582	17,431	23,300	22,811	7,116	4,911	18,620	20,391	21,022
Northampton County, Pennsylvania............................	297,017	2,323	1,189	6,118	8,453	8,178	1,288	2,020	6,012	6,806	7,626
Northumberland County, Pennsylvania............................	88,173	196	270	2,430	1,837	2,212	167	241	2,564	1,689	2,085
Philadelphia County, Pennsylvania............................	1,522,678	13,517	9,620	37,438	39,015	34,914	13,134	9,124	34,914	38,815	34,098
Schuylkill County, Pennsylvania....	137,543	651	746	2,850	3,670	3,574	777	205	3,641	2,751	3,921
Somerset County, Pennsylvania....	71,047	609	172	1,719	1,802	1,329	481	236	1,684	1,451	1,551
Washington County, Pennsylvania............................	200,641	2,358	1,282	5,062	4,497	4,471	1,396	1,426	4,993	3,122	4,556
Westmoreland County, Pennsylvania............................	340,038	2,468	1,389	7,807	7,594	7,260	2,581	1,967	6,184	6,596	7,677
York County, Pennsylvania...........	433,991	2,750	2,721	11,525	12,345	11,699	2,668	1,667	9,343	11,596	11,544
RHODE ISLAND....................	1,028,128	7,051	5,939	20,089	26,213	25,271	6,962	5,231	20,059	23,404	23,178
Kent County, Rhode Island...........	159,941	987	1,043	3,264	3,309	3,561	1,022	514	3,205	3,421	3,439
Newport County, Rhode Island......	79,971	771	39	937	2,298	1,528	691	0	1,460	1,889	1,556
Providence County, Rhode Island.............................	617,198	4,279	4,228	13,429	16,184	15,698	3,696	3,382	11,954	15,463	14,378
Washington County, Rhode Island.............................	123,418	450	175	1,759	3,439	3,098	1,222	876	2,660	1,423	2,232
SOUTH CAROLINA	4,976,415	31,388	30,866	128,036	134,044	130,200	28,193	31,149	120,697	130,786	123,606
Aiken County, South Carolina........	164,497	714	1,051	3,617	5,377	2,756	419	757	4,841	4,402	4,775
Anderson County, South Carolina................................	196,159	1,124	1,049	5,260	5,263	5,338	839	1,937	4,419	5,644	5,354
Beaufort County, South Carolina...	185,994	953	957	2,832	5,443	3,911	960	531	3,347	3,987	4,744
Berkeley County, South Carolina...	219,278	1,045	994	7,404	6,639	5,246	1,340	905	5,862	6,601	5,818
Charleston County, South Carolina................................	396,389	3,321	2,410	9,226	9,173	8,395	2,336	1,964	7,947	8,815	8,326
Darlington County, South Carolina................................	64,836	407	978	1,887	1,761	2,727	518	115	1,030	2,078	1,216
Dorchester County, South Carolina................................	156,530	1,174	730	4,842	5,304	4,213	661	542	6,466	3,521	4,531
Florence County, South Carolina...	133,654	497	1,121	4,089	3,361	4,620	744	1,252	2,150	5,183	2,683
Greenville County, South Carolina................................	504,231	3,697	2,385	14,667	13,712	13,205	2,979	3,418	13,843	13,984	12,117
Horry County, South Carolina	345,060	1,720	1,190	8,132	7,433	6,767	1,444	1,760	7,273	7,623	6,370
Kershaw County, South Carolina...	64,292	384	662	2,653	1,226	2,127	400	791	1,737	1,557	1,654
Laurens County, South Carolina....	65,245	280	546	1,764	2,130	1,582	478	492	1,648	1,855	1,183
Lexington County, South Carolina................................	289,611	2,139	2,687	6,211	9,562	7,848	1,903	2,536	7,815	7,923	8,103
Oconee County, South Carolina.....	77,900	50	581	2,014	1,938	1,567	225	300	2,199	2,676	1,559
Orangeburg County, South Carolina................................	84,049	320	227	2,894	2,161	2,859	64	661	2,156	2,477	2,785
Pickens County, South Carolina	123,059	569	1,067	2,263	2,318	2,885	370	564	2,816	2,480	2,848
Richland County, South Carolina...	401,500	2,954	2,777	8,640	10,559	12,762	2,759	2,876	7,603	9,440	11,576
Spartanburg County, South Carolina................................	306,564	1,982	1,835	9,014	8,595	8,347	1,504	1,988	8,791	7,749	7,934
Sumter County, South Carolina.....	103,341	1,352	1,603	3,659	2,508	2,145	752	649	2,809	2,699	3,353
York County, South Carolina	271,708	2,311	1,635	8,107	8,303	8,222	1,804	1,841	8,908	7,643	6,902
SOUTH DAKOTA	849,651	8,353	7,488	24,405	26,350	22,328	7,170	5,964	20,808	23,291	21,054
Minnehaha County, South Dakota .	184,729	2,247	1,905	5,620	6,397	5,016	2,593	634	4,810	4,854	4,015
Pennington County, South Dakota	109,729	759	654	3,702	2,706	2,735	781	384	2,340	3,390	2,555
TENNESSEE	6,586,649	47,454	43,357	161,981	183,203	179,876	41,441	38,804	159,506	173,331	162,225
Anderson County, Tennessee	75,112	173	671	1,780	1,713	1,746	310	926	1,717	1,469	1,819
Blount County, Tennessee.............	129,438	747	712	2,773	3,164	3,324	900	391	2,363	3,560	3,215
Bradley County, Tennessee...........	105,063	1,111	466	2,405	2,547	2,977	745	333	3,462	1,677	2,764
Davidson County, Tennessee.........	665,251	4,256	3,104	13,251	17,102	13,752	5,594	3,790	14,122	14,943	14,196
Hamilton County, Tennessee.........	354,553	2,750	2,618	8,795	8,555	9,119	1,663	977	7,164	9,657	8,400

Table C-4. Primary and Secondary School Enrollment, by Sex and Selected Counties, 2019—*Continued*

(Number.)

State/County	Population 3 years and over	Male — Nursery school, Pre-school	Male — Kindergarten	Male — Grades 1 to 4	Male — Grades 5 to 8	Male — Grades 9 to 12	Female — Nursery school, Pre-school	Female — Kindergarten	Female — Grades 1 to 4	Female — Grades 5 to 8	Female — Grades 9 to 12
TENNESSEE—(*Continued*)											
Knox County, Tennessee	456,736	4,187	2,890	11,123	10,726	10,517	3,551	2,863	10,236	11,086	11,544
Madison County, Tennessee	93,522	631	615	2,710	2,345	940	598	512	1,998	4,053	2,184
Maury County, Tennessee	93,344	1,572	346	1,385	2,916	3,175	772	1,045	2,156	2,471	1,048
Montgomery County, Tennessee	197,865	1,553	1,533	6,586	5,993	6,121	1,287	1,196	5,306	6,827	5,808
Robertson County, Tennessee	69,869	756	553	1,733	2,464	2,418	909	264	1,458	1,543	2,512
Rutherford County, Tennessee	320,723	2,465	2,423	7,964	11,028	10,816	1,614	2,135	6,784	11,083	9,368
Sevier County, Tennessee	94,669	141	69	2,391	2,563	1,872	138	277	2,538	2,607	1,667
Shelby County, Tennessee	896,007	8,388	6,695	27,239	26,718	26,596	6,905	6,445	24,913	26,634	24,198
Sullivan County, Tennessee	154,466	1,126	1,045	3,443	3,684	3,556	431	1,096	2,721	3,135	3,306
Sumner County, Tennessee	185,370	1,535	1,566	4,630	5,231	5,010	1,264	1,324	5,885	4,592	4,215
Washington County, Tennessee	125,189	386	771	1,720	3,244	2,986	423	492	3,069	3,143	2,385
Williamson County, Tennessee	231,749	3,078	2,097	7,827	8,585	8,334	2,705	2,016	6,803	7,254	9,314
Wilson County, Tennessee	139,673	1,157	1,190	3,197	4,976	4,033	597	835	4,042	4,130	3,447
TEXAS	27,854,473	239,123	212,834	804,544	902,549	845,952	227,182	202,033	800,581	833,335	822,955
Bell County, Texas	346,059	3,341	3,035	9,188	9,797	10,490	2,840	2,754	9,943	10,895	10,157
Bexar County, Texas	1,925,037	15,512	13,531	57,656	62,144	55,249	16,696	13,905	55,694	56,871	56,941
Bowie County, Texas	90,612	861	572	2,418	2,511	2,289	561	1,193	2,222	3,342	2,217
Brazoria County, Texas	360,103	2,889	1,742	11,239	13,213	10,434	1,399	1,717	10,236	12,630	12,856
Brazos County, Texas	220,888	2,661	1,354	5,304	5,346	3,334	1,198	472	6,107	4,715	5,286
Cameron County, Texas	404,164	3,538	3,890	13,299	15,600	14,040	5,708	3,436	12,771	14,316	14,787
Collin County, Texas	1,001,057	9,201	6,874	28,407	33,741	34,061	8,516	9,065	28,366	30,753	31,082
Comal County, Texas	151,641	780	1,073	3,424	4,574	3,931	1,575	376	4,252	4,423	3,678
Coryell County, Texas	73,324	688	473	1,893	1,817	1,978	873	509	2,299	1,666	2,860
Dallas County, Texas	2,523,190	21,253	19,303	66,816	87,500	77,609	20,292	17,396	74,079	77,490	72,661
Denton County, Texas	854,284	8,090	6,014	20,719	26,884	25,831	7,693	7,201	21,581	26,089	23,959
Ector County, Texas	157,300	876	1,443	7,102	5,086	4,670	1,138	1,137	6,057	4,628	4,931
Ellis County, Texas	177,935	1,658	1,146	5,283	6,316	6,545	1,313	1,683	4,691	5,064	6,550
El Paso County, Texas	801,881	7,127	6,977	26,930	25,860	24,967	5,815	6,124	25,687	24,799	24,875
Fort Bend County, Texas	780,369	8,232	4,809	26,727	28,304	28,417	9,241	6,340	24,083	24,205	25,972
Galveston County, Texas	329,374	2,003	2,037	9,040	9,401	10,021	2,234	1,985	8,675	9,194	10,271
Grayson County, Texas	131,040	779	812	3,511	4,682	4,555	760	1,388	3,706	2,959	2,916
Gregg County, Texas	118,818	1,503	598	2,616	4,624	3,656	1,376	820	3,366	2,870	3,228
Guadalupe County, Texas	162,245	2,375	1,230	4,502	4,263	5,015	1,524	861	5,440	4,397	4,490
Harris County, Texas	4,506,956	42,342	35,741	140,187	146,870	131,976	36,975	33,325	132,260	142,143	137,516
Harrison County, Texas	64,965	607	318	2,208	2,467	2,789	792	574	1,661	2,613	936
Hays County, Texas	223,466	1,503	1,079	5,907	5,187	6,293	1,653	1,160	4,683	5,332	6,716
Hidalgo County, Texas	825,313	5,493	10,254	31,415	34,205	31,975	8,136	8,304	29,253	33,265	30,718
Hunt County, Texas	95,047	933	646	2,635	2,892	2,041	239	575	2,768	2,299	2,488
Jefferson County, Texas	242,878	2,887	3,287	6,305	6,615	6,590	1,097	1,564	7,741	5,332	5,955
Johnson County, Texas	169,563	945	801	3,558	4,978	4,295	629	1,295	3,553	4,387	3,313
Kaufman County, Texas	130,171	1,859	1,148	4,403	3,943	5,005	905	2,018	3,804	4,037	3,443
Lubbock County, Texas	297,998	1,822	1,890	8,061	9,280	7,930	2,439	2,279	6,854	9,170	8,355
McLennan County, Texas	247,373	3,055	1,701	7,249	7,164	7,713	2,024	1,178	7,379	7,640	6,423
Midland County, Texas	168,103	1,048	1,509	6,402	5,658	3,288	2,510	518	7,358	4,544	4,974
Montgomery County, Texas	585,650	5,223	4,223	14,817	22,388	18,958	5,085	4,023	17,813	16,939	20,199
Nueces County, Texas	350,666	2,748	1,913	9,723	10,909	11,245	2,914	2,151	10,103	9,647	8,045
Parker County, Texas	137,951	618	1,295	4,266	4,120	4,946	1,392	1,179	3,752	3,866	4,166
Potter County, Texas	113,330	1,508	578	4,006	4,049	2,637	1,034	808	3,739	4,415	3,374
Randall County, Texas	132,815	709	274	4,084	3,911	4,292	454	1,132	4,524	3,159	2,857
Rockwall County, Texas	101,633	906	854	2,712	4,505	2,980	1,851	544	2,975	2,674	3,754
San Patricio County, Texas	64,112	910	652	1,769	2,277	2,595	522	300	1,834	2,088	2,402
Smith County, Texas	224,112	1,956	1,507	6,799	6,525	5,661	1,740	3,706	4,466	5,531	6,396
Tarrant County, Texas	2,018,960	18,684	16,682	56,993	69,291	63,193	15,131	13,550	58,709	62,011	63,436
Taylor County, Texas	131,808	671	1,112	3,344	3,991	3,781	1,382	815	2,755	4,347	4,272
Tom Green County, Texas	114,549	554	1,077	2,925	3,705	3,116	1,523	562	2,496	2,599	2,986
Travis County, Texas	1,228,820	11,030	7,766	31,262	30,330	27,034	11,111	6,901	28,427	29,778	28,544
Victoria County, Texas	88,584	744	215	2,770	3,209	3,139	316	1,190	2,700	2,010	2,333
Webb County, Texas	261,584	2,921	2,118	10,292	10,277	9,985	2,401	4,920	8,667	9,994	9,090
Wichita County, Texas	127,995	1,382	1,241	3,570	2,682	2,508	1,122	1,016	4,314	2,748	2,800
Williamson County, Texas	569,896	7,058	5,998	16,194	16,266	18,269	5,268	3,380	15,828	17,163	18,179
Wise County, Texas	67,100	518	253	1,933	2,451	2,449	484	269	1,823	2,092	1,481
UTAH	3,065,831	33,119	25,832	103,222	113,640	110,269	29,267	27,422	102,847	101,791	100,448
Cache County, Utah	122,061	1,455	962	4,422	4,477	4,129	1,348	1,113	4,713	3,885	3,987
Davis County, Utah	339,669	4,762	3,073	14,144	13,448	12,752	3,502	4,038	12,291	11,472	11,677
Salt Lake County, Utah	1,112,181	10,531	8,092	33,233	38,362	36,406	9,373	8,963	35,469	32,975	34,379
Utah County, Utah	602,660	7,041	5,761	23,489	24,239	23,811	7,080	6,461	21,368	23,294	22,552
Washington County, Utah	170,975	1,458	1,864	3,924	5,899	6,216	1,526	1,510	4,412	5,696	4,553

Table C-4. Primary and Secondary School Enrollment, by Sex and Selected Counties, 2019—*Continued*

(Number.)

		Male					Female				
		Enrolled in school					Enrolled in school				
State/County	Population 3 years and over	Nursery school, Pre-school	Kindergarten	Grades 1 to 4	Grades 5 to 8	Grades 9 to 12	Nursery school, Pre-school	Kindergarten	Grades 1 to 4	Grades 5 to 8	Grades 9 to 12
UTAH—(*Continued*)											
Weber County, Utah	248,521	2,752	1,818	7,460	9,303	7,610	2,259	1,228	8,180	8,859	7,204
VERMONT	606,267	4,973	2,926	12,525	12,820	14,874	4,417	3,372	12,564	11,821	13,701
Chittenden County, Vermont	159,003	1,566	663	3,333	3,419	3,448	799	656	2,973	2,975	3,595
VIRGINIA	8,239,980	67,559	46,778	212,107	217,148	223,837	65,041	46,530	197,359	208,772	211,763
Albemarle County, Virginia............	106,519	1,037	583	2,499	2,448	3,327	1,300	498	2,808	2,047	2,495
Arlington County, Virginia.............	229,615	2,367	1,215	3,977	6,076	2,908	2,256	1,242	4,218	5,823	4,232
Augusta County, Virginia..............	73,782	796	619	1,106	1,528	1,675	578	223	1,785	1,375	1,303
Bedford County, Virginia..............	76,569	877	289	2,578	1,428	2,010	358	448	1,296	2,083	2,528
Chesterfield County, Virginia	339,709	3,035	1,616	10,042	9,251	10,970	2,897	1,777	8,473	10,268	9,957
Fairfax County, Virginia	1,104,326	9,328	8,903	29,899	30,313	33,926	9,540	6,911	25,711	30,705	33,028
Fauquier County, Virginia	68,707	537	640	1,876	2,140	2,030	280	352	2,003	2,171	1,580
Frederick County, Virginia	86,487	944	170	2,304	2,997	2,782	736	306	2,064	3,241	1,599
Hanover County, Virginia..............	105,124	858	277	3,274	3,095	2,874	986	305	2,625	2,946	3,254
Henrico County, Virginia...............	319,854	2,399	2,174	8,273	9,959	9,203	1,967	1,194	8,988	8,886	8,410
James City County, Virginia	74,325	858	410	1,672	1,993	1,369	551	229	1,426	1,810	2,343
Loudoun County, Virginia.............	398,316	4,263	2,457	12,209	16,105	15,123	4,088	2,773	13,438	13,535	13,227
Prince William County, Virginia	448,945	3,133	3,169	13,419	16,960	14,361	3,860	3,075	14,374	14,447	14,125
Roanoke County, Virginia.............	91,312	344	131	1,660	2,919	3,629	730	352	1,898	2,210	1,876
Rockingham County, Virginia........	79,148	148	874	2,164	1,626	2,287	324	423	1,957	1,917	2,005
Spotsylvania County, Virginia........	131,175	1,466	860	3,835	4,030	4,390	345	1,205	3,201	4,949	3,418
Stafford County, Virginia..............	147,209	997	438	4,657	4,932	4,733	1,571	1,150	4,323	3,403	5,214
York County, Virginia....................	65,872	635	374	2,222	1,479	1,387	490	385	1,660	2,325	2,039
Alexandria city, Virginia................	152,832	1,587	618	3,924	2,356	2,997	1,049	393	3,022	2,775	2,574
Chesapeake city, Virginia.............	236,302	1,242	1,716	6,725	6,379	6,969	2,810	1,767	7,036	6,110	7,741
Hampton city, Virginia..................	129,012	1,049	796	2,823	3,256	3,936	966	625	2,876	2,249	3,734
Lynchburg city, Virginia................	78,954	613	437	1,606	1,840	1,579	164	339	1,668	2,352	1,064
Newport News city, Virginia	170,878	1,246	614	4,926	4,861	4,652	3,170	709	4,825	3,923	3,351
Norfolk city, Virginia....................	233,339	2,269	1,291	4,746	5,116	4,771	1,930	2,147	5,003	4,937	3,425
Portsmouth city, Virginia..............	90,384	969	349	2,757	1,933	1,719	745	258	2,418	1,876	3,217
Richmond city, Virginia................	221,548	1,634	1,268	4,957	3,416	3,965	1,639	1,697	4,187	3,444	2,894
Roanoke city, Virginia	96,117	681	284	2,593	2,327	2,043	881	648	1,820	2,273	2,438
Suffolk city, Virginia....................	88,779	1,598	875	2,470	2,279	3,131	1,057	225	2,503	2,746	2,521
Virginia Beach city, Virginia..........	432,895	4,600	2,387	11,984	10,566	10,638	4,451	1,700	10,662	10,503	11,794
WASHINGTON	7,351,064	63,366	47,774	181,800	192,339	187,212	58,863	47,959	169,690	185,180	182,812
Benton County, Washington.........	195,328	980	1,977	5,786	6,803	7,809	1,307	1,402	5,854	5,559	5,847
Chelan County, Washington	74,529	432	409	1,981	2,656	2,678	356	322	2,153	1,814	2,394
Clallam County, Washington	75,739	699	573	1,325	1,690	908	401	524	1,169	1,684	1,538
Clark County, Washington............	470,231	2,666	2,955	12,195	14,518	13,285	2,867	3,588	12,405	12,357	14,859
Cowlitz County, Washington.........	107,973	1,258	543	2,766	3,239	2,916	2,149	456	2,096	2,619	2,667
Franklin County, Washington	90,720	527	1,015	3,290	3,105	2,398	1,329	1,327	3,299	3,155	3,325
Grant County, Washington	92,812	606	1,099	3,964	2,342	2,393	546	1,256	2,689	3,600	3,675
Grays Harbor County, Washington	72,747	384	145	1,609	2,700	943	256	141	1,396	1,917	3,086
Island County, Washington	82,318	756	543	1,654	1,029	1,925	794	353	1,206	1,775	766
King County, Washington.............	2,178,347	20,540	12,973	49,381	52,483	47,677	19,871	10,402	46,052	52,130	48,091
Kitsap County, Washington	262,752	3,230	1,158	5,613	6,938	7,260	2,601	1,662	6,490	5,216	6,033
Lewis County, Washington	78,050	702	592	2,382	1,736	2,493	286	657	1,323	2,172	1,862
Pierce County, Washington	868,532	7,738	5,533	24,890	22,804	23,206	7,227	5,742	23,051	21,753	21,422
Skagit County, Washington	125,600	1,102	825	3,001	3,285	2,260	538	1,631	2,379	3,440	3,193
Snohomish County, Washington...	792,181	7,761	5,242	16,894	23,612	20,755	6,401	5,703	19,688	19,815	19,685
Spokane County, Washington	505,865	4,558	3,201	14,757	12,165	13,060	3,394	2,592	11,059	15,340	11,241
Thurston County, Washington......	280,276	2,895	2,287	6,723	5,886	7,630	2,266	2,600	5,748	7,055	6,716
Whatcom County, Washington......	223,297	1,381	1,445	4,172	4,507	5,565	1,095	1,213	5,354	3,876	4,957
Yakima County, Washington.........	240,672	2,431	1,670	6,607	7,998	8,500	2,367	3,220	6,694	7,682	7,454
WEST VIRGINIA	1,737,300	9,643	8,571	38,653	43,858	42,609	10,201	10,641	37,503	37,738	41,309
Berkeley County, West Virginia	116,087	596	890	3,711	3,115	2,739	1,028	987	2,639	2,872	2,810
Cabell County, West Virginia	88,442	380	106	2,516	2,107	1,922	404	535	1,725	1,287	1,892
Kanawha County, West Virginia.....	171,160	768	605	3,640	3,982	4,340	266	938	4,477	3,526	4,557
Monongalia County, West Virginia	102,911	744	194	1,549	2,175	1,733	807	257	2,307	1,436	1,854
Wood County, West Virginia	80,343	466	519	1,961	1,752	2,442	839	101	2,124	1,809	2,113
WISCONSIN	5,633,343	37,239	40,428	136,936	151,660	156,851	36,336	41,311	133,248	143,191	141,127
Brown County, Wisconsin.............	256,011	2,119	2,156	6,246	7,686	7,480	1,799	2,329	7,392	6,183	6,447
Dane County, Wisconsin	528,107	3,699	3,176	11,597	12,952	12,716	4,426	3,136	10,837	12,021	11,182
Dodge County, Wisconsin	85,720	688	365	1,757	2,119	2,264	715	681	1,787	3,145	2,430
Eau Claire County, Wisconsin........	101,285	1,150	312	1,967	3,342	2,357	599	878	2,529	1,723	2,384

Table C-4. Primary and Secondary School Enrollment, by Sex and Selected Counties, 2019—*Continued*

(Number.)

State/County	Population 3 years and over	Male — Enrolled in school					Female — Enrolled in school				
		Nursery school, Pre-school	Kindergarten	Grades 1 to 4	Grades 5 to 8	Grades 9 to 12	Nursery school, Pre-school	Kindergarten	Grades 1 to 4	Grades 5 to 8	Grades 9 to 12
WISCONSIN—(*Continued*)											
Fond du Lac County, Wisconsin....	99,210	886	696	2,440	1,500	2,025	421	1,014	2,384	2,210	2,636
Jefferson County, Wisconsin.........	82,065	590	217	2,521	1,773	2,052	456	602	1,772	1,729	2,167
Kenosha County, Wisconsin..........	164,413	1,421	1,082	4,715	4,064	5,268	1,035	694	3,906	5,113	4,839
La Crosse County, Wisconsin........	114,736	1,135	607	2,362	2,881	2,601	623	835	2,612	2,500	2,501
Manitowoc County, Wisconsin......	77,078	449	384	1,994	1,876	2,096	588	222	1,596	1,996	2,060
Marathon County, Wisconsin	131,548	922	880	3,775	3,410	3,871	1,308	666	3,068	4,302	2,833
Milwaukee County, Wisconsin.......	910,682	3,612	11,247	25,669	26,638	24,243	3,016	13,218	21,934	26,088	24,782
Outagamie County, Wisconsin	182,054	1,801	1,091	4,954	4,928	5,576	1,555	1,012	6,031	3,565	4,849
Ozaukee County, Wisconsin..........	86,598	495	996	2,014	2,337	2,528	435	260	2,111	2,657	2,077
Portage County, Wisconsin...........	68,673	411	592	1,581	1,706	1,521	483	397	1,606	957	1,517
Racine County, Wisconsin.............	188,704	768	955	5,089	5,570	5,771	1,829	1,140	4,719	5,292	4,625
Rock County, Wisconsin	156,691	798	921	3,647	5,054	4,534	851	887	3,157	4,128	5,060
St. Croix County, Wisconsin.........	87,311	519	905	2,093	2,926	2,899	486	627	2,289	2,895	2,410
Sheboygan County, Wisconsin......	111,787	810	507	2,968	2,861	2,865	858	1,388	2,853	2,986	2,155
Walworth County, Wisconsin	101,506	477	822	1,585	3,012	3,643	573	568	2,623	2,195	2,268
Washington County, Wisconsin	132,583	1,198	804	2,892	3,148	4,140	1,203	534	3,350	3,248	3,787
Waukesha County, Wisconsin	391,705	2,114	2,350	9,172	10,593	13,609	2,976	2,199	7,979	11,181	10,182
Winnebago County, Wisconsin	166,559	1,454	812	3,883	3,866	4,947	1,215	973	4,590	3,280	3,701
Wood County, Wisconsin..............	70,546	611	185	1,494	2,003	1,765	772	442	2,130	1,522	1,494
WYOMING...........................	559,758	4,132	3,918	16,951	15,752	14,699	4,028	2,797	16,462	15,555	14,308
Laramie County, Wyoming...........	96,591	892	1,212	2,338	2,376	2,483	663	278	3,140	2,935	2,383
Natrona County, Wyoming	77469	656	218	2,513	3,429	1,976	1,016	475	2,564	1,139	2,140

NOTES AND DEFINITIONS: COUNTY EDUCATION STATISTICS

Part C presents data items for selected counties, county equivalents, and independent cities. The District of Columbia is included as both a county and a state.

TABLES C-1 THROUGH C-4
Source: U.S. Census Bureau. *American Community Survey, 2019,* Tables S1701, S2701, S1501, B14004, and B14002. (ACS 1-Year Estimates) http://data.census.gov.

The population, characteristics, enrollment, and attainment data in Table C have been compiled from the detailed tables of the American Community Survey (2019 1-year) and can be found at data.census.gov on the Census Bureau's website.

ACS data are subject to sampling error, which can be especially large in small geographic areas or small population groups. Margins of error can be found on the Census Bureau website.

ACS gathers demographic, social, economic, housing and financial information about the nation's people and communities on a continuous basis, providing the detailed characteristics that have previously come from the sample long form of the decennial census.

GEOGRAPHIC IDENTIFICATION
A five-digit state and county code is assigned to each entity. The first two digits indicate the state; the remaining three identify the county. Within each state, the counties are numbered in alphabetical order, beginning with 001, with even numbers usually omitted. Independent cities follow the counties and begin with the number 510.

These codes have been established by the U.S. government as Federal Information Processing Standards and are often referred to as "FIPS codes." They are used by U.S. government agencies and many other organizations for data presentation. They are provided in this volume for use in matching the data given here with other data sources in which counties may be identified by FIPS codes.

Not all county equivalents are included in this publication.

County equivalents. In Louisiana, the primary divisions of the state are known as parishes rather than counties. In Alaska, the county equivalents are the organized boroughs, together with the census areas that were developed for general statistical purposes by the state of Alaska and the U.S. Census Bureau.

Independent cities. Independent cities are not included in any county; data are presented separately in this volume where available.

Maryland
  Baltimore (separate from Baltimore County)

Missouri
  St. Louis (separate from St. Louis County)

Virginia
  Alexandria
  Chesapeake
  Hampton
  Lynchburg
  Newport News
  Norfolk
  Portsmouth
  Richmond
  Roanoke
  Suffolk
  Virginia Beach

Highest Level of Educational Attainment.
People are classified according to the highest degree or level of school completed. The order in which degrees were listed on the questionnaire suggested that doctorate degrees were "higher" than professional school degrees, which were "higher" than master's degrees. The question included instructions for people currently enrolled in school to report the level of the previous grade attended or the highest degree received. Respondents who did not report educational attainment or enrollment level were assigned the attainment of a person of the same age, race, Hispanic or Latino origin, occupation, and sex, where possible, who resided in the same area or nearby. Respondents who filled in more than one box were edited to the highest level or degree reported. The question included a response category that allowed respondents to report completing the 12th grade without receiving a high school diploma. It allowed people who received either a high school diploma or the equivalent, such as those who passed the Test of General Educational Development (GED) and did not attend college, to be reported as "high school graduate(s)."

High school diploma or less. This category includes all persons who have not received a high school diploma, as well as those high school graduates who never attended college.

High school diploma or more. This category includes people whose highest degree was a high school diploma or its equivalent, people who attended college but did not receive a degree, and people who received a college, university, or professional degree. People who reported completing the 12th grade but not receiving a diploma are not high school graduates.

Bachelor's degree or more. This category includes people whose highest degree was a bachelor's, master's, professional, or doctoral degree. Master's degrees include the traditional M.A. and M.S. degrees and field-specific degrees. Some examples of professional degrees include medicine, dentistry, chiropractic, optometry, osteopathic medicine, pharmacy, podiatry, veterinary medicine, law, and theology. Vocational and technical training, such as barber school training; business, trade, technical, and vocational schools; or other training for a specific trade are specifically excluded.

Public and private schools. Public and private schools include people who attended school during the reference period and who indicated they were enrolled by marking one of the questionnaire categories for either "public school, public college" or "private school, private college." Schools primarily supported and controlled by a federal, state, or local government are defined as public (including tribal schools). Those primarily supported and controlled by religious organizations or other private groups are considered private, as are home schools.

School enrollment. People were classified as enrolled in school if they reported attending a "regular" public or private school or college during the three months prior to the interview. The question included instructions to "include only nursery school or preschool, kindergarten, elementary school, and schooling which leads to a high school diploma or a college degree" as regular school or college. Respondents who did not answer the enrollment question were assigned the enrollment status and type of school of a person with the same age, sex, and race/Hispanic or Latino origin whose residence was in the same or a nearby area. All persons 3 years old and over are included.

INDEX

INDEX